ENCYCLOPEDIA OF
ANTHROPOLOGY

To the memory of Marvin Farber

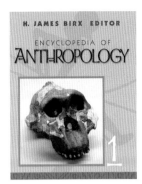
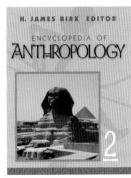
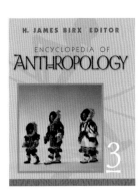

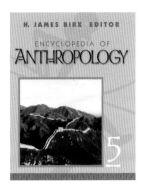

ENCYCLOPEDIA OF
ANTHROPOLOGY

H. JAMES BIRX ▪ EDITOR
Canisius College, SUNY Geneseo

2

A SAGE Reference Publication

SAGE Publications
Thousand Oaks ▪ London ▪ New Delhi

For information:

 Sage Publications, Inc.
2455 Teller Road
Thousand Oaks, California 91320
E-mail: order@sagepub.com

Sage Publications Ltd.
1 Oliver's Yard
55 City Road
London EC1Y 1SP
United Kingdom

Sage Publications India Pvt. Ltd.
B-42, Panchsheel Enclave
Post Box 4109
New Delhi 110 017 India

Printed in China.

This book is printed on acid-free paper.

Library of Congress Cataloging-in-Publication Data

Encyclopedia of anthropology / H. James Birx, editor.
        p. cm.
Includes bibliographical references and index.
ISBN 0-7619-3029-9 (cloth)
1. Anthropology—Encyclopedias. I. Birx, H. James.

GN11.E63 2005
301'.030—dc22
2005013953

05 06 07 08 09 10 9 8 7 6 5 4 3 2 1

Sage Reference:	Rolf Janke, Sara Tauber
Production:	Claudia A. Hoffman
Permissions and Image Research:	Karen Wiley
Typesetting:	C&M Digitals (P) Ltd.
Indexing:	Will Ragsdale
Cover Designers:	Ravi Balasuriya and Michelle Lee Kenny

3/5/07

CONTENTS

2

CHRONOLOGY

Date	Event	Refer to
1314 BCE	**Born:** Ramses II, pharaoh of Egypt	Abu Simbel, Pyramids, Ramses II, Rosetta Stone, Egypt
551 BCE	**Born:** Confucius, Chinese philosopher	Asia, Confucianism, Daoism, Great Wall of China
384 BCE	**Born:** Aristotle, ancient Greek philosopher and author of *The History of Animals*	Acropolis, Animals, Aristotle, Naturalism, Teleology
96 BCE	**Born:** Titus Lucretius Carus, ancient Roman philosopher and author of *On the Nature of Things*	Coliseum, Lucretius, Rome
1735	**Published:** *Systema Naturae* by Carolus Linnaeus	Carolus Linnaeus, Pongids, Primate taxonomy
1799	**Discovered:** Rosetta Stone in the Nile delta, west of Alexandria	Jean-François Champollion, Egyptology
1848	**Published:** *The Communist Manifesto* by Karl Marx and Friedrich Engels	Friedrich Engels, Karl Marx
1859	**Published:** *On the Origin of Species* by Charles Darwin	Charles Darwin
1871	**Published:** *Primitive Culture* by Edward Burnett Tylor	Edward Burnett Tylor
1908	**Discovered:** Venus of Willendorf figurine in Austria by archaeologist Josef Szombathy	Venus of Willendorf
1912	**Discovered:** Machu Picchu in Peru by Hiram Bingham	Machu Picchu, Peru
1921	**Published:** *Language* by Edward Sapir	Language and Culture, Edward Sapir
1922	**Published:** *Argonauts of the Western Pacific* by Bronislaw Malinowski	Bronislaw Malinowski
1922	**Completed:** *Nanook of the North*, a film by Robert J. Flaherty	Eskimos, Inuit
1922	**Published:** *The Andaman Islanders* by A. R. Radcliff-Brown	A. R. Radcliff-Brown
1922	**Discovered:** Tutankhamun's pharaonic tomb by Howard Carter in the Valley of the Kings, Egypt	Howard Carter, Egypt, Egyptology
1924	**Discovered:** Taung skull, the first Australopithecine fossil found in South Africa	Raymond A. Dart, Australopithecines
1928	**Published:** *Coming of Age in Samoa* by Margaret Mead	Margaret Mead
1934	**Published:** *Patterns of Culture* by Ruth Benedict	Ruth Benedict
1940	**Discovered:** Lascaux cave, with its magnificent Cro-Magnon cave murals, in France	Altamira Cave, Lascaux Cave, Ochre
1940	**Published:** *The Nuer* by Sir Edward E. Evans-Pritchard	Edward Evans-Pritchard
1940	**Published:** *Race, Language, and Culture* by Franz Boas	Franz Boas, Language, Culture
1949	**Published:** *Social Structure* by George Peter Murdock	George Peter Murdock
1953	**Proposed:** DNA molecule working model by James D. Watson and Francis F. H. C. Crick	DNA Molecule, RNA Molecule

Date	Event	Refer to
1955	**Published:** *Theory of Culture Change* by Julian H. Steward	Culture Change, Julian H. Steward
1956	**Published:** *Language, Thought, and Reality* by Benjamin Lee Whorf	Sapir-Whorf Hypothesis
1959	**Published:** *The Evolution of Culture* by Leslie A. White	Culture, Leslie A. White
1959	**Discovered:** *Zinjanthropus boisei* fossil skull by Mary D. Leakey at Olduvai Gorge in Tanzania	Mary D. Leakey, Olduvai Gorge, *Zinjanthropus boisei*
1960	**Published:** *Evolution and Culture* by Marshall D. Sahlins and Elman R. Service	Marshall D. Sahlins, Elman R. Service
1961	**Discovered:** *Homo habilis* by Louis S. B. Leakey at Olduvai Gorge in Tanzania	*Homo habilis*, Louis S. B. Leakey, Olduvai Gorge
1963	**Published:** *Anthropology: Culture Patterns and Processes* by Alfred Louis Kroeber	Alfred Louis Kroeber
1963	**Published:** *Race, Science, and Humanity* by Ashley Montagu	Ashley Montagu
1963	**Published:** *Structural Anthropology* by Claude Lévi-Strauss	Claude Lévi-Strauss, Structuralism
1963	**Published:** *The Mountain Gorilla: Ecology and Behavior* by George B. Schaller	Dian Fossey, Gorillas
1966	**Published:** *Religion: An Anthropological View* by Anthony F. C. Wallace	Anthropology of Religion, Anthony F. C. Wallace
1968	**Published:** *The Rise of Anthropological Theory: A History of Theories of Culture* by Marvin Harris	Marvin Harris, Theories
1972	**Discovered:** *Homo habilis* skull #1470 by Richard E. F. Leakey at Koobi Fora in Kenya	*Homo habilis*, Richard E. F. Leakey
1973	**Published:** *The Interpretation of Cultures* by Clifford R. Geertz	Clifford R. Geertz, Postmodernism
1974	**Discovered:** *Australopithecus afarensis* "Lucy" skeleton by Donald C. Johanson at Hadar in the Afar Triangle of Ethiopia	Australopithecines, Donald C. Johanson
1975	**Published:** *Reflections on Language* by Noam Chomsky	Noam Chomsky, Language
1975	**Published:** *Sociobiology: The New Synthesis* by Edward O. Wilson	Sociobiology, Edward O. Wilson
1976	**Discovered:** Laetoli footprints of *Australopithecus afarensis* by Mary D. Leakey in Tanzania	Bipedal Locomotion, Mary D. Leakey
1983	**Published:** *Gorillas in the Mist* by Dian Fossey	Dian Fossey, Gorillas, Primate Conservation
1983	**Published:** *In the Shadow of Man* by Jane Goodall	Chimpanzees, Jane Goodall
1983	**Published:** *Marxism and Anthropology: The History of a Relationship* by Maurice Bloch	Karl Marx, Marxism
1997	**Published:** *Bonobo: The Forgotten Ape* by Frans B. M. de Waal	Bonobos, Frans B. M. de Waal
2000	**Published:** *Extinct Humans* by Ian Tattersall and Jeffrey H. Schwartz	Hominid Taxonomy, Jeffrey H. Schwartz, Ian Tattersall
2003	**Completed:** Human Genome Project, working draft version	Human Genome Project
2005	**Completed:** Chimpanzee genome mapping	Chimpanzees, Bonobos
2005	**Published:** *The Great Apes* by Biruté Mary F. Galdikas	Apes, Pongids, Primate Conservation

CONVERSION CHART

Metric to Imperial

Length
mm	1 millimeter	= 0.04 inch (in)
cm	1 centimeter	= 0.40 inch (in)
m	1 meter	= 39.40 inches (in)
		= 3.28 feet (ft)
		= 1.09 yards (yd)
km	1 kilometer	= 0.62 mile (mi)

Area
cm^2	1 square centimeter	= 0.16 square inch (in^2)
m^2	1 square meter	= 10.77 square feet (ft^2)
		= 1.20 square yards (yd^2)
km^2	1 square kilometer	= 0.39 square mile (mi^2)
ha	1 hectare	= 107,636 square feet (ft^2)
		= 2.5 acres (ac)

Volume (Dry)
m^3	1 cubic centimeter	= 0.061 cubic inch (in^3)
m^3	1 cubic meter	= 1.31 cubic yards (yd^3)
		= 35.31 cubic feet (ft^3)
hL	1 hectoliter	= 2.8 bushels (bu)

Volume (Liquid)
mL	1 milliliter	= 0.035 fluid ounce (Imp)
L	1 liter	= 1.76 pints (Imp)
		= 0.88 quart (Imp)
		= 0.26 U.S. gallon (U.S. gal)
		= 0.22 Imperial gallons (gal)

Weight
g	1 gram	= 0.035 ounce (oz)
kg	1 kilogram	= 2.21 pounds (lb)
t	1 ton	= 1.10 short tons
		= 2,205 pounds (lb)

Speed
m/sec	1 meter per second	= 3.28 feet per second (ft/sec)
		= 2.24 miles per hour (mph)
km/h	1 kilometer per hour	= 0.62 mile per hour (mph)

Temperature
°F	degrees Fahrenheit	$= (°C \times {}^{9/5}) + 32$

Imperial to Metric

Length
in	1 inch	= 2.54 centimeters (cm)
ft	1 foot	= 0.30 meter (m)
yd	1 yard	= 0.91 meter (m)
mi	1 mile	= 1.61 kilometer (km)

Area
ft^2	1 square foot	= 0.09 square meters (m^2)
yd^2	1 square yard	= 0.84 meter (m^2)
ac	1 acre	= 0.40 hectare (ha)

Volume (Dry)
yd^3	1 cubic yard	= 0.76 cubic meter (m^3)
bu	1 bushel	= 36.37 liters (L)

Volume (Liquid)
oz	1 fluid ounce	= 28.41 milliliters (mL)
pt	1 pint	= 0.57 liter (L)
gal	1 gallon (U.S.)	= 3.79 liters (L)
gal	1 gallon	= 4.55 liters (L)

Weight
oz	1 ounce	= 28.35 grams (g)
lb	1 pound	= 453.6 grams (g)
ton	1 ton	= 0.91 ton (t)

Speed
ft/sec	1 foot per second	= 0.30 meters per second (m/sec)
mph	1 mile per hour	= 1.61 kilometers per hour (km/h)

Temperature
°C	degrees Celsius	$= (°F - 32) \times {}^{5/9}$

LIST OF ENTRIES

❖   Denotes sidebar accompanying main entry.

READER'S GUIDE

This list classifies main entries and sidebars into these categories: Applied Anthropology, Archaeology, Biography, Cultural/Social Anthropology, Evolution, Geography/Geology, Linguistics, Paleontology, Philosophy, Psychology, Physical/Biological Anthropology, Religion/Theology, Sociology, Research/Theoretical Frameworks. Some entries may appear in more than one category.

Applied Anthropology

Action anthropology
Aesthetic appreciation
Affirmative action
ALFRED: The ALlele FREquency
    Database
Anthropology and business
Anthropology and the Third
    World
Anthropology, careeers in
Anthropology, clinical
Anthropology, economic
Anthropology, history of
Anthropology, practicing
Anthropology, social
Anthropology, visual
Artificial intelligence
Bioethics and anthropology
Bioinformatics
Biomedicine
Biometrics
Carbon-14 dating
Counseling
Dating techniques
Dating techniques, radiometric
Dating techniques, ralative
Demography
Dendrochronology
Dispute resolution
DNA testing
Ecology and anthropology
Ecology, human behavioral

Economics and anthropology
Environmental ethics
Ethics and anthropology
Ethnoecology
Ethnomedicine
Ethnopharmacology
Ethnopsychiatry
Ethnoscience
Ethnosemantics
Field methods
Forensic anthropology
Forensic artists
Geomagnetism
Health care, alternative
Human rights and
    anthropology
Human rights in the
    global society
Intercultural education
Irrigation
Justice and anthropology
Law and anthropology
Law and society
Medical genetics
Multiculturalism
Museums
Native studies
New dating techniques
Paleomagnetism
Political anthropology
Political economy
Potassium-Argon dating

Rights of indigenous peoples
    today
Tutankhamun and Zahi Hawass
Twin studies
United Nations and
    anthropology
Uranium-Lead dating
Urban anthropology
Urban ecology
Women's studies
Y-STR DNA
Zoos

Archaeology

Abu Simbel
Acheulean culture
Acropolis
Altamira cave
Angkor Wat
Anthropology, history of
Archaeology
Archaeology and
    gender studies
Archaeology, biblical
Archaeology, environmental
Archaeology, maritime
Archaeology, medieval
Archaeology, salvage
Architectural anthropology
Atapuerca
Aurignacian culture
Axes, hand

Linguistics

Paleontology

Crime
Criminology and genetics
Cuba
Cultural convergence
Culture of poverty
Culture shock
Deviance
Durkheim, David Émile
Euthenics
Family, extended
Family, forms of
Family, nuclear
Feminism
Folk culture
Folk speech
Folkways
Friendships
Gangs
Genocide
Gerontology
Globalization
Gypsies
Homosexuality
International organizations
Israel
Labor
Labor, division of
Language use, sociology of
Mark, Karl
Marxism
Midwifery
Nationalism
Peasants
Population explosion
Rank and status
Sex identity
Sex roles
Sexual harassment
Sexuality
Slavery
Social anthropology
Social Darwinism
Social sturctures
Socialization
Societies, class
Societies, complex
Societies, egalitarian
Societies, rank
Societies, secret
Sociobiology

Sociolinguistics
Sociology
Speech, folk
Spencer, Herbert
Subcultures
Untouchables
Urban legends
Women's studies
Xenophobia

Research/Theoretical Frameworks

Alchemy
Alienation
Altruism
Anthropic principle
Anthropocentrism
Anthropology and business
Anthropology and epistemology
Anthropology and sociology
Anthropology of men
Anthropology of religion
Anthropology of women
Anthropology, characteristics of
Anthropology, humanistic
Anthropology, philosophical
Anthropology, subdivisions of
Anthropology, theory in
Anthropomorphism
Ape biogeography
Apollonian
Aquatic ape hypothesis
Arboreal hypothesis
Architectural anthropology
Art, universals in
Artificial life
Big bang theory
Cardiff giant hoax
Catastrophism
Chaos theory
Chaos theory and
   anthropology
Cladistics
Communism
Complexity
Computers and humankind
Configurationalism
Conflict
Cosmology and sacred landscapes
Creationism versus geology
Creationism, beliefs in

Critical realism
Critical realism in ethnology
Cross-cultural research
Cultural conservation
Cultural constraints
Cultural ecology
Cultural relativism
Cultural tree of life
Culture
Culture and pesonality
Culture area concept
Culture change
Culture, characteristics of
Cybernetic modeling
Cybernetics
Darkness in El Dorado
   controversy
Darwinism versus Lamarckism
Darwinism, social
Degenerationism
Determinism
Dictatorships
Diffusionism
Dinosaurian hominid
Education and anthropology
Egyptology
Emics
Enculturation
Enlightenment versus
   postmodernism
Enlightenment, age of
Entelechy
Environmental philosophy
Environments
Ethnocentrism
Ethnogenesis
Ethnohistory
Ethology and ethnology
Etics
Eve, mitochrondrial
Evolutionary anthropology
Evolutionary epistemology
Evolutionary ethics
Evolutionary ontology
Exobiology and exoevolution
Feminism
French structuralism
Functionalism
Future of anthropology
Futurology

EDITORIAL BOARD

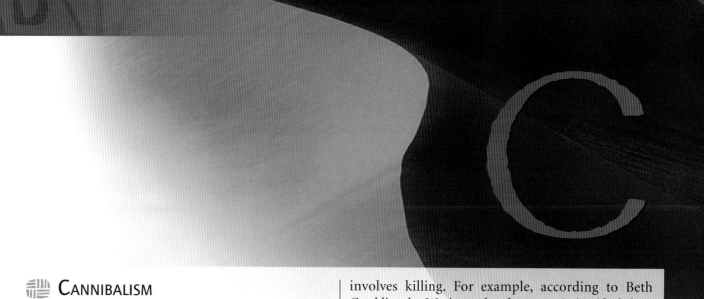

CANNIBALISM

Cannibalism is defined as the ingestion of members of one's own species. As used in zoology, it refers to species that prey on their own kind. In anthropology, it is used specifically to refer to the eating of humans by humans. Around the 16th century in English-speaking countries, the term cannibalism began replacing the Latin-derived term *anthropophagy*. The word *cannibal* is usually traced to the Caribbean and the voyages there of Christopher Columbus. Richard Hakluyt's *Divers Voyages Touching the Discovery of America and the Islands Adjacent* (1582) popularized the word in its English form.

Analytic categories of cannibalism vary. A recent archaeological study used the threefold classification of survival, funerary, and gastronomic cannibalism. Other categories commonly found in the literature, both anthropological and otherwise, include aggression, criminal, epicurean, nutritional, ritual, sexual, spiritual, and, less commonly, medical and autocannibalism.

Anthropologists usually focus on ritual cannibalism and often use the subcategories of *exocannibalism* to refer to the consumption of members from a culturally defined outside group and *endocannibalism* to refer to the consumption of members of one's own group. Hermann Helmuth suggests that exocannibalism was more common among agriculturalists and endocannibalism among foragers. In the folk model, exocannibalism is usually associated with the effort to strike fear in the enemy as well as to absorb the spirit of the enemy, and involves killing. Associated with an effort to maintain the group's identity, endocannibalism is often viewed as showing respect for the deceased. Obviously connected to burial ceremonies and sometimes called "mortuary cannibalism" or "compassionate cannibalism," endocannibalism rarely involves killing. For example, according to Beth Conklin, the Wari people of Amazonia justified their mortuary cannibalism with the belief that when they consumed the corpse, the spirit of the dead was absorbed by the entire tribe.

Cannibalism has a long history, ranging from 5th century BC writings of Herodotus to Bruce Knauft's documentation of three cases of cannibalism between 1978 and 1983 among the Gebusi in south central New Guinea. Probably the first full-scale treatment of cannibalism in English was Garry Hogg's 1958 *Cannibalism and Human Sacrifice*. More journalistic than anthropological, the book, nevertheless, was based on acceptable scholarship and remains a useful survey.

Recently, archaeologists working in the U.S. Southwest have provided incontrovertible evidence of cannibalism. For example, Tim White's extraordinarily meticulous account of cannibalism among the Anasazi in the U.S. Southwest uncovered the cannibalized remains from one site of 17 adults and 12 children. The number of cannibalized remains from other Anasazi sites is expected to exceed 100. Christy Turner and Jacqueline Turner concluded that cannibalism occurred in the Four Corners area for about four centuries, beginning about AD 900. In some Anasazi sites, human proteins have been identified as residues in cooking pots and in human feces. And preserved human waste containing identifiable human tissue was found at an Anasazi site along with osteological evidence of cannibalism.

The Naysayer

William Arens critically reexamined several anthropologically accepted accounts of cannibalism. Although he contended that he was simply investigating the connection between anthropology and cannibalism and not the existence of cannibalism itself, his writings have frequently been read as proposing that ritual cannibalism never existed.

The charge of cannibalism clearly has been used historically to impugn the reputation of certain groups, but Arens's notion that cannibalism is primarily a construction of European colonizers seems a peculiar instance of ethnocentrism; since Europeans did not do it, nobody did it. Unfortunately for Arens's position, Europeans did do it. Peggy Sanday briefly summarized the European medicinal cannibalism that existed from the first until at least the 19th century. And anthropology has never been as obsessively focused on the study of cannibalism, as Arens suggested.

Anthropologists before and after Arens have, indeed, considered the occurrence of cannibalism as quite obvious. One of the most vivid eyewitness accounts of cannibalism was written by Paul P. de La Gironière, from his travel in 1820 among the Western Kalingas of the North Luzon Highlands, also known as the Tinguians. The striking similarities between the details of his writings and the stories told to me by my elderly nonliterate Kalingas about what they had witnessed during their youth and the impossibility of any collusion between La Gironière and my informants convinced me of the truth of ritual exocannibalism among the Kalingas. And as one anthropologist stated, "The case for past cannibalism in parts of Papua New Guinea is no longer an issue for the majority of Melanesian scholars" (Goldman, 1999, p. 19).

Psychological, Symbolic, and Ecological Perspectives

After an exhaustive survey, the psychologist Lewis Petrinovich wrote, "Cannibalism is not a pathology that erupts in psychotic individuals, but is a universal adaptive strategy that is evolutionarily sound. The cannibal is within all of us, and cannibals are within all cultures, should the circumstances demand the appearance" (2000, p. vii). Psychologists offer many theories to explain cannibalism, most of them centering around the notion that the cannibal was overnurtured as an infant. Ethnographic evidence does little to support most of the psychological explanations.

Some of the more convincing symbolic explanations of cannibalism focus on the development of the Eucharist and the doctrine of transubstantiation in Europe in the Middle Ages, seeing in the ritual of ingesting consecrated bread and wine an association with theopagy (consuming the body/flesh of a deity).

While ritual cannibalism has been established beyond question, the origins and causes for the practice remain elusive. Previously ranging from obfuscations and elaborations of folk models to the phantasmagoric notions of psychoanalysis, analytic models were significantly advanced by the introduction of ecological perspectives. For example, Michael Harner famously proposed protein deficiency as the cause of Aztec cannibalism. With the careful reexamination of ethnohistoric accounts, the continuing gathering of ethnographies, and the important contribution of archaeology, anthropology and the public may expect still better explanations of cannibalism.

— *Robert Lawless*

See also **Anasazi; Religious Rituals; Taboos**

Further Readings

Arens, W. (1979). *The man-eating myth: Anthropology and anthropophagy.* New York: Oxford University Press.

Conklin, B. (2001). *Consuming grief: Compassionate cannibalism in an Amazonian society.* Austin: University of Texas Press.

Goldman, L. R. (1999). From pot to polemic: Uses and abuses of cannibalism. In L. R. Goldman (Ed.), *The anthropology of cannibalism* (pp. 1–26). Westport, CT: Bergin & Garvey.

Marlar, R. A., Leonard, L., Banks, L., Billman, B. R., Lambert, P. M., & Marlar, J. E. (2000). Biochemical evidence of cannibalism at a prehistoric Puebloan site in southwestern Colorado. *Nature, 407,* 74–77.

Petrinovich, L. (2000). *The cannibal within.* New York: Aldine de Gruyter.

Price, M. L. (2003). *Consuming passions: The uses of cannibalism in late medieval and early modern Europe.* New York: Routledge.

Turner, C. G. II, & Turner, J. A. (1999). *Man corn: Cannibalism and violence in the prehistoric American Southwest.* Salt Lake City: University of Utah Press.

CARBON-14 DATING

Radiocarbon is the best-known radiometric dating technique due to its successful application to problems in human history and prehistory for over 50 years.

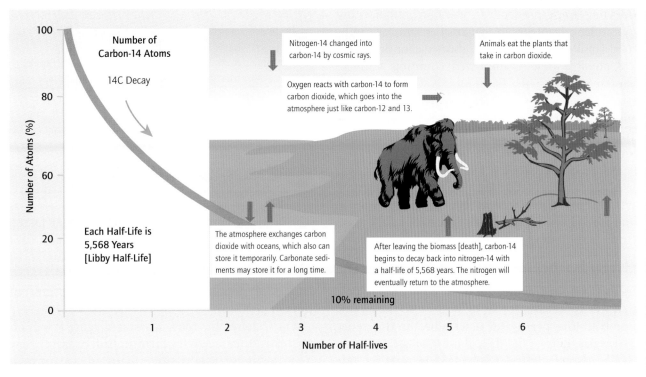

The decay of carbon-14 through 6.64 half-lives or 37,000 years, after which only 1% of the original carbon-14 remains. The production, mixing, and fate of the carbon-14 as part of the carbon cycle is shown in the insert.

Willard Libby's development of the technique in the late 1940s permitted relative time to be sorted radio-metrically in archaeological contexts in a manner that eclipsed the more traditional relative dating methods that had developed over the previous century.

Carbon-14 is a radioactive isotope produced in the upper atmosphere when cosmic rays generate neu-trons as they bombard that outer atmosphere. These neutrons can enter abundant nitrogen-14 nuclei (78% of the atmosphere), converting some of them to carbon-14. The carbon-14 combines with oxygen to form carbon-14 dioxide, which is assimilated by plants and the animals that consume those plants. The carbon-14 production is relatively constant over short periods of time and is in equilibrium with the carbon sinks in the environment (see figure).

The Libby radiometric clock is started when the organic item (animal or plant) dies. The clock is set to "0" at death and begins to tick, with a half-life of 5,568 years. After 5,568 years, one half of the original radio-carbon-14 remains; after 2 × 5568 years, one quarter is left, and so on. There are two methods employed today to determine the amount of radiocarbon remaining in a sample: (1) decay counting, the tradi-tional method, which relies on the decay of carbon-14 to nitrogen-14 with the emission of a beta ray that can be measured in decays per minute per gram and compared with a standard that has a decay rate of 15 decays per minute per gram; and (2) accelerator mass spectrometry (AMS), the atom-counting method, which counts the atoms of radiocarbon-14 in a sample and compares that result with those of a standard.

Libby made a fundamental assumption when he developed his technique. He assumed that the rate of carbon-14 production was constant through time. Subsequently, this assumption was shown to be untrue, but the difficulty could be overcome by insti-tuting a calibration that compared the radiocarbon age of an item with the radiocarbon age of a wood sample of known age. Today this calibration curve is known as the dendrochronological correction curve, and it allows the dated sample's age to be expressed either in calendrical years B.C. (or B.C.E.) or A.D. (or C.E.), or as a conventional radiocarbon-14 age expressed as B.P. (before 1950 in radiocarbon years). Today, there is a convention, not universally accepted, that radiocar-bon-14 dates that have not been dendro-corrected (for example, very old dates [> 40,000], groundwater dates, or atmospheric pollution dates) should be des-ignated with a lowercase bp (before present). AMS does not escape this dendro-correction limitation, but does offer advantages in that smaller samples can be used (milligrams vs. grams); shorter counting times are possible due to improved counting statistics (hours vs. days); the backgrounds associated with cosmic rays, which must be shielded against in the traditional method, are not a factor; and ages up to 70,000 years are measurable because of lower backgrounds and greater counting statistics.

A further complication in some kinds of materials used for radiocarbon dating is the issue of the natural introduction of old carbon into living organisms in and around oceans, due to the presence of old carbon from carbonate sources and upwelling water. A marine correction can be made for this effect in parts of the world where the offset is known. The standard method for determining this offset is to date a sample that was collected prior to 1950 (prior to the atomic bomb testing peak) and determine the difference between actual age and the radiocarbon age.

The two analytical methods exist side by side today, each having a specific market niche. While AMS may be preferred when samples are small or high precision dates (errors of less than 60 years) are required, the traditional beta decay method provides, at a reasonable price, perfectly acceptable results when sample size or high precision are not an issue. Not all laboratories are equal throughout the world, and *caveat emptor* should be kept in mind when choosing a lab from which to obtain results, for there exist those that are good, bad, and ugly. Surprisingly, this state of affairs has more to do with the chemistry of sample preparation, which varies greatly from lab to lab, than it does with either the AMS or decay systems themselves. There are slightly fewer than 100 active traditional radiocarbon dating labs throughout the world and more than two dozen AMS labs.

— *L. A. Pavlish*

See also **Dating Techniques; Dating Techniques, Radiometric; Dating Techniques, Relative; Libby, Willard**

Further Readings

Bennett, C. L., Beukens, R. P., Clover, M. R., Elmore, D., Gove, H. E., Kilius, L., et al. (1978). Radiocarbon dating with electrostatic accelerators: Dating of milligram samples. *Science, 201,* 345–347.

Libby, W. F. (1955). *Radiocarbon dating.* Chicago: University of Chicago Press.

Pavlish, L. A., & Banning, E. B. (1980). Revolutionary developments in carbon-14 dating. *American Antiquity, 45*(2), 290–296.

 ## CARDIFF GIANT HOAX

The Cardiff Giant hoax involved a large stone figure, advertised as a petrified giant man. The Giant is of anthropological interest both as a classic example of a hoax and as a source of insight regarding the interaction of popular and scientific conceptions of human prehistory.

On October 16, 1869, workers digging a well on William "Stub" Newell's farm outside Cardiff, New York, exhumed a gray stone figure of a giant man with contorted limbs and a serene facial expression. According to a contemporary advertisement, the Giant was 10' 4.5" (about 3.2 m) long and weighed 2,990 pounds (about 1,350 kg). Newell exhibited the Giant, charging 50¢ admission, for 2 weeks, and then sold a majority interest in it to a syndicate of businessmen from nearby Syracuse, where the Giant began to be exhibited on November 5. The Giant was of commercial benefit both to its exhibitors and to the city itself, which profited from the tourist trade.

Opinions about the Giant's provenance were divided. The popular view, encouraged by its exhibitors, was that it was a petrified giant, possibly one of the giants described in the Bible (for example, Genesis 1:6). It was sometimes called "the American Goliath," after the Philistine giant in Samuel 1:17. Scientific investigators, however, disagreed for a variety of reasons. The Giant was composed of gypsum, a soft stone that would not hold details for long when buried in wet soil; it displayed soft tissues, such as skin and muscle, which are incapable of petrifaction; and it appeared to bear the mark of sculpting tools. A minority thought that the Giant was a genuine ancient statue; most, including paleontologist O. C. Marsh and Andrew Dickson White, the president of Cornell University, regarded it as a recent hoax. Despite the opinion of the experts, the public remained fascinated by the Giant.

In December 1869, George Hull, a cousin of Newell's, admitted that he had commissioned the sculpting of the Giant and conspired with Newell to perpetrate the hoax. Motivated by a conversation with a Methodist minister who insisted on the literal truth of the Bible, including the stories about giants, Hull sought to expose—after profiting from—the gullibility of the religious. His admission was corroborated by the testimony of the sculptors. Not everyone was convinced, however; the Reverend Alexander McWhorter insisted, despite Hull's confession, that the Giant was a Phoenician statue.

The Giant remained popular after the hoax was exposed, spending the 1870s touring throughout New York, Pennsylvania, and New England. In New York City, during the winter of 1869 to 1970, it was in competition with a duplicate commissioned by P. T. Barnum, who advertised his as the "original" Cardiff Giant. (Barnum and Hull later collaborated on a similar hoax, "The Solid Muldoon," in Colorado.) As interest in the Giant dwindled, it changed hands a number of times; it is now on display at the Farmers' Museum in Cooperstown, New York.

Among the literary works inspired by the hoax are Mark Twain's "A Ghost Story" (1870), A. M. Drummond and Robert E. Gard's play *The Cardiff Giant* (1939), and Harvey Jacob's novel *American Goliath* (1997).

— *Glenn Branch*

See also **Hoaxes in Anthropology**

Further Readings

Dunn, J. T. (1948). *The true, moral, and diverting tale of The Cardiff Giant, or, The American Goliath.* Cooperstown, NY: Farmers' Museum.

Feder, K. L. (2002). *Frauds, myths, and mysteries: Science and pseudoscience in archaeology* (4th ed.). Boston: McGraw-Hill.

Franco, B. (1990). *The Cardiff Giant: A hundred year old hoax.* Cooperstown, NY: New York State Historical Association.

 CARIBS

The Caribs are a group of native peoples in the Lesser Antilles, after whom the Caribbean Sea was named. They are thought to have originated in the Orinoco River Basin of Venezuela and spread northward into the Antillean chain of islands. They spoke languages in the Carib family indigenous to South America, which are now widespread across northern South America from the mouth of the Amazon River to the Colombian Andes. The 29 living Carib languages are divided into a northern branch (21 languages) and a southern branch (8 languages). Some common words used in English were borrowed from the Carib language, such as *hammock, iguana,* and *hurricane* (after the Carib god of evil).

Archaeology suggests that pottery-making horticulturalists of South American origin spread from the mainland into the Lesser Antilles around 500 BC. These early Caribbean peoples are known from their distinctive Saladoid pottery, named after the Saladero site in Venezuela, some of which is intricately designed and decorated. They also brought with them crops for cultivation; the primary crop was cassava (also known as tapioca or manioc), a major staple for Amerindian groups, and various animals such as the dog, hutia, and the guinea pig (the latter of which is currently known only from Puerto Rico). These early settlements consisted of smaller villages and were largely focused on the coastlines. Research indicates that native groups incorporated both marine (for example, shellfish, turtle, fish) and terrestrial (for example, lizards, land crabs, birds) foods into the diet. Carib-speaking peoples continued to occupy the Lesser Antilles up until European contact and, according to some historical accounts, apparently killed, displaced, or forcibly assimilated with the Arawakan peoples who inhabited islands in the northern Caribbean, but who also originated from South America.

According to some of these same European accounts, the Caribs were aggressive, warlike, and cannibalistic. In fact, the English word *cannibal* comes from the Spanish *caníbalis,* which was recorded by Christopher Columbus from the earlier Carib word *karibna,* meaning "person." Although some Native Americans and other peoples around the world were known to practice cannibalism, Columbus's characterization of the Carib as eaters of human flesh probably reflected his and general European desire to represent them as savages: In 1503, Queen Isabella of Spain ruled that only cannibals could be legally taken as slaves, which encouraged Europeans to identify various Native American groups as cannibals.

Source: © iStockphoto/Regina Alvares.

The 1748 Treaty of Aix-la-Chapelle, between Britain and France, settled on control of the Lesser Antilles. Because of the formidable resistance mounted by the indigenous Caribs on the islands of Dominica and St. Vincent, they were left as "neutral" islands. This treaty was violated first by the French and later by the British, who obtained possession in 1783 and drove the existing Carib population to the mountains and Atlantic coasts.

In 1797, almost the entire population of 5,000 or more Caribs on St. Vincent were forcibly removed from the island by British troops and banished to Roatan Island, off the coast of Honduras. The Garifunas of Belize are their direct descendants today. The remaining Caribs on St. Vincent were allocated 233 acres by the British government for their subsistence. In Dominica, the Caribs lost control of their lands but were not forced to migrate. By 1764, the Caribs had jurisdiction over just 232 acres, in a remote area called Salybia on the east coast of Dominica.

In 1903, the British government, on recommendation of the British administrator, Sir Heskeith Bell, expanded the Carib reservation to 3,700 acres in northeast Dominica and officially called it the Carib Reserve. This was a paltry gesture by the government, considering that it amounted to only about 2% of the Caribs' original land on the island. The declaration that established the reserve officially recognized the authority of the Carib chief, but he was not given actual control of the area. Today, the Carib Reserve in Dominica is the only one of its kind in the Caribbean and has a population of around 2,700 people. Although it has helped the Carib community to maintain its own identity, the loss of language, cultural traditions, and lifeways as a result of European domination has severely impacted the Carib peoples.

— *Scott M. Fitzpatrick*

Further Readings

Farnsworth, P. (Ed.). (2001). *Island lives: Historical archaeologies of the Caribbean.* Tuscaloosa: University of Alabama Press.

Hulme, P., & Whitehead, N. L. (Eds.). (1992). *Wild majesty: Encounters with Caribs from Columbus to the present day: An anthology.* Oxford: Oxford University Press.

Wilson, S. M. (Ed.). (1997). *The indigenous people of the Caribbean.* Gainesville: University Press of Florida.

CARPENTER, C. R. (1905–1975)

During the 1930s, C. Ray Carpenter carried out the first modern studies of free-ranging primates. In its scope, duration, systematic data collection, and revelations about the naturalistic behavior of primates, his research went far beyond all previous studies, such as those by Bingham, Nissen, Zuckerman, and Marais. Although his 1931 doctoral dissertation was on the behavior of pigeons in captivity, he immediately switched to field research on free-ranging primates. Over the next decade, in Central America, Southeast Asia, and the Caribbean, he carried out landmark field studies of howler monkeys, spider monkeys, gibbons, and rhesus macaques. The rhesus were on Cayo Santiago, a small island off Puerto Rico, in a colony established in the late 1930s with monkeys that Carpenter shipped from India. In the years since then, that colony has been the subject of research by many scientists.

After completing his doctorate with Calvin Stone at Stanford (1931), Carpenter began his primate field studies under a 3-year postdoctoral appointment to Robert Yerkes's laboratory at Yale. Thereafter, he had professorial appointments in psychology at Columbia University (1934–1940) and in both psychology and anthropology, first at Pennsylvania State University (1940–1970), then at University of Georgia (1970–1975).

Although Carpenter was trained in psychology, his primate studies included a diversity of topics more characteristic of biology, including demography, manipulation and locomotion, foraging, ranging and territoriality, sexual behavior, mother-infant relationships, competition and cooperation, agonistic behavior, dominance relations, vocalization and communication, and grooming and play.

His field methods were essentially those of a descriptive naturalist, as he observed representative samples of populations on-site in their natural habitats and made accurate and detailed reports of his observations. He made several important contributions to the methodology of primate field studies, including (a) censusing groups as they progressed single file instead of when they were congregated; (b) breaking the complexity of ongoing interactions in a group into their more readily observed components, dyadic relationships; (c) gradually habituating animals to his presence and remaining at a distance at which he could observe them without undue disturbance; (d) taking advantage of available technology, including photography, sound recording, and playback equipment; (e) making objective records of behavior, often quantitative and checked when possible by repeated observation; and (f) taking representative samples, not just of the dramatic or unusual.

Carpenter was adamant about the potential of observational field studies to conform to the same canons of science that characterized laboratory research, including accuracy of records, adequate sampling, and data that permit "comprehensive description, measurement, interpretation and even prediction." He was interested in theoretical frameworks that might have the potential to encompass the complexities of primate social processes, and in his search for unifying principles, he turned, at various times, to sociometry, semiotics, mathematical models, design features of language, dominance hierarchies, homeostasis, and cybernetic functionalism.

In five articles published in 1942 (two), 1952, 1954, and 1958, respectively, Carpenter featured his generalizations about primate grouping and social processes. These eclectic articles include many revelatory statements. Here is a small sample, rearranged and edited for brevity. Most are from Carpenter's two earlier reviews, emphasizing his prescience and eclecticism, which went well beyond that of his contemporaries.

For the complete description of a group, each of the $N(N-1)/2$ paired interactions among N individuals should be minutely described and measured for a number of different characteristics. . . . The strength of the attachment between two individuals may be judged, or actually measured, by observing for a period of time the average distance which separates the two animals. (1942a)

A basic fact for primate societies is that all the individuals in a group are capable of perceiving and discriminating all the other individuals in the group and react discriminatively toward them. (1952)

A universal characteristic is that all social relations are, in varying degrees, reciprocal. . . . A relatively high degree of interdependence in natural groupings of primates is an important characteristic of their social life. Perhaps such expressions as mutual aid, altruism, cooperation, and social service are too anthropomorphic in connotation, and thus may becloud the actual relationships, by provoking controversy. (1942a)

Charles Darwin and many natural historians following him have so emphasized "the struggle for existence" and competition that the facts of interdependence in animal societies have not been accurately and fully represented. As a result, the formulated theories and principles of social behavior are faulty, since they are build on inadequate factual bases. . . . The survival and reproduction of groups of monkeys of a species depend on the social coordination—one may say cooperation—of all the individuals of the group. (1942b)

The monkey or ape in its natural group in the tropical forest has its freedom of movement strictly limited by the structure of its group. (1942a)

The ratio of adult males and females in a group seems to express a balance between the summed female sex needs or capacities in a group and the sexual capacities of the effective males available to satisfy the needs. (1942a)

Individuals in free-ranging organized groups deploy themselves in space in inverse relation to the strength of centripetal (cohesive) interactions and in direct proportion to the strength of centrifugal interactions. (1952, 1954)

There is no question but that groups of monkeys and apes are organized around several dominance gradients (1942b). . . . However, when multimale-multifemale groupings of monkeys and apes are observed under "free-range" conditions and for long periods of time, rarely if ever does one male have complete priority to all incentives at all times (1952). . . . Also, measures of dominance show wide individual variations in the magnitude of dominance, a variation which is not accurately indicated by describing an order of priority or general relative aggressiveness. (1942a)

In a concerted attack on the group, individuals may be killed, but this is incidental to the fact that the group survives and the species is perpetuated. (1942b)

In the years after completing his investigations of sexual behavior on the rhesus of Cayo Santiago, Carpenter's research was devoted primarily to educational films and television. He produced several documentary films on free-ranging primates, recensused the howler monkeys on Barro Colorado, and wrote several reviews of behavior in free-ranging primates. In 1971, Carpenter undertook his last fieldwork. He collaborated with José Delgado and others in their study of gibbons on Hall's Island, Bermuda. The object of the study was to induce lasting modifications of free-ranging behavior by means of remote, long-term stimulation of the brain.

Starting in the mid-1950s, research on free-ranging primates has been doubling about every 5 years, much faster than science as a whole, which doubles every 15 years. By comparison, at the time of Carpenter's early investigations, in the 1930s, no one else was actively engaged in such studies. Under the circumstances, his accomplishments are remarkable.

— *Stuart A. Altmann*

See also **Field Methods; Primate Behavioral Ecology**

Further Readings

Carpenter, C. R. (1964). *Naturalistic behavior of nonhuman primates.* University Park: Pennsylvania State University. [Note: Carpenter's major primate field study reports and several reviews are reprinted in this volume]

Haraway, D. (1983). Signs of dominance: From a physiology to a cybernetics of primate society, C. R., Carpenter, 1930–1970. *Studies in the History of Biology, 6,* 129–219.

Montgomery, G. M. (in press). Place, practice, and primatology: Clarence Ray Carpenter, primate communication and the development of field methodology, 1931–1945. *Journal of the History of Biology.*

Rawlins, R. G., & Kessler, M. J. (Eds.). (1986). *The Cayo Santiago macaques: History, behavior, and biology.* Albany NY: State University of New York.

CARSON, RACHEL (1907–1964)

The mother of the 20th-century environmentalist movement, Rachel Carson shed light upon the scientific as well as philosophical misconceptions embraced by Western society about humanity's relationship with the ecosystem. During an era in which the practices of science went almost unquestioned, Carson made known to all the hazardous effects of pesticides in her then-controversial book *Silent Spring* (1962). Not only did Carson spur the prohibition of such indiscriminate "biocides" as DDT (dichloro-diphenyl-trichloroethene), but even more awesome was the birth of the environmentalist movement that followed. Carson showed the world the true nature of our roles as participants within a delicate and intricate ecosystem.

Carson was foremost a writer and originally envisioned herself as an English major at Pennsylvania College for Women (PCW) (now Chatham College). She also held a strong love and interest for biology, which stemmed from her childhood in Springdale, Pennsylvania. There, she would accompany her mother on many of her bird-watches and nature studies along the Allegheny River. In school, with the support of a professor, she eventually switched her major to zoology. After completing her degree at PCW, she went on to receive her master's degree from Johns Hopkins University (1932) and soon after discovered her adoration for the sea, studying at Woods Hole Biological Laboratory and Johns Hopkins.

She began her career as a radio scriptwriter for the Bureau of Fisheries in 1935 (which became the U.S. Fish and Wildlife Service in 1939) and was given permanent appointment as junior aquatic biologist the following year. She held one of two professional positions occupied by a woman at the agency.

She published her first book, *Under the Sea-Wind*, in 1941, which entailed the story of a sea bird's arduous migratory journey from Patagonia to the Arctic Circle. It received great critical acclaim, but little public attention due to the ensuing World War II.

Carson became the editor in chief by 1949 of all publications put out by the agency and participated in major conferences regarding the latest scientific and technological developments. Slowed by her increased responsibilities with the agency, Carson published *The Sea Around Us* in 1951, 10 years following her first book. The book discussed the latest research in oceanography and earned Carson overwhelming critical acclaim as well as literary vogue. Her newly gained celebrity status made her following book, *The Edge of the Sea* (1955), an unsurprising best seller. Her literary popularity came from her ability to translate copious amounts of scientific information into lyrical prose that could appeal to the public eye.

Carson also had a secondary project she had been working on, dealing with the persistent ecological damage caused by the misuse of pesticides. She

submitted an article about the observed dangers of pesticides to 15 journals and periodicals, including *Reader's Digest* and *National Geographic*, and was rejected by all. Finally, *The New Yorker* recognized the importance of her work and serialized *Silent Spring* in 1962. Well before *Silent Spring* was published, Carson made her ecological campaign well-known and accordingly received abundant threats from not only pesticide corporations but colleagues as well. The threats proved futile against Carson's everlasting ardor for ecology.

Silent Spring and Carson's later testimonies before Congress challenged the government's approval of certain nonspecific pesticide usage and conveyed the uniquely ecological idea that humanity was just as susceptible to the hazards of pollution as any other element of the ecosystem. Just having ended World War II and with the advent of the Cold War, Western society was fixated upon the potentials of science and technology. This awe of industrial science heralded an ecological view of humanity as a controlling figure over nature, growing more and more omnipotent with every discovery and breakthrough. Carson humbled these sophisms with startling data about the affects of manmade pollutants on the ecosystem as well as the human body. Her work led directly to the prohibition of DDT and several other nonspecific "biocides" (a word she coined).

Prior to Carson, the field of ecology held little scholarly recognition for its broader take on the processes of the environment. Carson's writings not only gave the science scholarly legitimacy but also popularized it among the masses. So recognized were her writings that they inspired the beginnings of the modern environmentalist movement, which evaluates environmental issues from an ecological view. The significance of her work to humankind was monumental in presenting controversial concepts that today seem common sense to a generation born into an environmentally aware society. Rachel Carson was not the first to notice the encroaching dangers of our ecological malpractices, but she was the first to successfully and comprehensibly convey her concerns to a society too self-infatuated to notice on its own.

— *Andrew P. Xanthopoulos*

See also **Ecology and Anthropology**

Further Readings

Carson, R. (1989). *The sea around us* (Special ed.). New York: Oxford University Press.

Carson, R. (1998). *The sense of wonder.* (Reprint ed.). New York: HarperCollins.

Carson, R. (2002). *Silent spring* (40th anniv. ed.). New York: First Mariner Books.

Lear, L. (1997). *Rachel Carson: Witness for nature.* New York: Henry Holt.

CARTER, HOWARD (1874–1939)

There have been a number of momentous findings as a result of consistent and diligent archaeology efforts. However, certainly one of the most impressive and important of those findings is the excavation relating to the tomb of Tutankhamun due to the energetic efforts of Howard Carter, an individual who not only discovered a historical entity of great magnitude but also taught us lessons about the importance of continuing efforts to uncover the past in order to inform the present and future.

Howard Carter had an interesting background, which may have impelled him to his adult profession

Source: Courtesy of the Lear/Carson Collection, Connecticut College.

as an archeologist. He was born in a small town in Kensington, London, England, the son of a father who was an artist who specialized in animal paintings. Perhaps his father did influence him with this background, but the son who was later to become internationally famous found himself at the relatively young age of 17 going to Egypt, where he was hired to help record information about tombs. In 1900, he was appointed Chief Inspector of Antiquities to the Egyptian government for Upper Egypt, but a short time later, in 1904, took on another responsibility as Chief Inspector for Lower Egypt. In 1909, he became associated with the Earl of Carnarvon, who decided to finance some archeological work, and Carter was given the chance to again pursue his professional interests. His efforts in unearthing the famous Tomb of Tutankhamun followed the beginning of his association with the Earl of Carnavon and became perhaps became the crown jewel of his professional success.

We have much for which to thank this great archeologist by the name of Howard Carter. He has contributed lasting rewards about a subject that remains of immense interest to people throughout the world. Obviously, his findings have also increased knowledge about a time that few of us know a great deal. Of course, there is also a lesson that all of us can learn from Howard Carter no matter what our intellectual pursuit may be, and it is that diligent, persistent effort often does have its rewards.

— *William E. Kelly*

See also **Egypt, Ancient; Egyptology**

Further Readings

Ford, B. (1995). *Searching for King Tut.* New York: W. H. Freeman.

James, T.G. H. (2001). *Howard Carter: The path to Tutankhamun.* Cairo: American University in Cairo Press.

Reeves, N., & Taylor, J. H. (1993). *Howard Carter: Before Tutankhamun.* New York: Abrams.

Winstone, H. V. F. (1991). *Howard Carter and the discovery of the tomb of Tutankhamun.* London: Constable.

CASTE SYSTEMS

The term *caste* comes from the Portugese *casta* (breed, lineage) and was coined by Portuguese travelers to India in reference to the social, economic, and religious system they witnessed. The traditional Hindu term is *varna,* and its earliest meanings include color, covering, tribe, and species. The caste system is easily the most controversial aspect of the Hindu tradition. It is defended as a religious expression of one's progression toward liberation or as a formalized division of labor. Alternatively, it is condemned as a form of systematized oppression and racism. Either way, it generates emotional and rhetorical assertions on both sides of the discussion.

The first mention of the fourfold division of society that serves as the basis of the system is found in the Rig Veda, one of the most ancient and sacred of the Hindu holy writings. The earliest elucidation of the system appears in the *Laws of Manu,* the authoritative law book (3rd century BCE–3rd century CE) that sets forth the duties and restrictions for members of each *varna.* For orthodox Hindus, this text remains the ultimate authority in most caste matters. In addition to varna, there are several additional subcategories in the system, especially *jati* and *gotra.* Each category influences aspects of the lives of its members. Taken together, they have traditionally predetermined, to a large extent, almost every facet of the lives of Hindus in India.

Varna (caste)

It is uncertain as to when one's varna became determined by birth rather than occupation and role in the society. However, in early writings claiming to contain the words and teaching of the Buddha, already there are criticisms of the system and of deciding one's worth based on birth rather than actions. Nevertheless, once birth became the primary, or even sole, determinant, and caste became a closed group, it also came to determine, for the most part, one's occupation and possibilities for economic advancement, one's sphere of association and access to social involvement, one's marriage choices, and finally one's place in the developing religious hierarchy and access to religious activities and rituals.

The ancient system divided society into four varnas. The *Brahmin* was the priestly and learned caste. The duty of its members was to teach the others knowledge and wisdom and to oversee and lead the religious life of the community. The warrior and rule caste was called *Kshatriya.* The duties of its members were to protect and rule, in order to maintain a safe and stable society. The *Vaisya* were the agriculturalists and merchants. They grew and provided food and other necessities to the community. The lowest caste was the *Shudra,* which consisted of the laborers and servants. Their duty was to serve the other castes by doing all the menial and difficult physical tasks. Eventually, a fifth caste was added, the *Panchama,* or *Antyaja,* the "Untouchable." Members of this caste were actually placed outside the system *(avarna),* either because of alleged transgressions made against established rules of conduct or because of the defiling nature of their occupations. Their duties involved cleaning up after all the other castes and undertaking those tasks that were too impure and polluting for the others castes to perform.

Thus, of the five castes, only members of the upper four are considered varna Hindu. Of the four, only the upper three are called "twice-born." This term comes from a rite of passage ritual available to their male members, which qualifies them to learn Sanskrit, study the sacred scriptures, and participate in Vedic rituals. The mark of this status is the donning of the sacred thread, known as *yagyapavitra* or *janeu.* Of the three twice-born castes, the upper two are called "high caste," and some religious rituals and institutions have been limited to their male members only.

The religious justification for varna is closely tied to the concept of transmigration of the soul. It is based in the belief that the individual soul experiences countless lifetimes in its path to enlightenment and that one's birth in the present life is a direct consequence of knowledge gained and karma accrued from previous lives. Thus, one who has lived many lifetimes and has advanced on the path toward wisdom and enlightenment will be born into a higher caste, while a soul that is not as far along the path or that has accrued appreciable negative karma from past bad actions will be born into a lower caste. Therefore, the varna into which one is born reflects the dominant qualities of the individual, with those born into the higher castes having more positive and refined qualitites and characteristics, while those born into the lower castes have more base, negative, and unrefined characteristics.

Jati (subcaste)

The true functional unit of the caste system for everyday life in India is the *jati,* or subcaste, of which there are literally thousands. The development of individual jatis over the millennia is the result of many factors, including the assimilation of foreign groups who migrated to India in sufficient numbers to create their own communities, as well as the development of new religious sects that would also form their own endogamous communities. Primarily, however, jati formation seems to have been occupational. When a particular craft was developed, those families whose members focused on performing the skill would typically come to be identified with it, and eventually a new subcaste would form within the larger caste structure. In many ways, this development mimicked that of the European guild system, in which artisans and craftsman formed associations based on their specific skills and specializations. Because each craftsman tended to teach his skill to his offspring, one's craft was often the result of birth. In a similar fashion, jati, like varna, apparently began as a division of artisan professions but ended up a birth determined category. The elaboration of jatis brought with it the development of reciprocal relationships between the various subcastes, both within a particular varna as well as between them. The common Indian term used to refer to the system of occupational and reciprocal interrelationships is the *jajmani* system. Although there was a great proliferation of jatis, mostly within the merchant and servant castes, there was very little change in their status within the overall caste hierarchy. With exceptions, jatis within a caste have generally existed on a horizontal relationship with each other, as opposed to a vertical one.

Although many no longer pursue their traditional crafts, jatis continue to exist with their own distinctive customs, rules, and internal structural hierarchy. While there has always been, for various reasons, some degree of intermarriage between jatis in the same varna, they have tended to remain endogamous, which keeps the relationships of the members close-knit. Jatis are typically controlled by local and regional caste organizations and boards, or *panchayat*s, and leaders tend to have a great deal of influence in the internal functioning of the group and the activities of its members. For example, when Mahatma Gandhi wished to travel to England to get a law degree, his local subcaste leaders forbade him to do so. In his day, there was a religious restriction against crossing the ocean, since it was believed that one would not be able to adhere to purity rules on the journey. Gandhi went against the prohibition and was ostracized from his jati.

Gotra

Each jati is made up of multiple *gotra*s. A gotra (literally, cowshed) is a patrilineal clan group that claims ancestral lineage to famous ancient figures. Brahmin gotras, for example, trace their ancestry to one of eight sages believed to have been connected to portions of the Vedas, the ancient Hindu scriptures. Initially, the only varna that had gotra was Brahmin, but eventually all castes, nearly all jatis, and even Jains, adopted the tradition. Today, gotras number in the thousands, and some jatis have up to 100 or more.

Gotras are also important aspects of identity. In some, male members would wear distinctive garb or hairstyle to distinguish themselves from other gotras. Various orthodox rituals, especially rites of passage, require both name and gotra identification of the beneficiary as a part of the preparatory rites. When a jati panchayat meets, a member or leader of each gotra is supposed to be represented. When one has a dispute with another member of the same jati in a village, it is often the gotra heads who will be called upon to mediate. In some jatis, decisions by gotra heads carry the weight of law and are rarely disputed.

Because gotras are viewed as extended families, they are exogamous. Marriage, then, occurs within one's jati, but outside one's gotra. Like last name, a female adopts the gotra of her husband. Most jatis strictly prohibit marriage within one's gotra but allow marriage to a member of any other gotra within the jati. One of the only added limitations for most jatis is between offspring of a brother and sister, even though the children are of different gotra.

Caste as Indian, Caste as Hindu

There has been an ongoing debate for several decades on the role of caste in India, as opposed to caste in Hinduism. This is because caste can be found in non-Hindu religious traditions in the country as well. Although many will not admit it, caste plays a role in Buddhism, Islam, and Christianity in India. It is true that it is a holdover from caste consciousness among Hindus, but it has clearly become a reality in those traditions. At the same time, Hinduism outside of India is essentially caste free. Thus, caste as a social hierarchy and ranking has become more endemic to the land than to the religious tradition. For those who are against caste, this is both positive and negative. It is positive in that it shows that Hinduism can exist without caste, but it is negative in that it suggests that India may not be able to exist without it, at least rural India.

Caste in Modern India

The varna system continues to have its supporters, especially in the rural areas, especially those at the top of the hierarchy. They see it as necessary for social stability and for the maintenance of traditional values and institutions. At the same time, those who defend the system generally acknowledge that the long-standing and inherent prejudice against avarna Hindus should be removed. They envision a system that returns to one based strictly on a division of labor. The problem here is that occupational exclusivity of subcastes has been dying away since the 19th century. Some of the only professions that remain primarily caste or subcaste restricted include the work of priests at the top and most avarna occupations at the bottom. Those at the bottom of the system, on the other hand, see nothing positive in it at all. While the occupational elements of the system are ending, the inherent social prejudices connected with it are more resistant to change.

Diaspora Hinduism and Caste

In the early 1800s, the British government began the system of indentured servitude, whereby it sent more than one million impoverished, primarily rural, Indians to work British plantations in the Caribbean, Fiji, Mauritius, and South Africa, creating the Hindu Diaspora. The vast majority of Hindus who participated were from Shudra or Untouchable families and did so both for economic as well as social reasons. They sought to craft a new life for themselves in their new lands, and they left caste identity behind in the process. Consequently, Diaspora Hinduism is essentially caste free. Not only has this not hurt the practice of Hinduism in Diaspora lands, but it has benefited it in many ways. The intercaste tension and discrimination that seems natural and commonplace does not exist, and this allows Hindus in those lands to more freely interact, intermarry, and work together toward common goals.

Challenges to Caste

Ever since the early days of the development of Buddhism, more than two millennia ago, there has been criticism or the caste system. Buddha himself is said to have rejected the system for his followers. Nearly all the founders of new religious movements since that time, especially devotional movements, have echoed the Buddha's call for rejection of caste. Yet it persists. However, as Indian society is becoming more urban, adopting Western-style education and social values, the caste system is becoming less and less relevant. In the larger cities, socioeconomic class has become the basis for the hierarchy, and it appears that a similar pattern will eventually occur in villages as well. Nevertheless, the varna system still has a great deal of influence in India even though the original purpose of the system has been lost. For the most part, all that remains is a purposeless hierarchical structure that continues to keep those on top in power and those at the bottom relatively powerless.

— *Ramdas Lamb*

See also **Buddhism**

Further Readings

Kolenda, P. (1981). *Caste, cult, and hierarchy.* Merrut, India: Folklore Institute.

Sharma, K. L. (1986). *Caste, class, and social movements.* Jaipur, India: Rawat.

Zinkin, T. (1962). *Caste today.* London: Oxford University Press.

 # CATASTROPHISM

The principle of catastrophism states that all of the Earth's surface features and topography were produced by a few great catastrophes throughout history. These catastrophes were thought to have been so enormous in scale that no ordinary process could have initiated and supernatural forces had to be invoked. However, this was the philosophy of scientists in the 17th and 18th centuries, whereas the modern understanding of the principal relies very little on biblical providence. Not only were these land-altering catastrophes believed to be the fabricators of all the mountains, valleys, seas, and deserts, but the original catastrophism concept also implies that they need to have occurred in the relatively recent history so that they would fit the scriptural chronology of the Bible. The contemporary concept of catastrophism now allows for its rival principal, uniformitarianism, to overlap and combine to form a more accurate portrait of geologic change. Although the slow, uniform processes that operate in an almost regular, cyclic manner are responsible for most of the geology we observe on the planet, improbable and unique catastrophic events can and have radically altered this path of slow change.

When geologists study the vast extent of time recorded in the rock layers, evidence for catastrophes that would be improbable in the span of human history becomes highly abundant in the nearly 4.6 billion year history of the Earth. Evidence for such great catastrophes includes giant meteor impact craters from large bolide objects that have impacted the planet. This caused the vaporization and upheaval of large portions of land and earth that then fraught the atmosphere with accumulated soot and covered the earth, choking out the sunlight and slowly raining back down to earth. Another example would be huge volcanoes that have belched enormous amounts of noxious gas and dust into the atmosphere. It's easy to see how calamities such as these created havoc and instantly, in terms of geologic time, forced the extinction of entire ecosystems and many forms of life on Earth. Such events would assuredly bring about global change and permanently affect the course of geology and speciation on the planet. However, when catastrophism was first proposed as a singular reason for all the variety of land forms we see on Earth today, there was no evidence, aside from biblical accounts, for any such devastation having occurred. In the 17th century, there was little reason to worry about this void, simply because the secular view and the spiritual view of Earth were one and the same.

The leading champion, defender, and primary composer of the principle of catastrophism was Baron Georges Leopold Chretien Frederic Dagobert Cuvier (1769–1832). The French Cuvier was one of the leading geologists of his time, the foremost pioneer of comparative anatomy, as well the father to an entire branch of geology known as *vertebrate paleontology*. Although he did not accept evolution, but rather favored catastrophism, Cuvier was the first to authoritatively insist that species can go and have gone extinct. His high esteem in scientific society allowed Cuvier to suppress opposition to catastrophism while he was alive. He believed that the Earth was extremely old and that the conditions had changed relatively little since its formation; however, periodic "revolutions" would disturb the harmony and cause all of the changes we see in the fossil record. Living at the time he did, Cuvier was familiar with "revolutions," whereas he disliked the term *catastrophism* because of its supernatural distinction. Although he was a lifelong member of the Protestant church, Cuvier never identified any of his "revolutions" with acts described in the Bible. He regarded the turnovers as events with natural causes, but considered their causes a mystery and a geologic puzzle. Many later geologists, including the famous Rev. William Buckland from England, concluded from Cuvier's work that the most recent "revolution" must have been the biblical flood. This hypothesis was enjoyed until a former protégé of Cuvier, Luis Agassiz, determined that the "flood deposits" were actually glacial deposits from the last Ice Age. Cuvier's impact on geology, and science as a whole, can never be overestimated. Cuvier brought catastrophism to its height in the annals of science, where another student of his, Léonce Élie de Beaumont, carried it to nearly the end of the 19th century.

The harsh lack of evidence for these catastrophes has plagued the theory from its conception. The paradigm of uniformity held from 1850 to 1980, as most geologists supported catastrophism's rival, uniformitarianism, largely due to the lack of verifiable, concrete evidence for sudden devastation on a global scale. A dinosaur paleontologist named Walter Alvarez helped forge the ideas of uniformitarianism and catastrophism into the modern synthesis that is learned today. Alvarez was curious about a distinct clay layer a rough centimeter thick at Gubbio, Italy. The layer was highly enriched with a rare noble metal Iridium, which is normally completely absent from the crust of the Earth. This layer appeared nearly everywhere at what is known as the *KT boundary*. This boundary marks the demise of the dinosaurs 65 million years ago at the end of the Mesozoic and can be identified at over 50 separate locations on Earth. The source of such a concentration of this element could only be from the Earth's core or from a cosmic source such as a meteor. Alvarez eventually determined that the layer was created from an impact of a 10 km asteroid that accompanied the extinction of the dinosaurs. Soon after this discovery, a hunt for impact locations was launched that scoured the globe. Known meteor sites yielded evidence such as tektites (glass balls), stishovite, and shocked quartz grains, which were used to identify new impact craters. After several new impact craters were uncovered, the true culprit and murder of the Mesozoic was discovered at Chixculub of the Yucatan Peninsula in the Gulf of Mexico. This was a defining moment for catastrophism and for all of geology.

The modern synthesis of catastrophism has a history that stretches back to when humans first wondered why the land looks the way it does. Catastrophism has masked many philosophies and hidden agendas of persons from before geology was even a science. For 130 years, catastrophism has been shamed as religious fallacy and has now come full circle to be appreciated and accepted as part of Earth's geologic cycle.

— *Christopher Cody Matson*

See also **Big Bang Theory; Extinction**

Further Readings

Ager, D. (1993). *The new catastrophism.* New York: Cambridge University Press.

Albritton, C. C. Jr. (Ed.). (1975). *Benchmark papers in geology* (Vol. 13). Stroudsburg, PA: Dowden, Hutchinson & Ross.

Berggren, W. A., & Van Couvering, J. A. (Eds.). (1984). *Catastrophes and earth history.* Princeton, NJ: Princeton University Press.

CATEGORICAL IMPERATIVE

The concept of categorical imperative is one of the most important notions of Kant's practical philosophy. This concept falls under the Kantian project of the foundation of morality. To be precise, Kant does not attempt to create a new morality, but to propose a new formulation of it. From this point of view, the categorical imperative must provide a criterion that makes it possible for any human to differentiate with certainty the moral actions from those actions that are not moral.

Generally, Kant calls "imperative" the formula of a command, that is, the representation of an objective principle that is constraining for the will.

Since the human will is subjected to subjective motives that stem from the sensibility, the actions that are objectively necessary remain subjectively contingent so that their necessity appears for the agent as a constraint. Consequently, all imperatives are expressed by the word "ought" and indicate the relation of an objective law of reason to a will, the subjective constitution of which is not necessarily determined by this law.

Kant distinguishes two sorts of imperatives: hypothetical and categorical. When the imperative expresses the practical necessity of an action only in order to obtain something desirable, the imperative is *hypothetical* (these are imperatives of skill and of prudence). When the imperative expresses the practical necessity of an action as good in itself and for itself, the imperative is *categorical* and is a law of morality.

There is no difficulty in regard to the possibility of hypothetical imperatives: The constraint on the will is simply the application of the principle: "Whoever wills the end, wills also the means in his power that are indispensably necessary thereto." By contrast, the possibility of the categorical imperative presents a real difficulty because the necessity of this sort of imperative does not depend on any antecedent condition or of any consecutive end: This necessity unconditionally connects the will with the law.

To resolve this difficulty, Kant suggests considering if the conception of a categorical imperative would not supply the formula with it. Since beside the law, the categorical imperative contains only the necessity that the maxims shall conform to this law, and since the law contains no conditions restricting it, there remains only the general statement that the maxim of the action should conform to a universal law. Consequently the (first) formula of the categorical imperative is: *Act only on that maxim whereby thou canst at the same time will that it should become a universal law.*

The categorical imperative requires the ability to will that a maxim of one's action should be a universal law. To clarify this claim, we can take the four examples of maxims-duties (suicide, false promising, noncultivation of one's natural talents, and indifference to the misfortune of others) that Kant mobilizes. It appears in these examples that a maxim can be raised to the universality of a law, when we can conceive and/or want it without contradiction. Exactly, Kant distinguishes the action's maxims that cannot without contradiction be *conceived* as a universal law; these are the action's maxims that are *logically* contradictory (these maxims violate strict or rigorous [inflexible] duty, that is, the duty that admits no exception in favor of inclination), and the actions for which it is impossible to *will* that their maxim should be raised to the universality of a law; these are the actions maxims that are *practically* contradictory (these maxims violate the laxer, meritorious duty, that is, the duty whose application's modalities are left for the consideration of the agent). It is the practical noncontradiction, more than the logical noncontradiction, that makes it possible to distinguish the morally defended maxims of the morally allowed maxims (duties). It is thus false to consider, as Hegel does, for example, that the formal identity and the empty logicism of Kant's morality authorize the universalization of any maxim of action. From Kant's point of view, it is the will, more than the understanding, that must refuse to be contradicted by setting up certain maxims in universal laws.

From this first formula of the categorical imperative, Kant deduces three other formulae, which "are at bottom only so many formulae of the very same law and each of itself involves the other two": Act (2) as if the maxim of thy action were to become by thy will a universal law of nature; (3) as to treat humanity, whether in thine own person or in that of any other, in every case as an end withal, never as means only; (4) as if he were by his maxims in every case a legislating member in the universal kingdom of ends.

The four formulae of the categorical imperative are complementary. To say that our maxims must always be wanted, with regard to form, without contradiction (logical or practical) like universal laws of nature, to say that they must always respect the human dignity as end in itself or to say that they must always allow the will to represent itself as legislating member in the kingdom of ends, it is to say the same thing.

These four formulae are simply various manners of expressing the law of the autonomy of the will. So, the first two formulae of the categorical imperative privilege the formal criterion of the maxim, its conformity with the moral law, the fact that it can be desired without contradiction (logical nor practical) like an analog of a natural law. It is here that "Kantian formalism" takes shape: The will must be determined by the only *form* (universalizable) of its maxim, that is to say, by a independent rule of the objects of the will, abstraction made of the action's matter, of any material motive, by the pure respect for the *formal* principle a priori of the moral law.

On the other hand, the two last formulae privilege the subjective aspect of the ends, of the matter of the will. By giving to the maxims, morally allowed, for object the rational being as end in himself and as member legislator of kingdom of ends, the third and the fourth formulae underline the concrete dimension of the maxim.

Finally, the formalism of Kantian morality does not mean that our actions should not take place in the sensible world, but only that they should not originate there, that the moral action does not draw its value from the purpose which it reaches, but from the form (universalizable) and the quality (disinterested) of the maxim that determines the will. That being said, Kant does not claim that autonomy must regulate *all* our actions. Beside the categorical imperative, which provides us a certain criterion to recognize the actions that are moral and those which are not moral, there is place for hypothetical imperatives (technical and pragmatic), which include the inclinations and the human desires, the advancement of happiness.

Moreover, against the charge of formalism generally carried against Kantian morality, it is fundamental to see that Kant's practical philosophy is not reduced to a simply formalism, that the formal moment, the moment of the foundation, is only the first moment, that before it is to be *applied* the morality must be founded. The "formal" moment is the condition sine qua non of practical philosophy—only this moment guarantees its objectivity, universality, and apodicticity—but it does not exhaust it: It must be necessarily followed by a second moment, the moment of the application (metaphysics of morals and anthropology).

— *Sophie Grapotte*

See also **Kant, Immanuel**

Further Readings

Allison, H. (1990). *Kant's theory of freedom.* Cambridge: Cambridge University Press.

Beck, L. W. (1960). *A commentary on Kant's critique of practical reason.* Chicago: University of Chicago Press.

Nell, O. (1975.) *Acting on principle. An essay on Kantian ethics.* New York: Columbia University Press.

Paton, H. J. (1971). *The categorical imperative: A study in Kant's moral philosophy.* Philadelphia: University of Pennsylvania Press.

CAVALLI-SFORZA, LUIGI LUCA (1922–)

L. Luca Cavalli-Sforza was born on January 25, 1922, in Genoa, Italy, and is variously referred to as a pioneering population geneticist, the founder of genetic anthropology, the person who brought together modern genetics, archaeology, linguistics, and history, and one of the most distinguished geneticists in the world. He received an MD degree from the University of Pavia in 1944; went to Cambridge University for a few years, where he studied bacterial genetics; returned to Italy in 1950, where he served as director or chair of several genetic research positions; and in 1970 was appointed professor of genetics at Stanford University in Palo Alto,

California. He retired in 1992 but is a professor emeritus at Stanford, is the principal investigator at Stanford's Human Population Genetics Laboratory, and was a founder of the Human Genome Diversity Project, which seeks to collect a genetic database for medical purposes from throughout the world, especially from indigenous groups, which are relatively unmixed genetically. He is a member of the U.S. National Academy of Sciences and is a foreign member of Britain's most prestigious scientific organization, the Royal Society.

As early as the late 1940s and early 1950s, he was the first geneticist to suggest that genes of contemporary populations could be analyzed to obtain a historical record of humans. At first, he analyzed human blood groups, but then, as genetic research advanced, he changed to DNA for his analyses.

He introduced the methodology of studying gene frequencies in different locations to show the historical migrations of peoples throughout the world. He disagreed with archaeologists and cultural anthropologists who focused only on culture but emphasized that archaeology and the spread of agriculture were in agreement with migration patterns suggested by the analysis of gene distributions. He strongly supports a multidisciplinary approach and has analyzed the degree of relationship between genetic diversity and linguistic diversity. He argued for demic diffusion, that people with advanced knowledge introduced their knowledge and their subsequent reproductive success into an area via migration.

The African origins of modern humans, the migrations out of Africa that populated the world, the dates and locations that go with all major world migrations, and the contemporary distribution of genes in the world have all benefited tremendously from Cavalli-Sforza's genetic maps, genetic distance charts, and other publications. Nearly every recent book on human origins, evolution, or migration is based partly on Cavalli-Sforza's research.

Cavalli-Sforza has authored or coauthored a number of books, including *The History and Geography of Human Genes* (1994), a 1,000-page atlas of migrations and genetic diversity throughout the world. *The Great Human Diasporas: The History and Diversity of Evolution* (1995), written for the nonspecialist, summarizes the lifework of Cavalli-Sforza and uses genetic data to construct a tree of all human populations. *Genes, Peoples, and Languages* (2000) summarizes Cavalli-Sforza's lifetime work and shows how he has synthesized genetic, linguistic, and archaeological data. *Consanquinity, Inbreeding, and Genetic Drift in Italy* (2004) is based on a team project that Cavalli-Sforza began in 1951 and shows the results of a massive study of 8,000 communities in Italy on topics specified in the title. Other books also have furthered genetic knowledge.

— *Abraham D. Lavender*

See also **Genetics, Population; Human Genome Project**

Further Readings

Cavalli-Sforza, L. L. (2000). *Genes, peoples, and languages.* New York: North Point Press.

Cavalli-Sforza, L. L., & Cavalli-Sforza, F. (1995). *The great human diasporas: The history of diversity and evolution.* Reading, PA: Addison-Wesley.

Stone, L., &. Lurquin, P. F. (2005). *A genetic and cultural odyssey: The life and work of L. Luca Cavalli-Sforza.* New York: Columbia University Press.

 # CAVE ART

In the broadest sense, cave art is identical to rock art. In a narrow sense, it is painting on cave walls, ceilings, remote and hard-to-reach places; it is defined as nonmobile or monumental in contrast to small transportable objects like statuettes, bone engravings, and so on.

Origin and Evolution of Cave Art

The earliest displays of artistic activity or "natural creativity" of prehistoric populations are seen in Aucheulean times. In that period, the animal was used in ceremonies as an image of special kind. For that purpose, animal carcasses or bodies (or their most important fragments, often head only) were brought to the caves, where people lived, and usually were displayed at specially prepared places, situated at the central part of the cave or next to the entrance (Torralba in Spain, Leringen in Germany). Sometimes, numerous animal fragments were placed at caves used only for that purpose (i.e., Early Paleolithic Bear Caves—Drahelauh in Switzerland, Regourdout in France).

The next period of cave art evolution, or the stage of the "natural model," as argued by Russian archaeologist A. Stolyar, is marked by first attempts of animal body (or its fragments) simulation. It begins with the exhibition of the animal head on at first natural and later artificial rock platforms, which at the end of this stage were accompanied by primitive clay simulations of headless animal bodies; sometimes such compositions were covered by natural animal hide (Bazua in Italy, Peche-Merlet in France).

Such activity soon develops into the creation of three-dimensional sculptures made of clay (the "clay period"). Their size, at first close to real, decreased, leading to the bas-relief genre of visual art (Tuque d'Odoubert in France, Castere-Godena in Italy). This is most likely when statuettes and other forms of mobile art began to spring up (Dolni Vestonice, Pavlov).

The most brilliant examples of cave art in the form of paintings on cave walls are connected with the stage of "monumental animalistic masterpieces," after A. Stolyar, within the last 20,000 years of the Upper Paleolithic. During that time, prehistoric graphics went through many changes, which schematically could be represented as follows: profile contours of static "bipedal" figures shaped by stable line; inner shading, detailing of the contour; simple composition of similar animals or their pairs; painting of the contour in the form of monochromatic spots; "fresco" and color tone technique; appearance of dynamics and perspective, depth of image; complex compositions consisting of different figures (sometimes human being included) on the earth surface; and frontal perspective composition.

Function and Historical Interpretation of Cave Art

In contemporary prehistory, cultural anthropology, and art studies, there are few attempts to conceptualize cave art in all its historical, technological, and stylistic forms. Most existing cave art interpretations usually involve a separate case study, with scarce analogies in neighboring territories. Nonetheless, a series of theories and hypotheses have been elaborated.

The *magical (or ritual) explanation* for cave art was one of the earliest speculations of its function. The animal was the center of ritual activities (totemic, magic, and other forms) of Paleolithic hunter-gatherers; animal images on cave walls most probably were realistically identified with live animals. Inherent in the function of prehistoric cave art is the principle of analogy, which implies that one can control the object if one controls its image.

The *ideological explanation* is based on the stylistic homogeneity of cave art and the absence of painter personality. Most images are not connected with particular objects or animals and look like generalizations, with some slight variations. It testifies to the predominance of collective ideas and collective consciousness.

The *social (ethnic) identification* function of cave art is associated with its ideological explanation. As group symbols were the main subject of cave art, their creation could be used for expression of any form of collective identity (kin, community, ethnic, ritual) and were deeply connected with ritual activity of these populations.

The *communicative and memorial (or mythological) explanation* is associated with the previous theories but stresses that the symbols and images of art objects could reflect collective unity and integrity only if they expressed a connection with preceding generations, the early ancestors. It also implicates the informative function of prehistoric cave art and is the background for the cognitive explanation of cave art.

The *cognitive explanation* of cave art concentrates on the "information flow" throughout generations, which could be transmitted by images. Interpreting art in general as a peculiar form of world knowledge and information storage, it emphasizes that only important hunting species were the subject of cave pictures and that prehistoric painters were well-informed about animal anatomy and hunting means. Such information could be used in the preparation of adolescent members of the community for the various initiations. Contemporary postmodernists also suggest the cognitive significance of prehistoric cave art images, regarding them as texts that could be deciphered or images that could be read in order to comprehend past culture.

Source: © Kathleen Cohen.

The *ecological-demographic explanation* is based on the idea that climate deterioration resulting from the last glaciation (Middle Paleolithic), which caused food and other sources shortage and, in turn, had forced people to move to more suitable areas for their subsistence territories. Their concentration at a few niches demanded strict allocation of their foraging territories, which was accompanied with groups' inner integration and consolidation; thus the necessity of marking territory borders and the origin of cave art.

The *aesthetic explanation* ("art for art," or "game hypothesis") emphasizes that the broad emotional sphere of prehistoric populations displayed itself in the process of image stylization and creation of monumental animalistic compositions of high aesthetic value. It could not be ruled out, at the same time, that the artistic process was one of many forms of Paleolithic hunters' leisure.

In many modern case studies, researchers have tended to emphasize the primacy of the symbolic function of cave art and its connection with ritual activity of prehistoric communities. The complex character of such compositions, along with their remoteness, which ensured high secrecy of the process, supports this hypothesis. Later, with polychromatic images and improvement of forms and technique of image making, an aesthetic perception was forming, and it may be that only since that time can one argue the existence of "art." At the beginning of the 21st century, new discoveries of cave art in Australia, Asia Minor, and other parts of the world have caused many researchers to recognize the plurality of backgrounds, places, and reasons that influenced cave art origin and defined its historical function.

— *Olena V. Smyntyna*

See also **Petroglyphs; Pictographs; Rock Art**

Further Readings

Banh, P. G. (1995). Cave art without the caves. *Antiquity, 69,* 263.

Gamble, C. (1991). The social context for European Paleolithic art. *Proceedings of the Prehistoric Society, 57,* 1.

Mithen, S. J. (1991). Ecological interpretations of Paleolithic art. *Proceedings of the Prehistoric Society, 57,* 1.

Mithen S. J. (Ed.). (1998). *Creativity in human evolution and prehistory.* London: Routledge.

CAZDEN, COURTNEY B.

Courtney B. Cazden is an educational sociolinguist at the Harvard Graduate School of Education. Since the 1970s, she has been a key figure in the ethnography of schooling, focusing on children's linguistic development (both oral and written) and the functions of language in formal education, primarily but not exclusively in the United States. Combining her experiences as a former primary schoolteacher with the insight and methodological rigor of a trained ethnographer and linguist, Cazden helped to establish ethnography and discourse analysis as central methodologies for analyzing classroom interaction. Her work displays sensitivity and insight to the communicative demands made on both teachers and students in classroom settings, especially those involving ethnic minority students.

Formal schooling involves the mastery not only of academic content but also of the particular forms of discourse that are considered legitimate for classroom use. These forms are seldom explicitly taught; rather, they form part of the "hidden curriculum" of schooling. While they differ significantly from the forms of discourse that children customarily use in their homes and communities, the differences tend to be greater for ethnic minority children. Children who are U.S.-born, White, middle-class, native speakers of English are more likely to arrive at school already familiar with the parameters of classroom discourse, since these overlap considerably with the epistemological traditions, linguistic standards, and interactive patterns of White, middle-class communities. In contrast, African American, Chicano, low-income, and other "nonmainstream" children are likely to encounter greater discontinuities between the discourse of their home and community environments and that of the school. These discontinuities involve, among other things, ways of asking and responding to questions, structuring and interpreting oral narratives, and engaging written texts and can have a significant impact on students' learning opportunities as well as on teachers' perceptions of students' abilities.

Cazden's work has focused on the contours and effects of these home/school discontinuities and on what the discourse patterns of the classroom presume, foster, and ignore with regard to students' communicative competence. Inasmuch as discursive criteria partly determine "what counts" as knowledge and learning, they have important implications for student outcomes and the much-commented achievement gaps among students of different ethnicities, language backgrounds, and social classes. By making explicit the unconscious aspects of classroom discourse, Cazden has aimed to problematize classroom communication as a medium that is far from transparent or culturally neutral.

Throughout her career, Cazden has collaborated extensively with other distinguished scholars of language and education, such as Dell Hymes, Joshua Fishman, and Hugh Mehan. She is a past president of both the Council on Anthropology and Education and the American Association for Applied Linguistics, a member of the National Academy of Education and the Reading Hall of Fame, and recipient of various scholarly awards.

— *Aurolyn Luykx*

See also **Education and Anthropology**

Further Readings

Cazden, C. B. (1992). *Whole language plus: Essays on literacy in the United States and New Zealand.* New York: Teachers College Press.

Cazden, C. B. (2001). *Classroom discourse: The language of teaching and learning* (2nd ed.). Portsmouth, NH: Heinemann.

Cazden, C. B., John, V. P., & Hymes, D. (Eds.). (1972). *Functions of language in the classroom*. New York: Teachers College Press.

CEBIDS

Cebid refers to Cebidae, a family of New World monkeys distributed throughout Latin America. The family consists of three extant (living) subfamilies and eight genera that have been in South America since the Oligocene (about 3 million years ago). Cebids have long hairy tails used for counterbalance. Some species have semiprehensile tails, which are hairless on the bottom tip and can be used as a fifth limb.

The first subfamily, Aotinae, includes one genus, *Aotus.* The common name for this genus is owl monkey, night monkey, or douracouli. The name *owl monkey* comes from the low, owl-like hoots that the monkeys make, possibly to attract mates and/or maintain contact during nighttime foraging. Owl monkeys are the only higher primates that are nocturnal, and as a result, they have the largest sized orbits of any anthropoid (higher primate). Owl monkeys weigh around 1 kg and have slightly opposable thumbs. They are monomorphic, with males and females having similar body sizes. Owl monkeys live in monogamous families, and infants spend most of their time with the father, who carries them around and sleeps with them. However, unlike most monogamous primates, owl monkeys rarely groom each other. They are arboreal and eat mostly fruit, but also eat leaves and insects.

The second subfamily, Callithrichinae, is made up of three groups, the tamarins *(Saguinus, Leontopithecus),* marmosets *(Callithrix, Cebuella),* and Goeldi's monkeys *(Callimico).* Callitrichines are the smallest of the New World monkeys, weighing between 100 and 750 g. They often have brightly colored manes, moustaches, and coats. Although uncommon in higher primates, callitrichines have derived claws instead of nails, which allow them to cling to tree trunks to feed on exudates, insects, and fruits. Marmosets and tamarins usually give birth to dizygotic twins, while Goeldi's monkeys have single births. Although mating systems vary among callitrichines, many groups are polyandrous and contain a single breeding female and several adult males that help care for the young. Callitrichines can live in marginal and disturbed habitats.

The third subfamily is Cebinae, which consists of the capuchin monkeys (Cebus) and squirrel monkeys *(Saimiri).* Capuchins weigh an average of 3,000 g and live in multimale-multifemale groups of 8 to 30 individuals. They are arboreal and normally feed on many different types of fruits, leaves, and animal matter. Some capuchins use their proportionately large brains to obtain food not available to other species, such as the tufted capuchins' ability to break open the hard shells of palm nuts. Squirrel monkeys are smaller than capuchins, weighing between 554 and 1,250 g. They live in groups of 20 to over 50 individuals and are frugivorous and insectivorous. Squirrel monkeys, unlike capuchins, which have semiprehensile tails, have prehensile tails only as juveniles. In addition, squirrel monkeys often are used as laboratory animals. Furthermore, both squirrel monkeys and capuchins are easily recognized as pets on television, in films, and other forms of entertainment. A handful of Cebids are classified as vulnerable,

Source: © iStockphoto/Kevin Tate.

Golden Lion Tamarin

Source: Photograph copyright © by Gregory Scott Hamilton. Used by permission.

endangered, or critically endangered due to deforestation of vital habitat.

— *Lisa M. Paciulli and Adam M. Isaak*

See also **Marmosets; Tamarins**

Further Readings

Fedigan, L. M., Fragaszy, D. M., & Visalberghi, E. A. (2004). The *complete capuchin: The biology of the genus Cebus.* Cambridge: Cambridge University Press.

Fleagle, J. G. (1999). *Primate adaptation and evolution.* San Diego, CA: Academic Press.

Kinzey, W. G. (1997). *New World primates: Ecology, evolution, and behavior.* New York: Walter de Gruyter.

Rowe, N. (1996). *The pictorial guide to the living primates.* Charlestown, RI: Pogonias Press.

CELTIC EUROPE

Celtic Europe is that part of the Eurasian continent under the influence of the Celtic language family, a subset of the Indo-European group of languages. In very early Classical times, this included most of the European subcontinent west of a line running roughly between the modern cities of Gdansk, Poland, and Odessa, Ukraine, and north of the Alps, then south onto the Iberian Peninsula. In later Classical times, the area east of the Rhine and north of the Danube was considered Germanic; the area west of the Rhine and north of the Alps was considered Celtic, as well as Iberia. In the most strictly technical sense, the name *Celt* comes from a first millennium BCE tribe, the *Keltoi*, which occupied a very rough triangle of ancient Gaul, stretching north from a line between Marseille *(Massalia)* and Bordeaux *(Burdigala)* along the Garonne River, north of Aquitaine *(Aquitania)*, and east to Seine. Their name has been applied to the entire culture. The names of various Celtic tribes still survive today, disguised as modern European place names, for example, the *Parisii* gave their name to the city of Paris, and the *Boii* lent theirs to Bohemia. The modern Celtic parts of Europe are influenced more by an understanding of common origins and cultural elements, such as legends and music, and less by the Celtic language family; they include Scotland, Wales, and Cornwall on the island of Britain, Ireland, the Isle of Man, Brittany in France, and Galicia in Spain.

Ancient Celtic Europe

Pre-Celtic Europe in the Late Neolithic and Copper-Bronze Ages

Prior to the spread of Celtic culture from central Europe, Western Europe was occupied by Neolithic and Copper-Bronze Age farmers. These people farmed the land and built huge megalithic burial chambers, such as New Grange, in the Boyne Valley, and ritualistic and ceremonial centers, such as Stonehenge, in England, and Carnac, in France. Some of these sites may have served as calendrical devices or celestial observatories. It is unlikely that these Neolithic farmers were wantonly wiped out by the later Celtic invaders in a wholesale slaughter. Rather, it is more plausible that they were conquered and absorbed as the agricultural lower classes who supplied the food to an invading, pastoralist elite (see below), a story that repeats itself throughout the modern ethnographic literature as well. Quite possibly, some of the later megalithic people were speakers of a Celtic language themselves but had moved westward prior to the development of an Iron Age pastoralist economy. The influence of these early farming people can be seen in the continuation of an art style that emphasizes flowing tendrils and spirals from the Neolithic through the Iron Age, from the carvings on the great entry stone at New Grange, to the illuminated manuscripts in the *Book of Kells,* and the *Lindisfarne Gospels* nearly 4,000 years later. This art style may have influenced the later La Tène style, or led to its wide acceptance.

The Coming of the Celts From Central Europe: Their Earliest Archeological Appearances at the Iron Age Sites of Hallstatt and La Tène

The earliest (not the oldest) archaeological evidence for the Celts comes from two sites in central Europe, Hallstatt and La Tène. Hallstatt is a salt mine in Austria in which the 2,000-year-old brine-preserved body of a man was found in 1734.The body has been lost, the local people having assumed at the time that he was pagan and unworthy of Christian reburial. A century later, the area was excavated archeologically and found to have been an extensive Iron Age Celtic settlement that carried on long-distance trade in salt. Salt-preserved tools, clothing, and shoes have been excavated from this site. This mid-European mining culture may have developed out of the earlier Urnfield culture and been influenced by or converged with the equestrian Cimmerian peoples from north of the Black Sea, migrating onto the Hungarian Plain and up the Danube after being pushed west by the expanding Scythian people. During the Hallstatt period, we witness the development of mobile, warrior elite with several different centers of development from Spain to the areas north of the Danube. We know them from large pit burials that included four-wheeled wagons, long slashing swords, horse trappings, and, later, gold and Mediterranean trade items, such as are found with the rich burials of the "Princess" of Vix, in France, and the "Prince's" tomb from Hochdorf, near Stuttgart, Germany, which contained a magnificent 9-foot-long bronze couch supported by small human figurines who appear to be riding unicycles. The Hallstatt period came to an end around 500 BCE, when it was replaced by the La Tène era.

La Tène is the site of a prehistoric lake dwelling in Switzerland, as well as the name of an art style associated with the Celts. Celtic lake dwellings are known from Central Europe to Ireland, where they are called *crannogs.* They consist of artificial islands upon which homesteads were built on pilings and connected to the mainland by causeways, or in some cases by boats. Etruscan trade goods, especially bronze vessels and flagons, began to appear, and the burials now contained two-wheeled chariots, daggers, spears, and helmets in addition to the swords found in earlier graves. It was in the 4th century BCE that Pytheas of Marseille, the first European anthropologist, traveled into the northern and western regions and described the lands and their inhabitants (although labeled a liar by Strabo several centuries after the fact, Pytheas's observations since have been vindicated). It was during the early La Tène period that the Celts under Brennus invaded the Po Valley and sacked Rome in 390 BCE. A century later, Celts under another Brennus (hence H. D. Rankin's belief that it may have been a title rather than a name) invaded the Balkans following the death of Alexander, attacked Delphi, and invaded Asia Minor, where they settled and became known as the Galatians. Their Celtic identity remained distinct at least into the 1st century CE, when they were addressed as such in an epistle by Saint Paul.

By contrast to the archeological record that the Celts came from central Europe, the *Irish Book of Invasions (An Leabhar Gabhála Eireann)* states that the last protohistoric invaders of Ireland came from Spain: the Sons of Mil Espáine, or Milesians; Spanish Galician sources also reflect this point of view. Mil Espáine may be a corruption of the Latin, *miles Hispaniae,* a soldier of Spain. According to Daniel Bradley of Trinity College, Dublin, DNA analysis shows a common genetic link between the peoples of the Atlantic "Celtic Fringe" and Iberian populations. It is possible that the bulk of the people were descended from pre-Celtic or early Celtic Iberian settlers (based upon linguistic evidence) but that the elite culture came from the east with warlike Iron Age pastoralist invaders (see below). Rankin, however, believes that the linguistic evidence points to the mirror-opposite conclusion. Oxford archeologist Barry Cunliffe ties the Atlantic populations together into a separate subculture area from that of the mid-European Celts in a cultural line dating back before the Iron Age. He sees the rise of a mobile warrior elite during the La Tène phase that either spread out of development centers in central Europe or whose style influenced elites in other areas, leading to the spread of Celtic culture, if not necessarily chromosomes.

The Earliest Historical Sources and Linguistics

It is possible that Homer's equestrian Cimmerians in a cloudy land by a sea to the north may have been Celts. Some sources nominate the Cimmerians' neighbors, the Scythians, as the ancestors of the Celts on the basis of some linguistic cognates: The early Irish claimed that they were descended from the Scythians through their ancestress, *Scota;* thus, they were known as the *Scoti,* a name that transferred to north Britain when an Irish tribe, the *Dál Riada,* colonized it in the early Christian era, making Scotland the "land of the Irish." The Celtic love of horses is documented by classical authors, and a major goddess was horse-related, the Gaulish *Epona,* known to the Welsh as *Rhiannon* and to the Irish as *Macha.* A 6th-century BCE Greek description of a sea voyage, *Massiliote Periplus,* describes Celts living in Spain and France and mentions the two islands of *Ierne* (Ireland) and *Albion* (Britain). In the mid-5th century BCE, Herodotus calls them the Tin Islands because of their importance as sources of tin to make bronze. Herodotus says that the Celtic lands stretched from Spain to the Danube and that they were among the most western-living people in Europe. About 325 BCE, Pytheas of Marseille *(Massalia)* described the Irish and British *(Pritani)* as cattle and sheep pastoralists. The earliest historical sources provide linguistic evidence that ties the Greek *Keltoi* and the Roman *Galatai* as cognates. According to Julius Caesar, the people west and northwest of the Ligurians referred to themselves as *Celtae.* Caesar's division of the transalpine people into Celts and Germans may be somewhat arbitrary, as various tribes are believed to have been of mixed heritage, for example, the Belgae and the Aedui of northern Gaul; indeed, Nora Chadwick suspects that *Teutones* (Germans or Danes) and the Gaelic *Tuath* (a tribe or group of people) are linguistic cognates. Unfortunately, most of our early linguistic data come from Greek and Roman authors, as the Celts were a preliterate people, although there is a Celtic inscription from Egypt using Greek characters, and a calendar from France. It was not until the Common Era that the Celts began to develop a form of writing of their own, *Ogham,* which consisted of a series of horizontal and vertical slashes on the edge of a stone or piece of wood.

What is the common thread between the ancient *Gauls* and the modern Gaels, the areas of Galicia in both western Spain and eastern Poland, and Galatia in central Turkey? It is the linguistic cognate in these names: *Gaul, Galtee, Galatia, Galicia, Gaelic, Galati, Keltoi, Celtae,* and *Celt.* There are two main divisions in the Celtic language family; linguists distinguish between the "p" and "q" Celts, that is, the Brythonic versus the Goidelic speakers. At some point, the early Celtic speakers developed a linguistic shift in part of their language family from the hard "q" or "c/k" sound to the softer "p" or "b" sound, splitting proto-Celtic into Brythonic and Goidelic. As an example, the Picts of Northern Britain were known to the ancient Goidelic speakers, or "q" Celts, as *Cruithni.* Eventually the hard "c" softened to "p," *Pruithne.* Around 325 BCE, Pytheas called Ireland and Britain the *Pretanic* Islands and the people *Pritani,* from which we get the modern word, Britain. The main difference is in the hard versus the soft consonant. This difference distinguishes the Celtic languages to this day: Irish, Scots, and Manx are Goidelic; Welsh and Breton (as well as the now extinct Cornish, Brittonic, and Gaulish) are Brythonic. Galego, the language of Spanish Galicia, is a Romance language closely related to Portuguese, the indigenous Celtic language having been lost, although it is believed to have been Goidelic. The Breton language was brought to Armorica (Brittany) from Wales and Cornwall in the 5th century CE by refugees fleeing the Saxon invasions, giving Brittany its present name. Some sources say it may contain traces of the old Armorican Gaulish toward the east of the peninsula.

Economics and Politics

The pre-Romanized Celts elected their leaders from a pool of eligible aristocrats. Although some observers see this as an early form of democracy, it just as easily could be seen as analogous to the "big man" system in tribal Melanesia. The king, or chief, could choose a successor, who acted as a second in command but was not guaranteed succession should the electors prefer a different candidate. According to Poseidonius, the most renowned warrior at a feast could claim the "hero's portion," or best joint of pork, and any challenge could lead to a fight to the death, or tests of bravery, such as laying stretched out on the floor to see if anyone present had the courage to cut the hero's throat with a sword. This tradition is preserved among the Insular Celts in that portion of the Ulster Cycle known as *The Feast of Bricriu.* These pork prestations would serve to enhance group solidarity and reinforce the position of the chief through his ability to redistribute his wealth. Rankin compares them to the North American potlatch. The Celts were renowned in the Classical world for their drinking bouts and feasting, at which the Romans disingenuously (in light of their orgies) claimed to be shocked. There were at least four levels of society, although some authors consider only three; the aristocrats and an upper and lower level of free men and women. The fourth level were the slaves, whose existence, along with gold, tin, and amber, helped to provide a flourishing trade with the Mediterranean in exchange for finished jewelry, wine, and the jugs (amphorae) and vessels to ship, store, and serve it. Beverages also were served in elaborately decorated gold drinking horns.

There seems to be little doubt that the early Celtic peoples of Europe were headhunters, as described in legends such as the Irish *Táin Bó Culainge* or Cattle Raid of Cooley (which Cunliffe believes originated as a much older Continental La Tène tale because of its extensive descriptions of chariot warfare, which is archeologically unknown from Ireland. By contrast, according to Caesar, chariot warfare lasted in Britain centuries after it had been eclipsed on the Continent) and demonstrated archaeologically from such sculptures as the Celto-Ligurian sanctuaries of the Rhone Valley, as well as from numerous sculpted disembodied heads found throughout Western Europe. Likewise, boar hunting (and eating) was an important aspect of Celtic life in ancient times, as demonstrated in sculptures and legends. The backbone of the Celtic economy, though, appears to have been cattle pastoralism. This form of pastoralism is correlated in the anthropological literature with warfare and conquest of neighboring farming peoples to supply food, as the cattle represent wealth and are less likely to be eaten than are cultivated products. Indeed, this is what we find with the ancient Celts whose mixed farming economy left the warrior aristocracy battling over cattle, while the lower end of the social hierarchy was left to scratch the land to produce barley, wheat, and so on. Even into the late Middle Ages, the Irish aristocracy would spend the warmer months of the year moving from hunting camp to hunting camp, traveling with their cattle. Towns as a focus of Celtic life did not appear until about 200 BCE, in the form of the fortified, transalpine, Gaulish *oppida* as centers of iron working. Although they appear to be home-grown products of an indigenous cultural milieu,

possibly in response to increasing pressure from Germanic tribes, they may have been influenced by the Mediterranean region in the west. These *oppida*'s fortifications, what Caesar calls *murus gallicus,* nearly allowed the Gaulish king, Vercingetorix, to succeed in his rebellion against Rome during Caesar's first century BCE campaigns. Ireland did not develop towns until the Viking era more than 1,000 years later, when cities such as Dublin, Limerick, and Waterford were founded as Viking raiding camps.

Social Life

Classical authors from Pausanias to Plutarch speak with admiration and surprise about the status and size of Celtic women and their heroism in warfare. Tacitus describes the story of Boudicca, the queen of the British *Iceni,* who led a war of rebellion against the Roman invaders in the first century CE. In the *Táin Bó Culainge,* the boy hero, Cúchulain, is taught the warrior arts by a woman, Scathach. Free women among the ancient Celts had equal property rights with men and could make contracts freely, if they chose. During the early Christian era, women held equal status with men in the Celtic Christian church. Because of the lack of episcopacy in the Celtic church, the monastic system had female abbots, such as Brigid in Ireland, ruling over monasteries of mixed sex.

History and legend both show that upper-class women among the ancient Celts were willing to sacrifice sexual favors for political or military ends. Greek and Roman authors described the Celts as maritally promiscuous, incestuous, and cannibalistic. However, it is likely that some of the more outlandish reports by the classic writers were a combination of ethnocentrism, hearsay, and war propaganda, as other reports show admiration of the Celts' intense marital loyalty and codification of laws of conduct and morality. What was taken for incest very well may be a confusion of biology with kinship terminology, while reports of sexual license may be out-of-context religious rites associated with fertility and prosperity for the tribe, as in Geraldus Cambrensis's 12th-century report of a ritual in which a northern Irish king mated with a white mare, then drank a soup made from the sacrificed animal. At least we can say with little hesitation that they were patrilineal and patrilocal; the patrilineal assertion is borne out by amazement of the ancient Irish at the Picts' practice of matrilineal descent. The Celts may have practiced polygyny, and Caesar reports fraternal polyandry.

A woman's dowry had to be matched in wealth by her husband's, and this combined wealth was held in joint tenancy with rights of survivorship. Divorce was easy, and serial monogamy was known from the Celtic world even in the Christian era.

In early accounts of warfare with Celtic tribes, they are reported to have slaked back their hair with lime, giving them a frightful appearance. They also were reported to charge into battle naked (as shown by the statue, *The Dying Gaul,* a Roman copy of a Pergamene Greek original), screaming a terrifying war cry to the accompaniment of trumpet blasts. The frontline naked warriors, *gaesatae,* whose name derived from a type of javelin they carried, may have been a chronologically limited fad, however, as many other depictions show the Celtic military fully clothed in belted tunics and trousers, accompanied by armor. Both descriptions are attested by Polybius in the mid-2nd century BCE. In other instances, warfare was conducted from a safe distance with javelins, followed by single combat between champions, according to both the *Táin Bó Cuailnge* and reports of 4th-century BCE Roman encounters, in a parallel to the cattle pastoralist Zulu prior to Shaka's military innovations.

The ancient Celts shaved and washed their bodies with soap at a time when the Romans' hygiene had them scraping the sweat from their bodies, followed by oiling. Obesity not only was frowned upon, but there were penalties for being overweight. Men frequently are depicted wearing cloaks. Diodorus Siculus, writing in the 1st century BCE, describes their clothing as being dyed every color in stripes and small squares (plaid?). Some sculptures, such as those on the Gundestrup cauldron, show people wearing what appear to be two-piece knit or herringbone-weave outfits, consisting of long-sleeved shirts and knee-length trousers. Long, bushy moustaches were a common feature on men. Neck torques, solid metal necklaces open in the front, also were a common feature, as were winged or horned helmets, metal breastplates, and swords and daggers. Both men and women wore long linen shirts as undergarments. Women's clothing consisted of fringed tunics (visible on the dead wife on the sculpture *The Suicidal Gaul,* the companion piece to *The Dying Gaul*), covered by brightly colored cloaks decorated with jewelry or bells and held in place by large, elaborate brooches. Women further enhanced their appearance with makeup and hairstyles, from braids to raised coiffures styled using decorated mirrors. In contrast to the Greek and Roman penchant for sandals, well-made shoes, as found in burials, were an important feature for both sexes.

Religion, Druids

Ancient Celtic religious leaders were known as *druids,* after the Greek word for oak, *drus,* after the oak groves in which they performed religious ceremonies involving harvesting the parasite, mistletoe, from sacred oaks with golden sickles, according to Pliny the Elder. The different grades of druids were not only priests but scholars, judges (*brehon*), and diviners. Because the ancient Celts were a preliterate society, the druids spent decades memorizing all their knowledge of law, religion, and history in verse form, to be able to repeat it back without error. This ability was still found among rural storytellers among the Insular Celts until recent times. The power and importance of speech was such that druids (and in later times Bards) reputedly could kill with their use of satire, literally making their victims die of shame. Just as the British believed the Nuer prophets to be too-powerful a force inciting insurrection in their cattle pastoralist society, the Romans believed the druids to be too-powerful a force in Gaulish cattle pastoralist society. Tacitus reports that the Romans sent an expeditionary force to the druid college on Anglesey in Britain in the 1st century CE to massacre them, thus bringing about the fall of the old religious order in the Roman-held lands and unwittingly paving the way for the new religion, Christianity, to fill the vacuum. This attack preceded Boudicca's rebellion by one year and may have been related to it either by her allies' outrage over the sacrilege or incitement by the druid survivors.

An important ceremony held by the druids was the blessing of cattle on *Beltaine* (after the god *Belanos*), the feast of May Day. Pairs of bonfires would be built, and the herds would be passed between them while they were blessed. In addition to *Beltaine,* other Celtic feast days (determined by the druids' astronomical calculations) were *Imbolc,* February 1 (Christianized as St. Brigid's Day after a syncretism of the goddess *Brid* with a powerful early Christian abbess of the same name); *Lughnasa,* August 1, after *Lugh* (in Ireland, *Lludd* in Wales, and *Lugus* among the Britons and Gauls), whom some consider to be the Celtic Apollo; and *Samhain,* November 1, when the veil between this world and the Otherworld became thin and spirits could pass back and forth between the two worlds, the inspiration for the modern Halloween and All Souls' Day. The day after *Samhain* marked the Celtic New Year.

Lakes and other bodies of water held a special place in early Celtic culture, not just as defensible dwelling sites, but as holy places to reach the Otherworld and into which treasures, weapons, and sometimes people were thrown in sacrifice. Lindow Man, a young male member of the druidic class, was found sacrificed and preserved in a bog in Cheshire, and the bodies of apparently Celtic sacrificial victims were found in bogs in Denmark. To this day, holy wells are common places of prayer in rural Ireland. It is likely that the Celtic belief in an immortal soul aided the druids to convince their victims to become human sacrifices in much the same way that it aided the Aztec priests of Mexico a millennium-and-a-half later (too, many of the sacrificed were criminals or war captives). Tales about the Otherworld depicted it as a land of eternal feasting and dancing. Other stories, such as that of King Bran, whose head continued to talk after his decapitation, would have confirmed the belief in an afterlife. Some of the more sensational accounts of human sacrifice, such as Caesar's report of giant wicker human figures filled with living men and women and set afire, may have been exaggerations to justify conquest. In any case, even if accurate, they are bereft of their cultural and religious context and rationales.

Carved stone heads with three faces are known from the pre-Christian Celtic world. The Celts had a strong belief in spiritual triplicity, from tripartite gods to supernatural groupings of three, as in the three war goddesses, the *Morríghan*. The concept of a holy trinity is an ancient Indo-European belief found from India to Western Europe. A description of pre-Christian Celtic culture from folkloristic sources such as the *Táin Bó Culainge* demonstrates remarkable similarities with the early Vedic literature from India, showing the common Indo-European origins of both. Most of our knowledge of Celtic myths and legends comes from Ireland, where the Romans never settled, leaving the Irish free to continue the Celtic traditions for centuries after they had been lost on the Continent and, to a lesser extent, in Britain. Welsh myths and legends are very similar to those from Ireland, although the names and places have a Welsh context, as in the epic *Mabinogion*. Many stories tell of heroes under *geis*, a supernatural compulsion that occurs sometimes in hero tales of the Insular Celts. It cannot be ignored lest the hero come to some karmic

harm as a result. Possibly the *gaesatae*, the berserk, naked Celtic warriors of Galatia in Asia Minor, were operating under some form of geis that compelled them to sacrifice themselves, analogous to the Cheyenne contraries of the American Plains.

The Middle Ages Through the Enlightenment

Following the Christianization of Ireland by Patrick in 432 CE, and the fall of Rome 44 years later, the Insular Celtic monks, called *Peregrini,* established monasteries throughout Western Europe, beginning with Columcille's monastery on Iona. They and their converts kept learning alive in Medieval Europe, following the fall of Rome, through these centers of scholarship on the Continent, where they carefully reproduced classic texts, as well as recorded their own ancient myths and legends under a thin Christian veneer. Their work and the associated art styles in volumes such as the *Book of Kells* and the *Lindisfarne Gospels* give clues to the important spiritual aspects of the Celtic world.

Successive waves of invasions, conquest, and acculturation destroyed much of the Celtic heritage on the Continent and the English part of Britain. It was not rediscovered until the 16th century; in 1582, George Buchanan reintroduced the word *Celt* into history. Based upon classical works, he located them in northern Italy, France, and Spain. From Spain, some settled in Ireland and from there, in Scotland. England and Wales, according to Buchanan, had been settled by the *Galli* from Gaul.

In the 17th and 18th centuries, the study of Celts took on national importance in France and Wales as a means of establishing cultural identity. Ironically, during this same period, we had the end of the Gaelic political order in Ireland (the Flight of the Earls) and the defeat of the last Celtic (Stewart) king at the battle of the Boyne by William of Orange, an event that led to sectarian strife in the United Kingdom to this day. Celtic culture took on popular overtones during the Enlightenment when William Stukeley wrote *History of the Ancient Celts* and John Pollard wrote his *History of the Druids*. In France, authors wrote that all the megalithic monuments had belonged to the Celts. This "Celtomania," as Cunliffe calls it, led to the establishment of societies that put on invented, or at best reinterpreted, ceremonies, such as the Welsh *Eisteddfodau* and the various modern druidic societies.

Modern Celtic Europe

Prior to the Revolution, the French traced their origins to Germanic roots. In Napoleonic France, the Bonaparte government identified with the Celtic past to legitimize its new order rule. Napoleon III, a great admirer of the Celtic past, even had a statue erected in 1865 to honor Vercingetorix for his defiance of Rome in 52 BCE. The Germanic invasions of Gaul in the 5th century serve to reinforce the Bretons' assertions that they are the only true Celts in France, despite the rest of the country's reference to itself as "Gallic." Even the name, *France,* comes from that of a Germanic tribe, the Franks. Nonetheless, the Breton language began to decline in the 19th century because of what Cunliffe calls "the French official desire for homogenization." The desire for Breton autonomy received a black eye in the 1940s, when it was learned that *Parti National Breton* was going to negotiate with Germany for independence after its conquest of France. Newer groups, such as *Emgann* and the militant *Armée Révolutionaire,* have taken up the cause in recent years. Today, the relatively prosperous Brittany concerns itself with language preservation and plays host to several international folkloric and Celtic festivals.

The use of the Celtic languages was dying; the last native speaker of Cornish died in 1777 ("Revised Cornish" has been reconstructed from historical sources, aided by infusions of Breton and Welsh). Speaking Celtic languages was punished in schools in the areas of the British Isles, where it still was used. This was done to force the still defiant Celtic people to give up their quests for self-determination and assimilate into the new dominant culture of the United Kingdom. In Ireland, the Penal Laws were aimed at crushing Gaelic-Catholic culture and even excluded the native Irish from receiving education. The Irish language *(Gaeilge)* was almost destroyed by the Potato Famine of the 1840s, which struck hardest in the tuber-dependent *Gaeltact,* or Irish-speaking areas of western Ireland. The population of the island dropped by half in the 19th century, and with it went the Irish language.

Later in the 19th century, the establishment of the Abbey Theatre and the Gaelic League in Ireland brought about a linguistic, literary, and cultural revival, ironically among the Protestant Anglo-Irish elite. Ancient Hiberno-Celtic legends and themes became the subjects of books, plays, and poetry by Lady Augusta Gregory, William Butler Yeats, and John Millington Synge. In a parallel with Karl Marx's outline of the stages of revolution, soon after the cause (or at least the primitivistic glorification) of the oppressed lower classes was taken up by these members of the ascendancy, the home rule advocates took to the bandwagon, eventually leading to the 1916 Easter Rising, the Irish revolution, and establishment of the Free State under Éamon DeValera and Michael Collins. The recent sectarian violence in Northern Ireland is in part an outgrowth of this process, which led to the division of the island into a predominantly Protestant and industrial Northern Ireland, tied to the United Kingdom, and a Catholic and rural Republic in the south. In contrast to Ireland, the other Celtic areas in the British Isles, Scotland and Wales, have been earning their home rule more recently under the less bloody modern process of "devolution."

Today, learning the Irish language is required in schools, and students must take an examination on it in order to pass the "Leaving Cert.," that is, to graduate. Until recently, Irish civil servants were required to pass an Irish language examination to be hired, and all official documents must be printed in both Irish and English. *Raidió Teilifís Eireann,* the Irish national broadcasting company, broadcasts in Irish on one of its radio channels, *Raidió na Gaeltachta,* and on one of its television channels, TG4. The coastal islands, such as the Aran Islands and Tory Island, are considered the most "Irish" parts of Ireland, yet ironically, in recent years, the Irish motion picture industry has been filming popular films about traditional Irish culture not in Ireland, but on Mann (*Isle of Man*).

The Jacobite Rebellion and the Highland Clearances of the 18th and 19th centuries destroyed much of the Gaelic culture of Scotland, leading to mass emigration to America, like their Irish cousins in the later-19th century. What was left of traditional language and culture survived in the westernmost edge of the Highlands and on the islands. In the 19th century, Sir Walter Scott's adventure novels laundered the classical author's barbaric Celtic hordes into noble savages. It was during this time that the various Scottish clans were assigned the tartans with which we associate them today. This came about as a result of George IV's visit to Scotland in 1822; prior to this, individuals wore whatever tartan they chose. As representatives of the various clans came to the mills to order tartan fabric for the royal visit, they were assigned whatever was available or scheduled to be made, in the order in which they came in, and that association has lasted to this day. Today, Hebridean society is seen as retaining one of the "purest" forms of Scottish culture.

The Welsh Language Act of 1967 put the Welsh language on equal par with that of English in Wales, and Welsh is required to be taught in all schools. In a reversal of the 19th-century practice, one school requires students not to speak English on school property. A large part of the Welsh economy has been mining since prehistoric times; to this day, the Welsh people are identified with coal mining in Britain. BBC Wales maintains an all-Welsh television station, which can be watched on the Internet.

Galicia has a Celtic village at Santa Trega in which some of the houses have been reconstructed. To this day *castroes*, circular stone fortifications with concentric walls, may be seen. As in other Celtic areas, Galicia experienced a revival, the *Rexurdimento*, with political overtones in the 19th century. By the 20th century, the movement had solidified into political parties, the Autonomous Republican Organization and the Galeguist Party, which were persecuted by Francisco Franco's government. Galicia finally became a recognized Autonomous Community in 1981 under a 1936 Spanish law. Galician bagpipes *(gaita)*, similar to the Scottish Highland pipes, are gaining resurgence in popularity, as are traditional dances.

Today, the "Celtic Fringe" of Europe includes Ireland, Scotland, Wales, Mann, Cornwall, Brittany, and, arguably, Galicia. Besides having been possessors, if not currently speakers, of the Celtic languages, other common themes include bagpipes, the best known being the Highland pipes, then the Irish *Uillean* (elbow) pipes, played not with a mouthpiece, but with a bellows strapped to the arm, similar folklore and legends ("such as little people" and hero tales); low mountains and rocky soils; manufactured soils of seaweed, manure, and sand in the coastal areas; the importance of potatoes, swine, sheep, and dairying to the economies; deep religious feelings, a love of speech and music; poverty (the automobile manufacturing industry in Rennes is an exception to this) and a long history of emigration; seacoasts with excellent harbors; the wetness of the maritime climate; stem families with celibate adults; and, perhaps most strongly, a common sense of themselves as Celtic, distinct from the greater political communities of which they are parts. The Interceltic Congress, begun in 1867, still meets today, and international Celtic festivals play host to Scottish, Irish, Breton, Welsh, and now even Galician musicians, whose

Celtic bagpipe CDs can be purchased internationally. An international Celtic magazine, *Carn,* is designed to unite and inform the remaining Celtic communities of *Alba, Breizh, Cymru, Éire, Kernow,* and *Mannin* (respectively, Scotland, Brittany, Wales, Ireland, Cornwall, and Mann).

In the 20th century, anthropology began to look at folk communities in addition to preliterate, preindustrial societies. Some of the research turned to the Celtic countries; a sample of that work follows. One of the earliest community studies was Conrad Arensberg's and Salon T. Kimball's *Family and Community in Ireland.* Arensberg and Kimball studied three villages in County Clare, Ireland, in the 1930s, which they combined under the pseudonym, *Luogh.* It is a classic study of a now disappeared rural way of life. Isabel Emmett described her research in Llan in *A North Wales Village: A Social Anthropological Study.* In the early 1960s, John C. Messenger Jr. conducted research on one of the Aran Islands, considered one of the traditional parts of the country, at the mouth of Galway Bay. He described his research in *Inis Beag: Isle of Ireland,* with a focus on the rapprochements between religion, sex, and social life. Susan Parman described the island of Lewis in the Outer Hebrides in her book *Scottish Crofters: A Historical Ethnography of a Celtic Village,* which examined the crofting system, attitudes of the islanders to historic occurrences, such as the Highland Clearances, and to the intrusiveness of modern culture, as well as an examination of the history and current practice of the cottage industry of the island: weaving Harris Tweeds. Robin Fox examined marriage and kinship among the Tory islanders, off the coast of Donegal, in *The Tory Islanders: A People of the Celtic Fringe.* Nancy Scheper-Hughes wrote the controversial *Saints, Scholars, and Schizophrenics: Mental Illness in Rural Ireland,* describing her research into the connection between the traditional rural inheritance system and mental illness in County Kerry. Ellen Badone wrote *The Appointed Hour: Death, Worldview, and Social Change in Brittany,* about the cultural changes in Brittany since 1945.

Today, the homogenizing effect of television and other forms of mass communication is blurring the distinctions between communities on a global scale. The Celtic influence in the modern world, politics, and global economy always has been present, from the shipyards of Belfast to Andrew Carnegie's steel mills in America, but the dominant cultures always were given the credit for the innovations (for example, the *Titanic* was built in Belfast and made its last port of call in County Cork, Ireland, yet it is referred to as a British ship). Despite the homogenization of modern mass media, it has allowed the formerly "backward" areas to innovate in ways that the more industrialized regions have resisted on the grounds of the difficulty and expense of retooling. In the 1990s, the central west coastal area of Ireland, especially around Galway and Limerick/Shannon, became a major information-processing center for the world. The new information technology innovations have allowed the "Celtic Tiger" to become an international economic force in what used to be "poor Ireland," a country in which many households did not have telephones in the 1980s, but where now mobile telephones and personal computers are commonplace. For the first time since the 1840s, migration is in to Ireland rather than out of it.

— *Michael J. Simonton*

See also **Prehistory**

Further Readings

Childe, V. G. (1980). *Prehistoric communities of the British Isles.* New York: Arno Press.

Cunliffe, B. (2002). *The extraordinary voyage of Pytheas the Greek.* New York: Walker & Company.

Cunliffe, B. (2003). *The Celts: A very short introduction.* Oxford: University Press.

Eluère, C. (1993). *The Celts: Conquerors of ancient Europe.* New York: Abrams.

Raftery, B., & Clint, T. (Eds.). (2001). *Atlas of the Celts.* Buffalo, New York: Firefly Books.

Rankin, H. D. (1987). *Celts and the classical world.* London: Croom & Helm.

Squire, C. (1975). *Celtic myth and legend: Poetry and romance.* Newcastle: Newcastle Publishing.

 CERCOPITHECINES

Cercopithecines are primates that make up one of the two major groups of Old World monkeys. All Old World monkeys are members of a single primate family, Cercopithecidae, and so are referred to collectively as "cercopithecids." The family consists of two distinct subfamilies, Colobinae ("colobines") and

Cercopithecinae ("cercopithecines"), which separated about 14 million years ago.

About 73 species of cercopithecines are currently recognized. They range in size from dwarf guenons (females 745–820 g, males 1255–1280 g) to baboons, the largest monkeys (anubis baboon females 14.5–15.0 kg, males 22–28 kg). The cercopithecine group includes several species that are common in zoos, laboratories, and field studies, such as various species of macaques (including rhesus monkeys), baboons, drills and mandrills, guenons, and mangabeys. Currently, cercopithecines are the subjects of about two thirds of all non–in vitro research publications on nonhuman primates. The behavior, social relationships, group structure, ecology, and demography of various free-ranging cercopithecines have been the focus of many studies. As a result, we have, for the best-studied species, a large and rapidly expanding body of information about the lives of these animals in nature.

Distribution, Habitats, and Diets

Other than macaque monkeys, all species of wild cercopithecines are restricted to Africa, with one exception: a small population of hamadryas baboons along the southern edge of the Arabian Peninsula. Conversely, macaques are represented in Africa only by Barbary macaques, in the Atlas Mountain region, but in Eurasia by a series of about 15 species extending eastward across southern Asia to various islands of the south Pacific and north as far as the islands of Japan. The distributions of individual species of cercopithecines range in size from part of one peninsula of one Pacific island (Heck's macaque) to large portions of Africa (anubis baboons) and Asia (rhesus).

The habitats of various cercopithecine species differ widely: swamp forest, many other types of forest and open woodland, alpine meadows and bamboo thickets, savannah grassland, even Ethiopian rocky desert, and the Japanese island of Hokkaido, which is covered by snow in winter. A few species are primarily arboreal (for example, dwarf guenons) or terrestrial (patas monkeys, hamadryas, geladas), but most species are both, in varying proportions.

The two subfamilies of Old World monkeys are distinguished by various dental and skeletal features, but of particular ecological and behavioral significance are two distinguishing features of the animals' soft tissues: cheek pouches, found only in cercopithecines, versus a stomach with at least three enlarged fermentation chambers, found only in colobines. The cheek pouches of cercopithecines are used for short-term storage of relatively small but locally concentrated foods that can be harvested faster than they can be orally processed, thus reducing exposure to competition and predation. Later, at their leisure, the monkeys bring the foods back into the oral cavity for processing before swallowing them. Monkeys of this subfamily are sometimes referred to as "cheek-pouched monkeys."

Few cercopithecine primates are obligate food specialists. Most species can be characterized as eclectic omnivores, in that their foraging is very selective yet their diet is highly diverse. They feed selectively on a great variety of plant and animal foods that are available in their habitat, eating this part of a plant but not that, feeding on the fruit of one species but not that of a similar, closely related species, feeding on fruit that is fully ripe and ignoring fruit that is semiripe, removing acacia seeds from their pods, then the naked seeds from its seed coats, and so on. Baboons represent the extreme development of such highly selective omnivory. Their mastery of this mode of life has enabled them to become the most widespread and abundant primates on the African continent. Selection for traits that lead to such success are still present: among yearling baboons, differences in dietary intake of proteins and energy are accurate predictors of survivorship and lifetime reproductive success.

Grouping Tendencies

Most cercopithecine populations are partitioned into discrete, relatively closed and permanent social groups. Among the various groups within a local population, age and sex composition varies. Sizes of cercopithecine groups range from two individuals, in monogamous pairs of DeBrazzas monkeys, to 845 animals (mean 620) in hordes of mandrills. At any given time, group composition results from the population's history of seven processes: births and deaths, emigrations and immigrations across group boundaries, group fissions and fusions, and maturation. The first four of these processes can, under some conditions, result in populations having equal distributions of males and females among groups, and these sex distributions are consistent with observed distributions in several species of wild primates, including baboons. Such purely demographic models can indicate how the distribution of individuals among groups of a local population can remain largely unchanged over time and why group composition varies nonetheless. But they do not clarify the adaptive significance of species differences in group compositions. At present, the primary determinants of mammalian grouping patterns are considered to be ecological factors, particularly access to essential resources, such as food and mates, and reduction in exposure to hazards, such as predators.

For female cercopithecines, the characteristic numbers in groups of each species are thought to be determined largely by the spatial and temporal distributions of food and predation. For example, the smallest groupings (less than five adult females) are found among arboreal fruit and leaf specialists, such as mona monkeys and greater spot-nosed monkeys, which feed in trees on fruits and shoots; group size may be limited by the numbers of individuals that can feed together in one tree. Conversely, large groups with many females occur in species that may be particularly susceptible to predation, such as terrestrial species that range into treeless areas. In addition, large groups may have other advantages for females, including better conditions for child rearing, buffers against group extinction resulting from stochastic effects, and a larger pool of socially transmitted information.

In turn, the distributions of adult males among groups apparently are determined by the distributions of females: Males go where females are. Cercopithecine species with few females per group (average of six at most) always include just one adult male; species whose groups average more than 10 females never do. Overall, the number of males per group increases linearly with the number of females.

The dynamics underlying the distribution of adult males among the groups of a local population were revealed in a long-term study of group processes in the yellow baboons of Amboseli, Kenya. First, males that were reproductively less successful had shorter tenure in groups than males that were more successful. Second, the availability of cycling females and an individual male's own mating success were powerful predictors of male dispersal patterns. Males, whether natal or immigrants, were much more likely to emigrate in months when the number of males exceeded the number of cycling females, and they virtually never emigrated when cycling females were in excess. Similarly, the proportion of new immigrants in a group was approximately 4 times greater in months when cycling females were in excess. However, for a variety of reasons, such as the risks of dispersal, these intergroup migrations did not result in a perfect balance between the numbers of males and the numbers of cycling females. In several species of seasonally breeding guenons, males commonly move into groups at the time of year that females are receptive.

Several species of large, terrestrial cercopithecine primates live in small, one-male groups that merge into larger aggregations at various times. Such repeated fission and fusion of groups occurs daily in hamadryas baboons and geladas and has been reported to occur in pigtail macaques, drills, and mandrills. Among nonhuman primates, the hamadryas baboons of Ethiopia are the extreme example of multilevel, fission/fusion societies. Their basic social and reproductive groups are one-male units, each containing a single adult male, several females, and their offspring. (A few such female groupings, often termed "harems" in the literature, contain a second adult male who mates with the unit females only by stealth.) Two or three one-male units that are strongly associated constitute the next-higher unit, clans, within which each one-male unit remains intact. Social interactions are more common within clans than between. Mature males of a clan often bear a strong physical resemblance to each other and so are thought to be genetically related.

At the next-higher level of social organization, several hamadryas clans and some single males form bands. Band membership and clan membership are stable over many years. Bands are autonomous foraging units, but clans sometimes separate temporarily from their band as they feed on the sparse vegetation of their semidesert habitat. At night, members of a clan sleep on the same sleeping bluff. Several bands may congregate at one bluff, forming large herds (troops) of variable-band composition and sometimes numbering over 200 animals. These various levels of social organization in hamadryas appear to be adaptations to the spatial distribution of essential resources in their rocky desert habitat. Small, dispersed groups most effectively harvest sparse food, and large nightly aggregations provide safety in numbers on their large, dispersed night refuges.

Compared with hamadryas, the fission/fusion groupings of geladas show interesting similarities and differences, but again, probably representing adaptations to an extreme environment. For example, their daily fission/fusion cycle is the opposite of that of hamadryas: One-male, multifemale units of geladas in the Simien Mountains of Ethiopia sleep separately on the abundant cliff ledges during the night, then each morning coalesce into herds of hundreds of animals that feed on the lush alpine meadows.

Maternal Kinships and Social Relations

Selected aspects of cercopithecine kinship and social relationship—topics of particular interest to many anthropologists—are briefly discussed below. The patterns that are discussed here are based primarily on the most extensively studied cercopithecines, namely, yellow baboons, rhesus monkeys, Japanese macaques, and vervets. These primates are among the 25 species (out of 46 cercopithecines for which information on social structure is available) that live and breed in multimale-multifemale groups. Multimale bisexual groups are rare among mammals, and so there has been considerable speculation about why these 25 species—primarily macaques, baboons, and mangabeys—should be different. These multimale-multifemale groups are matrilocal: With rare exceptions, all females remain for their entire lives in the social group in which they were born. However, many males leave their natal group about the time that they reach physical maturity. Thus, each of these groups consists of clusters of matrilines (adult females and their descendants) and several adult males, most of whom have immigrated from other groups.

In these primates, adult females are the stable core of a group, not only because of their lifetime tenure in it but also because among them there is a "linear" (transitive and connected) dominance hierarchy that, with few exceptions, remains stable for many years, often for females' lifetimes. (Among baboon females, the primary exceptions are old females, some of whom drop in rank relative to their daughters.) Furthermore, each adult female ranks above all females of other matrilines that her mother dominates and above all female descendants of those females, again with few exceptions. In that sense, the female lineages themselves can be rank ordered.

In these species of baboons, vervets, and macaques, young females form strong, lifelong social bonds with their mother and other female relatives, and the resulting coalitions may contribute to stabilizing the dominance hierarchy. By contrast, maternal dominance has no discernable effect on rank acquisition among males, perhaps because in these species, the mother is not dominant over any of the other adult males. A few cases of adult females being dominant to

adult males have been reported, but in those groups, the relation of a son's rank to his mother's is currently unknown. Males tend to rise quickly in rank as they approach physical maturity, reach their highest rank in the next few years (about 2 years in yellow baboons), and then decline more slowly but steadily with age thereafter.

The pattern of strong matrilineal kinship effects described above has been found in provisioned Japanese and rhesus macaques, wild savannah baboons, and vervet monkeys but does not typify macaques of several other species studied in captivity (bonnet, Barbary, Tonkean, and stump-tailed macaques), in which females show little or no kin bias in affiliative interactions. Furthermore, in captivity, bonnet macaque females may come to outrank not only their mothers but also females dominant to their mothers. These species differences appear to be related to the extent to which the agonistic behavior of a macaque species can be described as "despotic" (rhesus and Japanese macaques), intermediate (long-tailed macaques), or "egalitarian" (Tonkean, bonnet, Barbary, and stump-tailed macaques), in that in the more despotic forms, kinship profoundly influenced social and dominance relations, whereas at the other extreme, affiliative interactions among nonkin were much more frequent, and little severe aggression was observed in egalitarian species.

In some species or populations of cercopithecines, a curious pattern of dominance relationships has been observed between sisters. Each new daughter of the matriarch takes on, as she approaches maturity, a dominance rank immediately below that of her mother but above that of her older sisters. Thus, sisters typically rank in reverse order of their ages. This pattern of "youngest ascendant" may result from the mother's agonistic support and defense of her infants against any others that the mother dominates.

Source: Photograph by Carol Berman from p. 69 in *Kinship and Behavior in Primates*, Bernard Chapais & Carol Berman, eds. Copyright © 2004 by Oxford University Press, Inc. Used by permission of the press.

Since 1958, when this pattern of "youngest ascendant" among sisters was first described in Japanese macaques by Masao Kawai and Shunzo Kawamura, it has also been observed in groups of wild baboons and vervets and in provisioned rhesus monkeys but, curiously, not in unprovisioned wild Japanese macaques.

Even in species in which the "youngest ascendancy" pattern predominates, exceptions have been observed. Several processes have been suggested as promoting these exceptions, including relative physical strengths of the individual females and availability of potential allies, as determined by demographic variables such as interbirth intervals, infant mortality, and competition for clumped food sources.

The tendency for matrilines within a group to be closely related to each other is augmented by two processes. First, when a group of baboons or macaques fissions into two or more new groups, they sometimes do so along kinship lines: Females of each matriline tend to go into the same new group. Second, in some groups, high-ranking females tend to produce a preponderance of daughters (who remain in the group), whereas low-ranking females tend to produce a preponderance of sons, many of whom will eventually leave their natal group. This rank-related sex bias or simply higher reproductive success among high-ranking females, combined with the tendency of daughters to rank just below their mother, results in a "push-down" system, in which low-ranking matriarchs do not produce as many female descendants, whereas an increasing proportion of the middle ranks come to be occupied by older daughters of high-ranking matriarchs as the lineages of their mother and their higher-ranking younger sisters continue to grow. In such groups, all females probably are related to one another to some degree.

Kinship relations are one of the most important factors influencing behavior and social relationships in female cercopithecine primates. They affect not only dominance relationships and access to resources but also patterns of affiliative behavior, such as spatial proximity, subgroup clustering, social grooming, alliance formation, conflict intervention, reconciliation, and cofeeding. However, females may also form affiliative relationships with supposedly unrelated females. For such cases in particular, rank proximity (closeness in dominance ranks) has been proposed as an alternative basis for attraction among females. Because rank proximity and kinship relatedness are positively correlated, this hypothesis has been difficult to test until recently, when appropriate statistical methods, based on matrix permutations, have been developed. By means of these methods, rank proximity has been shown to affect affiliative behavior independent of the effects of maternal kinship. An alternative and possibly correlated factor is a tendency of females to associate with their paternal siblings, discussed below.

Paternal Kinships and Social Relations

Savannah baboons, vervets, rhesus, and Japanese macaques are all polygynandrous: Males potentially mate with more than one female and females with more than one male, even during a single reproductive cycle. Thus, although the mother of each infant can be identified in the field unambiguously on behavioral grounds, the father cannot, and so until recently, only maternal kinship relationships could be positively identified in field studies. However, development of noninvasive methods for genetic analysis of free-ranging animals using hair or feces has made possible the identification of fathers.

In 1979, Jeanne Altmann pointed out the potential importance of paternal sibships in nonhuman primates. A subsequent series of studies of yellow baboons in Amboseli, Kenya, carried out by Susan Alberts, Altmann, and their colleagues have shown, first, that consortships between siblings involve less sexual but more affiliative behavior than those between nonsibs; second, that adult female paternal sisters are at least as affiliative as maternal sisters; and most recently, that baboon fathers preferentially support their own young, even though an infant's father may not have been the only male to mate with the mother during the fertile part of the cycle in which she became pregnant. Similarly, rhesus females that are paternal sibs and are close in age maintain stronger affiliations with each other than with nonkin.

Thus, these monkeys appear to have an ability to recognize not only their maternal kin but also their paternal kin, that is, to react differentially to them. Beyond that, several experiments, carried out both on group-living captive animals and in the wild, strongly suggest that cercopithecines can also recognize kinship relationships among other individuals in their group. For example, when the distress call of a juvenile vervet monkey was played back, the mother of the infant looked toward the loud speaker, as expected, but the other adult females looked toward the mother. After a group-living, captive, long-tailed macaque was conditioned to respond when shown photographs of a mother and her offspring, she correctly matched photos from her group of mothers and their infants. In agonistic encounters, captive bonnet macaque males consistently recruited support from males that outranked their opponent. In playback experiments, wild chacma baboons responded more strongly to call sequences mimicking dominance rank reversals between matrilineal families than within. In several species (Japanese and pigtail macaques, vervets), monkeys that have recently been threatened will frequently "redirect" aggression by threatening a third party, often specifically targeting a close matrilineal relative of their recent opponent.

The mechanisms for kin recognition by cercopithecines have not yet been identified, but suspects include social familiarity and spatial proximity during development (ultimately based on the mother-infant bond) and phenotype matching, including distinctive odors controlled by genes of the major histocompatability complex. From the standpoint of Hamiltonian kin selection, the essential issue is the result: kin-biased behavior.

Research on paternal kinship is adding a new and unexpected perspective to kinship effects on primate social systems and will lead to reevaluation of the proximate mechanisms whereby social relationships develop.

— *Stuart A. Altmann*

See also **Baboons; Macaques; Monkeys, Old World**

Further Readings

Chapais, B., & Berman, C. M. (Eds.). (2004). *Kinship and behavior in primates.* Oxford: Oxford University Press.

Fa, J. E., & Lindberg, D. G. (Eds.). (1996). *Evolution and ecology of macaque societies.* Cambridge: Cambridge University Press.

Glenn, M. E., & Cords, M. (Eds.). (2002). *The guenons: Diversity and adaptation in African monkeys.* New York: Kluwer Academic.

Groves, C. (2001). *Primate taxonomy.* Washington, DC: Smithsonian Institution.

Kappeler, P. M. (Ed.). (2000). *Primate males: Causes and consequences of variation in group composition.* Cambridge: Cambridge University Press.

Rowe, N. (1996). *The pictorial guide to the living primates.* Charlestown, RI: Pogonias.

CHACHAPOYA INDIANS

The Chachapoya Indians, often described in popular media as Peru's ancient "Cloud People," inhabited the Andean tropical cloud forests between the Marañon and Huallaga River valleys prior to their rapid cultural disintegration after the Spanish conquest in AD 1532 (see Figure 1). In anthropology and in the popular imagination, the Chachapoya represent the quintessential "lost tribe," founders of a "lost civilization," and builders of "lost cities" now abandoned and concealed by cold and rainy tropical cloud forests. In world archaeology, the Chachapoya resemble the ancient Maya and Khmer civilizations insofar as they challenge conventional anthropological wisdom regarding theoretical limitations on cultural development in tropical forest environments. The Chachapoya are most widely recognized for their distinctive archaeological remains. These include monumental clusters of circular stone dwellings 4 to 10 m in diameter and built on terraced, and often fortified, mountain- and

ridgetops. The most famous include ruined settlements at Kuelap, Vira Vira, and Gran Pajatén, and elaborate cliff tombs like Los Pinchudos, Laguna de los Condores, and Revash, set high above mountain valleys. Chachapoya settlements typically yield few surface artifacts, but cliff tombs nestled in arid microclimates afford a rare glimpse of perishable Andean material culture, including preserved mummies, textiles, wooden statues, carved gourds, feathers, cordage, and even Inca string-knot records called *quipu*.

Both scholars and lay authors have attempted to reconcile the paradox of a cosmopolitan, urban, Chachapoya "civilization" seemingly isolated within Peru's most remote and forbidding eastern Andean cloud forests. The fortified urban complex at Kuelap contains over 400 circular stone constructions sitting atop a 600 m stretch of prominent ridge top that its builders flattened and entirely "encased" with massive masonry walls up to 20 m high (see Figure 2). Buildings ornately decorated with stone mosaic friezes at Gran Pajatén and Los Pinchudos have been granted World Heritage status by the United Nations Educational, Scientific, and Cultural Organization (UNESCO), and are widely considered masterpieces of pre-Columbian monumental art (see Figure 3). These contradictions, coupled with the scarcity of historical documentation, have led to much romanticizing, mystification, and pseudoscientific speculation regarding Chachapoya cultural and "racial" origins. Even most scientific theories posit external origins for Chachapoya populations, based on the assumption that tropical montane forests cannot support dense populations and complex social and political structures. Such theories postulate that brief periods of cultural and artistic florescence were externally subsidized by the Inca state. The fall of the Inca is widely believed accountable for the demise of the Chachapoya and other dependent eastern-slope societies, and the rapid abandonment of regions now blanketed in montane forest. Only within recent decades are archaeologists beginning to construct a reliable Chachapoya culture history and to understand the economic and sociopolitical systems that evidently supported autonomous Chachapoya societies.

The name *Chachapoya* (often written as *Chachapoyas* or *Chacha*) is extrinsic, referring to the administrative province established by Inca conquerors around AD 1470, and later described by Spanish chroniclers like Garcilazo de la Vega and Cieza de León. Scholars now use the term *Chachapoya* to refer to the people and *Chachapoyas* in reference to their

Figure 1   Map of northern Peru with locations of Chachapoya territories and major sites

probably exceeded 300,000 individuals, but by AD 1650, they had declined far in excess of 90%. Demographic collapse, coupled with a lack of sustained Spanish interest in a remote region with no indigenous labor pool, has left scholars with scant historical evidence with which to reconstruct Chachapoya language and culture.

The scale and magnitude of monumental constructions widely distributed across the northern cloud forest have led some to propose the existence of a unified, pre-Inca Chachapoya state or kingdom. Based upon its extraordinary scale, a few scholars have viewed Kuelap as the paramount Chachapoya political center. The settlement's population has been estimated at approximately 3,000 prior to the Inca invasion. News media descriptions of Gran Vilaya (La Congona) and Gran Saposoa reported by explorer Gene Savoy as "metropolises" covering 120 and 26 square miles, respectively, are sensational exaggerations, as they conjoin distinct sites with no obvious interrelationships. The documentary evidence portrays the Chachapoya as a patchwork of autonomous polities that frequently warred upon one another when not confederated against a common outside threat such as the Inca. Historical evidence further indicates a clear lack of political and even military unity during defensive and insurgent actions against the Inca and factional conflicts between local leaders after Spanish conquest. Because of scant documentary evidence, much of the burden for reconstructing Chachapoya culture has fallen to archaeologists. Inspection of the archaeological record likewise reveals regional variation in architecture, ceramics, and iconography. In terms of settlement design and details of building architecture, no two Chachapoya sites are identical.

The paltry ethnohistorical evidence for Chachapoya culture contained in major colonial period chronicles and scattered administrative and ecclesiastical records

pre-Hispanic homeland. The former appears to be an Inca-inspired amalgamation of a local tribal name Chacha with the Inca (Quechua language) term for "cloud," *puya*. As such, cultural affiliation implied by Chachapoya is an artifice referring only to local populations grouped together by the Inca on the basis of cultural similarity for the purposes of administration. Archaeological research within the region corresponding to the Inca province reveals broadly shared cultural attributes that evidently reflect the emergence of a regional cultural identity predating the Inca conquest, perhaps by AD 900. Because scholars have been slow to recognize the degree to which cultural and demographic transformations wrought by Inca conquerors permanently altered indigenous social and political structures, they have used the term Chachapoya loosely to refer to pre-Inca, Inca period, and Spanish colonial period cultural identities that are quite difficult to disentangle. Colonial period cultural identities may be the least accessible. By the time of sustained Spanish contact in 1536, the Inca had already exiled large numbers of rebellious Chachapoya, and diseases introduced from the north, west, and east had begun taking a high toll. Chachapoya populations once offers information of variable reliability. Scholars generally view Garcilazo de la Vega's reproduction of Jesuit priest Blas Valera's description of Chachapoya culture under Inca domination as reliable. Spanish chroniclers typically describe the Chachapoya romantically as renowned for their fierce warriors and powerful sorcerers. Repeated references to Chachapoya women as "white," "beautiful," and "gracefully proportioned" have become fodder for racist theories. The explorer Savoy adds "tall and fair-skinned, with light hair and blue eyes" to buttress

Figure 2   The perimeter walls at the fortified settlement of Kuelap reach 20 meters high

his assertion that the Chachapoya reside in mythical Ophir as descendents of Phoenician maritime traders and King Solomon's miners. Unfortunately, such misinformation regarding Chachapoya origins and racial affiliations disseminated by charlatans and profiteers often sells more copy than scientific treatises, and it abounds on the World Wide Web. By styling themselves in the cinematic molds of Indiana Jones or Allan Quatermain, pseudoarchaeologists such as Savoy have built impressive private fortunes by attracting international media attention to periodic "discoveries" of sites well-known to villagers and archaeologists. Contemporary ethnohistorian Waldemar Espinoza's more sober interpretation of Chachapoya culture is based upon analysis of some administrative documents, but he presents some conjecture as fact, and he does not reveal all of his sources. Jorge Zavallos, Duccio Bonavia, Federico Kauffman Doig, Arturo Ruiz Estrada, Alfredo Narvaez, Daniel Morales Chocano, Peter Lerche, Inge Schjellerup, Gary Urton, Sonia Guillen, and Adriana von Hagen are among other contemporary historians and anthropologists who have published significant interpretations of Chachapoya society and culture history. Today, archaeologists strive to document Chachapoya settlements and cliff tombs prior to the arrival of highland colonists, uncontrolled adventure-tourists, and looters, which are rapidly destroying the archaeological

record. What follows is a brief outline of present scientific knowledge of the so-called Chachapoya distilled from ethnohistory and archaeology.

Location, Environment, and Territory

The Inca province of "Chachapoyas" encompassed approximately 25,000 sq km of mountainous terrain between the Marañon and Huallaga Rivers. This territory trended north and south from the lower Utcubamba river valley near 6° S. latitude, approximately 250 km to the modern boundary separating La Libertad and Huánuco departments at 8° S. latitude. From east to west, it begins in dry thorn forests in the Marañon canyon, near 78° 30′ W. longitude, and straddles moist montane, alpine, and wet montane rain forest ecological zones of the cordillera, to end somewhere in the lower montane rain forests of the Huallaga Valley, near 77° 30′ W. The deep Marañon river canyon provided a natural boundary to the west. The other boundaries, especially the eastern boundary, are much harder to locate precisely. Politically, Inca-period Chachapoyas covers portions of the modern Peruvian departments of Amazonas, San Martin, and La Libertad. Today, populations cluster between 2,500 and 3,000 m, where they produce staple grains, legumes, and tubers on deforested intermontane valley slopes, while periodically tending

Figure 3   The cliff tombs of Los Pinchudos viewed with a fish-eye camera lens exhibit four hanging wooden statues and characteristic Chachapoya stone mosaic friezes

cattle in higher alpine valleys. Fruit, coca, and chili peppers are cultivated at lower elevations. In pre-Hispanic times, however, Chachapoya populations were much greater and concentrated above 3,000 m on prominent ridgetops along the Marañon-Huallaga divide or between 2,800 and 2,000 m on lower eastern slopes now cloaked in tropical forest.

In general, documentary sources and archaeological evidence still provide scant clues to identify pre-Inca cultural boundaries, which must have shifted frequently with changing social alliances and cultural identities. Enough data are accumulating to begin identifying cultural variability within Chachapoya territory. Documentary sources describe a major Inca and colonial period administrative boundary between northern and southern divisions that shifted between Leymebamba and Cajamarquilla (now modern Bolivar). Archaeologically studied population concentrations and settlement types can be grouped into three imperfectly understood divisions. The first is evident along the Utcubamba-Marañon River divide and throughout the upper Utcubamba watershed. It includes ancient settlements at Kuelap, Caserones (perhaps ancient Papamarca), and Pirka Pirka above Uchucmarca. The second division stretches from Bolivar, southward along the Marañon-Huallaga

divide as far as modern Pias, and includes Gran Pajatén and Cunturmarca. Limited exploration of the Huallaga side of the cordillera suggests that this division's demographic core may have lain on the now forested slopes. An apparently distinctive third division lies between Buldibuyo and Huancaspata, centering around the Parcoy and Cajas River tributaries of the Marañon River, and including the sites of Charcoy and Nuñamarca. This third, southernmost area is often excluded from recent considerations of Chachapoya territory, but documentary evidence suggests that it was part of Chachapoyas as the Spanish understood it. Archaeologically, the latter two divisions are the least known. This tripartite grouping may be more apparent than real, as vast stretches of remote and forested terrain remain unknown to science. Even the best-known areas have been inadequately sampled.

The eastern Andean cloud forest habitat of the Chachapoya, often called the "Ceja de Selva" or "Ceja de Montaña" (literally edge, or eyebrow, of the jungle), coincides with a major cultural boundary between highland societies participating in Andean cultural traditions and tropical forest lowlanders practicing Amazonian traditions. Geographers regard this sparsely inhabited region as the last forested South American wilderness. Indeed, the cloud forest represents an environmental transition of unparalleled magnitude. Much 20th-century literature depicts an equally rigid cultural dichotomy, split by the eastern "frontier" where Andean civilization ends and the "uncivilized" world of Amazonia begins. However, archaeologists have begun to recognize that the perceived dichotomy between civilized and savage worlds never existed prior to successive imperial conquests by the Inca and Spanish. The Chachapoya and many other poorly known eastern-slope societies left ample evidence of pre-Hispanic settlement in what was thought to be an "empty" wilderness with scattered pockets of highland colonists tending coca fields. Archaeological and ethnohistorical analyses of the so-called Andean frontier now acknowledge the presence of elastic, fluid, and sometimes ephemeral series of social boundaries at this major cultural interface, where interaction was constant. Such boundaries shifted in response to circumstances both local and regional, endogenous and exogenous, as societies in each region offered rare and desirable natural or manufactured commodities to societies in other regions throughout the prehistoric past. A vast amount of archaeological evidence of pre-Hispanic settlement and economic activity is masked today by thick forests, which capitalist ventures repeatedly fail to exploit successfully in any sustainable fashion.

Biological Origins

Biological data from skeletal populations recovered by archaeologists remain paltry but promise to shed light on persistent questions of origins. Preliminary analyses of skeletons from Laguna de los Condores, Laguna Huallabamba, and Los Pinchudos document rather typical Native American physiognomies that may reflect variation within the parameters of Andean populations. Not a shred of evidence supports the notion of "White" Chachapoya populations of European or Mediterranean descent. In fact, studies of DNA from mortuary remains at Laguna Huallabamba linked one cadaver to a living descendent in the nearby village of Utchucmarca, a case demonstrating biological continuity between ancient and modern populations not unlike Britain's "Cheddar Man." The problem of origins of the very earliest Andean populations currently remains an issue of contention among archaeologists. Archaeological excavations at Manachaqui Cave in southern Chachapoyas unearthed stone tools and radiocarbon evidence demonstrating human occupation at the edge of the cloud forest by the end of the Pleistocene Epoch, as early as anywhere else in the highland Andes. Although the Manachaqui sequence is not uninterrupted, it yields cultural remains evincing remarkable stylistic continuity through the late pre-Hispanic centuries of Inca imperialism. Of course, cultural continuity does not necessarily reflect biological continuity. Continued biometric research on Chachapoya skeletal samples should address competing hypotheses related to transregional migrations, population interactions, and the antiquity and continuity of human occupation on the eastern slopes of the Central Andes.

Cultural Origins

Anthropology discovered Chachapoyas with the arrival of Adolf Bandolier at the end of the 19th century, while the first scientific archaeology in the region was conducted by Henri and Paula Reichlen during the 1940s. Throughout the 20th century, archaeologists addressed the question of Chachapoya origins, and opinions became divided as they pointed to either highland or lowland sources. Until the mid-1980s, and archaeological fieldwork coordinated by the University of Colorado and Yale University in the United States and Peru's Universidad Nacional de Trujillo, the notion that the Chachapoya Indians descended from late pre-Hispanic migrants from the neighboring highlands remained the predominant interpretation. Early radiocarbon dates from Gran Pajatén and Manachaqui Cave produced unassailable evidence that humans had occupied the montane cloud forests since 200 BC, and the greater eastern slopes by the end of the Paleo-Indian period. As data accumulate, the archaeology of Chachapoyas has begun to resemble that of other Central Andean regions, but the pre-Hispanic population density, the scale of landscape transformation, and the abundance of monument construction in this extremely wet and steep environment still defy intuition. The extraordinary architectural achievements at monumental sites like Kuelap and Gran Pajatén would garner world attention regardless of their geographical contexts. These characteristics, coupled with isolation from modern Peru's coast-centered economy, add to the mystique that has nourished pseudoscientific speculation on Chachapoya origins. But it must be borne in mind that the abandonment of this populated region began with early colonial period demographic collapse and forced-relocation programs. It became permanent with the alteration of indigenous social formations and modes of production and the extinction of cultural memories.

The characterization of pre-Inca Chachapoya boundaries previously offered should introduce the reader to the complex problem of identifying the origins of cultural identities such as the Chachapoya. The Chachapoya "culture," or cultural tradition, was comprised of practices and traditions that converged piecemeal and only crystallized when subjected to particular internal or external forces that remain to be identified. This time of ethnogenesis, when the Chachapoya first appear archaeologically as a regional tradition with shared architectural, ceramic, and mortuary styles, is to some extent an "artifact" of archaeological visibility. Radiocarbon dates suggest that Chachapoya practices of building circular stone dwellings on terraced mountain tops and interring their dead in masonry cliff tombs date to around AD 1000, while more tenuous evidence suggests one or two centuries of additional antiquity. At Manachaqui Cave, the origins of diagnostic Chachapoya-style coarse brown pottery with appliqué decoration and folded rims can be traced all the way back to 1500 BC, when pottery first appears in the Andes.

The ceramic sequence from stratified deposits excavated from Manachaqui shows gaps between 400 BC and 200 BC, and AD 700 and AD 1000, yet basic shapes and decorative norms persist from earliest times to the European conquest. The Chachapoya preference for promontory settlement locations probably dates to centuries between AD 200 and AD 400, when settlement patterns shifted to higher mountain- and ridgetops all along the eastern slopes. The shift likely reflects a new emphasis on camelid pastoralism at higher altitudes, adoption of llama caravan transport technology, and entry into broadened spheres of Andean interregional exchange. Diagnostic Chachapoya architecture, cliff tombs, and iconography still lack radiocarbon evidence to establish a precise developmental chronology. Hence, the full fruition of the complete constellation of cultural attributes that scholars have come to identify as Chachapoyas remains poorly dated. However, it is already clear that Chachapoya "culture" did not simply arrive from elsewhere, but instead developed locally through processes similar to those that governed the development of other, better-known Andean cultures.

Language

The identification of the pre-Inca, indigenous Chachapoya language or dialects would contribute important information to resolve issues of Chachapoya origins. Unfortunately, recognition of these has been obscured by the Inca imposition of Quechua between AD 1470 and AD 1532 as the imperial lingua franca. The demographic collapse of the 16th and 17th centuries further contributed to the virtual extinction of aboriginal languages in the region. Evidently, there was no ecclesiastical interest in recording local languages for indoctrinary purposes, and the only surviving evidence of Chachapoya languages consists of names of individuals and places appearing in historical and modern records and maps. Analysis of these by several specialists has yielded inconclusive results. Most intriguing are recent suggestions of relationships to Jivaroan languages, which are presently spoken in the forested lowlands to the northeast. A distribution overlapping lowland and highland foothill environments would not be unprecedented, since the ethnohistorically documented Palta and Bracamoro of the southeastern Ecuadorian Andes spoke Jivaroan dialects. It is possible, perhaps likely, that several unrelated languages were spoken across pre-Incaic Chachapoyas and that a widely used trade jargon blended elements of these with pre-Incaic north Peruvian highland Quechua and minority language groups like Culle. While this proposal is speculative, it would help account for the extraordinarily murky picture of historical linguistics emerging from the region.

Economy

Documentary sources offer little to suggest that Chachapoya subsistence strategies differed greatly from those of other highland Andean societies. Cieza de León's observation that the Chachapoya kept substantial herds of camelids (llamas and alpacas) may reflect his surprise at finding these ubiquitous Andean herd animals in such extreme environments. Evidently, Chachapoya settlements were located to facilitate access to herds, as well as to fields for cultivating a typical mix of Andean staples, especially high-altitude tubers like potatoes, and maize, legumes, and squash from lower slopes. Remaining at issue is the question of whether the Chachapoya, or at least those "Chachapoya" populations settled deep in the eastern montane forests, were largely self-sufficient with regard to subsistence needs. The vast extent of terracing systems on eastern valley slopes attests to labor organization and agricultural production on a large scale. Although many scholars believe that such terraces were constructed for monocropping of maize and coca under imperial Inca direction, the emerging picture of the Chachapoya would instead suggest a long history of local economic and subsistence autonomy predating Inca hegemony. Of course, no Andean economy was ever entirely self-contained, as all societies relied to some degree upon interregional exchange of items crucial to the maintenance of domestic and political systems.

In the moist soils at Chachapoya archaeological sites, food remains do not ordinarily preserve well, but recovered samples of charred potatoes, maize, and beans support documentary evidence. Studies of floral and faunal remains from the subalpine rockshelter Manachaqui Cave (3,650 m), coupled with paleoecological data from sediment cores recovered at nearby Laguna Manachaqui, suggest that local populations intensified the cultivation of high-altitude grains, like quinoa, by 2000 BC. Remains of maize and beans likely cultivated at lower altitudes appear around 800 BC, and camelids enter Manachaqui's archaeological record between AD 200 and AD 400. With the exception of the relatively late introduction of llamas and alpacas, these data exhibit a developmental sequence resembling those recovered from other Central Andean regions. Evidently, local populations did not adopt domesticated camelids as sources of meat and wool, as did Andean populations in neighboring regions. Instead, the appearance of camelids correlates with other evidence suggesting utilization of llamas as beasts of burden in broadening networks of Andean interaction.

Economic activities that lie at the heart of Chachapoya cultural development relate to the geographically privileged location of these societies. Poised strategically between populations that anthropologists typically dichotomize as "Andean" and "Amazonian," the Chachapoya supplied a crucial link in long chains of interregional communication and exchange. Because of its unusually deep penetration into the Central Andes, archaeologists have long believed that the Upper Marañon River valley west of Chachapoyas served as a major "highway" for migrations and trade throughout Andean prehistory. However, the role of the upper Marañon may be overrated, as its canyon is narrow and steep and the river is only seasonally navigable by balsa rafts through the canyon above the mouth of the Utcubamba River. By land, entry to the Central Andes from the northeastern lowlands can be gained only by traversing the populated ridgetops of Chachapoyas. By river, greater penetration of the Central Andes could be gained by canoe navigation up the Huallabamba River into the heart of Chachapoyas or by navigating the southward course of the Huallaga River as far as Tingo María in Huánuco Department. The latter route bypasses Chachapoyas, but also bypasses most of northern Peru. Scattered references to paved roads and Inca outposts in the forested Huallabamba valley further indicate that this was a major gateway to the Central Andes. During the mid-16th and 17th centuries, Chachapoyas was the jumping-off point for expeditions to Amazonia in search of mythical El Dorado. Ethnohistorical analyses describe the lowland Cholones and Hivitos Indians as trade partners living along the middle Huallaga. Products typically traded across the eastern slope would include feathers, wax, honey, stone and metal axes, coca, cotton, wool, vegetal dyes, hardwoods, slaves, medicinal herbs, and a host of products that do not ordinarily preserve in archaeological sites.

Although the Chachapoya are renowned as inhabitants of a remote and isolated region, the archaeological record attests to intensive interaction through extensive exchange networks stretching toward all points of the compass at one time or another. Evidence of long-distance interaction is evident in projectile point and pottery styles shared across considerable distances from earliest times. Studies at Manachaqui Cave reveal that exchange relations with populations to the north and east were particularly important prior to AD 200, when Chachapoya populations intensified their trade relationships with Central Andean societies in Cajamarca, Huamachuco, and the Callejón de Conchucos. Cajamarca trade ware and small amounts of Huari pottery attest to uninterrupted participation in Central Andean exchange networks through Inca times, when even coastal Chimu pottery finds its way into Chachapoya tomb assemblages. However, it was the trade linkages with lowland neighbors in the Huallaga Basin that the Inca coveted to the extent that they conquered, and reconquered, the Chachapoya at great expense. Extensive Inca constructions at sites like Cochabamba and Cuntur Marca reflect the importance of these localities as major entryways to the eastern lowlands. Chachapoyas is remote only to the degree it is isolated from Peru's national infrastructure. The archaeological evidence demonstrates that Chachapoya societies occupied an enviable position at one of South America's most important pre-Hispanic crossroads.

Sociopolitical Organization

Very little is known with certainty regarding indigenous Chachapoya sociopolitical organization, and especially the basis for "Chachapoya" cultural identity prior to Inca conquest. Documentary evidence attests to unification of autonomous, small-scale polities with the imposition of Inca authority and its attendant political, economic, and religious infrastructure. In the context of empire, the Chachapoya amounted to an ethnic group, which, like other such Andean groups, was recognized by particular clothing and headwear. Current interpretations depict pre-Incaic Chachapoyas as a patchwork of "chiefdoms," or *curacazcos* in Andeanist parlance, led by local chiefs, or *curacas*. These, in turn, were based upon Andean kin-based corporate groups called *allyus* specific to certain settlements, or local clusters of settlements. The small circular dwellings typical of the Chachapoya suggest nuclear family habitations and bilateral descent. Virilocal residence patterns have been suggested. Espinoza's use of the medieval Spanish term *behetias* to describe Chachapoya polities may seem inappropriate as a concept borrowed from the Old World. However, it may be more accurate than "chiefdom" in characterizing political systems in which leadership status could be achieved as well as ascribed. Some pre-Inca Chachapoya polities may have indeed been "rank societies," conforming to the classic "chiefdom" model. However, a graded series of leadership statuses, including the kind of ad hoc and situational varieties described by Espinoza, likely characterized some Chachapoya communities. Archaeological evidence should speak to this problem, but neither chiefdomlike site hierarchies nor elite housing have been positively identified. Both documentary and archaeological evidence make clear that the Chachapoya were far more fractious and unruly than the Central Andean Wanka and other "classic" Andean chiefdoms.

After Inca conquest around 1470, imperial administrators installed a nested hierarchy of *curacas* and lower-level lords overseeing tributary units portioned in accordance with the Inca decimal accounting system. The Inca divided the new Chachapoya province into several *hunos* (groups of 10,000 tribute payers each), split into northern and southern divisions. Following the European conquest, a great deal of litigation occurred in Leymebamba in 1574, where local lords installed or displaced during decades of imperial machinations vied for legitimacy under the viceroyalty. The Inca had been forced to reconquer the rebellious Chachapoya at least twice, and repeated changes in political authority exacerbated factionalism, which further hinders ethnohistorical identification of pre-Inca political structures. A permanent state of political instability was the unintended result of consolidating local populations that subsequently forged a united resistance to Inca imperial authority. The resulting ethnogenesis of a unified Chachapoya group actually fortified an insurgent movement that leapt at the first opportunity to ally itself with Pizarro's Spanish forces against the Inca.

Religion

Documentary and archaeological sources render a picture of Chachapoya *ayllus* venerating ancestors, which they interred in "open" sepulchers built into cliff faces. Los Pinchudos, Laguna de los Condores, and Revash provide examples of mausolea where prominent kin groups maintained access to mummies and consulted with the dead on earthly matters. From these promontories, the ancestors "oversaw" community lands dotted with sacred landmarks central to memories of the mythical past. Mountains, prominent rocks, trees, and other natural features in the landscape could embody ancestor spirits that bestowed water and fertility upon the land. *Ayllus* looked to lakes, springs, and caves as places where their original "founding" ancestors emerged. A less typical Chachapoya mortuary practice was the enclosure of individual seated cadavers in conical clay capsules arrayed in rows along cliff faces. The most famous of these *purunmachus* are found at the site of Karajía, where the clay sarcophagi exhibit modeled heads and faces and elaborate red-painted decorations. Mortuary ritual included the painting of pictographs, usually large red concentric circles, on the rock above tombs. In short, the Chachapoyas landscape was animated with local ancestors, prompting Inca efforts to superimpose imperial symbolism through landscape modifications and new constructions. In this way, they legitimized their presence in Chachapoyas territory and exerted a measure of ideological control.

Although the details of Chachapoya mortuary practices are unique, local religious beliefs were evidently not unlike those of other Andean cultures. The Chachapoya were purportedly unified in their belief in a common deity, which, if true, may reflect construction of regional Chachapoya cultural identity through the metaphor of common descent from a single apical ancestor. Chroniclers mention the local worship of serpents and the condor as principal deities. The serpent is the single most prevalent image in Chachapoya iconography, appearing in pottery and architectural embellishments. Details of other local deities and cyclical rituals performed to propitiate agriculture remain unknown. Apparently, the Chachapoya did not build temples dedicated to indoor ritual, although outdoor spectacles and feasts certainly took place in central plazas. Excavations in prominent buildings at the sites of La Playa and Gran Pajatén did yield quartz crystals, rare metals, and other evidence for ritual activities, perhaps within elite habitations, but no similar evidence has yet been reported elsewhere in Chachapoyas. Chronicles provide an inordinate number of references to powerful sorcerers, or "shamans," in this region. The importance of Chachapoya shamanism likely has local roots and probably relates to the accessibility of herbs, narcotic plants, and esoteric knowledge at a major gateway to the Amazon lowlands where the greatest shamans reputedly dwelled. However, social and political chaos during the colonial period probably led to widespread increase in the hostile sorcery witnessed by the Spaniards.

Art and Expressive Culture

Chachapoya art and iconography as we know it present themes of war, male sexuality, and perhaps shamanic transformation into alter egos, such as felines. Much expressive culture surely relates to ancestor veneration and agricultural propitiation, but such interpretations rely heavily on indirect evidence. The Chachapoya are most widely known for their stone carving and architectural skills, yet they have been described by chroniclers as among the greatest of Andean weavers. Still, Chachapoya textile arts remained virtually unknown until archaeologists rescued approximately 200 mummy bundles in 1997 from ongoing looting at the cemetery at Laguna de los Condores. The extraordinary preservation at the cliff cemetery now permits experts to unravel the details of Chachapoya weaving techniques and iconography. Designs on textiles, pyro-engraved gourds, and other media typically include representations of serpents, felines, and other fanged creatures, and feline-human hybrids. Anthropomorphic wooden sculptures accompany the dead at the Laguna and hang from ingenious wooden hinges beneath the eaves of mausolea at Los Pinchudos. Because of preservation conditions, wooden sculpture remains unknown elsewhere in the Andean highlands. An obsession with human heads,

most frequently carved in stone and incorporated into building masonry, may represent concern for ancestors or trophy heads taken in war. These are among the most significant finds in a growing corpus of artistic media that promises to shed new light on Chachapoya culture. Unfortunately, the problem of looting at Chachapoya tombs is expanding, and sustained scientific archaeology in the cloud forest is a difficult and expensive enterprise.

— Warren B. Church

See also **Peru**

Further Readings

Church, W. (1994). Early occupations at Gran Pajatén. In *Andean Past, 4,* 281–318. (Latin American Studies Program, Cornell University, Ithaca, NY)

Schjellerup, I. (1997). *Incas and Spaniards in the conquest of Chachapoyas* (Series B, Gothenburg Archaeological Theses No. 7). Göteborg University, Sweden.

von Hagen, A. (2002). Chachapoya iconography and society at Laguna de los Condores, Peru. In H. Silverman & W. Isbell (Eds.), *Andean archaeology II: Art, landscape and society* (pp. 137–155). New York: Kluwer Academic/Plenum.

 # CHAGNON, NAPOLEON (1938–)

Napoleon Chagnon is biosocial professor emeritus in the Department of Anthropology at the University of California, Santa Barbara. Chagnon was born in 1938 in Port Austin, Michigan. He earned his PhD in anthropology at the University of Michigan in 1966. There, he studied unilineal cultural evolution under Leslie A. White. Chagnon tested White's assertions that changes in technology played a primary role in social evolution when he gathered ethnographic field data among the Yanomamo Indians of Venezuela and Brazil. When Napoleon Chagnon began his study of the Yanomamo in 1964, few Whites had interacted with them, and none for extended periods of time. Chagnon was able to document the effects of Yanomamo acculturation to outside cultures, particularly the political and technological impact of trade goods. Chagnon also documented the effects of diseases and epidemics introduced by lumbermen and miners on the Yanomamo population and social organization. In 1988, Professor Chagnon established a survival fund with nonprofit organizations to develop health care programs for the Venezuelan Yanomamo. The Yanomamo are victims of scourges like influenza and water pollution as a result of their contact with an influx of illegal miners.

Chagnon became world renowned for his analysis of Yanomamo warfare and his participant observation field research techniques. He is also widely respected for his international advocacy for Yanomamo land rights, environmental protection, and human rights. The nature of Yanomamo warfare and violence between villages has been the subject of much of Chagnon's research. Chagnon's most important observations of the Yanomamo include their use of hallucinogenic drugs in shamanistic healing rituals and the violent practice of fighting with axes. The "Ax Fight," captured on film, is a popular ethnographic CD-ROM for college students. Chagnon explains Yanomamo violence and warfare as a result of a shortage of wives, perpetuated by female infanticide and cycles of vengeance. In response to protein-shortage explanations for warfare asserted by other anthropologists, Chagnon and partner Raymond Hames measured the amount of protein in several Yanomamo villages. They did not find a correlation between protein levels in local diets and violent warfare.

Chagnon continues to gather field data among extremely remote Yanomamo villages contacted in the early 1990s.

In 1993, Chagnon was part of a team that investigated the violent murders of Yanomamo women and children by illegal miners. The massacre of the women and children followed the Yanomamo shooting of Brazilian miners who had killed Yanomamo men over territorial disputes. In 1999, Patrick Tierney alleged fieldwork misconduct on the part of Chagnon early in his research career, in a sensational book titled *Darkness in El Dorado*. The American Anthropological Association engaged in a detailed investigation in 2001 of the charges that Chagnon and geneticist James Neel had been the cause of a measles epidemic among the Yanomami people. All major allegations made by Tierney were shown to be not only false, but deliberately fraudulent.

Chagnon is currently engaged in computer-assisted longitudinal analysis of Yanomamo demography, settlement patterns, geography, and warfare patterns. He seeks to further understand and explain differences in Yanomamo village life and warfare intensity over time and place.

— *Elizabeth A. Dyer*

See also **Darkness in El Dorado Controversy; Participant-observation; Yanomamo**

Further Readings

Chagnon, N. A. (1967). Yanomamo social organization and warfare. In M. Fried, M. Harris, & R. Murphy (Eds.), *War: The anthropology of armed conflict and aggression*. New York: Natural History Press.

Chagnon, N. A. (1997). *Yanomamo: The last days of Eden* (5th ed.). San Diego: Harcourt, Brace, Jovanovich.

Chagnon, N. A., & Hames, R. (1979). Protein deficiency and tribal warfare in Amazonia: New data. *Science, 203*(4383), 10–15.

CHANTS

Chanting is an important linguistic act that is part of many secular and religious practices throughout the world. Many political rallies, sporting events, collective religious services, and private religious devotions involve some form of chanting. In general, chanting is distinct from other speech activities by having a unique rhythmic structure, by having distinctive stress and intonation patterns, and by being limited in significance to specific social situations.

The primary purpose of chants, in most cases, is to put the mind beyond words and into an altered state of consciousness in order to, for example, achieve enlightenment, to personally experience God, or to enter into the spirit world. Chanting such as this may be done alone or in a group. Anyone who has ever repeated the same word over and over again has noticed that any repeated word, or string of words, eventually seems to become strange and meaningless. Chanting like this can be found in Buddhist meditation, Christian devotions, shamanistic rituals, and in other religious contexts. Since chanting like this seeks to affect the individual—even if done in a group—its orientation is toward the self, or ego.

In other cases, while the consciousness of the participants may still be altered, the ultimate purpose of the chanting is to express group solidarity and cohesiveness. Here, the chanting attempts to create oneness and unity in a group, so, its orientation is toward the assembly, or community. Liturgies and rituals in many different corporate religious prac-

Source: © iStockphoto/Vicky Bennett.

tices use chanting as a way to bring participants into the ritual space and to define the community and everyone's place in it.

Chanting that is oriented toward the community may be part of a larger complex sociolinguistic ritual. For example, in the liturgy of the Coptic Orthodox Church, the deacons, congregation, and the priest responsively chant for most of the time between the recitation of the Orthodox Creed and communion. This chanting is led by the priest. The deacons and the congregation must respond by chanting in the same language used by the priest. In Egypt, the languages used in the liturgy are Arabic, Coptic, and a little Greek. In Coptic Churches in the United States, the languages used are Arabic, Coptic, English, and a little Greek. The chanting is rhythmic, and the beat is maintained by deacons, who play the cymbals and triangle. The overall effect after only a short time is to induce an altered state of consciousness, in which the participants are drawn into the community of believers and prepared spiritually for the communion.

Communally oriented chanting like that of the Coptic Orthodox Church is meaningful, however, only when the community is gathered and the social roles of priest, deacon, and congregation are all represented. Chanting not only alters the consciousness of the participant but also acts to key different frames and, by so doing, defines the event, act, role, and genre of every event, action, and person in the Coptic liturgy. In this sense, chanting is a powerful sign that keys, or signals, the meaning of various symbols and symbolic acts in the liturgy. The action of a priest walking in a circle around the altar on a weekday, when there is no liturgy, has a different meaning than the same priest walking around the altar during the liturgy against a background of liturgical chant.

The use of chants is not restricted to religious settings. Chanting is also part of many secular activities, such as sporting events and political protests. Such chanting can be done to the point where it alters consciousness, but more frequently in these kinds of contexts, it is done to communicate idea and/or build emotional consensus in a group.

Throughout history, humans have explored many ways to extend the boundaries of linguistic thought and experience: alcohol, hallucinogenic drugs, folk riddling, fasting, exposure, and self-mortification, to name a few. Many instances of chanting can be viewed in a similar way, as an attempt to extend human cognitive experience. The fact that chanting, in some form, is nearly universal across cultures is not surprising. Language is also present across all cultures. So, similar linguistic boundaries are placed on all of humanity. Chanting, whether performed for personal enlightenment or to strengthen the bonds of community, is an effort to go beyond words to get to a transcendent awareness and/or feeling.

— *Richard R. Jones*

See also **Buddhism**

Further Readings

Abdel-Massih, E. T., Melika, Fr. M. M., & Michail, Fr. R. S. (1982). *The divine liturgy of St. Basil the Great.* Troy, MI: St. Mark Coptic Orthodox Church.

Bauman, R. (1977). *Verbal art as performance.* Rowley, MA: Newbury House.

Goffman, E. (1974). *Frame analysis.* New York: Harper Colophon Books.

Leach, E. (1976). *Culture and communication: The logic by which symbols are connected: An introduction to the use of structuralist analysis in social anthropology.* Cambridge: Cambridge University Press.

CHAOS THEORY

Chaos theory describes the motion of certain dynamical, nonlinear systems under specific conditions. Chaotic motion is not the same as random motion. It is especially likely to emerge in systems that are described by at least three nonlinear equations, though it may also arise in other settings under specific conditions. All of these systems are characterized by a sensitivity to initial conditions within bounded parameters. Chaotic systems must also be transitive (any transformation in period t_1 will continue and overlap in period t_2), and its periodic orbits are dense (for any point in the system y, there is another point with a distance $d = y$ in the same periodic orbit).

The history of this branch of study is a complex, interdisciplinary affair, with scholars in different fields working on related problems in isolation, often unaware of research that had gone before. One of the most important characteristics of chaotic systems is their sensitivity to initial conditions. In 1961, one of the fathers of chaos theory, Edward Lorenz, accidentally discovered this principle while studying a simple model of weather systems constructed from no more than 12 parameters. Wishing to review a certain set of results, he manually reentered values for these parameters from a printout and started the simulation again in midcourse. However, the new set of predictions that the computer made were vastly different from the first series that had been generated. After ruling out mechanical failure, Lorenz discovered that that by reentering the starting values of the parameters, he had truncated the decimals from five places to three. Lorenz and his colleges had assumed small variance in the inputs of a set of equations would lead to a likewise small variance in the outcomes. Yet in a system of complex or chaotic movement, very small variance in initial conditions can lead to large difference in outcomes. This property is popularly referred to as the "butterfly effect."

Theoretical Implications

While chaotic motion may make long-range forecasting of certain systems impossible, it is important to point out that it does not imply randomness. Rather, *chaos,* as the term is used in experimental mathematics, describes systems that are still deterministic that yield complex motion. Furthermore, patterns of predictable, or recurring, aperiodic motion may emerge out of this chaos.

It then follows that one way to visualize a complex system is by *attractors,* or *strange attractors,* which track the motion of the system through a three-dimensional space. In a truly random structure, the value of the system could be at any point in the three-dimensional space. With deterministic chaotic motion, the system's values are all found within a bounded subset of space. The shape of this bounded space will vary in predictable ways as the values of the initial parameters are increased in a proportionate series characterized by "Feigenbaum numbers." One of the most famous of these shapes is the "Lorenz attractor," which has been characterized as a set of linked concentric spirals that resemble either the eyes of an owl or butterfly wings. This was one of the first strange attractors characterized and is often remarked upon for its beautiful and complex fractal pattern.

Implications of Chaos Theory for the Social Sciences

While chaos theory is often characterized as a branch of experimental mathematics, it has important implications for many other fields of study. Early researchers in the development of chaos theory addressed issues in areas as diverse as physics, meteorology, ecology, and even understanding variation in cotton prices over time. Biologists and anthropologists working on ecology or population dynamic problems are no doubt already aware that simple logistic models of population growth can yield chaotic outcomes when starting parameters are moved beyond certain levels.

Evolutionary biologists have wondered if certain strange attractors have phenotypical expression. For instance, it's interesting to note that not all possible forms can be reached through evolution. While there are certainly great variations in physical form between creatures, not all possible variations are expressed. The giant pangolin from Africa and the giant armadillo from North America look quite similar, but it is not because they are closely related. Rather, the phenomenon of convergent evolution raises the question of whether there are strange attractors for body types.

The social sciences could benefit much from chaos theory precisely because its area of study is often characterized by complex, nonlinear systems. Obviously, this has implications in formalized areas such as economics and game theory. It is also interesting to note that this may also have implications for other sorts of theorizing as well. For instance, teleological theories, such as those advanced by Hegel or Marx, predict that systems move toward a future steady state in which actions may happen but the nature of the system is not disrupted. These future states might be conceptualized as strange attractors for social systems.

One of the traditional misconceptions about teleology stems from the role of the end states. Objections are often raised to the idea that future end states can cause effects in the present (known as "backward causation"). Chaos theory provides a systematic argument for how the same parameters that cause the emergence of a strange attractor also select for a certain set of behaviors in the agents. Therefore, it is not the end state itself that generates change. This also has implications for how agency is conceived in social systems. The movement of a system from a state of random, or indeterminate, behavior to deterministic, or chaotic, behavior will affect the scope of individual agency. Nevertheless, a certain amount of agency remains in these explanations, not only in that a wide range of behavior remains possible once a strange attractor has been reached, but the principle of sensitivity to initial conditions means that much room may exist for agents to determine how the system develops.

— *Benjamin N. Judkins*

See also **Chaos Theory and Anthropology**

Further Readings

Alligood, K. T., Sauer, T. D., & Yorke, J. A. (1996). *Chaos: An introduction to dynamical systems.* New York: Springer.

Byrne, D. (1998). *Complexity theory and the social sciences.* New York: Routledge.

Gleik, J. (1987). *Chaos: Making a new science.* New York: Viking.

Kiel, L. D., & Elliot, E. (Eds.). (1996). *Chaos theory in the social sciences: Foundations and applications.* Ann Arbor: University of Michigan Press.

Wendt, A. (2003). Why a world state is inevitable. *European Journal of Political Science, 9,* 491–542.

 # CHAOS THEORY AND ANTHROPOLOGY

Confusion is the word we have invented for an order which is not understood.

— Henry Miller, *Tropic of Capricorn*

For those who are familiar with anthropology, the themes of chaos and complexity might seem intuitively related to the field. Immersion in unfamiliar cultures is understood to produce disorientation, confusion, and perceptions of the foreign culture as "chaotic." Consequently, the relevance of chaos theory and complexity theory to anthropology might not require a detailed justification. Here, we make those connections explicit and suggest ways in which chaos theory and complexity theory might be useful in anthropological inquiry.

Chaos Theory

Both chaos and complexity theories have their roots in the development of systems theory, which emerged in the period during and after World War I. In particular, open systems were defined as "open" because they exchanged resources with their environment and "systems" since they were composed of a variety of interconnected and interacting components. The movement to systems theory might be thought of as the "holistic turn," which marked a departure from the reductionist or atomistic approach that sought to break things down into smaller and smaller pieces in an effort to uncover their essence. In contrast, systems thinking can be characterized as the recognition that the whole is more than the sum of its parts. The parts can, in a sense, be understood as holographic representations of the whole, which, when combined create through their interaction a new and unique entity.

The development of chaos theory began in the 1970s with the work of Edward Lorenz, a meteorologist whose interest in modeling weather patterns led to the discovery that miniscule differences in initial conditions can have tremendous effects on outcomes. The observation became known as the "butterfly effect," described here by Ian Stewart (1989):

> The flapping of a single butterfly's wing today produces a tiny change in the state of the atmosphere. Over a period of time, what the atmosphere actually does diverges from what it would have done. So, in a month's time, a tornado that would have devastated the Indonesian coast doesn't happen. Or maybe one that wasn't going to happen, does. (p. 141)

While positivistic science would typically dismiss small differences as bothersome detail or noise, in chaos theory, these small differences became the subject of intense interest. Over time, this phenomenon became known as "sensitive dependence on initial conditions." What this meant for Lorenz and his interest in weather modeling at the time of his initial experiments was that accurate prediction of the weather was impossible.

A second important observation by Lorenz came through his search for a simplified version of his original experiment. The resulting phenomenon illustrates again that slight differences in initial conditions bring about vastly different outcomes. However, this time, there was something new: What initially appeared to be random behavior turned out not to be random at all. James Glieck, who introduced chaos theory to the general public in 1987, describes the Lorenzian water wheel:

> At the top, water drips steadily into containers hanging on the wheel's rim. Each container drips steadily from a small hole. If the stream of water is slow, the top containers never fill fast enough to overcome friction, but if the stream is faster, the weight starts to turn the wheel. The rotation might become continuous. Or if the stream is so fast that the heavy containers swing all the way around the bottom and up the other side, the wheel might then slow, stop, and reverse its rotation, turning first one way and then the other. (p. 29)

Anyone can observe the workings of a simple water wheel. What Lorenz showed was that the seemingly chaotic behavior of this simple device was actually ordered. Until this time, scientists recognized two types of order: steady state and periodic order. Steady state order describes behavior in which the variables never change, resulting in a repetitive pattern. Periodic order describes a pattern of a single loop that repeats itself indefinitely. Yet when the results of Lorenz's experiment were graphed, a third type of order emerged.

The results of the equations in Lorenz's experiment were also ordered, but neither steady state nor periodic. Never settling on a single point, the patterns did not repeat themselves. What appeared at first to be chaotic was in fact ordered, a phenomenon that became known as the "Lorenz attractor." Within the Lorenz attractor, the butterfly wings image shows both chaos and order: chaos in that the pattern is never repeated twice, and order in that the patterns fall within parameters.

The results of Lorenz's experiments were published in 1963. However, since his work appeared in a meteorological journal, his findings didn't reach a wide audience. It was years before those outside meteorology would hear about his work. Over time, individuals from fields including mathematics and biology reported similar phenomena in experiments with the flipping of a coin, the growth of populations, fluctuations in cotton prices, and coastline measurement. What these experiments brought to light were hidden and surprising aspects of behavior that were to become important concepts in chaos theory.

One of the key developments that emerged from continuing studies of chaos was the concept of the fractal, a graphic representation that embodies the attribute of self-similarity. The term *fractal* comes from *fractional*. Examples of fractals include bifurcation diagrams of Mandelbrot's population equation, the Lorenz attractor, and the Koch curve. Each of these figures exhibits some paradoxical feature that reveals the hidden order within apparently chaotic systems. For example, the Koch curve illustrates how each time new triangles are added to the outside of a triangle, the length of the perimeter line gets longer. Yet the inner area of the Koch curve remains less than the area of a circle drawn around the original triangle. Essentially, it is a line of infinite length surrounding a finite area. Benoit Mandelbrot, a mathematician studying self-similarity, used this concept to explore anomalies in measuring the length of coastlines.

Developments in chaos theory were aided by advances in computation and measurement technologies. The introduction of high-speed computing had an effect similar to the impact made by the electron microscope. Both allowed scientists to see deeper into the nature of things that had previously been obscured because of the limitations of human vision and capacity to perform massive calculations. And while they allowed us to look deeper inside, they also expanded the scope of our vision: The bigger picture revealed obscure aspects of behavior that challenged long-held assumptions about the universe and the nature of life itself.

The implications of chaos theory would be taken up by researchers from a wide range of disciplines, who continued to evolve new theories. The following section introduces complexity theory and explains its relationship to chaos and other theories that emerged from the intellectual ferment of the early 20th century.

Complexity Theory

There is a close relationship between chaos theory and complexity theory. As previously noted, both grew out of the interest in holism and gestalt theories, followed after World War II by cybernetics and systems theory. What these intellectual movements had in common was the desire to replace reductionism with an appreciation for modeling interactions instead of simplifying them away. Described as strikingly similar to systems theory regarding environmental interaction and awareness, the three states defined by systems theory—organized simplicity, organized complexity, and chaos—are mirrored in the typologies of complexity theorists Stephen Wolfram and Chris Langdon: stability, Edge of Chaos, and Chaos.

Chaos theory, cybernetics, catastrophe theory, and general systems theory share a common interest in deterministic dynamic systems in which a set of equations predicts how a system moves through states from one point in time to another. What distinguishes complexity theory from the others is that it provides an alternative method for exploring regularities that emerge from the interactions of individual components within systems. In combination, these components form what is referred to in complexity theory as *complex adaptive systems* (CAS). One of the key contributors to the development of complexity theory, Murray Gell-Mann, identified four elements common to CAS: agents with schemata, self-organizing networks, coevolution to the Edge of Chaos, and recombination and systems evolution. As the examples of their application in the next section will attempt to demonstrate, each of these characteristics can be related to research topics in anthropology and the social sciences.

According to Robert Axelrod, known for his work on competition and collaboration involving Prisoner's Dilemma (a type of game in which two people engage in a scenario in which the successful strategy is one of cooperation based on reciprocity), complexity theory is the study of many actors and their interactions. Actors or agents might be people, organizations, nations, fish, populations, atoms, or simulated creatures, and their interactions can include any activity from warfare, alliance building, and new product development to mating.

This wide range of application has been cited as evidence to argue that there is no consensus on a definition of complexity science. Moreover, some argue that we cannot refer to complexity as a science or theory at all but should, instead, think of it as a paradigm or discourse, similar to Martin and Frost's characterization of postmodernism. Yet despite this debate, the application of constructs and concepts from complexity theory continues. The growing volume of related literature suggests that complexity is more than a theme. And, as with any new science, defining its parameters requires ongoing scholarly discourse.

A recognizable set of core concepts and principles has emerged to give form and substance to complexity theory. Many of these have worked their way into mainstream academic and practitioner literature. Examples include the Edge of Chaos, emergence, fitness landscapes, phase transitions, adaptive self-organization, and nonlinear feedback loops with mutual causality. The concepts of adaptive self-organization, coevolution, and agents have particular applicability to anthropology and are covered in some detail throughout this section. When applied to anthropological problems, each of these concepts provides new insight to the nonlinear dynamics of complex adaptive systems and the environments from which they emerge, develop, mature, and pass out of existence.

For anthropology, this means the opening of potential channels to investigate complex social systems, which are characteristically dynamic in nonlinear ways.

The risk inherent in applying constructs from complexity theory is that of allowing these concepts to degenerate into descriptive language or metaphor. Referred to as "soft complexity science," the use of complexity concepts and language helps to visualize or "see" the complexity inherent in social systems and sociotechnical organizations. Some complexity theorists refer to the lack of rigor in the use of complexity thought and language as "pseudoscience," which is thought to describe much of the work in complexity theory. While the value of metaphor is indisputable, there is much more that can be done in the way of applying complexity theory to the investigation of complex adaptive systems.

The maturation of new sciences (complexity science) involves the development of research tools and techniques. Rather than simply applying the concepts of complexity theory as a metaphorical lens, more rigorous approaches in the form of agent-based modeling and simulation are producing valuable insights across many scientific domains, including anthropology. Simulation allows researchers to model and demonstrate how the seemingly simple behavior of interacting agents can generate large-scale effects or "emergent properties" as they adapt to changing conditions in their environment.

It is important to stress that the objective of agent-based modeling and computer simulation is not to reproduce realistic models of empirical data. The goal instead is to bring to light the emergent recurring patterns of behavior that bring about a reordering of a complex system. It is important to have a deeper understanding of the dynamics of interaction that reappear across a wide range of diverse circumstances. So, rather than characterizing complexity theory by *what* is studied (i.e., societies, organizations, economies), Stephan Phelan argues that the focus should be on new methods for studying regularities or patterns such as those revealed by Axelrod's work with agent-based models of competition and collaboration.

Where traditional science has focused on simple cause-effect relationships, complexity science seeks to detect simple "generative" rules that cause complex effects. Generative rules are few and simple; they have been used to demonstrate how a group of artificial agents, such as cellular automata in the "Game of Life"

or computer-generated flocking patterns ("boids"), will behave over time in a virtual environment.

In Phelan's words, "Complexity science posits simple causes for complex effects." In CAS, this behavior is referred to as *autogenesis,* or self-organizing behavior, which is generated by a set of relatively simple rules that govern the interactions between agents over time ("time t influences conditions at time t + 1"). These rules, in turn, create structure. According to Philip Anderson, "Rules generate structure because the state that is the output of one application of rules becomes the input for the next round." Structure evolves from ongoing interaction between agents within the unit itself, between the unit and other units with which it interacts, and within the larger systems to which it is related. Complexity theorists refer to as *coevolution,* a dynamic process through which components of a system known as "agents" not only adapt to their environments, but shape them over time. The conceptual overlap with cultural ecology and systems theory is clear.

It must be emphasized that models of adaptive behavior are significantly different from so-called rational choice models. The optimizing strategies that support rational choice models, such as those used in classic economics, are based on assumptions of rationality from which the consequences of specific choices can be deduced. In contrast, advocates of agent-based modeling and computer simulation argue it provides a more realistic representation of reality. Multiple agents following a few simple rules will often produce surprising effects, since anticipating the full consequence of even simple interactions is impossible. Although interaction is determined by the set of rules that generate the behaviors of individual agents, Anderson notes that agents need not be prisoners of a fixed set of rules. This notion of infinite variability and surprise is a common characteristic of complexity theory in computer and physical sciences, as well as in the application of complexity theory to social phenomena. In the domain of social phenomena, we can equate this to the capacity of human actors for choice, what Giddens refers to as "agency."

Understanding the central role and functions of the agent in agent-based models is essential to appreciating how complexity can be applied as a theoretical framework in anthropological research. Depending on the level of analysis, agents can be defined as individuals, groups, families, units, firms, or any other entity distinguished by their differentiation from some "other." The key characteristic of agents is their ability to interact with other agents. The response of each agent is based on the responses of other agents, and their interaction results in the phenomenon of "coevolution." The "adaptive landscape," the field in which they interact, is constantly shifting. This connectivity is what gives CAS their dynamic nature.

Chaos, Complexity, and Anthropology

With its primary interest being the study of human societies and cultures, anthropology undoubtedly qualifies as a science interested in complex systems. The conceptualization of culture from the systems view can be discerned in the work of many of anthropology's key contributors to anthropological theory, notably Malinowski and Radcliff-Brown (functionalism), Steward and White (cultural ecology), and Lévi-Strauss (structuralism). More recent versions of cultural ecology have expanded on this systems view.

Despite obvious correlations, the systems view has been criticized by social science researchers for its mechanistic, deterministic overtones, which did not reflect the often messy reality of social systems. Its unpopularity can also be linked to the influence of postmodernism and distrust of theories of culture that hint at a unified theme. However, more recent iterations of systems thinking, such as chaos theory, have revealed dimensions within the randomness (or messiness) of apparently disordered systems that are found upon closer examination to be ordered, what Glieck calls the stable chaos of self-organizing systems. Complex systems such as social systems can give rise to both turbulence and coherence at the same time. Emergent order within apparent chaos is at the core of both chaos and complexity thinking. Modeling and simulation are the tools that have been developed by complexity scientists to explore this phenomenon.

In applying agent-based modeling to the investigation of complex social systems, it is important to establish the distinction between human responses to routine, known situations and those that address uncertain, complex, and unknown situations. This distinction highlights the critical difference between a closed system, in which equilibrium is maintained through routine responses without regard to external influences, and an open system that must respond to an unpredictable and constantly changing environment.

Although it can be argued that the closed-system model might have been appropriate for traditional anthropological studies of single, small-scale, and relatively isolated populations, it is clearly not adequate for the highly integrated, globalizing world that faces contemporary anthropologists. Chaos and complexity science provide not only a theoretical framework but also unique methods and tools useful in investigating how discrete parts of complex social systems, such as indigenous populations within developing countries or divisions of a multinational firm, relate to and are integrated within the larger environment as a whole. The interest in part-whole relationships is also a primary concern of anthropologists working in the social-cultural ecology framework.

The theme of interaction is consistent within systems and ecological approaches that share a common concern with the dialectic interplay between sociocultural systems, their environments, and reciprocity, or feedback causality, in which both the sociocultural system and environment influence each other. Environment has an active, selective role in shaping the evolution of culture; culture, in turn, influences the characteristics of its environment. This understanding of the relationship between environment and culture relates directly to the notion of coevolution, a key concept from complexity theory.

From the systems perspective, culture is conceptualized as a system of socially transmitted behavior patterns that serve as mechanisms that "adjust" human communities to their environments. Closely aligned to the concept of coevolution described in the previous section, manifestations of this perspective as sociotechnical or sociocultural systems tend to revolve around the notion of reciprocity and feedback. These concepts were also noted in earlier references to Axelrod's work with patterns of competition and cooperation.

The blending of variations of the systems view, chaos theory, and complexity science with anthropological theory provides new avenues for research. Within contemporary anthropology, the complexity of cultural multiplicity has become a prominent theme. Notions of negotiated cultures and nested cultural layers have developed through ongoing dialogue since postmodernism first challenged the assumptions of traditional anthropological thought. Hamada and Jordan explain that the classical concept of nature that explains differences between small, relatively homogeneous societies is challenged by social groups without boundaries and whose memberships in these groups may overlap, causing shifting allegiances depending on the situation.

While complexity is a hallmark of contemporary social systems, as Hamada and Jordan suggest, the application of complexity theory is not limited to anthropological research on contemporary topics such as the effects of globalization on indigenous communities. Because of its capacity to bring to light emergent patterns within complex and seemingly chaotic systems, complexity theory has the potential to provide the theoretical framework and analytical tools required to accommodate research on complex social systems, regardless of their historic timestamp.

The village simulation model developed by Tim Kohler to study of the collapse of complex social systems and Robert Reynolds's work with cultural algorithms serve as examples. Developed using data collected from sedimentation and other archeological findings from the Mesa Verde region, the village simulation model was initially designed as an approach to understanding the behavior of pre-Hispanic inhabitants. It was hoped that the model would bring to light possible explanations for their disappearance, evidence of which is based on archeological studies of the region. The simulation produced evidence that suggested that more than environmental factors were involved in shaping the social history of the region.

Using Kohler's agent-based model of the Mesa Verde pre-Hispanic Pueblo region, Reynolds employed a framework for modeling cultural evolution. With the addition of cultural factors, Reynolds applied cultural algorithms to explore the emergent properties' impact. If the social system was brittle, it was hypothesized that any factor that induced stress could cause its collapse. By investigating the impact of environmental variability on the formation of social networks, Reynolds and coresearcher Ziad Kobti looked at how the spatial distribution of agricultural land and the temporal distribution of rainfall affected the structure of the social system.

Reynolds and Kobti were able to show how the distribution of agricultural resources was conducive to the development of so-called small-world networks, which depended on the existence of conduits or agents whose connectivity was sufficiently powerful to link the small worlds together. Without the conduits, the small-world network would be prone to collapse. Experiments suggest there was, in fact, a major decrease in these conduits, which would have had a negative impact on the resiliency of the small-world network.

Applicability of Chaos and Complexity Theories

What is particularly noteworthy about the development of both chaos theory and complexity theory is their widespread applicability to phenomena across diverse fields, ranging from computer science to the physical and social sciences. Both theories are inherently interdisciplinary with demonstrated relevance for investigating the workings of complex systems, meaning that the principles are applicable across a diverse spectrum of systems. For example, Joseph Sussman's characterization in 2000 of a complex system describes transportation, but it could also be applied to an economy or a society:

> A system is complex when it is composed of a group of related units (subsystems), for which the degree and nature of the relationships is imperfectly known. Its overall emergent behavior is difficult to predict, even when subsystem behavior is readily predictable. The time-scales of various subsystems may be very different.... Behavior in the long-term and short-term may be markedly different and small changes in inputs and parameters may produce large changes in behavior.

The closed-system perspective is, at best, an inaccurate lens for investigating the complex interactions and nested systems that characterize contemporary societies. For similar reasons, theoretical and methodological boundaries that limit the capacity of anthropologists to embrace the scope and depth of their research topics should be transformed by new theoretical paradigms that have proven in other fields to provide valuable insight on a wide range of complex adaptive systems. The recent works in archeology by Koehler and Reynolds serve as examples of how concepts from chaos theory and the methods and tools of complexity science can be applied.

Chaos theory and complexity theory offer anthropologists new areas of exploration and cross-disciplinary collaboration, especially important as the signature concept of anthropology (culture) and core methodology (ethnography) are being appropriated by other disciplines. Anthropologists are remarkable in their ability to apply their unique skills, methods, and tools to other fields of research, for example, medicine, business, and engineering. However, we could be better at communicating and making explicit what Diana Forsythe called the "invisible" aspects of anthropological work.

Computer simulation has become a common research tool in applying complexity theory to the study of complex adaptive systems across a wide range of disciplines.

Engaging in interdisciplinary research, presenting at academic conferences outside anthropology, and coauthoring journal publications with colleagues from other fields all serve to enhance appreciation for the relevance of anthropology and value that anthropologists can bring to the study of crucial human problems and challenges confronting the world today.

The quote by Henry Miller that opens this entry suggests that order lies hidden beyond the state of confusion in which all appears chaotic. This encapsulates the basic premise of chaos theory and reflects an underlying approach to the investigation of phenomena that is compatible with the basic tenets of anthropology.

Exploring new research perspectives such as chaos and complexity theory provides opportunities for interdisciplinary discourse that both broaden anthropology's research perspective and further a wider understanding of the philosophical and theoretical underpinnings that form the foundation of anthropological inquiry.

— *Christine Z. Miller*

See also **Chaos Theory**

Further Readings

Alliare, Y., & Firsirotu, M. E. (1984). Theories of organizational culture. *Organizational Science, 5*(3), 193–226.

Anderson, P. (1999). Complexity theory and organizational science. *Organization Science, 10*(3) 216–232.

Axelrod, R. (1997). *The complexity of cooperation.* Princeton, NJ: Princeton University Press.

Glieck, J. (1987). *Chaos: Making of a new science.* New York: Penquin Books.

Hamada, T., & Jordan, A. (1990). Cross-cultural management and organizational culture. *Studies in Third World Societies, 32.*

Martin, J., & Frost, P. (1999). The organizational culture war games: A struggle for intellectual dominance. In S. Clegg & C. Hardy (Eds.), *Studying organization theory & method.* London, Sage Publications.

Phelan, S. E. (2001). What is complexity science, really? *Emergence, 3*(1), 120–36.

Reynolds, R. G. (1979). *An adaptive computer model of the evolution of agriculture for hunter-gatherers in the Valley of Oaxaca, Mexico.* Ann Arbor: University of Michigan.

Stewart, I. (1989). *Does God play dice? The mathematics of chaos.* Cambridge, MA: Blackwell.

Sussman, D. (2000). *Ideas on complexity in systems: Twenty views.* Cambridge: MIT Engineering Systems Division.

CHICHÉN ITZÁ

Chichén Itzá emerged as a principal political player following the Late and Terminal Classic "collapse" of Maya polities in the southern and central lowlands. Situated in the northern lowlands of Yucatán, this center dominated as a regional power until the end of the Early Postclassic period (ca. AD 1200). Key to Chichén Itzá's success were its military accomplishments, blending of old and new cultural traditions, and emphasis on commercial transactions that extended beyond regional borders. Consequently, inhabitants of Chichén Itzá are characterized by their cosmopolitan attitudes manifested in art and architecture, religion, and politics.

Details about the earliest occupation of Chichén Itzá are poorly understood. We do know that in the site's southern section, Terminal Classic inhabitants (ca. AD 800–900), the Yucatec Maya, constructed Puuc-style buildings resembling those erected at Uxmal. One striking example is the Caracol, a spherical building set atop an earlier-constructed rectangular platform. A spiral staircase inside of the Caracol accesses an upper-level observatory. The building's unique design and orientation are believed to have facilitated viewing of astronomical events like planetary movements.

By the end of the 9th century, the Itzá, a Putún Maya group from Tabasco in Mexico, had established a formidable presence at Chichén Itzá. Consequently, this Mexicanized-Maya group instigated dramatic

Source: © iStockphoto/Justin Horrocks.

cultural change through hybridization. The architecture of this later period at the site is particularly innovative in this respect and references Toltec styles. Buildings concentrated in the site's northern section, like the Temple of the Warriors and the Castillo, displayed colonnades, images of warriors and feathered serpents, and *chacmools* (three-dimensional sculptures of reclining figures).

Aside from art and architectural styles, cultural hybridization also affected political organization at Chichén Itzá. Unlike Classic dynastic rulership, political authority in the Early Postclassic period (ca. AD 900–1200) was delegated to a group of elites who ruled jointly. Increased interregional contacts with groups throughout Mexico also occurred during this period, as a consequence of commercial and military endeavors.

By the end of the Early Postclassic period, Chichén Itzá's power had waned. There is evidence that the site had been sacked, quite possibly by inhabitants of Mayapan, a center that filled the political void after Chichén Itzá's demise. The city was abandoned by the beginning of the Late Postclassic period (ca. 1250 AD), though pilgrims continued to visit the Sacred Cenote.

In fact, visitation to *cenotes,* or natural limestone sinkholes, remains the one constant throughout Chichén Itzá's history. *Chichén Itzá* translates into "opening of the wells of the Itza." The presence of two at the site, the Xtoloc Cenote and Sacred Cenote, may have attracted early occupants. Cenotes offered a stable source of water and also functioned as sacred conduits to the underworld. Modern dredging of the Sacred Cenote has yielded human sacrifices and 30,000 objects, including gold artifacts from Panama and Costa Rica, copper from Mexico, and jade and obsidian from the Guatemalan highlands. The tremendous nature of this find underscored the sacred space's long-standing ceremonial usage.

Even today, Chichén Itzá has not lost its pull as a pilgrimage site. Religious obligations have been replaced by the siren songs of scientific inquiry and tourism. Future work at the site may further clarify question marks about chronology, ethnicity, and demography.

— *Pamela L. Geller*

See also **Mayas; Mexico**

Further Readings

Coggins, C., & Shane, O. C. (Eds.). (1984). *Cenote of sacrifice: Maya treasures from the sacred well at Chichén Itzá.* Austin: University of Texas Press.

Miller, M. E. (1996). *The art of Mesoamerica.* New York: Thames & Hudson.

Sharer, R. J. (1994). *The ancient Maya.* Stanford, CA: Stanford University Press.

CHILD ABUSE

Child maltreatment has occurred throughout history and across cultures. Anthropology's cross-cultural approach has contributed to efforts to define and explain aggressive or inadequate treatment of children.

Child maltreatment was brought to public and professional attention when it was identified in the medical and social work literature in the United States and Europe during the 1960s and 1970s. The landmark publication by pediatrician C. Henry Kempe and his colleagues coined the term *the battered child syndrome* and is frequently viewed as initiating the field. The International Society for Prevention and Treatment of Child Abuse and Neglect was founded in the late 1970s, seeking to bring worldwide attention to the problem.

Many nations had similar experiences of first denying the existence of child maltreatment within their boundaries, only to later "discover" its existence. This stimulated interest in the broader cross-cultural record. Anthropology's cross-cultural perspective has contributed to understandings of definitions and etiology of and a literature on culturally competent responses to child maltreatment.

Defining Child Abuse and Neglect

Criteria for defining and identifying child abuse and neglect were developed in European and North American societies by professionals working primarily in clinical settings. Early definitions of child maltreatment centered on physical harm resulting from acts of omission or commission by parents and other caretakers. Over the next 40 years, definitions expanded in both the national and international literatures to encompass a broad range of harms to children. The four basic categories of child maltreatment are *physical abuse, physical neglect, emotional maltreatment,* and *child sexual abuse.* Neglect may also include *medical neglect* or *educational neglect. Munchausen's Syndrome by Proxy,* an illness fabricated by a parent that can cause harm to a child, is also generally included in the spectrum of child maltreatment. *Fatal maltreatment,* in which a child dies from a repetitive pattern of abuse and/or neglect, is often a separate category in the professional literature.

As international work in child abuse expanded, additional definitional categories were added. Even though these problems exist in Euro-American nations, the international literature brought them more to the forefront. These include *child labor* that extends beyond family-based subsistence and is exploitative, and *child prostitution.* In addition, *selective neglect,* or *underinvestment,* has been identified in international demographic data through patterns of differential mortality in which some categories of children are less likely to thrive or survive due to medical, nutritional, and other forms of inattention and neglect.

Establishing culturally valid definitions of child maltreatment has been complex. Identification of child maltreatment relies on a complex interaction of (a) harm to the child, (b) caretaker behaviors that produced or contributed to that harm, and (c) societal or cultural assignment of responsibility or culpability. Just as there is no absolute standard for optimal child rearing that would be considered valid cross-culturally, there has been difficulty in establishing a universal definition of abusive or neglectful behavior. Three definitional levels have been suggested for culturally informed definitions of child maltreatment. First, cultural practices vary, and what one group considers abusive, another group may consider well within the normative range of behavior. Differences in definitions of child maltreatment that can be ascribed to differences in normative cultural beliefs and practices are not, strictly speaking, abuse, since they are not proscribed, at least by the group in question. This does not preclude discussions and evaluations of the relative harm and benefit of different culturally accepted practices but puts different practices in context. Second, idiosyncratic departure from cultural standards and norms affords an intracultural view that highlights those individuals who violate the continuum of acceptable behavior. And third, societal-level maltreatment of children is sometimes confused with culturally acceptable behaviors. Societal neglect refers to the level of harm or deprivation, such as poverty or war, that a larger political body (nation) tolerates or inflicts on its children. Because child maltreatment has not always been labeled as such in other cultures, some anthropological works have examined physical punishment or emotional climate, as maltreatment requires that behaviors meet three criteria. First, the behavior must be proscribed by the culture in question. Second, it must be proximate to the child and caretaker and not be harm that results from broader conditions beyond parental or care-taker control, such as warfare or famine. And third, it must be potentially preventable.

Incidence and Demographics

In the United States, between 800,000 and 1 million children are identified as abused or neglected each year as a result of reports to child protection agencies. Between three and five children die from fatal maltreatment each day, and homicide by parents is a leading cause of trauma-related death for children under 4 years of age. Between one half and two thirds of child maltreatment cases are neglect. Children under 3 years of age have the highest rates of victimization. Victimization rates are similar for males and females, with the exception of child sexual abuse, in which approximately three to four times more girls than boys are involved.

There is limited data on incidence and prevalence of child maltreatment cross-culturally. While the available evidence suggests that child maltreatment occurs, or has the potential to occur, in all societies, the differential distribution is difficult to estimate. Definitional issues discussed above increase the difficulties in making valid cross-cultural or cross-national comparisons. Despite increasing international awareness, child abuse and neglect are often difficult to recognize or make sense of in the small populations often studied by anthropologists. Because child maltreatment is a low base-rate behavior, it may be rare in a small population during a single year of fieldwork. Rare cases that seem at odds with more general cultural patterns, then, may not find their way into the literature. In addition, it often is difficult to estimate the incidence or prevalence of child maltreatment in societies with high infant and child mortality rates due to disease or malnutrition.

In the United States, there is controversy about whether there are differential rates of child maltreatment across ethnically diverse populations. Questions remain as to whether a higher proportion of reports in poor ethnic minority populations is due to stresses associated with poverty leading to maltreatment or due to increased scrutiny by public welfare agencies leading to higher reports.

Etiology

The etiology of child abuse and neglect is poorly understood, even within those nations that have the longest history of research and policy attention to the problem. More sophisticated etiological models stress the importance of an ecological framework, with risk and protective factors transacting across the ecological levels of individual factors, family factors, community factors, and factors in the larger sociocultural environment. These complex theoretical models, however, have rarely been adequately subjected to empirical testing and research.

A cross-cultural perspective has the potential to enhance understanding of the complex interaction of risk and protective factors that contribute to or prevent the occurrence of child maltreatment. It is not currently known whether common or divergent pathways lead to child maltreatment across diverse populations. For example, does the interaction of poverty and an individual history of child maltreatment have different consequences in different community contexts? Etiological factors should have explanatory power both within and between cultures.

The cross-cultural record sheds some light on categories of children at risk for maltreatment. Even in cultures in which children are highly valued and rarely punished, some children may receive a lesser standard of care than other children. These categories of children may be identifiable through demographic analyses that suggest differential survival by factors such as gender or birth order. Identification of categories of children at risk also requires knowledge of cultural values on specific child behaviors or traits.

Circumstances in which children have diminished social supports or in which social networks are lacking or deficient have also been suggested as increasing the risk of maltreatment. Social networks can act either to prevent child maltreatment or to exacerbate the risk of its occurrence. Social networks, on the one hand, provide the context for assistance with child care, for redistribution of children who may be at risk for maltreatment, and for the establishment, scrutiny, and enforcement of standards of child care and treatment. These functions of social networks should diminish the likelihood of child abuse and neglect. On the other hand, some abusive or neglectful families may be embedded in closely knit but maladaptive networks. Abusive parents may engage with others whose child-rearing attitudes and behaviors are similar to their own. Networks in which attitudes and behaviors toward children tend toward the aggressive or neglectful may provide precisely the kind of role models that facilitate abuse. Network members may be hesitant to intervene or to report maltreatment because their own behavior is similar. They may be fearful that if they report others, they risk reporting themselves. In addition, network members may be isolated from community facilities and supports and therefore may not know how to access supports or services for themselves or for an abusive parent in their midst. Inequality of power between parents has also been implicated in the etiology of child abuse cross-culturally.

Consequences of Child Abuse and Neglect

Child abuse and neglect has been associated with increased risk of adverse outcomes. Not all abused and neglected children suffer immediate or lasting consequences beyond their immediate injuries. Nevertheless, abused and neglected children are at increased risk for a range of physical, mental/emotional, and social/behavioral difficulties. The pathways to these outcomes are complex. Cross-culturally, children who are treated with rejection rather than with warmth and acceptance by their parents and caregivers display negative psychological outcomes.

Cultural Competence in Child Maltreatment

Child abuse and neglect was originally identified in European and Western nations, and many of the formulations about its definitions, causes, and consequences stem from these origins. Anthropology has offered broader understandings of the issues by applying the cross-cultural record both internationally and for diverse populations within multicultural nations. This is a field with many possibilities for future research.

— *Jill E. Korbin*

Further Readings

Handwerker, H. P. (2001). Child abuse and the balance of power in parental relationships: An evolved domain-independent mental mechanism that accounts for behavioral variation. *American Journal of Human Biology, 13,* 679–689.

Korbin, J. (1987). Child maltreatment in cross-cultural perspective: Vulnerable children and circumstances. In R. Gelles and J. Lancaster (Eds.), *Child abuse and neglect: Biosocial dimensions* (pp. 31–55). Chicago: Aldine.

Korbin, J. (1987). Child sexual abuse: Implications from the cross-cultural record. In N. Scheper-Hughes (Ed.), *Child survival: Anthropological perspectives on the treatment and maltreatment of children* (pp. 247–265). Dordrecht, Holland: D. Reidel.

Korbin, J. E. (1997). Culture and child maltreatment. In M. E. Helfer, R. Kempe, & R. Krugman (Eds.), *The battered child* (5th ed., pp. 29–48). Chicago: University of Chicago Press.

Korbin, J. E. (1998). "Good mothers," "babykillers," and fatal child maltreatment. In N. Scheper-Hughes & C. Sargent (Eds.), *Small wars: The cultural politics of childhood* (pp. 253–276). Berkeley: University of California Press.

Levinson, D. (1989). *Family violence in cross-cultural perspective.* Newbury Park, CA: Sage.

National Research Council. (1993). *Understanding child abuse and neglect.* Washington, DC: National Academies Press.

Rohner, R. (1986). *The warmth dimension: Foundations of parental acceptance-rejection theory.* Beverly Hills, CA: Sage.

Scheper-Hughes, N. (Ed.). (1987). *Child survival: Anthropological perspectives on the treatment and maltreatment of children.* Dordrecht, Holland: D. Reidel.

Scheper-Hughes, N., & Sargent, C. (Eds.). (1998). *Small wars: The cultural politics of childhood.* Berkeley: University of California Press.

CHILDBIRTH

Until recently in the history of human beings, childbirth has been the exclusive work of women, who labor and bear down with their uterine muscles to deliver their babies from their wombs into the larger world of society and culture. Today, however, increasing

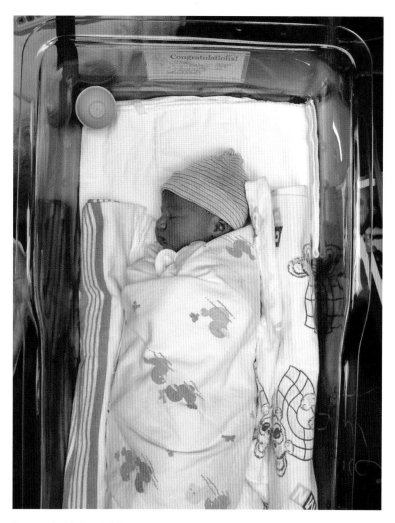

Source: © iStockphoto/Erick Jones.

Mexico's Yucatan, originally published in 1978, was the first to comprehensively document the wide cultural variations. Her biocultural approach focused on the cultural definition of birth, the place of birth, birth attendants, artifacts to facilitate or control birth, and differences in knowledge systems about birth.

Among these, place of birth has emerged as most salient for how birth happens. In home settings across cultures, from huts to mansions, childbirth flows according to the natural rhythms of labor and women's social routines. In early labor, women move about at will, stopping their activities during the 45 seconds or so per contraction and continuing their activities, which may include doing chores, chatting, walking, eating, singing, dancing, and so on. Such activities subside as they begin to concentrate more on the work of birthing, often aided in this labor by massage and emotional support from their labor companions, who are usually midwives. Many cultures have rich traditions about who should be present (sometimes the father, sometimes only women, sometimes the whole family and/or friends), how labor support should be provided, what rituals should be performed to invoke the help of ancestors or spirits, and what herbs and hand maneuvers may be helpful to assist a birth or stop a postpartum hemorrhage. When birth is imminent, women at home usually take upright positions, squatting, sitting, standing, or on hands and knees, often pulling on a rope or pole or on the necks or arms of their companions, and work hard to give birth, rewarded by the baby in their arms. Postpartum practices vary widely: Some cultures encourage early breast-feeding; some code colostrum as harmful and feed the baby other fluids until the breastmilk comes in. Steam and herbal baths and periods of postpartum confinement are often culturally prescribed, varying in length from a few to 40 days.

Where freestanding birth centers exist, whether staffed by traditional or professional midwives, the experience of birth is resonant with the experience of birthing at home—a free flow. There are no absolute rules for how long birth should take. As long as the

numbers of the world's women deliver babies via the medical establishment's use of forceps, vacuum extractors, surgery through cesarean section. The medical definition of *birth* is the emergence of a baby from a womb, a definition that minimizes women's involvement and agency. This definition and its implications encode the challenges faced by social scientists who study childbirth.

Anthropologists have consistently shown that, although childbirth is a universal fact of human physiology, the social nature of birth and its importance for survival ensure that this biological and intensely personal process will carry a heavy cultural overlay, resulting in wide and culturally determined variation in childbirth practices: Where, how, with whom, and even when a woman gives birth are increasingly culturally determined.

Brigitte Jordan's comparative study of birthing systems in Holland, Sweden, the United States, and mother's vital signs are good and the baby's heartbeat is relatively stable, trained attendants allow birth to proceed at its own pace.

Birth in the hospital is a different experience. The biomedical model that dominates hospital care demands that births follow familiar patterns, including cervical dilation of 1 cm per hour—an arbitrary rule unsupported by science but consistent with industrial patterns of production. Ensuring a consistent labor requires frequent manual checking of cervical dilation, which, if determined to be proceeding too slowly, may be augmented by breaking the amniotic sac and administrating the synthetic hormone pitocin (syntocinon) intravenously to speed labor. In Western-style hospitals, staff may monitor the strength of the mother's contractions and the baby's heart rate. At the moment of birth, the vaginal opening may be deemed too narrow to permit an easy birth and so an episiotomy may be performed to widen the vaginal outlet. Such surgeries may be medically unnecessary in as many as 90% of births, but some researchers interpret such routine obstetric procedures as symbolic of the core values of the technocracy, which center around an ethos of progress through the development and application of ever-higher technologies to every aspect of human life, including reproduction.

In a world where the high technologies of Western medicine are valued, many developing countries destroy viable indigenous birthing systems and import the Western model even when it is ill-suited to the local situation. Western-style hospitals built in the third world may be stocked with high-tech equipment but lack the most basic supplies. Hospital staff may have little understanding of or respect for local birthing traditions and values, resulting in local women avoiding such hospitals whenever possible. From Northern India to Papua New Guinea to Mexico, indigenous women echo each other's concerns about biomedical hospitals and clinics in both rural and urban areas: "They expose you." "They shave you." "They cut you." "They leave you alone and ignore you, but won't let your family come in." "They give you nothing to eat or drink." "They yell at you and sometimes slap you if you do not do what they say." Ironically, none of the rules and procedures these women find so alarming are essential to good obstetric care; rather, they reflect the importation of the culturally insensitive technocratic model.

This Western-style model of childbirth, sold to governments as "modern health care" and to women as "managing risk" and "increasing safety in birth," has resulted in an unprecedented explosion of technological interventions in birth, including cesarean sections. Despite the World Health Organization's (WHO) demonstration that nowhere should cesarean rates be above 15%, cesarean rates for Taiwan and China are at 50%; for Puerto Rico at 48%; for Mexico, Chile, and Brazil at around 40%; for the United States at 27.6%; and for Canada and the United Kingdom at 22%. Other factors in the rise of cesarean births include physician convenience and economic gain and deeply ingrained medical beliefs that birth is a pathological process that works best when technologically controlled. The Netherlands meets the WHO standard with a cesarean rate of 12%, reinforced by the excellence of birth outcomes in that country. This success is entirely cultural: In combination with Dutch cultural values on family, midwifery care, and careful attention to scientific evidence, the definition of birth in the Netherlands is as a normal, physiological process, resulting in minimal interventions in hospital birth and the high home birth rate of 30%. In contrast, in most of the developed world, home birth rates hover around 1%, despite its demonstrated efficacy and safety.

The disparity between the scientific evidence in favor of less intervention in birth and the increasing interventions of actual practice reflects

widespread acceptance of the Western technocratic model of medicine as the one on which to base developing health care systems

the political and economic benefits to physicians and technocrats from the imposition of this model

the forces of globalization and their concurrent trends toward increasing technologization

women's concomitant faith in this model as the safest practice for birth

Nevertheless, many contest this model's domination. In addition to the thousands of local birthing systems, three primary models for contemporary childbirth exist throughout the world: technocratic, humanistic, and holistic. The technocratic ideology of biomedicine views the body as a machine and encourages aggressive intervention in the mechanistic process of birth. The reform effort located in the humanistic model stresses that the birthing body is an organism influenced by stress and emotion and calls for relationship-centered care, respect for women's needs and desires, and a physiological, evidence-based approach to birth. The more radical holistic model defines the body as an energy system and stresses spiritual and intuitive approaches to birth. In dozens of countries, humanistic and holistic practitioners and consumer members of growing birth activist movements use scientific evidence and anthropological research to challenge the technocratic model of birth. They seek to combine the best of indigenous and professional knowledge systems to create healthier, safer, and more cost-effective systems of birth care.

Yet from an anthropological point of view, all three paradigms are limited by their focus on the care of the individual. For example, mortality resulting from birth is widely recognized as a massive global problem. Biomedicine identifies conditions such as hemorrhage and toxemia as major causes of maternal death, and it advises investment in doctors, hospitals, and rural clinics to provide prenatal care to prevent toxemia and active intervention immediately after birth to prevent hemorrhage. In contrast, anthropological research in countries with the highest maternal mortality rates highlights the general poor health of women, who suffer from overwork, exhaustion, anemia, malnutrition, and a variety of diseases resulting from polluted water, showing that the most important interventions required for improving women's health and for increasing safety in birth are clean water, adequate nutrition, and improved economic opportunities for women.

— *Robbie E. Davis-Floyd*

See also **Midwifery**

Further Readings

Davis-Floyd, R. E., & Sargent, C. (1997). *Childbirth and authoritative knowledge: Cross-cultural perspectives.* Berkeley: University of California Press.

DeVries, R., van Teijlingen, E., Wrede, S., & Benoit, C. (Eds.). (2001). *Birth by design: Pregnancy, maternity care, and midwifery in North America and Europe.* New York: Routledge.

Jordan, B. (1993). *Birth in four cultures: A cross-cultural investigation of childbirth in Yucatan, Holland, Sweden, and the United States* (4th ed.). Prospect Heights, OH: Waveland Press.

CHILDE, VERE GORDON (1892–1956)

Vere Gordon Childe was a 20th-century archaeologist whose work concentrated on European prehistory, social evolution, and origins of the archaic state.

Born in Sydney, Australia, in 1892, Childe moved to Britain to begin his studies at Oxford University in 1914. After brief involvement in left-wing politics in his native Australia, he returned to England to work in the library of the Royal Anthropological Institute, where he came to publish his first book, *The Dawn of European Civilization* (1925). In 1927, Childe accepted the Abercromby Chair of Archaeology at the University of Edinburgh, where he concentrated his writings on European and Near Eastern prehistory. At this time, he conducted excavations throughout Scotland and published widely on his results, notably, *The Prehistory of Scotland* (1935). Childe left Edinburgh in 1946 to become director and professor of European archaeology at the University of London's Institute of Archaeology. Childe retired in 1956 and returned to Australia, where he fell to his death during a survey of rock formations later that October.

Collectively, Childe's earliest works on European prehistory argue that such cultural innovations as agriculture and metallurgy were developed in Egypt and Mesopotamia and later spread through trade and migration to prehistoric Europe, then a patchwork of heterogeneous societies. Arguing against popular notions that saw European civilization as racially and cultural "pure," Childe insisted that Europe benefited from external influences that upset the status quo and introduced new cultural practices into the region. Europe had adopted the Near East's advancements and reconfigured them in such a way that the student soon surpassed the teacher.

By the 1930s, archaeologists had become dissatisfied with cultural relativism and historical particularism and sought alternatives for explaining why cultures change. Childe introduced a modified social evolutionary framework, multilinear evolutionism, in which a culture followed a trajectory of increasing/decreasing categories of social complexity (usually band, tribe, chiefdom, and state). While he did not disregard diffusion, Childe sought broader political and economic contexts in which to explain transformations in cultural practices. Change occurred because the role that political and economic institutions played in a society resulted in tensions between progressive and traditional practices. The influence of Marxism, especially historical materialism, on Childe is evident in his explanation of change as a product of conflict.

Toward the end of his career, Childe sought explanations for the origins of the archaic state. With more efficient agricultural practices, he argued, communities produced beyond their everyday necessities, creating a need to manage and distribute this surplus. Efficiency in agricultural production created a role for full-time specialists such as craftsmen and bureaucrats, who engaged in recursive relationships with agriculturalists. Citing the need to supervise large public works such as irrigation canals along with the need to resolve social conflict, Childe suggested a demand for a centralized organization (i.e., the state) to effectively coordinate this complex infrastructure. Childe set out 10 characteristics of archaic states: (1) increase in settlement size, (2) urban dwelling, full-time specialists, (3) taxation for surplus building purposes, (4) monumental architecture, (5) the emergence of a class-stratified society, (6) recording systems, (7) the development of counting, measuring, and calendrical systems, (8) an advancement in artistic expression, (9) the growth in long-distance trade in luxuries, and (10) a politically organized society based on territory rather than kinship.

— *Benjamin W. Porter*

See also **Political Economy; Social Change**

Further Readings

Childe, V. G. (1951). *Man makes himself.* New York: New American Library of World Literature. (Original work published 1936)

Harris, D. R. (Ed.). (1994). *The archaeology of V. Gordon Childe: Contemporary perspectives.* Chicago: University of Chicago Press.

Trigger, B. G. (1980). *Gordon Childe: Revolutions in archaeology.* New York: Columbia University Press.

 # CHILDHOOD

Since the Industrial Revolution, most Western societies have come to consider childhood as a time of innocence rooted in biological processes that gradually progress from infancy, childhood, and adolescence into adulthood. In this concept, all youth are defined as minors who are dependent upon adult guidance and supervision; accordingly, youth are denied legal rights and responsibilities until they reach the age that legally defines adulthood. Progressive social scientists view childhood as a concept dependent upon social, economic, religious, and political environments. Rather than see childhood as a time of nonparticipation and dependence, social constructionists see childhood as an expression of society and its values, roles, and institutions. In this sense, childhood is conceptualized as an active state of participation in the reproduction of culture. Indeed, constructionist views of childhood state that childhood is not a universal condition of life, as is biological immaturity, but rather a pattern of meaning that is dependent on specific sets of social norms unique to specific cultural settings.

Childhood can be characterized as the interplay and conflict of and between institutions, individuation, and individualization. Childhood is positioned within this triangulation, revealing how institutions such as day care and kindergarten are rooted in women's labor issues, creating a pull between the pedagogical needs of children versus the economic needs of adults. Individuation is the process by which individuals become differentiated from one another in society. This process identifies childhood as the target for the attention of the state and produces institutions and care providers who delimit the individuality of children. Therefore, a basic tension exists between individual development and collective needs, between the real needs of children and the economic and political needs of adults. Hence, childhood is kept within specific boundaries defined by institutions administered by adults. Therefore, children can be seen to be at the beginning of the process of individualization, long ago achieved by men and only recently achieved by women.

It has been suggested that childhood constitutes a social class, in that children are exploited in relation to adults, who determine and define the needs of childhood according to adult terms. This forces us to place the analysis of childhood in a political-economic frame and shows how children are actually buried in the ongoing division of labor within the adult world.

Childhood Reflects Structures of Power and Domination

The Industrial Revolution in 19th-century Europe resulted in major transformations in economic and social relations. These transformations resulted in the concentration and penetration of capital, which generated two distinct classes: bourgeoisie and proletariat. With this transformation, we see the separation of childhood as distinct from adulthood. Children were differentially affected by industrialization according to class and family relations. Innocence, purity, protection, and guidance define the children of the bourgeois class, while children of the proletariat were considered to be miniature adults who constituted a reserve pool of labor power in early and middle industrial capitalism. Children of the upper classes received private education that trained them for positions of leadership and power, while children of the working class were often put to work alongside adults in factories and sweatshops in industrial Europe.

Economics

A key step in redefining childhood beginning in the mid-1800s was the removal of children from the public sphere. The state, religious, and civil societies each had particular interests in redefining childhood and in removing children from their exposure to the adult world. Growing industrialism demanded an unimpeded free labor market, where child labor was plentiful and cheap. However, toward the end of the 1800s, new reformist attitudes about the detrimental effects of child labor were forming. Protestant Christians and social reformers' concerns about the physical and emotional hazards of child labor helped to initiate the welfare movement and led to debates about the desirability and feasibility of controlling the child labor market.

Childhood Changes Culturally

Conceptualizing childhood in diverging cultural settings requires an anthropological perspective that sees children and childhood as windows into societies. Unfortunately, anthropologists have not taken childhood and children seriously enough, focusing instead on adult society as the locus of interest and change.

Currently, there is a growing movement in social science to view children as active agents who construct meanings and symbolic forms that contribute to the ever-changing nature of their cultures. Not only are children contributing to the complex nature of cultural reproduction, they are accurately reflecting the unique nature of their specific culture.

Margaret Mead's *Coming of Age in Samoa* (1928) explored the theoretical premise that childhoods are defined by cultural norms rather than by universal notions of childhood as a separate and distinct phase of life. The term *youth culture* was introduced in the 1920s by Talcott Parsons, who defined the life worlds of children as structured by age and sex roles. Such a definition marginalized and deindividualized children. The work of Whiting and Edwards, during the 1950s to late 1970s, in diverse cultural settings, developed methodologies to explore what they exemplified as cross-societal similarities and differences in children. Their attempts at producing a comprehensive theory about childhood development, cognition, and social learning processes were informative and groundbreaking. Their work linked childhood developmental theories to cultural differences, demonstrating that children's capacities are influenced as much by culture as by biology. By the 1980s, social research had moved into predominately urban studies, where youth groups and gangs were conceptualized and defined by American sociologists as deviants rebelling against social norms. Current authors such as Qvortrup, Vered Amit-Talai, Wulff, and Sharon Stephens are recasting global research on childhood by defining children as viable, cogent, and articulate actors in their own right. Such research has spawned strident debates concerning the legal rights of children versus the legal rights of parents.

Managing the Social Space of Childhood

Reform of child labor laws required that the needs of poor families, reformers, and capitalists be balanced. In this equation, public education became a means by which children could be removed from the public sphere and handed over to the administrative processes of the state. Statistics from the late-19th-century censuses reveal the effectiveness of the reformers: In England, by 1911, only 18% of boys and 10% of girls between the ages of 10 and 14 were in the labor market, compared with 37% and 20%, respectively, in 1851. Economically, children moved from being an asset for capitalist production to constituting a huge consumer market and a substantial object of adults' labor in the form of education, child care, welfare, and juvenile court systems. Although reformers and bureaucrats could claim a successful moral victory in the removal of child labor from the work force, in reality, children had been made superfluous by machinery and the requirement that industrial work be preserved for adult male and female laborers. In this respect, culture is not only perpetuated by children, but changed by it. The late-modern constructions of childhood acknowledge that children are placed and positioned by society. The places that are appropriate for children to inhabit have widened, and children are now seen as targets of media and marketing campaigns, though children as individuals and as a class have few legal rights.

The definitions of childhood as a state of innocence and purity follow long historical cycles of economic change that correspond to the development of capitalism as it spread within the world system. Immanuel Wallerstein's world systems theory describes historical economic relations in terms of exchanges between the core, semiperiphery, and periphery states. The evaluation the role of children in the world system has led to an agreement by many social scientists that childhood is historically and culturally relative. Recent anthropological political economy theory demonstrates how relations between nation-states and the development of capitalism affect growing child poverty. In addition, these relations determine the role of children economically, socially, and educationally throughout the world, affecting policy development at both the state and federal levels, particularly in the areas of child poverty and child development. Social scientists should turn their attention to a generational system of domination analogous to the gendered oppression that has captured the attention of feminist scholars for the last several decades. If successful, this agenda will advance the legal status of childhood globally, freeing future generations to participate as viable actors within political, economic, and legal realms within their unique cultures.

Recent research on street children around the world demonstrates that childhood is a social construction dependent on geographical, economic, ethnic, and cultural patterns. Patricia Márquez, in *The Street Is My Home* (1999), explored how street youth in Caracas, Venezuela, are brought together because of economic scarcity and social violence, by describing

Source: © Photo provided by www.downtheroad.org, The Ongoing Global Bicycle Adventure.

the ways in which these youth are able to gain financial resources and material wealth through the creation of meaningful experiences and relationships in their lives. Tobais Hecht, in *At Home in the Street* (1998), portrayed street children in Recife as socially significant themselves, acting as both a part of and a reflection of the concerns of adults. He found that Recife's street children took pride in working and earning an income.

Social reality may be seen as a process of constructing one's social world through the skillful actions of everyday life. Alongside the development of the constructionist view of race, gender, and ethnicity, childhood is simultaneously viewed as dependent on location. Historically, theoretical views of childhood have profoundly affected how children are positioned socially, politically, economically, medically, and legally. Due to the recognition of the ways in which both popular and academic views of childhood have impacted children, recent social science research now seeks to redefine childhood as a time of agency and self-directed learning and participation in society, while developing new theoretical paradigms that view children as subjects worthy in their own right, not just in their social status as defined by adults.

— *Marcia Mikulak*

See also **Childhood Studies; Enculturation; Socialization**

Further Readings

Amit-Talai, V., & Wulff, H. (Eds.). (1995). *Youth cultures: A cross-cultural perspective.* New York: Routledge.

Blanc, S. C. (1994). *Urban children in distress: Global predicaments and innovative strategies.* Grey, Switzerland: Gordon & Breach.

James, A., & Prout, A. (1997). *Constructing and reconstructing childhood: Contemporary issues in the sociological study of childhood.* London: Falmer Press.

Mickelson, A. R. (2000). *Children on the streets of the Americas.* New York: Routledge.

Qvortrup, J., Bardy, M., Sgritta, G., & Wintersberger, H. (Eds.). (1994). *Childhood matters: Social theory, practice, and politics.* Brookfield, VT: Avebury.

Rogers, R., Rogers, S., & Wendy, S. (1992). *Stories of childhood: Shifting agendas of child concern.* Toronto, Canada: University of Toronto Press.

Scheper-Hughes, N., & Carolyn S. (Eds.). (1998). *Small wars: The cultural politics of childhood.* Berkeley: University of California Press.

Stephens, S. (1995). *Children and the politics of culture.* Princeton, NJ: Princeton University Press.

CHILDHOOD STUDIES

Childhood studies refers to a reorientation in the interdisciplinary study of children and childhood. The study of children and childhood has a long history in many disciplines, including anthropology, but childhood studies seeks to expand and reorient how the study of children and childhood is conceptualized and approached. Anthropology's role is central to this reorientation because childhood studies builds, in large part, upon anthropology's traditional interests in understanding culture and society from the *emic* (insider, participant) perspective. While children have been the object of a long history of cross-cultural research, the emic perspective of children has received less attention than that of adults. Most anthropological research on children has sought to understand children through the adults charged with their care, usually parents, teachers, and other caregivers. This is also true of the social sciences more broadly. There is a tradition of anthropological work, however, that has actively sought the child's perspective, dating from the foundational work of Margaret Mead (1928) and extending to the present day. This reorientation is similar in some ways to the increased anthropological interest specifically in women that emerged alongside women's studies in recent decades.

Childhood studies also arises from interests that accompanied the 1989 United Nations Convention on the Rights of the Child (UNCRC) that by 2004 had been ratified by all but three nations (the United States, Somalia, and Timor-Leste). The UNCRC has three basic principles: *protection* of children from a range of harms (from intrafamilial abuse to war-related traumas); *provision* of what children need (from the basic physical needs for food and shelter to emotional needs for love and caring); and *participation* by children themselves in matters concerning them insofar as their developmental capacity permits (from family dissolution to educational issues). The UNCRC stimulated a reorientation of thinking about children and childhood. It was clear that children around the world suffered from a range of insults to their development and well-being. It was also clear that children's voices were rarely sought, and thus rarely heard, on issues of basic concern to them. The UNCRC stimulated a body of research, largely in European countries that had ratified the convention, that sought to make children a more integral part of research and to give credence to the child's perspective.

Basic Principles of Childhood Studies

The following are concepts and ideas that form the basis of childhood studies.

Multiple ChildhoodS: Franz Boas transformed the idea of a singular Culture, with a capital C, to the multiplicities of cultureS, with a capital S. Similarly, in childhood studies, a core assumption is that there is no single version of "childhood," but that "childhoods" vary across time and culture. Furthermore, the experience of childhood varies within any culture by variables such as age, gender, and socioeconomic status. Childhood studies, in a reaction against the paradigm of universal child development, argues against privileging any one version of childhood, usually a Western-oriented model of optimal development. Childhood studies, such as earlier work from the Whiting School, recognizes that the experience of childhood may show equal or greater variability intraculturally as interculturally. One of its central missions of childhood studies, therefore, is to describe and explain multiple childhoods.

Source: © Photo provided by www.downtheroad.org, The Ongoing Global Bicycle Adventure.

Distinguishing Among Childhood, Children, and the Child: Childhood studies distinguishes between terms that are often used interchangeably. *Childhood* is defined as a position in social structure, *children* as the group of individuals who occupy that position, and *the child* as both a whole, complex, and rights-bearing citizen and an idealized entity. Childhood is both a permanent and temporary space in the sociocultural context. It is permanent in that all cultures and societies have a life course stage defined by its immaturity, both physical and social. It is constantly shifting in light of larger sociocultural change. It is also constantly changing because each cohort of children, along with the parents and other adults involved with their rearing, bring with them a set of individual and group differences from the cohort before them. Childhood studies takes as a given that childhoods are culturally constructed.

Children as Competent Social Actors and Active Participants: Childhood studies promotes the idea that children are competent social actors who shape their worlds, take action on behalf of themselves and others, participate in decisions that affect them, and define the directions and processes of their own development. The topic of *agency* has in recent years also become increasingly prevalent in studies of the child, as reflected by the right to *participation* in the UNCRC.

The Child's Perspective: If children are regarded as competent social actors, then they must also be regarded as research participants whose perspectives must be sought. Childhood studies has a central mandate to bring in children's voices, studying children in ways that reveal the experiences and perspectives of the child, from the child's point of view, and in his or her own words.

Methods for Studying Children: Methodologically, childhood studies' interests in the child's emic perspective stimulated interests in methods to obtain that perspective. Anthropological methods such as participant observation and ethnographic interviewing have been important in obtaining children's perspectives. Involvement of children and adolescents in the research enterprise has also been an innovation in childhood studies research.

The Social Spaces of Childhood: The field of childhood studies is concerned with how children inhabit, navigate, and negotiate their social worlds. These studies consider a range of both public and private spaces with varying levels of adult control and supervision and varying levels of direct involvement of children in designing and creating those spaces. Peer cultures established independently of adults have been of interest in this regard, for example, in preschools or medical settings, even though there is the wide recognition that no age group is entirely independent. In addition to social spaces, childhood studies has stimulated interests in how children use and regard the physical spaces they occupy.

Children, Childhood, and the Interdependence of Generations: The field of childhood studies, even in emphasizing agency and social participation, has cautioned against going too far in promoting the notion of the autonomous and independent person, as if it were possible to be human without belonging to a complex web of interdependencies. There is much to learn about how generational phenomena are played out at family and societal levels. Trends across these levels need not be complementary, but may be contradictory. A balance of research is needed on both the views of children as well as those who are linked to them.

The Complexity of Contemporary Childhood: Childhood studies recognizes the complexity of modern childhood. For every trend in one direction, there is a trend in another direction, especially when we take a global view. For example, in many parts of the world, a pressing question is how childhood will maintain its space/position in society as the childhood population decreases. There will be fewer children to fill the social space of childhood and a greater proportion of adults, particularly elders. There are also increasing numbers of couples and singles who choose childlessness. What is the impact on childhood of "child-free" housing, for example? While this is often seen as of greater salience for wealthy nations, it will be increasingly important for developing countries seeking to control their populations. Shifting age profiles will have a huge impact on societies and childhoods within them. In a contrasting direction, at the same time, in other parts of the world, children remain a majority, or even increasing proportion, of the population. Demographic patterns as well as warfare and disease have altered the population structure, with wide-ranging consequences for the nature of childhood.

— *Jill E. Korbin*

See also **Childhood; Enculturation; Socialization**

Further Readings

Christensen, P., & James, A. (2000). *Research with children: Perspectives and practices.* London and New York: Routledge/Falmer.

Corsaro, W. (2003). *"We're friends, right?" Inside kids' cultures.* Washington, DC: Joseph Henry Press.

James, A., & James, A. (2004). *Constructing childhood: Theory, policy, and social practice.* Houndmills, UK, and New York: Palgrave Macmillan.

James, A., & Prout, A. (1997). *Constructing and reconstructing childhood. Contemporary issues in the sociological study of childhood.* London: Falmer.

Woodhead, M., & Montgomery, H. (2003). *Understanding childhood. An interdisciplinary approach.* Chichester, UK, and New York: Wiley & Sons.

CHIMPANZEES

The chimpanzee (*Pan troglodytes*) belongs to the Pongidae family of the Primate order. They have a wide distribution, extending across central Africa from Senegal in the west to Tanzania in the east. There are three subspecies of common chimpanzee recognized. They are the western subspecies, *P. troglodytes verus*, the central species, *P. t. troglodytes*, and the eastern subspecies, *P. t. schweinfurthi*. A fourth subspecies from Nigeria and Cameroon may soon be added.

North of the Zaire River, the common chimpanzee has been known of since the 17th century. Captive chimpanzees have been studied since the 1920s, beginning with German psychologist Wolfgang Kohler conducting behavioral research. Most famously, Jane Goodall's research at Gombe Stream National Park in Tanzania has been going on for nearly 40 years and is the longest study of a wild species ever conducted.

Anatomy

Chimpanzees are well-known for their strength and ability to walk upright on two feet or bipedally for short distances. They are human's closest living relatives, sharing more than 98% of the same DNA and with similarities in immune functions and blood composition. Human and chimpanzee lineages separated about 6 million years ago. We are also their closest relatives of all of the living primates, except bonobos. This means that they can contract any infectious disease that a human can be infected by and has led to exploitation by biomedical research institutions. Bonobos and chimpanzees are thought to have shared a common ancestor from whom they split approximately 3 million years ago. Chimpanzees diverged from gorillas 7.5 million years ago and orangutans 16 million years ago.

Chimpanzees live in a variety of habitats, from densely forested jungles to savannas that are believed to closely resemble the environment that human ancestors would have had to endure. Chimpanzees are well suited for life in the trees, where their quadrupedal dexterity and opposable thumbs allow them easy movement, and on the ground, where they knuckle-walk like the other African apes. Male chimpanzees are approximately 1.2 m (4 ft) tall and weigh 60 kg (132 lbs). Females are 1.1 m (3.5 ft) tall and weigh 47 kg (103.6 lbs). Chimpanzees live an average of 30 to 40 years in the wild and longer in captivity.

Chimpanzees have stout bodies with relatively long arms. They have a round head with large, projecting ears and small, forward-facing nostrils on a prognathous muzzle. The top of a chimpanzee skull is flat and is without a sagittal crest. Chimpanzees have large teeth when compared with humans, but have the same dental formula: 2123/2123 = 32. Chimpanzee senses are similar to human senses; however, they have more effective olfactory functions.

There are 13 different categories for chimpanzee calls that range from soft grunts to loud pant-hoots and shrieks. Chimpanzee calls are distinguished from bonobos by being a lower pitch.

Chimpanzees exhibit a high degree of sexual dimorphism. Males are larger and stronger, with characteristically large testes and prominent genitalia. Sexually mature females can be recognized by the pink swellings of perineal skin that are present during the estrous cycle. The estrous cycle is when a female is sexually receptive and fertile. This period lasts for 2 to 3 weeks and occurs every 4 to 6 weeks. Captive females reach sexual maturity at 8 to 9 years of age and give birth for the first time at 10 to 11 years of age. Wild females mature and give birth 3 to 4 years later than captive females.

Male chimpanzees engage in some sexual activity at 2 years of age. They begin to engage in more mature courtship rituals around 3 to 4 years old. These courtship rituals consist of displaying an erect penis, swaggering with hair bristling, and branch shaking and leaf stripping. Receptive females respond by approaching the males and presenting their sexual swellings for inspection.

There is no breeding season for chimpanzees, but females are sexually attractive and receptive only during their estrous cycles, which occur throughout the year. At the beginning of the estrous cycle, females will mate up to six times a day with different individuals. Near the end of the estrous cycle, more exclusive partnerships, called *consortships,* are formed. A consortship, consisting of one receptive female and a male, will often disappear into the forest for several days or even for weeks or months. Sexual activity during this time in the estrous cycle likely results in pregnancy.

The gestation period of a chimpanzee is 8.5 to 9 months long. After birth, the infant is helpless. The female will not be receptive again for 3 to 4 years, when her offspring has been weaned. Unlike bonobos, chimpanzees do not engage in sexual activity during pregnancy or lactation.

Within a few days of birth, infants are able to cling to their mother's underbelly, and they will ride on her back at 5 to 7 months of age. Young chimpanzees are weaned around 3 years of age, and by 4 years of age are walking separately from but always near their mothers. Female chimpanzees leave their natal group when they reach sexual maturity, but males remain in their birth group and maintain close relationships with their mothers and maternal siblings.

Chimpanzees live in colonies of up to 150 individuals. The range of a community is 10 to 50 sq km, with a core area of 2 to 4 sq km. The core area is inhabited 80% of the time. Colonies may have overlapping ranges, but not core areas. Males will regularly patrol the boundaries of their territory. They will chase and attack intruders.

Foraging for food is not an entire group activity. Chimpanzee males will forage in a group of three to six individuals, while females forage alone or with their offspring. Chimpanzees eat ripe fruit for up to 4 hours a day. They also eat soft pith, tree seeds, galls, resin, bark, and young leaves. They have been observed to eat up to 20 different species of plant in

1 day and over 300 different species in 1 year. They are also known to use some plant species for medicinal purposes.

Chimpanzee diets also consist of up to 5% animal protein, which is taken in by foraging for insects and hunting small mammals, including other primates. Females spend twice as much time searching for insects, and males are more active in hunting small mammals, such as monkeys, pigs, small antelopes, and occasionally birds. Different populations of chimpanzees may eat very different diets, depending on their habitats and the traditions of the group. For instance, the chimpanzees of Gombe eat a high percentage of palm oil nuts, while those at nearby Mahale do not. Chimpanzees do not store any food.

Chimpanzee Hunting

Jane Goodall's discovery in the early 1960s that chimpanzees actively engaged in and were successful at hunting small mammals, especially primates, such as colobus monkeys and other mammals, shocked the world of primatology. Since then, different hunting strategies have been observed in various communities, but the most frequently employed technique is based on subgroup cooperation. When prey is spotted, the lead hunter will head silently into the forest to where the monkeys are roosting. The lead hunter is often, but not always, the alpha male. The rest of the hunting troop, a subgroup of the entire troop, follows the lead hunter into the forest. Usually, two of the members will sprint to the periphery of the monkey troop, climb to their level, and act as side blockers. Several other blockers run ahead on the ground to get in front of the fleeing monkey troop and climb high into the canopy to prevent the less heavy prey from getting to an unreachable vantage point, effectively closely the trap.

While this may sound very strategic and organized, a successful hunt is often chaotic. The panicking monkeys dart throughout the canopy, with some of the males staying behind to delay the chimpanzees, even attempting to fight them. When a monkey is captured about 40% of the time at Gombe, the entire chimpanzee troop is brought to a frenzy of excitement. The one who possesses the carcass at this point, which is not always the individual who actually captured the prey, will share the meat with his friends and allies, both male and female. This individual is often not the alpha male, and there is a notable change in the social dynamics of the group during the distribution of the spoils of the hunt.

One possible byproduct of predation, or failed attempts at predation, has been infanticide. In seven instances with the Mahale Mountain National Park chimpanzee group, over several years, the kidnapping, killing, and eating of a male infant followed the stress caused by a failed hunt. The mothers of the victims were fairly new transfers to the group. Therefore, the infanticide might be explained as a result of uncertain paternity and the alpha male's natural desire to get rid of any new infants he suspects are not his own. However, in one case, the mother had been with the group for more than 5 years.

Questions remain as to whether or not the newcomers were seen as threat from the time they joined the group and were intended to be killed. The adult males may have seen the failed hunt as an opportune time to snatch an infant from an excited and distracted mother. Or it is possible that the infants were only viewed as prey in the excitement and disappointment of a failed hunt. Infanticide has finally been accepted as an event that occurs regularly in many species. Our own relationship to chimpanzees and other primates makes it a difficult subject for many to discuss and study without bias. Interestingly, infanticide has not been observed or suspected to occur in bonobo societies.

Social Behavior

In chimpanzee troops, adult males at the top of the social hierarchy are a formidable and overpowering force. The alpha male and several subordinate males dominate and control the troop, often by force and aggression. Physical displays and confrontations reestablish their position on an almost continual basis, which can make life for lower-ranking individuals very stressful. They reestablish and reinforce their positions several times a day. For example, when a chimpanzee troop reaches a food source, the alpha male will usually put on a physical display of his strength by crashing around, reaffirming his dominance by threatening the others. Feeding will then proceed under his watchful eyes, in a hierarchical order, with the least-dominant individuals waiting their turn for and often receiving the least amount of nourishment.

The coalition of adult males is usually intolerant of neighboring troops and are much more territorial than bonobos. Chimpanzees are known to patrol their territorial range and chase or attack any intruders. Jane Goodall observed a war, the "4-year war," between two troops that had originally been one at Gombe. The original troop systematically searched for and attacked all of the individuals from the splinter group. It is believed that the entire splinter group was killed during the 4 years.

Despite the overwhelming evidence for an aggressive existence, chimpanzees are very affectionate with each other. They are known to frequently embrace their friends when nervous or after a stressful encounter and to reinforce bonds and curry favor from dominant individuals. They will also embrace the individual they were at odds with in order to diffuse the tension of a fight and reconcile. Frans DeWaal has done extensive research on the coalition-building and reconciliation habits of chimpanzees.

Tool Use and Chimpanzee Culture

Chimpanzees are well-known for their ability to make and use tools, in the wild and in captivity. In fact, different tool-making traditions, which some scientists consider primitive cultures, have developed at different locations. These traditions are passed on from one generation to the next by observation, imitation, and even instruction. An example of this process at one location is the use of tree roots and rocks as a hammer and an anvil to crack open palm oil nuts. For this technique to be successful, the chimpanzee must be very selective about the hammer and anvil materials and also must master the cracking technique with strength and aim. They have been observed to carry a good hammer from one feeding site to another.

Some of the tools made and used by chimpanzees are as simple as a termite "fishing stick," which requires the toolmaker to pick an appropriate length of stick, strip it of leaves, and poke it into the right termite mounds. As simple as this sounds, it is a skill that is learned. Some chimpanzees are better at it than others. The fisher must patiently wait for the termites to grab ahold of the wood before removing the stick with a bounty of protein attached. Chimpanzees make other tools from their natural environment, such as chewing leaves and moss and using the wad as a water sponge.

Another example of the various primitive cultures of chimpanzees at different locations includes the

Source: © iStockphoto/Kevin Tate.

hand-clasp grooming technique. Grooming partners clasp hands overhead while facing each other, as if to hold up the arm for better access to the body. However, not all chimpanzees engage in this grooming practice. The habit seems to have originated with one troop and followed an emigrant into another troop, transmitting the culture to the troop that did not originally practice the hand-clasp grooming technique. The technique is even used by a captive group that seems to have learned it from a newly introduced wild chimpanzee.

Ape Intelligence

Chimpanzee cognitive abilities are evident in the fact that they pass the self-recognition mirror test. For this test, a red dot is painted on an anesthetized individual. When the individual wakes up and is presented with a mirror, it begins to inspect its image and touch the dot on its own face, recognizing that the image in the mirror is its own and not another being. Other primates, such as monkeys, do not have this ability.

One of the most significant demonstrations of chimpanzee intelligence has been well documented through ape language studies. Sue Savage-Rumbaugh and her husband, Duane, work with apes at the Language Research Center at Georgia State University, in Atlanta. The experiments that Savage-Rumbaugh conducts include teaching symbolic representations, called *lexigrams,* of English words to chimpanzees and bonobos. As a result of this work, the apes have shown that they are able to combine meaningful lexigrams to demonstrate a rudimentary understanding of language. Other scientists and institutions are engaged in similar research using sign language.

Some scientists, such as Steven Pinker of York University in Toronto, who studies language acquisition in children, are not convinced the apes actually understand what they are doing. Pinker believes the language skills of Savage-Rumbaugh's subject are little more than circus tricks. Fortunately, ape language acquisition research continues with positive results and star pupils in each new study.

Spontaneous communication, especially when not in regard to food or within an immediate experiment, is what most researchers believe is the best evidence of language comprehension by chimpanzees and bonobos. In one instance, one of Savage-Rumbaugh's chimpanzees, Panshiba, wanted to communicate with her, alone. Panshiba took her aside to describe an event that the chimpanzee had overheard in another cage earlier in the day. An adolescent chimpanzee, Austin, had bitten his mother and caused a commotion. Panshiba appeared to want to gossip about the incident by telling Savage-Rumbaugh what had happened.

The emotional lives of chimpanzees are more difficult to research and document. However, they have been observed getting excited, rushing about, and shrieking when they encounter a waterfall or it begins rain. Researchers call this a "rain dance" and believe the chimpanzees are capable of an emotion comparable to human awe of nature. Unlike their bonobo relatives, chimpanzees are usually afraid of standing water, and they despise rain.

Conservation

If chimpanzees share more than 98% of the same DNA as humans, sense their habitat with the same

functionary capabilities, and even behave in similar ways to humans, it should logically follow that they have nearly equal emotional and intellectual capabilities. However, this would mean that they are more humanlike than many would like to believe or that we are more animal-like. Whatever position is taken, even those who exploit chimpanzees and their habitats cannot deny the fact that their numbers are dwindling due to the encroachment of humans for agriculture and forest products, as well as hunting them for the bushmeat trade and the live-animal market. Chimpanzee populations today equal a mere 5% of the numbers in existence at the turn of the century.

Like humans, chimpanzee infants are slow to develop and have long periods of dependence. Coupled with a fairly low birth rate, which is not able to keep up with death rates that are influenced by external forces, chimpanzees and the other African apes are in dire need of habitat protection and the enforcement of hunting and selling bans. We have learned so much about or closest relatives in the past decade, yet the knowledge we have amassed is negligible compared with what is still available through continued long-term, intensive studies. If we believe that chimpanzees and bonobos are an important model for our own evolution, we must preserve their well-being in order to continue researching their origins, as well as our own. As the natural conditions are destroyed, so to are the natural behaviors from which we wish to learn.

— *Jackie L. Orcholl*

See also **Chimpanzees and Bonobos, Differences; Chimpanzees, Saving; Goodall, Jane**

Further Readings

Boesch, C., Hohmann, G., & Marchant, L. F. (Eds.). (2002). *Behavioural diversity in chimpanzees and bonobos.* Cambridge: Cambridge University Press.

De Waal, F. (1990). *Peacemaking among primates.* Cambridge, MA: Harvard University Press.

De Waal, F. (1996). *Good natured: The origins of right and wrong in humans and other animals.* Cambridge, MA: Harvard University Press.

De Waal, F. (2000). *Chimpanzee politics: Power and sex among apes.* Baltimore: Johns Hopkins University Press.

Goodall, J. (1986). *The chimpanzees of Gombe: Patterns of behavior.* Cambridge, MA: Belknap Press, Harvard University Press.

Goodall, J. (2000). *In the shadow of man.* New York: Houghton Mifflin Company.

Nichols, M., & Goodall, J. (1999). *Brutal kinship.* New York: Aperture Foundation.

Wrangham, R. W., Heltne, P. G., McGrew, W. C., & De Waal, F. B. M. (Eds.). (1996). *Chimpanzee cultures.* Cambridge, MA: Harvard University Press.

CHIMPANZEES AND BONOBOS, DIFFERENCES

Chimpanzees, the most socially diverse group of apes, are represented by two species, the common chimpanzee *(Pan troglodytes)* and the pygmy chimpanzee, or bonobo *(Pan paniscus).* Both species are found in the tropical forests of equatorial Africa. Sharing approximately 98% of their genes with humans, chimpanzees are genetically more closely related to humans than they are to any other ape group. For this reason, the chimpanzee has been important to the study of human evolution and behavior.

The common chimpanzee is found in many parts of equatorial Africa, inhabiting the forested regions of 22 countries. The variation in flora and fauna between these different areas has enabled the common chimpanzee to evolve into at least three separate subspecies that are localized to specific regions. The three subspecies are *Pan troglodytes troglodytes* from central Africa; *Pan troglodytes verus* from western Africa; and *Pan troglodytes schweinfurthii* from eastern Africa. Two other subspecies, *P. troglodytes vellerosus* from Nigeria and *P. troglodytes koolokamba* from Cameroon and Gabon, have been proposed, yet these designations are considered more controversial.

The common chimpanzee lives in multimale-multifemale polygynous groups with a single dominant male, several mature males, and several mature females and their offspring. Males tend to remain in their natal groups while females emigrate. This sets up a social dynamic in which males often form alliances with other males, usually related individuals, and females only form loose bonds with each other. Like other polygynous primates, chimpanzees display significant sexual dimorphism, with males weighing on average 60 kg (132 lb) and females weighing 47 kg (104 lb). The social interactions between members of this species include vocal, physical, and gestural-visual behaviors, some of which are typical of most primates and others that are specific either to the species or local population.

The second species of chimpanzee is the bonobo or "pygmy chimpanzee" from the central Congo Basin. Male bonobos weigh on average 45.0 kg (99.2 lb), while females weigh 33.2 kg (73.2 lb). This species, which is the more gracile cousin of the common chimpanzee, not a smaller version, has been little studied compared with the more popular common chimpanzees studied by Jane Goodall and others. However, the little that is known about this species indicates that it is very different from any other ape species in terms of behavior.

Bonobos live in multimale-multifemale groups where the group hierarchy appears to be divided between a dominant male and a dominant female. As opposed to the more aggressive interactions seen in the common chimpanzees, bonobo behaviors are more docile. The social interactions of this species include vocal, physical, and gestural-visual behaviors. However, these behaviors appear to be more complex than that of their cousin, the common chimpanzee, in that there are few displays of dominance, and many physical displays have a sexual component tied to them. As Frans de Waal and other researchers have found, bonobos and chimpanzees lead significantly different social lives.

In common chimpanzees, females mate only when they produce conspicuous sexual swellings as they come into estrus. This advertises their receptivity to males in the group, who spend much of their time engaging in aggressive behaviors in order to gain mating access to females. Bonobos, however, have evolved a different strategy, in which females are continually receptive. In addition, bonobos use sexual activity as a part of normal social interactions. As such, bonobo groups are more cohesive, with males and females interacting more frequently than is seen in the common chimpanzee, where males rarely interact with females who are not in estrus.

Much of what is known about the behaviors of the closest living relatives of humans has been conducted by researchers such as Jane Goodall, Richard Wrangham, Takayoshi Kano, and Frans de Waal. From their studies, it has been discovered that chimpanzee behavior mirrors that of humans more closely than previously thought. For example, Goodall discovered that chimpanzees engage in war to expand their territory and eliminate any competitors. Goodall also found that chimpanzees are capable of producing rudimentary tools to crack open nuts or fish for termites. However, these behaviors are not universal among common chimpanzees. Rather, each localized population possesses its own suite of behaviors, including toolmaking. This has led some researchers to suggest that chimpanzees possess culture in the human sense.

Based on studies of bonobos, it has been found that humans are not unique in engaging in sexual activity for pleasure. Bonobos have also demonstrated an exceptional ability to grasp complex tasks, such as learning a rudimentary language, which is also shared by common chimpanzees but not to the same degree of proficiency. The capacity of both species for learning may relate to their ability to engage in deception and other cognitive tasks that require associative processing above the reactionary responses seen in other primate species. These and other ongoing studies continue to demonstrate that many of the features once thought unique to humans have their origins in their closest living relatives, the chimpanzee and bonobo.

— *Douglas C. Broadfield*

See also **Apes, Greater; Bonobos; Chimpanzees, Saving; Goodall, Jane**

Further Readings

Boesch, C., Gottfried, H., & Marchant, L. F. (2002). *Behavioural diversity in chimpanzees and bonobos.* Cambridge: Cambridge University Press.

Goodall, J. (1986). *The chimpanzees of Gombe: Patterns of behavior.* Cambridge, MA: Belknap/Harvard University Press.

Wrangham, R. W., McGrew, W. C., De Waal, F. B. M., & Heltne, P. G. (Eds.). (1996). *Chimpanzee cultures.* Cambridge, MA: Harvard University Press.

 # CHIMPANZEES, SAVING

At the beginning of the 20th century, more than 2 million chimpanzees flourished in the forests of 25 African countries. Today, only 4 nations have significant populations. Population estimates for 1999 show that common chimpanzee numbers have dwindled to between 150,000 to 235,000 individuals. Most of the remaining animals are found in the Central Africa forests of Zaire, Gabon, Congo, and Cameroon. There are many factors that have contributed to the decline of wild chimpanzee populations. The largest contributor to the chimpanzee crisis is the threat made by the overpopulation of *Homo sapiens.* Large encampments of human population create a stress on the environment by consuming resources. Harvesting the environment for fuel and raw material results in deforestation and loss of habitat. Harvesting the environment for food results in the bushmeat trade.

The Pan African Sanctuary Alliance (PASA) is an alliance of 16 primate sanctuaries from all over Africa. PASA suggests a need for general guidelines for the establishment of authorities, site location, long-term sustainability, management practice, primate management, and health issues. Norm Rosen, a member of the PASA advisory board and a professor of anthropology at California State University Fullerton, coordinated a study on the extinction rate of the wild chimpanzee. The results of this research suggested that certain subspecies of chimpanzee could become extinct within the next two decades. The *Pan troglodytes vellerosous* is one of four chimpanzee subspecies, and it is estimated that only 8,000 remain in the wild. According to Rosen, the situation is critical; the rising number of orphaned chimpanzees is indicative of the decrease in population. There are a variety of reasons why wild chimpanzee populations are dropping dramatically.

The tropical rain forests of West and Central Africa cover an area of over 2 million sq km. Timber companies enter into untouched areas in search of the valuable trees that are scattered throughout the forest. The building of roads into unlogged areas heavily fragments the forest and opens it up to hunters. Logging companies introduce a large new workforce that increases the demand for meat. Furthermore, logging vehicles are used to transport bushmeat to the market, where the precious delicacy can satiate the demands of the masses. The vehicles facilitate the process, which results in more demand: more mouths to feed and ultimately far fewer chimpanzees in the wild. The logging companies make it easy and profitable for their workers to enter into the commercial trade for bushmeat.

Economics drives the bushmeat crisis. Growing demand for meat in most cities provides new economic opportunities for people whose traditional sources of income have disappeared and where jobs have become scarce. A majority of people who eat bushmeat do so because it is cheap or free and easily accessible. Hunting is vital to families without access to agricultural markets. Hunting is also woven into many societies. Animal parts, such as horns, feathers, or bones, are a crucial part of many cultural and religious ceremonies.

Source: Photograph by Gregory Scott Hamilton, Honolulu Zoo.

Central Africans typically eat as much as many Europeans and North Americans (30–70 kg/person/year). Approximately 30 million people live in the forests of Central Africa, and they eat approximately 1.1 million tons of wildlife each year. The estimated annual value of the bushmeat trade in West and Central Africa could exceed 1 billion U.S. dollars. A hunter can make $300 to $1,000 per year from commercial hunting, which, in that economic reality, is a lot of money. As the urban populations create more of a demand, more people will be attracted to the bushmeat trade.

Logging companies can potentially have a large role in curbing the bushmeat trade. Not only are they crucial in determining forest habitat management in the region, but they can also establish policy that would reduce the strain on the environment. The majority of large, relatively intact blocks of forest outside of protected areas currently comprise less than 6% of the landscape in Central Africa. These regions are already being logged or earmarked for logging. It is critical that logging companies modify their policies to minimize the impact on wildlife. It is also important that the protected areas have sufficient funding to ensure the long-term existence of forest fauna. To facilitate this, the government along with the logging companies need to establish long-term wildlife management plans, set aside unlogged refuges for rare or threatened species, halt the transportation of hunters and bushmeat of logging vehicles, deny hunters road access to logged forests, and seek ways to provide local populations with alternative sources of protein.

Economics will play a key role in developing resolutions to the environmental tragedy of bushmeat. Cooperative efforts should be made to increase law enforcement and to tax commercial trade in the bushmeat. Local production of economically affordable bushmeat alternatives is vital, to stop the unsustainable levels of hunting. We need to reduce the amount taken out of the forests and shift the demand to the local alternatives. Unless people have economically viable alternatives, they will continue to demand wildlife as an affordable source of food, which is perceived as an inexhaustible and abundant resource. Local government also needs to promote the use of family planning by providing the resources to curb the growth of population.

Not all chimpanzees are pulled out of the wild for bushmeat; some are used in the black-market pet trade and in biomedical research. The Great Ape Project Census 2001 revealed over 3,100 great apes living in captivity in the United States, ranging from modern zoos and sanctuaries to carnivals and laboratories. The census found great apes living in 37 states, 1,280 in biomedical research laboratories. Up to 90,000 chimpanzees a year were once used by biomedical research in the United States. Labs today rely on their captive breeding policy to provide new individuals, reducing the demand for wild-caught chimpanzees. Chimpanzees are one of the 61 primate species prohibited from commercial trade by the Convention on International Trade in Endangered Species (CITES). Although they are illegal to sell, chimpanzees are still bought and sold in the underground pet trade.

We as humans have to be responsible in how we treat our environment and our neighbors. We need to set aside forests for our closest living relative and properly manage what forests remain. We need to find viable alternative food sources so that all local fauna does not get consumed as food. We need to come up with realistic alternatives for income generation, such as ecotourism. In the long term, the bushmeat trade is not economically viable. It is limited and nonsustainable, and at the current rate of proliferation, the chimpanzee will not exist in the wild in 10 to 15 years.

— *Gregory Scott Hamilton*

See also **Apes, Greater; Chimpanzees**

Further Readings

Bushmeat Crisis Task Force. (2000, April). *The role of the logging industry* (Fact sheet). Silver Spring, MD: Author.

Great Ape Project Census (2001). www .greatapeproject.org

Grolimond, G. (2004). *Alarming study reveals chimpanzee extinction crisis.* Montreal, Canada: Jane Goodall Institute of Canada.

Gunn, C., Liffick, M., & Mathis, J. (2001). *Biological diversity 2001: Chimpanzee.* http://www .earlham.edu/~mathijo/chimp.htm

CHIMPANZEES IN CAPTIVITY

Biological anthropologists closely study chimpanzees, which share 98% of their DNA with humans. Chimpanzees have been particularly useful in helping scientists identify and treat diseases of the liver. As a result, some 1,600 chimpanzees are being used in biomedical research in the United States alone. In addition to medical research, chimpanzees have received a good deal of attention from researchers and the general public in response to Jane Goodall's (1934–) anthropological and conservation work with chimpanzees in the Gombe Game Reserve in Africa. The sale of chimpanzees has been banned since 1977 by international treaties. However, it is believed that 40 to 50 baby chimpanzees continue to be sold each year on the black market. Chimpanzees have also begun to receive the unwelcome attention of hunters from local tribesmen due to the bushmeat crisis in Africa. Hunters trap adult chimpanzees and sell them for meat to be used as food for logging camps or to be shipped all over the world on the black market. Perhaps in retaliation for human violence, chimpanzees in Tanzania and Uganda have stolen and killed 10 human babies, and several others have been seriously injured in attacks.

Because hunters have focused on female chimpanzees in groups of 5 to 10 at a time, they leave thousands of young chimpanzees orphaned and not always able to care for themselves in the wild. Goodall has headed a campaign designed to provide sanctuaries for orphaned chimpanzees. Established in 1983, the Chimfunshi Wildlife Orphanage in Chingola has become such a refuge for motherless chimpanzees. The refuge area was financed by donations from the United States, the United Kingdom, and Germany. The largest primate refuge in the world, Chimfunshi has designated 1,500 acres as a reserve for the 100 or so chimpanzees in its care. In June 2004, officials at the orphanage released 12 chimpanzees that had been held in cages into a 150-acre protected enclosure populated with fruit trees and open grasslands. In addition to those orphaned chimpanzees that are rescued and placed in sanctuaries, many more are lost to death, the black market, laboratory research, and humans who keep them as pets. In addition to Chimfunshi, at least 11 other sanctuaries have been established in Africa. A couple hundred rescued chimpanzees also live in private homes or in halfway homes awaiting transfer to reserves.

In June 2004, anthropologist Norm Rosen of California State University at Fullerton announced at the conference of the Pan African Sanctuaries Alliance that illegal hunting and rapid deforestation have placed chimpanzees in danger of extinction.

The number of chimpanzees has also been reduced drastically by the fact that chimpanzees in reserves are on birth control because unchecked population growth would make it impossible to care for them. Scientists believe that the most vulnerable subspecies of chimpanzees, the *troglodytes vellerosus,* of which only some 8,000 remain, could become extinct by the end of the first quarter of the 21st century. By the middle of the 21st century, all species of chimpanzees could become extinct if the current rate of attrition continues.

— Elizabeth Purdy

 CITY, HISTORY OF

A primary focus of urban anthropology and the archaeology of complex societies is the history of the concept of a *city.* Scholars generally cite the first city as emerging in 3500 BC in Mesopotamia. Discussions of the city have emerged in anthropological literature in association with that considered urban, both as process and spatial locus. Useful distinctions, first drawn by Kemper within this context, are between anthropology *in* cities versus anthropology *of* cities. Equally important are those distinctions between the preindustrial, modern, and postmodern exemplifications of the city. Understanding the process, growth, or history of the city includes consideration of the public and private use and organization of space, architecture, and the economic and sociopolitical life of the inhabitants.

Scholarship focusing on the city began with sociologists locating "society" as being indicative of changes collective humans underwent that ultimately became the city. Early urban sociologists included F. Tonnies (1887), who established the difference between *Gemeinschaft* (community) and *Gesellschaft* (society); E. Durkheim (1897), who introduced the concepts of mechanical and organic society; M. Weber (1904), who considered the social structure of a city; L. Wirth (1938), who developed a theory of the characteristic influences of urban life on social organization and attitudes; and R. Redfield (1947), who built on Wirth's ideas to introduce the folk-urban continuum concept. It was in the 1920s that the Chicago School of Urban Ecology (with R. Park at the University of

Chicago) began to focus on issues such as demography, census information, interviews, and historical data, with an emphasis on the social problems within cities, as opposed to the theory of processes of urbanization.

Early Cities in the Old World

The earliest examples of cities in the archaeological record are found in the Old World and date to the Chalcolithic and Early Bronze Age. Located close to waterways, these cities show evidence of increases in population, centralization of power, organization of trade, and the development of communication and mobility.

In explaining the urban phenomenon, archaeologists first looked to prime movers for theories on why the geopolitics of river valleys would lead to the emergence of a city. Key prime movers were increase in population, the technological advancement of irrigation systems (K. Wittfogel's "hydraulic society"), and warfare. As opposed to single-factor and linear reasoning, multicausal theories explaining the development of settlements to urban sites are now commonly accepted. One of the key texts for archaeologists has been V. Gordon Childe's *The Urban Revolution* (1950), which lists criteria for considering a site "urban." This list includes domestication of agriculture, change to sedentary lifestyle, monumental and public architecture, burials, craft specialization (ceramic and metal), and the centralization of power. Sites in the Old World such as Jericho, Catal Höyük, and Mehrgarh are generally thought of as illustrative of the development of urbanism. The first cities are located within river valley civilizations during the Bronze Age: Mesopotamia (Ur), Egypt (Abydos), the Indus (Harappa), and China (An'Yang). These cities were engaged in the storage of surplus, centralization of power, urban planning, and the establishment of long-distance trade.

Early Cities in the New World

In the Oaxaca Valley, one of the earliest examples of settled trading communities is the Zapotec Culture (2000 BC). Monte Alban was an administrative center that was architecturally developed and politically dominant; however, it was abandoned by 750 BC. In lowland Mesoamerica, the Olmec Culture preset the oncoming Maya as a political force. The city of Tikal (c. 800 BC–AD 900), one of the largest Maya cities, emerged as a powerful political force in Central

America. In the highlands, one of the largest cities that emerged in the Valley of Mexico was the site of Teotihuacán (200 BC– AD 750). Teotihuacán is over 21 sq km, and has over 600 pyramids built in its city limits.

In South America, the site of Caral, Peru, demonstrates some of the earliest dates for a city in the New World. Recent dates suggested date Caral to 2600 BC. This 150-acre site consists of a complex of pyramids, plazas, and residential buildings. Other early cultures that demonstrated urban processes were those of El Paraiso (800–500 BC), Chavin (1500–300 BC), and Nazca (600 BC–200 AD). These cities illustrate civic planning and monumental architecture, in addition to evidence of trade and agricultural surplus.

Early Cities: Mediterranean

A major political innovation in Greece (800–700 BC) was the development of the city-state, or *polis*. These political units were centrally based on a single city. A main characteristic of the city-state was its small size, which allowed for political experimentation. It was within this framework that democracy (primarily during Periklean government, ca. 462–431 BC) first came to be developed as a system where free male citizens constituted a small enough body that policy decisions were able to be made effectively.

Concurrently, in Italy, the Etruscans had established city-states, which ultimately formed into confederacies. These became powerful through trade and political connections. Scholars contend that Etruscan city-states provided the framework for the later Roman Empire. It was during the Roman Empire that individuals living in cities commented upon its sociological effects. Writers such as Cicero (106–43 BC) and Livy (64 or 59 BC–AD 17) began to discuss the various hazards of living in cities (such as Rome), including problems with the lack of urban planning, traffic, noise pollution, predominance of unsanitary areas, fires, collapsing buildings, theft and general crime issues, expressing the need to find meaning in life through "retreats" from city life.

Preindustrial Cities

After the fall of the Roman Empire, city-states such as Venice began to flourish around the 6th century AD. The city became associated with maritime powers and controlled trade that flowed from East to West, and vice versa. Venice, as a city-state, was never part of the old Teutonic Empires, but rather maintained its allegiances for centuries with Byzantium. As a city, the interesting aspect of Venice are the more than 200 canals that network the city, increasing internal mobility.

Another example of a varied concept of the city is found in the Vijayanagar Empire (AD 1336–1565), which provides the blueprint for a cosmic city in South India. The planned city of Vijayanagara reproduces, in material form, a pattern that can exist in the cosmic realm and a pattern of celestial authority, characterized by three features: a clear orientation and alignment with the cosmos, a symbolism of centrality, and the throne of the sacred king. The city of Vijayanagara is one of the most architecturally elaborate examples of the cosmic city in the world today.

It should be noted that some early scholars of urban anthropology (mis)used the term *preindustrial cities* to refer to third-world cities in the modern world instead of as a chronological marker, as used in this context.

Industrial Cities

One of the key examples of the progression to an industrial city is that of Chicago. Chicago was incorporated as a city in 1837. Soon after, the railroad arrived, and Chicago became the chief railroad center for the United States. Due to rapid overpopulation and factory booms, new industrial cities were always in danger of fires. This was an acute problem for cities such as Chicago and Philadelphia, because adequate water systems had still not been put into place, nor were fire houses close to some areas of the city. Chicago saw its big fire by 1871. By the time Ford Motors began the factories for the building of motor vehicles, Chicago had rebuilt itself, extended itself out, and created some of the first evidence for a suburban sprawl. The development of the city of Chicago, and of the diametrically opposite inner cities and suburbia, was directly related to the industrialization of the city and the booming of factory businesses.

Urban Planning

The establishment of a planned city is indicative of centralized control and power. Many ancient cities demonstrate evidence of planning and standardization, although the type of urban planning varies region to region. The Indus cities of Mohen-jo-Daro and Harappa are good examples of standardization of building materials and of main aerial streets off which smaller streets emerge. Ancient Rome is another example of the manner in which urban planning was used for civic convenience and military defense purposes. This is in contrast to cities that emerge from organically settled clusters. Despite the ancient illustrations of planned cities, the 5th-century Greek architect Hippodamus (planned the Greek city of Miletus) is often called the "father of urban planning." Modern examples can be found in most capitals of nations. "New Towns" in Great Britain were developed by long-term loans from the central government and were first authorized by the New Towns Act of 1946. The idea is traced back to a book by E. Howard on garden cities (1898). Other examples of planned cities are Chandigarh, India (planned by Le Corbusier); Brasilia, Brazil (planned by Niemeyer Soares); Queenstown, Singapore (planned through the "New Towns" initiative); and Philadelphia, Pennsylvania (initially planned by William Penn).

The Global City

The concept of the "global city" brought forth by S. Sassen (1991) refers to a type of city that is a prominent center for trade, banking, finance, and, most important, markets. These global cities have much more in common with each other than with other cities within their own countries. For example, cities such as New York City, Tokyo, London, Karachi, Paris, and Moscow would be considered global cities. This type of city clearly privileges economics over other forms of sociocultural affiliations. Sassen's typology, however, may be extended into various genres of global cities; for example, cities of high religious importance might be grouped into Vatican City, Mecca, Varanasi, Jerusalem, and so on.

Current research on cities extends from ancient cities to the cities of tomorrow. Such research must combine understandings of the histories of both the theory of the city and the illustration of urban phenomenon with the spatial location. Definitions of the city depend on the context; however, in each, the core understanding of an urban space remains.

— *Uzma Z. Rizvi*

See also **Economics and Anthropology; Harappa; Tikal; Urban Ecology**

Further Readings

Hannerz, U. (1980). *Exploring the city: Inquiries towards an urban anthropology.* New York: Columbia University Press.

Low, S. (Ed.). (1999). *Theorizing the city: The new urban anthropology reader.* New Brunswick, NJ: Rutgers University Press.

Sassen, S. (1991). *The global city: New York, London, Tokyo.* Princeton, NJ: Princeton University Press.

GHOST TOWNS

One of the essential elements of folklore in the American West is the ghost town, the forlorn remnant of a thriving outpost of civilization from the days of the great silver and gold mines of the old West. Yet not all ghost towns died: Some went on to become successful, reinventing themselves to meet a new era. Tombstone, Arizona, the scene of the famous gunfight at the OK Corral in October 1882, between the Earp brothers and the Clantons and McLowerys, went on to become a major tourist attraction, bringing its heritage to thousands of tourists each year.

The town has been helped by the continued interest in the Wyatt Earp saga, in motion pictures from John Ford's *My Darling Clementine,* to *Wyatt Earp* by Kevin Costner, and *Tombstone,* which starred Kurt Russell as Earp. Both *Wyatt Earp* and *Tombstone* came out in the same year, 1994. Tombstone, the former ghost town "too tough to die," was also immortalized in Hugh O'Brien's 1950s television series *Wyatt Earp,* which was a hagiographic view of the tall frontier gunman based on the biography by Stuart Lake. Walter Noble Burn's *Tombstone* gave a slightly less biased historical account of the hellacious life of the town.

Even today, those who go to the town, which has faithfully restored the frontier buildings of yore, are heatedly divided in their views about the gunfight and what led up to it. One school of thought holds that the gunfight was essentially between two gangs, the Earp and Clanton factions, which were fighting to control the lucrative cattle trade of the area and the gambling dens of the town. Another view says that the Earps represented the law-and-order faction in the town and that the Clantons and the McLowerys were basically cattle rustlers, abetted by their ally, Tombstone's sheriff Johnny Behan.

Yet another view is political: The Earps and the businessmen supporting them were Republicans, and Behan and his allies were Democrats, and the entire feud was a bloody version of a Philadelphia or Boston political ward struggle. Yet another theory was that the Earps were from the North in the Civil War and that the Clantons and their comrades had supported the South, and both groups had brought the festering hate from that struggle west. Whatever the reasons, on October 26, in 1881, Virgil, Morgan, and Wyatt Earp, with that deadly dentist, John "Doc" Holliday, met the Clantons, Billy Claiborne, and the McLowerys near the OK Corral and Camillus Fly's Photography Studio. After the gunfire ceased, Billy Clanton and Tom and Frank McLaury were all killed, and "Doc" Holliday, Virgil, and Morgan Earp wounded. Billy Claiborne and Ike Clanton ran away; Ike was killed rustling cattle later on. Only Wyatt Earp remained unscathed. The history of Tombstone—and the entire American West—would never be the same.

— **John F. Murphy Jr.**

URBAN ANTHROPOLOGY

Although the term *urban anthropology* was coined only in the 1960s, anthropology and urban studies have always been closely associated. As Chicago sociologist Robert E. Park put it in his founding text of American urban studies, *The City* (1915), the same methods of observation that anthropologists had used to study "primitive" peoples "might be even more fruitfully employed in the investigation of the customs, beliefs, social practices, and general conception of life" in the different neighborhoods of American cities.

Louis Wirth, a colleague of Park in Chicago, greatly influenced the development of urban anthropology through his essay, "Urbanism as a Way of Life." Wirth theorized that urban life exerted a clear influence on social organization and attitudes. To Wirth, urban life is marked by impersonal, instrumental contacts that tend to free individuals from the strong controls of such primary groups as the extended family, yet at the same time, this freedom of individual action is accompanied by the loss of collective security. The Chicago School's early reliance on interviews, ethnographic work, and life histories is particularly evident in founding texts of urban anthropology, such as Carolyn Ware's *Greenwich Village, 1920–1930;* W. Lloyd Warner's *Yankee City;* and William Foote Whyte's *Street Corner Society.*

With its proposed shift from the study of "primitive" civilizations to urban cultures, urban anthropology stands in opposition to colonial anthropology that assumes "primitive" people as being essentially different from Western civilization. This opposition, urban anthropologists claim, is no longer valid, as there has not been a single society that has remained untouched by the process of industrialization.

The new subject of analysis required anthropologists to reassess their methodology. The traditional form of participant observation that put the researcher in a close relationship with a small community for a certain period of time was no longer viable in an urban context. Anthropologists working in the field have had to expand their scope to include other materials, such as surveys, historical studies, novels, personal diaries, and other sources. The rise of urban anthropology in the 1960s reflects the acknowledgment that traditional target groups of anthropological research, such as tribal and peasant people, became increasingly integrated in an urbanized world. Topics such as rural-urban migration, urban adaptation, ethnicity, poverty, and other social problems have been particularly important in urban anthropology, which has increasingly been integrated in the discourses of other social sciences.

— Luca Prono

 ## CIVIL DISOBEDIENCE

Civil disobedience refers to the willful challenge and disruption of law or the orderly flow and process of daily social activity. The intent of such action is to foster change in perceived unjust, immoral, or unethical government policies, mandates, or procedures. Civil disobedience is usually a nonviolent but officially discredited means to resolve citizen grievance. These grievances are generally politically based issues that a segment of the population considers unjust and in which the government is viewed as resisting a suitable resolution.

There are several different methods of civil disobedience that are not criminal by statute, but are nonetheless disruptive. Public speeches, public statements, letters of opposition, petitions, and public declarations are all formal statements that openly deliver an opposing plea. Similar acts such as group representations, symbolic public acts, pressure on individuals, processions, public assemblies, action by consumers, noncooperation with social events, strikes, and rejection of authority are only a few of the equally effective noncriminal tactics available to motivated citizens.

The use of noncooperation and civil disobedience has been widely studied by political philosophers and theorists. Primary questions at the root of civil disobedience are: How sacred is the law of the state, and what are the limits of the authority government can assert over its citizens; also, do citizens have a responsibility to obey bad laws? The fundamental debate is whether government should be responsive to the desires of the people or if the people should absolutely obey the directives of government without challenge.

Two universal truths exist regarding government in civilized countries. The first is whether the creation of laws by government should exist for the welfare of the people. The second is to sustain civility; government is an imperfect but necessary condition. The essential component for a country to remain orderly is citizen respect for the law and the recognition of the authority of some lawmaking body. Each citizen must see himself of herself as a member of the community, and as such, each member has an obligation to respect and obey the law. Certainly as important is the belief that if laws are in place on the behalf and interest of all citizens, then it is the responsibility of the citizens to reshape untenable laws. However, most changes are usually conducted willingly by the government, either by the process of internal or external review. Consequently, when citizens take it upon themselves to violate certain laws, not out of either convenience or self-interest, but rather the larger calling of an ethical or moral good, then their willful disobedience becomes an instrument of change. Any violation of law places offenders under the assessing scrutiny of the justice system, a potential recipient of punishment. Usually those who deliberately commit civil disobedience are prepared for the anticipated judicial response with a defense strategy. An often essential component of the strategy is their arrest and punishment, which draws wider attention and endorsement for their cause. Ideally, others will become polarized and inspired to disobey as an act of both protest and support. As the number of disobedient citizens grows and the impact of their actions spirals into greater social disruption and the corresponding cost to the government increases to intolerable levels, alternatives and compromises will begin to look more attractive to those in power.

Civil disobedience has other qualities that distinguish it from typical criminal behavior. An act of civil disobedience that breaks the law is, of course, as criminal as promoting or to conspire to commit a crime. Those who commit acts of civil disobedience may claim (and often do) a compelling moral duty as citizens. This claim is especially valid in a democratic system, where citizen participation in lawmaking is a cornerstone of the government ideal. When civil disobedience is employed to provoke change, the defense used is that the wrongful act committed is less harmful than the existence of unjust law and should mitigate the criminal charge. This argument has a greater validity if the government has been aware of the existing injustice, that it has had the opportunity to end the harm, and has failed to act or to act adequately.

Another quality of civil disobedience is that it is a public act. The citizen, in full comprehension of committing a punishable offense, acts in the public service in a clear and open protest and defiance to the government. The disobedience loses its value and message if conducted in secret or covertly, as in the example of one who paints seditious statements of protest on government buildings under the cover of night. In this situation, no matter how well intended, the act takes on the status of simple criminal mischief or vandalism, and the perpetrator, identified or not, assumes the role of a common criminal. The achievement of such public behavior is sometimes hailed as a means for acquiring personal notoriety, self-acclaim, or attention seeking. To some extent, this is true. The actor seeks attention, however, only to bring the illuminating spotlight of public review to the cause they champion. Ultimately, the individuals become synonymous with their cause, and the issue at hand receives greater review, particularly as the transgressors move through the various stages of the legal system.

Another characteristic of civil disobedience as an instrument of change is that the lawbreaking act must be a nonviolent act. Violence and inflicting injury are incompatible with the concept of civil obedience as a means of fostering change. In fact, any interference with the civil liberties of others is unacceptable with this mode of citizen political action because it obscures the message or purpose of the disobedience. Furthermore, an act of violence or injury attaches a distinctly negative sentiment to the political issue or cause. Such a sentiment is counterproductive because it acts to disperse rather than unite citizens in an act of forced change. At the heart of civil disobedience is the desire to inspire the righteous indignation of the complacent citizenry and to incite action.

Another trait of civil disobedience that separates it from most other forms of citizen action to promote change is that while civil disobedience is an expression of disobedience to the law, it also is at the same moment fidelity to the law. It is the fidelity that serves as a message from the minority to the majority of the population that their act is truly political, and separates their act of lawbreaking from mean-spirited aggression. By avoiding violence, the disobedient citizens exhibit a moral foundation and establish themselves as legitimate citizens provoking change, rather than a disorderly and unfocused band of troublemakers.

The last distinguishing trait of civil disobedience is that unlike crime, it has a place and function in civilized societies. This is especially true in countries that embrace democratic principles as the foundation of their government. In nations such as monarchies and totalitarian states, the citizens may plead their cause; however, they cannot disobey if their request is denied because to do so is an act of rebellion against the legitimate authority. In this situation, the ruling authority may have decided unwisely, and the citizens do not have the right to correct the error. However, with a constitutional-based government, where the structure is founded on mutual cooperation of equals, an imposed injustice does not require absolute obedience. Just like free elections and an independent judiciary, civil disobedience, though often illegal, when employed with proper judgment and limitations serves to maintain fair-spirited societies. While remaining faithful to the intent of law in a free democratic society, restrained nonviolent civil disobedience provides stability through a social/political outlet for dissent, challenge, and public voice.

— *Richard M. Seklecki*

See also **Altruism; Social Change**

Further Readings

Debenidetti, C. (1990). *Give peace a chance.* Syracuse, NY: Syracuse University Press.

Feinberg, J., & Hyman, G. (1980). *Philosophy of law.* Belmont, CA; Wadsworth.

Ginsberg, B. (1986). *The captive public.* New York: Basic Books.

Kronenwetter, M. (1994). *The peace commandos.* New York: New Discovery Books.

Peterson, T. (2002). *Linked arms.* Albany: State University of New York Press.

Seaton, C. (1996). *Altruism and activism.* Landham, MD: University Press of America.

Terkel, S. (1996). *People power.* New York; Lodestar Books.

CLADISTICS

Cladistics is a method of reconstructing phylogeny without necessary recourse to either fossils or molecular distances. It is required to trace the evolutionary changes within a group of organisms (a series of taxa), and the following stages are followed.

First, one or more outgroups are selected; these are taxa that are known to be outside the group under study (the ingroup), but not too distantly related to it. Second, the characters that vary among taxa of the ingroup are listed. Third, the character states (the ways in which the ingroup taxa differ) are listed as objectively as possible, and the corresponding states of the outgroup(s) are also listed. The states shared by the outgroup with members of the ingroup are deemed to be most plausibly inherited from their common ancestor: They are called *symplesiomorph*, or shared primitive. States that occur only in one or more members of the ingroup and not with the outgroup(s) are deemed to have evolved since the ingroup came into being: They are called *apomorph*, or derived. Some of these apomorph states are confined to a single member of the ingroup: These are called *autapomorph*, or uniquely derived. Other apomorph states are shared between different members of the ingroup: These are called *synapomorph*, or shared derived. It is the synapomorph states, of course, that are evidence for phylogenetic relatedness.

The simplest case reconstructs the phylogeny of just three ingroup members (the three-taxon problem). An example in anthropology might be the reconstruction of the phylogenetic relationships of human, gorilla, and baboon. We might take the lemur as a sensible outgroup; it is acknowledged that lemurs are phylogenetically more distant from the members of the ingroup than they are from each other. We can list a few characters that vary in the ingroup, and their states in the different taxa, as follows:

In Characters 2 and 4, human is different from the outgroup, but uniquely so: The states are autapomorph (uniquely derived). These two characters therefore show how unusual human is, but not which of the other two ingroup members it more resembles. But if we take Characters 1, 5, and 6, we see that though human is again different from the outgroup, it shares the derived states with gorilla; these states are therefore synapomorph (shared derived) and are evidence that human and gorilla

Character	Human	Gorilla	Baboon	Lemur (outgroup)
1. tail	no	no	yes	yes
2. canines	short	long	long	long
3. body hair	very sparse	sparse	dense	dense
4. locomotion	biped	quadruped	quadruped	quadruped
5. thorax	wide	wide	narrow	narrow
6. frontal sinus	yes	yes	no	no

are phylogenetically closer to each other than to baboon. Finally, Character 3 is a special case; it has three states, not just two, and logically, the gorilla state (sparse) is intermediate between that of baboon and the outgroup (dense) and that of human (very sparse).

The deduced primitiveness or derivedness of the character states is called their *polarities*. The character states are typically coded; in the above case, all the characters have States 1 and 2, except for Character 3, which has States 1, 2, and 3. One then has the option of whether State 2 is to be treated as intermediate between 1 and 3 (ordered) or whether all three states are equidistant.

We arrive, then, at the phylogeny shown in this figure:

At Node A, the human/gorilla synapomorph states of Characters 1, 3, 5, and 6 appear. Between Node A and human, the human autapomorph states of Characters 2, 3, and 4 appear.

We refer to gorilla and human as a *clade* (branch) with respect to baboon and the outgroup, while of course gorilla, human, and baboon together form a clade. Human and gorilla are sister groups (or if they are species, sister species); the human-plus-gorilla clade is the sister group of baboon.

We can then add other taxa to the analysis: chimpanzee, orangutan, gibbon, for example. The more taxa we add, the more unwieldy the analysis becomes.

What renders it yet more difficult is the existence of *homoplasy*. This is where an evolutionary event occurs more than once. The three types of homoplasy are:

- Convergence: two rather different taxa independently evolve the same character state
- Parallelism: the same character state evolves independently in two descendants of the same ancestor
- Reversal: a more apomorph state, after evolving, is lost again

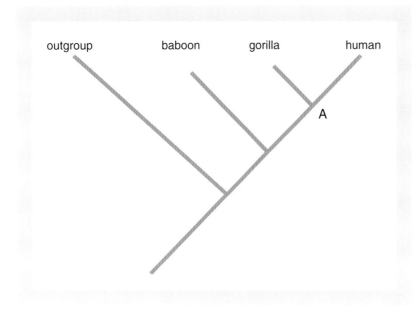

outgroup   baboon   gorilla   human

A

Phylogeny of Three Taxa

Homoplasy can easily be mistaken for *homology* (the unitary occurrence of an event); when two taxa share an apomorphic state, generally the only way to deduce whether they share it by homology or by homoplasy is by parsimony. On the assumption that an evolutionary change is a rare event, an apomorphic state is more likely to have occurred once than twice or more. The cladist will count up the apparent synapomorphic states between taxa A and B, and those between A and C and between B and C, and will usually suppose that the two that share the largest number are the sister groups. The smaller numbers of shared states that are incompatible with this conclusion are deemed to constitute homoplasy.

When a large number of taxa are being analyzed, using a large number of characters, then cladistic analysis simply cannot be performed without the aid of a computer. There are several computer packages available to perform cladistics quickly and efficiently, giving the number of steps (evolutionary changes) and several indices that record the amount of homoplasy (consistency index, retention index, and so on). When the true phylogeny is already known, or suspected, most of these computer packages can compare the analyzed phylogeny against the known one and so test the assumption of parsimony. In some cases, the result has revealed that homoplasy is unexpectedly frequent.

There is no reason why fossil taxa should not be included in a cladistic analysis. The results often have a bearing on the potential ancestral position of a given fossil, although it is important to appreciate that the function of a cladistic analysis is to discover sister group relationships, irrespective of whether one of a pair of sister groups might actually be an ancestor.

The assumption behind character counting is, of course, that each change of state represents a mutation. If there is reason to think that a state change is more complex than this, then different characters can be given different weights, so that one counts more in an analysis, and another less. Finally, molecular data can be analyzed cladistically as well as by distance methods.

The subject of cladistics is a complex one, with its own language and methodologies. Its influence on evolutionary anthropology has been enormous. A separate question is whether the results can be directly plugged in to make a taxonomic scheme or whether taxonomy should be more than simply a representation of phylogeny.

— *Colin Groves*

See also **Evolution, Organic**

 # CLANS

The anthropological term *clan* comes from Gaelic *clann* and Old Irish *clann* or *cland*, denoting a group claiming descent from a common ancestor. The word was extended to refer to similar kinds of groups in other cultures at least from the early 16th century, and by the 1860s it had entered into sociological and anthropological usage. Anthropologists have given a number of different labels to groups recruited by filiation or descent: for example, *gens* (plural *gentes*) by Morgan and *sib* by Lowie, who reserved gens for the patrilineal form and clan for the matrilineal form. Clan has become the preferred term, however.

In anthropological usage, a clan is a social group whose members share a doctrine of common ancestry but who do not necessarily trace descent from a common ancestor by known genealogical links. A clan may consist of more than one lineage whose members trace descent from a common ancestor by known (but possibly fictive) genealogical links. The group may be recruited by patrifiliation to form a patrilineal clan, by matrifiliation to form a matrilineal clan, or by a combination of these to form a cognatic clan. Adoptive links may be important. There may be a difference between the descent ideology and actual practice, as in parts of Papua New Guinea, where a matrifilial link becomes converted to a patrifilial one.

Clans may be exogamous; that is, a member ought to marry someone from a clan other than his or her own. Clan organization may articulate with other forms: Two or more clans may cluster into phratries; clans may be distributed between two moieties; or clans may be distributed between four semimoieties. A number of clans may form a larger entity, such as a phratry, tribe, or language group. This hierarchical structure of identities is most elaborate in models of segmentary lineage systems applied to societies of the southern Sudan.

Societies vary in the predominant lineality of clans; in some societies, patrilineal or patrifilial groups are predominant, while in others (though more rarely) matrilineal groups are the most common form. Some societies combine patrilineal and matrilineal clans in a system of double descent. Groups in Polynesian societies draw on ambilineal or cognatic descent to form groups in which an individual has potential claims in a number of groups, through both parents and four grandparents, although only one claim is likely to be activated.

Clans and other kinds of groups coexist with kinship, which is normally bilateral. The form of kin classification, however, may be strongly shaped to fit lineage and moiety identities. In the case of unilineal groups, each individual is often connected to the other parent's clan through complementary filiation, yielding rights that are not transmitted to the next generation.

In general, clan organization has been found in societies in which kinship and descent have provided the main bases for the organization of society,

although it can be combined with hierarchical forms of organization. It has persisted in many areas with colonial and postcolonial state structures.

Clans and Hierarchy

Clan organization is capable of elaboration to incorporate various forms of hierarchy. According to the model of the conical clan, which has been applied to descent groups in parts of Polynesia, the birth order of ancestors ideally determines the rank order of their descendant lineages, although a good deal of manipulation is possible, especially where these groups are ambilineal or cognatic. Raymond Firth applied the term *ramage* to the ambilineal Polynesian clan. Hunter-gatherer societies of the northwest coast of North America were hierarchical. Among coastal Tshimshian, for example, the four matrilineal clans were ranked in order, and members of each clan were ranked, with chiefs, who possessed honorific titles, at the top of the rank order.

In some chiefdoms, royal clans and lineages were distinguished from commoner ones. Among Bantu peoples of southern and central Africa, such as the Zulu, Swazi, and Bemba, the descendants of a chief's clan form a ruling caste, and clans are ranked according to the tradition of original migration into the area or the degree of relationship with the chief's descent group.

Clans in Social Theory

The concept of clan has featured in general theories of social organization. For example, the 19th-century theory of totemism outlined an ideal type of "primitive" society in which each exogamous clan was linked to a totemic species. In his outline of the evolution of the division of labor, Émile Durkheim contrasted "segmental structure" associated with a minimal division of labor and "mechanical solidarity," with a more generalized structure of permeable groups associated with a greater division of labor and "organic solidarity."

The concept of clan became linked with the concepts of corporation and corporate group, deriving from the legal history of Henry Maine and Max Weber's theory of the *verband,* but with its ultimate origins in Western law of incorporation. A corporate clan is thus a descent group whose identity persists beyond the life of any individual member and that holds some kind of property as a group, such as land and/or totemic insignia. In the structural functionalist anthropology of Africa, the clan became one variety of the unilineal descent group, theorized by anthropologists such as Meyer Fortes. Thus, in structural functionalist anthropology, "clan" and related concepts were linked to descent theory, in which descent was seen as a major component of social structure. This approach contrasted with alliance theory, associated with Claude Lévi-Strauss, in which groups such as clans were linked in various ways by marriage exchange.

Critiques of the Concept

From the early 1960s, cultural and social anthropologists, including John Barnes, Robert Barnes, Ian Keen, Adam Kuper, and Roy Wagner, have criticized lineage theory and the use of concepts such as clan and sib on the grounds that the assumptions and metaphors implicit in the concepts distort ethnographic reality. The concept of clan is perhaps best thought of as a model that approximates the constitution of social identities and their entailments to varying degrees.

— *Ian Keen*

See also Social Structures; Totemism

Further Readings

Kuper, A. (1982). Lineage theory: A critical retrospect. *Annual Review of Anthropology, 11,* 71–95.

Wagner, R. (1974). Are there social groups in the New Guinea Highlands? In M. Leaf (Ed.), *Frontiers of anthropology* (pp. 95–122). New York: Van Nostrand.

 # CLINES

Clines are gradations in biological features over geographic space. They refer to continuous degrees of difference in either phenotype or genotype across or within human populations. A given cline consists of the gradient in frequency of a single trait over space. This graded change is often associated with a gradually changing environmental factor. Thus, gradients in the appearance or function of a trait represented by a cline can correspond with graded alterations in the environment. Clines are useful to biological, medical, and other anthropologists interested in depicting and analyzing human variation.

When a cline is graphically portrayed, portions of the distribution of the trait that have the same value are connected by a line. On either side of the line appear other lines representing progressively greater and lesser frequency of the trait. Thus, the graph of the cline resembles a weather map, with bands of varying temperature or pressure occurring over space. A map of a cline effectively illustrates how the distribution of the trait is gradual and continuous rather than abruptly different from one area to the next.

Gene flow is one evolutionary process that can generate a clinal trait distribution. Population movements can result in a trait pattern of highest frequency where the population originated and decreasing frequency with greater distance from the ancestral home. Frequencies of the ABO blood group in Europe and Asia provide a good example of this effect of gene flow. The prevalence of Type B is greatest in Asia and declines as one moves west. This pattern is attributable to population movements by Asian nomads who spread to eastern and central Europe in several waves over the last 2,000 years. The dissemination of Type B was less with the smaller groups who migrated farthest, and the concentration of Type B remained greatest in the regions of origin. A second cline of the ABO blood group in Europe and Asia exists with Type A, which is greatest in Europe and decreases as one moves east, a pattern opposite to that of Type B.

In addition to gene flow, an evolutionary process that can produce clines is natural selection. If selective forces vary geographically, responding trait distributions can be clinally patterned. Ancestral skin color provides an example of clines that reflect natural selection. Average skin pigmentation reveals a notable pattern that varies with the selective force of ultraviolet radiation. Darkest skin color is seen at or near the equator, and amount of pigmentation becomes increasingly less as distance from the equator increases. Specifically, in the Old World, the cline of skin color shows gradients that decrease more readily as one moves north of the equator than as one moves south. The general pattern of pigmentation decline holds in both hemispheres, but it is more pronounced for a given latitude in the northern than in the southern hemisphere. A plausible explanation for this difference is that UV radiation is less in the northern than in the southern hemisphere at comparable latitudes. In the New World, pigmentation clines exist that do not reflect the forces of natural selection, but rather the historical effects of population movements. For example, the mass, forced withdrawal of West Africans during the period when slaves were traded placed human groups in new geographic areas. The resulting trait distributions were not linked to UV radiation as they had been in the ancestral homes.

Other clines revealing an influence of natural selection relate to body size and shape. Climate exerts strong selective pressures on certain body parameters.

As far as size, a cline for mean body mass demonstrates that body mass for a given stature is higher as latitude increases and average annual temperature declines. Concerning body shape, mean body breadth can be assessed by the width between the crests of the two ilia (hipbones). This body breadth measurement shows a latitudinal cline, with breadths wider as latitude increases and average annual temperature falls. A second latitudinal cline for body shape involves mean limb length. Arms and legs are shorter for a given stature or trunk size as latitude increases and average annual temperature declines. Collectively, these three gradients for body size and shape constitute adaptive strategies related to thermoregulation. Through alterations in body form, surface area per unit mass is decreased in colder climates to reduce heat loss, while it is increased in warmer environments to enhance heat dissipation.

With the accumulation of data on gene frequencies in various world regions, clines are sometimes redrawn. The increased knowledge of trait distributions enables clinal maps that have greater detail and smaller increments in trait frequency among neighboring areas. Another ongoing consideration with clines is that as human groups migrate and interbreed with others from different major geographic regions, connections between phenotypes and geography can be weakened.

As an approach to studying human diversity, clines are useful for investigating worldwide and regional distributions of traits and interpreting these distributions. A clinal orientation can be viewed as an alternative to a racial, or typological, perspective on human variation. For example, researchers of clines focus on only one or a few traits at a time, not on combinations of traits that are expected to differ together, as a racial orientation requires. Also, clinal analysis looks at the continuity of trait distributions, rather than the discontinuity that characterizes a racial viewpoint. Furthermore, in explaining the distribution of traits, a clinal approach focuses on evolutionary forces such as natural selection and gene flow that increase and decrease variation within and among human groups. Such an outlook contrasts with the static nature of human diversity assumed by the race concept.

Some anthropologists believe that the clinal approach is most valuable when it is applied in combination with a population focus. It is important to recognize that traits do not exist in isolation, but rather are part of the entire genetic endowment of humans. Thus, while single genotypes and phenotypes can demonstrate a clinal distribution, the overall patterning of traits is fundamentally linked to the behavior of individuals and populations.

— *Penelope A. McLorg*

See also **Gene Flow; Genetics, Population; Selection, Natural**

Further Readings

Cavalli-Sforza, L. L., Menozzi, P., & Piazza, A. (1994). *The history and geography of human genes.* Princeton, NJ: Princeton University Press.

Molnar, S. (2002). *Human variation: Races, types, and ethnic groups* (5th ed.). Upper Saddle River, NJ: Prentice Hall.

Ruff, C. B. (1994). Morphological adaptation to climate in modern and fossil hominids. *Yearbook of Physical Anthropology, 37,* 65–107.

CLINICAL GENETICS

Whereas medical genetics is the study of the genetics of human disease, *clinical genetics* deals with the direct clinical care of people with genetic diseases. Clinical genetics encompasses the scientific methods and their application in clinical practice, with the focus on human diseases caused by genetic variation. The principal concerns of clinical genetics include clinical evaluation, diagnosis, genetic counseling, and therapeutic management of genetic disorders. Genetic disorders are typically complex, multiorgan, and systemic in nature, requiring a coordinated approach to the care of affected individuals and their families.

Clinical geneticists are physicians who typically have training in a medical specialty, such as pediatrics, medicine, or obstetrics and gynecology, with extended training in medical genetics. Clinical genetics is now a medical specialty in the field of medical genetics, with board certification and standards of care.

The conditions with which clinical geneticists have traditionally been concerned include chromosomal abnormalities, single-gene disorders, and birth defects. Many conditions are now identified through prenatal diagnosis or genetic screening. But most often, genetic disorders are diagnosed through the referral of an individual to a clinical geneticist by his or her physician. Today, clinical genetics is extended increasingly to common later-onset diseases, such as familial cancer, diabetes, and cardiovascular disease, with more emphasis on preventive measures and behavior modification to delay the onset of the disease.

Areas in which the field of clinical genetics relates to anthropology concern both cultural and biological issues. It is increasingly evident that genetic health care services need to be provided by professionals who are culturally competent. Providers of genetics health care should understand culture-based beliefs and attitudes about disease, including genetic disorders, in order to deal effectively with the needs of families. In the assessment of individuals, clinical geneticists often use anthropometric measurements, a traditional tool of biological anthropology, especially in the evaluation of craniofacial dimensions that are important in the diagnosis of many genetic disorders. In addition, clinical geneticists evaluate the physical growth of children, the focus of a traditional research area in biological anthropology, as body growth and size frequently vary from the norm in genetic disorders.

Perhaps there never has been a stronger contribution to the field of clinical genetics than the Human Genome Project (HGP). It is estimated that there are now almost 1,000 diseases for which genetic tests are available. Included in this estimation are a number of the common, complex diseases such as cardiovascular disease and cancer. The HGP has created a human genome map with approximately 35,000 human genes. Almost one third of these genes have been discovered, with many of the gene loci, allelic variants, functions, and disease associations described. The HGP has enabled researchers to identify errors in genes that may contribute to or cause certain diseases. By the year 2010, predictive genetic testing might be available for more than 25 common diseases, such as diabetes and hypertension. This very expectation will impact genetic counseling and testing, in which individuals will seek information to take steps to reduce the risks for certain genetic diseases. For example, cardiovascular disease is a complex interaction of genetic factors (gender, family history, single-gene abnormalities of lipids, diabetes, obesity, and hypertension) that interact with nongenetic risk factors (smoking, physical inactivity, stress, and increasing age). In the future, an individual might seek genetic counseling and testing to determine susceptibility to cardiovascular disease in order to make lifestyle modifications. More important, the identification of disease-related genetic variation plays a role in the prevention of disease and will reshape the future of health care.

— *Kathy Prue-Owens and F. John Meaney*

See also **Human Genome Project; Medical Genetics**

Further Readings

Davies, K. (2001). *Cracking the genome: Inside the race to unlock human DNA*. Baltimore: John Hopkins University Press.

Nehring, W. M. (1999). Clinical genetics: An overview. *The Journal of Cardiovascular Nursing, 13,* 19–33.

Wilson, G. N. (2000). *Clinical genetics: A short course.* New York: Wiley-Liss.

 # CLOVIS CULTURE

The antiquity of humans in the New World had been a controversy during the 19th and early 20th centuries. Insight into just how long ago the incursion of people into the Americas occurred came in 1927, when lanceolate projectile points were found with the remains of extinct bison near Folsom, New Mexico.

Then, in 1932, similar but distinctive stone points were found at Dent, Colorado, this time associated with the mammoth. These artifacts appeared to be related to the Folsom points, both of them bearing axial channels ("flutes") at their bases for hafting. The Dent points were different, however, in being larger and thicker and having proportionally shorter axial channels and coarser flake scars. Clearly, humans were in North America by at least the late Ice Age.

In the mid-1930s, Dent-type points were found near Clovis, New Mexico, at a site called Blackwater Locality No. 1, beneath an unconformity (a break in the vertical deposition sequence). Above the unconformity were Folsom points. This stratified sequence showed that the Dent-type artifacts (thereafter referred to as "Clovis" points, for the nearby town) were older than the Folsom points. Clovis points, or points closely resembling them, are now known from most of North America. They, and the other artifacts found with them, have come to represent a cultural complex that bears the same name.

Clovis is the oldest clearly defined culture known in North America, with radiocarbon dates concentrating in the range of 11,200–10,900 years BP (before the present) (though a few sites have yielded dates three to four centuries older). Its most characteristic artifact, the Clovis projectile point is lanceolate (axially elongate with roughly parallel sides curving to a point), with a concave base, and one or more elongate axial flakes removed from each side of the base, presumably to facilitate hafting to a shaft. The edges of the lower sides and the base were commonly blunted by grinding, in order to avoid severing the binding. The artifact was made remarkably thin through a process called "overshot flaking" (*outre passé*), which involved removing a flake from one side of the artifact clear across to the other side. These points, or ones closely resembling them, occur in North America from the East to the West Coast, and from the Canadian plains to central Mexico and possibly even Panama. The Clovis lithic industry is also typified by blades, end scrapers, side scrapers, pièces esquillées, and gravers. Burins, while present, are generally rare, and microblades are absent.

While the Clovis fluted projectile point is distinctive, it does show a degree of variation. This is strikingly illustrated by eight points found at the Naco site in Arizona. They were associated with a mammoth skeleton and are believed to reflect a single hunting event. The points differ markedly in length (approx. 11.6 to 5.8 cm), though less so in width and in the profile of the edges. One of the longest Clovis points known is a 23.3 cm chalcedony artifact from the Richey-Roberts Clovis Cache, at East Wenatchee, Washington State.

Clovis blades, most common in the southeastern United States and the southern Great Plains, are large, triangular in cross section, and thick toward the distal end. No microblades have been found at Clovis sites.

The use of bone, ivory, and antler as raw material for toolmaking was an important aspect of Clovis technology. From these were made what have been interpreted as awls, punches, choppers, scrapers, scoops, fleshers, and points. Osseous rods with beveled, cross-scored ends are known from sites widely distributed throughout the United States. Some of them have been interpreted as foreshafts, short cylinders to which points were bound and that, in turn, were inserted as needed into the socketed end of the main spear shaft. It has also been suggested that these beveled osseous rods served as levers for tightening the ligature of a hafted tool as it was used to slice.

While most Clovis osseous tools appear to be expedient, a clearly formal tool, probably made from mammoth long-bone cortex, appears to have served as a wrench for straightening spear shafts (similar to devices used by Eskimos). It is shaped as a ring with a long, straight handle extending from it. The inner edges of the ring are beveled. A shaft 14 to 17 mm in diameter would be the best fit for the ring, concordant with what would be expected to haft the fluted points found in the area. This artifact, from the Murray Springs site in southeast Arizona, was found with Clovis points near a mammoth skeleton.

Because it was first recognized and characterized in that region, the Clovis complex *sensu stricto* is best known in the western United States. As researchers move outside this area, however, defining a true Clovis site becomes more difficult. The term has been used informally to include whatever sites have yielded Clovis-like projectile points. As was demonstrated by the eight Naco points, however, there can be variation in the form of points from a single site. On the other hand, points from widely separated localities can be remarkably similar. Also, the very broad geographical distribution of apparent Clovis points spans a wide range of environments and of associated floras and faunas.

The fluted points themselves show stylistic variation that within a given region has been interpreted as reflecting changes over time. In the northeastern United States and southeastern Canada, for example, the Gainey type of point most resembles the western Clovis point, while the Barnes and Crowfield types are thought to be later styles.

Another criterion that may be useful is the presence of Pleistocene megafauna, especially proboscideans (mammoth, mastodon), since the type Clovis occurrence is associated with animals (especially mammoth) that disappeared from that area at the same time that the Clovis complex was replaced by Folsom. In Michigan, the northern limits of early Paleo-Indian fluted points and of fossil proboscideans nearly coincide along an east-west demarcation midway up the Michigan peninsula, the so-called Mason-Quimby Line.

Discoveries at the Hiscock site in western New York, however, show that use of this association for such interpretive purposes requires caution. While Clovis-like Gainey points co-occur here with abundant mastodon bones, some of which were used to make tools whose radiocarbon dates are coeval with Clovis, there is no clear evidence that these people were hunting mastodon. On the other hand, there is evidence that they were retrieving bones found at the site and using them as raw material for toolmaking. Thus, the man-beast relationship may not have been "personal," and the chronological separation between the people and the megafauna is difficult to gauge.

While there had been a long-standing belief that the Clovis people were the first humans to enter the New World, the last few decades have cast some doubt on this. A scattering of sites in North and South America have yielded radiocarbon dates associated with non-Clovis cultural remains that predate Clovis. Monte Verde, in Chile, contains evidence of human presence somewhere within the range of 12,000–12,500 radiocarbon years ago. Mammoths may have been butchered near Kenosha, Wisconsin, and a tortoise in Florida at around the same time. Radiocarbon dates in cultural contexts, reaching back to 16,000 years BP, have come from the Meadowcroft rockshelter in southwest Pennsylvania. It seems likely that there were humans in the New World some time prior to Clovis, though the paucity of their traces suggests the populations were quite small and scattered.

Clovis Lifeways

Several aspects of Clovis life are reflected by the varied archaeological sites attributed to this culture. Habitation or campsites were small in comparison with those of the Folsom complex (which succeeded Clovis on the Great Plains). Hearths are represented by depressions less than 3 m in diameter and up to 20 cm deep, containing charcoal. These hearths were not lined with rocks. The presence of well-drained soil and nearby water seem to have been desirable traits for habitations. For example, at the Aubrey site (northeast Texas), a Clovis camp was situated on sandy soil, 1 m above an adjacent pond.

With regard to water, the Hiscock site (western New York) is instructive. This locality featured active springs during the late Pleistocene, and the abundance of bones indicates that animal life here was plentiful. Yet while archaeological artifacts demonstrate the presence of Clovis (or Clovis-contemporary) Paleo-Indians at the site, there is no evidence of significant habitation. This may be due to the fact that Hiscock was a mineral lick, and probably not an appropriate source of drinking water.

There are a few very large, artifact-rich habitation sites that appear to have been occupied repeatedly and/or for extended periods of time (the Gault site in Texas, the Arc site in New York). These are suggestive of places where several bands would come together periodically, a practice that may have been important for the long-term survival of wandering, sparsely distributed human populations.

At sites where prey animals were killed and butchered (or sometimes perhaps scavenged), butchering tools were resharpened on the spot, leaving concentrations of debitage. The Murray Springs site (Arizona) contains a mammoth and a bison kill, along with a hunting camp. A partial mammoth long bone and a tooth found in the camp links it with the mammoth remains. Refitted impact flakes matched with damaged projectile points similarly link the bison kill site with the camp.

Quarry workshops were sources of rock suitable for toolmaking (typically chert), where the raw material was reduced in size and shaped to make it more portable. There were also "bone quarries" (the Hiscock site) where bones, teeth, and antlers were sufficiently abundant to be gathered as raw material for tools.

Clovis people valued chert, obsidian, and other aphanitic rocks that were attractive and of high quality. Many lithic tool collections reflect raw materials obtained from multiple sources within several tens of kilometers of each other, and sometimes from 300 km and even more distant. A point from the

Kincaid Shelter site in central Texas was made from obsidian obtained 1,000 km away, in central Mexico. Of course, it is uncertain to what extent the origins of these various rocks reflect mobility of the people and how much is attributable to serial trading. Nevertheless, the frequent occurrence of raw material from distant sources has generally been taken as evidence of a nomadic way of life for the Clovis people.

Concentrations of stone and bone tools, commonly in good condition and sometimes of remarkable aesthetic quality, have been found at several sites (the Richie-Roberts Clovis Cache in Washington State). These have been interpreted as caches, representing either spiritual offerings or emergency stocks left by nomadic people for retrieval in emergencies.

The wide dispersion of their projectile points, and the fact that they are made from chert that was sometimes obtained from distant sources, suggests that the Clovis people were nomadic hunters. When a Clovis site contains animal remains, proboscidean bones are commonly among them, and in the "typical" western Clovis sites (Naco, Dent, Blackwater Locality No. 1, Murray Springs), these belong to mammoths. Clovis people also used mammoth bones to make tools. Hence, the Clovis have been thought of as mammoth hunters.

The exploitation of mastodon on a similar scale by Clovis hunters has been less widely accepted, with only a few sites providing evidence for predation on this species.

Mammoth and mastodon appear to have occupied different habitats (mammoth favoring more open land such as plains and tundra, mastodon being more associated with wooded areas), so it was thought this led to a preference for mammoth hunting. Beginning in the 1980s, however, there have been reported mastodon skeletons in the Great Lakes region in which marks on the bones and peculiarities in the distribution of skeletal elements in peat bogs (former ponds) strongly implies that the animals had been butchered.

Most of the putatively butchered mastodons were young and middle-aged males, animals in the prime of life. Significantly, virtually all of them had died between midautumn and early winter. This nonrandom pattern suggests hunting rather than scavenging. Among modern elephants, males are excluded from the security of the herd around the time when they reach sexual maturity. If this was the case with

mastodons (an uncertain proposition, since mastodons were not true elephants, as were mammoths), the pattern suggests that Clovis hunters stalked isolated males as winter approached, knowing that they would have spent the summer and fall storing up fat and other nutrients. Following a successful hunt, they would butcher the carcass and store those parts not used immediately in the bottoms of cold ponds to secure them from scavengers and decomposition. They could be retrieved during the winter for food resources. It has also been suggested that the hunters had filled mastodon intestines with sediment and used them to anchor the meat to the floor of the pond. Mammoth bone piles at Blackwater Locality No. 1 (New Mexico) and Colby (Wyoming) have also been interpreted as winter meat caches. An aggregation of large boulders at the Adkins site (Maine) has been asserted to be a meat cache, though no bones were found associated with it.

It is not clear how a Clovis hunter would have used a spear in a hunt. While spear-throwers (*atlatls*) dating from the Archaic are known from dry caves in the western United States, none have been found in a Clovis archaeological context. Nevertheless, impact fractures on some Clovis points at the Murray Springs bison kill area indicate sufficient force to suggest they were propelled. Experiments on fresh carcasses from an elephant cull in Zimbabwe demonstrated that a spear tipped by a Clovis point can inflict a lethal wound with the aid of an atlatl. Thrusting with a spear could have done the same, although less reliably. Needle-sharp ivory and bone points, found in Florida underwater sites, may have been useful as lances for reaching the heart. Simple stone tools have proven effective experimentally in performing butchery tasks, and concentrations of chert debitage at kill sites show that stone tools were resharpened and sometimes reshaped during processing.

Most mammoth kills in the West were in low watering places, such as springs, ponds, and creeks. A skilled elephant tracker today can harvest a wealth of information about individual animals and their condition from their trackways, the composition and condition of their dung, and other evidence. It seems reasonable that Clovis hunters would have developed and used similar skills in hunting the proboscideans, which were evidently an important component of their subsistence.

Clovis or early Paleo-Indian hunters seem to have used the local landscape to their advantage. At the Vail

Site (Maine) there is a camp and nearby kill and butchery sites. These lie near the narrowing of a river valley, which could have concentrated migrating caribou herds, affording an opportunity for ambush. Similarly, at the end of the Pleistocene, the Hiscock site, in western New York, lay on the edge of a 3-km-wide emergent area that formed a corridor breaching a 153-km-long belt of ponds and wetlands. The site itself was a salt lick and contains abundant bones of mastodon and caribou, as well as early Paleo-Indian tools. This location may have been a reliable area for monitoring the passage of herd animals.

Dogs appear to have been present at late Paleo-Indian localities in the western United States (Folsom component of the Agate Basin site, eastern Wyoming). It seems reasonable, then, that they accompanied Clovis bands, perhaps assisting in their hunts.

Animals other than proboscideans were also hunted by Clovis people. Bison were one of the prey animals at Murray Springs. This site also includes a possible horse kill. Bear and rabbit bones, some of them calcined (burned), occur in hearth areas at the Lehner site (Arizona). Similarly, calcined bones of caribou, hare, and arctic fox were associated with a pit feature at the Eudora site (southern Ontario). Fish bones were found in a hearth at the Shawnee-Minisink site (Pennsylvania).

How large was a Clovis band? The eight Clovis points at the Naco site (Arizona), associated with a single mammoth, are thought to represent one kill or possibly a mammoth that escaped a hunt and succumbed later to its wounds. Four to eight hunters may have been involved in this hunt. If they constituted 20% of their band, then a band size of 20 to 40 people would seem reasonable.

It is assumed that Clovis people traveled primarily by foot. If they had dogs, these animals may have been used, as by later American Indians, to help carry or otherwise transport items, but there is no surviving evidence to support or negate this.

The presence of Paleo-Indian sites on what would have been islands at that time strongly suggests that these people were able to make some sort of watercraft when the need arose. Certainly, some Old World Pleistocene people (Australian aborigines) lived on lands that could have been reached only by boat or raft, so the technology for making watercraft was likely understood by Clovis people.

Little remains to attest to Clovis aesthetic sensibilities. This is rather surprising, as there is a rich artistic legacy in Late Pleistocene archaeological sites of central and eastern Europe, with which the Clovis culture otherwise seems to have a remarkable number of links (see below). Sculptures and cave paintings, as found in Europe, have not been found at Clovis sites. What have been found are simple beads. A roughly cylindrical bone bead was found in the Clovis component of Blackwater Locality No. 1. One from the Hiscock site, in New York, was made from a crudely rounded piece of gray sandstone, about 8.5 mm in diameter and 6 mm thick, pierced by a lumen just under 2 mm wide. This lumen, which must have been produced by a very fine stone spike, was drilled about three quarters of the way through the piece of sandstone, and then finished from the other side to avoid rupturing the bead. Other beads from Paleo-Indian sites are made from bone as well as stone, although not all date from Clovis times. Presumably, these were worn on cords of animal hide or plant fiber.

Other examples of Clovis artistry are inscribed linear designs and patterns on various hard materials. A bevel-based ivory point from an underwater site in the Aucilla River (Florida) has a zig-zag design engraved along its length on one side. A bevel-ended bone rod from the Richey-Roberts Clovis Cache (Washington State) bears a zipperlike series of short, transverse lines along most of its length. While this latter pattern may have been aesthetic or symbolic, it might also have been functional, for example, to prevent a winding cord from slipping along its axis. Several limestone pebbles with complex patterns of inscribed, intersecting lines were found at the Gault site in central Texas.

Clovis people seem to have devoted much of their aesthetic attention to the manufacture of their fluted biface points, some of which are remarkably large and made from attractive stone. In some cases, the stone was obtained from a considerable distance and may have been valued for its appearance.

Religious beliefs of the Clovis people are hinted at by a small number of discoveries. At the Wilsall (Anzick) site in Montana, the crania of two juvenile humans, one of them stained with red ocher (a form of the mineral hematite), were found with ocher-stained Clovis age artifacts. Because the site's stratigraphy had been extensively disturbed before it could be properly excavated, the relationship of the two crania and the artifacts was uncertain. The stained cranium proved to be 10,500 to 11,000 radiocarbon years old, a reasonable fit with the artifacts. (Later radiocarbon dating showed that the unstained bone was 8,000–9,000 radiocarbon years old, and thus fortuitously associated with the older cranium.) Ocher staining has been found in conjunction with burials at widespread prehistoric sites in the Old World, suggesting that this may have been a burial with artifacts left as an offering.

Evidence of the ritual destruction of lithic artifacts was found in southwestern Ontario, at the Caradoc site. Although the artifacts reflect a Paleo-Indian culture later than Clovis (the estimated age of these items is somewhere between 10,500 and 10,000 radiocarbon years BP), it seems reasonable to hypothesize such behavior among earlier Paleo-Indians. Apparent caches of lithic tools at a number of Clovis sites, especially the one associated with the possible burial at the Anzick site, suggest that these people attributed significance beyond the simply utilitarian to the stone implements they crafted. At Caradoc, at least 71 artifacts had been deliberately smashed. The tools were mostly made of Bayport chert from the Saginaw Bay area of Michigan, about 175 to 200 km from the Caradoc site.

Clovis Origins

Where did the Clovis culture originate? Its roots may lie among Aurignacian and Gravettian hunters, who were in Eastern Europe beginning 24,000 to 26,000 years ago, using mammoth for food and for materials to produce tools, art, and even houses. The environment in which humans interacted with these animals and other megafauna, called the "Mammoth Steppe," extended into eastern Siberia and picked up again in central North America. A number of archaeological links between the eastern European Upper Paleolithic cultures of the Mammoth Steppe and the Clovis culture have been cited: bifacially flaked projectile points with thinned bases, bevel-based cylindrical bone points, knapped bone, grave goods with red ocher, blades from prismatic cores, end scrapers, unifacial flake tools, bone shaft wrenches, bone polishers, hearths in shallow depressions, and circumferentially chopped and snapped tusks. The percussion bulb was removed from a Murray Springs (Arizona) flake tool by pressure flaking, a common feature in the Old World Late Paleolithic.

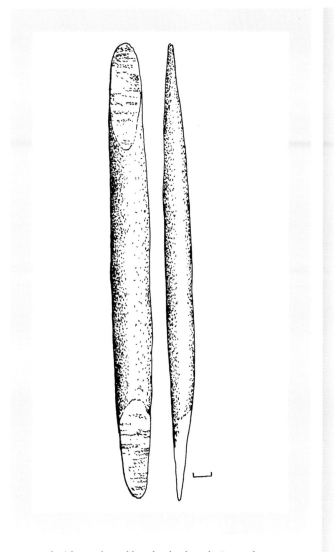

Bone rod with roughened bevel at both ends. Bar scale = 1 cm

At Mal'ta, near Lake Baikal (southeastern Siberia), was found an 18,000-year-old burial of two children with red ocher and cylindrical bone points. Though it is much older, this material is strikingly similar to what was found at the Anzick Clovis site in Montana.

Most researchers have looked to northeast Asia as the region from which humans first entered the New World and Alaska as the place of their initial arrival. Since much of the earth's water was transferred from the ocean basins to continental and alpine glaciers during the last glacial maximum, the sea level dropped dramatically. An area of exposed sea floor joined eastern Siberia and Alaska into a vast region called *Beringia*, whose greatest areal extent existed between 15,000 and 20,000 years ago. The steppe-tundra of Siberia and its

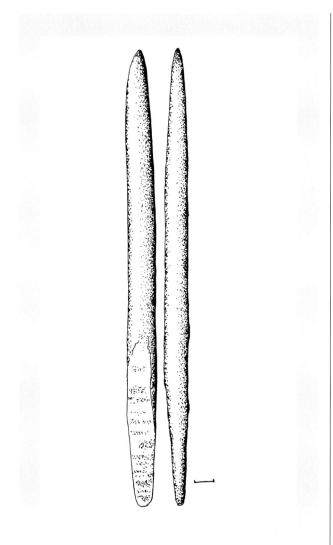

Bone rod with roughened bevel at one end and point at the other. Bar scale = 1 cm.

fauna expanded into this region and were presumed to be followed by human hunters.

Archaeological evidence shows that people arrived in eastern Beringia (central Alaska) sometime between 12,000 and 11,000 radiocarbon years BP. Once they had occupied this region, however, when did they enter central North America? Until recently, it was thought that the Cordilleran and Laurentide ice sheets of North America separated as early as 25,000 years ago, providing access to the south via an ice-free corridor. More recent evidence, however, indicates that such a corridor did not exist until about 11,000 BP, and that the glacial mass would have blocked inland access from Beringia to the unglaciated southern regions. On the other hand,

the presence of land mammal fossils (such as brown bear and caribou) along the northwest coast of North America indicates that this area was ice-free back to at least 12,500 years BP. This has led some researchers to favor a coastal route, using watercraft, for entry into the south.

Two toolmaking traditions have been found at Late Paleolithic sites in Beringia. One is based on wedge-shaped cores and microblades, which are believed to have been set into grooves carved along the sides of elongate pieces of bone or antler to produce sharp-edged projectile points and other tools. This tradition is found in China and northeast Asia, and it reached Alaska and the northwest coast (where it is called the "Denali complex") by about 12,000 years BP. Microblades, however, have not been found at Clovis sites, and Denali is generally not considered closely related to Clovis.

A second industry that included bifaced projectile points and large flakes struck off of cylindrical cores (the Nenana complex) existed in the central Alaskan region of Beringia around 12,000 to 11,500 years BP. This tradition thus preceded and may have slightly overlapped Clovis, and it has characteristics from which its proponents believe the Clovis tool industry could indeed have been derived.

The Mill Iron site of southeast Montana, a possible Clovis contemporary, contains unfluted, concave-based points. Nenana bifaced projectile points in Alaska are also unfluted. The fluted Clovis point, then, may have developed south of the continental ice sheet in the mid- to late 11,000s BP, rapidly spreading from coast to coast and into Central America. It has been suggested by some researchers that this innovation originated in southeastern North America, where fluted points are unusually abundant and varied, possibly evolving from the Suwanee-Simpson point.

On the other hand, some researchers have pointed to striking similarities between Clovis and the Upper Paleolithic Solutrean and Magdalenian complexes of northern Spain and southern France, which together date to 21,000 to 11,000 years BP. Solutrean points, while unfluted, share other traits with the Clovis form, including the use of overshot flaking. Core blade technology is also similar, and there is even a counterpart to the Murray Springs Clovis shaft wrench. While the European complexes predate Clovis, proponents of a relationship claim that artifacts from putative pre-Clovis North American sites (Meadowcroft in Pennsylvania; Cactus Hill in Virginia) do have Solutrean features.

These researchers envision the first North Americans as having come west across the Atlantic, perhaps along the edge of the North Atlantic ice pack.

The Environmental Context of Clovis

The Clovis culture was contemporary with some of the most dramatic environmental changes—in climate, hydrology, flora, and fauna—since the Sangamon Interglacial. The oldest Clovis dates may coincide with, or slightly predate, the end of the Intra-Alleröd Cold Period (IACP), at a time of reversion to the general warming of the Bølling-Alleröd Interstadial. This brief warm period (lasting roughly 200 years) brought with it widespread drought in the Western United States and possibly east of the Mississippi River as well. The large proglacial and pluvial lakes that had formed during rapid melting of the ice sheets were greatly reduced in size, and water tables fell. The dryness is reflected in a 140-cm-deep cylindrical well at the Blackwater Draw site (New Mexico) dug during Clovis times. When the water tables finally rose again in the Southwest, the Clovis complex was gone, as was the Pleistocene mammalian megafauna (with the exception of *Bison antiquus*). This return to wetter conditions is taken to reflect the beginning of the Younger Dryas Cold Period, about 10,900 or 10,800 radiocarbon years ago. The Clovis culture was now replaced by Folsom bison hunters on the Great Plains.

While this scenario may hold for the western states, Clovis sites occurred in such a wide variety of environments that the end of the culture was almost certainly a complex affair, leaving much yet to be learned by archaeologists.

— *Richard S. Laub*

See also **Folsom Culture; Paleontology**

Further Readings

Boldurian, A. T., & Cotter J. L. (1999). *Clovis revisited*. Philadelphia: University of Pennsylvania Museum.

Collins, M. B. (1999). *Clovis blade technology*. Austin: University of Texas Press.

Fiedel, S. J. (1999). Older than we thought: Implications of corrected dates for Paleoindians. *American Antiquity 64*, 95–115.

Gramly, R. M. (1990). *Guide to the Paleo-Indian artifacts of North America*. Buffalo, NY: Persimmon Press.

Haynes, G. (2002). *The early settlement of North America: The Clovis era*. New York: Cambridge University Press.

Soffer, O., & Praslov, N. D. (1993). *From Kostenki to Clovis: Upper Paleolithic-Paleo-Indian adaptations*. New York: Plenum Press.

 COLISEUM

"The Roman People," wrote the satirist Juvenal in the first few decades of the second century CE, "once used to rule . . . but now they wish for two things only: Bread and Games." And the Roman people had been amply provided with both: the *frumentationes* (free distribution of grain to between 200,000 to 300,000 members of the *plebs*) had been going on since the beginning of the Republic, and magnificent buildings and sites such as the Coliseum and the Circus Maximus offered entertainment many times a year. The emperors supplied the grain, the games, and the impressive buildings, aware of the efficiency of these means of social control.

The Roman Coliseum was built in less than 10 years. Planning was begun in 69 CE, after the death of Nero in 68, and finished in 80 CE, under the reign of Titus, one of the sons of the popular Emperor (Titus Flavius) Vespasianus, who died a year before its inauguration. The construction was paid for by the spoils of the Judaic war, which provided much gold and many captives, who were sold as slaves. The poet Martial, alive at the time, praised the monument and made clear that from its planning stages throughout its execution, the Coliseum was always meant to rival the other seven wonders of the world, such as the Pyramids or the Hanging Gardens of Babylon. Coins were struck that carried its image. It was known as the "Flavian amphitheater" until the 8th century CE, when its current name gradually came into use. It was called "the colossus" after the giant 100-foot-tall statue of Nero that had been

Source: © iStockphoto.

placed beside it, Nero's head having been replaced with the head of Apollo. The Coliseum was built on the site of Nero's Golden House, more precisely, on the site of his private lake. Nero had confiscated this land for his own use after the great fire of Rome in 64 CE, and by returning it to the people, Vespasianus gained enormous popularity.

The inaugural festivities lasted 100 days and involved gladiatorial games and mock hunts *(venationes)*, which called for tigers, elephants, lions, antelopes, cranes, and many other animals. In one day, 5,000 animals and men are said to have been killed. Some events were reenactments of myths: for instance, Orpheus, supposedly calming wild animals with his music, was torn limb from limb by a wild bear.

The normal course of events would be a *pompa*, or procession, led by the sponsor of the event, followed by the animals, gladiators, and criminals with placards around their necks announcing their crimes. The *pompa* gave spectators the opportunity to place bets on the competitors. Once in the arena, hunts and executions of criminals by wild animals would be first, followed during lunchtime by some more executions and some less bloody performances, for instance, clowns and jugglers, and then the main gladiator contests in the afternoon. The sponsor or the public would decide on the fate of the defeated gladiators. The dead would be carried out of the arena through a special gate by someone dressed up as the god of death (Pluto), or Charon, the ferryman of the underworld. The winner would receive a crown, a cash prize, and other gifts. Many gladiators had fans and were considered "stars," in the modern sense of the word. Gladiators would specialize in different weapons and gear and sometimes would be (mis)matched against each other or against animals for greater excitement. Over time, expenses related to putting on shows rose so high that several laws were enacted in an attempt to keep costs down. A list from the 4th century CE indicates the maximum amounts that could be charged for imported animals, such as lions, ostriches, lionesses, leopards, deer, wild boars, and wild asses. Crocodiles, rhinoceroses, monkeys, big dogs, and hippopotamuses were also popular.

The gladiatorial contests are believed to have originated in funeral games in the Campania, an area near Rome. At the time of the inauguration of the Coliseum, Rome is calculated to have had about 1 million inhabitants. The Romans themselves knew that the *munera* (duties, or obligations) were blood sports to appease the spirits *(Manes)* of the underworld. They believed that originally slaves or captives would have been sacrificed on the tombs of important men, and that over time this practice developed into contests, always ending in killing. The Coliseum was a permanent place to stage such events, which during the 2nd century BCE became detached from funerals and turned into secular staged shows to entertain (and buy) the masses. The games spread from Rome all over the conquered world: Permanent buildings or amphitheaters, also called *spectacula* because they allowed unimpeded views, are found in France, England, Germany, Spain, and North Africa. Already existing theaters in the Middle East were adapted to accommodate gladiatorial games and executions.

Most amphitheaters are elliptical in shape, to allow for better viewing, as the architect Vitruvius had already suggested in his *De Architectura.* The Roman Coliseum is believed to have had a capacity of 50,000 to 75,000 spectators. For comparison, the Circus Maximus, where horse races were held, could accommodate up to 250,000. The center part where the action takes place is called the *arena* (or sand), and the tiers where the public is seated are called the *cavea.* The area underneath the *arena* is hollow, and contained *carceres,* or cages, for wild animals, tunnels, and other rooms and areas, which allowed quick changes in the scenery by means of pulleys and lifts. Complex plumbing and draining systems characterize all amphitheaters. The multiple entrances and exits were clearly marked, as were the seats, so that spectators of different class and status need never mingle. The emperor, the nobility, and ruling class had the better seats lower down, and the higher up the seat, the less important the spectator. Thus, the seating in the Coliseum reflected a virtual microcosmos of Rome, enforcing group allegiance by the joint witnessing of executions and the transgression of social laws, such as killing for pleasure. An awning covered most of the audience against the sun, since games would last all day; it was operated by experienced sailors.

Many earthquakes and fires damaged the Coliseum over time; repairs were undertaken occasionally. The last gladiatorial games took place during the 5th century; the *venations,* or hunting games, stopped about 60 years later. It is thought that it was the high expense of giving games, rather than moral beliefs, that put an end to these events. In addition, foreign invasions, lightning, plagues, famines, and general population decline—only a few tens of thousand inhabitants occupied Rome in the 6th century CE—accelerated decay. The valley of the Coliseum now lay outside the city limits. The building was variously used as a quarry, as a thoroughfare between the valleys of Rome, as stables, refuge for criminals, storage area, and a fortification for different noble families. In the 14th century, all knowledge of its previous use had been lost, although it continued to symbolize Roman (pagan) power, and was believed to be a place where evil spirits and ghosts gathered. No efforts to protect the structure were made, and quarrying continued. Some archeological work was undertaken in the 15th century, and old channels were identified. At the beginning of the 18th century, Pope Clement XI planned to have a church built inside the Coliseum in honor of the martyrs, which Christians erroneously believed to have been sacrificed there. This belief saved the Coliseum from further destruction. During the 19th and 20th centuries, numerous restorations were undertaken; nevertheless, during World War II, it was used as a shelter and weapons depository for German paratroopers. During the last three decades of the 20th century, further archeological investigation was undertaken; the building is now under control of the Office of Archeological Superintendence of the city of Rome. Approximately 3 million people visit per year.

— *Thérèse de Vet*

See also **Rome, Ancient**

Further Readings

Gabucci, A. (Ed.). (2001). *The Colosseum* (M. Becker, Trans.). Los Angeles: Getty Museum.
Quennell, P., et al. (Eds.). (1971). *The Colosseum.* New York: Newsweek.

 COLLECTORS

Collecting, also referred to as "gathering" or "foraging," is a broad anthropological term used to describe a food production strategy. Collectors rely on identifying and harvesting native plants and animals rather than engaging in agriculture or animal husbandry. Collectors migrate in small extended-family bands within fixed boundaries or home ranges in search of food and water. They are successfully adapted to their local environments due to highly detailed knowledge of plant and animal life in particular regions and their sensitivity to the carrying capacities of these resources. Collectors gather only what they need for a few days at a time. If food becomes scarce in an area, due to seasonal variation or weather conditions, the band moves, sometimes over a great distance.

Collectors have few material possessions, which vary according to the resources they gather. Some live in deserts and subsist on the roots and wild plants gathered by women and the wild animals hunted by the men. Some live in forests, where women collect nuts, berries, and other wild plants and the men hunt wild animals and fish. Some live on plains and subsist on wild grains, fruits, and vegetables. Others live near ocean waters, which supply fish and other aquatic animals. These resources define the materials from which collectors build their temporary shelters and make their clothing. Natural resources also define the nature of the food production technologies developed by collector cultures. This includes simple hunting, fishing, grinding, and cooking tools and techniques.

The social organization of collector cultures is simple. Small bands of 100 or less people control their populations in response to local natural resources. This ensures that resources will not be overused and that people will not suffer starvation. All collector cultures are characterized by a gendered division of labor. The temporary base camp is the center of daily food processing and sharing. Collectors are egalitarian and view the accumulation of wealth as unnecessary, if not actually undesirable. Reciprocity, which is the exchange of goods and services to benefit all in need, is a key element of a collector culture. Members of band societies learn to live and cooperative with one another and their environment in order to survive. They are led, as least spiritually, by a shaman.

Among the best-known collector groups of the modern world are the Aborigines of Australia and the Inuit peoples of Greenland, Canada, Alaska, and northern Siberia. The San (Bushmen) of Botswana, Namibia, and southern Angola formerly subsisted as collectors until their territories were taken from them and their resources destroyed. There are many lesser-known groups of collectors or former collectors in all geographic regions of the world. They find it increasingly difficult to live by their traditional collecting strategies. The pressure from governments and settled neighbors to surrender their lands for commercial development makes it necessary for them to adapt to new social and natural environments. In the process of modifying their traditional food production strategies, collectors sometimes join political movements with others who struggle against overwhelming political and economic forces. Despite romantic support of their causes, their numbers are small, and their cultural survival is threatened.

Anthropologists study collectors to understand the detailed knowledge they have of marginal environments. Despite their simple lives, collectors are well fed, generally healthy, free of stress, and comfortable. Anthropologists argue that collectors represent the most sustainable and successful of all human adaptive strategies. They can teach complex societies much about the long-term benefits of living simply.

— *Barbara J. Dilly*

See also **Aborigines; Inuit**

Further Readings

Bodley, J. H. (1997). *Cultural anthropology: Tribes, states, and the global system.* Mountain View, CA: Mayfield.

Jorgensen, J. G. (1990). *Oil age Eskimos.* Berkeley: University of California Press.

Wilson, D. J. (1999). *Indigenous South Americans of the past and present.* Boulder, CO: Westview Press.

 COLOBINES

Colobine primates make up one of the two major groups of Old World monkeys. All Old World monkeys are members of a single family, Cercopithecidae, consisting of two subfamilies, Cercopithecinae (the cercopithecines) and Colobinae (the colobines). About 54 species of colobines are currently recognized. Like cercopithecines, colobines are widespread both in Africa and across southern Asia and various islands of the southwest Pacific. They range in size from the West African olive colobus (average adult males 4.7 kg) to Himalayan grey langurs (19.8 kg) and proboscis monkeys (21.2 kg). Most colobines are long-tailed, long-legged, primarily arboreal inhabitants of moist, lowland tropical forests. Most species seldom come to the ground, except to cross openings in the forest. A few species are partly terrestrial; grey langurs of the Indian subcontinent spend up to 80% of the day on the ground and obtain much of their food there.

Food and Digestion

Colobine monkeys differ from cercopithecines in having large, multi-chambered stomachs, an anatomical feature closely related to their behavior and ecology. Anterior sacculations of the fore-stomach are fermentation chambers. They contain bacteria capable of digesting the celluloses and hemicelluloses of dietary fiber. In the forest habitat that most colobines favor, leaves are the most obvious and abundant high-fiber food, and the colobines are sometimes referred to collectively as the "leaf-eating monkeys." However, the digestive system of colobines does not confine them to a completely folivorous (leaf-eating) diet. Less than a tenth of studied species have diets with more than 30% leaves, and when feeding on leaves, they tend to select the youngest ones. Fruits and seeds/nuts are other major constituents of their diets, making up more than a third of the annual diets of several species. Seed storage tissues, whether carbohydrate or lipid, are richer sources of energy than are young leaves. However, seed storage tissues are also substantially tougher than young leaves. Colobines have molar teeth whose shapes and sizes appear to be well adapted to chewing both leaves and tough seeds.

A second possible function of colobines' fermentation chambers is that they may lower the gut's concentrations of various toxic compounds that are produced by plants as a defense against destructive plant eaters. For example, detoxification may account for the ability of purple-faced langurs to eat the toxic fruits of *Strychnos* trees, which contain toxic alkaloids such as strychnine. Conversely, *Strychnos* fruits are avoided by toque macaques, which are cercopithecine monkeys that also have access to these fruits but do not have highly developed fermentation chambers in their guts.

The fermentation chambers of colobines enable them to process relatively indigestible forest foliage when other foods are scarce, thus enabling them to attain unusually high biomass. In many forest communities, the biomass of colobine monkeys is greater than that of all other primates combined.

Social Groups

Colobine monkeys of many species live in relatively small social groups, consisting of a single adult male, several adult females, and their offspring. In other colobines, social groups range from small, monogamous associations to groups of over 200 with many adult males. Compared with cercopithecine primates, aggressive and other interactions occur

Source: © iStockphoto/Holger Ehlers.

infrequently among females in forest-dwelling colobines. This difference in behavior has been attributed to leaves as a key food resource for many colobines. The abundance and dispersion of leaves within large tree crowns allows several animals to feed together without competition. In contrast, foods of cercopithecine monkeys tend to be more clumped: to occur in smaller, more dispersed patches. In cercopithecines, cheek pouches, which colobines do not have, may be an adaptation to the relatively clumped distribution of fruits and other foods that they commonly eat, enabling them to take quantities of foods into their mouths faster than they can chew and swallow them, thereby reducing competition.

The infrequency of aggressive behavior in colobines may be related to another feature of many species: conspicuous fur color in infants, a common trait in those species in which infants are frequently held and handled by females other than the mother, so-called allomothering. If, when that occurs, mothers can

Hanuman langurs near Ramnagar, Nepal, fishing for aquatic plants

Source: Photograph © by Carola Borries.

quickly locate and monitor their infants visually, they may be less likely to try to retrieve them.

Infanticide

After taking over a one-male group, some colobine males kill the infants present in the group at the time. Infanticide in primates was first described among Hanuman langurs by Yukimura Sugiyama in 1965. It has since been reported in a wide variety of other primates and various other mammals. In langurs, it has been regarded by some as a social pathology, an accidental by-product of heightened aggression resulting from higher population densities in populations provisioned by humans. Others consider it a sexually selected adaptation, a male reproductive strategy, in that without a nursing infant, females come into estrus sooner. This would thereby increase the new male's breeding opportunities, particularly if the new male, in turn, might otherwise be deposed before any females have come into estrus. However, this would

not be the case in seasonal breeders, in which the male would, in either case, have to wait until the next breeding season. Thus, any reproductive advantage to the males of being infanticidal would depend on the distribution of males' takeover times relative to breeding seasons, the distribution of males' tenure in groups, and a propensity to kill the infants of other males but not their own. In 1999, Carola Borries and her colleagues, using DNA analysis to determine langur paternity, presented the first evidence that male attackers were not related to their infant victims, and in all cases, they were the likely fathers of the subsequent infants. This study strongly supports the interpretation of infanticide as an adaptive male reproductive tactic.

Of course, for infants and their deposed fathers, infanticide is clearly disadvantageous. For mothers, it may not be from the standpoint of their biological fitness—not, for example, if the greater toughness and aggressiveness of the deposing male is inherited by the sons that he sires. If, as adults, these new sons breed more successfully, then more of their mothers' genes may be passed on to future generations than if their sons by the deposed male had survived.

— *Stuart A. Altmann*

See also **Monkeys, Old World**

Further Readings

Davies, A. G., & Oates, J. F. (Eds.). (1994). *Colobine monkeys: Their ecology, behaviour, and evolution.* Cambridge: Cambridge University Press.

Lambert, J. E. (1998). Primate digestion: Interactions among anatomy, physiology, and feeding ecology. *Evolutionary Anthropology, 7,* 8–20.

Van Schaik, C. P., & Janson, C. H. (Eds.). (2000). *Infanticide by males and its implications.* Cambridge: Cambridge University Press.

INTERSPECIES COMMUNICATION

Interspecies communication occurs when there is communication of thoughts or emotions between species. Interspecies communication studies examine whether and how different species communicate with each other. Throughout history, people have always observed that animals communicate with their own kind. Mating rituals among birds, or even insects, involve communication of signs. Parenting by many species of birds and animals involve extended periods of interaction between parents and their young.

It has long been observed that animals can be taught in domestic situations to cooperate with one another. The first and most obvious is between humans and animals. Humans have domesticated and trained animals for thousands of years. Signals such as hand movements, whistles, or other actions clue the animal that the human trainer wants a particular behavior performed. One example is hunting behavior in falcons or dogs. Communication may involve applying force in the cases of horses and elephants. These communications are in a human-language-based (HBL) code. In recent decades, the question has been asked: Can HBL or a code comprehended by animals be developed for rational communication?

Attention has been focused on communications between different animal species and, more important, communication patterns that seem to be like human communication. For example, studies have been done of several kinds of birds to understand how they learn new sounds or arrange sounds in their songs. In these studies, attempts have been made to teach animals language that can be understood by humans. Extended studies have been made of dolphins. Dolphins have been trained by the U.S. Navy to locate explosive sea mines and scout enemy vessels, especially submarines.

Studies have also been made of great apes. For example, Kanzi and other Bonobos at the Yerkes Center and Koko at the Gorilla Foundation have participated in studies that involve learning language. Koko is a gorilla who speaks sign language. The development of animal sign language is a goal of researchers. It would be used in a variety of situations, including online communications such as the one hosted by Koko on April 29, 1998: the first interspecies Internet chat.

Computers are now being used to aid studies of speech recognition sensors that transmit signals, comprising units of communication. At issue is: What is the degree of rationality that informs symbolic intelligence?

— Andrew J. Waskey

SUSAN SAVAGE-RUMBAUGH

Susan Savage-Rumbaugh is a lead scientist at the Great Ape Trust of Iowa, where she does language research with bonobos. For 23 years, she was associated with the Language Research Center at Georgia State University, where she studied communication among primates. She also carried out research at the Yerkes Primate Center in Atlanta. She is the author of *Kanzi: The Ape at the Brink of the Human Mind* (1996) and, with Stuart G. Shanker and Talbot J. Taylor, has coauthored *Ape Language and the Human Mind* (1998). Both volumes detail Savage-Rumbaugh's discoveries about African bonobos, apes that closely resemble chimpanzees, which apparently use complex trail markers to silently communicate among themselves. Her conclusions contrast with the belief of many scientists that apes lack the brain structure for the use of symbolic language in complex communications.

Observing the behavior of apes in the forest, Savage-Rumbaugh concluded that they could keep their groups together only through communication. Even though bonobos live in groups of more than 100 and the trails are only barely marked, each night they still manage to gather for their rest. This, she argues, is possible only thanks to the signs that they leave for each other at crucial points. For example, she noticed that whenever a trail crossed another trail, the lead group would stamp down vegetation or rip off large leaves and place them carefully. These marks occur only at the junctions of trails, and thus, the lead group is obviously leaving them for those who come after.

Savage-Rumbaugh has also directed her experiments to demonstrate that chimps can acquire language skills in their interaction with humans. Studying the behavior of Kanzi, the pygmy chimp, Rumbaugh has argued that the primate has been able to achieve relatively flowing two-way communication by using symbols that are associated with words and manipulating an electronic keyboard that then generates English words. According to the tests carried out by Savage-Rumbaugh, Kanzi has reached the linguistic competence of a 2½-year-old child and has also demonstrated understanding of some grammatical rules such as word order. Critics charge that these experiments are overinterpreted and that apes are just mimicking what humans do. Yet the story of Kanzi has decisively contributed to the revival of ape language studies.

— Luca Prono

 # COMMUNISM

Communism entered world history in a number of forms, of which we may distinguish the following: a vision of ideal human association, a multistranded political movement, a modular set of state systems run by nominally communist parties, a Cold War counter-idea ("the communist menace"), and a widespread human striving. At each of these levels, communism massively shaped the politics of the last 150-odd years. As a consequence, it also shaped the environment in which modern anthropology established itself. And at each level we can trace the intersection of communism and anthropology.

The Vision of Primitive Communism

Communism features neither in Aristotle's famous typology of governmental forms (monarchy, aristocracy, and constitutional government) nor in his list of respective governmental perversions (tyranny, oligarchy, and democracy). It is not until around 1840 that the word finally appears in print. Like its slightly older cousin socialism, communism announced itself from the start as an antidote to the toxins coursing through the veins of early capitalist society: its pauperism, crime, landlessness, war, despotism, injustice, and moral corruption. The instability endemic to the new bourgeois mode of production, and the legacies of Enlightenment reason and the French Revolution, exposed these ancient poisons as not only intolerable but unnecessary. They could be abolished. A new humane and self-legislating social order was possible. And it belonged to humanity by right.

At the center of existing society, and the source of its ills, according to the communists, was the exploitation of one person by another. It was class society, with its pampered rich and its destitute working masses, which had to be overcome. If the source of the power of the bourgeoisie was private property, the manipulation of the state to enforce their alleged property rights, and the reduction of each laborer's working life to an item to be sold to the highest bidder, then the communist antivenin, as it were, must eventually entail the abolition of money, the withering away of the state, and the holding of all productive property in common.

The mid-19th century also saw the emergence of modern anthropology, and it was in the work of some of the fathers of the new discipline that Marxist communists in particular looked for evidence that communism might be possible. This evidence was of two sorts. In anthropological accounts of the variety of human societies, they found confirmation that capitalism was not in fact the natural order of things. And in descriptions of the earliest forms of human society, they found confirmation that humanity had once organized itself into associations that could fairly be given the name "primitive communism."

The cumulative picture arising from the researches of Johann Jakob Bachofen (1815–1887) and Lewis Henry Morgan (1818–1881), in particular, was one in which the early human societies were egalitarian, property was shared, classes were nonexistent, and sexual relations were unrestricted. Basing his arguments principally on investigations into the Iroquois, Morgan emphasized the matrilineal character of Iroquois kinship, seeing it as evidence for an original and universal matriarchal order. He also proposed an evolutionary schema that attempted to account for humankind's departure from its egalitarian beginnings and its ascent to civilization (a journey he did not wholeheartedly applaud).

Karl Marx (1818–1883) and Friedrich Engel's (1820–1895) interest in anthropological themes had already shown up in their early coauthored work *The German Ideology*. But so significant was the material evinced by Morgan and other anthropologists that it would claim much of Marx's attention in his last years (his observations would eventually be published by Laurence Krader in 1974 as *The Ethnological Notebooks of Karl Marx*). Working up Marx's notes, Engels wrote the first and still most influential "anthropological" book by a Marxist, *The Origin of the Family, Private Property and the State*. Here, preliterate hunter-gatherer society was conceived as an early and rudimentary form of communism in which people lived without prohibitions or jealousies. In the light of this prehistory, the domination, exploitation, and inequality of subsequent social forms had to be seen not as human universals but as specific outcomes of the historical process.

The idea of primitive communism has received its share of criticism, whether for the quality of Morgan's evidence, for his speculations about early promiscuity and matriarchy, his linear model of cultural evolution by stages, his view that goods were once shared and property held in common, his supposition that production was originally simply for "use," or for his assumption that contemporary tribal and band societies could provide direct evidence about the earliest modes of human organization. For many communists, however, the idea has seemed worth arguing for. Certainly there was an empirical case to be made, and various anthropologists, most notably Eleanor Burke Leacock (1922–1987), made it well.

But quite apart from the facts of the matter, primitive communism functioned as an existential guarantee (what once was may come again) and as a germinal model for a future society. In a passage Engels does not fail to quote, Morgan spoke of the democratic era to come as "a revival, in a higher form, of the liberty, equality, and fraternity of the ancient gentes." For the anthropologist Stanley Diamond (1922–1991), writing in the 1970s, any better future for humankind was inconceivable without reference to the primitive egalitarianism now interred under the foundations of civilization.

Movement

Communism, as ideology and as movement, spread rapidly beyond its West European birthplace. By the mid-20th century, regimes from Warsaw to Beijing and capitals farther south were headed by parties calling themselves communists. Meanwhile, the pressures and opportunities created by superpower rivalry, and frequently by the presence of domestic guerilla insurgencies, affected political, economic, and cultural life in what came to be known as the Third World.

Not the least of the consequences for ethnographers was that their fieldwork sites might be traversed by these struggles. This fact could of course be ignored: Robert Redfield (1897–1958), working within earshot of militant Mexican communists in Tepoztlan in the mid- to late 1920s, was undistracted by their struggles. But it could also provoke sympathy and political commitment: when Pierre-Philippe Rey did his initial fieldwork in Congo-Brazzaville, the exposure to local Marxist revolutionaries transformed his understanding of the significance of anthropology.

Although no methodological creed unites communist anthropologists, one common feature is a greater interest in contemporary political forces than is typical of many of their colleagues. Writing of Peru in the 1960s and 1970s, Orin Starn accuses most anthropologists of having missed the revolution that was brewing there. He contrasts the focus on the customs and rituals of Andean highland communities typical of ethnographic accounts with what can be revealed to an anthropologist with an eye for the economic linkages, labor migrations, poverty, brutalization, and protest endemic in the countryside. One such eye was that of Antonio Díaz Martínez. His book *Ayacucho: Hunger and Hope* clearly anticipated the insurgency to come. Unlike Starn himself, Diaz was a communist. Indeed, within a few years, he had crossed from interpretation to action, joining the leadership of the Maoist Sendero Luminoso (Shining Path).

Official Communist Anthropology

A continuous line of intellectual descent connects the writings of the later Engels to those of his student Karl Kautsky (1854–1938), from there to the father of Russian Marxism Georgi Valentinovich Plekhanov (1857–1918), and from Plekhanov to his younger colleague Vladimir Ilyich Lenin (1870–1924). In this manner, the enthusiastic Morganism of Engels was transmitted to the academic tradition of anthropology in Russia and subsequently to all the societies steering themselves by the twinkling star of Marxism-Leninism.

Outside of Central Europe, these societies went through more or less cataclysmic paroxysms associated with forced modernization. Like every other field of inquiry, anthropology in such conditions was compelled to be immediately useful, its analyses geared to the overriding task of building communism. This ought to have been a straightforward matter, as all these societies were governed, openly or in practice, by one-party states equipped with a scientific ideology capable of resolving every intellectual problem. As it turned out, the party line tended to describe a zigzag course, with yesterday's "rightist deviation" making way for today's "self-criticism" and tomorrow's rejection of "vulgar egalitarianism."

Not all of these "really existing socialist" countries had a preexisting tradition of anthropology but all had largely preindustrial economies and predominantly agrarian populations. Many contained ethnic minorities whose cultural trajectory intersected uncertainly or perhaps not at all with the communist future. In the Soviet Union, with its extensive "multinational" territory, Marxism proved a mercurial guide for ethnographers. Many ethnic cultures, for instance, showed few signs of having evolved according to Morgan's developmental stages. And in any case, was it the task of communists to protect them from assimilation to the ways of the "imperial" Russian ethos or to find ways to expedite their escape from backward kin-based forms of authority and social organization?

As Yuri Slezkine has shown, these and many other questions became flash points for bitter disputes between anthropologists (or ethnologists, as they were more often known), particularly in the 1920s and 1930s. Later, in the post-Stalin era, the disputes became both less bitter and less dangerous, but all positions had to keep in touch with the prevailing doctrinal assessment of the country's needs. All the same, as Ernest Gellner (1925–1995) reminded an English-speaking audience in 1980, even under these conditions important studies continued to be published throughout the Communist period.

No attempt will be made here to sum up the anthropological achievements of the countries run by communist parties over the better part of a century. Mention may be made, however, of one of the most interesting figures from the founding period of Soviet anthropology, the ethnographer Lev Shternberg (1861–1927). A political prisoner under the tsar, in the mid-1920s he would become the dean of the Ethnography Department within the Geography Division of Leningrad University. Despite having fairly moderate politics in the context of the times, Shternberg's moral and intellectual authority was second to none among Soviet ethnologists. Not only had he been a revolutionary martyr, but during his exile on the island of Sakhalin he had contrived to conduct an ethnography of the native Gilyaks. These were a people who impressed Shternberg as simultaneously communistic, nonauthoritarian, and individualistic. His discovery, as he supposed, of "survivals of group marriage" among the Gilyak attracted great interest and was rapidly noticed by none other than Engels (who, like Marx, had troubled himself to learn Russian). As Sergei Kan has documented, Shternberg himself read Engels's *The Origin of the Family* while in exile. Engels in turn paid Shternberg the ultimate compliment of translating a report of Shternberg's findings as an addendum to the next edition of his own book. Shternberg, it seemed, had found living evidence of the group marriage and primitive communism posited by Morgan.

Anticommunist Views of Communism

Twentieth-century regimes run by communist parties were responsible for mass killings of their own populations on a scale to rival the worst horrors with which human history is replete. Yet these crimes were not the original cause of anticommunism. More basic was antipathy to the very idea of empowerment of the lower orders. When the socialist, anarchist, communist, and republican Communards took over the administration of Paris in 1871, some 30,000 were slaughtered in the street by the troops of the Third Republic. Before the Russian Revolution was a year old, 21 foreign powers had joined the White armies to ensure, as Winston Churchill put it, that Bolshevism was "strangled in its cradle."

During most of the 20th century, Western officialdom, and a goodly slice of Western populations, saw in communism only the menacing visage of totalitarianism. With the end of World War II and the division of Europe into East and West, this anticommunist definition of communism once again became a presupposition of Anglo-American domestic and international politics (though less so on the Continent). As with many other intellectuals, anthropologists were sometimes drawn into the struggle, and here their detailed local knowledge could make their contributions much more than "academic."

When the reformist government of Jacobo Arbenz Guzmán (1913–1971) was overthrown with CIA help in 1954, it was an anthropologist with close knowledge of Guatemalan society who reported secretly to the U.S. State Department on the political leanings of those taken prisoner during the coup. As studies by David Price, Thomas Patterson, and Roberto Gonzalez establish, cooperation between anthropologists and the CIA has not been uncommon in Southeast Asia and other areas of intimate concern to the U.S. administration.

Erik Wakin provides a blow-by-blow description of the uproar in the American Anthropological Association in 1970–1971, when it was alleged that certain anthropologists might have been secretly helping the U.S. government's counterinsurgency effort in Thailand. That such involvement was a scandal at all owed much to the ideological strength of the New Left at the time.

Twenty years earlier, when the Western left was still largely either social democratic or Soviet-aligned, McCarthyite anticommunism had set the tone. In this period American communist and socialist anthropologists felt the pressure to adopt Aesopian language. If their colleagues in the U.S.S.R. had to pepper their articles with obligatory references to Marx, in the United States Eleanor Leacock, Stanley Diamond, Leslie White (1900–1975), Gene Weltfish (1902–1980), and other distinguished anthropologists learned that although Marx was good to read, he was hazardous to cite.

Inner Strivings

Now that the sun of capitalism illumines every corner of the globe, it may be easy to underplay the geopolitical impact made by communism. In fact, this impact was tremendous and must remain inexplicable if account is not taken of a final dimension of the concept. As the urge to discover a "primitive communism" in the past might indicate, this modernizing and often avowedly "scientific" ideology drew much of its strength from the fact that it crystallized a series of perhaps immortal longings. These would include the wish to find that our ends will connect us back to our beginnings; the hope that human history, with all its dreadful and apparently senseless destruction, will not have been a tale told by an idiot; the dream of overcoming the antagonism between nature and culture; the pining for true mutual recognition and understanding; and the demand for a world where finally people will live as free and equal comrades and not as one or other species of predator and prey. All these are forms of the desire for social self-completion, and as such for the overcoming of the antagonistic splits that separate us from what somehow we are meant, as social and natural creatures, to be.

Communism, then, has been the name for a widespread set of human desires. That they are only widespread and not universal can be read off from the fact that many human societies never conceived of any opposition between "nature" and "culture," did not conceive of themselves as "historical," and never sought redemption for their "alienated" condition in an eschatological future.

Yet in societies where some of these elements were present, images of past golden ages have been common. In a letter to his friend Arnold Ruge (1802–1880), the young Marx commented that "the world has long been dreaming of something that it can acquire if only it becomes conscious of it." That something was communism. Of course, from the perspective of modern ethnography, the "world" Marx knew had its limits. But perhaps it was not so limited as a world that thinks to have killed that dream.

— *Sebastian Job*

Further Readings

Díaz Martínez, A. (1969). *Ayacucho: Hambre y Esperenza.* [Ayacucho: Hunger and hope]. Ayacucho, Peru: Ediciones Waman Puma.

Gellner, E. (Ed.). (1980). *Soviet and Western anthropology.* New York: Columbia University Press.

Gonzalez, R. J. (2004). *Anthropologists in the public sphere: Speaking out on war, peace and American power.* Austin: University of Texas Press.

Kan, S. (2001). The "Russian Bastian" and Boas or why Shternberg's *The social organization of the Gilyak* never appeared among the Jesup Expedition publications. In I. Krupnik and W. W. Fitzhugh (Eds.), *Gateways: Exploring the legacy of the Jesup North Pacific Expedition, 1897–1902* (pp. 217–251).Washington DC: Smithsonian Institution.

Leacock, E. (1981). *Myths of male dominance.* New York: Monthly Review Press.

Marx, K. (1974). *The ethnological notebooks of Karl Marx: Studies of Morgan, Phear, Maine, Lubbock.* (L. Krader, Transcriber and Ed.). Assen, Holland: Van Gorcum. (Original work published 1880–1882)

Patterson, T. C. (2001). *A social history of anthropology in the United States.* Oxford, UK: Berg.

Price, D. (2002). Interlopers and invited guests: On anthropology's witting and unwitting links to intelligence agencies. *Anthropology Today, 18*(6),16–21.

Redfield, R. (1930). *Tepoztlan: A Mexican village: A study of folk life.* Chicago: University of Chicago Press.

Starn, O. (1992). Missing the revolution: Anthropologists and the war in Peru. In G. E. Marcus (Ed.), *Rereading cultural anthropology* (pp. 152–180). Durham, NC: Duke University Press.

Wakin, E. (1992). *Anthropology goes to war: Professional ethics & the counterinsurgency in Thailand* (Monograph No. 7). Madison: University of Wisconsin Center for Southeast Asian Studies.

COMMUNITIES

The concept of community developed mostly in sociology to refer to an organic whole whose components are tied together by a common and innate moral order. Classical literature on community emphasizes its homogeneity in terms of the beliefs and activities of its members, who are interrelated in face-to-face relationships and whose allegiance and belonging are clearly defined. Seminal studies across social sciences depict community in a nostalgic fashion ("Oh, the good old days"), while the nature of modernity is presented as impersonal and bureaucratic. Anthropology, to a certain extent, has contributed to this view because of anthropologists' strategic insertion and approach to the field as a unified and self-contained whole. From the rise of anthropology as a discipline in the 19th century until recently, the most privileged areas carved for ethnographic investigation remained the "exotic others" living in non-Western societies, where ecology and social organization combined with research interests to generate a particular unit of analysis conceived of as "community," endowed with a quasi-ontology. It is within this paradigm that after World War II, community studies in Latin America, the Caribbean, Africa, Southeast Asia, and even in the United States became popular among anthropologists in their quest to grasp discrete worlds (communities) that could escape the capillary power of the nation-state.

During the end of the 1960s through the mid-1970s, the rising voice of multiple currents within anthropology and cultural studies culminated in the concept being reevaluated. This reevaluation resulted from the effect of sociopolitical movements that gave voices to different segments of society and expression of identities. The idea of "community" as an organic whole disallowed thinking about community as a site of violence, political struggle, or multiple hierarchies. Feminist critics questioned how traditional analysis embedded gender inequality to romanticize oppressive structures and omit in its narrative sites of contestation, including the arbitrariness and fixity of the ideas of belonging and allegiance of members to "their" community, as constructed in analytical texts. Critical race theorists brought into the debate the issue of exclusion when it comes to fulfilling the idea of freedom and equality for all in the nation. Postcolonial theorists questioned the oversimplification and the inequality of relationships embedded in the imposition of the concept of community to refer to large complex processes (for example, community of nations, Caribbean community); this oversimplification, they contend, masks new modes of alienations and oppressions implicit to these impositions (for example, economic exploitation and political dominations exercised by powerful nations over weaker ones within the same regional or international community).

Today, new patterns of circulation of people and capital have led to the development of new forms of identity communities and political struggles where articulated movements of networks give way to new modes of belonging and allegiance (for example, experiences of identities among diasporic populations). Given these dynamics, anthropologists as well as some currents in social sciences have come to view alternative narratives of experiences of communities as occurring in a complex web of shifting power relations. As such, the concept of diaspora constitutes a creative medium to give account of immigrants' experiences of differences, marginalization, place, and mobility as well as their political implications in a wider transnational process. Central to this approach is the critical role of complexity in the processes of belonging to multiple communities or larger collectivities. Emerging ways of understanding "communities" call upon anthropologists to reevaluate the classical categories that used to sanction totalities and modes of relationships that used to fall outside anthropology's domain of appreciation. Contemporary anthropology attempts to grasp and render meaningful these emerging strategies of fluid relationships in ever-reconfiguring settings by recalibrating its conceptual tools and incorporating ideas of hierarchies, power, and diversity in its perspectives.

— *Louis Herns Marcelin*

See also **Subcultures**

Further Readings

Anderson, B. R. O' G. (1991). *Imagined communities: Reflections on the origin and spread of nationalism.* New York: Verso.

Brubaker, R. (2004). *Ethnicity without groups.* Cambridge, MA: Harvard University Press.

Redfield, R. (1962). *The little community: And peasant society and culture.* Chicago: University of Chicago Press.

COMPLEXITY

The concept of complexity seems to be simple and elusive at the same time. Everyone understands what we mean when we call an object "complex," but if we define this attribute clearly and distinctly, we encounter many difficulties.

The first difficulty arises when we want to specify to what aspect of an object we refer by calling it "complex." Does this mean that an object has a rich structure that cannot be described easily? Or that it fulfils a difficult function? Or that it is intricate to generate this object?

Those three aspects of an object—its structure, its function, and its generative history—do not have to be equivalent in respect to complexity. Let us show this by some examples.

- A part of most intelligence tests are sequences of numbers that appear to be irregular (i.e., to have a complex structure). The task of the test person is to find out the rather simple mathematical formula that produced the sequence in question. Here, we have a complex structure but a simple generative process. In addition, this generative process is performed to fulfill a complex function, namely, to contribute to the quantification of intelligence, which is a much-debated psychological concept.
- A geometrically simple artifact like a parabolic mirror for an optical telescope is intricate to make; for example, it needs different time-consuming steps to polish it. Here, we have a simple structure but a complex generative process. Moreover, the function of such a mirror is, from a physical point of view, rather simple: It has just to focus the incoming rays of light.
- Locks have also a simple function, namely, to hinder burglars from breaking into a house. But in order to fulfill their function, they must show a complex inner structure so that it is not too easy to pick the lock.
- Mathematical set theory has a rather simple structure, which can be defined by a few axioms, but it is used to fulfill complex functions, for example, to talk in a clear way about very abstract philosophical problems, such as: Do there exist different kinds of infinity?

We can remark on a common feature of all these examples: The more space and time we need (or seem to need) for describing the structure, the function, or the generative history of an object, the more complex this object is in respect to its structure, its function, or its generative history.

The next difficulty consists in finding a good quantitative characterization of the relation between, on one hand, the time and space needed for describing an object and, on the other hand, the degree of complexity we ascribe to it. Such a correlation must be as abstract as necessary in order to be principally applicable to any kind of object, but it must also be as concrete as possible in order to be practically applicable to specific objects, their structure, their function, and their generative history.

The best available proposal for an abstract conceptual framework into which all those aspects can be integrated so that the complexity of a specific object can be concretely measured is based upon the idea of computation. By "computation," we understand an ordered sequence of mathematically describable operations that is effective for solving a problem and that can be executed by a computer if it is formulated as an algorithm in a programming language. To sum up two ratios is as well a computation in that sense as the meteorological modeling of tomorrow's weather.

The computational problem to be solved in our complexity-theoretic context is to find an adequate description of the structure, the function, or the generative history of some object. Since the "natural" language of a computer is coded in binary form, we refer from now on by "description" only to strings of zeroes and ones stored in the computer.

To define complexity measures on the basis of the idea of computation, we have to look at the physical resources a computation requires to solve our problem. The first such resource that can be used for measuring complexity is the minimal time a program needs to compute a solution (i.e., to output a description of a chosen object). An important question that arises in this context is: How much does the running time of a computation depend upon the descriptive length of the problem? Is it possible to define different classes for the dependence of the running time of a program upon that length? As a central part of computer science, the theory of computational complexity tackles this problem.

The theory of algorithmic complexity focuses not on time, but on space, namely, on the minimal computer storage required for a program that can solve our problem (i.e., that outputs a description of a chosen object). Its complexity is then defined as the number of bits of the shortest program that carries out this task. The longer this program is, the more complex the object is. Of course, the concrete value depends also upon the type of computer on which the program is run.

Time and space needed for a computation are taken together into account to define the algorithmic depth of an object. This complexity measure is defined as the average running time of all programs that output a description of a chosen object, whereby the respective contribution of a program to this value is weighted inversely proportionally to its running time.

The theory of complexity analyzes the above-mentioned and many more measures of complexity. It belongs, like cybernetics, information theory, and semiotics, to the structural sciences. These sciences try, on one hand, to construct formal systems (like all possible machines in cybernetics and all possible codes in semiotics), without taking into account the specific nature of objects that might realize those systems. On the other hand, structural sciences have a clear orientation toward the application of their models upon a wide variety of empirical phenomena. Therefore, it is not surprising to find mathematicians (like Kolmogorov), information scientists (like Chaitin), computer scientists (like Bennett), physicists (like Murray Gell-Mann), biologists (like Bernd-Olaf Küppers), cognitive scientists (like Allen Newell), economists (like Herbert A. Simon), and social scientists (like Niklas Luhmann) among those people that are much interested in complexity. These scientists have contributed to the foundations of the theory of complexity, which today is a network of formal models that help to describe the various aspects of complexity in different empirical contexts.

— *Stefan Artmann*

See also **Chaos Theory and Anthropology**

Further Readings

Davis, M. (1982). *Computability and unsolvability.* New York: Dover.

Gell-Mann, M. (1994). *The quark and the jaguar: Adventures in the simple and the complex.* New York: W.H. Freeman.

Kauffman, S. A. (1995). *At home in the universe: The search for laws of self-organization and complexity.* New York: Oxford University Press.

COMPUTERS AND HUMANKIND

Computers and Evolution

At first glance, the average person would be familiar with only the last 30 years of computer history. In fact, the origins of the computer, in the way of simple counting aids, date back at least 2,000 years. The abacus was invented around the 4th century BC, in Babylonia (now Iraq). Another device called the *Antikythera* mechanism was used for registering and predicting the motion of the stars and planets around the 1st century BC. Wilhelm Schickard built the first mechanical calculator in 1623, but the device never made it past the prototype stage. This calculator could work with six digits and carry digits across columns.

First-generation computers (1939–1954) used vacuum tubes to compute. The simple vacuum tube had been developed by John Ambrose Fleming, in 1904. The vacuum tube was used in radios and other electronic devices throughout the 1940s and into the 1950s. Most computer developments during this time were used for military purposes. During World War II "the Colossus" (December 1943) was designed in secret at Bletchley Park to decode German messages. The ENIAC (Electronic Numerical Integrator Analyzor and Computer) was developed by Ballistics Research Laboratory, in Maryland, in 1945. This computer was used to assist in the preparation of firing tables for artillery. The UNIVAC (Universal Automatic Computer) was developed in 1951, by Remington Rand. The UNIVAC was the first commercial computer sold. The Census Bureau purchased the UNIVAC on June 14, 1951. It contained a magnetic storage system and tape drives and was so large it was housed in a garage-sized room. The UNIVAC contained 5,200 vacuum tubes and weighed about 29,000 pounds. The UNIVAC I, which was an upgrade of the original UNIVAC, was used to calculate and predict the winner in the 1952 presidential campaign. Interestingly, TV networks refused to trust UNIVAC I's prediction results.

Second-generation computers (1954–1959) used transistors rather than vacuum tubes. Dr. John Bardeen, Dr. Walter Brattain, and Dr. William Shockley developed the first transistor in December 1947. Transistors were developed in an attempt to find a better amplifier and a replacement for mechanical relays. The vacuum tube, although it had been used for nearly 50 years, consumed lots of power, operated hot, and burned out rapidly. Transistors provided a new, more efficient method of computing. International Business Machines (IBM) dominated the early second-generation market. IBM, with Tom Watson Jr. as CEO, introduced the model 604 computer in 1953. This computer used transistors. The 604 developed into the 608 in 1957. This was the first solid-state computer sold on the commercial market. IBM had a number of other significant developments during the same time frame. They developed the 650 Magnetic Drum Calculator, which used a magnetic drum memory rather than punched cards. IBM also developed the 701 scientific "Defense Calculator." This series of computers dominated mainframe computers for the next decade. Although IBM dominated the second generation, several other companies developed computer systems. In 1956, Bendix sold a small business computer, the G-15A, for $45,000. This computer was designed by Harry Huskey.

Third-generation computers (1959–1971) were built with integrated circuits (IC). An IC is a chip made up of many transistors. Three companies played major roles in the development of third-generation computers. The first IC was patented by Jack Kilby, of Texas Instruments (TI), in 1959. Although IC development started in 1959, it wasn't until 1963 that a commercial IC hearing aid was sold. IBM again played a major role in the development of computers during the third generation. They produced SABRE, the first airline reservation tracking system for American Airlines. IBM also announced the System/360. This computer was an all-purpose mainframe computer, which used an 8-bit character word. Digital Equipment Corporation (DEC) introduced the first "mini-computer" in 1968. This was a smaller-sized version of normal computer systems of the day and was called the PDP-8. The "mini-computer" was named after the "mini-skirt" of the 1960s. Early computer applications were also developed during this time. In 1962, Ivan Sutherland demonstrated "Sketchpad," which was installed on a mainframe computer. This program provided engineers the ability to make drawings on the computer using a light pen. Doug Engelbart demonstrated (1968) an early word processor. Toward the end of the third generation, the Department of Defense started development of Arpanet (the precursor of the Internet), and Intel Corp started producing large-scale integrated (LSI) circuits.

The microprocessor was developed in the early 1970s. From 1971 through the present is generally known as the fourth generation of computer development. There have been many developments in computer technology during this time. In 1971, Gilbert Hyatt, at Micro Computer Co., patented the first microprocessor. Ted Hoff, at Intel Corp., introduced the first 4-bit processor in February of that year, the 4004. In 1972, Intel developed the 8-bit 8008 and 8080 microprocessors. The 8080 was the microprocessor design IBM used with its original IBM PC sold commercially in the early 1980s. Control Program/Microprocessor (CP/M) was the earliest widely used microcomputer operating system. This language was used with early 8-bit microprocessors. Many of the components seen on modern computers were developed in the 1970s. IBM developed the first sealed hard drive in 1973. It was called the "Winchester," after the rifle company. It had a total capacity of 60 megabytes. Xerox developed Ethernet in 1973. Ethernet was one of the first environments that allowed computers to talk to each other. The Graphical User Interface (GUI) was developed by Xerox in 1974. Common GUIs seen today are Apples' Mac OS and Microsoft's Windows Operating System. In 1976 one of the companies that revolutionized microcomputer development was started. Apple was a startup business in 1975–76. Jobs and Wozniak developed the Apple personal computer in 1976. In 1977, the gaming industry started. Nintendo began to make computer games that stored data on chips on the inside of game cartridges. A few of the early popular games included "Donkey Kong" (1981) and "Super Mario Brothers" (1985). Probably the most significant software occurrence was the contract between IBM and Microsoft's Bill Gates in 1980. In 1980, IBM offered Microsoft a contract to build a new operating system for IBM's new desktop PC. Microsoft bought QDOS from Seattle Computer and eventually developed MS-DOS. This contract formed the beginnings of Microsoft, which is now the largest software company in the world. Another important event took place in 1987, when Bill Atkinson of Apple Computer developed a program called "Hypercard." Hypercard used hypertext and was a predecessor of the graphical environment used on the World Wide Web today.

Fifth-generation computing (the present and beyond) encompasses common use of the Internet, World Wide Web, virtual reality, Artificial Intelligence, and daily use of sophisticated technological innovations.

Several important events set the stage for fifth-generation computing. Among these was the development of the World Wide Web in 1991, by Tim Berners-Lee; the first Web browser, "Mosaic," in 1993; the release of Netscape Navigator in 1994; and the release of Internet Explorer by Microsoft in 1996. Today, technology and computing are moving forward at an ever-increasing rate. The World Wide Web is the common program to browse the Internet. As computers increase in power, virtual reality is becoming common as well. Doctors can use virtual reality to operate on a patient prior to a real surgery. Pilots log hundreds of hours in flight simulators before ever setting foot in the cockpit of an airplane, and astronauts can train for complex maneuvers before takeoff. Computers are becoming smarter as well. Artificial Intelligence and expert systems are being developed daily. The increase in technology has spun off numerous computer-like devices, such as smart cell phones, MP3 players, and many more personal portable computers.

It's interesting to note that as the computer has evolved to support ever more sophisticated software applications, computers are now used to simulate and model everything from the evolution of man to the weather. Information gathered from anthropological finds can be entered into computers, enabling the simulation of prehuman-to-human evolution. By understanding human evolution, scientists can learn, in addition to other benefits, more about natural selection and the processes all life goes through in the evolutionary process. Computers develop climate change models by analyzing environmental data gathered from sensors around the world. These models can forecast what the environment might be like in 50 or 100 years and help humankind prepare for future environmental shifts.

The fast pace of increasing technology has led to serious human physical and psychological conditions. Since the computer has become a necessary component of everyday business, the work environment has seen an increase in repetitive stress injuries (RSI). RSI include carpal tunnel syndrome (CTS), tendonitis, tennis elbow, and a variety of similar conditions. The field of computer ergonomics attempts to improve worker productivity and reduce injuries by designing computer equipment that will be able to adjust to the individual's natural body positions. *Technostress*, a term originally popularized by Sethi, Caro, and Schuler, refers to stress associated with the continually changing and uncertain technology environment individuals are faced with either at work or home. As a result of the rapid and uncertain change in technology (resulting in technostress), humans, probably more so than at any point in history, must have the ability to quickly adapt to new situations and environments.

As the computer continues to change the world, we will undoubtedly see more technological innovations in the near future. The computer is indeed quickly evolving into a new form that, today, we cannot imagine.

Computers and Research

In the past, research required significantly greater time to complete than today. Data had to be gathered, then analyzed by hand. This was a very slow, tedious, and unreliable process. Today, computers take much of the manual labor away from research. Primarily, computers assist researchers by allowing them to gather, then analyze, massive amounts of data in a relatively short period of time.

Even though scientists began identifying and understanding DNA in depth in the 1950s, detailed analysis could not be performed until technologies were able to analyze and record the volumes of data associated with DNA research. The Human Genome Project began in 1990 and was coordinated by the Department of Energy (DOE) and the National Institutes of Health (NIH), resulting in the coding of the human genetic sequence. The goals of this project were to *identify* all the approximately 30,000 genes in human DNA, to *determine* the sequences of the 3 billion chemical base pairs that make up human DNA, to *store* this information in databases, to *improve* tools for data analysis, to *transfer* related technologies to the private sector, and to *address* the ethical, legal, and social issues (ELSI) that may arise from the project. The Human Genome Project was originally intended to last 15 years but was completed in just 13 due to computer technology advances.

Technologies such as distributed computing (thousands or millions of computers working on the same project at the same time) and the Internet have aided in the development of new research methodologies. For example, when a home computer is turned on, its microprocessor is sitting idle most of the time regardless of the task the user is performing. Distributed processing takes advantage of the idle time by running programs in the background. The user is usually never aware another program is running. The SETI@Home project is one example of how distributed processing can be used in research. This project uses a screen-saver program, designed for home computers, that analyzes radio signals from outer space for patterns or other signs of alien life. Individuals volunteer to use their home computer as part of the program. Each home computer receives data from a radio telescope in Puerto Rico. The home computer then analyzes the data and returns the results. The screen-saver program is the distributed program interfacing through the Internet with the radio telescope. Mainframe computers are typically used to analyze this type of data but can be very expensive to use. Research costs are significantly reduced using distributed computing.

Computers can be used for modeling. Modeling is similar to building a virtual prototype. For instance, rather than an auto manufacturer physically building a new car, then testing it for safety, a computer model is virtually created. That model can then be tested as though it were a real car. The modeling process is quicker and less expensive than traditional methods of testing car safety and performance and allows for a greater variety of tests in a short time frame.

Computers are also used to assist communication between researchers located at geographically separated locations. Researchers in Puerto Rico can easily and instantly communicate with researchers in Hawaii. Researchers from eastern European countries can easily collaborate with their peers from the West. The ability to share resources and knowledge creates an environment where people from many different geographical areas, backgrounds, and experiences can effectively merge, creating a more productive research team.

Computers are being used in education research to better understand how individuals learn. By knowing how individuals learn, educational programs can be tailored so each person can learn more efficiently.

Ironically, computers are being used in research to learn how humans interact with computers. By understanding the interaction process, software can be designed so it is more intuitive and easier to use. This increases user satisfaction and productivity-boosting efficiencies.

Computers impact every facet of research, from education to space research. The ability of the computer to quickly analyze and store massive quantities of data has been a key to the success of the computer in research.

Computers and Genetics

The field of genetics, or the study of genes, is incredibly complicated and contains massive amounts of data. Biotechnology is the study of genetics aided by computers. Computers are an absolute necessity in the field of biotechnology.

Computers help scientists get a three-dimensional visualization of long strings of DNA. Before the advent of computer use in genetics, scientists were able to make only rough guesses as to the makeup of DNA structure.

Computer technology is necessary in managing and interpreting large quantities of data that are generated in a multitude of genetic projects, including the Human Genome Project and companion efforts, such as modeling organisms' genetic sequences. Information in all forms of biotech databases, such as the nucleotide sequence, genetic and physical genome maps, and protein structure information, has grown exponentially over the last decade. As the quantity of data increases, computers become even more important in managing access to information for scientists worldwide. Around the world, there are hundreds of large databases used in genetic research. For researchers to obtain accurate information, it is often necessary to access several different databases.

Computers are able to interface between different types of databases using programs such as Entrez for text term searching. Entrez is a tool used for data mining (searching many databases for specific information such as trends or patterns). Entrez has access to nucleotide and protein sequence data from over 100,000 organisms. It can also access three-dimensional protein structures and genomic-mapping information. Access to this data is important for scientists to understand the DNA structure of organisms. There is similar software used for sequence similarity searching, taxonomy, and sequence submission.

Among the benefits computer technology has brought to the field of biotechnology is the ability to increase the rate at which pharmaceutical drugs can be developed. Screening is a process by which researchers learn how a chemical or natural product affects the disease process. Using computer technology, researchers are now able to screen hundreds of thousands of chemical and natural product samples in the same time a few hundred samples were screened a decade ago. Modern computer technology has enabled the discovery of thousands of new medicines in an ever-shortening time frame.

In the future, computers will be able to simulate cells at two different levels. Computers will be able to simulate cells at the atomic level, allowing scientists to learn how proteins fold and interact. It's important to understand this basic interaction, since proteins are the building blocks of all life. On a larger scale, computers can simulate biochemical compounds, where they can learn more about cell metabolism and regulation. By understanding how the cell works and being able to simulate cells, scientists would then be able to build larger biological models. Rather than test the effects of drugs on animals or humans, scientists would be able to simulate the same test on virtual organisms. Scientists could even create a simulated model of an individual testing the effect medications have on the human system. This technology would enable doctors to treat patients more effectively.

Organizations have been established to create and maintain biomedical databases. The National Center for Biotechnology Information (NCBI) was created in 1988 toward this purpose. A few of NCBI's responsibilities are to conduct research on fundamental biomedical problems at the molecular level using mathematical and computational methods; maintain collaborations with several NIH, academia, industry, and governmental agencies; and foster scientific communication by sponsoring meetings, workshops, and lecture series.

Computers and Education

Computers have changed the face of education. Basic computer skills are becoming more necessary in everyday life. Every facet of education has been affected by computer technology. English, philosophy, psychology, and history teachers now have a wide range of informational and educational resources and teaching tools accessible through the Internet. Mathematicians use computers to better understand equations. Science teachers use computers to gather and analyze large quantities of experimental data. Health and human performance (physical education) teachers are able to use computers to model human anatomy, which provides insight to the cause and prevention of sports injuries. Computer science instructors teach a variety of skills, such as programming, networking, and computer applications. Education in each discipline is important to the success of children worldwide.

The advent of the computer in education has changed many teaching methods. Teachers have traditionally used textbooks and lectured about a particular topic. Today, computer technology has brought interactive learning methodologies into the classroom. Computer simulations are common. Using the Internet for research is common as well.

Computers in education provide students with a wide array of diverse learning techniques. Some students excel at individually paced courses, while others learn better working in groups. Computers provide a means of improving the learning environment for each type of learner. For example, individual students can use a program on compact disc (CD) that provides course content, complete with quizzes and exams. This enables students to work at their own pace, mastering each unit and then continuing with subsequent lessons. Computers and the Internet can be used by groups of students as a tool for collaboration, enabling them to work together even though they are geographically separated.

In today's busy world, many individuals are taking classes online in order to advance their education and careers. Distance courses provide supplemental classes to high school students and lifelong learners. Distance education is becoming more prevalent as computer technology improves. Home computers with network connections to the Internet are now faster and easier to use. Students enrolled in distance courses today can expect to take part in discussions and chats, view images and video, and be provided with a long list of course-specific Internet resources. Courseware (a program used by teachers to organize and deliver online course content) is becoming very friendly and efficient to use to organize and present course material. Courseware is not only making distance learning easier but is also used to supplement onsite courses as well.

Children with special needs benefit from computer technology in the classroom. A general class of computer technologies that helps children with special needs learn and function is called "assistive technologies." There are many ways assistive technologies help children with disabilities to learn. For instance, applications provide cause-and-effect training activities, which is a beneficial learning style for special needs children. In more severe cases, assistive technologies offer students with cerebral palsy and other debilitating conditions a way to learn through the use of speech-generating devices (augmentative and alternative communication, or AAC). Assistive technologies also assist those who are hearing and visually impaired by using computers as an interface to learning environments.

Computers have changed the face of education in business as well. Today, keeping up with current technology is necessary for companies to remain competitive in a global market. Employees must continually upgrade their skills in order to remain valuable to the company. Computers allow individuals to update their skills through both online professional development and computer-based training applications. Some companies have developed extensive industry-specific curricula, creating a unique learning environment that is partly online and partly onsite. In this example, industry employees are able to learn computer-networking concepts in a combined-media format, containing elements such as text, image, audio, video, and simulations. High school and college students may also participate in this online learning environment.

Computers are used to provide a variety of assessments. These range from the computerized versions of the traditional quiz or exam to interactive-skills-based exams. Individuals have a variety of ways they learn best. Some are visual. Some are better able to memorize information. The computer has provided the means to create a wider variety of assessments, enabling teachers to better determine students' knowledge and skill in a particular discipline or content area. Once individuals are assessed, computers can then analyze the data. Administrators and teachers can monitor and analyze learning trends.

With the world becoming more technical, it is necessary to learn about computers in every educational grade. Whether it is learning about computers or using computers to teach other disciplines, computers are key in the success of today's children as well as adult learners. Computers are the way we work today. With the world and technology changing ever more quickly, it is more important than ever that computers be included in every facet of education.

Many third-world countries are now in the process of developing internal networking technologies, and the world continues to get smaller. The Internet has enabled children around the world to collaborate and communicate with each other. It has brought similar teaching methodologies to the forefront worldwide, creating the most unique learning environment the world has thus far seen.

Computers and the Global Village

The world is continually shrinking thanks to the advent of electronic mediums such as radio and television and, more recently, the computer and the Internet. These technologies have electronically interconnected the world. Marshall McLuhan first coined the phrase "global village" in the early 1960s. McLuhan was a professor at the University of Toronto's St. Michael's College. He studied the effects of mass media on behavior and thought. McLuhan wrote several books about the effect of the media on humankind. He first predicted world connectivity in 1965.

What is the global village? We'll start by defining the word *village*. What is a village? A village is local. You pass villagers each day on the street. You live next door to villagers. You discuss neighborhood events with the villager who lives next door. Villagers with common interests gather for meetings at the local public school. They gather to socialize at restaurants and other locations. Everyone in the village is connected in some way. This village can be your neighborhood or the city where you live. News, gossip, and community events are known commonly throughout the village. Fires, deaths, and other important community news spread rapidly throughout the community. The village is geographically limited in size.

The global village has been created through the use of the electronic medium. From the 1920s through the 1960s, it was represented by radio, television, movies, and the telephone. One could experience events around the world through these mediums. Regardless of the individual's physical location in the world, they were able to experience the stock market crash in 1929, the Japanese attack on Pearl Harbor in 1941, the Cuban missile crisis of 1963, and the social movements that took place in the late 1960s, in much the same manner as individuals in a village experience their local events within the community. The 1970s saw the development of Arpanet. Arpanet was a U.S. Department of Defense project that connected computers together from several geographical areas across the United States into one network. The modern-day Internet was built upon the technologies and concepts of Arpanet. The introduction of the personal computer in the early 1980s combined with the growth of computer networks and the Internet for business use initiated the socialization of the "net" (Internet) in the 1990s. The World Wide Web (1993) has enabled this socialization, creating a common, easy-to-use interface that became the standard way to navigate and use the Internet.

Throughout the latter part of the 20th and first part of the 21st century, the Internet has developed into the "global village" McLuhan spoke of in the 1960s. The Internet has created a social and information culture similar to the traditional village, yet in a virtual environment. You communicate or chat daily with individuals who are online. You purchase goods through online auctions. You write letters that contain pictures and movies and send them to family and friends through the use of electronic mail. You check the headlines on the daily paper, perhaps the *New York Times* or the *Scotsman*, while living in rural Montana. Through telecommuting, you can work in large urban areas and live in less crowded rural settings. The global village concept extends to education as well. You can take a course to further your education or career from any university in the world that offers distance learning, all from the comfort of you home. This new global village, through the Internet, enables you to be a participant in worldwide events, regardless of location.

The global village has changed how we interact with information. Traditional books are being supplemented by e-books, Web sites, and other electronic sources. McLuhan said reading a book is an individual personal experience. The e-book or Web site (or other electronic medium) becomes a group experience due to the nature of the medium. The information you read is being read by perhaps 100 or 1,000 other individuals at the same time who are physically dispersed around the globe, just as you are.

The global village has in part grown out of a need for socialization. Although it is more personal to interact with individuals face-to-face, career and family needs take a significant amount of time out of our daily lives. Social interaction is an important component of healthy individuals' lives. In today's world, it is normal that both parents have to work to support the family. In one-parent homes, it is difficult to make ends meet with just one job. A parent will often have two or more jobs. Family obligations then take priority once the workday is done. The Internet acts to meet socialization needs. When parents are busy at work, children are home alone until the parents get off work. Children can browse the Internet and take part in chats with friends. After the children are in bed, parents can go online e-mailing or chatting with family and friends. Individuals who live outside a family setting take advantage of the Internet as a social tool as well. Many of these individuals work long hours and haven't the energy or desire to socialize away from home. The Internet meets this socialization need as well by creating a virtual meeting place right in your home.

Since the world is virtually growing smaller, individuals are becoming more aware of issues such as politics and culture. It has become easy and inexpensive to post information and propaganda on a Web site. This has given a voice to politically oriented groups, regardless of cause. People with similar interests gather on the net, creating communities. Communities can be created based on hobby, gender, nationality, or any other preferences. Most often, chats and discussion groups are the preferred means of community interaction within the global village. Culture (cyber, ethnic, and racial) plays an important role on the Internet. Due to its global nature, the Internet has users from many ethnic and racial groups, who form communities based upon their similar interests. Like villages or neighborhoods, cultures form within the Internet. *Cyberculture* is a general term for the subcultures that have developed on the Internet.

The "global village" has changed the world we live in. Although most concepts remain constant, the methods of communication change with advances in technology. In every example given, the Internet has enabled the creation of our modern global village with its specific technology, moral, ethical, and social aspects. Every aspect of the physical village is contained in the global village. Communities form regardless of the physical location or medium, and individuals with similar interests will associate with each other. Books will still be printed, but the medium used by the global village will change the way we use the printed traditional book. Politics contain the same message, but the global village carries the message farther. Culture develops and changes the way we interact with each other both online and off.

The global village has extended our reach. It enables individuals to reach out and participate in world events instantaneously. Our friends are now global. Our education is now global. The (online) communities we are involved in are global. Social interaction has departed from the more personal face-to-face environment to the new cybercommunity. The global village is changing the way we work, learn, communicate, and interact with others. For all the benefits the new village brings, however, there are negative aspects as well. Some say that within the cyberworld, the traditional personal environment is being supplanted with an almost isolationist mentality.

Through the use of real-time multimedia, the Internet will evolve into a more personalized experience. Internet and electronic medium tools will become more intuitive. The Internet will become the facilitator of the global village, the new village nearly every individual on the Earth will interact within. In the future, the global village, created by electronic media, will merge with the traditional village setting, creating a new experience somewhere between the real and virtual.

Computers and Intelligence

Artificial Intelligence (AI) is the science and engineering of making intelligent machines, especially intelligent computer programs. So, how does human intelligence differ from AI? AI is being developed to enable machines to solve problems. The goal in the development of AI isn't to simulate human intelligence; it is to give machines the ability to make their own decisions based on specific criteria. Researchers in AI have suggested that differences in intelligence in humans relate to biochemical and physiological conditions such as speed, short-term memory, and the ability to form accurate and retrievable long-term memories. Modern computers have speed and short-term memory but lack the ability to relate experience to problems. They are unable to compare current problems to past events ("memories" based on experience).

Alan Turing, a mathematician, started researching AI in 1947. By the late 1950s, many scientist were attempting to develop AI systems through a software design approach. Turing developed a test to evaluate intelligence in machines, to see whether a machine could "pass as human" to a knowledgeable observer. He theorized the test could be made with the observer communicating with a computer and a person by teletype (the teletype was prevalent in the 1950s). Essentially, the observer was attempting to discern which was human and which wasn't. Although the "Turing test" was never conducted in full, some test components have been used.

Although some AI researchers' goals are to simulate human intelligence, others feel that machines do not have to be "intelligent" in the same way humans are to be able to make decisions. Using traditional software programming, researchers at IBM developed "Deep Blue." Deep Blue is a computer system that was designed with the intelligence to play chess without human assistance. Many researchers claim the breadth of Deep Blue's knowledge is so narrow that it doesn't really show intelligence since the computer only examines and then responds to chess moves. They claim that Deep Blue doesn't actually understand a chess position. Other AI researchers claim there is an intelligence involved in Deep Blue. How does a human brain work to enable the individual to make a decision? The brain works because each of its billions of neurons carries out hundreds of tiny operations per second, none of which in isolation demonstrates any intelligence at all. As a result of the background computations going on in your brain, the individual is able to complete conscious thoughts, which lead to intelligent decisions. Essentially, although very narrow in scope, Deep Blue computes millions of chess moves, as a background thought, then will determine the best strategic move. Is this process intelligence? The human mind computes, then determines chess moves. The computer mind computes, then determines chess moves. It would seem that there is at least a level of intelligence within Deep Blue.

Epistemology is a branch of philosophy that studies the nature of knowledge, its presuppositions and foundations, and its extent and validity. Cybernetics uses epistemology, theoretically enabling computers to intelligently understand problems and determine decisions. Cybernetics and AI are similar but use different means to theoretically achieve intelligence in computers. AI involves the application in the real world of knowledge stored in a machine, implying that it is essentially a soft-coded, rule-based expert system (programmers give the computer intelligence). Cybernetics, by contrast, has evolved from a "constructivist" perspective. Under this theory, a computer learns from past experience. The computer builds a database of experiences, then correlates these to solve problems. Cybernetics calls for computers to learn, then change their behavior based upon past experience. Although AI has been at the forefront of computer intelligence for the last 50 years, there is currently renewed interest in cybernetics due to limitations in the ability to further develop AI programs.

AI researchers have attempted to bridge the computer intelligence gap by developing new technologies such as "neural nets." NASA is working on developing "fuzzy logic" and "neural net" technology for use with the Mars Technology Program, attempting to create robots that can make human decisions. Fuzzy logic is closer to the way human brains work, and its approach to problems duplicates how a person would make decisions. A neural network is a processing device used for solving problems using a step-by-step

approach, as humans do. This method will allow a robot such as a Mars rover to choose a course on its own, and remember it, without the aid of a remote driver, acting according to logic, not just mechanics.

Many philosophers believe true AI is impossible. Some believe it is immoral. Despite the negative aspects of AI, researchers continue to move forward, attempting to develop a humanlike artificial intelligence. There are many uses for AI, ranging from game playing (such as chess), speech recognition (as in automated telephone systems), to expert systems as well as intelligently guiding and steering vehicles on other planets in our solar system. Researchers are continually working to improve the intelligence of computers and robots.

Computers and the Space Age

Computers have been an integral part of the space program since the National Aeronautics and Space Administration's (NASA) founding in the late 1950s. Today, computers are used in every facet of space exploration. They are used for guidance and navigation functions, such as rendezvous, reentry, and midcourse corrections, as well as for system management functions, data formatting, and attitude control.

Throughout the years, NASA's computing focus for manned space flight has been to take proven technologies and adapt them to space flight. The reliability of proven technologies is of primary importance when working in the manned space flight program. In unmanned programs, NASA has been able to be more innovative and has encouraged innovative new technologies.

There are three types of computer systems NASA uses in the space program: (1) ground-based, (2) unmanned onboard, and (3) manned onboard computer systems. Ground-based systems do the majority of computing, being responsible for takeoffs, orbital attitudes, landings, and so on. Unmanned onboard computers are usually small computers that require little energy and can operate on their own without failure for long periods of time. NASA's Cassini-Huygens mission to Saturn was launched in October of 1997 and arrived in July of 2004. The specialized computer systems on Cassini-Huygens project has worked flawlessly in deep space for over 7 years. Manned onboard systems control all aspects of the manned spacecraft. As in space shuttle missions, once the ground computers at NASA release control of the spacecraft, the onboard computers take control. The shuttle is a very complicated spacecraft. There are literally thousands of sensors and controls spread throughout it. Information from these sensors is fed into the shuttle's computer systems, enabling real-time navigation, communications, course control, maintenance of the living environment, reentry, and many additional functions. There are typically many smaller computer systems on manned spacecraft that are networked together. This allows for real-time processing of massive amounts of data. System reliability is one of the most important features of the onboard computer systems. If a system crashes, the astronauts will lose control of the spacecraft.

The Mercury project was America's first man-in-space effort and took place in the early 1960s. NASA subcontracted the development of the Mercury spacecraft to McDonnell-Douglas. The Mercury capsule itself was designed in a bell shape. The capsule wasn't able to maneuver on its own and was barely large enough for one astronaut to fit into. A ground system computer computed reentry, then transmitted retrofire and firing attitude information to the capsule while in flight. The ground system computer controlled every part of the Mercury mission; therefore, an onboard computer was not necessary.

The first onboard computer systems were developed by IBM for the Gemini project of the late 1960s and early 1970s. The onboard computer was added to provide better reentry accuracy and to automate some of the preflight checkout functions. The computer IBM developed was called the "Gemini Digital Computer." This computer system functioned in six mission phases: prelaunch, ascent backup, insertion, catch-up, rendezvous, and reentry. Due to the limited amount of space on the Gemini capsule, the size of the computer was important. The Gemini Digital Computer was contained in a box measuring 18.9 inches high by 14.5 inches wide by 12.75 inches deep and weighed 58.98 pounds. The components, speed, and type of memory were influenced due to the size limitation of the computer. Gemini VIII was the first mission that used an auxiliary-tape memory. This allowed programs to be stored and then loaded while the spacecraft was in flight.

One of NASA's primary challenges in the early days of space exploration was developing computers that could survive the stress of a rocket launch, operate in the space environment, and provide the ability to perform increasingly ambitious missions.

On May 25, 1961, President John F. Kennedy unveiled the commitment to execute Project Apollo in a speech on "Urgent National Needs."

The Apollo program's goal of sending a man to the moon and returning him safely, before the decade was out, was a lofty and dangerous one. One of the most important systems of the Apollo spacecraft was the onboard guidance and navigation system (G&N). This system played the leading role in landing the lunar module on the moon at precise locations. The G&N performed the basic functions of inertial guidance, attitude reference, and optical navigation and was interrelated mechanically or electrically with the stabilization and control, electrical power, environmental control, telecommunications, and instrumentation systems. The inertial guidance subsystem sensed acceleration and attitude changes instantaneously and provided attitude control and thrust control signals to the stabilization and control system. The optical navigation subsystem "sighted" celestial bodies and landmarks on the moon and Earth, which were used by the computer subsystem to determine the spacecraft's position and velocity and to establish proper alignment of the stable platform.

The computer and astronaut communicated in a number language. Communication was through a device called the "display and keyboard unit" (or "disky," abbreviated to DSKY). This unit was different than modern keyboards and monitors in that it had a 21-digit display and a 19-button keyboard. Two-digit numbers were programs. Five-digit numbers represented data such as position or velocity. The command module had one computer and one DSKY. The computer and one DSKY were located in the lower equipment bay, with the other DSKY on the main console. The Apollo command module and the lunar module had nearly identical computer systems.

The space shuttle has flown 46 shuttle flights since the mid-1980s. The shuttle's computer system has been upgraded through the years and has become very complex. This computer maintains navigation, environmental controls, reentry controls, and other important functions.

Adapted computer hardware and software systems have been developed to support NASA's exploration of our solar system. Autonomous systems that to some extent "think" on their own are important to the success of the Mars rovers Spirit and Opportunity. NASA has also made use of power sources such as nuclear and solar to power spacecraft as they explore

Source: Courtesy of NASA.

adopt this technology, giving them strategic and competitive advantages. The development of Arpanet, the forerunner of the Internet, initiated the Internet's development by connecting remote computers together into one global network. In the late 1970s, Jobs and Wozniak's Apple computer brought computers to each person's desktop, starting the microcomputer revolution. Today, we see computers in all forms. Some computers resemble the first Apple and still sit on the user's desktop, but others are now more portable and can be built into nearly every device, such as personal digital assistants, automobiles, phones, and even kitchen appliances. Each of these computers either does or will eventually have the ability to be connected through a network enabling the user or appliance to communicate with others worldwide.

In the future, we will see computers playing an even greater role in our world. Computers will be even more essential in education and business and will become a necessity in the home, enabling individuals to control functions and the environment within the home. Utilities and "smart appliances" will be connected to a controlling computer. Lights, heating, cooling, security, and many other utilities will be controlled through a central computer by kiosks (displays) located strategically around the home. Entrance may be controlled by the main computer through voice or fingerprint authentication. When a person enters the home, that individual's preference in lighting, temperature, television programming, music, and more will be adjusted accordingly. Appliances will be networked through the Internet. For instance, if you are returning home at night and would like the lights turned on, connect to your home's controlling computer by using your wireless personal digital assistant, which has software that enables you to turn on the lights and increase the temperature. You will also be able to check your appliances and settings remotely. Perhaps you are

the outer edges of our solar system. The computer systems onboard these spacecraft are built to use the least amount of power possible while still remaining functional. Redundant systems, or multiple systems that can perform the same function in case of a system failure, are important in deep-space exploration. Again, reliability and system hardware and software survivability are important, not just to manned spaceflight but also to missions that may last as long as 10 or 15 years.

Without computer technology, NASA would not have been able to achieve its long list of accomplishments. Computers use distributed computer systems that provide guidance and navigation functions, system management functions, data formatting, and attitude control. Without this functionality, it would be impossible to place satellites and astronauts in orbit, explore the Martian landscape, or take photos of Saturn's moons.

Computers and the Future

In the past 60 years, the development of the computer has had a more profound impact on civilization than any other technological advance in history. In the 1940s, development of the computer was spurred on by the technological advantages it gave the military. After World War II, the business world learned to concerned you left the oven on when you left for a business trip; turn your oven off by connecting to it through your personal digital assistant's wireless connection to the Internet. Refrigerators will be able to scan the items within it, then automatically order items over the Internet. You will never run out of milk or butter. Computers, in one variety or another, will inundate the home of the future.

Computers will continue to play an active role in education. It will be even more important in the future to teach our children useful technology skills. Education's role will not only be to teach through the use of computers but also to teach the theory and skills necessary for students to use technology in their personal and professional lives. Just as in the home, computers will be everywhere in the school. The Internet will still be used for research but to a much greater degree than today. Computers will be able to teach complete courses, transforming the teacher into a facilitator rather than a provider of knowledge. In this classroom, the computer may give an initial test determining the students' basic skills, then teach the entire course, using feedback as a learning indicator and customizing each lesson accordingly. Although common today, distance education will continue to grow. The quality of distance education instruction will continue to improve by giving teachers more and better tools with which to teach. These tools will comprise higher Internet bandwidths, the ability to bring higher-quality multimedia (video, audio, and others) to the students' desktop, and software that will create an easy-to-use interactive learning environment. Classrooms will be "wired" in more ways than ever. Computers are providing an ever-increasing knowledge base for students. They will be able to bring simulations to life in a three-dimensional holographic way, enabling students to be active participants in their own learning.

Computers will also continue to play a major role in business. Many of the current business trends will continue and improve, with integrated electronic commerce systems, online bill paying and customer services, improved communications, and telecommuting enabling a mobile workforce and instant access to information such as sales and marketing forecasts. Business will continue to develop and use advanced technologies to build cars more efficiently and to fuel them with inexpensive, nonpolluting fuels. Computers will enable the business professional to stay more connected than ever.

Computers will play an even larger role in the military. The military computer system is essential in the management of warfare. Without the military computer system, missiles will not fire or may miss their targets, navigation systems will not work, intelligence gathering is inhibited, and battlefield supply and maintenance becomes impossible. Computers will "attack" enemy computer systems using viruses, denial of service, and other types of cyberwarfare. Computers from warring nations will attempt to attack civilian sectors as well, such as power plants, financial institutions, and other strategic targets.

Robotics is a developing technology that is currently in its infancy. There is incredible potential for robotics in the future. Robots will assist surgeons because they are more steady and precise. Although robots are being used to explore our solar system today, their role will become more significant and complicated in the future. Robots will be used to clean your home or take you to work, using AI to make humanlike decisions on their own. Robots are currently being used to manufacture items such as automobiles, but given AI, they will also be able to design cars for maximum efficiencies in both production and use. Intelligent robots will also be used for dangerous jobs or on military missions. Currently, technology is not advanced enough and distances in space are too great to be explored by humans. In the more-distant future, robots with AI will be used to colonize planets at the edge of or outside of our solar system.

The science fiction of *Star Trek* may become reality in the future. The U.S. Air Force is investigating teleportation (moving material objects from one location to another using worm holes). Beginning in the 1980s, developments in quantum theory and general relativity physics have succeeded in pushing the envelope in exploring the reality of teleportation. Computers are mandatory in exploring the practicality, possibilities, and application of such new technologies.

The trend toward smaller, faster computers will continue. Currently under early stages of development by IBM and several research partners are "quantum computers." Quantum computers work at the atomic level rather than on a "chip" or "circuit" level, as in computers of today. They will be able to work on a million computations at one time, rather than just one, as current technology allows, increasing computing power and decreasing size requirements dramatically.

Computers in the future will enable Marshal McLuhan's vision of the "Irresistible Dream," already beginning to be realized through the Internet, of connecting all computers in the world into one large network, like a global nervous system. This network will be distributed so that there is not one central location of control. This network will be able to reconfigure itself, solve unanticipated problems, be fault tolerant, and always accessible. Users will be able to access any kind of information almost instantaneously, anywhere, anytime.

The use of computers in our world will continue to grow. For the foreseeable future, we will need faster and smaller computers to satisfy the ever-growing need for computing power, either for research, business, education, or for our own personal use. Computer-aided artificial intelligence will give robots the ability to think and perform tasks for the convenience of humans. One comprehensive global network will allow individuals to connect to the resources of the world. Technologies are currently being developed that will make these visions a reality.

— Shaun Scott

See also **Artificial Intelligence; Globalization**

Further Readings

Caro, D. H. J., Schuler, R. S., & Sethi, A. S. (1987). *Strategic management of technostress in an information society.* Lewiston, NY: Hogrefe.
McLuhan, M. (1964): *Understanding media.* New York: Mentor.
McLuhan, M., & Fiore, Q. (1968): *War and peace in the global village.* New York: Bantam.
Minsky, M. (Ed.). (1968). *Semantic information processing.* Cambridge: MIT Press.

COMPUTER LANGUAGES

Anthropologists who study the field of synthetic anthropology have much to learn from the development of computer languages. While the first major computer language surfaced in 1957, with the development of FORTRAN (FORmula TRANslating System), the entire field owes a great debt to an early 19th-century scientist and mathematician Charles Babbage (1791–1871), known by various sources as the father, grandfather, or godfather of computing. Babbage's "Difference Engine," which was designed to make tabulating figures error free, is the first recorded instance of a computer programming language. There is no doubt that Babbage was a genius, but his lack of diplomacy doomed his invention. Despite the fact that by 1834, Babbage had raised $1 million to build his first version of the Difference Engine, the project stalled when Babbage quarreled with his engineer and failed to maintain political support for the project.

In the mid-1980s, a group of scholars, historians, and computer experts, led by Doron Swade of London's Science Museum, became interested in the idea of building the second version of Babbage's Difference Engine in time to celebrate the anniversary of his 200th birthday. Made up of some 4,000 parts, the machine performed calculations by manual rotation of a mangle-like handle. At a cost of some $500,000, the finished product was 11 feet long, 7 feet tall, and weighed 3 tons. The cost of building the accompanying printer was considered impractical until Microsoft's Nathan Myhrvold promised to underwrite printer costs in exchange for having an identical Difference Engine built in his home in Seattle, Washington.

Initially, computer languages commanded programs to perform particular functions. In Babbage's case, his computer language was directed toward commanding his inventions to perform certain physical motions. An operator was needed to manually shift gears for the Difference Engine to perform additional functions. By 1942, the U.S. government had built the ENIAC computer, which depended on electrical signals rather than a human operator to shift functions, employing principles developed by Babbage over 100 years before. Beginning with the work of John Von Neumann of the Institute for Advanced Study in 1945, the technology behind computer languages advanced so that functions could be used across programs.

Babbage also designed but never built the Analytical Engine, which, according to today's estimates, would have been roughly the size of a locomotive. The Analytical Engine had much in common with computers of the later 20th century, including separate processing and memory units, looping, microcopying, and punch cards.

Founded in 1978, the Charles Babbage Institute (CBI) of the University of Minnesota, named after the computing pioneer, serves as a link between the ever-expanding field of computer technology and the historical celebration of information technology and information processing. In November 2003, with National Science Foundation (NSF) sponsoring, CBI completed the Web-based "Building a Future for Software History," which included a dictionary of software history, an electronic journal on software history, and an oral history project consisting of interviews with pioneers in the field of software history and programming languages.

— Elizabeth Purdy

COMTE, AUGUSTE (1798–1857)

Usually labeled the "founder of sociology and positivism," Auguste Comte was one of the most important 19th-century French philosophers. Born Isidore-Auguste-Marie-François-Xavier Comte on January 19, 1798, in Montpellier, he began life in the chaos of the last years of the French Revolution and spent his life dealing with the problems the revolution had bequeathed.

Sharing the bourgeois values of frugality, routine, and work, Comte's family was profoundly Catholic and counterrevolutionary. Comte had two younger siblings but apparently was no closer to them than he was to his parents. "The correspondence between him and his family members is characterized by constant feuding, demands, reproaches, and slights" (Pickering, 1993, p. 17).

Admitted to the exclusive École Polytechnique in Paris in 1814, he developed a lifelong interest in mathematics. An intellectually superior but rowdy student, Comte was expelled 2 years later.

Living an ascetic life in Paris, Comte studied the writings of Benjamin Franklin and became enamored with the new nation of the United States, where he expected to teach geometry. He also absorbed the works of Montesquieu and Condorcet. The position in the United States never materialized, and instead he went to work for Comte de Saint-Simon as a political journalist. Despite having acquired a mistress, daughter, mentor, and occasional teaching positions that allowed him to write, Comte was often depressed.

Around 1820, Comte began refining his famous concept of the three evolutionary stages of explanation, the theological, metaphysical, and positivist. In 1824, the first signed publication of Comte's signaled his break with the elderly Saint-Simon. About this time Comte became impressed with the German philosophers, especially Johann Gottfried Herder and Immanuel Kant, as well as with the Scottish philosophers.

In 1825, Comte married a strong woman who was not awed by his intelligence. He described his married life as painful, and his writings became rather misogynous. He had a nervous breakdown in 1826 and attempted suicide a year later. His interpretation of his mental problems became incorporated into his three-stage system, and in 1830, he sent the first volume of his magnum opus (often referred to simply as the *Cours*) to the Academy of Sciences.

Comte's mother died in 1837, and he unsuccessfully attempted a reconciliation with his family. His difficulties with his wife and friends continued as he worked on the remaining volumes of the *Cours*. In 1838, he had a second nervous breakdown, but in 1841, he began a remarkable correspondence with John Stuart Mill. Within a few years, Comte was well-known among English intellectuals, and Mill published an influential book on Comte and positivism (1866). He completed the *Cours* in 1842, though his wife left him in the same year.

In 1845, he became emotionally involved with a young woman, who died 16 months later. The last stage of his life has been described as "rapture and absorption in the ideal" (Marvin 1937, p. 43), and nothing of note in positivism came from this period.

Almost always in poor health, constantly in debt, and often dealing with the scandals of his family and his wife's family, Comte died in Paris on September 5, 1857.

— *Robert Lawless*

See also **Positivism**

Further Readings

Marvin, F. S. (1937). *Comte: The founder of sociology.* New York: Wiley.
Pickering, M. (1993). *Auguste Comte: An intellectual biography* (Vol. 1). Cambridge: Cambridge University Press.
Thompson, K. (1975). *Auguste Comte: The foundation of sociology.* New York: Wiley.

CONDORCET, MARQUIS DE (1743–1794)

A member of the radical enlightenment in France, Marie-Jean-Antoine-Nicolas de Caritat Condorcet (b. Ribemont dans l'Aisne, September 17, 1743) believed humanity capable of infinite progress and sought to inject reason into social affairs. Ironically, Condorcet was declared, on March 13, 1794, *hors la loi* (and hence to be executed without trial if apprehended, along with any who aided him). He died of a hemorrhage (Bourg La Reine, March 29, 1794) within a few days of leaving his Paris refuge to protect those who had sheltered him.

Educated at the Jesuit college in Reims and the College of Navarre, where he studied mathematics, he became secretary of the Academy of Sciences in 1777 and was elected to the French Academy in 1782 and the Academy of Sciences in 1789. Condorcet published a biography of Turgot (1786) and Voltaire (1789). When Turgot became Controller General of France in 1774, he appointed Condorcet as Inspector General of the Mint (a post he held until 1791). Condorcet married Sophie de Grouchy, a renowned beauty, in 1786.

Condorcet was a prodigious reader with a superb memory who acquired from working with Turgot a firm belief in economic laissez-faire policies supplemented by state intervention in cases where the market was not developed enough. He knew many of the prominent intellectuals of the age and advocated religious toleration, legal and educational reform, and the abolition of slavery, but his poor rhetorical skills hurt his causes and made him enemies. Condorcet had a major role in writing the first (Girondin) moderate constitution for revolutionary France, but this prejudiced his case when Robespierre and the Jacobins took over.

Condorcet's inveterate optimism showed most explicitly in his last great work, *Esquisse d'un tableau historique des progrès de l'esprit humain* (Sketch of an Historical Canvas of the Progress of the Human Spirit), written while in hiding and largely without a library (1795). Like others, Condorcet imagines humanity progressing from a state of savagery up through a number of stages of civilization. His theme influenced many, including Hegel, but Condorcet's originality lay in his description of a final tenth stage,

M. J.ᴺ A.ᴺ N.ᴺ CONDORCET.

Source: Courtesy of the Library of Congress.

in which inequality between nations and individuals will disappear and human nature will be perfected intellectually, morally, and physically.

Condorcet's most original contribution may in the end have been in mathematics. He wrote several treatises on calculus (1765, 1772, and a manuscript just before his death) but he gained fame in 1785 with his *Essai sur l'application de l'analyse à la probabilité des décisions rendues à la pluralité des voix* (An Essay on the Application of Probability Theory to Majority Decisions), which radically clarified the mathematics of voting. He was one of the first to point out that preferences of pluralities are not transitive (a plurality may prefer A to B, B to C, and C to A). He developed what has been called a "Condorcet criterion" for winning, in which the result satisfies the criterion that the majority would prefer the winner to any other single candidate. Condorcet demonstrated the mathematical advantages of what has come to be known as a ranked-pairs method of determining a winner from binary preferences (for example, 9 of 11 prefer A to B), by progressively accepting preferences from greatest plurality to least if and only if they do not entail an inconsistency with those preferences already accepted.

— *Thomas K. Park*

Further Readings

Condorcet, Marquis de (1979). *Sketch for a historical picture of the progress of the human mind* (J. Barraclough, Trans.). Westport, CT: Greenwood Press. (Original work published 1794)

 ## CONFIGURATIONISM

Most often associated with the work of Ruth Benedict (1887–1948), configurationism focuses on understanding phenomena as organized wholes rather than as aggregates of distinct parts. A reaction to European diffusionism, which dealt with isolated traits, configurationism instead stressed the integration of traits with the other elements of culture. Benedict best expressed this approach in her immensely popular book *Patterns of Culture* (1934), which focused on a comparison of three peoples: the Zuñi of New Mexico, the Kwakiutl of Vancouver Island, and the Dobuans of Melanesia. As Benedict (1934) stated, "The basic contrast between the Pueblos and the other cultures of North America is the contrast that is named and described by [Friedrich] Nietzsche in his studies of Greek tragedy" (p. 78), that is, Apollonian (harmonious and restrained) and Dionysian (megalomanic and unrestrained). While Greek tragedy had both, some Native American cultures, according to Benedict, focused on one or the other.

For example, in their search for supernatural power, the dionysian Kwakiutls (and Plains Native Americans) induced visionary experiences by individualized fasting, self-torture, and the use of drugs, while the apollonian Zuñi (and other Pueblo Native Americans) harmoniously grouped together and recited by rote an extensive ritual, numbing their minds and allowing the supernatural to take over. The Dobuans were paranoid, secretive, and treacherous. In each case, all beliefs, behaviors, and cultural institutions were shaped and interrelated by the one dominant configuration.

Benedict (1934) clearly thought that cultures could be adequately described by psychological terms and that "a culture, like an individual, is a more or less consistent pattern of thought and action" (p. 46). Although she traced her intellectual ancestry to the psychologist Wilhelm Dilthey and the historian Oswald Spengler, Franz Boas was her mentor, and she dwelt on Boasian themes of cultural determinism and cultural relativism.

Echoing the appraisal of many anthropologists, H. Sidky stated (2004), "What Benedict provided in her *Patterns of Culture* was description, not explanation" (p. 156). Her scholarship was more humanistic than scientific, idiographic rather than nomothetic. Benedict (1934) explicitly accepted the circular argument that cultures are different because they are different when she approvingly quoted a "chief of the Digger Indians" saying, "God gave to every people a cup . . . but their cups were different" (pp. 21–22). She apparently drew no causal connections among ecology, subsistence, and culture. The unkindest reading of Benedict is that her writings are an obfuscation and elaboration of stereotypes springing from a folk model. And her work did, indeed, create an industry of anthropologists and journalists traipsing off to New Mexico to find drunken Indians and off to British Columbia to find somber ones.

Beautifully written (Benedict was an accomplished poet), *Patterns of Culture* is probably the most widely read book in anthropology. Translated into more than a dozen languages, it is still in print. As Alan Barnard (2000) has pointed out, "Her premise that culture determines both what is regarded as correct behaviour and what is regarded as a normal psychological state, remains one of the strongest assertions of relativism in anthropology" (p. 104). And *Patterns of Culture* did introduce the anthropological concept of culture to the lay public.

— *Robert Lawless*

See also **Benedict, Ruth; Culture, Characteristics of; Kwakiutls; Zuni Indians**

Further Readings

Barnard, A. (2000.) *History and theory in anthropology.* Cambridge: Cambridge University Press.

Benedict, R. (1934). *Patterns of culture.* Boston: Houghton Mifflin.

Mead, M. (1959). *An anthropologist at work: Writings of Ruth Benedict.* Boston: Houghton Mifflin.

Mead, M. (1974). *Ruth Benedict.* New York: Columbia University Press.

Modell, J. S. (1983). *Ruth Benedict: Patterns of a life.* Philadelphia: University of Pennsylvania Press.

Sidky, H. (2004). *Perspectives on culture: A critical introduction to theory in cultural anthropology.* Upper Saddle River, NJ: Pearson Prentice Hall.

 CONFLICT

Conflict involves antagonistic relations of ideas, interests, and persons. It occurs at different levels, including internal, interpersonal, small groups, large-scale sectors, organizations (such as states), and broad social principles. Furthermore, conflict takes many forms, from sullen silence to verbal debate, from interpersonal violence to organized warfare. Important forms of conflict are tacit rather than open, involving differences in concepts and interests buried in the flow of social life. Paying attention to these distinctions is important, for a typical and troubling confusion is explaining organized violence, such as warfare, as a simple extension of interpersonal aggression without attention to the different causes, scales, and activities involved. Anthropology, with its wide comparative scope, is suited to distinguishing among kinds of conflict and exploring each one as part of a complex whole.

Conflict and consensus form a principal axis of theories in the social sciences. Conflict theories explore patterned conflict forming the architecture of social relations. Some conflict theories stress individual actors engaged in competition and maneuvering, out of which social patterns emerge; market and transaction models are typical ones. Other conflict theories emphasize broad social groups acting on profoundly different interests and ideals; Marxist class struggle models exemplify these. Consensus theories, on the other hand, emphasize shared ideas and interests, resulting in coordinated social activity. Social functionalist and cultural pattern approaches are major consensus theories in anthropology. Conflict and consensus are not, however, mutually exclusive—a good example being the enormous level of coordination required for large-scale warfare—and key conflict theories draw on consensual phenomena, and vice versa.

Humans have a biological capacity for conflict, including vertical relations of domination and resistance and horizontal relations of rivalry, broadly shared with other primates. There are important elements of antagonism within the most intimate of relationships, such as between mates or parents and children. But these conflicts are arranged, expressed, and suppressed in highly varied ways, and models that attribute to humans a singular drive to dominance, for example, miss the remarkable flexibility that characterizes the human adaptation. One of the richest—if most debated—biosocial case studies of conflict concerns ritualized violent fighting and extensive intervillage raiding among the Yanomami peoples of the Guinea Highlands of South America. Napoleon Chagnon argues that increased mating and thus reproductive fitness drives violence among men. Others dispute this biosocial interpretation, however. Marvin Harris emphasized group-level conflicts over scarce protein in the rain forest, while Brian Ferguson questioned the context of the ethnographic evidence, pointing to the direct and indirect effects of frontiers of state-level societies on "tribal" peoples. Also, other ethnographers of small-scale societies, such as Robert Dentan, documented alternative cases in which public expression of conflict (especially violence) is highly repressed.

Indeed, the flexible human relation to conflict is most evident in the widespread mechanisms designed to avoid or attenuate it. These include the recourse of splitting groups rather than fighting, and the extensive networks of gift friendships and marriages, which Claude Lévi-Strauss suggested was instrumental in the emergence of human culture. Classic consensus theories, such as British structural functionalism, often found their evidence in mechanisms for resolving public disputes, but otherwise they ignored open and suppressed conflicts. Developed as a reaction to structural functionalism, the Manchester school explored conflict theory approaches to social structure. Their "extended case" method started with an open-conflict situation and traced outward the connections, group alignments, and ideas surrounding the specific case. Max Gluckman argued for a cyclical view, in which rituals first opened up and then reunified social cleavages (for example, between women and men), but his students explored transformative conflicts, such as the struggles against colonialism and racial hierarchy in southern Africa. An important analytical transition thus took place: from conflict as needing control within an overall emphasis on static culture/society to conflict as a basis for the construction and reconstruction of society/culture over time.

Source: © Photo provided by www.downtheroad.org, The Ongoing Global Bicycle Adventure.

War and class relations are two of the main grounds for the social scientific study of conflict. Although it is heavily debated, many anthropologists today reserve "war" for organized violence in stratified societies and thus distinguish it from general aggression and interpersonal violence (such as inter-village raiding). The question then becomes: What is the social context for war? War sometimes (but not always) involves strategic geography and control over resources, but its most fundamental association seems to be with centralization of political power. For example, the modern democratic nation-state, including its key status of "citizen," comes into being (in part) through taxation for and recruitment of mass militaries.

Class relations are part of a set of conflicts based on differentiated and unequal social relations (gender is another one, though it involves different dynamics). Karl Marx saw class struggles as the driving force of social arrangement and change over time. But his notion of struggle was inherent in the unequal nature of the relationship and only periodically emerged in open conflicts, such as revolution (also, Marx saw conflict not just as a matter to be resolved, but as a driving force of change to new relationships). To anthropologists, orthodox Marxism has serious flaws, such as an insufficiently cultural conceptualization of interests and social groups, but neo-Marxist social science provides us important insights into conflict.

James Greenberg, for example, delineates alternative explanations of violent feuding in indigenous rural Mexico, concluding that it principally stemmed from struggles over different concepts of the morality of capitalist accumulation and exchange upon the advent of commercial coffee production. James Scott likewise explores conflicts beneath the seemingly placid surface of Malaysian village life. Rural class relations were undergoing rapid change, due to new varieties of rice and mechanization of former hand labor jobs (the "green revolution"). Poor peasants could not afford to rebel openly, but they struggled against rich peasants and landlords in subtle ways—insults, gossip, malingering, feigned incompetence, theft, and petty vandalism—what Scott memorably terms "weapons of the weak." In each case, a level of normality and consensus reigned on the surface, and the analytical task was to show the hidden cleavages and struggles in a process of fundamental social change.

— *Josiah McC. Heyman*

See also **Aggression; War, Anthropology of**

Further Readings

Greenberg, J. B. (1989). *Blood ties: Life and violence in rural Mexico.* Tucson: University of Arizona Press.

Haas, J. (Ed.). (1990). *The anthropology of war.* Cambridge: Cambridge University Press.

Vincent, J. (1990). *Anthropology and politics: Visions, traditions, and trends.* Tucson: University of Arizona Press.

CONFUCIANISM

Confucianism is a Chinese system of thought that originated with the teachings of *Kong Fuzi*. Literally "Master Kong" and latinized as "Confucius," *Kong Fuzi* is an honorific for *Kong Qiu* (alias *Zhongni*, 552–479 BC), who served in minor official posts during his lifetime. Confucianism is philosophical as well as spiritual. Historically, its rise paralleled that of the Western philosophical tradition represented by Socrates, Plato, and Aristotle. Since its ascent to the status of state orthodoxy during the Former Han Dynasty (206 BC–AD 8), Confucianism has molded the spirit of Chinese civilization.

What is known as Confucianism actually grew out of contributions from both Confucius and his major followers, such as Mencius (ca. 371–289 BC) and Xunzi (ca. 313–230 BC). The basic Confucian canon consists of two parts. One contains the "Four Books," including the *Analects*, the *Mencius*, the *Great Learning*, and the *Doctrine of the Mean*. The other part contains the "Five Classics," including the *Book of Changes*, the *Book of History*, the *Book of Odes*, the *Spring and Autumn Annals*, and the *Book of Rites*. There is general consensus that the *Analects* is probably the only reliable source of teachings delivered verbatim by Confucius himself.

Philosophical Tradition

Confucian thought is humanistic and rational. It maintains that everyone has the mental and moral potential to fully realize themselves in the fulfillment of their social roles and that the world can be understood through the use of human reason alone. This is why Confucius sought to promote "education without class" and is remembered as the "greatest teacher of all time" in China. If Confucius implied only that human nature was good, Mencius took it a step further to declare that man was equipped with innate knowledge and ability to do good. In contrast to Mencius's Idealistic Confucianism, Xunzi adopted a position known as Realistic Confucianism, and he argued that humans were born selfish and asocial. Nevertheless, both believed in the perfectibility of all humans through education.

At the heart of the Confucian intellectual tradition is a social, political philosophy that centers on "government by virtue." To govern is to correct. Confucius compared two different ways to achieve this end: government by regulations and punishments versus government by moral examples and persuasion. His conclusion was that there would be shameless evasions under the former, but shame and correctness under the latter. Government by virtue was one of benevolence. Three tenets figure large in its building: self-cultivation, rectification of names, and the *Doctrine of the Mean*.

Self-Cultivation

Benevolence, or *ren*, was central to Confucian morality, which also included such virtues as righteousness, loyalty, filial piety, fraternal love, devotion, courtesy, and so on. Self-cultivation involved engaging in an unwavering pursuit of virtues, practicing industry and hard work, and exercising control over desires and emotions. Asceticism was a necessary ingredient of self-cultivation, and not everyone could go through the arduous journey to complete moral perfection and become a *junzi*, or profound person. In Confucian political thought, it was the privileged responsibility of the profound person to assume a position of leadership and render public service to society. Behind the Confucian stress on self-cultivation was a moral idealism that identified the cultivation of virtues with ideal statesmanship. Not only did this moral idealism advocate a political elitism, but it also linked Confucianism to the state through the civil service examinations that were based on Confucian texts.

The moral examples set by the profound person were expected to include the practice of *li*, literally "rites," and the adherence to the *Dao*, literally "Way." People became truly human as their raw impulse was shaped by *li*. Used this way, the meaning of *li* extended beyond "rites" to denote the "rules of propriety" that were generated by the entire body of tradition and convention. The Master believed that the practice of *li* was instrumental in promoting conformity to proper moral values and social behavior and bringing about a civilized society. In fact, the content of benevolence was often defined in terms of ritual behavior; it was in association with *li* that Confucius gave the golden rule: "Do not do to others what you do not want them to do to you." As for the *Dao*, it was the path that led from human nature in the raw to human nature fulfilled. The Way was knowable by the human mind. But adhering to it called for a tenacious commitment to lofty goals, and people could use a role model from the profound person.

Rectification of Names

To rectify names was to specify moral obligations and behavioral codes for people in various social roles, that is, "names." Confucius identified three most basic bonds of society in the ruler-subject, father-son, and husband-wife relationships. Two more social relationships, namely, elder brother–younger brother and friend-friend, were added to the foregoing "Three Bonds" to yield the "Five Cardinal Relations." Modeling after the traditional Chinese family system, reciprocal obligations and behaviors were specified for each set of relations. However, there was an asymmetry of status, with authority assigned to the first party in each set of relations except that of friend-friend.

The exercise of authority was dependent on the fulfillment of responsibilities, a principle that applied to ruler as well as father, husband, and elder brother. Failure to fulfill their responsibilities nullified the obligation of allegiance by subject, son, wife, and younger brother. The Son of Heaven, for instance, must rule virtuously or risk the loss of his Mandate of Heaven. Confucian thought provided no formal checks against the abuse of power by the government. Rather, the exercise of power by the government rested on the consent of the governed. The rectification of names served to sanction a social hierarchy in moral terms and to institutionalize its behavioral code through state sponsorship. With this, Confucius hoped to see the prevalence of social stability that he had envisioned for an ideal society.

The *Doctrine of the Mean*

The ultimate justification for self-cultivation and the rectification of names consists in the *Doctrine of the Mean,* a tenet that relates moral behavior and good government to the Way of Heaven. The Chinese for this tenet is *zhong yong,* where *zhong* means "centrality," and *yong* denotes "universality" or "commonality." Instead of conjoining to teach moderation and balance, as in the *Analects,* they represent a doctrine expounding what is central in the cultivation of virtuous behavior and how it harmonizes with the universe. The *Doctrine of the Mean* begins as follows:

What Heaven imparts to the humankind is called human nature. To follow human nature is called the Way. Cultivating the Way is called teaching. The Way cannot be separated from us for a moment. What can be separated from us is not the Way. Therefore the profound person is cautious over what one does not see and apprehensive over what one does not hear.

The Human Way, which originated in Heaven, is inherent in the nature of everyone. Since there is a unity of the Heavenly Way and the Human Way, a natural way, as is preached by Daoism in separation from humanity, is not the Confucian Way. Exemplifying the Confucian personality, the profound person is watchful of the process whereby his inner humanity is to be manifested as the Way. It is a process of increasing self-knowledge that gives one an acute awareness of imperfection until the full discovery of one's inner self. In addition to the centrality of its role in the discovery process, self-knowledge must be realized in a state of mind that transcends emotions and desires in pursuit of self-realization. Ultimately, the centrality of self-knowledge is defined in transcendental terms.

As the self-knowledge of the profound person is employed to guide society, moral behavior becomes a way of life. People are ruled by persuasion, ethical examples are followed, the family system is maintained, and rites and rituals are practiced in honor of the social hierarchy and behavioral codes. In short, the universal values of humanity are translated into common, prevalent behavior. Among them are benevolence and justice, which are built into the government system, and filial piety and ancestor worship, which are accepted as the basis of the fundamental human relatedness. In this idealized fiduciary community, there is affection between father and son, righteousness between ruler and minister, separate functions between husband and wife, proper order between the old and young, and faithfulness between friends. Such is the Human Way, which reflects human nature, harmonizes with the Heavenly Way, and is universally true.

What brings humans and Heaven together is *cheng,* meaning "sincerity" or strong commitment in the cultivation of self-knowledge and self-realization. But in the *Doctrine of the Mean,* the notion of *cheng* goes far beyond a state of mind. A lengthy discussion takes it on a ride of ever-deepening subjectivity to denote a metaphysical force that changes and transforms things in addition to facilitating human perfection. As this metaphysical force works for the realization of both humans and all things, moral order and cosmic order are literally two in one. In both cases, *cheng* marks the beginning and end of the quest for Heavenly truth and is used as the idiom of ultimate reality. With this, *cheng* becomes a counterpart of the omnipotent principle of Daoism: the Way.

Neo-Confucianism

The *Doctrine of the Mean* has a twin, namely, the *Great Learning*, which discusses the steps of self-cultivation within an overarching framework of scholarship, moral perfection, and fulfillment of social obligations. Originally two chapters in the *Book of Rites*, they were selected by Zhu Xi (1130–1200), the leading scholar of neo-Confucianism, as two of the "Four Books" that would become the basic texts for civil service examinations between 1313 and 1905. Neo-Confucianism was a response to the growing popularity of Buddhism and Daoism of the time. It started to gather momentum in the second half of the 11th century, when neo-Confucianism received formative impact from a conscious appeal to mysticism, on one hand, and a rationalistic reinterpretation of Idealistic Confucianism, on the other.

Classic Confucianism has a simple tripartite cosmology of Heaven, Earth, and Humans. In the drive to revitalize classic Confucianism, efforts were made to enable it to address the fundamental problems of human life, for which people had turned to Buddhism or Daoism. Out of these efforts grew the neo-Confucian metaphysics, which gave new life to the explanatory power of the Confucian cosmology. It recognized *qi*, or "cosmic energy," as a material force in the universe, which was solely responsible for the existence of reality. Mistakenly called "nonbeing" by the Daoists, *qi* gave form to all being and was in a constant state of change. Clearly the development of this metaphysics was indebted to Daoism and Buddhism. But its purpose was purely Confucian, that is, to reaffirm the reality of human existence and provide a metaphysical basis for the teaching of Confucian ethics in rejection of Daoism and Buddhism.

Parallel to the concept of *qi* is the tenet of *li*, or "principle." Principle is that which informs *qi* in the creation of everything. As such, it comprises the eternal laws of creation and manifests itself in the products of *qi*. Both *qi* and *li* have their roots in the Great Ultimate *(taiji)*, the source of all being, which also exists in every individual. This doctrine is named the "Cheng-Zhu School of Principle," in recognition of the contributions from both Cheng Yi (1033–1107) and Zhu Xi (1130–1200). Following Mencius's idealistic interpretation of human nature, they agreed that humans were born good. Nevertheless, the material endowment from *qi* varied from individual to individual, causing differential obstruction to the manifestation of one's true nature. By cultivating moral attitudes, however, everyone could overcome the limitations of material endowment to attain the enlightenment of a sage.

As a principal method for self-realization, Zhu Xi proposed the "investigation of things." The observation and discovery of principles inherent in things would lead one to conform to them. Intellectual and rationalistic, this approach reinforced the Confucian emphasis on learning and scholarship. Not only was Zhu Xi the most influential neo-Confucian, but he was also the most brilliant synthesizer of his time. He grouped the "Four Books" and wrote commentaries on each of them. His extensive exegesis on Confucian teachings is highly regarded for its rational approach, which gave Confucianism new meaning, and for its conscientious adherence to orthodox Confucian thought. Zhu Xi has profoundly impacted Chinese thought as well as the thought of Korea and Japan.

Spiritual Tradition

There is a strong spiritual component in Confucian thought. This is because what is moral is also spiritual in the Confucian quest of self-realization. The *Mencius* has a famous saying that describes this grueling journey:

> When Heaven is about to confer a great responsibility on any man, it will exercise his mind with suffering, subject his sinews and bones to hard work, expose his body to hunger, put him to poverty, place obstacles in the paths of his deeds, so as to stimulate his mind, harden his nature, and improve wherever he is impotent.

The description is meant to summarize the making of a profound person or sage. It is important to note that according to Idealistic Confucianism, Heaven is not external to the individual, but abides in everyone's human nature. So Mencius is virtually describing an internal process. Indeed, contrary to the idea that Confucian moral values are just social, they are really the manifestation of a spiritual quest in the first place. One does what one's conscience commands one to do, and the value realized is entirely internal to one's conscience. It follows that this value is primarily spiritual.

To the extent that self-realization is spiritual, it is also transcendental. Confucius compared the experience to meeting Duke Zhou, an ancient sage, and to fathoming the Mandate of Heaven. The soul-searching led him to believe that there had existed an ideal ancient era against which contemporary realities could be judged. It was his mission to restore the ideals of that golden age. In the process, Confucius went over the old to find the new. But he claimed to be a messenger rather than a creator, implying that the ideals had crystallized to him from conformity to the Way of Heaven. Confucian transcendence is anchored in the awe of Heaven. Despite the Master's reluctance to talk about supernatural beings and forces, he seemed to acknowledge an interaction between humans and a higher order. Thus, he conceded that the ruler was governing on the Mandate of Heaven. To the disappointment of the Master, his sociopolitical ideology failed to win official sponsorship in his lifetime. Sadly, Confucius attributed it to a lack of good timing ordained by Heaven.

After Confucianism came to dominate the system of social values in China, it replaced the ethical function of religion. Confucius was officially elevated to the status of patron saint for the literati. In AD 630, the emperor of the Tang Dynasty (618–907) decreed that all prefectures and districts build Confucian temples in order for the local scholar-officials and scholar-gentry to offer sacrifices to the Master. With the rise of neo-Confucianism during the Song Dynasty (960–1279), the spirituality of Confucian thought was further mystified. The metaphysics of *qi* played an important role in this process and so did the theory of the mind developed by Wang Yangming (1472–1529), a prominent neo-Confucian thinker whose influence was second only to that of Zhu Xi. To Wang, neither principle nor things are external to the mind. To discover principle is to rectify the mind by eliminating from it what is incorrect. As the mind essentially means the will, sincerity of the mind is more crucial than the investigation of things. Under the impact of Wang's idealism, meditation increasingly became a standard practice in the neo-Confucian

quest of self-realization, and spiritual enlightenment was sought after.

When Confucianism is juxtaposed with Buddhism and Daoism as the "Three Teachings," it reads *rujiao*, meaning "literati religion." But scholarly disagreement has persisted over whether Confucianism is a religion. On one hand, Confucianism has functioned as a belief system that assigns meaning to life, provides an ethics-based order for society, has sacred space and time, and inspires a sense of religious awe, albeit to different degrees over time. In view of all this, Confucianism is characteristically an ethico-religious tradition. On the other hand, Confucius is typically worshipped as a sage rather than a deity; his moral concerns have a clear "this-worldly" orientation, and his teachings, stripped of the ideological impositions by the ruling class and elite, are primarily philosophical.

Challenges to the Confucian Tradition

Confucian thought has been constitutive of Chinese mores and ethos for over 2,000 years. The vicissitudes of Confucianism in dynastic China show that its moral idealism was vulnerable to disillusionment in times of protracted warfare, national disunity, or invasion from without. But once social order was restored, Confucianism was put back on the pedestal again. This pattern ground to a stop in modern times, when Confucianism had to face challenges from the Western ideology that called its fundamental rationale into question, as in China after the overthrow of the Qing monarchy (1688–1911), in Japan during the Meiji Reforms (1867–1912), and in Korea at the end of the Choson Dynasty (1392–1910).

Modern critics of Confucianism found a loud-and-clear voice in the May Fourth Movement of 1919, a patriotic student campaign that, in protesting against an imminent sellout of national interest, deepened its critical spirit to press for an intellectual modernization of China. Briefly, the root cause of China's backwardness was believed to lie in Confucianism, which dictated blind obedience to authority, promoted servile adherence to the status quo, and provided unconscionable justifications for social inequality and injustice, especially through the Confucian family system. China was badly in need of reinvigorating itself with assistance from "Mr. Democracy" and "Mr. Science," but the authoritarian and conservative nature of Confucian institutions stifled the quest of freedom, individualism, and originality.

"Down with Confucius and Sons!" became a new battle cry of the May Fourth Movement. What some of its leaders wanted, however, was a total rejection of China's past in favor of wholesale Westernization.

After the Chinese communists came into power in 1949, a new round of attacks was mounted on Confucian thought. But these assaults were engineered by an ideology that was critical of Western freedom and democracy as much as of Confucian "benevolence" and "self-cultivation." Confucius was denounced publicly, and Confucian values were declared decadent for fear that they would undermine "socialist ethics." The anti-Confucian mentality culminated during the "Cultural Revolution" (1966–1976), when a violent, destructive vendetta was unleashed against any "remnants," real or suspected, of Confucianism. It was not until the mid-1990s that the Chinese Communist Party started to retreat from its radical iconoclasm and attempted to reclaim the right to speak for China's Confucian heritage.

The rise of industrial East Asia has directed attention to the role of Confucian heritage in modernization. For many researchers, the point of entry is culture as an integral part of economic dynamics. Known as the "Sinic World," East Asia evidences a pervasive influence of Confucian values. Japan and the Four Mini-Dragons (South Korea, Taiwan, Hong Kong, and Singapore) are all situated in this cultural universe. A number of Confucian factors have been proposed in connection with the successful transformation of East Asia: strong government with moral authority, the centrality of the family in capital formation, power politics and moral education, the scholar-official mentality that makes the best minds available for public leadership, duty consciousness, encouragement of learning, good work ethic, and so on.

Explanations have been attempted for the retention of Confucian values in the modernization of East Asia. According to one explanation, Confucianism has a critical spirit and the potential to transform itself, as in its promotion of social reforms by neo-Confucian scholars Wang Anshi (1021–1088) and Kang Youwei (1858–1927). In the East Asian drive toward modernization, Confucian thought has reemerged as a "humanistic rationalism." Another explanation identifies three components in Confucian thought: philosophical insight, political ideology, and popular values. It argues that the first component may prove useful in bridging the philosophical gap between the East and the West, the second must be discarded, and the third is very much alive in the East Asian experience of modernization. A third explanation stresses that modernization in East Asia entails the mobilization of local resources, including the Confucian tradition. As this tradition impedes, facilitates, and guides the process of modernization, it is also being rejected, revitalized, and fundamentally restructured. But there is tradition in modernization, and it is time to redefine modernization in light of its successes outside of the West.

Ethnography on modern China has contributed significantly to the awareness that there is dynamic interaction between the Confucian tradition and modernization. More specifically, it is instrumental in revealing the contemporary metamorphosis of traditional familism in kinship and descent, marriage and gender roles, household economy, economic reforms, lineage organization, local politics, migration, corporate property, resource management, and so on. Since the Confucian tradition happens to hold out most tenaciously in these areas, ethnographic findings are invaluable for the study of its dynamic articulation with modernization. But such findings are possible only if the field researcher rises above the thinking that the Confucian tradition is just a thing of the past.

— *Zhiming Zhao*

See also **Buddhism; Daoism**

Further Readings

Chan, W.-T. (1963). *A source book in Chinese philosophy.* Princeton, NJ: Princeton University Press.

de Bary, W. T., Chan, W.-T., & Watson, B. (1960). *Sources of Chinese tradition.* New York: Columbia University Press.

Fingarette, H. (1972). *Confucianism: The secular as sacred.* New York: Harper & Row.

Jochim, C. (1986). *Chinese religions: A cultural perspective.* Englewood Cliffs, NJ: Prentice Hall.

Tu, W.-M. (1996). *Confucian traditions in East Asian modernity.* Cambridge, MA: Harvard University Press.

Wright, A. F. (1965). *Confucianism and Chinese civilization.* New York: Atheneum.

Yang, C. K. (1961). *Religion in Chinese society.* Berkeley: University of California.

CONSCIOUSNESS

Consciousness in a very general sense is thought to be merely the state of awareness. However, the definition of what consciousness *is* has received numerous contributions from many different fields of study. For example, psychology, psychiatry, neurophysiology, anthropology, behavioral science, and a new field called "cognitive science," which is the study of the nature of various mental tasks and the processes that enable them to be performed, all have donated some variation to the growing definition of what consciousness is.

A steadfast definition of *consciousness* is that it is the totality of our awareness of bodily sensations, perceptions, emotions, thoughts, and recollections at a particular moment of time. This tends to be considered more of a psychological definition of what consciousness is. However, a biological definition, which has been subdivided by Gerald Edelman into what is called "primary consciousness" and "higher-order consciousness," displays a difference in degrees of consciousness.

Primary consciousness is thought to be the state of being mentally aware of things in the world, of having mental images in the present, but is not accompanied by any sense of a person with a past or future tense. This type of consciousness is thought to be possessed by animals that are nonlinguistic and nonsemantic; it is referred to as "creature consciousness."

Higher-order consciousness is different from primary consciousness in that it involves the actual recognition of an individual's own actions or affections (i.e., we are conscious of being conscious). It also embodies a model of the personal and of the past and the future as well as the present; this is also known as "mental state consciousness." In addition, higher-order consciousness exhibits direct awareness, the noninferential or immediate awareness of mental episodes without the involvement of sense organs or receptors. According to Edelman, it is believed that humans possess both primary and higher-order consciousness and that the two coexist and couple the actions of each other.

Throughout the ages, there have always been "theories of consciousness" addressing who or what possesses consciousness. The "anthropistic theory" holds that consciousness is peculiar only to man; this is philosophically the opinion that Descartes upheld.

Another theory known as the "neurological theory" or the "Darwinian theory" holds that consciousness is a result of "progressive evolution" (i.e., the centralization of the nervous system) and is therefore possessed only by man and higher mammals with this anatomical tendency.

Some theories hold that all animals, but not insects, plants, or other life forms, possess consciousness. This is known as the "animal theory." Animal consciousness at the present is loosely defined. The reason for this is most likely because when the concept of animal consciousness is addressed, the following two questions remain unanswered: How can we definitively know which animals, besides humans, possess consciousness (this is known as "the distribution question")? Is it possible for humans to understand what the conscious experience of other animals is like (this is known as "the phenomenological question")? Also, due to the many varieties of species, it would be difficult to differentiate the different types of consciousness that may exist.

The "biologic theory" is another definition that is more liberal and holds that all organisms inherently possess consciousness. A more extreme extension of the biologic theory is the "cellular theory," which believes that consciousness is a vital property of every cell. The final type of theory holds that consciousness is an elementary property of all atoms; this is known as the "atomistic theory." Philosophically, the atomistic theory could imply that each molecule of DNA (which is composed of atoms) may be conscious in a way that is not known to us, and may in fact exert a will of its own. Thus, it is conceivable that "DNA consciousness" may exist. Perhaps this could have been the driving force behind evolution. Of course, each of these three theories is conceivable; however, they all hold a burden of proof and lack an experimental model for evaluation, in addition to our lack of technology to explore these possibilities.

New questions regarding consciousness tend to focus more on an empirical description of the conscious experience and what it is. The most well-known philosophical theory is "Cartesian dualism," which was proposed by Descartes. This model proposes that things in the physical world occur in an extended form in the brain but are then somehow condensed into a nonextended form where thought occurs. This allows for a type of indirect perception due to sense organs and proposes that there is an extended model of the sights and sounds of the physical world in the brain and this model in the brain is then somehow condensed into a nonextended place where thoughts happen (which is nonmaterial). Therefore, Cartesian dualism proposes that thought, which is nonmaterial, is different from the physical world, which is material, and the two coexist together.

Another theory known as "naive realism," unlike Cartesian dualism, does not distinguish between the mental experience and the physical world. It upholds that an individual's perception is identical to the physical objects that are perceived. However, this is unlikely to be fully acceptable, because it is known physiologically that our special senses—eyes, ears, and tongue, for example—receive input that is deciphered by the brain. Therefore, we experience a neurochemical copy or stimulus of those physical objects, and our brain interprets what that sensory information means neurologically and perceptually.

Another notion is known as "epiphenomenalism," which is a theory that proposes that there may in fact exist a geometric form in the brain (called a "ghost in the machine") that is not considered a direct physical part of the processes in the brain and is only involved in the experience of the things arranged in space. Epiphenomenalists also uphold that there is little conscious involvement in any of the processes occurring in the body or the brain and that all aspects of consciousness regarding events and decisions occur after they have happened. Therefore, epiphenomenalism is a form of dualism that regards mental happenings as a nonphysical phenomenon, which occurs in the physical world but cannot have a direct effect upon it.

The evolution of consciousness, which would mostly likely be defined as a progression from a basic or primary form of consciousness to a higher-order form of consciousness, is inherently dependent on changes in neuroanatomy and physiology. Studies of the human skull have implicated a gross transformation of brain distribution during the course of evolution. It is observed that in *Australopithecines,* there is a much larger occipital region of the brain and a smaller frontal region, as compared to the skulls of modern *Homo sapiens,* which possess a markedly smaller occipital region and a larger frontal region.

This is significant because the frontal lobes of the brain are involved with more higher-cognitive and executive functions (for example, planning and social behavior). An increase in the frontal lobe region would imply a higher-order form of consciousness. Larger and more complicated brains with larger frontal lobes would have provided the neuroanatomy and physiology for a more complicated form of consciousness. In addition, these changes in neuroanatomy, in accordance with changes in degrees of consciousness, support the notion that consciousness has the potential to evolve.

One question that arises is: What caused these changes in early hominid neuroanatomy and physiology? One hypothesis is that the drive to support cortical expansion was fueled by an increased demand for more complicated social behavior. The cooperative behavior and socialization of early hominids provided many benefits (for example, communication could have provided easier access to food). Increased access to better food would, in turn, provide adequate nutrients to support the metabolism of a larger and more complicated brain. The access to better food is an important concept, because even though a larger frontal lobe can provide significant advantages, it comes at an absorbent metabolic cost. Therefore, the increased demand for social behavior to acquire access to better food could have provided the drive for these changes in neuroanatomy and physiology.

This biological "trade-off" for a bigger brain can be seen today in many animals by comparing the size of their brains versus the food source and length of the gastrointestinal tract required to digest that food source. For example, animals that procure easily obtained foods, such as leaves, have smaller brains and a much longer gastrointestinal tract, which is required to digest it. Comparatively, animals that utilize their bigger brains to procure more nutritious but harder to obtain food have much smaller gastrointestinal tracts.

Another biological factor provided early hominids with the opportunity to evolve bigger, more complicated brains (i.e., neuroplasticity). The old view of the brain was that after the first few years of our developmental age, the brain ceased to form new neuronal connections. However, it is now known that the brain continues to reorganize itself by forming new neural connections far after our developmental age; this is known as neuroplasticity.

These reorganizations in the brain involve changes in the connections between linked neurons and are achieved by mechanisms such as "axonal sprouting"; this is where an undamaged nerve can grow a new nerve ending to reconnect to neurons whose attachments were damaged. This allows the brain to compensate for any damage that may occur.

Neuroplasticity occurs not only in response to neuron damage but has also been observed to occur with an increase in stimulus and increase in performing skills. Therefore, it is conceivable that receiving communication input and performing communication skills sparked neuroplasticity to reorganize the hominid brain. Thus, neuroplasticity and the availability to more nutritious food sources enabled frontal lobe expansion in hominids, paving the way for a new form of consciousness.

It is also worth pointing out that the brain of *Homo sapiens sapiens* has changed over time and, as a result, changed our type of consciousness. Therefore, it is also possible that our consciousness could once again evolve into a newer form of consciousness. It is interesting to speculate what factors would drive this evolution.

More modern approaches attempt to incorporate the foundations of "the scientific study of consciousness." This is an effort to describe consciousness in terms of understanding the physical/material world around mankind and how the brain processes it. However, it must be noted that scientific theory should imply that this attempt to describe the physical world is only a description based on our analytical observations, not the physical world itself.

New advances in technology and growing volumes of scientific research, more specifically in neuroscience, have created a great deal of understanding about the neurobiology of consciousness. These understandings have included the role of neurotransmitters and specific regions of the brain that are necessary for consciousness to occur in humans.

Up until now, much has been discussed about frontal lobe expansion and its relevance to developing higher degrees of consciousness. However, what areas of the human brain are primarily responsible for the process of human consciousness?

The cerebral cortex is the largest part of the brain and is subdivided into four regions: the frontal lobe, the occipital lobe, the parietal lobe, and the temporal lobe. All of these lobes in the cerebral cortex consist of neurologically specialized areas that receive sensory information and process different aspects of sensation and motor control. The cerebral cortex also creates mental models, which create a model of the world around us and within us based on sensory data and associations of that data in our memory. However, numerous neurophysiologic experiments confirm that consciousness can exist with damage or ablation to regions of the cerebral cortex but consciousness is abolished when damage or ablation occurs to the thalamus.

The thalamus is subdivided into numerous small and medium-sized nuclei and is connected to the entire bottom layer of the cerebral cortex. These neuronal connections are called "thalamocortical" and "corticothalamic" connections, which receive signals through the "internal capsule" and allow the thalamus to receive input from every sensory and motor process in the nervous system.

Studies involving "persistent vegetative states" (this is physical wakefulness without awareness to one's surroundings) have shown that the overall cortical (cerebral cortex) metabolism remains constant during a vegetative state. This is because the metabolism in the prefrontal cortex is dependent on the activation of the thalamic intralaminar nuclei. This confirms that it is the thalamocortical connections that are responsible for consciousness to occur, not cortical activity by itself.

The location of the thalamus is perfectly placed for integrating all of the brain's activity; thus, it is involved in the global integration of cortical activity and controls consciousness. The intralaminar nuclei are more notably the most profound site of the conscious experience in the thalamus, but neurophysiologists cannot yet say how it works.

Medically, variation in normal states of consciousness can occur, known as "altered states of consciousness." These are changes in our neurobiology that cause perceptual changes and cognitive impairments that are different from our normal state of consciousness. Certain drugs or medications can cause these changes. Also, impairments in one's physical conditions can cause states of delirium or dementia. Delirium is typically seen is cases of drug intoxication, for example, alcohol intoxication. Dementia is more likely to be seen in a patient with a neurodegenerative disease (e.g., Alzheimer's).

Some individuals consider dreams to be a state of altered consciousness. This is an interesting topic, and new researchs is being done in this field. Also, much has been written about shamanism and meditation in respect to individuals intentionally entering an altered state of consciousness. However, at this point, not much legitimate neurological data has been gathered.

The field of "exobiology" is the study of possible biological life in the universe. It would be interesting to examine other types of consciousness that may exist elsewhere and how they may differ from forms of consciousness existing on our planet.

Much has been written and debated regarding human consciousness and other possible forms of consciousness that we are not aware of. Also, neuroscience has compiled an impressive amount of information that still falls short of a comprehensive definition. However, future development in technology and open-mindedness may help us discover the answers that we seek pertaining to our consciousness.

— *John K. Grandy*

See also **Brain, Human**

Future Readings

Bear, N., Bear, M. F., Connors, B. W., & Paradiso, M. A. (2002). *Neuroscience: Exploring the brain* (2nd ed.). New York: Lippincott, Williams & Wilkins.

Blackmore, S. (2003). *Consciousness: An introduction.* New York: Oxford University Press.

Edelman, G. M., Tonomi, G., & Tononi, G. (2001). *A universe of consciousness: How matter becomes imagination.* New York: Basic Books.

Kandel, E. R., Schwartz, J. H., & Jessell, T. M. (2000). *Principles of neural science* (4th ed.). New York: McGraw-Hill Medical.

Koch, C. (2004). *The quest for consciousness: A neurobiological approach.* New York: Roberts & Co.

 # CONTINENTAL DRIFT

Dating back to the early history of science, it was long thought that Earth was a static, stable planet whose surface remained largely unchanged through time. This view radically changed during the 1960s, as an array of improved analytical techniques and an influx of new observations revealed that Earth's surface is in a state of constant change. This new approach to understanding the Earth is known as *plate tectonics* and is composed of two basic processes: sea floor spreading and continental drift. Although these two processes are coupled, the notion of continental drift has allowed scientists to understand the evolution and distribution of many plant and animal groups, including primates.

The first suggestions of continental drift were offered by 16th-century philosophers and geographers, who noted the congruence between the coastlines of Africa and South America. In 1596, the geographer Abraham Ortelius argued that the Americas were once conjoined with Europe and Asia, but later "torn away" by earthquakes and other catastrophes. In recent years, historians of science have revealed nascent hints of continental drift in the writings of Francis Bacon and noted French scientist Comte de Buffon. However, it wasn't until the early 20th century that a coherent hypothesis of continental drift was presented to the scientific community. This hypothesis was articulated by Alfred Lothar Wegener, a German meteorologist who assembled widely divergent lines of evidence into an understandable theory of continental motion.

Like the early geographers before him, Wegener was intrigued by the closely matching coasts of South America and Africa. After reading a paper describing similar Paleozoic fossils from these two continents, Wegener launched a massive literature search in the hopes of finding additional data to support continental drift. The data he uncovered were varied and wide-ranging. Wegener discovered that South America, Africa, India, Australia, and Antarctica shared a suite of unique Mesozoic fossils, including a signature fern flora and several reptiles. Modern animals do not range across all continents, because it is often impossible to disperse across oceans and other barriers. This suggested to Wegener that these continents were linked during the Mesozoic and have since moved to their present, widely divergent positions. Other evidence gathered by Wegener included closely matching rock units shared by Africa and South America and geological evidence indicative of former equatorial climate belts and past glaciations that made little sense if the continents have always occupied the same positions.

Wegener presented his hypothesis in a series of lectures and journal articles in 1912. Three years later, he outlined his ideas in a short, 94-page book, *Die Entstehung der Kontinente und Ozeane*, which was subsequently revised three times and translated into English as *The Origin of Continents and Oceans*. The notion of continental drift, which overturned much of the conventional geological wisdom of the day, was initially dismissed by critics as untenable, largely because Wegener could provide no plausible mechanism for continental motion. When Wegener died during a 1930 expedition to Greenland, his hypothesis was openly ridiculed and his scientific credibility scorned.

Although Wegener would never know it, his hypothesis was later verified as a new age of science dawned in the shadow of World War II. Over the course of the 1960s, a handful of earth scientists from across the

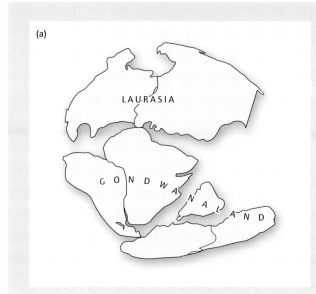
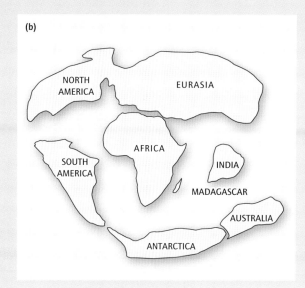

Source: Hespenheide Design.

globe instituted a scientific "revolution" that saw the birth of plate tectonics. Important data supporting this new theory came from studies of paleomagnetism. As lava cools into solid rock, tiny crystals of the magnetic mineral magnetite are "locked" into position, thereby recording the strength and direction of Earth's magnetic field at the time of the rock's formation. Using trigonometric equations, geologists can take this data and determine the latitude at which a certain rock formed. This procedure was applied to igneous rocks across the globe, and it was discovered that the latitudes at which the rocks formed were different than the latitudes they occupy today. This, along with an avalanche of additional data, strongly supported Wegener's original hypothesis of continental drift, which today is regarded as an important tenant of plate tectonics.

Although important to geologists and other Earth scientists, continental drift is also relevant to studies of primate evolution and distribution. Understanding the patterns of continental motion greatly enhances our comprehension of biogeography, the study of the distribution of living species. As continents move over time, they carry with them living organisms, which evolve as the continents collide and drift apart. The distribution of both fossil and living primates, including members of the human lineage, is illuminated by continental drift.

Primates originated between 85 and 65 million years ago, at the same time that the southern landmass of Gondwana, comprising present-day Africa, South America, Australia, Antarctica, India, and Madagascar, was rapidly fragmenting. Thus, it is likely that the initial evolution and divergence of primates was closely linked with continental drift. The extinct adapoids, a group of primitive primates, are only known from North America, Europe, Asia, and Africa, which is explained by a long-lived land connection between North America and Europe. Continental drift also helps explains the split between Old World and New World primates, including how early human ancestors evolved on an isolated African-Arabian continent and later dispersed after collision with Asia. The distribution of the more primitive prosimians is also elucidated by continental drift, but is somewhat complicated. Patterns of continental motion help explain why prosimians are limited to Africa, Asia, and Madagascar, but do not adequately describe why Madagascar is home to an abundance of species. Several hypotheses have attempted to answer this puzzle, many relying on continental drift, but there is no current consensus among researchers. Interestingly, purely geological processes associated with continental drift have enabled the preservation of important hominid fossils in Africa. The African continent is currently rifting, or splitting in two, as is manifested by the Red Sea and the line of East African lakes, such as Victoria and Malawi. This rifting is associated with volcanism and the formation of valleys, which have enabled preservation of early human fossils in Kenya and surrounding countries.

Continental drift has both revolutionized geology and enabled a better understanding of plant and animal distribution. Primates originated and evolved as continents moved and collided, which has affected modern primate distribution and habitats. As older primate fossils are discovered and more is discerned about the evolution of primate groups, the patterns of continental drift are becoming increasingly important to primatologists.

— *Stephen L. Brusatte*

See also **Fossil Record**

Further Readings

Hallam, A. (1973). *A revolution in the earth sciences.* Oxford: Oxford University Press.

Hartwig, W. C. (Ed.). (2002). *The primate fossil record.* Cambridge: Cambridge University Press.

Wegener, A. L. (1924). *The origin of continents and oceans.* New York: Dutton.

Coon, Carlton S. (1904–1981)

American physical and cultural anthropologist Carlton Coon dealt with the origin of races within the species *Homo sapiens sapiens*. Born and raised in Wakefield, Massachusetts, Coon's early developmental progress was within the patriotic, yet segregated, New England community. A community where religion was the principal factor in the determination of social status, the religious dichotomy often created a hostile environment. Considered an intelligent and a high-spirited youth, Coon's destructive and intolerable behavior was the cause of legal problems. Much to his parent's dismay, these behavioral problems were carried over to Wakefield High School, where an incident caused him to be expelled. Finishing his education at Andover, the environment was well suited for a person of his demeanor. After graduating from Andover, Coon went to Harvard. At Harvard, Coon was exposed to anthropology under Earnest Hooton, American anthropologist. This resulted in an academic shift from English to anthropology, thereby continuing his anthropological education until his graduation in 1925. Coon remained at Harvard to continue his education in anthropology. During his

term at Harvard, he married Mary Goodale in 1926, siring two children within the marriage. Mary accompanied him throughout his travels as Coon did research for his dissertation. Coon received his PhD from Harvard in 1928.

After receiving his PhD, Coon remained at Harvard to teach until the outbreak of World War II. During the war, he served with the Office of Strategic Services in Africa. Returning to Harvard after the war, Coon found himself in disagreement over several issues, particularly concerning the topics of race and culture. For Coon, a full professor, the possibility and eventual leaving from Harvard was seen as a relief from the academic politics within the department. Approached by Ephraim Speiser of the University of Pennsylvania, Coon soon accepted the position of curator of the University Museum in 1948. While curator, he constructed the Hall of Man (1949–1950). Within this presentation, his contribution was a logarithmic chart depicting time against human energy use. Essentially, innovations in technology stem from the organization of human society. Besides research and duties as curator, Coon partook in the TV series *Summer School* and *What in the World,* along with being a consultant for *Life.* He finished his career with a combined 20 books and monographs, mostly known for *Tribes of the Rif* (1931), *The Races of Europe* (1939), *Races* (1950), and *The Origin of Races* (1962). After an illustrious yet controversial career, Coon died on June 6, 1981.

Contributions and Perspectves

Even though human classification (for example, races) has been utilized scientifically for over 100 years, the issue is wrought by either scientific obscurity or cultural bias. Thankfully, modern science within an evolutionary framework is beginning to unravel the mystery concerning genetic variation. Coon, venturing on a teetering scale between scientific truth and biased predetermination, understood the essential contributing factors among climate, culture, and genetic variation. In an evolutionary framework, these factors surely contribute to the process of adaptation. However, Coon supported not only the traditional "man the hunter" but also the erroneous process of natural eugenics. From these superior and intelligent individuals, a band or small tribe may become what is now termed a *race.*

Though today the term *race* is noted as being a social construct, Coon took a liberal or radical view concerning it. Associating individual specimens with places, breeding habits, and behavior, the term *race* begins to take on the more known social stigma. The nature of genes, genotypes, blood groups, and mutation were known by Coon; yet the majority of racial determining factors and associated accomplishments always seemed to possess some Caucasoid phenotypic features. These attributes were not assigned arbitrarily, but conceived by the interpretation of the process that accounts for all life, that being evolution.

Source: © Photo provided by www.downtheroad.org, The Ongoing Global Bicycle Adventure.

Understanding the importance of bipedality, Coon drew the sharp distinction among the varieties of *Homo erectus* and the geography of modern human populations. Viewing the arterial grooves, cranial capacity, and complexity can be used to draw sharp distinction among *Australopithecus, Pithecanthropus,* Negro *Homo erectus,* and *Sinanthropus.* Within the continent of Africa, the primary races are Caucasoid, Capoid, and Congoid, whereby the other races evolved from their perspective geographical hominid form. The progression from *Homo erectus* to *Homo* was not seen in a Darwinian sense. Coon stated a clear jump from one form to another, saltation via *supervention.* This process resulted in the deciding factor that gave our species an advantage, the large and complex cerebral hemisphere. These complexities led to greater complex thought and social organization. According to Coon, evolution places the Caucasoid as the oldest *sapiens* race, followed by Capoids and Congoid. Although the origin of modern human in the Far East is obscured and polarized by two positions, evolution of regional forms and occupation by Neandertal migration, the biological and cultural adaptations resulted in the division or classification of modern *Homo sapiens sapiens.*

In Coon's later works, he held the belief of five distinct races: Caucasoid, Mongoloid, Australoid, Congoid, and Capoid. Each race held certain phenotypic traits that determined their classification. Caucasoid possesses skin whose tones varies from pinkish to nearly black; hair color ranges from varying degrees of blonde, red, and black; eye color ranges from blue, grey, brown, and black. Morphological features include narrow nasal passages and deep eye sockets. The Mongoloid and Capoid races possess varying degrees of yellow skin; black hair; eye color is either brown or black; low nasal passages and flush eyes. The Australoid and Congoid races posses skin color that ranges from brown to black; eye color is either brown or black; hair color is black and curly. Variations among these attributes are due to the evolutionary principles that created the variation and the selective forces found within nature. It was held that this process, along with the added element of culture, decreased his number of races from 30 to 5.

Whether or not Coon's view can be determined as possessing extreme prejudices or just simply overstated, the contributions of his research and insights are incontrovertible. His eye for detail, intelligence, and adventurous spirit furthered the knowledge concerning the detailed analysis of variations in phenotypic expressions of our own species. However, his evolutionary principle was determined by cultural and unknown biological factors, essentially taking an evolutionary principle from scattered and differentiated leaps in biology and culture via energy. Causality always being problematic, the combined view serves only to skew the unity of our species and its own created ontology and self-directed teleology.

— *David Alexander Lukaszek*

See also **Evolution, Models of**

Further Readings

Coon, C. S. (1977). Overview. *Annual Review of Anthropology, 6,* 1–10.

Coon, C. S. (1981). *Adventures and discoveries.* Upper Saddle River, NJ: Prentice Hall.

Coon, C. S. (1982). *Racial adaptations.* Chicago: Nelson Hall.

 COPPER AGE

The Copper Age, or Chalcolithic time period, generally refers to circa 5000 BCE to 2000 BCE. This typology was initiated by Dane Christian Jurgensen Thomsen in 1807 as a three-age system of classifying human prehistory based on toolmaking technologies (i.e., Stone Age, Bronze Age, and Iron Age). These categories were later refined by John Lubbock in 1865. The term *Chalcolithic* ("copper-stone") is derived from the Greek *chalcos* (copper) and *lithos* (stone). The Chalcolithic time period is significant in Old World contexts because it coincides with the beginnings of craft specialization, development of agriculture, long-distance trade, and increased sociopolitical complexity.

Central and Northern Europe

The Copper Age in Central and Northern Europe overlaps heavily with the Middle and Late Neolithic periods. The Middle Neolithic/Copper Age I (4500–4200 BC) is best illustrated by the Tiszapolgar Culture. The first farmers of the Northern European plains, of the Funnel Beaker Culture (4200–2800 BC), settled in southern Norway to the Czech/Austrian border, and from the Netherlands to Ukraine during the Late Neolithic/Copper Age II (4200–3750 BC). Evidence for the first wheeled carts occur in Germany and Poland during this time. Northern Europe developed agriculture, plow tools, copper tools, and monumental architecture. The Corded Ware/Single Grave Culture (2800–1850 BC) continued in the same areas and expanded eastward. Scholars suggest the development of Indo-European language groups at this time. The Corded Ware Culture was followed by the Bell Beaker Interaction Sphere, based on bell-shaped pots found from the Middle Danube to the Iberian Peninsula and from Ireland, Great Britain, and Denmark to Sicily and North Africa. Depending on the location, this sphere may be considered part of the Late Copper Age or Early Bronze Age (2900–1700 BC).

The Levant

The Chalcolithic in the Levant dates between the late 5th and early 4th millennia BC (5000–3500 BC). The chronology and periodization of the Chalcholithic in the southern Levant has long been a contentious topic, resulting in significant overlap between Copper Age material and the Early Bronze Age material. Key to understanding the Chalcolithic in the Levant is the shift in settlement patterns, simultaneously illustrating an increase in sociocomplexity and metallurgy. Examples of sites with Chalcolithic material include Arad, Byblos, Ghassul, Gilath, Jawa, Khirbet Querin (North), Tell Teo, and Tell Um Hammad.

Central Asia and China

The Chalcolithic in Central Asia exhibits the first uses of copper and indications of organized agriculture. In western Central Asia, the typological phase Anau IA (late 6th–early 5th millennia BC) illustrates the use of copper tools at Chakmakli-depe and Mondjukli-depe. Subsequently, the Namazga sequences at these sites define the chronology of the developed Chalcolithic period (4th–2nd millennia BC). This period in western Turkestan represents the first organized agricultural villages in Central Asia, and during the Namazga Chalcolithic, craft (metal and ceramic) specialization became an economic factor linking Central Asia to the Near East and South Asia. Unlike the Namazga sites, the Keltiminar groups of Khoresmia developed separately due to the barrier of the Kyzl Kum desert. Autochthonous developments are also seen in societies north of the Caspian Sea, along the Volga and Ural rivers, such as Tripolye and Sredny Stog (ca. 4000–3500 BC), which represent sedentary communities employing mixed economies of hunting, fishing, animal domestication, and limited agriculture. Similar to those communities, the Botai and Tersek (Ural Mountains and Tobol River in Kazakhstan) show local affiliations and interaction.

In China, the Chalcolithic period (3000–2000 BC) is best represented by three main cultures: Qijia culture, with settlements following the upper course of the Yellow River; Longshan culture, distributed along the middle and lower Yellow River; and Liangzhu culture, with the settlements clustering around Lake Tai. Whereas in the former two cultures, brass developed with the use of copper, the Liangzhu culture is known for jade artifact production. The Chalcolithic levels mark the beginning of urbanism and a move toward extensive trade networks in East Asia.

South Asia

The Chalcolithic in South Asia is divided into five main regions. The Indus Civilization sites (such as Mohen-jo-Daro and Harappa) have Chalcolithic levels that demonstrate the use of copper/bronze, intensification of agriculture, and the development of trade networks. Other Chalcolithic settlements illustrate a range of subsistence strategies, from hunting/gathering to agropastoralism, at sites in northwest India, northeast India, Saurashtra, and Central India (Deccan and Vidarbha). The Chalcolithic period appears to be absent in the southern parts of India, where the chronology leaps from the Neolithic to the Iron Age. In northwest India, cultural areas such as the Ganeshwar-Jodhpura Cultural Complex and the Ahar-Banas complex existed during the 3rd to 2nd millennia BC. At sites such as Bagor, evidence exists for settled agricultural communities alongside more mobile populations, where copper tools joined the continued use of microlithic tools. In Madhya Pradesh, there are over 40 Chalcolithic sites (late 3rd millennia). Northeast Chalcolithic excavated sites include Golbai Sasan, Randu Rajar Dhibi, and Chirand. Over 70 Chalcolithic sites have been identified in West Bengal. The sites in Saurashtra, considered Sorath Harappan, include sites such as Rojdi and Lothal. These sites share traits with the Indus sites, although they carry distinct ceramic styles. The Deccan Chalcolithic is divided into four periods: Savalda (2000–1800 BC), Late Harappan (1800–1600 BC), Malwa (1600–1400 BC), and Jorwe (1400–1000 BC). These are considered early farming communities with hunters and gatherers living alongside one another. In addition, there are a large number of copper hoards that are found throughout Northern India and across the Deccan. Usually found apart from settlements, these hoards are associated with a particular type of ceramic, dating to approximately 2650 BC to 1180 BC.

The Chalcolithic period indexes the first widespread use of metal by human society, replacing the exclusive use of stone tools. In many parts of the world, this technological advancement marks the transition from a pastoral society to a more agricultural and urban one. This change simultaneously allows for a significant increase in interaction between various regions. Illustrations of the Chalcolithic may be found worldwide, such as in Africa (Egypt and the Eastern Coast), Asia Minor, Mesopotamia, and the Mediterranean, to name a few.

— *Uzma Z. Rizvi*

See also **Prehistory**

Further Readings

Bagolini, B., & Schiavo, F. L. (Eds.). (1996). *The Copper Age in the Near East and Europe.* Forli, Italy: International Congress of Prehistoric and Protohistoric Sciences.
Maddin, R. (Ed.). (1988). *The beginnings of the use of metals and alloys.* Cambridge: MIT Press.
Maisels, C. (1999). *Early civilizations of the Old World: The formative histories of Egypt, the Levant, Mesopotamia, India, and China.* New York: Routledge.

COPTIC MONASTICISM

Christianity was introduced into Egypt in the 1st century and found itself in competition with two other religions: Judaism and the Hellenized native religion. By the 4th century, Christianity was the religion of the majority of the people in Egypt. By the end of the 5th century, the last of the ancient temples and priesthoods were gone.

Christianity originated as a sect of Judaism and, consequently, shares similar traditions and myths. St. Mark brought Christianity to Alexandria early in the first century, which at that time had a large Jewish population. Not surprisingly, early Christianity established itself first among those Jews. Christianity also had a mythology that was similar to many aspects of Egyptian mythology. The stories of Osiris, Isis, and Horus in many ways parallel the Christian story of God, Mary, and Jesus: Jesus defeats Satan and is the champion of his father, God; Horus defeats Set and is the champion of his father, Osiris; Both Jesus and Osiris are killed and resurrected, and so on. The

Source: © iStockphoto/Pierrette Guertin.

and St. Antony (ca. AD 251–356), the two earliest ascetic hermits in Egypt. They established the pattern for later anchoritic practice, where monks lived alone in the desert. The second type began with St. Pachom, who instituted a communal, or cenobitic, form of monasticism in AD 320, in Upper Egypt, by building a monastery organized according to military-like rules and order. Both forms of monasticism quickly merged to form a semicenobitic kind of monastic practice that is still practiced today. Monks in contemporary Egyptian monasteries spend some of their time in solitary spiritual pursuits, often still in caves or shelters in the desert, while the remainder of their time is spent living as part of a community within a monastery.

ability to find common ground with Judaism, and with the native Egyptian religion, gave Christianity an advantage that no doubt contributed significantly to its eventual success.

Some religious practices already in Egypt influenced Christianity when it was introduced. Philo described an ascetic community that existed in Egypt during the 1st century near Alexandria that was probably Jewish. Also, the life of priests and priestesses in the native Egyptian religion was cloistered and ritualized in some ways that later Christian monastic practice would emulate.

Christian monasticism began in Egypt during the latter part of the 3rd century. The increasing tax burden imposed by the government, and the practices of the civil religion, which were repugnant to many Christians, along with increasing persecutions of Christians, caused many people to leave the cities and villages for the wilderness. Some of those people moved into even more remote areas to lead solitary ascetic lives. People flocked to many of these desert hermits as they developed reputations as healers and teachers. A type of religious revitalization ensued during the beginning of the 4th century that resulted in monastic practice first being institutionalized, and then taking control, within the Orthodox Church in Egypt.

Two types of monasticism developed in Egypt. The first type began with St. Paul (ca. AD 228–343)

Many monks of the Coptic Orthodox Church are also saints. There is an extensive oral and written hagiography of the lives of many of those desert fathers. Coptic monks, in general, are depicted as champions of orthodoxy, and historically, the monks of Egypt did, indeed, defend the church against numerous heresies. Coptic monks were important participants in the first four Ecumenical Councils.

The development of the Coptic Orthodox Church and Coptic Orthodox Monasticism took place during four major periods. The first period was from AD 284 to AD 451. During that time, Coptic Monasticism was institutionalized, and the first four Ecumenical Councils defined the doctrines of the church. The Coptic Orthodox calendar began in the year AD 284. The second period was from AD 451 to AD 1517. During that time, Coptic culture in Egypt flourished until the Islamic conquest in AD 642, after which Egypt was ruled by a succession of Islamic dynasties. The Coptic language, a form of late Egyptian spoken during Pharonic times, was eventually replaced by Arabic as the spoken language. Coptic was relegated to liturgical use in the church. The third period was from AD 1517 to AD 1798. During that time, the ethnic and cultural identity of the Coptic people was forged under Ottoman rule. The fourth period, from AD 1798 to AD 1920, saw European influence dominate Egyptian culture and, eventually, the rise of Arab nationalism as the Ottoman Empire collapsed.

Today, the Egyptian Christian Church is referred to as the "Coptic Orthodox Church." The name came from the Greek words *Aigypt/Aigyptios* (Egypt/Egyptian), which became *qibt/qibtii* in Arabic, and *Copt/Coptic* in English. The Patriarch of Alexandria (currently Baba Shenouda III) is head of the Coptic Orthodox Church. Upon the death of the patriarch, a new patriarch is chosen from among the monks of Egypt's monasteries by the bishops of the church. The bishops are also monks who have been chosen and appointed to their sees for life. Consequently, monks, who are also priests, control the entire upper hierarchy of the church. Parish priests, who oversee the operation of the churches and who serve the more immediate liturgical and spiritual needs of Coptic congregations, are married and form a separate hierarchy within the church.

Although exact numbers are impossible to determine and official numbers vary in terms of reliability, there are probably nearly 10 million Copts in Egypt today, about two dozen or more monasteries, and over 1,000 monks in the Coptic Orthodox Church. There is also one Coptic Orthodox monastery in Southern California.

— *Richard R. Jones*

See also **Religion and Anthropology**

Further Readings

Jones, R. R. (1997). *An ethnohistory of Coptic monasticism.* Doctoral dissertation, Wayne State University, Detroit, MI.

Yonge, C. D. (1993). *The works of Philo.* Peabody, MA: Hendrickson.

COSMOLOGY AND SACRED LANDSCAPES

Cosmology is literally the "science of nature," from the physics of Aristotle and Newton to the mythical cosmograms of Tibet. A cosmology is any composition or cultural construct relating to the structure and process of systems of creation. Included are the origins of physical elements of earthly or astronomical spheres, the genesis of the material world, and the order and function of the observable universe, including the planets, the solar system, and celestial bodies. Quite simply, a cosmology is any cultural belief related to the creative forces responsible for the composition of the universe.

Landscapes are integral to any cosmology, though not all cosmologies emphasize that landscapes are sacred. *Landscape* is a powerful term, with considerable utility for describing and giving context to cultural beliefs and worldview regarding the natural world in which people live. Hence, it is important in the context of cosmology. People live in landscapes, but landscapes are more than social space. Long the domain of geographers who fashioned "landscapes" from "spatial-scientific" or "structural" geographical theory, broader understandings of non-Western cosmologies have brought deeper comprehension of landscape and its relationship to cultures.

For the anthropologist, landscape has two primary meanings: It is a "framing convention" that provides the backdrop for how a study is presented, and it is a means to attribute the ways that local people view their cultural and physical surroundings. As a spatial element, landscape is intertwined with time, in that it is not a static or abstract entity, but a part of social practices. The term *landscape* dates to the renaissance. In art history, it is based on a geometric perspective in media renderings meant to be viewed in a way that projects a picture involving some aspect of geographic features that can be perceived in a realistic fashion.

Anthropologists have long recognized that many indigenous people view and map landscapes differently than is done in the West and that often conceptions of land and landscape are permeated with notions of the sacred. Among the Andonque of the Columbian Amazon, the land is conceptualized as specific features identified as being both within and outside of their territory. These features include mountains, hills, flat savannahs, and rocks. Each feature has been purposely named by a religious specialist, is "owned" by a specific supernatural force, and is identified socially by specific mythic events that occurred there. This landscape extends well beyond the actual territory of the community. This conception of the world is not fixed or permanent. Shamanic intervention in the form of specialist communication with specific landscape features results in symbolic remodeling of both the landscape and the ceremonial ways people interact with and are influenced by it.

Specifics about the sacred landscapes are learned: As people grow, they become aware of the relationships between land and ancestors, as well as their social responsibilities, by physically moving through the land. There are dramatic indications of links between memory, ancestral power, and the land. Recently, residents of northern Australia visiting southeastern parts of the continent identified features in the natural environment as being part of their ancestral landscape. This is particularly relevant in that the individuals in question had never been to southeastern Australia before, and little was known about the mythology of the area or the original inhabitants, who had been forcibly removed in the 19th century. This knowledge is part of an ancestral grid, learned through interaction with and observation of highly ritualized activities, and then experienced by traveling to different places. Each place is connected in this chainlike grid, which reflects an individual's current kinship group as well as ancestral validation of links to the land. The landscape is seen as composed of segments that reveal ancestral ties to specific areas of the land. "Because ancestral beings not only created the landscape, but also placed people in a particular relationship to it as perpetuators of the ancestral inheritance, the landscape is viewed simultaneously as a set of spaces for people to occupy" (Morphy, 1995, p. 192). Even in land disputes, such as when a group moves into a new land and takes over, they view this as the land taking over the people, thus preserving the continuity. When previously unoccupied land (or that for which direct links are no longer articulated) is settled, there exist "mechanisms for creating or recreating the linkages" (Morphy, 1995, p. 186).

Temporality has been an important concept in anthropological studies of sacred landscapes. Landscapes are perpetuated through and imbedded in memory, which makes them more processes than objects. Landscape is a crucial element in enculturation, defining the limits of social space in ways that are both transmitted between people and fluid though time. Because concepts of sacred and secular landscapes are culturally constructed, they clearly have different meanings to different people at different times. The temporality of landscape is not the analytical category devised by anthropologists to set distance between them and that which they study through the use of terms like *archaic, Stone Age, and primitive,* which are employed as distancing devices. This is not to say that there is not a duality to time. Like space, which can be experienced differently from emic or etic perspectives, the temporality of landscape also has elements of objective process and subjective representation. It is impossible to deal with the multiple ways humans interact with the social and natural world using only one particular concept of time.

Time can be a dynamic historical marker of place. In Fijian notions of landscape, place is both a location and a temporal identifier. Historical time is marked by the succession of locations for villages occupied in the past, each named for an apical ancestor. Social forms have ways of extending into time and space, which creates forms of time and space that are socially conditioned. For the Wakuénai and other indigenous people of the Upper Río Negro of Venezuela and Columbia, space and time can be transcended in powerful ways. The playing of sacred musical instruments in different places can resituate centers of social power present in indigenous mythohistorical accounts. The relationship between landscape and temporality has been the subject of numerous specific studies, most of which utilize phenomenological interpretations. These studies focus on the way landscape has a synergy among its parts that make up the whole.

Sacred landscapes are often associated with political interests, especially in cases where ritual space becomes a location where human agency is integrated with divine activity. Ritual mapping of territory through naming is done in Northwestern Amazonia, where political Wakuénai mythic narratives and ritual performances continue to emphasize the ethnopolitical centrality of this headwater area as sacred and political space for Arawak-speaking peoples who live north of the Amazon River. This is a complex issue that articulates itself differently in different places. In India, sacred space is often separate from political centers. In historical context, natural sacred spaces are often the focus of political interests, not the locus: Political capitals may change location, even within a territory, while sacred locations maintain stability over time.

— *Keith M. Prufer*

Further Readings

Bakker, H. (1992). Introduction. In H. Bakker (Ed.), *The sacred centre as the focus of political interest* (pp. vii–xi). Groningen, The Netherlands: Egbert Forsten.

Hill, J. (2002). Made from bone: Trickster myths, musicality, and social constructions of history in the Venezuelan Amazon. In G. Schrempp & W. Hansen (Eds.), *Myth: A new symposium* (pp. 72–78). Bloomington: Indiana University Press.

Hirsch, E., & O'Hanlon, M. (Eds.). (1995). *The anthropology of landscape: Perspectives on place and space.* Oxford: Clarendon Press.

Morphy, H. (1995) Landscape and the reproduction of the ancestral past. In E. Hirsch & M. O'Hanlon (Eds.), *The anthropology of landscape: Perspectives on place and space* (pp. 184–209). Clarendon Press, Oxford.

Thomas, J. (1993). The politics of vision and the archaeologies of landscape. In B. Bender (Ed.), *Landscape politics and perspective* (pp. 19–48). Providence, RI: Berg.

Toren, C. (1995). Sign into symbol, symbol as sign: Cognitive aspects of a social process. In P. Boyer (Ed.), *Cognitive aspects of religious symbolism* (pp. 147–164). Cambridge: Cambridge University Press.

Ucko, P. J., & Layton, R. (Eds.). (1999). *The archaeology and anthropology of landscape: Shaping your landscape.* London: Routledge.

COUNSELING

The profession of counseling is dynamic, adaptive, and centered on meeting the needs of individuals in their particular environment. The goals of the counseling profession are directed toward assisting individuals to become self-sufficient and capable of managing their problems in efforts to lead productive, fulfilling lives. Moreover, the counseling process provides a therapeutic context to help individuals recognize and effectively use unused or underused resources and opportunities. Hence, through the process of counseling, individuals become effective and empowered self-helpers as they learn how to manage problem situations and develop life-enhancing opportunities. Counseling is a collaborative, two-way process that involves active involvement between client and counselor. According to

Gerard Eagan, the process of counseling represents an "-ing" word that illustrates active engagement and involvement in a series of therapeutic activities or interventions that will create and elicit constructive change. The art of counseling involves a process in which skilled counselors assist individuals to develop tailored programs that will encourage constructive change in efforts to live more fully. Individual counseling is driven and determined by client needs and is effective to the degree that the needs and concerns of clients are successfully met.

According to Carl Rogers (1902–1987), the counseling relationship is characterized as a relationship in which one person has the objective to promote growth, development, and maturity in another person with the goal to assist the other person to learn how to effectively cope with life. The counselor's role is to facilitate self-growth in individuals and to make individuals aware of possible alternatives or choices available in their lives. Counselors have the responsibility to ascertain by means of conducting a thorough assessment which counseling interventions, services, and treatment modalities will most likely lead to positive outcomes. In particular, competent counselors will amalgamate research with practice in efforts to afford quality service to clients. The goals of counseling, regardless of the occupational setting, involve behavioral, cognitive, and lifestyle change; insight and self-knowledge; and amelioration of suffering and symptomatolology. Professional counselors provide an array of services that promote mental health and well-being through a variety of counseling practices that range from individual counseling, to couples and family counseling, to group counseling.

The profession of counseling is rooted in a variety of disciplines, which has led to the development of a variety of counseling specialties, in the fields of marriage and family counseling, school counseling, rehabilitation counseling, college counseling, and addiction counseling, to name a few. Hence, counselors work in a variety of occupational settings, from private practice; to community mental health agencies; to medical, educational, jail, and prison settings; to business settings, and they offer a wide range of services to a diverse population of individuals.

Historical Perspective of Counseling

The profession of counseling is considered to be a relatively new occupation. Prior to the 1900s, professional counseling took the form of advice or deliverance of information. The evolution of counseling can be traced back to important historical events of the 20th century. The counseling profession developed and emerged consequent to the convergence of societal problems that plagued the United States at the turn of the 19th century, most notably the Industrial Revolution and the urbanization of America. Other factors that contributed to the growth and advancement of counseling in America include the advent of World War I and World War II, the Great Depression, the science and development of psychology as an occupation, the mental hygiene movement in the early 1900s, the mental health movement in the mid-1940s, the vocational guidance movement in the late 19th and early 20th centuries, and continued emphasis in vocational counseling. Government involvement also influenced the course of professional counseling by means of government-sponsored counseling services.

Theories of Counseling

Psychoanalytic Theory

Psychoanalysis evolved from the work of Sigmund Freud (1856–1939), founder of psychoanalytic therapy in the late 19th century. A dedicated student, Sigmund Freud completed medical school at the University of Vienna in 1881. Freud's initial occupational endeavors and contributions to the medical profession consisted of neurological research that focused on the brain and spinal cord. However, Freud's research focus shifted as he became interested in the work of Josef Breuer, a famous physician who practiced in Vienna, Austria. Breuer specialized in treating individuals who suffered from emotional disorders and implemented the use of hypnosis and verbal expression as methods of treatment. During this time, Freud began to invest his professional energies into the study and treatment of neurotic disorders. As Freud began to involve himself in researching and counseling clients who suffered from psychological disorders, he eventually came to emphasize the importance of human sexuality, sexual expression, as well as dreams as key to understanding human nature.

Prior to Freud, the discipline of psychology was regarded as both a philosophy and a study of psychophysiological processes. The notion of scientific thinking as it related to the study of the human mind and human motivation began to define the practice of psychology with the commencement of psychoanalysis. The historical timeline of psychoanalysis can be divided into three periods, dating from the late 19th century and continuing into the present day. The initial period that marks the beginning of the psychoanalytic movement was dominated by Freud in the late 19th century and continued until the end of World War I. To understand the fundamental tenants of psychoanalysis that developed out of the work of the early psychoanalytic pioneers, it is first essential to recognize the social context the dominated Western Europe and Viennese society in the late 19th century. During this time, Victorian society was governed by strict adherence to defined social norms, particularly as they related to human sexuality. Above all, female expression of sexuality was strictly confined and governed, which, in turn, encouraged repression or denial of sexuality among women. At the turn of the 20th century, the first psychoanalytic society was organized in Vienna; shortly thereafter, psychoanalysis began to gain momentum and recognition, which led to the formation of the International Psychoanalytical Association.

The second historical period of psychoanalysis began shortly after World War I, from 1918 to 1939. The emergence of psychoanalytic training institutes and psychoanalytic societies worldwide mark this period. It was during this time that scientific literature and case studies that demonstrated the work of psychoanalysts began the expansion of psychoanalytic thought and study. The third period of psychoanalysis began post–World War II (1945–) and continues into the present day. The significance of this period is marked by continued international expansion of psychoanalysis, as well as an expansion of psychoanalytic thought beyond Freud's traditional psychoanalysis. New theories of ego, object relations, and self psychology have emerged as contemporary, modern theories of psychoanalysis.

Psychoanalysis is recognized and defined as a *depth psychology*. The goals of psychoanalysis are aimed at resolving conflicts that reside at the unconscious level in efforts to change personality. Furthermore, psychoanalysis places emphasis on problem resolution and enhancement of coping resources in order to equip individuals to learn how to effectively manage their lives and to live in relation to others in a meaningful way. Intervention strategies that comprise the psychoanalysis process revolve around working through unresolved developmental problems. Interventions that are widely employed in psychoanalysis involve free association, analysis of dreams, analysis of transference, resistance, interpretation, and the study of the dynamic relationship between client and counselor. Other analytic techniques include interpretation, which involves bringing into conscious awareness of unconscious material, confrontation, clarification, and working through. The process of working through is a significant analytic procedure and refers to the continued analysis of resistance (form of psychological defense) once clients gain insight and awareness of their well-established unconscious conflicts. The procedure of working through helps clients to unblock and erode unconscious repressive or defensive mechanisms in efforts to create lasting change in personality and character structure.

Recent developments in the delivery of health care in the United States have had a well-defined impact on the current practice of professional counseling. Most notably, the rise of managed care has created significant changes in the funding and delivery of mental health treatment. A salient implication in how the practice of counseling has been impacted by managed care rests in the increased use of time-limited brief therapies and solution-focused interventions. Given that psychoanalysis is recognized as an extended, long-term depth psychology that requires both time and money, the practice and incorporation of psychoanalysis has lost popularity and favorability in the United States.

Cognitive-Behavioral Theories

Cognitive-behavioral theories are a set of related theories that have emerged from the clinical experiences, scholarly writings, and empirically based studies that were conducted by psychologists who studied and conceptualized human behavior from both behavioral and cognitive theoretical orientations. Cognitive-behavioral theories represent an extensive theoretical system within the profession of counseling. Theories that are cognitive-behavioral represent an amalgamation of both cognitive and behavioral oriented approaches to counseling people. Cognitive-behavioral theoretical orientations place emphasis on the mutual influence between cognitions and behaviors within individuals. These theories do not place importance on clients' feelings, insight, or the exploration of unconscious processes. Furthermore, cognitive-behavioral theories are concerned with present issues and place little value on exploring childhood issues or on past histories of individuals. The basic philosophy that underlies the cognitive-behavioral approaches suggests that cognitions are mediators of behavior.

Since cognitive-behavioral theories represent an amalgamation of behavioral and cognitive theories, the evolution and development of cognitive-behavioral treatment modalities trace back to the 1950s, with the earlier works of behaviorists and cognitive therapists. Behavior therapy was defined, shaped, and prevailed as an approach to counseling and psychotherapy from the contributions and works of three leading behaviorsts: John B. Watson (1878–1958), an American psychologist who is also referred to as the "father of behaviorism"; B. F. Skinner (1904–1990), an experimental psychologist; and Joseph Wolpe (1915–1997), a South African psychiatrist. By the 1980s, behavior therapy had gained status and recognition among the mental health profession. Albert Ellis (1913–), an American psychoanalysis, and Aaron Beck (1921–), an American psychiatrist, are considered to be two of the most influential contributors in the development of cognitive therapy. Cognitive-behavior theories emerged as a result of the integration of both cognitive and behavioral theories.

Just like there are a wide range of cognitive-behavioral theories, there are a number of cognitive-behavioral treatment interventions. Cognitive-behavioral interventions are considered to be structured, goal directed, didactic, and time limited in nature. Cognitive-behavioral strategies may include the use of humor, homework, risk-taking exercises, systematic desensitization, bibliotherapy, and stress inoculation training. The application of cognitive-behavioral interventions incorporate both behavioral (reinforcement, positive reinforcement, negative reinforcement, extinction, shaping, and stimulus control) and cognitive interventions (identifying distortions in thinking, thought stopping, positive self-statements, cognitive restructuring) that emphasize the importance of cognitive processes and behavior mediation. In essence, cognitive-behavioral theories place emphasis on identifying cognitive and behavioral deficits and excesses.

Family Therapy Theories

According to Samuel T. Gladding, a *family* is defined as individuals who are bonded through historical, emotional, or economic connections and who perceive themselves as being biologically and/or psychologically related to each other. This definition of family encourages a wide conceptualization in defining who comprises a family unit as well as acknowledging the varying compositions of family life.

Family counseling is considered to be a relatively new profession in the mental health field. The evolution of family theory can be traced back to the mid-20th century. Prior to the 1940s, family theory was nonexistent within the counseling profession due to the popularity and preeminence of individual psychoanalysis and behaviorism. The fruition of family theory evolved as a result of multiple historical events that transpired in American life during and after World War II. In the advent of World War II, many families experienced considerable stress and systemic changes as family members were geographically separated from one another. World War II also challenged traditional gender-specific roles as women were expected to work outside the home in factories to support the war efforts. In addition, mass casualities, as well as physical and emotional disabilities, added further strain to family life. Post–World War II, women began to reject their roles as housewives and began to reevaluate their status in society, which marked the advent of women attending college. It was during this time that courses in family life education gained popularity. Another hallmark event that influenced the evolution of family therapy was the development and appreciation of professional marriage counseling.

The practice of family therapy began to flourish in the 1970s. Consequently, as family theory and family counseling gained momentum and professional recognition in the United States, mental health professionals began to have new ways to conceptualize human behavior and individual psychopathology. The advent of family counseling marked a shift in the way that individual pathology and symptomatic behavior were explained and understood. Family theories emphasized the etiology and maintenance of pathology as existing within a larger social system, that being within the family. Such a systemic perspective invited a shift from treating the individual family member to treating the entire family.

The practice of family therapy is based in systems theory, which conceptualizes families as living social systems who seek to maintain homeostasis through patterned and predictable transactional patterns. Systems theory contends that change in any part of a system subsequently creates deviation from the status quo and, in turn, affects the entirety of a system. When applied to family counseling, systems theory recognizes that family dysfunction is meditated by maladaptive interactions between family members that subsequently have an effect on the whole family system. Family counselors incorporate techniques throughout the course of family counseling in efforts to elicit the process of change that will accordingly transform the basic structure of the family system.

There are several family therapy theories and approaches to counseling families. The majority of family theories focus on interpersonal dysfunction and maladaptive interactional patterns, whereas individual counseling targets intrapersonal dysfunction. The primary goal of family theory is best perceived as eliciting structural change within the whole family system. This concept of systemic familial change represents a sharp deviation from that of individual counseling, in which the primary objective is intended to initiate behavioral, cognitive, and affective change of an individual. The term *family theory* houses a wide variation of distinct family therapy approaches, with each ascribing its own family counseling theory and approach to counseling families. In general, the application of family counseling consists of identifying dysfunctional communication and relational patterns within the family system, as well as ascertaining issues related to hierarchy, power dynamics, and problems within the family structure. Furthermore, family counseling identifies boundary problems, dysfunctional transactional patterns, and family role conflicts.

To date, there are a number of family therapy theories, such as conjoint theory, strategic theory, structural theory, transgenerational theory, and narrative theory, which all approach family counseling from different frames of reference. Each theory integrates different techniques and interventions when counseling families. It is important to note that no matter what family theory a family counselor is counseling from, the fundamental goal of family therapy is the restructuring of some part of the family system.

Brief-Therapy Theories

Toward the late 20th century, the counseling profession and practice of counseling began to shift and embrace the use of brief therapies in response to the limited mental health resources and pressures from managed care organizations to contain rising costs of mental and medical health care. The advent of managed-care systems has created substantial implications for professional counselors, most notably in the number of counseling sessions that are allotted and approved and in the selection, deliverance, and implementation of clinical duties and counseling interventions. Brief therapy can be quantified as time-limited treatment that typically consists of 8 to 12 counseling sessions.

Brief, time-limited counseling is an all-encompassing topic that incorporates many different theories. It will be illustrated through the time-limited counseling modality of brief solution-focused therapy (BSFT). The practice of BSFT is considered a time-limited, cognitive-behavioral treatment orientation that focuses on individual strengths and resources. The process of BSFT is collaborative in nature between client and counselor in efforts to assist clients in developing solutions to resolve personal difficulties. Key constructs of BSFT illustrate the creation of meaning, use of language to assess how individuals perceive and create the world around them, responsibility for self, and utilization of unused resources.

Counselors who practice from a BSFT modality believe that individuals create meaning in their lives and construct reality through the use of language. A fundamental belief of BSFT is that objective reality is nonexistent, since the construction of reality and mere act of describing experiences require interpretations that are rooted in the subjective. Brief solution-focused therapy counselors ascribe to the beliefs that individuals are the experts of their own lives, are capable of initiating change, and espouse self-corrective inclinations. The clinical practice of BSFT places emphasis on competence rather than on pathology or character deficits. Furthermore, BSFT acknowledges that focusing on problems is not beneficial nor is it helpful for individuals; rather, counselors collaborate with individuals to help them define and create solutions. In doing so, the change process pivots around solution talk rather than problem talk.

Current Trends Within the Counseling Profession

The profession of counseling is an ever-evolving occupation that is constantly changing and shifting to meet the growing demands and needs of society. Societal issues that continue to be salient to the counseling profession in the early 21st century are advancements in media and technology; issues pertinent to wellness, health promotion, spirituality, social justice, diversity, and advocacy; and issues related to managed care and health maintenance organizations. Other current trends within the counseling profession that highlight prominent concerns and shed light on complex societal and multifaceted issues include poverty, violence, and social unrest. In response to heightened incidents of school violence in the forms of school bullying and school shootings, counselors are becoming increasingly concerned with the need to develop crisis plans and methods of intervention that will stop acts of violence and bullying within school settings. Hence, issues of promoting and maintaining school safety represent pressing issues for counselors in the 21st century.

Of these noteworthy issues that have had a pervasive impact on the delivery of counseling services, one of the most defining moments that has shaped the course of the counseling profession was the terrorist attacks on September 11, 2001. This momentous event has had a profound impact on the mental health community, most notably, the demand and large-scale need of crisis intervention services. Following the aftermath of September 11, 2001, when terrorists crashed commercial airliners into the World Trade Center in New York City and into the Pentagon in Washington, D.C., issues pertinent to immediate responsive actions to traumas, tragedies, and crises took on a new meaning within the mental health community. Specifically, such a defining moment highlighted the need for counselors to be trained and competent in implementing and delivering crisis services to individuals affected by large-scale trauma and tragedy.

Other noted salient issues within the counseling profession in the new millennium include dealing with poverty, family discord, workplace violence, funding of mental health services, and caring for the aging.

Wellness

Wellness is not a new concept. Dr. Halbert Dunn first coined the term *wellness* in 1961, and he defined it as unified functioning directed toward maximizing an individual's potential. Dunn defined complete well-being by focusing on the interrelatedness among mind, body, family, and community. The concept of high-level wellness is conceptualized as optimal functioning of the individual.

Wellness is a basis of life quality and involves embracing health-enhancing values and lifestyle behaviors that promote health or illness-free states.

The tenant of wellness revolves around the concepts of health promotion, disease prevention, and well-being. Furthermore, the concepts of wholeness, integration, purposeful living, and good health are used to conceptualize the construct of wellness. Perhaps the most salient aspect of a wellness philosophy is that it challenges the long-established belief of repairing something only when broken. A wellness approach attempts to move beyond such a reparative conceptualization by focusing on prevention rather than on remediation. Wellness is viewed as pertaining to the total person and is conceptualized as existing on a continuum throughout the life span. Thus, wellness is a lifelong, continuous, and proactive process rather than a one-time prescription. Such a deliberate health-conscious process is construed as an ideal, dynamic, fluctuating state of being. Positive wellness is to be attained through concerted, purposeful efforts to promote optimal functioning, rather than a state that exists succeeding reparative work related to a deficit in one's state of wellness. The notion of "well-being of the many" underscores the holistic perspective of wellness and gives emphasis to the idea of wellness of individuals, community context, and societal structures.

A wellness movement has gained momentum across the United States as a result of the pressing realities of increasing health care costs and alarming rates of premature morbidity and mortality due to unhealthy lifestyle behaviors. The wellness movement signifies a cost-effective and humane paradigm shift that is a distinct departure from a medical system that has exhausted the nation's financial resources.

A contemporary paradigm of wellness has emerged within the last decade that has provided a refreshing approach to health and wellness. During the late 20th century, Dr. Jane Myers and Dr. Tom Sweeney considered the notions of prevention and well-being as they related to individuals' overall total health. These two researchers and counselor educators have proposed and created several wellness models in efforts to view wellness from a holistic, multifaceted frame of reference. Most notably, their *indivisible self* model of wellness represents a contemporary, evidence-based model of wellness that highlights the reciprocal interactions between environmental factors and human behavior. The indivisible self model of wellness conceptualizes wellness across the life span and consists of 17 discrete dimensions of wellness; 5 second-order factors, identified as the essential self, social self, creative self, physical self, and coping self; and 1 higher-order wellness factor. The essential self consists of 4 dimensions, including spirituality, self-care, gender identity, and cultural identity. The creative consists 5 factors, including thinking, emotions, control, positive humor, and work. The social self consists of friendship and love. The physical self consists of exercise and nutrition. The last factor is the coping self, which consists of realistic beliefs, stress management, self-worth, and leisure.

Counseling and Wellness Promotion

Inherent to the role of professional counselor is the promotion of wellness and enhancement of quality of life. The American Counseling Association (ACA) in 1992 underscored the significance of wellness promotion as the foundation to the counseling profession. Counseling for wellness pivots around the salient belief that wellness constitutes purposeful choice and decision making regarding lifestyle and healthy living; individuals who make healthy lifestyle choices will experience greater happiness, life satisfaction, longevity, and overall well-being.

A primary function that counselors have in the promotion of wellness is to encourage and endorse the process of client self-awareness, self-acceptance, and responsible living in efforts to promote a healthy lifestyle. By espousing and introducing a holistic wellness approach to the counseling process, professional counselors can further perpetuate the guiding philosophy of wellness, that being an acknowledgment of the whole person. The profession of counseling is rooted in a strength-based approach when working with clients, much like the underpinnings of wellness paradigms that also focus on engendering a sense of self-empowerment and optimal functioning. The nature of the counseling profession requires that counselors create and maintain a safe and supportive therapeutic environment that will encourage positive growth and desired change. Moreover, professional counselors are committed and obligated to enhance and increase clients' knowledge base regarding holistic health, wellness, and creative living.

The emerging paradigms of health and wellness embrace prevention, early intervention, and alternative interventions. With the growing importance on wellness and holistic health care in the 21st century, the popularity of complementary and alternative medicine has significantly increased among U.S.

adults in recent years. More Americans are relying on alternative paradigms in health care in efforts to treat ailments, promote wellness, delay aging, and protect against illness.

Perhaps the first mental health professionals who embrace and adhere to a wellness approach in understanding, designing, and implementing a preventive orientation that focuses on positive human growth, optimal functioning, holistic health, and well-being are professional counselors. Counselors are in a leading position to promote health and affect wellness among a diverse population of individuals.

— *Holly Tanigoshi*

See also **Ethnopsychiatry; Psychology and Genetics**

Further Readings

Ardell, D. B., & Langdon J. G. (1989). *Wellness, the body, mind, and spirit.* Dubuque, IA: Kendall/Hunt.

Capuzzi, D., & Gross D. R. (1999). *Counseling and psychotherapy.* Upper Saddle River, NJ: Prentice Hall.

DeJong, P., & Berg, I. K. (1998). *Interviewing for solutions.* Pacific Grove, CA: Brooks/Cole.

Eagan, G. (1989). *The skilled helper.* Pacific Grove, CA: Brooks/Cole.

Ellis, A. (1995). *Better, deeper, and more enduring brief therapy.* New York: Brunner/Mazel.

Gladding, S. (2002). *Family therapy: History, theory, and practice.* Upper Saddle River, NJ: Prentice Hall.

Gladding, S. T., & Newsome, D. (2004). *Community and agency counseling.* Upper Saddle. River, NJ: Prentice Hall.

Myers, J., Sweeney, T., & Witmer, J. M. (2000). The wheel of wellness counseling for wellness: A holistic model for treatment planning. *Journal of Counseling and Development, 78,* 251–266.

COUSTEAU, JACQUES-YVES (1910–1997)

Jacques-Yves Cousteau (1910–1997) was the father of modern underwater exploration as well as a pioneer of underwater photography. A marvelous visionary and inventor, he designed the first underwater breathing system, the *aqualung,* as well as depth record-breaking submarines and underwater research stations. A passionate and groundbreaking filmmaker, Cousteau created over 100 films, winning him three Academy Awards for best documentary, including for his debut underwater documentary, *The Silent World* (1956). Cousteau's foremost passion, the flame that sparked all other interests in his life, was for the preservation and exploration of marine environments. Cousteau envisioned and created technology that allowed him to explore previously unreachable marine worlds and shared his love for these places with his films, books, and philanthropic endeavors. He opened the doors for humanity to discover and understand the previously misunderstood and underappreciated ecology and biodiversity of marine life.

Cousteau's passion for exploration and travel began from childhood, when he often accompanied his father on his many seabound travels. His love for film was also rooted in his childhood, as he made his first film at age 13 and went on to produce several more short melodramas, in which he always has the role of the villain. By the age of 22, Cousteau had joined the French naval academy and was traveling all over the world aboard the *Jeanne d' Arc,* all the while filming the cultures and peoples me met. At 25, he enrolled in the aviation school, but after a car accident that nearly cost him an arm, he was forced to leave and return to the naval academy. Once returned, he avidly swam and snorkeled to help recuperate his arm with several of his academy friends. Even here, Cousteau was not without a camera, and he soon makeshifted one he could use for underwater filming. He was, however, frustrated at his time limitation for having to swim up for air. This inspired him to design a device that would make extended underwater exploration for individuals possible. With the help of an engineer, Cousteau brought his design to life and in 1943 successfully tested and filmed the first scuba equipment, then called the aqualung.

During World War II, the aqualung was at first used for military purposes, but after the war, Cousteau used it primarily for scientific exploration. The invention would be the beginning of a new era in marine exploration, with Cousteau at the helm.

In 1950, he acquired an old converted minesweeper called the *Calypso.* The ship would serve as his primary research vessel for 46 years and became the

Source: Courtesy of the Library of Congress.

mascot of his travels. Aboard the *Calypso*, Cousteau came across the first extensive underwater archeological dig, led countless scientific dives, submerged and tested scientific submarine prototypes, and filmed his award-winning television series, *The Undersea World of Jacques Cousteau*. He directed the engineering of numerous submarines and underwater research stations, all designed to help scientists better study marine life.

In 1958, Cousteau first became aware of the negative human affects on marine ecosystems when he revisited a site where some of his first filmings had taken place along the French Riviera. He reacted by forming the Cousteau Society, a nonprofit organization aimed at the conservation of marine ecosystems, in 1974. The Cousteau Society leads important efforts in international lobbies for better marine conservation as well as scientific evaluations of marine wellness all over the world. Cousteau's environmental efforts did not go unnoticed, as he received the U.S. Medal of Freedom from President Ronald Reagan and the National Geographic Gold Medal for Exploration from President John F. Kennedy.

Through his inventions, films, and books, Jacques Cousteau not only created the modern world of marine exploration but brought it to the eyes and ears of millions across the globe. His efforts to raise awareness over conservation issues reached and inspired people all over the world and played an essential role in modern environmental issues, both politically and culturally. Cousteau envisioned and sought after a global society that would collaborate on all issues, including environmental. He helped catalyze this process by raising awareness and concern over marine health endangerment. Such environmental issues fall under no political boundaries and, so, called for international cooperation. Cousteau's love for the sea showed him the necessity for a global society and thus spurred his life's efforts toward this goal. After his death in 1997, French President Jacques Chirac noted Cousteau as being "a great Frenchman who was also a citizen of the world."

— *Andrew P. Xanthopoulos*

See also **Environmental Philosophy**

Further Readings

Cousteau, J. (1985). *The ocean world*. New York: Abrams.

Cousteau, J. (2004). *The silent world*. New York: National Geographic Adventure Classics.

Cousteau, J., & Sivirine, A. (1983). *Jacques Cousteau's Calypso*. New York: Abrams.

 CRANIOMETRY

The technique of measuring the human body for the purpose of describing or comparing individuals and groups of individuals is known as *anthropometry*. Anthropometry includes four basic subject matters: somatometry, cephalometry, osteometry, and craniometry. Craniometry is the measurement of the skull (cranium and mandible), especially measurements on dry bone. Craniometry has a long history in the biological sciences, as some of the earliest works on skeletal biology focused on measurements to complement descriptions of materials.

At the end of the 19th century, Anders Retzius created the cephalic index, sparking large-scale efforts to measure populations of living people. The cephalic index is a simple formula that divides the maximum head breadth by the maximum head length, and multiplies by 100. The cephalic index is used on living individuals and is distinguished from the cranial index, which is the same measurements on dry bone. On the basis of these measurements, attempts were made to differentiate between local populations from which an individual was descended. The basic premise underlying this methodology is that individuals with shared ancestry share similar cranial shape, due to morphology being strongly determined by genetics.

The data accrued from such studies was used for a variety of purposes, ranging from genuine scientific inquiry to justifying racial stereotypes, immigration laws, and arguments of racial superiority. There were even attempts to relate the shape of one's head to criminality, and pseudosciences such as phrenology gained widespread use as a "civilized" tool for justifying racism. A backlash against misuse of biomeasurements led to many works that sought to dispel these notions, such as the research of Franz Boas and Ales Hrdlička on Eskimo skeletal morphology. In the early 20th century, Boas published his seminal work, *Changes in Bodily Form of Descendents of Immigrants,* which compared cranial measurements of thousands of immigrants to those of their children, who had grown up in the United States. He concluded that the children of immigrants did not show sufficient affinities to their parents to support the notion that genetics played the major role in determining the shape of the skull of individuals. This work was a major blow to biological determinism and to the importance of cranial measurements as a distinguishing characteristic between populations.

Despite criticisms from various fronts, Boas's work became a fundamental part of anthropology and modern society, underpinning such documents as the first United Nations Educational, Scientific, and Cultural Organization (UNESCO) statement on race. However, while his research has remained a strong component of the argument that the environment is the primary determinant of morphology (rather than genetics), the validity of craniometrics has become well established in the field of forensic anthropology, paleoanthropology, and archaeology. Forensic anthropology has developed a number of statistical methods using craniometric data that distinguish both sex and racial affiliation, and these interpretive frameworks have been used extensively in paleoanthropology to sex and type specimens and distinguish between closely related species. In addition, archaeological research uses these methods in the determination of group affiliations of skeletal material, in order to map migration patterns in prehistory.

Rather than simple measures of cranial length versus breadth, researchers have developed a suite of osteometric points that correspond to functional features of the cranium. Measurements are taken as chords between points, and multivariate analysis of the resulting measurements compares the shape of the skull with known samples in order to evaluate probably ancestry. The inherent limitation of this method is context, meaning that when particular regional variations (not necessarily correlated to "races") have not been sampled, correct identification is impossible. Normal population variance also results in individuals that do not fit particularly well, since identification is based on probability rather than qualitative characters. In addition, individuals of mixed ancestry often do not fit well into a particular category when looking at cranial measures. Despite such limitations, craniometry remains extremely useful in forensic contexts for identification of human remains.

Craniometry is a probabilistic method of discriminating between possible ancestries of an individual. The utility for identification of human remains in forensic contexts has resulted in the continued refinement of formulae and procedures over more than a century, and the principles have extended into related aspects of physical anthropology, such as archaeology and the discrimination of paleontological species.

— *Christopher David Kreger*

See also **Anthropometry; Osteology, Human**

Further Readings

Bass, W. M. (1987). *Human osteology: A laboratory and field manual.* Columbia: Missouri Archaeological Society.
Buikstra, J. E., & Ubelaker, D. H. (1994). *Standards for data collection from human skeletal remains.* Fayetteville: Arkansas Archeological Survey.
Gill, G. W., & Rhine, S. (1990). *Skeletal attribution of race.* Albuquerque: University of New Mexico: Maxwell Museum of Anthropology.

CRANIOMETRY

For centuries, anthropologists have studied the craniometry of humans in order to determine whether or not brain formation can be used to identify race, sex, intelligence, criminal tendencies, and other physical characteristics. The science of craniometry has been particularly helpful in allowing scientists to identify human remains in the study of anthropology. Scientists have also used craniometry to unlock the secrets of fossils. In August 2004, scientists reported that brain X-rays of an archaeopteryx, one of only nine such fossils to exist, has revealed that this winged and feathered creature may have been able to fly, making it the world's oldest known bird. The archaeopteryx, which lived some 150 million years ago, has also been identified as a dinosaur. While the archaeopteryx's brain and inner ear displayed characteristics similar to birds of contemporary times, other traits such as a full set of teeth and a long, bony tail placed the archaeopteryx solidly in the dinosaur family. In the early 1990s, ornithologist Alan Feduccia of the University of North Carolina announced that his examination of the claws of the archaeopteryx had revealed that they were tree dwellers rather than ground dwellers, offering the information as additional evidence for the theory that the archaeopteryx was a bird and not a dinosaur.

In 2004, paleontologist Timothy B. Rowe and his team at the University of Texas at Austin used computerized tomography (CT) to scan the brain of an archaeopteryx to try to solve the puzzle. The more than 1,300 images they produced provided the necessary information to workers at the Natural History Museum in London, who reconstructed the brain of the fossil. Paleontologist Angela C. Milner guided the efforts that resulted in the discovery that the cerebellum of the archaeopteryx covered nearly half of the animal's brain. The information gathered from the CT scans also led scientists to believe that the archaeopteryx possessed excellent eyesight and hearing, in addition to well-developed muscle coordination, characteristics shared by all birds. This information, coupled with a 2003 discovery by Larry Witmer of Ohio University at Athens that pterosaurs also possessed large brains and optic lobes, has excited those who are interested in the origin of flight. Pterosaurs have been identified as flying reptiles that lived some 235 million to 65 million years ago. In 2003, while doing postgraduate work at the University of Calgary, Nick Longrich discovered evidence that the archaeopteryx used its legs to help it fly, leading to some speculation that birds glided before they actually flew.

Both the British Museum in London and the Berlin Museum in Germany have nearly completed skeletons of the archaeopteryx, which when full grown is approximately the size of the contemporary magpie or grackle. Other archaeopteryx fossils have been partially reconstructed. Since the first fossilized archaeopteryx was discovered in 1861 in the Solnhofen region of Bavaria in southern Germany, scientists have been unsure whether more than one species of this dinosaur existed. They had been tentatively identified as the *Archaeopteryx recurva*, the *Archaeopteryx siemensii*, the *Archaeopteryx bavarica*, and the *Archaeopteryx lithographica*. In April 2004, Phil Senter and James Robins of Northern Illinois University applied regression analysis to compare six skeletons, determining that all known specimens of the archaeopteryx should be identified as *Archaeopteryx lithographica*.

— Elizabeth Purdy

PHRENOLOGY

Although phrenology has been discounted by anthropologists now, there was a time in the early 1800s when many people believed it was a science. Phrenology, sometimes known as cranioscopy, was the study of the structure of the human skull in order to read the person's character and mental capacity. Phrenologists believed that mental faculties were located in brain "organs" on the brain's surface, which could be felt if you ran your hands over the person's head. It was believed that brain organs grew larger as they were used, so those who used the organs a lot would create bumps on their skulls.

Phrenology came from the theories of Franz Joseph Gall, a Viennese physician in the late 1700s and early 1800s. He stated that the size of an organ in the brain was a measure of its power and that the development of various organs dictated the shape of the brain. Therefore, the surface of the skull was an accurate index to a person's psychological aptitudes and tendencies. From the mid 1790s to approximately 1810, Gall and his disciple, J.G. Spurzheim, were the only practitioners of the science. The English-speaking world learned about phrenology from a review condemning it in the prestigious *Edinburgh Review*. Many people became interested. A phrenological society was founded in 1820 in Edinburgh. Many others followed throughout Britain and America in the next few decades. During the 1830s and 1840s, phrenology was very popular in America.

Phrenology was always controversial, and never widely accepted as an actual science. By the middle of the 19th century, it had been almost totally discredited as a science in Europe, although the idea continued to flourish in America for quite some time. Phrenology was subscribed to by such illustrious people as Ralph Waldo Emerson, Horace Mann, and Thomas Edison. Even as late as 1934, many people still believed in the pseudoscience. Henry C. Lavery and Frank P. White invented a machine, called a psychograph, that did a phrenological reading with a printout. The psychograph was made up of 1,954 parts and measured 32 mental faculties. The owners of one of the machines netted about $200,000 with the device at the 1934 Century of Progress Exposition in Chicago.

Phrenology did have some correct assumptions about the human brain. Such things as intellect, emotions, and perception are located in the brain. Also different parts of the brain are responsible for different functions.

— Pat McCarthy

CREATIONISM VERSUS GEOLOGY

Creationism is the belief that our universe came into being in exactly the way described in the Bible's book of Genesis. This literal interpretation of the Bible's accountings of our beginnings has been embraced by some—but not all—Protestant Christians and Catholics. Many levels of the Catholic Church give Genesis a more allegorical or symbolic meaning, and Pope John Paul II publicly accepted the theory of evolution.

A History of the Debate

Since antiquity, humankind has tried to apply science to the Bible's description of creation, eventually giving rise to the *science of origins* and a *natural theology*, which considered that the marvels revealed by science through nature confirmed religion. In 1748, Count Buffon proposed that the Earth could be millions of years old, an idea that outraged the theological authorities at Sorbonne, who forced him to publicly recant. Buffon went on to define seven geological eras, in accordance with the days in Genesis.

In the first part of 19th century, naturalists such as Louis Agassiz, Georges Cuvier, and Alcide d'Orbigny supported the idea of a series of successive extinctions and creations. Their *catastrophism* was used to integrate and reconcile the scientific discoveries of geology with the Bible's doctrine. But the Archbishop Ussher had established that the date of creation was 4004 BC, and the new data demonstrated that the Earth was many years older. Today's creationists consider the Great Flood responsible for all fossils, but early catastrophists did not.

By the middle of the 19th century, James Hutton's *actualism* and Charles Lyell's *uniformitarism* began to overtake catastrophism. Geology was an emerging science, and its paradigm questioned some of the constructs of creationism: the Great Flood, the direct creation of all animals by God, and the creation of human beings from clay. Lyell, particularly, presented theoretical foundations that set the stage for Charles Darwin's *natural selection* in the transformation of species and the theory of evolution. Only a few fossils were known in Darwin's time, and scientists could not find support to corroborate the evolutionary process using palaeontology until Simpson demonstrated the value of fossils to document the *synthesis theory* of evolution.

Acceptance of Darwin's theory of evolution has been gradual. At the end of the 19th century, some renowned scientists remained opposed to the theory. Some, such as the geologist James D. Dana, defended evolutionism but supported the specific creation of human beings and the comparison between day and geological era. Others, including Arnold Guyot, a naturalist from Princeton, and the Canadian geologist John W. Dawson not only compared day and era, but attempted to harmonize science and the Bible by invoking a singular creation for matter, life, and humankind.

In 1909, C. I. Scofield published a version of the Bible that enforced Thomas Chalmers's idea that there were long intervals of time between the events described in verse 1 and verse 2 in the first chapter of Genesis. This explanation allowed the time required by earth sciences between the first destruction and a new creation. At the same time, geologist and Protestant minister George F. Wright began a text on Christian opinions about evolution. In the 1920s, evolutionists in some parts of the United States were persecuted, and various professors resigned.

In 1923, a geology textbook by George McCready Price gave the Great Flood credit for producing all the rocks and fossils at the same time through catastrophe. Price, a Seventh-Day Adventist, also wrote other books disputing the theory of evolution, the first time that a creationist took on evolution through a scientific—rather than Biblical—approach. Today, we consider Price a pioneer who inspired the scientific creationists of the 1960s, especially Henry M. Morris.

The Debate in the United States

In the United States before 1925, 37 states approved laws that prohibited teaching evolution in public schools. In 1925, professor John Thomas Scopes went on trial in Tennessee for teaching the theory of evolution. In a case that would become known as the Monkey Trial, the conviction carried so light a sentence that creationists could claim no victory. Still, writers of school textbooks feared an antievolution backlash, and the theory of evolution nearly disappeared from texts. It took 40 years for the antievolution laws to be declared unconstitutional and repealed.

Particularly in the U.S., creationists organized and formed societies to fight evolutionary theory. These included the Religion and Science Association (1935),

the Society for the Study of Creation, the Deluge, and Related Science (1938), and the American Scientific Affiliation (1948). At the latter's convention in 1953, Henry M. Morris, a professor of hydraulic engineering, gave a speech on "Biblical Evidence of a Recent Creation and a Universal Flood" based on Price's geology of the Great Flood. In 1957, the theologian John C. Whitcomb wrote *The Genesis Flood.* In 1958, the Seventh-Day Adventists created the Geoscience Research Institute in Loma Linda, California to study the scientific evidence about our origins. In 1961, Whitcomb, in collaboration with Morris, published a well-received work of scientific creationism. In 1963, creationists formed the Creation Research Society in Michigan based on a committee of scientific experts and nonscientific members (such as Whitcomb). This society's members believed that the Bible was the written word of God and historically and scientifically true.

In 1970 in San Diego, California, the Creation-Science Research Center directed by Morris and Gish was formed to spread the idea that evolutionism and creationism are two concurrent scientific hypotheses. In his book *Evolution, the Fossils Say No!* (1972), Gish attempted to discredit the value of fossils in what amounted to an attack on paleontology. In Whitcomb's 1972 book *The Early Earth,* he revives the idea of long time intervals for the days described in Genesis. This time-interval approach led to the 1981 laws passed in Arkansas and Louisiana that granted equal treatment in the schools for the theory of evolution and the science of creationism. When many American scientists protested the enactment of similar laws in other states, these laws were rescinded in 1987.

In the U.S. today, polls show that half the population believes that God created human beings in our current form less than 10,000 years ago. In 1996, members of the education committee of the State of New Mexico eliminated all references to evolution in the *State's Standards for Science Education* in public schools. Creationists continue to publish antievolutionary works: The Geoscience Research Institute alone publishes *Origins,* a magazine about the history of the Earth; *Geoscience Reports,* a newsletter for the general public; and *Ciencia de los orígenes* for the Hispanic community. The Creation Research Society, still directed by Morris and Gish, publishes the magazine *CRS Quarterly* and the bimonthly newsletter *Creation Matters.*

The Debate in Australia

In Australia, in 1989 Rhondda E. Jones warned about the dangers of creationism in teaching science and proposed that scientific creationism was one of the best illustrations of pseudoscience. In 1994, the director of the Department of Geology at the University of Newcastle, R. Plimer, wrote *Telling Lies for God, Reason vs. Creationism* and soon filed suit against a creationist who claimed to have found Noah's Ark through scientific analysis; Plimer's case was rejected.

The Debate in Europe

In Europe, the Catholic sect *Cercle Scientifique et Historique* was created to spread the word of the diluvian leader, Fernand Crombette. One of the sect's most outspoken members, French sedimentologist Guy Berthault, in 1988 discredited evolution by denying the main principle of the superposition of strata. In 1991, another active leader, Dominique Tassot, concluded that evolutionary prehistory is illogical, irrational, and a permanent fraud. Furthermore, Tassot claimed that only the Bible's trilogy of the Creation, the Descent, and the Flood is simple, complete, and factual. In Spain, creationists may remain Catholic but sympathize with scientific creationists. Professor of geology Indalecio Quintero published *Adam and Eve Were Alive* in 1986 in an attempt to integrate scientific data and the Bible. In 1996, Alejandro Sanvisens Herreros, a Catholic professor, published *The Whole Truth About Evolution* through the University Publishing House of Barcelona. It attacks evolution using the same arguments as Morris and Gish. The creationist publishing house founded in Tarrasa (Barcelona) and directed by Santiago Escuain has translated and published many articles and books written by U.S. creationists.

The Geological and Paleontological Perspective

Historically, data from geology and paleontology have not well served creationists. Scientists such as Kitcher, McGowan, Berra, and Birx, as well as geologists and paleontologists such as Newell, Gould, Gastaldo and Tanner, Eldredge, and Molina have defended evolutionism. Recent data indicate that the Earth is thousands of millions of years old, and that, over this time, slow geological processes—almost imperceptible in the short length of a human life—have molded the Earth's surface, giving rise to the current geological and geographical configurations. Paleontology has demonstrated that, throughout these millions of years, life has evolved from the smallest and most simple cells, in the Precambrian, to the most complex and intelligent animals. In addition to the biological data, fossils are the best evidence of evolution and its mechanisms.

— *Eustoquio Molina*

See also **Big Bang Theory; Darwin, Charles; Evolution, Arc of; Evolution, Disbelief in; Fossils; Monkey Trial (1925)**

Further Readings

Eldredge, N. (Ed.). (2000). *The triumph of evolution and the failure of creationism.* New York: Freeman.

Gillispie, C. (1996). *Genesis and geology. A study in the relations of scientific thought, natural theology, and social opinion in Great Britain, 1790–1850.* Cambridge, MA: Harvard University Press.

Molina, E. (2000). Evolution and "scientific" creationism in the earth sciences. Geological and paleontological arguments. In H. J. Birx & E. I. Kolchinsky (Eds.), *Science and society* (pp. 246–252). St. Petersburg: Russian Academy of Sciences.

CREATIONISM, BELIEFS IN

Creationism is a surprisingly complex and diverse position that has had resurgence in the first part of the 21st century. Initially a stance taken in response to the development of evolutionary sciences in the 19th century, Creationism is usually based on three fundamental positions:

- A superior being created all out of nothing.
- The doctrine of the essentialism of species.
- A divine being creates individual human souls.

While creationism is most often cited as a position held by certain Christian groups, there are also a number of non-Christian, Jewish, Islamic, Vedic, and indigenous groups that maintain creationist positions. And, although creationism has often been reduced to a simple antiscientific stance, it is an area that actually contains a wide range of ideas and formulations. These can be divided into Christian-based beliefs, non-Christian, and "great tradition" beliefs.

Christian-Based Creationism

1. One of the oldest associations of creationists is the *Flat Earth Society*. While a seeming anachronism today, the Flat Earth Society maintains a lively discussion based on a literal translation of the biblical account of Noah and the Flood. Their view is that the earth is covered by a solid dome (firmament) and that attempts to "prove" the earth is round are biased, politically driven propaganda.

2. *Geocentric creationists* have had a resurgence in the past 20 years, notably led by Tom Will's movement to reform the Kansas school system curriculum. This version of creationism posits the earth as spherical but argues that the Earth, and not the sun, is the center of the universe. Using a literal interpretation of the Old Testament Hebrew cosmological assumption, the geocentric creationists have lobbied extensively to ban references to evolution, earth history, and scientific methods from public school textbooks and classrooms.

3. A controversial but influential work by the famed English naturalist, P. H. Gosse, *Omphalos*, published in 1857, united *Christian fundamentalism and uniformitarianism*. Gosse argued that our perception of age influences the way we see the earth. Predating Darwin's work by 2 years, Gosse maintained that the earth appears old to us but is really quite young. While he managed to affront both fundamentalists and scientists with his theories, it remains a work that is discussed in literature (Borges) and in science (Stephen Jay Gould) and by creationists.

4. *Restitution creationists,* or "gap creationists," interpret the two creations of Genesis (Gen. 1 and Gen. 2) to account for the age of the Earth, and the relatively recent creation of life. According to this tradition, God created the ancient world in Genesis 1, and millions of years passed. Genesis 2 is God's recreation of the world, accomplished in a literal 6 days. This would then account for the age of the earth geologically, and for the recent arrival of human beings.

5. *Day-age creationists* interpret the 6 days of creation as a metaphor. Rather than a literal 24-hour day, each day stands for millions of years. In this way, they account for God's ongoing creation as well as the age of the earth.

6. *Progressive creationists* view modern science as providing evidence of God's power at work in the universe. The big bang theory is accepted in that it explains the Creator's immense grandeur. However, modern biology and evolutionary sciences are viewed with extreme skepticism, and this school maintains an essentialist position concerning the development of species.

7. An extremely influential book published by William Paley in 1802 has formed the basis of much creationist thought in what is termed *intelligent design*. In *Natural Theology: or, Evidences of the Existence and Attributes of the Deity, Collected from the Appearances of Nature,* Paley laid out the nature of intelligent design in the universe, or natural theology. The work echoes elements of Thomistic theology, adding to the spiritual philosophy elements of microbiology, mathematics, and logic. This area of creationism is especially adroit in its attacks on evolutionary science and scientific methodology and maintains that evolutionary sciences are in fact a form of materialist philosophy. Some influential groups that argue this position include the Discovery Institute and The Center for Renewal of Science and Culture.

8. *Evolutionary creationism* is yet another Christian-based school of thought that is based on a literal interpretation of the story of Genesis. It adds to this an acknowledgment of scientific objectivity. However, while all of nature depends on the will of God for its beingness, Creation took place before time as, we now experience it, was in place. Thus, there were biological human creatures prior to Adam and Eve, but Adam and Eve were the first spiritually aware beings.

9. *Theistic evolution* is a Christian position that is held by the larger Protestant denominations and by most Roman Catholics. In their creationist account, God created and is present in the evolutionary process. Most of contemporary scientific method and theory is acceptable here, as these disciplines shed light on how God works in human history. The Bible is generally used as an interpretive document that needs to be explained in light of new discoveries and insights. Thus, these creationists still posit a God that is outside the realm of science, and is unknowable in some areas (e.g., the creation of human souls).

10. *Young Earth* creationists are often referred to as "scientific creationists." This can cause some confusion, as their methodology is not scientific. Again, they rely on a literal interpretation of the Bible and follow Bishop Ussher's calculation of a 4,000-year-old Earth. And while they accept the concept of a heliocentric solar system, all of the Earth's processes are reduced to (a) the result of Noah's flood and (b) the sin of Adam and Eve.

The term *scientific creationism* is derived from the work of George McCready Price, a Seventh-Day Adventist who was deeply influenced by the visions of the prophetess, Helen White. Gaining a wide audience in the 20th century by melding science with Biblical interpretations, Price remains an important icon long after his death (ca. 1963). The basics of scientific creationism are similar to the above schools; that is, God created the universe, and biological life was created in its essential form. The first humans were a special creation at a certain point in time. Again, the evidence of geological history is proof of the Great Flood of Genesis. And while nature must obey fixed laws, the Creator can intervene at any time. The science of this form of creationism is essentially a study of teleology; humans are supposed to study creation in order to understand our ultimate destiny. In most cases, this is posited as a finite Earth and an apocalyptic ending.

Summarizing the major points of most Christian creationists, the following points are pertinent:

1. Creation is the work of a Trinitarian God.

2. The Bible is a divinely inspired document.

3. Creation took place in 6 days.

4. All humans descended from Adam and Eve.

5. The accounts of Earth in Genesis are historically accurate records.

6. The work of human beings is to reestablish God's perfection of creation though a commitment to Jesus.

Christian creationism was most infamously displayed in the Scopes Trial of 1925. Clarence Darrow defended John Scopes, the high school biology teacher, from the fundamentalist position of William Bryan. The national attention that this brought to evolution is usually overshadowed by the fact Scopes was convicted and fined for teaching evolutionary theory. The political nature of the creationist position continues today in numerous constitutional challenges to scientific teaching in public schools. Most often cited in recent debates in the Schemp Opinion (1963, *Abington School vs. Schemp*), which ruled that evolutionary teaching could represent overt antagonism to religious ideals. The revival of creationist efforts to influence public education in the 21st century has been seen in challenges in Georgia and Oklahoma school systems.

Non-Christian Creationism

It would be a mistake to classify all creationists as Bible-based or Christian-based positions. For example, *methodological materialists* argue that while God did start creation, God does not actively interfere with evolutionary process. Agnostic in a sense, this school uses scientific methodology for explaining the creative influences in natural developments and denies the activity of a supernatural entity in natural processes.

Other examples of non-Christian creationists are *Raelians,* who claim life came from another planet. They attribute alien scientists and UFOs for life that we have on earth. The *Panspermians* claim that bacteria and other microorganisms were carried here from other solar systems by meteors and other naturally occurring phenomena. And *catastrophic evolutionists* maintain that evolution was quick, driven in quantum leaps by extreme conditions in the very recent past. Each of the above theoretical positions has produced cultlike followings, such as Heaven's Gate and Solar Temple, that lie outside most organized religious creeds.

Great Traditions Creationism

Other major world religious traditions exemplify a wide spectrum of creationist thought. While Christianity has dominated the arena for some time in the West and has used its political power to influence public discourse on theory, science, and evolution, Islam, Judaism, Hindi, and indigenous religions also have commented on, and are concerned with, creationist ideals and discussions.

In the Hebrew tradition, a strict literal interpretation of the Torah is difficult to maintain. Unlike the fundamentalist translations that are part of the Christian tradition, Hebrew tradition maintains the importance of four levels of interpretation. Referred to as "PRDS" (garden, or paradise), creation in the Hebrew tradition is viewed as a complexity of (a) *Pshat,* the literal meaning and intent of the verses; (b) *Remez,* the particular grammar, spelling, syntax, and sentence structure that indicates deeper meaning; (c) *Drash,* the homiletical level of interpretation (on this level the metaphorical potential of the verse for each individual life is important); and (d) *Sod,* the secret, mystical level of interpretation. Therefore, in the Hebrew tradition of creationism, a weaving of theology and philosophy can coexist with pure science in a manner that does not explicitly deny evolutionary explanations. Still, the explanation for all life is attributed to Yahweh and to the special relationship of Yahweh to the Hebrew people. Creation, then, took place outside of ordinary time, and the Genesis story exists to relate a story about relative values.

For the Islamic community, Genesis does not have the moral ascendancy as does the Koran. So, while Islam can tend to a more literal tradition of scriptural interpretation, it is not as rigid as Christian creationism. The Koran accounts of creation are quite vague, allowing a representation of diverse interpretations. The essential notion is that Allah created all, and Allah is all-good. Thus, the Islamic creationists exhibit a wide spectrum, from literalistic to the more liberal, especially depending on the area where the particular Islamic tradition is practiced.

Since much of the Islamic world remains an area where the theory of evolution has not yet taken hold, traditional Islamic beliefs regarding creation remain dominant. As more Western influences penetrate traditional areas, however, elements of intelligent design creationism are allied to Islamic teachings and science. Some fundamental Islamic groups have attached themselves to the Turkish writers Harun Yahya and Fethullah Gulen, who criticize Western evolutionary sciences as leading to moral corruption. Areas that illustrate particular allegiance to more Koran fundamental creationist ideals are Indonesia and Malaysia, citing the decadence of Western culture and society as evidence of the dangers of evolutionary thought.

According to the Hindu Vedic texts, the Earth is ancient, undergoing periodic transformations lasting billions of years. While the science of evolution and the Vedic teachings of creation appear to be conflicting, actually, the Avatars of Vishnu are viewed as close to Darwin's theories of evolution. The theological/philosophical basis of Hindu cosmology is based on a cyclical notion of time, with periodic creations, rebirths, and deaths. While the above major religions have shown evidence of sometimes quite volatile reactions to the concept of evolution, the creationism of Hindu is accepting of the theories within their own traditional way of knowing.

Indigenous Creationism

Various indigenous groups voice a strong challenge to the sciences of evolution today. In North America, the contemporary Native American movement criticizes the scientific community as being racist and biased toward a Eurocentric explanation and worldview. Calling upon their own tribal traditions of creation, many Indians maintain that they have always been in North America and were specially created to care for the Earth. In particular, many Indians discard the out-of-Africa notion and the spread of human beings through Asia, Europe, and the Pacific as an example of European control and domination. Along with this critique are arguments that the Ice Age and Beringia theories are scientific myths. For Native Americans, in general, the Great Spirit created the first people here, and they have always been here in order to care for the world. Vine Deloria Jr. has been particularly vocal about what he views as the ongoing colonization of thought by Western science and the abuse of indigenous epistemologies of creation.

Creationism, then, is a multifaceted epistemology that seeks to find the roots of human existence and the Earth's existence in a spiritualized, nonscientific milieu. The strength of the movement has been particularly strong in the West, where scientific-style analysis of the Bible has taken place in the last 100 years. For while many denominations had for centuries viewed the Bible as the literal, unerring word of God, the critical analysis opened the door for a more systematic interpretation of the documents. This, in addition to the ascension of the scientific paradigms, brought concern about cultural changes and the seemingly atheistic turn to secularism. Among indigenous peoples, the influence of Nativistic movements has raised consciousness about their own traditional ways of knowing and skepticism about the ability of Western paradigms to provide essential answers to their ways of life. The creationists are united in their common cause to keep a sense of the mystical, nonscientific explanation for existence in the public discourse.

Creationism beliefs can also be viewed as reactionary movements to maintain a place within the rapidly shifting cultural environments today. As noted above, many Christian-based creationists are returning to a literal interpretation of Scripture and a call to return to older sets of biblically based values. Similarly, the creationist movements in Islam and Judaism tend to be fundamentalist reactions to the secularization of world cultures. And in the case of indigenous peoples and their need to maintain sovereignty and to maintain a critical place within a globalized culture, the recalling of creationist myths establishes their unique place in world history.

Creationist studies can be appropriate to the field of anthropology on several levels. For one, the examination and analysis of creation stories have consistently been an important area of folklore scholarship. Understanding the cosmology and cosmogony of a culture provides an insight into the way a society structures its institutions. In addition, the literary nuances of creationist concepts provide scientists with alternative ways of examining the merits of evolution over a wide spectrum. For example, Native American criticism of the ice-free corridor and the Clovis-first theories have continued to bring about alternative theories to new evidence of very ancient human occupation of the Americas. On the other hand, the scientific theoretical models that are integral to evolutionary sciences do not attempt to answer the same sorts of questions that the creationists are concerned with, such as the existence of God and a spirit world. Thus, while science is a powerful paradigm for explaining facts, it remains very important for anthropologists to be aware of and conversant with creationist accounts of existence, as well. This will enable the discipline to adapt to alternative worldviews and to continue to be sensitive to a wide spectrum of cultural phenomena.

— *Ted Fortier*

See also **Big Bang Theory; Darwin, Charles; Darwinism, Modern; Evolution, Arc of; Evolution, Disbelief in**

Further Readings

Deloria, V. Jr. (1995). *Red earth, white lies: Native Americans and the myth of scientific fact.* New York: Scribner.

Eve, R. A. (1990). *The creationist movement in modern America.* Boston: Twayne.

Kaiser, C. B. (1991). *Creation and the history of science.* Grand Rapids, MI: Eerdmans.

Moore, J. A. (2002). *From Genesis to genetics: The case of evolution and creationism.* Berkeley: University of California Press.

National Academy of Sciences, Committee on Science and Creationism. (1984). *Science and creationism: A view from the National Academy of Sciences.* Washington, DC: National Academy Press.

Zabilka, I. (1992). *Scientific malpractice: The creation/evolution debate.* Lexington, KY: Bristol Books.

 # CRETE, ANCIENT

A stunning civilization arose in Crete between 1950 BCE and 1200 BCE, only to collapse for reasons that are as yet not clearly understood. What caused this civilization to flourish, and then mysteriously disappear? What were its links to events on the mainland of Greece? Since the early 1900s, archaeologists have uncovered monumental buildings and evidence suggesting that Crete presents a clear case of early state formation. What remains unclear is who the people were and what language they spoke. Also found were three prealphabetic writing systems, two of which remain to be deciphered. The third writing system, Linear B, is derived from the first two and proved to be early Greek; it was deciphered during the 1950s by the English architect Michael Ventris. The information received from the Linear B clay tablets forced scholars to rewrite the history of early Greek civilization. The other two represent an unknown language: If deciphered, what would they tell us?

Crete was a mysterious place for the ancient Greeks as well: It was believed to be the birthplace of their god Zeus. Minos, the legendary king of Crete, was the son of Zeus and Europa, a princess kidnapped from Asia Minor. Minos later became a judge in the underworld. According to Athenian legend, the Minotaur, a bull-like creature, lived in the labyrinth and demanded human sacrifice: Seven maidens and seven young men had to be sent on a yearly basis. Finally, the cycle was interrupted by the hero Theseus, who seduced Minos's daughter Ariadne into helping him out of the maze. Crete was also the dwelling place of Daedalus, the

Source: © iStockphoto/Paul Cowan.

clever artist and the first man to fly: Unfortunately, his son Icarus came too close to the sun and fell into the sea en route to Sicily.

Geography and History

Crete is a mountainous island in the eastern Mediterranean, extending along an east-west axis. It is approximately 160 miles long and 40 miles wide in the middle, narrowing toward both ends. A number of valleys crisscross the island, facilitating communication from the earliest times. The highest mountain is Mount Ida, at approximately 8,000 feet.

Crete was first occupied during the Neolithic (ca. 7000 BCE), as archeological finds have shown.

The first inhabitants are believed to have come from Anatolia; they brought agriculture and sheep and goats. For the first three millennia, settlements remained quite small, no more than 50 individuals, and relied on agriculture; between 4500 BCE and 3500 BCE, there were population increases, possibly due to immigration from the Cyclades, a group of islands to the north, which were slowly being populated for the first time. The number of inhabitants at Knossos, a settlement located in the center of the north coast, could have been as high as 1500. Burials in circular graves (tholoi), which were often used for centuries, indicate an egalitarian lifestyle.

During the early Bronze Age, between approximately 3000 BCE and 1900 BCE, a complex civilization began to develop simultaneously at several sites. This period is commonly referred to as the "Prepalatial era." Settlements at Knossos and Phaestos, a community located to the southwest of Knossos near the southern coast, and several smaller ones grew in size and importance.

A second period, the "Protopalatial," lasted from approximately 1900 BCE until 1700 BCE, when the palaces were destroyed, possibly by earthquakes. Generally, the palaces consist of many rooms around several paved courtyards. The palaces had large storage facilities for agricultural surpluses. Clay tablets have been found in one of the earliest hieroglyphic scripts (still not deciphered), which are assumed to be inventory lists. Numerous seals to secure storage rooms have also been found, some bearing the same script. Burials of the Protopalatial period show social stratification, perhaps under the influence of increased contacts and trade with the civilizations of the eastern Mediterranean.

Trade with the surrounding areas intensified during this period, establishing Crete as one of the first thalassocracies, a term first used by the 5th-century BCE Greek historian Thucydides (ca. 460–400 BCE) to indicate absolute power over the seas. The historian Strabo (63 BCE–24 CE) uses the term directly to explain the early supremacy of Crete. Metals were imported from the Greek mainland, Anatolia, and Syria; gold, ivory, and precious stones came from

Egypt; and one mention is found in the palace at Mari on the Euphrates about goods expected from a place called Kaptara: cloths, a fine inlaid sword, and a pair of shoes for the King of Mari to give to Hammurabi of Babylon. According to the tablets of Mari, a Cretan tin buyer also seems to have been living in Ugarit, which was an important transit station for the tin trade.

Craft production, such as weaving and goldsmithing, also seems to have been located at the palaces. Cretan Kamares (bright polychrome) pottery has been found in Egypt, near Elephantine and in Byblos. Minoan pottery was also found at Ugarit, Beirut, Qatna, Hazor, and Cyprus. It is also thought that wood, grain, wine, oil, and textiles may have been exported on Cretan ships, but no traces of those perishable products remain. The influence of Cretan pictorial art has been found in Egypt and in the Near East; Egyptian influence can also be seen in the frescoes on Crete.

Rebuilding took place during the "Neopalatial" period, 1700 BCE to 1450 BCE. The walls of these new palaces were handsomely decorated with paintings of everyday scenes and religious events. The famous "bull-leaping" frescoes date from this era, in which youth (it is unknown whether male or female) are shown to be somersaulting over the backs of bulls, either grabbing the horns of an oncoming bull or leaping between the horns to land on the back and vault off. It is not known whether this formed part of initiation rites or was a sport or part of a cult. Bull leapers also appeared on seals, on boxes, on gold rings, and on pottery; one bronze statue depicting a youth on the back of a bull is at the British Museum. Bull-leaping scenes are also found on the Greek mainland; the last ones most likely were created during the decline of Mycenae. During the Neopalatial period, villalike buildings started to appear in the countryside, suggesting that the control of the palaces may have weakened somewhat. The Linear A script was now used everywhere on the island for administrative purposes. A second era of destruction followed, perhaps again caused by earthquakes combined with foreign invasions.

The final and "Postpalatial" period lasted from 1450 BCE until ca. 1200 BCE, the end of the Late Bronze Age. The original inhabitants appear to have sought refuge in the mountain areas, which leads archeologists to believe that foreign invaders (most likely mainland Mycenaeans) are to be blamed.

Others suggest internal conflict may have caused the destruction of all inhabited sites: In fact, Knossos remained undamaged for about a century after the other centers were destroyed. Whatever may have been the causes, many inhabited areas were abandoned, and the population seems to have crashed. The writing systems fell into disuse, not only on Crete but also on the Greek mainland (Pylos), where tablets with the same Linear B script were found by the archeologist Carl Blegen in 1939. The entire area was plunged into a Dark Age, which lasted until 800 BCE.

Dating of Events and Periods

Scholars continue to adjust the dating of events in Crete, a difficult task, because a difference of several decades can change the presumed causes of the mysterious destructions of the palaces and Minoan culture. For instance, archeologists believe that the cataclysmic volcanic eruption that destroyed the flowering civilization of Thera (present-day Santorini), the southernmost island of the Cyclades, just 60 miles north of Crete, took place around 1520. They assume that the explosion was also responsible for the decline of agriculture on Crete and augured the subsequent collapse of the Neopalatial period. Scientists, however, put the date for the cataclysm at around 1628, too soon to explain the destruction of the palaces. Absolute dating has also been attempted by comparisons with Egypt (Crete is mentioned in some Egyptian records), by the sorting of local pottery and pottery styles, Mycenaean events, C14, and tree ring analysis, as well as the chronology of developments on the nearby Cycladic islands, whose inhabitants may have migrated to Crete on occasion.

Religion and Cult Sites

Mountaintops and caves were important cult sites from the beginnings of Cretan civilization, and numerous terracotta statues (mostly representing slim-waisted goddesses in long skirts), typical double axes, horns of consecration, and other offerings have been found in those locations. Many frescoes in the palaces show depictions of human figures, who may or may not have represented gods and goddesses, in peaceful nature settings, surrounded by animals and flowers. The palaces are thought to have been important cult sites or to have contained shrines and rooms where rituals were carried out. Other sites offer some evidence of human sacrifice: The crushed bodies of a victim, a priest, a female attendant, and one other person were found at Anemospilia, near Knossos. They were apparently surprised inside the building when it collapsed during an earthquake, the same one that may have caused extensive damage around 1700 BCE.

The cave on Mount Ida where Zeus was believed to have hidden from the murderous intent of his father Kronos was an especially sacred place; religious tourists visited the site at least until the Roman era.

Archeology

The civilization of Crete was called "Minoan" by Sir Arthur Evans, the first excavator of the city of Knossos, after the mythological king Minos. His aim was to distinguish Cretan civilization from the one discovered by Heinrich Schliemann on the Greek Peleponnese, which was called "Mycenaean" after the city of Mycenae, the stronghold of (the mythical) King Agamemnon. Evans chose this name to emphasize his belief that Cretan civilization was non-Greek and non-Mycenaean: He believed that the palaces, the storage rooms, and the necessary quest for copper and tin (required to make bronze) indicated that Cretan civilization must have been more closely related to the countries of the Middle East than the Greek mainland. Evans turned out to be only partially right: The tablets found at Pylos on the Peloponnese show that the Mycenaeans had close contact with the inhabitants of Crete during the Postpalatial period, even though their civilizations show differences. At the same time, their records written in Linear B showed that the Mycenaeans were Greeks, as were the people that inhabited the Cretan palaces during the last phase of Minoan civilization. Until the discovery and the decipherment of the Linear B tablets, it was commonly believed that the Mycenaeans were non-Greek.

— *Thérèse de Vet*

Further Readings

Dickinson, O. (1994). *The Aegean Bronze Age.* Cambridge: Cambridge University Press.
Fitton, J. L. (2002). *Peoples of the past: Minoans.* London: British Museum Press.
Marinatos, N. (1993). *Minoan religion: Ritual, image, and symbol.* Columbia: University of South Carolina Press.
Robinson, A. (2002). *The man who deciphered Linear B: The story of Michael Ventris.* London: Thames & Hudson.

 # CRIME

Crime, in the strictest sense, is the willful commission and/or omission of established codified laws of a society, nation, or culture. A less formalized understanding of crime includes the committing of any commonly recognized prohibited act worthy of punishment as established by the norms, mores, and values of a given population. Crime has been widely studied because it is considered a phenomenon when members of a community knowingly commit offenses either against another citizen or against the community or state. The study of crime is essentially grounded in two different perspectives, which are environmental based and biological based. Biological-based theories are concerned with all potential influencing external forces endemic to the social world.

To better understand crime, one must have some understanding of the fundamental social-based theory regarding the power dynamics behind the creation of law and how laws impact crime. Most people think of laws as a means to create fairness and equality for all members of law; however, law may also reflect the controlling interests of the sovereign (government) or those with influence in that society. For an act to be relegated to the status of a crime, it must generally have the condemnation of the majority or those in authority to mandate it into law. In any society, there are those who have greater personal power, due to their wealth, class, official position, or social affiliations. Such persons have the ability to influence the creation of laws that satisfy a personal need or augment and strengthen their social status. This is to say, laws can favor the powerful and actually serve to keep other members of a society at a disadvantage. An act or specific behavior cannot be a criminal offense and the offender cannot be punished unless the act has formal criminal status.

The creation of laws or governing rules within any population of people must therefore be understood as a social process with potentially complex interrelationship and motivations. Consequently, committing crimes and casting certain members of a society as disobedient offenders can have very serious outcomes. Consider how the Christians were effectively labeled as both social deviants and enemies of the state by the ancient Romans. The wholesale persecution and execution of an entire group of people followed solely due of their spiritual beliefs. Such persons, in the current common parlance of criminology, are referred to as a criminal "subgroup." Many contemporary studies of deviants

Source: © iStockphoto/Liv Friis-Larsen.

as a criminal subgroup have been examined as an outcome of social power with respect to who does the labeling, who generates the label, and how the labeled persons are affected. One of the findings is that a key determinant of the labeling process is how effectively those in power can apply the deviant label so the majority population reacts to and the subgroup in question accepts the label.

Consistent with the influence of social power differences is the effect of social structure. Social structure theories maintain that members of the lower class are involved in more crime than those of the upper or middle class. Social structure theories are divided into three areas: strain theory, cultural deviance theory, and social disorganization theory. Strain theory emphasizes that persons of the lower class are unable to attain higher goals or values and this restriction is due to their economic limitations. Their inability to achieve these goals causes strain, which leads some people to reject the established social standards of behaviors. The inability to cope with strain causes some individuals to proceed through life without norms or values to guide their behavior, leading to eventual criminal transgressions. Social disorganization theory maintains there are geographic areas within urban centers that are far more transitional with respect to establishing a sense of community. Such transitional neighborhoods are characterized by light industry and lower-class worker residences that tend to be in a deteriorating and disorganized condition. The disorganization leads to juvenile delinquency and juvenile gangs and ultimately to increased levels of crime. Cultural

deviance theory holds that criminal behavior is simply an act of conformity to lower-class values based upon their differences with the dominant cultural norms and standards. For members to obey the laws and rules of the dominant culture, lower-class members (usually racial and ethnic minorities) are placed in conflict with their class peers.

Social interaction theories address crime from four perspectives: social learning, social control, symbolic interaction, and labeling. Social learning theories maintain criminal behavior is the result of socialization, where peers are taught criminal acts are not only acceptable, but preferable to socially approved acts. Social control theories begin with the belief that human nature is the motivating force behind criminal behavior. The presence of some form of social control keeps humans within the range of acceptable social behavior. However, in the absence of suitable controls, humans are permitted to engage in criminal conduct. Symbolic interaction theories place emphasis on the perception and interpretation of situations, which influence the response. It is theorized that humans will respond in the role or demeanor that others have characterized them. Within the scope of this theory, then, all behavior is a function of self-perception as individuals believe others perceive them.

Biological theories address factors that are not within the environmental-based family of explanations of crime. Beginning with the work of Richard Dugdale in 1877, researchers have sought a biological explanation to criminal behavior. Dugdale's early studies focused on heredity to establish a genial connection of family degeneration. He researched families with histories of criminal involvement, poverty, and mental health problems. His belief was that the family lineage was defective and persons of degenerated criminal stock would produce similar socially defective offspring. His work was sharply criticized as incomplete and unreliable.

An Italian physician named Cesare Lombroso developed a theory known as *atavism*, which held that criminals are predisposed at birth to criminal behavior. Criminals were considered genetic throwbacks to primitive man, with underdeveloped brains. In addition, Lombroso identified several physical characteristics that were indicative of a distinct "criminal type." Some examples of these include large jaws or cheekbones, unusually small or large ears, abnormal teeth, long arms, fleshy lips, and receding chins. Following Lombroso, Charles Goring conducted comparisons of English convicts and noncriminal citizens. He concluded that criminals were shorter and weighed less. This research was challenged because Goring failed to account for the differences in environment. In 1939, Ernest Hooten's study found that convicts tended to have physical characteristics such as low foreheads, long necks, and crooked jaws. Like Goring's research, Hooten's work was criticized for being methodologically flawed.

The efforts of William Sheldon to establish a biological connection to crime is especially significant because it was the first time that a quantitative grading system was developed to gauge the physical traits of criminality. Sheldon found that all people have some elements of three distinct body types: endomorphic, ectomorphic, and mesomorphic. The mesomorphic qualities or traits were determined as especially representative in criminals. His quantitative approach assigned a number on a scale with a 7-point maximum. The three body types were each assigned a number depending on how strongly or significant traits were exhibited in a given individual. This quantification is called a *soma type* and might look like this: 4.6 2.1 5.4. The center figure is always the mesomorphic figure. Naturally, the shortcoming of this approach is that the body type assessment is very dependent upon the interpretation of the assessor and is therefore subjective and unreliable.

There have been a number of other approaches to studying potential biological relationships to criminal behavior. One that was popular for a while was the belief that those who committed crimes were less intelligent than other individuals. This generated research into the intelligence test scoring of delinquencies. The standard IQ test score comparisons created a great deal of controversy because the tests were considered invalid across racial and class lines. Studies also explored chromosome abnormalities with respect to the "XYY" syndrome's relationship to violent crime. It was theorized that the Y chromosome is the designated "male" chromosome and that males are far more violent than females; the extra Y chromosome in some males may reveal an increased proclivity toward violent behavior. However, the studies were unable to confirm any such relationship.

— *Richard M. Seklecki*

See also **Aggression; Deviance; Eugenics; Norms**

Further Readings

Denno, D. (1985). *Biological, psychological, and environmental factors in delinquency and mental disorders.* Westport, CT: Greenwood Press.

Downes, D. (1982). *Understanding deviance.* Oxford: Clarendon Press.

Guenther, A. (1976). *Criminal behavior and social systems.* Chicago: Rand McNally.

Johnson, E. H. (1974). *Crime, correction, and society.* Homewood, IL: Dorsey Press.

CRIMINOLOGY AND GENETICS

During the 20th century, it was not only the Nazis of Adolf Hitler's Germany who embraced the doctrine of eugenics, which held that some groups of people were genetically superior and others genetically inferior. Eugenics had its diehard adherents in the United States as well. One of these was the influential American scientist Henry Goddard. To further actual social policy, Goddard wrote about the Kallikak family. They lived in a region of the country still mysterious to many, the Pinelands, or the Pine Barrens, of New Jersey.

According to Goddard, some 200 years earlier, the Kallikaks had split into an uplifted half and a morally and socially degraded clan. The split came when Henry Kallikak impregnated a degenerate tavern girl. Thus, he combined two of the era's greatest "hot button" issues: eugenics and prohibition against alcohol. According to Goddard, Henry Kallikak's progeny descended into a social morass of immorality, depravity, and crime. The last of the "bad" Kallikaks, a woman, was living confined in the Vineland, New Jersey, School for Feeble-Minded Boys and Girls. The Kallikaks seemed to be a living representation of what George William Hunter had written in his 1914 *A Civic Biology,* "It is not only unfair but criminal to hand down to posterity" such an unwholesome set of genes. The only remedy was to sterilize those who were considered as being such genetic "carriers." In the cause of eugenics, untold hundreds, perhaps thousands, of patients were sterilized in mental institutions throughout the United States—all without their consent.

Goddard's account became an accepted part of American sociology and psychology textbooks as late as the 1940s. There was only one problem, however: Goddard had fabricated the entire story to prove his point. There never had been any Kallikaks. Goddard's prostitution of science to serve his own theories rings even more true today. Increasingly, powerful psychiatric drugs have been prescribed for apparently disturbed young people, both here and in the United Kingdom. A major category has been antidepressant medications. Yet, in the early 2000s, a frightening wave of suicides caused Great Britain to virtually enact a legal ban on the use of such drugs for young people, and a movement is afoot toward the same goal in the United States. (On February 13, 2005, a policy was announced to further study the risk of suicide among adult users of the antidepressant drugs.)

— John F. Murphy Jr.

FORENSIC ARTISTS

Forensic artists, it can be said, are those who truly enable the dead to speak to the living and bring their murderers a critical step toward final justice. The pioneer in the field lived almost a century ago, the Swiss Wilhelm His. He was presented with a skull that was supposed to be that of the composer Johann Sebastian Bach. His did such a superb job and the likeness was so good that the skull was declared to be definitely that of Bach. No one knows for sure at this point whether it really is.

Sometimes, however, forensic artists can work in the opposite direction: They can produce images of the murderers themselves. On December 7, 1971, in New Jersey, the murder of the List family shocked the state. As reported in newspapers such as the *Atlantic City Press,* police found a massacre at the List house in Westfield, New Jersey. Helen List, 45; Patricia List, 16; John List Jr., 15; Frederick List, 13; and Alma List, a venerable 85, were all found brutally murdered. Suspicion soon centered on the father, John List, the only family member not found in the slaughterhouse that was now 431 Hillside Avenue.

The police investigation unveiled that List had cleverly conceived the murder plot and had shot his entire family on November 9, 1971. He had informed his pastor, Reverend Rehwinkel at Redeemer Evangelical Lutheran Church, after he slaughtered his family, that they were in North Carolina and that he would be joining them there. Then, John List disappeared—for over 15 years. By 1985, Police Captain Frank Marranca had inherited the "cold case" file of the List murders in Westfield. In 1988, Marranca took the extraordinary step of contacting the executive producer of the television show *America's Most Wanted,* Frank Linder. Linder contacted Philadelphian Frank Bender, who was a forensic artist who had reconstructed the images of murder victims. Working with Richard Butler, a forensic psychologist, Bender produced an image of John List, aged to how he would look at that time.

With the show's host John Walsh explaining the murders, the List story was aired on May 21, 1989. Some 300 calls came in to the television show's crime line, including one from Wanda Flannery, who had been for some time suspicious that her neighbor, Robert Clark, was indeed the missing fugitive. Flannery was right. Clark was arrested, and through fingerprints, he was positively identified as John List. On April 12, 1990, he was sentenced to four consecutive life terms for the murders he had committed almost two decades earlier.

— John F. Murphy Jr.

PHYSIOGNOMY

Physiognomy, a pseudoscience related to phrenology, is the practice of reading faces. Physiognomists believe they can determine personality traits by studying the features of a person's face. This is not a new development, but one that dates back to Aristotle, who is credited with writing a treatise on the practice. He believed that certain characteristics were derived from certain types of features.

In the 14th century, people such as Giambattista Della Porta and Barhele Cocles believed you could evaluate people's faces by determining what animal they most looked like. For example, if you looked like a pig, you were sloppy and brutish. Cocles believed physiognomy was a science. He said that "People with snub noses are vain, untruthful, unstable, unfaithful, and seducers."

Physiognomy is sometimes associated with astrology and has been used as a method of divination. In 1743, when King George II was king, Parliament passed a law forbidding the practice of physiognomy. Those caught practicing it could be publicly whipped or imprisoned. Novelists of the 18th century used physiognomy when creating characters for their novels. Physiognomy can be used as a form of fortune-telling, along with graphology, phrenology, and palmistry. Proponents of physiognomy used it as a method of detecting criminal tendencies in the 18th and 19th centuries. Racists still use it to judge character and personality.

Dr. Edward Vincent Jones, a U.S. Superior Court judge in the 1920s, began studying physiognomy. Fascinated by similarities in people he met in the courtroom, he developed a list of 64 physical traits that he believed were accurate indicators of a person's character. Jones believed that tolerant people had a space equal to the width of an eye between their eyes. These people he believed were good-natured, easy-going, and inclined to procrastinate. He thought a fold of skin over the eye identified a person with an analytical mind. An exacting person had a small line or two between the eyes. Intolerant people had eyes close together and were perfectionists.

Also in the early 20th century, Holmes Merton believed he could match a person's character to a suitable job with his Merton Method. Many large corporations used his system in the first half of the 20th century. Although physiognomy is now considered a pseudoscience, many people still believe in the practice of face reading.

– Pat McCarthy

 ## CRITICAL REALISM

Critical realism is best understood as the philosophy that maintains that we can know things about the world because we can gain reliable knowledge about it, although always with the proviso that we must not be overly confident or naive about the quality of the information we bring in. *Critical realism* as an identifiable term arose in the United States as an answer both to idealism and to earlier rejections of idealism. Critical realism was first identified and articulated as a coherent philosophy by the American philosophical naturalist Roy Wood Sellars (1880–1973), in a book called *Critical Realism*, published in 1916. The same year, a collection of essays began to take shape to develop the idea. The book was delayed by the exigencies of war and was published in 1920 under the title *Essays in Critical Realism* (1920). Several prominent American thinkers, or people who went on to become prominent thinkers, contributed to this work: As well as Sellars, contributors included George Santayana (1863–1952), Arthur O. Lovejoy (1873–1962), and Durant Drake (1878–1933).

Durant Drake, whose essay was placed first, argued that critical realism escaped the problems of both "epistemological monism and epistemological dualism." The critical realists agreed with the pragmatists, for instance, that evidence for the existence of the external world was overwhelming, primarily because the evidence "worked." But they were suspicious of the monists' quest for too certain a link between the external world and our knowledge of it. The critical realists were naturalists without being reductive materialists. As Sellars put it: "Physical things are the objects of knowledge, though they can be known only in terms of the data which they control within us." Several of the contributors to *Essays in Critical Realism* went on to articulate further their ideas, the most notable results being Lovejoy's *The Revolt Against Dualism* (1930) and Sellars's *A Philosophy of Physical Realism* (1932).

But if the critical realists knew what they were against, they were less clear what they were for. The contributors to *Essays in Critical Realism* straddled a variety of opinions across the metaphysical, social, and political divide. And during the 1930s, the focus shifted away from the epistemological questions of the *Essays* toward social and political questions. And after World War II, the intellectual trends moved further away from critical realism when philosophy took the so-called linguistic turn. An important voice for critical realism, without using the term, was the American philosopher Marvin Farber (1901–1980), the latter part of whose philosophical career was spent criticizing some of the more extravagant implications of phenomenology. In the United Kingdom, critical realism has been championed by the philosopher Roy Bhaskar (1944-), who was also instrumental in the establishment of the International Association for Critical Realism in 1997. The IACR seeks to further the aims of critical realism and facilitate contact between critical realists around the world.

The foundation of the IACR is one manifestation of the reemergence in the 1990s of critical realism as an important philosophy. Once again, it has emerged largely as a reaction to the excesses of earlier trends. Today's critical realists are reacting to the perceived follies and excesses of postmodernism. A worthwhile example of the recent styles of critical realism can be found in a collection of essays edited by José López and Garry Potter. Heavily influenced by Bhaskar, the critical realism as outlined by López and Potter claims that we can have good, rational grounds for believing one theory rather than another. It is not simply an arbitrary choice, as postmodernists argue. Furthermore, we can have these grounds because some theories give better accounts of reality than others do. Critical realists accept that knowledge is constructed in society and that it is built up with language and that all these construction methods are fallible. But it refuses to then leap to the conclusion that no objective knowledge or truth is possible. And notwithstanding all the objections that could be made about the ways science gathers its knowledge, the fact remains that is does have the best track record of producing reliable knowledge about the world and that we ignore this at our peril.

Another, stronger, version of critical realism has been advanced by the philosopher John Searle, when he spoke of "external realism," which he defines as the view that there is a way things are that is logically independent of all human representations. Searle calls facts about the external reality "brute facts," which have logical priority over what he calls "institutional facts," which are about the institutions human beings create, such as marriage or money. External realism functions as part of the taken-for-granted part of our surroundings. Searle argues that the very first step in combating irrationalism is to defend the notion of external realism and refute arguments against it.

More recently still, Susan Haack has spoken of "critical common-sensism," which is even closer to critical realism than Searle's external realism. Haack outlines critical common-sensism as referring to the idea that there are objective standards of better and worse evidence, that observation and theory are independent, that scientific theories are either true or false, and that the determinants of evidential quality are objective even when the judgments of them are perspectival or dependent upon situation or context.

Searle and Haack, López and Potter, are all reacting against the radically skeptical, even nihilist implications of the postmodernist attacks on objectivity, science, and reason over the past 30 years. And as several commentators have noticed, the epistemological questions raised by critical realism are very relevant to the discipline of anthropology, cultural anthropology in particular. Many commentators have noted the serious divisions over questions of the construction of social reality, the evaluation of rival claims, and the politics of research. Lawrence Kuznar is one among many who has articled what could be described as a critical realist appeal for an anthropology that takes science seriously. Related to the epistemological challenge articulated by Kuznar, anthropologists like H. James Birx have spoken of what he calls "dynamic integrity" as the motivational agent behind the critical realist approach.

— *Bill Cooke*

See also **Critical Realism in Ethnology; Postmodernism**

Further Readings

Archer, M., Bhaskar, R., Collier, A., Lawson, T., & Norrie, A. (1998). (Eds.). *Critical realism: Essential readings.* London & New York: Routledge.

Haack, S. (2003). *Defending science—Within reason.* Amherst, NY: Prometheus Books.

Kuznar, L. A. (1997). *Reclaiming a scientific anthropology.* Walnut Creek, CA: Alta Mira.

López, J., & Potter, G. (2001). (Eds.). *After postmodernism: An introduction to critical realism.* London & New York: Athlone Press.

Searle, J. (1996). *The construction of social reality.* London: Penguin.

CRITICAL REALISM IN ETHNOLOGY

Critical realism is a social science metaphilosophy that offers ethnology an ontological grounding necessary to realize its full potential as the study of humanness. Humanness is a feature of the world derived from, but not reducible to, evolution by natural, sexual, and kinship modes of selection. An emergent feature of humanness is the ability to glean, winnow, and trade on information for sustenance in natural and social environments. Thus, any philosophical grounding of ethnology must explicitly accord due roles, in the interaction of matter and ideas, to both evolutionary structure and personal and social agency. The interaction of structure and agency, or dialectical process, centers on human experience. Experience, in turn, has a nature. It has certain properties and powers not derived from, or limited to, particular culturally specific worldviews. Critical realism intends to describe both the precultural world and the dialectics of sociocultural forms, that is, to delineate the real conditions that make ethnology possible. Because critical realism has emerged in part to surmount ills of positivism on one hand and hermeneutics on the other, describing it is inherently historical and contrastive.

Ethnology's Ambivalence Toward Ontology

The Absence of Ontology From Culturism

A significant strain of some but not all ethnology has for many decades lacked grounding in a defensible ontology. In place of an ontological basis for human affairs, this strain has tried to pose culture, and for this reason, it may be referred to as *culturism.* The term applies to any ethnology that either (a) neglects to theorize reality or (b) denies it, tacitly or explicitly, in any of three general ways: (1) regarding the world as unknowable or irrelevant, (2) believing the only referent of any proposition is some further aspect of culture, not the world, or (3) denying the capacity of evolved experience to access truth about reality. In addition, this disparate school often blurs the definition of culture, sometimes characterizing it in such ways as "traits," "traditions," elements," or "the meaningful world." This last phrase illustrates the problem, for does "culture is the meaningful world" mean that culture comprises those limited parts of the world certain subjects find meaningful? Or is it that the meaningful world is the only one knowable by them? Is culture the meaning? Or is culture the world itself, which is found meaningful, or even created by meaning?

Culturism typically does not probe such ontological distinctions, and large bodies of ethnological hermeneutics, reflexivity, constructionism, poststructuralism, and postmodernism all circle around it. These tend to see culture as a local mode of epistemology, that is, as meanings, ideas, and values. While not wrong in itself, the view is, in addition, hypostatized so that culturalized epistemology is placed in opposition to philosophical and scientific ontology. It claims that culture is an irreducible filter between people and any possible real objects of perception or conception. In such presentations, these objects themselves thus fade from consideration, to be replaced by representations without due links to concrete referents. The existence of culture is thus, self-contradictorily, said to preclude pursuit of knowledge about ontology; culture intercedes between humankind and whatever reality might lie behind it and ends up replacing reality with particular cultural views. These views then become the primary object of ethnological study, which turns out to investigate culture at the expense of the very people that culture informs. As a leading ethnologist of this persuasion recently wrote, ethnology should be the "genealogy of secondary descriptions." That is, ethnology should concern texts and their relations, not people.

This culturist view misses two points emphasized in critical realism. First, ideas and culture are not wholly epistemic merely because they do concern knowledge. They also have an ontic status in their own right. Ideas themselves are real, as known from their possible and actual observable effects on humans and the world. For example, the idea of personal honor can underlie people's structuring of many highly consequential behaviors, cooperative and agonistic. Likewise, the idea of justice can motivate people to redistribute social and economic goods. To claim that the ideas behind these effects are not real is to render the motivation behind the effects, and thus the effects themselves, partly causeless and unexplained. Second, ideas can be referred to as such. Were they not real, this would be impossible. When one person cites, however tacitly, what another just said as a reason for his or her own part in a dialogue, that person acknowledges the statement's reality and renders the dialogue coherent. So, ideas are real conceptual tools with which real people really leverage reality.

To draw the sharpest heuristic contrast here, critical realism notes a contradiction within culturism, that it first hypostatizes culture by denying its connection to independent reality, then at the same time tries to locate culture in place of the world. The culturist freezing of culture above the flow of dialectical process amounts to theorizing the primacy of worldview over practice. Since worldviews are variable and fractious, humanness has almost gotten lost in the debacle, the breakup of ethnology, known as "cultural studies." Cultural studies expressly rejects any possible grounding in theorized reality. To the extent that some warmer versions of culturism do melt into reality, they only prove its inescapability and the need for due theorization. But whether such engagement is even possible is a topic some try to rule out of court. The introduction of evidence concerning reality existing in its own right is often equated with reductionism, scientism, biologism, progressivism, racism, sexism, conservatism, empiricism, and/or Westernism. Culturism actually wishes to preserve humanness for humans, but the attempt to do so by isolating culture from anything material turns culturism instead into a kind of spiritualism, in which people are defined by something absolute, ineffable, essential, unassailable, and immaterial. Culture itself is placed beyond critique. So, culturism generally skirts the crucial issue of what the precultural world must be like for ethnology itself to be possible. Yet we know there is such a world precisely because the capacity to develop and use knowledge evolved in it.

Though stressing worldview, culturistic ethnology nonetheless remains haunted by the sub-rosa realization that viewpoints can and often do have consequences. It therefore sometimes hedges on the question of reality, invoking untheorized presuppositions about it when an argument calls for them, yet discounting this very move by putting "reality" in quotation marks. The most ardent culturists even contend that there is no reality, that all is just viewpoint, interpretation, discourse, and politically motivated self-interest. Such reverse absolutism, that absolutely no view can access truth about the world, leads culturism to routinely commit three additional sorts of errors, as noted and avoided by critical realism: (a) self-contradiction, (b) theory-practice inconsistency, and (c) the epistemic fallacy. The self-contradiction appears in culturism's declaring what is possible in a world it denies. The theory-practice inconsistency lies in proclaiming all knowledge cultural, while casuistically admitting precultural reality ad hoc. Also inconsistent is culturism's presupposition that its own views are indeed materially consequential, for if they weren't, they literally wouldn't "matter." Then, culturism would have no reason to argue them. Critical realism, by contrast, holds that if views can matter, there must be a world they matter in and it should be theorized.

Finally, the epistemic fallacy is the claim that what is real about the world can be adequately reduced to what is known, that knowledge alone establishes what is effectively real. The world as posited by a given cultural view is the only one relevant to it and may exist in epistemically grounded contrast to neighboring worlds. That claim is easily refuted by the mere fact that knowledge, as a general human capability, evolved in the matrix of reality as it was obtained in the environment of evolutionary adaptation, not vice versa. Knowledge is an adaptation; it is humankind's occupation of the epistemological niche in nature. Nature itself contains information for creatures able to access it, and intelligence, the use of knowledge, evolved to exploit that possibility. A creature capable of accurately inferring the existence of a far-off edible carcass from the mere sight of wheeling vultures has a great advantage over one not so capable. But there's the rub. Many ethnologists do not acknowledge evolutionary theory, hoping that humans can be shown to be exempt from its constraints.

Culturism's Errors Regarding Evolution

The misgivings culturism has about evolution, coupled with its misunderstanding of evolutionary theory, together explain its weaknesses regarding reality and ontology. Such doubts first arose around the turn of the century, especially among Franz Boas and his students, who opposed an errant social Darwinism trying to co-opt the power of evolution by means of natural selection on behalf of social engineering. Social Darwinism posited group and even "racial" survival as an index of group "fitness," and fitness as an indication of rightness in the moral sense. Rightness, in turn, implied a "natural" entitlement. Its conclusion was that more powerful groups should, by one means or another, weed out the less powerful. This provided an ostensible justification for some of colonialism's and national socialism's most heinous depredations.

But it only did so by profoundly distorting the evolutionary notion of fitness. Properly understood, "survival of the fittest" is an utterly amoral, nonevaluative, purely descriptive, nonprescriptive statement that notes the ex post facto contingent results of selective processes. It is neither good nor bad, in the hypothetical eyes of nature, that any life form should exist at any given time. Most that have ever existed are now extinct, including three genera and perhaps 10 species of pre-*sapiens* hominids. Evolutionary theory shows that which traits contribute to fitness always depends on the actual existing environment, and environments change. Thus, the adaptiveness of any specific traits may wax or wane. Because the detailed characteristics of future environments with which humans might be forced to cope are uncertain, we cannot accurately foresee what future fitness will entail. Thus, we do not now know with any precision what specific traits will be adaptive and selected for, other than general, basal, reality-linked intelligence, mobility, and creativity. For this reason alone, it is not justified to presume, with social Darwinism, that the aggrandizement of some present modes of power is "morally" enjoined.

But social Darwinism also fails a second time, and again on evolutionary grounds. We do know that future human environments will contain humans and that all humans have basic rights founded on nothing more than their humanness per se. Human rights are not culture dependent—though not all cultural practices are equally defensible in the court of human rights. Rights must be adjudicated, for intentions and outcomes vary. But it is indubitable that the legitimate idea of legitimate rights exists and that all peoples have a sense of natural entitlements. Moreover, though the full content of the category, "rights" can be argued; and critical realism holds two human

rights to be grounded in the reality of humanness. They are liberty, that is, the right to be free of oppression, and the right to learn. Liberty inheres in humanness because social categorical distinctions between individuals are cultural impositions, despite often being propounded on the basis of supposed links between certain people and natural forces. Such suppositions can be attributed to personal merit evinced by good fortune, long tradition, class privilege, racial ascription, divine right, and so on, none of which prove essential to humanness. If such categorical distinctions are not natural, then rights ostensibly deriving from them cannot be natural either. Thus, liberty is the natural right to choose the social constraints under which one agrees to live. Learning, in turn, is essential to humanness because *Homo sapiens* evolved precisely as an information-seeking creature. By their very nature, humans exploit real information by means of evolved intelligence. Thus, to structurally deny anyone the opportunity to learn is to block the realization of his or her own humanness and violates a fundamental human right. Together, liberty and learning go far toward eudemonism, or pan-flourishing, which humanness itself thus enjoins as the final aim of human endeavor.

In this way, humanness is seen to have an inherent moral component, which establishes the real basis for rights to liberty and learning. It is important to demonstrate the ontic nature of morality per se, its existence prior to being given particular content, for only by so doing can the culturist claim that all morality is cultural, and none ontological, be thwarted in principle. This is done as follows: Humans are conscious; consciousness entails the ability to envision alternate actionable possibilities; mutually exclusive alternatives must be selected between; intentional selection demands, and implies the existence of, evaluative criteria; and criteria necessarily entail notions of preferable and not preferable, approach and avoid, "better" and "worse." Thus, morality per se inheres in humanness. And two of its aspects, the twin rights of liberty and learning, also qualify as ontic, that is, existing prior to any culturalized inflection of humanness. Beyond liberty and learning, however, the ethical content of criteria informing any given strategy is not given in nature. Even the two natural rights are often more than a little difficult to operationalize. But all humans know that rights and wrongs exist as a categorical reality, regardless of the content variably ascribed to them. So although in prehuman nature, doing the "wrong" thing is not possible, because morality does not exist in prehuman nature, its possibility emerges when humanness does. Morality is an emergent property of the world, and its existence, the reality of moral naturalism, delegitimizes any attempt to exterminate people, whose right to liberty may be justifiably restricted only to the extent that they, by committing crimes, say, thwart the liberty and learning of others.

This evolutionarily grounded delegitimization of social Darwinism accomplishes two important things for ethnology. First, it allays fears that it might be evolutionary theory per se that, by "biologizing" people, robs them of their humanness. Quite to the contrary, it is precisely evolutionary theory that accurately describes humanness and its moral place in nature. By denying human nature, culturism unwittingly subverts its own best means of establishing rights. Second, to clarify the relation between humanness and reality is to free ethnology for its true task, the description of intelligibilia and their relation to consequential, morphogenic processes. "Intelligibilia" includes anything graspable by the human mind, anything intelligible, and it is the critical realist definition of culture. Culture, through agents' appropriation and refashioning of intelligibilia, interacts morphogenically with real conditions to engender subsequent new conditions of either continuity or change.

Boasian objections to social Darwinism spawned the culturist, antibiology backlash that still distorts the culture concept itself. It tries to put culture in place of biology as humanity's prime mover, when the solution in fact lies in realism, the dialectic of biology and culture, what has been called "coevolution." This concept was first most clearly articulated by William Durham, and though the details of cases are highly complex, the prima facie contention that ideas and matter are coconstitutive in humanness is incontestable. But early 20th-century Boasian culturism and its latter-day adherents held and hold that everything from warfare to gender relations, childhood development, and religion are functions of culture unmodified by any proclivities rooted in nature. Now many ethnologists treat such tenets as received wisdom. The sole alternative seems reduction of humans to creatures of base instinct, incapable of channeling their appetites. Yet there aren't even any animals that fail to channel their appetites, and humans obviously do channel them routinely.

By midcentury, another purported reason to eschew evolution appeared to an ethnology already committed to the hegemony of culture. Culturism's stance against social Darwinism convinced it of the utter insupportableness of any mode of selection above or below the level of the individual. Thus, when William Hamilton posited his model of kin selection, culturism ruled it anathema. Kin selection shows that selection operates at both the level of specific genes and genetically related individuals (i.e., small groups). The new term *sociobiology*, used to describe the interaction of biology and culture in human affairs, was wrongly taken to imply that social circumstances were all mere epiphenomena of inviolable biological mechanisms. Such misunderstandings, and misrepresentations by some of sociobiology's early proponents, created the impression that sociobiology intended to reduce humanness to biological drives. Again, that humans obviously do alter their behavior and conditions in light of many considerations should have sufficed to allay such fears. But in an overreaction to sociobiology's attention to our species' evolutionary background in nature, culturism sought to denature humans by discounting evolution's role in shaping humanness. Conversely, it also sought to make nature a purely human construct, something dependent on culture for its existence. Again, that such a thoroughly plastic world is, by all evidence, not the one we inhabit should have warned culturists off this course.

Learning, Liberty, and Practice

Thus, the implications of culturism are the very opposite of what most culturists intend. The antidote to totalitarianism is not culturism but eudemonism, pan-flourishing, the fostering of conditions that support the common weal through learning and liberty. These are natural rights and are conjoined very simply: Humans are information-seeking creatures that naturally wish to absent constraints on their happiness. Our innate craving to learn is a conative adaptation to the need to exploit information in the social and natural environments, motivating us to be active seekers of information. When drinking water is scarce and thirst creates dissatisfaction, humans seek information in and about the world. They mentally construct virtual models that hypothesize as to water's possible whereabouts. Such basic approaches to human needs are not dependent on culture, though culture may constrain who in a group seeks water where, how, and when. But no humans willingly brook what they regard as unwarranted constraints on their liberty.

Even beyond this level of basic needs, a great deal of everyday practical behavior is also comprehensible to humans by virtue merely of their being human. A person of Culture X seeing a person of Culture Y paddle a canoe will already understand much of the paddler's present and near future experience, even though the person of Culture X may never before have seen a canoe. He will understand that the canoeist is an intentional being, the canoeist is male or female, he or she is of an approximate age, she wants to go a certain direction, he exhibits a certain level of accomplishment, the boat is floating, the river has a current, it's easier to paddle with the current, the water will rise if it rains, rain comes from above, if the paddler falls out she will get wet, he will not be able to breathe under water, when the canoe disappears around the bend it disappears for everyone (not just those of a certain worldview), when night falls it will be harder to see, paddling will then be more difficult, the canoe will have to be secured for the night, the canoeist will likely be tired and hungry, and on and on. Such practically based knowledge comprises by far the better part of what is necessary for both successful paddling and the understanding of it. For this reason, critical realism highlights the primacy of practice and rejects the purported, culturist primacy of worldview. Culturally particular worldviews are irrelevant to the basic practice of getting a canoe upriver, precisely because intentionality, sex, age, floating, the current, rain, wetness, breathing, darkness, the laws of motion, gravity, fatigue, and so on are the same for everyone. This does not deny culture its own importance.

Dialectics and Reflectionism

But general flourishing, eudemonism, can be a guiding principle only under the recognition that both what flourishing entails and how to achieve it are subject to constant dialectical revision, and for two reasons. Both have to do with the philosophical, critical realist description of the pre-cultural world. First, both natural and social systems are inherently open. They are not experimentally closed to limit variables; they are subject to input from outside local systems; and they are subject to the emergence within them of novel properties and powers. This means that the best descriptions of them are always provisional

and cannot be reified, for they must change with changes in the systems themselves. Second, human concepts and strategies are inherently fallible. We can make mistakes, these being our constant reminder that reality does indeed lie behind all possible conceptions of it. Eudemonism is thus not to be conceived as an absolute condition, for it is predicated on both the ongoing dialectic of structure and agency and the dialectic's companion feature of reality, the human ability to learn.

One thing most humans learn quickly is that some models of reality are better than others precisely because they fit it better. The best matches make the best models, and so they also work the best, a fact of which no practically inclined indigene needs to be convinced. This position thus directly contravenes the absurd but prevalent culturist contention that knowledge does not, and cannot, "reflect" reality. This error results from the fallacy that a model must be perfect in every respect, that reflection must be an utterly undistorted image of reality, to be any adaptive good at all. But because errors are in fact part of the game, no model meets such specifications. Culturism mistakenly inflates this feature of models, that they are inherently imperfect, into the notion that all models must be completely arbitrary. Culturism thus adheres to a stanch antireflectionist philosophy. To debunk this position, just one telling difficulty will suffice: that people operating under grossly faulty descriptions of reality eventually fail to thrive.

In fact, a hypothetical reliance on errant views of real conditions in the environment of evolutionary adaptation would have prevented hominid intelligence from evolving in the first place. The grasping hand reflects the structure of tree branches for brachiating and, fortuitously, also that of stones that can be turned into tools. The grasping mind is ultimately no less beholden to real conditions for its adaptiveness. For evolutionary reasons, then, it is patently not the case, as Richard Rorty, a culturist philosopher, has put it, that no description of the world can be invalidated, on the grounds that the supposed invalidation would be just another redescription, under which no real world reposes. For Rorty and this school, the world is just texts all the way down. But from a due evolutionary position, it is obvious that any human group grounding its attempts to adapt to real conditions on arbitrarily selected descriptions of them, on the premise that no description can possibly be better or worse than any other, would soon be trying to comprehend the all-too-real speed of its demise. It is only because culturism has repressed the adaptive imperative, and repressed adaptation because culturism irrationally eschews evolution by natural selection, that it could paint itself into such a corner.

How Real? Why Critical?

Critical realism is realism because it theorizes the real social and natural dimensions of the world that exist apart from human knowing. As critical realism's founder, Roy Bhaskar, describes it, the social world consists of a three-layered ontology, each with its own properties and powers: structural tendencies, as known by their effects; causally engendered events in time and space; and personal experience. The natural world consists of a four-layered ontology comprised of chemical, physical, biological, and conscious reality. Each layer is derived from, but not reducible to, prior layers. Emergent features are common, as when automobility emerges from life and cities emerge from productive socioeconomic structures. Sociocultural processes in which structure and agency relate dialectically are summed by Margaret Archer as "morphogenesis." In morphogenic processes, agents deploy and/or invent concepts to exert leverage on existing structures on behalf of their perceived interests. Such sociocultural phenomena are not culturally particular, for humans have agentive powers merely by virtue of being human, and they deploy them in and on the conditions they face.

Next to such matters—for matter is indeed what grounds practice—culture appears as a later and secondary development, which is exactly what it is in the evolutionary sense. Hominids did not suddenly lose their existing, practical, adaptive skills when and as culture emerged. Rather, culturally inflected values also evolved alongside practical activities that had sufficed on their own as adaptive schemes for millennia prior to culture's emergence. Still, when culture emerges and is deployed, duly modified structures of society and nature become the real preexisting conditions that future agents will have to contend with. And at the conceptual level, ideas themselves have structural relations of compatibility, as in capitalism and market expansion, or incompatibility, as in mysticism and empiricism. Beyond this, critical realism theorizes many additional conceptual relations independent of culture, and demonstrates their possible sociopolitical correlates for interested agents. Both people and society have notable, emergent, culturally nonspecific properties and powers, and the details of the morphogenic model are to be found in Archer's works.

Immanent Critique

Critical realism is critical because it recognizes that inherent in the best, most accurate descriptions of existing conditions lies an immanent critique of them. Right within a fact, an accurate description, is often expressed a value. This widely accepted observation is yet little known in ethnology, which still largely clings to the Humean posit that fact and value are utterly disjunct, that no "ought" can be derived from any "is." Were this true, cultures could establish their own unassailable values and projects, in utter independence of the very world that makes them possible. Here lies another culturist self-contradiction. Yet most ethnologists are quite familiar with the prototypical immanent critique, Karl Marx's description of capitalism. Marx simply showed that owners of capital were co-opting the surplus value of worker's labor. This social and economic fact, in and of itself, both implied and violated an implicit value, that of fairness. It also implied an agentive course of action: redress. Critical realism argues the moral imperative of producing the best possible descriptions of social and natural conditions, so that the immanent critique of conditions contrary to eudemonism can be expressed and acted on.

Scholarly sociocultural models that allow either structure or agency to predominate misrepresent actual sociocultural process. Structures dominating agency reduce people to mere bearers of culture, making them its pawns. Despite Claude Lévi-Strauss's immense contribution to ethnology, his overall model exhibits just this bias. Real people are missing from it. On the other hand, if agency dominates structure, conditions become largely irrelevant; indeed, would-be agents could encounter no real, resistant conditions on which their programs, strategies, or intentions could even be applied. This is the trap that hermeneutics, cultural relativism, and postmodernist discourse theory together all step into. They imagine culture as an omnipotent bellwether capable of leading docile conditions into any and every pen. A third error regarding the relation of structure and agency is found, for example, in Anthony Giddens's "structuration." This concept tries to conflate structure and agency, positing each as immediately constitutive of the other, to account for the influence of both in actual behavior and cognition. But conflation precludes the analytical disentangling of the respective roles of agency and structure, and confounds the processual dialectic of material and idea as people use ideas in the attempt to work their will.

Philosophical Anthropology

Once anthropology itself was just philosophy. Philosophy was the investigation of humanness at a prescientific time when knowledge was still developed by deduction from first principles. Such a deductive principle was that humans are sinful, soul-bearing, instantaneously fabricated, immutable creatures of God. The span of this deductive approach to humanness, even outside the church, centered on the Enlightenment but stretched from well before it to the Victorian era just prior to the ethnographic revolution led by Bronislaw Malinowski. Philosophers from Descartes to Hegel pronounced on the nature of humankind. Cartesian dualism, Hobbesian strife, Rousseauian isolation, Lockean contracts, Humean experience, Kantian idealism, and Hegelian dialectics of the spirit all posited a kind of human being philosophically deduced. Such accounts remained clouded by the long shadow of medieval scholasticism. This largely precluded an investigation refigured, from the bottom up, as ethnographic description, to be followed by the induction of testable covering laws. Even Lewis Henry Morgan, Herbert Spencer, Edward Tylor, and James Frazer, despite a notable turn to the actual social world to enrich their models, were still essentially deductivists. They posited the nature of humanness, then adduced evidence cohering with the position.

Eventually, the naturalism of nascent science, powered by awareness of the ineluctability of natural and sexual selection, did induce investigators to take up the challenge of fieldwork. If it were true that humans are creatures subject to the same natural laws of selection as others, it called for the investigation of social forms as adaptive means. So, although anthropology was still philosophy, it had become philosophy by other means. The nature of humanness could no longer be deduced; nor, on the other hand, could ethnology be the mere acknowledgement of theory demanded by the force of raw data. The human study of humanness is dialectical, for our own understandings themselves become real and have real effects on the very social and ecological relations we study. Humanness evolved as the increasingly intelligent exploitation of available resources. This led to the eventual emergence of technological capacities geared to modifying reality in the interest of extracting yet more resources from it. Through fieldwork, in other words, the early ethnographers discovered culture.

Referential Detachment and Reflectionism

As we now would say, humanness is the adaptation that exploits the epistemological niche in reality. In 1872, the same year Charles Darwin published *The Descent of Man*, and well prior to the ethnographic revolution, A. Lane-Fox Pitt-Rivers appropriately defined culture as "emanations of the human mind." Such a view accepted that things can be known about the world, that people can know them, and that knowledge comprises humankind's chief adaptive tool. However, the fact that culture does emanate from the mind, that it leaves the mind, and that culture escapes its creators and takes on properties of its own creates the vexing problem of referential detachment. The links between culture and the world become problematic because no logical necessity demands that culture—ideas—must fit nature like glove fits hand. People can devise understandings and create social forms that turn out to be maladaptive because they do not match reality. The possibility of maladaptive behaviors, taken by itself, makes humans no different than any creature. But the human capacity to comprehend has an entailment that cultural forms, though their evolutionary emergence was initially prompted by selective pressure from the hominid natural and social environment, become referentially detached objects of knowledge in their own right. Cultural forms are real in the three senses that they have observable effects, can themselves be objects of reference, and their effects, even when maladaptive, can reveal truth about both humanness and the world.

The discovery of culture and its property of referential detachment thus became for ethnology very much a two-edged sword. It enabled ethnology to flourish as an independent mode of inquiry and to contribute greatly to the store of human knowledge. At the same time, the seductions of referential detachment created the possibility of culturism. This soon became no longer the investigation of human adaptation to the real world, but the courting of notions detached from any possible reality. War, gender, adolescence, personality, religion, and much else were held, especially by still influential Boasianism, to be strictly functions of culture, behaviors that could and would change if socialization did. It was thus akin to behaviorism, its congener in psychology, and did not contravene positivism as it claimed to do.

Positivism explored the possibility that causation in social forms could be reduced to mechanics akin to chemical reactions. Though culturism despised the reduction of people to imitations of molecules, its own platform of socialization, or enculturation, presupposed just such a mechanical notion of cause in human affairs. Culturists seeking to free people from material constraints ended up fixing them to enculturation processes. The elaborate particularization of cultures did not change this central error, though it became a hallmark of culturism for the second half of the 20th century. Now, in partial recognition of the erroneous relegation of reality to the status of an epiphenomenon, some cultural relativists are backtracking, and emphasize only methodological relativism, the due suspension of judgment about alien lifeways in the interest of accurately describing them. Nonetheless, culturism has yet to theorize the reality it thus furtively lets in the back door, having long ago turned it away from the front.

What this antiscientism misses is that no adaptation need be perfect to prevail. It need only offer its bearers a competitive advantage, however slight, and it will spread through a socializing and/or breeding population. In the final analysis, it is culturism's posited impossibility of reflectionism that is impossible. Knowledge could not have evolved did it not provide a sufficiently accurate, and fallible, model of reality. Critical realism recognizes that fallibility is not merely an incidental feature of human modeling, but essential to it. Without fallibility, neither critique nor effective revision could obtain.

Of late, some culturism, finding no escape from its self-contradictions, has sought refuge in postmodernist irony. It avers that there is no truth, and no reality about which truth claims can be made. Culture is said to be the veil that humans create between themselves and whatever untheorized something it might once have been that prompted the rise of knowledge in the first place. Some maintain as a first principle that truth is but culture's attempt at self-validation, behind which no reality resides. Thus, the human capacity for judging the merits of alternative

views—a capacity inhering in consciousness, and not subject to dismissal—is dismissed. Critical realism, by contrast, maintains that the truly liberatory resides in dialectically pursued eudemonism, in which judgmental rationalism is essential in deciding what values have merit and what courses to them are worth pursuing.

The Inner Conversation and Experience

If, as critical realism maintains, there is indeed some central link between humans and the world, communities and landscape, persons and place, word and world, past and present, structures and agency, how are we to conceive of it? The process in which these linked facets of reality are processually coconstitutive is capsulized as morphogenesis, the dialectic of structure and agency. Archer identifies the central link as the individual's internal conversation. In silent inward deliberation, constraints and volition briefly meld in informing thought and action, after which newly modified personal and social constraints and possibilities obtain. This formulation can profitably be augmented by John Dewey's notion of natural experience.

Archer holds that all conscious humans have an inner domain of mental privacy, where the intentionality necessary to drive sociality is generated. Agents have a silent say in what strictures and strategies they will deem actionable. This life of the mind is essentially private, not amenable to "extrospection." Even "introspection" inadequately describes the phenomenon, because it is not a matter of passively gazing into internal darkness to see what glimmer of self might catch the mind's eye. The self is, in fact, the inner conversation. This belies the culturist tenet that all varieties of human selves are entirely matters of cultural artifice, such that some humans may not have selves at all. But however it might be culturally inflected, the phenomenological self is actively deliberative, and shot through with evaluations of practical and moral import. "What should I do?" is no mean aimless rumination, but the most fraught consideration anyone faces.

As most ethnologists recognize, it is insufficient to claim that in traditional societies, culture largely answers this question on behalf of the individual, who thus could get through life robotically. Even those who are normally compliant must continually decide whether and how earnestly to be so. Not infrequently, some decide to opt out one way or another, as when disgruntled hunter-gatherers leave the parent group to found a new settlement. No intentional, practical activity would be possible for a creature that did not have a sense of itself as an ongoing, agentive being with certain properties and powers. This is the universal, accurate sense that the individual is both distinct from his or her environment and can also affect it. The actual inner conversation merely comments on this reality and on the options it engenders.

Archer notes that all agents must respond to perceived conditions, assess their own aims and ambitions, and consider likely consequences for social stability or change. That is, being human, all people inwardly exercise discernment, deliberation, and dedication. Though modally subjective, the inner conversation is an ontic feature of human existence. It is the dialogical, dialectical realization of the relation of mind to world, for all humans must negotiate realities pertaining to nature, practice, and society. Yet the concrete situations deriving from these overlapping spheres of reality do not impinge mechanically on agents. They are mediated by the agent's own concerns and processed in the internal conversation, the nexus of structure and agency. This mediation works to dialogically bring structure and agency together in the interests of individuals, as they understand them. It does not work, as would culture as posited by culturism, to first barricade people from, and then obviate, the world. It is precisely real consequences that people are concerned with and on which they inwardly deliberate. Agency meets structure both in the internal conversation and in practice. By addressing the work of Charles Sanders Peirce and William James, Archer duly considers the natural links this mature practice theory has with pragmatism. Other recent work in critical realism suggests that the pragmatic linchpin of morphogenesis is experience as Dewey, another pragmatist, has theorized it.

In this view, the priority and centrality of experience derives from the fact that it is precisely about experience, had and likely, that the inner conversation takes place. Dewey was often at pains to disabuse his critics of the misconception that he equated experience with sense impressions, the psychological usage of the term. He meant, instead, the conjunction of humanness and the external world as realized in and through a given individual. Such a view of experience may be characterized, on Dewey's behalf, as the personalized register of what takes place, and clarified as follows. The personalized register of what takes place is not limited to the particular consciousness of the hypothetically self-contained individual; it leaves room for shared experience, the sociality that in turn informs an individual's consciousness. The register need not even be fully conscious, for input and output via the unconscious are also real, as known from their effects. The phrase "personal register" encompasses corporeal modes of registration, though in some ways, these may bypass cognition, for their effects will bear on future experience.

Finally, the fact that experience is the personal register of what happens duly recognizes the many parameters conditioning personhood. These include evolution, history, sociality, culture, the environment, and life course development. With these qualifications, experience becomes the crux of sociocultural process, that is, of morphogenesis. This recognizes that the inner conversation takes place with regard to experience and that practice, in part, is the result. Though it is indeed the individual who is the experiencer, of necessity, the strings of experience are tuned also to social and natural refrains.

Ethnological Investigations of Reality

Because philosophy and anthropology have the investigation of humanness as their common axis, there is a continuum from one to the other that takes as its parameter the adaptationist imperative. Adaptation is a tacit, post hoc imperative, because failure to adapt is ultimately failure to exist. It does not imply that any and all particular human endeavors are adaptive or that humans can necessarily know the difference between what may or may not prove adaptive in the long run. But sooner or later, in Archer's phrase, reality will have its revenge. And because humanness is adaptively informed, evolutionary theory underwrites many subdisciplinary modes of ethnology. Critical realism's embrace of the evolutionary paradigm makes it largely compatible with any anthropological mode of inquiry that grounds humans in reality. But more than mere compatibility is at stake. Critical realism intentionally theorizes what is often taken for granted, that conditions of the real world structure human endeavor. Thus, it accommodates social science to naturalism. Paleoanthropology, primatology, population genetics, and archaeology all implicitly exploit knowledge of the stratified ontology critical realism describes. Here follows a brief sample of modes of inquiry also immediately relevant to ethnology and the bearing of critical realism on them.

Evolutionary Epistemology

The plain conjunction of evolution and philosophy yields evolutionary epistemology. This field recognizes that knowledge exists because it evolved, and evolution can thus be presumed to have left its mark on the general structures of human knowing. As Dewey also emphasized, knowledge must be capable of being about the world, because the world spawned it. Just as the light-sensitive motility of a paramecium models the reality of sunlight and the bird's wing models the resistance of air—those realities do have the properties from which such adaptations as motility and flight derive—so the representations made possible through consciousness also reflect pertinent structures of reality. These include space, time, location, motion, relation, contrast, cause, event, change, vitality, growth, and death. Thus, where Immanuel Kant posited a transcendental idealism in which categories of thought, such as space and time, imposed themselves on reality, which was thus rendered utterly inaccessible, critical realism properly sequences the real horse and the ideal cart it pulls. It is the world that shapes the structures of consciousness, a view that evolution substantiates. So, critical realism is a transcendental realism.

Beyond the basic structures of the world and human knowing, evolutionary epistemology theorizes that ideas evolve under the same selective principles as do life forms, namely, variation, selective retention, and transmissibility. In the long run, ideas that perdure are those experience shows to have been the most apt reflections of reality. Throughout this process, conceptual and theoretical mistakes are legion, as are vital "mistakes" in nature. The workers of the Soviet Union, let alone those of the world, never did meaningfully unite, because people's primary attachments are not to class distinctions, and no amount of reculturalization could make them so. People's primary attachments are to familiars and locale, as predicted in the evolutionary model of humanness. Richard Dawkins has advanced the concept of "memes," on an analogy with genes, to account for the apparent attractiveness and consequent transmissibility enjoyed by certain ideas. Such features may be explained at least in part by the mind's evolutionary preparedness to hold and convey them, a preparedness grounded in their previous adaptive effects. Pascal Boyer has usefully applied a similar model to the particular nature of religious ideas as found cross-culturally. He thus accounts for the attractiveness of notions that posit ostensible phenomena that are salient because unusual, yet not so bizarre as to be preposterous, at least by the terms of a given cultural milieu.

Evolutionary Psychology

A step closer to ethnology per se is evolutionary psychology, a vibrant and expanding subdiscipline descended from an earlier sociobiology. Like everything evolutionary, it has dedicated opponents of its recognition that key determinants of human affect, cognition, and behavior are not pure products of utterly malleable socialization but are also proclivities inherited because the genes underwriting them got transmitted at higher rates in the environment of evolutionary adaptation. The idea was first outlined by Darwin, who by the principle of sexual selection accounted for the existence of the apparent adaptive liability that peacocks carry in their cumbersome, unwieldy, energy-consuming, predation-inviting tails. The answer lies in peahens' preferential selection of such long-tailed males as mates. Handsome tails are informational proxies for a healthy inheritance; females mating with such males tended to produce more surviving offspring.

Despite much research intending to demonstrate that female humans, to the contrary, select mates on principles that vary haphazardly with culture, the vast preponderance shows that they too tend to select males for traits associated with vigor and power. Likewise, young men tend overwhelmingly to select mates on the basis of due female proxies for healthy genes, these being lush hair, clear skin, prominent breasts, a high waist-hip ratio, and the absence of visible disease and deformity—all components summarized as "beauty." These observations largely hold true across cultures, for all such signs suggest a female's fitness to bear and nurse children. Beauty has evolved to be inherently attractive to a male because mating with a healthy woman affords his genes a selective advantage. Power is attractive to females because mating with a good provider affords her genes a selective advantage. Because men often compete for preeminence, critics have uncomprehendingly faulted evolutionary psychology, or sociobiology, with justifying violence. The further irritant to such critics is that is has partly been female choice over the millennia that has produced male humans more than ready to indulge in violent competition, as witnessed by the near ubiquity of war.

But the sociobiological, evolutionary psychological claim is neither that men cannot control themselves, which in general they obviously can, nor that women are forced beyond measure to beautify themselves. The evolutionary theory only accounts for the obvious cross-cultural proclivities in play, understanding that can help establish such sociopolitical constraints as may be deemed appropriate. By many such examples, including the contribution to group fitness made by otherwise problematic phenomena such as depression and phobias, evolutionary psychology demonstrates that the human psyche is a product of evolution and that reality-based evolutionary theory is pertinent to everyday behaviors affecting societies in general. Its pertinence to critical realism is that it demonstrates the morphogenic process, as soma, psyche, and sociality coevolved.

Prospect–Refuge Theory and Cultural Ecology

Both prospect–refuge theory and cultural ecology capitalize on realities of the human–world relation. Prospect–refuge theory derives from Jay Appleton's work in human geography. It predicts that humans will show marked preferences for landscapes that signify the availability of exploitable resources, exploitable refuges from potential danger, or the possibility of safe exploration for either. Thus, the response to narrow defiles is expected to be averse, to protected promontories favorable, and to winding paths through open country one of enticement. Psychological research has born this theory out, as the anthropologist would expect, given that humans evolved in hazardous environments to be omnivorous, hunting, information-seeking, colonizing, conflict-prone creatures. To say that humans are by nature colonizing creatures is only a due description of the fact that humans have, through exploration and the intelligent use of information gleaned from dispositional properties of reality, colonized every corner of the globe. It neither celebrates colonialism nor holds sociocultural aggrandizement to be an uncontainable passion.

While it is no doubt true that many people simply prefer familiar landscapes to unfamiliar ones, the principle of familiarity does not obviate people's selective preference, within a given environment, for features promising prospects or refuge. In fact, it would be virtually impossible for intelligent creatures not to have developed discerning capacities due to selective pressures at work on their forebear's choices of landscapes within which to provision, travel, or dwell. The dispositional, informational properties of nature, transformed into knowledge and exploited by humans as they occupy the epistemological niche, lie immediately in features of nature themselves. People do not give landscape its property of being able to conceal a person or reveal a resource; those properties are in the landscape. Humans turn such information to account by realizing, in both senses of the word, what those properties are. Caves can protect; defiles can trap. Intelligence realizes such properties first by becoming aware that they exist—independent of anyone's knowing—and second by enabling humans to practically avail themselves of them. This ability to recognize and use information about reality, in particular, abilities involving high perspicacity in the assessment of landscape affordances, has duly evolved in humans. It is the ability Dewey described as experience, the pragmatic phenomenon of mining reality for practical information regarding its real dispositional properties.

Cultural ecology uses the principle of adaptation to describe, assess, and compare various human modes of production and sociopolitical organization. It is the socioeconomic perspective on the human–world relation, albeit one that readily incorporates both beliefs and history. Cultural ecology is in some ways the offspring of models of cultural evolution advanced in midcentury by Leslie White and Julian Steward. Such models have been considered both sophisticated and, nonetheless, problematic. Although they take an adaptationist view, the clear trend they reveal is one of increasing socioeconomic complexity, which can be misconstrued. White, for example, related cultural evolution to the amount of energy that a mode of production could harness and intentionally deploy. Since this amount has, in general, clearly increased through time, it leaves the impression that more-powerful societies are more adaptively advanced and less-powerful ones "backward."

In fact, less-powerful societies usually have a quite viable adaptation of their own. Absent the intrusion of extrinsic forces, such systems most often exist in a cybernetic balance both with natural resources and neighboring socioeconomic systems. In the 1960s, Roy Rappaport showed that multiyear cycles of ritual, warfare, and pig production in highland New Guinea coincided in a cybernetic system that, overall, effectively related population size to carrying capacity. Today, cultural ecologists produce some of the most substantive studies of human adaptive modes, with clear implications for the future of humanity at large. The many instances of socioecological collapse, for example, as documented in the archaeological record, and ongoing processes of ecological degradation that can be studied now should give pause to advocates of policies for continued increases in resource exploitation.

Moral Naturalism and Material Culture

Moral naturalism has been arrived at independently by both philosophical critical realism and anthropology, which thus complement each other. The critical realist argument for moral naturalism has been given above and resides in the ontic ineluctability of choice, and thus justification, on the part of intelligent creatures. Evolutionary anthropology approaches the problem from the analysis of altruism, the apparent prevalence of other-benefiting, self-jeopardizing behaviors among humans and some other species. If genuinely altruistic behavior aids another to the actor's own detriment, how could genes underwriting its continued behavioral manifestation be preserved? Altruists and their behavioral proclivities should be weeded out by natural selection, but they aren't. Aside from the problem that what may appear altruistic from one perspective might actually be self-serving from another, the answer to the real problem that altruism poses lies in kin selection.

In the environment of human adaptation, bands of hominids would largely be comprised of kin in the first place. And specific, close kin recognition, evident among nonhuman primates, can be accomplished by a juvenile merely noticing to which other individuals its own mother provides care. Individuals do not need to be able to mathematically calculate degrees of relatedness in order for their behaviors benefiting kin to perdure, for those kin share some of the altruist's genes, quite apart from any knowledge of the fact. So genes underwriting altruism can get passed on even if altruists die as a result of their own behavior. Such proclivities are not tantamount to biological reductionism, for humans can obviously choose, in the moment, whether to act altruistically or not. But altruism remains a genetically possible behavior because genes underwriting it pass collaterally through kin whom altruism benefits. Culturists have

not answered the question of how morality divorced from matter could matter. And if morality does have material consequences, those consequences must have selective entailments.

At the other end of the naturalistic spectrum from moral naturalism lies material culture. This consists of objects, artifacts, buildings, tools, artwork, trash, icons, texts, roads, and all sorts of tangible products of consciousness working on reality. Such objects manifest and exemplify the leverage exerted by intelligibilia derived through reality-based experience. Items of material culture easily become objects of cathexis and in their embodiment of intelligibilia thus morphogenically exert further leverage on sociocultural conditions. Possessions shape the behavior of their possessors and so in a sense turn around to possess the possessors. This phenomenon remains just as true of people such as hunter-gatherers, who have very few possessions. If one's only tool is a stone axe and it is lost, one either makes another axe or has an immediate, serious, existential problem. This contradicts the widespread culturist premise that materialism is a Western cultural phenomenon. The focus on materials for survival is a human trait; capitalism merely capitalizes on it, albeit in an extreme and often damaging form.

Critical realism is not without its limitations. The first is the difficult writing style of its chief exponent, Roy Bhaskar. This may have discouraged many from deciphering his reality-based model of human sociality, which does repay the effort. The second is a recent "spiritual turn" by some critical realists, which may have more to do with desired realities than ones demonstrably inhering in the world.

— *Derek P. Brereton*

See also **Critical Realism; Evolutionary Epistemology**

Further Readings

Archer, M. (2000). *Being human: The problem of agency.* Cambridge: Cambridge University Press.

Archer, M. (2003). *Structure, agency, and the internal conversation.* Cambridge: Cambridge University Press.

Bhaskar, R. (1975). *A Realist theory of science.* London: Verso.

Bhaskar, R. (1989). *Reclaiming reality.* London: Verso.

Brereton, D. P. (2004). Preface for a critical realist ethnology, Part I: The schism and a realist restorative. *Journal of Critical Realism, 3,* 77–102.

Collier, A. (1994). *Critical realism: An introduction to Roy Bhaskar's philosophy.* London: Verso.

Sayer, A. (2000.) *Realism and social science.* Thousand Oak, CA: Sage.

CROIZAT, LEON C. (1896–1982)

As one of the last great Victorian naturalists and iconoclasts of the 20th century, Leon C. Croizat explored conceptual and methodological questions in the fields of botany, zoology, biogeography, anthropology, evolution, taxonomy, archeology, linguistics, and philosophy. Few other 20th-century biologists have had such a significant impact on the integration of evolution, systematics, and biogeography, the three principal elements of the historical sciences. Born in Turin, Italy, Croizat seemed destined for a life of jurisprudence, although his lifelong interest was in the natural sciences. During his early years, Croizat was exposed to a prominent circle of local Italian naturalists, including the early exponent of cladistic systematics Daniele Rosa.

In 1924, to escape the rise of Italian fascism, Croizat immigrated to the United States, where his formal training in Italian jurisprudence provided him with few professional opportunities, particularly during the Great Depression. He eventually became acquainted with Elmer Drew Merrill, director of the Arnold Arboretum, and was employed there as a technical assistant. Croizat availed himself of the arboretum's extensive research library, where he was able to review the research fields necessary to write on biogeography, evolutionary theory, and botanical evolution. In 1947, Croizat's position was terminated when Merrill lost a power struggle with the botanist Irwin Widmer Bailey, who was intolerant of Croizat's heterodoxy. Croizat emigrated once again, this time to Venezuela at the invitation of Henri Pittier. In the 1950s, Croizat retired from teaching to devote his time to research, while his wife took up professional landscape gardening. In 1972, the Croizats moved to Coro, where they were appointed codirectors of the new *Jardín Botánico Xerófito "Dr. León Croizat."* While developing the *Jardin,* Croizat continued his research and publishing until his death at the age of 89.

Often at radical variance with prevailing and popular views about evolution and biology, Croizat's writings are often ignored by prominent and influential scientists. However, they have withstood the test of time, with many of his ideas either being adopted or reflected in later research. Croizat is best known for his new approach to biogeography. In the 1950s, he did what no one else had ever thought of doing before. He tested Darwin's theory of evolution through biogeography. In so doing, he was able to demonstrate that Darwin's theory of centers of origin and dispersal failed to predict global patterns of distribution and their correlation with tectonics. Long before continental drift and plate tectonics became the accepted worldview for geologists and evolutionists, Croizat used animal and plant distributions to successfully predict the geological structure of regions such as North and South America and the Galapagos Islands. The subsequent corroboration of his predictions by geologists demonstrated the progressive nature of panbiogeography over the prevailing Darwinian theory.

As an alternative to Darwinism, Croizat proposed the biological synthesis known as *panbiogeography.* This evolutionary framework rested on the foundations of biogeographic analysis to understand species, speciation, and biological differentiation in space, time, and form as a single synthesis rather than as the disparate conglomeration of disconnected hypotheses exemplified in Darwinism. His panbiogeography also provided for a concept of biological evolution that did not require natural selection or any form of teleology to "explain" organic differentiation and speciation. Adopting the term *orthogenesis,* Croizat, like Rosa and other biologists before him, viewed the generation of novel variation as a process biased by the existing genetic and developmental types of organization. Adaptation was seen as a consequence of evolution rather than a cause, and his orthogenetic approach eliminated the unscientific narrative approach to evolution prevailing then, as now, in Darwinian theory that explains the origin of an adaptation by its ability to meet a future goal such as the resulting advantage or utility. Croizat's orthogenetic framework also anticipated subsequent developments in molecular and developmental genetics.

Far less recognized are Croizat's contributions to anthropology and archeology, particularly for biogeographic aspects of human evolution and cultural development. He proposed a biogeographic context for the origins of modern humans along a sector ranging between South Africa, Europe, and East Asia, which contrasted to Darwinian notions of an original birthplace followed by a concerted and sequential outward dispersal. Croizat saw human evolution as a combination of migration and stabilized differentiation around two principal focal areas: what he called "Cro-Magnon" in Africa and Europe and "Austro-Melanesian" in East Asia. In the 1970s, he also produced a comprehensive analysis of the biogeographic origins of American Indians that anticipated current theories by proposing seafaring colonization (coastal theory) by people who were not modern Asians in appearance (now implicated in studies of skulls such as the Kennewick Man), and arrival before the Clovis culture (upward of 40,000 years ago that compares well with the 20,000–30,000 now predicted by some anthropologists). He also predicted the American Indians are principally derived from seafaring coastal Asian Austro-Melanesian people rather than from continental Asians.

— *John R. Grehan*

See also **Biogeography**

Further Readings

Craw, R. C., Grehan, J. R., & Heads, M. J. (1999). *Panbiogeography.* New York: Oxford University Press.

Croizat, L. (1964). *Space, time, form: The biological synthesis.* Caracas, Venezuela: Author.

 # CROSS-CULTURAL RESEARCH

Almost by definition, cultural anthropology *is* cross-cultural research. The search for an understanding of what culture is has meant undertaking research with an eye for comparing ethnographic data generated in different societies. Anthropological fieldwork has been driven as much by the desire to test a particular theory about culture as it has been about documenting another unknown group of people.

In current convention, however, *cross-cultural research* refers to a specific approach to cultural anthropology, namely, using data from multiple cultures to test hypotheses using statistical methods. This quantitative approach developed out of the *culture and personality school* of anthropology and grew through the work of George P. Murdock, who first organized the Human Relations Area Files (HRAF), a database that today consists of nearly 400 different ethnographies of cultural groups, indexed by over 700 different topics.

The lasting value of the statistical cross-cultural comparison using HRAF has been that it has allowed cultural anthropologists to ask the "big" questions that other kinds of research are ill-equipped to handle: What are the causes of warfare? Why do states form? Why do states collapse? What are the causes of social inequality?

The very earliest anthropologists interested in cross-cultural comparative work were out of the evolutionary mold: E. B. Tylor, Herbert Spencer, and Lewis Henry Morgan. These late-18th-century anthropologists compared cultures and ordered them in an evolutionary sequence, called *unilineal evolution,* based upon their presumed level of development. In analytical and methodological terms, Morgan was the most sophisticated. He conducted actual fieldwork (with Seneca Indians) and collected data from nearly 70 other American Indian tribes in the United States. Indeed, one of his main contributions to comparative cross-cultural research was the discovery of classificatory kinship systems. As might be expected, then, Morgan's evolutionary scheme was the most sophisticated, based upon a culture's technical capacity and material technology.

Nevertheless, the rejection of evolutionism and the kind of comparative work it engendered by Franz Boas and his students pushed cross-cultural comparative work into the background of cultural anthropology for nearly 40 years. When comparative work reemerged in American anthropology, it was the intellectual descendants of Morgan and Tylor who were responsible for it.

Another source of the contemporary statistical model of cross-cultural comparison emerged out of the *basic and modal personality* school of anthropology. This brand of cultural anthropology included scholars such as Ralph Linton, Ruth Benedict, Edward Sapir, Cora Du Bois (all Boasians), and Abraham Kardiner (a psychoanalyst). This orientation toward culture and personality studies was essentially the application of psychoanalytic theory to the study of culture: Cultural anthropologists presented their fieldwork data, and Kardiner provided a profile of that particular culture.

The working assumption of the approach was that every society had a "basic personality," a common denominator of personality types. There was a clear understanding that basic personality was formed based on the cultural institutions involved in child socialization. Cultural patterns, such as mythology, marriage patterns, and gender relations, were believed to be projections of basic personality.

The problems with the approach were that all of these "studies" were conducted after the fact, so there was no real testing of data. Cora Du Bois, however, conducted fieldwork with the Alorese during 1937 to 1938, collecting data specifically to test basic personality. Her work refined the understanding of culture-personality relationships. Unfortunately, the methodological improvements in her research design and execution were lost on most culture and personality anthropologists, who later became enamored of the national character studies.

At Yale, however, the methodology for investigating psychology using anthropological approaches did become more sophisticated, through the interaction of psychologists John Dollard and Clark Hull and anthropologists Edward Sapir, George P. Murdock, and John Whiting.

George P. Murdock was the most influential figure of cross-cultural analysis, a student of William Graham Sumner, which makes Murdock one of the rare American anthropologists of the early 20th century to be trained by someone outside of the Boasian tradition. Indeed, Murdock's intellectual ancestors were from the line of Tylor, Morgan, and Spencer. Murdock first developed the Cross-Cultural Survey during the 1930s and 1940s, which in 1949 became the HRAF. Murdock is best known for this work and for his studies of kinship systems.

Whiting earned his PhD at Yale in 1938 and returned there following military service during World War II to conduct, with Irvin Child, a large-scale, systematic study of child training and personality using Murdock's Survey. Published in 1953 as *Child Training and Personality,* the work was noteworthy because it tested a model very much like basic personality on a sample of 39 different cultures, using basic statistical procedures to analyze the data. The results were not all that encouraging (the correlation between child training and personality was not strong), but the method led to a number of other examinations of child training and personality, among them Barry, Bacon, and Child's classic *Relation of Child Training to Subsistence Economy,* which demonstrated that subsistence mode and environment were important influences in how children were raised.

There were, however, notable problems with HRAF. One of these problems was that studies tended to lose information through the coding process. That is, coding a society for a particular trait ignores any variability that might have existed within that society. A second problem was that large-scale, complex societies were either underrepresented or ignored entirely, simply because most anthropological fieldwork was done with small-scale, primitive societies. A third problem was that not all ethnographies were of equal value.

Whiting was aware of all of these problems, but most especially the last, because many ethnographies made no comments at all on child training and child development, Whiting's primary research interest. To address this issue, he and his wife, Beatrice, devised the Six Cultures Project, a study designed to collect similar, directly comparable data from six cultures: the United States (in Massachusetts), Philippines, Japan, Kenya, Mexico, and India. Research results began to be published in 1963, but the project is most famous for *Children of Six Cultures,* published in 1975.

The HRAF have, however, been consistently upgraded, improved, and expanded. Significant work using the HRAF has expanded the anthropological understanding of complexity, kinship, marriage, and descent; the social correlates of particular subsistence modes; socialization; religion; warfare; and numerous other subjects. A great deal of what cultural anthropologists teach in an introductory course in anthropology is based on work done using the HRAF.

— *Peter Collings*

See also **Anthropology, Cultural; Murdock, George Peter; Sumner, William Graham; Tylor, Edward Burnett**

Further Readings

Levinson, D., & Malone, M. J. (1980). *Toward explaining human culture: A critical review of the findings of worldwide cross-cultural research.* New Haven, CT: HRAF Research Press.

Murdock, G. P. (1949). *Social structure.* New York: Macmillan.

Whiting, B., & Whiting, J. W. M. (1975). *Children of six cultures: A psycho-cultural analysis.* Cambridge, MA: Harvard University Press.

CUBA

Cuba is an island nation known for its beautiful tropical beaches, intoxicating musical rhythms, and rich cultural heritage and diversity. Some 90 miles off the coast of Florida Keys and the largest island in the Caribbean, Cuba is 48,800 square miles, or 110,860 sq km, just a bit smaller than the U.S. state of Louisiana. Along with the main island, Cuba includes the *Isla de Juventud* and more than 4,195 small coral cays and islets, which makes up approximately 3,715 km. Cuba is a coveted strategic location, which has been fought over throughout its history. Situated at the convergence of the Atlantic Ocean, the Gulf of Mexico, and the Caribbean Sea, it is positioned along the most powerful maritime passage in and out of the Caribbean.

Geography and Nature

Approximately one third of the island is made up of forested mountains, including the Sierra Maestra in the Oriente, the Guaniguanco chain in the western province of Pinar del Rio, and the Escambrey to the south in the province of Las Villas. The remainder of the island is made up of plains used for cattle ranching and the growing of sugar cane. In addition, the island includes coastal regions of estuaries, swamps, and marshes, along with offshore islets and keys. Some 6,000 species of plants are on the island, over half of which are endemic. Forests include semideciduous, mangrove, pines, and tropical rain forest. Cuba's national tree is the royal palm *(Reistonea regia)* of which there are 20 million in Cuba, reaching up to 40 m tall. Cuba has an abundance of reptiles, including crocodiles, iguanas, lizards, and snakes. The largest indigenous mammal is the tree rat or the *jutía,* measuring approximately 60 cm long. Also, Cuba is home to some 350 species of birds, including the world's smallest bird, the bee hummingbird, or *zunzuncito;* the males weigh only 2 g, with the female slightly larger.

The capital, Havana, or *La Habana,* is the largest city in the Caribbean and an important port city, home to some 2.2 million people. Havana is the country's center of government, education, medicine, trade, tourism, and communication. Many of the houses in the city are in a state of charming disrepair.

The second-largest city is Santiago de Cuba, located in the Oriente province, which also serves as an important political, economic, military, and cultural center of the island.

Demographics and Identity

Presently, Cuba is home to 11 million people. The majority of Cubans speak Spanish exclusively, in a dialect typical of other Caribbean islands. Nearly 51% of the people are considered mulatto (both African and European descent), about 37% are considered White, while 11% are Black. The remaining 1% of the population are the descendents of the Chinese-indentured servants, who replaced the labor lost after the cessation of slavery in 1853. Much of the culture is strongly influenced by West African traditions brought over by slaves during the mid- to late 1800s. Slaves became an important labor resource with the rise of the sugar industry and loss of indigenous labor. The largest population imported to Cuba came from the Yorubá people of Nigeria.

Music and Dance

There are strong expressions everywhere of Afro-Cuban art, religion, music, and dance. To be Cuban means many things to many people, and the idea of "Cubanness" is difficult to define. Cubans are comfortable regarding close bodily space, and physical contact and affection are readily displayed. Socialization and dancing take place in streets and in lines for food, goods, or ice cream. Afro-Cuban cultural forms of music and dance dominate the modern conception of Cuban identity. Cuban music is the island's most well-known export worldwide. Cuban music is a blending of West African rhythms and ritual dance with the Spanish guitar, further fused with American jazz. The most popular Cuban music today is *Son,* first created in the Oriente region, combining string instruments, bongos, maracas, and claves. Mambo, bolero, salsa, and cha-cha all contain elements of Cuban *Son.*

Cuban dance has important links to Santeria, an Afro-Cuban religion, which combines West African deities, beliefs, and rituals with Catholicism. Catholic saints, especially the Virgin Mary, are associated with Yoruban *orishas.* In this way, early slaves were able to

Source: © iStockphoto/Arjan Schreven.

have reached the island approximately 5,000 years ago from South America. Their primary subsistence strategies included fishing, hunting, and gathering. The later arrivals of Tainos were horticulturalists, who introduced the cultivation of sweet potatoes and manioc. During this time, the greatest concentration of people was centered around the Bahía de Nipe, on the eastern part of the island. By the time Columbus arrived in the late 15th century, most people who inhabited the island were Taino-speaking Arawaks.

The indigenous population was quickly exterminated or forced into slavery by the Spanish. Those enslaved were made to work in mining and agricultural projects. This system of *encomiendas* entitled Spanish landowners to the indigenous labor force in the region in return for their Christianization. Prospecting for gold was also an important agenda for the Spaniards, but proved to be inadequate. Those who wished that Cuba would bring them instant wealth were quickly disappointed because the island did not hold large deposits of gold or other minerals. Meanwhile, the unhappy indigenous labor force organized many uprisings against the conquistadors.

keep their traditions while ostensibly practicing the Christian faith. The religion consists of male priests, *babalawo,* who cure the sick, offer advice, and protect their petitioners. Offerings of food, herbs, and blood are presented to stones in which the spirit of the *orisha* resides, and rituals are performed at religious gatherings.

Cuban History

Columbus first spotted Cuba in 1492, and it was quickly colonized by the Spanish. By 1511, the first permanent settlement was established near Baracoa, on the eastern tip of the island. Pre-Columbian populations numbered 112,000 and comprised mainly Arawaks or Taino and sub-Taino peoples. Earlier populations of Guanahatabey and Siboney are said to

Spain referred to Cuba as the "Fortress of the Indies" and the "Key to the New World," acknowledging the island's influential position in controlling the development of the New World. The Caribbean was an arena for European rivalries, including England, France, and the Dutch, who went to war to protect their strategic and economic interests. Caribbean islands became the pawns in international conflicts and were captured in times of war and returned at the peace table. In the case of Cuba, this meant disruptions in trade, increased taxation, and great human suffering.

In the late 1800s, the great poet and statesman José Martí, the "father of the Cuban Nation," who is considered the country's most famous literary figure, became a national hero for both his liberal ideals and martyr's death. He represented a great human rights figure, who spoke out against inequality and is sometimes compared to Martin Luther King Jr. Martí worked from the United States, where he was in exile, to form a revolution to remove Spanish occupation from Cuba. The United States supported Cuba's freedom from Spain only because it wanted the island to be defenseless against an economic invasion by capitalists. Since the late 1400s, when Columbus reported the existence of Cuba, it remained a colony of Spain until the invasion in 1898 by the United States. Consequently, Cuba became a de facto colony of the United States, which had both military and corporate interests there.

The war began in the Oriente in 1895, when the population rebelled against the colonial government. For 3 years, guerilla warfare ensued. However, an explosion that sank the *U.S.S. Maine* in the Havana harbor incited the United States to declare war on Spain and invade Cuba. In 1898, under the Treaty of Paris, the United States claimed the remaining Spanish colonies of Cuba, Puerto Rico, and the Philippines. The imminent victory of Cuban freedom fighters was stolen by the colonial power of the United States, and the Cuban people protested to no avail.

The United States agreed to withdraw from Cuba in 1901, keeping a 99-year lease on the Guantánamo naval base in the Oriente, along with other demands drawn up in the Platt Amendment. In the early 1900s a U.S. corporation called the "Cuban Colonizing Company" also sold lands to non-Cubans, much to the dismay of the majority of the inhabitants of the island. In 1924, without U.S. protest, Gerado Machado y Morales made himself dictator of the island and led a corrupt and violent government until 1933. In 1934, and again in 1952, Fulgencio Batista seized power and ruled Cuba under his dictatorship, with the support of the United States. During this time, the United States corporate and military interests dominated Cuban government, corporate expansion, and life until the triumph of the revolution on January 1, 1959, liberating Cuba for the first time in its history.

The first attempt to overthrow the corrupt government of Batista came on July 26, 1953, at Moncada and was led by Fidel Castro, a brazen man who had organized and trained a guerrilla army after Batista's coup d'état the previous year. The rebels were defeated, and almost half of the men died in battle, while more were subsequently executed. Despite their defeat, the revolutionaries reorganized and named their movement *Movimiento 26 de Julio*. In 1955, Castro and his brother Raul organized members, who were set to sail from Mexico to Cuba for another rebellion. It was during this time that Castro met Ernesto Che Guevara, the 27-year-old revolutionary from Argentina, who was trained in medicine and known for his intelligence and his considerable knowledge of Latin American social and political movements. On December 2, 1956, the group assembled off the coast of Santiago in a small ship named *Grandma*. Many of the revolutionaries were captured, but some managed to escape into the Sierra Maestra mountains in the Oriente, where they were joined by thousands of other Cubans. The rebel army with the support of the local population and knowledge of the terrain launched an attack on the Batista regime. In 1959, the guerrillas and supporters of Castro toppled Batista's government, and he fled to Miami with more than $300 million (U.S.) of embezzled funds.

Fidel Castro and the Revolution

Before 1959, Cuba was considered a stable Latin American country. It ranked third in life expectancy, fourth in electricity consumption per capita, and fifth in per capita income, $353 (U.S.) in 1958. The people of Cuba owned consumer products, such as televisions and cars, and by economic indicators, it appears that Cubans lived well. However, the distribution of wealth and quality of life was heavily skewed in favor of the rich class. The actual income was $270 and lower per year. Moreover, racial discrimination was rampant and Blacks found it more difficult to earn a living before the revolution. In the rural regions, more than one quarter of the people were landless peasants. Land ownership was held by a few rich families with large land holdings or by North American companies, and 8% of the population held 79% of the arable land. Farmers could work for months on these plantations and still not have enough money to buy food for their starving families. The rural population represented extreme poverty, with 25% of the people unemployed, 45% illiterate, 84% percent without running water, and 54% without indoor plumbing.

From a balcony in Santiago de Cuba, on January 2, 1959, Fidel Castro delivered his first speech. The choice of this city was deliberate and designed to evoke memories of the humiliation inflicted upon Cuba in 1898 by the United States. Castro announced "the Revolution begins now," and "this time it will not be like in 1898 when the North Americans came and made themselves masters of our country. This time, fortunately, the Revolution will come to power." It is said that two white doves landed on Castro's shoulders during this speech, reinforcing the idea for many Cubans that he was divinely guided.

Fidel Castro is considered to be a fascinating figure of his generation; in his youth, he was a successful athlete and a brilliant orator destined for politics. Castro has proven to be one of the most intriguing men of the 20th century. The bearded revolutionary, sporting his signature combat fatigues, went against the most powerful nation in the world and was successful. More than 40 years later, the struggle of power has continued, as the George W. Bush administration tightened U.S. sanctions and Castro rejected the U.S. dollar in an economic countermove. Today, both Fidel Castro and Che Guevara are viewed by many Latin American libertines as heroes, who fought against economic imperialism. One has only to scratch the surface of U.S. and Latin American economic policies to understand their emotions.

North-American-owned oil and fruit companies have gone into many regions of Central and South America and taken the natural resources, polluted the soils and rivers, and exploited the people for their labor. Consequently, the populations have been left in far worse economic and social situations than they were before the arrival of the companies. Though the companies made promises, their ultimate aim was to create a large profit despite the adverse affects on the locals. For example, in Ecuador, Texaco ignored safety precautions and polluted enormous portions of the Amazon Basin, leaving the indigenous people disease ridden and unable to continue their subsistence farming because of the contaminated air, water, and soils. In a recent study of health in the Amazon region, the population rated 30% higher than the national average in diseases such as cancer and respiratory infirmities.

There are, however, many people unhappy with Castro's policies. The majority of those who oppose him were the wealthy business and landowners of Cuba, whose assets were seized and redistributed after the revolution. These people eventually left the island to settle in the United States. Two of the most populated states of exile communities include Florida (Miami) and New Jersey. Of the 1,500,000 Cuban immigrants who live in Cuba, 700,000 of them live in southern Florida. Powerful lobbyists, who strongly influence U.S. policies toward Cuba, these communities hope to return to a "Castro-Free" Cuba one day.

The Bay of Pigs Invasion

Since the inauguration of Castro's Revolution, the U.S. government, along with Cuban exiles, has tried without success to overthrow Castro's government. For instance, in April of 1961, Cuban exiles with the backing of the U.S. Central Intelligence Agency (CIA) launched the Bay of Pigs Invasion, *Bahía de Cochínos* (named for the wild pigs that roamed the region), on the south side of the island, west of Trinidad. Castro knew that an attack was inevitable after the destruction of a sugar mill in Pinar del Rio and the bombing of a department store in Havana called "El Encanto" by counterrevolutionaries from within the island. It was at this point that Castro leaned toward his Soviet Union alliances and in a speech following the attacks described his government as a "socialist revolution," defining the nature of the revolution for the first time. Two days later, on April 17, exiles landed on the shores of Playa Girón and Playa Larga. Castro's militia attacked by air and land in defense of the island and defeated the invaders, leaving 100 exiles dead and 1,200 captured. Cuba lost 160 defenders in the attack. The invasion has become known in U.S. history as a poorly organized major blunder that only reinforced the momentum of Castro's movement.

The Cuban Missile Crisis

In the aftermath of the Bay of Pigs disaster, the Kennedy administration appointed General Edward Landsdale in charge of "Operation Mongoose" to help the exiles bring down the Castro regime, including plotting the assassination of Castro. Castro learned of the conspiracy, and to end the threats to his Revolution, he formed an alliance with the Soviet Union to arm the island against possible U.S. invasion. In October 22, 1962, the United States woke up to the reality of the threat of a nuclear missile attack. For several months, the United States had detected through the surveillance of military spy planes that Cuba was building Soviet-style nuclear arms installations on the island. With the help of Nikita Khrushchev, in what is known as code name "Operation Anadyr,"

Soviet missiles and troops were assembled on the island throughout the summer of 1962, with the nuclear warheads arriving in October. Castro urged Khrushchev to make a public announcement about their plans to let the United States and the world know that they were taking steps to arm themselves and that the two countries had signed a defense treaty. Castro sent Guevara to convince the Soviet leader to go public, but Khrushchev refused, assuring him that everything was on schedule.

On the night of October 22, 1962, Kennedy appeared on television to inform U.S. citizens that there was a Soviet buildup of nuclear weapons on Cuba, with warheads capable of striking Washington, D.C., and other cities in the United States. During this "Cuban Missile Crisis," President Kennedy, along with his brother, Robert, met with defense secretary Robert McNamara to discuss their options of dealing with the situation. McNamara discouraged an operational air strike, citing the possibility of thousands of casualties. Instead, President Kennedy decided to implement a naval blockade and during his television speech stated, "All ships of any kind bound for Cuba from whatever nation or port will, if found to contain cargoes of offensive weapons, be turned back." Kennedy concluded by saying: "To the captive people of Cuba, your leaders are no longer Cuban leaders inspired by Cuban ideals, but are puppets and agents of an international conspiracy." Castro went on television the following evening and responded to Kennedy's comments:

> Our progress, our independence, and our sovereignty have been undercut by the policy of the Yankee government. The Americans had tried everything: diplomatic pressure, economic aggression, and the invasion at Playa Girón. Now they are trying to prevent us from arming ourselves with the assistance of the Soviet camp. The people should know the following: we have the means to which repel a direct attack. We are running risks, which we have but no choice to run. We have the consolation of knowing that in a thermo-nuclear war, the aggressors, those who unleash thermo-nuclear war, will be exterminated. I believe there are no ambiguities of any kind.

Tensions between the two countries' leaders mounted, and finally on October 26, Khrushchev sent a letter to Kennedy, stating that he'd sent missiles to Cuba to prevent another exile invasion like the Bay of Pigs. He would withdraw the weapons if Kennedy agreed not to invade. The U.S.-Soviet agreement also stipulated that the United States would remove U.S. missiles in Turkey. By the end of November, Kennedy announced that the crisis was over; the naval blockade was lifted, and "Operation Mongoose" was dismantled.

The Special Period

The fall of the communist states of Eastern Europe put unimaginable strains on the Cuban economy. Prior to the collapse, the Council of Mutual Economic Assistance (COMECON) of the Soviet Union had subsidized the Cuban economy by selling them oil at below-market prices and allowing them to resell for a profit. In addition, the Soviet Union purchased 63% of Cuba's sugar, 95% of its citrus, and 73% of its nickel, which constituted the three main industries. The economic disaster created when this excessive contribution ended and the country was forced to rely on its own unstable industry was without precedent. Cuba was now forced into the global economy based on cash transactions that did not create allowances for their idealistic policies. Though the island had experienced economic slumps in the past, during the depression of the 1930s, after the revolution, and during the time of economic transformation of the early 1960s, none could compare with the disintegration of the economy in the 1990s. Exiled Cubans living in the United States believed that this was the end of the Castro regime—but not so.

Both fuel and food were in desperately short supply. Agricultural lands were being used for cattle ranching and sugar, and Cuba had relied on imported foods supplied by Eastern Europe. The country now had to seek out immediate ways to grow crops at home and become self-sufficient. Food programs were introduced, along with new means of restarting the economy. Two important industries came out of this transitional period: investing in biotechnology or medical products and the tourist industry.

Industry and Commercial Activity Today

Under the extreme conditions of the Special Period (after 1989), the state found it necessary to decentralize economic activities and encourage private enterprise on a small scale. In the early 1990s, constitutional amendments recognized more than 100 new categories of privatization. Today, commercial activity is a mixture of both private and commercial ownership of the major economic industries. For example, lands are owned in small parcels by individual agriculturalists, but larger farms are operated by the state. The result of this new configuration is a return of social stratification that had been equalized by Castro. With new markets opening, those able to capitalize on them have become a marginally privileged class with access to luxury items.

Though sugar has historically been the mainstay of the economy, tourism has become an important industry. Another impact of the Special Period was the opening of Cuban borders to foreign visitors, as President Castro declared that tourism would become its main source of income. Now it accounts for more than 50% of its hard currency, and more than 2 million foreign vacationers were expected to visit the island in 2004. Cuba has much to offer to foreign travelers in the form of natural resources, and culturally, Cuba is imbued with a combination of West African and Spanish traditions that offer a rich authenticity of music, dance, food, arts and crafts, and unique worldview. All of these resources have been harnessed to promote Cuba as a world traveler's destination.

The tourist industry gave a much-needed boost to the economy during the Special Period but left gross disparities of earning among Cubans. Where a bellhop or waiter can make between $150 and $1,000 (U.S.) per month, a physician or lawyer is making only $30. These differences in income have caused resentment among Cuban professionals, and today it is not uncommon to see a doctor working for a hotel to earn cash.

Because the local currency, the Cuban peso, is not convertible on the world market, the state adopted the U.S. dollar in 1994. However, 6 days after President George W. Bush was reelected, in 2004, and sanctions were tightened on Cuban trade, Castro converted to a national peso that would be easily exchangeable with the Eurodollar. Previously, though, pesos were sold on the black market, along with other goods, such as agricultural products, for American dollars.

Political Structure

Cuban government structure is based on a Marxist-Leninist theory, combined with a struggle for sovereignty and social justice. José Martí was an integral figure who shaped Cuban history and influenced the great socialist thinkers by writing about the importance of forming national unity by creating the Cuban Revolutionary Party (*Partido Revolucionario Cubano,* or PRC). Martí's observations from living in the United States led him to the conclusion that corrupt capitalist elections were "bought" by large corporations that supported candidates who represented only the elite. His ideas called for a new political party that represented the majority of Cubans. Martí believed the working masses were necessary for change. Castro, in his famous speech, "History Will Absolve Me," outlined the goals of national independence and social justice, which shaped his more than 40-year revolution.

The Constitution of 1976 created a National Assembly of the People's Power (*Asamblea Nacional del Poder Popular*), whose members are elected every 5 years. In 1992, the electoral system was amended to facilitate more efficient popular participation and decision making. Half the candidates are nominated by mass organizations, and the other half of the candidates are chosen by elected municipal delegates. In the past, all candidates were nominated by the Communist Party committees. The National Assembly is the sole body with legislative authority. There is only one candidate for each assembly seat, and a negative vote of 50% is enough to reject a candidate. The National Assembly elects a 31-member Council of State, and the council's decisions must be ratified by the National Assembly. The Council of the State determines the composition of the Council of Ministry, and both bodies constitute the executive arm and cabinet of government.

Cuba is divided into 169 municipalities, including the Special Municipality of Isla de la Juventud, and 14 provinces. The municipal assemblies are elected every 2½ years, and these, in turn, elect their own executive committees.

Land Tenure and Property

The society does not value private space as in the United States, because Cubans are accustomed to living in cramped quarters. Few new constructions have been built since 1959, since construction materials are always in short supply. Since 1970, the construction of new homes has been carried out by "microbrigades," or groups of 30 people who assemble prefabricated high-rise buildings for apartment-complex-style housing. Since 1960, rents were converted into mortgages, and nearly half a million Cubans gained title to homes and lands. The sale of houses is prohibited, but exchange without currency is admissible. In the rural regions, land reforms such as the Agrarian Reform Law of 1959 divided lands and redistributed them to 200,000 farm workers without land. In 1975, the National Association of Small Farmers worked at creating cooperatives, and by the mid-1980s, three quarters of private farmers were cooperative members. Membership incentives include goods such as seed, fertilizers, machinery, social security, and tax breaks. In addition, small farmers no longer lived with the threat that they would be kicked off of their lands.

The Future of Cuba

Cuba will remain throughout history as a country of intrigue and fascination. Painted indelibly with a colorful past, dominated by three colonial powers, each of which has left their mark, has influenced the culture and way of life. The Revolution has changed the status of the country by marking it as an independent nation, and today, Cuba has emerged a self-determining country with a unique sense of identity. The world is waiting to see what will happen to Cuba "after Fidel Castro." Raúl is next in line to lead. He is already in charge of the armed services, and has been since 1959. In addition, Ricardo Alarcón, president of the National Assembly of the People's Power, has served as Cuba's political expert in negotiations with the United States. Over the past 15 years, members of the Cuban government have been selected from the younger generations, people in their 30s who follow socialist philosophy. Cuba has already been ruled for many years by a post-Castro government, competent individuals who are capable of successfully running the island. Castro, in the autumn of his life, presides over the government that he has created—still an idealistic man with remarkable conviction.

— *Luci Latina Fernandes*

See also **Communism**

Further Readings

Gott, R. (2004). Cuba: *A new history.* New Haven, CT: Yale University Press.
Perez, L. A. Jr. (1995). *Cuba: Between reform and revolution.* New York: Oxford University Press.
Saney, I. (2004). *Cuba: A revolution in motion.* Manitoba, Canada: Fernwood.
Stanley, D. (1997). *Cuba: Survival guide.* London, UK: Lonely Planet.
Suchlicki, J. (1997). *Cuba: From Columbus to Castro and beyond* (4th ed.). Washington, DC: Brassey's.

CULTIVATION, PLANT

Plant cultivation includes a whole range of human behaviors, from watering, to weeding, to the construction of drainage ditches, which are designed to encourage the growth and propagation of one or more species of plants. Cultivated plants are distinguished from domesticated plants, which show morphological changes, indicating that they are genetically different from their wild ancestors. In many cases, early domesticated plants are so different from their wild progenitors that their reproduction depends on human interference. For example, in wild cereal plants, the rachis, the axis of the plant to which the grains are attached, is brittle. When the cereal grains ripen, the rachis shatters, allowing the grains to disperse and the plant to reseed itself. Early domesticated cereals have a nonbrittle rachis and depend on humans for their propagation. While plant cultivation is certainly an early stage in the process of plant domestication, plant cultivation does not always lead to domestication.

Recovery of Archaeological Plant Remains

To study plant cultivation and plant domestication, archaeologists must be able to recover plant remains from archaeological sites. A technique known as *flotation* is generally used to recover archaeological plant remains. Flotation, or water separation, uses moving water to separate light organic materials, such as seeds and charcoal, from archaeological soils. Most flotation machines include a large tank with a spout that pours water into a fine mesh strainer. A large tub with a screened bottom fits inside the tank. The screen, which is often made of window screening, is used to catch heavier artifacts, such as stone tools and pottery shards. When a measured sample of archaeological soil is poured into the flotation machine, the light

of grasses. However, the barley remains from Netiv Hagdud were morphologically wild. Based on the large quantities of barley remains that were recovered, the excavators of the site have suggested that Netiv Hagdud's economy was based on the systematic cultivation of wild barley. In this case, plant cultivation represents an intermediate point between the plant-gathering economies of the Late Pleistocene and true plant domestication. Morphologically domesticated barley has been recovered from many later Neolithic sites in the Near East, and domesticated barley and wheat became the dominant cereal grains throughout later Near Eastern prehistory.

organic materials floats to the top of the tank. Moving water carries this material down the spout and into the fine mesh strainer. The resulting material is known as the light fraction and generally includes small fragments of carbonized seeds, other plant parts, and wood charcoal. The plant remains recovered through flotation are usually studied by specialists known as *archaeobotanists*.

Archaeological and Ethnographic Examples of Plant Cultivation

One of the best-known archaeological examples of plant cultivation comes from the site of Netiv Hagdud in the West Bank. The site originally covered about 1.5 hectares and has been dated to between 9,900 and 9,600 uncorrected radiocarbon years BP. Three seasons of excavation at Netiv Hagdud, under the direction of Ofer Bar-Yosef and Avi Gopher, produced the remains of several small oval houses with stone foundations, as well as storage pits. The stone tools and other artifacts from Netiv Hagdud indicate that it was occupied during the Prepottery Neolithic.

The excavations at Netiv Hagdud also yielded over 17,000 charred seed and fruit remains, including the remains of cereals, legumes, and wild fruits. Barley was by far the most common cereal recovered from Netiv Hagdud, making up about 90% of the remains

Ethnographic studies of traditional Aboriginal plant use in northern Australia provide similar examples of what might be termed plant management, or even plant cultivation. When Australian Aborigines in the Cape York province region of northern Australia harvested wild yams, they often replanted the tops of the tubers in the holes. The top of the yam is the portion of the plant from which regeneration takes place. Yams were also planted on islands off the coast of Australia, to extend the range of these plants and to serve as stores for visitors who might be trapped on these islands. These essentially horticultural behaviors were observed among people classified by anthropologists as hunter-gatherers.

Australian Aborigines also used fire to increase the productivity of cycads, whose seeds were collected for food. Many of the dense stands of cycads seen in northern Australia today may be a result of Aboriginal burning. The use of fire to control the distribution of plants (and animals) is well documented in the ethnographic and archaeological record of Australia. Other prehistoric hunter-gatherer populations who used fire to control the distribution of plants and game include the Mesolithic foragers of northern Europe and the Archaic hunter-gatherers of eastern North America.

From Foraging to Farming

The transition from hunting and gathering to agriculture is one of the most important changes in all of human prehistory. Archaeological evidence from sites such as Netiv Hagdud suggests that plant cultivation may have represented an important stage in the transition from foraging to farming. However, hunter-gatherers sometimes practiced behaviors that may be interpreted as plant cultivation, since they were designed to encourage the growth of favored plants. These data suggest that plant cultivation may not always have led to plant domestication.

— *Pam J. Crabtree*

See also **Agriculture, Origins of; Horticulture**

Further Readings

Bar-Yosef, O., & Gopher, A. (Eds.). (1997). *An early Neolithic Village in the Jordan Valley, Part I: The archaeology of Netiv Hagdud.* Cambridge, MA: Peabody Museum of Archaeology and Ethnography, Harvard University and American School of Prehistoric Research.

Cowan, C. W., & Watson, P. J. (1992). *The origins of agriculture: An international perspective.* Washington, DC: Smithsonian.

Lourandos, H. (1997). *Continent of hunter-gatherers: New perspectives in Australian prehistory.* Cambridge: Cambridge University Press.

Sobolik, K. D. (2003). *Archaeobiology: Archaeologist's toolkit.* New York: Alta Mira.

 Cults

The term *cult* stems from the Latin *cultus,* to worship. The term is difficult to define, as it is used to denote various actions and situations. In common parlance, cult brings to mind specific groups or sects who hold unorthodox religious beliefs. In anthropology and archaeology, the term *cult* tends to be conflated with ritual and religion. A study entitled "an archaeology of cult" will invariably discuss religion and ritual, while an anthropological study by the same title is likely to focus on religious and magical rituals.

Colin Renfrew defines the *archaeology of cult* as the system of patterned actions in response to religious beliefs, noting that these actions are not always clearly separated from other actions of everyday life. Indicators that may point to cult and ritual archaeologically are attention-focusing devices, a boundary zone between this world and the next, the presence of a deity, and evidence of participation and offering.

Thus, Renfrew notes that ritual locations will be places with special and/or natural associations (for example, caves, groves, and mountaintops) or in special buildings set apart for sacred functions (temples). The structure and equipment used will have attention-focusing devices (altars, special benches, hearths, lamps, gongs, vessels, and the like), and the sacred zone is likely to contain many repeated symbols (i.e., redundancy). In terms of boundaries, while rituals may involve public displays, they may also have a hidden aspect. Ruth Whitehouse focuses on this hidden dimension of ritual in her study of Neolithic caves in Italy. The sacred area may often show strong signs of cleanliness and pollutions (pools and basins).

The deity may be reflected in the use of cult images or represented in an abstract manner. Ritual symbols will often relate to the deity and associated myths. These may include animal and abstract symbolism. Rituals generally involve prayer and special gestures. These are rarely attested archaeologically, except in iconography, and it is anthropology that provides information on dances, music, the use of drugs, and so on.

Other rituals may involve the sacrifice of animals and humans, the consumption of food and drinks, and votive offerings. All of these have been attested to both archaeologically and anthropologically. The equipment and offerings may reflect a great investment of wealth and resources, although this is not always the case.

To assist in elucidating the problems involved in such analyses, which range from attribution in cultures without direct ethnographic parallels to being self-referential, archaeologists have traditionally turned to anthropology. Here, studies of cult focus on religious and magical rituals, in particular shamanism and specific aspects of rituals (termed a cult, for example, a fertility cult). Following Émile Durkheim and Mircea Eliade, such studies focus on the sacred (as opposed to the profane). The sacred is set apart from the normal world and may entail knowledge that is forbidden to everyone but the cult leaders. This knowledge is generally associated with magical forces, spirits and deities, and the distinction is often blurred.

While it is no longer fashionable to classify belief systems, there are a few important key concepts. Animism is the belief in spirits inhabiting mountains, trees, rivers, and so on. Next is totemism, a complex concept that broadly means the symbolic representation of social phenomena by natural phenomena. There are various kinds of totem, for example, individual totems, clan totems, and sacred-site totems. Their significance varies cross-culturally, and some anthropologists (for example, Claude Lévi-Strauss) maintain that there is no such thing as totemism because it is not a single phenomenon. Yet one of the most debated topics in both archaeology and anthropology remains studies of shamanism. Briefly, a shaman is a type of religious expert who mediates between the human and spirit world. In archaeology, there has been plenty of work on shamanistic practices with relation to rock art, for example, the work of David Lewis-Williams and Anne Solomon in South Africa.

Cargo cults, on the other hand, are another widespread phenomenon, which deals with the end of the world. These beliefs are especially found in Melanesia and the Pacific, where people believe that at the dawn of a new age, their ancestors will return with a "cargo" of valuable goods. The story of Captain Cooke has been explained in this manner; his arrival corresponded to the belief of the arrival of a powerful god. Cult studies may also include witchcraft (a malevolent magical practice), sorcery (similar but is learned rather than inherited), sacrificial cults, and various rites of passage.

In dealing with monotheism, cults assume another nature, and attention is devoted to specific aspects of a religion that is deemed a cult. Examples include Ancient Egyptian cults (for example, the cult of Isis) and, in the modern world, certain Christian groups (for example, those following the neo-Catechumenal way; adherents and other sectors of the church deny that this is a cult or sect). Which brings us to "cult" as used in common parlance, an often controversial term. By defining cults as unorthodox, they are immediately placed into the category of "the other." To noncult members, cults are groups that generally practice mind control, demand total submission, and, most often, take a member's money. To cult members, a particular cult is generally seen as either the "one true way" and/or a safe haven.

There is no agreement on which particular group is a cult or not (for example, Jehovah's Witnesses). However, there are three main features of any given cult. The first is the need for a charismatic leader (for example, David Koresh, leader of the Branch Davidians). Second is a philosophy of "us versus them." Cults generally demand that members alienate themselves from the outside world. Finally, cults are strictly hierarchical, and leaders employ varying degrees of indoctrination and demands of strict obedience.

Many cults are known to be dangerous and subject members to stress, fatigue, and humiliation. Isolation, peer pressure, and the causing of fear and paranoia are used to control and manipulate subjects. Cults may harm both members and nonmembers; for example, the Aum Shin Rikyo cult masterminded a deadly gas attack on the Tokyo subway system in 1995.

Common misconceptions on cults include that followers must be mentally instable and/or mad. However, while a leader may exhibit signs of mental instability, there is no prerequisite for followers to do likewise. Indeed, followers find a sense of belonging and protection in a particular cult. Very often, a member may feel this is the only way to salvation.

Whichever way one defines cult, what is important is to state at the outset is how the term will be used. While in archaeological and anthropological literature, usage is taken for granted, neither has offered a satisfactory distinction between cult and religion.

— *Isabelle Vella Gregory*

See also **Animism; Religion and Anthropology; Religious Rituals; Totemism**

Further Readings

Barnard, A. (2000). *Social anthropology: A concise introduction for students.* Taunton, MA: Studymates.

Novella, S., & DeAngelis, P. (2002). Cults. In M. Shermer (Ed.) & P. Linse (Contributing Ed.), *The skeptic encyclopedia of pseudoscience* (Vol. 1). Santa Barbara, CA: ABC-CLIO.

Renfrew, C., & Zubrow, E. B. W. (Eds.). (1994). *The ancient mind: Elements of cognitive archaeology.* Cambridge: Cambridge University Press.

CULTURAL CONSERVATION

Cultural conservation refers to systematic efforts to safeguard traditional cultural knowledge, customs, and materials and the natural resources on which they are based. The primary goals of cultural conservation projects are to sustain cultural and ecological diversity within modernizing communities and landscapes, to promote the active engagement of community members in local resource management, and to mobilize government support for the preservation of regional heritage. Anthropologists, folklorists, historians, and cultural geographers have advanced these goals in recent years by assessing the relevance of expressive traditions among social groups and by encouraging an appreciation for the cultural heritage within the communities they study.

Traditional cultural resources may be tangible, such as vernacular architecture, sacred landmarks, ethnic foodways, and folk arts. Others are intangible, such as regional music and dance, storytelling, games, and expressive oral traditions. While heritage preservation is concerned with the continuation of all aspects of traditional culture, it extends beyond the restoration of historic sites and the documentation of social customs. Cultural conservation is a highly cumulative, multidisciplinary process that entails the careful assessment of the consequences of industrialization and relocation of cultural traditions with symbolic and historic significance.

Over the past three decades, the conservation of traditional culture has become increasingly urgent. This is particularly true in the rural United States, where urbanization is rapidly changing the character of traditional lifestyles, and in some cases accelerating the decline of folklife altogether. Frequently, rural people relinquish folk traditions in favor of more cosmopolitan goods and services. Anthropologists call this process "delocalization," and one of the tasks facing scholars interested in cultural conservation is to identify the socioeconomic factors responsible for the erosion of cultural heritage and folk technology. Subsequent efforts by state and federal historic preservation agencies can benefit from this information by creating sensible strategies to maintain traditional innovations for the benefit of future generations.

A number of federally funded programs, such as the National Endowment for the Humanities and the American Folklife Center, are active supporters of cultural conservation research. Cultural conservation is most successful when implemented on a community level, using a "grassroots" approach to identify local pathways to heritage preservation. For example, cultural knowledge of medicinal plants in the Ozark Mountains is most endangered in communities that have shifted from subsistence farming to more progressive, service-based economies. While urbanization has brought modern health care services to underserved areas, economic development has hastened the abandonment of valuable folk medical expertise in exchange for more conventional approaches to health care. By working locally to promote ecological awareness of medicinal flora through educational workshops and by developing programs to encourage health care practitioners to integrate traditional healing alongside scientific medicine, the preservation of folk medical knowledge can ultimately be possible in modernizing communities of the rural Ozarks and elsewhere in regional American cultures.

Cultural resources are malleable, and as such, they can be reconstituted and presented to the public as nostalgic expressions of "living history." Region-specific customs and materials have persevered as tourist commodities, such as sea grass baskets in coastal South Carolina, Amish-made quilts in central Pennsylvania, maple syrup in upstate Vermont, or woven blankets sold on Navajo reservations. Visitors to folk cultural regions can now visit theme parks and museums demonstrating romantic and mythical images of past ways of life. While the promotion of cultural resources for mainstream consumption may seem to undermine their authenticity, "heritage tourism" can indeed reaffirm cultural cohesiveness and thus help ensure the rejuvenation of living traditions and expressions. Accordingly, the manipulation of tradition is not degenerative to cultural continuity, but an adaptive response to commercialization.

Some scholars have surmised that folk technologies can and do undergo revivification for more cerebral reasons. The eminent anthropologist John Roberts, for example, has surmised that that folk knowledge and skills are frequently held on "ready reserve" as functional alternatives, should modern technology eventually fail to serve the community's needs for survival. People also retain historic innovations as a way to reconnect with their collective past and as powerful expressions of cultural identity.

Numerous examples of cultural resource revival can be found in regional cultures in the United States, such as the widespread popular appeal of traditional hunting and fishing methods in the upper South. Here, as in other regions of the United States, people are returning to more historic approaches to wild game hunting, despite the industry-driven attempts to promote expensive and complex equipment for wildlife procurement. Examples of these techniques include traditional longbow archery, the use of muzzleloading black-powder rifles, and anachronistic angling methods such as cane-poling and handfishing. The recent implementation of these traditional techniques is evidence of a renewed appreciation for the guardianship and continuity of folk creativity and craftsmanship.

Despite the recent progress in heritage revitalization projects, there are a number of challenges to cultural conservation. The agendas of social scientists occasionally conflict with those of community members, particularly with regard to environmental policy and stewardship. Federal land managers may envision forests as aesthetic resources or national parks where wildlife and woodsmanship can flourish as part of the local recreational culture. Conversely, native people may prioritize industrial and economic development over ecological preservation of natural landscapes. Such conflicts, however, can engender a much-needed awareness among policymakers of the need to reconcile public and private agendas in cultural intervention programs.

For cultural conservation projects to succeed, they must culminate with sensible models that link natural resource conservation with the survivorship of cultural traditions. This can ultimately be made possible if anthropologists collaborate effectively with community members and listen closely to their concerns and remain sensitive to their needs. Through the realization that cultural and ecological conservation are interdependent processes, social scientists can continue to discover how living traditions are imagined, maintained, and rendered meaningful by people in their daily lives.

— *Justin M. Nolan*

See also **Cultural Ecology; Folk Culture**

Further Readings

Feintuch, B. (Ed.). (1988). *The conservation of culture: Folklorists and the public sector.* Lexington: University of Kentucky Press.

Howell, B. (Ed.). (1990). *Cultural heritage conservation in the American South.* Athens: University of Georgia Press.

Hufford, M. (Ed.). (1994). *Conserving culture: A new discourse on heritage.* Urbana: University of Illinois Press.

 ## CULTURAL CONSTRAINTS

Anthropologists Clyde Kluckhohn and William Kelley claim that by "culture," we mean those historically created selective processes that channel men's reactions, both to internal and to external stimuli. In a more simplistic way, culture is the complex whole that consists of all the ways we think and do and everything we have as members of society. Culture may thus be conceived of as a kind of stream, following down to the centuries from one generation to another. When we think of it in this way, culture becomes synonymous with social heritage. Each society has its own culture. The process of acquiring the culture of a different society from one's own is called "acculturation." We popularly refer to this process as the "melting pot." The culture of all people includes a tremendous amount of knowledge about the physical and social world. Even the most primitive societies have to know a great deal simply in order to survive. Their knowledge is more practical, like knowledge of how to obtain food and how to build shelters. In advanced societies, sciences and technologies create complex and elaborate cultures.

Although culture is abstract and intangible, its influence is far from superficial. A food *taboo* can be internalized so deeply that the digestive system will revolt if the taboo is violated. The involuntary physiological responses to embarrassment—blushing, stammering, and so on—are, in effect, controlled by culture, because the proper occasions for embarrassment are culturally defined. Thus, culture puts constraints on human behavior, thinking processes, and interaction. *Cultural constraints* are either prescriptive (people should do certain things) or proscriptive (people should not do certain things). Cultural constraints go a long way toward telling people what they can do; where they can choose; and with whom, where, and how they can interact; and they also help solve the problem of having to compare things that are seemingly incomparable. In addition, traditional constraints on choice may tell people in which domains of their lives the principles of rational choice are allowed to operate. Thus, cultural constraints serve as a kind of preventive medicine, protecting people from themselves. Cultural constraints affect not only the choices individuals make but even how the individual—the self—is constituted. The boundaries that separate the self from others are very much culture dependent. In cultures such as the United States, the self is construed as an independent entity. The boundaries between the self and others are clear and distinct. Independence, autonomy, and self-determination are prized, and the values and preferences of each individual are given a status that is independent of the values and preferences of others. However, in other, even industrial cultures such as Japan, the self is construed as an interdependent entity. Significant others form a part of the self, and their values and preferences are one's own.

Biologist Jacob Von Uexkull has noted that *security is more important than wealth* to explain how evolution shaped organisms so that their sensory systems were exquisitely attuned to just those environmental inputs that were critical to their survival. Thus, biology seems to supply the needed constraints on choice for most organisms. For human beings, those constraints come from culture. The interference of cultural constraints in the developmental process of the young humans, particularly the cognitive-ordering processes entailed in naming and word association, have worked to release the grip of instinct over human nature and to break up its fixed patternings, which carry significance in the world. In other words, cultural constraint through the process of internalization of habit and externalization of ritual is mostly indirect constraint that remains mostly subconscious, below the level of our conscious awareness. Such indirect constraints channel our lives along the grain because they confer a sense of regularity, predictability, subjective inevitability, and efficacy to all that we think, say, and do and without which our lives would be made to seem haphazard, chaotic, uncontrollable, and somewhat contrived. Cultural constraints include sanctions, laws, and taboos.

Sanctions: Sanctions are the supporters of norms, with punishments applied to those who do not conform and rewards given to those who do. Negatively, they may be anything from a raised eyebrow to the electric chair; positively, they may be anything from a smile to the honorary degree. There are more or less subtle ways in which disapproval of action may be expressed.

One of the less subtle ways is ridicule. However, it is a powerful social sanction because no one likes to be considered to be ridiculous by those whose opinions he or she values. One likes to stand in well with others, especially with those who constitute his or her intimate groups, and such a sanction, therefore, has an immediate and direct effect when promptly applied to those who do not conform. Thus, ridicule is so effective in some primitive groups, it is the only negative sanction needed to induce people to abide by the customs of the society. The ultimate negative sanction for both the mores and folkways is ostracism, a studied refusal to communicate with violators, the banishment of offenders from the groups to which they want to belong, sending them to coventry. Individuals do not like to be exiled from groups they consider their own, from their circle of intimates and friends. Ostracism is thus one of the cruelest social punishments known to men.

Laws: There are legal constraints, too, which are the negative sanctions applied to violators of the laws. These constraints are clear, familiar, and stated in the laws themselves. They include fine, imprisonment, deportation, and, for some offenses, death.

Taboos: Taboo means prohibition against an item, person, or type of behavior. In religious taboos, the forbidden item is believed to be unclean or sacred, and the taboo is imposed for protection against the item's power. Prohibition against incest and marriage within certain groups are examples of behavioral taboos. The most universal prohibition of such taboo is that on mating among certain kinds of kin: mother-son, father-daughter, brother-sister. Some other taboos are more concerned with social relationships, as in the obsrvance of caste or class rules or use of language among family members.

— *Komanduri S. Murty and Ashwin G. Vyas*

See also **Incest Taboo; Law and Society; Taboos**

Further Readings

Chick, G., & Dong, E. (2003, April 6–8). Possibility of refining the hierarchical model of leisure constraints through cross-cultural research. *Proceedings of the 2003 Northeastern Recreation Research Symposium,* Bolton Landing, NY.

Lewis, H. (1993). *Anthropologia.* Whitter, CA: Lewis Micropublishing.

Nanda, S. (1994). *Cultural anthropology* (5th ed.). Belmont, CA: Wadsworth.

CULTURAL ECOLOGY

Cultural ecology is the study of the adaptation of a culture to a specific environment and how changes in that environment lead to changes in that specific culture. It also focuses on how the overall environment, natural resources available, technology, and population density affect the rest of the culture and how a traditional system of beliefs and behavior allows people to adapt to their environment. Interplay between any population and their environment is the subject of *ecological studies.* Cultural ecologists study how humans in their society and through specific cultures interact with the larger environment. In the case of human beings, much of the behavior involved in interaction with the environment is learned behavior that has become part of the reserve of learned skills, technology, and other cultural responses of a people in a society.

Marx

Much of cultural ecology was founded on Marx's methodology. Marx claimed there are real regularities in nature and society that are independent of our consciousness. This reality changes, and this change has patterned consistencies that can be observed and understood. Tensions within the very structure of this reality form the basis of this change. These changes add up until the structure itself is something other than the original organization. A new entity is then formed with its own tensions or contradictions.

When studying a society, the research should begin with a people's interaction with nature. Humans, through their labor, produce the means of their own survival. The environment, natural and social, in which people provide the basis of their own survival, becomes central to the analysis of a society.

Through the means of production, which includes technology, environment, population pressure, and work relationships, a people are able to take from nature what they need to survive; this, in turn, creates what is possible for the various parts of the *superstructure.* Any study of the historical change of a people must assume economic factors will be of first importance. The economic primacy is not absolute, however, because each of the various parts of a society has its own continual influence on the social whole.

Researchers who study noncapitalist societies become aware that major differences do exist between individual noncapitalist societies. One major difference that is noticed by social scientists is the degree of complexity in social structures between one society and another. It is argued that the differing degrees of complexity of the social relations are directly related to different productive levels, including how efficiently a technology can utilize a particular environment to support the people of that social structure.

With changes in the organization of labor, there are corresponding changes in the relationship to property. With increasing complexity of technology and social organization, societies move through these diverse variations to a more restrictive control over property, and eventually, with a state society, there develop restrictions on access to property, based upon membership in different economic classes.

A social system is a dynamic interaction between people, as well as a dynamic interaction between people and nature. The production for human subsistence is the foundation upon which society ultimately stands. From the creation of the specific methods of production of an economic system, people, in turn, establish their corresponding set of ideas. People are the creators of their social ideologies. People are continually changed by the evolution of their productive forces and of the relationships associated with these productive forces. People continuously change nature, and thus continually change themselves in the process.

The study of history begins with the material or objective organization of people living their everyday lives. This is set into motion by means of a people's relationship with nature, as expressed in their social and cultural lives. Through these relationships, humans produce their own *means of subsistence.* Each generation inherits and reproduces this means of subsistence and then changes it to fit their changed needs. This historically and culturally specific setting shapes individual human nature. This means that how people are organized and interact is determined by production.

Production molds all other social relations. This includes the relation of one nation to another as well as the internal social structure of a single nation. With every new change in the forces of production, there exists corresponding change in the relations of production. These changes lead to changes in the division of labor. With changes in the division of labor, there are changes in the property relations of the nation. Ultimately, this means ideological changes as well.

The first historical act is the production to satisfy material life. Following the first historical act is the production of new needs that are the practical result of satisfying the needs of material life. People reproduce themselves, their families, and their culture daily. These acts of production and reproduction are prearranged by the historical past of a people, but this very activity changes both the people and their culture. With the changes, the needs of a people are changed; old needs are redefined or eliminated, and new needs are created. With these ever-changing needs, the development of human life is both social and natural. Humans are both the animal creations of nature and the social creations of society. With this, each society creates its own social organization based upon its own historical *mode of production.* The nature of society is based upon the mode of production and consciousness. People's relations to nature mold their relations with each other. People's relations with one another affect their relations to nature. Borrowing from Marx, then, production, human needs, population pressure, and change make up cultural ecology.

Julian Steward

Julian Steward coined the term *cultural ecology,* which is a continuation of his theory of *multilinear evolution.* Multilinear evolution searches for regularities in cultural change. Cultural laws can be defined that explain these changes. Determinism is not the issue, but patterns of historical change follow patterns of an interaction between parts of a society and the larger environment. Cultural traditions have distinctive elements that can be studied in context. Similarities and differences between cultures are meaningful and change in meaningful ways. The evolution of recurrent forms, processes, and functions in different societies has similar explanations. Each society has its own specific historical movement through time. This prefaces cross-cultural studies.

Cultural ecology is the adaptation by a unique culture modified historically in a distinctive environment. With this definition, Steward outlined a creative process of cultural change. Steward focused on recurrent themes that are understandable by limited circumstances and distinct situations. This helps to establish specific means of identifying and classifying cultural types. *Cultural type* is an ideal heuristic tool designed for the study of cross-cultural parallels and regularities. This analytical instrument allows assembling regularities in cultures with vastly different histories. This type of classification is based upon

selected features. It is important to pick out distinctive configurations of causally interdependent features of cultures under study. These features are determined by a particular research problem within its own frame of reference. The researcher chooses specific physiognomies that have similar functional interrelationship with one another.

For example, economic patterns are important because they are more directly related to other social, cultural, and political configurations. This is the *cultural core.* These comparative associations are the particular attributes of patterned organization in an evolutionary sequence. Universal evolutionary stages are much too broad to tell us anything concrete about any particular culture. The changes from one stage to another are based upon particular historical and cultural ecological arrangements unique for each society. Exceptionalism is the norm. Global trends and external influences interact with a locally specific environment, causing each society to have a unique evolutionary trajectory.

Cultural ecology is a look at cultural features in relation to specific environmental circumstances, with unique behavioral patterns that are related to cultural adjustments to distinctive environmental concerns.

Cultures are made up of interrelated parts. The degree of interdependence varies in the ways in which some traits have more influence than other characteristics. The *cultural core* is grouped around subsistence activities and economic relationships. Secondary features are more closely related to historical contingencies and less directly related to the environment. Cultural ecology focuses upon attributes immersed in the social subsistence activity within the specific environment in a culturally directed fashion. Changes are in part alterations in technology and productive arrangements as a result of the changing environment. Whether these technological innovations are accepted or not depends upon environmental constraints and cultural requirements. Population pressure and its relative stability are important. Also, internal division of labor, regional specialization, environmental tension, and economic surplus create the cultural conditions in which technological innovation becomes attractive, leading to other cultural changes. These social adaptations have profound effects upon the kinship, politics, and social relations of a group.

Culture, according to Steward, is a means of adaptation to environmental needs. Before specific resources can be used, the necessary technology is required. Also, social relations reflect technological and environmental concerns. These social relations organize specific patterns of behavior and its supportive values. A holistic approach to cultural studies is required to see the interrelationship of the parts.

The researcher begins with the study of the relationship between technologies of a people and how they exploit their environment for their survival. To use these technologies within an environmental setting, certain behavior patterns are established. The interaction between labor (behavior patterns) and the connection between technology and the environment has a reciprocal relationship with other aspects of culture, including ideology.

Cultural Materialism

Marvin Harris expanded upon cultural ecology and called his approach "cultural materialism." Human communities are fused with nature through work, and work is structured through social organization. This is the basis of the industry of all societies. Social science must reflect this if it is to understand the deeper underlying connections between specific social actions and global trends. In this, industry, commerce, production, exchange, and distribution establish the social structure, which, in turn, gives birth to the ideological possibilities of any culture. Along these lines, social-economic classes are determined by the interaction between technology and social organization in a particular environment. The needs of every society and the individuals in that society must be met; this, in turn, creates its own ideological support. With the development of capitalist society, for example, science develops to meet the needs of its economic requirements. Even more important, science is established as the integrating principles of modern industrial capitalism. This is possible because the principal ideas of any class society are that of the ruling class. Those who control the material forces of society also define the values and beliefs of that society. Workers are subject to those ideas, while the dominant ideology reflects the dominant material relations of the society. In this, Marxism, cultural ecology, and cultural materialism have similar thoughts on the subject.

The complex relationships between the material base of technology, the environment, population pressure, and the ideological superstructure are a constant factor in studying social change. The *social consciousness*, while being the product of real material relations of society, in turn has an impact on those social relations. This feedback loop is central to understanding the historical dynamics of society. Social consciousness becomes the collective reflection of *social relations.* Through social consciousness, people become aware of and act upon nature and society. Even though forms of social consciousness reflect a specific social existence, this social whole is not a static or passive relationship. The *ideological superstructure* is different in each community and changes as the economic relations of that society change. More precisely, there is an interactive relationship of all the parts of society. Economics is the most important of all these interactive parts. From this, the forms of commonly held feelings, religious expressions, ways of thinking, and, over all, worldview, including the different forms of property relations, are established. The ideology of a society reflects the social conditions of its existence.

Through the means of production, which includes technology, environment, also called *infrastructure,* and work relationships, called *structure,* a people are able to take from nature what they need to survive. This interaction, in turn, creates what is possible for the various parts of the superstructure. The superstructure includes not only the ideology but also the social psychology of a people. The superstructure and structure are ultimately molded and limited by the infrastructure. The infrastructure sets the limits of what is possible for both the structure and superstructure.

The interaction between social organization (structure) and the use of a technology within an environment (infrastructure) can be used to understand many particulars about the total culture. The evolution from band-level society to tribal-level society, tribal to chiefdom, and chiefdom to state-level society has to take into consideration changes in the organization of labor, including the growing division of labor and, ultimately, changes in the technology used by a people. With changes in the organization of labor, there are corresponding changes in the relationship to property. With increasing complexity of technology and social organization, societies move through these various stages to a more restrictive control over property, and eventually, with a state society, there develop restrictions on access to property, based upon membership in economic classes.

Marxism, cultural ecology, and cultural materialism all agree that a social system is a dynamic interaction between people, as well as a dynamic interaction between people and nature. The production for human subsistence is the foundation upon which society ultimately stands. In producing what people need to live, people also produce their corresponding set of ideas. People are the creators of their ideologies, because people are continually changed by the evolution of their productive forces; they are always changing their relationships associated with these productive forces. People continuously change nature and thus continually change themselves in the process.

Cultural Core as Used After Steward

Cultural core is the central idea of cultural ecology. Current scholars in the field add the use of symbolic and ceremonial behavior to economic subsistence as an active part of the cultural core. The result of cultural beliefs and practices leads to long-term sustainability of natural resources. The symbolic ideology becomes as important as economics in the cultural core. Through cultural decisions, people readapt to a changing environment. This opens the door for a critical anthropology; the anthropologist can act as an advocate for groups threatened by corporate agricultural concerns. The humanistic approach does not negate anthropology as a social science. The new anthropology has a new activist approach by recognizing that different agents may have competing interests in resource management. Any historical analysis of important issues must include indigenous knowledge in maintaining not only long-term sustainability but also protecting the rights of those most vulnerable.

— *Michael Joseph Francisconi*

See also **Anthropology, Economic; Cultural Conservation; Culture Change; Economics and Anthropology; Marxism; Materialism, Cultural; Steward, Julian H.**

Further Readings

Bodley, John H. (1999). *Victims of progress* (4th ed.). Mountain View, CA: Mayfield.
Bodley, J. H. (2000). *Anthropology and contemporary human problems* (4th ed.). Mountain View, CA: Mayfield.
Foster, J. B. (2000). *Marx's ecology: Materialism and nature.* New York: Monthly Review.

Harris, M. (1980). *Cultural materialism: The struggle for a science of culture.* New York: Vintage Books.
Harris, M. (1998). *Theories of culture in postmodern times.* Walnut Creek, CA: Rowman & Littlefield.
Netting, R. M. (1977). *Cultural ecology.* Menlo Park, CA: Benjamin/Cummings.
Steward, J. H. (1955). *Theory of culture change: The methodology of multilinear evolution.* Urbana: University of Illinois Press.

CULTURAL RELATIVISM

Cultural relativism is the idea that beliefs are affected by and best understood within the context of culture. It is a theory and a tool used by anthropologists and social scientists for recognizing the natural tendency to judge other cultures in comparison to their own and for adequately collecting and analyzing information about other cultures, without this bias. Cultural relativism was born out of and can also be applied to epistemology, which is the philosophical study of human knowledge. Empiricism is the theory that knowledge and understanding come from experience with the world. Cognitive relativists claim that differing belief systems are equally valuable, such as theories about what exists and how people interact with the world. Epistemological relativism acknowledges the role one's environment plays in influencing an individual's beliefs and even the concepts behind the words contained in a language.

Moral relativism is often mistakenly assumed to be the same concept as cultural relativism. While there are similarities, there are also key differences. Relativistic moral judgments are determined relative or according to the values and beliefs held by a particular culture. In the extreme sense this implies that there is no universal right and wrong in ethics. Most ethicists consider relativistic theories to be inferior to stricter normative, or rule-directed, theories that prescribe how a person ought to act. (If there is no absolute right and wrong, then there is no purpose in debating ethical questions. Morality would be empty and instead just describe how people act rather than how they *ought* to act.) Many people operate with a relativistic approach, however, in an effort to avoid the dangers of ethnocentrism—the same pitfall that anthropologists sought to correct through cultural relativism. Ethnocentric thinkers focus on the values of their own group as superior to those of others. Behaviors and beliefs in a different culture are compared and judged according to a narrow idea of what is normal. Cultural relativism—also sometimes called "pluralism"—cautions against unfairly condemning another group for being different and instead respects the right for others to have different values, conduct, and ways of life. Cultural relativism approaches awareness of cultural differences as a tool for appreciating and analyzing other cultures without assuming one's own group to be superior.

The concept of cultural relativism was developed by Franz Boas (1858–1942) and his anthropology students. Boas sought to study cultures of people in terms of how they interacted with their environment, and he acknowledged that rather than holding a single set of unchanging core beliefs, the ideas valued by most cultures changed over time. He observed that individual members of a community both affect and are affected by the larger whole. The implication of this changed the way anthropologists approached what were formerly understood to be distinctions between modern and traditional cultures. Because the interactions between the individual and the society were active in both directions, there was no longer a basis for assuming traditional cultures to be unchanging and modern cultures exclusively dynamic, or in motion. Boas proposed that there was room for both progress and enduring values in both types of society. Furthermore, because of the potential for rapid change, his theories encouraged anthropologists to conduct their studies from within the culture itself, or ethnographically. Thus began a new paradigm for methods of collecting and analyzing cultural data.

In addition to ethnography, the method of ethnology was inspired by cultural relativism in anthropology. Ethnology is the study of a wide collection of cultural subjects within the same study. In-depth data are collected detailing the unique characteristics of each culture and then considered as part of a larger pool of several cultures. By expanding the distribution or range of cultures studied, a new picture of human history began to develop. Anthropology shed the centuries-old ethnocentrism that celebrated particular Western-focused societies, no longer presuming one's own group to be the most advanced and all others primitive. Subsequently, with this broader purview, anthropology emerged as the unique field that studies the overall development of human culture.

Anthropologist Ruth Benedict (1887–1948), a student of Boas, saw the role of anthropology as studying human cultures from an unbiased perspective, much in the same manner that an astronomer studies stars or a biologist studies cells. The role of the scientist is that of objective observer; however, there is also a deeper understanding of one's own culture to be gained in the recognition of how values are instilled in other cultures. Her 1934 book *Patterns of Culture* advanced the term *cultural relativism* and compared three distinct groups in search of the universal trait that all cultural groups have in common. Her work with the U.S. government during World War II identified distinct differences in the attitudes of Japanese and American soldiers and civilians. Cultural relativism in this manner serves as an instrument of diplomatic relations.

A potential difficulty with cross-cultural comparison is incompatible values. It is possible that a phenomenon occurring in one group is so unique that is does not have a parallel in another culture, or as Margaret Mead (1901–1978) realized following her studies of Polynesian teenaged girls, the values revealed through anthropological study can be controversial. In 1928 her Western readers were shocked to learn that premarital sexual exploration was widely practiced in Samoa among even respectable members of society. Such a reaction demonstrates ethnocentric tendencies; in this case, religious-inspired American views saw anything other than sexual abstinence as immoral. The reaction also demonstrates the challenge of cross-cultural comparison. There is a universal feature of each culture having particular codes of acceptable social and sexual behavior. Where they differ is in the application, in what specific behaviors are acceptable for whom at certain times. Adolescent sexual activity in these two diverse societies could appear to represent conflicting values. Cultural relativism instructs the anthropologist to consider the cultural context instead of judging. The beliefs of either group are necessarily affected by the individuals and the evolving community itself. The cultural relativist steps outside the home group's perspective to gain a less biased understanding of the cultural dynamics of the subject group.

— *Elisa Ruhl*

Further Readings

Boas, F. (1928). *Anthropology and modern life.* New York: Norton.

Mead, M. (1934). *Patterns of culture.* Boston: Houghton Mifflin.

Rapport, N., & Overing, J. (2000). *Social and cultural anthropology: The key concepts.* London: Routledge.

CULTURAL RELATIVISM

While cultural convergence implies the merger of the cultures of two or more groups, most often because one of them is dominant and coerces the merger, cultural relativism on the other hand could stand for the acceptance of what is best and most valuable in each of the cultures. The famous anthropologist Franz Boas may have been the first to use the term after his work among the Eskimo (Inuit) on Baffin Island. In a sense, where cultural convergence would create a cultural melting pot, cultural relativism would lead to a cultural mosaic. An interesting case of this took place in the American West in the latter half of the 19th century, among both laymen and Catholic and Protestant missionaries serving with the Native American tribes of the western Great Plains. By this time, the messianic fervor for conversion among European Americans had begun to give way to an appreciation, in no small part to the work of anthropologist Boas, of the intrinsic worth of Native American religion and customs. Long gone were the days when Puritan divines in Massachusetts Bay had urged the slaughter of the indigenous population as demons in the 1630s.

Representative of this "new wave" of European Americans was John G. Neihardt. Born near Sharpsburg, Illinois, in 1881, Neihardt went to teachers' college at the Nebraska Normal School, where he graduated with a Bachelor of Science degree at the age of 16. It was in Nebraska that he began work among the Omaha Indians. Not until 1930, as Neihardt writes, did he become acquainted with Black Elk, a holy man, or *wasicu,* of the Oglala clan of the Sioux tribe on the tribe's Pine Ridge reservation in South Dakota. From that meeting, one of the most creative collaborations in the history of American anthropology began. Black Elk immediately recognized in Neihardt a kindred spirit. As Black Hawk said of Neihardt, "He has been sent to learn what I know, and I will teach him." It was a charge that Neihardt did not take lightly; as he explained, "Always I felt a sacred obligation to be true to the old man's meaning and manner of expression."

Being illiterate, Black Elk dictated his thoughts and memories to Neihardt, who published their collaboration as *Black Elk Speaks* in 1932. Although at first reaching a small audience, it soon even gained the attention of the famed psychologist Carl Jung. Eventually, during the decades to come, *Black Elk Speaks* was republished in many editions. It is a landmark in the development of cultural relativism, and an appreciation that all men and women—of all cultures—are bonded together by the same hopes, loves, and dreams.

— **John F. Murphy Jr.**

 ## CULTURAL TRAITS

Culture is that complex whole that includes knowledge, belief, art, morals, law, customs, and other capabilities acquired by man as a member of society. Culture consists of abstract patterns of and for living and dying. Such abstract patterns are learned directly or indirectly in social interactions of two or more people. In anthropological theory, there is not what could be called closed agreement on the definition of the concept of culture. However, for the present discussion, we want to note three prominent key elements. First, the culture is transmitted. It constitutes a heritage for social tradition. Second, the culture is learned. It is not a manifestation of man's genetic constitution. Third, the culture is shared. It is, on one hand, the product of and, on the other hand, the determination of systems of human social interaction. When talking about a very small bit of culture, anthropologists use the terms *trait* or *item*. A sparkplug, for example, is an item of material culture; the notion the world is round is an item of ideational culture; and the practice of shaking hands with acquaintences is an item of nonmaterial culture classified as *norm*. Anthropologists are inclined to use the term *item* when referring to material culture and *trait* when referring to nonmaterial culture. There is nothing precise about this usage, nor is it standardized in the literature.

Cultural Traits

Norms: A norm is a rule or a standard that governs our conduct in social situations in which we participate. It is a social expectation. It is a cultural specification that guides our conduct in society. It is a way of doing things, the way that is set for us by our society. It is also an essential instrument of social control. A norm is not a statistical average. It is not a mean, median, or mode. It refers not to the average behavior of number of persons in a specific social situation, but instead, to the expected behavior, the behavior that is considered appropriate in that situation. It is a norm in our society, for example, to say "Please" when requesting a favor and "Thank you" when a favor is received, but no statistical count of the actual frequency of occurence of these polite expressions is available. Nor would such a count be relevent. The norm is considered the standard procedure, whether or not anyone confirms to it, follows it, or observes it in a specific situation. The principle function of the norm for the individual is thus to reduce the necessity for decision in the innumerable social situations that he or she confronts and in which he or she participates. Without them the individual is faced from moment to moment with an almost intolerable burden of decision. Norms are both prescriptive and proscriptive—that is, the norms both prescribe or require certain actions and proscribe or prohibit certain other actions. We are required to wear clothes in our society and forbidden to go naked in the street. Frequently, the prescriptions and proscriptions come in pairs; that is, we are required to do something and forbidden not to do it, or forbidden to commit an act and required to omit it. Proscriptive norms when they are not legal prohibitions are known a *taboos*. There are many kinds of norms, such as folkways, mores, traditions, belief system, rules, rituals, laws, fashions, manners, and ceremonies, some of which are discussed here.

Folkways: It is a term introduced by the late William Graham Sumner. The term means literally the ways of the folk, the ways people have devised for satisfying their needs, for interacting with one another, and for conducting their lives. Folkways are norms to which we conform because it is customary to do so in our society. Conformity to the folkways is neither required by law nor enforced by any special agency of society. And yet we conform even without thinking. It is matter of custom, matter of usage. Each society has different folkways, and they constitute an important part of the social structure and contribute to the order and stability of social relations.

Mores: The mores differ from the folkways in the sense that moral conduct differs from merely customary conducts. Our society requires us to conform to the mores, without, however, having established a special agency to enforce conformity. The word *mores* is a Latin word for *customs* and it is also the Latin source of the word *morals*. Sumner introduced this word into the sociology literature as those practices that are believed conducive to societal welfare. Folkways, on the contrary, do not have the connotation of welfare.

Laws: Laws are associational norms that appear in the political organization of society. Asociations other than the state have their rules and regulations, too, and these requirements are also classified as associational norms.

Belief System: Cultural belief systems can be divided into two parts. One is *existential beliefs,* which include (a) empirical-science and empirical lore, (b) nonempirical-philosophical and supernatural lore, and (c) specialization of roles with respect to investigative interests. Second, *evaluative beliefs* include (a) ideologies, (b) religious ideas and traditions, and (c) role differentiation with respect to responsibility for evaluative beliefs. Religious beliefs are nonempirical ideological beliefs. By contrast with science or philosophy, the cognitive interest is no longer primary, but gives way to the evaluative interest. Acceptance of religious beliefs is then a commitment of its implimentation in action in a sense in which acceptance of a philosophical belief is not. Thus, religious beliefs are those concerned with moral problems of human action, the features of human situations, and the place of man and society in the cosmos, which are most relevant to his moral attitudes and value-orientational patterns.

In the past 60 years, the development of the computer has had a more profound impact on civilization than any other technological advance in history. In the 1940s, development of the computer was spurred on by the technological advantages it gave the military. After World War II, the business world learned to adopt this technology, giving them strategic and competitive advantages. The development of Arpanet, the forerunner of the Internet, initiated the Internet's development by connecting remote computers together into one global network. In the late 1970s, Jobs and Wozniak's Apple computer brought computers to each person's desktop, starting the microcomputer revolution. Today, we see computers in all forms. Some computers resemble the first Apple and still sit on the user's desktop, but others are now more portable and can be built into nearly every device, such as personal digital assistants, automobiles, phones, and even kitchen appliances. Each of these computers either does or will eventually have the ability to be connected through a network enabling the user or appliance to communicate with others worldwide.

In the future, we will see computers playing an even greater role in our world. Computers will be even more essential in education and business and will become a necessity in the home, enabling individuals to control functions and the environment within the home. Utilities and "smart appliances" will be connected to a controlling computer. Lights, heating, cooling, security, and many other utilities will be controlled through a central computer by kiosks (displays) located strategically around the home. Entrance may be controlled by the main computer through voice or fingerprint authentication. When a person enters the home, that individual's preference in lighting, temperature, television programming, music, and more will be adjusted accordingly. Appliances will be networked through the Internet. For instance, if you are returning home at night and would like the lights turned on, connect to your home's controlling computer by using your wireless personal digital assistant, which has software that enables you to turn on the lights and increase the temperature. You will also be able to check your appliances and settings remotely. Perhaps you are

mascot of his travels. Aboard the *Calypso,* Cousteau came across the first extensive underwater archeological dig, led countless scientific dives, submerged and tested scientific submarine prototypes, and filmed his award-winning television series, *The Undersea World of Jacques Cousteau.* He directed the engineering of numerous submarines and underwater research stations, all designed to help scientists better study marine life.

In 1958, Cousteau first became aware of the negative human affects on marine ecosystems when he revisited a site where some of his first filmings had taken place along the French Riviera. He reacted by forming the Cousteau Society, a nonprofit organization aimed at the conservation of marine ecosystems, in 1974. The Cousteau Society leads important efforts in international lobbies for better marine conservation as well as scientific evaluations of marine wellness all over the world. Cousteau's environmental efforts did not go unnoticed, as he received the U.S. Medal of Freedom from President Ronald Reagan and the National Geographic Gold Medal for Exploration from President John F. Kennedy.

People of a society conform to normative traits for various reasons. One is that people have been indoctrinated to do so. From earliest childhood, they are taught to observe the norms of their society. Second, people have become habituated by norms. Habituation reinforces the norms and guarantees the regularity of conformity. Third, norms have utility value. As reflective individuals, we can see that norms are useful, that they enable us to interact with others in a way conducive to the best interest of all, and that they contribute to the ease of social exchange. Finally, norms serve as means of group identification. This is the phenomenon of what Robert Merton called "reference group."

— *Komanduri S. Murty and Ashwin G. Vyas*

See also **Cultural Constraints; Enculturation; Folkways; Norms; Taboos**

Further Readings

Bierstedt, R. (1970). *The social order* (3rd ed.). New York: McGraw Hill.
Johnson, H. (1966). *Sociology: A systematic introduction.* Bombay, India: Allied.
Merton, R. K. (1957). *Social theory and social structure.* Glencoe, IL: Free Press.
Parsons, T. (1951). *The social system.* New York: Free Press.

 # CULTURAL TREE OF LIFE

Within anthropology, the "tree of life" concept can be viewed from either a biological or a cultural perspective. The cultural tree of life is generally linked to religious beliefs and actions. Symbolic reference to trees as sacred entities can be found in Christianity, associated with the Garden of Eden and with the cross of crucifixion. In Viking myths and legends, according to Kenneth Johnson in *Jaguar Wisdom*, the shaman is said to have "hung like a sacrifice in search of wisdom" from a tree limb.

In the Americas, the ancient Mayan civilization made great use of their own version of the life-giving tree. With the Maya, the tree of life was interpreted on several levels, one being as a conduit or umbilical cord linking one area of space with another. The Mayan lords traveled inside the tree to reach destinations in the sky and also into the underworld of Xibalba and death. As Linda Schele and David Freidel set forth in *A Forest if Kings,* supernatural spirits moved freely from one realm to another via the sap of the trees, much as human blood, upon which they devoted much religious ritual, coursed through the human body. On the great sarcophagus lid of the Maya Palenque, Lord Pacal is carved traveling up the great world tree called *Wacah Chan.* Pacal is depicted as being in transition, moving up from the dark world of Xibalba and the Maw of the underworld, through the realm of earthly existence, to the celestial bird positioned at the top of the great tree, where he will next move up into the sky. The tree is laden with blood bowls and spirit-reflecting mirrors, representing the link between the natural and supernatural worlds.

Moojan Momen in the text *The Phenomenon of Religion* shows that in Siberia, the Buryatia are known to elaborately decorate sacred trees with pieces of ribbon and paper upon which they have written wishes, dreams, and desires, in hopes that they may influence spirits, residing in specific trees, to grant their requests. Momen also includes a description of the often convoluted and weblike structure of the Sephiroth tree of the Kabbalist, within which is formulated its 10 interconnected circles where the "unknowable godhead" representing the "horizons of eternity" resides.

Anthropomorphized deities are included, such as the Buddha Amitoyus, who is known as the "tree of life" and is illustrated with a tree for a body. On several occasions, the great God Zeus, as described in Van Der Leeuw's writing *Religion in Essence and Manifestation,* was drawn with the body of a tree. The Egyptian sycamore tree was known to encircle supernatural gods or have the limbs that serve as a throne for the gods.

James Frazer devoted an entire section in *The New Golden Bough* to life-giving embodiment and life-taking qualities of trees and their resident spirits depicted in a cross-cultural perspective. Included is the belief that contact with specific tree species can increase changes of female fertility capabilities and the ability of tree spirits to ensure abundant crop growth, also connected to fertility. Within the Māori Tuhae tribe, there is the belief that trees are the umbilical cords of mythical ancestors. The Tanga coastal peoples of East Africa believe that specific tree spirits can cause or cure illness and misfortune.

Philip Peek in *African Divination Systems* shows how for the African Yaka, the tree is a symbol of marital bonding across lineage lines, where households simultaneously both deliver and hold onto their fertile females when physically transferring them to other tribes. Each limb and branch of the life-giving tree reflects the interconnectedness of the continuing alliances across lineage lines and the transmission of continued tribal life as grandmother, mother, and daughter each produce successive generations.

Whether symbolizing Germanic myths of the Oden as shaman, the power of the Garden of Eden, the Mayan conduit or the Hindu and African fertility rites, the life-giving tree is a powerful cross-cultural symbol connecting life, death, time, and space and is worthy of further exploration.

— *Beverly J. Fogelson*

See also **Anthropomorphism; Fertility**

Further Readings

Johnson, K. (1997). *Jaguar wisdom*. Minneapolis, MN: Llewellyn.

Momen, M. (1999). *The phenomenon of religion*. Oxford: OneWorld.

Peek, P. M. (Ed.). (1991). *African divination systems*. Bloomington: Indiana University Press.

Schele, L., & Freidel, D. (1990). *A forest of kings*. New York: Morrow.

Van Der Leeuw, G. (1986). *Religion in essence and manifestation*. Princeton, NJ: Princeton University Press.

 CULTURE

Culture is a system created by human activity comprising spiritual, organizational, and material items and expanding within the Earth's nature at the expense of this very nature. People mostly understand human culture in several ways: (1) as an acquired characteristic of human behavior, (2) as a spiritual culture, (3) as a better view of civilization, and (4) as a continuation or refinement of nature. These various understandings are supported by the original antique meaning of the Latin words *colo, colere*, which signified, approximately, the same as the current words *till, educate,*

grow, cultivate. The understanding of culture as a spiritual culture, as an acquired feature of human behavior or as a cultivation of nature, becomes perplexing and hardly tenable in the confrontation with the current environmental situation. Culture should be rather understood evolutionally, as a system, that is, as a result of the Cultural Revolution, as an artificially constituted system within the biosphere. Cultural evolution, ignited by humans, is the other possible means of the new ontical (real) structure origination on the Earth, besides the natural, cosmic evolution.

Culture is then a human-created, artificial system with its own internal information—the spiritual culture, that is, human knowledge, opinions, convictions, values, and beliefs. Spiritual and material cultures belong one to another; they are two sides of the same open, nonlinear system of the regional or global culture. The relationship between the spiritual and material cultures is therefore analogous with the biological relationship between the genotype and phenotype in spite of the variant ontical character of cultural and live systems. Understanding culture as a system opposing nature and containing its own internal information and evolution makes it possible to distinguish not only the origins and characteristics of the current environmental crisis but also ways for the alleviation and resolution of this crisis. So far the cultural expansion within the biosphere has resulted in an ever-faster retreat of the original nature and a decrease in the original order of the Earth.

Essential dependence of culture upon nature is primarily determined by the fact that the cultural evolution within nature is generated by humans as a biologic species. Yet culture is dependent on nature and opposes nature and it is also comparatively young and time limited. Humans have not been on the Earth from its beginning and they will not be here until its end. Due to a biologic predisposition to an aggressive adaptive strategy, humans are the only universally active animal species that have managed to ignite another evolution on the Earth occupied with life: This was the cultural evolution—the competitor of the natural evolution. And this artificial evolution, structuring nature differently from the inside, has started not only the conspicuous human era but, unfortunately, also a critical period in the Earth's history. Human artifacts are "baked from the same flour" as natural structures. And since this imaginary flour (elements of the periodic table) has been embedded in live and inanimate structures of the Earth's surface by the natural evolution, the expansion of the cultural existence causes destruction and replacement of this natural existence—it causes a reduction in the natural order of the Earth, including a mass extinction of biologic species.

A serious problem with the currently fast-expanding culture on this finite Earth, leaving aside the raw material and fuel exhaustion and waste and pollution matters, lies in the retreat of and damage to the biosphere, in the loss of the territory occupied

Source: Photo provided by www.downtheroad.org, The Ongoing Global Bicycle Adventure.

by life. Spatial expansion of the elements of the material culture (for example, fields, highways, factories, and cities), which are as material and spatial as the natural ecosystems, is realized only by means of destroying or limiting the evolutionarily established natural order. Even though the cultural order expansion doesn't directly change the genetic information in live systems, it shatters and destroys the original environmental order, impairs living conditions for many populations, and is the main cause for the current mass extinction of biologic species. In comparison to the natural ecosystems, which do not contain any free natural information, the cultural ecosystems are much more integrated, systematically more resistant, and therefore also more life destructive. Culture is therefore not only a reconstruction of nature that is rather advantageous for our species, but it is also a shortsighted supplant of the original natural existence that used to be in harmony with humanity.

Ontical opposition of culture against nature mostly results from the fact that culture is a system containing different internal information than nature. Culture, as well as any open nonlinear system with internal information, originates by means of materialization of its own constitutive information, its specific "genome," its spiritual culture. The biologic carrier of the spiritual culture is not the highly objective genetic memory (DNA) but the less specific and rather species-colored (selfish) human epigenetic, neuronal memory. Yet only a channeling, development, and language encoding of

the human, natural, neuronal information give rise to the actual genome of the cultural system, to the social, spiritual culture.

A deeper understanding of the opposition between culture and nature requires answering the following question: What is the connection between the character of the current culture and humans, their neuronal knowledge, and the contents of the spiritual culture? It is clear that the direct connection with humans as a biologic species is determined by a special structure of human body and human psyche, by the aggressive type of the social adaptive strategy of humans as a species. Lack of human biologic specialization, determining the universality of human interests, transforms humanity's external environment not only into the subject of satisfying their biologic needs, language-encoded learning, and aesthetic evaluation but also a subject of ownership and unlimited exploitation. Humans, as a species with an aggressive adaptive strategy, experienced the world primarily for the purpose of surviving by means of reproduction and development of their own nonbiologic body—the culture. And since culture is a system with its own internal information, the conflict between culture and nature is "causally" connected with the contents and purpose of the social spiritual culture. This social spiritual culture, as internal information of the cultural system, as its genome, determines and reproduces the form of the current antinatural culture. A change in the cultural genome

Source: Photo provided by www.downtheroad.org, The Ongoing Global Bicycle Adventure.

species evolution, has never been independent: On the one hand, it has defended the valid claims of human organism, and on the other hand, it has submitted to system requirements of various cultures. Only today do we come across evidence that all human interpretations are influenced by hidden pragmatic motives, not only the individual and group ones, which is a generally accepted fact, but also the generally cultural and species-specific ones, which is a suppressed fact.

Therefore, even the scientific conceptual knowledge, which currently so strictly specifies, as far as information is concerned, the elements of the microelectronic technics and of the developed material culture, doesn't describe the world in its objective order, ontical creativity, and complexity. It shows, for example, that science is still connected with the prescientific division of the world, with language and experience. Yet to survive with our special biologic equipment, we have had to see and interpret the world in a species-biased way from the time of the first hominids. The world was mostly what we were interested in, what we could learn through our conservative biologic constitution and through our culture in the particular epoch. And since we were evolutionarily adapted to the external reality with our bodies and genomes, we have never needed to know what nature and life were, what was culture, and what was the position of culture within nature. Such knowledge, an adequate theoretical model of the development of culture within the biosphere, is needed only today. You can find the reason for this in the comparison between the evolution of the biosphere and culture: the development of the planetary life was able to gradually wipe out the abiotic conditions that had caused its origination, yet the development of culture, its whole future existence, will always depend on the preservation of the biologic conditions that had been required for the origination of the very culture. Until the end of its existence, the human culture will depend on the faultless biologic reproduction of humanity; it will be bound to a sufficient scope and structure of the quaternary biosphere supporting this reproduction.

(contents of the spiritual culture) is therefore the key requirement for the alleviation and resolution of the current crisis. If we want to change a system with internal information (memory), we will have to change its information, because the old constitutive information of the system is able to reverse any phenotype changes.

The cultural system, as well as other natural ecosystems, includes strictly information-specified elements (for example, technics, structures, and consumer objects), but as a whole it cannot be a strictly information-specified system. Even though it also originates through succession (in the course of time sequence), it significantly differs from the natural ecosystems: Besides the integral constitutive information, it also contains the free information—the dispersed spiritual culture. This spiritual culture, as a memory permitting information changes, holds out hopes that the current antinatural culture could be transformed in a biofile way, that it could be naturalized.

Yet it isn't easy to discover the roots of the antinatural character of culture, which is connected with the structure of the human psyche. To achieve that goal we would have to admit that our culture has originated as a materialization of the spiritual culture and that the conceptual interpretation of the world, which we establish by means of the neural equipment of our animal ancestors, is not a true reproduction of reality. The cognitive component of the human psyche, which was the fastest to develop during our

Source: © iStockphoto/Santiago Batiz Benet.

The current highly technical global culture is spiritually anchored in a partial scientific rationality is well as in harmony with some cognitive functions of the human psyche, but it irretrievably destroys those natural structures that the whole human constitution had been adapted to. This significantly consumer culture is based on a technological experience of nature, and it doesn't really care about the value, integrity, and claims of the natural development of the biosphere. Even though there come into existence technologies that are less environmentally aggressive and more energy and waste efficient, the general human approach toward nature remains unchanged. The speed of establishing more environmentally friendly manufacturing processes is equaled by the speed of the environmentally reckless consumption—the new common characteristic of the current human lifestyles. This focus is in harmony with the traditional liberal right of individuals to own their properties, their right for an unlimited personal consumption.

Physical globalization of the human culture, that is, the material-energetic and information interconnection of formerly isolated regions, accompanied by a planetwide migration of people, fast exchange of technologies, goods, inventions, services, and so on, has brought about a situation humanity has never encountered before. Inside the global biosphere, at the expense of this biosphere, there grows a global technosphere, global economy, global division of labor, and global cooperation. This not only deepens the cooperation between physically distant people and cultures, but it also disturbs the beneficial effects of the biosphere upon the globalized culture that had once optimized the local cultural structures and eliminated social disturbances and crises. And therefore the globalization finally turns not only against nature but also against culture. It multiplies its pressure upon nature and it forces the destabilized biosphere—if we can put it like this—to change its strategy: If the live nature cannot defend itself by means of dominance and force, it will do so by means of its vulnerability and fragility. It doesn't have enough power anymore to maintain its most complicated structures, but it can establish a new system integrity and get rid of those live forms that are no more "needed" in the new context. Humanity and culture can be just an easily removable obstacle for the continuing natural evolution.

For the first time in history, humanity and their culture are endangered by the weakened maternal environment of the planet that had once made their origination possible. Even politicians, who are mostly interested in power, economic growth, and conditions of human liberty, will be soon forced to make decisions under the pressure of the endangered future. They will have to leave the narrow anthropologic, social, and technologic viewpoints and accept a global evolutionally ontological view of the world: For the first time they will be responsible for the human existence as a species.

The antinatural cultural system originated from the essence of the human constitution; it had originated spontaneously, and its development had taken a comparatively long time. The program of the aggressive cultural strategy therefore not only materialized in this system, but it has also entered the ethnical languages, human education, and upbringing. Its resistance to the biofile social-cultural information feels like an interspecies information barrier or an immunity system: Since our current cultural system didn't originate as a materialization of the environmental social-cultural information, people have been ignoring it, refusing to listen to it, and they don't understand its future significance and cultural self-preservation contents.

The planetary solution of this crisis, which is not based in a change in the human constitution but in a philosophic identification of its roots and the possibilities of a biofile cultural strategy, must be therefore prepared by a high theory. Therefore, the positive environmental transformation of the existentially endangered culture by means of its new constitutive information represents an unprecedented attempt of humanity to end the unchecked stage of the antinatural cultural evolution. It could start an intentionally biofile-anticipative stage of the antinatural cultural evolution. Our hope in the success of this attempt is supported by the fact that the conditions for the environmental change automatically ripen due to the crisis development of the current antinatural culture. Yet this crisis must become even more pronounced; the habitability of the Earth must unfortunately become even more complicated to force the current shortsighted party politics to accept the program of the necessary changes that is currently definitely better understood by common people than by bankers, businesspeople, and political representations.

Since we were not prepared for such changes in the reactions of nature either by our natural or our cultural development, we are failed in the confrontation with the wounded nature not only by our biologic constitution: We are failed also by our basic cultural archetypes. No culture can cooperate with a weakened and destabilized biosphere. No political subject could possibly handle it in a delicate way in the current, economically competitive environment. And since there is no adequate philosophical concept of the crisis, even the intellectuals don't understand what has actually happened and what will have to be done to secure human survival on the Earth. If humanity is to survive, it will have to deliberately surrender to nature, and the antinatural spiritual and material cultures will have to be naturalized.

People appeared on the Earth teeming with life at the end of the Tertiary period. They couldn't have philosophically understood the live nature they were evolutionally adapted to. The human psyche, which managed the process of conquering nature, was adapted to the fight for survival and not to compassion with life and care for other species. Spontaneously originating cultures following up the human species' predispositions broke up the natural ecosystems and occupied the Earth. This Earth is currently conquered by culture, the tissue of its life is disturbed with tilled soil, it is encircled with highways and cities, pushed back with buildings, concrete, and pavement. There can be no nobler task for science and philosophy, together with ethics, law, and politics, than preparing an irreversible future change: a rescue of the natural order of the planet, the indispensable condition for a long-lasting and feasible culture.

— *Josef Šmajs*

Further Readings

Barkow, J. H., Cosmides, L., & Tooby, J. (1992). *The adapted mind.* New York: Oxford University Press.

Blackmore, S. (1999). *The meme machine.* Oxford, UK: Oxford University Press.

Capra, F. (2003). *The hidden connections.* London: Flamingo.

Eagleton, T. (2000). *The idea of culture.* Oxford, UK: Blackwell.

Edgar, A., & Sedgwick, P. (Eds.). (2002). *Cultural theory. The key concepts.* London: Routledge.

Mulhern, F. (2000). *Culture/Metaculture.* London: Routledge.

Pinker, S. (2002). *The blank slate.* London: Allen Lane.

Ridley, M. (2003). *Nature via nurture.* London: Fourth Estate.

Šmajs, J. (1997). *The threatened culture.* Dobromysl: Slovacontact.

Smith, M. J. (2000). *Culture.* Buckingham, UK: Open University Press.

Sperber, D. (1996). *Explaining culture.* Oxford, UK: Blackwell.

CULTURE AND PERSONALITY

"Culture and personality" has been perhaps the most mythologized and misunderstood of American anthropology's interdisciplinary endeavors. Ruth Benedict and Margaret Mead, the two anthropologists most closely associated with "cultural and personality," have often been understood to equate culture with personality.

While views of this sort are common, there is little, if any, evidence in Mead's writings or papers supporting such contentions; Mead used the rubric seldom, and then descriptively rather than methodologically. Despite clearly articulated differences in temporal scale, at best Benedict's writings show an analogy between personalities and cultures. Furthermore, such views are not easily reconciled with Benedict's and Mead's differing concepts of deviance.

Lawrence Frank, a sociologist at the Rockefeller Foundation, seems to have coined the phrase "culture and personality" for an interdisciplinary conference Mead attended in Hanover, New Hampshire, during the summer of 1934. Nonetheless, in April 1935, Mead wrote to John Dollard that Frank's phrasing seemed "ridiculous." In a 1946 overview of the cultural study of personality, Mead held that the "and" that had been used to join the two distinct subjects had introduced a number of "methodological embarrassments."

Instead of "culture and personality," Mead preferred to discuss the "individual in culture." As early as 1928, her work was replete with discussions of named individuals living in specified, described societies. Mead taught a seminar entitled "The Study of the Individual in Culture" in 1935. This emphasis upon the individual in culture should rightly be traced back to Edward Sapir.

In 1925, Sapir sought to keep Mead from undertaking research in Samoa, and she, equally resolutely, went off to her first fieldwork. This falling-out between Sapir and Mead along with Benedict continues to influence the development of psychological anthropology. To the extent that the writing of the history of anthropology is closely tied to the work of A. Irving Hallowell, this falling-out has also shaped anthropology's useable past.

Hallowell was an associate of Sapir's. His assessments of the field largely ignored Mead's contributions; Mead was not among those invited to contribute to a volume edited by Hallowell, among others, dedicated to Sapir's memory. Concomitantly, Mead elided the contributions of Hallowell, as well as others of Sapir's students and protegées, in her 1946 encyclopedia article.

Edward Sapir

In 1917, Sapir responded to A. L. Kroeber's essay "The Superorganic," wondering whether anthropology required such an idea at all. But if culture is not superorganic, as Hegel's Spirit and Durkheim's Society are, then the psychological processes of cultural life only arise as real (that is, organically singular or individual) people live and act together. Those individuals influence the course of their cultures, even as that culture will be for them genuine or spurious in Sapir's terms (i.e., emotionally sustaining or not).

In bringing the notion of the individual in culture to the fore, Sapir also transformed the meaning of the term *psychological*. Previously, American anthropology had used the term *psychological* to describe cultures considered synchronically rather than historically. After Sapir, it became possible to think of cultures and personal or dynamic psychologies together.

Primarily a linguist, Sapir felt that for human beings, language was the "medium of expression for their society." Their specific language was not merely a means of communication or reflection, but rather an essential means to their adjustment to the world and to social activity; languages, as both signs and phonemes, were psychological realities. Hence, as languages differed, so too psychologies could differ. Benjamin Lee Whorf would subsequently develop this line of Sapir's reasoning.

Besides his much praised linguistic work, Sapir's outstanding contribution was to begin a critique of the concept of culture that attended to the psychological lives of individual people. In conjunction with Harry Stack Sullivan and Harold Lasswell, Sapir sought to bring anthropology, sociology, and psychology together in mutually informative ways, particularly through a series of conferences in Hanover funded by the Rockefeller Foundation; the conference Mead attended in 1934 followed from those Sapir had earlier taken part in.

In the summer of 1925, Sapir taught a seminar on the psychology of culture. He reprised this seminar several times at Yale before his death in 1939. Many who would later teach psychological anthropology were either Sapir's students or the students of his students; as his interdisciplinary activities faded, these protegées and students became Sapir's legacy.

The examples in Sapir's lectures and essays on the subject may have come from his social milieu and that of his students, but Sapir did not provide explicit cultural context for the examples he used or use examples from other cultural worlds; these luminous works contain no real people living real lives in real cultures.

However, these lectures, like Sapir's ostensible "last testament" on culture and personality, included attacks upon Benedict and Mead. According to Sapir, Mead and Benedict not only relied on too few persons but also conflated their informants' subjective, even idiosyncratic, views of social interaction with broader cultural patterns.

Ruth Benedict and Margaret Mead

Benedict and Mead were closely associated for many years; their respective work owed much to the other's influence. This has contributed to a general tendency to treat these two as if they agreed on all or most matters, with Benedict's work being largely more fashionable. It is equally important to understand how Benedict and Mead disagreed on two crucial topics: deviance and the open or closed set of possible configurations.

The term *configuration* was a translation of the German *struktur,* a technical term brought into the American intellectual world in 1925 with the translation of Kurt Koffka's *The Growth of the Mind,* a classic of Gestalt, rather than idealist or behaviorist, psychology. For Koffka, such structures initially arose as the infant's nervous system adapted itself to the wider world and its shifting stimuli through the infant's active perceiving of that world. The structures themselves were organizations of apperception including both the perceiving individual and the stimulative world into a single whole not reducible to its parts.

Benedict first used the term *configurations* in the early 1930s. In *Patterns of Culture* of 1934, citing the Gestalt school, but not Koffka personally, Benedict dissented from earlier views of cultures as amorphous, anomalous sets of traits haphazardly brought together through diffusion. While not a foregone conclusion, some cultures succeeded in transforming a slight preference into a largely integrated, articulated whole not reducible to the selected traits. In ways analogous to persons, cultures tended to select from the traits available to them, making use of some and not others; here, Benedict prefigured Claude Lévi-Strauss's notion of *bricolage.*

As Clyde Kluckhohn noted, Benedict was not so much interested in inductive analysis of a given society as in using behavioral details illustratively, to exemplify a configuration and its influence on local life or as a counterpart to an ideal pattern. As such, common criticisms of Benedict that took her to be writing about invariant patterns of behavior were inapt.

Benedict intended her four descriptive terms— apollonian Hopi, dionysian Plains Amerindians, paranoid Dobuans, and megalomaniac Kwakiutl— to sum up her expositions. While she borrowed the terms *apollonian* and *dionysian* from Friedrich Nietzsche, Benedict's Hopi and Plains accounts were largely based on her own researches; she used materials from the work of Reo Fortune and Franz Boas for the Dobuans and the Kwakiutl, respectively.

Not all the behavior manifest in a given society necessarily accorded well with that society's accepted standards, whether that society was well integrated or otherwise. From the vantage of a particular society, such discordant, unacceptable behavior was deviant; those who behaved in deviant fashions locally understood could often be subject to stigmas locally applied. Benedict's best-known example compared homosexuality in the West of her day and the *berdache,* men who dressed and lived as women, among some Amerindian groups.

Where Benedict's notion of deviance concerned discordant, unacceptable behavior at odds within a specific cultural gestalt, Mead's notion, though often expressed behaviorally, concerned personalities at odds temperamentally or characterologically with the ethos of a given society.

Neither Benedict nor Mead gave any indication that deviance or its local contraries were statistical matters; nor did Mead, in particular, understand either neurosis or psychosis as deviation from a society's statistical norms. Their notions must be distinguished from other ideas such as A. F. C. Wallace's understanding of a modal personality and Abram Kardiner's notion of a culturally basic personality structure. Whatever the theoretical problems posed for Wallace by the presence of multiple modal personalities among the Tuscarora, to Mead or Benedict, Wallace's Tuscarora would likely have appeared as a not terribly well-integrated society.

Benedict repeatedly commented upon the sheer variability of elements upon which one society or another could elaborate an integrated pattern. Where Benedict perceived endless combinations, however, Mead's thought concerned a limited set of types.

Both approaches allowed for a rigorously comparative anthropology. Strictly speaking, however, Mead and Benedict were not comparing quite the same phenomena. Benedict's patterns were akin to Oswald Spengler's destiny ideas or Wilhelm Dilthey's notion of *Weltanschauung:* a worldview that is also a philosophy of or feeling for life. Such a view is psychological insofar as it implies a human interiority. But Benedict's was neither a particularly nor necessarily dynamic psychology. Where Mead had little feel for what Bateson called *eidos,* or the structure of ideas, Benedict similarly had little feel for Freudian and neo-Freudian genetic psychologies organized around a set of stages, focused upon some portion of the body and the individual's mode of engagement therewith.

Both Mead and Benedict have been criticized for empirical lapses. Similarly, some have held that deviance was effectively a catchall category into which anything that did not fit their analyses could be consigned. These latter views largely ignore or misrepresent Benedict's and Mead's understanding of deviance arising integrally out of local social concerns.

Margaret Mead and Gregory Bateson

For Sapir, no amount of familiarity with the psychological literature could undo the flaws in Mead's work.

Mead received both her bachelor's and master's degrees in psychology. She was trained in many aspects of psychology, including the development of psychological tests, before she took up anthropology. Late in life, Mead thought she had remained within psychology's ambit ever after.

Many of the ideas she developed derived from the psychology of her student years. She reworked William McDougall's notions of temperament (innate, heritable constitutional predisposition) and character (the pattern of learned habits developed over a lifetime). Mead remained particularly fond of June Etta Downey's idea of load (psychological inertia) and freedom therefrom. These ideas are no longer familiar to many psychologists and were perhaps never that familiar to most anthropologists.

Mead was a dedicated, methodologically innovative fieldworker; she undertook studies in Samoa, Manus, among the Omaha, in New Guinea among the Arapesh, Mundugumour (now Biwat), and Tchambuli (now Cambri), as well as in Bali and among the Iatmul, all initially between 1925 and 1939. Her Omaha study was perhaps the first ethnography to portray a North American Native society as largely broken in the wake of its colonial encounter; her New Guinea ethnographies introduced the notion of the "Big Man" and portrayed several peoples as part of a larger mytho-ceremonial order: the tamberan. Mead's and Gregory Bateson's Balinese and Iatmul researches of 1936 to 1939 made greater use of photography than any others to that date, while integrating those materials, more conventional field notes, and both Balinese and Iatmul language texts into an unusually extensive and deep body of ethnographic materials.

Perhaps influenced by Boas's resistance to grand theory, the young Mead sought more to test psychological ideas in various cultural contexts than to debunk them. Mead's early fieldtrips to Samoa and Manus involved explorations against the background of work by G. Stanley Hall on adolescence, as well as Sigmund Freud and Jean Piaget on the purported similarities between the mentality of primitives and children. Mead thought the Freudians and neo-Freudians largely correct about psychological mechanisms but that these mechanisms were much more variable than the psychoanalysts imagined. She explicitly rejected any equation of culture with the superego, but had praise for Geza Roheim's work among Australian Aborigines.

Mead and Bateson began developing their unpublished theory of the so-called squares while among the Tchambuli during March of 1933. The terms of that hypothesis organized the arguments in *Sex and Temperament in Three Primitive Societies* of 1935, a book better known now for its discussion of gender *avant la lettre,* the rationale for Mead's and Bateson's research among the Balinese and their restudy of the Iatmul between 1936 and 1939, as well as *Balinese Character* of 1942. Mead's debt to Bateson's epistemological concerns, contributions to learning theory as well as his evolving emphasis upon both the generative and destructive qualities of interactive encounters, manifest in his work on schismogenesis, steady states, and eventually double binds, should not be underestimated.

Mead and Bateson recognized four primary types of temperament, each constituting a pole of one of two axes. The two types opposite one another on a given axis were dialectically related to each other. One axis (in Mead's diagrams running north to south) emphasized the qualities of relations with other people she termed "possessing" and "being possessed." The other axis (running east to west) emphasized the individual's relations with the broader world, or introversion and extroversion. They also recognized four intermediate types, each combining qualities of the adjoining primary types and dialectically related to its opposite. Perhaps following Erich Fromm, in some 1935 versions of the squares, Mead also distinguished a central position, which combined qualities of all the other types. Taken together, these types formed a structural set that Mead and Bateson utilized to compare and contrast individual temperaments as well as cultural ethoi.

For the Mead of this period, the individual's personality was a temporary phenomenon arising within the conjunction of constitutional or temperamental inheritance each person receives from their direct ancestors, the operations of the so-called genetic process, the order and accidents of their upbringing, as well as the particular culture in which the person lived. In ways similar to Erik Erikson's notions, Mead and Bateson understood the genetic processes generally characteristic of our species to unfold differently for people of differing temperaments in differing cultural environments. These divergent patterns of human development posed variable demands upon and difficulties for a person's character, hence various life problems, especially for people of one temperament living in a culture whose ethos was more congruent with another temperament. Mead's interest in and debts to the Gestalt psychologists are most apparent here.

Under some circumstances, a given society could stabilize a particular conjunction of temperament and character such that this conjunction provided an organizing pattern for emotional life in that society or, in Bateson's terms, the society's ethos. The society would have to be reasonably endogamous; problems posed by recessive genes, and their influence upon possible temperaments, would have to be limited; the population would have to have become well adapted to the local foods and diseases; the society would have to be able to withstand the economic and military threats posed by outsiders; new forms of knowledge and technological advances or their inverses would have to be more or less consistent with the preexisting social order.

For Mead, such stabilizations were fragile cultural achievements, easily disturbed as well as difficult to produce and reproduce. Any event, personal or more broadly societal, that affected the lives of adults affected the lives of the developing children those adults raised.

Mead explicitly disavowed any theory advancing a mechanical reduction of later adult character to local child-rearing practices. While the external techniques of child rearing prevalent in a given society (swaddling, premastication, and so forth) influenced the course of a child's development, both its health and especially the attitude of the child's caregivers were more important. In this sense, but with a firm recognition of temperament as an integral element of personality, Mead and Bateson agreed with Sapir that psychology arises only in the interactions of individuals.

Not all aspects of the phenomena postulated by the squares hypothesis were observable using ethnographic methods. The biology of the period did not as yet have an adequate theory or the methods necessary to contribute to any such study. As the America of the period was still largely legally segregated and racism was common, Mead, following the advice of both Benedict and Boas, chose not to publish their theory explicitly. This choice contributed greatly to the misunderstanding of Mead's work, including Derek Freeman's characterization of Mead as an extreme cultural determinist.

Aftermath

Sapir, Benedict, Mead, and Bateson were not the only anthropologists interested in psychological matters broadly conceived. W. H. R. Rivers, Bronislaw Malinowski, John Bayard, and the Seligmans all had psychological interests; the psychologist Frederick Bartlett had serious anthropological interests. Among the Americans, aside from those previously mentioned, John Whiting undertook a study of the Kwoma; Cora DuBois worked among the Alorese; Ralph Linton collaborated with Kardiner, DuBois, and Kluckhohn, though the Apache as described by Kluckhohn did not easily fit Kardiner's models; Paul Radin translated works by Alfred Adler.

By the late 1940s, two volumes of readings on the subject had been brought out. But the rigors of professionalization and the differences between the disciplines Sapir and Frank had hoped to bring together began to tell. Sapir, Sullivan, and Benedict were dead, as were several of the major Gestalt psychologists. Bateson had left anthropology to work among schizophrenics, and eventually on animal communication. Mead was not teaching and had further become embroiled in misunderstandings attendant upon national character studies, especially Geoffrey Gorer and John Rickman's swaddling hypothesis. Melford Spiro and Harold Orlansky had written essays critical of the earlier work.

Sapir's students and protégées were ascendant. Of these, Hallowell was probably the most important. In Hallowell's hands, Sapir's ideas and Koffka's influences, reconfigured as "the behavioral environment of the self," began to prefigure anthropological semiotics as he studied self and perception among the Ojibwa. Most of his work appeared well after the heyday of so-called culture and personality studies.

Bateson, and particularly his notion of *eidos,* would influence cognitive anthropology. Perhaps because her psychology largely concerned worldview without necessarily being dynamic, Benedict could appeal to the more semiotically minded. Like Sapir's, Mead's influence is everywhere and nowhere at the same time.

— *Gerald Sullivan*

See also **Benedict, Ruth; Mead, Margaret; Sapir, Edward**

Further Readings

Bateson, G., & Mead, M. (1942). *Balinese character.* New York: New York Academy of Sciences.

Benedict, R. (1934). *Patterns of culture.* Boston: Houghton Mifflin.

Haring, D. G. (Ed.). (1956). *Personal character and cultural milieu* (3rd ed.). Syracuse, NY: Syracuse University Press.

Kluckhohn, C., Murray, H. A., & Schneider, D. M. (1953). *Personality in nature, society, and culture.* (2nd ed.). New York: Knopf.

Mandelbaum, D. G. (Ed.). (1949). *Selected writings of Edward Sapir in language, culture, and personality.* Berkeley and Los Angeles: University of California Press.

Mead, M. (1946). The cultural approach to personality. In P. L. Harriman (Ed.), *Encyclopedia of psychology* (pp. 477–488). New York: Philosophical Library.

Spier, L., Hallowell, A. I., & Newman, S. S. (Eds.). (1941). *Language, culture, and personality: Essays in memory of Edward Sapir.* Menasha, WI: Sapir Memorial Publication Fund.

CULTURE AREA CONCEPT

The culture area concept was developed in the early 1900s, at a time when American anthropology was in its infancy. Franz Boas and his students were collecting enormous amounts of data about the "disappearing" native cultures of North America. There was no framework for organizing this data, however. The concept of the culture area was first applied by ethnologist Clark Wissler in order to provide a theoretical framework for the information being generated. A culture area was defined as a geographical/cultural region whose population and groups share important common identifiable cultural traits, such as language, tools and material culture, kinship, social organization, and cultural history. Therefore, groups sharing similar traits in a geographical region would be classed in a single culture area. This concept has been vociferously criticized over the last century. The notion of the culture area has been viewed as being ethnocentric because it ignores adaptation or biology and appears to rely on diffusion as an explanation for similar cultural traits (especially inventions) in a single geographic area. The underlying idea of this concept is that by spatially tracing traits, it is possible to understand the history of an institution. By defining the idea of a "culture core," or the group in the culture area that produces the most complex traits and then shares those with other nearby groups, this concept provided a powerful explanatory tool. This concept, as defined, is therefore very selective in the kinds of traits on which it focuses. As a result, local and regional differences are virtually ignored, and the concept of independent invention was often discarded. An additional criticism is that anthropologists cannot agree on the number of culture areas and how groups should be classified within those divisions. The current division of culture areas tends to be the most popular; however, there are certainly variations on this scheme: Arctic, Subarctic, Pacific Northwest, Northeast, Southeast, Great Plains, Southwest, Plateau, Great Basin, and California. This was readily apparent in archaeology, where culture areas were seen as archaeological equivalents to ethnographic "cultures" and this concept was used to narrowly define and explain similarities in material culture of the past. Similarly, museums organized data, catalogued artifacts, and created displays based on this concept.

Despite its apparent faults, anthropologists continue to use the culture area concept. As an explanatory tool, this concept falls short; however, the concept still provides a mechanism for organizing a multitude of data. In addition, the idea of a culture area certainly illustrates the interaction between neighboring groups of people. Comparisons of groups within and between culture areas allow anthropologists and archaeologists to examine those common environments and historical processes that may link groups or and create similarities and differences between them. The culture area concept also provides a common language for anthropologists working in a particular area. It is often the case that studies are focused by region, and the literature will be equally focused. In addition, research questions and theoretical issues tend to link anthropologists working in a particular culture area. This concept has therefore both divided and united anthropologists.

— *Caryn M. Berg*

See also **Anthropology, Cultural; Cultural Ecology; Wissler, Clark**

Further Readings

Erickson, P. A., & Murphy, L. D. (2003). *A history of anthropological theory* (2nd ed.). Peterborough, Canada: Broadview Press.

Kroeber, A. L. (1931). The culture-area and age-area concepts of Clark Wissler. In S. A. Rice (Ed.), *Methods in social sciences* (pp. 248–265). Chicago: University of Chicago Press.

Trigger, B. G. (1989). *A history of archaeological thought.* Oxford: Cambridge University Press.

 # CULTURE CHANGE

Human beings are the bearers of culture; therefore, it is important to study how humankind has evolved over time as a basis to understand culture change. Periods of culture change indicate the direction in which the strengths and values of said cultures survive and maintain their existence. How to study culture change may be difficult at best because theoretical ideas concerning culture have created a schism among proponents and opponents of cultural evolutionism.

The literature suggests that Charles Darwin's theory of evolution was central to the understanding of how societies evolved over time. Darwin's main point focused on species survivals, that is, the individuals who were best suited to their environment transmitted cultural survivals from generation to generation. However, a biological framework is not progressive in that it can suffice to explain cultural survivals in terms of social structures, hierarchy, social justice, intergenerational poverty, and the like. To this end, rather than to rely upon biology alone, it became important to theorize about how humans "think." Therefore, it is equally important to examine the social world of humans and the coexistence of mental and material phenomena, perhaps in symbolic interactionism.

With respect to symbolic interactionism, symboling and socialization are inextricably linked. Human beings make sense of their reality through symbol manipulations, and thus they behave accordingly. Both concepts can be viewed as a system of rules and regulations. As noted by Talcott Parsons, human beings must achieve compatibility and integration among cultural, social, personal, and biological systems. Therefore, culture and culture change can be examined and theorized through human interactions as well as human responses to environmental influences.

Environmental influences or the "web of life," as coined by Julian Steward, refers to other human communities, plants, animals, and climatic changes that impact and influence how human beings and nature participate in a dance of survival. Furthermore, the question is: Who or what wins the proverbial prize of the ultimate survivor?

For the purpose of this entry, I will use Leslie White's concepts regarding culture. For White, culture has four key foci. First, it is ideological, in that humans relate to one another based upon shared knowledge, beliefs, and values that are transmitted from one generation to another. Second, it is sociological, in that it governs the laws and those institutions whereby codes of ethics are formulated and advanced in terms of appropriate and inappropriate behaviors. The third element of culture deals with the subjective expressions in human society, in other words, the attitudes or sentiments of the realities that are constructed through the ability to symbol. Finally, the technological aspect of culture explains how human beings developed tools in order to adapt to the environment as well as to survive the forces of nature. In summation, the four elements of culture as explained by White provide a holistic explanation of how culture is produced and changes over time due to a need to survive. White contends that human beings produce culture and that one's understanding of culture is through symboling or a sharing of values and meaning.

Culture change is inevitable. No matter how we as human beings resist or accept it, change of every kind is inevitable. Present-day society is experiencing an accelerated period of culture change. I will focus on technology as an agent of change. Technology has had an immense impact upon our society. The media (for example, television, radio, print media, and computers) tend to shape values and visions of the "self" in terms of what is acceptable and what is not acceptable (such as material wealth and/or physical attributes). Mental images are flashed before our eyes at a rate of speed too fast to compute, yet not fast enough that the mind does not absorb the intended subliminal messages of self-worth or lack thereof. Cell phones have largely replaced public phones. E-mail has replaced letters. The traditional means of communication, the U.S. Postal Service, has competition from the computer. Ironically, the religious community is adapting to the rapid changes in culture. Amazingly, nuns are selling products that are synonymous with beauty for the pure supplementation of personal finances. The Catholic Church now recognizes that the vow of poverty cannot withstand the medical and retirement needs of an aging population of clergy. In addition, cell phone users are not exclusive to people in the workplace, but include people from every strata of society despite social class, ethnicity, age, gender, occupation, or religion, all for the purpose of organizing the day-to-day activities.

Furthermore, religious communities reflect acceptance of changes that have occurred within our culture in order to keep up with the demands of a fast-paced and growing circle of people who are in need of quick fixes. Technology delivers messages of spiritual uplift through the use of the cell phone, the fax, and/or the computer at a rate faster than the speed of light. Technology is redefining the concept of "time." Operational "time" serves to regulate individuals' comings and goings. However, the cell phone user's interpretation of "time" is manipulative in that time can be saved by making a call to provide an explanation of what is late or early or on time. In fact, for some, technology has served to become a controlling device, in that one is forced or seduced into paying bills online rather than by standing in lines to remit. Moreover, cyber-promiscuity and child pornography are becoming uncontrollable vices.

As previously stated, technology has changed and is changing the face of society. It is, however, difficult to determine when technology became such a dominant cultural system, because the story of humankind and one's tools has a long history, dating as far back as before Christ (BC). Clearly, technology has served to preserve humankind in its struggles with nature and the environment. Nonetheless, the fundamental question is: To what extent has technology become a disservice to humankind? And how can there be a healthy balance?

An analysis of cultural change presents multiple interpretations and evolutionary stages and adaptations in and of society depending upon the focus. Technology, as a rule, has shaped and defined culture. In other words, how technology is used and how it serves humankind shape the attitudes surrounding it. White's theory of technological determination is relevant here. Within this theme, technology influences the ways in which people perceive and interact within their environment. In essence, technology in and of itself cannot explain emotions or the social elements of culture. However, the impact of technology upon the social elements of culture can be explained through observable behaviors brought about by the production and possession of materials. Accordingly, a second theme of importance is economic determinism.

In general, a distinctive way of life is determined by social and economic status. For example, Marxism produces an explanation for the impact that material production has had on the social consciousness of the individual. Regardless of privilege and power, the forces of production conflict with and complement the needs of society. On one hand, technological materialism and the production of tools are specifically designed for the purpose of meeting human needs. On the other hand, material production impacts social relations positively or negatively, contingent upon the intent. Consequently, the more an individual or particular group experiences material wealth (capitalism), political power, and privilege, the less socially conscious one may become concerning others.

Modern conveniences, dependent upon the individual's position on the economic ladder, shape definitions of labor both inside and outside the home environment. In terms of employment, new technology equals increased output and savings over outdated technology. On a personal level, economic status dictates to what extent technology defines one's social image, and one's acquisition of advanced technology (for example, expensive modes of transportation, Internet access via personal computers, and even using a remote control to change the channel versus getting up to do so). Marxism provides a deeper understanding of economic relations; equally important, Marxism, like technological determinism, focuses upon human relations. Power and privilege within the context of social class relations provide a deeper understanding of social consciousness (i.e., there is a social divide between the haves, have-nots, and those who have least of all). As Marvin Harris notes, "materialism is what happens to you when you abandon your ideals and sell out." To put it differently, technological materialism serves to produce unequal relations among people rather than to strike a balance between humankind and nature for the sake of survival.

Modern conveniences have indeed changed survival modes. With a shift in physical labor came a preoccupation with self-image and thus understanding the authentic "self" and the soul's life purpose. The latter served to offset the pressures of succumbing to the emotional pressures to fit into an ideal that may or may not be attainable. Specifically, White correlates ideals of beauty (for example, with respect to women) to technology. In some cultures, where the food supply is not technologically driven and the stock is scarce, voluptuous women are regarded as beautiful; conversely, where there is an abundance of food, those same women in another culture would be deemed unattractive. There is also a correlation between social class and voluptuousness. In the first example, voluptuousness is an indicator of wealth, whereas the latter is regarded as poor to working class.

Burniske and Monke assert that online activities challenge the very notion of "self" and complicate issues of identity among the youth population. The youth population, like a blank canvas, is deficient in life experience and therefore falls victim to others' interpretations of them. Here, online activities breed isolation and the lack of critical thinking and critical analysis of the information presented via the Internet. Technological culture, in this sense a threat to collaboration, eliminates face-to-face discourse and guidance to facilitate authentic or possibilities of authentic self-definition. In other words, opportunities to seek truth, think out loud, or a space to mull over ideas in order to construct more satisfying answers to questions and more authentic definitions of "self" are nullified by technology.

The interrelationship between culture and technology has altered the spirit of collaboration. As Neil Postman informs us, the United States, for example, has evolved from a technocracy to become a "technopoly." As a technopoly (i.e., totalitarian technocracy) every realm of life is regulated through technology. For instance, most inquiries concerning the day-to-day activities that affect financial stability or instability are directed to computerized simulacra of humans without emotions ("Press zero if you'd like to speak to a customer service representative"). Interestingly, Postman equates technocracy with industrialization, inclusive of humankind and an enduring sense of spirituality. In other words, pretechnological man was loosely controlled by social customs and religious traditions. As an illustration, pretechnological man was less mechanical and more in touch with a moral dependency upon God (or the possibility of things coming into being due to a higher power) if not dependency upon one another. Accordingly, technology is chipping away at the human element that guides the emotions, leaving less regard for the human spirit. Technology is paving the way for a culture that is an insult to self-respect, such that the word "thank you" is becoming an anomaly. Postman argues that technocracy (tradition) and technopoly as two opposing worlds coexist (technology being the dominant worldview), and thus are redefining the symbols of culture (religion, community, politics, history, truth, and privacy).

Culture change takes place to accommodate human beings in their immediate environment. There is at times evidence of resistance to change and individuals who do their best to preserve elements of the culture through law enforcement. However, accommodations for the changes that do occur within our culture shape our very survival. In the final analysis, technology is just one aspect of culture change, yet because people are highly dependent upon technology, its influence is felt in every aspect of daily living.

Burke and Ornstein refer to the talented people who changed our lives, presumably for the better, as the "axemakers." Furthermore, they argue that in exchange for their innovations, the axemakers gained control of our minds and redefined our beliefs and values. The very use of their innovations is seductive and addictive due to its image-producing powers.

In addition, Burke and Ornstein suggest that technology has both improved the quality of life in some societies, while generating a negative effect within and outside these societies. For instance, in Jamaica, in order to support tourism, businesses are eroding those spaces where individuals could once grow crops for individual and commercial use. Thus, natural resources that were once readily available for the taking are no longer accessible to the less fortunate. Here, opportunities for economic growth, while available for "big" business, deny the very livelihood of others. With respect to culture change, technology is the gift that packs such a deep sense of dependency and control that people feel as though without it, they cannot function. However, Burke and Ornstein inform us that the changes that are taking place within our world need not be beyond our control. The key to surviving periods of culture change is to become acquainted with the processes involved within the change. It is very important to be mindful of our most valuable resource, our children, and the environment in which their lives and minds are shaped and developed. Through our children, we stand to take back our power and reshape our future our way.

— *Virginia A. Batchelor*

See also **Cyberculture; Social Change; Steward, Julian H.; Technology**

Further Readings

Burke, J., & Ornstein, R. (1997). *The axemaker's gift: Technology's capture and control of our minds and culture.* New York: Putnam Books.
Burniske, R. W., & Monke, L. (2001). *Breaking down the digital wall: Learning to teach in a post-modern world.* Albany: State University of New York Press.

Harris, M. (1993). *Cultural materialism: The struggle for a science of culture.* New York: Vintage Books.
Postman, N. (1993). *Technopoly: The surrender of culture to technology.* New York: Vintage Books.
White, L. A. (1959). *The evolution of culture: The development of civilization to the fall of Rome.* New York: McGraw-Hill.

CULTURE OF POVERTY

Social scientists credit Oscar Lewis (1914–1970), an American anthropologist, with introducing the concept of a culture of poverty. He first suggested it in 1959, in his book, *Five Families: Mexican Case Studies in the Culture of Poverty.* The concept refers to the ideas and behavior developed by poor people in some capitalist societies as they adapt to urban circumstances. Lewis conceptualized the culture of poverty as having its own structure and rationale and as consisting of a way of life that is passed down from generation to generation along family lines.

The view advanced by Lewis emphasized that the culture of poverty in capitalist societies was not simply a matter of economic deprivation or the absence of something. Rather, it is also something that provides individuals with a framework for interpreting their lives and the problems they encounter in their daily existence. Furthermore, the culture of poverty transcends regional, rural-urban, and national differences to produce remarkable similarities in family structure, interpersonal relations, and value systems in different societies.

Poverty and the Culture of Poverty

Lewis recognized that there are degrees of poverty and many kinds of poor people. Not all societies have a culture of poverty. Lewis argued that a culture of poverty is more likely in societies with a certain set of conditions. First, these societies have a cash economy, wage labor, and production for profit. Second, they have a persistently high rate of unemployment and underemployment for unskilled labor. Third, there is the presence of low wages. Fourth, these societies fail to provide social, political, and economic organization either on a voluntary basis or by government imposition for the low-income population. Fifth, there exists a bilateral kinship system rather than a unilateral one. In a unilateral kinship system, one traces descent either through males or through females. In a bilateral system, one traces descent through males and females without emphasis on either line. Sixth, the values of the dominant class stress the accumulation of wealth and property, the possibility of upward mobility, and thrift, and they explain low economic status as the result of personal inadequacy or inferiority.

The way of life that develops among some of the poor under these conditions constitutes the culture of poverty. Lewis described this way of life in terms of some 70 interrelated social, economic, and psychological traits. These traits represent a reaction of the poor to their marginal position in a class-stratified, highly individuated, capitalistic society. They represent an effort by the poor to cope with feelings of hopelessness and despair that develop from the recognition of the improbability of achieving success in the larger society. The number of traits and the relationship between them could vary from society to society.

Lewis theorized that the culture of poverty is not only a present adaptation to a set of objective conditions of the larger society. Rather, once it comes into existence, it tends to perpetuate itself from generation to generation because of its effect on children. For example, Lewis argued that by the time slum children are age 6 or 7, they have usually absorbed the basic values and attitudes of this culture of poverty and are not psychologically geared to take full advantage of increased opportunities that occur in their lifetime.

Traits of the Culture of Poverty

Lewis derived the essential features or traits of the way of life he termed the *culture of poverty* from an extensive collection of life histories and psychological tests with families. For example, in his classic work, *La Vida* (1966), he described the culture of poverty in terms of poor families in Puerto Rico and New York. From these studies, he suggested that social scientists could identify and study the traits that formed the culture of poverty from a variety of points of view: (a) the relationship between the culture of poverty and the larger society, (b) the nature of the slum community, (c) the nature of the family, and (d) the attitudes, values, and the character structure of the individual.

The Culture of Poverty and the Larger Society

Lewis argued that one of the crucial characteristics of the poor in a culture of poverty is their lack of effective participation and integration in the major institutions of the larger society. This characteristic results from a variety of factors, including lack of economic resources; segregation and discrimination; fear, suspicion, or apathy; and the development of local solutions for problems faced by the poor. While the poor "participate" in some of the institutions of the larger society as inmates in prison, as recipients of welfare, or as soldiers in the armed services, participation in such institutions perpetuates the poverty and sense of hopelessness.

The low wages and chronic unemployment and underemployment of the poor lead to lack of property ownership and an absence of savings. These conditions reduce the likelihood of effective participation in the larger economic system. In addition, a constant shortage of cash and inability to obtain credit results in borrowing at high rates of interest, use of secondhand clothing, and furniture and pawning of personal goods.

Lewis also reported that people with a culture of poverty have a low level of literacy and education, are not active members of political parties, and make very little use of community resources such as banks, hospitals, museums, or art galleries. Moreover, they have a critical attitude toward some of the basic institutions of the dominant classes. For example, they may dislike the police, hold a mistrust of the government and those in high positions, and display a cynicism that extends even to the church.

While people with a culture of poverty are aware of middle-class values, Lewis argued that they largely do not live by these values. For example, the poor typically do not marry, although they consider marriage an important ideal. Lewis thought that this was largely a consequence of their economic condition. Men with no steady jobs or other sources of income want to avoid the expense and legal difficulties of marriage. Women believe that consensual unions are also better for them. They believe that marriage ties them down to men who are immature, abusive, and unreliable, and, in addition, by not marrying, they have stronger ties to their children and exclusive rights to a house or any other property they own.

The Nature of the Slum Community

Lewis referred to the place where the poor resided as "slum communities." Poor housing conditions, crowding, and a minimum of social organization beyond the level of the family characterizes slum communities. While one can find occasional voluntary associations or neighborhood gangs present in these communities, it is the low level of organization that gives the culture of poverty its marginal quality when contrasted with the complex, specialized, and organized larger society.

However, even in slum communities, one may find a sense of community or esprit de corps. The development of this sense of community depends on several factors, such as the size of the slum community, incidence of home ownership, low rents, stability of residence, ethnicity, kinship ties, and the slum's location in terms of the larger city. For example, Lewis's research indicated that when there are barriers that separate slums from the surrounding area, when rents are low and stability of residence is great, when the population constitutes a distinct ethnic or racial group, and when there are strong kinship ties, then a strong sense of community can develop. However, even when these conditions are absent, a sense of territoriality develops that demarcates the slum neighborhoods from the rest of the city.

Source: © iStockphoto/Mary Marin.

The Nature of the Family

Lewis's studies indicated that people with a culture of poverty tend to form common-law marriages or cohabiting arrangements. Abandonment of families by fathers is common, and consequently, there is a high incidence of female-centered families and strong ties with maternal relatives. Crowded living arrangements foster a lack of privacy, and scarcity of resources creates competition for limited goods. Sibling rivalry is common, as is rivalry for maternal affection.

Children in these families begin adult activities earlier in their life cycles compared with children from middle-class families. For example, they are more likely to have early initiation into sex and are less likely to complete high school, thus entering the job market sooner than their middle-class counterparts.

Attitudes, Values, and Character Structure of the Individual

Individuals living in a culture of poverty share a set of traits that differentiates them from the rest of society. These traits are behavioral or psychological; the family perpetuates these traits as it passes them down from generation to generation through its psychological impact on children.

Lewis argued that the major individual characteristics are a strong feeling of marginality, helplessness, dependence, and inferiority. People with a culture of poverty also display a sense of resignation and fatalism, present-time orientation, lack of impulse control, weak ego structure, sexual confusion, and the inability to defer gratification. They also are provincial, locally oriented, and have very little sense of history. Typically, they are unable to see the similarities between their problems and those like them in other parts of the world.

Critique of the Culture of Poverty

The term *culture of poverty* became well-known in the social sciences and in the political arena as well. During the 1960s, for example, Michael Harrington utilized the phrase in *The Other America* to emphasize how the economy and social structure limited the opportunities of the poor and produced a culture of poverty that the poor did not choose. However, criticisms of the concept also emerged. Two criticisms are especially important.

First, the media and politicians frequently used the concept in a manner different from Lewis's initial conceptualization. The connection between the political economy and the culture of poverty was frequently absent in their descriptions of the poor. The behavioral, psychological characteristics of poor individuals were emphasized, as well as the problems created by the family structures of the poor. The larger society often blamed the poor for their circumstances because analysis of the poor presented only the culture of poverty. The ties to the economic and structural dimensions of society theorized by Lewis were frequently forgotten. Scholars and activists attacked this "blaming the victim" for being in poverty and continued to conduct research and present policy proposals that link the behavioral outcomes of the culture of poverty to social structural factors.

Second, Lewis presented a view of urban poverty that argued that the urban poor develop their own adaptation that is fundamentally different from the culture of the rest of society. However, an alternative point of view emphasizes that the urban poor share many values of the larger society around them. This view emphasizes that the "subculture" of poverty is part of the larger culture of the dominant society. While one may find in the poor the traits described by Lewis, one also finds that the poor may share values of the dominant society. For example, research reports individuals among the poor who possess a strong work ethic passed on through extended-family networks, only to confront the structural reality of limited job opportunities in the urban ghetto.

Poverty and Culture

The culture of poverty remains an important scientific idea. It refers to one way of life shared by poor people in given historical and social contexts. The concept enables us to see that many of the problems we think of as distinctively belonging to one society also exist in other societies. The concept also enables us to see that poverty can exist without the culture of poverty. Finally, Lewis argued that because the traits associated with the culture of poverty are passed on from generation to generation through the family, elimination of poverty per se may not be enough to eliminate the culture of poverty, which is a whole way of life.

— *Patricia E. Erickson*

See also **Economics and Anthropology**

Further Readings

Allen, V. L. (1970). *Psychological factors in poverty.* Chicago: Markham.

Auletta, K. (1982). *The underclass.* New York: Random House.

Gans, H. J. (1995). *The war against the poor.* New York: Basic Books.

Harrington, M. (1962). *The other America.* New York: Macmillan.

Lewis, O. (1959). *Five families: Mexican case studies in the culture of poverty.* New York: Basic Books.

Moynihan, D. P. (Ed.). (1968). *On understanding poverty: Perspectives from the social sciences.* New York: Basic Books.

Myrdal, G. (1965). *Challenge to affluence.* New York: Vintage.

Wilson, W. J. (1987). *The truly disadvantaged: The inner city, the underclass, and public policy.* Chicago: University of Chicago Press.

 # CULTURE SHOCK

Culture shock refers to feelings of uncertainty and discomfort experienced by an ethnographer during fieldwork in a different culture. Confronted by a new environment, strangers, and many new behaviors and ideas, almost all ethnographers react emotionally, some with unusual anxiety, anger, sadness, fear, or disorientation. Culture shock tends to resolve over time but may be reawakened when ethnographers return to their own cultures and discover that "the normal" now has become strange in light of their changed perspectives. For many cultural anthropologists, culture shock is a necessary part of learning about culture's power to shape human experience. Understanding culture's influence directly shapes the ethnographer and is one reason ethnographic fieldwork is so significant to cultural anthropology.

Culture shock, defined broadly, includes adjustments to surroundings that are felt physically by ethnographers as well as psychological discomfort that results from more subtle differences to which they must adapt. Thus, ethnographers find new food and ways of eating, lack of Western-style plumbing, sleeping on the floor, wearing unwashed clothes for days, different modes of urination and defecation, constant insects, and even unexpected weather as annoying, exasperating, and tiring conditions that must be faced early in fieldwork. Often, it is not so much the conditions themselves as that ethnographers are unsure about correct behavior and are afraid they unwittingly may offend their hosts. The combination of physical adjustment and uncertainty or fear often dominates the initial fieldwork period.

Perhaps of greater long-term significance are various psychological accommodations that ethnographers often continue to make throughout the fieldwork period. These may enable ethnographers to realize how much they have integrated their own culture's values in their everyday lives and identities. Privacy and independence are difficult if not impossible to achieve when most people around them do not understand them and routinely live immersed in family and kin group loyalties. Ethnographic work itself with its associated values of education and literacy may be irrelevant or not comprehensible to informants. Often, culture shock leads to insights that challenge deeply held cultural assumptions. For example, U.S. ethnographers may hold notions of child rearing that emphasize egalitarianism and nurturing. Yet ethnographers may discover that favoritism of a first or last child is the norm in the culture being studied or that children are differentiated by gender as well as age in the form of care provided. Insights gained from culture shock often lead to the reformulation of research questions by the ethnographer in the field.

Many scientific accounts of other cultures traditionally contained impersonal descriptions of subsistence patterns, social organizations, and religious practices rather than discussion of culture shock and the emotional toll of fieldwork. Accounts of emotional upheaval were left to anecdotal conversation, the field diary, and occasionally to introductory remarks in the ethnography itself. The situation began to change by the late 1960s and even more so with the advent of postmodern ethnography in the last quarter of the 20th century. Bronislaw Malinowski's posthumously published diary provides an example of loneliness and discontent by the fieldworker often credited as the originator of modern participant observation.

— *Audrey C. Shalinsky*

See also **Ethnographer; Malinowski, Bronislaw; Participant-observation**

Further Readings

Bock, P. K. (Ed.). (1970). *Culture shock: A reader in modern cultural anthropology.* New York: Knopf.

Chagnon, N. (1996). *Yanomamö* (5th ed.). Fort Worth, TX: Harcourt Brace.

Malinowski, B. (1989). *A diary in the strict sense of the term* (2nd ed.). Palo Alto, CA.: Stanford University Press.

CULTURE, CHARACTERISTICS OF

The first complete definition of culture in anthropology was provided by Edward Tylor, who defined the concept as "that complex whole which includes knowledge, belief, art, morals, law, custom, and any other capabilities and habits acquired by man as a member of society." This definition is taken from *Primitive Culture,* Tylor's 1871 cultural evolutionary account of human development. Though the 19th-century cultural evolution model has long been rejected by anthropology, the main elements of Tylor's definition of culture remains. Tylor defined culture in a much more open and holistic manner than his contemporary, Matthew Arnold, who defined culture in 1869 as "high culture," which is defined in terms of the "best that has been said or thought in the world." Most anthropologists would share with Tylor a definition of culture that examines ordinary daily life as opposed to the production of the "elite."

Though culture seems like a simple concept, the challenge is studying culture in all its complexity. Culture has both an ideational/symbolic axis as well as a material/behavioral axis. By ideational/symbolic, this refers to the fact that culture exists in our minds: Culture includes the idealized norms and values that we hold in our minds and the symbolic nature of culture, which is understood and interpreted by individuals. Though culture could be conceived of as an ideal existing in thought, it is expressed through material production and direct human interaction. Culture is characterized, then, by what people think and what they do; that culture is based in symbols, both those that exist in thought and those that are expressed in material culture and social life.

Some of the common characteristics that are common to all definitions are the fact that culture is *shared,* that culture is *learned,* and that culture is an *integrated* whole.

By shared, this means that even though no two individuals will have exactly the same culture knowledge and life experience, both will share enough to make social life possible. That is to say, as cultural beings, individuals can predict and understand the behavior of others, thus enabling social life. Culture shock precisely occurs when all that is taken for granted (i.e., shared within your own culture) no longer applies.

Not only is culture shared, it is also learned. This recognizes the fact that humans do not live by instinct alone; rather, culture mediates our adaptation to the physical environment. To survive, humans acquire culture. By learned, this presumes that culture will be in large part acquired in the first years of a child's life (enculturation), but it does not imply that humans ever stop learning culture. As culture is constantly in a state of flux, humans have the ability to acquire new knowledge and to generate new culture over the course of their lifetimes.

Finally, culture is an integrated whole, or to paraphrase Clifford Geertz, a web of meanings and significance, whereby every element of culture is connected in this web of significance to everything else in that culture. On a more practical level, this means that culture is an interrelated whole and that to truly study culture, it is necessary to look at the larger context. This means that a study of political life would entail an analysis of kinship and marriage, looking at how authority and power are often transferred between generations; economics and the ways in which politics shapes production, distribution, and consumption as well as the ways in which large economic considerations shape the distribution of political power and authority; religion

and the ways in which the sacred is called upon to justify or legitimate power; and finally, language and communication and ways in which power can be achieved through the use of metaphor and language.

Though contemporary anthropologists rarely write monographs that purport to describe an entire culture or population, anthropology will still seek to understand any aspect of culture or social life as existing in a much larger and complex whole whereby changes in one quadrant may possibly bring about unexpected changes elsewhere in that culture. Likewise, anthropology will not see culture as a shopping list of features or norms, rather as a continually changing mass of ideas and behaviors, in which culture is imperfectly shared between individuals in a social group, but equally between social groups.

— *Michel Bouchard*

See also **Anthropology, Cultural; Cross-Cultural Research; Culture Shock; Societies, Complex; Social Structures; Tylor, Edward Burnett**

Further Readings

Arnold, M. (1869). *Culture and anarchy: An essay in political and social criticism.* London: Smith, Elder.

Geertz, C. (1973). *The interpretation of culture: Selected essays.* New York: Basic Books.

Haviland, W., Fedorak, S., Crawford, G., & Lee, R. (2005). *Cultural anthropology* (2nd Canadian ed.). Montreal, Canada: Nelson.

Tylor, E. (1871). *Primitive culture: Researches into the development of mythology, philosophy, religion, art, and custom* (2 vols.). London: J. Murray.

CYBERCULTURE

The advent of the personal computer combined with the development of the Internet and easy-to-use, Internet-based computer applications has created a new virtual environment in which new forms of social interaction occur. Adding new technologies to social behaviors has created an environment that has changed individuals, cultures, and the world. Due to the dynamic nature of the Internet, individuals can communicate with others who have the same interests worldwide. A new world culture has formed. The overlying culture is different from previous cultural development in nature and scope. The development is of a virtual nature and (or will) encompasses every individual worldwide. Never before have new global cultural forms emerged so quickly.

Culture is defined in several ways: (a) the totality of socially transmitted behavior patterns, arts, beliefs, institutions, and all other products of human work and thought; (b) the patterns, traits, and products considered as the expression of a particular period, class, community, or population; and (c) the predominating attitudes and behavior that characterize the functioning of a group or organization. *Cyber* refers to computers. *Cyberculture* can then be defined as the transforming of social behavioral patterns, arts, beliefs, institutions, and all other products of human work and thought in which humans interact with computers and computer networks.

Culture plays a role in society and societal issues. Barnouw stated that society is a more or less organized group of people of both sexes who share a common culture. Loosely "society," in this context, refers to issues such as meeting food, shelter, reproductive, and other basic needs. Das stated that a society typically has only one culture. Ember and Ember, and Nanda stated that two different societies cannot possess the same culture. Das again stated that this implied that if cyberculture is a distinct culture, then it should form one particular separate society. Cyberculture is unique in that it is essentially one distinct and separate subculture of many global societies. This societal cultural extension is the same globally but is connected to societies with different values, ethics, and morals. For instance, Europe, America, and Asia all have different societies, with each having its own unique culture. The culture of cyber, transported through the Internet, is identical regardless of physical location. Beliefs, behaviors, patterns, traits, and predominating attitudes are nearly identical whether the individual is in New York, London, Hong Kong, Moscow, or Munich. Cyberculture is then intertwined with the local culture and society, extending the physical world into the virtual world. North has called cyberculture a "pan-societal superstructure." Cyberculture, unlike traditional cultures, is freed of the responsibilities of providing a number of properties that can reasonably be expected from any

mainstream society by virtue of the fact that its members are also members of the traditional mainstream societies that supply basic societal needs (food, shelter). According to Das, the Internet society has become a melting pot of different societal components, such as economics, socialization, politics, and entertainment.

The Internet and cyberculture have brought about a shift in values from those accepted in traditional societies. Although multimedia components such as audio, pictures, and video are becoming a more important (and more abundant) component of the Internet for the personal user, its first decade in existence was primarily based on simple text as a form of communication between the majority of users. When this form of communication is used, it removes the traditional way societies judge one another and places a new value on one's worth. Traditionally, societies judge people by appearance, gender, race, wealth, dress, occupation, and so on. In the Internet culture, individuals are judged on their contributions to the new culture. For instance, prestige is earned by what an individual writes or by performing some other service such as maintaining discussion groups or websites.

Another interesting benefit from the Internet and cyberculture is its reciprocity to the user. Traditionally, as the number of individuals in a society increases, the resources available to that society, per person, decrease. The opposite is true in the Internet culture. As more individuals use the Internet, each person brings more resources into the societal pool. These resources are of a humanitarian nature, such as providing information, advice, writings, and software. As a result, the larger the Internet grows, the more resources are available for individuals to use, which, in turn, attracts more users.

Just as in mainstream society, there are rules of use for the Internet. All users are expected to conform to these rules. *Netiquette* is the term used to refer to these rules. If members of mainstream society do not follow typical societal rules, usually, but not always, an authority figure (such as the police) is responsible for punishing the individual. In fewer and less severe cases, neighbors might ostracize a particular member of its local society for breaking societal rules. The Internet is interesting in that the authoritarian role is reversed. In cyberculture, unacceptable behavior is usually dealt with by the offending user's peers. This is primarily through written chastisement, and converse to mainstream society, in a minimal number of cases, police action is sometimes taken if the infraction contains criminal activity. There are 10 basic Netiquette rules: Rule 1: Remember the Human; Rule 2: Adhere to the same standards of behavior online that you follow in real life; Rule 3: Know where you are in cyberspace; Rule 4: Respect other people's time and bandwidth; Rule 5: Make yourself look good online; Rule 6: Share expert knowledge; Rule 7: Help keep flame wars under control; Rule 8: Respect other people's privacy; Rule 9: Don't abuse your power; and Rule 10: Be forgiving of other people's mistakes.

There are negative aspects in all cultures and societies. Cyberculture has been criticized for its effect on individual socialization. Since the Internet is essentially a world of its own, many users become socially isolated from the physical society at large. These users spend the majority of their time online, with very little socializing in the traditional manner. Research has shown that these individuals are more likely to be depressed and are agitated and irritable when offline. Cyberspace can also lead to expensive compulsive behaviors, such as online gaming, online auctions, and pornography. Often, when individuals excessively use the Internet, problems with real-world relationships occur, resulting in counseling for the affected individuals. There are also physical dangers for those individuals who use the Internet excessively. Physical activity is important for human health. Excessive use of the Internet creates a sedentary lifestyle in which the individual is physically inactive. Physical inactivity leads to greater stress and increased risk of heart disease. There are resources available on the Internet that will assist with these issues.

The Internet is made up of many components, applications, and services affecting the culture of the net. Electronic mail (e-mail), instant messaging, chatting, and the World Wide Web (WWW) are important parts of the modern-day Internet.

There are several common communication methods in which users interact on the Internet using various types of messages. Electronic mail was the first widely used form of communication on the Internet. E-mail is a form of asynchronous communication by which a user enters a text message consisting of several sentences or paragraphs and sends it to another individual somewhere on the Internet. If the receiver is not currently online, the message will be held until the receiver picks up or retrieves his or her e-mail from the e-mail server. That individual can then respond at a time of convenience. Instant messaging usually consists of not more then a sentence or two. Both users must be online at the same time in order to communicate. The sender will enter the message and "instantly" send it to the receiver. Chatting requires that both parties be online at the same time. Users exchange messages in a synchronous environment, where all members in the "chat" can send text at essentially the same time. The information sent in this environment is usually a few words to a sentence. Discussion groups are another common method of communication on the Internet. A discussion list is like a bulletin board. One user "tacks" up a message on the board, and everyone can see it. In the online world, the users submit messages to a discussion list. Everyone who accesses the list can view the original message and respond to it. Usenet newsgroups are one of the oldest parts of the Internet. Originally, a message board/forum system was used mainly by academics and scientists. Discussion groups (newsgroups) are the modern-day message board systems and have become one of the most common forums for communication exchange. There are over 100,000 forums in use today on every topic imaginable with millions of users.

The WWW, an Internet-based hypermedia initiative for global information sharing, was developed by Tim Berners-Lee in 1989 while he was working at the European Particle Physics Laboratory (CERN). Berners-Lee wrote the first Web client (Web browser) in 1990, called "WorldWideWeb." After several years, this browser was renamed "Nexus." In 1991, there was just one Web server; by 1993, there were 50 Web servers worldwide. Mosaic, one of the first browsers with a graphical interface, was released in February 1993. Interest in the World Wide Web grew exponentially over the next year, with over 1,500 Web servers registered in June 1994 (1000% increase over January 1993). The following several years brought even more growth to the WWW and the releases of two of the most popular Web browsers, Netscape Navigator and Internet Explorer.

In simplest terms, the growth and ease of use of the WWW combined with communication technologies, such as e-mail, instant messaging, chatting, and discussion groups, has led to this new Internet-based culture. The resulting environment has enabled individuals across the globe to communicate and create communities formed around common interests. The Internet has fostered the growth of personal and professional relationships that go beyond traditional geographical boundaries. The Internet has brought immeasurable quantities of information to the fingertips of users worldwide. The Internet is a cyber "neighborhood" and has become a virtual society. As in any society, a cultural identity forms. Cyberculture defines the social behavioral patterns, arts, and beliefs that individuals assimilate while using the Internet.

— *Shaun Scott*

See also **Computers and Humankind; Culture Change; Globalization**

Further Readings

Das, T. K. (1999, March 18). *The impact of net culture on mainstream societies: A global analysis.* http://in.arxiv.org/abs/cs.CY/9903013

Nanda, S. (1991). *Cultural anthropology* (4th ed.). Belmont, CA: Wadsworth.

North, T. (1994). *The Internet and Usenet global computer networks.* Masters thesis, Curtin University of Technology, Perth, Australia.

Silver, D. (2003). *Introducing cyberculture.* http://www.com.washington.edu/rccs/intro.asp

 # CYBERNETIC MODELING

Cybernetics is the study of control and self-organizing processes in systems, including living organisms, human organizations, and machines. Cybernetic modeling is the attempt to use math or visual symbolic representations of system components and processes to understand the effect of feedback on a given system's potential states of organization or performance.

The term *cybernetics* can be traced to Aristotle's metaphorical reference to ship navigation to describe political governance. The industrial revolution of the 1700s produced rapid technological advances in self-regulating machinery, especially James Watt's steam engine, and the notion of self-regulatory systems now permeates Western thought. In the 1940s,

a group of engineers, biologists, psychologists, and others began to meet regularly to solidify disparate notions of systems theory and applied the term *cybernetics* to their work. Norbert Wiener, whose early interests included self-correction in antiaircraft guns and tanks, was perhaps the most influential. Anthropologists Margaret Mead and Gregory Bateson were core members of the group. The group's ideas were heavily influenced by the Austrian biological and social theorist Ludwig von Bertalanffy. Many of the group's early works were published in the *General Systems Yearbook.*

Among cybernetic principles, *homeostasis* is the tendency of a biological or social system to resist change and maintain itself in a state of equilibrium. The household thermostat is a common metaphor for *negative feedback,* which keeps processes in equilibrium. *Positive feedback* increases deviation from a goal or equilibrium. Cybernetic theory has strongly influenced social science, engineering and physics, psychology, mathematics, communications, organizational management, biology, artificial intelligence, and the computer revolution. The concept of "feedback" has become so pervasive it is now used in common parlance.

It is difficult to identify the complete effects that cybernetic theory has had on anthropology, because the idea of "social systems" is so prevalent in Western thought, but cybernetic theory is clearly discussed in psychological and ecological anthropology. Gregory Bateson influenced the emerging field of psychological anthropology through his theories of mental illness. Rather than treat the human mind as an individual entity, he considered it part of a culturally created system with positive or negative feedback. In the 1950s, Howard T. Odum and Eugene Odum applied cybernetic modeling to ecosystems research in ecology. Archeologists and cultural anthropologists adopted these tools to model human ecosystems. Perhaps best known is Roy Rappaport, who modeled Maring spirituality, nutrition, social organization, and natural resources as a system of feedback mechanisms that regulate ritual and warfare. Critics claimed that the focus on equilibrium precluded an explanation of how social systems change over time, artificial boundaries used to define systems were meaningless, and choices of which system components to model were arbitrary. Cybernetic theorists now focus more on system components that lead to change. New theories of complexity, chaos, and resiliency share the notion that relationships between components of a system may determine the future direction of a system but specific outcomes are difficult to predict because the relative importance of initial conditions cannot be identified. Some anthropologists focus on the unique histories of social systems rather than universal components that should be modeled and are experimenting with computer models that include individual agency as a component of system complexity.

— *David G. Casagrande*

See also **Chaos Theory; Functionalism; Mead, Margaret; Rappaport, Roy; Societies, Complex**

Further Readings

Heims, S. J. (1991). *Constructing a social science for postwar America: The cybernetics group.* Cambridge: MIT Press.

Kohler, T. A., & Gumerman, G. J. (Eds.). (2000). *Dynamics in human and primate societies: Agent-based modeling of social and spatial processes.* New York: Oxford University Press.

Rappaport, R. (1984). *Pigs for the ancestors: Ritual in the ecology of a New Guinea people.* New Haven, CT: Yale University Press.

CYBERNETICS

One of the most important developments in cybernetics today is in *nanotechnology*, which may be to the 21st century what the discovery and exploitation of atomic energy and the computer were to the 20th century. According to the Institute of Nanotechnology, "A nanometer is a billionth of a meter, that is, about 1/80,000th of the diameter of a human hair, or 10 times the diameter of a hydrogen atom." It is on such a small scale that the future of cybernetics may be made. The institute notes that nanotechnology "encompasses precision engineering as well as electronics; electromechanical systems (known as lab-on-a-chip devices) as well as mainstream biomedical applications in areas as diverse as gene therapy, drug delivery, and novel drug discovery techniques."

In nanotechnology, there seems to be no limit to what can be envisioned or created. As the institute explains, "In 2000, the barrier between man and machine is as thin as a strand from the double helix. As computer equipment, surgical tools and communications pipelines shrink ever smaller, the next step in engineering is to merge biological and mechanical molecules and compounds into really, really small machines."

In the area of health care, nanotechnology provides, along with genetic engineering, the promise of a coming revolution in medical efficiency. Not too many years from now, heart pacemakers will be able to communicate electronically with hospitals in order to help health care professionals monitor the hearts of those patients. By being able to keep closer watch on such patients, not only will the health of the patients be better monitored, but also health care and insurance costs may be limited as well.

With such new advances in medicine through nanotechnology, there will also be new questions raised in bioethics, that field that studies the effect growing medical technology has on the individual and society. The institute notes, "Ethical issues in merging with computers go beyond the 'weird' factor into a whole new kind of problem: What happens if human beings are made from nonhuman parts? Is a baby made from cloned DNA, gestated in a bubble, and connected to a cellular phone still human? The answer matters because it is no longer obvious what it means to call something or someone 'normal' or a 'person,' even in the world of medicine." Indeed, nanotechnology is heading truly to a "brave new world," to use the title of Aldous Huxley's famous novel. Not only will nanotechnology present us with an amazing new technology—but also ethical questions on how to use it.

— John F. Murphy Jr.

DANILEVSKY, NIKOLAJ JAKOVLEVICH (1822–1885)

The main place amongst Russian antagonists to Charles Darwin's theory of evolution, and especially his conception of descent of man, belonged to Nikolaj Jakovlevich Danilevsky (1822–1885), the prominent Russian naturalist, economist, historian, philosopher, a head of the late Slavophils, and the author of the original conception of exclusive types of mankind cultures and natural laws of their development. His two-volume work *Anti-Darwinism* (1885, 1889) directly split the biological community by giving rise to heated controversy between advocates of the evolutionary theory and its antagonists. Twenty years earlier, his book *West and East* (1869) predetermined, to a great extent, further development of the theory of "cultural-historical types" that had been, for the first time, formulated by the German historian Henrich Rükkert.

The work of Danilevsky, in the environment of pre-revolutionary Russia, supported the official religion and monarchy as the most suitable for the existing cultural-historical type of Russian ethnos, taking into consideration all forms of religious, political, social, economic, and cultural activities.

From Socialism to Rational Use of Natural Resources and Preservation of the Environment

Nikolaj Jakovlevich Danilevsky was born in November 28, 1822, in his father's village, Oberets, in Orlovskaya province. The beginning of his life was traditional for noble families of his time. In 1842, Danilevsky graduated from the privileged Tsarskoselsky Lyceum and was appointed to the Military Ministry Office. He could not be satisfied with a military career, though, and, at the same time, without having the formal status of student, he began to attend university, natural department of the physics and mathematics (1843–1847). Having achieved the status of candidate, Danilevsky successfully passed master exams in 1849, and prepared to defend his dissertation on flora of the Black Sea zone of the European part of Russia.

While studying at the university, Danilevsky began to visit Mikhail V. Petrashevsky, who organized Friday gatherings at his home, where participants were making close study of the works of French socialists and exploring the possibilities of revolution in Russia. Danilevsky was considered an expert on the works of Charles Furrier. In 1849, all the participants, including the well-known writer Fyodor M. Dostoyevsky, were arrested, and the most active of them were sentenced to death, replaced at the last minute by imprisonment for life.

Danilevsky was arrested, too, and, after 100 days of imprisonment in the Peter and Paul Fortress, sent to Vologda, where he had to live under surveillance of police, and where from May 1850 he worked for province administration. In 1852, he was sent to Samara and appointed to take part in the expedition to explore the conditions of fishery on Volga and Caspian Sea (1853–1857). The supervisor of the expedition was Karl E. Baer, the prominent zoologist, embryologist, geographer, and anthropologist.

Acquaintance with Baer was crucial for Danilevsky, who was assigned in 1857 to the Agricultural Department of the State Property Ministry. After that, for more than 20 years, Danilevsky supervised expeditions exploring fishery and seal trade on the White Sea, Black Sea, Azov, and Caspian Seas, and Arctic Ocean.

Thus, he examined almost all the waters of the European part of Russia and became the biggest expert on rational use of natural resources. Accumulated by Danilevsky, materials were published in the book *Examination of Fishery Conditions in Russia* (1872), later underlying Russian fishery law. Danilevsky headed the commission for working out the rules for use of running water in Crimea (1872–1879), Nikitsky Botanical gardens (1879–1880), and in 1880s was a member of the commission for combating grape plant louse (philloxera). As a member of Geographical Society, Danilevsky published in its papers quite a few articles devoted to climatology, geology, geography, and ethnography of Russia. He was awarded with a Big Golden Medal. However, in due course, his positivism was slowly growing into objective idealism and providentialism.

Anti-Darwinism and Divine Origin of Man

Danilevsky's views on evolution were strongly influenced by his collaboration with Baer, who had already formulated, in the 1820s, a teleological conception of evolution under the influence of some inherent factor *Zielstrebigkeit,* and in 1873 criticized the theory of Darwin. In the1880s, Danilevsky himself joined the critics of Darwinism. He called his views "natural theology." In his monumental work *Darwinism: Critical Research* (1885), more than 1,200 pages length, Danilevsky made an attempt to summarize all the arguments against Darwinism collected during 25 years of its existence. Unfortunately, he did not manage to redeem his promise to present his own arguments in the second volume of this work. His death in 1885 prevented Danilevsky from fulfilling his plan and giving the picture of evolution a unity of substance and spirit. The second volume, published after the death of the author (1889), presented only some preparatory work on the problem of the descent of man, which he explained as an act of supreme reason.

The criticism of Darwinism by Danilevsky was not essentially new; he merely summarized the points that already existed in literature: (a) the analogy between variability of wild and domestic animals is not correct, because the variability among domestic animals is much higher; (b) varieties could not be considered as new species, because varieties have quantitative and not qualitative distinctions; (c) variability among domestic animals never oversteps the limits of species; (d) Darwin exaggerates the role of artificial selection in the origin of new breeds; (e) struggle for existence is not so violent in the natural world and cannot produce new forms; (f) natural selection cannot accumulate useful changes, because of "blended inheritance"; (g) Darwin's theory does not explain the appearance of useless or even harmful traits; and (h) there are no transition forms in paleontological chronicles.

To explain evolution, Danilevsky adopted Baer's concept, *Zielstrebigkeit*; also, he attached religious meaning to this concept. He contended that there was intellectual reason behind the creation of the world; evolution is predetermined and conforming to the will of the Creator—while Darwinism is based on the belief in "blind chance." Having replaced static expediency with dynamic expediency, Danilevsky proposed ontogenesis as a model of phylogenesis, using Baer's research of ontogenesis, which implied that in processes outside of organisms and also inside an egg or womb, some forms develop into other forms and both supplement and substitute for each other.

The Theory of Historical-Cultural Types

In 1869, Danilevsky published in the journal *Zarja* his treatise of "Russia and Europe: A Look at the Cultural and Political Relations of the Slavic World to the Romano-German World," which was republished many times as a separate book, making him a world-famed thinker, historian-philosopher, and culturologist. In this book, he disproved of the idea of existence of the commonality of all mankind/civilizations. He developed a conception of exclusive "cultural-historical types" of mankind, that is tribes and nations united by common language and culture, with their own civilization that could not be passed to another "type," or borrowed from it. For Danilevsky, mankind was abstraction, and the nation was reality.

Danilevsky determined 4 categories of cultural-historical activities (religious, political, sociopolitical, and cultural) and 10 cultural-historical types (Egyptian, Chinese, Assiro-Babilonian, Jewish, Greek, Roman, Muslim, Slavic, Romano-German). He applied the biological idea of predetermined evolution of each type going through certain stages to his theory, assuming that each civilization had periods of youth, adultness, and old age; the last period would once and for all exhaust the cultural-historical type.

Danilevsky believed that the Slavic type was in youth period, in the making. In connection to this thinking, he considered the reforms of the Emperor Peter the Great as attempts to impose alien, European values on Russian culture; he stood for liberation from "paralyzing and inimical European influence." For Danilevsky, supremacy of the common cultural type (Romano-German) meant degradation. That is why, he thought, unification of the Slavic world was more important than freedom, science, and education. To fulfill this plan, it was necessary to create a pan-Slavic union, with the capital in Constantinople, a historical center of Eastern Christianity, headed by an Orthodox Emperor who would guarantee the cultural balance and secure against Western aggression. Here pan-Slavism by Danilevsky develops into an apology for monarchism.

Although this theory was politically engaged, it was based on Karl Baer's theory of four main types of animals and predetermined evolution within these types. It is not accidental that Danilevsky limited the terms of existence of these types and that their development looked like ontogenesis.

Danilevsky died on November 7, 1889 in Caucasus, Tiflis (modern Tbilisi, the capital of Georgia), and was buried in his own estate, Mshanka, on the south coast of Crimea, directly opposite Constantinople.

Danilevsky's Works

The works of Danilevsky gave rise to lively discussions in Russian literature. Those philosophers who adhered to the position of teleology and idealism took the part of Danilevsky, one of them being Nikolaj N. Strakhov (1886, 1889). At the same time, he was criticized by Alexander S. Famintsin (1889) and Kliment A. Timirjazev (1887, 1889). The articles of these two leading biologists among supporters of evolutionary theory produced a strong impression on the scientific community and even convinced it that objections to Darwinism were, using the words of Nikolaj A. Kholodkovsky (1889), "absolutely groundless." Later, however, one could find the ideas of Danilevsky in the theory of nomogenesis by Lev S. Berg (1922), historical biogenetics by Dmitrij N. Sobolev (1924), typostrophism by Otto Schindewolf (1936, 1950), works by Pierre Teilhard de Chardin (1965), and some other contemporary supporters of orthogenetic and saltationistic conceptions of evolution.

The book *Russia and Europe* also provoked heated controversy. It was spoken about enthusiastically by world-famed writer Fyodor M. Dostoevsky, who considered himself a student of Danilevsky, and philosophers-Slavophils Konstantin S. Aksakov and Konstantin N. Leontjev. The famous writer Leo N. Tolstoy was also sympathetic with this work. On the other hand, representatives of the "western wing," historians and sociologists Nikolaj I. Kareev, Piotr N. Miljukov, and Nikolaj M. Mikhailovsky, criticized the book using sharp words. Nevertheless, the book became a prototype for subsequent conceptions of exclusive, cyclically developing cultural types: the two-volume edition of *The Decline of Europe,* by Oswald Spengler (1918–1922), and the 12-volume edition of *A Study of History,* by Arnold J. Toynbee (1934–1961). Nowadays, the influence of the book can be traced in the theory of the multipolar world and antiglobalism.

It is worth emphasizing that biological ideas about the existence of certain stages in the development of civilizations were later used to give proof to different philogerontical theories and explain that any taxon passes the same stages of youth, adultness, old age, and death, as an individual. Interestingly, there was a visible correlation between the increasing popularity of these theories in biology and philosophy and the crises of the 20th century, such as wars, revolutions, and economic disaster.

— *Eduard I. Kolchinsky*

See also **Biological Anthropology and Neo-Darwinism; Darwinism, Social; Evolution, Models of; Teleology**

Further Readings

Danilevsky, N. (1995). *Russia and Europe.* St. Petersburg, Russia: Glagol.
Toynbee, A. J. (1935–1961). *A study of history* (12 vols.). London: Oxford University Press.

 # DAOISM

Daoism is a Chinese way of thinking that is best understood as being composed of two traditions, philosophical Daoism and religious Daoism. Both traditions are primarily derived from texts of archaic antiquity. Among them are the *Dao De Jing* (Classic of the Dao and Its Power) and the *Zhuang Zi* (Master Zhuang).

As the major inspiration and authoritative source of Daoism, the *Dao De Jing* is a combination of poetry, philosophical reflection, and mystical speculation that is composed of some 5,200 words. Given its present form, this classic was probably completed in the third or fourth century BC. However, its original title is *Lao Zi* ("Old Master"), which attributes the authorship to a legendary figure who was born around 602 BC. It is likely that a good part of the book was edited from much older texts at the time of rendition and put in the mouth of *Lao Zi*. Profound and abstruse, this philosophical treatise is the most translated of all classics, next to the Bible.

Central to Daoism is the notion of *Dao* (*Tao* as in non-pinyin romanization, which also yields *Taoism*). The profound revelation that grew out of Daoist elaboration on the *Dao* or "the Way" is the key to a real appreciation of the Chinese worldview on the universe, society, and life. It impacted all other Chinese belief systems, including Confucianism. In expounding the meaning of the *Dao*, Daoism and Confucianism ran through Chinese thought like two powerful streams side by side until modern times. If Confucianism concentrates on social order and active duties, Daoism focuses on individual life and tranquility. While the former preaches conformity to a man-made social order, the latter emphasizes conformity to natural order. Daoism contrasts Confucian worldliness with a transcendental spirit that is by no means escapist. Not only does Daoism have a social, political ideology that rivals that of Confucianism, but its discourse also goes much deeper into the Way of life.

Philosophical Daoism

Two themes stand out in the *Dao De Jing*—life and government. Philosophical Daoism is concerned with how to live a meaningful life and institute a sage rulership. In addressing the issues that arise from these two questions, Daoism subscribes to a philosophical approach that puts more faith in nature than in humanity. This naturalism finds expression in a number of principles whereby the *Dao* is to be discovered, appreciated, and followed.

Simplicity of Life

To live simply and plainly is to exist close to nature, where the *Dao* rules without any interference from man-made social, moral, and political orders. It is a state in which people have direct access to the observation of the Way. Simplicity of life, or *pu*, also purifies the mind so that it becomes a clean mirror to capture everything clearly and enhance the reflection of the *Dao* in human awareness. For the mind to be purified, however, it must be emptied of social self, traditional wisdom, and mundane desires. Therefore, the *Dao De Jing* urges people to "return to the state of childhood," "discard wisdom," and be "free of desires."

Lao Zi is literally "old child" in Chinese. In fact, all humans are believed to be the children of the *Dao*. To discover the *Dao*, people should return to their natural conditions as found in infancy or childhood. The journey is not going to be easy. It involves self-effacement and the practice of asceticism before a state of tranquility that is free from desires, passions, and moral distortions can be restored. The *Dao De Jing* condemns all learning that leads people to become self-important and impose their will on nature; the only learning encouraged is of the laws of nature.

Simplicity of life is the gateway to sagehood. A sage is a Holy Person (*shengren*) who identifies with the *Dao*, knows its principles, respects its power, and behaves accordingly. The liberation gained from such union with the *Dao* caught the seminal imagination of Zhuang Zi (ca. 369–286 BC), another major founder of philosophical Daoism. The opening chapter of the *Zhuang Zi* exalts the ecstasies of transcending the limited experience of man, the narrow bounds of conventional knowledge, the fragility of man-made standards, and the artificiality of logic to roam freely across the universe with the Creator. Notwithstanding the poetic license of the *Zhuang Zi* to fantasies, Daoist sagehood is naturalistic, stressing *Dao*-centered ethics. The *Dao De Jing* is scornful of the human-centered Confucian ethics, such as humanity or benevolence. Human behavior becomes moral if and only if it acts in harmony with the will of nature. Humanity has no place in Daoist morality, as natural operations are not meant to feel benevolent or show preference for humans.

The Relativity of Opposites

How does *Dao* operate? Attention is called to the workings of *yin* and *yang*, which generate everything in the universe. This process is known as the "*Dao* with name," meaning the *Dao* manifested in operation. It is important to note that as two material forces, *yin* and *yang* are polar opposites. The former is typically feminine, dark, cold, and debilitating, whereas the latter is typically masculine, bright, warm, and invigorating. Their opposition is self-evident. But in Chapter 2 of the *Dao De Jing,* it is stressed that no opposition is absolute and that invariably, opposites are complementary:

Difficult and easy complete each other;

Long and short contrast each other;

High and low distinguish each other;

Sound and voice harmonize with each other;

Front and back follow each other.

Much as the opposites contrast categorically, they also are in a symbiotic relationship. What is *difficult* is meaningful only relative to what is *easy,* and vice versa. By the same token, *front* and *back* have meaning only in relation to each other. Semantically, there is mutual causality between two opposites. One cannot exist meaningfully without the other. It is in this sense that the opposites "complete" and "follow" each other as much as they "contrast" and "distinguish" each other.

From the mutual causality of opposites, the doctrine "relativity of opposites" is inferred. Each state of being is relative in the sense that it will change to its opposite in due time, just as day is bound to become night and the young are bound to grow old. Because everything in the universe eventually produces its opposite, cyclic change is characteristic of the way that *Dao* operates. Furthermore, opposites coexist rather than exclude each other during cyclic change. To bring about prosperity in life or society is not a nonstop drive to replace *yin* with *yang.* Rather, it involves achieving a combination of *yang* and *yin* in their right proportions so that harmony will prevail. Then again, there are elements or seeds of discordance in harmony, and sooner or later they will grow, causing harmony to change to its opposite: dissonance.

With the doctrine known as the "relativity of opposites," Daoism entertains a dynamic worldview, recognizing that nothing stands still and that the whole universe is in a constant flux of change. The relativity doctrine is also incorporated into the Daoist cosmogony. It is assumed that the universe began as a primordial mass and took shape only after the two material forces *yin* and *yang* were born and started to interact in the presence of *qi,* or "cosmic energy," to generate everything in the universe. As the evolution of the universe followed the laws of a natural *Dao,* it had nothing to do with divine creation. Were it not for the Daoist belief of cyclic change that creates an impasse for the metamorphosis of species, this cosmogony would be more in tune with evolutionary thinking.

Being and Non-Being

The *Dao* is knowable by the human mind. But it exists in two forms: the *Dao* that can be named and the *Dao* that is nameless. The former is *being,* and the latter is *non-being.* As being, the *Dao* with name is phenomenal, gives form to everything, and lends itself to observation and naming. As non-being, the *Dao* without name is obscure to observation and defies naming and description. In the opening chapter, the *Dao De Jing* remarks:

The *Dao* that can be told of is not the eternal *Dao;*

The name that can be named is not the eternal name;

The nameless is the origin of Heaven and Earth;

The named is the mother of all things.

Therefore let there always be non-being, so we may perceive its subtlety,

And let there always be being, so we can observe its outcomes.

Everything under Heaven is born of being, and being is born of non-being.

Attainment of the *Dao* boils down to grasping the principles and laws of non-being that accompanied the beginning of time and are eternal. In non-being lies the ultimate reality, which resembles a void, seemingly empty but replete with contents and potentials. The principles and laws of non-being are deeply embedded in the products of being. This is why the *Dao De Jing* goes on to note, "Being and non-being produce each other."

The dichotomy of being and non-being became a focal point when scholars pored over philosophical Daoism to look for its "affinity" with Confucianism during the Period of Disunity (221–589). In an influential commentary, Wang Pi (226–249) argued that non-being was actually pure or imperceptible being. Known as "Mystery Learning," such revisionist attempts are held to be beside the point by some contemporary scholars. Confucianism seeks to find a constant *dao* that guides social behavior infallibly. But in Daoist thought, a constant *dao* requires constant naming. Since there are many possible standards, it is arbitrary to pick out one of them as the constant guide to naming. The Daoist notion of non-being is not necessarily asocial. Rather, it rejects any arbitrary *dao* in favor of a natural *dao* that is truly profound.

Nonaction

The *Dao* is to be translated into behavior through the sage, who makes an ideal ruler and practices non-action (*wuwei*). Nonaction means taking no action against the flow of Nature. Almost a third of the *Dao De Jing* is devoted to the art of government and sage rulership. Repeatedly, the role of nonaction in statesmanship is defined as "acting without competing (against the will of nature)," and the text of the *Dao De Jing* also ends its last chapter on this note. If Daoist nonaction is meant to refrain from interference in the operations of nature, it does not mean withdrawal from society.

In practice, nonaction is symbolized by the flow of water, which takes the path of least resistance. Meddlesome behavior is pointless in the sense that other than endangering oneself, it achieves nothing in its attempt to change the natural law. Therefore, the sage ruler "governs without governing" and delegates the duties to his ministers, who are expected to do the governing by rejecting arbitrary and calculated decisions in favor of spontaneity (*ziran*). Under this laissez faire approach, decision making is made in harmony with the *Dao,* interference in the natural course of things is minimized, and the government is kept lean.

The Daoist advocacy of nonaction had its precursor in the political ideology attributed to the mythical *Huangdi* (Yellow Emperor). In recognition of contributions from both *Huang Di* and *Lao Zi*, the doctrine of nonaction is known as the *Huang-Lao* art of government. It was adopted by the early rulers of the Han Dynasty (206 BC–AD 220) and had a considerable impact on the Legalists, who, in arguing for the rule of law, agreed that the ruler should be detached, but remain perfectly aware and responsive.

Religious Daoism

As an indigenous religion, Daoism has its roots in the classical religion of the Zhou period (1122–221 BC), which featured popular practices of shamanism, ancestor worship, occult arts, magical cults, and the veneration of Heaven as the supreme power commanding a pantheon of deities.

However, Daoism did not emerge as a voluntary and organized religion until the 2nd century, when it received formative impact from two peasant uprisings. One was the rebellion of "Great Peace Daoism" (*Taiping Dao*), which broke out in AD 184 in what is now Hopei Province of northern China. It united a large number of communities under a Daoist hierarchy of governance. This politico-religious movement quickly spread to a large part of the country under the leadership of its founder Zhang Jue (ca. AD140–188). Known as the "Yellow Turbans" because of its distinguishing headdress, the rebel army was eventually crushed. The year AD 189 saw another rebellion erupt under Zhang Daoling or Zhang Ling (34–156), who had founded the Five-Bushel Sect of Daoism in Sichuan. This movement soon came to be known as "Celestial Masters Daoism" (*Tianshi Dao*) and was able to establish a local rule that would last over two decades.

The Rise of an Organized Religion

Unlike the classic religion that was communal, Daoism was a voluntary religion. Its membership was no longer ascribed by inherited affiliation with a community, but based on voluntary conversion of the individual believer. In the midst of the two aforementioned rebellions, Daoism was transformed into an organized religion complete with a system of theology, a set of teachings and rituals of its own, and a hierarchical priesthood.

The "Yellow Turbans" were inspired by the theology of the *Taiping Jing* (Scripture of Great Peace), which prophesized a messianic and millenarian restoration of the utopian reign of Great Peace. "Celestial Masters Daoism" developed its theology based on the *Dao De Jing* and a revelation from *Lao Zi* that preached universal brotherhood in opposition to the existent social order. Its local rule was administered by a hierarchy of priest-officials. As they regularly held masses for spiritual purification, faith healing, and the redemption of sin, a liturgical tradition of the community was initiated. Individual ritualistic practices included the performance of magic cults that promised invincibility in the battlefield and the exercises of dietary and sexual hygiene that promised to deliver meritorious men from the finality of death to immortality. When "Celestial Masters Daoism" surrendered its local rule in AD 215, it was allowed to disseminate its teachings peacefully, and its hierarchy of Daoist priesthood was officially recognized in China.

With the rise of Daoism as an organized religion, its philosophical stock was profoundly changed. Different magical, religious, and philosophical traditions were grafted to it. This process featured two strategies: a syncretism with borrowings from rival belief systems and a continual accommodation of indigenous practices. After all the dust had settled, religious Daoism came to possess three distinct dimensions: mystical, liturgical, and canonical.

Mystical Dimension

Religious Daoism claims efficacy in providing direct connection with the supernatural beings or cosmic forces. Technically, its practices can be divinatory, respiratory, gymnastic, meditative, hygienic, sexual, or alchemical. Functionally, its aim is either to enact communication with the supernatural or to nourish life. A repertoire of mystical practices was developed to cater to the desire to have one's life energy preserved and nourished. These practices, in turn, are attributable to two beliefs.

One relates to the Daoist philosophy that urges a return to the state of childlike simplicity and the land of the *Dao*. But this spiritual quest is reinterpreted as a way to recover life energy. Using meditative or other means, Daoist adepts envisage the process of their gestation as a new embryo to their rebirth as an infant. By so doing, it is believed, one's lost energy would be recovered. A second belief relates the human body as microcosm to the universe as macrocosm. Since one is the replica of the other, the human body can rejuvenate itself as nature does. In both cases, life thrives on the concentration of *qi*, or cosmic energy. Mystical Daoist practices are supposed to provide a way of enriching life-rejuvenating *qi* and helping the human body to tap into its sources.

The quest for immortality is an epitome of Daoist mysticism. In Chinese, an immortal is called *xian* or *xianren* (divine-human), who could choose to remain invisible to the human eye or appear in mortal form to enlighten the virtuous and punish the wicked. There were two approaches to the attainment of immortality, external alchemy and internal alchemy. The end product of external alchemy was an elixir made primarily from gold and cinnabar. External alchemy gave way to internal alchemy during the Song Dynasty (AD 960–1279). An internal elixir was to be generated by

the inner circulation of *qi* according to the Daoist microcosmology of the body. In a meditative mood, one circulated one's *qi* in such a way that it went through channels supposed to connect the vital parts of the body. This would enhance one's Essence (*jing*) and Spirit (*shen*) to bring about longevity of life. To enrich one's *qi*, the observance of calisthenic exercises and dietary practices must also be included.

Daoist meditation is typically employed to achieve a mystic union with one's true Self: the inner child who has direct access to the *Dao* and cosmic forces. The skill is passed on from master to disciple through an apprenticeship that is based on teaching without words. The transmission of instructions is intuitive, going from mind to mind without the intervention of rational argumentation in conceptual terms. This antilanguage teaching is thought to have inspired the *Chan* (Zen) tradition, a religious school that shuns scripture learning and subscribes to intuitive meditation as a principal means to attain enlightenment. *Chan* is a transliteration of the Sanskrit *dhyāna*, but its tradition is distinctively Chinese. Drawing on Daoist mysticism, this religious school emerged as a reaction to the scholastic and formalistic preoccupations of Mahayana Buddhism and contributed to the rise of *Chan* Buddhism subsequently.

Liturgical Dimension

The two main functions of the Daoist master are the protection of the mundane world against the attacks of evil spirits and the performance of rituals on behalf of individuals, families, and communities. Both functions are liturgical. They turn religious Daoism into the liturgical organization of the country and make its rituals and rites most visible at the grassroots level of society.

In the Daoist theology and liturgy, the highest divinity consists of five gods: the "Three Pure Ones" (a triad of the Heavenly Venerables of the Primordial Origin, the Numinous Treasure, and the *Dao* and its Power), Jade Emperor (who is the Supreme Celestial Sovereign), and his deputy, Purple Empyrean Emperor. The basis for the Daoist priest's control over these gods and a pantheon of deities is a form of "name magic." Assisted with a performance of ritualistic chanting and dancing, he can summon and dismiss the divinities by virtue of his knowledge of their names, descriptions, and functions.

Symbolism is an integral part of the Daoist liturgy. One most important symbol is *fu,* the talisman or magical charm that is enacted into efficacy by cabalistic writing. A sort of moral contract is implied with the writing of *fu*. People pledge not to sin in return for the assurance that they would never become ill or fall victim to evil spirits. Another important symbol is *dou*, meaning "bushel" or "container," which symbolizes the Big Dipper constellation and, by extension, the Great Ultimate *(taiji)*. As the Dipper is a heavenly clock marking the cycle of days, seasons, and major turning points in life, it is ritualistically potent and often invoked symbolically in Daoist dancing. Representing the Great Ultimate, the symbol is present everywhere, on the Daoist's sword and crown and in the naming of vital bodily parts. Turning to the Daoist *dou*, it is a receptacle in which ritual instruments are purified, and votive oil and rice are consecrated. Then there is the "Step of Yu." Legend has it that this dance enabled Yu the Great, a legendary hero, to gain command over spirits of nature when he was out there saving his people from the Deluge. Through this dance, the Daoist outlines a celestial constellation to take possession of its power.

The Daoist liturgy offers two major services, *zhai* (fasts) and *jiao* (offerings). Each may last 3 days or longer, and both have four components: rituals for the consecration of ritual space, rituals for obtaining merits through penitence (rites of fasting), rituals of communion and covenant (rites of offering), and rituals for the dispersal of sacred space. The rituals involved may differ in contents from *zhai* to *jiao*. The *zhai* service is more somber, for it is designed to cleanse the living of their sins or to deliver the souls of the dead and bring them salvation as a part of the funerary rite. The *jiao* service is always communal and designed to petition for favors, such as, rainfall in time of drought, or offer thanksgiving for favors received. Invariably, it also performs rituals to appease lonely spirits and hungry ghosts lest they harass the living.

It is small wonder that exorcism has a role in both *zhai* and *jiao* services. The priest who officiates at this rite undergoes self-transformation to become one with the Dao. Then, he takes a symbolic journey to the heavens for an audience with the gods. To overpower demons, he summons the assistance of deities and dances the "Step of Yu," in synch with the counting of his thumb on finger joints, and brandishes his sword to make the decisive strike. When embedded in *zhai* and *jiao*, all this is done to the accompaniment of acolytes burning incense, chanting hymns, and playing instruments.

Canonical Dimension

Religious Daoism has a classical canon that provides a standard of orthodoxy and a basis for Daoist religious practices. The Daoist Canon is immense, containing 5,385 volumes under about 1,500 titles. Only three complete sets of the 1445 edition of this Canon appear to have survived the vicissitudes of time and the anti-Daoist rule of the Qing Dynasty (AD 1644–1911). Each set has an addendum that was published in 1607. The Canon is entitled *Daozang*, in emulation of the Buddhist Tripitaka *Sanzang*. First compiled by Lu Xiujing (AD 406–477) in AD 471, it was the response of Daoism to the growing challenge and competition of Buddhism. The corpora of the Daoist Canon are divided into "Three Grottoes" and "Four Supplements."

The first Grotto is based on texts of the Mao Shan School or *Shangqing* (Supreme Purity) tradition, and the most significant of these texts is the visionary experiences revealed to and transcribed by Yang Xi between AD 364 and AD 370. The second Grotto features scriptures of the *Lingbao* tradition, *Lingbao* (Sacred Treasure) being the Daoist name of "holy books." This school incorporated the psalmody of holy books into the liturgical ritual in the belief that deities, who were not pure enough to behold holy books, had heard them recited by the Heavenly Venerable of the Primordial Origin, the highest anthropomorphic emanation of the *Dao*. The third Vault is built around scriptures of the *Sanhuang* tradition, *Sanhuang* (Three Sovereigns) being the cosmic lords of heaven, earth, and humans. The Three Grottos are taken to represent different stages of initiation that form a progression of increasing spiritual purity from the *Sanhuang* to the *Shangqing*.

Each Grotto of the Canon is divided into 12 sections so that the basic texts, such as talismans, commentaries, diagrams, genealogies, and rituals, are grouped under separate categories. But over the centuries, there were substantial departures from this ideal arrangement. The confusion worsened when more texts were included, and the catalogue was edited and reedited, not to mention the vicissitudes that the Canon went through in the course of history. It gave rise to the well-known lack of organization in the Daoist Canon.

The Four Supplements were added in the 6th century, containing works related to the established traditions, except for the last Supplement. At the core of each of the first three Supplements are the *Dao De*

Jing, the *Taiping Jing,* and alchemical texts, respectively. The fourth Supplement is devoted to scriptures of the *Zhengyi* (Orthodox One) school, which is the oldest Daoist religious tradition dating back to Celestial Masters Daoism of the 2nd century. However, a large amount of materials collected in the Daoist Canon are neither spiritual nor religious. Their inclusion merely underscored Daoism as an indigenous religion vis-à-vis Buddhism as an alien one. Among these materials is the *Bencao Gangmu* (Pharmacopoeia of the Flora), attributed to the mythical ruler *Shen Nong* (Divine Farmer). Such materials are highly valuable for research into the history of Chinese natural sciences and philosophies.

Religious Daoism and Popular Religion

Religious Daoism is often regarded as a degenerate form of philosophical Daoism. Confucian scholar-officials not only tended to equate religious Daoism with superstition but also thought that it was politically dangerous. After Daoism spread to Korea and Japan between the 4th and 7th centuries, its religious practices were put under government control. The early Daoist temples in Korea and the bureau of Daoist divination in Japan were state sponsored. Daoism never established itself as an organized religion in Korea or Japan, and its impact found expression mostly in their folk beliefs and popular religions.

Religious Daoism has a much closer tie with Chinese popular religion. Its liturgy plays an important role in the religious life of the community and in more recent decades has provided the framework that enables local cults to expand and develop in Mainland China. Through the shared use of indigenous divinatory arts, such as the *yin-yang* cosmology, the hexagrams, and the Five Elements ideology, religious Daoism has an affinity with fortune-telling, physiognomy, and geomancy. Daoist masters, for instance, are likely to be skillful geomancers. Furthermore, they readily perform rites and rituals to assist in individuals' quest of fortune, wealth, and longevity of life in this world. Nevertheless, Daoist masters seek to transcend the mundane desires themselves, and they are members of a religion that is organized and other-worldly oriented.

— *Zhiming Zhao*

See also **Buddhism; Confucianism**

Further Readings

Chan, W.-T. (1963). *A source book in Chinese philosophy.* Princeton, NJ: Princeton University Press.

de Bary, W. T. (1960). *Sources of Chinese tradition.* New York: Columbia University Press.

Dean, K. (1993). *Taoist ritual and popular cults of southeast China.* Princeton, NJ: Princeton University Press.

Hansen, C. (1992). *A Daoist theory of Chinese thought: A philosophical interpretation.* New York: Oxford University Press.

Largerwey, J. (1987). *Taoist ritual in Chinese society and history.* New York: Macmillan.

Maspero, H. (1981). *Taoism and Chinese religion* (F. A. Kierman Jr., Trans.). Amherst: University of Massachusetts Press.

Schipper, K. (1993). *The Taoist body* (K. C. Duval, Trans.). Berkeley: University of California Press.

 # DARKNESS IN EL DORADO CONTROVERSY

Late in the year 2000, an intellectual tsunami hit anthropology in America and beyond. It was generated by the controversy surrounding the publication of a book by Patrick Tierney called *Darkness in El Dorado: How Anthropologists and Journalists Devastated the Amazon.* Five years after its publication, this unprecedented controversy was still rife with debate and far from settled. Moreover, it goes to the very heart of anthropology, with broad implications for every anthropologist. Primarily, it is a matter of professional ethics and more generally, of values.

Values have been a sincere concern of various practitioners of anthropology since its beginnings about 150 years ago. For example, many anthropologists have demonstrated their humanitarian commitment through advocacy work in promoting the survival, welfare, and rights of indigenous societies struggling under the pressures of Western colonialism and the genocide, ethnocide, and ecocide often associated with it. On the other hand, to this day, many anthropologists pursue science as if it were entirely amoral and apolitical.

The largest professional organization of anthropologists in the world, the American Anthropological

Association (AAA), was established as early as 1902. However, the articulation of formal guidelines for professional ethics came decades later and grew only intermittently, through a succession of occasional declarations beginning with the brief "Resolution on Freedom of Publication," issued in December 1948; then, a more extensive "Statement on Problems of Anthropological Research and Ethics," in March 1967; next, the "Principles of Professional Responsibility," in May 1971; and, most recently, the "Code of Ethics," in June 1998. It was not until 1971 that the AAA finally established a standing Committee on Ethics, although by 1996, its function was reduced mostly to education. Usually, any concern with professional ethics within American anthropology has been more reactive than proactive, and more a matter of defensive maneuvering than constructively grappling with the issues head-on. Ethical concerns, and sometimes even actions, arise mostly during periods when scandals or controversies erupt, especially if they reach the public to threaten the image of the profession; but soon they decline, if not disappear completely, except if a publication record remains and/or through the research of historians. Many of these tendencies are exhibited in the most recent ethical crisis in the AAA, although it goes to the very heart of the discipline, with some enduring implications for every anthropologist.

This crisis exploded in late 2000, only partially subsided by the middle of 2002, and then erupted again in early 2005. It is characterized by unprecedented magnitude, complexity, difficulty, and ugliness. (An extensive archive is available on the Douglas W. Hume Web site.) The crisis arose in response to investigative journalist Patrick Tierney's book, with its provocative title and subtitle, *Darkness in El Dorado: How Anthropologists and Journalists Devastated the Amazon.* His painstakingly detailed book is based on more than a decade of field and archival research. Tierney tried to document numerous and diverse allegations of violations of professional ethics and even of human rights by Napoleon A. Chagnon and his associates in their field research with the Yanomami. Some points in the book were challenged after investigations by various individuals and organizations. Nevertheless, many other points were confirmed by the AAA Task Force on Darkness in El Dorado and other researchers.

This task force was established at a meeting of the AAA Executive Board, February 3–4, 2001. The AAA had no choice but to initiate a serious inquiry because of the firestorm that erupted around the book in the international media and cyberspace, which became a public relations disaster. (Tierney's publication received several prominent awards, from the *Boston Globe, New York Times,* and *Los Angeles Times* as well as a finalist for the National Book Award.) After more than a year of systematic and meticulous inquiry into selected issues on May 18, 2002, the task force issued a final report that subsequently was posted on the Web site. Members of the task force included Janet M. Chernela, Fernando Coronil, Raymond B. Hames, Jane H. Hill (Chair and former AAA president), Trudy R. Turner, and Joe E. Watkins. However, at a late stage of the inquiry, Hames resigned to avoid any appearance of a conflict of interest, because he was a former student of Chagnon and is a long-term associate in his research, grants, and publications.

This scandalous controversy pivots around Chagnon, who accumulated a total of about 5 years in the field with Yanomami, in the Venezuelan Amazon, over a period of nearly three decades, starting in 1964. Through various publications and films, he garnered a reputation in the United States and beyond as the primary ethnographer in the study of the Yanomami, whom he depicted as one of the most traditional "primitive" cultures surviving in the whole world. However, usually ignored is the fact that several other anthropologists lived with the Yanomami much longer, such as Kenneth R. Good for more than a dozen years, and Jacques Lizot for about a quarter of a century.

Unlike many other anthropologists who have worked with the Yanomami in Venezuela and Brazil, Chagnon persistently characterized them as "the fierce people," in a manner reminiscent of Thomas Hobbes's caricature of "savages" with nasty and brutish lifeways. Many of the other anthropologists who have lived with the Yanomami, such as Good and Lizot, have opined that Chagnon became obsessed with the violence in that society and exaggerated it to the point of gross distortion. Moreover, Leda Leitao Martins in a book edited by Robert Borofsky exposes irrefutable evidence that this image was publicized in the Brazilian media and then used by some unscrupulous government and military officials as part of the rationalization for their efforts to undermine the rights of the Yanomami to their ancestral territory. This became, and remains, a major ethical issue, since Chagnon failed to speak out about the misuse of his statements and to defend the human rights of the Yanomami in Brazil, according to the Brazilian Anthropological Association and other critics. Moreover, after some 4 years of controversy, Chagnon has yet to really speak out in his own defense, although he has had numerous opportunities to do so.

When the controversy over this and many other serious allegations in Tierney's book exploded in the world media, a small but vocal group associated with Chagnon quickly came to his defense. Among his defenders in various degrees and ways are James S. Boster, Lee Cronk, Irven DeVore, Jeffrey D. Ehrenreich, Kent V. Flannery, Robin Fox, Thomas A. Gregor, Daniel R. Gross, Raymond B. Hames, Kim Hill, William G. Irons, Jane B. Lancaster, A. Magdalena Hurtado, Andrew D. Merriwether, Stuart Plattner, Lionel Tiger, John Tooby, and Trudy R. Turner. Some of Chagnon's defenders have repeatedly disseminated misinformation and disinformation, even when repeatedly challenged with contradictory facts. Some defenders, like Gregor and Hurtado, have asserted that the controversy and AAA inquiry ignore the sources of the more serious suffering among the Yanomami. However, Tierney's book was mostly about the alleged abuses committed by Chagnon and his associates, and the executive board charged the task force to conduct an inquiry about them. Other avenues within the AAA, such as the Committee for Human Rights, have taken action repeatedly, although Hurtado disparaged that in an earlier article in the March 1990 *AAA Anthropology News*. Also, the Pro-Yanomami Commission, an anthropological advocacy organization in Brazil, has been the most effective organization in addressing Yanomami health problems, this, in collaboration with the French group Doctors Without Borders.

Defenders of Chagnon have accused his critics of being merely jealous, failed anthropologists, anti-science, antievolution, antisociobiology, and/or post-modernists. Among the critics of Chagnon who have worked most closely with Yanomami for many years are Bruce Albert, Gale Goodwin Gomez, Kenneth R. Good, Jacques Lizot, and Alcida R. Ramos. Other critics of Chagnon over the decades variously include Nelly Arvelo Jimenez, Timothy Asch, Gerald D. Berreman, Manuela Carneiro da Cunha, R. Brian Ferguson, Carolyn Fluehr-Lobban, Clifford Geertz, Marvin Harris, Timothy Ingold, David H. P. Maybury-Lewis, Laura Nader, Jacob Pandian, Linda

Rabben, Marshall D. Sahlins, Nancy Scheper-Hughes, Leslie E. Sponsel, and Terence S. Turner. The publications and reputations of these various critics do not accurately reflect the accusations of Chagnon's defenders. More important, many of the points these critics raised over a period of three decades never attracted serious attention from the AAA and many individual anthropologists until Tierney summarized them in his book. Had the various criticisms been given serious consideration by the profession and Chagnon as they arose, then Tierney's investigation and the subsequent public scandal and ensuing embarrassment to the AAA and profession might well have been avoided.

The main political tactic of Chagnon's defenders has been to distract attention from questions about the abuses of professional ethics, and thereby violation of Yanomami human rights in some of the instances, by focusing mostly on the causes of the measles epidemic during the 1968 expedition of Chagnon and his associates. During that expedition, the scientists attempted to continue to conduct research despite a rapidly spreading epidemic of measles. Geneticist James V. Neel was the leader of the expedition. He sacrificed only a small portion of the research time for himself and the other medical doctors on the team to administer some limited health care to sick and dying Yanomami. The defenders claim that this medical attention saved numerous Yanomami lives. Probably it did so, although this has never been documented. However, as some critics have pointed out, by the same reasoning, probably many more lives would have been saved had the medical doctors fully honored their Hippocratic Oath and along with other team members temporarily suspended all of the data collection to give their full time and attention to the needs of the Yanomami in this dire medical emergency. In any case, although by now more than 4 years have transpired since Tierney's book, most of the defenders of Chagnon have yet to seriously address most of the questions about the violation of professional ethics and human rights.

To date, the AAA and profession in general have yet to adequately address many of the allegations made by Tierney. Yet as mentioned before, many of his allegations are not new by any means. Only when Tierney summarized and amplified them and added others in his book did the AAA and profession in general begin to be concerned. For instance, 5 years before Tierney's book, in a meticulous systematic analysis of the political history of the Yanomami, R. Brian Ferguson asserted that Chagnon increased intervillage aggression by giving large concentrations of steel tools to selected villages in payment for cooperation in his data collection during brief visits. No uproar followed. Later, Tierney discussed this issue, but the task force neglected to investigate it, even though it was among his most serious allegations, and the fifth of the five general allegations that the executive board requested be pursued in their inquiry.

There has also been much constructive discussion and debate among other anthropologists who were able to transcend the particulars, including any personal differences and animosities, to deal forthrightly with the serious implications for the Yanomami as well as the broader ramifications for professional practice and ethics. Some of this discussion even transpired within the AAA. For instance, a very useful set of six briefing papers developed by the Committee on Ethics is available on the association's Web site. A far more expansive and useful arena for discussion on this controversy is the Web site for Public Anthropology developed by Borofsky.

The top leadership of the AAA claimed that the association did not have any formal procedures to legally sanction, morally censure, or reprimand an American anthropologist for serious violations of ethics, unlike the professions of law and medicine. Nevertheless, in late spring 2002, the AAA Executive Board publicly denounced Chagnon's proven violations of professional ethics and abuses of the human rights of the Yanomami by accepting the final report of the AAA Task Force on El Dorado. The AAA disapproved of Chagnon's conduct regarding at least five matters: (1) He failed to speak out against misuses by others of his negative characterization of the Yanomami as "the fierce people" to block the Yanomami reserve in Brazil and thereby undermine their ancestral territorial, land, and resource rights. (In fact, this reflects an ethical principle already enunciated at least as early as 1948 in the AAA "Resolution on Freedom of Publication"); (2) he failed to obtain adequate informed consent for taking blood and other biological samples from the Yanomami, and he failed to honor the promise that these would provide future medical benefits; (3) he made unfounded and damaging public attacks, including in the Brazilian press, on Yanomami leaders and spokespersons as well as on advocacy anthropologists and nongovernmental organizations assisting the Yanomami and promoting their human rights, this, in the midst of the catastrophic illegal invasion of gold miners into the southern territory of the Yanomami; (4) he collaborated with corrupt politicians in Venezuela engaged in criminal activities designed to create a much-reduced Yanomami reserve to facilitate illegal mining and to develop a private territory for his own research; And (5) he repeatedly transported groups of outsiders with Venezuelan public funds into Yanomami communities without proper quarantine precautions, thereby risking and probably causing outbreaks of serious illnesses among the Yanomami.

This final report and the controversy in general had at least seven positive effects: (1) The AAA proved to be capable of carrying out an inquiry into violations of its Code of Ethics by particular individuals and their specific actions, despite initial denials by the leadership and partisans of the alleged violators; (2) an aroused and engaged membership overcame attempts by the AAA leadership to whitewash, cover up, and otherwise divert the investigation. For instance, the AAA administration was forced to provide a Web page on the association's Web site for open discussion following the release of the preliminary report of the task force, from February 10 to April 19, 2002 (that report was removed from the Web site after the final report was posted); (3) the release of a public document by a research unit of professional colleagues reporting findings of unethical conduct negated the protestations that the AAA could not apply meaningful sanctions (at the time of this writing, that report is being challenged by a referendum to rescind it introduced by Gregor and Gross for a vote on the March ballot of the AAA); (4) the misrepresentation of ethnographic and historical reality in the service of an anthropologist's theories that demean the Yanomami culture and people was held to have negative consequences that fall under the Code of Ethics; (5) the responsibility of anthropologists to speak out publicly against uses of their work by others to damage the interests of their research subjects was affirmed; (6) it was explicitly recognized that science, as an anthropological project, not only deals with objective facts and building theory, but is a social activity with effects on the research subjects and host community that may have ethical implications; and (7) a more general constructive outcome of the controversy has been a flurry of several edited books on professional ethics in anthropology. However, some contain contents that further propagate misinformation and disinformation, thereby generating additional ethical problems.

It should also be noted that other inquiries into Tierney's allegations were conducted by the American Society of Human Genetics, the International Genetic Epidemiology Society, the National Academy of Sciences, the Society for Visual Anthropology, and overseas, by a medical team of the Federal University of Rio de Janeiro in Brazil and a special commission of the Venezuelan government. However, these inquiries were much more limited in scope and duration than that of the AAA; they produced conflicting conclusions regarding the few allegations by Tierney that they pursued; they did not take into account the AAA inquiry, since they were conducted and reported prior to the release of the final report of the task force; and the inquiry in Venezuela remains incomplete and therefore inconclusive. Albert edited the report in Brazil, and the others can be found through links at the Web sites of the AAA, Chagnon, and Hume.

Another central figure in this controversy besides Chagnon has remained almost completely silent in the years following the initial explosion of discussion and debate: Tierney. Various inquiries have exposed problems with many points in his book, although many other points have been confirmed. To date, Tierney has not addressed all of the problems by revising the book for a new third edition, although this may be forthcoming. Science, academia, and other fields progress through a cumulative process of identifying and correcting errors, discovering gaps and addressing them, noting weaknesses in an argument and strengthening them, and so on. Nevertheless, undoubtedly Tierney has made a major contribution to anthropology by generating ethical awareness, concern, discussion, and debate in the profession like never before. It is embarrassing that the catalyst came from outside of the profession and that this transformation has been obstructed by some of Chagnon's defenders and by the apparent apathy of a silent majority.

In 1996, more than 4 years before the El Dorado controversy exploded, Myron Perez Glazer asserted that any anthropologist genuinely concerned with professional ethics must inquire about the ethics of power, reciprocity, respect, and accountability. In his perceptive review of professional ethics in anthropology, Glazer raises these penetrating questions: Are researchers invariably exploiting the people they study, and if so, how can this be minimized? Do the subjects benefit from the research in ways that they themselves consider meaningful and fair? Does the researcher adequately respect the integrity of the subjects' culture, avoid undue interference, and minimize disturbance? How are anthropologists held accountable for their behavior, research, and publications?

The above and many other ethical questions have yet to be adequately explored, let alone resolved, in the case of the controversy over Tierney's multitude of diverse allegations. However, a new book is by far the most thorough, penetrating, balanced, and fair assessment of the entire controversy. The editor, Robert Borofsky, provides an overview not only of the controversy but also of its broader implications and ramifications. This is followed by a series of detailed roundtable discussions by six authors who have had various lengths and types of experience with the Yanomami and who reflect the opposing sides in the controversy: Bruce Albert, Raymond B. Hames, Kim Hill, Leda Leitao Martins, John F. Peters, and Terence S. Turner. The book is also unique in its pedagogical devices, which assist students and other readers in wrestling with the numerous and diverse questions and issues involved in this convoluted controversy. This book is intended to generate some genuine deep soul-searching in the profession and perhaps even some fundamental transformations. Meanwhile, the Yanomami continue to suffer from threats to their land and resource base as well as disease and epidemics, among other serious problems. Borofsky writes that any royalties from the book will go to a health fund for the Yanomami, a very rare ethical consideration that more anthropologists might well emulate.

This unprecedented scandalous controversy will probably simmer for decades and occasionally boil over, and then subside, like others such as the supposed hoax involving the Tasaday in the Philippines. In any case, by now, there is ample literature on professional ethics, including case study material as well as on the El Dorado controversy in particular. Thus, there is absolutely no excuse for any future researcher, teacher, or student to not be familiar with these subjects and to not seriously consider various ethical guidelines in their own work. Still, seldom can anyone actually specify to an individual precisely what to do in any particular situation; that must be left to the professional maturity, moral character, and common decency of the individual. On the other hand, it should be obvious that some actions are just plain unprofessional and unethical, as revealed by instances in this El Dorado controversy.

There are many lessons to be learned from this controversy that also have much broader relevance for the profession. Perhaps the most important one of all is the lesson that many ethical problems might have been avoided had the dignity and rights of the Yanomami as humans been fully recognized and respected. Instead, clearly, they were viewed as some "primitive" survivors of the evolutionary past. Among several other places, this attitude is documented in the film by Neel, Chagnon, and Asch, called *Yanomama: A Multidisciplinary Study*.

Ultimately, the bottom line for professional ethics in anthropology, as elsewhere, is to avoid harm, and to do good. Fortunately, many other anthropologists have been ethically responsible and socially relevant in their work with the Yanomami. For instance, in 1991, President Annette Weiner and the Executive Board of the AAA established a special commission to investigate the situation of the Brazilian Yanomami. The members of this international commission included Bruce Albert, Jason Clay, Alcida Rita Ramos, Stephan Schwartzman, Anthony Seeger, and Terence S. Turner (Chair). Special consultants included Claudia Andujar, Manuela Carneiro da Cunha, and Davi Kopenawa Yanomami. The report of this Commission; an OpEd in the *New York Times* by Turner on June 18, 1991; and a letter protesting Brazilian government policy drafted by Schwartzman and signed by eight U.S. Senators, which was sent to President George H. W. Bush, all combined to influence a positive change in the policy of the Brazilian government, especially its proposed archipelago scheme. (The latter was to be a series of 19 separate minuscule reserves that would markedly increase Yanomami community size, while greatly reducing the natural resource area available to each as well as facilitate penetration of miners, together guaranteeing a catastrophe for the Yanomami.) Thus, the Yanomami commission's action may have helped to make the difference between survival and extinction of the Yanomami in Brazil. This commission was the largest single case of intervention that the AAA has ever undertaken in the defense of the cultural rights of an indigenous group. Another example of ethical responsibility is provided by Bruce Albert and Gale Goodwin Gomez, who together researched and authored a bilingual Portuguese-Yanomami health manual to aid medical personnel to more effectively communicate with Yanomami in treating their medical problems. Such initiatives demonstrate that the pursuit of scientism and careerism alone is (or should be) an anachronism that is no longer tolerable and honorable in anthropology. When people are suffering and dying from epidemic diseases and/or have other serious problems, then "research as usual" is simply untenable. Science without conscience is a monstrous pursuit in any situation. Fortunately, a tectonic shift may be in the making for professional ethics in anthropology.

— *Leslie E. Sponsel*

See also **Chagnon, Napoleon; Ethics and Anthropology; Yanomano**

Further Readings

Asch, T., Chagnon, N., & Neel, J. (1971). *Yanomama: A multidisciplinary study.* Washington, DC: U.S. Atomic Energy Commission Film.

Berwick, D. (1992). *Savages: The life and killing of the Yanomami.* London: Hodder and Stoughton.

Borofsky, R. (Ed.). (2005). *Yanomami: The fierce controversy and what we can learn from it.* Berkeley: University of California Press.

Chagnon, N. A. (1997). *Yanomamo* (5th ed.). Fort Worth, TX: Harcourt, Brace, Jovanovich.

Ferguson, R. B. (1995). *Yanomami warfare: A political history.* Santa Fe: School of American Research Press.

Fluehr-Lobban, C. (Ed.). (2003). *Ethics and the profession of anthropology: Dialogue for ethically conscious practice.* Walnut Creek, CA: Alta Mira Press.

Good, K., with D. Chanoff. (1991). *Into the heart: One man's pursuit of love and knowledge among the Yanomami.* New York: Simon & Schuster.

Gregor, T. A., & Gross. D. R. (2004). Guilt by association: The culture of accusation and the American Anthropological Association's investigation of *Darkness in El Dorado. American Anthropologist, 106,* 687–698.

Ramos, A. R. (1995). *Sanuma memories: Yanomami ethnography in times of crisis.* Madison: University of Wisconsin Press.

Salzano, F. M., & Hurtado, A. M. (Eds.). (2004). *Lost paradises and the ethics of research and publication.* New York: Oxford University Press.

Sponsel, L. E. 1998. "Yanomami: An arena of conflict and aggression in the Amazon." *Aggressive Behavior, 24*(2), 97–122.

Sponsel, L. E. (2001). Advocacy in anthropology. In N. J. Smelser & P. B. Baltes (Eds.), *International encyclopedia of social and behavioral sciences* (Vol. 1, pp. 204–206). Oxford: Pergamon Press.

Tierney, P. (2000). *Darkness in El Dorado: How anthropologists and journalists devastated the Amazon.* New York: Norton.

Tierney, P. (2000, October 9). The fierce anthropologist. *New Yorker,* 50–61.

Turner, T. (2001). *The Yanomami and the ethics of anthropological practice* (Latin American Studies Program Occasional Paper Series, Vol. 6). Ithaca, NY: Cornell University Press.

Turner, T. (Ed.). (2005). *Biological anthropology and ethics: From repatriation to genetic identity.* Albany: State University of New York Press.

DARROW, CLARENCE (1857–1938)

During the peak of his career, Clarence Darrow was the most well-known criminal lawyer in the United States. It is a fact that not one of Darrow's clients ever received the death penalty under his defense, including the infamous murder trial of Leopold and Loeb, sons of rich socialites. A brilliant maneuver at the last minute of the trial and a two-day long summation spared the two boy's lives. Also in Darrow's extensive résumé was his defense in the "trial of the century" where he defended John T. Scopes for teaching evolution and the thoughts of Charles Darwin to his students; this case has been nationally remembered as the "Monkey Trial" and was the cornerstone of the transformation from traditionalist ideals to the recognition of scientific evidence.

Clarence Darrow's origins were, at best, humble. He was born in Kingsman, Ohio, on April 18, 1857, the fifth child of Amirus and Emily Eddy Darrow. The town of Kingsman had only 400 inhabitants and was not even labeled on contemporary maps of the area. Amirus Darrow manufactured and sold furniture and was the town's undertaker. Emily Eddy Darrow played the traditional role of running the household; she died when Clarence was only 15 years old. Although the Darrows lived a meager existence in the smallest of towns, they had a love for books; they read Jefferson, Voltaire, and Thomas Paine, and this love of books was force-fed to their children.

Despite Clarence Darrow's humble origins, he went to Allegheny College, from which he graduated. After a brief time of fruitless jobs, he attended the University of Michigan Law School, where he gained his juror's doctorate in law. Darrow did badly in school, mostly because he was not disciplined; he failed to prepare for and to contend with unexciting works, which would hurt him in his future legal career. He relied on luck, inspiration, and his uncanny ability to "rise to the occasion."

Clarence Darrow laid claim to many victories in court, but none were more recognized than the "Leopold and Loeb" case and the "Monkey Trial." The Leopold and Loeb trial happened in the summer of 1924, in the city of Chicago. Richard Loeb, age 17, the son of the vice president of Sears, Roebuck, and Company, and Nathan Leopold, age 18, also the son of a wealthy family, conspired to commit the perfect murder. They lured a friend into a rented car. Once in the vehicle, the two boys proceeded to stab the young boy with a chisel and strangle him with rope. After dumping acid on the boy to make identification difficult, Loeb and Leopold disposed of the body in a swamp. After the body was disposed of, they proceeded to mail a letter to the murdered boy's family and asked for a ransom, with the promise that the boy would be unharmed. Although the young murderers thought they had pulled it off, they soon found out that their scheme was far from perfect.

Police discovered the young boy's body soon after Loeb and Leopold disposed of it, and were able to identify the body. A crucial mistake by the boys was that Nathan Leopold had dropped his spectacles where the body was disposed; these spectacles had special hinges on them that were sold to only three people in all of Chicago, one of those being Nathan. Ten days after the murder, Loeb and Leopold were brought in for questioning; both cracked under pressure and confessed to the murder, though both confessed that the other did the actual killing.

The murder attracted national media attention due to the defendants' social status as sons of upper-class families. The common belief was that only uneducated, poor, and vile people committed these types of crimes—yet two young boys from "good," wealthy families had committed this atrocious premeditated offense. Clarence was called in to represent Loeb and Leopold. The media immediately criticized Darrow for defending these two boys solely for materialistic gain. With a full-fledged confession by both boys and an insurmountable amount of evidence against them, Darrow was hired to save their lives from the death penalty, which in Illinois was death by hanging. Darrow, who was an avid spokesperson against the death penalty, had almost an impossible case to win.

From the beginning, Darrow knew that the only way to attain a sentence of life imprisonment for Leopold and Loeb was to try the case before a judge in a bench trial, because there was no possibility of attaining an unbiased jury. Darrow originally had the boys plead not guilty, with the intention of changing this plea to guilty, which would force the judge alone to sentence Loeb and Leopold to death, and use the element of surprise to throw off the prosecution.

In a dramatic two-day summation, Darrow downplayed the murder, while focusing on the boys' mental abnormality as well as the fact that the crime was senseless, motiveless, and mad. He also attacked the prosecution because of their persistence for the death penalty in light of his clients' economic class and the national exposure to the case. When he made his verdict, Judge John Calverly disagreed with many of the points that Darrow made, but was swayed nonetheless by the summation and especially the boys' young ages. He gave them both life sentences for kidnapping and murder. Although Darrow was criticized for materialistic gain in this case, the families of Leopold and Loeb at first refused to pay Darrow any money; after much debate, the families paid Darrow a total of $100,000, which in no way compensated Darrow as well as his staff for the time and work they had put into the case.

The trial of John T. Scopes took place in July 1925. Clarence Darrow defended Scopes for free, and it was the first and last time he would ever do so in a case. He waived his fee and defended Scopes only because the prosecutor in the case was William Jennings Bryan, a well-known rival. Bryan was the nation's leading fundamentalist, and three-time presidential candidate. John T. Scopes was arrested for teaching evolution and the theories of Charles Darwin at Dayton High School, in Dayton, Tennessee. Scopes was not actually a biology teacher, but rather a physics teacher; only after Scopes had substituted in the biology class and gave a reading assignment dealing with evolution was he charged.

The jury in the "Monkey Trial" had never heard of Charles Darwin, and all but one were fundamentalists. Bryan was considered a "man of God," while Darrow was disliked as "the devil." The prosecution led by Bryan motioned that no expert testimony be allowed for either side of the trial. The judge ruled in favor of the prosecution, almost crippling the defense's case. Although not his idea, Darrow called Bryan himself to testify on his religious beliefs and evolution. Bryan agreed to this blindly and took the stand before Darrow. Clarence humiliated Bryan by subjecting him to question after question, targeting the many miracles and inconsistencies of the Bible while Bryan testified unwavering to his strict beliefs. The judge ultimately threw out the testimony, but Bryan was embarrassed and was criticized throughout the nation for his behavior.

Darrow, along with his defense team, consisting of Dudley Field Malone and Arthur Garfield Hays, knew that because they were not allowed to introduce expert testimony and Bryan's testimony was thrown out, there would be no way to win the case against a fundamentalist jury. To save face and not allow Bryan to fight back against the humiliating display, Darrow chose not to make a closing statement—in Tennessee, the law stated that the prosecution must also waive closing statements along with the defense.

John T. Scopes was convicted under the antievolution law, but the guilty verdict was later reversed by the Supreme Court of Tennessee on nonconstitutional technical grounds. Although Darrow was unsuccessful with this case, this led to other cases dealing with the unconstitutionality of the teaching of evolution. The "Monkey Trial" actually stimulated other states to pass anti-evolution laws, which had not been established before. This case was about the freedom of expression and the value of scientific evidence. The whole country knew that John T. Scopes broke the law, but the question was whether the law was just. And more important, was the law constitutional? In 1968, the U.S. Supreme Court ruled that statutes prohibiting the teaching of Charles Darwin's theory of evolution were unconstitutional because it violated the prohibition on the establishment of a state religion. Clarence Darrow died on March 13, 1938, but his legacy will remain because of his unwavering defense of those who would not be heard because of prejudice and bigotry.

— *Eric C. Chadwick*

See also **Creationism, Beliefs in; Law and Society; Monkey Trial; Scopes, John**

Further Readings

Boyle, K. (2004). *Arc of justice: A saga of race, civil rights, and murder in the jazz age.* New York: Henry Holt.

Cowan, G. (1993). *The People v. Clarence Darrow: The bribery trial of America's greatest lawyer.* New York: Time Books.

Darrow, C. (1932). *The story of my life.* New York: Grossett's Universal Library.

Tierney, K. (1979). *Darrow, a biography.* New York: Fitzhenry & Whiteside.

DART, RAYMOND A. (1893–1988)

Australian anatomist and anthropologist Raymond Dart was known for his discovery and analysis of the fossil hominid *Australopithecus africanus.* Born in Toowong, Brisbane, Australia, Dart was one of nine children born to strict and religious parents. Living and working on his parents' Australian bush farm, Dart's pioneer life and naturalistic inclinations would influence both his decision to leave the farm and to pursue a course of relevant academic interest. After attending Ipswich Grammar School, Dart won a scholarship and attended the University of Queensland, where he studied zoology. Proving his academic merit, Dart won a residential scholarship to St. Andrew's College in Sydney, where he studied biology.

After his graduation in 1917, Dart went to wartime England to serve in the medical corps. This would give Dart the opportunity to study in London, England. While at University College, London, Dart studied anatomy under Elliot Smith. During this period of study, Dart was presented with an opportunity to study in America. Due to the generous contributions of the Rockefeller Foundation, Dart went to Washington University, St. Louis, United States, to study histology. Between studies and research, Dart met and married Dora Tyree, before returning to England in 1921. Upon returning to University College, Dart was appointed head of histology. During his remaining time at University College, the influence of neurologist Dr. Kulchitsky, former Russian Minister of Education and political refugee, served to strengthen Dart's ability in both microscopic and gross anatomy. With the encouragement of Elliot Smith and Arthur

Keith, Dart accepted the chair of anatomy at the University of Witwatersrand, Johannesburg, South Africa, in 1922. However, accepting the chair was not tantamount to his research and position at University College. The city of Johannesburg was thriving, but the department at the university was not. Since the University of Witwatersrand severely lacked both equipment and literature, Dart renewed his interest in anthropology.

Contributions and Perspectives

During the time when Asia was thought to be the cradle of humankind, the discovery at Taung in the Bechuanaland Protectorate rekindled the Darwinian speculation that Africa was the origin of our species. Recovering fossils lying in limestone (through the aid of both Dart's students and miners at the Taung mines), Dart began to evaluate the specimens that were sent. One of the first specimens was an endocranial cast that was bigger than a baboon or chimpanzee (with a cranial capacity around 520 cc) but less than what can be considered as primitive for the human species. With small canine teeth and a more forward *foramen magnum,* the morphological features would indicate that the specimen could be considered as the "missing link" between the human species and the common ape. When comparing and contrasting any significant features, what was of real importance was that the specimen possessed two distinct furrows, *lunate* and *parallel sulci,* the latter of which are found in primitive humans. Given the geographic location, this species would indicate a deviation in the previous thought concerning the habitat of our early ancestors. What was more striking and controversial than the origin was the possibility concerning the depth of the australopithecine's Osteodontokeratic culture.

Finding and correctly interpreting behavior via material culture is problematic at best. Facing conflicting theoretical constructs and related terminology, the possibility for a conclusive definition may seem elusive, whether it is applied to either our remote ancestors or our living cousins, the chimpanzees. The imposing question remains: Does the manufacturing of tools become a sole indicator of hominid intelligence and related culture? Or may the possibility of utilizing, and perhaps slightly modifying, preexisting material for intentional be seen as a cultural indicator? For Dart, this question was not

Source: From the R. A. Dart Collection, University of Witwatersrand Archives.

problematic. The australopithecines did possess a rudimentary form of culture. The implication concerning hominid behavior was staggering: No longer were our ancestors seen as passive and humble creatures of the forest canopy. Rather, they were depicted as aggressive and intelligent hunters on the open plains and grassy savannas. This translated into a unique view of this hominid form.

According to Dart, the South African man-apes utilized many existing bones as tools. Similar to the evidence found at Choukoutien, Dart came to the conclusion that this hominid form expressed its behavior in the same way. Using an antelope thigh bone or arm bone as a club or sharp ends of broken bones as daggers, the australopithecines became a formidable predator. Although the evidence at Taung was attempted to be dismissed as being a product of hyenas (which itself is a myth), the faunal remains (buffalo, saber-toothed tiger, and giant porcupine) suggest that these hominids must have had the ability to effectively communicate and execute complex maneuvers. Such dangerous confrontations would have had to necessitate both higher forms of technology (beyond arbitrary implements) and social structure. However, the world of academia would be reluctant to extend many of the attributes to the Osteodontokeratic culture.

The contribution made by Dart was considerable. Besides his insights into anatomical evaluation of the specimen at Taung (especially in viewing the endocranial cast), the extending of human qualities continues to raise philosophical questions. This can be divided into two issues, one being taxonomical and the other being cultural. In view of the morphological characteristics of the australopithecines, the adoption of an erect posture promoted bipedality. This fact, along with an increase in cranial capacity and the free use of hands, made the australopithecines more reliant on their larger brains (some past the "Rubicon" of 750 cc) than brute strength. Although this "missing link" was not capable of articulate speech, the physiological characteristics of their brains do suggest greater complexity than was seen in earlier hominid forms. The placement of these hominids among the array of other hominid forms provided the Darwinian view of gradualism and continuity. With their more complex brains and bipedal gait, the development of culture becomes a necessity. The defining attributes of culture, similar to that of characteristics in general, become subjective to the anthropocentric evaluation of our species. The reluctance to credit this hominid form, as with our primate cousins, tends to obscure the evolutionary progression of our own humanity. Granting that the extent by which this can be called culture is not great as compared to the advancements of modern humankind, Dart's evaluation forces us to reevaluate humankind's place within nature.

— *David Alexander Lukaszek*

See also **Australopithecines; Hominids; Hominization, Issues in; Missing Link**

Further Readings

Dart, R. (1956). The myth of the bone-accumulating hyena. *American Anthropologist, 58,* 40–62.

Dart, R. (1958). Bone tools and porcupine gnawing. *American Anthropologist, 60,* 715–724.

Dart, R. (1960). The bone tool-manufacturing ability of *Australopithecus prometheus. American Anthropologist, 62,* 134–143.

Dart, R. (1982). *Adventures with the missing link.* Philadelphia: Institutes for the Achievement of Human Potential.

DARWIN AND GERMANY

We can analyze Charles Darwin's influence in Germany by examining four connections. These include, first, Darwin's relationship to social Darwinism and, in particular, to Hitler and the Third Reich, as many people still tend to see a strong link between these two movements. While we cannot regard Darwin as connected to the cruelties of the Third Reich, there is a relationship between Ernst Haeckel, the main defender of Darwin's theory of evolution in Germany, and some aspects of Third Reich politics. The second connection is Darwin's influence on two major German zoologists, August Weismann and Ernst Haeckel. Third, we can focus on the influence Darwin has had on the ideas of German philosophers and philosophical anthropologists, including David Friedrich Strauss, Karl Marx, Friedrich Engels, Friedrich Nietzsche, Georg Simmel, Ernst Cassirer, Max Scheler, Nicolai Hartmann, Helmuth Plessner, Arnold Gehlen, and Vittorio Hoesle. Fourth, we can examine how Darwin is seen in Germany today.

Darwin, Social Darwinism, and the Third Reich

When the name "Darwin" comes up in discussions in Germany, it still happens that people mention Social Darwinism and Darwin's influence on Hitler and the Third Reich. Therefore, there is the necessity of making two brief remarks about this issue.

First, it has to be said that Hitler, like Darwin, saw himself as a defender of the "will of nature." However, Hitler linked the concept of the "will of nature" with a particular people and infers from this the necessity of aggressive behavior toward inferior races ("Aryans" versus "Jews"). Such an element cannot be found within Darwin's theory.

Second, it needs to be said that Darwin does not promote measures against contraselection. Contraselection takes place within a civilization when the struggle for existence cannot be active in an appropriate manner, as inferior, weak, and lazy people are supported and are taken care of, and such circumstances are supposed to lead to the transmission of weak hereditary dispositions. Of course, it is a matter of dispute whether there is such a phenomenon as contraselection or not. Measures against contraselection were demanded by Ernst Haeckel, further promoted from some race hygienists (*Rassenhygieniker*) and later on carried out by Hitler and the national socialists. I say more about this in the section on Haeckel. At this point, it has to be stressed that first, contraselection cannot follow from Darwin's theory of selection, as the individuals who win the struggle for existence within his theory are by definition the most suitable whatever the cultural conditions are; and second, Darwin never demanded that one should refrain from helping the weaker.

Given the above comparison between Darwin's and Hitler's ideas, we must conclude that Darwin should not be seen as an intellectual precursor of the German national socialist movement.

Darwin and Two Major German Zoologists

The first zoologist I deal with here is August Weismann (1834–1914). At the 100th anniversary of Darwin's birthday, Weismann pointed out the importance of Darwin by stressing that before Darwin zoology, botany, and anthropology existed as separate sciences, but with Darwin's theory of evolution, a connection between these various sciences was established. Weismann is regarded as the first proper Darwinist and as the founder of neo-Darwinism, although originally he believed in Lamarck's theory of the transmission of acquired traits. What is significant for neo-Darwinism is that it combines our knowledge of genetics with Darwin's theory of selection. Weismann combines the theory of cells, embryology, and genetics with another, and interprets the result by means of the theory of selection. He transfers the principle of natural selection from the macroscopic to the cellular perspective, which implies that the cellular plasma (*Zellplasma*) is transmitted from generation to generation and thereby becomes potentially immortal. The cellular plasma is also the basis for the soma or bodily plasma. Today, we would use the expressions *genotype* and *phenotype*. To clarify this position a bit further, we could say that for the neo-Darwinists, the genotype is the basis for transmission and the phenotype follows from it, whereas for a Lamarckian, the phenotype is the basis and the genotype develops from this. In addition, I wish to make clear that it was important for Weismann to stress that given the theory of selection, it does not follow that the beastly tendencies should govern human

Source: © iStockphoto/Michael Blackburn.

beings, but that for human beings it is particularly the mind or spirit that matters, rather than the body.

The next scientist we discuss is the zoologist and philosopher Ernst Haeckel (1834–1919). I have already alluded to some of his ideas in the first part of this article, and I return to them later in this section. Before comparing Haeckel's ideas to Darwin's I need to point out that in 1863, Haeckel wrote a letter to Darwin informing him that he wished to dedicate his life to Darwin's theory of evolution, which he did by taking the theory of descent and the principle of selection for granted, and then applying these theories to the various areas of biology.

First, I wish to mention that Haeckel clearly expressed that none of the living great apes is the ancestor of the human race, as they died out long ago. Today, we believe that the last common ancestor of human beings and great apes lived about a couple of million years ago. It seems to me that even today, many people believe that the living apes are actually our ancestors. Haeckel clearly recognized this problem of understanding. Second, Haeckel managed to relate phylogenesis and ontogenesis to one another. According to him, the ontogenesis is a short and fast repetition of the phylogenesis, which means that an embryo passes through the various phases of our ancestors via fishes to higher mammals. One can find this relationship between ontogenesis and phylogenesis already within Darwin's works, yet it comes out clearly for the first time in the writings of Fritz Mueller (1822–1897), Johann Friedrich Meckel (1781–1833), and in particular Ernst Haeckel.

All of Haeckel's above-mentioned observations were very perceptive, yet it also has to be noted that he and some other German scientists, like Carl Vogt or Fritz Mueller, were far more extreme and axiomatic than Darwin. For example, Haeckel boldly and loudly expressed his opinion: "There is no God, and no immortality." Considering this aspect of Haeckel's personality, we can now return to the topic of the first part, where Haeckel was already mentioned. According to Haeckel, it is the most important task of the practical philosophers of his times to develop and bring about a new ethics. The only ethics that he was able to regard as consistent with Darwinism was neither democratic nor socialist, but aristocratic. Given this belief, it makes it easier to understand why Haeckel was in favor of measures against contraselection, such as recruiting ill people for the military, the death penalty for criminals, or murder of ill and weak children. Twenty years later, his ideas with respect to contraselection were taken up again by race hygienists (*Rassenhygienikern*) such as Wilhelm Schallmyer (1857–1919), who wrote the first book dealing with the hygiene of a race in 1891, and Alfred Ploetz (1860–1940), who in 1895 created the notion "hygiene of a race" (*Rassenhygiene*). Both refer directly to Haeckel. In numerous publications after 1933, Haeckel is seen as a thinker closely related to national socialism, his demands concerning eugenics were praised, and indirectly via the race hygienists, he influenced the ideology of the national socialist. One can even find related ideas in Hitler's *Mein Kampf.*

To make the orientation easier for someone interested in the German reception of Darwin within the fields of biology and anthropology, I mention the most important German biologists and anthropologists who were significantly influenced by Darwin in this section. The most notable German biologists in the 19th century besides the one already mentioned were Naegeli, Hermann, and Fritz Mueller. For the 20th century, E. Baur, Rensch, Timofeef-Ressovsky, Zimmermann, and Schindewolf have to be mentioned. The most important German anthropologists in the 19th century were Rudolph Wagner, Carl Vogt, Hermann Schaaffhausen, Karl Ernst von Baer, Robert Hartmann, and Gustav Schalbe. Rudolf Virchow and Johannes Ranke Extremely were critical of Darwin. Concerning 20th-century anthropologists who were significantly influenced by Darwin, Hermann Klaatsch, Gerhard Heberer, Winfried Henke, and Hartmut Rothe have to be mentioned. In addition, one should not forget the Social Darwinists Alfred Ploetz, Wilhelm Schallmeyer, and Otto Ammon. After having shown Darwin's influence on two major German zoologists, and having mentioned the most important 19th- and 20th-century German biologists, and anthropologists who were significantly influenced by Darwin, I now come to the relationship between Darwin's theory of evolution and the ideas of German philosophers and philosophical anthropologists.

Darwin, Philosophers, and Philosophical Anthropologists

Within this section, I progress in chronological order, starting with the earliest thinkers influenced by Darwin and ending with the last notable thinker. It has to be noted that most of the thinkers listed were active during the first half of the 20th century.

The first thinker I wish to mention is the theologian David Friedrich Strauss (1808–1874). He was the author of the famous book *The Life of Jesus,* which was very influential, especially in the 19th century. David Friedrich Strauss admitted that Darwin's theory was irresistible to those who thirsted for "truth and freedom."

More famous and influential than Strauss are the next two thinkers, namely Karl Marx (1818–1883) and Friedrich Engels (1820–1895). The following story has often been told when the relationship between Darwin and Marx was discussed. "And when Marx proposed to dedicate to him [Darwin] *Das Kapital,* he firmly refused the honour, explaining that it would pain certain members of his family if he were associated with so atheistic a book" (Himmelfarb, 1962, p. 383). However, in recent times, doubt has been shed on the truth of this story. Bowler (1990), for example, said, "It is perhaps worth noting that the once popular story that Karl Marx offered to dedicate a volume of *Capital* to Darwin is based on a misinterpretation of the relevant correspondence" (p. 206).

What is certain is that both Engels as well as Marx had been deeply impressed by Darwin's theory of evolution, as the topic comes up very often in their correspondence, and both Engels as well as Marx were usually full of praise for it. Engels once wrote that Marx's theory of history can be compared to Darwin's theory of evolution, whereby it has to be assumed that he was referring to the scientific value of both theories. In another letter, which Engels wrote to Marx in November 1859, he praised Darwin for destroying the then still very strong teleological worldview. Here, he was referring to the principle of selection, which is indeed consistent with a mechanistic description of the world. In December 1860, Marx says in a letter to Engels that although Darwin's works are very English, he regards them as containing the basis for their own work. Of particular interest has to be Engel's letter to the Russian journalist Lawrow (1875), who was a strong opponent of Darwinism. In this letter Engels makes clear that he accepts Darwin's theory of evolution, although he has doubts with respect to his methodology. For Engel, it was not possible to base all activity within this world on the "struggle for existence," and he compared Darwin's theory in this respect to the positions of Hobbes and Malthus. Engels believed that all worldviews containing the idea of the "struggle for existence" theory must have come about by means of the following mistake. The respective thinkers must have observed the realm of plants and animals and expanded the observed forces to the human world. This, however, cannot be done, according to Engels, as human beings have developed the capacity to produce things, and this capacity cannot be found anywhere else in nature except in human beings. Therefore, it cannot be justified to apply observations of the realm of plants and animals to the human world. This seems to have been Engel's main point of criticism.

After having dealt with the relationship of Marx and Engels to Darwin, I now come the most important philosopher of the second half of the 19th century in

Germany: Friedrich Nietzsche (1844–1900). Birx (2000) correctly pointed out that "The scientist Charles Darwin had awakened the philosopher Friedrich Nietzsche from his dogmatic slumber by the realization that, throughout organic history, no species is immutable (including our own)" (p. 24). In addition, Birx also explained, "As with Thomas Huxlex, Ernst Haeckel and Darwin himself, Nietzsche taught the historical continuity between human beings and other animals (especially the chimpanzees)" (p. 24). However, Nietzsche was not unconditionally affirmative of Darwin. Nietzsche's most important criticism was, like Engel's, directed toward Darwin's "struggle for existence" theory. He did put forward many types of arguments against the theory of the "struggle for existence," and he also explains why he regards the aspect of power as more important than the aspect of pure existence. One of the better arguments can be found in an aphorism titled "Against Darwinism." Here, Nietzsche pointed out that Darwin overestimated the outer situation and forgot to take the inner form giving force into consideration. This creative force leads to the feeling of becoming stronger, which again is what human beings are after. This is one of the reasons why Nietzsche did not regard the "struggle for existence" but the "will to power" as the basis of all human actions. Finally, concerning the relationship between Darwin and Nietzsche I wish to mention that Nietzsche did not read much by Darwin himself, but a lot of secondary literature about him.

Georg Simmel (1858–1918) is the next thinker with whom I am concerned. He is a philosopher and one of the founders of sociology, and besides many other subjects, he also dealt with evolutionary epistemology. This theory of knowledge considers that human beings are the result of a long natural process of evolution, since it regards this fact to be relevant for our way of understanding and getting to know the world. Through Simmel and the Austrian ethnologist Konrad Lorenz who was heavily influenced by Darwin, the idea of an evolutionary epistemology was transmitted to the present, in which it has become an influential stream of philosophy that is the subject of intense philosophical debates.

Another philosopher of culture deeply indebted to Darwin's ideas is Ernst Cassirer (1874–1945). This neo-Kantian philosopher has often referred to the role of 19th-century biology with respect to the breakthrough of historical thinking within the field that is concerned with knowledge of nature. The 17th century was dominated by a mathematical ideal of the natural sciences. However, in the 19th century, the historical approach became more and more important, according to Cassirer. Especially because of Darwin's theory, the historical approach to knowledge of nature has been able to reach a new level of importance, and it has become obvious that scientific and historical thinking do not have to be contradictory, but can complement one another, to attain a useful symbiosis of these two streams of thinking.

The Catholic Nietzsche and founder of philosophical anthropology Max Scheler (1874–1928) is the thinker with whom I deal with next. He studied with Ernst Haeckel in Jena, who influenced him significantly with respect to Darwin's theory of evolution. Within his mature philosophy, he accepted that with respect to their "physis," human beings are constructed according to the same fundamental plan as animals. However, with respect to the mind, there is an enormous difference between men and animals. Yet it is not the case that animals do not have a mind, according to Scheler, but they have it to a much lower degree. This difference alone would not grant human beings a special status in the world. It is because of something else that men have such a special status, which I explain soon.

From the above remarks alone, one can see that Scheler's thought was closely linked to the sciences. Yet he was not the only one who was so strongly influenced by the natural sciences. According to him, all educated Europeans think within the tradition of the following three cultures when they are asked what comes to mind when they think about human beings: the Jewish-Christian tradition, the ancient Greek cultural realm, and the field of modern natural sciences, particularly the theory of evolution and genetic psychology. However, these three realms exist parallel to one another within our civilization without there being a link between them. Scheler tried to find a solution to this problem, and Cassirer in 1944 took up the same problem but without accepting Scheler's solution. Scheler's solution goes as follows. According to him, given the theory of evolution that Scheler accepts, human beings (men as *Homo naturalis*) cannot have a special status within nature, as mentioned before. He developed a model where the organic realm is separated into various stages, yet this cannot justify that men have a special status, as human beings and animals do form a strict continuum. However, Scheler thought that there is something that separates us from the natural realm. Here, the notion of *Weltoffenheit* (openness to the world) comes in. By this notion, he means our ability to be relatively free from our instincts and forces, and therewith our ability to choose for ourselves which type of life we wish to live. In this way, he introduced a dualism within his philosophy, which was rejected by the later philosophical anthropologists Helmuth Plessner and Arnold Gehlen.

Often, Darwin's theory has been criticized on the grounds that selection is a tautology and, as such, cannot be regarded as a scientific theory, as it cannot be falsified. While this was reason enough for many people to doubt Darwin, Nicolai Hartmann thought the plausibility of this principle revealed its status as a priori knowledge. Spencer, too, had emphasized the a priori status of the principle of selection.

After Hartmann, we can come back to the philosophical anthropologists again, and so we reach Helmuth Plessner (1892–1985). Although he agrees with Darwin on many points—like the one that there is only a very small difference between men and animals, but not a substantial difference, only a gradual one—he is very critical of Darwin as well. For example, he does not accept that at the basis of all actions is the "struggle for existence." It also needs to be mentioned that Plessner grants the principle of selection also an a priori status.

Another important philosophical anthropologist who was influenced by Darwin is Arnold Gehlen (1904–1976). There are quite a few similarities in their theories. Darwin regarded the biological weakness of human beings as probably their greatest strength, as it brought about that men work together and form communities, and it enabled men to adapt themselves to the various possible situations and to develop great spiritual capacities. Gehlen referred to the same phenomenon with the expression *Maengelwesen* (defective creature), whereby he alluded to Nietzsche, who in the "Gay Science" described human beings as "wayward animals." Human beings need culture, and, as Gehlen says, institutions in order to be capable of living well, as they are lacking the appropriate instincts. Like Darwin, Gehlen held that there is only a gradual difference between men and animals. However, he neither attributed a lot of importance to the "struggle for existence" nor granted any relevance to the principle of selection.

The last great philosopher who has dealt with Darwin is Vittorio Hoesle (1960-). Together with the biologist and philosopher Christian Illies, he wrote the very philosophical and clear introductory book titled *Darwin* (1999). However, within his own understanding of history, he is much closer to Hegel than to Darwin.

Darwin in Germany Today

The attitude toward Darwin in Germany today is still ambiguous. The following two aspects have to be stressed. On one hand, there is the "bad Darwin," who is related to Social Darwinism and eugenics, and on the other hand, there is the "good Darwin," who is the great observer of nature, clear writer, and role model for any natural scientist. Two recently published articles represent good examples for each of these attitudes.

The first article, *"Reine Rasse"* ("Pure Race") (Franke, 2001), deals with the questions of gene diagnosis, cloning, and euthanasia. It was mainly inspired by the fact that just before Easter, the Dutch Parliament passed a law that legalized active mercy killing, or euthanasia, which brought about a massive and emotionally charged discussion in Germany. Within this article, Darwin was mentioned as someone who realized the problem of a surplus population but accepted that nothing can be done about it. However, it was also said that many of his followers have taken a different view, and it was implicitly expressed that the danger of a solution different from Darwin's was clearly contained within Darwin's ideas, as he himself had realized the problem of a surplus population. Although the author could have given a much worse description of Darwin, here one can still find the picture of the rather "bad Darwin."

The second article, "Mit Darwins Augen" ("With Darwin's Eyes"), was written by Durs Gruenbein (2001), a famous German writer. In it, Darwin was portrayed as the role model of a natural scientist. His ability to express the results of his research to the public was praised, and positively compared to the capacities of the present generation of natural scientists. It was made clear that he had the calmness, the perseverance, the patience, and just the right eye for being a clear and rigorous observer of nature, from whom all natural scientists could learn something.

It is fair to say that although we can still find the "good" and the "bad" Darwin within German contemporary culture, it seems that the positive aspects dominate. What we must consider, however, is that even in Germany, we find creationists with posts at good universities again, a fact that should make us question whether creationism will become more influential.

— *Stefan Lorenz Sorgner*

See also **Biological Anthropology and Neo-Darwinism; Creationism, Beliefs in; Darwinism, Modern; Neo-Darwinism, Origin of; Selection, Natural**

Further Readings

Birx, H. J. (2000, October/November). Nietzsche & evolution. *Philosophy Now, 29.*

Bowler, P. J. (1990). *Charles Darwin: The man and his influence.* Cambridge: Cambridge University Press.

Darwin, C. (1998). *The descent of man* (Intro. by H. James Birx). New York: Prometheus Books.

Darwin, C. (1999). *The origin of species: By means of natural selection or the preservation of favoured races in the struggle for life.* New York: Bantam.

Franke, K. (2001). Reine Rasse [Pure Race]. *Der Spiegel, 29,* 128–134.

Gruenbein, D. (2001, June 23). Mir Darwins Augen [With Darwin's Eyes]. *Frankfurter Allgemeine Zeitung, Bilder und Zeiten,* p. 1.

Himmelfarb, G. (1962). *Darwin and the Darwinian revolution.* New York: Norton.

Sorgner, S. L. (1999). Metaphysics without truth: On the importance of consistency within Nietzsche's philosophy. In N. Knoepffler, W. Vossenkuhl, S. Peetz, & B. Lauth (Eds.), *Muenchner Philosophische Beiträge.* Munich: Herbert Utz Verlag.

DARWIN AND INDIA

Charles Darwin (1809–1882) was the British naturalist who became famous for his theories of evolution and natural selection. He believed that all the life on earth evolved over millions of years from a few common ancestors. He went on expeditions around the world from 1831 to 1836, studying and collecting plants and fossils. Upon his return to London, Darwin conducted thorough research of his notes and specimens. Out of this study grew several of his related theories: (a) Evolution did occur; (b) evolutionary changes were gradual, requiring thousands of millions of years; (c) the primary mechanism for evolution was a process called *natural selection;* and (d) the millions of species alive today arose from a single original life form through a branching process called *specialization.* Darwin's theory of evolution holds that variation within species occurs randomly and that the survival or extinction of each organism is determined by that organism's ability to adapt to its environment. Although he avoided talking about the theological and sociological aspects of his work, other writers used his theories to support their own theories about society and humankind.

Darwin's theory of evolution is rooted in a philosophical commitment to naturalism or materialism, which assumes that all reality is ultimately physical or material. Thus, in his theory, mind or spirit is reducible to material reality, and God and religion are vanished to the land of irrelevance. This contradicts India's Hindu philosophy of life, its existence, and development.

Hindu philosophy believes in different types of origins of humankind than what Darwin prescribed. In one of the earliest literatures of Hindu social thought, *Purushasukta,* a reference has been made to the four orders of society as emanating from the sacrifice of the primeval being. The names of those four order are given there as *Brahmana, Rajanya, Vaisya,* and *Sudra,* who are said to have come respectively from the mouth, the arms, the thighs, and the feet of the creator. This origin of the four classes is repeated in most of the later works with slight variations and interpretative additions. For example, the *Taittiriya Samhita* ascribes the origins of these four classes to the four limbs of the creator and adds an explanation. The *Brahmins* are declared to be the chief because they are created from the mouth. The *Rajanyas* are vigorous because they are created from vigor. The *Vaisyas* are meant to be eaten, referring to their liability to excessive taxation because they were created from the stomach, the receptacle of food. The *Sudra,* because he was created from the feet, is to be the transport of others and to subsist by the feet. In this particular account of the creation, not only is the origin of the classes interpreted theologically, but also a divine justification is sought to be given to their functions and status. The creation theory is here further amplified to account for certain other features of their social classes. In Hindu social thought, God is said to have created certain deities simultaneously with these classes. The *Vaisya* class, the commoners, must have been naturally very large, and this account explains that social fact by a reference to the simultaneous creation of *Visvedevas,* all and sundry deities, whose number is considerable. Also, no deities were created along with the *Sudra,* and hence, he is disqualified for sacrifice. Here again, the social regulation, which forbade *Sudra* to offer sacrifice, is explained as an incidental consequence of the creation.

The theory of the divine origin of the four classes is often repeated with special stress on the origin of the *Sudra* from the feet of the creator. In the *Mahabharata,* a slight material change is introduced in this theory, where we are told that the first three classes were created first and the *Sudra* was created afterward for serving others. In the *Bhagavadgita,* the creator is said to have apportioned the duties and functions of the four classes according to the inherent qualities and capacities of individuals. This theory of origin, even though it fails to explain how the individuals at the very beginning of the creation came to be possessed of peculiar qualities and capacities, tries to provide a rational sanction for the manifestly arbitrary divisions. God separated people into four classes not merely because they were created from different limbs of his body, nor again out of his will, but because he found them endowed with different qualities and capacities.

Darwin explains the concept of sexual selection by examining one of the social customs practiced in India. He maintains that infanticide was probably more common in earlier times, practiced by "Barbarians" who killed off children they were not able to support. Darwin gives many examples of tribes formerly destroying infants of both sexes. He further notes that wherever infanticide prevails, the struggle for existence will be less severe, and all the members of the tribe will have an almost equally good chance of rearing their few surviving children. In most cases, a larger number of female than of male infants are destroyed, for it is obvious that the latter are of more value to the tribe, as they grow up and aid in defending it. This was a practice in some tribes of India, particularly in a village on the eastern frontier, where Colonel MacCulloch found not a single female child. However, practice of infanticide in India, unlike Darwin's argument, did not stem from the struggle for existence. Rather, it was rooted in the traditional customs and spiritual practices. It was believed that when natural calamities, such as droughts and epidemics, took a toll on (tribal) communities, it was their moral duty to offer sacrifices to God to gain his mercy and blessings. Female infants were preferred over male infants for sacrifices because of their purity and superior quality as the source of creation. In ancient Hindu epics, one female infant is equated with three male infants—indicating that God will be pleased as much with the sacrifice of one female infant as he would be with three male infants. Thus, female infants were thought to be the premium offerings to God. Not all infants were qualified for sacrifice. There were certain criteria in selection of an infant for sacrifice—such as, the chosen infant must be healthy, beautiful, and belong to a noble family of the tribe. In this practice of sacrifice, the strongest and fittest infant was the one more at risk of being sacrificed than the weakest and nonfittest, contrary to the Darwin's theory of the survival of the fittest. These sacrifices were conducted in an orderly form for the noble cause of the welfare of the entire tribe, rather than as a routine practice of mere killing of infants for the struggle for existence.

Darwin further contemplates that the practice of infanticide created scarcity of marriageable women, which, in turn, resulted in polyandry. Whenever two or more men, whether they are brothers or strangers, are compelled to marry one woman, such a marriage system is referred to as *polyandry.* Darwin gives the example of the Toda tribe of India who practiced polyandry. However, there is convincing evidence that this was never a common form of marriage practiced in India. In India, the polyandry form of marriage is supposed to have once been a trait of the culture, from the classic instance of *Draupadi* having the five *Pandavas* of the *Mahabharata* fame as her husbands, and some vague allusions to polyandry in the *vedic* mythology. However, *Draupadi's* case does not appear to be as clear evidence of polyandry as it is generally supposed to be. According to the *Mahabharata,* the five *Pandava* brothers, after the death of their father, King *Pandu,* found themselves at odds with their cousins, the *Kauravas.* The long-drawn enmity between them compelled the *Pandavas* to stay hidden after their escape from the palace. During their exile, they lived on alms, which they collected and shared with their mother. One day, the sage *Vyasa* came and informed them that King *Drupada* of Panchala had invited kings to make their claims for the hand of his daughter *Draupadi.* The king had pledged her hand to the hero who successfully performed the feat of piercing a fish suspended on a post by taking his aim looking at its shadow in the water. *Vyasa* further asked them to attend the function in the guise of Brahmans. *Arjuna,* the third among the *Pandavas,* successfully performed the feat and became the suitor of *Draupadi*. The *Pandava* brothers, on their return home with *Draupadi*, found the house door closed. They merrily asked their mother to open the door and receive them who had returned with pretty alms that day. Not knowing what alms they referred to, she asked them from behind the door to divide it amongst themselves. *Draupadi* thus became the common wife of the five *Pandavas*. When mother *Kunthi* saw *Draupadi* instead of alms, she realized the blunder she had committed and was taken aback. *Draupadi's* marriage to the five brothers raised a storm of protest from her relatives. Her father could not think of his daughter being the wife of five brothers, and he denounced it as irreligious, being against the *Vedas* and usages. Her brother attacked it with vehemence and asked *Yudhishtira* how he, as an elder brother, could marry the wife of his younger brother.

Thus, polyandry seems to have been discredited as a cultural trait from the time of the *Aitareya Brahmana* (800 BC), when it was said that a man could have many wives but a woman could have only one husband. The *Mahabharata* reiterates that this tradition to have many wives is no *adharma* (injustice) on the part of man, but to violate the duty owed to the first husband would be great *adharma* in the case of a woman. To sum up, polyandry has been found with the joint family not only among the *Todas,* as claimed by Darwin, but also among the *Kotas, the Coorgs, the Iravans, the Nairs, and the Khasa* community in India, but it was in different contexts and with different significance. Some of these communities considered *Pandavas* as their Gods and embraced the tradition of *Pandava* polyandry.

— *Komanduri S. Murty and Ashwin G. Vyas*

See also **Biological Anthropology and Neo-Darwinism; Creationism, Beliefs in; Darwinism, Modern; Hinduism; India, Philosophies of; Neo-Darwinism, Origin of; Selection, Natural; Polyandry**

Further Readings

Darwin, C. (1859). *On the origin of species.* London: John Murray.
Darwin, C. (1871). *The descent of man* (2 vols.). London: John Murray.
Ghurye, G. S. (1957). *Caste and class in India.* Bombay: Popular Book Depot.

Kapadia, K. M. (1958). *Marriage and family in India* (2nd ed.). Bombay: Oxford University Press.
Ruse, M. (2001). *Mystery of mysteries: Is evolution a social construction?* Cambridge, MA: Harvard University Press.
Satguru, S. S. (1997). *Dancing with Siva: Hinduism's contemporary catechism* (5th ed.). Kauai, HI: Himalayan Academy.
Vyas, A. (1991). *Social stratification and third world countries.* Berkeley, CA: Folklore Institute.

DARWIN AND ITALY

The history of the interrelation between Charles Darwin and Italy begins long before Darwin's main works were published. In 1814, the Italian natural scientist Gianbattista Brocchi published his *Concchiologia fossile subappenina con osservazioni geologiche sugli Appenini e sul suolo adiacente,* in which he supported the theory that species can disappear and do actually become extinct, based on his detailed examination of the fossilized remains of crustaceans. With this theory, he contradicted Carl von Linné, J. E. Walch, Georges Cuvier, and Jean Baptiste Lamarck, who all, in their different ways, ruled out the possibility that a species could disappear entirely. Brocchi explained the disappearance of species by analogy with the life cycle of an individual. Just as an individual is born, grows old, becomes weaker, and finally dies, he believed that species became increasingly weaker down the generations. Brocchi believed he could prove that before they disappeared, extinct species had become smaller and smaller from one generation to the next and then finally died out. In this way, Brocchi saw the tiny spiral snail as the last stage of development of the originally much larger ammonites. Strangely, although Brocchi drew these parallels between the life of the species and the life of the individual, he did not use them as the basis to explore further what would seem the next obvious question about the origin of the species. He therefore accepted a gradual aging of species irrespective of exceptional external changes (catastrophe theory) but rejected Lamarck's theory that one species could develop into another.

Through Charles Lyell's *Principles of Geology* (1830–1833), in which Brocchi's theories were examined at length, Charles Darwin came into contact in the 1830s with Brocchi's theory that species could change independently of external influences and gradually disappear. This caused him to doubt the claim made in *Natural Theology* (1802), by William Paley, that the species were contrived to be perfectly adapted, and eventually brought him to the theory of transformism.

In 1830, the famous dispute between Cuvier and Isidore Geoffroy Saint-Hilaire took place at the Académie des Sciences in Paris about whether there were several designs in nature (Geoffroy Saint-Hilaire) or just one basic design (Cuvier), a debate behind which was the fight between fixism (Cuvier) and Lamarckism (Geoffroy Saint-Hilaire). In 1859, Darwin's *On the Origin of Species* was published. In the period between these two important dates, the question of the origin of the species played only a minor role among natural scientists in Italy. This was because, with a few exceptions like Franco Andrea Bonelli and Carlo Porro, they were occupied mainly with questions of systematics and classification. Bonelli, Francesco Baldassini, F. C. Marmocchi, and some others responded positively to Lamarck's theories, while natural scientists like Camillo Ranzani and Filippo Parlatore rejected them with the arguments previously produced by Cuvier against Geoffroy Saint-Hilaire as "pantheistic" and therefore unchristian. As early as 1856, Carlo Luciano Bonaparte, on the other hand, claimed the variability of species within a geological period and classified human beings in the order of the apes. Faced with the choice between fixism and Lamarckism, many natural scientists in the Italian states chose to tread a third path: Returning to the model of a "Great Chain of Being," which had already been discussed in the 18th century, they assumed a gradual difference and consequently a relation between the species, but without regarding this as chronological evolution. Among others, Filippo De Filippi Parlatore and Gabriele Costa also advocated a nonevolutionary, systematic connection of this kind between the species, although in a different form. It is important to remember that many extremely different evolutionary theories inspired by natural philosophy were circulating at that time within the scientific community in the Italian states. These theories bore reference to Johann Wolfgang von Goethe, Friedrich Wilhelm Joseph Schelling, Georg Wilhelm Friedrich Hegel, and Carl Gustav Carus, among others. This demonstrates that numerous attempts were made to reconcile creationism and evolution.

The publication of Darwin's *On the Origin of Species*, which had already been circulating in Italy since 1862 in French translation, was at first received with relative composure, since the innovativeness of Darwin's approach was not initially recognized among natural scientists. Rather, Darwin's theory was received simply as one of many that were circulating at the time. He excited interest mainly with regard to the possibility he suggested of a genealogical system of species.

The public discussion about Darwin began in Italy in 1864, with De Filippi's famous lecture on *L'uomo e le scimmie* (Man and the Apes), in which he attempted to reconcile Darwinism with Christian dogma by classifying human beings in a separate fourth kingdom of nature alongside the mineral, plant, and animal kingdoms. Although this was after the appearance of Thomas H. Huxley's *Man's Place in Nature* (1863), Lyell's *The Antiquity of Man* (1863), and Carl Vogt's *Vorlesungen über den Menschen* (1863), it was 7 years before Darwin's *The Descent of Man* (1871) was published. In the same year, Giuseppe Bianconi gave a lecture at the Accademia delle Scienze in Bologna, in which he assumed an "independent emergence" of human beings and took the view that there was absolutely no genealogical relationship between man and animals. Alexander Herzen's lecture *Sulla parentela fra l'uomo e le scimmie* (On the Relationship Between Man and Ape), in 1869, in Florence, then also caused a sensation. Raffaello Lambruschini and Niccolò Tommaseo opposed Herzen. In response to the accusation that Darwinism was attempting to degrade humans by making them into apes, Herzen pointed out in his reply that neither he nor Darwin had ever claimed that man originated from the apes, but only that both man and ape originated from the same ancestor. The dispute between Herzen and Lambruschini also had more of a political character, since Lambruschini supported the theory of the "Great Inquisitor" in Dostoevsky's *The Brothers Karamazov*, namely, that it was not right to deprive the people of their belief in religious myths as it would cast them into despair. Herzen, on the other hand, insisted that scientific truth by its inherent merit must not be concealed.

After 1859, numerous natural scientists declared their support for Darwin, including Michele Lessona and Leonardo Salimbeni. One of the most important supporters of Darwinism in Italy was the natural scientist Giovanni Canestrini, from Trento, who had translated *The Descent of Man* into Italian with Salimbeni in 1864. Strangely, the translators from English corresponded with Darwin in French and German, and peculiarly, there are several errors of translation in the Italian version that can also be found in the French translation of 1862. One example is the incorrect translation of the English word *metaphorical* in Darwin's explanation of the term *natural selection* into *metafisico* (i.e., metaphysical). As in the French version, *selection* was also translated into the Italian *elezione,* which is approximate to "choice or election," which encouraged an interpretation with problems.

In 1866, that is to say, 5 years before Darwin's *The Descent of Man,* Canestrini's monograph *L'origine dell'uomo* (The Origin of Man), dedicated to the same subject, was published. In this work, he defended Darwin against criticism, by Giuseppe Bianconi for example, in Italy. On the other hand, he deviated from Darwin's opinions in several areas. Unlike Darwin, who had been much more cautious in this area, Canestrini believed that evolution was a process of advancement to things more complex and elevated. As far as systematics is concerned, Canestrini does not classify man in the same order as apes. He claims that man is not descended from apes, but that ape and man are descended from one common ancestor.

In the same year, Geminiano Grinelli attacked Canestrini in his publication *L'origine divina e non bestiale dell'umanitá* (The Divine and Not Animal Origin of Man), and in 1874, Giuseppe Bianconi published in French his book opposing Darwin's theory of descent, *La théorie Darwinienne et la création dite indépendante* (Darwin's Theory and the So-Called Independent Creation). In this work, the dispute surrounding Darwin is not so much about the dispute between creationists and evolutionists as about the fight between an "idealistic" evolutionism inspired by "natural philosophy" and Darwin's evolutionism, which is considered to be empirically materialistic. In his work published between 1872 and 1875, in Bologna, *I tipi animali* (Typology of the Animals), the Hegelist Angelo Camillo De Meis summed up the situation at the time perfectly when he wrote: "Even non-Darwinians admit to evolution, but they understand it as a necessary and rational process since, according to them, mutation first occurs ideally in the substantial form and then subsequently in the natural form." Augusto Verra also objected to Darwin's "empiricism" in his *Il problema dell'Assoluto* (The

Problem of the Absolute), which was published in Naples in 1882.

Two years after Darwin was appointed a member of the Accademia dei Lincei in 1875, Luigi Bombicci published his *Il processo di evoluzione nelle specie minerali* (The Evolutionary Process of Minerals), in which he describes evolution as a general process of both animate and inanimate nature. In the same year, the work by Pietro Siciliani, *La critica nella filosofia zoologica del XIX secolo* (Criticism in the Philosophical Zoology of the 19th Century), appeared, which was somewhat more critical about Darwin. In 1880, Giacomo Cattaneo published his *Saggio sull'evoluzione degli organismi* (Essay on the Development of Organisms) and 2 years later, the Darwin obituaries by Paolo Mantegazza and Salvatore Tommasi appeared. The latter had already published an important essay, *Sul moderno evoluzionismo* (On Modern Evolutionism) in 1877, in the periodical *Rivista Europea.* Now, in his obituary, he summed up the decision for or against Darwin in this way: "either evolution or miracle."

In 1883, a few months before his death, Francesco de Sanctis, one of the most important intellectuals in the new Italy, also took up the cause of Darwin and emphasized his extreme importance, not only in the field of natural science but also in all levels of human life. This makes De Sanctis one of the first people to realize the significance and the possible consequences of Darwin's theory. In his lecture *Darwin e l'arte* (Darwin and Art), given by De Sanctis in 1883 in several Italian towns, he said: "There may be people who do not know his books and have never heard the name of Darwin but still live surrounded by his teachings and under the influence of his ideas."

Francesco de Sarlo covered at length possible "applications" for Darwinism in chemistry, astronomy, philology, and sociology in his *Studi sul darwinismo* (Studies on Darwinism), published in 1887. In his essay *Darwinismo ed evoluzionismus* (Darwinism and Evolutionism), which appeared in 1891 in *Rivista di Filosofia Scientifica,* Enrico Morselli also spoke in favor of an extension of Darwinism into other disciplines. In this article, Morselli attempted to link Darwin and Herbert Spencer and demonstrate the broad applicability of Darwinism. Not only this, he also supported the irreconcilability of Darwin with a "mystic, theological and finalistic evolutionism" as argued by Antonio Fogazzaro in Italy and Asa Gray in the United States. Morselli described the United States in this connection as "a country that tends towards every form of abstruse mysticism." Among others, Alberto Sormani and Achille Loria examined the political consequences of Darwinism. In 1894, Enrico Ferri published his work *Socialismo e scienza positiva, Darwin-Spencer-Marx* (Socialism and Positive Science, Darwin-Spencer-Marx), in which he describes socialism as the logical extension of Darwin's and Spencer's theories. Of great importance in the question of the relationship between Darwinism and Marxism in Italy are Antonio Labriola's *Saggi sul materialismo storico* (Essays on Historic Materialism), published in 1896.

In his work *La teoria di Darwin criticamente esposta* (A Critical Account of Darwin's Theory), published in 1880, Giovanni Canestrini not only opposed Darwin's theory of "sexual selection," he also, and above all, opposed Darwin's theory of pangenesis as expounded in his *The Variation of Animals and Plants Under Domestication* (1868). Despite his admiration for Darwin, Canestrini preferred Lamarck's theory of inheritance, which he considered proven by numerous reports and observations.

Federico Delpino, Darwin's most important direct contact in Italy, also disputed the theory of pangenesis. In 1869, Delpino's essay *Sulla darwiniana teoria della pangenesi* (On Darwin's Theory of Pangenesis) appeared in the Italian periodical *Rivista contemporana*. This impressed Darwin so much that he had Delpino's text translated in the same year at his own cost and published in the English periodical *Scientific Opinion*. Referring to empirical assumptions about the unbelievably large number of "gemmules" that an organism would have to pass on in reproduction, Delpino, who took a spiritual position, objected that this would only be possible if the "gemmules" were immaterial substances. Assuming the empirical refutation of pangenesis, Delpino attempted in this way to reconcile Darwin's theory of evolution with a spiritual finalism. According to Delpino, the evolution of the species did not take place gradually, but rather erratically and teleologically. He believed a "forming principle" governed evolution and guaranteed the harmony of nature, which could be seen, for example, in the parallel development of blossom and pollinating insects.

Finally, as far as the notorious "Anthropologia criminale" by a certain Cesare Lombroso is concerned, this is based entirely on pre-Darwinian theories and cannot, as Lombroso himself stated, be attributed to Darwin in any way.

Darwin last appeared in the headlines of the Italian newspapers in 2004, when it was announced that the Ministry of Education intended to remove the theory of evolution from the school curriculum, where it had not even been introduced until 1978, because it apparently placed excessive demands on children. However, the ensuing outcry by the general public and the scientific community finally led to a withdrawal of this suggested reform, and Darwin's theory of evolution has remained a fixed part of the school curriculum.

— *Martin G. Weiss*

See also **Biological Anthropology and Neo-Darwinism; Creationism, Beliefs in; Darwinism, Modern; Neo-Darwinism, Origin of; Selection, Natural**

Further Readings

Corsi, P., & Weindling, P. (1984). The reception of Darwinism in France, Germany, and Italy. A comparative assessment. In D. Kohn (Ed.), *The Darwinian heritage: A centennial retrospective* (pp. 683–729). Princeton, NJ: Princeton University Press.

Giuliano, P. (1991). *Darwin in Italy: Science across cultural frontiers* (Rev. ed., R. B. Morelli, Trans.). Bloomington: Indiana University Press.

Paul, H. W. (1974). Religion and Darwinism: Varieties of Catholic reaction. In T. F. Glick (Ed.), *The comparative reception of Darwinism* (pp. 403–436). Austin & London: University of Texas Press.

DARWIN, CHARLES (1809–1882)

Charles Robert Darwin (1809–1882) is one of the greatest naturalists in the history of science. His theory of organic evolution delivered a blow to traditional thought by offering a new worldview with disquieting ramifications for understanding and appreciating the human species within natural history. The geobiologist had presented his conceptual revolution in terms of science and reason (i.e., his evolutionary framework is based upon convincing empirical evidence and rational arguments). As a result of Darwinian evolution grounded in mechanism and materialism, philosophy and theology would never again be the

Source: Courtesy of the Library of Congress.

same; just as the human species is now placed within primate history in particular and within the organic evolution of all life forms on this planet in general, religious beliefs and practices are now seen to be products of the sociocultural development of human thought and behavior.

The implications and consequences of biological evolution for the human species were both far-reaching and unsettling. It is no surprise that the brute fact of organic evolution disturbed Darwin himself, because he had been trained in theology at Christ's College, Cambridge, where he had become interested in William Paley's *Natural Theology* (1802). A strictly mechanistic and materialistic view of the emergence of humankind in terms of evolution challenged the most entrenched religious beliefs, for example, the existence of a personal God, human free will, the personal immortality of the soul, and a divine destiny for moral persons: If evolution were a fact, then the human animal would be an evolved ape, not a fallen angel.

Naturalists were becoming aware of the unfathomable age of this planet. Incomplete as they were (although ongoing scientific research is closing the gaps), the geological column and its fossil record argued for the heretical idea that species are, in fact, mutable throughout organic history.

For the theist, this universe was created by, is sustained by, and will be completed by a personal God, a perfect being that loves our species as the cosmic center of His divine creation. It is impossible, however, to reconcile materialistic evolution with traditional theology; science and reason have challenged the belief that earth history and the process of evolution are the result of a preestablished plan within the alleged order and design of this dynamic universe. Consequently, it is not surprising that some biblical fundamentalists and religious creationists reject the scientific theory of organic evolution and desire to discredit it and prevent both evolutionary research and the teaching of evolution. For others, it takes an extraordinary leap of faith and speculation to believe that a personal God could be both the beginning and the end of cosmic evolution. Biological evolution is a process that is long and complex, with pain and suffering as well as death and species extinction (five recorded mass extinctions on a global scale) pervading organic history, not to mention the endless appearance of deleterious mutations involving physical characteristics and behavior patterns. Surely, philosophy and theology now have a difficult time in maintaining teleology and essentialism as built-in aspects of cosmic evolution in general and the emergence of life forms (including the human animal) in particular.

Darwin was the pivotal thinker in establishing the fact of evolution. His heretical theory shifted an interpretation of this world from natural theology to natural science, a direct result of giving priority to empirical evidence and rational argumentation rather than to faith and belief. It was Darwin's naturalistic orientation that led him to explain evolving life forms in terms of science and reason, an interpretation independent of theology and metaphysics.

Discovering Evolution

The young Darwin was interested in geology and entomology; he enjoyed studying rocks, collecting beetles, and taking field trips with accomplished naturalists. But over the years, his primary interest would shift from geology to biology, and he came to doubt both the fixity of species and the biblical account of creation. There was no early indication of his genius for descriptive and theoretical science. Yet a convergence of ironic and fortuitous events over a period of

7 years would result in his theorizing that all species are mutable in nature and slowly evolve (or become extinct) due to natural causes over vast eons of time.

How was Darwin able to deliver this blow to traditional thought in terms of evolution? For one thing, the young naturalist had a free, open, curious, and intelligent mind that had not been indoctrinated into any religious creed or philosophical framework. That is to say, he was able to reinterpret the living world in terms of his own experiences (unique events that were critically examined in terms of science and reason). Darwin also had an exceptional ability to analyze natural objects (orchids, barnacles, and earthworms), as well as to synthesize vast amounts of empirical evidence into a comprehensive and intelligible view of organic history. Furthermore, he had an active but restrained imagination that allowed him to envision the process of biological evolution gradually taking place over vast periods of time as a result of natural forces.

Besides his unique psychological makeup, Darwin was greatly influenced by the writings of Charles Lyell, whose three-volume work, *Principles of Geology* (1830–1833), placed historical geology on a scientific foundation. While reading the entire work during his trip as naturalist aboard the HMS *Beagle,* Darwin slowly accepted Lyell's sweeping geological framework of time and change within a naturalistic viewpoint of earth history. One may even argue that Lyell was the single most important influence on Darwin because without this vast temporal perspective, the geobiologist might never have questioned the eternal fixity of species or, subsequently, thought about life forms in terms of their mutability throughout organic history. Simply put, the dynamic framework of Lyellian geology, with its changing environments, implied a process view of plants and animals. Having become convinced that Lyell was right, Darwin then began both to doubt a strict and literal interpretation of Genesis and to question more and more the alleged immutability of flora and fauna types on this planet. Briefly, Lyell's dynamic interpretation of rock strata throughout geological history clearly argued for an evolutionary interpretation of life forms throughout biological history.

Another major influence on Darwin's worldview was, of course, his voyage of discovery on the HMS *Beagle.* During this 5-year circumnavigation of the globe (1831–1836), the young naturalist experienced the extraordinary diversity of plant and animal species in the Southern Hemisphere (particularly the insects of a Brazilian rain forest) as well as the provocative discovery of giant fossils in the geological column of Argentina. Slowly, he began to imagine the tree or coral of life throughout organic history. Of special importance was Darwin's comparing and contrasting life forms on oceanic islands with their counterparts on the mainland of South America. He was struck not only by their differences but also even more so by their similarities. These similarities suggested that groups of species share a common ancestor. Thus, throughout space and time, Darwin envisioned the historical continuity and essential unity of all life on this planet. Certainly, in retrospect, it was his 5-week visit to the Galapagos Islands (September 15 to October 20, 1835) that caused this naturalist to acknowledge the crucial relationship between the physical characteristics and behavior patterns of an organism and its specific habitat.

No doubt, Darwin was puzzled by the belief that a personal God had created so many different species of a specific animal form for the same archipelago: Why would there be different species of finches, mockingbirds, tortoises, and iguanas throughout the Galapagos Islands? For Darwin, the obvious answer, supported by the empirical evidence, is that there was neither a single divine creation only 6,000 years ago nor a sequence of special creations over this same period of time. Instead, science and reason argued for a natural (not supernatural) explanation for the origin, history, diversity, and extinction of life forms on the changing earth.

Darwin was willing to doubt the myth of Genesis, while taking seriously both the new facts and the new concepts in several earth sciences (geology, paleontology, biogeography and comparative morphology). At the end of the voyage, he was convinced that species are mutable and began to keep notebooks on his theory of "descent with modification"—an evolutionary interpretation of organic history. Unfortunately, he did not as yet have an explanatory mechanism to account for biological evolution in terms of a naturalistic framework. Nevertheless, he steadfastly committed himself to the mutability of species as an incontrovertible fact of the living world.

In 1838, by chance, Darwin read Thomas Malthus's scientific monograph, *An Essay on the Principle of Population* (1798, 1803), which described life as a struggle for existence. According to Malthus, this ongoing struggle for survival in nature results from the discrepancy between the arithmetic increase of plants and the geometric increase of animals (especially the human species). Malthus's book gave the naturalist his major explanatory mechanism of natural selection or the "survival of the fittest" (as the philosopher Herbert Spencer had referred to it). Now, Darwin had both a theory and a mechanism to account for the history of life on earth: The scientific theory is organic evolution, while the explanatory mechanism is natural selection. This was a strictly mechanistic and materialistic interpretation of the biological world.

Admittedly, Darwin himself was concerned neither with the beginning of this universe and the origin of life nor the future of our species and the end of the world. He left it to other thinkers to grapple with those philosophical questions and theological issues that surround the scientific fact of organic evolution.

Darwin's Thoughts

In the first and second editions of *On the Origin of Species* (1859), Darwin did not refer to God as the creator of the world. But encouraged to do so by the geologist Lyell, the last four editions of the *Origin* volume contained only one simple reference to God:

> There is grandeur in this view of life, with its several powers, having been originally breathed by the Creator into a few forms or into one; and that, whilst this planet has gone cycling on according to the fixed law of gravity, from so simple a beginning endless forms most beautiful and most wonderful have been, and are being evolved.

Nonetheless, Darwin's *Autobiography* makes it perfectly clear that he was publicly an agnostic (if not privately an atheist). Briefly, Darwin's own cosmology is agnostic, while his theory of evolution is atheistic.

Realizing how disturbing his epoch-making *Origin* book would be, Darwin did not wish to add to the growing controversy surrounding biological evolution by writing about the emergence of our own species. Interestingly enough, then, Darwin does not discuss human evolution in his major work on the theory of evolution. In fact, one may argue that it was the devastating ramifications of organic evolution for the human animal that actually caused the uproar over Darwinian evolution.

Grappling with the implications of evolution, Thomas Huxley in England coined the word "agnostic" to express his own noncommittal position concerning the existence of God, while Ernst Haeckel in Germany advocated pantheism to express his dynamic worldview free from religion and theology. In doing so, both naturalists had acknowledged that the scientific fact of organic evolution has wide-ranging conclusions for those entrenched values of Western civilization that are grounded in traditional philosophy, religion, and theology. At Harvard University, the botanist Asa Grey supported theistic evolution.

For over a decade, even Darwin himself had been reluctant to extend his theory of evolution to account for the origin and history of the human species. After 12 years, he published his other major work, *The Descent of Man* (1871). It is in this book that the naturalist writes about human evolution, although both Huxley as comparative morphologist and Haeckel as comparative embryologist had already lectured on and written about the evolution of our species within the history of the primates.

Darwin wrote that the human animal is closest to the African pongids, the chimpanzee and the gorilla (the existence of the bonobo was unknown to the naturalists of that time). He held that our species and these two great apes share a common ancestor, which would be found in the fossil record of that so-called Dark Continent, which has, since the middle of the 20th century, shed so much light on the history of humankind. Moreover, Darwin claimed that the human species differs merely in degree, rather than in kind, from the pongids, there being no structure or function in the human animal that does not already exist to some degree in the three great apes known to him (orangutan, gorilla, and chimpanzee). That is to say, even intelligence and emotions exist to some degree in all the pongids, which now include the bonobo.

For Darwin, it was the moral aspect in the human being that elevates it above—but does not separate it from—the apes. Even so, this moral aspect has also evolved throughout primate history from even lower beginnings, in earlier animals. Philosophers and theologians cannot ignore the reality that human beings themselves have created ethics, morals, and values within a natural environment and sociocultural milieu; one may speak of a human being as the evaluating animal, thereby distinguishing the human species from all the apes and monkeys.

Likewise, Darwin claimed that the naturalistic basis of human morality had had its origin in those social instincts and altruistic feelings that have enhanced the adaptation and reproduction of evolving fossil apes, and later protohominids, followed by bipedal hominids. These instincts and feelings are visible in the behavior patterns of living primates, particularly in the great apes.

The Evolutionary Worldview

Clearly, scientific evolution both challenged and superseded the ideas and frameworks of Plato, Aristotle, Aquinas, Descartes, Kant, and Hegel (among many others). The certainty of previous values grounded in God-given laws or divine revelations could no longer be upheld by rigorous naturalists. As a result, the Darwinian conceptual revolution in science resulted in the emergence of both evolutionary ethics and pragmatic values in modern natural philosophy, as well as an evolutionary interpretation of the origin and history of human societies and their cultures (including languages and beliefs).

For the rigorous scientist, evolution requires at least reinterpreting or rejecting the old beliefs in God, free will, immortality, and a divine destiny for our species. For decades, ongoing evolutionary research in the areas of paleoanthropology and primate ethology has clearly supported the fact of human evolution, as well as a naturalistic explanation for the so-called brain/mind problem in philosophy.

It is not surprising that Darwin was an agnostic, but he did not deal directly with the religious implications and theological consequences of the fact of evolution. No doubt, he himself was disturbed by the ramifications of evolution for Christianity. The power of science and reason had demolished the traditional beliefs concerning this universe, life on earth, and the place the human species occupies within dynamic nature. Neither this small planet nor the human animal on it could still be held to be absolutely unique within cosmic reality.

In summary, Darwin developed his theory of evolution as a result of the convergence of three important events: accepting Lyell's geological perspective, reflecting on his exceptional experiences during the global voyage of HMS *Beagle,* and benefiting from Malthus's insightful theory of population growth. It is to Darwin's great credit that his analytic abilities were supplemented by a rational imagination. Through abduction, the creative interrelationship of facts and concepts, he was able to elevate his own methodology above a strictly empiricist approach to investigating the natural world in terms of the earth sciences. This open orientation of synthesis allowed him to bring about a conceptual revolution in terms of the biological evolution of all life on this planet.

There is a crucial distinction between evolution and interpretations of this process. Darwin was able to replace myopic opinions and naive superstitions with science and reason. For him, vitalism and theism were no longer needed to explain human existence in terms of organic evolution. As such, the theory of evolution has provoked philosophers and theologians alike to accept a dynamic interpretation of this universe and a new conception of the creation and destruction of life throughout organic history.

Darwin's scientific writings make no appeal to a personal God to account for organic evolution or the emergence of our own species. Darwin was an agnostic in a cosmological context but an atheist within the evolutionary framework. We might wonder what his thoughts on religion and theology were when, as an aged naturalist, Darwin took those daily strolls down the Sandwalk behind his residence, Down House, in Kent, England. His reflections on scientific evidence must have caused him to doubt every aspect of theism, and perhaps in his later years, he was a silent atheist who kept his disbelief to himself, just as his own free-thinking father, Robert Waring Darwin, had kept his atheism from influencing the other members of the Darwin family.

It may be argued that Darwin himself demonstrated a failure of nerve in his own unwillingness to clearly state an atheistic position. Nevertheless, as an iconoclastic scientist and transitional naturalist, he paved the way for the pervasive materialism of modern times.

Consequences of Evolution

Although a shy and gentle apostate in science, Darwin had opened the door onto a universe in evolution. Of the countless millions of species that have inhabited this planet, most of them now extinct, only one life form has been able to philosophize on both its own existence and the natural environment: We may speak of *Homo sapiens sapiens* as this evolving universe conscious of itself. More and more, through science and technology, the human species is capable of directing its ongoing evolution as well as determining the future destiny of plant and animal forms on the earth and elsewhere. Today, we witness emerging teleology as a result of human intervention. This incredible power of control over life dictates that human beings make value judgments that could affect their adaptation, survival, enrichment, and fulfillment. What we may learn from evolution is that, as a species-conscious and evolution-aware form of life, humankind needs other plants, animals, and a suitable environment for its ongoing existence. And the inevitability of extinction is a brute fact for all life.

Clearly, Darwin had both intellectual and personal integrity; he was willing to change his scientific interpretation of nature as the integration of empirical evidence and rational concepts dictated. He exemplifies an open-minded and courageous naturalist whose commitment to organic evolution challenged both the engrained Aristotelian philosophy of fixed species and the Thomistic theology of divine causality.

In his autobiography, Darwin writes about his extraordinary global voyage on the HMS *Beagle* and subsequent productive life at Down House, despite chronic illness. Five chapters focus on the preparation, publication, and critical reviews of *On the Origin of Species* (1859), the naturalist's major contribution to evolutionary thought. Interestingly, his wife Emma Wedgwood Darwin had deleted the references to God and Christianity from the posthumously published *Autobiography*. Not until 1958 did an unexpurgated version of this significant work appear in print.

In Chapter 3, Darwin presented his final thoughts on religion and theology. It is clear that this evolutionist and materialist was reticent to express his own beliefs. Even so, his personal thoughts neither verify nor falsify the evolved claims of religionists and theologians. It suffices that Darwin's theory of evolution is strictly naturalistic, both in principle and intent.

— *H. James Birx*

See also **Creationism, Beliefs in; Evolution, Models of; Selection, Natural**

Further Readings

Browne, E. J. (1996). *Charles Darwin: Voyaging.* Princeton, NJ: Princeton University Press.
Browne, E. J. (2003). *Charles Darwin: The power of place.* Princeton, NJ: Princeton University Press.
Darwin, C. (2000). *Autobiography.* Amherst, NY: Prometheus Books. (Original work written May–August 1876, first published in 1887, first unexpurgated edition published 1958)

Dennett, D. C. (1995). *Darwin's dangerous idea: Evolution and the meanings of life.* New York: Simon & Schuster.
Mayr, E. (1991). *One long argument: Charles Darwin and the genesis of modern evolutionary thought.* Cambridge, MA: Harvard University Press.
Moorhead, A. (1969). *Darwin and the Beagle.* New York: Harper & Row.
Ridley, M.(Ed.). (1996). *The Darwin reader* (2nd ed.). New York: Norton.
Weiner, J. (1995). *The beak of the finch: A story of evolution in our time.* New York: Vintage.

DARWINISM, MODERN

Modern Darwinism, also known as the "modern synthesis" or "neo-Darwinism," is a comprehensive theory of evolution that combines Darwin's theory of natural selection with principles of Mendelian genetics. Although the theory was established in the 1920s to 1940s and biology has undergone profound and rapid changes since that time, neo-Darwinism is still considered to be a generally accepted paradigm of biological evolution.

A basic idea of neo-Darwinism is that it is a two-step process. The first step is a random generation of genetically determined variance in population of individuals, followed by second step, the selection of those individual variants by environments that are relatively more successful to survive and reproduce. In recent years, we have been witnessing an expansion of neo-Darwinian principles beyond biology: to cosmology, medicine, economics, computing, neurology, psychology, psychiatry, modeling of cultural development, and history of science. Neo-Darwinian algorithm is applicable not only to living organisms but also to any system (whether made of molecules, organisms, digital strings) if the following conditions are satisfied:

1. There is a population of entities capable of multiplication and variation.

2. There is a process of selection by a limited environment in which better-adapted entities multiply faster than others.

The Reconciliation of Mendelism and Darwinism

Soon after the publication of *On the Origin of Species,* the Achilles heel of the whole theory of evolution via natural selection was recognized in an inheritance theory used by Darwin. Darwin worked with the blended-inheritance theory commonly accepted by his contemporaries, which, however, logically undermines the very nature of the evolutionary mechanism as suggested by Darwin, an accumulation of a small inherited adaptive changes through a long time. If inheritance is blended, any accumulation of inherited variations, which is a key element in the gradual building of complex adaptive structures, is impossible. For if heredity is of a blending type, any new variation is halved in every generation, and in fact it disappears very soon. Darwin tried to answer the problem by his own ad hoc theory of heredity (called *pangenesis*), a totally speculative one. He flirted with his own version of the inheritance of acquired characteristics (despite the fact that he was strongly critical of Lamarckian theory of evolution), but he never was happy with it. Paradoxically, at the same time, the right answer was already there—in Gregor Mendel's theory of inheritance. Mendel came up with the idea of hereditary "atoms" (he called them "factors"), which cannot blend, but can only combine in a particular rations. Mendel's work was published in 1865, but unfortunately it remained unknown (although not inaccessible to Darwin, as well as to almost all his contemporaries) until it was rediscovered two decades after Darwin's (1882) and Mendel's (1884) deaths at the beginning of 20th century.

German biologist August Weismann (1834–1914) is now known as a forerunner of neo-Darwinism, since he recognized that the Darwinian mechanism of evolution can work perfectly without any kind of Lamarckian inheritance of acquired characteristics, and all it needs is a generation of random changes in hereditary material and selection of those individuals who carry not the best possible adaptations, but better than their competitors.

When principles of Mendelian genetics were rediscovered and accepted by biologists during the first two decades of the 20th century, they were first completely misunderstood as a crucial argument not in favor but (paradoxically from today's perspective) against Darwinism. The argument went like this: Mendelian ratios of inherited characteristics display nonblended discrete inheritance, which is also responsible for discrete differences not only between individuals within a species but also between species. New species are generated by a big change in hereditary material, which is responsible for large differences in phenotypes, and therefore natural selection is not needed to explain speciation.

However, the schism between Mendelian genetics with mutational saltationisms at one side and natural selection with gradualism at the other side did not last for a long time. A reconciliation between Darwinism and Mendelism was achieved by the independent theoretical works written around 1930 by Ronald A. Fisher (1890–1962), John B. S. Haldane (1892–1964), and Sewall Wright (1889–1988). As early as 1918, R. A. Fisher published a paper in which he showed that continuous character distribution in populations as observed by biometricians can be explained by discrete Mendelian genetics. He expanded his mathematical exploring of evolution in the book *The Genetical Theory of Natural Selection* (1930). In a similar way, J. B. S. Haldane summarized a series of his theoretical papers on evolution in his book *The Causes of Evolution* (1932), and S. Wright published a long paper called "Evolution in Mendelian Populations" in 1931.

These works inspired other biologists in the 1930s to 1940s from a variety of different biological disciplines to contribute to this project of reconciliation: from field and laboratory studies in population genetics (T. Dobzhansky, E. B. Ford), paleontology (G. G. Simpson), and systematics (E. Mayr). The reconciliation is now known under several names: neo-Darwinism, the synthetic theory of evolution, and the modern synthesis.

Changes of Gene Frequencies in Gene Pools

The key concept for the modeling of evolutionary dynamics is the gene pool, a concept that comes from quantitative population genetics and became a main conceptual tool of reconciliation between Mendelism and Darwinism, mentioned above. A gene pool is a collection of all genes, in fact, all gene variants (alleles), shared by all members of population. From a philosophical point of view, Darwin is thought to have brought population thinking into species conceptualization in order to replace traditional typological species concept. For him, species were populations of different individuals.

A gene pool is a scientific abstraction, since genes do not actually exist freely in some sort of pond, but they always exist within living organisms. As with every abstraction, the gene pool model presupposes a set of ideal conditions, which are hardly met in nature. Despite this, the model is no less successful than other useful population models in descriptions of a real population of organisms and in predictions of the dynamics of its change, as for example, a concept of ideal gas in physics. In fact, ideal conditions of the gene pool helped biologists to recognize quantitative limits for stability and evolutionary change of real populations. These conditions are as follows: the absence of mutation; no migration of genes from other gene pools; the population size is large enough (effectively infinite), so there is no a sampling error in a process of setting up a new gene pool by reproduction; combinations of gene variants into genotypes (as result a of mating) are random; and finally, there is no selection—all gene variants have the same probability to have their own copies in next generation. As it was shown independently in 1908 by English mathematician G. H. Hardy and German physician G. Weinberg, if these conditions are met, frequencies of gene variants in gene pool are stable through generations and there is no evolution, the statement known as the Hardy-Weinberg theorem. It can be demonstrated that the stability of gene frequencies in successive gene pools is a result of bionomic distribution.

Slower or rapid changes in gene frequencies of population are the results of parameter values of processes destabilizing the Hardy-Weinberg equilibrium: mutation, migration, nonrandom mating, limited size of population, and selection.

An objection can be raised that all changes of allele frequencies in a gene pool are only of small importance for evolutionary theory, because they explain what is called "microevolution," or changes within borders of the same species. But "true" evolution has to do with the origin of a new species, and big changes. The neo-Darwinian answer to this objection is that gradual accumulation of microevolutionary changes over a long period of time leads to big changes, so big that new species arise. For example, a new gene pool can be set up by the gradual accumulation of microevolutionary processes after an original population divides into two subpopulations that are isolated geographically. In such a way, they in fact form two separate gene pools, which differ in their gene compositions so much that they cannot fuse together later when geographic barriers disappear and populations physically unite (allopatric speciation). Or a breeding barrier can arise within the original population in a way that a new gene pool is set up inside the old one (sympatric evolution), without geographic isolation. Evolutionary biologists spent some time quarreling over which type of speciation is the right one, until they found that both are present in nature.

Impact of Molecular Approach to Modern Darwinism

Since early the 1970s, the use of modern molecular biology techniques such as gel electrophoresis, restriction fragment length polymorphism (RFLP) analysis, and recently, DNA fingerprinting with the help of polymerase chain reaction (PCR), protein, and mostly DNA sequencing, all together with the use of computer power, have revolutionarized our understanding of past evolutionary history and Darwinian mechanisms of the evolutionary process.

Molecular phylogenetic studies have helped to settle some issues of phylogenetic relationships that were impossible to solve using traditional methods of comparative morphology, anatomy, physiology, or behavior. The range of molecular approaches in reconstructing phylogenies is incredible—from very rapid recent evolution of viruses like HIV to the origin of the three domains of life (bacteria, archea, and eukaryotes). New phylogenetic trees based on protein or DNA sequence homology were constructed. In many cases, they were in good agreement with trees constructed by traditional methods; however, in some important cases, they revealed surprising differences, as, for example, in the case of human evolution. Based on various molecular data, scientists estimated that African apes and humans diverged from each other about 5 million years ago, not 15 or even 30 million years ago, as it had been estimated from fossil record evidence. These data suggest that human lineage diverged after the separation of the orangutan lineage, but before the separation of chimpanzees and gorillas.

Analysis of sequence differences in mitochondrial DNA coming from recent human populations from around the world led to a reconstructed phylogenetic tree with a single root, which represents a common maternal ancestor ("mitochondrial Eve"), living 120,000 to 300,000 years ago. A new powerful technique (mostly PCR) enables scientists late in the 20th century to isolate fragments of mitochondrial DNA from the Tyrolean Ice Man, an Egyptian mummy, or a Neandertal skeleton (so-called molecular paleontology). Since Neandertal DNA differs from human DNA about 4 times more than the difference between living humans, it is reasonable to conclude that Neandertals must have diverged from a common ancestor with humans about 550,000 to 690,000 years ago, which means that Neandertals were probably a separate species.

Although there is still an ongoing debate about the methodology of molecular approach (for example, how accurate is "a molecular clock"), and much more data are needed, there is no doubt that molecular anthropology is receiving growing respect among scientists as their methods are rapidly improving.

Neutralist-Selectionist Controversy Over Molecular Evolution

One of the most important conceptual challenges to neo-Darwinian paradigm came from the theory of neutral molecular evolution proposed by Japanese geneticist Motoo Kimura (1924–1994) in November 1967, and published a year later. It started with the controversy over how to interpret available first indirect estimates of genetic variability based on protein polymorphism, which had started to be measured by gel electrophoresis. According to Kimura, the level of measured protein variability was too high to be explained by natural selection, and he believed that the overwhelming majority of genetic variability at the molecular level (DNA, RNA, and proteins) is due to random accumulation of selectively neutral mutations. With the help of population mathematical models, he tried to demonstrate that the way these neutral mutations are lost or fixed in gene pools is due to a sampling-error process (called "random genetic drift"). It has been known before that sampling errors are at work when offspring gene pools are created from gene pools of parents, but it was thought that it is significant only in small populations undergoing population bottlenecks. But Kimura pointed out that sampling errors are significant even in large but finite populations. He was not rejecting the role of natural selection on genes responsible for adaptations to the environment. But according to him, a process of neo-Darwinian selection is responsible for only a small fraction of observed genetic variability

and the great majority of mutant substitutions at the molecular level are due to random fixations of selectively neutral mutants.

The support for the theory of neutral molecular evolution came later from the revealing of noncoding sequences of DNA as introns (nontranslated spacers within genes) and pseudogenes (a sort of gene wreck). These DNA sequences ignored by natural selection are accumulating mutations at a higher rate than coding sequences, as it was predicted by neutral theory. At present, the neutral theory is a widely accepted theory for the evolution of those parts of DNA that are selectively neutral.

Punctuated-Equilibrium Theory

In 1972, American paleontologist Niles Eldredge and Stephen Jay Gould opened the discussion about the tempo of macroevolutionary changes. They argued that the paleontological evidence does not support a classical Darwinian view of gradual transitions. They insisted that what is actually seen in fossil records are long periods of morphological stability (stasis), which are punctuated by short (in geologic terms) periods of rapid changes. They believed that this pattern cannot be explained in a satisfying way, referring to gaps in fossil records, but that in fact this fossil pattern reflects an evolutionary process itself in which new forms appear rather suddenly. They proposed a new model of evolution called "punctuated equilibrium."

In the debate that followed, biologists discussed whether "revolutions" in phylogeny caused by micro-mutations (small changes in DNA sequences like base-pair substitutions, deletions, and insertions) or larger genetic changes (macromutations), such as various chromosomal rearrangements or movements of transposable genetic elements across a genome, are needed in order to explain large morphological changes. Critics of the punctuated-equilibrium model argued that revolutionary changes are not in fact revolutionary and it all is a question of scaling. They were theoretically demonstrating that periods of "sudden" changes are long enough to be explained by the accumulation of micromutations and that gaps in fossils series really reflect incompleteness of the records.

A new perspective was brought to the debate by a recent advance in interdisciplinary research in evolutionary developmental biology, or "evo-devo." On one hand, it supports the view that very small genetic changes can become amplified during organismal development into major morphological differences at the order of higher taxons. On the other hand, it also started to provide growing evidence showing how various macromutational changes, such as gene duplications, chromosomal rearrangements, and genome reshapings, could be responsible for major evolutionary events.

Neutral theory and punctuated-equilibrium theory were proposed as theories of "non-Darwinian" evolution, and they are a fundamental challenge to neo-Darwinism if we understand it in the narrow sense of a few limited ideas. But if we understand modern Darwinism in the sense of a broader framework for the evolutionary theory that combines randomness with selection, then both challenging theories can be incorporated into it. Randomly generated micro- or macro-mutations are fixed in gene pools either randomly, if they are selectively neutral, or by natural selection.

— *Peter Sykora*

See also **Biological Anthropology and Neo-Darwinism; Genetics, Population; Selection, Natural**

Further Readings

Lewin, R. (1997). *Patterns in evolution.* New York: Scientific American Library.

Majerus, M., Amos, W., & Hurst G. (1996). *Evolution: The four billion year war.* Edinburgh: Longman.

Ridley, M. (2003). *Evolution.* Oxford: Blackwell Science.

Strickberger, M. W. (2000). *Evolution.* Sudbury, MA: Jones & Bartlett.

Wen-Hsiung, L. (1997). *Fundamentals of molecular evolution.* Sunderland, MA: Sinauer.

DARWINISM VERSUS LAMARCKISM

In the sometimes almost fratricidal debate between Darwinians (proponents of gradual evolution over many generations) and Lamarckians (proponents of evolution who believe traits acquired during the lifetime of an organism can be passed on to offspring), Charles Darwin had few champions as

persistent or superb as Ernst Mayr, who died in February 2005. Mayr had, during his career, become perhaps the foremost interpreter of Darwinism in Europe. In his obituary (posted by Michael Ruse on the academic Internet site "Philosophy of Biology"), it was noted that Mayr had "met and became close friends with a group of men who were determined to put evolutionary studies on a new and proper foundation. Most important of all was the Russian-born geneticist Theodosius Dobzhansky, closely followed by the brilliant paleontologist George Gaylord Simpson."

Ambroise Tardieu direxit

Mayr, who was converted to Darwinism at least in part by Dobzhansky, wrote his own opus, *Systematics and the Origin of Species* in 1942, at a time when the theory of Social Darwinism was being put to a brutal test by the fascist dictatorships of Europe during World War II. As the obituary explained, "His main contribution was to demonstrate beyond doubt the variation that exists in nature, and how everything points to gradual change—a key plank in the Darwinian program. Particularly important was the evidence of groups that range all the way from good species (interbreeding populations, isolated from others), to species-in-the-making, with subgroups starting to break apart, and on to fully defined separate species."

Moreover, much of the work at systematizing evolution and making it a permanent part of scientific inquiry was done by Mayr as well. As the founding editor of *Evolution* magazine, he provided a public forum for a discussion of the discipline. As one who had been educated in philosophy in his native Germany, he also saw the links between evolution and other sciences and worked greatly in his later career to bring scientific disciplines closer together to collaborate more and compete less. Perhaps the most significant achievement of this part of his career was his role in the foundation of the Department of the History of Science at Harvard University. As Ruse wrote of Mayr, "Above all, Mayr was a holist, meaning that he thought breaking things down to small components is not only not necessarily the right way to go in biological science, it is often positively exactly the wrong way to go."

— John F. Murphy Jr.

DARWINISM, SOCIAL

Social Darwinism is the theory that human beings have a natural tendency to compete and that the strong will overcome the weak. The name comes from its association with Charles Darwin's (1809–1882) biological theories of evolution and natural selection. Like many social theories that attempt to explain human behavior, Social Darwinism can best be seen on a continuum; that is, the application of the ideas in actual practice range between extremes, some well-intentioned and others discriminatory. Generally, the label of "Social Darwinism" is not a positive one, though there have been some prominent defenders and the principles still present themselves in contemporary socioeconomic theory.

It is misleading to reduce all of the ideas that were advanced by Charles Darwin to a single theory of "Darwinism." Through the biological study of humans and other animals, he drew several conclusions, including that organisms in the world are constantly evolving, have descended from common ancestry, and abide by a natural selection process that considers genetically inherited traits and adaptation to the environment. It is equally misleading to presume that Social Darwinism is a deliberate extension of his theories. Social Darwinism was not developed by Darwin himself, but represents the social attitudes of many people from his time, especially the decades following the 1859 publication of *On the Origin of Species*. The common aspect between Darwin's work and Social Darwinism is natural selection.

Background

The English philosopher Herbert Spencer (1820–1903) in the years before Darwin's fame developed a theory of social evolution whereby the best form of society is one where individualism prevails. Spencer, not Darwin, coined the phrase "survival of the fittest," and he applied this concept to human beings and societies, not just to particular plant and animal species. For humans to prevail in nature, the society must be as strong as it can be; this leaves no room for weak members. If this theory is descriptive, it observes that this is the state of nature and attempts to explain what happens on its own. Spencer, however, used the theory prescriptively; that is, he endorsed the application of eliminating the weakest links as a theory of ethics. What is morally right, in this view, is what advances the species as a whole. Society is strengthened when composed of the strongest individuals. Those too weak to fend for themselves, those who suffer from illness or disability, even those who find themselves in disadvantaged social circumstances such as poverty would best serve humankind if left behind. Spencer extended this principle to a liberalist political view that valued the rights of individuals over government power. He was influenced by the French philosopher Jean-Baptiste Lamarck (1744–1829), who proposed that environmentally inspired human traits were transferred from parents to children during their own lifetimes through the theory he called the "inheritance of acquired traits."

Most noted for his support of social contract theory, English philosopher Thomas Hobbes (1588–1679) similarly emphasized the importance of the individual. For Hobbes, human beings are naturally self-interested. Every action and decision is based upon what will ultimately serve the best interests of the individual. Society is a collection of individuals who agree to give up some of their personal rights and liberties in order to benefit all individuals within the group. In agreeing to abide by social laws, each citizen agrees to a "contract." In addition, Hobbes proposed that without government, humans would compete against one another in a brutal "state of nature" not unlike the struggle Social Darwinists claim to be natural. Hobbes was rebuffed by French philosopher Jean-Jacques Rousseau (1712–1778), who asserted that good and bad behavior are both attributable to one's civilization, an emphasis of nurture over nature that would present itself again over the next centuries. Spencer nevertheless recognized the self-interested human nature that Hobbes observed but placed it in evolutionary terms. The most effective contract would be with oneself and representative of those interests to the point of disregarding the weaker members of society. Spencer believed that this is the way of nature: that the strong will survive through competition and by disregarding, rather than helping, the weak.

Like Hobbes, the English mathematician, minister, and economic theorist Thomas Robert Malthus (1766–1834) believed that individual restraint could serve to benefit society. He saw this less through social contract, however, than through individual commitment to avoiding vice, such as excessive reproduction (he advocated abstinence). The betterment of the world's human population could only arrive by limiting its growth. In fact, Malthus predicted that overpopulation would lead to increased demands for resources that society would be unable to produce. A shortage of food, in particular, would result, he claimed, as the population needs outgrew the supply, and the weakest members of society would die of starvation. To avoid famine, civilization would regress to subsistence level with an emphasis on agriculture—producing just enough food to survive—in what has come to be known as a "Malthusian catastrophe." There is a balance that must be maintained in nature. The evolutionary cycle of society offers a means of controlling human excess and weakness of will.

Social Application

The theories of Hobbes and Malthus are considered the predecessors to Social Darwinism. They influenced both Darwin and Spencer; Darwin himself accredited Malthus with inspiring *On the Origin of Species.* Successors have endorsed similar philosophies in more of a social application than Darwin's biological account of human evolution. The American entrepreneur Andrew Carnegie (1835–1919) hosted Spencer in a visit to the United States and implemented the ideas of Social Darwinism into his extensive philanthropic projects (by the time of his death, he had donated over $350 million). While Carnegie was not above providing financial assistance to others—in fact, he believed that those with wealth had an obligation to support their societies—he was selective in choosing the recipients. In his 1900 book, *The Gospel of Wealth,* he expressed the Social Darwinist idea that money should be used for cultural enrichment rather than charitable handouts to the poor. Most of his public projects provided services for the intellectual growth of individuals, such as libraries, music halls, and institutions of higher education. He insisted on local accountability and maintenance of these projects, and his approach would be recognized today as a merit-based, rather than entitlement, system. The individual was responsible for his or her education. Carnegie encouraged access to tools for growth, but only those with the desire to improve their own lives would truly benefit.

This same principle—that individuals should be responsible for their own welfare and accomplishments—is associated with the laissez-faire political theory, where the government intrudes as little possible and leaves individuals to their own resources. This concept is applied in economics, social policy, and ethics; any behavior is acceptable until it infringes on the rights or welfare of others. Economically, the motivation is to inspire accountability, and this is the driving force behind capitalism. Critics complain that Social Darwinism can lead, however, to economic exploitation and class divisions. The wealthy become wealthier by profiting from the work of the labor force. Because the working poor need money, they work menial, sometimes dangerous jobs, for excessive hours and with substandard benefits. Strong individuals achieve further success, while those who are weak remain in the working class. Social Darwinism claims this is not a bad thing, that unfavorable finances are motivation for self-empowerment, and that those who do not rise above disadvantage do not deserve to enjoy the benefits of the higher classes.

Discrimination

Because labor distinctions are often drawn along ethnic lines—with minority populations working low-wage jobs—there is potential for discrimination that follows racial lines. The National Socialist Party that rose in Germany before World War II began with the hope for a unified Germany and economic prosperity for workers amidst industrial and technological change. A poor economy, however, was blamed on minorities and foreigners, particularly Jewish immigrants who did not share German ancestry. In a vivid display of Social Darwinism taken to an extreme, the Nazi regime under Adolf Hitler (1889–1945) sought to improve German society by first ejecting, then eliminating, what were considered to be inferior races. The Jewish people were considered so weak, so low among the classes of humans, as to be no more valuable than animals. Social Darwinism here provided justification for seizing property, imprisoning without cause, using humans involuntarily as test subjects in gruesome mutilations and medical experiments, and ultimately exterminating approximately 6 million human beings. This was done with the intention of weeding out the weak, the members of society considered an obstacle to the progress of German culture and the master human race that was destined to rule the world.

Racist ideas were not uncommon to American thought in the late 19th century, with intellectuals such as John Fiske (1842–1901) and Darwin himself publicly endorsing racial supremacy. Fiske said that the domination of British and American Caucasians over the rest of the world, be it civilized or what was understood as "barbaric" at that time, attested to the superiority of the Anglo-Saxon race. Darwin believed that women were inferior to men and that Blacks (or African Americans) were among the least evolutionarily developed human beings. Social Darwinists frequently referenced this assertion when defending the application of their theory to justify racism, including later Nazi efforts to advance the perfect race and Jim Crow laws that endorsed discrimination through segregation in the southern United States through the 1960s, 100 years following the official end to slavery in this country.

Racial purification is only one possible end of *eugenics*, the term Darwin's cousin, Sir Francis Galton (1822–1911), gave to the concept of improving human society through reproductive controls. Galton was a pioneer in studies on hereditary traits, researching genetic patterns in traits such as fingerprints. *Eugenics* is from the Greek word *eugenav*, which means "well-born." In its least controversial forms, this could mean

choosing partners for procreation who have particular desirable traits, such as strength, health, and intelligence. It becomes more questionable when individuals and then groups of people are categorically denied the right to reproduce, such as through the sterilization of mental patients. Social Darwinism, in seeking to eliminate the weaker members from the gene pool, justifies denying these individuals the right to reproduce. A healthy society would be free of disease. If certain diseases, temperaments, and even work ethic and productivity habits are determined to be heritable traits, then denying these traits from being passed on to future generations would be toward the improvement of the society as a whole. If the weak are destined to be eliminated through natural selection regardless, then actions toward this end are neither contrary to nature nor outside of the right of stronger individuals to impose. The evolutionary account of human development places people within the animal kingdom biologically. Humans are not outside of nature. People are agents who can act and make decisions according to their own will, but anything we do is within the bounds of nature, regardless. Social Darwinism sees eugenics as simply hastening the inevitable natural selection process.

Biology and Culture

Darwin's ideas were revolutionary because they radically altered the way most sciences proceeded from that point forward. They also were taken as an affront to many who were religious, because human evolution seems to conflict with creationism, the belief that humans were designed by the intelligent being recognized as God. Many critics reduced Darwinism to a theory that failed to distinguish humans from apes. In fact, his main claim was that animals, including humans, had evolved, based upon the biological evidence he had collected through fossils.

Social Darwinism looked to biological features as an explanation for social behavior. If it was natural for only the best-suited traits to be passed on to offspring—or even for one species of plant or animal to eliminate another—then it was also natural for the best-adapted humans to survive, thrive, and dominate the weaker members, who were naturally destined to die off. Inheritable traits were determined to be the cause of physical conditions, good and bad, through the theory that is called "genetic determinism." Developmental theories were inspired, some more legitimate than others. Phrenology mistakenly attempted to identify criminal behavior according to the shape of the human head. Psychology justly looked to neural connections in the brain to explain emotional and affective states.

Anthropologist Franz Boas (1858–1942) reemphasized the cultural component of social research, however, encouraging science not to disregard the historical aspects of the human experience individuals and societies cannot be explained purely in terms of biological features or evolution. Rather, Boas and successors noted the extent to which individuals are affected by their environment, and society by the actions of the individuals. Boas's approach advocated the abandonment of one's own bias when studying other cultures. In this regard, it is the opposite of the Social Darwinist trend of emphasizing the qualitative differences between individuals and groups of people. The idea of not relying solely on genetics and, rather, recognizing the dynamic influence of culture was shared by the 20th-century behaviorist psychological movement, which observed the ways in which one's society could profoundly affect, or condition, individual patterns of response.

The 1950s work of James D. Watson (1928-) and Francis Crick (1916–2004) again swung the scientific emphasis back toward Darwin's biological foundations with their proposal for the double-helix structure of DNA and their studies of the genetic code. Certain human traits, after all, can to an astonishingly intricate degree be attributed to genetic inheritance. With the understanding of genetic structure on the molecular level, medical science now can take a new direction in the path of eugenics: therapeutically altering gene structure to prevent and treat genetic diseases. Where rabid Social Darwinists endorsed a "live and let die" approach to human ailments and frailty, natural biology now has the tools to combat genetic flaws, not just for future generations, but within the individual. Somatic gene therapy in this way treats only the cells recognized as being dysfunctional. Gametic or germline therapy corrects only the hereditary components, thus preventing the particular dysfunction from being spread through reproduction. Opponents claim that gene therapy, particularly gametic therapy, reeks of the ruthless social cleansing practices enacted by early Social Darwinists and proponents of eugenics. There is the threat of a slippery slope, that allowing some forms of genetic manipulation, even with the best of intentions for helping to treat patients who currently suffer from disease, is only steps away from the trail blazed by Nazi scientists and others. Social Darwinism becomes complicated here, with two possible applications to contemporary genetics. If it is natural for society to move toward constant improvement through survival of the best-adapted traits, then perhaps somatic gene therapy is wasteful in the same way that Social Darwinists claimed we should exert neither money nor energy on weak or inferior individuals. To be consistent with this thought, most medical treatment would be equally wasteful, since essentially it gives artificial assistance to people nature is not inclined to favor. At the same time, however, genetic manipulation, particularly gametic, works toward improving overall society by eliminating undesirable traits. Carriers of an affliction would reserve the right to reproduce, but the offending condition would not be passed on to future individuals. An extreme Social Darwinist view might claim nonetheless that disease carriers—treatable or not—do not serve the best interests of future humanity.

—Elisa Ruhl

See also **Darwin, Charles; Eugenics; Genocide; Hobbes, Thomas; Selection, Natural**

Further Readings

Carnegie, A. (1962). *The gospel of wealth and other timely essays.* (E. C. Kirkland, Ed.). Cambridge, MA: Belknap Press. (Original work published 1900)

Darwin, C. (1964). *On the origin of species.* Cambridge, MA: Harvard University Press. (Original work published 1859)

Darwin, C. (1997). *The descent of man* (2nd ed.). Amherst, NY: Prometheus Books. (Original work published 1871)

Dawkins, R. (1990). *The selfish gene* (2nd ed.). Oxford: Oxford University Press.

Degler, C. N. (1992). *In search of human nature: The decline and revival of Darwinism in American social thought.* Oxford: Oxford University Press.

Hofstadter, R. (1944). *Social Darwinism in American thought.* Boston: Beacon Press.

Kevles, D. J. (1995). *In the name of eugenics: Genetics and the uses of human heredity.* Cambridge, MA: Harvard University Press.

Spencer, H. (1967). *The evolution of society: Selections from Herbert Spencer's principles of sociology* (R. L. Carneiro, Ed.). Chicago: University of Chicago Press.

SOCIAL DARWINISM

Social Darwinism has come to represent a conservative stance in the debate on human nature and society. Although the term was coined at the end of the 19th century, it still serves today to describe aggressive individualism, racism, laissez-faire capitalism, and social determinism. The label of Social Darwinism has been used to describe phenomena as distant in chronological terms as the free-market economy, Nazi eugenics, and sociobiology. Therefore, social Darwinism is best described not as a homogeneous school of thought, but rather as a worldview assigning biological factors a leading role in the creation and collapse of species and in shaping social and psychological features of humankind.

As defined by cultural historian Richard Hofstadter in his study *Social Darwinism in American Thought* (1944), social Darwinism applies to human affairs key ideas derived from Charles Darwin's *On the Origin of Species* (1859), such as the struggle for existence, the survival of the fittest, and natural selection. To leading social Darwinists such as Herbert Spencer (1820–1903) and William Graham Sumner (1840–1910), human beings followed the same laws as animals and plants. Both theorists misused Darwin's ideas to justify economic individualism and to call for minimal state interventions in social matters. The controversial social conditions of the period were natural and could not be changed. To Sumner and Spencer, the rapid growth of an impoverished working class, the huge gap between rich and poor, and the spread of urban slums were factors that highlighted that society was functioning. Social Darwinists like Sumner claimed that social existence was a competitive struggle among individuals possessing different natural capacities and traits. Those with better traits, the fittest, succeeded, becoming wealthy and powerful, while those who were unfit were condemned to poverty. Government intervention in economic and social matters must be minimal. Improving the condition of the poor would only preserve bad traits: To Sumner, the only alternative to the survival of the fittest was the survival of the unfittest.

Social Darwinism was again in the spotlight after the rise of free-market economics during the 1980s. Media started to use the phrase with reference to capitalist abuses and racial discrimination. Some scholars have also challenged the notion that social Darwinists misinterpreted Darwin's ideas. In his controversial *Darwin's Metaphor* (1985), Robert Young claimed that Darwin's theories themselves drew on capitalist, racist, and imperialist assumptions, thus making him the first Social Darwinist. The reviving of social Darwinism has prompted a renewed focus on the urgency of constructing community movements at both local and global levels.

— Luca Prono

 ## DATING TECHNIQUES

Dating is nothing more than ordering time. Time is the quintessential sorter of events. All living beings go through life being on occasion acutely aware of its transient yet eternal, ceaseless yet tenacious quality. Time is the omnipresent judge that indicts all life for existence and condemns it to death. Thus, for the greatest portion of human history, time was seen in terms of an individual or series of lifetimes, with a clear beginning and a clear end. This view of the world applied as much to the wonders of nature as it did to the human being, with such phenomena as the rising and setting of the sun, the moon, and important stars and the passing of the seasons. The ancient Egyptian proverb, "All things fear time; but time fears the pyramids" summarizes the essence of time's role in human history. Time has always been an enigma somehow understandable to the individual but incomprehensible and unexplainable to others. With the advent of high civilization, time was ordered by the actions of leaders, and a number of king's lists have survived in the written record to assist the modern scholar in the very difficult task of attaching dates to events of the near-distant past.

This ordering of time throughout the ages serves a purpose, to answer the question: "What is the age?" Or, "How old is it?" In anthropological research, time has always been the great sorting mechanism. Collectors and travelers of classical times, such as Herodotus, studied historic monuments and produced speculative accounts of prehistory. In fact, several dozen classical authors in the first millennium BC ordered time as a succession of ages based on technological progress. A three-age system encompassing the Stone, Bronze, and Iron Ages was the most common time-sorting methodology, but there were variations with copper and gold. Lucretius (95–53 BC) summarized these Western views of dating the past. Yuan K'ang (ca. AD 50), a Han Dynasty Chinese scholar, wrote an account of the historical development of toolmaking, from the use of stone/ jade through bronze to iron.

The principle of a systematic organization of ex situ archaeological materials started with the understanding of the three-age system in the 16th century by Michael Mercati (1541–1593), who was the superintendent of the Vatican gardens and adviser to Pope Clement VIII. The combination of his Renaissance education, his substantial mineral and fossil collections, and his access to the newly acquired American ethnographic artifact collections permitted Mercati to formulate the foundations of modern archaeology. His observations, which were not easily accessible until the 18th century, are all the more remarkable when one considers the intellectual milieu of that era. In Europe during this era, inquiry into the prehistoric past was discouraged, because the Bible was regarded as the supreme authority on human history and the early history of the earth. For example, creationism dominated scholarly writings on the origin of the universe and humanity, and during this period, fossils of marine organisms that were sometimes found in mountains were described as being washed up by the Great Flood. Ancient arrow points and other prehistoric stone tools were thought to have been produced by thunderbolts and other natural phenomena. Prehistoric stone arrow points and axes were believed to have fallen from the sky at the moment when thunder stuck. These implements were called thunderstones, *ceraunia,* or *pierre de foudre.*

It generally was believed that all living plant and animal species were survivors of the Great Flood and that with careful biblical research, especially on the book of Genesis, it was possible to calculate the age of the earth. For example, in 1642, Dr. John Lightfoot, the vice-chancellor of Cambridge University, calculated that the universe was created in 4004 BC, on October 23, at 9:00 am, coincidental with the beginning of the Fall Term. Later in 1658, Archbishop James Ussher refined this estimate and suggested that the earth was actually created on the evening preceding October 23, 4004 BC. This is the kind of pedantic (to us) debate that took place, so that although historical sites were being studied, prehistoric archaeology was being interpreted in light of the Bible.

It was only in the early part of the 19th century (1837) that Mercati's concepts were applied rigorously to a museum collection in Denmark by Christian Thomsen (1788–1865). The material culture in "cabinets" and museums could be now sorted relatively. But, in situ materials also required theory for relative sorting, and this was provided by the Danish atomist and geologist Bishop Nicholas Steno (1638–1686). He was the first to clearly state the three principles of stratigraphy, which have come to be known as Steno's Laws. They are: the Principle of Superposition: In a sedimentary sequence, the older beds are on the bottom, and the younger beds are on the top; the Principle of Original Horizontality: Sediments tend to be deposited in flat, horizontal layers; and the Principle of Original Lateral Continuity: a flat layer will tend to extend for a considerable distance in all directions. The first principal (superposition) is the one employed in conjunction with fossil markers by early geologists William "Strata" Smith (1769–1839) and Charles Lyell (1797–1875) and archaeologists Pitt Rivers (1827–1900) and Boucher de Perthes (1788–1868) to sort materials stratigraphically, with an assumption of a time progression.

Through human ingenuity, the last 150 years have been witness to great number of techniques for sorting time applicable to the scientific study of the past. These various dating techniques fall into one or more of three categories: absolute, relative, and radiometric. Absolute techniques of varve analyses and dendrochronology are only such when they can be clearly calibrated to a known year; in all other cases, they are relative dating techniques. Relative dating techniques permit chronological relationships to be ascertained through physical and/or chemical seriation (cation exchange ratio, fluorine dating, patination, pollen analysis) based on spatial relationships (stratigraphy and cross-dating), differential abundances, technological variations, or combinations thereof. Some techniques (for example, obsidian hydration, archaeomagnetism) require a radiometric technique for calibration; all benefit from their use. Other relative dating techniques require dated historical information (astronomical dating).

Basic information on some dating techniques, sorted from most to least reliable.

Technique	How it Ticks	How it Is Set	How it Is Read	Basic Assumptions
Dendrochronology	Tree ring and width pattern	Growth in life, ring	Count rings and measure	1 ring = 1 year; no duplication or missed rings; regional comparability
^{14}C	Radioactive decay and atom counting	Wound in life Set in death	Count beta decay or ^{14}C per unit volume	$t^{1/2}$; $^{14}C/^{12}C$ is known. Exchange with atmosphere and production rate are constant
$^{40}K/^{40}Ar$ & $^{40}Ar/^{39}Ar$	Radioactive decay & buildup of daughters	Rock formation heating	Measure ratios of $^{40}K/^{40}Ar$ or $^{40}Ar/^{39}Ar$	No ^{40}Ar to start; none lost
U/Pb	Radioactive decay and buildup of daughters	Rock formation	Measure U and Th and Pb isotope ratios	No U, Th, or Pb loss
Varve, Ice, and Deep Sea Cores	Systematicdeposition	Deposition	Count layers and measure	Assume annular deposiition and rate are constant
U Series	Radioactive decay and buildup of daughters	Rock formation differential solution	Measure U & Th	No losses in series radon gas not an issue
Fission Track	U fission to I and Br	Last heating	Count tracks per unit volume	There has been no track annealing
Archaeomagnetism	Field intensity & direction	Cooling	Measure field direction	Field is responsible; object not moved; last firing is known
Geomagnetism	Magnetic field reversals	Cooling to where the field is "frozen"	Measure field direction	One knows the age of the reversals [All?]
Thermolumin-escence [TL]	U, Th, and K decay energy trapping	Last heating or formation	Heat sample and measure light output	Energy stored in linear manner; no secondary heating; no bleaching
Obsidian Hydration	Water diffusion	New surface by material removal	Measure hydration layer thickness	Diffusion rate constant; temp. of burial known; at least 1 date ^{14}C known
Archaeo-Astronomy	Alignment and movement	Alignment when constructed	Compare alignments	Assume alignments were used
Electron Spin Resonance [ESR]	U, Th, and K decay energy trapping	Heating or formation	Measure the length of time trapped electron takes to relax	Traps filled in linear manner; there is no loss from traps
Geochemical [U, F, N]	Diffusion degradation	Determined rate begins at time of deposition	Absolute measurement of relative amt. or amount vs depth	One can know the physical, chemical, biological conditions
Patination	Chemical alteration on object surface	Begins at time that fresh surface exposed	Depth &/or intensity	Sample in same environment throughout life
Calcium Diffusion	Chemical diffusion	Construction of clay/cement interface	Measure depth into clay of Ca diffusion	Assume diffusion rate is independent of environs
Glass Layer	Hydration	Chemical change at the surface	Thickness and/or number of layers	Assume layer per year & a constant environment
Cation Exchange	Soil chemical process	Begins with soil formation processes	Measure, e.g., Na concentrations as a function of depth	Assume constant rate of movement of e.g., Na need ^{14}C date to cal
Amino Acid Racemization	Biochemical transformation	Wound in life Set in death	Determine L and R Isomer ratio	Racemization is constant temp constant [rare]

Materials, time ranges, and limitations for dating techniques.

Technique	Material	Range (Ky)	Limits
Carbon-14 [^{14}C]	organics		sampling
beta decay		35	contamination
atom counting		65	backgrounds
^{40}K/^{40}Ar or ^{40}Ar/^{39}Ar	volcanic rock	unlimited	availability
	or minerals	coarse calibration	preparation
U Series [^{234}U, ^{230}Th, ^{231}Pa]	coral, molluskas	30-300	contamination
	travertine		few facilities
			very controversial
			contamination
Fission Track	minerals	unlimited	technical
	U content	coarse	problems
Geomagnetism	undistorted	unlimited	limited
	seds. or volcanic	but coarse	facilities
Archaeomagnetism	kilns & hearths	2	calibration
Obsidian hydration	obsidian	~35	limited application
	tephra		calibration
			regional framework
Thermoluminescence [TL]	pottery, stone, and bone	1,000	range of error
			few facilities
Geochemical dating	[F & U]	relative	site specific
Amino Acid	bone, shell	~200	experimental
Racemization			few facilities
Varves, Ice, Deep Sea Cores	sediments	150	limited
Dendrochrology	tree rings	13.5	region specific
Archaeoastronomy			stratigraphic
			sequences
Patination		supported	cross-correlations
Cation Exchange		by	seriations
Calcium Exchange			typologies
Calcium Diffusion			index artifacts
ESR			botanical dating
			phase botany
			vertebrate
			palaeontology
			volcanic action
			playa lakes
			soil zones & hard pans

Contrary to popular belief, radiometric dating techniques, whether they are based on the exponential decay of a radioactive element or the ionizing damage effects of radiation, are only relatively absolute as they can only give a statistical approximation of an absolute age. Radiometric dating techniques that rely on radioactive decay include potassium-argon dating, radiocarbon dating (Carbon 14), and uranium-thorium dating. Radiometric dating techniques that rely on the buildup of damaging ionization from radioactive decay include thermoluminescence dating, optically stimulated luminescence, electron spin resonance (ESR), and fission track dating.

Basically, all dating techniques can be seen as clock types. The analyst must know some basic information about each clock: How does the clock tick? How is the clock set? How is the clock read? With these fundamentals, all dating clocks have the potential to provide a chronological framework. Some dating techniques are shown in Table 1 with respect to their clock functions. Unfortunately, not all dating procedures are created equal, and some methods are more reliable than others.

All dating techniques have limitations with respect to the material within which they function and the age range over which they are applicable. Table 2 lists material and limits for some dating techniques.

— *L. A. Pavlish*

See also **Dating Techniques, Radiometric; Dating Techniques, Relative; Dendrochronology; Potassium-Argon Dating**

Further Readings

Göksu, H. Y. (1991). *Scientific dating methods.* New York: Kluwer Academic.

Gräslund, B. (1987). *The birth of prehistoric chronology: Dating methods and dating systems in nineteenth-century Scandinavian archaeology.* Cambridge: Cambridge University Press.

Herz, N., & Garrison, E. (1998). *Geological methods for archaeology.* Oxford: Oxford University Press.

Rutter, N. W., & Catto, N. R. (Eds.). (1995). *Dating methods for quaternary deposits.* St. John's, Canada: Geological Association of Canada.

NEW DATING TECHNIQUES

Some dating techniques have been in use for hundreds of years and are still used today. They work well for certain time periods. Dating techniques are divided into two types: relative dating and absolute dating. Absolute dating determines the actual age of an object or stratigraphic layer, while relative dating puts artifacts and layers into sequence, without determining an actual date. Until the 20th century, only relative dating techniques were available.

Radiocarbon dating has been widely used since 1949, when it was developed by J. R. Arnold and W. F. Libby. It provides a means of absolute dating, without taking into account artifacts or local stratigraphic sequences. An unstable isotope of carbon, Carbon 14 (or C-14) is formed when nitrogen is broken down by cosmic radiation. This carbon is absorbed by plants and the animals eating them. After a plant or animal dies, the ratio of C-14 to the stable C-12 begins to decrease. Scientist know the rate for this decrease, so are able to determine the age of an object by finding the ratio of C-14 to C-12 contained by that object.

Luminescence dating was developed in North America in the 1950s and 1960s. In 1985, scientists developed optically stimulated luminescence dating techniques, using laser light. These techniques are used for dating sediments.

The potassium-argon method also relies on measuring radioactive emissions. It was first used at Olduvai Gorge, and more recently a modification of this method, known as argon-argon dating, was used at Pompeii.

Obsidian hydration is used to determine dates in volcanic glass. After a new fracture, the new break is covered with a rind, which grows at a constant rate. This is only useful for dating older fractures, as it takes several centuries for a detectable rind to grow.

Archaeomagnetism and paleomagnetism dating techniques were originated by geologists. These methods were first used in the United States in the 1960s and have been useful in the American southwest.

Oxidized carbon ratios is one of the newest methods. This is a chemical procedure, developed by Douglas Frink. It has recently been used to date the construction of Watson-Brake.

Another recently discovered technique is electron spin resonance, which measures the decay of uranium that has soaked into buried bones and teeth from groundwater. Another newer technique, amino acid racemization, studies decay of proteins encapsulated in hard tissues of fossil animals. Since the introduction of new dating techniques, many sites and fossils in Africa have been determined to be older than previously thought.

— Pat McCarthy

DATING TECHNIQUES, RADIOMETRIC

Radiometric dating became a possibility with Becquerel's discovery in 1896 of natural radioactivity. Rutherford postulated that radioactivity could be used to determine the age of the Earth. His and Soddy's discovery (1902) of the transmutation of the atom became the basis for understanding exponential decay and the evolution of decay products ("daughter" elements). Age estimates for the Earth that had been determined by rate of heat loss (Lord Kelvin) now had to make allowances for the heat energy associated with radioactive decay. Thus, scholars were able to argue for great antiquity of the rocks on Earth. It was really with the advent of data collection technologies after World War II that the radiometric dating field began to develop with rapidity.

Radiometric dating must be viewed as having two forms: (1) techniques that rely on the decay of an isotope of an element, the production and decay of daughter decay products (radiocarbon dating, potassium-argon, argon-argon, and uranium-lead, uranium series) and (2) the techniques that rely on the crystal damage that is generated by the ionizing radiation generated by the decay of radioactive elements (thermoluminescence, electron spin resonance, and fission track).

All radiometric-dating determinations are a function of a statistical distribution of one or more sets of decay data that must be viewed as a probability result, approximating a particular age with an error attached to it. These errors in age determinations are usually expressed as standard deviations from a mean age value. These standard deviations are probability statements that a determined age actually will fall somewhere within the age distribution defined by the standard deviation. One standard deviation, often termed *one sigma,* means that 68% of the time, the determined age will fall between the range defined by that standard deviation. In the same manner, two- and three-sigma standard deviations mean the determined age will fall somewhere between the defined age range 95% and 99.6%, respectively. Therefore, it is immediately apparent that it would be a misnomer to suggest that these radiometric dating techniques were methods of absolute dating.

Radiocarbon-14 is the best known of the radiometric techniques and is in fact an established method that relies only on the decay of an isotope (14C) formed from the outer-atmosphere comic-ray-generated neutron bombardment of Nitrogen-14 (14N) without reference to daughter production. In this respect, it is the most straightforward of the radiometric dating techniques. Living organisms incorporate 14CO2 and maintain an equilibrium until death, at which time the radiocarbon clock begins to tick as the 14C decays exponentially with a rate known as the *Libby half-life* (5,568 years). A simple ratio measurement of the amount of 14C remaining versus the amount present when the organism left the living biomass yields a radiocarbon age, which can be converted to calendrical years with a dendrochronological curve that corrects for the cosmic ray fluctuations that have taken place in the past. This ratio of original-to-remaining 14C is obtained in one of two ways: (1) The direct decay of the 14C back to 14 yields a beta ray that can be detected in a shielded Geiger counter; and (2) the actual counting of the individual 14C atoms present in a sample compared with the stable 12C in that sample and an accompanying standard. The atom-counting method affords an advantage in some dating situations (for example, shorter counting times, smaller sample sizes, no cosmic ray backgrounds, and the extension of the age range from less than 40,000 years to 70,000 years). Potassium-argon (40K/40Ar) and argon-argon dating (40Ar/39Ar), uranium-lead dating (U/Pb), and uranium series dating are all dependant upon both the exponential decay of a "parent" radioactive isotope and the buildup of one or more "daughter" isotopes, which may or may not themselves be radioactive. The ratio of the "daughter" to the "parent" permits an age estimate to be made. These techniques tend to have an age range orders of magnitude greater than radiocarbon (for example, age of the Earth), because they use half-lives that are very long in comparison to radiocarbon (t½ for–40K: 1.28×10^9 yrs; 238U: 4.47×10^9 yrs; 235U: 7.038×10^8 yrs; 232Th: $1.41 \times 1,010$ yrs), though uranium series disequilibrium dating has a dating range of a few days to about 20 million years.

Thermoluminescence (TL), electron spin resonance (ESR), and fission track are dating techniques that rely on the accumulation of radiation damage in materials from the decay of radioactive isotopes. TL and ESR depend on the #945, #946, and #947, decay of 40K, 238U, 235U, and 232Th in the natural environment and the consequent buildup of age information in the form of trapped electrons removed from their valence bands by the ionizing radiation. TL recovers this information by heating the sample or by optically measuring the trapped energy, or optically stimulated luminescence (OSL). ESR identifies radicals that have been formed by ionizing radiation in liquids and solids and electron traps in minerals. ESR measurement is accomplished by applying a microwave frequency to the sample that permits the amount of radiation damage to be quantified. The radiation environment within which a sample was exposed must be known well for both TL and ESR to be effective techniques. Both OSL and ESR techniques do not destroy the signal, as does the TL heating, permitting remeasurement of a sample multiple times. These techniques assume that there is a direct linear relationship between the ionizing radiation flux and the quantity of trapped electrons or radicals and that there are no secondary losses.

Fission track relies on the spontaneous fission of 238U into two heavy elements that travel through the mineral, creating track damage. The number of tracks present is a function of the original 238U concentration and the time that has elapsed since the mineral was formed or last heated. Once the tracks are counted, the mineral is heated to anneal the tracks and irradiated with neutrons to induce spontaneous fission in the 235U. By counting these induced tracks to determine the 235U content, the 238U concentration can be deduced and compared with the original track count to determine the age of the mineral. The method's success assumes the fission tracks have not been subject to partial annealing.

— L. A. Pavlish

See also **Dendrochronology; Potassium-Argon Dating**

Further Readings

Göksu, H. Y. (1991). *Scientific dating methods.* New York: Kluwer Academic.

Herz, N., & Garrison, E. (1998). *Geological methods for archaeology.* Oxford: Oxford University Press.

Rutter, N. W., & Catto, N. R. (Eds.). (1995). *Dating methods for quaternary deposits.* St. John's, Canada: Geological Association of Canada.

DATING TECHNIQUES, RELATIVE

The oldest and the simplest relative dating method is stratigraphic dating. Relative dating, properly applied to sedimentary materials, carries no implied rate of change in time. An isolated event can only be deemed to have occurred either before or after another isolated event. This situation obtains because rates of deposition are rarely constant over long periods of time. There will be breaks in the buildup of sediments, and there may be differential removal of material. These depositional activities create unconformities that are understandable when one considers that the physics of any geomorphic process is the result of two physical laws of Nature (gravity and Bernoulli's principle) as they apply to sediment particles in two media of transport (water and wind). The complexity of geomorphic dynamics precludes long-term constant depositional rates and any accompanying assumptions that relative time can be calculated in any other manner than relationally.

Prior to the 20th century, research in the fields of archaeology, paleontology, and geology was based on and limited by this general form of dating that relied on the inferred, time-based, relative relationships that were perceived to exist between phenomena or entities of interest. In other words, the sorting of time was a very subjective exercise, strongly influenced by the mental template of the practitioner.

Both before and after the invention of writing, there were undoubtedly countless attempts to date absolutely events that occurred before recorded history. Without a factual method of quantifying time, these endeavors were doomed to failure. The ever-changing four-season year, based on nature's rhythms, the king's lists, logging parts of human lives, and the "age systems" that were founded on assumed technological and cultural progression, were all employed at one time or another by classic scholars throughout the world. These approaches, which were often clouded by religious dogma, gave a functional, if imprecise, perspective of the past.

It was with the coming of the Renaissance and the Age of Enlightenment that a real attempt at the understanding of dating in a relative sense was undertaken. Objects by themselves and those still within a relational context could now be sorted chronologically. There were two contributions that led the way for this dating improvement: (1) Michael Mercati's

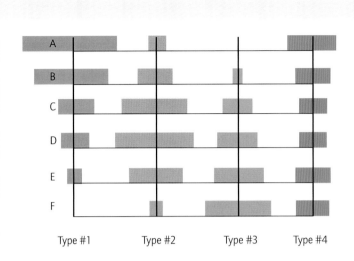

or material culture sequences permitted a wider application of the relative dating concept known as cross-dating. When the index fossils or artifacts were not totally distinct in unrelated stratigraphic sections, the relative abundance of an index item might be used in many instances to relatively date the sections based on the assumption that natural or cultural materials have a lifetime of their own, in which they begin at a point in time and become popular and eventually fall out of use. These distributions are called "battleship curves" and are a form of seriation dating (see Figure 1). Over the last century

(1541–1593) systematic organization of ex situ archaeological materials in the Vatican collections based on an understanding of the "three-age system," which had its origins in the classical literature, and (2) Nicholas Steno's (1638–1686) treatise, known today as the "three principles of stratigraphy" or Steno's Laws, which is directly applicable to the relative dating of in situ materials.

Christian Thomsen (1788–1865) applied the three-age system to museum collections in Denmark in the early 19th century, demonstrating that cultural materials could be now sorted relatively and, most important, he publicized the approach. When this concept was combined with the Steno-based advances in geological understanding taking place at the same time, non-biblically based estimates of relative time sequences became possible.

In this way, early geologists like James Hutton (1726–1797), William "Strata" Smith (1769–1839), and Charles Lyell (1797–1875) and archaeologists like Pitt Rivers (1827–1900) and Boucher de Perthes (1788–1868) were able to employ the principle of superposition in conjunction with fossil or cultural markers to sort materials stratigraphically, with an accompanying assumption of a time progression. In this manner, practical relative dating had been developed. A vertical fossil succession now placed its encapsulating rock in a relative sequence in a manner analogous with a series of vertically buried cultural materials. The ability to meaningfully associate totally independent stratigraphic sections with similar fossil

and a half, a great number of techniques have been developed for the relative sorting of past events. These relative dating techniques permit chronological relationships to be ascertained through physical and/or chemical seriation (such as cation exchange ratio-http://www.mnsu.edu/emuseum/archaeology/dating/dat_florin.html, patination, or pollen analyses) based on spatial relationships (stratigraphy and cross-dating), differential abundances, technological variations, or combinations thereof. Some techniques (e.g., obsidian hydration, archaeomagnetism) require a historic event or a radiometric technique for calibration; all benefit from their use. Other relative dating techniques require dated historical information. Astronomical dating requires that an event be recorded both spatially and chronologically, but there are usually several historical events as well as celestial ones that can be made to fit a particular set of criteria. Paleography is based on the relative changes that take place in writing styles through time and has application in authenticity as well as dating. Codecology is a relative dating technique that is based on the way in which scrolls and books are assembled. For example, two millennia ago, scrolls that had been bound in vertical pages were bound horizontally from right to left. Therefore, it is apparent that any artifact or event that can be placed in a context in relationship to other artifacts or events can be relative dated.

This figure graphically depicts seriation, showing a series of idealized "battleship curves" with relative time being shown as the abundances of artifacts, with the oldest at the bottom and youngest at the top. We may view this as the differential distribution of Artifact Types #1 to #4 through stratigraphic layers A though F at one sampling site (archaeological or pale-otological) or as the ordering of differentially distributed Artifact Types #1 to #4 obtained from sampling sites A through F. In both the single and multisite results, the relative sequencing of the Artifact Types provides a method of relative dating based on their differential abundance. Artifact Type #1 appears in layer or site E and continues through A, becoming relatively more abundant. Artifact Type #2 shows a classical "battleship" abundance distribution covering an almost complete cycle from inception to discard. Artifact Type #3 shows a consistent decrease in abundance with a final cessation. This distribution would suggest that digging deeper or finding other sites may provide the other half of the curve. Artifact Type #4 shows a constant abundance through the section or sites.

— *L. A. Pavlish*

See also **Dating Techniques, Radiometric; Dendro-chronology; Potassium-Argon Dating**

Further Readings

Pavlish, L. A., & Litherland, A. E. (2003). Physics and archaeometry (Foreword, special issue). *Physics in Canada, 59,* 222–225.
Zeuner, F. E. (1946). *Dating the past.* London: Methuen.

DAWKINS, RICHARD (1941–)

An English ethnologist and evolutionary biologist, Richard Dawkins was born in Nairobi during the onset of World War II. Spending his formative years in a biologically diverse environment of Africa, the young Dawkins probably cultivated his naturalistic perspectives in East Africa until his family returned to England in 1949. After what can be considered as being a traditional English education, Dawkins continued his education at Oxford, whereby he graduated in 1962. After graduating from Oxford, Dawkins remained and received his doctorate in ethnology under the eminent ethnologist Dr. Niko Tinbergen. Pursuing a career in teaching, Dawkins was appointed to an assistant professorship of zoology at the University of California at Berkeley in 1967. Upon completion of this appointment, he returned to Oxford in 1969 as lecturer in zoology and was elected a fellow of the New College in 1970. Dawkins holds the Charles Simonyi Chair of Public Understanding of Science (1995).

Richard Dawkins is noted for his ability to relate highly scientific knowledge, such as genetics, to the general public. His most noted books include *The Selfish Gene* (1979), *The Extended Phenotype* (1982), *The Blind Watchmaker* (1986), *River out of Eden* (1995), and *Climbing Mount Improbable* (1996). He has also published multitude of articles, coauthored books, and book reviews. Dawkins has lectured internationally and has received multiple awards and honors. He also received honorary doctorates in both science and literature.

Contributions and Perspectives

In the area of science, particularly concerning the processes of biological evolution, the general public has been given an array of theoretical interpretations concerning the biological mechanisms that explain the diversity of life on this planet. Acknowledging the cultural influence on these interpretations (e.g., religious or vitalistic beliefs), Richard Dawkins continues to provide the public with an understandable materialistic explanation of complex scientific knowledge that was attained during the last century. Although he is not considered a philosopher of science, his materialistic interpretation of biological processes has caused severe criticisms, essentially labeling him either a biological determinist or an extreme reductionist. Being a defender of Darwinian evolution, Dawkins poses a plausible relationship between biological processes and expressed behavior within an evolutionary framework.

Taking a purely materialistic view of concerning the processes of evolution, the process of adaptive radiation and speciation has accounted for both the diversity and complexity of organic life found on this planet. Although Dawkins himself supports a Darwinian gradualist's view of the evolutionary process, he does hold that a momentary punctuation in evolution could be supported by several factors, among them being mutations, extinctions, and exponential growth of more suitable organisms within an ecological niche. Though in this manner, life may seem to possess a creative teleology stemming from a complex design, the implications from the deoxyribonucleic acid (DNA) molecule dissolves any remote theological plausibility. The four base units, adenine, thymine, cytosine, and guanine (A, T, C, G) is the first cause and only cause from the outgrowth of the symbiotic relationship among the various cells and/or tissues within an organism. Essentially, we are replicators (vessels) for our genes. Within the processes of life, the DNA is beyond the scope of good or evil; their existence drives us to action and replication.

With the concept of the *Selfish Gene* (1976), Dawkins illustrates the extensive and influential role that biology has on behavior. The strategy is simple; establish a productive cost-benefit analysis that would increase the chances for both survival and reproduction. Since an organism has only a limited amount of energy, any expenditure of energy would ultimately dictate an organism's behavior. Examples could be seen through out the diversity of life, including our species. For a "moral" species, the implications become evident; there are no metaphysical dimensions with altruistic intentions. This would certainly have great philosophical and theological implications. We do not act out from either natural law or some Kantian sense of duty, rather, our uncanny ability to recognize the genetic proximity of our genes and related acts of reciprocity that follow (cost-benefit analysis). The symbiosis between cells and the underlying genetic foundation within phenotypic expressions are critical within this process. Genes influence more than the organic material in which they inhabit and control.

Indirectly, genes influence the external world in which the organism exists. This directly opposes the traditional view of our species speculated by Aristotle (theologically by Thomas Aquinas) or by Immanuel Kant (1724–1804). This mechanistic view, by which our species operates, along with a real united view of our species in relation to nature, redefines our ontological and teleological status, which is currently held as being philosophically or theologically infallible. It is the biologically based emotive/psychological properties (for example, desires for immortality) and cultural capabilities that create the reluctance for a philosophical shift. This fact withstanding, it is the driving intention that forces our species to be in control of any perception or perceptive qualities that

becomes a point of our consciousness. Essentially, it is the individual's psychological components that become an adaptive mechanism that accounts for the continuous "strategy" based on environmental interaction and modification. The adaptive response indicates an ongoing reciprocal relationship between the encapsulated genes and their extended environment.

Every organism has an impact on the ecology in which they live. Our species, by comparison of other species, has the greatest impact on the global environment. The reason for this global impact is due our species' ability to adapt and survive in most environments found on this planet; all impart to the cultural capabilities of our species. In Dawkins's theory on *The Extended Phenotype* (1982), he makes a clear point on how our genes have the ability to influence the environment around them. This is done through culture. Culture and cultural transmissions can be seen in terms of memes. *Memes*, units of imitation, are bits of information transmitted from brain to brain through human interaction. In this manner, memes are exposed to the same theoretical principles of evolution. The replication vessels of information, for example, both memes (resulting in complex thought) and their respective physical representations, are exposed to various selective forces. These selective processes can be either cultural (e.g., philosophically ritualistic) or random propagation of mutated memes. Although the implementation of the written word has reduced the possibility concerning the change in the original transmission, the creative ability and personal interpretation can itself become cultural adaptation (e.g., cultural transformation of mythology and various technologies). With the ability for greater ability for contemplation, the greatest implication resides in our species' epistemology and resulting ontology and teleology.

The subtle underlying theme concerning the epistemology of our species becomes evident. Though there maybe behavior that is indicative of a biological nature as opposed to behaviorism, our species' resulting behavior does not come into existence with either previous knowledge or knowledge separate from the biological components within the human brain. It is human consciousness that emerges from organic matter that allows for the ability for free acts of creativity and disposition for control. This position negates the claim of biological determinism that is often attributed to him by critics. The bases of the objections are not from critical analysis or the exploration of other possible suggestive scenarios; rather, the objections rendered are from the implications that severely question and nullify both the claims of spiritual dimension and the dualistic influences from René Descartes (1596–1650). Questions pertaining to mind and behavior can be explained in purely materialistic explanations. Cultural complexity, as seen with biological complexity, does not have any spiritual dimensions, even though it may have metaphysical connotations. The uncovering of motives or intensions within a biological framework (e.g., selfish memes), threatens the psychological stability of a sensitive creature within a dynamic and violent universe. This, in turn, somehow challenges the perception of our humanity in a qualitative manner, especially in terms of personhood, aesthetics, and emotion. Erroneously, it is claimed that our species loses its humanity by accepting what science has already deemed as being highly probable. The philosophical implication for psychology, and to a greater extent theology, denies the mind/body dualism or the existence of the soul. It is in the human manipulation of these memes, especially in their propagation, that makes the natural selective process of evolution precarious (from the human standpoint), for overspecialization can lead to either personal or specieswide extinction.

Our species, which remains locked into an endless cycle of inquiry, seeks out answers that are more psychologically comforting than what is scientifically plausible. While acknowledging the impossible claims given by traditional religions and accepting the evidence given by science, some individuals seek untraditional answers that provide the same results given by traditional religions, an ontological and teleological design by an unknown, perhaps unknowable, designer. Their belief structures stem from the complex and creative processes, indicating complexity itself reflects a greater process that entails and encompasses the unknown. For these individuals, complexity is itself an indicator of something more grand and complex. Both design and designer have replaced Descartes's mind and body and traditional theological answers concerning the philosophical implications for scientific discovery.

With the rise of human consciousness, the resulting cognitive processes have entailed our species to posses a greater degree of self-awareness. This greater self-reflective ability has resulted in the progressive concepts of the soul. Based on both metaphysics and human desire to transcend death, the resulting

ontological and theological memes are resilient. As innovations and scientific discoveries are made, human imagination and creativity become apparent. For the theists and vitalist, the argument for design (ultimately, a designer, e.g., God) has become the answer to the materialistic interpretation of Darwinian evolution. In *The Blind Watchmaker* (1986) and *Climbing Mount Improbable* (1996), Dawkins gives an evolutionary account for complexity (e.g., the human eye), without any teleological sediment. Just as with organic evolution, the complexity found within nature is the expression of genetic information. Accumulative selection and intricate symbiotic relationships have resulted in the human eye, bodily development, and perhaps more important, consciousness rising from the human brain. All life on this planet owes its existence to the immortal coils of DNA.

In viewing Dawkins's approach for our species, it is understandable why his critics erroneously label him a determinist or reductionist. The implications of his writings, as with Darwin, have far-reaching consequences for our species ontology and teleology. Challenging the traditional cosmologies, Dawkins gives a united materialistic account for life on this planet. His unique perspective concerning culture and behavior has brought our own species back to a naturalistic and evolutionary framework. When comparing our species' behavior with other species, the traditional and sometimes spiritual position of our species within nature has greatly diminished. No longer can our species' position be deemed separate and completely unique in nature. Our species, when compared, only differs in degree and not in kind. This implication can be seen stemming from Darwin's scientific discovery of organic evolution. With the evolution of the human brain and memes, artificial intelligence has become more than a source of science fiction. This artificial intelligence may someday contribute or succeed our species for existence in this universe and beyond. As illustrated by Dawkins, no matter what will be involved, whether it is DNA or programmable microchips, the resulting product will always be subjected to the never-ending process of evolution.

— *David Alexander Lukaszek*

See also **Dennett, Daniel C.; Evolution, Molecular; Evolutionary Epistemology**

Further Readings

Dawkins, R. (1989). *The selfish gene.* Oxford: Oxford University Press.

Dawkins, R. (1995). *River out of Eden.* New York: Basic Books.

Dawkins, R. (1996). *The blind watchmaker.* New York: Norton.

Dawkins, R. (1996). *Climbing Mount Improbable.* New York: Norton.

Dawkins, R. (1998). *Unweaving the rainbow.* New York: Houghton Mifflin.

Dawkins, R. (1999). *The extended phenotype.* Oxford: Oxford University Press.

Dennett, D. C. (1991). *Consciousness explained.* New York: Back Bay Books.

Dennett, D. C. (1995). *Darwin's dangerous idea.* New York: Touchstone.

Sterelny, Kim. (2001). *Dawkins Vs. Gould: Survival of the fittest.* Cambridge: Totem Books.

 DE ANGULO, JAIME (1887–1950)

Jaime de Angulo (1887–1950), the eccentric amateur anthropologist, helped to move the field of anthropology away from armchair theorizing with decades of intense linguistic fieldwork among, most notably, the Achumawi or Pit River Indians of Northern California. De Angulo collected and studied a wide range of severely endangered languages from the American West and Mexico during the 1920s and 1930s, a period of time during which formally trained, and funded, anthropologists were scarce. Through the study of American Indian languages and the collection of folklore, de Angulo attempted to elicit the worldview of those he studied and preserve their cultural identity.

Born to Spanish parents in Paris, France, de Angulo became disillusioned by his strict Jesuit upbringing and struck out to make his fortune in the United States at the age of 18. De Angulo worked a grueling life as a cowboy in the Western United States and underwent a series of misadventures in South America before pursuing formal education in medicine. While at Johns Hopkins University, de Angulo took an interest in anthropology after reading works by Lewis Henry Morgan and Franz Boas. Later, while de Angulo was living with his first wife, Cary Fink, in Carmel, California, he met his earliest anthropological mentor,

Alfred Kroeber. In 1920, de Angulo accepted Kroeber's offer to teach two summer classes at Berkeley on Levi Brühl's notion of the primitive mind and the use of psychoanalytic theory in studies of primitive culture.

De Angulo was impacted greatly by Edward Sapir's introductory text, *Language,* and began a lifelong correspondence with him concerning his own linguistic research. With support from wealthy friends, his first, and his second wife, Nancy Freeland, de Angulo investigated various linguistic research projects among the Achumawi, whom he first met during a ranching venture in Alturas, California, and Taos Indians without university support. In 1922, with recommendation from Kroeber, Sapir, and Boas, de Angulo began working for the Department of Anthropology of Mexico, under Manuel Gamio, investigating the languages of the Zapotecan region. Organized in 1927, the Committee on Research in Native American Languages, headed by Franz Boas, Edward Sapir, and Leonard Bloomfield, granted de Angulo paid research projects to record those American Indian languages they thought to be nearest to extinction. De Angulo received more funding from the committee than any other researcher and was appointed to the advisory board in 1929. During his years of fieldwork, de Angulo studied 30 Native American languages and attempted to devise writing systems for the Pomo and Taos Indians in order that each may transcribe their own language.

De Angulo is best known for his ethnography of the Achumawi, *Indians in Overalls,* in which he detailed their present way of life and his introduction to the structure of their language. De Angulo used his Spanish heritage and cowboy experience to his advantage during his fieldwork; his informers equated his Spanish background with his being Mexican and were impressed by his rugged nature. He enthusiastically participated in their rituals, gambling bouts, singing, and heavy drinking, to the shock of many professional anthropologists at the time. De Angulo's work reveals a genuine appreciation for the language and culture of the Achumawi.

De Angulo's *Indian Tales,* a unique collection of folklore texts of the Northern California Indians seamlessly bound within de Angulo's fictional narrative, was first broadcast over the radio in 1949 as a series of "Old Time Stories" read by de Angulo himself. While much of de Angulo's salvage linguistic research and his exploration of language titled *What Is Language?* remain unpublished to this day, readers of *Indians in Overalls* and *Indian Tales* can appreciate de Angulo's bold fieldwork strategies and profound reverence for the American Indian way of life.

— *Katherine Lamie*

See also **Language and Culture; Native Peoples of the United States; Sapir, Edward**

Further Readings

de Angulo, G. (1995). *The old coyote of Big Sur.* Berkeley, CA: Stonegarden Press.

de Angulo, J. (1953). *Indian tales.* New York: Hill & Wang.

de Angulo, J. (1990). *Indians in overalls.* San Francisco: City Lights Books.

Leeds-Hurwitz, W. (2004). *Rolling in ditches with shamans: Jaime de Angulo and the professionalization of American anthropology.* Lincoln: University of Nebraska Press.

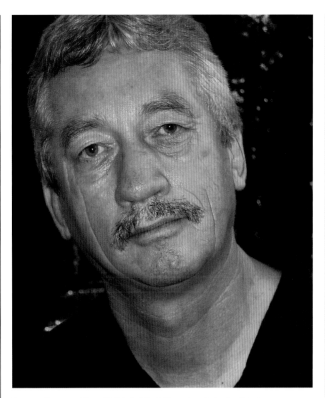

Source: Courtesy, Frans B. M. de Waal. Photo by Catherine Marin.

DE WAAL, FRANS B. M. (1948–)

Frans De Waal was born in the Netherlands in 1948. He received his training as a zoologist and ethicist from three Dutch universities, earning a PhD in biology from the University of Utrecht in 1977. De Waal moved to the United States in 1981, accepting a research position at the Wisconsin Regional Primate Research Center in Madison. In 1991, de Waal moved to the Psychology Department at Emory University in Atlanta, where he is currently a Charles Howard Candler Professor of Primate Behavior.

In 2004, De Waal received one of the most prestigious honors in the scientific community by being elected to the National Academy of Sciences. He is also the director of the Living Links Center for the Advanced Study of Ape and Human Evolution at the Yerkes Primate Research Center (YPRC), established in 1997. The YPRC of Emory University is a National Primate Research Center, which is funded by the National Institutes of Health. It is at the forefront of biomedical and behavioral studies with nonhuman primates.

De Waal has several published scientific articles and books, which include *Peacemaking Among Primates,* a 15-year study of conflict resolution and reconciliation among the captive chimpanzees *(Pan troglodytes)* of

the YPRC, for which he received the *Los Angeles Times* Book Award. De Waal's research has had an unquestionable effect on understanding the complexity of human social behavior and the evolution of morality in humans, as well as in other animals. His studies investigate the development and complexity of ethical behaviors and morality with results that suggest animals other than humans have an innate awareness of what is considered right or wrong.

De Waal has also challenged the idea of human culture by showing different adaptive strategies to conflict within various communities of the same species, suggesting that other animals have the ability to evaluate the situations they are presented with rather than being completely driven by instinct. This is well demonstrated by a study of combining a juvenile group of rhesus monkeys *(Macaca mulatta)* and stump-tail monkeys *(M. arctoides).* The more aggressive rhesus monkeys learned to be more passive from interacting with the stump-tail monkeys, which dominated the group. The two species became friends, interacting and grooming on a much less aggressive level than is usual for the rhesus monkey. De Waal is also interested in food sharing and social reciprocity.

While De Waal is best known for his behavioral research and theories on the origins of morality, the recognition of right and wrong in humans and other animals, he has also helped to shed light on the fascinating lives of bonobos *(Pan paniscus)*. The bonobo is the chimpanzee's lesser-known, yet seriously endangered, counterpart. Although there are several international experts on the bonobo, de Waal and photographer Frans Lanting have published the most comprehensive study of bonobos to date.

De Waal continues his research in Atlanta but has also traveled the world in order to make cultural reflections on the nature of humans and nonhuman primates in other cultures. He has been funded by such esteemed organizations as the National Science Foundation, the *National Geographic* Society, the National Institutes of Mental Health, the National Institutes of Health, and the Wisconsin Regional Primate Research Center in Madison.

— *Jackie L. Orcholl*

See also **Bonobos; Primatology**

Further Readings

De Waal, F. (1989). *Peacemaking among primates.* Cambridge, MA: Harvard University Press.

De Waal, F. (1996). *Good natured: The origins of right and wrong in humans and other animals.* Cambridge, MA: Harvard University Press.

De Waal, F. (1997). *Bonobo, the forgotten ape.* Berkeley: University of California Press.

De Waal, F. (2000). *Chimpanzee politics: Power and sex among apes.* Baltimore: Johns Hopkins University Press.

De Waal, F. (2001). *The ape and the sushi master, cultural reflections of a primatologist.* New York: Basic Books.

De Waal, F. (2002). *Tree of origin: What primate behavior can tell us about human social evolution.* Cambridge, MA: Harvard University Press.

De Waal, F. (2003). *My family album: Thirty years of primate photography.* Berkeley: University of California Press.

DEATH RITUALS

Death is a universal inevitability, but human responses are different. How people deal with death has always been closely studied by anthropologists.

Death-related beliefs and practices provide a window for viewing a society's social organization, cultural values, and worldviews. With a long-term perspective, this window can also allow us to see mechanisms of culture change and cultural adaptation to new socioeconomic circumstances.

Ethnographic record shows that there exist a wide variety of death rituals in the world. Death rituals usually start when a person stops breathing or is pronounced dead culturally. The body may be first washed, shaved, combed, painted, or perfumed. Then, it may be dressed or left naked, covered with blankets or adorned with jewelry. Finally, it may be buried, cremated, kept in the house, preserved by smoking or pickling, dismembered to feed animals or birds, thrown into river or sea, exposed as carrion, or even eaten, raw or cooked. Family, friends, and neighbors may get together to express grief by weeping, wailing, singing dirges, beating the breast, or tearing the hair. How the body is treated and disposed and how family, friends, and neighbors should behave for a specific period of mourning are all determined by cultural guidelines.

Anthropological Perspectives of Death Ritual

The study of death-related beliefs and practices has been of crucial importance to anthropology from its beginning. In archaeology, remnants from burials are often the only data surviving from early paleolithic cultures. They have provided evidence of cultural activities for the world's oldest civilizations and religious practice of prehistoric people. Mortuary structures have produced impressive and revealing evidence about ancient ways of life. The huge pyramids in Egypt and the magnificent tombs in Greece and China have yielded a plethora of information about the ideologies and values of ancient societies in those countries.

In sociocultural anthropology, interest in death-related beliefs and practices can be traced to the cultural evolutionists of the 19th century who attempted to construct grand evolutionary schemes of social development in the world. Edward Tylor and Sir James Frazer, for example, focused their attention on beliefs associated with death and existence thereafter. They argued that early humans' contemplation of death and deathlike states, such as sleeping and dreaming, was the origin of the concept of the soul and that the belief in its continued existence after death lead to the origin of all religions.

The evolutionary approach of Tylor, Frazer, and others has been discredited because of its ethnocentric scheme of universal cultural evolution, its faulty use of the comparative method, and its unsupported speculations concerning the origin of various institutions, beliefs, and practices. However, the subject of death-related behaviors continued to play an important role in the anthropological study of religion. In the 20th century, anthropologists interested in the study of religion shifted their attention from its origins and evolution to the study of basic functions that religion serves in human society. The functional approach to religion had its origin in the works of French sociologist Durkheim, developed further in the works of his students such as Robert Hertz, and in the works of British social anthropologists such as Radcliffe-Brown and Malinowski. These functionalists, through the analysis of death-related behaviors, attempted to demonstrate how a religious system serves to affirm and preserve the social system by establishing equilibrium and maintaining social solidarity.

Émile Durkheim in *The Elementary Forms of the Religious Life* (1912) put forth the theory that funeral rituals, and other rituals as well, are expressions of the unity of a society. He asserted that the function of those rituals is to recreate the society or the social order by reaffirming and strengthening the sentiments on which social solidarity and therefore social order itself depend. His student, Robert Hertz, in his study of the second burial in Indonesia (particularly the island of Borneo), also pointed out that the continuity and permanence of a society is threatened by the death of one of its members and that at the death of a member, the society, disturbed by the shock, must gradually regain its balance. It is only through the performance of death rituals during the period of mourning after the death that the society can recover its peace and triumph over death. For Hertz, death ritual is a long transformative process consisting of different stages.

The works of the Durkheimian school strongly influenced British functionalists. Radcliffe-Brown wrote in 1933 in his study of the funeral customs of the Andaman Islanders that a person's death constitutes a partial destruction of the social cohesion. The normal social life is disorganized. The social equilibrium is disturbed. After the death, the society

has to organize itself anew and reach a new condition of equilibrium. This view was also clearly expressed by another British anthropologist, Malinowski, who pointed out that death in a "primitive society" was much more than the removal of a member. The ceremonial aspect of death counteracted the centrifugal forces of fear, dismay, and demoralization caused by the death and reintegrated the group's shaken solidarity.

The functional approach has been seriously criticized for its excluding not only a large range of data such as indigenous interpretation of ritual acts but also important theoretical questions, such as how rituals convey meaning. It has been criticized for ignoring the role of the individual in society. It has also been criticized for being incapable of dealing with the dysfunctional components of religious behaviors and their contribution to the transformation of cultural systems.

In 1908, a French social anthropologist Van Gennep published *The Rites of Passage,* in which the funeral is regarded as one of a large class of rituals concerned with transitions from one state to another. He argued that all these rites of passage share a common tripartite structure, involving, first, separation from one status, then a transition or liminal period, followed by reincorporation into a new status. He pointed out that in death ritual, transition plays a dominant role.

Victor Turner brilliantly elaborated Van Gennep's notion of liminality. Building on Van Gennep's concept that the transitional phase sometimes acquires a certain autonomy from the rest of the ritual, Turner developed a view of a "state of transition," in which the inhabitants are "betwixt and between" normal social status. Based on his intensive study of life crisis rituals among the Ndembu of Zambia, Turner regarded this liminal or transitional phase as ambiguous, inversive, ludic, and a source of the intensive, effervescent camaraderie that he described as "communitas."

Turner's works represent a trend in anthropological studies of ritual that shifted emphasis from seeking for function to meaning in 1960s and 1970s. Symbolic and interpretative anthropology developed out from this trend and have had tremendous influence on anthropological studies of death ritual. They have sought to understand symbols and rituals primarily through the indigenous interpretation of the society in question. Victor Turner defined ritual as an

Source: © iStockphoto/Nicholas Belton.

aggregation of symbols, with the symbols being the smallest unit of ritual that still retains the specific properties of ritual behavior. From this definition, we can see a crucial feature of his methodology, which works from discrete ritual symbols ("storage units," "building blocks," and "molecules of ritual") to their incorporation in ritual systems, and then to the incorporation of such systems in the whole social complex being studied. He stressed the common diachronic profile or processual form in rituals, that is, the sequence of ritual acts in social contexts. He treated ritual symbols not as static, absolute objectifications but as social and cultural systems, shedding and gathering meaning over time and altering in form. This emphasis on social process distinguishes him sharply from his own background in British social anthropology, which focused primarily on structure and static functionalism.

Turner outlined a method to analyze symbols. Symbols, according to him, should be examined in terms of three levels of meaning: exegetical, operational, and positional. Exegetical meaning consists of how indigenous people consciously understand a symbol, as well as the symbol's linguistic derivation, social history, and material substance. Operational meaning centers on how a symbol is used—in what institutions, by what groups, and so on. Positional meaning has to do with a symbol's relationship to other symbols both within a particular ritual and within the framework of a total ritual system.

Clifford Geertz advocated an interpretive approach to the study of symbols and rituals. He argued that the analysis of culture is not an experimental science in search of law but an interpretive one in search of meaning. He believed that culture should be understood to consist of socially established structures of meaning embodied in systems of symbols. It is through these structures of meaning, these webs of significance, that we order our experience and make sense of the world we inhabit.

Ritual, according to Geertz, is such a system of symbols, which stand for values, codes, and rules. Ritual interpretation is a process that integrates theorists' abstract conceptual categories and the cultural particularity of a rite. The theorists' conception should be based on the natives' view. Their perceptions and knowledge are melded to those of the indigenous people. Geertz believed that what we call our data are really our constructions of other people's constructions of what they and their compatriots are up to. In a word, Geertz's model in ritual study illustrates that ritual participants act, whereas those observing them think. The observers' understanding of the ritual behavior should be based on the performers' own emic views. The title of one of Geertz books, *Local Knowledge,* signifies his view of seeking knowledge by starting from the base of indigenous knowledge and combining it with that of the observer.

The influence of Turner and Geertz can be seen in two anthropological books on death rituals: *Celebration of Death,* by Huntington and Metcalf, and *Death and the Regeneration of Life,* edited by Bloch and Parry. The first book, based on the authors' ethnographies of the Bara of Madagascar and the Berawan of Central Borneo, attempts to interpret the relationship between the symbols of death and sexuality and rebirth. The second book contains seven articles that incorporate the sociological, symbolical, and psychoanalytic approaches to explain the significance of symbols of fertility and rebirth in death rituals.

Death Rituals in Sanyuan Village, China

Sanyuan Village lies at the northeast edge of Chongqing Municipality of China. It is an administrative unit, consisting of 10 natural villages or hamlets. Four of them are located on the plain over the Dahong River Valley, and the rest are down in the valley by the river, whose fields are often submerged by the flooding river in spring and summer. Its economy depends on rice farming.

In Sanyuan Village, every family holds elaborate funerals for its members who die, except children who die before reaching adulthood. They are regarded as *gui erzi* or *gui nuer* (son or daughter of devils) and are doomed to die. Any family who gives a deceased child a full formal funeral will suffer from misfortune or even the death of other members in the family.

Preparation for Death

Preparation for death usually starts when a person is over 60 years old. A coffin may be made or purchased for him or her, or coffin money may be collected from his or her children for future use. Aged villagers may have their *shouyi* (grave clothing) sewn in the eventuality of their death. A *shouyi* consists of a coat and a pair of pants. The number of the *shouyi* depends on the wealth of the family. It is always an odd number, varying between three and nine pieces. Seven is considered the ideal, because *qi* (seven) is a homophone for the abundance of descendants, harmony, and prosperity of the family. The color of the *shouyi* is either black or white for all, regardless of gender difference. But the outerwear is always black. With the coffin purchased and *shouyi* made, the predeath preparations for funeral are completed.

Initial Ritual

When a person is seriously ill and near death, his or her *houren* (offspring) will be summoned and gathered around him or her. Before he or she breathes the last breath, the patient will be moved into a chair in his or her room, facing the door. To die in bed is considered as harmful because the soul of the newly deceased cannot easily leave the bed. To die in a chair is considered as the most dignified death, with all the descendants kneeling down around the chair and the spouse, brothers, and sisters standing around. The oldest son holds the ill person upright. Last words are exchanged between the dying and the surrounding persons. The local terminology for this process is *songzhong* (sending off the dying).

As soon as the dying person breathes a last breath, the descendants, especially women, burst into a loud wailing. Firecrackers are set off to scare away hungry ghosts who might be wandering around the house. The loud wailing and firecrackers also inform the community that a death has occurred, so that the other families can take proper measures to eliminate bad effects of the death. *Daotou fuzi* (paper money bound in small rectangular bundles with the names of the deceased and donors written on the cover) is burned to provide the deceased with traveling expenses on the way to the world of the dead. Messengers are sent out immediately to inform other relatives of the death in the family.

Treatment of the Body

After a person dies, he or she is placed on a wood board in the *tangwu* (living room) and is prepared for *mahang* (ritually washing the deceased). *Aishui*, which literally means "love water" (water boiled with eucalyptus leaves or tea), is prepared. The sons' clothes are soaked in the *aishui*. It symbolizes the *ai* (love) of the descendants to the deceased. This specially boiled water is to clean the dead body ritually and to drive away any evil spirits that might have possibly attached to the body.

Two or three elders in the village are invited to wash and dress the deceased. They soak a piece of white cloth in the *aishui* and move it across the body three times from head to feet. The cloth does not necessarily touch the body. After this, they dress the deceased with *shouyi* (grave clothes), tie up the deceased's feet and waist with black threads, put the corpse into a coffin set up on two benches in the *tangwu*, and fix the corpse tightly so that it will not shift when the coffin is moved out of the village to the grave site. A *shoubei* (a very small cotton-wadded quilt) is put on top of the body. The coffin is half closed, with only the head end open, so that the face of the deceased can be seen. A piece of white cloth is laid over the face. An incense pot and a kerosene lamp (called *changming deng*) are set on the top of the coffin. A ceramic pot or iron basin is put under the coffin for burning paper money.

Preparations by Specialists

A funeral in Sanyuan Village involves several groups of specialists. A bereaved family needs to hire Daoist priests to conduct funerary rituals, a funeral band to play mourning music, a feng shui master to look for a grave site, a local scholar to write a eulogy, and one or two craftsmen to make a miniature paper house, paper furniture, and other items of daily necessity for the deceased to use in the otherworld.

Priests usually arrive at the bereaved house in the afternoon. They generally spend the afternoon preparing for their rituals. The most important items they make for the funeral are a *lingpai* (soul tablet) for the deceased, a *fan* (a lanternlike object), passports to the otherworld, written documents addressed to certain deities in the otherworld, five tablets representing east, south, west, north, and center directions, a *xiao dan* (a list of all filial descendants), and many bundles of *fuzi* (paper money).

After making the soul tablet, *fan,* and other items, the priests set up a *tan* (altar) with two dining tables in the *tangwu* against the wall facing the door. Four benches are placed by the two sides of the altar for the priests to sit on. A tablet for the ancestors of the bereaved family, the soul tablet of the deceased, two kerosene lamps, and incense holders are placed on the altar. With the altar set up, the priests are ready to start their ritual performance.

Ritual Performance

All the rites performed by priests are accompanied by percussion music, produced by drums, gongs, *mu yu* (wooden sound boxes), and brass ringing bowls, and by chanting of scripts by the chief priest alone or by all the priests in chorus with their percussion music. Their performance usually lasts all night. Though different priests may conduct rites in different order and in various styles, their performance consists of the following rites:

1. Rite of *Pobai* (breaking the white). After the sun sets, priests start their performance. They chant their scripts first. Their chants point out that life is hard and death is unavoidable. They inform the deceased that the descendants are all heartbroken. They ask the *xiaozi* (filial descendants) to kowtow toward the soul tablets. Then, they tell the *xiaozi* to put on *xiaofu* (mourning clothes, usually a long piece of white cloth) to show their filial piety to the deceased. As soon as the *xiaozi* put on mourning dresses, they officially enter the mourning stage.

2. Rite of *Qingshui* (fetching water). The priests lead all the *xiaozi* to a well or a river nearby, accompanied by the funeral band. When the troupe reaches the well or the riverside, the priests plead to the dragon and guardian spirits of the water for permission to fetch their water. Paper money and incense sticks are offered to them by being burned. The eldest son or other siblings in his absence then fills a bottle with water. The burning of paper money suggests that the water is purchased from its sacred guardians. So it is *shengshui* (sacred water) and is used by the priests symbolically.

3. Rite of *Jingzao* (worshipping the Stove God). The priests lead the *xiaozi* into the kitchen. The soul tablet, a passport, and a copy of a written document are put on the top of the stove. Incense sticks are burned on the stove. The chief priest chants scripts. He pleads the Stove God to report the death to the Jade Emperor. *Xiaozi* then kowtow to the stove. Paper money is burned. The purpose of this rite is to inform the Stove God of the death and to appeal for his protection for both the deceased in the *yinjian* (the underworld) and the living members in the *yangjian* (this world) by providing them with abundant food. It is believed that this rite facilitates admittance of the soul of the deceased into the world for the dead.

4. Rite of *Kai Wufang* (opening the way). There are two kinds of *kai wufang*: a grand one and a little one. For the former, at least six priests are needed; for the latter, one to three priests. The priests lead all the *xiaozi* into the courtyard to dance around five tables that stands for five directions in the universe: east, south, west, north, and center. Paper money, incense, and food are offered, respectively, to five gods who are in charge of those directions. Five paper tablets of the directions are burned one by one, suggesting the gods have received the offerings and have opened up all the directions for the deceased to travel. Then, the priests lead all the *xiaozi* to cross a bridge built in the courtyard. The bereaved family can choose to construct *gao qiao* (high bridge) or *ping qiao* (flat bridge). For the high bridge, 11 to over 40 square tables are needed. The tables form a pyramid-like shape, with one on the top. The flat bridge can be built with three or five tables placed on the same level. Under the bridge, the priests put a bronze snake (actually made of bamboo), an iron dog (made from bamboo and paper), a paper boat, and a blood basin (basin with red color water). They symbolize the bloody river that separates the living world and the world of the dead. The bridge is called *Laihoqiao* that symbolically connects the two worlds. The priests and all the *xiaozi* (with the

eldest son carrying the soul tablet of the deceased) will cross the bridge three times, suggesting crossing three bridges. If the little *kaifang* is chosen by the family, the priests will let the eldest son move the soul tablet across three paper tablets on a long bench that symbolizes *Laihoqiao.* Crossing these bridges suggests that the deceased has entered the world of the dead and will be judged by the gods there.

5. Rite of *Yingwang Anwei* (welcoming back the soul of the deceased). A priest puts a kerosene lamp at the front door of the house to light the way for the soul of the deceased to return home. A temporary bathtub is improvised by using a bucket or basin full of water. The sacred water purchased from the gods earlier is poured into the tub. The tub is enclosed by a straw or bamboo mat. The soul tablet of the deceased and another red tablet representing ancestors are moved over the bucket of water, indicating that the deceased and his or her ancestors have taken a bath before entering home. The bath washes away dirt they carry and refreshes them up. Then, the two tablets are set at the head of the altar, ready to receive offerings and prayers. Food and liquor will be placed in front of them.

6. Rite of *Tuanfu* (praising the deceased). First, the eulogy writer reads his writing with great emotion in the *tangwu.* All the *xiaozi* should kneel down on the ground, while other senior relatives stand around listening. The eulogy usually covers the whole life of the deceased, from the birth to the death, emphasizing his or her contributions to the family, the sufferings and achievements in his or her life. Then, the chief priest reads *Shi Yue Huaitai* (Ten Months of Pregnancy) or *Shi Er Xifu Bu Xiao Niang* (Ten Daughters-in-Law Don't Observe Filial Piety to Their Mother-in-Law) for a female client. The first is a rhymed account of the happiness and sufferings that a mother has experienced in her 10 months of carrying a baby and in nursing the baby for the first 3 years after the birth. The second one describes various unfilial behaviors of 10 daughters-in-law and the great sufferings their mother-in-law has experienced. If the deceased is a man, the priest reads *Shier Dian* (Twelve Large Houses). It is a story about the sufferings of a father who strives all his life to build houses for his 12 sons.

7. Rite of *Baican* (praying to gods for the deceased). The bereaved family invites old women from the village to sing laments in the *tangwu.* They kneel down on cushions or mats on the ground in front the altar in the *tangwu.* They kowtow toward the altar as guided by the priests. They sing laments (a combination of weeping, singing, and speaking) to mention many good deeds the deceased has done in this world and to pray for the gods to release him or her from all of his or her crimes or misdeeds committed in this world. It is believed that the deceased at this time is going through the 10 courts in the *diyu* (the hell or underworld) and is being judged by magistrate, secretary-attendants, and demonical monstrous underlings of each court. *Baican,* and *tuanfu* as well, are intended to seek mercy for the deceased so that he or she may not be punished too severely and can go to the Western Heaven of Paradise.

8. Rite of *Chushang* (the funeral procession). Early in the following morning, the bereaved family checks the coffin and the body. If the deceased is a woman, her brother or relatives from her own natal family are invited to make the final check to make sure that the body is set at the right place and no unwanted object such as nails are placed inside the coffin. Then, the chief priest knocks at the coffin with an ax, without chopping it, while chanting scripts to wake up the soul of the deceased. He uses rooster blood to write a few magic spells on the coffin to drive away any hungry ghosts and evil spirits. After the priest's performance, the coffin is closed and sealed by old men from the village. Eight selected villagers carry the coffin on their shoulders. Firecrackers are first set off to scare away ghosts and give courage to the deceased on his or her way to the Western Heaven of Paradise. The funeral parade sets out for the gravesite. At the head of the parade is an old villager carrying a torch, which symbolizes a light in the otherworld for the deceased. Next is the *fan* carried by a son or nephew of the deceased. The soul tablet of the deceased is at the third position carried by the eldest son. The funeral band follows the soul tablet. Next comes the coffin. Following the coffin are the *xiaozi,* relatives, friends, and neighbors. Relatives and friends carry *jizhang* (pieces of cloth offered to the deceased by relatives and friends, which are put up on bamboo sticks like flags and on which the names of the donors and the deceased are written). The priests and the feng shui master are at the end of the parade. At the gravesite, the feng shui master first drops some rooster blood into the pit to drive away any hidden ghosts and demons, and then cleans the pit with a few drops of

the sacred water before the coffin is moved in. He then orients the coffin in the most beneficial direction to secure the best feng shui that will determine the future prosperity of the bereaved family. He shovels some soil on each corner of the coffin before the *xiaozi* throw dirt on the coffin with their hands. With this done, the *xiaozi* hurry home, taking a different route in order to evade the soul of the deceased in case it follows them. Two or three villagers stay behind to fill the grave pit with soil first and then pile up the soil into a cone-shaped tomb. Later, the bereaved family will cover up the tomb with a layer of stone to prevent the mound from erosion. They may set up a stone monument in front of the tomb with the deceased's name and the time of birth and death.

9. Rite of *Shao Huotang* (burning paper house, the *fan*, and the soul tablet). Returning from the gravesite, the bereaved family provides a final feast to all the participants. Food and drink are offered to the soul tablets of the recently deceased and the ancestors at the altar in the *tangwu*. This is the last meal for all of them at home. After the feast, the priests ask the *xiaozi* to remove the two soul tablets out of the house to an open space. A miniature replica paper house made by craftsmen is also moved there. The soul tablets are placed inside the paper house. The *fan* is placed against the paper house. Paper furniture, paper TV sets, and any other paper objects are placed either inside the paper house or outside. They are set on fire. Measures are taken to ensure that they are completely burned up. This is called *ciling* (sending away the souls of the deceased and other ancestors). Burning the two tablets suggests that the deceased now has joined his or her ancestors. After burning down the paper objects, the chief priest asks for a rooster, some food and liquor, and a bundle of sorghum heads. Having chanted scriptures, the priest puts a drop of rooster blood into a bowl of liquor and read the patterns to see if the deceased is pleased with the funeral. He then picks up the bundle of sorghum heads and uses it as a broom to symbolically sweep the floor for the bereaved family and the village. This drives away all hungry ghosts that wander around the house and the village after the death, and the villagers can resume normal life. This marks the end of the funeral.

Postburial Ritual

Burial does not end the descendants' obligation to the deceased. The bereaved family observes a period of mourning for 49 days. On every 7th day, the family members go to the tomb to offer food and paper money to the deceased. Locally, this is called *shaoqi*. On the last 7th day (the 49th day after the burial), the bereaved family prepares a banquet and invites relatives and friends for the banquet. Priests are hired to chant scripts. This marks the end of the mourning period for the bereaved family. After that, the bereaved family makes offerings to the deceased on the 100th day after the burial, the deceased's birthday, the death anniversary, and festivals such as the Chinese New Year.

Significance of Death Ritual

The death ritual in Sanyuan Village serves to reinforce family and kin group cohesion. It enhances cooperation and harmony in a community. It facilitates grieving and helps reduce fear and anxiety. It teaches villagers to observe filial piety to their parents and to take good care of their children. It provides principles to regulate human behaviors and interpersonal relationship. It displays economic and social resources that a bereaved family can utilize at a time of crisis. It transforms the discontinuity of biological death into social continuity and the corpse into an ancestor. It helps the deceased to adjust to the new environment and helps the living to understand that the deceased has become one of their ancestors. It ensures harmony between the living and the dead, and between the dead and supernatural beings. It celebrates death.

— *Gang Chen*

See also **Geertz, Clifford R.; Religious Rituals; Rites of Passage; Tylor, Edward Burnett**

Further Readings

Bell, C. (1997). *Ritual: Perspectives and dimensions.* New York: Oxford University Press.

Doty, W. G. (1986). *Mythography: The study of myths and rituals.* Tuscaloosa: University of Alabama Press.

Geertz, C. (1983). *Local knowledge: Further essays in interpretive anthropology.* New York: Basic Books.

Huntington, R., & Metcalf, P. (1991). *Celebrations of death: The anthropology of mortuary ritual.* Cambridge: Cambridge University Press.

Malinowski, B. (1954). *Magic, science and religion and other essays.* Garden City, NY: Doubleday Anchor Books.

Tylor, E. B. (1871). *Primitive culture.* New York: Putnam.

Watson, J. L., & Rawski, E. S. (1988). *Death ritual in late imperial and modern China.* Berkeley: University of California Press.

DEGENERATIONISM

There have been elements of degenerationist thinking for many centuries, although the term only arose in the 19th century in a specific context of evolutionary theory. Many ancient cultures understood their times as degenerate remnants of a golden age. For example, traditional Chinese history spoke of the golden age of the philosopher-king who is said to have ruled China with exemplary wisdom in ancient times. The name and dates of the philosopher-king differ according to which school of Chinese philosophy one consults, but they all agree that subsequent ages are ages of decline. Egypt, India, Greece, and Rome all had variations of the myth that current ages are degenerate survivals from a long-lost golden age. For example, Hesiod, the Greek poet and contemporary of Homer, outlined the classical Greek view of a golden age of gods and men living in harmony, which was followed by the silver, bronze, and iron ages, each one successively more grim for humans. The Christian religion continued this myth with the story of the expulsion of Adam and Eve from the Garden of Eden, and all subsequent humanity living with the consequences of their sin.

Variations of these mythologies of degeneration held the field with little change until the 19th century, when a new crop of degeneration theories arose. The Swiss historian Jacob Burckhardt (1818–1887) became an influential proponent of the idea that most of the ideas and trends characteristic of modern civilization were harbingers of a leveling barbarism. Friedrich Nietzsche (1844–1900) took Burckhardt's pessimism further, seeing the degeneracy as endemic to European civilization as a whole.

But it was developments in science that stimulated the most original variations on the old theme of degeneration. Evolution, particularly as it was expressed in the first half century after Darwin, was overwhelmingly progressionist in tone, being widely regarded as a process whereby organisms, including humans, move from simple to more complex forms of organization. When this was applied to human evolution, many people assumed that this meant history operated in a linear progression from backward states toward civilization. Furthermore, this progression upward was widely held to be a permanent condition.

The scientific variation of degeneration theory was, on the surface at least, a respectable enough idea: While most species move from the simple to the more complex, some move in the opposite direction toward more simple, or degenerate, forms. This idea was applied for a while to the study of ants and microorganisms and had a brief vogue in the 1870s before falling away in the face of the overwhelming consensus that evolution involved progress.

It was in the application of degeneration theory to human evolution that it had found a more congenial home. Degenerationism soon found an important role in the non-Darwinian brands of evolutionism now known as *Social Darwinism.* It was suggested, for instance, that the races held to be the most primitive, the Fuegians, Bushmen, and Australian Aborigines, had all at some time degenerated from more advanced forms. Social Darwinists were prone to appeal to the White races to adopt some attitude or other so as to avoid a similar fate. Variations of degenerationism also had a brief vogue among supporters of eugenics, and among those who studied criminology. The Italian criminologist Cesare Lombroso (1836–1909) was particularly influential in this area. Another early exponent of aspects of degenerationism was the German biologist Anton Dohrn (1840–1909). Dohrn's legacy, it has to be said, was far wider than his digression into degenerationism; he made important contributions to several areas of experimental biology. But degenerationism among scientists declined as Social Darwinism and eugenics declined as credible aspects of evolutionary theory.

In the English-speaking world, the most comprehensive 19th-century attempt at a theory of degeneration came from Phillip Gosse (1810–1888). In *Omphalos* (1857), Gosse, who was a biblical literalist, divided time into what he called diachronic, or historical time, and prochronic, or unreal or virtual, time. Gosse argued that even 20 minutes after the

Creation, the Garden of Eden would have shown signs of the passage of time that in real time had not taken place. In this way, the trees would have had annual rings commemorating years that had not passed, and Adam would have sported a navel from a birth that had not taken place. This bedrock of prochronic time, Gosse argued, was a necessary foundation for subsequent diachronic time to proceed from.

Gosse's book failed entirely to convince people, even other Christians concerned with the consequences of evolutionary theory. It was soon recognized that the arguments in *Omphalos* were unscientific in that they were quite untestable.

Gosse's book had been motivated in part by his religious orthodoxy, but his failure to harmonize religion and science did not deter other defenders of religious orthodoxy from employing variations of degeneration theory to support their religious beliefs. For instance, a noteworthy minority of 19th-century missionaries spoke in degenerationist terms with regard to subject peoples. Not only were the "savages" degenerate by virtue of beings descended from the sin of Adam, as all humans were thought to be, but they shared an extra helping of degeneracy by virtue of their very savagery. Unlike the Christians, savages had degenerated still further into devil worship, cannibalism, and all the other horrors that confronted the missionaries. Classified in this way, the missionaries were able to see their role as entirely beneficent and kindly.

While degenerationism came and went within two generations in the areas of science and religion, perhaps its most long-lasting legacy can be found in literature. Two early examples would include Robert Louis Stevenson's *Dr. Jekyll and Mr. Hyde* (1886), which explored the notion of an evolutionary duality in man, with modern man being confronted with an atavistic, inner-savage alter ego, and H. G. Wells's hugely influential *The Time Machine* (1895), which told of a future world where most humans have degenerated into Morlocks, living a spectral existence as toilers and providers for the ruling Eloi. The cultural pessimism that is so influential in much of contemporary literature and social theory is a direct descendant of the degenerationism of the 19th century.

— *Bill Cooke*

See also Darwinism, Social; Eugenics; Gosse, Philip

Further Readings

Bowler, P. (1992). *The non-Darwinian revolution.* Baltimore & London: Johns Hopkins University Press.

Gosse, E. (1970). *Father and son.* London: Penguin Books. (Original work published 1907)

Gosse, P. (1998). *Omphalos: An attempt to untie the geological knot.* Woodbridge, CT: Ox Bow Press. (Original work published 1857)

Herman, A. (1997). *The idea of decline in Western history.* New York: Free Press.

DELEUZE, GILLE (1925–1995)

Deleuze was a philosopher deeply influenced by his French predecessor Henri Bergson and early on by philosophical phenomenology, though he moved away from the latter in his most famous work. The pattern of his most influential work emerged in *Nietzsche and Philosophy* (first published in 1962), where he read Friedrich Nietzsche as the opponent of dialectic and negativity in Hegelianism. What Nietzsche offered as an alternative was an approach based on the affirmative, on forces, and on chance. After this, Deleuze's work becomes more individual and quirky, less systematic and formal in approach. His style now gives the impression of forces overflowing conceptual boundaries and in which he practiced the philosophical theory he had put forward in relation to Nietzsche. In accordance with Nietzsche, he tries to overturn the Platonist-metaphysical heritage in Western thought. He questions Plato's hierarchy of ideal forms, objects as imitations of forms, and our perceptions as imitations of those objects, by suggesting that such a hierarchy makes the forms dependent on their being copies of the forms. If the existence of the forms rests on the possibility of there being copies of them, then the metaphysical priority of forms over objects and perceptions is undermined. If Platonist metaphysics is undermined by the possibilities of difference and repetition of metaphysical forms, then all conceptual rigidities are undermined by the way that sense always runs into contradictions. I cannot even name anything without being caught in the contradiction between claiming that the name is connected uniquely with what it names and claiming that names and objects are distinct entities.

Deleuze was able to advance into a rich affirmative alternative to logical-metaphysical philosophy through a collaboration with the psychoanalyst Félix Guattari. The central result was the project *Capitalism and Schizophrenia,* which appeared as two books: first. *Anti-Oedipus* (first published in 1972), and then its sequel, *A Thousand Plateaus* (first published in 1980). It is the latter book that has become the standard reference point for Deleuzians. *Capitalism and Schizophrenia* superficially seems to weave together Freudianism and Marxism, but it is at least as much an attempt to collapse the Marxist and Freudian systems as it is an application of them. Deleuze and Guattari jump between literature, philosophy, psychoanalysis, anthropology, physical sciences, and all domains in an approach that takes force and the direction of force as its basis. Force appears in production, but production produces antiproduction as it forms itself into different kinds of machines. As in Bergson, there is an emphasis on constant flows and becoming in an approach that aims at being both transcendental and materialistic, "transcendental materialism." The materialism is transcendental because it does not refer to fixed forms, but to the constant transformations of forces. There is no deep structure behind what we sense, there are just endless multiplicities of levels, or plateaus, where energies appear, transform, and move between plateaus.

The social levels are defined through production of machines by machines and the ways in which that flow of force always breaks itself up, creating static despotic and paranoiac systems as we try to encode the Earth. As production encodes, the codes are unstable, interrupt production, and must collapse as codes are scrambled and new codes are produced. This approach is sometimes explained in terms of Benedict de Spinoza's philosophy of the complete immanence of being, that is, being as what exists only in the material world. It is also brought into discussions of literature, painting, cinema, and Michel Foucault. Foucault wrote the preface to *Anti-Oedipus,* but there was a later conflict and a critical though appreciative book by Deleuze on his old associate.

— *Barry Stocker*

See also **Bergson, Henri**

Further Readings

Gilles D. (1983). *Nietzsche and philosophy.* New York: Columbia University Press.
Gilles D., & Guattari, F. (1983). *Anti-Oedipus: Capitalism and schizophrenia.* Minneapolis: University of Minnesota Press.
Gilles D., & Guattari F. (1987). A thousand plateaus: Capitalism and schizophrenia. Minneapolis: University of Minnesota Press.

DELORIA, ELLA CARA (1889–1971)

Ella Cara Deloria, also known as *Anpetu Waste Win* (Beautiful Day Woman), was a noted Yankton Dakota (Sioux) anthropologist, linguist, educator, and novelist. With her intimate knowledge of the Lakota and Dakota dialects combined with an understanding and interest in her own culture as well as the world around her, she worked to preserve the riches of Native culture while representing those riches to outsiders in a dignified manner.

Ella Deloria's mother was Mary Sully Bordeau Deloria. Her father, Philip Deloria, grew up in the traditional camp circle and was educated in seminary. He became one of the first Dakota ordained an Episcopal priest. The family's roots were Yankton (central) Dakota, as well as Irish and French. Ella was born in the White Swan district of the Yankton reservation in eastern South Dakota. Both parents were previously married; each had two daughters, making Ella their first child in a family of five girls. The couple's other children were Philip, who tragically died at 10; Mary Susan, who became an artist; and Vine, who also became an ordained Episcopal priest.

Ella was raised at Wakpala on the Standing Rock Reservation, where she attended school at the mission founded by her father. Growing up, she spoke the Yankton dialect of Dakota at home and learned the Lakota dialect from her playmates on the Standing Rock Reservation. She also mastered the eastern dialect of Dakota, English, and later, Latin. She grew up immersed in traditional and Christian Lakota culture.

Ella continued her schooling in 1902 at All Saints Boarding School in Sioux Falls, another Episcopal institution. She attended the University of Chicago for a short time, won a scholarship to Oberlin

College, in Ohio, where she attended for 2 years, and then transferred to Teacher's College, Colombia University, in New York City, where she earned her bachelor of science degree in 1915. There, Deloria met the eminent anthropologist Franz Boas and began a fruitful though sometimes difficult collaboration, also working with Boas's students, anthropologists Ruth Benedict and Margaret Mead.

Ella Deloria saw the enactment of kinship roles as key to the integrity and continuation of Dakota society—an understanding that was not simply an intellectual construct, but a lived reality for her. After graduating from college, she returned to care for her aging parents and for her sister Mary Susan, who suffered from brain tumors. Committed to education, Deloria taught at All Saints beginning in 1915 until she went to Haskell Indian School in 1923, where she taught dance and physical education. In 1916, her mother died, and Ella took over the care of her sister Mary Susan and of her brother Vine, as well as her aging father.

Deloria began conducting formal research on Dakota language and culture in 1927. Sponsored by Franz Boas, she traveled between South Dakota and New York, making both geographical and cultural transitions as she had done from her earliest years. At Boas's request, she checked the work of James Walker, an early ethnographer of the Lakota, with contemporary Lakota people knowledgeable in the culture from 1896 to 1914. She translated the Lakota language texts of George Bushotter, a Lakota who moved from South Dakota to Washington, D.C., and worked at the Bureau of American Ethnology under James Owen Dorsey in 1887 and 1888. She also translated the Santee Dakota texts of missionary linguists Gideon and Samuel Pond and checked the accuracy of missionary linguist Stephen Return Rigg's Dakota dictionary. Deloria's collaboration with Boas lasted until his death in 1942.

At the same time, Ella Deloria had her own interests in studying language and culture and actively pursued them. Never formally trained as an anthropologist, as she was not able to muster the considerable financial resources and free time required to complete an advanced degree; most of her personal and financial resources were committed to the support of her family, a factor that sometimes brought her into conflict with Boas, who felt she should have been more available for research. Nevertheless, Deloria had a deep commitment to scholarship and to the documentation and continuity of her own culture and carried on an extensive correspondence with Boas, Benedict, and Mead. These documents are particularly interesting to anthropologists, as they transcend Deloria's writings about Lakota and Dakota culture and give vital insights into her own personal history, her understanding of her two worlds, as well as depicting her personal and scholarly struggles.

In addition to her anthropological research and to caring for her family, Ella Deloria worked at a wide variety of occupations. In addition to early teaching positions, she worked for the Campfire Girls and the Young Women's Christian Association and gave various lectures and demonstrations on Native culture. She collaborated on a study of the Navajo sponsored by the Phelps-Stokes Fund and the Bureau of Indian Affairs. She consulted with the Lumbee Indians in Pembroke, North Carolina, writing a pageant in consultation with them. She won the Indian Achievement Award in 1943, the highest honor at the time, from the Indian Council Fire in Chicago. She returned to St. Elizabeth's in Wakpala as an administrator from 1955 to 1958, and later became an instructor for the Nebraska Teachers Corps and St. Mary's Indian School for Girls in Springfield, South Dakota, with positions at the Sioux Indian Museum in Rapid City, South Dakota, and as assistant director of the W. H. Over Museum, in Yankton, South Dakota. At the end of her life, she was compiling a Siouan dictionary. In recognition of her considerable intellectual ability as well as meticulous scholarship, she received grants from the Wenner-Gren Foundation in 1948 and from the National Science Foundation in the 1960s. Ella Deloria suffered a stroke in 1970 and died the next year of pneumonia.

Today, her importance has grown, not only in her legacy of anthropological interpretation from a female Dakota perspective, but in the interpretation and translation of her own life and scholarly production generated by other scholars interested in Native and women's studies, marginality, postcolonial studies, literary criticism, cultural resistance and accommodation, and the contested ground between traditional and Christian beliefs. She is important not only for what she recorded, translated, and interpreted but also for who she herself was: a Yankton Dakota, a woman, and a member of an extended kinship group who both assisted and inspired her relatives (and was in turn inspired by them) and whose members include her artist sister Mary Susan; her Episcopal priest brother, Vine Deloria Sr.; her scholar/activist nephews

Philip S. Deloria and Vine Deloria Jr.; and her historian grand-nephew Philip J. Deloria.

Ella Deloria's published works included linguistics *Dakota Grammar* (published with Franz Boas), Native language folk stories, Dakota texts, ethnographies such as *The Sun Dance of the Oglala Sioux,* a popularized portrait of Dakota history and culture entitled *Speaking of Indians* (1944), and her novel *Waterlily,* published posthumously in 1988. The majority of her research and correspondence, yet unpublished, is archived in places such as the American Philosophical Society in Philadelphia; Vassar College Special Collections, Poughkeepsie, New York; and the Dakota Indian Foundation in Chamberlain, South Dakota. Beatrice Medicine, herself a Lakota ethnographer, knew Ella personally and has written on her life, as did Raymond J. DeMallie and her nephew Vine Deloria Jr. The most extensive biography of her life was written by Janette Murray. The written scholarship on Ella Deloria herself and her scholarly output continues to grow.

— *Raymond A. Bucko*

See also **Boas, Franz; Native Peoples of the United States; Women and Anthropology**

Further Readings

Deloria, E. (1998). *Speaking of Indians* (Introduction by V. Deloria Jr). Lincoln: University of Nebraska Press. (Original work published 1944)

DeMallie, R. (1980). Ella Cara Deloria. In B. Sicherman (Ed.), *Notable American women, the modern period: A bibliographical dictionary* (pp. 183–185). Cambridge, MA: Harvard University Press.

Medicine, B. (1988). Ella Cara Deloria. In U. Gacs, A. Khan, J. McIntyre, & R. Weinberg (Eds.), *Women anthropologists: A biographical dictionary* (pp. 45–50). New York: Greenwood Press.

Murray, J. K. (1974). *Ella Deloria: A biographical sketch and literary analysis.* Doctoral dissertation, University of North Dakota.

 # DEMENTIA

The term *dementia* entered the English language from the French in a rendering of French psychiatrist Pinel's (1745–1826) word "démance" (from *Treatise on Insanity,* 1806). Its ultimate source is Latin, meaning "loss" (or out) of "mind" or "reason." Some forms of dementia are transitory, while others are neurodegenerative and fatal. Dementias may co-occur or present independently. They include Alzheimer's disease (AD) and vascular dementia (VaD) (formerly, multi-infarct dementia [MID]), the two most common; dementia with Lewy bodies (DLB); Pick's Disease (PD); and dementias due to other medical conditions such as HIV disease, Huntington's Disease (HD), Parkinson's Disease (PaD), and dementia due to Creutzfeldt-Jakob Disease. Dementias also derive from toxic substances and brain or head trauma.

Dementia, as opposed to delirium, which appears rapidly and fluctuates, denotes a progressive loss of mental powers in multiple domains, including memory, language, and reasoning from previous levels of functioning. Difficult behaviors and psychiatric symptoms (BPSD) also may develop. The brain/behavior contrast leads to conflict between psychiatry and neurology about which has proper authority over the disorder. Differential diagnoses may involve clinical and instrumental assessment, neuroimaging, laboratory, genetic investigation, and ultimately, brain autopsy. However, the neuropathology may not accord with clinical symptoms.

In the early 1900s, *senile dementia* was an unremarkable finding among seniors. The 1901 encounter between German psychiatrist, Alois Alzheimer (1964–1915), and his patient, Auguste D. (died 1906), led to a reformulation because of her comparative youth (51 years). Alzheimer's first papers concerning her (1906, 1907) led to the bestowal of the eponym "Alzheimer's Disease" by the eminent psychiatrist Emile Kraepelin. As a *presenile dementia,* so distinguished by Kraepelin, AD took some time to gain ground and did so in part by expanding its application from presenile to senile cases.

Today, AD is understood as involving the deposition of amyloid plaques and the development of neurofibrillary tangles in the brain, in line with Alzheimer's findings. These characteristic features have independent developments with little overlapping distribution. However, researchers have incomplete knowledge of their relationship to clinical symptoms. Here, we note that Alzheimer's second diagnosed case of AD, Johann F., did not exhibit the tangles.

The lack of specificity problematizes pharmacological research strategies, as well as the elucidation of distinct disease etiologies even in the rare cases of the familial AD (about 2% of cases) and where there is an increased risk (e.g., with apolipoprotein 4). Increasingly, researchers suggest that AD is brain aging, not a disease process.

Social science interest in dementia centers on AD and sees related biomedical theory and research as cultural practice. Research areas include the decreasing clarity of disease differentiation and etiology; the promotion of ill-defined precursor states and their ethical challenge; the cross-cultural variation in the meaning and roles of cognition, memory, seniority, and caregiving; the evident sociocultural and political features of the development of AD as disease; gender issues in research and its interpretation; the role of pharmaceutical companies in disease conceptualization; dementia narratives, and the study of the medical sciences such as genetics within the cultural studies of science from medical anthropology.

— *Atwood D. Gaines*

See also Medical Genetics

Further Readings

Cohen, L. (2000). *No aging in India.* Berkeley: University of California Press.

Growdon. J., & Rossor, M. (Eds.). (1998). *Blue books of practical neurology series: The dementias.* Woburn, MA: Butterworth Heinemann.

Hinze, S. W., Atwood D. G., Lerner A. J., & Whitehouse, P. J (1999). An interdisciplinary response to the Reagan Center Report on women and AD. A*lzheimer Disease and Associated Disorders, 13,* 183–186.

Post S. G., & Whitehouse P. J. (Eds.). (1998). *Genetic testing for Alzheimer disease: Clinical and ethical issues.* Baltimore: Johns Hopkins University Press.

Whitehouse, P. J., Gaines A. D, Lindstrom H., Graham J., & ADWG (Anthropology and Dementia Writing Group). (2004). Dementia in the anthropological gaze: Contributions to the understanding of age-related cognitive impairment. *The Lancet Neurology 3*(12).

Whitehouse, P. J., Maurer K., & Ballenger J. F. (Eds.). (2000). *Concepts of Alzheimer disease: Biological, clinical, and cultural perspectives.* Baltimore: Johns Hopkins University Press.

 # DEMOGRAPHY

Modern demography seeks to characterize populations or subgroups of populations based upon statistical commonalities or differences between them. Clearly, some of these may be largely cultural (e.g., age of marriage, total fertility, socioeconomic status) or largely biological (e.g., resistance to particular strains of malaria, skin cancer risk, mean height), while others may be almost entirely cultural (e.g., knowledge of contraceptive technology) or almost entirely biological (e.g., presence or absence of particular inheritable genes). The disentanglement of biology and culture in group characteristics has proved to be complex.

While human societies are always conditioned by demographic characteristics, thinkers such as Malthus or, later, Boserup have made sweeping claims for the fundamental role of population growth as the key independent variable. Malthus, famously, argued that population inevitably grew quickly to exhaust resources regardless of the rate of growth in the latter, due to the superior power of a geometric series compared to an arithmetic one. This flawed perspective was unfortunately used as the basis for population policies biased against the poor and aimed at protecting social surpluses for the upper classes. Many have long found this claim unconvincing both in its mathematical formulation as well as in its biological, sociological, and technological naïveté. Scientific claims mixed with an uncritical stance toward the power structure unfortunately characterized demographic writing long after Malthus.

Demographers, with few exceptions, have tended to be atheoretical or uncritical, from a social science perspective, and to decontextualize variables such as mortality rates and fertility rates or even to devise demographic models purportedly applicable to many times and places. By contrast, anthropologists and historians argued throughout the 20th century for the need to recognize the complexity of the interactions between demographic, epidemiological, cultural, political, and environmental factors.

Perhaps the most influential demographic model, that of the demographic transition (introduced in 1929 but tailored to address U.S. policy objectives in 1945), is a case in point. This model uses fertility rates and mortality rates as dependent variables, differentially impacted by a variety of other factors, to explain the major demographic growth displayed by many societies since the advent of modern public health as well as the recent arrival at very low population growth levels by, for example, Germany or Japan. The demographic transition models the change from high fertility rates and high mortality rates (close to static population levels) to high fertility rates plus lower mortality rates due to public health measures (leading to longer average life spans and rapid population growth). It then charts a period of increasing prosperity and state social security policies motivating smaller household sizes, leading to another equilibrium (again roughly static population) at lower fertility and mortality rates.

The model seems to fit the trajectory followed by many modernizing countries but falls considerably short, even at the statistical level, of a universal model for industrial societies, as the significant differences between German and U.S. demographic trends in the 20th century would suggest. What it most particularly lacks is any critical reflection on the necessity or current or future desirability of conformity to such a model. Barely below the surface of the model is the Malthusian assumption that U.S. concerns about a third-world population explosion are beyond criticism and that public health, economic liberalization, democracy, and family planning efforts will have their primary justification in slowing population growth in the poorer regions of the world. Predictably, despite the historical evidence that changing economic conditions caused demographic changes in Europe, the focus for poorer countries was placed on family planning. The forced sterilization campaigns in India from the 1950s to the 1990s were linked to this policy yet supported by the Indian government. The parallels between this view and the more overtly racist views of many demographers earlier in the 20th century largely obviate the differences.

In the latter part of the 20th century, demographers moved away from the highly criticized transition theory to attempt to incorporate culture. With the exception of institutional demography, which focused on the influence of historical social institutions (family systems, community organization, patriarchy, and so on) on demographic variables such as fertility, demographers nevertheless continued to be largely Eurocentric, ahistorical, and apolitical building, on diffusion theory, a branch of modernization theory, to predict the spread of European technology for fertility control to supposedly less enlightened areas.

Demographic models by nondemographers have had different agendas. The problem of explaining historical increases in agricultural production (per unit area) led Boserup to argue that technical progress in agriculture was historically motivated by demographic pressure. Boserup proposed a universalistic model in which increasing population pressure led humans to gradually ratchet up the intensity of agriculture (equated with frequency of land use) from slash-and-burn through gradual stages to annual production, characterized at each stage by lower returns to labor (primarily due to soil exhaustion or the extra labor needed to maintain fertility). The model proposed that these diminishing returns to labor were acceptable only because higher returns per unit area were achievable and were necessitated by demographic pressure. Thus, demographic necessity was the mother of technological invention and individual maximization the driving force. Few believe matters are this simple. The ancient custom of flood recession agriculture, where nature annually renews fertility, followed a different trajectory, more easily fitting political economy models than demographic or individual maximizing ones. When irrigated agriculture obtained long-term multiplier impacts from infrastructure, this also necessitated complex political change enabling choices between long, and short-term benefits, not simple individual responses to population pressure.

If Boserup made politics a mere response to demography, Carneiro suggested that population pressure was the proximate cause of state formation. In his model, states occur where populations are circumscribed by ecology such that their eventual concentration leads to conflict, which, in turn, necessitates some form of higher organization. Provided that productivity is high, such as along navigable river systems, population growth brings ever-greater population pressure and ever-greater need for political resolution of conflict, and eventually this leads to state creation. Carneiro incorporated the idea that agricultural technology itself is relative and so levels of demographic pressure leading to conflict are themselves dependent on the capacities of the technology, as applied to the natural resources, to support population growth. While Carneiro proposed this model as a general theory of state formation, subsequent archaeological work has not sustained its specific premise that population pressure preceded the development of hierarchy, nor its general claim for the foundational role for population circumscription and demographic pressure in state formation.

A contextualized historical demography brings specialized techniques that social scientists in many fields rely on to understand both human and animal populations. Ratios of males to females and age distributions can often be reconstructed and used to chart major economic and social change. Even tabulating household composition solely in terms of age and gender tells us a great deal about any society. If we add to this study of disease, nutrition, and DNA (human, animal, and microbe), also discernable from skeletal material, a vast array of insights into social structure, kinship, and migration of past societies can be gleaned from the most basic demographic materials.

Societies differ enormously in terms of the availability of ancillary materials of demographic importance, and these may vary from evidence of dwelling spaces, refuse heaps, or potshards all the way to several hundred years worth of birth and death records for each parish in a country (as in France). Surface surveys focusing on potshards in the Fertile Crescent (Mesopotamia) have provided one of the simplest reasonably reliable methods for estimating local population trends. Brinkman notes that although surface surveys are less than perfect, they provide one of the few ways to survey large geographic areas, and they exhibit enough internal consistency to support significant demographic arguments. Thus, they suggest that between 2100 BC and 625 BC, the population of lower Mesopotamia declined dramatically and did so differentially with an approximate 75% decline in the northern sector and a 25% decline in the southern regions. The same data also suggest that between 2700 BC and 625 BC a much larger percentage of the total population in lower Mesopotamia came to live in small towns and villages. These conclusions, and the associated details of regional patterns of habitation, obviously have many broad implications for an understanding of the period even if by themselves they raise more questions than they answer.

Anthropologists attempting to reconstruct historic or ancient population patterns have used demographic tools with their own research agenda without attempting a full scale rethinking of demography's assumptions or history. Recent attempts to reconstruct the peopling of the new world exemplify research driven by the assumption that in key respects, the indigenous inhabitants of the Americas resemble populations at similar technological levels elsewhere. In an attempt to gain precision on where these peoples came from, how (mainly but not entirely across Beringia, a land bridge existing in particular periods), and when (9–13,000 BC or substantially earlier), scholars have focused on genetic markers that distinguish particular subpopulations. This first step leads directly to a consideration of the many factors that may have influenced the fertility and mortality of each subpopulation.

The actual genetic analysis is heavily weighted toward the use of statistics gleaned from geographically based studies of modern populations in the Americas or Siberia to extrapolate to degrees of historical proximity. Little serious effort has been done to model the implications of culture specific marriage patterns in the Americas or to apply such models to past demographic analysis even though statistically significant parallel or cross-cousin marriage would impact the rates of change in genetic markers carried in male or female lines.

The Atlantic slave trade and the conquest of the New World, with its huge significance in increased mortality, brought major transformations to the Americas that in some sense obscure the dynamics of indigenous demographics. Both processes have thus directly tied research into ancient demographics in the New World to similar research in the historic period beginning with the conquest. The scarcity of pre-contact skeletal remains has meant that modern populations with indigenous ancestries need to be used as proxies. This raises many issues, since most Native Americans have their own origin stories, do not subscribe to an Asian origin, and view the enterprise as potentially weakening remaining rights to land.

While demographers and physical anthropologists now regularly use sophisticated statistical and biological techniques to study health, disease, migration, and nutrition among different populations, many social scientists still view the field with lenses colored by a perception of the field's history of apolitical or even overtly racist research. The modern preoccupation of private insurance companies with eliminating risk has raised a modern concern about the potential misuse of demographic statistics. This touches on the more general issue of human subjects protection within academia and the very real difficulties and risks, including legal risks to researchers, associated with collecting large databases of DNA even for the most worthy of causes. It may become increasingly difficult to do demographic research. If this leads to critical reflection and debate on research agendas, it may have a positive outcome, while if demographic research is simply stifled, much of great value will be lost.

— *Thomas K. Park*

See also **Genetics, Population; Malthus, Thomas**

Further Readings

Crawford, M. H. (1998). *The origins of Native Americans. Evidence from anthropological genetics.* Cambridge: Cambridge University Press.

Greenhalgh, S. (1996). The social construction of population science: An intellectual, institutional, and political history of twentieth-century demography. *Comparative Studies in Society and History, 38*(1), 26–66.

McNicoll, G. (1994). Institutional analysis of fertility. In K. Lindahl-Kiessing & H. Lundberg (Eds.), *Population, economic development, and the environment* (pp. 199–230). Oxford: Oxford University Press.

Salzano, F. M., & Bortolini, M. C. (2002). *The evolution and genetics of Latin American populations.* Cambridge: Cambridge University Press.

DENDROCHRONOLOGY

Dendrochronology is the study of the dating of trees by their annual rings and, subsequently, other objects, both historical and environmental events and processes. Because of some tree species' long life spans and growth responses, a reliable pattern of temperature and precipitation has been recorded in their woody tissue. Just beneath the bark of a tree is a tissue called the vascular cambium, a thin layer of cells that is responsible for the growth in diameter of the trunk. This tissue rapidly divides in two directions, with the outer cells forming the phloem, the transport system that carries food from the photosynthetic tissues to the other parts of the tree and also provides storage and support. The inner cells produce the xylem cells, which are thick-walled cells with perforated or missing end walls, resulting in the continuous vertical transport of water. The size of these cells is dependent on the seasons of the year and its concomitant availability of moisture and fluctuating temperatures. In the spring, in temperate climates, when days are cool and soil moisture is more plentiful, the cambium layer produces large-diameter xylem cells. As the summer temperatures increase, it produces smaller cells. This cycle repeats itself each year, resulting in distinguishable growth rings of large, dark spring wood and the smaller, lighter summer wood. By counting these rings, the age of the tree can be determined.

The method of extraction, after locating appropriate trees and sites, is to use a borer, a threaded hollow tube that is screwed into the trunk of a tree and an extractor inside the borer shaft that enables the dendrochronologist to pull the sample from the tree. Generally, a second bore is made on the opposite side of the tree, taken to the laboratory, and sanded until the cell structure of the wood is visible under a microscope.

Astronomer Andrew E. Douglass, of the University of Arizona, is credited with the modern-day study of tree rings. While studying sunspot cycles, solar energy, and climate, he speculated that these cycles should be evident in the growth of trees. Further study established the pattern of the varying tree ring widths with climate. Subsequently, he used a process called *cross-dating* to establish exact dates of specimens in an historical perspective. By comparing the pattern of rings of trees in which life spans partially overlap, these patterns can be extended back in time, whether in the same region or in distant locations. Using intact and overlapping sections of living, recently, or long-dead trees or timbers, researchers have been able to construct an unbroken record, stretching back nearly 9,000 years, using the bristlecone pines in the American Southwest. In Europe, oak and pine chronologies reveal an 11,000-year-old record. With this information, scientists can accurately fix calendar dates to tree rings against a known chronological reference point.

Growth processes functioning within a geographical area are influenced by a variety of environmental factors, including water, temperature, slope, wind, sun, canopy removal, fire, and snow accumulation. Growth is at its best within a geographic area that is constrained only by the environmental factor that is most limiting. Trees with an ample supply of soil moisture show a minimal effect of climate on the ring width, but sites that have limiting factors favorable for growth show the largest degree of effect on the rings. The former rings are called *complacent*, and the latter *sensitive.* For example, trees are more sensitive to changes in their environment along the margins of their natural range and, therefore, display the widest variations in their annual ring sizes. The bristlecone pine has been extensively studied because of its long life span and sensitivity to drought conditions. The oldest known living specimens are almost 5,000 years old, surviving in marginal habitats in the arid mountainous regions of California, Nevada, and Utah in the United States, at an elevation of over 9,000 feet. These locations, where water supply is the main limiting factor, result in extremely slow growth patterns and, therefore, provide data about the climate over past ages.

Wood is organic and, as such, is biodegradable, but certain conditions, such as dry climate, waterlogging in bogs and swamps, and fossilization, preserve the dead wood for hundreds and even thousands of years, thus providing a means to extend tree ring chronologies beyond living organisms.

In addition to the record of climates, tree ring chronologies have assisted in the interpretation of data from many archaeological sites. Douglass's early expedition to Pueblo Bonito, a prehistoric Native American settlement in the southwest United States, analyzed the wood used in its construction to determine its existence some 800 years before European arrival, exploration, and settlement on the North American continent. Exact dates of timbers, campfires, and artifacts from the ruins of many ancient sites have been established by tree ring study, together with evidence of the impact of natural events such as floods, fire, and droughts on Native human populations, history, and migration patterns. Cross-dating has also enabled the confirmation of times of construction of early structures of many buildings, barns, bridges, wells, and boats.

Prior to the study of tree rings, there was no way to independently confirm dates using radiocarbon methods. What was once an important assumption underlying radiocarbon dating, namely, that the amount of carbon 14 in the atmosphere had remained constant throughout history, had to be altered because tree ring evidence pointed to fluctuations in the amount of carbon 14 during different ages. While a green plant is alive, carbon 14 is incorporated into the organism by the photosynthetic reaction using carbon dioxide directly from the atmosphere. It stops when the organism dies because this atmospheric exchange ceases. The rate of decay is then calculated, but within a very large range. Instead of roughly dating an artifact within several centuries, scientists can use tree ring calibrated radiocarbon measurements that are within tens of years of the origin of organically derived archeological objects.

Fire scars are also evident in tree rings as a result of naturally occurring wild fires over the past centuries and have enabled scientists to reconstruct their frequency, extent, and effect on ecosystems and, subsequently, the impact on human populations.

Other recent areas of study using the principles of dendrochronology extend to solar variability, earthquakes, volcanism, erosion and deposition rates, glacial movement and moraine deposits, insect damage and geographic extent, and a variety of atmospheric pollutants, changes in the composition of the atmosphere, and other possible effects of hazardous wastes brought about by human interference with the natural processes.

— *Paul A. Young*

See also **Dating Techniques**

Further Readings

Douglass, A. E. (1920). Evidence of climatic effects in the annual rings of trees. *Ecology, 1*(1), 24–32.
Fritts, H. C. (1976). *Tree rings and climate.* New York: Academic Press.
Webb, G. E. (1983). *Tree rings and telescopes: The scientific career of A. E. Douglass.* Tucson: University of Arizona Press.

DENNETT, DANIEL C. (1942–)

American philosopher, Daniel C. Dennett focuses on the philosophical problems concerning science, particularly in the areas of mind and consciousness within an evolutionary framework. Born in Boston, Massachusetts, Dennett received his BA from Harvard in 1963 and his PhD in philosophy from Oxford in 1965. After graduation, Dennett taught at the University of California at Irvine as both an assistant professor (1965–1970) and associate professor (1970–1971) until accepting a position at Tufts University (1971). At Tufts University, Dennett was promoted from associate professor to currently held position of professor (from 1975). During his tenure, he has held the position of chairman of the philosophy department (1976–1982) and received several distinguished positions, including both visiting associate professor/professor at other universities. Dennett has also lectured both nationally and internationally. Aside from lecturing, Dennett was both cofounder and codirector of the curricular Software Studio at Tufts. Amid his scholastic endeavors, Dennett holds memberships of several organizations (both national and international).

Throughout his academic career, Dennett has become a prolific writer with great philosophical contributions to science. He has published 11 books and multiple score of academic articles. Of his published books, *Content and Consciousness* (1969), *The Mind's I: Fantasies and Reflections on Self and Soul* (1981), *Consciousness Explained* (1991), *Darwin's Dangerous Idea* (1995), and *Freedom Evolves* (2003) reflect a historical account of cognition and implications it has concerning our species' epistemology, ontology, and teleology. Savoring the deepest philosophical questions, Dennett attempts to explain the implications stemming from a materialistic explanation of cognition. While searching for an inclusive paradigm, interests in computer design (developed from the computer revolution) and subsequent programming have become a point of special interest.

Contributions and Perspectives

Questions concerning epistemology and phenomenology have deep philosophical implications for our species ontology and teleology. These interdependent sources of human inquiry are the basis for our species cognitive existence. Drawing upon physical attributes with rational speculation, the ancient Greek philosophers Plato (ca. 428–348 BC) and Aristotle (384–322 BC) attempted to construct the processes by which human beings exist in the external world. Through this philosophical inquiry, the birth of metaphysics provided the necessary explanations that would replace both myth and superstition. After metaphysics became adopted and modified by natural theology, the Enlightenment provided an opportunity for explanations to be independent of religion and theology. The philosophical positions of both the rationalists and the empiricists movement provided fertile groundwork for all facets of psychology and their philosophical implications, especially in the area of cognition. With the advancements made both in biology and evolutionary theory, a deeper understanding of biological processes has replaced or modified previously held theoretical positions about all processes of cognition, including our species' derived ontology, epistemology, and self-directed teleology.

Dealing with these issues, Daniel C. Dennett attempts to provide answers for the questions that are derived from human consciousness. His blended intellectual inquiries span from the philosophical spectrum of old (e.g., epistemology, phenomenology, ontology, and teleology), with recent advancements in both the cognitive sciences and artificial intelligence (AI). In the process of contrasting today's philosophical perspective with scientific evidence, his resulting interpretation provides a unique staring point by which a holistic understanding of personhood can be attained. Strengthened by the understanding of Darwinian evolutionary theory, Dennett's philosophical perspective also gives a dynamic materialistic explanation of our species in relation to the rest of nature, resulting in philosophical controversies that give cues to the remaining influences of the philosophers of the Enlightenment.

The philosophical impact of René Descartes (1596–1650) upon psychology's theoretical foundation has been very profound. With the introduction of dualism, the separation of mind and body served to rationalize human cognition with spiritual implications. Although cognitive psychologists reject this idea of a separation of mind and body, the given materialistic explanation still has dualistic properties. This stems from the personal narrative or perspective of the self-aware individual (e.g., first person). It is both the singularity of incoming perceptions and first-person perspective, via centralized processing (e.g., central executive), that gives the phenomenological problem in what Dennett calls "Cartesian materialism." To neutralize this phenomenological problem, Dennett poses a third-person narrative or heterophenomenological stand that is similar to processes used in the scientific method. In this perspective, Dennett suggests that an individual, through the senses, creates multiple scripts by which the intentional stance of the individual can choose a point of focus (e.g., notional world). The initial discrimination of incoming stimulus need happen only once, whereby the resulting information creates the perception of a "virtual world" of continuous time and space. This unique perspective may have solved the problems that cognitive theorists (e.g., Broadbent) have dealt with since the beginning of World War II. This would leave the primary filter factors to the physical limitations of the central nervous system and the focus of attention to intentions of the individual. It is the existence of intentions or intentional stance, in conjunction with the biological hardware, which may serve to both answer philosophical questions and give direction toward a united theory of cognition.

On a philosophical level, proving the existence of other minds by a priori means is impossible, not to mention promoting a sense of materialistic dualism. Though this Cartesian feat does nothing but to obscure and mislead areas of critical inquiry, evaluating intentions in an evolutionary framework starts to give a unique starting perspective. When dealing with the philosophical questions concerning whether other minds exist and aid in explaining the resulting behavior, Dennett utilizes an intentional stance of an object, whether human or machine (AI), to determine the teleological and to an extent ontological status. It is during this assessment of intentions that we attribute *belief* and *desires* to a particular organism or object by which varying degrees of rationality are expressed.

When addressing intentional systems, there are multiple orders of intentional systems. For example, zero order reflects the basic biological processes (e.g., fight/flight mechanism), often associated with basic survival. Beliefs and desires have no basis on this level. The first-order intentional system has beliefs and desires but has no reflections of these beliefs and desires. The second-order intentional system has reflective abilities concerning beliefs and desires. Third-order intentional systems have the capabilities, based on desires, of transmitting those beliefs in others. The fourth order is more complex. The fourth-order intentional system allows for the ability for understanding of these intensions. Although the construction of these orders is nebulous, whereby numbered class and characterization are moot, the orders by which these intensions are constructed reflect the biological designs and capabilities of the organism. These beliefs and desires, upon it being assumed, give the expression of freedom. Regardless whether freedom is an illusion, as sometimes portrayed in primate behavior, it is the ability of our species' syntax and semantic capabilities (internal and external) that enable and express this belief and desire in action, including the art of deception. Although both *design stance* and *physical stance* have certain objective benefits, it is the *intentional stance* that opens the "black box" of Skinner's behaviorism. In the long run, our species cannot be reduced to pure cause and effect. Just as culture (e.g., Dawkins's memes), thwarted our genetic disposition, the intentional stance frees our species from the blind deterministic outcome. Theoretically, the two are complementary, if not integrated by degree. The resulting processes, expressed in varying degree, are based on the predictive powers of rationality of the intentional system.

Throughout the history of philosophy, rationality has become a cornerstone of human ontology, teleology, and to an extent epistemology. As for Dennett, rationality is not some decisive and divisive deciding factor. Systems, by an evolutionary process, must operate by some principles of logic, even though it may not be readily apparent. Regardless if the system is biochemical or silicon based, rationality, though not total, is an adaptive strategy that allows for survival and reproduction in an environment. Though design and physical stance precede existence (evolutionarily speaking), it is the evolutionary-tested rationality of the intentional stance that allows for the possibility of prediction. Prediction is the key to understanding the intentional system of the object in question. For example, the a priori assumption of logic is given to Object A. If the object has been encountered prior, a posteriori cue in memory of past behavior gives behavioral predictability. If the object is new, perceptual cues within a logical framework (e.g., physical form and behavior) become encoded in memory in order for prediction to become possible. Evolutionary success is based upon the ability to predict such outcomes. The degree to which prediction can be utilized is based on the degree of physical (biological) complexity, signifying the evolutionary "leap" in the cognitive functions of our species. Although terms of belief and desires are expressions of freedom due to intentional systems, the inquiry nevertheless shows the complexity by which human systems operate in comparison to other species.

While treating systems as intentional systems, the mental processes by which human systems operate are a point of conjecture. The process of deriving the "mind" from organic matter boarder on determinism; after all, intention does not imply freedom of choice. As Dennett clearly points out, the algorithmic process of mental activity, the same algorithmic process that can account for the evolutionary process of our species (including chance or random occurrences), may seem to leave little room for free will. Yet human action and interaction has the sensible qualities of freedom found within the array of beliefs and desires. The relationship among biology, mind, and the mind's intention are expressed within our species' unique expression of culture, above all, including language and materialistic expressions.

The impact of culture upon our species' ontology, and thus teleology, is essential to our own epistemological understanding. Just as natural selection (or as Dennett humorously depicts Mother Nature) produced our design, culture enables our species to modify it. Dennett, utilizing Richard Dawkins's storm of memes, realizes the impact that culture has on both the environment and phenotypic expressions, the resulting behavioral modification necessitated by changes in the environment (e.g., memes act as a selective factor). In the process of enculturation (the transmission of memes from one individual to another), the active processing of exposed memes tends to modify the individual's selectivity. Emotional responses to cultural, including aesthetical qualities, has an active role in behavioral expressions. Dennett, even while contemplating Dawkins's stance on the *Selfish Gene,* believes the behavioral characteristics of genetics can be subverted by the exposure of memes. Though not advocating blind determinism (the disappearing self) or behaviorism, Dennett provides the connection among these factors. Through logical progression (all that varies by degree) of mental activity, the overarching biological factors are either subdued or enhance by the cultural phenomenon. Directed by belief and desire, the opportunity for choice (even as simple as yes or no) is present, an indicator for existence of freedom. When viewed in its entirety, the combination produces something, evolutionarily speaking, unique—that being personhood.

Questions pertaining to personhood are just as problematic as proving the existence of other minds. Combinations of design stance, physical stance, and intentional stance interact with environmental factors that produce the dynamics of human personality. These characteristics, by which intensions can be revealed, possess a contextual element of value judgment. On a basic level, these value judgments are neither good nor evil (by traditional religious standards). They are amoral decisions that are utilized to

promote the genetic welfare whereby these decisions are expressed by the variation (sometimes conflicting) of cultural expressions (e.g., mores and laws). The defining qualities or constituents of being a person have no magical or transcendental properties. The expressive use of language in practical reasoning can account for the necessitated views of ontology and teleology. In the course of human development, issues concerning causation and control over an individual's actions were given to free will via a divine source. With the discovery of organic evolution by Charles Darwin (1809–1882), the groundwork was set for a naturalistic explanation of human existence. In time, new scientific discoveries launched new areas of research and development. Dealing with these formable issues, Dennett continues to provide insight into the human condition. Advancements in AI and the cognitive sciences may someday aid in the evolutionary direction of our species. Through the views of philosophers such as Dennett, the "essence" of our humanity will evolve with great insights provided by science. In terms of personhood, our species will redefine its own ontological status in light of a self-directed teleology.

— *David Alexander Lukaszek*

Further Readings

Dennett, D. C. (1984). *Elbow room.* Massachusetts: Boston: MIT Press.

Dennett, D. C. (1987). *The intentional stance.* Boston: MIT Press.

Dennett, D. C. (1991). *Consciousness explained.* New York: Back Bay Books.

Dennett, D. C. (1993). *Brainstorms.* Boston: MIT Press.

Dennett, D. C. (1995). *Darwin's dangerous idea.* New York: Simon & Schuster.

DERRIDA, JACQUES (1930–2004)

Derrida has become a figure of extreme fame and extreme notoriety, neither of which phenomena has aided the evaluation of his work. Despite a later reputation for purposeless obscurity or creatively going beyond conceptual truth, depending on the point of view taken, Derrida started off as a scholar of the very formal and rigorous phenomenological philosopher, Edmund Husserl. His first notable publication was a long commentary on Husserl's short essay "Origin of Geometry." Derrida claimed that a close study of Husserl was bound to show contradictions between elements that emphasized the historical origin of geometry and the abstract structures of geometry as a discipline. For Derrida, the contradictions cannot be removed without destroying Husserl's position. This is not something unique to Husserl; all philosophy and all thought rest on contraction. Everything I say is an attempt to communicate the contents of my consciousness to another individual, who cannot grasp the contents of my consciousness. I cannot even grasp the contents of my own consciousness, since during the time of the act of grasping the contents of my consciousness, the contents of my consciousness have changed. The process of time means I may have died before my words have reached the listener or before I have finished grasping the contents of my own consciousness. The possibility of death always undermines claims to transparency of communication and consciousness for Derrida, and awareness of death is a constant factor in his philosophy, drawing on the discussion of death in G. W. F. Hegel and Martin Heidegger.

Philosophy, and all thought, have necessarily tried to ignore and repress contradiction in order to create systems of thought and stable ways of thinking. The repression of contradiction follows a pattern: One of the contradictory terms is regarded as superior, as truth, and the other is regarded as inferior. In the history of philosophy, being has been preferred to non-being, truth to falsity, oneness to difference, and so on. This may not look immediately harmful, but we cannot refer to being without referring to non-being and that gives non-being a being of some kind, as Plato recognized. We cannot escape from the lower term, as it must appear when we are discussing the higher term. The most important discussion in Derrida of this refers to speech and writing as aspects of language and meaning. He examines the privileging of speech over writing in Plato and Rousseau. Plato condemns writing as orphaned from its father, the originator of the words, who remains constantly present in speech. Writing has to be interpreted without reference to the original meaning and is therefore not a reliable expression of truth. Truth is only reliably present in speech, as we know what someone who is speaking means, and we can ask if we are not completely sure. For Derrida, the reduction of language to the presence of truth is "logocentrism," the centrality of "logos" as the living word of truth. The privileging of speech over writing is "phonocentrism," the centrality of the spoken word, and is a form of "logocentrism." "Logocentrism" is another word for metaphysics, and Derrida belongs to a tradition that questions the metaphysical elements of philosophy, while regarding them as unavoidable.

Derrida situates himself with regard to Friedrich Nietzsche and Martin Heidegger, both of whom he regards as precursors of his own deconstructive philosophy. Deconstruction aims to unveil the metaphysical oppositions and hierarchies underlying our thought, and then reverse the hierarchy in order to show its limits. Writing is therefore given priority over speech in Derrida's texts on that topic, but not with the intention of creating a new metaphysical hierarchy. There is a strategy that shows that all the negative things Plato attributed to writing are in speech, which can therefore be referred to a secondary form of writing, for strategic purposes. Nietzsche and Heidegger are taken as different aspects of deconstruction: Nietzsche as the playful affirmation of difference outside any possible unity in being, Heidegger as the nostalgia for being which can never be brought into presence but is always guiding our thought as an unavoidable presupposition. Jean-Jacques Rousseau has a similar role to Heidegger, in opposition to Nietzsche, as Rousseau's thought is dominated by a nostalgia for an always-absent nature. The questions of logocentrism and metaphysics are not restricted to philosophy at all. Derrida sees these questions as present in all thought and systems of knowledge. The particular target for him in this field was structuralism in the humanities. Structuralism in linguistics, literary studies, and anthropology are full of logocentric metaphysics, according to Derrida.

The most important work Derrida did on the social sciences is in *Of Grammatology* (first published in1967), which focuses on Rousseau and the relation of Rousseau with the linguistics of Ferdinand de Saussure and the anthropology of Claude Lévi-Strauss. He claims that Saussure's linguistics rests on assumptions on Rousseau's assumptions about language, in which the inside of language, what belongs to it metaphysically, is the naturalness of the spoken word. Derrida's discussion of Lévi-Strauss provides the opportunity to question the naturalness and the inwardness of speech compared with writing. Lévi-Strauss looks at "primitive" peoples as natural, which includes a capacity for speech combined with a lack of writing. Lévi-Strauss's view of primitive tribes is read as following Rousseau's vision of natural self-containment. However, according to Derrida, Lévi-Strauss's own texts demonstrate that primitive individuals have writing of a kind and exteriority of a kind (the capacity to see themselves in objects of creation). Writing appears in the examples of wavy lines given by Lévi-Strauss, which are drawn on when the chance to use paper and pen is offered. These lines refer to marks on the body, so there has always been writing of some kind. Exteriority can be seen in the genealogies memorized by Levi-Strauss's primitives. The genealogies demonstrate that they cannot be living in the natural historyless immediacy of the present that Lévi-Strauss mentions.

For Derrida, all societies, all language, and any kind of self-aware consciousness require exteriority, time, and writing as preconditions. The opposition of nature to society is untenable, since if we can make this distinction, then we are presuming a movement from the natural to the social. If the social emerges from the natural, then there is something in nature that brings about the social. What brings about the social is already social. Derrida argued for this in detail through readings of Rousseau, Saussure, and Lévi-Strauss, by showing the necessary appearance of contradiction in the transition from the social to the natural.

Despite accusations that Derrida is an extreme relativist and a nihilist, the purpose is certainly not to deny the possibility of knowledge, but rather to show that contradictions are at the heart of knowledge and that the constitution of structures of any kind creates a transcendental system opposed to the differences inherent in the empirical. The empirical is full of the variety and transformations of material forces, which contradict any rationality, since rationality contains the transcendence of the empirical. Derrida aimed to challenge the transcendental aspects of philosophy, and all thought, with the empirical but not to deny that this rationalization and system building is necessary. We cannot define the empirical without reference to the transcendental, but we can say that the transcendental is never a pure transcendental universal, it is always a particular force acting on empirical, and is part of this irreducibility of difference.

— *Barry Stocker*

See also **Anthropology, Philosophical; Saussure, Ferdinand de**

Further Readings
Jacques D. (1978). *Writing and difference.* Chicago: University of Chicago Press.
Jacques D. (1989). *Introduction to Husserl's origin of geometry.* Lincoln: University of Nebraska Press.
Jacques D. (1997). *Of grammatology.* Baltimore: Johns Hopkins University Press.

 DETERMINISM

Determinism, from the Latin *determino* or define, is a basic philosophic theory about general interdependence and interconditionality of phenomena and processes. The idea was pronounced for the first time in ancient natural philosophy, in particular, in notions about primary origins and elements. Later, it was developed by Persian poet Omar Khayyam, Italian naturalist G. Bruno, and others who believed in existence of cause-and-effect rational consequence.

Laplace's determinism was the first attempt to generalize and theoretically interpret general deterministic ideas, proposed by Pierre-Simon Marquise de Laplace, the 18th-century naturalist and philosopher. According to his variant of determinism (sometimes called "strict" or "mechanistic" determinism), everything in the contemporary world (and human beings ourselves, taken as biological and social creatures) is caused completely by previous facts and events. He believed that unidirectional and dynamic connection of any phenomenon's states could be described with the help of laws of physics and mechanics. According to Laplace, the universe is utterly rational, and complete knowledge of any given situation permits us to experience with certainty the future and the past of any unit.

Further development of such kind of deterministic theory is connected with conceptualization of causality notion (Spinosa's ideas about inner causality, Leibniz monadology, Darwinian evolutionary theory, Hegel dialectic theory).

Geographic determinism as particular form of strict deterministic theory approves geographic environment as principal determinant of social layout and cultural development. As early as at the middle of 4th century BCE, it had been designed as peculiar direction of philosophic thought (Hippocrates, Phoukidid, Xenofont) with at least two extreme schools: one of climatic psychology (Hippocrates, Aristotle) and one of climatic ethnology (Hippocrates, Polibius).

Enlightenment and modern ideology had given us the chance to reconsider these ideas in framework of establishment of general regularities of livelihood systems, social sphere, ideology, and political organization development in historical retrospection (Ch. Montesquieu, L. Mechnikov, H. Sample, E. Huntington).

During the 20th century, geographic determinism notion was concerned mainly with theories trying to explain the unevenness of social and cultural development of separate countries and peoples exclusively by peculiarities of their natural habitats.

Today, the influence of geographic space on political decision making is the subject of scientific modeling of geopolitics, regarded as a special discipline bordering anthropogeography, political geography, and political science.

Marxist determinism emphasizes total objectiveness, interdependence, and interconditionality of objects, facts and phenomena of the real world, which is based on the matter inner regular development. Apart from causal interrelations, Marxist determinism presumes the existence of a wide spectrum of interconnections of different kinds, such as spatial and chronological correlation, functional dependence, symmetry connection, system elements interaction, mutual determination of part and the whole, and connection of states in development and movement. In such contexts, social life regularities define the mainstream of historical process, but do not determine the whole diversity of individual and group activity. So, freedom in purpose formulation is ascribed to the human being and to the social group as well.

In its Marxist variant, economy is regarded as a sphere of human activity that determines or at least influences character and the essence of political and social processes. On this basis, we could conceptualize historical development through the series of socioeconomic formations (primitive, slavery, feudal, capitalistic, and communist). In such a context, state, ideology, politics, and culture are regarded as expression of economic basis, which, in its turn, reflects interests of dominative class and results from the mode of production.

Statistic and system determinism in the 20th century has brought new insight into deterministic ideas, thanks to statistic and probabilistic methods of scientific research. Statistic regularities had been revealed and conceptualized in the framework of a wide spectrum of probabilistic world theories. Statistic determinism is widespread in the context of sociology, demography, and other social sciences. It presumes that, in large sets of social phenomena, we can trace statistic regularity or the general tendency of development. In such a context, we interpret character of social connection as possibilistic and regular at the same time.

Determinism's oppositions: Deterministic ideas are withstanding indeterminism, which denies existence of objective causal regularities. Its origin at the first quarter of 20th century was stimulated by development of statistic methods of scientific prognosis. Another determinist's opposition is teleology, according to which all process flow is predestined by action of nonmaterial (ideal) purpose-defining principle.

— *Olena V. Smyntyna*

Further Readings

Darwall, S. (Ed.). (2003). *Deontology.* Oxford: Blackwell.

Krause, S. J. (1964). *Essays on determinism in American literature.* Kent, OH: Kent State University Press.

Von Wright, G. H. (1974). *Causality and determinism.* New York: Columbia University Press.

 # DEVIANCE

Sociologists define *deviant behavior* as behavior that violates social norms. Norms are expectations or prescriptions that guide people into actions that produce conformity. Norms make social life possible because they make behavior predictable. While members of a society do not have to agree on all the norms of a society, conformity to norms rests upon agreement by most members of society. Therefore, deviant behavior is behavior that most people in a society find offensive or reprehensible. It generates disapproval, punishment, or condemnation of the behavior. Society applies sanctions to deviant behavior to reinforce social norms.

Sociologists conceptualize norms into three categories: folkways, mores, and laws. Folkways are everyday norms based on custom, tradition, and etiquette, such as standards of dress and eating behavior. Violation of these norms does not generate serious condemnation but may cause people to consider the violator as odd. Mores are norms based on important societal morals. Upholding these norms is critical to the fabric of society because their violation threatens the social order. Drug addiction, for example, constitutes a moral violation that generates strong social condemnation. Criminal laws are the most serious norms of a society and are supported by formalized social sanctions. People who violate them are subject to arrest and punishment. A person convicted of robbery, for example, will usually serve a term of imprisonment. While criminal behavior and deviant behavior share some common features, they are not interchangeable terms. Clearly, some behaviors in a society, such as murder, are both criminal behaviors and deviant behaviors. However, not all deviant behaviors are criminal behaviors. Inappropriate eating behavior, for example, is not usually considered criminal behavior.

Explanations of deviant behavior are a central task of the field of sociology. In addition to sociological explanations, scholars have also formulated biological and psychological explanations. Biological, psychological, and sociological theories of deviant behavior try to answer one of two questions: (1) Why are some individuals more likely than others to engage in deviant behavior? and (2) Why do certain behaviors become defined as deviant, and how does society enforce nonconformity to norms? Sociological explanations attempt to answer both questions, while biological and psychological explanations focus on answering the first question.

Biological Explanations

Biological explanations attempt to identify characteristics of people that predispose them to engaging in deviant behavior. Primarily, these theories are concerned with attempting to identify those factors associated with criminal behavior. For example, physician and criminologist Cesare Lombroso (1835–1909) formulated one of the earliest biological explanations. Basing his explanation on the measurement of bodies of men in prisons, Lombroso theorized that criminals

were atavists, or throwbacks, to an earlier stage of evolution. Lombroso's assumption that criminals were biologically defective influenced the work of anthropologist Earnest Hooton (1887–1954). Hooton also studied male prisoners and theorized that criminals are biologically inferior and should be sterilized and exiled to reservations. In 1949, William Sheldon (1898–1977) introduced his theory of somatology, theorizing that people's body shapes affect their personalities and therefore the crimes they are likely to commit. More specifically, Sheldon identified the body shape of the mesomorph as a type that is muscular and athletic and more likely to engage in criminal behavior. While scholars criticized the research methodology and conclusions of these early biological explanations, the assumption that criminals are biologically different continued to guide research on crime. Researchers noticed that crime runs in families and assumed that criminal tendencies are inherited. Their research included, for example, studying identical twins or nontwin siblings separated by birth and raised by different parents. However, these studies were not able to conclusively establish that a genetic basis for crime exists.

Biological research has also investigated chromosomal abnormalities as an explanation for criminal behavior. The pattern that has been of most interest to researchers is the XYY variety; however, the rarity of occurrence of this pattern means that it would account only for a small fraction of the crime that is committed. Other researchers have focused on neurotransmitters and hormones as the predisposing factors for violent criminal behavior; however, researchers have not reached any definitive conclusions regarding the biological role in offending.

Psychological Explanations

Psychological explanations of deviant behavior are concerned not only with criminal behavior but also with other kinds of deviant behavior, such as mental illness, sexual deviance, and substance abuse. Psychologists refer to deviant behavior as "abnormal behavior"; that is, it is behavior that is maladaptive to the culture in which it occurs. Psychology utilizes many perspectives to explain abnormal behavior; however, generally, these explanations emphasize the importance of negative childhood experiences, especially within the family, as the cause of later problematic behavior.

Sigmund Freud (1856–1939), the founder of psychoanalysis, developed one of the first explanations of the relationship between the human mind and behavior. Freud posited that all individuals have natural drives and urges repressed in the unconscious, which include abnormal or deviant tendencies; however, through the process of childhood socialization, individuals develop internal controls. The improperly socialized child may develop a personality disturbance that causes abnormal or deviant behavior. Contemporary psychoanalytic theory relies on case histories of individuals under treatment or samples of individuals in mental institutions or prisons as the basis for their conclusions about the causes of deviant behavior. Social scientists view the reliance on a patient or institutionalized population as a limitation of the conclusions from this research.

Psychological explanations of deviant behavior include an explanation of moral development proposed by Lawrence Kohlberg (1927–1987) that emphasized the role of reasoning in explaining deviant behavior. Kohlberg theorized that individuals pass through several stages of development in which they develop their ability to reason morally. He argued that not everyone completes all the stages of moral development and, because of that limitation, not all individuals develop what we refer to as a "conscience." Therefore, a lack of conscience explains why individuals pursue criminal and other kinds of deviant behavior. However, critics of this theory point to the fact that criminal behavior as well as other kinds of deviant behavior may result from other factors, such as peer pressure.

Contemporary psychologists have also formulated theories about the relationship between personality or temperament and abnormal behavior. Personality research uses inventories, usually the Minnesota Multiphasic Personality Inventory (MMPI) and the California Psychological Inventory (CPI). Psychologists administer these inventories to samples of incarcerated juvenile and adult offenders. These studies find differences between offenders and nonoffenders that psychologists assume are responsible for the offending behavior. However, as with psychoanalytic research, critics charge that since most research occurs in institutional settings, offenders' personality problems may be he result of their institutionalization.

Finally, contemporary psychological research also focuses on childhood temperament, examining the association between temperament problems during childhood and behavioral problems during childhood and also delinquency problems during adolescence. Psychological research demonstrates that children with temperament problems such as impulsiveness, hyperactivity, and coldness are more likely to become delinquent in unstable families marked by inadequate parenting, than in stable families. However, while this research often does not control for the factors of socioeconomic status and education, researchers believe that it offers a valuable understanding of deviant behavior at the individual level of analysis.

Sociological Explanations

Sociologists study deviant behavior from many different perspectives. They examine the forces in society that shape the creation of norms. They also examine deviant behavior in terms of what groups are likely to engage in deviant behavior and the reasons for their deviance. Finally, sociological explanations also may include an analysis of how society enforces nonconformity to norms. Embedded within these varied perspectives are two distinct approaches for studying deviance as a social phenomenon. In the first approach, sociologists view deviance as an objectively given phenomenon; in the second approach, sociologists study deviance as a subjectively problematic phenomenon.

Sociologists who study deviance as objectively given phenomenon assume that there is widespread consensus in society about what expectations constitute the norms of the society and, consequently, that it is relatively easy to identify what constitutes deviant behavior. They also assume that deviant behavior typically evokes negative sanctions, such as arrest and imprisonment for criminal behavior. Finally, they assert that the punishment given to the deviant serves to reaffirms the norms of the society. Therefore, the focus for sociologists who follow this approach is to examine the sociological conditions that are likely to produce deviant behavior.

Sociologists who approach the study of deviance as a subjectively problematic phenomenon focus on social definitions and social interaction. They emphasize that deviance is a label that is applied at a given place and time. The subjectively problematic approach espouses a relativist view of deviance and examines whether and why a given act is defined by society as deviant. It also emphasizes the process by which a person is defined and stigmatized as deviant. Rather than studying the causes of deviant behavior, this approach tends to study the people, such as police, who define others as deviants, and its research often demonstrates that there is often a lack of consensus on whether a particular person should be treated as a deviant. This view also examines the perspective and reactions of the person defined as deviant.

Major Sociological Theories

There are many sociological explanations for deviant behavior that conceptualize deviance as either objectively given or subjectively problematic. The dominant sociological theories of deviant behavior include functionalism, social disorganization, anomie/strain theory, differential association theory, labeling theory, control theory, radical criminology, and feminist theory.

Functionalism

The functionalist approach to the study of deviant behavior is a perspective that posits that some behaviors that are widely condemned in society are in actuality functional or beneficial in terms of their effects. Sociologists credit Émile Durkheim (1858–1917) with developing the functionalist approach in sociology. While Durkheim understood that society must prohibit certain behaviors because they harm society and its members, he asserted that deviant behavior is also a normal phenomenon that occurs in every society. He argued that deviant behavior contributed to maintaining the social solidarity of society because punishment of deviant behavior clarifies social norms and reinforces social ties among societal members. Durkheim also believed that deviant behavior plays an important role in social change, because without deviant behavior, freedom of thought would not exist; hence, social change would not be possible.

Social Disorganization

In the 1930s, a sociological approach emerged at the University of Chicago that advanced a structural explanation of deviant behavior. Developed by W. I. Thomas (1863–1947) and Florian Znaniecki (1882–1958), it emphasized the relationship between crime and the social disorganization of certain neighborhoods in certain areas. This approach posited that as a city grows, its sense of community breaks down, and as social disorganization in an area increases, crime also increases. However, not all neighborhoods are equally disorganized; rather, those areas in which the population is

geographically unstable, moves a great deal, is composed of a variety of different racial and ethnic groups, has a high proportion of immigrants, and lacks neighborhood controls are the neighborhoods in which deviant behavior frequently occurs. Robert E. Park (1864–1944) and Ernest W. Burgess (1886–1966), two other sociologists at the University of Chicago, advanced an ecological analysis of Chicago neighborhoods and identified the areas in which deviant behavior frequently occurs as zones of transition.

Anomie/Strain Theory

Émile Durkheim first utilized the term *anomie* to refer to disturbances in the social order that caused deviant behavior. In particular, Durkheim studied the relationship between anomie and suicide. In the 1930s, Robert Merton (1910–2003) further conceptualized anomie as a disjunction between culturally defined goals and structural available opportunities. Merton posited that culturally defined goals are ones that society expects all of its members to embrace. In Western societies, the primary culturally approved goals are monetary and material success. However, Merton argued that every society places limitations on how to achieve culturally defined goals. The conflict between cultural goals and the differential opportunity to achieve these goals creates pressure to commit deviance. Merton identified five different types of responses (modes of adaptation) that could result: conformity, innovation, ritualism, retreatism, and rebellion.

Differential Association Theory

In the 1930s, Edwin Sutherland (1883–1950) developed a major theory of criminology that he called the "theory of differential association." Its most important proposition is that criminal behavior is learned. Sutherland advanced nine propositions to explain how criminal behavior is learned. Among these propositions are the ideas that criminal behavior is learned through face-to-face interaction between people who are close or intimate with one another and that the earlier in one's life one is exposed to attitudes and values favorable to committing crimes, the greater the likelihood that one will in fact commit crime. Sutherland did not argue that it was necessary to associate with individuals who had committed criminal acts; rather, only exposure to definitions favorable to criminal actions is necessary.

Sutherland's theory posits that a person becomes delinquent or criminal because of an excess of definitions favorable to the violation of the law over definitions unfavorable to the violation of the law.

Labeling Theory

Labeling theory is an approach to studying deviant behavior that developed in the 1960s. Labeling theory does not try to explain why an individual initially commits deviant acts. Rather, labeling theory posits a relativist definition of deviant behavior; it assumes that there is nothing about a particular behavior that makes it deviant. Howard Becker (1899–1960), one of the originators of labeling theory, argued that deviance is not the quality of the act the person commits, but rather a consequence of the of the rules or sanctions applied by others. Labeling theory also argues that people in positions of power impose definitions of deviance on the behaviors of those without power. Therefore, some people and behaviors are more likely labeled than others. Labeling theory also stress that labeling someone deviant can produce a deviant self-image that may result in the individual committing more deviant acts.

Control Theory

Control theorists focus on criminal behavior and examine the role an individual's ties to conventional institutions play in discouraging the person from acting on criminal motivation. One of most widely known and researched control theories is Travis Hirschi's social control theory. This theory asserts that delinquency results when an individual's bond to society is weak or broken. Hirschi examined four interrelated elements of the social bond: attachment, commitment, involvement, and belief. In testing the theory, Hirschi found that attachment itself is critical in preventing delinquency. His most important finding was that there was no relationship between social class and delinquency. Other studies have focused on various aspects of Hirschi's conceptualization of the social bond. For example, in reexamining the issue of involvement and its relationship to delinquency, research indicates that leisure activities may influence all four elements of the social bond.

Radical Criminology

Radical criminologists focus on crime and propose that we can explain crime by examining the patterns of economic organization in a society. Many of the ideas contained in radical criminology have their roots in the works of Karl Marx (1818–1883) and Friedrich Engels (1820–1895). From this perspective, law, law enforcement agencies, and government itself are perceived as instruments of the ruling class designed to maintain the status quo. Radical criminologists also examine the disparity between the written law and law as it is actually applied. In this regard, radical criminologists especially emphasize the role of social class in the application of criminal law. Some radical criminologists, such as Richard Quinney, see crime as one of the many forms of violence perpetuated in American society. They argue that we must end suffering if we want to end crime and in order to end suffering we must fundamentally transform our social structure.

Feminist Theory

There are several feminist perspectives on crime. Although there is no single feminist perspective, all feminist theories share assumptions about the gendered nature of crime, criminal victimization of women, and the bias of criminal justice processing in patriarchal societies. Liberal feminism attributes gender differences in crime rates to the different ways men and women are socialized. Marxist feminism views women's subordination as resulting from the capitalist mode of production. Radical feminist criminologists are distrustful of the legal system because it is male dominated. They focus their research on the violent victimization of women. Socialist feminist criminologists examine how class inequality and gender inequality operate together to shape criminal opportunities, victimization experiences, and responses of the criminal justice system.

Sociologists study deviant behavior utilizing a variety of theoretical perspectives. Each seeks to present an explanation that relates deviance to norm violation. Whether the theory assumes deviance is objectively given or subjectively problematic, each theoretical perspective examines deviant behavior from a social process or social structural perspective. Research findings from each perspective enhance our understanding of deviance in society.

— Patricia E. Erickson

See also **Conflict; Crime; Durkheim, Émile; Functionalism; Norms**

Further Readings

Adler, P. A., & Adler, P. (2002). *Constructions of deviance: Social power, context, and interaction.* Belmont, CA: Wadsworth.

Barkan, S. E. (2001). *Criminology: A sociological understanding.* Upper Saddle River, NJ: Prentice Hall.

Goode, E. (2004). *Deviant behavior.* Upper Saddle River, NJ: Prentice Hall.

Pontell, H. N. (2002). *Social deviance: Readings in theory and research.* Upper Saddle River, NJ: Prentice Hall.

Renzetti, C. M., & Curran, D. J. (2001). *Theories of crime.* Boston: Allyn & Bacon.

Rubington, E., & Weinberg, M. (2004). *Deviance: The interactionist perspective.* Boston: Allyn & Bacon.

DeVore, Irven (1935–)

It's not often that a boy from a small town in Texas gets to become a renowned Harvard professor, but Irven Devore is one who was able to do this. His preparation for the academic world began at the University of Texas where he received his BA degree in philosophy and anthropology. He furthered his professional interests later by graduating from the University of Chicago with an MA degree and a PhD in anthropology.

After his university student days, Devore was able to make several important contributions to the discipline of anthropology not only by his extensive and interesting research concerns but also by other responsibilities associated with the academic profession. He is the recipient of impressive academic rewards and fellowships and has had the honor of being selected to participate in several professional organizations. Although he has served at Harvard as a professor and as chairman of the anthropology department, Devore has also lectured at a number of other prominent educational institutions, such as Stanford University and the University of California at Berkeley. A casual perusal of his impressive résumé makes one readily understand why he has such a prominent reputation in the field of anthropology.

His research interests have focused on animal behavior. In particular, he has focused on what we can learn from the behavior of monkeys and apes.

Understandably, in order to conduct his research, Professor Devore has engaged in numerous field studies, which provided him with important insights about the subjects of his research. As a result of his research, he has produced a number of interesting articles, with titles such as the "Social Behavior of Baboons and Early Man," "The Evolution of Social Life," and "The Natural Superiority of Women." He is also the author of various scholarly books concerning his special interests within the discipline of anthropology.

After a long and productive scholarly career, he is presently continuing to make important contributions to the discipline of anthropology by serving as the curator at the Harvard University Peabody Museum. Hence, we can expect to hear more about his interests as time goes by.

— *William E. Kelly*

See also **Primatology**

Further Readings

DeVore, I. (Ed.). (1965). *Primate behavior: Field studies of monkeys and apes.* New York: Holt, Rinehart & Winston.

DeVore, I., & Eimerl, S. (1965). *The primates.* New York: Life Natural Library, Time.

DeVore, I., & Lee, R. B. (Eds.). (1968). *Man the hunter.* Chicago: Aldine.

DeVore, I., & Lee, R. B. (Eds.). (1976). *Kalahari hunter-gatherers.* Cambridge, MA: Harvard University Press.

Dewey, John (1859–1952)

John Dewey was an American philosopher, educator, psychologist, public intellectual, social critic, and political activist. He was a major figure in American intellectual history and one of the great minds, deserving, according to his biographer G. Dykhuizen, the title of the "spokesman of humanity." Born in Burlington, Vermont (1859), he died in New York City (1952). His multivolume works comprise writings from all areas of philosophy and also from psychology, education, political science, and the arts. As a philosopher, he is recognized worldwide as one of the founding fathers of the distinctively American

Source: © Bettmann/CORBIS.

philosophical school of pragmatism, with his own version, titled "instrumentalism." As an educator, he is renowned for his system of teaching through experimental observation (a progressive system in education focused on learning by doing), which in the 20th century has become internationally influential for decades in many countries, including Japan, China, Turkey, and the former Union of Soviet Socialist Republics. As a psychologist, he was a pioneer in functional psychology. As a public intellectual, social critic, and political activist, he was involved in numerous cultural, social, and political actions and movements, including founding and presiding over the American Psychological Association, the American Philosophical Association, the New School for Social Research, and the Commission of Inquiry into the Charges Against Leon Trotsky; issues of community and democracy; domestic and international political affairs, such as presidential elections and world peace; woman's suffrage; school reform; and academic freedom. All of these activities were directed by Dewey's reconstructed conception of philosophy as an intellectual enterprise, whose mission is to solve the problems of men and women, rather than the purely academic problems of philosophers themselves. Such a philosophy must be substantially practical in making human life and activity more creative and intelligent and serving the "construction of good," by which he means the shared communicative experience. By understanding democracy as a creative "way of life" rather than simply the method of government, he has earned the title of true "philosopher of democracy."

While from the start being interested in empirical psychology, Dewey's thought has undertaken an early move, according to his own expression, "from absolutism to experimentalism," after having dealt with German philosophers such as Leibniz, Kant, and particularly Hegel. The Hegelian flavor, stripped from idealism, has remained with Dewey for the whole subsequent career, in the sense of its unifying and organic character, and moreover its dialectics as a form of evolutionary paradigm. Dewey was an organic holist from the start. The idea of dynamic, open, evolving unity remained a guiding principle of his philosophy. His further move toward naturalistic experimentalism was substantially prompted by the revolutionary input of Darwinism. The theory of natural selection also continued to have a lifelong impact upon Dewey's thought, while he explicitly rejected Social Darwinism with its self-serving and antidemocratic rhetoric about the survival of the fittest. Thus, both Hegel and Darwin had become the particular and lasting sources of Dewey's antidualism, that is, the search for overcoming of all traditional philosophical dualisms, such as between culture and nature, subject and object, theory and practice, psychical and physical, mind and world, and individual and society. Dewey's critical stance toward past efforts in this area was expressed by his conceptions of "experimental experience," "experimental teaching," and even "experimental logic" in the middle stage of his career, which had provided him with an empirically based theory of knowledge that was in line with the developing American school of thought known as "pragmatism."

Darwinism had suggested the idea of interaction between the human organism and its environment when considering questions of psychology and the theory of knowledge. Dewey understood human thought naturalistically, as the product of the interaction between organism and environment, and knowledge as having practical instrumentality in the guidance and control of that interaction. Hence, he adopted "instrumentalism" as the original name for his own pragmatist philosophy. Instrumentalism consists of taking ideas as tools or instruments with which to cope with a given situation. Moreover, various modes and forms of human activity are also instruments developed by human beings to solve multiple individual and social problems. Since the problems are constantly changing, the instruments for dealing with them must also change. Even the educational philosophy of Dewey reflects Darwin's theory of evolution. Education is also evolutionary. In a constantly evolving universe, it is an endless experiment wherein humans create ways of actively transforming themselves to secure the most complete and effective adaptation possible.

Dewey's contention that human life as a part of nature follows the patterns of nature is the core tenet of his naturalistic outlook. There is a "natural" continuity between nature and human experience. Humans are not the spectators of nature but active participants in it. We live in the world that is both precarious and stable, and we must help to survive the former with the aid of the latter. It is how our intelligence, whose purpose is the creative adaptation to natural and human condition, works. The intelligence, reflecting creatively on past experience, adapts as a means to new experiments in order to test their value. The search for absolute and immutable world and values as separated this world of process and events is, however, a futile old-fashioned business of classical metaphysicians that has to be abandoned. There is no such thing as changeless being. Dewey is an antimetaphysicist for whom the only reality is nature in its serial process of events. Also, truth, evolutionary in nature, partakes of no transcendental or eternal reality and is based on experience that can be tested and shared by all inquirers.

Such a Deweyan pragmatic approach to human affairs, showing that knowledge is a product of an activity directed to the fulfillment of human purposes, has ample important anthropological consequences. In the place of an example, let us take, for instance, his four-phase theory of human inquiry, which also serves as the theory of human problem solving. To begin with, humans encounter the problematic situation as a practical and experiential situation that triggers all further cognitive development in order to fulfill human needs and desires. In the second phase, humans gather all kinds of data available for clarifying the situation. The third phase involves the reflection and imagination in order to create all possible variants of solutions, which are also entertained in the abstraction. Finally, a practical solution is achieved by implementing the preceding. However, this is not completely the final phase, either, since action means "transaction" (rather than merely "interaction") between humans and their environment, meaning the transformation and change on both sides. Although this new situation contains elements implied in the former, it is richer because of its new meaning and greater complexity. Such human conduct, which enriches the life via transformation of natural condition and provides the growth of humanity, Dewey is not reluctant to call "art" in the broadest sense of a term.

Dewey applied the method of intelligence and an experimental approach to problems of practice also in the realm of human social existence. He insisted that the human individual is a social being from the start and that individual satisfaction and achievement can be realized only within the context of social habits and institutions that promote it. Even the human mind is a social rather than a purely biological phenomenon, according to Dewey. In one of his anthropologically most significant works, *Human Nature and Conduct* (1922), which provides a comprehensive statement of his conception of human nature, he focused on the key role of habits in forming the dispositions of action and the importance of reflective intelligence as a means of modifying them. Through creative intelligence, one of whose highest achievements is creative and evolutionary democracy, we can transform the world according to our desires. Dewey conceived of democracy as a primary ethical value, and he did much to formulate the working principles for such a democratic society.

Dewey's philosophical influence has been changing over the decades. While during the first half of the 20th century, he was a prominent figure of American and even international philosophical scene, his work, not exempt from misunderstandings, has provoked many critics (notably B. Russell among them) to raise objections against his theory of inquiry and logic. Dewey himself was not reluctant to develop the key concepts further in the course of time; one of the most anthropologically significant corrections he intended to accomplish concerned the substitution of the term *culture* for the term *experience* in the title and content of his opus magnum, *Experience and Nature* (1925).

After the eclipse of the whole pragmatist philosophy around the middle of the 20th century, Dewey's influence began so have a considerable renaissance. Recent developments have shown many of his ideas to continue to be rich and inspiring into the 21st century. During his lifetime, the very first volume of the spectacular *Library of Living Philosophers* was devoted to him (1939), and *The John Dewey Society* was established in 1935. The Center for Dewey Studies at Southern Illinois University at Carbondale was established in 1961, whereby a 37-volume set based on Dewey's manuscripts was published from 1969 to 1991. Other resources for studies in Dewey's philosophy are being stored and offered to many Deweyan scholars all over the world. In addition to figures of contemporary world philosophy such as Richard Rorty, Jürgen Habermas, Hilary Putman, and others, the growing school of "neo-Deweyans" in philosophy and social thought represent the enduring relevance of his innovative and seminal version of naturalistic pragmatism.

— *Emil Visnovsky*

See also **Pragmatism**

Further Readings

Campbell, J. (1995). *Understanding John Dewey.* Chicago: Open Court.

Dewey, J. (1969–1991). *The collected works of John Dewey* (J. A. Boydston, Ed.). Carbondale and Edwardsville: Southern Illinois University Press.

Hickman, L. (Ed.). (1998). *Reading Dewey. Interpretations for a postmodern generation.* Bloomington and Indianapolis: Indiana University Press.

Hickman, L., & Alexander T. M. (Eds.). (1998). *The essential Dewey* (2 vols.). Bloomington and Indianapolis: Indiana University Press.

Rockefeller, S. (1991). *John Dewey: Religious faith and democratic humanism.* New York: Columbia University Press.

Ryan, A. (1995). *John Dewey and the high tide of American liberalism.* New York: Norton.

Westbrook, R. B. (1991). *John Dewey and American democracy.* Ithaca, NY: Cornell University Press.

 # DIAMOND, JARED (1937–)

As a social scientist, Jared Diamond is interested in how human societies have developed and fared over the millennia, and he has continually striven to understand the broad patterns of human behavior across the globe. For him, answering questions about how and why different human societies evolved over time under various environmental and social conditions is critical, and approaching these issues using data from a number of disciplines is essential.

Diamond was initially trained in the biological sciences and later began studying the ecology, evolution, and biogeography of birds in New Guinea in the 1960s. He subsequently led nearly 20 expeditions to New Guinea and nearby islands to study bird species (including the rediscovery of the goldenfronted bowerbird) and developed a conservationist plan for Indonesian New Guinea's national park system. His commitment to analyzing and preserving the environment led him to becoming a founding member of the board for the Society of Conservation Biology and a member of the Board of Directors for the World Wildlife Fund (USA).

Because of his efforts, Diamond was inducted into the National Academy of Sciences, the Academy of Arts and Sciences, and the American Philosophical Society. He is also the winner of several prestigious awards, including the National Medal of Science, a MacArthur Foundation Fellowship, and the Tyler Prize for Environmental Achievement. Perhaps most important, however, is his determination to make complex ideas and theories accessible to a wide audience.

During the 1980s, Diamond became fascinated with environmental history and began integrating the disciplines of anthropology, linguistics, history, biology, and history to investigate the technological advances of humans worldwide. In particular, he was concerned about the social and environmental factors that led to certain outcomes or disasters. One of Diamond's first major works to explore these issues was *The Third Chimpanzee: The Evolution and Future of the Human Animal.* In this book, he focused on how the human species (which shares much of the same genetic material as chimpanzees), developed the unique ability to form religious thought; create language, art, and science; and form complex civilizations. He noted the irony that these advancements have also allowed humans to acquire the means to instantly destroy these achievements. He has authored eight books and hundreds of scientific articles, many of which have recently focused on the role environment plays in the rise and fall of ancient civilizations.

In his Pulitzer-Prize-winning book *Guns, Germs, and Steel: The Fates of Human Societies* (1999), for which *The Third Chimpanzee* is considered a precursor, Diamond explores the geographical and environmental reasons why some human groups have prospered more than others. His most recent book, *Collapse: How Societies Choose to Fail or Succeed* (2004), tries to explain why ancient societies such as the Anasazi of the American Southwest fell apart and what modern society can learn from the fates of others.

Although not specifically trained as an anthropologist, Diamond has contributed significantly to discussions of how human societies have evolved and the unfortunate outcomes that result when populations fail to see the errors of their ways. As one of the leading scholars in understanding environmental-human relations, he has brought many social issues into the forefront of public interest and inquiry and brought forth new ways of understanding how the evolution of our species took place and how we can use the past to teach us about both the present and the future.

— *Scott M. Fitzpatrick*

See also **Anasazi; Archaeology, Environmental**

Further Readings

Diamond, J. M. (1992). *The third chimpanzee: The evolution and future of the human animal.* New York: Perennial.

Diamond, J. M. (1999). *Guns, germs, and steel: The fates of human societies.* New York: Norton.

Diamond, J. M. (2004). *Collapse: How societies choose to fail or succeed.* New York: Viking Press.

 # DICTATORSHIPS

The 20th century certainly had its share of political problems. Some have come, some have gone, and some are still with us in a new century. Dictatorships have been a big problem for a number of reasons,

including their effects on a people, a society, a country, and the international sphere. The 20th century saw a substantial number of dictators, such as General Noriega of Panama, Castro of Cuba, Ceausescu of Romania, Jean-Claude "Baby Doc" Duvalier of Haiti, Marcos of the Philippines, Pol Pot of Cambodia, and Quathafi of Libya. However, three of the most evident in history have been Benito Mussolini in Italy, Adolf Hitler in Germany, and Joseph Stalin of Russia. Mussolini and Hitler represented a fascist type of dictatorship, and Stalin represented a communist type of dictatorship. Both types represent a threat to the United States, Western democracies, and other societies that are trying to practice activities that conform to expected equitable norms.

It is interesting that not all individuals may refer to these persons as dictators. Perhaps that shows the reality of the fact that dictators have been viewed differently by citizens. For example, although the Americans have usually referred to Stalin as a dictator, he had a large number of supporters in his country until his death. Perhaps the same may have been said of Mussolini and Hitler if they had not had untimely deaths and political misfortunes such as lost wars.

A dictatorship need not just refer to one person. It may also refer to a country directed by a small group of persons. However, whether it is a dictatorship of one person or a dictatorship of a number of individuals, it seems to have a number of characteristics associated with it. For example, Carl Friedrich and Zbigniew Brzezinski in their work, *Totalitarian Dictatorship and Autocracy,* have identified six. They are (1) an official ideology, (2) a single mass party, (3) a system of terroristic police control, (4) a technologically conditioned near-complete monopoly of control, (5) a near-complete monopoly of control of all means of effective armed combat, and (6) a central control and direction of the entire economy. What a dictatorship appears to come down to is major control of society by a leader or leaders, little freedom for opposition to the ruling individual or people in political power, and a strong impetus from the government to conform to its norms or face serious punishment.

Obviously, a dictatorship is not always a continuing phenomenon in a country. It may come and go, as we have seen in some countries. However, there are a number of factors that may be cited to inhibit the development of a dictatorship in a society. For example, the allowance of political opposition or the presence of political parties each advocating a different political policy would be methods of keeping the probability of a dictatorship from developing quite low. Along with this political situation is the allowance of free expression among the populace so that different views regarding government policy may be expressed and come to the attention of the mass of citizens. It would also be a good idea to have civilian control of the military, as is found in the United States, to prevent a coup and takeover of the government, as we have seen in many Latin American countries in the last century. Of course, a satisfied public has its advantages of preventing a dictatorship from coming about. This is especially true in situations where the general public realizes that all of us have the opportunity to improve ourselves in life without fear of prejudice based on race, religion, or political affiliation. Other factors that might inhibit the development of a dictatorship include a healthy economic situation in a country and the absence of international conflict that could result in a lost war. When people are hungry and frustrated, as they are in severe economic depressions, and see that their country has been defeated in war, as the Germans experienced after World War I, it is easy to understand that they might be more likely to accept a person like Hitler as their political leader. Perhaps it would have been much more difficult for a person like Hitler to obtain power in Germany if the economic and political situation had been different in that country following World War I.

The 21st century may be one in which we see a continuation of dictatorships around the world, as is evidenced by North Korea and China. If history has shown us anything about international politics, it is that dictatorships pose a potential and real problem for nondictatorships. Hence, countries have to be continually on guard so that they may not be unduly influenced by them. Yet, it is also important to keep the lines of communication open between those countries that are led by a dictatorships and those that are not. This is important because regular communication may lessen the negative impact of dictatorships. They are not immune from being influenced, and influence can come about in many ways. For example, it may be that international public opinion could be important to them. Hence, when their behavior is projected in a negative way on a worldwide basis, this may have the effect of weakening their role in an international sphere of activity. In addition, constant monitoring of their activity and military capabilities has value in that it may prevent such dictatorships from extending their political influence outside of their immediate environment.

As we progress in the 21st century, we can expect to encounter the presence of dictatorships. It would be ideal if they were to cease in existence and be replaced by democratic elements. However, the reality of the situation is that some old ones will continue to exist, some new ones will develop, and some will change their form of a government to a more acceptable type.

— *William E. Kelly*

Further Readings

Brooker, P. (2000). *Nondemocratic regimes: Theory, government, and politics.* Houndmills, UK: Macmillan.

Fulbrook, M. (1995). *Anatomy of a dictatorship: Inside the GDR.* New York: Oxford University Press.

Olson, M. (2000). *Power and prosperity: Outgrowing communist and capitalist dictatorships.* New York: Basic Books.

DIFFUSIONISM

Focusing on the notion that similarities among cultures resulted from components spreading from one culture to another, diffusionism is often seen as a reaction to the paradigm of classic unilinear evolutionism, which traced cultural development to the ability of cultures to innovate independently. The major names in the early years of diffusionism worked in the great museums of central Europe, studying the distribution of artifacts and coming to the conclusion that cultures were patchworks of traits, with each trait having its own origin and history. Grounded in museum empiricism and relatively modest in theory, diffusionism successfully attracted scholars away from evolutionism in the first few decades of the 20th century.

Some diffusionists, mostly German- and English-speaking, thought they could discover the earliest forms of human behavior by mapping the distribution of cultural traits in non-Western societies; the most widely distributed traits would be the oldest. Some diffusionists were determined to prove that all human culture originated in one place and then spread through diffusion, such as Englishmen G. Elliot Smith (1871–1937) and W. J. Perry, who created what is often called the" pan-Egyptian" or "heliolithic" (sometimes known as the "heliocentric") school. The German-Austrian culture historical or culture circle (also known by the German word *kulturkreis*) school and the American historical particularists were more restrained. Since the North American school is usually discussed separately, the entry will concentrate on the English and German-Austrian approaches.

Heliolithic Hilarity

An anatomist distinguished for his work on the brain, Smith traveled to Egypt to study mummies. When he returned to Cambridge University, he noticed the triangular similarities between the English megaliths and Egyptian pyramids. He then observed that variations of the triangular form appeared widespread in many cultures, including Native American burial mounds.

Beginning in 1911, he published articles and books that concluded that all civilization had originated in Egypt and had diffused to the rest of the world beginning in about 4000 BC. Smith wrote that after observing seeds sprouting out of the fertile soils along the Nile River, the ancient Egyptians began planting seeds on their own. After learning to predict the river's floods and developing irrigated agriculture, they invented the technologies of civilization, along with cities, government, and a religion that centered on sun worship and burial of sun kings in pyramids. Seeking gems for these burials, they navigated the globe and brought their superior civilization to other cultures. Until the diffusion of the triangular form, and along with it all the accoutrements of civilization, prepyramid cultures were abjectly primitive.

Kulturkreislehre

Building on the work of the geographer Friedrich Ratzel (1844–1904), who suggested that traits had unique forms that would allow investigators to trace them, the early diffusionists constructed a worldwide template of trait routes and culture contacts. The major figures in the culture circle school were Leo Frobenius (1873–1938), Fritz Graebner (1877–1934), and Wilhelm Schmidt (1868–1954). A noted authority on prehistoric art, Frobenius led 12 expeditions into Africa between 1904 and 1935. Trained as a historian, Graebner worked in museums in Berlin and Cologne and developed a surprisingly accurate prehistory of Oceania that involved six successive cultural stages: Tasmanian, Australian boomerang, totemic hunters, two-class horticulturists, Melanesian bow culture, and Polynesian patrilineal culture. Each of these culture circles had counterparts in Africa and elsewhere, and as the traits migrated, they blended, disappeared, grew, borrowed, and accommodated. To describe these diffusions, Graebner constructed an elaborate and often arcane jargon consisting of primitive, secondary, and tertiary circles, each containing a variety of subcircles, such as marginal, peripheral, and overlapping subcircles. Graebner's 1911 *Methode der ethnologie* is the classic of the evolutionists (in English, however, there exists only a seven-page summary in V. F. Calverton's 1931 *The Making of Man*).

In a sophisticated way, the diffusionists combined data from biological anthropology, historical documents, historical linguistics, and stratigraphic archaeology to construct the culture circles, which were essentially aggregates of traits arranged spatial and temporally. An elaborate statistics program was applied to uncover significant associations among the traits. This impressive enterprise acknowledged the influence on diffusion of conquest, cultural predispositions, geographic barriers and conduits, personalities, religious proselytization, trade, socioeconomic differentiation, and a variety of other factors.

Although most diffusionists assumed that the culture circle would grow naturally out of an analysis of the data, Schmidt, who was a Jesuit priest, thought that all foragers believed in a supreme god and that this pristine Christian-like belief was later corrupted by animistic notions. Schmidt also believed that Pygmies represented the original humans and that they had populated the world by emigrating from Tasmania. He wrote a 12-volume work of world prehistory titled *Der ursprung der gottesidee*, published between 1926 and 1955 (which has not been translated into English except for a one-volume summary).

Legacies

In addition to its erroneous interpretation of data, the position of the heliolithic school rests largely on the unacceptable notion that the simple triangle is a unique form that could be invented only once. Although the heliocentric approach no longer exists in anthropology, it is found in the folk models of Western societies, especially in England, where W. J. Perry popularized the approach in his 1923 book, *The Children of the Sun.*

The culture circle school generally has had bad press in the English-speaking world, though Clyde Kluckhohn and Robert Lowie gave it favorable reviews. Although Graebner and Schmidt conducted no fieldwork, they did inspired scholars to do serious research among Pygmies, such as that done by Paul Schebesta. Some of the diffusionist principles are used by art historians, and distribution approaches remain an important technique in archaeology. Anthropologists are still interested in studying the diffusion of ideas and innovations, especially as they spread from the major industrial powers to the rest of the world.

Pioneers in quantitative anthropology, the diffusionists also introduced a relativism that seeped rather unacknowledged into U.S. anthropology, for their patchwork, nonunilineal argument meant that there were no straightforward connections between, for example, technological and theological complexity. The diffusionists also emphasized detailed empirical investigations and comparative methods, both of which became hallmarks of modern anthropology.

— *Robert Lawless*

See also **Cultural Traits; Migrations**

Further Readings

Brandewie, E. (1990). *When giants walked the earth: The life and times of Wilhelm Schmidt, SVD.* Fribourg, Switzerland: University Press.
Graebner, F. (1931). Causality and culture. In V. F. Calverton (Ed.), *The making of man* (pp. 421–428). New York: Modern Library.
Koppers, W. (1952). *Primitive man and his world picture.* London: Sheed & Ward.
Lowie, R. (1937). *The history of ethnological theory.* New York: Holt, Rinehart & Winston.
Perry. W. J. (1923). *The children of the sun: A study in the early history of civilization.* London: Methuen.
Schebesta, P. (1933). *Among Congo Pygmies.* London: Hutchinson.
Schmidt, W. (1931). *The origin and growth of religion.* London: Methuen.
Schmidt, W. (1939). *The culture historical method of ethnology: The scientific approach to the racial question.* New York: Fortuny's.
Smith, G. E. (1915). *The Ancient Egyptians and the origin of civilization* (Rev. ed.). London: Harper.

DINOSAURIAN HOMINID

Contemplating "what if" questions about the extinction of nonavian dinosaurs has long been a pastime of scientists and the general public alike. If the dinosaurs hadn't died out, how would they have evolved, and could they have developed sentience? It is just those questions that paleontologist Dale Russell and model maker/taxidermist Ron Séguin attempted to address in proposing a hypothetical hominid-like dinosaur they called a "dinosauroid." This musing appeared as an addendum to a 1982 paper that detailed the process of skeletal reconstruction and modeling behind the construction of a mount of the dinosaur *Stenonychosaurus* for the National Museum of Natural Sciences in Ottawa, Canada. From the beginning, Russell and Séguin frequently referred to hominid evolution, comparing *Stenonychosaurus* to the recently discovered hominid specimen "Lucy" in terms of completeness and importance. (This comparison overstates the case: there are more relatively complete theropod fossils than hominid fossils, and *Stenonychosaurus* did not add as much to paleontological knowledge.)

Stenonychosaurus is a theropod dinosaur belonging to a group called troodontids. Theropods are the group of predominantly carnivorous dinosaurs that include such famous members as *Tyrannosaurus, Allosaurus,* and *Velociraptor;* the omnivorous and herbivorous ornithomimids, oviraptorids, and therizinosaurids; and birds. Troodontids are small, gracile, possibly omnivorous theropods closely related to dromaeosaurs (such as *Deinonychus* and *Velociraptor*) and avialans (the lineage that includes *Archaeopteryx* and birds). Like dromaeosaurs, troodontids have enlarged claws on their second pedal digit and a semilunate carpal in the wrist. Troodontids also possessed elongate feathers on their hands and tails; in many ways, they were quite avian-like. *Stenonychosaurus* was about 1.2 m long and probably weighed about 70 kg. It was bipedal and had a tridactyl hand, with a somewhat opposable first digit. It also had large eyes and a narrow muzzle, allowing for stereoscopic vision, and relatively enlarged cerebral hemispheres.

Four features of *Stenonychosaurus* impressed Russell and Séguin: its stereoscopic vision, its high encephalization quotient, what they took to be its opposable digits, and the fact that its bipedality freed the hands from use in locomotion. These are all features that might plausibly be thought to be required for intelligence in humans. On this basis, they suggested that if dinosaurs had continued to evolve, troodontids such as *Stenonychosaurus* were the most likely dinosaurs to attain a human level of intelligence. Hence, their hypothetical dinosauroid.

Regarding stereoscopic vision, nonavian maniraptor dinosaurs, such as troodontids and dromaeosaurs, do indeed have narrow muzzles, and troodontids couple that with very large orbits, suggesting large eyes. Furthermore, because of the narrow muzzle, the eyes can be directed forward, allowing for some degree of stereoscopic vision. However, this vision is not equivalent to that of primates because the long snout would have still obstructed their field of vision, giving them a stereoscopic vision more akin to that of dogs than primates.

Of all the evidence cited, the encephalization quotient (EQ) is most interesting. The EQ is the ratio of an animal's brain weight to the brain weight of a "typical" animal of the same body weight. Russell and Séguin calculated *Stenonychosaurus*'s EQ at about 0.34, comparable to that of galliform birds, armadillos, insectivores, and—most significant from their perspective—the Mesozoic ancestors of humans. But given the uncertainty about the weights of the body and the brain in fossil organisms, the calculations contain a large potential for error, and having a high EQ does not necessarily mean that an organism will evolve "intelligence" in a hominid sense.

Russell's proposal that *Stenonychosaurus*'s first and third digits were opposable was incorrect, however. Functional studies of the hands of theropods show that they are incapable of the kind of digit opposability that we see in primates. Furthermore, the structure of the hand would make evolving true opposability unlikely, because the first metacarpal (which rotates in primate opposability) is tightly appressed to the second metacarpal and the fused distal carpals in *Stenonychosaurus* thus cannot move independently.

The only joint free to evolve opposition would be between the first metacarpal and its first phalanx.

The most problematic part of Russell and Séguin's argument is bipedality. Assuming that the vertically bipedal form seen in hominids is the ideal form for sentient organisms, they conclude that selection for sentience would directly lead to a hominid-like set of body proportions in dinosaurs. While bipedality and sentience may be related, it seems unlikely that such hominid-like proportions would evolve in theropod dinosaurs, which start out with a body plan fundamentally different from that of nonhominid primates. In both theropods and hominids, the form that bipedality takes is the result of the skeletal structure (long bodies with proportionally short limbs in theropods, short bodies with proportionally long limbs in hominids). Hominid bipedality is the result of the body plan and proportions of arboreal apes that hang from branches and thus takes on the shape dictated by the skeleton. In theropod bipedality, the body is cantilevered between the legs, with the pelvis acting as a fulcrum and counterbalance provided by a long tail and neck. As detailed by Russell and Séguin, in order to assume a hominid-like bipedality, a theropod would have to shorten its tail and neck, reorient its skull articulation and its pelvis, reorganize its legs, and flatten its feet. This would take a large degree of skeletal and muscular reorganization, and since the intermediaries would be ungainly at best, the idea that theropod dinosaurs would give up the highly efficient counterbalanced bipedalism for the more inefficient vertical bipedalism of humans makes little selective sense.

In the end, Russell and Séguin's hypothesis was less science than science fiction, a congenial genre for such musings. The science fiction and fantasy literature has a number of examples of bipedal hominid-like dinosaurs, probably the most famous of which appear in Harry Harrison's *Eden* series, which features humans living alongside (and in conflict with) hominid-like dinosaurs. Eric Garcia's *Anonymous Rex* series features incognito dinosaurs wearing human costumes. Space-traveling hominid-like dinosaurs descended from hadrosaurs appeared in the *Star Trek: Voyager* episode "Distant Origin" (Season 5). It could be argued the "Sleestacks" of Sid and Marty Croft's 1970s television show *Land of the Lost* were hominid-like dinosaurs; they look a lot like Russell and Séguin's dinosauroids.

— *Alan D. Gishlick*

Further Readings

Dixon, D. (1988). *The new dinosaurs: An alternative evolution.* New York: HarperCollins.

Russell, D. A. (1969). A new specimen of *Stenonychosaurus* from the Oldman Formation (Cretaceous) of Alberta. *Canadian Journal of Earth Science, 6,* 595–612.

Russell, D. A. (1981). Speculations on the evolution of intelligence in multicellular organisms. In J. Billingham (Ed.), *Life in the universe: Proceedings of the Conference on Life in the Universe, NASA Ames Research Center, June 19–20, 1979* (pp. 259–275). Cambridge: MIT Press.

Russell, D. A., & Séguin, R. (1982). Reconstructions of the small Cretaceous theropod *Stenenychosaurus inequalis* and a hypothetical dinosauroid. *Syllogues, 37,* 1–43.

DISEASES

The trajectory of the word "disease" in anthropology from the 20th century through to the present reflects as much about the constitution of the discipline as it does the discipline's transformation in focus and paradigms. Following World War II, anthropology began to move away from its conventional objects, and the resultant encounters with non-Western medical systems called anthropologists' attention to the intersection between medicine, culture, and health and led them to analyze the hegemony of biomedical systems in places where it is critical to understand the indigenous etiologies of diseases and illnesses. Anthropologists mapped out different etiologies and ethnotheories of diseases-illnesses in non-European countries and developed a hierarchy of etiologies from natural to supernatural and even mystical. This focus became the domain of medical anthropology. Biomedicine has always used the word *disease* to designate the physiological abnormalities or pathological states identified by its diagnostic strategies. Until the 1970s, it was common for medical anthropologists to rebuff the term to the domain of biomedicine while using the concept of illness to give account of individual symptoms and experiences of disease. For many professionals in the field, a clear understanding of the etiology of diseases provides a base for public health prevention, and, in the case of infectious diseases, some even challenged the view that the indigenous causes

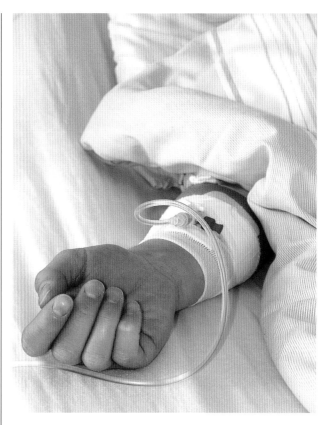

Source: © iStockphoto/Elena Korenbaum.

attributed to contagious diseases are fundamentally different from Western allopathic medicine.

More recently, the division between disease and illness has led to substantial critique by some anthropologists who deconstruct these concepts on social and cultural grounds. Disease, they contend, is not merely a physiological disturbance but takes place in wider social, ecological, political, and cultural processes that are experienced by the whole body. This perspective has given rise to an important line of investigation of diseases in critical medical anthropology, a subsegment of medical anthropology. According to this model, disease is viewed within the larger framework of the political economy of health and what its proponents call "critical biosocial causality."

In this approach, diseases are located in terms of the loci of social inequality and power differentials within local groups or in the relationship between local groups and wider regional, national, or global structures. As part of this newer approach, the experience of the sufferer is central, and sufferer narratives have been mobilized in efforts to fight the hegemonic worldview of biomedicine. Others are concerned with understanding the underlying social processes that explain the re-emergence of old diseases, as, for example, the appearance of multidrug-resistant tuberculosis, as well the contexts of emerging new pathogens, such as HIV, and their impact on the lives of socially vulnerable populations. With the advance of globalization, anthropologists are introducing new approaches for unveiling underlying processes of global inequities and local public inadequacies to deal with emerging plagues, as well as the intertwining of diseases in vulnerable populations, a phenomenon medical anthropologists call *syndemics*. Within the Western world, some anthropologists are taking the new vantage point offered by advances in various technologies and data collection (for example, the human genome project) to investigate configurations of genetic diseases. By moving away from traditional representations of the non-Western world and incorporating new analytical tools and strategies to account for diseases and their complex interconnections with the political economy of health and sociocultural contexts, anthropology is helping shape new understandings of situations of inequities and actively informing local as well as global health programs.

— *Louis Herns Marcelin*

See also **Human Genome Project**

Further Readings

Augé, M., & Herzlich, C. (1995). *The meaning of illness: Anthropology, history, and sociology.* New York: Harwood Academic Publishers.

Green, E. C. (1999). *Indigenous theories of contagious disease.* Walnut Creek, CA: AltaMira.

Singer, M., & Amityville, H. B. (1995). *Critical medical anthropology.* New York: Baywood.

 # DISPUTE RESOLUTION

Dispute processes, those that initiate disputes and those that operate to resolve them, are cultural processes. These must be analyzed and understood within the social and cultural context of a community rather than as a matter of individuals' rights and wrongs according to a logical political system of standardized jurisprudence. The anthropological study of dispute resolution is not different from an ethnography of community life. Community life consists of relationships among neighbors and kin, and involving economic, political, religious, and environmental resources. And all of these can be the subject of disputes.

Disputes involve a contested interpretation of shared principles of community life. These principles, or structural elements, are themselves not contested. A dispute is related to the manner in which a person has acted in relationship to these principles, as this has impinged upon the interests and affairs of other community members. Thus, the members of a community may share the general belief that the products of a garden are the property of the person who worked it, that gardens should be fenced, and that pigs, watched by a swineherd, roam and forage freely. A person who has a garden raided by another person's pigs then may initiate a dispute with the pigs' owner. Neither may propose that pigs should be penned nor that garden products are not owned by their farmers. The gardener may argue that the pig owner, via the swineherd, did not watch the animals carefully, and the pig owner may argue that the gardener did not construct a durable fence.

Disputes are embedded in the recurring life events of a community; each dispute has a trajectory out of past events, including prior disputes, and proceeds encumbered with the baggage of a wider context of community affairs. The gardener and the owner of the pigs may be rivals for community resources and have been involved in prior disputes. The garden may be placed in an area where pigs are often taken by swineherds; this herd of pigs is usually taken to forage close to gardens, and so forth.

Moreover, it is likely that any dispute can be viewed as impacted by a supernatural agency. Pigs that overcome a well-built fence or that were able to eat an unusually large amount of produce may have been assisted by a supernatural agent. The gardener may have angered these and become vulnerable, or the pig owner may have facilitated their involvement.

Disputants, in a sense, must agree to dispute, and the community must agree that there is a valid dispute. A person who raises an objection to pigs roaming free to forage or who objects to farmers having ownership of the produce of their farm work would be ridiculed, or at least find no community support. One of the unsettling results of social change is the introduction of unfamiliar principles as a basis for disputes.

Are humans inherently contentious? There is no easy answer to this question. Humans are inherently social and socially sensitive creatures. We creatively construct our cultural behavior daily from our traditional experience and in concert with our fellow community members. And we mutually dispute our varying creative versions. It is unlikely that creatures as complex as humans and as adept at symbolic reinterpretation could live in a dispute-free condition. The continuous potential of disputing, however, does not lead to a continuing condition of social disruption.

The social organization of communities also enables the means to resolve disputes. These range from inaction, avoidance or relocation by the persons involved to formal processes of adjudication by authorities vested with sanctioning powers. These processes are themselves normative properties of the community's social system. The ways in which they are applied are often also the source of disputes. However, community members who do not abide by them in good faith may be viewed as less-than-desirable community members. The farmer whose garden has been invaded by another's pigs and who in response seizes and kills several of the pigs, or who goes in the night and takes a corresponding part of the pig owner's garden may likely be in violation of community values regardless of his apparent loss. Indeed, witchcraft or sorcery is usually viewed as an improper tactic by an aggrieved person. The response is often to identify the witch (witch "doctors" are skilled at reading patterns of community disputes) and then try to resolve, in appropriate fashion, the dispute at the root of the attack.

Anthropology has tended to examine resolution processes that are located within communities or within a superordinate entity accepted by the community, such as a chiefdom. This is in contrast to processes imposed on the community based on foreign concepts and administered by strangers (such as those established by European administrations and kept by those assimilated to European culture). However, given the reality that these processes are embedded firmly in new nations, more anthropologists include national resolution procedures, typically formal adjudication.

There is a range of resolution processes. Some involve the two disputants in personal negotiation, but more usual is some kind of mediation or arbitration with a third party directing or even deciding on the nature of a settlement. It is also common for the resolution process to be part of a ritual procedure. Ancestral figures, but also other supernatural agencies, are disturbed by disputing (especially if it has led to conflict). Community misfortune may result unless resolution, specifically in a ritual setting appreciable by the supernatural agency, is completed. Mediators are often religious specialists.

Is resolution effective? It may be, insofar as both parties believe that their positions have been justified and fairly dealt with. The "aggrieved" party should believe that restitution (even apology) has been made, and the "aggrieving" party should believe that their actions were held to be understandable, even though assessed as requiring some adjustment to the other party. The contemporary judicial approach of restorative justice holds that disputes (especially those involving injury) cannot be truly resolved unless all parties—victims, perpetrators, and other community members—participate, accept responsibility and work together to make the community's life right again.

In fact, resolution probably achieves only a temporary result. Compromise may leave both parties discomfited. An explicit judgment that one party has acted wrongly, even foolishly, leaves that person vulnerable to community approbation. The person awarded a judgment may not feel that it was sufficient. Ritual resolution, even with its powerful supernatural incentive for reconciliation, may not last. Given the human condition, resolution should not be expected to eliminate disputes, but rather to ameliorate them. The success of a community's dispute resolution repertoire must lie in its capability to provide continuing temporary remedies, whether or not these are completely acceptable.

— *John Rhoades*

See also **Conflict; Law and Society; Sorcery; Witchcraft**

Further Readings

Caplan, P. (Ed.). (1995). *Understanding disputes: The politics of argument.* Oxford: Berg.

Gulliver, P. H. (1979). *Disputes and negotiations: A cross-cultural perspective.* New York: Academic Press.

Nader, L. (1965). The anthropological study of law. *American Anthropologist, 67*(6, Part 2), 3–32.

DNA Molecule

DNA (deoxyribonucleic acid) is a complex molecule that expresses, stores, and replicates all of the genetic information that is contained in eukaryotic cells. This genetic information is responsible for all the characteristics expressed in a particular species (e.g., color, size, and gender). In addition to physical characteristics, information pertaining to behavior and intelligence is also stored in the DNA molecule.

The DNA molecule is composed of two long strands (which are sugar-phosphate) and repeating units called *nucleotides.* Each of these nucleotides has three components: a 5-carbon sugar (which is deoxyribose in DNA vs. ribose in RNA), a phosphate group, and a nitrogenous base. Four nitrogenous bases make up the DNA molecule: two purines, adenine and guanine, which are composed of two nitrogenous rings, and two pyrimidines, thymine and cytosine, which are composed of one nitrogenous ring.

By forming hydrogen bonds, adenine pairs with thymine, and guanine pairs with cytosine. These pairs are known as *base pairs* and are responsible for the structure of the DNA molecule. The two adjacent polynucleotides are wound into two spiral-shaped strands called a *double helix.*

These long stands of the DNA molecule are organized by various proteins into individual units called *chromosomes.* Chromosomes are located in the nucleus of all eukaryotic cells. There are 46 chromosomes in each human cell, except in the sex cells (i.e., the eggs and the sperm), which have 23 chromosomes. On the chromosomes, there are regions of DNA, called *genes,* which are responsible for individual inheritable characteristics. A gene carries the actual biological information and can be as short as 999 base pairs to as long as several hundred thousand base pairs. It was estimated in 1996 that 30,000 to 40,000 genes exist in the genetic make up of *Homo sapiens.* However, upon the completion of the Human Genome Project in 2003, it is now postulated that only 20,000 to 25,000 genes exist.

The history of the discovery of the DNA molecule is an interesting one. It first began with the idea that physical traits of species are actually inherited in a predictable pattern from the parents to offspring. However, it was not until the middle of the 20th century that scientists began to actually identify the mechanism of inheritance and its molecular basis.

Gregor Mendel, a mathematician, known as "the father of genetics," conducted many scientific experiments involving pea plants, which he began in 1857. The results of his experiments illustrated that pea plants distributed characteristics to their offspring in a mathematically predictable pattern. Mendel postulated that these characteristics (e.g., height of the plant) were inherited by the parent plant. However, at this time, the term *character* was used to define a heritable feature, such as the color of a flower. These characters vary among individuals. Each variant of a character is called a trait, such as purple or white. Even though he could not physically prove the biological foundation of this phenomenon, his work dramatically increased interest in the study of genetics.

In 1928, Frederick Griffith hypothesized that a molecule responsible for inheritance must exist. His work involved experiments using mice and the bacteria *Streptococcus pneumonia.* First, a virulent strain of *S. pneumonia* was injected into a mouse, and the mouse died. Second, a nonvirulent strain of *S. pneumonia* was injected into a mouse, and the mouse did not die. The next phase of his experiments involved heating up the virulent strain to denature and kill it; then, this killed strain was injected into a mouse, and the mouse lived. Finally, he injected a mouse with nonvirulent *S. pneumonia* that had not been heated up together with a virulent *S. pneumonia* that had been heated up, and the mouse died. Griffith postulated the killed virulent bacteria had passed on the virulent characteristics to the nonvirulent strand to make it virulent. He called the passing on of the inheritance molecule "transformation."

A scientist named Oswald Avery revisited Griffith's experiment 14 years later. Avery attempted to identify the inheritance molecule. In Avery's experiments, he selectively destroyed different molecules in the virulent *S. pneumonia* (e.g., carbohydrates, proteins, lipids, and ribonucleic acids). After the destruction of these molecules, transformation still occurred—until he destroyed deoxyribonucleic acid, and transformation did not occur. Avery had at last isolated the inheritance molecule, DNA.

In the 1940s, a scientist named Erwin Chargaff discovered that the DNA molecule is composed of four bases: adenine (A), guanine (G), cytosine (C), and thymine (T). In addition, he found that the amount of adenine is almost equal to thymine and that the amount of guanine is almost equal to the amount of

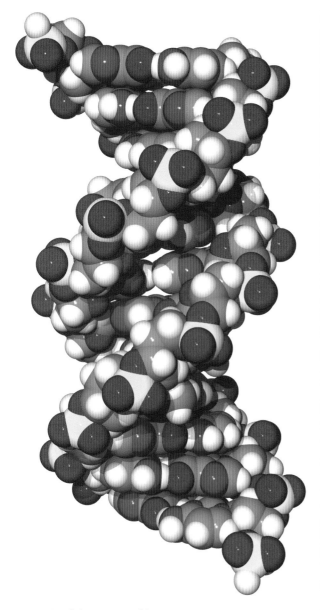

Source: © iStockphoto/Magnus Ehinger.

cytosine. Therefore, Chargaff postulated that A = T and G = C. This became known as "Chargaff's rule."

Two scientists named Rosalind Franklin and Maurice Wilkins attempted to crystallize and make an X-ray pattern of the DNA molecule, in order to understand its structure. Their results showed a pattern that appeared to have ladder-like rungs in-between two strands that were arranged side by side. In addition, the X-ray results showed an "X" shape and that the DNA molecule had a helical shape.

In 1953, two scientists, James Watson and Francis Crick, were working together and tried to put together a model of the DNA molecule. By examining the X-ray results of Franklin and Wilkins's picture, they produced a model of a double helix that had rungs connecting the two strands. The rungs were actually the bases of the nucleotides that were paired together using Chargaff's rule, so that all the adenine bases were paired with all of the thymine bases and all of the guanine bases were paired with all of the cytosine bases. These pairs are held together by a sugar-phosphate backbone, which makes up the double helix of the DNA molecule.

Watson and Crick also discovered that thymine and adenine each had two hydrogen bonds available and this is why they readily pair together. In addition, they discovered that guanine and cytosine each had three hydrogen bonds and this is why they pair together. Therefore, thymine can pair together only with adenine, and guanine can pair only with cytosine. Thus, one side (or strand) of DNA is a complement to the other side, which is made up of the corresponding base pairs.

The DNA molecule performs two functions: *replication,* where the DNA molecule "unzips" and makes an identical copy of itself (described below), and *transcription,* which is a process in which the DNA unzips and produces an mRNA molecule that ultimately produces a protein molecule (a process called *translation*).

These nucleotides are grouped side by side in threes (triplets), called *codons* (e.g., ATT or CGA); this is also known as "the triplet code." Each codon codes for a particular amino acid, and usually 2 to 4 codons will code for the same amino acid. Amino acids are the organic molecules that serve as the building blocks for proteins. Some codons initiate a start or stop point on a particular segment of DNA.

How exactly is protein produced from DNA (i.e., how do we go from gene to protein)? During the process of transcription, a molecule called *RNA polymerase* helps to unzip the two strands of DNA by breaking the hydrogen bonds between the base pairs. The RNA polymerase knows where to begin by locating the start codon (called "the promoter"); it does this with the help of other proteins called *transcription factors.* Once it attaches and separates the two strands of DNA, the exposed bases attach with newly available complementary bases, forming a complementary strand of "mRNA." This mRNA will continue to grow until the stop codon (and terminator sequence) is reached. Transcription ends after the RNA polymerase releases the newly made strand of mRNA and then detaches itself from the DNA after it has zipped it back up.

After transcription is complete, the mRNA molecule leaves the nucleus of the cell and makes its way to a ribosome, which uses the mRNA to synthesize protein. This process is called *translation*. During translation, mRNA slides through the ribosome, while a molecule called "tRNA" serves as an interpreter and brings the appropriate amino acid to the corresponding codon on the mRNA molecule. Each tRNA contains what is called an *anticodon,* which attaches to the codon on the mRNA; on the other end of the tRNA is an amino acid. The mRNA transcript is secured on the ribosome and will temporarily bond with the appropriate tRNA. Once this bond takes place, the tRNA transfers its attached amino acid to the chain of amino acids, which is growing as the mRNA is being read. This continues until the stop codon is reached, at which time termination of translation occurs, and a free polypeptide is released into the cytoplasm of the cell.

In addition to protein synthesis, it is important to note that the structure of the DNA molecule provides a reliable mechanism of heredity. This is based on the fact that genes carry important biological information. They must be copied accurately each time the cell divides, to form two identical daughter cells in order for successful transmission of inheritable characteristics to take place. This is done during *replication,* which is the process by which the DNA molecule replicates itself.

Replication begins when the DNA molecule is unwound and prepared for synthesis by the action of several types of molecules. Some of these are DNA gyrase, DNA helicase, RNA primers, and single-stranded DNA-binding proteins. These molecules work together to separate the two strands of the double helix, forming a "replication fork." Single-stranded DNA-binding proteins work to stabilize the unwound DNA. The replication fork moves in one direction, and only one strand, called the *parental DNA,* is replicated; the newly replicated stand is called *the leading strand.* This leading strand is synthesized in a continuous direction known as the *5 prime to 3 prime* direction, which is directed by DNA polymerase. The other strand called the *lagging strand* (travels in a 3 prime to 5 prime direction), which is not replicated continuously and produces short discontinuous replication products called *Okazaki fragments* (named after the Japanese scientist who discovered them). These fragments, which are formed by DNA polymerase, are usually 100 to 200 nucleotides long and are joined together by a molecule called *DNA ligase.*

During the replication of DNA, enzymes "proofread" the DNA and repair damage to existing DNA. This is done in two ways: Proteins proofread replicating DNA and correct errors in base pairing; this is called *mismatch repair.* The other way DNA is repaired is called *excision repair;* this is where repair enzymes actually fix DNA that is damaged by physical and chemical agents (including ultraviolet light).

The DNA molecule contains segments that are "noncoding." These sequences are called *introns* (short for *intervening sequences*). The regions that do code for the translation of protein synthesis are "coding regions" and are called *exons* (because they are expressed). The exons are separated from one another by introns (i.e., the sequence of nucleotides that codes for proteins does not exist as an unbroken continuum).

The DNA molecule differs from the RNA molecule in several ways. First, the DNA molecule is composed of two strands, or is "double stranded," whereas the

RNA molecule is composed of only one strand or is "single stranded." Second, the actual molecular compositions in their structure are different. The nucleotides that compose the RNA molecule are adenine, guanine, cytosine, and uracil, while in DNA, uracil is replaced by thymine. Like thymine, uracil is also a pyrimidine and pairs together with adenine during the processes of transcription and translation. Another structural difference between DNA and RNA is the type of sugar (a pentose sugar) found in the sugar-phosphate backbone. The DNA molecule contains deoxyribose, whereas the RNA molecule contains ribose. The final and most important difference between DNA and RNA is in their function. The DNA molecule makes RNA, and the RNA molecule synthesizes proteins.

Up to now, the DNA molecule has been presented as a highly organized unit that can replicate itself without error. However, a phenomenon called *mutation* can take place. A mutation is a change in the DNA of a gene; that is, the actual nucleotide sequence of the DNA is altered. An example of this would be if ATG changed to AAG. This change, no matter how small or drastic, will do one of three things: First, it could serve as a benefit by enhancing that specie's physical or biological attributes. This could increase a specie's ability to propagate and flourish, eventually becoming a permanent trait in that species. Second, it could cause an adverse effect in that specie's physical or biological attributes. This could hinder and decrease the specie's ability to survive or propagate an inferior version of the species, eventually leading to its extinction. Third, it could have no effect at all. Regardless of what effect a mutation has, it ultimately creates genetic diversity. All gene pools have a large reservoir of genetic mutations.

Because the DNA molecule is responsible for our genetic makeup and influences our physical totality all the way down to our cells, it in effect links all *Homo sapiens* together. The species *Homo sapiens* has a wide variety of genetic diversity, from height to skin and eye color. However, the common denominator of our species remains the similarity of our DNA molecules. DNA also in this effect links all biological life on this planet.

Due to the DNA molecule's many activities, which appear to be influenced by biochemical feedback, it appears to take on a life of its own. This new notion is becoming known as "molecular consciousness," or more specifically, "DNA consciousness."

It is also worth mentioning that even though we now know a great deal about DNA, there is still much that we do not understand. In addition, we also have to reserve anticipation for the possibility of life forms in other regions of the universe. What type of molecules will be at the root of their existence? Will they have a molecule similar to DNA or RNA, or will these other life forms possess an entirely different molecule?

Recent advances in bioengineering will have many fascinating implications in regard to the DNA molecule. For example, many genetic diseases can be detected with screening tests that can identify a very specific gene that is responsible for that disease. DNA testing can also be used to determine if an individual is or is not the father of a child with up to 99.9% accuracy in forensic anthropology. In the future, an individual's DNA will determine what type of medication will yield the maximum therapeutic results, increasing the quality of health in the population at large.

Finally, recombinant DNA technology, which involves techniques that can allow for the isolation, copying, and insertion of a new DNA sequence into a cell, could potentially give rise to new species or modified versions of existing species in the future. This is becoming more of a reality with the completion of the Human Genome Project.

— *John K. Grandy*

See also **DNA Testing; Genetic Engineering; Genetics, History of; Human Genome Project**

Further Readings

Alberts, B., Johnson, A., Lewis, J., Raff, K., Roberts, K., & Walter, P. (2002). *Molecular biology of the cell* (4th ed.). New York: Garland.

Butler, J. (2005). *Forensic DNA typing: Biology, technology, and genetics behind STR* markers (2nd ed.). New York: Academic Press.

Micklos, D., & Freyer, G. A. (2003). *DNA science: A first course* (2nd ed.). New York: Cold Spring Harbor Laboratory Press.

Watson, J. (2001). *The double helix: A personal account of the discovery of the structure of DNA*. New York: Touchstone.

Watson, J., & Berry, A. (2003). *DNA: The secret of life*. New York: Knopf.

DNA TESTING

DNA (deoxyribonucleic acid) testing is a scientific method used to distinguish among living entities through the variations between strands of DNA. It is hard to believe that the use of DNA testing first entered the forensic world just 25 years ago. From the criminal cases shown by the media to the new popular television series *CSI*, the importance of DNA analysis is well-known.

The advancement in science and technology has allowed the development of DNA testing techniques, allowing scientists to solve questions once deemed unsolvable. Not only are we able to determine who the rightful father is in a parental dispute or the guilty party in a criminal investigation, but technology now has the ability to uncover the identity of thousands of body fragments from the September 11, 2001, terrorist attack on the World Trade Center, in New York City.

Furthermore, the use of DNA testing has played a significant role in tracing back human ancestry. By following mitochondrial DNA back through time, one is able to track the migration of specific genes through maternal lineages. DNA testing has greatly enhanced human curiosity and our understanding of the world in which we live.

Genetics and Molecular Biology

DNA is the foundation of life. Within each living cell, there is a nucleus that holds thousands of paired genes within structures called chromosomes. In human beings (who are considered normal), there are 46 chromosomes composed of strands of DNA, which include 22 pairs of non-sex-determining chromosomes (autosomes), along with one pair of sex-determining-chromosomes; an X chromosome from the mother and an X or Y from the father. The sex chromosomes determine whether the child will be male (XY) or female (XX). Except for sperm and egg cells and cells that do not have a nucleus, such as blood cells, the genetic makeup of our entire body is in every cell.

The double-helix "rope ladder" structure of DNA was discovered by James Watson and Francis Crick in 1953. They found that within each chromosome are strands of DNA, which are composed of long chains of base pairs: guanine (G), adenine (A), thiamine (T), and cytosine (C). The chemical properties allow Base A on one strand to pair with T on the other, and G to pair with C. Thus, depending upon the specific order and pairings, a gene that consists of various lengths of base pairs encodes for specific proteins. This instructional ability does not include every length of DNA, for the majority of DNA has no known function. The locus is the molecular location of a gene along a strand of DNA, and every chromosome contains a specific order of loci, which is the same in all humans. For example, on Chromosome 7 in every human, there is a gene that, if altered, may cause cystic fibrosis.

The Advancement in Testing Techniques

The first method of DNA testing used by forensic labs was restriction fragment length polymorphism (RFLP). Although it was first discovered in 1980 by David Botstein and coworkers, it was Sir Alec Jeffreys (English biochemist) who first discovered its application in "DNA fingerprinting." Jeffreys brought DNA fingerprinting into the criminal justice system to identify criminals and/or determine innocence of those wrongfully convicted. This technique is based on distinguishing variation in the length of DNA at particular loci (location on the chromosome). Thus, it is able to determine whether two different samples are from the same source. Although RFLP has the ability to discriminate a large number of loci, it has a number of drawbacks. It requires a large amount of DNA and has difficulty using degraded or old samples, which are quite common in forensics. In addition, it is a long and difficult task to perform; therefore, it will eventually be a technique of the past. Other early techniques included the human leukocyte antigen analysis (HLA DQAI), which examined only one locus; the AmpliType PM+DQA1 system; and amplification fragment length polymorphisms (AMFLPs).

With advancement in technology, new techniques were developed that were less strenuous, faster, and had the ability to target mitochondrial DNA, X and Y chromosome markers, and short tandem repeats. A variable-number tandem repeat (VNTR) is a region of DNA that differs in the number of consecutive DNA sequences that are repeated throughout a chromosome. The first of the two main techniques, VNTR typing, utilizes the extensive variation of VNTRs among individuals along with regions of identifiable length to help differentiate humans. In 1983, Dr. Kary Mullis developed the polymerase chain reaction (PCR), in which large amounts of DNA can be replicated from a small sample of DNA (from a strand of hair or on a stamp). Once the DNA is amplified, the process continues similar to that of VNTR. The PCR method has a few drawbacks that can reduce its efficiency. Initially, if the genes are contaminated, then the process will amplify the wrong DNA. And second, because some of the loci used in PCR are functional genes, there is a higher probability that they would be influenced by natural selection, thus changing the frequencies of various genes throughout the human genome.

Typically, the DNA is amplified and then analyzed for specific characteristics. With the advances in technology and the Human Genome Project, a third method known as "DNA sequencing" or the "Sanger method" was developed. This technique is able to unravel specific DNA sequences base by base, to be used for making detailed comparisons to determine similarities and differences between strands.

Uses, Accuracy, and Limitations

The most common purpose for DNA testing is in criminal cases to identify and confirm a suspect's innocence or guilt. This is extremely important, because some cases would not be solved without DNA evidence. With enhanced techniques and decreased costs, testing is now used not only for murder and rape cases, but for everyday disputes, including pet ownership, burglaries, marital infidelities, and so forth. Parental testing for identifying the rightful father of a child is a common use in custody cases. In addition, preserving children's DNA in commercial kits will assist in helping to identify lost children who are found. Many more uses include following genetic disease incidence, prenatal testing, genetic mapping, the Human Genome Project, identifying human remains (soldiers, victims of the World Trade Center), among others. The use of DNA testing has proven crucial to many aspects of society today.

The world of forensics has assisted in the rapid improvement in DNA-testing techniques that are available today. In only a few decades, technology has advanced in such a way that DNA analysis has gone from taking months to conduct to being able to perform within a few hours. The technical aspect of DNA analysis has consistently proven itself; however, there are a few limitations. The primary weakness has been found through human error within procedure and lab methods. For example, there is error when testing two samples that are shown to originate from the same source when they actually are not from the same source. DNA testing may produce false positive or negative results. False positive results occur when testing results show a suspect sample is that of the forensic sample when it is not. False negative results are when testing results show suspect DNA is not the same as forensic sample when it actually is. However, there is no exact error rate, because error cannot be predicted, nor will it remain constant. The statistics show that in a trial, the source of the DNA is 1 million times more likely to be the suspect's than another random person's with the same genetic profile.

The FBI has strict standards and regulations on DNA testing and validity for "accuracy, precision, and reproducibility." These regulations include documents that characterize the loci of genes on a subject's DNA and the distribution of genes within the population from which to compare. Furthermore, evidence samples must be collected in an appropriate manner and handled according to procedure, while labs are to use reputable methods and techniques to analyze and interpret DNA samples. The FBI uses statistics to determine if DNA information is valid and unique to the suspect. Consequently, if the profile frequency of the suspect compared to the entire U.S. population is less than $3.9 \times 10^{(-11)}$, it is 99% certain the DNA in question did not come from another individual.

Identifying Humans

In tragedies such as the World Trade Center attack, victims' bones and body parts are compared with DNA from their toothbrushes, hairbrushes, razors, and so forth, to allow DNA sequence comparison in order to be able to give remains to relatives. Also, DNA (along with proteins and lipids) from ancient organisms is able to be accessed through fossils, soil, and rocks to help bring greater understanding of biological history. This brings together the disciplines of archaeology, paleontology, molecular biology, geology, and chemistry.

If enough DNA from an ancient organism is discovered and the damage to the DNA was not severe, the possibility of cloning would still exist. The cloning process takes certain portions of DNA from one species and inserts it into that of a host organism that is similar to the organism in question. Utilizing the host's natural ability to grow and reproduce, the organism could modify the donor DNA with the ancient DNA, creating a larger segment of DNA, and the organism can gradually "rebuild" the ancient organism. This can provide evidence to show relations of organisms to one another and help to rebuild species ancestry, a "phylogenetic tree."

Scientists also use DNA analysis to look at tissue remains on skeletons from mummified bodies. Since mummies underwent rapid drying, it was thought that rehydration of tissues could allow visualization of nuclei and subsequently genetic material could be extracted. For example, in 1981, nucleic acids from a preserved liver from a 2,000-year-old Han Dynasty corpse were isolated by G. Wang and C. Lu.

The mitochondrial (mt) DNA studies have had a significant impact on tracing human ancestry. These studies are based on the assumption that mtDNA is solely inherited from the mother and does not undergo genetic recombination. For example, the mtDNA analyses of the "Iceman" found in the Tyrolean Alps of Italy determined that he was an ancestor of current Europeans living north of the Alps. If the assumptions are true, then mtDNA studies will continue to increase our knowledge of maternal lineages and human evolution.

The most common use of DNA technology involves the collection of blood, semen, skin, and hair samples at crime scenes that are used to extract DNA and identify the donor. The DNA is first isolated, and amazingly, even if there is a trace amount of blood present at the scene, DNA can still be extracted and suspended in a liquid with the proper use of chemicals and heat. Once analyzed, DNA is stored in databases so that in the future, DNA profiles can be searched.

Criminal Investigations

After being convicted based on circumstantial evidence and/or eyewitness testimony, many criminals have been sent to prison or put to death. Within the legal system, there have been many cases in which the guilty have been set free and the innocent have been put behind bars or even placed on death row. Since 2002, there have been 102 cases in which men were wrongly convicted and freed from death row because of DNA technology.

Ronald Jones spent 10 years on death row after he was convicted of a 1989 rape and murder of a woman from Chicago. Jones was one of the first to be proven innocent by DNA testing. The trial almost did not occur because Judge John Morrissey dismissed Jones's request; however, the Illinois Supreme Court ordered DNA testing to take place, which proved his innocence. Another example is Robert Earl Hayes of Broward County, Florida, who was convicted of rape and murder and put on death row in 1991. The difference in this case is that it was due to faulty DNA technique that lacked proper validity. After Hayes had been on death row for 4 years, his DNA was retested using more acceptable methods of analysis. Hayes was finally acquitted in 1997. Furthermore, in 1987, in a rape case in which semen was tested from a victim's vagina, Tommie Lee Andrews became the first American to be convicted due to DNA evidence.

Future

Since the discovery of forensic DNA analysis, a new perspective has changed the history and future of mankind. This is clearly illustrated in a wide variety of cases, whether it is a "criminal" being freed from prison or the identification of passengers of the *Titanic*. It has reached a point where it is nearly impossible for someone to not leave physical evidence wherever they go.

For example, in cases where DNA samples do not include sperm and only the identification of the suspect as male is present, Y chromosome analysis can be used to find specific genetic loci specific to an individual. At the present time, labs have the equipment and expertise to look at more than 20 specific DNA loci; however, this number will increase with technological advances. It has been predicted that by the year 2010, one will be able to examine loci that determine physical traits.

Advances in technology may lead to handheld DNA devices for quick identification of a suspect for arrest. Furthermore, a research team consisting of scientists and engineers at the University of Michigan has developed a "lab on a chip" that electronically analyzes DNA samples. This inexpensive glass silicon chip is portable, extremely efficient, and is one of the latest advances in DNA technology.

Furthermore, genetic engineering and cloning have come together to be able to clone animals with specific traits. Once the gene for a particular trait is discovered, then it is only a matter of time before the gene is manipulated to change or eliminate its effect. For example, the gene Fel d1 in cats that produces a protein that causes an allergic reaction in humans has been identified. Thus, alteration of that gene may one day help many people who suffer from cat allergies.

The formation of a completed national and world DNA database in the future will be of great assistance in solving crimes. It is certain that the future of DNA testing will continue to ride the wave of technology into the future.

With increasing knowledge and technology, the future of DNA testing will continue to influence mankind. Today, the use of DNA testing in criminal cases and paternal decisions has become widespread. For instance, if it were not for the advancement of DNA analysis, more than half of the World Trade Center victims would not have been identified. In addition, in the war against terror, DNA databases will continue to help track and capture members of al Qaeda, especially Osama bin Laden.

With the latest advances, one can only imagine the impact DNA testing will have on human life over the next century. Researchers have already begun putting missing pieces together to uncover some of the unanswered questions from our past. For example, DNA analyses have already been conducted on U.S. presidents such as Thomas Jefferson and James Madison in an attempt to determine whether they fathered children by female slaves.

The field of genetics is extremely fascinating, with new developments and discoveries happening everyday. However, being able to uncover the "blueprint of life" may also be frightening at times. Depending upon the views of society and the laws of the land, difficult issues that have an impact on individual privacy will continue to arise. As promising as a national database may seem, have we really thought about the ethical implications on members of society? Whether dealing with genetic diseases and biological warfare cases such as anthrax or putting criminals behind bars, DNA testing has and will certainly continue to become an important aspect of humanity.

— *Joshua Zavitz and Carrie Wannamaker*

See also **DNA, Recombinant; Evolution, Molecular; Genetics, Human; Human Genome Project**

Further Readings

Cohen, S. (2003). *The wrong men: America's epidemic of wrongful death row convictions.* New York: Carroll & Graf.

Jones, M. (2002). *The molecule hunt: Archaeology and the search for ancient DNA.* New York: Arcade.

Lee, H. C., & Tirnady, F. (2003). *Blood evidence: How DNA is revolutionizing the way we solve crimes.* Cambridge: Perseus.

Palmer, L. J. (2004). *Encyclopedia of DNA and the United States criminal justice system.* Jefferson, NC: McFarland.

Rudin, N., & Keith I. (2002). *An introduction to forensic DNA analysis* (2nd ed.). New York: CRC Press.

DNA, RECOMBINANT

Recombinant DNA, also written as rDNA, is the combining of genes from two or more organisms. The procedure is to construct a DNA molecule in vitro and then insert it into a host cell or organism. The product of the procedure usually is defined as being *genetically engineered,* although the two terms *genetically modified* or *transgenic* are also used. Recombinant DNA is one of three types of cloning and often is mistakenly identified with one of the other two types: reproductive cloning and therapeutic cloning, although there is overlap.

Reproductive cloning (*cloning* is from the Greek word for twig) has been used for plants since ancient times, as a twig from a plant would be put in the ground and grow. But the first cloned animal, a tadpole, did not occur until 1952. Much popular attention has been given to reproductive cloning, largely since the cloning of a sheep, "Dolly," in 1997, by the Roslin Institute in Scotland. Since then, a number of other animals have been cloned (e.g., mice, cows, pigs); attempts to clone some other animals (e.g., monkeys, cats, dogs) have been unsuccessful; and the possible cloning of humans has become a major topic of concern, with much opposition. Mice are the main source of animal-cloning experiments, but cloning of pigs is a goal because their tissues and organs are similar to those of humans. Reproductive cloning is very expensive, and most experiments are not a success.

The most popularly known example of therapeutic cloning is stem cell research, which first became a controversial political issue in the United States during the 2004 presidential election, when President George W. Bush opposed the furtherance of the small amount of stem cell research the United States has sponsored and his Democratic challenger, John Kerry, supported an increase in stem cell research. Because an embryo is destroyed in the process, some people object to stem cell research on religious grounds, as being similar to abortion. Possibilities are cures for cancer, heart disease, Alzheimer's, and other serious medical conditions. In the same 2004 election, California voted to provide $3 billion over 10 years for stem cell research, 12 times as much annually as the nation's 2004 funding. The hope is that in the future, entire organs can be produced from single cells and be used to replace defective organs.

Recombinant DNA has not received the controversial emotional and political coverage received by animal cloning and stem cell research. However, it does exert an important role in the success of biotechnology and has led to many successful advances. Crucial vaccines are in the pipeline. Foods, for example, have been produced that can resist insecticides, pesticides, or viruses, provide more nutritional value, grow faster and larger, or resist bad weather conditions.

The 1953 discovery, by James Watson and Francis Crick, of the structure of DNA started the continuing explosion of genetic research, including recombinant DNA technology. In 1962, Watson, Crick, and Maurice Wilkins received the Nobel Prize for Physiology and Medicine. Rosalind Franklin, the fourth discoverer, had died in 1958 at age 37. Among other examples of the explosion, the genetic code was cracked in 1966. In 1972, Paul Berg pasted two DNA strands together, forming the first recombinant DNA molecule; and the following year, Stanley Cohen, Annie Chang, and Herbert Boyer produced the first recombinant DNA organism by splicing a recombinant DNA molecule into bacteria DNA. In 1975, at Asilomar, California, an international conference of scientists asked the government to regulate recombinant DNA experiments, and in 1976, many types of experiments were restricted. The recombinant DNA Advisory Committee was established by the U.S. National Institutes of Health. The same year, two famous scientists founded Genentech, Inc., a biotechnology company whose goal was to develop and market recombinant-DNA-based products.

The controversy over whether private businesses should be able to patent new knowledge would be bitter and long-lasting, but a very expensive and competitive entrepreneurial race had begun, largely by medical, pharmaceutical, and agricultural concerns. In 1977, the U.S. Congress failed at attempts to pass more regulations, and in 1980, the United States allowed Exxon to patent an oil-eating microorganism. In 1988, the first patent was awarded for a genetically altered animal, a mouse highly susceptible to breast cancer. In 1989, the National Center for Human Genome Research, with James Watson as head, was created to oversee the Human Genome Project's goal to map and sequence all human DNA by 2005. The center was formally begun in 1990, and that year, anthropologists and the public also saw the book, *Jurassic Park,* which increased public interest and concern through a story of bioengineered dinosaurs running amuck, with dangerous results. The book became a popular movie in 1993.

How will recombinant DNA affect the future? The possibilities are great for medical advances, for helping fight starvation, for improving the environment, and for other areas. There are numerous biotechnology companies, with many successful and unsuccessful research projects. But there are and will continue to be serious ethical controversies. A major amount of opposition will come from people who because of their religious beliefs view recombinant DNA technology as changing their supreme being's definition of life. A cultural lag between knowledge and allowable application of that knowledge will continue to exist in many areas. There also is a fear that unknown and very negative results might arise from combining different life forms.

Other concerns are over the treatment of animals, the tremendous knowledge and financial benefits that might go to a selected few individuals or governments, the probability that poorer countries might have their natural resources exploited but receive no benefits, the confusion that people will experience because of the complexities of new products and results, and the possibilities of unexpected negative medical reactions.

Despite concerns, biotechnology has been safe; recombinant DNA has more precise methods than traditional biotechnology; and oversight has become more flexible. The Human Genome Project was completed in 2003, ahead of schedule, and will continue to provide much more helpful genetic information far into the future.

— *Abraham D. Lavender*

See also **DNA Testing; Evolution, Molecular; Genetics, Human; Human Genome Project**

Further Readings

Cranor, C. F. (Ed.). (1994). *Are genes us? The social consequences of the new genetics.* New Brunswick, NJ: Rutgers University Press.

Relethford, J. H. (2001). *Genetics and the search for modern human origins.* New York: Wiley-Liss.

Watson, J. D. (with A. Berry). (2003). *DNA: The secret of life.* New York: Knopf.

DOUGLAS, MARY (1921–)

British social anthropologist Mary Douglas developed theories about human behavior and culture that have been influential in many disciplines, including anthropology, psychology, political science, religious studies, economics, literature, biblical criticism, risk analysis, and folklore. Douglas, a symbolic anthropologist, focuses on how people understand the world in which they live and how this understanding influences their cultures. Douglas is also concerned with the interactions between people and within their culture's institutions. She is notable for developing theories that can be applied to people in all cultures and societies.

In the early part of her career, Douglas's work centered on Africa, but by the mid-1960s, she began examining theoretical issues on a broader scale. In Douglas's book, *Purity and Danger* (1966), she outlined her theory that people organize their social lives based on categories of purity and impurity. Moreover, in societies where beliefs of pollution and cleanliness are particularly strict, Douglas argued there are also religious and other cultural practices and prohibitions to reinforce these ideals of purity, which apply not only to physical cleanliness but moral health as well.

In *Natural Symbols* (1970), Douglas outlined her grid/group theory, which has been particularly influential throughout many disciplines. Douglas believes that all societies can be understood and compared on the basis of both "grid" and "group." Grid refers to the extent to which the status of an individual in society is ascribed based on specific social distinctions and divisions, such as race, ethnicity, sex, descent, and caste status. Group, in this case, relates to the degree to which people in a particular society are motivated based on the good of the society as a whole or whether they are driven by their own individual beliefs. Therefore, in societies with a strong grid and group, the good of the group is used as an explanation to divide people in the society into clearly delineated structures. These social divisions, whether they are based on caste, age grades, or race, are believed to be necessary to sustain the society. In societies with low grid and low group, individuality has a greater level of importance, and an individual's role within society is variable.

In her more recent work, Douglas has focused on a variety of current issues, including HIV/AIDS, social justice and awareness, environmental issues, religious revivalism, and economics.

Douglas earned her PhD in 1951 from Oxford University. She was awarded honorary doctorates from University of Uppsala, University of Notre Dame, Jewish Theological Seminary, University of East Anglia, University of Essex, and University of Warwick.

Douglas has had an illustrious career in the field of anthropology that includes appointments at Oxford University, University of London, Northwestern University, Princeton University, and the Russell Sage Foundation, where she worked as the director for research on culture. Douglas continues her research as a professor emeritus at University College London. In addition to the two books mentioned previously, Douglas has published numerous books and articles exploring her theories and applying them to a wide variety of topics.

— *Kristine McKenzie Gentry*

See also **Cross-Cultural Research; Taboos**

Further Readings

Douglas, M. (1966). *Purity and danger: An analysis of the concepts of pollution and taboo.* London: Routledge & Kegan Paul.

Douglas, M. (1970). *Natural symbols: Explorations in cosmology.* New York: Vintage Books.

Fardon, R. (1999). *Mary Douglas: An intellectual biography.* New York: Routledge.

DOWRY

Dowry is a custom practiced mostly by intensive agri-culturalists with significant inequalities in wealth. It is a form of marital exchange occurring in 5% of the societies studied by anthropologists in Europe, Southern Asia, and the Middle East, the most well-known being the Indian Hindus. Generally speaking, it involves the transfer of property, money, or goods, such as household wares, jewelry, cars, and clothing from the bride's family to the bride, groom, or groom's family. The dowry is actually the daughter's inheritance and functions to mark the social status of both the spouses and their offspring and solidify the marriage contract. Much of the dowry is pre-sented on the wedding day, but the bride's parents and maternal uncle provide gifts periodically through-out the marriage. In patrilocal societies, where the bride goes to live with the groom's family, dowry pay-ments transfer money to the bride's new residence and are a public announcement of the new alliance between families.

In Hindu culture, dowry or *daan dehej* is consid-ered a matter of religious duty, or *dharma,* referred to in religious texts, such as the *Manusmriti.* It creates an atmosphere in which women are seen as property, governed first by their father and later by their husband. Though there are some "love matches," in which couples ask for negotiations to begin between family representatives, marriages are usually arranged by the parents through kin and other networks but can also be established from want ads placed in the newspapers. These advertisements, placed by the parents, include attributes such as age, income, occu-pation, physical features, kinship ties, family back-ground, place of residence, personality, consideration of dowry, time and type of marriage, and language, through which the families evaluate potential family alliances.

The institution of dowry in India has resulted in a high incidence of violence against women. Advances in medical technology that can determine the sex of the fetus have introduced the practice of selective female abortions. Because dowry payments are a drain on the bride's family, female children are less valuable and therefore considered expendable. Statistics from a 2001 census show that there are now 933 women to every 1,000 men. Furthermore, rates of female suicide have increased in cases where the families cannot afford to produce a dowry. However, most violent acts occur after the marriage has taken place, with additional demands from the groom or groom's family. If these demands cannot be met, the results are the abuse and torment of the wife, which ultimately end in her death. "Bride burning" is a practice during which the woman is burned to death in kerosene, the fuel typically used in kitchen stoves. A hospital in Delhi typically sees three to four burn victims a day who report having "fallen onto a stove" as the cause of their injuries. While in the hospital, the groom's family still harasses and threat-ens these women to keep them from telling the authorities what really happened.

In 1961, the Dowry Prohibition Act made the practice illegal; however, it has proven to be ineffec-tive in combating this social issue. Because the victims rarely incriminate their attackers and the custom is entrenched in the society, the law is not easily enforced. There are some women who act out against the demands and call the police, and on these occasions the men are arrested and sent to prison.

Trends suggest that it is in the urban areas of Northern India that the occurrence of "bride burn-ing" is the highest. Because of the lack of social con-trols that are more obvious in the rural areas, the groom's family is able to act with impunity. In smaller communities, the husband and family are held accountable for their actions. Also, women in these areas are more involved in the family's economic production and are consequently more valuable. This custom and the social issues surrounding it continue today.

— *Luci Latina Fernandes*

See also **Bride Price; Hinduism; India, Rituals of**

Further Readings

Bailey, G., & Peoples, J. (2002). *Essentials of cultural anthropology.* Belmont, CA: Wadsworth.

Murdock, G. P. (1949). *Social structure.* New York: Macmillan.

Van Willigen, J., & Channa, V. C. (2004). *Law, custom, and crimes against women: The problem of dowry death in India.* In N. F. Bellantoni & L. L. Fernandes (Eds.), *Anthropologists at work: An introductory Reader* (2nd ed.). Cambridge, UK: Pearson.

DRYOPITHECUS

Dryopithecus is one of 40 genera representing up to 100 species of extinct apes that lived during the Miocene (22.5 to 5.5 million years ago). The fossils of *Dryopithecus* have been found in the region ranging from Spain to the Republic of Georgia. *Dryopithecus fontani* was the first fossil great ape discovered. It was discovered in Saint Gaudens, France, by Édouard Lartet in 1856.

Dryopithecus species (referred to as dryopithecines) flourished in Europe between 13 and 7 million years ago. About 9 million years ago, the climate became cooler and dryer, causing a disappearance of tropical regions in Europe. Many of the Miocene apes became extinct at this time. *Dryopithecus* was one of two lineages (*Sivapithecus* and *Dryopithecus*) that survived this climatic change. Dryopithecines presumably survived by migrating with their preferred ecological zones to Africa.

Many dryopithecine fossils have been discovered, and much of the skeleton is represented. Like all living apes, dryopithecines possessed relatively large brains. They also show apelike characteristics associated with a reduced reliance on smell and an increased emphasis on vision: they had shortened snouts and forward-facing eye sockets with overlapping fields of vision. Like all living apes, dryopithecines also lacked a tail. The skeletal remains indicate that dryopithecines were quadrupeds, walking on four legs. They also possessed adaptations to suspensory locomotion: Their stable yet fully extendable elbow joint allowed them hang and swing below branches. In addition, remains of the hands and feet show that they possessed powerful grasping capabilities. All of these characteristics suggest that *Dryopithecus* moved about the forest canopy in a way that is similar to modern great apes.

The lower molar teeth of *Dryopithecus* have long had significance for paleoanthropologists. Their five cusps are arranged in a pattern that is observed in all fossil and recent apes as well as humans. It is known as the *Y-5 pattern*, because the fissures separating the five cusps form a "Y." This is one of many characters that are used to distinguish apes from monkeys. The size and shape of the other teeth, including large incisors and bladelike canine teeth, suggest that dryopithecines were adapted to a diet of soft, ripe fruits. Aspects of the skeleton that reflect life history variables, including tooth microstructure and brain size, suggest similarities to living apes. Dryopothecines apparently lived relatively long lives, matured relatively slowly, and gave birth to one large offspring at a time.

The place of *Dryopithecus* in human and ape evolution is still debated. A recent discovery (1999) of a new *Dryopithecus* skull from Hungary shows that the cranium is more similar to that of African apes and early fossil humans than to Asian apes. Thus, scientists suggest that *Dryopithecus* (or its close relative *Ouranopithecus*) was the likely ancestor of African apes and humans. If this were the case, the common ancestor of African apes and humans would have originated in Eurasia and later migrated to African to establish separate African ape and human lineages sometime during the late Miocene.

— *Shara. E. Bailey*

See also **Primate Morphology and Evolution**

Further Readings

Begun, D. (2003). Planet of the apes. *Scientific American, 289*(2), 74–83.
Kordos, L (2000). New results of hominoid research in the Carpathian Basin. *Acta Biologica Szegediensis, 44,* 71–74.
Kordos, L., & Begun, D. (2001). A new cranium of *Dryopithecus* from Rudabánya, Hungary. *Journal of Human Evolution. 41,* 689–700.

DUBOIS, EUGENE (1858–1940)

A Dutch anatomist and geologist, Eugene Dubois was known for his discovery of *Pithecanthropus erectus.* Born in the Netherlands in 1858, Dubois cultivated his naturalism with interest in the natural sciences. With support from his family, he studied medicine at Amsterdam University, whereby he received his doctorate in 1884. After graduating, Dubois was appointed as lecturer of anatomy in 1886. It is believed that his interest in evolution developed rapidly during this appointment. Perhaps believing that Asia was the cradle of human evolution, Dubois began to critically assess the possibilities of moving to the Dutch colony. The following year Dubois went to the Dutch East Indies (Indonesia) as a military surgeon. Although the island of Sumatra yielded few fossils, the move to the island of Java (Trinil) in 1890 would prove to be of great significance, ultimately yielding the fossil *Pithecanthropus erectus* (Java man) that would change both hominid taxonomy and secure Dubois's place in the scientific community.

After careful examination of the fossil evidence, Dubois published his findings 4 years (1894) after his arrival in Java. In 1895, he returned to Europe to discuss and defend his interpretation of the fossil evidence. Although the scientific community was open to new evidence concerning evolution, most disagreed with his methodology and interpretations concerning the placement of this hominid form. During this time, Dubois became a professor of geology at the University of Amsterdam. Lecturing and traveling throughout Europe, he continued to defend his analysis of Java man. Unwavering in his interpretation, Dubois remained firm in his belief that *Pithecanthropus erectus* was an intermediate form between simian ancestry and humankind. The similarities of the morphological features of then recent discoveries in Java had increased the Java controversy. Regardless of his scientific demeanor and interpretation, physical anthropology benefited from Dubois's quest for human ancestry.

Contributions and Perspectives

From 1891 to 1892, Dubois discovered a deposit of fossil bones at Trinil. In the strata that would date to the Pleistocene, the lapilli layer would yield a third molar (second molar found in October 1892), cranium, and a left femur. Besides the hominid evidence, other fossil remains of extinct creatures were recovered, among them being Stegodon, *Bos elephas,* rhinoceros, sus, felis, and hyena. Viewing the evidence as a whole, a picture of a bygone time emerged through the rock strata. Among the hominid fossil bones that were recovered, the interpretation of the thighbone and cranium led him to conclude that the specimen was an intermediate form between man and ape. Although he first referred to this new find as *Anthropithecus erectus,* he later renamed this hominid form as *Pithecanthropus erectus.*

Characteristically, Dubois (1896) assessed that the femur possessed both human and simian-like

Source: The New York Academy of Medicine Library.

qualities. The differences between a human femur and that of *Pithecanthropus erectus* involved the following characteristics: increased rounded form of the inner side of the shaft, a round convex popliteal area, and more simian-like trochanteric line. Although the femur does have humanlike characteristics, Dubois asserted that the evidence must be evaluated in its entirety, including the other simian-like (perhaps a giant gibbon form) fossil bones that were discovered along with the femur. The calveria is measured at 185 mm (length) and 130 mm (breadth). According to Dubois, the skull is also simian in character. The cranial capacity is estimated at being around 1,000 cc, receding forehead, *torus occipitals,* and the pronouncement of the frontal bone's orbital indicates a marked difference from human. Although similar to other anthropoid apes and some human characteristics (e.g., cranial capacity), Dubois continued to maintain that *Pithecanthropus erectus* was not a microcephalic idiot as some claimed, but a distinct and extinct hominid form between humankind and ape, an intermediate form that has Hylobatoid characteristics and is close to the genus *Homo.* The exact relationship and interpretation concerning the evidence was the center for agitated discussions, only to resurface with other hominid finds.

Discoveries of fossil hominids in both China (Peking man) and Java renewed interest in Dubois's discovery and interpretation. According to the evaluations of then newly discovered evidence, the fossil remains appeared to be very similar to that of *Pithecanthropus erectus*. However, Dubois defended the independence of *Pithecanthropus*. Dubois claimed that the newly discovered fossil in Java was, in fact, *Homo soloensis*. Dubois stated that *Homo soloensis* is proto-Australian and that both Solo man and Rhodesian man are a primitive type of *Homo sapiens*, all of which are distinct from *Homo neanderthalensis*. Considering the cranial vault, low cranial capacity, pulp cavities of the teeth, and slender bones, the specimens of *Homo soloensis* and *Homo rhodesiensi*, and *Sinanthropus* are the most primitive type of *Homo* by which all human races can be derived. Any variation found among these types is due to cultural influences. In a reevaluation of *Pithecanthropus* in 1937, Dubois gave his reevaluation.

Dubois stated very clearly that *Pithecanthropus*, though not human, was a gigantic genus close to the gibbon. The morphological features of the calvaria are similar to anthropoid apes; however, the essential features of the femur indicates an erect position and gait. For these reasons, Dubois had given the name *Pithecanthropus erectus*. Furthermore, the lack of the parietal vertex and cranial capacity would be expected if a siamang gibbon had the body weight of *Pithecanthropus* (estimated using the dimensions of the femora). The increased cranial capacity, in Dubois's opinion, was a product of *progressive cerebration by great leaps* (his italics), a law of phylogenic growth of the psychencephalon. Last, Dubois alluded to the conclusion that *Pithecanthropus erectus* may have undergone a *transformation* (his italics) toward human organization, whereby slight modifications of form could result in greater transformations. However, he still retained that this form was unique as well as extinct.

Despite Dubois's academic and professional energies to maintain the distinctness of *Pithecanthropus erectus*, the expenditure was futile. Today, *Pithecanthropus erectus* is classified as *Homo erectus*, a hominid phase in human evolution that is 1.6 million years old. This phase in human evolution could be found in China, Indonesia, Java, Northwest Africa, Olduvai, and the Turkana Basin. Although there is still controversy concerning the defining characteristics, number of lineages, and rates of change, *Homo erectus* signifies a major segment in human evolution. It is unfortunate that Dubois, before his death in 1940, never accepted the diversity of *Homo erectus* that his specimen partly represented. Regardless of his known idiosyncrasies, Eugene Dubois had made important contributions in both discoveries and thought-provoking analysis to the understanding of human evolution.

— *David Alexander Lukaszek*

See also **Hominization, Issues in; Hominids; Homo Erectus; Missing Link; Primate Morphology and Evolution**

Further Readings

Birx, H. J. (1988). *Human evolution*. Springfield, IL: Charles C Thomas.

Dubois, E. (1896). On Pithecanthropus erectus: A transitional form between man and the apes. *The Journal of the Anthropological Institute of Great Britain and Ireland, 25,* 240–255.

Dubois, E. (1937). On the fossil human skulls recently discovered in Java and Pithecanthropus Erectus. *Man, 37,* 1–7.

Shipman, P. (2001). *The man who found the missing link: Eugene Dubois and his lifelong quest to prove Darwin right.* New York: Simon & Schuster.

DURKHEIM, DAVID ÉMILE (1858–1917)

David Émile Durkheim was a French sociologist and philosopher concerned with establishing the domain of sociology, that is, how sociology is different from other academic disciplines. He was also committed to establishing sociology as a science that could compare with the standing of the natural sciences. Scholars regard Durkheim as one of the founders of sociology and one of the most important sociologists in the history of the field of sociology.

Durkheim's central thesis was that sociology's domain lies with the study of social phenomena, that is, the study of society. Durkheim posited that social phenomena have an existence in and of themselves; they are sui generis. They arise when individuals create a reality that cannot be understood in terms of the properties of the particular individuals; that is, social phenomena are not reducible to psychological or biological explanations. Rather, social phenomena are "social facts" and are caused by other "social facts." The role of sociology is to discover the laws or "social facts" that maintain societies. Durkheim further developed a functionalist approach to the study of "social facts." This approach emphasized the roles that institutions and processes play in maintaining social order.

Scholars describe Durkheim's approach as macrosociological, because he was concerned with studying the characteristics of groups and structures. Durkheim applied the macrosociological approach in such works as *The Division of Labor in Society* (1893), *The Rules of Sociological Method* (1895), *Suicide* (1897), and *The Elementary Forms of Religious Life* (1912). For example, in *The Division of Labor in Society*, Durkheim examined how social order is maintained in societies by focusing on differences in the division of labor in traditional and modern societies. Durkheim held that traditional societies have a simple division of labor and are held together by common values. There is a correspondence between collective consciousness and individual consciousness. Durkheim referred to this type of social order as "mechanical solidarity." Modern societies, however, are characterized by a complex division of labor in which specialization of labor and social roles create dependency that ties people to one another. Durkheim referred to this type of social order as "organic solidarity." Furthermore, in modern societies, the complex division of labor produces an individual consciousness that is distinct from collective consciousness. Modern societies may also experience rapid social change that can produce a breakdown of norms regulating behavior that Durkheim referred to as state of *anomie.*

In *Suicide* (1897), Durkheim examined the breakdown of norms regulating behavior by analyzing the suicide rates of different groups, such as Protestants and Catholics. He posited that differences in suicide rates are a function of differences in social cohesion. He demonstrated that suicide varies inversely with the degree of social cohesion. Durkheim explained that when people are well integrated into a group, they participate in activities and hold values that bind them together. Hence, their integration serves as a kind of buffer from the stresses of life, and they are less likely to commit suicide. Using this analysis,

Source: © Bettmann/CORBIS.

Durkheim explained the higher rates of suicide among Protestants when compared with Catholics by noting that Protestantism had fewer common beliefs and practices.

— *Patricia E. Erickson*

See also **Norms; Social Structures**

Further Readings

Farganis, J. (Ed.). (2004). *Readings in social theory: The classic tradition to post-modernism.* New York: McGraw Hill.

Giddens, A. (Ed.). (1972). *Émile Durkheim: Selected writings.* New York: Cambridge University Press.

Nisbet, R. A. (1974). *The sociology of Émile Durkheim.* New York: Oxford University Press.

Source: © Photo provided by www.downtheroad.org, The Ongoing Global Bicycle Adventure.

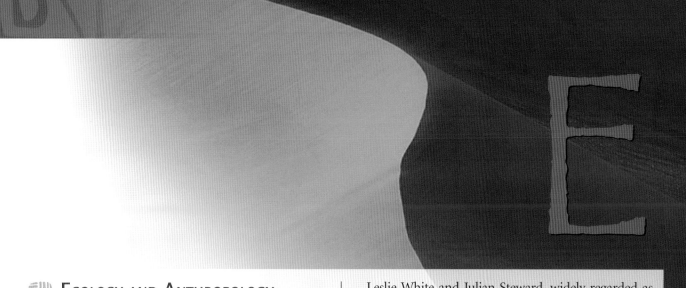

ECOLOGY AND ANTHROPOLOGY

The study of ecology and anthropology, here termed *ecological anthropology*, is at its most basic level the examination of the relationship between humans and the natural environments in which they live. Although the nature of how anthropologists approach this relationship has changed and varied considerably over the past century, ecological anthropology is best characterized as a materialist enterprise. Studies of ecology and anthropology have at their core an implicit assumption that human societies are the products of adaptation to specific environmental conditions. In addition, the human capacity for culture is most often seen as a primary mechanism for achievement of successful adaptation. Despite this general framework, however, contemporary approaches to ecological anthropology range from the very materialist application of evolutionary theory to approaches like historical ecology, which incorporate traditional humanistic approaches to the study of human-environment relations.

Ecological anthropology has a long history within anthropology, dating to the origins of the discipline. However, because the writers of the early 19th century believed that environmental conditions absolutely determined particular cultural constructions, a perspective called *environmental determinism*, the emergence of a rigorous approach to the study of culture through systematic data collection, championed by Franz Boas, virtually eliminated ecology as a worthy focus of anthropological investigation. Known as *historical particularism*, an approach devoted to the study of culture areas, it regarded cultures as unique and ultimately incomparable. Broad theorizing about culture origins and development was rejected outright.

Leslie White and Julian Steward, widely regarded as the fathers of contemporary ecological anthropology, were both trained within the Boasian paradigm. They were, however, led by their early professional experiences to reject the Boasian paradigm in favor of addressing the processes of cultural evolution and the principles that underlie cultural similarities and differences.

For White, appointment at the University of Buffalo in 1927 and subsequent work with local Seneca Indians led him to read Lewis Henry Morgan's writing about the Iroquois. For White, this entrée into 19th-century evolutionism fostered a deep interest in general cultural evolution. White believed that cultural evolution was driven by increased energy use per capita. His lasting contribution to ecological anthropology was the reintroduction of evolutionary thinking into anthropology.

Julian Steward's work with the Great Basin Shoshone in the 1930s demonstrated the direct relationship between environment, technology, population density, and social organization. His work ultimately led to the development of cultural ecology, an approach to the study of culture that advocated the investigation of the relationship between the culture core, which he defined as a society's environment, technological capacity, and social organization, and all other aspects of culture.

The deterministic nature of Steward's work stimulated new thinking about human-environment relationships. Pioneered by anthropologists Frederik Barth, Robert Carniero, Marvin Harris, Robert Netting, and Andrew Vayda, among others, the recognition of the ways in which ecology influences cultural formulations, especially the evolution of complexity, stimulated new interest in the interplay between ecology, politics, economy, and religion. This new perspective is perhaps best exemplified by Elman Service's *Primitive Social Organization* and Morton Fried's *Evolution of Political Society*.

Roy Rappaport's *Pigs for the Ancestors,* an examination of the relationship between ritual cycles, warfare, and ecology among the Tsembaga Maring of New Guinea, highlighted another interest among ecological anthropologists. Rather than being simply an adaptive tool, culture began to be recognized as a mechanism regulating the human-environment relationship, promoting homeostasis and long-term survival.

The neoevolutionary and neofunctional approaches of the 1960s and early 1970s, however, were criticized on numerous grounds. Neoevolutionary arguments were deficient either because of vagueness surrounding units of measurement and selection or because of a reliance on outdated evolutionary theory, such as group selection. Neofunctional approaches were criticized both for their lack of historical depth and their naive assumptions that culture and nature automatically tend toward stability.

Since the middle of the 1970s, then, what has been termed here as ecological anthropology has advanced in a number of seemingly disparate directions, although all have at their core a concern for understanding human-environmental relationships as a process that occurs over both short- and long-time scales, for example, the formation of specific adaptive strategies, for explaining variability not only between but also within cultural systems, and for forging links across traditional disciplinary boundaries.

Political ecology developed during the late 1970s and early 1980s as anthropologists combined ecosystem approaches and actor-based decision-making models with political economy models often used by anthropologists. The result has been a greater understanding of power relationships between state societies and local peoples, particularly regarding issues of sustainability, resource management, political and economic decision making, and subsistence economies.

Human behavioral ecology incorporates evolutionary theory from biology and ecology and applies it to the study of humans. The study of foragers using optimal foraging theory, the motivation for reciprocal sharing arrangements, human mating systems, mate choice and marriage transactions, and parental investment in offspring are some avenues of exploration. These kinds of investigations have provided new insights into traditional anthropological topics. The central concern of this work is in understanding how contemporary human behavior reflects our own history of natural selection.

Historical ecology perhaps pays the most attention to time scales and processes of change between humans and their environments. Much effort has been spent in understanding the processes by which humans develop new strategies for coping with dynamic environments. There is, however, equal attention paid to the impacts that human activity has on local ecology and to the effects that human-induced change has on ecology and on humans living in those altered environments. In particular, work in this direction focuses on questioning the degree to which a presumed natural environment has been artificially created, the impacts of environmental degradation on human societies, and how specific cultures conceptualize and interact with their particular habitats.

Environmentalism and anthropology parallel some of the work of the political ecologists through the examination of power relations between state societies, multinational corporations, developers, and local people. However, while issues of sustainability, conservation, resource management, and development predominate within this work, a keen interest in how local environmental movements have developed, and how these movements integrate with national movements is one avenue of exploration. Another topic of interest to anthropologists working within this domain is environmental rights. What are indigenous people's rights to particular territories? What rights of access do local and state agents have to particular resources? What is the nature of intellectual property law regarding rights to indigenous knowledge?

— *Peter Collings*

See also **Cultural Ecology; Environmental Philosophy; Rappaport, Roy**

Further Readings

Balee, W. (Ed.). (1998). *Advances in historical ecology.* New York: Columbia University Press.

Cronk, L., Chagnon, N., & Irons, W. (Eds.). (2000). *Adaptation and human behavior: An anthropological perspective.* New York: Aldine de Gruyter.

Netting, R. McC. (1986). *Cultural ecology* (2nd ed.). Prospect Heights, IL: Waveland Press.

Human behavioral ecology (HBE) applies to principles of evolution by natural selection to explain behavioral and cultural diversity in human populations. It explores how features of social and physical environment constrain the suite of behaviors or "strategies" of individuals and applies the logic of optimization to make formal predictions about the conditions that favor or disfavor particular behaviors. The main focus of HBE is to explain behavioral variation within and among populations. Its intellectual forbears include developments in biology (evolutionary biology, animal behavior, population and community ecology, life history theory), anthropology (cultural ecology, hunter-gatherer studies), and economics (microeconomics of consumer choice). Since HBE's formulation in the late 1970s, it has been referred to as human sociobiology, Darwinian anthropology, evolutionary or behavioral ecology, and biocultural and biosocial anthropology. Currently, HBE shares common goals and foundations with evolutionary psychology and cultural transmission theory but differs in specific goals and methods. Initially focused on understanding foraging behavior among hunter-gatherers, HBE has expanded over the past 25 years to cover a wide scope of themes and problems, using a broad range of observational, ethnographic, and experimental methods.

Natural Selection and Behavior

Natural selection will influence the frequency of traits when there is sufficient phenotypic variation in traits across individuals, when such variation is inheritable, and when it has an impact on biological "fitness" or reproductive success, via the ability to differentially survive or reproduce in a specific environment and population. Heritability of traits occurs through genetic transmission from parent to offspring and through individual or social learning of information and behavior. HBE therefore focuses on behavioral and cultural "traits" that are likely to have fitness consequences. These include the suite of foraging, mating, parenting, and costly social behaviors found in all populations. People everywhere in all cultures develop ways to extract resources from their environment; find mates; defend access to resources; protect, feed, and care for offspring; and form and maintain social partners and alliances and must often trade off time and energy among these tasks. While evolution can also occur due to founder effects in small populations, random mutation, and gene flow, only natural selection can produce directional change or complex, adaptive design.

HBE treats observed behaviors or traits of interest (phenotypes) as if they were controlled by a simple genetic system, even though most behaviors are multicausal and involve networks of many genes and their interaction with stimuli from local environments. Biologist Alan Grafen has referred to this methodological tactic as the "phenotypic gambit." Behavioral ecologists usually assume that most fitness-related behaviors are sufficiently flexible, and so a safe working assumption is that behaviors can be examined without regard to the particulars of the form of inheritance.

Optimization

Most HBE research employs a hypothetico-deductive methodology, where explicit hypotheses are derived from theoretical models and tested using information collected from fieldwork among living populations. Models are usually mathematical formulations of fundamental adaptive problems. Models balance tractability with realism and specify key relationships among variables believed to best capture the theoretical dynamics of a problem. Two common approaches are optimality models and game-theoretic models. Optimality models examine conditions favoring an optimal behavioral "strategy" from a suite of available strategies, with the goal of maximizing some currency under a set of ecological constraints. The currency may be direct biological fitness, typically measured as the number of children surviving to some later age. The currency is often a proxy of direct fitness, such as foraging efficiency, growth rate, and fertility. While optimality models typically examine costs and benefits from the perspective of a single individual without any reference to what others in the population are doing, the success of strategies in game-theoretic models depends upon the frequency of other strategies in the reference population. For example, a lone cooperator may not fare well in a world populated by defectors.

Models are useful for generating qualitative or specific quantitative predictions. One of the first models used in HBE was the prey choice model (see below). This examines the set of food resources that should or should not be observed in the optimal diet of a forager, who attempts to maximize the currency of net energy gained per unit time, given the finding rate and expected energetic returns from pursuing each specific resource type in the forager's environment. As with many optimality models, the currency used is not direct fitness, but rather a proxy, which is better suited for the specific problem at hand. More food per unit time or the same amount of food in less time each result in a higher rate of energy gain and in many circumstances should positively correlate with fitness.

HBE has been applied to an increasing number of broad topics, such as foraging and subsistence practices, altruism and cooperation, resource conservation, mating and marriage systems, parental care of offspring, status and resource competition, and short-term and long-term life history patterns. Several themes highlighting the HBE approach are outlined below.

Foraging Behavior

Studies of human foraging patterns focus primarily on the set of resources that compose diets and the choice of profitable resource patches and habitats. Group mobility and group size are also considered, as each has been modeled as flexible responses to ecological variables. The prey choice model predicts that, upon an encounter with any kind of food resource, a forager should attempt to acquire it if the expected gain from doing so outweighs the expected gain from continued search (i.e., the long-term rate of caloric gain). This simple model has been used to predict the suite of resources people target in local environments in ethnographic and archaeological samples. Adjustments to the models have been made to fit characteristics of many human groups. Recent model specifications emphasize the importance of consuming macro- and micronutrients, cognitive limitations of the forager, information gathering, and the division of labor by sex and age. Changes in technology that increase the average caloric return rate, such as shotguns instead of bows and arrows, or trucks and snowmobiles instead of on foot, have been shown to increase the number of resource types people acquire in their diet. Similarly, reduced processing or handling costs of certain resources such as seeds and grains raises the profitability of those resources, and so they enter the optimal diet. Declines in the abundance of very profitable resources, such as megafauna in North America, over historical time have been

implicated as fundamental in the subsequent adoption of plant and animal domestication.

The patch choice model examines the suite of patches where individuals forage and the length of time they spend in each of these patches before moving on to the next. The qualitative prediction is that optimizing foragers should leave a patch and proceed to the next patch before the former is depleted. Rather than reflecting a strategy of conservation, such behavior is consistent with the goal of caloric-rate maximization. In a similar vein, foraging theory has recently been invoked to evaluate the validity of competing claims regarding the conservation ethic of indigenous populations. A conservationist might target fast-reproducing species, males, juveniles, and older animals, such that future long-term gain is maximized, whereas according to foraging theory, an individual is more likely to target whichever resources maximize more immediate energy gain.

Altruism and Cooperation

Altruism refers to the conferring of benefits upon others at personal cost. The prevalence of costly altruistic acts is a conundrum because exploiters, cheaters, or free riders should out-compete selfless altruists in a Darwinian world. Consistent with evolutionary theory, altruism is expected when donor and recipient are close biological kin (kin selection), when recipients today send return benefits as donors in the future (reciprocal altruism), when giving acts honestly advertise phenotypic quality or the intent to cooperate (costly signaling), when forced to do so by others (despotism), and when simultaneous mutual benefits can be gained (mutualism or trade). Altruism has been most studied in the context of collective production and distribution of food and services among small-scale hunter-gatherers and agriculturalists, group defense and warfare, wealth inheritance across generations, adoption of nongenetic offspring, and volunteerism and philanthropy in modern societies. Although evolutionary theory has shed much insight on the conditions that tend to favor more or less altruism in a particular context in small-scale societies, there is increasing evidence that some types of large-scale cooperation found in modern nation-states cannot be adequately explained by any of the above models. Alternatively, several forms of cultural group selection have been proposed where social norm compliance is enforced by punishment within cooperative groups.

Mating and Marriage

The widespread variation in the ways that mating is publicly formalized as marriage across the globe has been examined as a function of the ecological interplay between the benefits men receive from investing their time and energy into parental care versus the gains of staying in the mating market, as well as the level of variation in mate "quality." Because women usually benefit more from increased access to resources than from increased access to mates, it is usually assumed that women's primary interests are coincident with child welfare. Pair bonds are expected when both parents have large positive effects on child welfare and when extra-pair mating opportunities are few. These pair bonds should be monogamous when the wealth differences among men are few, and polygynous when some men monopolize valuable resources, such as arable land and cattle. Women in polygynous societies thus become second or third wives to rich men who own more resources rather than first wives to single men with few resources. Polyandry is rare and occurs only in extreme environments, where two or more men, usually brothers, share sexual access to one woman.

As described above, the payoffs to investments in parental care are an important feature of mating systems across and within societies. In environments where high parental investment can increase child fitness (via reduced mortality and increased likelihood of gaining necessary skills, education, and mating opportunities), and where paternity can be reasonably assured, higher paternal investment is likely. Higher investments by both parents in few children have been invoked as a crucial component in the fertility reductions so common in modern, industrialized countries and among the wealthy in poorer countries. Such "demographic transitions" are seen as consequences of declining mortality and a competitive skills-based labor market, where there are potentially few perceived diminishing returns to investments in a small number of children by educated and wealthy individuals.

Life History

The timing and development of important fitness-related events, such as birth, maturation, marriage, and death, constitute an individual's life history. At the species level, humans take a comparatively long time to become physical and functional adults, have large, costly brains, and have very long life spans, much of which is spent in a postreproductive state. Extended childhood has been explained as a time to develop the abilities and knowledge necessary to become an efficient adult food producer or a socially shrewd adult. These explanations explore how the complex human foraging or social niche requires a long time to master, and they help to explain the buildup and maintenance of our large, costly brain. Extended childhood has alternatively been described as a functionless artifact of humans having an extended life span. A long postreproductive life span is explained as a form of indirect reproduction, in which older individuals positively impact descendant kin via food provisioning, direct care, education, and reconciliation, at a cost of reduced investments in reproduction earlier in the life span. There is strong evidence that the transfer of resources across and within generations may be a critical feature that shapes the life histories of humans and other social animals.

Life history variation has also been explored among individuals reared in different environments or exposed to different sets of circumstances and opportunities. These differences can impact the ways that people trade off present benefits against future costs or present costs against future benefits. Thus, a life history perspective has been used to investigate topics such as age at marriage and first birth, teenage pregnancy, infanticide and abortion, exercise and drug use, time preferences, and cooperation.

Future Directions

Behavioral ecologists evaluate the adaptiveness of behavior given the set of constraints and options in the natural, social, and cultural environment. There has been a renewed appreciation for the ways in which cultural history can provide insight into the content and form of these constraints and help to explain behavioral variation among peoples living in similar ecologies. Cognitive aspects of human decision making have also received increased attention in helping to formulate the ways that people internalize, evaluate, and engage important parameters in typical models. Future directions will continue to integrate aspects of cultural anthropology and cognitive psychology with behavioral ecology.

— *Michael Gurven*

See also **Adaptation, Cultural; Anthropology, Cultural; Altruism; Collectors; Selection, Natural**

Further Readings

Alvard, M. (Ed.). (2004). *Socioeconomic aspects of human behavioral ecology.* Amsterdam: Elsevier.

Barrett, L., Dunbar, R., & Lycett, J. (2001). *Human evolutionary psychology.* London: Palgrave Macmillan.

Cronk, L., Chagnon, N., & Irons, W. (Eds.). (2000). *Adaptation and human behavior: An anthropological perspective.* Hawthorne, NY: Aldine de Gruyter.

Hill, K., & Hurtado, A. M. (1996). *Ache life history: The ecology and demography of a foraging people.* New York: Aldine de Gruyter.

Krebs, J. R., & Davies, N. B. (Eds.). (1997). *Behavioural ecology: An evolutionary approach* (4th ed.). Oxford: Blackwell.

Low, B. S. (2000). *Why sex matters: A Darwinian look at human behavior.* Princeton, NJ: Princeton University Press.

ECONOMICS AND ANTHROPOLOGY

From the inception of the discipline of anthropology, ethnographic monographs have dealt with the economies of the people under discussion as a matter of course. The evolutionists were fundamentally interested in levels of technology and environmental "adaptations," and functionalists interpreted all social systems in terms of the satisfaction of basic human needs. Subsequently, anthropologists influenced by Marx would see a given society's "mode of production" as determinant, at least in the last instance, of politics, law, and ideology. Even though none of these theoretical paradigms dominates the field today, it is generally accepted that compelling accounts of social and symbolic behavior must relate them to the material organization of society. Ironically, it appears that economic anthropology loses relevance as a subdiscipline as the larger discipline concerns itself with economics.

Formalism Versus Substantivism

Malinowski's study of the Trobriand Islanders set the tone for an anthropological approach to economic phenomena with his functionalist analysis of the marvelous inter-island *kula* exchange system. He described this symbolically charged system of transacting shell armbands and necklaces in great detail, explaining *kula* practice in relation to cultural values other than material advantage. Malinowski used his Melanesian data to challenge the supposed universality of "economic man"—the egotistical schemer of Bentham's utilitarianism. As Firth pointed out, however, Malinowski's straw "economic man" was already an outmoded figure for economics by the time the latter was making his argument.

Firth argued that the distinctions Malinowski made were invalid: Economics was a question of means, not ends, and economic relations were simply a component part of the social relations that it was anthropology's job to study.

Anthropology has, clarified Burling, alternately taken the economy to be (a) a primitive society's technology and material culture or (b) that range of things that are priced by the market in our own society. There is nothing, he maintains, in the definition of economic behavior that limits it to material ends. There is nothing, to return to the Trobriander, to justify considering the choice to maximize reputation or adhere to custom as antieconomic. The idea that economics consisted in techniques for analyzing behavior regardless of its content—hence "formalist"—was articulated with increasing precision by both anthropologists and economists. It formed one pole of the heated "formalist-substantivist" debate that polarized economic anthropology for at least a decade and, it is argued, made the subdiscipline intellectually inhospitable.

The subject of economics, according to the formalists, is a kind of behavior—"economizing"—that is universally applicable to situations where only limited means are available for achieving a range of ends. Herskovits endorsed this position in the 1952 reissue of his 1940 text *The Economic Life of Primitive Peoples.* Scarcity, he maintained, is universal, as is maximizing behavior on the part of the individual. It is only the cultural matrix within which these occur that varies. The same means are everywhere applied to achieve different ends.

The opposing view was championed by Polanyi and a group of his students from Columbia University. Polanyi analyzed the identity of the economy in contemporary capitalist society and argued that the extent of its autonomy was an absolutely novel historic development. Therefore, not only could other societies not be assumed to have assigned the same independence to economic processes, but the science premised on that independence was, *ipso facto,* only appropriate to our own society. The difference between the industrial capitalist economy of the West and both contemporary and historic premarket economies was one of substance—hence "substantivist"—and different forms of economy were not susceptible to analysis by a uniform method.

Polanyi defined the economy as "an instituted process of interaction between man and his environment, which results in a continuous supply of want-satisfying means." The "institution" of an economy or, more famously, its "embeddedness" is subsumed under three general "forms of integration": reciprocity, redistribution, and market exchange. Under systems characterized and provided stability by means of reciprocal exchange or redistribution, the rates of exchange are set by the imperatives of the larger social institutions—such as in the obligation in the Inca Empire for every subject community to make offerings to the son of the sun, which could then be redistributed by the center. Neale and Mayhew pointed to the ongoing tradition of institutionalist economics, which had long been considering nonmarket societies and mechanisms of economic change and noted that the formalism-substantivism distinction was operating within the discipline of economics as well.

Dalton was one of Polanyi's proponents, using his volume on *Markets in Africa* to work out Polanyi's ideas about the different social and political circumstances for trade and elaborating ideas about the separation of the various functions of money in nonmarket societies. He also devoted room in the volumes of *Research in Economic Anthropology* under his editorship to elaborations or defenses of Polanyi's ideas. Halperin is another former student who promoted and defended Polanyi's ideas. Sahlins labeled himself a "substantivist" in *Stone Age Economics* (1972), but, in fact, he employs neo-classical means to analyze the choices made by hunters and gatherers there.

Formalists bitterly disputed the substantivists' emphasis on the irreducible particularities of economic systems. At issue, in the claims of neoclassical analysis to be able to model economic behavior the world over, in part, was the authority to direct "development." Economists could initially dismiss anthropology's contributions to the larger practical task at hand because, "in addition to a lack of interest in social change, [Anthropology] has been marked by

lack of a theory of change powerful enough to have practical consequences." Similarly, economists and anthropologists disagreed about whether development would be achieved by a given increase in productivity and consumption *tout court* or whether development involved the strengthening of institutions that could direct resources toward socially and culturally desired ends.

All sides to the debate had numerous chances to refine their theoretical apparatus as development schemes failed throughout Africa, Asia, and Latin America. However, the most potent critiques of "development" and its sociological version "modernization" theory were coming from political economy and development studies.

Marxist Anthropology

Although he had read Marx, Polanyi stopped short of identifying regular rules underlying the relationships between economies and different social institutions or attempting to account for the motors of social change. The Marxist anthropologists of the 1960s and 1970s made much more profound theoretical attempts to wrestle with noncapitalist economies.

Althusser's structuralist reading of Marx identified the analytic tools that might be extracted from Marx's study of the rise of industrial capitalism and applied to alternative social formations. Meillassoux is considered the first anthropologist to analyze a precapitalist society in Marxist terms with his study of the Guro of Côte d'Ivoire (1964). Rather than applying Marx's unsatisfactory prefabricated constructs of "Asiatic" or "slave" mode of production, he identified a lineage mode of production by analyzing the direction of surplus extraction in Guro society. In this work and in his subsequent *Maidens, Meal, and Money* (1981), Meillassoux pointed to the central importance of biological reproduction as a means of production in a situation of abundant land and relatively capital-poor technology. Terray commended Meillassoux for his breakthroughs but argued for a larger vocabulary of "modes of production." Terray made the historical materialist point that a kinship system is the reflection of social relations of production rather than (contra almost all of British social anthropology except Edmund Leach) a first-order principle.

Rey described the articulation of the capitalist mode of production with the lineage mode of production, including in his analytical frame the world-historical changes taking place in the Congolese society he studied. In Godelier's work in Oceania, he attempted to show the inseparability of mental and material in both economic base and social superstructure—criticizing Althusser's layercake image and paralleling the cultural Marxism of someone like Raymond Williams.

From Cultural Ecology to Political Economy

With some exceptions, American anthropologists never adopted a Marxist problematic in the way that French and some British anthropologists did. There was, however, a turn to materialist principles of explanation in the 1960s and 1970s, as the ecological determinisms of an earlier period (Julian Steward, Leslie White) were revisited. Orlove categorized this work as neoevolutionist (Elman Service, Marshall Sahlins) and neofunctionalist (Marvin Harris, Andrew Vayda, Roy Rappaport). The latter group tended to view human societies and their environments as interactive systems, taking inspiration from the systems theory. Marshall Sahlins described a state of primitive abundance, calculating the resources required for hunters and gatherers to supply their needs and observing that their societies did not induce scarcity of want-satisfying means. Marvin Harris and Elman Service worked out different versions of the evolution of human society and culture in terms of adaptations to environmental constraints, the former tending to a techno-environmental determinism. Roy Rappaport derived the ecologically adaptive functions of various religious and ritual observances. Although materialist and evolutionary, none of this work was historical or dialectical.

Eric Wolf emphatically introduced history when he turned to dependency and world systems theory for a reappraisal of anthropology's modus operandi. Dependency theory had been elaborated by radical economists working in Latin America and Africa who argued, against development and modernization theory, that global integration was serving to underdevelop peripheral regions of the globe at the expense of the capitalist "core." Wallerstein examined the ways European imperialist expropriations had financed the industrial revolution at the expense of the colonies. The new attention to global interconnection took anthropology by storm. Though reactions to the top-down, center-out determinism of dependency theory were quick to appear, the emphasis on the global relations of power that intersect anthropology's "local" has been tremendously influential.

The move from economics to political economy paved the way for an analysis of the interrelation between power and value at even the most local level. Keith Hart identified the significance of the state in undergirding the value of exchange tokens. Parallel insights have enabled John and Jean Comaroff, James Ferguson, and Sharon Hutchinson to think about the value of cattle in relation to competing political economies.

Exchange and Value

In *The Social Life of Things,* Appadurai made an appeal for the utility of examining exchange independently of production (although it might be argued that this is what non-Marxist anthropology has been doing since Malinowski reported on the *kula* ring or since Paul Bohannan brought back proof of Polanyi's ideas about the social embeddedness of trade from the Tiv). For a Marxist anthropologist, to look at exchange without considering production is to participate in ideological mystification. For most anthropologists, however, exchange processes offer a rich field for examining the cultural construction of meaning and value. Much anthropological and ethnohistorical work has addressed the historical exchange of objects across cultural space, where the meanings of the objects transacted are a matter of contest.

In the early part of the century, Mauss drew widely on existing ethnographic sources to describe a kind of exchange in "archaic" societies that was essentially the opposite of the commodity fetishism of capitalist exchange. Anthropologists have taken up Mauss's ideas about the relationships of debt and obligation created through gift exchange as a fundamental mechanism of social cohesion. Apart from Gregory's attempt to ground gifting in specific social relations of production and reproduction, most of the theoretical impact of gifting seems to have been registered outside of the subdiscipline of economic anthropology.

In a general way, the concept of the gift has been helpful in providing insight into processes of incomplete or unstable commodification. The inability of "money" to fully shed its associations with particular people, things, or productive processes and, therefore, to fully close a particular transaction of the type C-M-C (in Marx's famous notation) has been usefully looked at in terms of the *hau* of the gift in the nonmarket economy. Anthropologists have also revisited theoretical understandings of "money," turning to phenomenological philosopher Georg Simmel as well as to Marx and Polanyi to understand various ways in which money fails to operate as a perfect abstraction or fails to be correctly "fetishized." Taussig describes a case where the money commodity is seen to embody magically generative properties. Jane Guyer argues that precolonial African polities valued people, not as labor power, but as the bearers of unique and irreducible knowledge, who served as critical technologies of production and reproduction. She offers a description of a social imaginary in which value is not ultimately measured in terms of "money"—an abstract, quantifiable medium—primitive or otherwise.

Consumption

Consumption has also been looked at as a meaning-making practice. Veblen interpreted a wide range of behavior in turn of the century North America in terms of the concept of conspicuous consumption. Bataille proposed that the potlatch be viewed with sacrifice, rather than with trade, as the expression of a quasi-natural law of "expenditure." Douglas and Isherwood collaborated to produce a general theory about consumption as symbolic, communicative behavior. Bourdieu used the language of markets to analyze processes of cultural consumption as well as to analyze linguistic production, exchange, and accumulation.

The Subdiscipline of Economic Anthropology

Keith Hart argues that the first economic anthropologists—Karl Marx, Friedrich Engels, Vladimir Lenin, Rosa Luxembourg, Karl Kautsky, and Nikolai Bukharin—were anthropologists of the capitalist transition in the West. Certainly, the classics of economic anthropology were often meant as critiques of industrial capitalism, whether as explicitly, as in Malinowski and Mauss, or not.

Given this, it is perhaps ironic that as a subdiscipline, economic anthropology seems currently to be largely constituted by applied anthropology and development studies. A great deal of anthropological work on exchange, in particular, is not generally classified as economic anthropology, nor are studies that examine changes in consciousness that result from and underpin changes in political economy.

Some of this can be attributed to historical accident and terminology, but it seems that, in a larger sense, the science of economics has swallowed the subdiscipline of economic anthropology theoretically—and anthropology deals in its subject matter at the cost of conceding the term. The pages of economic anthropology texts are filled with attempts to understand entrepreneurial behavior across the globe in terms of calculations of marginal utility, opportunity costs, and game theory. When anthropology looks deeply and imaginatively at production, exchange, accumulation, distribution, and consumption, these become "symbolic," "linguistic," or just "cultural" phenomena.

— *Molly Roth*

See also **Anthropology, Economic; Malinowski, Bronislaw; Marxism; Political Economy**

Further Readings

Appadurai, A. (Ed.). (1986). *The social life of things: Commodities in cultural perspective.* Cambridge: Cambridge University Press.
Douglas, M., & Isherwood, B. (Ed.). (1979). *The world of goods: Towards an anthropology of consumption.* New York: Routledge.
Halperin, R. H. (1988). *Economies across cultures.* London: Macmillan.
Hutchinson, S. (1996). *Nuer dilemmas: Coping with money, war, and the state.* Berkeley: University of California Press.
Meillassoux, C. (1981). *Maidens, meal, and money: Capitalism and the domestic community.* Cambridge: Cambridge University Press.
Neale, W. C., & Mayhew, A. M. (1983). Polanyi, institutional economics, and economic anthropology. In S. Ortiz (Ed.), *Economic anthropology: Topics and theories* (pp. 11–20). Lanham, MI: University Press of America.
Schneider, H. K. (1975). Economic development and anthropology. *Annual Review of Anthropology 4,* 271–292.
Thomas, N. (1991). *Entangled objects: Exchange, material culture, and colonialism in the Pacific.* Cambridge. MA: Harvard University Press.
Valensi, L. (1981). Economic anthropology and history: The work of Karl Polanyi. In G. Dalton (Ed.), *Research in economic anthropology* (Vol. 4, pp. 3–12). Greenwich, CT: JAI Pre.

EDUCATION AND ANTHROPOLOGY

Human beings are curious by nature. In that way, we are all anthropologists in the sense that we possess the universal trait of "curiosity." From the time that a child asks his mother, "Where did I come from?" human beings question why we were made, why we were born, and where we will go. We exhibit curiosity about the origin of humankind and how our early ancestors communicated, interacted, and survived. We reach out to learn from whence we have come and how life has changed and evolved over time.

Originating from the Greek words, *anthropos,* meaning "human or man," and *logia,* meaning "study," the term anthropology defines itself. Anthropology, then, can be understood as the study of humankind from the dawn of man to the present day. It explores early and modern human beings and their cultures, comparing their ways of living and their ways of learning. Anthropology allows us to uncover the roots of our common existence and the sources of our differences. Essentially, anthropology seeks to understand the total premise of human existence from the study of culture and social relations, to human biology and evolution, to languages, to music, to art, to architecture, and to the vestiges of human habitation.

Imagine, for a moment, living in a vanilla world. Surrounded by vanilla flavors and colors, we would be at a loss to understand vanilla in that we would have no grasp of the color or the flavor, nor would we have any means to compare vanilla with chocolate. For the anthropologist, the diversity of humankind provides a colorful basis for understanding any single facet of life or learning in any given individual or community. Among other variables, anthropologists note diversifications in size, shape, language, culture and customs, garb, religion, and worldview.

The Link Between Education and Anthropology

Consider the close link between education and anthropology. Both fields share common roots in their desire to decipher the human experience and our history as a species. Our common interests include, among other things, time, change, creativity, and diversity. Time is a precious commodity. Man is subject to the passing of time. He has attempted to harness time, recording it, and giving it shape and meaning. Time is the tooth that gnaws. Today's educators create curriculum guidelines, and, working against the clock, parcel out time for instruction to prepare for testing and assessment, certification and graduation. How much time is necessary for learning to take place remains a key question. Similarly, change or evolution is key to the anthropologist and to the educator in terms of history, immediacy, and destiny. Jean Baptiste Monet de Lamarck noted that traits are acquired through use and disuse. Simply stated, traits that are not used fall away, and traits that are used develop, thrive, and evolve. In education, effective teaching strategies are preserved, while less effective strategies are discarded. Over time, change and evolution are apparent in physical traits as well as in knowledge and educational processes.

Creativity has its origin in our primate ancestors. They were the ones who began using and later fashioning crude implements in order to simplify their lives. As an emergent species, man retained this ability and through our enhanced brain, imagined and designed better and more useful tools. Education is furthered as a result of imagination and creativity on even the most basic classroom level. At the classroom level, teachers are challenged to work with diverse populations, thus necessitating creative and imaginative approaches to delivering curriculum. New and innovative ideas for presenting information not only keep the course of study interesting for the student but also refresh the material for the educator. As each child comes to the classroom with his own history, belief system, and learning issues, it is inherent in the responsibilities of the teacher to diagnose and prescribe programming ranging from remediation to acceleration. Educating the public is a daunting task. While externally, it may seem that education and anthropology diverge, in application, they function in the same way; to better understand the human condition. Understanding our beginnings in both the anthropological and educational sense is an effective way to enrich our lives. Anthropologists have alerted us as to how our own culture has shaped our lives. To exclude others' cultures from our lives, or the lives of the students being taught, is a detriment to our society. Because our culture is changing and will continue to change, a cross-cultural environment open to curiosity, creativity, diversity, and tolerance is needed in American schools.

Areas of Anthropology

Traditionally, anthropology explores four main areas or branches that focus on how our species evolved and revealed the differing strata of the human experience. The four areas may be classified as: (1) physical or biological, (2) archaeological, (3) cultural or social, and (4) linguistic. With the exception of physical anthropology, anthropology centers on self-initiated human characteristics. A fifth area, (5) is termed *applied anthropology.* Education is one aspect of applied anthropology that delves into the teaching/learning dynamic and is of paramount importance in the schools.

Physical and Biological Anthropology

Physical and biological anthropology supplement one another and assist in the study of our animal origins, evolutionary development, and genetic diversity. It is concerned with understanding the way humans have evolved from their hominid ancestors as well as the extent to which we share genetic characteristics with primates such as the great apes (gorillas and chimpanzees). This branch of anthropology extends to a study of human variations, human nature, and how people adapt to different environments. Of great interest to educators is the attempt to understand the evolution of the brain and the nervous system and how it impacts teaching and learning.

Archaeology

Archaeologists have been able to unearth human artifacts that go back almost 3 million years. From cave dwellers, to ancient Greece, Rome, and Egypt, to 21st-century America, archaeologists analyze, interpret, and evaluate small pieces or fragments of objects to determine their origins and their history. These researchers study cave paintings, pictographs, discarded stone tools, earthenware vessels, religious figurines, and baskets from long ago, many in tatters, remnants of ancient societies. Information gathered is evidence of our past, preceding and complementing the human record written in alphabets and books. Archaeology is of critical importance in the field of resource management and to governments interested in preserving architectural, historical, cultural, and thus, our educational heritage.

Cultural and Social Anthropology

Considered the largest branch of anthropology, cultural and social anthropology, simply stated, seeks to describe and analyze human knowledge, values, and learned traditions that have been passed on from generation to generation by way of words, concepts and symbols. A subdiscipline, termed *ethnography,* is practiced by anthropologists who venture out to observe, compare, and interpret what they see and hear as they study various cultures and societies, resulting in an understanding of behaviors that, on the surface, may seem bizarre or without meaning. Ethnology, a comparative and theoretical branch of anthropology, is concerned with cultures in their traditional forms and in their adaptations to ever-changing conditions in modern society. Dimension is given to hypotheses and theories concerning causes of past and present cultural similarities and differences. Ethnology attempts to describe culture, custom, language, and structures of people and their products. A holistic approach to understanding, ethnology impacts significantly upon education by examining all aspects of the school community as a whole in order to have a global understanding of students' institutional and instructional needs and desires. Moreover, by understanding each culture in its uniqueness, educators may ascertain students' different learning styles based upon their cultural backgrounds. Educators who desire to avoid the tendency to relate foreign customs to preconceptions embedded in their own cultures employ the holistic, multi-variable collective process used by cultural and social anthropologists to understand their diverse school populations. As anthropologists analyze groups in distant settings in terms of material and economic conditions, social organization, intellectual life, and expressive traditions, so do teachers view students in these terms in order to address educational issues that relate to their students. Educators, like anthropologists, view learning in terms of individual process and collective behavior. It can be said that educators and anthropologists have very similar mind-sets. The perspective of anthropologists is to view and define societies as coherent wholes. Likewise, a teacher's goal is to understand and influence individuals so that they may become whole, rational, and productive citizens.

Linguistic Anthropology

Of great import to educators is linguistic anthropology. Language is the hallmark of our species. It is the responsibility of teachers to help transmit information across generations through written and verbal language. It is upon language that culture relies and within language that human knowledge resides. Linguistic anthropology attempts to trace the background of all languages spoken by human beings.

Anthropologists compare language forms and concern themselves with the relationship between the evolution of languages and the evolution of various cultures. Links between societies and contextual use and meanings of verbal concepts shed light on the social and political relationships among people being studied. Linguistic anthropologists work to make associations among language, brain, and behavior. Using their knowledge and insight derived from language study, anthropologists aim to understand the way people perceive, think about, and react to the world in which they live. Educators often behave as sociolinguists to study the social forces inherent in language in order to more successfully instruct African American students who speak Ebonics, Hawaiian students who speak Pigeon, or other students who are learning English as a second language.

Applied Anthropology

Applied anthropology is significant because it utilizes the findings of physical, archaeological, cultural, and linguistic studies to solve practical problems affecting the security, prosperity, health, and education of human beings within cultures. Applied anthropologists strive to discover the general principles of behavior that apply to differing human cultures and communities. From that perspective, education became an academic subfield of anthropology in the 1970s as it applies to different communities and cultures existing within the educational system. For example, students, parents, faculty, and administration represent different communities, and by using anthropological theories, we can understand the current conditions of education and conceive applications for the future. The importance of applied anthropology to education is spotlighted as we gain understanding of classroom dynamics with respect to an increase of diversity, special needs students, and technology in the classroom. Concepts of race, gender, ethnicity, and nationality are especially relevant as students develop their sense of identity as members of groups. These concepts are critical as schools look to deal with conflict and promote positive intergroup relations. As anthropologists cut across disciplinary boundaries and question conventional wisdom, educators also cut across curricular boundaries to make relevant connections in order for students to achieve an understanding of and an appreciation for the human experience. With insight extracted from anthropologists, education and anthropology work together to alleviate behavioral difficulties, dropout rates, violence, and other negative influences that potentially impact upon the school, and ultimately, the individual.

Education cannot be reduced to simple information processing and the classification of knowledge. The objective of education is to assist learners to construct meaning. Making meaning requires an understanding of the prevailing culture, whether the subject is literature, social studies, or science. Effective education is based upon positive social interaction among all those involved in the school community. Teachers who build their practice on anthropological understandings and methodologies will leverage this knowledge to improve student attitude and achievement.

Value of Anthropology to Education

The classroom environment is a microcosm of the larger society. There, students are active learners and participators within a framework of rules, codes, beliefs, and ethics. Teachers act like anthropologists in that they are asked to understand the "internal logic" of the classroom society. Teachers who develop an anthropological outlook foster a cooperative environment where students' similarities and differences are accepted and their interdependence is recognized. The anthropological societies established by teachers embrace their diverse members and manifest the sharing of ideas, experiences, theories, discoveries, and expertise. Teachers arm students with global information and thinking skills critical to following various career paths to success in 21st-century business, research, teaching, advocacy, and public service.

With this in mind, the connections between education and anthropology become extremely important, and the fields bear more in common than might be realized. Key skills that are taught and refined in the study of anthropology are germane to the study of education. These include seeking multiple perspectives, rational speculation, dialogue, scientific inquiry, analytical reading, data collection, comparing and contrasting, testing hypotheses, and applying theories. Attention is given to research methodology, logic and reasoning, detailed record keeping, and clear thinking. Notably, the analytical categories and processes that are used to understand tribal and small-scale societies can be useful in understanding the culture of schoolchildren and undergraduate students.

Anthropology has been applied to education dating back more than a century, when Hewett published his thoughts on education in the *American Anthropologist.* However, the connection between education and anthropology remains a relatively new frontier. To some degree, historically, the education profession revised old programs and practices, renewing and renaming them, and implementing them in what had been hoped to be a new way. A more anthropological approach to change is to study the old programs and practices in light of their relative success, break old molds, design innovations, and implement new and revolutionary practice based on the research. Clearly, this approach precludes that it is the responsibility of the educator to teach social skills and to interact with cultural and ethnic groups other than their own. In turn, this will allow students to study in collaborative situations leading to social acceptance, self-discovery, and the ability to take risks within the learning environment. More and more, education and anthropology aspire to similar goals and utilize similar methods of research and discovery.

Mutual Goals Promote Diversity

One area of anthropological research that has had great impact on education and inspired great innovation is seen in the programs that have recently been incorporated in American schools to celebrate human diversity, multiculturalism, and ethnicity. Strides have been made not only in the way that we teach children about ethnicity and diversity but also in the way we instruct children from other cultures. One excellent example is in a New Jersey high school where a program was developed by the school counselor to inform students and staff about human rights and tolerance. As a student advocate, the counselor created a six-page booklet concerning diversity within the school. A tolerance and diversity committee was formed, resulting in attention to Human Rights Week, Martin Luther King's birthday, Black History Month, Women in History Month, and workshops on "Critical Issues." Nonetheless, research continues to reveal statistical data, case studies, and analyses of how many Black and other minority students have become underachievers in the American educational system.

The complexity of humanity directs anthropologists and educators to work in concert. Equipped with a satchel of scientific and academic armaments, professionals are prepared to crack the smallest kernel of misinformation. Together, anthropologists and enlightened educators deploy devices such as scientific inquiry and logic and creative reasoning to go about "solving" the problems that we face in our lives, studies, and classrooms. A huge mutual goal is to determine how we can consistently and successfully manipulate such tools, challenging America's youth and changing how American youth process their inherent positions and perceptions. A typical United States public school classroom houses many nationalities. It is of utmost importance to educate all students to understand differences: cultural, socioeconomic, psychographic and demographic. By expanding the horizons of our students, we are likely to invest in the notion that we are all different despite not being similar in appearance, ability, or possessions.

Prejudice and ethnocentrism are the products of fear caused by a lack of knowledge and lack of understanding of differences. These conditions have shaped society. Throughout the ages, an attitude of "banish or perish" has launched attacks of humanity upon humanity. In the middle of the 20th century, the development of third-world countries was seen as a precursor to positive interethnic relations. Melting-pot theorists predicted that as poor nations advanced in their development, ethnicity would become obsolete and peace would follow. This view was challenged by conflictual modernization theory, and development was seen for a time as a cause of conflict. As the world approached the 21st century, development was again considered to be a precondition for peace. Today, bias, prejudice, bigotry, conflict, and ethnocentrism continue to contaminate society, and these hazards trickle down into the classroom.

The teaching of scientific inquiry, therefore, is significant when students learn to question circumstances and problems as they arise. Students need be taught to question and respond profoundly, beyond transactional or procedural questions or the typical short answers to teachers' questions. It is suggested that a learner's questions identify both naive and complex thinking as they focus either on conceptualizations or minutiae and detail. Helping children to question situations may make a student successful, but bringing students to understand that different people think of different ways to question is the greater lesson. This lesson brings with it an appreciation that people of other ethnicities and cultures may bring drastically different questions to bear on a given situation. Situations of small or large consequence may be solved collaboratively and skillfully when participants accept and appreciate the contributions of others.

Charles Darwin

Charles Darwin recalled his father once telling him, "You care for nothing but shooting dogs and rat-catching, and you will be a disgrace to yourself and all your family." It was an inauspicious indictment of one of history's greatest thinkers. Born in 1809 in Shrewsbury, England, young Darwin did poorly in a traditional school setting and preferred to collect specimens of animals, plants, and minerals that he would experiment upon in his brother's chemical laboratory. He was, by today's definition, a hands-on, tactile-kinesthetic learner. At age 16, with urging from his father, Darwin entered the School of Medicine at Edinburgh University, where he found lectures boring, cadaver dissections horrible, and surgeries, without benefit of anesthesia, gruesome. After graduation, the reluctant Darwin enrolled in Cambridge with the notion of becoming a clergyman. While at Cambridge, Darwin was inspired by the "personal narrative" of Alexander von Humboldt, the German, who wrote about his travels in South America and his discoveries in geology, geography, and mineralogy.

Having been invited to set sail on HMS *Beagle*, a frigate designed for scientific research, Darwin embarked on a 5-year expedition to chart the coastlines of South America. Onboard ship, he read intently and was influenced greatly by the geological systems described by Charles Lyell. The *Beagle* reached Brazil in February 1832, and Darwin began to answer the call of the wild. He spent months observing and collecting plants, animals, minerals and fossils and keeping careful and detailed records of his discoveries. Moreover, he was astounded to find marine fossils high in the Andes Mountains, thus hypothesizing that the land had once been covered by water. Earthquakes in Chile, experienced by Darwin, satisfied his belief that the earth's topography is always changing. Subsequently, arriving in the Galapagos Islands, Darwin discovered many life forms that were not found anywhere else in the world. He was intrigued by the numerous species of birds found there, and he noticed how various species of finch had developed specialized beaks that aided them in gathering and consuming food. Darwin further noted that organisms on the island seemed similar, yet different, from those on the mainland.

From his experiences on HMS *Beagle,* Charles Darwin began to question the idea of creationism and the belief that a supreme god created immutable organisms to populate the unchanging world. He used the comparative method to challenge concepts, introduce new facts and values, and construct his extraordinary evolutionary framework. In brief, all living things compete for space and sustenance while being constantly challenged by threats from their changing environment. Later, in *On the Origin of Species* (1859), Darwin explained his theory of natural selection as "grounded in the belief that each new variety, and ultimately each new species is produced and maintained by having some advantage over those with which it comes into competition; and the consequent extinction of the less-favored forms almost inevitably follows." Essentially, he implied that all life on earth, including human life, is the result of evolution over millions of years of adaptations to changing environments. Darwin concluded, "having been originally breathed by the Creator into a few forms or into one, and that, whilst this planet has gone cycling on according to the fixed laws of gravity, from simple a beginning endless forms most beautiful and most wonderful have been, and are being evolved."

Darwin and Education

Charles Darwin saw the magnificence of all living things, including man, and his theory impels us to respect one another despite any or all differences. The convergence of Darwin's evolutionary framework points to the precarious position of our species and the essential need for mutual respect, global understanding, and planetary interdependence. As a species, we are constantly competing for space and sustenance. Opposing forces such as insurrection, disease, poverty, ethnocentrism, and racism threaten us. Shifts in the environment, climatic changes, depletion of natural resources, and pollution challenge us. For these reasons, we must come together as one unified, diversified species, evolved from a common ancestor and aware of the interconnectiveness of the global society.

Educators have been influenced profoundly by Charles Darwin, his research, his methodologies, and his theories. Far from being a disgrace, in the 200 years since his birth, Darwin has become a model of optimism, unification, and hope for the future as we look ahead through his penetrating eyes. Darwin tells us: "It is a world of wonderful similarity and change among all living things; where the tiniest flea is directly, organically related to the most massive elephant; where the struggle and even death make for progressive evolution in which good useful characteristics develop to benefit every species." Thanks to Darwin, present-day teachers respect the similarities and differences in their students more than ever and view them as an "evolving species," which will grow and develop into productive adults. Teachers also consider themselves to be an "evolving species," capable of adapting teaching styles and strategies to meet the diverse needs and desires of their students. Through the intersection of education and anthropology, humanity has its greatest hope of survival as we advance scientifically, morally, philosophically, technologically, and academically.

Darwin and Dewey

In the same year that Charles Darwin published his seminal work, *On the Origin of Species,* John Dewey (1859–1952) was born into a Burlington, Vermont, family. Son of a Civil War veteran and an evangelical congregationalist mother, Dewey grew to become the most influential philosopher of modern times. His influence is most viable in political and educational forums. The founder and renowned "father of progressive education," Dewey built his philosophy around his own life experiences as well as the emerging philosophy and scientific thought of the times.

Upon graduation from the University of Vermont in 1879 and unsure of his future, John Dewey was tutored in philosophy for 3 years while he earned his living as a high school teacher. He then applied to and matriculated at Johns Hopkins University for graduate work. Studying under George Sylvester Morris, who followed Hegelian philosophy, Dewey wrote his dissertation on Hegelian idealism and earned his PhD in 1884. In time, Dewey rejected absolute idealism, which suggested that fact and thought are connected in that facts develop from thought. However, Dewey evolved a more naturalistic, pragmatic philosophy that was refined and supremely influenced by the works of Charles Darwin. Darwin's theory of natural selection provided a form for Dewey's naturalistic approach to the theory of knowledge. *On the Origin of Species* introduced a mode of thinking that would ultimately transform the logic of knowledge and hence the treatment of morals, politics, religion, and education. Rejecting supernatural explanations for the origins of species, Dewey adopted Darwin's naturalistic account and then considered the development

of knowledge as an adaptive response (i.e., the product of the interaction between man and his environment). Dewey saw knowledge as having a practical instrumentality in the dominion and administration of that interaction. He termed his new philosophical approach "instrumentalism." Clearly stated, if problems are constantly changing, then the instruments for dealing with problems must change. It follows, then, that if truth is evolutionary in nature, it does not have an eternal reality.

The influence of Charles Darwin on John Dewey's philosophy of education was immeasurable. In his own practice, Dewey taught at the University of Minnesota and then at the University of Michigan. He achieved greatness as chairman of the department of philosophy, psychology, and pedagogy at the University of Chicago. He became president of the American Psychological Association in 1889 and the president of the Philosophical Association at Columbia University from 1905 until his retirement in 1930.

John Dewey's philosophy of education has had far-reaching effects on teaching and learning. His pragmatist stance suggested that schools should prepare individuals for participation in community life and overcome barriers between school and community to provide education that satisfies the needs of a truly participatory democracy. Dewey favored practice over theory, based on his belief that learning best occurs when students are free to generate their own experiments, experiences, questions, and creations. He believed that under the direction and guidance of a good teacher, children could learn ways to cope with situations and conditions that might occur in the unpredictable future. Dewey believed strongly that schools should take on societal responsibilities. He was convinced that acculturation of immigrants was the responsibility of the schools. Therefore, like Darwin, Dewey showed respect for diversity and saw individuals as valuable contributors to society.

In 1896, John Dewey established laboratory schools where he highlighted the scientific method for problem solving and where students, in workshop settings, took ownership of their own learning. The role of the teacher was that of facilitator, not director or instructor, designers of educational experiences that guided learning through doing in areas of children's real interests. Dewey's pedagogy contrasted sharply with traditional teacher-centered methods of isolation, study, and recitation. Dewey's theories became very popular. However, progressive education began to take on tangential forms. Dewey's Laboratory School in Chicago and Manhattan's The Lincoln School both closed primarily because progressive education was misinterpreted and secondarily because the cold war advanced conservatism and the rigorous study of math and science. Today, applications of the progressive movement are flourishing in many American schools as well as international schools, and action research, open classrooms, schools without walls, multiage groupings, looping, block scheduling, and cooperative learning are integrated forms of this movement. Emphasis on multiculturalism, hands-on learning, and participation in authentic learning experiences with real-world audiences reflect the pedagogical contributions of John Dewey. Notably, as Darwin inspired Dewey, so have Dewey's contributions inspired other movements of import to education (contextualism, empiricism, humanism, and naturalism). A study of Deweyan philosophy is especially relevant in the postmodern age as we come to terms with immigration, globalization, and extensive cultural diversity. Clearly, Dewey stands with Darwin as one of the greatest thinkers of our time.

Vygotsky

In 1896, when John Dewey was opening the laboratory schools where group work was fostered as a meaningful way to learn, another teacher was born in present-day Belarus, a place that would later become part of the Union of Socialist Soviet Republics. A Russian educational psychologist, Lev Semenovich Vygotsky was recognized early on to be a brilliant and original thinker, and his novel ideas about teaching and learning were respected by the intelligentsia within the Soviet Union. Vygotsky spent his short life in Marxist Russia, but his theories did not conform to communist ideology. The Soviet government banned the publication of Vygotsky's work after his untimely death from tuberculosis in 1934. Unfortunately, Vygotsky's work remained in obscurity until his books were printed in the West during the 1960s.

Vygotsky's views on teaching and learning are founded on the premise that human intelligence is not a fixed characteristic, but instead, it is a dynamic entity that can be enhanced by social interaction and collaborative work. Central to Vygotsky's views on learning is the belief that knowledge is not directly transferable from teacher to learner. Rather, through social interaction, the learner constructs his or her own meaning. This constitutes the theoretical basis for cooperative learning, a method that has now found favor throughout the United States, Canada, and other countries around the world. To comprehend Vygotsky's views as they relate to cooperative learning, it is necessary to understand his concept of the zone of proximal development (ZPD). The ZPD may be described as the dynamic range of intelligence that characterizes any individual. If we were to envision two concentric circles, or double rings, then the large space in the center of the inner ring would represent an individual's current developmental ability to solve a problem while working alone. This area or zone may be likened to what would be measured by an intelligence test. The space between the first and second rings represents where an individual solves a problem when being guided or coached by a more capable peer or a teacher. This, according to Vygotsky, represents the ZPD. As individuals solve problems with assistance, this zone is expanded, and another ring encircles and defines a new ZPD. What did lie within the original zone of proximal development has been subsumed into the initial, and now expanded, current developmental level of abilities (the enlarged center of the circle) and is encircled by a new and enlarged ZPD. Naturally, there are problems that cannot be solved despite the best help from others, and some tasks lie outside of the individual's current zone of development. However, those tasks remain proximate and may be learned with more experience, or they may be found to be unattainable.

Cooperative Learning

When assigning problems for cooperative-learning groups to solve, it is essential that they be within students' ZPD. If the task is too simple, then it poses no challenge to the group. The work could be done independently and so does little to enhance intelligence. A task that is too complex for any member of the group lies outside the boundaries of the ZPD and cannot be solved with any amount of appropriate assistance. In that situation, all the students would be functioning at the frustration level. Ideally, tasks should be assigned at the outermost area of the ZPD for the most capable students in the group, where everyone on the team may be challenged to produce a solution to the problem. The newly discovered knowledge is shared within the group, and each group member constructs meaning according to his or her understanding of the information. In this manner, all team members increase their zones of actual development and their ZPDs. Continual expansion of the ZPD is accomplished by a process that is often termed "scaffolding." Scaffolding involves reaching out and sometimes down to assist another member of the group to broaden his or her level of understanding. Through scaffolding, students are able to accomplish more complex assignments as the ZPD evolves and expands.

Undoubtedly, cooperative-learning classes are progressive, and students are encouraged to interact, share experiences, and participate in their own learning. In effective cooperative-learning settings, thought is continually being expressed through language, and students are engaged in a social-constructivist process, creating concepts through conversation. Teachers fill the role of facilitator, circulating among the learners to provide assistance as needed. Cooperative-learning classes minimize the time that students spend sitting passively and taking notes while their teacher solves problems for them. Conversely, cooperative-learning classes maximize the time that students spend interacting with others to solve problems for themselves. A sense of optimism, hope, and power is infused in Vygotskian theory when we realize that what children can do with assistance today, they can do independently tomorrow. It remains uncertain whether Dewey influenced Vygotsky directly, yet their philosophies of education are compatible and are found at the heart of anthropological and educational thought and practice.

Howard Gardner

A prominent leader in the field of education and brain research, Howard Gardner extensively investigated and documented cross-cultural studies on human intelligence. Gardner employs anthropological methods, and his research reflects a respect for science, the value of experience, and an acceptance of change that was intrinsic in the work of Charles Darwin, John Dewey, and Lev Vygotsky. Currently a psychologist and professor at Harvard University School of Education, Howard Gardner developed the theory of multiple intelligences. In *Frames of Mind*, published in 1983, Gardner theorized that there are seven equally important components of intelligence. In 1999, two additional components of intelligence were introduced in *Intelligence Reframed*, and recently Gardner revealed a ninth intelligence.

Traditionally, intelligence has been seen as cognitive capacity, established at birth, "fixed" and uniform across a lifetime. Like Dewey and Vygotsky, Gardner disputes that intelligence is fixed, and his research illustrates that individuals exhibit unique variations of intelligence. If we were asked who is most intelligent—William Shakespeare, Albert Einstein, Salvador Dali, Condoleezza Rice, Jesse Owens, Igor Stravinsky, or H. James Birx—we would be prone to name Shakespeare or Einstein. Our own thinking, however, tells us that all of the individuals listed are geniuses in their respective fields, and they exhibit superior mental abilities in the areas of language, mathematics, art, leadership, athletics, music, and philosophical anthropology. Inappropriately, intelligence was and continues to be measured in terms of verbal-linguistic and logical-mathematical concepts. Most schools test students' competencies through the administration of short-answer standardized tests. Often, students qualify or fail to qualify for gifted programs on the basis of these largely verbal and mathematical scores. Howard Gardner suggests that educators broaden their traditional and narrow conception of giftedness.

Gardner conducted his research through intensive interviews and in-depth analyses of the brain function of hundreds of subjects including stroke victims, prodigies, autistic individuals, and individuals who are classified under the heading of "autistic savant." While involved in Harvard University's Project Zero, Gardner studied the cognitive development of average, gifted, and brain-damaged children. As a result, Howard Gardner views intelligence as consisting of three specific components: (1) ability to invent a useful product or offer a service that is valued within a culture, (2) skill to solve real-life problems, and (3) potential to find or postulate new problems for consideration in the light of new knowledge.

Multiple Intelligences

Gardner delineates his theory of pluralistic intelligence into what are, at this point in time, nine ways of knowing. Criteria for identifying the existence of an intelligence is grounded in neuroanatomy, developmental psychology, cognitive psychology, and anthropology. An intelligence, therefore, has a developmental pattern and a base in the physiology of the brain; it is ignited by stimuli native to the particular intelligence, and it depicts ideas in a universally symbolic manner, as with music, words, or formulae. To date, Gardner has revealed nine intelligences, of which two, intra-personal intelligence and interpersonal intelligence, are person related. Four others, mathematical-logical, visual-spatial, naturalist, and bodily-kinesthetic intelligences, are object related in that they are activated by objects in the environment. Verbal-linguistic, musical-rhythmic, and existentialist intelligences are not connected to objects.

Howard Gardner hypothesizes that individuals are born with and possess a unique compilation of all nine intelligences, which may be strengthened through experience and effort. Realistically, students learn more readily when instruction is geared to their strongest intelligences. Gardner's understandings have had an immediate and dramatic effect on how curriculum is designed and delivered. Educators are internalizing a more flexible perception of intellectual development, and they are striving to incorporate some of the intelligences into each of their lessons as entry points to facilitate learning. Teachers who construct brain-compatible classrooms anticipate future findings resulting from the research of Howard Gardner and others who realize that intelligence is definitely not fixed at birth.

Looking to the Future

Anthropology is both a mirror and a window for education. The mirror reflects our common humanity: our wants, our needs, our desires, our conflicts, and our resolutions. Anthropology reflects the human condition and offers the tools to ensure our survival as a species. The window opens to the future. Through science and technology, the world is becoming increasingly more interconnected. The "global village" is experiencing the migration of people around the world. In the centuries to come, anthropology will continue to be relevant to education due to man's acute curiosity about cultural differences. New directions will be taken as educators stay abreast of all the research that impacts upon their pedagogy. Overall, it is evident that taking a holistic anthropological approach to education has greatly benefited in the improvement of students in terms of academic achievement. It allows educators to look at all aspects of teaching and learning in a critical manner and to adjust or change methods as needed.

Both anthropologists and educators enthusiastically welcome change. Instead of debating the legitimacy of their theories, they progress. As researchers, they are task specific, and they anticipate the further evolution of science and technology, psychology, and neuropsychology. Educators are cognizant of the impact that Charles Darwin has had upon science and education down through the generations. John Dewey said that Darwin's influence on philosophy came from having conquered the phenomena of life for the principle of transition, thereby freeing us to apply logic to "mind and morals and life." The new logic inspired Dewey to invest in schools as centers for social responsibility and interaction, thus providing the intersection of education and anthropology. Darwin's understanding of the earth and its populations to be ever evolving and never fixed in nature underlies the philosophies of Lev Vygotsky and Howard Gardner. It stands to reason that if man evolves, then his intelligence will evolve and expand through experience. Vygotsky based his notion of the ZPD on the theory that an individual's zone of actual development can be enlarged by working with others. Gardner, in developing his theory of multiple intelligences, recognized the new logic inspired by Darwin when he defined nine equally important components of dynamic intelligence.

As we look into the future and the possibility of life on other planets, both educators and anthropologists will have to develop a wider cosmic perspective of culture that will engulf our current earthly perspective. Differences among earth's peoples will be trivialized, and all traces of anthropocentric conceits will evaporate as we encounter the rise of comparative exoevolution. *Exovolution* is a term coined by H. James Birx, to "complement the notion of exobiology, which is the search for the existence of life elsewhere in this universe." Birx theorizes that if exobiology exists, then exoevolution exists also. It is incumbent upon us to develop what Birx terms an attitude of dynamic integrity as we actively aspire to understand the enormity of the universe and our relatively miniscule role as agents of change. As we develop creatively and grow intellectually, we become living evidence of the evolutionary process. As agents of change, anthropologists and educators can affect our small but colorful world. It is advances in education that will guide our species as it further evolves on earth and among the stars.

— *Suzanne E. D'Amato*

See also **Darwin, Charles; Dewey, John; Vygotsky, Lev Semenovich**

Further Readings

Birx, H. J. (1991). *Interpreting evolution.* Amherst, New York: Prometheus Books.

Bruner, J. (1999). *The culture of education.* Cambridge, MA: Harvard University Press.

Darwin, F. (Ed.). (1958). *Autobiography of Charles Darwin and selected letters.* New York: Dover.

Dewey, J. (1956). *The child and the curriculum* and *the school and society* (Combined ed.). Chicago: University of Chicago Press.

Gardner, H. (1993). *Multiple intelligences: Theory in practice.* New York: Basic Books.

Ianni, F., & Storey, E. (1993). *Cultural relevance and educational issues: Readings in anthropology and education.* Boston: Little, Brown.

Lee, C., & Smagorinsky, P. (Eds.). (2000). *Vygotskian Perspectives on literacy research: Constructing meaning through collaborative inquiry.* Cambridge, UK, New York: Cambridge University Press.

Ornstein, A. C., & Levine D. U. (2003). *Foundations of education.* New York: Houghton Mifflin.

Schumar, W. (2004). Making strangers at home: Anthropologists studying higher education. *The Journal of Higher Education, 75*(1).

EGYPT, ANCIENT

Ancient Egyptian civilization lasted from approximately 3000 BC until the date of the last known hieroglyphic inscription in 395 AD. Though many cultures invaded and at times ruled Egypt, its character survived largely the same until the Roman Period, and many aspects of ancient Egyptian civilization remained through the Coptic Period. Egypt did not attain international prominence until the time of the Old Kingdom (ca. 2686–2125 BC) and increased in power until its height of the New Kingdom (ca. 1550–1069 BC), when its empire stretched from present-day Sudan to the Euphrates River and eastern Turkey. The fortunes of Egypt have always been intertwined with the Nile River and its canals, along with expeditions to gain precious resources in remote neighboring regions.

Egyptology as a discipline did not fully develop until Jean-François Champollion's decipherment of ancient Egyptian in 1822, and since then, it has dealt with all aspects of ancient Egypt, including language and literature, architecture, archaeology, art, and overall historical developments. Major finds, such as the tomb of Tutankhamun, the workmen's village at Giza, and, more recently, the origins of the alphabet have fueled public interest in Egyptology and the field as a whole. With archaeologists and historians making great discoveries every year, the perceptions of key issues in ancient Egyptian civilization continue to change.

History of Egyptology

Ancient Egypt has never been completely lost to the world, and the concept of its rediscovery is largely through Western eyes. It remained a popular place to visit during Roman times, with many items on the ancient itinerary remaining the same today, including the pyramid fields and the ancient capital city of Memphis. Numerous pilgrims visited St. Catherine's monastery, in South Sinai, during medieval and crusader times. Many early Muslim scholars held ancient Egypt in high regard and wrote treatises on its language and architecture. Though largely incorrect, these papers give insights into the importance of ancient Egypt long after its hieroglyphic system of language went out of use.

European crusaders returned with many stories of their travels, inspiring others to take the same journey to see the wonders of the ancient Near East. The idea of the pyramids as the "granaries of Joseph" has its origins in the writings of Julias Honorus and Rufinus, as well as a 12th-century depiction in one of the domes of St. Mark's Cathedral in Venice. This and other tales renewed interest in the history of the pagans during the Renaissance. With the creation of the printing press and increased protection for travelers after Egypt fell under Turkish Ottoman rule in 1517, travelers soon became antiquarians, collecting artifacts and manuscripts for libraries and museums.

Egyptology has its roots in the Napoleonic expedition to Egypt in 1798, when Napoleon's army, accompanied by engineers, draftsmen, artists, botanists, and archaeologists, mapped the whole of Egypt. Along with documenting modern and ancient Egypt, they collected artifacts and specimens over a 3-year period and produced a series of volumes entitled the *Description de L'Egypte.* With Champollion's decipherment of hieroglyphs and increasing interest in

Source: Courtesy, Wikipedia.

the culture of ancient Egypt, numerous collectors flocked to Egypt, including Henry Salt, Giovanni Belzoni, and Bernardo Drovetti, all of whom contributed to the growing collections of the British Museum, in London; the Musée de Louvre, in Paris; and Museo Egitzio, in Turin.

Archaeological expeditions increased in frequency as well, with investigations led by Auguste Mariette, Gaston Maspero, and Eduard Naville. William Mathews Flinders Petrie, considered by many to be the father of Egyptian archaeology, pioneered detailed recording methods in the late 19th and early 20th centuries. American and European scholars conducted numerous other studies, and Egyptology experienced increased interest after the discovery in 1922 of a virtually intact tomb of a relatively minor 18th dynasty pharaoh, Tutankhamun, in the Valley of the Kings, in Luxor, by Howard Carter and his patron, the Earl of Canarvon. Today, over 400 foreign expeditions work in Egypt alongside many local excavations, under the auspices of the Supreme Council for Egyptian Antiquities.

Geography

Egypt is characterized by the Nile river floodplain between harsh desert lands composing its eastern and western frontiers. Long considered the breadbasket of the ancient world, Egypt relied upon Nile floods to sustain its agricultural economy. Even during ancient times, Egyptians called their country *kemet,* meaning "black land," referring to the rich silts deposited annually by the Nile inundation. The harsh desert world, dominated by chaos and inhabited by liminal creatures, was known as *deshret,* or "red land." The interplay of the dual concepts of black land and red land, order and chaos, symbolize parts of ancient Egyptian religion and mythology.

The Nile River is 6,670 km long and covers 34 degrees of latitude, from 2 degrees south of the equator to 32 degrees north in Egypt's delta, and then drains into the Mediterranean. The waters of the Nile come from Lake Tana in the Ethiopian plateau (at 1,830 m elevation) and Lake Victoria in East Africa's lake district (at 1,134 m elevation). These lakes connect to the Blue and White Nile basins in sub-Saharan Africa and before the phases of Aswan high dam construction (in the early 1900s and 1960s) relied on annual monsoon rainfalls to fill these basins for good flood levels. Higher flood levels meant a good harvest, good fishing, and better grass for grazing. Floods were so important to the ancient Egyptians that they connected the annual flood to the religious myth of the wandering eye of the sun, which told the story of the goddess Hathor bringing annual inundation waters from the south. The rise and fall of different aspects of ancient Egypt are also closely connected to flood levels. Predynastic material culture first starts to appear after a period of high then low floods around 4,200 BC to 4,000 BC. The end of the Old Kingdom was potentially connected with a series of disastrous flood years followed by drought. Ancient Egyptians measured flood levels by a series of Nilometers, several of which survive to this day.

The eastern and western deserts represent outside areas with many mines and trade routes. The eastern desert has many mines, including alabaster and quartzite quarries, and numerous rock inscriptions. The western desert contains the oases of Dakhla, Farafra, Kharga, and Bahiriyah, which contain important trading settlements and outposts guarding the western desert from invading forces. Sinai represents an important region for copper and turquoise mining at Serabit el-Khadim and Wadi Magahra, while north

Sinai existed as part of the "Way of Horus," an ancient fortification route connecting Egypt to Syria-Palestine.

History and Chronology

An Egyptian priest named Manetho in the 3rd century BC divided ancient Egypt into 30 dynasties, which current Egyptologists generally retain in their historical analyses. Though this method of dating continues, it is slightly passé with current discoveries in ancient Egyptian chronology and the utilization of radiocarbon dating. More emphasis has been placed on socioeconomic trends and less on political events. Periods are no longer understood only in historical events, but in terms of material culture shifts. Three approaches mark the way in which Egyptologists deal with ancient Egyptian chronology, which include relative dating methods (such as seriation with pottery or coffins, or stratigraphic phases), absolute chronologies (including astronomical and calendrical events in ancient texts), and radiometric methods (radiocarbon dating and thermoluminescence).

A unified Egyptian state did not appear until 3200 BC, but it had its origins in the preceding Naqada culture, which lasted from about 4000 BC to 3200 BC and lay to the north of present-day Luxor. Petrie found 3,000 graves dating to the Naqada I Period. They represented simple burials in pits with wooden or ceramic coffins. The Naqada II Period saw an increase in funerary offerings, as well as painted pottery, showing the early development of ancient Egyptian art and artisans. During the Naqada III Period, Egypt unified into a large state with major political consolidation, and there were increases in cereal production with improvements in the irrigation system. The unification between Upper and Lower Egypt took place through a combination of warfare and alliances, yet throughout ancient Egyptian history, an emphasis was placed on the divided nature of the country, with one of pharaoh's titles being "King of Upper and Lower Egypt." Important artifacts showing warfare and kingship around the time of unification include the Narmer Palette and Macehead, and early international relations can be seen at tomb U-j at Umm el-Qa'ab, Abydos, with 40 imported jars, possibly from Palestine.

Egypt's early dynastic state emerged about 3200 BC, with Memphis as an important political center and Abydos as a central cult center. Though evidence for some early cities survives, most of Egypt would have existed as small settlements during this time. Basin irrigation gave way to large state-controlled irrigation, allowing for increased crop growth. Writing was introduced during this time, used in art, administration, and for the economy, and the iconography of power and kingship developed as well. Cult centers linked towns and regions, while the tombs of the Dynasty 1 kings developed in form and function at Abydos. Archaeologists discovered early body preservation techniques at Saqqara, with an increase of the use of wooden coffins seen at the end of Dynasty 2. Taxation and increase of state power led to more expeditions being sent to Nubia, Sinai, Palestine, and the Eastern Desert for acquisition of goods. This led to a formalization of the bureaucratic structure that formed the basis of Egyptian society for much of its history.

Egypt's Old Kingdom (Dynasties 3–6) did not differ much politically from the early dynastic period, with the royal residence still located at Memphis, yet architectural innovations reveal the overall growth and consolidation of state power. The construction of Djoser's step pyramid complex at Saqqara and the development of the true pyramids at Giza, Medium, and Abusir demonstrate the internal organization and power of kingship needed to effectively join its people and resources. Artisans, scribes, architects, and skilled laborers became essential parts of ancient Egypt's societal fabric, and religion developed, with royal mortuary cults and increasing importance of the god Ra. Nomes began at the start of the Old Kingdom and divided the country into regional administrative units, with 22 nomes in Upper Egypt and 20 nomes in Lower Egypt led by nomarchs, or regional governors. A breakdown in royal administration with the 94-year rule of Pepy II (ca. 2278–2184 BC) and growth in the power held by the nomarchs led to the "collapse" of the Old Kingdom, as well as important environmental factors, including a period of drought.

The following First Intermediate Period (ca. 2160–2055 BC), Dynasties 7/8 to mid-11, represents a time of political upheaval and unrest in ancient Egypt. The royal residence shifted from Memphis in the north to Herakleopolis in central Egypt, with an opposing band of rulers emerging at Thebes in the south. Although the overall political structure may have changed, development took place on a local level, with tombs, pottery, funerary models, and mummy masks. War raged between the Theban and Herakleopolitans (who connected themselves to the Memphite court traditions) for control of Egypt, with local rulers taking the place of pharaohs for care of

Deir el-Bahri

their people. The Theban "royalty" took over the Herakleopolitans stronghold at Asyut, followed by their capital at Herakleopolis, and thus the beginning of the Middle Kingdom and late Dynasty 11.

While late Dynasty 11 ruled from Thebes, the court of the 12th Dynasty and the first half of Dynasty 13 moved to the Fayoum in the period known as the Middle Kingdom (ca. 2055–1656 BC). Known as the "renaissance" period in ancient Egyptian history, the Middle Kingdom had many developments in art, architecture, and religion. Nebhepetre Montuhotep II (ca. 2055–2004 BC) reunited Egypt and increased construction projects, including his mortuary temple at Deir el-Bahri and developments in art, and dispatched commercial expeditions once again into Sinai and Nubia. His son, Mentuhotep III, sent the first Middle Kingdom expedition to Punt (eastern Sudan and Eritria) for incense. In Dynasty 12, the capital moved to Ijtawy, near the Fayoum, under the reign of Amenemhet I, to administer a reunited southern and northern Egypt. The government became more centralized, with a growth in bureaucracy and in town organization. Osiris became an increasingly important god, and mummification became more widespread.

In the succeeding Second Intermediate Period (ca. 1650–1550 BC), Egypt divided into two kingdoms, with the capital in the Fayoum moving to Thebes (southern Egypt), while an Asiatic kingdom (The Hyksos) arose in the Delta through graduated migration, settlement, and some invasions in the east. Evidence exists for a widespread Asiatic (Hyksos) material culture in Lebanon, Syria, Palestine, and Cyprus, as early as the Middle Kingdom. They ruled from Avaris in the eastern Delta during Dynasties 14 and 15, while a rival Egyptian kingdom (Dynasties 16 and 17) ruled from Thebes. The Hyksos controlled northern Egypt from the Delta to Hermopolis, with Cusae in Middle Egypt marking the southern frontier. Military might grew again in Thebes, with the ruler Kamose controlling the gold routes to Nubia and incorporating mercenaries into his army. Kamose began a 30-year war against the Hyksos, continued by his son Ahmose, who attacked Tell el-Hebua (the eastern military headquarters) and then Avaris, to drive out the Hyksos for good.

Ahmose initiated the New Kingdom (ca. 1550–1069 BC), a period of great renewal and international involvement. The New Kingdom saw additional military action and colonization in Nubia, and campaigns to the Euphrates River in Syria under Thutmose I. These campaigns intensified under Thutmose III, who consolidated Egypt's empire in the Levant. Improvement in mummification occurred, and the Valley of

Deir el-Medina

the Kings became the location for royal burials. The village of Deir el-Medina housed the workmen for the Valley of the Kings. Karnak temple and the cult of Amun-Re grew in size and prominence during the reign of Hatshepsut, daughter of Thutmose I; she built her famous mortuary temple at Deir el-Bahri. Additional military successes in Nubia and Syria-Palestine brought additional wealth pouring into Egypt's coffers, allowing Amenhotep III to build on unprecedented levels during his reign. His son Amenhotep IV, or Akhenaten, broke away from a polytheistic religious tradition to found a new capital city at Tell el-Amarna, in Middle Egypt, and implemented a worship of primarily one god: the Aten (the sun's disk). This move and religious shift affected cultural and religious traditions for a long period of time. Tutankhamun moved the capital back to Memphis, reinstated the cults of other gods, and returned Thebes and the cult of Amun to their positions of prominence. Late Dynasty 19 and 20 represented the Ramesside Period, during which Seti I built new temples and conducted several large military campaigns against a new enemy, the Hittite empire. Ramses II led campaigns as well, and built a new capital at Pi-Ramses in the eastern Delta. Egypt's Levantine empire and other

east Mediterranean cultures fell to a mass migration of Sea Peoples, sea raiders, and displaced refugees, with Ramses III saving Egypt from invasion. Egypt declined slowly under Ramses IV through XI, losing its empire, power, prestige, and cultural unity.

Foreign incursions and economic weakening led to civil war, and the start of the Third Intermediate Period (ca. 1069–664 BC). When the viceroy of Kush (governor of Nubia) invaded Egypt, Dynasty 21 began in the north at Tanis under Smendes (ca. 1069–1043 BC), while the high priest at Thebes effectively ruled in southern Egypt, albeit acknowledging the sovereignty of Dynasty 21. Sheshonq (ca. 945–924 BC), a Libyan, started Dynasty 22 and reaffirmed the political power of the king. Dynasties 22 through 24 are called the Libyan Period, which ruled primarily from the western Delta. Dynasty 25 started when the Kushites invaded from Nubia and took over Egypt through military might. The Kushites reverted to more traditional religious practices and copied Old Kingdom art in a form of archaism, to reaffirm their rule.

The period of the Assyrian empire and sporadic invasions of Egypt spanned Dynasties 25 through 26 and the beginning of the Late Period (ca. 664–332 BC). Dynasty 26 covers the Saite reunification of Egypt

decree written during the reign of Ptolemy V in 196 BC, describing homage paid to the ruler after he endowed Ptolemaic temples.

The native Egyptian culture and accomplishments declined after the reign of the famous queen Cleopatra VII, a brilliant and shrewd leader who spoke many languages (including Egyptian). Her affairs with both Julius Caesar and Marc Antony led to Egypt's defeat by Rome at the Battle of Actium in September of 31 BC. Though the Romans controlled Egypt, its culture continued, with additional temples constructed and its religion becoming a Romano-Egyptian hybrid. This culture lasted until Christianity was adopted in the 3rd century AD, and by the time of the Islamic invasion in AD 662, it had ceased to exist.

Language

Egypt's language went through many stages in its development, and continuing advancements in textual and grammatical studies are helping to elucidate key historical issues. Muslim scholars in medieval times correctly identified 10 letters in its alphabet, while attempts to translate the language in the 1600s and 1700s produced a broad range of theories, many of which had humorous results. Despite serious studies by a Jesuit scholar, Athanasius Kirchener, the first serious efforts to translate the language took place with Thomas Young and Jean-François Champollion. Champollion, a linguistic genius who had long been a scholar of Coptic, studied what became known as the "Rosetta stone," discovered by Napoleon's army in the western Delta. This stone has three inscriptions, in Greek, Demotic, and Egyptian hieroglyphs. Champollion used his knowledge of Greek to translate the names of Ptolemy and Cleopatra in hieroglyphs, and proceeded to hieroglyphs based on his newly found knowledge of the alphabet. His results allowed scholars access to a language that had been dead for over 1,400 years.

Proto-Egyptian hieroglyphs have been found on seals from tomb U-J at Abydos, with the language developing Old, Middle, and Late Egyptian forms. There are 24 letters in the ancient Egyptian alphabet, with the language using alphabetic, phonetic, and ideographic signs as well as determinatives at the end

under the rule of Psamtik, who made Sais his capital in the western Delta. After a brief period of Saite imperialism, the first Persian occupation of Egypt, Dynasty 27, took place when Cambyses defeated Psamtik III in the Battle of Pelusium in around 525 BC. In Dynasties 28 through 30, Egypt gained independence from around 404 BC through 434 BC. Increasing Persian threats added to the growing instability of ancient Egypt. In the second Persian occupation period, from around 343 BC through 332 BC, Artaxerses III assaulted Egypt and fought against and defeated Nectanebo I and II, the last pharaohs of dynastic Egypt.

Alexander the Great invaded Egypt in around 332 BC and founded Alexandria, a major center of wealth, knowledge, and intellectual activities. After his death, control of Egypt went to his general Ptolemy, which began the Ptolemaic Period (ca. 332–30 BC). This period was marked by a series of short-lived rulers, of whom Ptolemy I was the only ruler to die of natural causes. The great Rosetta stone, later responsible for allowing the deciphering of ancient Egyptian, was a of words. In total, there are over 4,000 hieroglyphic signs. The cursive form of ancient Egyptian, known as Hieratic, became the script used in business matters, while Demotic developed in the 5th century BC. Coptic was the last stage in the development of ancient Egyptian, though the form spoken by the ancient Egyptians, the Sahidic dialect, has now been replaced by the Bohairic dialect. The language survives today in numerous forms: on temple

and tomb walls, on ostraca (usually limestone and pottery fragments), and on papyrus, in religious, economic, and political documents.

Religion

Ancient Egyptian religion took many forms, including formal state religion maintained by priests in temples and in annual festivals, and more regional and personalized religious traditions in village shrines and homes. Ancient Egypt had several creations myths; in one, Egypt began by rising out of a watery nothingness as a primeval mound, upon which life sprouted forth. Another myth involves the god Ptah creating the world, while another myth related that the god Amun-Ra had created the world beginnings. Priests played important roles in temples to the gods and deified kings, while the pharaoh represented a living embodiment of the god Horus on earth, acting as an intermediary between the gods and humanity.

A number of ancient Egyptian religious documents survive, providing a religious code and enabling the deceased's soul to safely and successfully journey to the afterlife. These books are known as the Pyramid Texts, Coffin Texts, and Book of the Dead (the mortuary texts from the Old, Middle, and New Kingdoms), while the New Kingdom religious compositions include the Book of the Heavenly Cow, Book of the Gates, and other underworld books. Select scenes and passages from these documents occur on tomb walls, sarcophagi, and mummy cases. Personal piety increased during the New Kingdom after the Amarna Period, and amulets representing different aspects of

deities were worn on occasions. Household shrines played an important role in the daily lives of ancient Egyptians, and local shrines offered a chance for commoners to participate in religion on a regional scale. Certain aspects of ancient Egyptian religion lasted through the Coptic Period, but most ancient practices died out with the introduction of Islam in AD 662.

Temples and Funerary Monuments

Numerous temples appear throughout Egypt, but none are as well known as the temple of Karnak, on the east bank of the Nile in Luxor. It was the temple of Amun-Re, creator of all things, known as "the place of majestic rising for the first time." Karnak was simultaneously the divine residence of the god and an ever-growing cult; it played important roles in social, economic, and political events. Its construction began in the Middle Kingdom, and it grew continuously until Ptolemaic-Roman Periods. Over 80,000 people worked at Karnak Temple during the time of Ramses II (Dynasty 19). The temple itself has an east-west axis, with a main pillared hall, numerous pylons (twin towers flanking entryways), courts, and jubilee halls. The complex was dedicated to the Amun-Mut-Khonsu triad, with adjacent temples complexes constructed for Mut and Khonsu.

Five kilometers south of Karnak is another major temple, Luxor Temple, which was dedicated to Amun of Luxor, a major fertility figure. Built originally by Amenhotep III, Ramses II added a pylon, an outer court, and two obelisks. The Beautiful Feast of Opet was celebrated at Luxor Temple annually to celebrate

protected and remote valley, the royal tombs still suffered robbery, mostly during the New Kingdom. The large *quern* or hill overlooking the region functioned as a focal symbolic pyramid. Today, over 1 million people visit the Valley of the Kings annually, making it one of the most popular archaeological sites in the world.

Numerous royal mortuary temples from the New Kingdom lie on the west bank in Luxor, built separately from the tombs in the Valley of the Kings. Over 20 were constructed in a 500-year period. Called "the mansion of millions of years" for each king, few remain standing today.

Settlement Archaeology

Egypt's major settlements and provincial and national capital cities existed as political, cultural, and religious centers during key periods of Dynasties 1 through 30. In particular, the cities of Abydos, Memphis, Thebes (Luxor), and Alexandria formed particularly significant settlements for most of the pharaonic era.

Abydos, located 145 km north of Luxor, represented the burial place for the kings of Dynasties 1 and 2, with 10 known associated funerary enclosures. The subsequent Old Kingdom pyramid complexes originated from the royal cemetery at Umm el-Qa'ab, while the north cemetery at Abydos functioned as the burial place for commoners during the Middle Kingdom. The ancient settlement of Abydos is located at Kom es-Sultan, which spanned the Old Kingdom to the First Intermediate Period. Royal cult foundations existed at Abydos in both the Middle and New Kingdoms. For instance, the Osiris Temple of Seti I was constructed during Dynasty 19, with seven sanctuaries called "The House of Millions of Years."

the birth of the king's *ka* (spirit) and to regenerate his divine kingship. Luxor Temple was later used as a Roman military camp, and the mosque of Abu el-Hagg was constructed on its grounds. Today, numerous sphinxes from the reign of Nectanebo line its entrance. There are still major finds within its grounds; an excavation in 1989 discovered many votive statues of divinities and kings buried in its courtyard to make room for new votive statues.

The Valley of the Kings and Valley of the Queens lie in western Thebes. The latter place represents the place for Pharaoh's wives and children. The Valley of the Kings, known as "The Great Place," or Wadi el-Biblaan el-Malik, "The Valley of the Gates of the Kings," contained the burials for the kings of the Dynasties 18 through 20. In the Valley of the Kings are 62 known tombs, alongside 20 pits or unfinished shaft tombs. Despite the high-quality limestone of the hills and the

Memphis, which lies 25 km south of central Cairo on the east bank of the Nile, usually represented the capital of Egypt. Founded in about 3100 BC, its placement at the apex of the Delta, between southern and northern Egypt, and its access to desert trade routes made it an ideal administrative center. Memphis was the capital of Egypt in the Old Kingdom, lying near the Dynasty 12 capital at el-Lisht. In Dynasty 18, it was a powerful bureaucratic center, and in the Late Period and Ptolemaic Period, kings were crowned at Memphis. It existed as a religious center of pilgrimage for many years.

Luxor, or ancient Thebes, has archaeological material beginning in the Middle Kingdom. In the New Kingdom, it became a religious center for all of Egypt, containing major temples, tombs, and funerary monuments. It was known in ancient times as "the city" (much like New York today), with many

festivals taking place throughout the year. Today, the modern city covers much of the ancient one, but excavation is starting to reveal the broad extent of Thebes at the height of pharaonic power.

Alexandria was founded in 332 BC at the northwest edge of the Delta opposite the Island of Pharos. It was five km long and 1.5 km wide, with the city divided into three equal parts. The famous lighthouse lay at the end of a bridge across the bay. Over 1 million people lived in Alexandria during its height, and it continued to be a major city throughout the Ptolemaic and into the Roman Periods. The library, housing tens of thousands of important scrolls and documents, appears to have burnt down during the conquest of Alexandria by Julius Caesar. In the late 4th century AD, Alexandria suffered extensive modification and destruction when temples became churches and many earthquakes damaged the city. The modern town covers much of ancient Alexandria, and new building construction continues to bring to light many important aspects of the city.

Future Directions

Modern urban developments, coupled with an increasing population, threaten many of Egypt's archaeological sites. The rising water table is causing damage to innumerable monuments throughout the Nile Valley, and much is lost each year to the agricultural needs of the populace. Fortunately, the Egyptian government is working in partnership with many foreign expeditions in heritage management and conservation efforts. A new part of the Egyptian Supreme Council of Antiquities, the Egyptian Antiquities

Information Service, is attempting to document every known archaeological site in Egypt and aims to preserve as much as possible.

Technology is also playing an important role in the location, preservation, and reconstruction of archaeological sites, including remote sensing (both on the ground and in the air), 3-D modeling and mapping of sites, and digital scanning of monument inscriptions and reliefs. With many wonderful discoveries gracing the pages of newspapers and journals each year, Egypt's past continues to offer much to its present.

— *Sarah Parcak*

See also **Egyptology; Pyramids**

Further Readings

Allen, J. (1999). *Middle Egyptian: An introduction to the language and culture of hieroglyphics.* Cambridge: Cambridge University Press.
Bard, K. (Ed.). (1999). *Encyclopedia of the archaeology of Ancient Egypt.* London: Routledge.
Kemp, B. (1994). *Ancient Egypt: Anatomy of a civilization.* London: Routledge.
Redford, D. (2002). *The ancient gods speak: A guide to Egyptian religion.* Oxford: Oxford University Press.
Shaw, I. (Ed.). (2000). *The Oxford history of Ancient Egypt.* Oxford: Oxford University Press.
Shaw, I., & Nicholson, P. (2000). *Ancient Egyptian materials and technology.* Cambridge: Cambridge University Press.
Wilkinson, R. (2000). *The complete temples of Ancient Egypt.* London: Thames & Hudson.

ABU SIMBEL

The extensive temple complex of Abu Simbel near Aswan, Egypt, has attracted the attention of archaeological anthropologists around the world since the 1820s, when noted French archaeologist Jean-François Champollion, the "founding father of Egyptology," first deciphered inscriptions on the temple. Archaeologists have been especially interested in the fact that Abu Simbel was carved out of mountainous, living stone rather than the more traditional freestanding temple. Ostensibly, Ramses II (1290–1224 BCE) built the temples to glorify the Egyptian deities Re-Harakhta and Re Amon. However, the temples have served as lasting monuments to Ramses II (who had the distinction of negotiating the first antiaggression pact in recorded history) and to his favorite wife, Nefartari.

Since the completion of the restoration project that began in the 1960s and saved the Abu Simbel temple complex from being overrun by the proposed Aswan Dam, tourists have flocked to the ancient temples to see depictions of the pharaoh surrounded by his wife and the children. The temples give visitors a glimpse of daily life as well as portrayals of Egyptian military life and ancient Egyptian religions. Visitors to Abu Simbel are fascinated by the temple's special construction, which allows the gods in the inner sanctum to be lit by the rising sun for two days each fall.

In the aftermath of the terrorist attacks and the subsequent war in Iraq in the early 2000s, tourism in the Middle East dropped dramatically. Initially, visitors canceled 50% of the scheduled reservations to Abu Simbel and the surrounding area. However, unlike other tourist meccas in the Middle East, Egyptian tourism rebounded. By the summer of July 2003, Egypt was reporting that 6 million tourists had visited the country, with a jump of 16.4% over 2002.

Survival of the Abu Simbel temple complex is currently being threatened by the environmental dangers of fire, smog, and corrosive winds that continue to damage this relic of ancient Egyptian life, causing the stone to become brittle and making it more likely to crumble. The fire and smog are caused by nearby rice farmers who burn chaff in the Nile delta. In addition to this enveloping blanket of smog and fire, archaeologists believe that since its relocation, Abu Simbel has become more exposed to corrosive winds, resulting in a gradual wearing down of the inscriptions. The Egyptian Environmental Affairs Agency has launched an effort to protect Abu Simbel and other such relics of ancient Egypt from these new dangers.

— Elizabeth Purdy

TUTANKHAMUN AND ZAHI HAWASS

The figure of the pharaoh Tutankhamun has always been shrouded in mystery. The discovery of his intact tomb in 1922 has increased sinister speculations about this historical character and his supposed curse, which struck all those involved in the expedition and the excavation. The death of the Egyptian king, who ruled from 1333 BCE to 1323 BCE, has also been the subject of much speculation. Because he lived in a turbulent period in Egypt's history, many archaeologists have argued that the pharaoh, who died before he was 20 years old, was murdered. Historians have suggested that Ay, Tutankhamun's prime minister, had murdered him or had him killed because he was seeking greater independence.

A different group of scholars believed that a high priest called Pa-Nahesy killed him after accusing him of blasphemy. The evidence for this theory was the recovery of bone fragments in his skull that were found in 1968, when a team led by Professor Ronald Harrison, of Liverpool University, was allowed to x-ray the mummy. The bone fragments in his skull suggested a blow to the head. Yet in 2005, Tutankhamun's mummy was removed from its tomb and analyzed

through the use of more modern computerized technologies by a group of Egyptologists, led by the archaeologist Zahi Hawass, the outspoken secretary general of the Supreme Council of Antiquities in Cairo.

The scan of the mummy revealed that Tutankhamun was not murdered but that he probably died after breaking his leg in an accident and then picking up an infection in the open wound. The scans supervised by Hawass confirmed the presence of two fragments of loose bone in the skull. Yet the team concluded the skull could not have been fractured before the pharaoh's death. Otherwise, the fragments would have become stuck in the embalming fluid that was poured into the head at burial after the removal of the brain. The skull must have been damaged during the embalming process or by Howard Carter, who discovered the tomb. The team led by Hawass also discovered a fractured left thighbone. The fracture had not started to heal, and embalming fluid was located inside the wound. These two pieces of evidence supported the hypothesis that the fracture in the leg may have happened shortly before death. The idea of the accident is also confirmed by the possibility that the right kneecap and right lower leg may also have been fractured.

— Luca Prono

 # EGYPTOLOGY

Egyptology is defined as the study of Ancient Egypt from the *Badarian*, circa 4500 BCE, to the Muslim invasion of Egypt in AD 641. (Identified in Upper Egypt by Brunton and Caton Thompson in 1928, the *Badarian* is contemporary with *Fayum A* in Lower Egypt.) This brought the "Great Tradition" cultural practices that had coalesced during Egyptian civilization's 5,000-year existence to an end (pyramid building and other related monumental architecture, worship of the pantheon of Egyptian deities, dynastic succession, hieroglyphic writing, and mummification).

Egyptology should not be confused with "Egyptomania," which refers to the fascination with "all things Egyptian" that took place after Howard Carter discovered the tomb of Tutakhenaten (who ceremonially changed his name to Tutankhamun shortly before his death), in the early 1920s. In this case, "Egyptomania" disrupted the systematic study of the artifacts by trained Egyptologists; bizarre interpretations of ancient Egyptian civilization remain with us today as a result (for example, the popular book *Chariots of the Gods* claimed that the pyramids were probably built by extraterrestrial beings, not by the indigenous people of Africa). However, the general public's interest is certainly beneficial to Egyptology; few patrons can forget the impact of an Egyptian exhibit after visiting a museum like the Metropolitan Museum of Art or the Cairo Museum. Remarkably, Ancient Egyptian civilization continues to be compelling, and relevant, in the postmodern world.

A History of Egyptology

Although Athanasius Kircher made a valiant attempt to decipher Egyptian hieroglyphs in the mid-1600s, the modern phase of the study of Ancient Egypt is believed to have commenced after Napoleon Bonaparte's invasion of Egypt in 1798. Napoleon employed a number of artists and scholars, an estimated 167 in total, who formed the Commission des Arts et des Sciences, which included Claude Louis Berthollet, Gaspard Monge, Jean Michel Venture de Paradis, Prosper Jollois, Edmé François Jomard, René Edouard Villers de Terrage, and Michel-Ange Lancret; more than 30 from the commission died in combat or from disease. A new organization to focus on the study of Egypt, the Institut d'Egypte, was formed by Napoleon in August of 1798, with Gaspard Monge serving as its president. Baron Dominique Vivant Denon (1742–1825) was urged to join Napoleon's expedition by his protectress Joséphine de Beauharnais, who would later marry Napoleon. Denon was a diplomat, playwright, painter, and renowned society conversationalist; his drawings of Medinet Habu are considered to be some of the most important in the history of Egyptology. Baron Joseph Fourier (1768–1830), who was an outstanding mathematician, facilitated the publication of *Description de l'Égypte* upon his return to France, and he held a number of prestigious posts, including prefect of the Isère Département, in Grenoble, and Director of the Statistical Bureau of the Siene; Fourier's publication represents an early attempt at compiling the tremendous amount of Egyptian material that was being discovered apace, making it widely available for other scholars to examine.

The British invaded Egypt shortly afterward and took possession of the priceless "Rosetta stone," which had been discovered in 1799 near a city known as *Rashīd* (meaning "Rosetta"), in 1801 when the French capitulated. The Rosetta stone was inscribed with three scripts—Egyptian hieroglyphic, Egyptian demotic, and Greek—thus Greek served as a conduit between the ancient Egyptians and the modern world. Thomas Young, a British physicist who had mastered 12 languages by the time that he was 14 years old, is responsible for some of the first creditable decipherments of ancient Egyptian writing, and he shared his findings with Jean F. Champollion, who later became famous as the preeminent figure of the decipherment effort.

A multitalented circus performer, strongman, and artist-turned-explorer named Giovanni Battista Belzoni (1778–1823) conducted archaeological excavations at Karnak between 1815 and 1817, and he entered Khafre's pyramid at Giza in 1818, making him the first known person to enter the temple in modern times. In 1820, Belzoni published *Narrative of the Operations and Recent Discoveries Within the Pyramids, Temples, Tombs, and Excavations, in Egypt and Nubia*. Belzoni's association with Henry Salt, the British Consul General who had retained him to procure Egyptian antiquities for the British Museum, often causes scholars to regard him as a treasure hunter. Belzoni's lack of "scholarly" credentials and his questionable archaeological agenda generate a measure of concern and derision among Egyptologists. Girolamo Segato (1792–1936) went to Egypt in 1818 as well, and he crossed Belzoni's path, uncovering elusive artifacts that had been overlooked. Segato was a chemist, naturalist, and draftsman, and he was the first person to enter the Step Pyramid of Djoser in modern times (the pyramid had been plundered, presumably in antiquity, like most of the pyramids). Segato was a prolific mapmaker, in the service of Ismail Pasha, with his work leading him well into the Sudan, where he encountered the Kingdom of Chiollo and Wadi Halfa during a 40-day walk. Although most of Segato's drawings were lost to fire and his Egyptian treasures lost to shipwreck, he published *Pictoral, Geographical, Statistical, and Cadastral Essays on Egypt* in 1823, and *Atlas of Upper and Lower Egypt* with Domenico Valeriano in 1837.

The most noteworthy contributors to the establishment of Egyptology as an academic discipline are Ippolito Rosellini, diplomat, explorer, and collector Bernardino Drovetti (1776–1852), Emmanuel vicomte de Rougé, Jean Jacques Rifaud (1786–1845, Drovetti's artist), James Bruce (1730–1794), Owen Jones, Samuel Birch, Ludwig Borschardt, Heinrich Brugsch, Emile Brugsch (1842–1930), Adolf Erman, Hermann Grapow, Carl Richard Lepsius, Somers Clarke (1841–1926), Emile Armélineau (1850–1915), Jean Capart (1877–1947), Gaston Maspero (1846–1916), Edouard Naville (1844–1926), Victor Loret (1859–1946), Sir John Gardner Wilkinson, Sir Alan H. Gardiner, Sir William Matthew Flinders Petrie (Seriation at Abydos), James Henry Breasted, Auguste Mariette, Amelia Edwards (1831–1892), Ernest Alfred Thompson Wallis Budge (1857–1934), George Andrew Reisner (1867–1942), Howard Carter (1874–1939), Jaroslav Cerný (1898–1970), Dorothy Louise Eady (1904–1981), and Walter B. Emery (1903–1971).

Sir John Gardner Wilkinson (1797–1875) went to Egypt in 1821 to study tombs in the Valley of the Kings, the site of Karnak, and the sacred Gebel Barkal in Nubia, a mountain that appears to be

Source: © FreeStockPhotos.com.

shaped like a *uraeus* (the cobra that fronts the Egyptian king's crown). Wilkinson made contributions to Egyptian epigraphy by copying inscriptions and being the first to identify the names of the kings with whom they were associated.

Rosellini (1800–1843) and his brother Gaetano accompanied Champollion on an expedition to Egypt in 1828 and directed the Italian committee as head archaeologist, while Champollion directed the French committee; supported by Leopoldo II, grand duke of Tuscany, and Charles X, King of France, their field study was called the Franco-Tuscan Expedition. Naturalist Guiseppe Raddi, artists Alessandro Ricci, Alexandre Duchesne, Albert Bertin, draftsman Nestor L'Hôte, and Pierre Lehoux were major contributors to the project. Champollion and Rosellini published the results of their expedition in *Monuments de l'Égypte et Nubie*. This visionary title clearly suggests that these scholars surmised that there was a significant relationship between Nubia and Egypt; however, its significance has been overshadowed until recent times. Today, we know that Nubia's influence on Egypt was far greater than many Egyptologists had suspected. For example, Nubian pottery has been unearthed and dated at 8000 BCE, which provides evidence that sedentary life in Nubia predates the *Badarian*, when Egyptian civilization began to coalesce; a great deal of effort has been directed at creating a rigid separation between the two areas, or populations. Importantly, metals like gold were virtually nonexistent above the Second Cataract (*cataracts* are the whitewater regions of the Nile); therefore, it was mined at Buhen or other Nubian sites and carted off to Egypt by the ton. Thus, Egypt's reliance on Nubian products was perpetual, from the emergence of dynastic Egypt around 3250 BCE until the invasion of the Persian Archaemenid Dynasty in 525 BCE.

Owen Jones (1809–1874), a British engineer and draftsman, traveled to Egypt in 1832, made substantial drawings of Karnak, and published *Views on the Nile from Cairo to the Second Cataract* in 1843. Samuel Birch (1813–1855) wrote the introduction to Jones's elaborate volume, which contained engraver George Moore's lithographs of his original drawings, accurately documenting the architectural details of the various structures that Jones had encountered during his expedition. After collaborating with Joseph Bonomi and Samuel Sharpe, Jones published *A Description of the Egyptian Court* in 1854. Scottish artist David Roberts (1796–1864) went to Egypt shortly after Jones's expedition, in 1838. Roberts believed that Abu Simbel was the most impressive of all Egyptian temples, and his various paintings became the most popular of his time.

Lepsius (1810–1884) led an expedition to Egypt from Germany, commissioned by Friedrich Wilhelm IV of Prussia, in 1842. Lepsius was accompanied by artist Joseph Bonomi and architect James Wild, and he published *Denkmäler aus Ägypten und Äthiopien, 12 vol.* in 1859 (Egyptian and Ethiopian Monuments), which rivaled the work published by Fourier in scale. Emmanuel vicomte de Rougé (1811–1872) worked with Lepsius to formulate a method for interpreting new Egyptian discoveries in a consistent manner. De Rougé was also curator of the Egyptian section at the Louvre in Paris.

Brugsch (1827–1894) collaborated with Mariette (a cousin of Nestor L'Hôte) in the 1850s, and his major contribution to Egyptology is his work on the decipherment of the demotic script; Brugsch worked at the Berlin Museum as well, and he held a number of posts related to Egyptology, including Founder and Director of the Cairo School of Egyptology. Mariette (1821–1881), an archaeologist known for virtually destroying archaeological sites, went to Egypt in 1850 to look for ancient manuscripts; however, he excavated Saqqara and Memphis instead, working in Egypt and sending antiquities to the Louvre until 1854. After returning to Egypt in 1858, he remained in Egypt and established the Egyptian Museum, after convincing the Ottoman Viceroy of Egypt of its merit. Mariette unearthed the temple of Seti I, as well as other temples at Edfu and Dendera. His work exposed material that dated back to the Old Kingdom, extending the range of Egyptian history that scholars could analyze.

Amelia Edwards (1831–1892) was a successful journalist who went to Egypt in 1873 and became enthralled with what she saw. Edwards published *A Thousand Miles Up the Nile* in 1877 and in 1882, founded the Egypt Exploration Fund (now known as the Egypt Exploration Society) to rescue ancient Egyptian monuments from decay, neglect, and vandalism. A wealthy British surgeon, Sir Erasmus Wilson, supported Edwards's efforts until her death, shortly after she completed an American speaking tour that consisted of 115 lectures, in 1889. Edwards strongly endorsed Sir Flinders Petrie in her bequest for the establishment of a chair of Egyptology at University College in London; it contained a proviso that "Flinders Petrie should be the first professor." Petrie (1853–1942) is considered to be "the father of modern Egyptology" by some Egyptologists. In conjunction, the archaeological methods that he developed extended beyond the Egyptian sites and are used by many of today's archaeologists. Petrie excavated Naqada, Tanis, Naucritis, Tell-al-Amarna, the pyramids of Senusret II and Amenemhat II, and the cemetery at Abydos, from 1895 to 1899 (see the Methods in Egyptology section that follows).

Erman (1854–1937) elucidated and emphasized what he believed to be significant connections between ancient Egyptian language, the Coptic language, and Semitic languages. Three of Erman's publications are considered to be among the most important that have ever been written on Egyptology: *Ägyptische Grammatik* (Egyptian Grammar), *Wörterbuch der ägyptischen Sprache* (Dictionary of the Egyptian Language), and *Neuägyptische Grammatik* (New Egyptian Grammar). Grapow (1885–1967) was a protégé of Erman, and his publications focused on ancient Egyptian medicine. Gardiner (1879–1963), a student of Erman, is well-known for his interpretation of the *Narmer Palate* and his seminal 1927 publication, *Egyptian Grammar*, which is considered required reading for Egyptologists today.

Breasted (1865–1935) published the five-volume *Ancient Records of Egypt* in 1906, *A History of Egypt* (1905), *Development of Religion and Thought in Ancient Egypt* (1912), and *A History of the Early World* (1916) before his 1919 expedition to Egypt, while he was a professor of Egyptology and Oriental History at the University of Chicago. With the financial support of John D. Rockefeller, Jr., Breasted established the Oriental Institute at the University of Chicago, in 1919.

A number of other archaeologists, artists, authors, and architects could certainly be included among these important figures in the history of Egyptology, and their contributions to the discipline's development must be acknowledged. Many of the Egyptologists who are working today will undoubtedly become part of this illustrious historic record.

Methods in Egyptology

The systematic study of Ancient Egypt has provided a wealth of information; however, it is of a relatively recent vintage. The Edict of Milan, which was issued in AD 313 by the Roman Empire, established Christianity as the empire's official religion. As a result of this decree, representations of Egyptians gods and deities were attacked as symbols of "devil worship," and Egyptian artifacts were zealously destroyed by Christians.

By the time Napoleon's scholars arrived in Egypt to conduct systematic studies, significant damage to Egypt's artifacts had already taken place. Egyptologists were forced to assess what remained with the understanding that looters, vandals, zealots, and adventurers had gotten to the sites ahead of them. When Sir William Matthew Flinders Petrie arrived in Egypt to excavate Abydos near the end of the 19th century, he was horrified by the methods and practices that he observed used by Mariette at Khafre's temple, which is documented in Lorna Oakes and Lucia Gahlin's *Ancient Egypt.*

Mariette excavated the Serapaeum at Memphis as well, where the sacred Apis bulls had been buried. Mariette's methods included the use of dynamite, which inherently destroys aspects of an archaeological site that may have been of importance. By intentional contrast, Petrie invented *seriation,* a method used by archaeologists to determine the sequences of artifact development, change, and frequency (or lack of frequency) in the layers of a site's strata. For example, artifacts found in the lower levels of the strata are considered to represent an earlier technocomplex or habitation period in relation to the upper levels of the strata; seriation is a *relative-dating* technique. Petrie first used seriation at Naqada, Hu, and Abadlya, and his method is now widely used by modern archaeologists; at the very least, in this way, Egyptology certainly contributed to the study of humans as a whole. B. G. Trigger, B. J. Kemp, D. O'Connor, and A. B. Lloyd described Petrie's method in their groundbreaking *Ancient Egypt: A Social History,* which was first published in 1983.

Petrie cut 900 strips of cardboard, each measuring 7 inches long, with each representing a grave that he had excavated; on each strip, Petrie recorded the pottery types and amounts, as well as the other grave goods, which allowed him to compare the grave's contents and develop a relative chronology. Petrie's meticulous method represented a watershed event in both Egyptology and archaeology, and seriation has undoubtedly enhanced the effort to analyze, preserve, and curate countless antiquities. In conjunction with seriation, a variety of methods are now used by Egyptologists to locate archaeological sites, including aerial photography, electromagnetic acoustic sounding radar, resistivity measurement, and thermal infrared imagery to indentify geological anomalies that merit further investigation. Polymerase chain reaction (PCR, a method of DNA molecule duplication that yields more material for analysis) and CAT-scans are now used to study the genetic relationships, or the lack thereof, between the human remains that have been unearthed and the pathology of their diseases. Computer programs that allow users to create 3-D reconstructions of sites and that allow users to type hieroglyphs are widely used by researchers, epigraphers, and students of Egyptology today. Relative dating methods, like stratigraphic palynology, and absolute dating methods, including thermoluminescence (TL), Radiocarbon (C-14), and electron spin resonance (ESR), are among the methods that can now be used to date artifacts, faunal, or floral material that is associated with Egyptian archaeological sites. These investigative tools have definitely enhanced Egyptologists' ability to study the world of the ancient Egyptians.

A new method that is available to Egyptologists yielded some compelling results in August 2004. Gilles Dormion and Jean Yves Verd'hurt reported that they had found an unknown corridor that leads to a burial chamber in the tomb of Khufu, by using ground-penetrating radar; if they are correct, they may have solved an age-old mystery as to where Khufu was actually buried. However, as of now, Dormion and Verd'hurt have not been given permission to excavate.

Major Sites of Study

Mariette's discovery of the Serapaeum at Memphis, and Khafre's temple at Giza were major sites of study in the 19th century. Abydos, the center of the Osiris cult, was found to be equally significant. The Abydos site continues to be one of the most important in Egyptology. Based on the archaeological excavations of Dr. Gunter Dreyer from the 1990s, it appears that during the Gerzean, pharonic Egypt and hieroglyphic writing began at Abydos, about 3200 BCE. With the discovery of the tomb of King Scorpion (Sekhen), Dreyer found many of the markedly Egyptian cultural practices that would become definitive, including the mastaba, the ivory sceptre, the symbol of Horus, and the bulbous crown that symbolized a ruler's dominion over Upper Egypt.

In conjunction, Dr. John Coleman Darnell and Deborah Darnell discovered the Scorpion Tableau nearby at the Jebel Tjauti site, which appears to be the earliest known example of the "smiting of the king's enemies" mural that later Egyptian kings would commission. Karnak and Thebes (Luxor) are among the most studied sites of Upper Egypt, in conjunction with the Valley of the Kings, Deir el Medina, Hierakonpolis (where many ancient kings claimed to have been born), and Naqada. Dr. Kent Weeks is now conducting the Theban Mapping Project that is focusing on KV5 where Ramses II built interconnected tombs for his sons, which probably numbered over 50. KV5 represents an architectural project from antiquity that is completely unique. Egyptian kings were buried in the Valley of the Kings from about 1500 BCE to 1000 BCE, and the number of tombs located there is somewhat staggering, to say the least. At least six kings from the Ramesside Period were also buried in the Valley of the Kings, along with Merenptah, Tawosert and Sethnakhte, Seti I and II, Tuthmosis I, III, and IV, Siptah, Horemheb, Yuya and Tuya, and of course, Tutankhamun. Deir el Bahri in Western Thebes, the site of both Mentuhotep II and Hatshepsut's tombs, continues to be a major site of interest to Egyptologists as well; the location of Hatshepsut's tomb, which was built nearly 500 years after Mentuhotep II's, exemplifies the later pharaoh's desire to identify with and surpass her predecessor.

Some of the major archaeological sites of Lower Egypt are the illustrious Giza Plateau, Bubastis, Sais, Heliopolis, and Tanis. In the delta region, natural preservation is more problematic; however, astonishing finds associated with the 21st Dynasty have been unearthed. The silver coffins that were made during the Tanite Dynasty and its successors are exceptionally impressive, although this period in Egypt (29th–23rd Dynasties) may have been relatively chaotic, in view of the archaeological and historical records.

The major archaeological site of Middle Egypt is Tell al-Amarna (Akhetaten in antiquity), a city that was purposely built in the desert, in iconoclastic fashion, by king Akhenaten for his worship of the Aten. This site may represent the first example of a monotheistic king and state; however, Akhenaten's motive may have been twofold. By abandoning the pantheon of Egyptian gods and deities that were in place, Akhenaten may have wanted all power to reside in him.

Many discoveries have been made as a result of restudies of sites that were already known. In this way, Upper, Middle, and Lower Egyptian sites provide perpetual enrichment for Egyptologists. For example, the Abusir site was excavated by Ludwig Borschardt (1863–1938) from 1902 to 1908; however, it is now being worked again, and its remarkable complexes are providing today's Egyptologists with more knowledge about the lives of Raneferef, Sahure, and other kings from the 5th Dynasty.

In conjunction, the modern-day boundaries of Egypt do not correspond with the boundaries of the Old Kingdom, Middle Kingdom, or New Kingdom. Therefore, Egyptian influence was prevalent below the First Cataract to areas south of the Third Cataract, and the number of pyramids in Nubia (modern-day Sudan) actually exceeds the number of pyramids that were built within the boundaries of modern Egypt. After Tuthmosis I (ca. 1504–1492 BCE) invaded Nubia, Amenhophis III built a well-known temple at Soleb. Akhenaten built a temple at Sesibi, which marks the southernmost point of the New Kingdom's conquest of the Kushites.

Major Discoveries and Areas for Research in Egyptology

The discovery of the Rosetta stone in 1799 was one of the most critical of all discoveries, because it allowed Egyptologists to communicate with the ancient Egyptians. Without the Rosetta stone, much of what Egyptologists believe would probably be dependent upon conjecture. Therefore, the decipherment of hieroglyphic writing has clarified a great deal about antiquity, and it represents a major benefit for all researchers.

Djoser's pyramid, Egypt's first stone building, which consists of a series of stacked mastabas; the pyramid of Khufu (Cheops) at Giza; the Red Pyramid at Dashur; and the Kushite pyramids discovered at el-Kurru represent merely a few of the major architectural achievements of this culture area. Karnak Temple, Abu Simbel, and other examples of monumental architecture demonstrate the undeniable brilliance of ancient Egyptian mathematicians, engineers, architects, and workmen.

Recent discoveries in the Valley of the Kings are no less than remarkable, because Egyptologists are learning so much more about a site that some archaeologists considered to be exhausted about a 100 years ago. In conjunction, the inadvertent discovery of the blue lotus's similarity to Viagra, in 2001, has transformed Egyptologist's interpretation of Egyptian paintings. The virtually ubiquitous use of the plant has medical, sensual, and cultural implications that are now being studied.

Interpretations of the Evidence and Recent Theories

New theories about the mysterious Egyptian have now emerged that merit further scrutiny. Dr. Bob Brier has been examining the circumstances of King Tutankhamun's early demise and his physical remains. For Brier, foul play is evident, based on a cranial anomaly and the political climate of the time. Some forensic scientists are not convinced; however, the evidence continues to be examined critically, and this research may broaden our understanding of the 18th Dynasty's machinations in significant ways.

In 2000, Robert Bauval hypothesized that the configuration of the pyramids at Giza was aimed at replicating the heavens on earth; each pyramid represented a star, and it was to be placed in alignment with the constellation now known as Orion. By superimposing a scale model of the Giza Plateau upon a photograph of the constellation Orion, a correspondence between the alignment structures and the stars can be observed. If Bauval is correct, this would explain why the Egyptians invested so much effort in building projects that would propel them into the afterlife, at least in part.

Egyptologists cannot say exactly how the pyramids were built, and theories abound as to how such a feat could have been accomplished without the use of modern equipment. Dr. Maureen Clemmons, a Professor of Aeronautics at the California Institute of Technology, surmised that the ancient Egyptians may have built their pyramids by using kites and wind power. Overcoming a number of technical obstacles and setbacks in her field tests in the Mojave Desert,

and with the assistance of Morteza Gharib and Emilio Graff, the team was able to raise a concrete obelisk that weighed about 3.5 tons in less than 5 minutes, using sails, wood, rope, and pulleys that would have been available to the ancient Egyptians. If Clemmons is correct, this would appear to be one of the most cogent explanations for how so many tons of stone could have been moved in antiquity.

Are these theories mere conjecture, or will they eventually enhance our understanding of the ancient Egyptian, who scholars have been struggling for centuries to understand? There are Egyptologists who take differing positions on these, and other, theories; however, divergent theoretical orientations serve as the foundation for scientific inquiry, and they often lead to breakthroughs, as Thomas Kuhn suggested in *The Structure of Scientific Revolutions.*

Preserving the Evidence/Sites

The rescue of the temples at Abu Simbel represents one of the most remarkable efforts known to Egyptologists. Ramses II built the two temples in Nubia; however, the rising level of the Aswan Dam, which was built in the 1950s, was about to flood their location and submerge the monuments forever. Through the efforts of UNESCO (United Nations Educational, Scientific and Cultural Organization), about $36 million was raised from international sources in order to move the temples to higher ground, and the temples were salvaged between 1963 and 1970. Clearly, this was a visionary undertaking, since the massive stone temples had to be dismantled in sections for future reassembly.

Tourism is a major sector of modern Egypt's economy; however, numerous measures have been enacted to limit the deleterious effects upon the visitation sites. Humidity within the structures is now monitored, and the number of people who are allowed in per day is regulated. The natural decay of structures, like the Amenhotep III temple at Thebes, has been a recurrent problem since ancient times. Traffic and pollution have both served to hasten the deterioration of the Sphinx and other ancient monuments. Thus, human activities continue to be a threat to the cherished artifacts of this unique civilization, and this has been recognized by Dr. Zahi Hawass, Chief Inspector of Antiquities for the Egyptian government. Hawass engaged in numerous restoration and preservation projects at Edfu, Kom Obo, and

Luxor, in conjunction with building tourist installations that are located a safe distance away from the sites, the use of safe zoning that separates a site from a town, and open-air museums. Taken together, these measures will complement the preservation efforts of the archaeologists who have permits to work alongside Egypt's vital tourist industry.

The Value of Egyptology to Anthropology

Egyptology offers exceptionally fertile areas of study for all four of anthropology's subfields. Physical anthropologists have gleaned a wealth of information about human adaptation, disease pathology, mating, and medicinal practices from ancient Egyptian remains; as for archaeologists, Egypt has exerted a substantial influence on their field considering the impact of seriation, which is widely used, developed by Egyptologist Sir Flinders Petrie.

The vibrant cultural array of Ancient Egypt and Nubia, including their pantheons of gods, philosophies, mating systems, and geopolitical interaction spheres, continues to be of interest to cultural anthropologists, with no evidence of abatement. And for linguists, the discovery of a unique, unpointed (written without vowels) language with a full compliment of written symbols has proven to be irresistible, at least since medieval times.

An incalculable number of anthropologists have drawn inspiration from Ancient Egyptian civilization, and they will probably continue to do so, while preserving its legacy for future generations of scholars and enthusiasts alike.

— *Larry Ross*

See also **Egypt, Ancient; Pyramids**

Further Readings

Bongioanni, A., & Croce, M. S. (Eds.). (2001). *The treasures of Ancient Egypt from the Cairo Museum.* New York: Universe.

Hawass, Z. (2004). *Hidden treasures of Ancient Egypt.* Washington, DC: National Geographic Society.

Johnson, P. (1999). *The civilization of Ancient Egypt.* New York: HarperCollins.

Oakes, L., & Gahlin, L. (Eds.). (2003). *Ancient Egypt.* New York: Barnes & Noble Books.

Shaw, I. (2002). *The Oxford history of Ancient Egypt.* Oxford: Oxford University Press.

Siliotti, A. (1998). *The discovery of Ancient Egypt.* Edison, NJ: Chartwell Books.

Trigger, B. G., Kemp, B. J., O'Connor, D., & Lloyd, A. B. (1983). *Ancient Egypt: A social history.* Cambridge: Cambridge University Press.

Watterson, B. (1998). *Women in Ancient Egypt.* Gloucestershire, UK: Sutton.

JEAN-FRANÇOIS CHAMPOLLION

French linguist and scholar Jean-François Champollion greatly advanced the field of archaeology by founding the field of Egyptology, allowing researchers to discover the secrets of ancient Egyptian life, language, and culture. Determined that he would be the one to encipher Egyptian hieroglyphics, in 1821, Champollion used the writing on the Rosetta stone to break the code that had eluded scholars for centuries.

In early 2003, new information about how Champollion was able to accomplish his task came to light when a portfolio of watercolors and drawings were discovered in Kingston Lacy, the Dorset County home in England that had belonged to William Bankes, a disgraced English politician. Between 1815 and 1819, Bankes had meticulously documented Egyptian monuments, including the temples of Dabod and Abu Simbel. In an effort to remind posterity of who had been involved in uncovering the mysteries of ancient Egypt, Bankes scratched his name on the leg of one of the colossi at the entrance to Abu Simbel.

Kingston Lacy was also home to an Egyptian obelisk that Bankes had transported from Philae Island near Aswan. The inscriptions on this obelisk were integral in Champollion's deciphering of the hieroglyphics. To the end of his life, Bankes believed that Champollion had taken all the credit for deciphering ancient Egyptian writings without acknowledging publicly that he had built on the work of British scholars who had given him free access to their work. After fleeing England to escape arrest on charges of sodomy, Bankes died in exile in 1855. His contributions to Egyptology were relatively unknown until archivists at the British Museum decided to organize and publish his notes and drawings after the discovery at Kingston Lacy.

Unlike Bankes, the contributions of Champollion to Egyptology have been documented for two centuries, and his contributions are clearly evident in resources on the subject today, including the Internet. More than 1 million sites are available, ranging from those aimed at the general public to those designed for serious scholars.

On the site of the Egyptian Supreme Council of Antiquities (http://www.sca.gov.eg/index.html), for example, it is possible to virtually examine artifacts at Egypt's Alexandria Library Museum or learn about the expanding field of underwater archaeology. For those who prefer to visit ancient Egypt more directly, the Internet offers a sampling of displays at museums that may be closer to home. Such displays include those at the Museum of Fine Arts in Boston (http://www.mfa.org/egypt/explore_ancient_egypt/index.html), the Poznan Archaeological Museum in Poland (http://www.muzarp.poznan.pl/muzeum/eindex.html), and the Louvre in Paris (http://www.louvre.fr/francais/collec/ae/ae_f.htm).

With a few clicks, it is possible for archaeologists and would-be archaeologists to gather information on possible digs taking place in Egypt (http://www.newton.cam.ac.uk/egypt/dig.html) or take a virtual tour of particular sites such as the Odyssey in Egypt site (http://www.website1.com/TheDigSite/), offering information on the excavation of the Monastery of St. John the Little at Wadi Natrun.

Although Champollion died at the age of 42, long before he had accomplished all that he meant to do, the field of Egyptology has served as a monument that continues to expand its reach to new generations who understand the importance of learning about the past and the part that such knowledge plays in understanding the present.

— Elizabeth Purdy

EL CERÉN

Located in the highlands of central El Salvador, El Cerén, or Joya de Cerén, has been described as the "Pompeii of the Americas." Discovered by accident in 1976, the Classic Maya site was covered with more than 5 meters of ash from an eruption of the Loma Caldera volcano circa AD 600, leaving this hamlet in an outstanding condition of preservation. It is registered with United Nations Educational, Scientific and Cultural Organization (UNESCO) as a World Heritage Site.

At the time of the Loma Caldera eruption, Cerén was a hamlet on the banks of the Rio Sucio. Data from several years of excavation suggest that people were just finishing their evening meal when the first signs of danger appeared. People fled the site, leaving buildings and belongings as they were. No human remains have been encountered at the site as a result of the disaster, though it is uncertain whether or not the people of Cerén actually escaped the many waves of intense explosions or not.

Outside of the eruption that preserved it, village life at Cerén was not unique. It was one of many villages and towns under the influence of the Classic Maya center at San Andres. San Andres served as the major religious and political center as well as providing a market where people from Cerén could have bartered for needed and desired items such as obsidian, shell, and salt. Life at Cerén however, focused on agricultural production of corn, with some specialized production of ceramics and other crafts.

Excavations at Cerén are notable for three major reasons. First, the sudden abandonment of the site left it in an unparalleled state of preservation. This led to an ongoing series of field projects directed at understanding the details of daily life in a Classic Maya village. Investigations have provided evidence for domestic and public architecture; where and how food was stored, prepared, and consumed; specialized tasks conducted by residents; agricultural practices; as well spatial arrangements within and between dwellings. It was because of the research potential of this unprecedented preservation that Cerén was nominated to UNESCO's list of World Heritage sites.

Second, Cerén has been both a testing ground and a model for interdisciplinary research and applications of technology in archaeological research. The challenges of conducting excavations of a substantial and deeply buried site promoted the use of remote-sensing technologies, such as resistivity and ground-penetrating radar, and opened up opportunities for collaboration with a variety of natural scientists. Excavation techniques for recovering and analyzing fragile remains of house posts, roof thatching, and growing corn developed over many seasons of fieldwork.

Third, Cerén stands as a model of diplomacy and international cooperation. Initial excavations at Cerén took place during intense conflict and political instability in El Salvador, during which project leaders successfully negotiated for the safety of excavators and the site itself. In addition, the Cerén project became one of the best-documented and most accessible archaeological projects in the world, with a well-maintained site museum and many field reports, photographs, and field specimen lists available through an official Cerén Web site.

— Jo Ellen Burkholder

See also **Mayas**

Further Readings

Lewin, J. S. (2002). *An interactive guide to Cerén before the volcano erupted.* Austin: University of Texas Press. http://ceren.colorado.edu

Sheets, P. D. (1992). *The Cerén site: A prehistoric village buried by volcanic ash in Central America.* Fort Worth, TX: Harcourt, Brace, Jovanovich.

Sheets, P. D. (2002). *Before the volcano erupted: The ancient Cerén village in Central America.* Austin: University of Texas Press.

 # ELDERS

Humans are the primate species with not only the longest life span (120 years) but also the greatest proportion of those years spent in social and biological maturity. The evolutionary legacy of aging also includes a powerful biological dimension of programmed senescence. Despite this, cross-cultural psychiatrist David Gutmann suggests elders exist not because of our species' technical ability to keep the weak alive; instead, we attained our humanity through the very existence of elders and the significance of their postparental roles.

The simplest way of conceptualizing elders and elderhood is as the age cohort relatively older than yourself or the generation with more years than anyone else in the community. Cultural construction of this older-adult category typically combines the path of biological maturity, the developmental kinship and family cycle, and broader notions of social generation. Elderhood more often than not focuses on the latter two factors, although for women, menopause can function as an important status-turning point, signaling eligibility for elder status. However, as Rasmussen notes for the Tuareg, the ending of reproductive capacity complexly impacts the unfolding of female personhood through realignment of kin hierarchies and other social strata affecting both males and females.

In essence, cultures are more apt to see elderhood as a marker of a social rather than a biological or time-based maturity. This is clear when we see persons, especially males, enter the beginning ranks of elder in their late 20s and early 30s among Africa's age set societies as well as in Australian Aboriginal tribes. From another perspective, an abundance of years without the culturally prescribed markers may allow individuals never to be socially considered an elder. For example, in Peterson's study of African American working-class women in Seattle, she found that female elders were designated by the word "wise," a term given to women who have not only borne children, but have raised kids who, in turn, have their own offspring. In this community, the label "wise" could be attained while a woman was in her late 30s. However, females who might be in their eighth decade of life but had not accomplished the required social tasks of maturity would be considered in the same generation as teenagers.

Age along with gender and kin relations stand as the three universal bedrocks of how all human societies construct a framework of social order and biocultural succession. Passage of human populations through the life span is translated into notions of social time, created by transit through successive age-based statuses marking the cultural mapping of the life cycle. Linguistic variants of child, adult, and elder become social boundaries in virtually all societies, marked by such things as variations in dress, comportment, modes of speech, and deferential gestures. Sometimes, actual physical boundaries can be involved, such as in the traditional Irish peasant pattern of moving elders into the sacred west room of the house, where younger kin could not enter without permission. An even more dramatic and negative case is that of the Fulani, West African pastoralists. Here, after a couple's last child has wed, the elders are regarded as socially dead. They live as dependents of their oldest son, moving separately to different outer edges of his house compound, symbolically residing over their future grave sites.

The societal definition of elder status is often differentiated from "oldness" or the cultural constructions of old age. The latter terms are more keyed to biological maturity of an individual in combination with some social aspect of one's relative position in society. In an indigenous, Nahuatl-speaking Mexican peasant community, Sokolovsky found that elderhood was attained by having shouldered important community rituals and becoming a grandparent, or *culkn.* To be considered old, or *culi,* required at least several grandchildren plus signs of physically slowing down, such as using a cane to walk around. A more debilitated stage of oldness, where one seldom ventures far from the home, is called *Yotla Moac,* literally "all used up."

One of the earliest efforts to mine anthropological data on the contribution of elders to their societies came from Leo Simmons's classic work, *The Role of the Aged in Primitive Society* (1945). He showed the wide variety of ways elderly function in society, including knowledge bearing; child care; economic support; and ritual, judicial, and political decision making. Numerous ethnographies have validated how a combination of deep knowledge held in older adults' heads and their nurturing actions toward younger generations sustains human societies. Among the Akan of Ghana, there is no adjective that exists to describe a human as old, but those who have grandchildren and are older adults are referred to by the verb *nyin,* to grow. Such individuals who acquire wisdom based on experience and use this for the benefit of others receive the honorific of *payin,* or honorable, composed, and wise. As van der Geest relates in a 2004 journal article, an Akan saying is that a "*payin* has elbow so that 'when you are in the chief's palace and you are saying something which you should not say, a *payin* will . . . touch you with his elbow to stop you from saying that which might lead you into trouble.' The proverb means if the *payin* has nothing at all, he has wisdom, he can give advice to people."

Globally, elderhood is less celebrated in ritual than the beginning phases of social maturity, adolescence, and adulthood. Yet in some societies, age is a predominant means of ordering social life, such as in Africa's age set societies, where passing into elderhood and even exiting active elderhood are marked by powerful rituals. Here, persons progress through the life cycle collectively and form tightly bound groups, performing specific tasks. Societies where age groupings play such a powerful role in ordering social life have been found in Africa, among certain Native American groups, Australian Aborigines, and Papua New Guinea, but their global occurrence is relatively rare. The most elaborated forms of such cultural systems are found among East African nomadic herders, such as the Samburu of Kenya or the Tiriki.

Age set organizations for women in non-Western societies are reported much less frequently than for males. Well-documented examples include the Afikpo, Ebrie, and Mbato peoples of West Africa. It is likely, as Thomas suggests, that the paucity of age sets for females is related to the difficulty of male ethnographers learning about a realm of culture purposely kept secret from men.

— *Jay Sokolovsky*

See also **Family, Extended**

Further Readings

Aguilar, M. (Ed.). (1998). *The politics of age and gerontocracy in Africa: Ethnographies of the past and memories of the present.* Lawrenceville, NJ: Africa World Press.

Albert, S., & Cattell, M. (1994). *Old Age in global perspective.* New York: G. K. Hall.

Ikels, C., & Beall, C. (2000). Age, aging and anthropology, In R. Binstock & L. George (Eds.), *The handbook of aging and the social sciences* (5th ed., pp. 125–139) San Diego, CA: Academic Press.

Sokolovsky, J. (Ed.). (1997). *The cultural context of aging* (2nd ed.). New York: Bergin & Garvey.

Van Der Geest, S. (2004). "They don't come to listen": The experience of loneliness among older people in Kwahu, Ghana. *Journal of Cross-Cultural Gerontology, 19,* 77–96.

 # ELIADE, MIRCEA (1907–1986)

As novelist, philosopher, and humanist, Mircea Eliade advocated a unique perspective in his primary work as historian of religions, a field in which he was universally recognized as a brilliant and enthusiastic scholar. By means of his creative and controversial approach to the religious expression of humankind, he attempted to bridge the gap between the contemporary, secularized world and archaic or more traditional cultures, where the sacred dimension has held a higher profile. By any standard, Eliade had a significant impact on his field and related academic disciplines, but the debate about Eliade as "problem" or "prospect" is still quite lively. As a leading historian of religions, he mastered a vast array of data, but became, and still remains, the subject of considerable inquiry himself.

Eliade was born in Romania and was educated as a philosopher at the University of Bucharest. He was an avid reader (in several languages) and learned English to gain better access to James George Frazer's *The Golden Bough,* a classic in the anthropological study of religion. While in Italy doing research on Renaissance philosophers, he became interested in Indian philosophy and took an opportunity to study for 4 years at the University of Calcutta. This time in India, which included an extended period in an Himalayan ashram, changed Eliade's life in several ways. He returned to Bucharest and received the doctorate in 1932 for a dissertation on yoga (later published as *Yoga, Immortality, and Freedom*), but he also returned to the West with a profoundly different understanding of the East, including Eastern religious traditions.

Like Frazer's work, Eliade's writing was marked by illustrations drawn from the wide range of religious traditions, from the broad sweep of history. Though he produced several specialized studies on religion (such as yoga, shamanism, Australian religions), Eliade called for "learned generalists" that could identify and interpret parallel thoughts as expressed throughout the history of humankind. Of course, he was aware of the historical contexts of religious events, objects, and words but had a special interest in the recurring forms or patterns of religion. Such wide-ranging research led to the compilation of a major theoretical work, *Patterns in Comparative Religion* (1958), and toward the end of his life, the completion of his three-volume *A History of Religious Ideas* (1978–1986).

Through his cross-cultural and historical approach, Eliade documented what he claimed were universal patterns, and his search for common ground in the world's religious traditions led him to advocate a new humanism. He was aware of the more rationalistic perspective on religion, but some students of Eliade's hermeneutic detect a postmodern slant in his approach.

He left Romania in 1940 because of political turmoil and more promising circumstances and spent the rest of his life teaching and writing in Europe and America. This exile included time in Paris, where he lectured at the Sorbonne and formulated some of his central concepts. Eliade became a professor at the University of Chicago in 1956, where he succeeded Joachim Wach and served with many illustrious colleagues for 30 years, until his death in 1986. In Eliade's earlier days, he published numerous novels (including *The Forbidden Forest*), which focused on great philosophical themes and fantasy and included slightly veiled references to his Indian experience. Taken as a whole, the literary legacy of Mircea Eliade is remarkable; he wrote over 1,300 items (beginning with an article at age 14), including many books that are still held in great esteem and some that are regarded as classics in the field. Other important titles in the Eliade oeuvre include *The Myth of the Eternal Return* (an analysis of the human experience of history and time); *The Forge and the Crucible* (a byproduct of Eliade's lifetime interest in alchemy); and *The Sacred and the Profane* (a study of how the holy has manifested itself in some cultures). In 1961, he was instrumental in launching the prestigious journal *History of Religions;* he also served as editor in chief of the 16-volume *Encyclopedia of Religion* (1987), an important reference set that reflects Eliade's own encyclopedic range of interests.

The intellectual forces that shaped Eliade (through the written word or through his many friendships) were numerous and varied (for example, Rudolf Otto, Surendranath Dasgupta, Gerardus van der Leeuw, George Dumézil, Raffaele Pettazoni, C. J. Jung, Paul Tillich). His background in philosophy and lifelong interest in Eastern religions and mythology (among other subjects) are evident at every turn. Eliade's analyses of religious phenomena (as historian, phenomenologist, and interpreter) always reflect his academic background, but the reader of an Eliade book can easily detect the author's energy, creativity, and curiosity. Much of that creativity was channeled into an intriguing technical vocabulary, without which it is impossible to understand what Eliade means. Sometimes he adopted (and adapted) these technical terms from ancient or medieval writers or his own scholarly predecessors, but some words were defined in specific ways for a book and serve as keys to its main points (for example, axis mundi, coincidentia oppositorum, ganz andere, hierophany, homo religiosus, homo symbolicus, illud tempus, imago mundi, sacralize, theophany). Eliade promoted his humanist agenda by asking readers to recover meaning and truth in a "desacralized" world—by discovering the sacred, the "wholly other," in its various hierophanies—and to accept religious phenomena within their own frame of reference.

— *Gerald L. Mattingly*

See also **Religion and Anthropology**

Further Readings

Eliade, M. (1963). *Patterns in comparative religion.* New York: World Publishing.
Rennie, B. S. (1996). *Reconstructing Eliade: Making sense of religion.* Albany: State University of New York Press.
Saliba, J. A. (1976). *"Homo religiosus" in Mircea Eliade: An anthropological evaluation.* Leiden, The Netherlands: Brill.

 ## EMICS

Emics is a term used by some cultural anthropologists to denote descriptions and explanations of human beliefs and behaviors in terms relevant to the native practitioners of the culture in question. The linguist Kenneth Pike coined the term emics from the linguistic term *phonemics,* the study of the system of sound contrasts used by speakers of a language to construct meaningful units: words and so forth. Pike used emics to denote a level of description of human behavior based on categories meaningfully relevant to the people performing the behavior.

Marvin Harris and other cultural materialists popularized the term within anthropology by using it to refer to native or folk explanations for cultural beliefs and behaviors. One of Harris's best-known examples is his analysis of the Hindu Indian cattle complex. Hindus revere cattle as sacred and claim that their religion prevents them from killing or eating the cattle. This is, in Harris's terms, an emic explanation for Hindus' treatment of cattle. The emic level of explanation can be further divided into two categories corresponding to (conscious) belief and behavior: *emic-mental* (cattle are not killed or eaten because the Hindu religion has declared them to be sacred) and *emic-behavioral* (cattle are not killed or allowed to starve to death).

It is important to emphasize that in Pike's original formulation, emics (along with etics) represented a level of description. Pike saw behavior, like speech, as composed of waves; humans, however perceive, categorize, and react to behavior in terms of particles, or contrastive units, which in the case of language correspond to phonemes. In more contemporary terms, we might say that behavior is analog, while human mental processing of behavior is digital. Pike's goal of emic description of any human behavior is to present that behavior in terms and categories relevant to the native participants in the behavior. Harris and some other anthropologists use the term to represent a level of explanation. Emic explanations correspond very approximately to what some other anthropologists refer to as "folk models" or folk "explanations."

— *Ronald Kephart*

See also **Etics; Language; Models, Anthropological**

Further Readings

Harris, M. (1987). *Cultural materialism: The search for a science of culture.* New York: Random House.
Headland, T. N., Pike, K. L., & Harris, M. (Eds.). (1990). *Emics and etics: The insider/outsider debate.* Newbury Park: Sage.
Pike, K. L. (1971). *Language in relation to a unified theory of the structure of human behavior.* The Hague: Mouton.

 ## EMPEDOCLES (495–435 BC)

Empedocles was a Greek pre-Socratic philosopher and a poet. He was born circa 495 BC in the Sicilian city of Acragas (recently Agrigento) and died, according to a famous but unproven story, by throwing himself into the active volcano Mount Etna in Sicily circa 435 BC, thus intending to demonstrate his personal immortality.

Empedocles is said to have been personally extravagant, practicing magic, medicine, rhetoric, and politics. His philosophy was fundamentally inspired by, and is a reaction to, the teachings of another two major pre-Socratics, Pythagoras and Parmenides. Empedocles provided the first comprehensive vision of the pluralistic and dynamic unity of the universe in Western philosophy. He sought to put all diversity of being into one system, to unite nature with human soul, physics with psychology, lifeless things with living bodies, even competing and contradictory powers and processes into one cosmic cycle of endless flux of formation and dissolution.

His two major works, philosophical poems *On Nature* and *Purifications,* survive in one of the largest corpus of fragments of all pre-Socratics. Empedocles's basic philosophical doctrine presupposes that there are four irreducible physical elements or roots (earth, air, fire, and water), from which the whole cosmos is created. To explain this creation as well as any kind of movement, change, and evolution, Empedocles postulates, in addition to four elements, two basic cosmic forces or principles, one of which is constructive (love, *philia*), another destructive (strife, *neikos*), as a means by which the elements are combined and separated. The elements themselves, being the earliest version of particle theory, though eternal and unchanging, are by no means mechanistic and involve their own creative potential within, since they are also divine and sentient. This potential comes into actual being by their intermingling in endless mixtures, which are constantly reconfigured without losing their elementary building blocks. The active powers, remaining rather magical and mythical in Empedocles's conception, that secure this reconfiguration of stable and rather passive elements are of two kinds: Love brings all together, harmonizes and unites, while strife separates, dissolutes, and divides. The results of both attraction and distraction processes are bodies, plants, organisms, and living creatures and their decomposition back into parts and elements. This shows the powerful analogy between the evolution of the universe and the evolution of life and makes a link to Empedocles's biological explanations of zoogeny (the origin of species), which is also anthropologically relevant and

later influenced Plato and Aristotle. According to Empedocles, life is the consequence of an evolutionary process.

— *Emil Visnovsky*

Further Readings

Guthrie, W. K. C. (1962–1978). *A history of Greek philosophy.* Cambridge: Cambridge University Press.

Kirk, G. S., Raven, J. E., & Schofield, M. (1983). *The pre-Socratic philosophers.* Cambridge: Cambridge University Press.

Wright, M. R. (1981). *Empedocles: The extant fragments.* New Haven, CT, and London: Yale University Press.

ENCULTURATION

Enculturation is the process by which children are socialized to the standard modes of thinking, feeling, and behaving considered appropriate for an adult in a given society. Because language is the primary means of communication, it is one of most important components of the enculturation process, and because cultural information is encoded in language, children acquire knowledge about their society through verbal interaction with adults. Even before birth, a fetus can differentiate its mother's voice from other sounds. Though an infant is born with the ability to produce any sound and learn any language, they are shown to prefer their mother's native tongue, which they hear prenatally. Later on in their development, an infant begins to discriminate between sounds, producing those that are heard most often. In addition, they learn speech patterns and syntax as adults use intonation and rhythmic sounds. Once toddlers have the ability to communicate ideas and a cognitive awareness of their surroundings, adults begin to define their world and its important aspects. For example, children in Western societies learn the many dangers of modern conveniences, including light sockets, hot irons and stoves, and traffic.

Furthermore, children begin to learn the social rules of behavior as they interact with other members of their society. American children learn the value of directness and independence, while Japanese children learn that indirectness and circumscribed behavior are more appropriate. Children also learn about the concepts of status and roles with which they must be familiar. For example, in patrilineal societies, the father is the main source of discipline and authority, while in matrilineal societies, this role falls to the mother's brother, and the child responds to each accordingly. Children also learn gender roles, including the expectations of each sex as they mature. In Australia, fathers give boys tasks that bring them outside, while mothers solidify the concept of the women's domain in the home. Other aspects taught are the attitudes, feelings, and emotions of the culture. Displays of affection are regarded differently depending on social background. In Ecuador, men and boys hug and kiss as a sign of friendship and goodwill. However, in other parts of the world, this behavior would make men the objects of ridicule.

Anthropologists began studying this phenomenon in the late 1800s. Unlike psychologists, they did not automatically assume that the enculturation process was identical cross-culturally. Influenced by Freud, the early work focused on set stages encountered in the first 3 years. Freud believed that each individual experience in early childhood formed adult personality and any deviation from a set pattern produced psychosis. However, in Margaret Mead's classic study, *Coming of Age in Samoa* (1928), child-rearing studies showed that Freud's stages were not universal; even the concept of adolescent angst was foreign to the Samoan teenagers. Mead argued that no stage was common to all cultures nor inevitably faced by a growing child. Children growing up in Samoa developed different personality traits because their characters were formed by different enculturation processes.

— *Luci Fernandes*

See also **Childhood Studies; Family, Nuclear; Socialization**

Further Readings

Bailey, G., & Peoples, J. (2002). *Essentials of cultural anthropology.* Belmont, CA: Wadsworth Thomson Learning.

Lenkeit, R. E. (2004). *Introducing cultural anthropology.* New York: McGraw-Hill.

Rosman, A., & Rubel, P. G. (2004). *The tapestry of culture: An introduction to cultural anthropology.* New York: McGraw-Hill.

NATURE AND NURTURE

For centuries, scientists have debated whether nature or nurture has more influence on human behavior. The basic argument was whether human differences are historic and the result of genetics or whether they are environmental and therefore changeable.

In the 19th century, nature was widely believed to be dominant over nurture. Those who held with this belief thought that inherited traits accounted for most human behavior.

Much of the fuel for nature advocates has come from studies of twins who were separated at birth and raised in different environments. When they meet as adults, they are found to have many of the same mannerisms and habits. It seems plausible that something in the genetic makeup of the individual determines such mannerisms, considering that the twins were reared in entirely different environments.

Much of the literature in recent years that calls itself evolutionary psychology or behavioral genetics has held that most human behavior has been programmed into the human genes by natural selection. This point of view has been popularized in recent years by MIT psychologist Stephen Pinker and others. In January 2003, this view was challenged by a pair of prominent Stanford University scientists, Paul R. Ehrlich and Marcus W. Feldman. Both are members of Stanford's department of biological sciences' faculty and both are considered pioneers in genetics and evolutionary biology and have recently written separate books on those topics. Their article "Genes and Cultures: What Creates Our Behavioral Phenome?" challenges Pinker and others, whom they say "overestimate how much of human behavior is primarily traceable to biological universals that are reflected in our genes."

Ehrlich and Feldman argue that evolutionary psychologists such as Pinker fail to acknowledge the importance of cultural evolution and of interactions. They accuse these psychologists of promoting the idea that human nature is genetically fixed, while they themselves suggest that circumstances and experiences contribute a great deal to each person's individual nature.

Their publication was met by many rebuttals from leading anthropologists who accused the two men of name-calling and wrongfully criticizing the methods used by geneticists and evolutionary psychologists. Many believe it is not necessary to take an extreme position on either side of the nature-nurture controversy. Most scientists agree that, to some degree, heredity and environment work hand-in-hand to develop the personalities or natures of human beings.

— Pat McCarthy

ENDOGAMY

From the Greek εντὸζ + γαμώ ("in" + "to marry"), endogamy is the marital rule according to which the spouses are selected from within the same social group (kindred, religious, ethnic, etc.). It is the opposite of *exogamy.*

Through endogamy, social groups aim to preserve their constitutive elements (for example, power, wealth, religion, language) and transmit them to the following generations, in order to perpetuate their existence.

Each society may be endogamic in one or more aspects and exogamic in others. For instance, the Aborigines in Australia are exogamic as to the *clan* (a social group the members of which acknowledge a common ancestry and whose relationships are ruled by solidarity) but endogamic as to the *tribe* (wider than a clan group that owns a territory and is homogeneous and autonomous from a political and social viewpoint).

Kindred Endogamy

One form of endogamy is the one taking place within the kindred group (but beyond the boundaries of incest, which may be different for each society). Such a case is *preferential marriage,* that is, marriage with a close relative, such as between the children of a brother and sister (*cross cousins*). In practice, this translates to a man marrying his mother's brother's or father's sister's daughter. Such marriages are encountered in Southeast Asia, New Guinea, the Aborigines in Australia, and native South Americans.

Another case of kindred endogamy is the so-called lineage endogamy, that is, the marriage between "relatives" who are beyond the boundaries of kinship (and therefore of incest) set by their society but still maintain a memory of kinship. This is a marriage that, although desirable, is by no means mandatory. Such a marriage is usually performed on a *lineage* level (hence the term *lineage endogamy*), that is, within the wider group of individuals beyond the family who are interconnected through consanguineal kinship either patrilinealy or matrilinealy and who acknowledge a common ancestor. It may often result in the women having the same family name before and after marriage (*patronymic endogamy*), since it usually occurs in *patrilineal* lineages, where their prime constituents (such as the family name) are transmitted via the father. Such marriages are often arranged at the birth of the future spouses and serve to reinforce "family" ties. They are a very common strategy in Mediterranean societies, for example, in rural France, the Mediterranean Arab societies, and certain societies in Greece, such as the Maniates in west Mani and the Arvanites in Ermionida, both in the Peloponnese. The Arvanites are groups spread across Greece and characterized mainly by their language, Arvanitika, an archaic Albanian dialect they speak in parallel with Greek. The figure records a particular case of *lineage endogamy* from the village of Didima in Ermionida. The predominant explanation for such a marriage is that it allows for the patrimony to remain in the lineage. If the girls married outside of it, a part of the patrimony would leave the lineage in the form of the dowry.

In other societies, the endogamic rule, according to which, following the death of a spouse, the second husband must be a brother of the first (*levirate*) or the second wife a sister of the first (*sororate*), is in place. For example, the mosaic law dictates that should the husband die, the wife must marry his brother. The children born from this marriage are considered to be the dead man's children. This ensures the continuation of the dead husband's family.

The rule of *kindred endogamy* is also applied in the case of *fraternal polyandry* (the most common form of polyandry, where a woman can simultaneously have more than one husband, provided they are all brothers). In this case, endogamy shows which lineage the children originate from, which would be impossible if the husbands were not brothers.

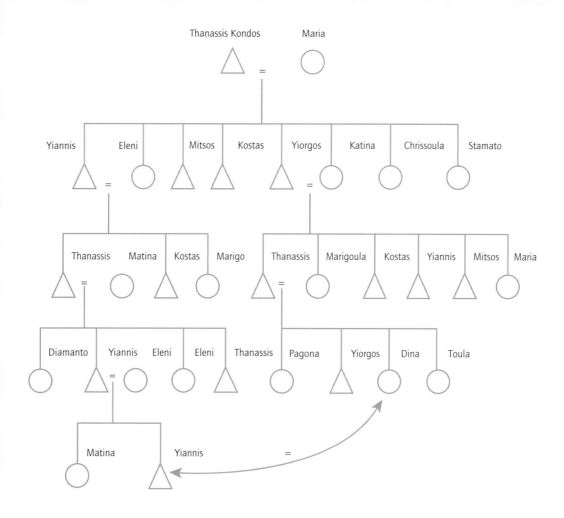

Lineage endogamy (Didima, Greece). The marriage of Dina and Yiannis was not only desirable but also allowed, as the forbidding rule of incest extends only to second cousins

Religious Endogamy

Religious endogamy is a universally enforced form of endogamy, according to which the spouses must belong to the same religion. Religious endogamy is especially strong because religion and marriage are intimately intertwined. Marriage is usually validated by a religious ritual, which must be accepted by the spouses; this can only happen when they both embrace the same religion. If this requirement is not fulfilled, the marriage cannot take place.

A particularly strict form of endogamy takes place within the castes in India (i.e., hierarchical groups in which individuals are hereditarily placed for life), as dictated by the Hindu religion.

Local and Ethnic Endogamy

The preservation of the cohesion (and consequently the perpetuation) of the *local community* (social group the members of which share goods and interests and live together in general), the *ethnic group* (the group of individuals belonging to the same culture and acknowledging themselves as such), and even of the *nation* are the main reasons behind the choice of the spouse from within the same local community, ethnic group, or nation. These forms of endogamy are particularly widespread and powerful.

The following saying, used throughout Greece with respect to spouse selection, aptly summarizes the preference toward local endogamy: "[Get] a shoe from your place even if it's patched," that is, it is better to choose a local spouse despite his or her short-comings (implying that selecting a nonlocal spouse may have unpredictable consequences). Thereby, in Didima (Peloponnese), on a local community level and according to marriage records, between 1928 and 1939, 93.7% of grooms and 90.0% of brides were locals. From 1940 to 1988, these percentages continuously fall, reaching 56.7% and 83.6% respectively between 1980 and 1988. This trend shows the gradual decline of the rule of local endogamy.

— *Maria Velioti-Georgopoulos*

See also **Exogamy**

Further Readings

Goody, J. (1983). *The development of family and marriage in Europe.* Cambridge, UK: Cambridge University Press.

Lévi-Strauss, C. (1949). Endogamy et exogamy. In *Les structures élémentaires de la parenté* (pp. 49–60). Paris: PUF.

Segalen, M. (1972). *Nuptialité et alliance. Le choix du conjoint dans une commune de l'Eure.* Paris: Maisonneuve et Larose.

 # ENGELBRECHT, WILLIAM ERNST

Dr. William Ernst Engelbrecht, the son of Waldo Ernst Engelbrecht and Margaret Patricia Schall, is an archaeologist whose primary focus continues to be on Northern Iroquoian peoples. After completing his bachelor of arts in anthropology at Northwestern University (1965), where he studied under Sally Binford, Paul Bohanen, Ronald Cohen, Creighton Gable, Bruce Trigger, and Oswald Werner, Engelbrecht entered the University of Michigan in pursuit of his doctorate. At the University of Michigan, he continued his studies while taking classes taught by James B. Griffin, Arthur Jelinek, Frank Livingston, Jefferey Parsons, Roy Rappaport, Marshall Sahlins, Robert Whallon (Engelbrecht's dissertation adviser), and Leslie White.

In 1965, Engelbrecht received funding from the National Science Foundation, which allowed him to attend a field school in Hay Hollow Valley (Arizona) that was under the direction of Paul Martin. Building on this experience in Arizona, he completed a variety of fieldwork, including his participation (1966) in the Teotihuacán Mapping Project, which was initiated by William Sanders from Penn State and continued by Jeff Parsons. In 1967, Engelbrecht completed fieldwork in Saginaw, Michigan, and in southeastern Missouri.

Engelbrecht was hired by Marian White to run the Highway Salvage Archaeology program at the State University of New York at Buffalo in 1969 while finishing his degree at the University of Michigan. White, an archaeologist who was responsible for the identification, examination, and preservation of prehistoric and historic sites throughout the western New York region, provided Engelbrecht with additional direction and an enduring friendship that still motivates and guides Engelbrecht. While overseeing the Salvage Archaeology program, Engelbrecht gained a strong familiarity with the Niagara Frontier and the peoples whose activities in the region preceded any European excursions. The job also provided him with an opportunity to familiarize himself with archaeological collections in the western New York region.

After finishing his graduate studies and obtaining a PhD in anthropology (1971), Engelbrecht received a teaching position at Edinboro University in Pennsylvania, where he remained until 1973. In 1973, he was hired as an assistant professor in the anthropology department at Buffalo State College. He served as department chair for 6 years and retired in 2003. During his tenure, he taught an assortment of courses, which allowed him to incorporate his research and field experience into courses focused on human origins, the indigenous populations of North America, ancient civilizations, and archaeological examinations of North America. He also directed 17 archaeological field schools that focused on the excavation of the Eaton Site. Eaton is a multicomponent site located in western New York, which includes a Late Woodland Iroquoian village site occupied circa AD 1550. In conjunction with these field schools, Engelbrecht taught multiple seminars in archaeology that prepared and assisted students in the research and analysis of material from the Eaton Site.

Engelbrecht continues to analyze material collected from the Eaton Site and assist graduate and undergraduate students examining the material. Throughout his career as an educator, he advised countless students in their educational and career pursuits, assisted and encouraged students in their efforts to conduct and publish research, and served as an outside dissertation reader for 19 graduate students. His dedication to his students was recognized in 1990 when he received the Chancellor's Award for Excellence in Teaching.

Engelbrecht's research and publication interests varied, but his primary focus remains on Northern Iroquoian peoples, particularly the nations of the Haudenosaunee Confederacy (the Iroquois). His PhD dissertation itself, *A Stylistic Analysis of New York Iroquois Pottery* (1971), was a study of Iroquois ceramic trends that served as a continuation of Robert Whallon's study of Owasco and Iroquois ceramics. The examination and analysis of Iroquoian ceramics was a continual focus for Engelbrecht, resulting in additional publications between 1971 and 2003. During this time, he also analyzed and published a large volume of data from the Eaton Site and other sites in the northeastern North American region. Of this work, he placed a considerable amount of attention on the effects of contact between Native Americans and Europeans and the "disappearance" of Iroquoian nations, particularly peoples from the St. Lawrence region. Engelbrecht's work also included studies of Paleo-Indian "watercraft" (work and publication coauthored with Carl Seyfert) and population changes and social organization among Native American nations. Through it all, however, the Haudenosaunee Confederacy remained a primary interest, leading to Engelbrecht's comprehensive 2003 publication, *Iroquoia: The Development of a Native World*.

— *Neil P. O'Donnell*

Further Readings

Engelbrecht, William E. (1971). A stylistic analysis of New York Iroquois pottery. (Doctoral dissertation, University of Michigan, 1971). *University Microfilms International.*

Engelbrecht, William E. (2003). *Iroquoia: The development of a native world.* Syracuse, New York: Syracuse University Press.

Engelbrecht, William E., & Grayson, Donald K. (Eds.). (1978). *Essays in Northeastern anthropology in memory of Marian E. White. Occasional Publications in Northeastern Anthropology,* 5.

ENGELS, FRIEDRICH (1820–1895)

Friedrich Engels was born November 28, 1820. Engels's father was a wealthy German entrepreneur. In his early 20s, he moved to Manchester, England, to supervise the family cotton factory. While managing the plant, Engels was shaken by the poverty of his workers. This became the data for his book *Condition of the Working Classes in England* (1844). He also became associated with the Chartist, an English working-class movement for political and economic reforms. In 1844, in Paris, Engels became part of a radical journal *Franco-German Annals,* which was edited by Karl Marx; the two men became close friends. Together they wrote *The Holy Family* and *German Ideology.* On January 25, 1845, Marx was deported from France for radical activities. Engels and Marx from then on would always be seen as part of a larger European community of revolutionaries. Marx, together with Engels, moved to Belgium. With Engels's financial support, Marx had the opportunity to put together his economic and political theories in written form.

In July 1845, Engels and Marx traveled to England. There, they met with Chartist leader George Julian Harney. In Brussels, in 1846, Engels and Marx established the Communist Correspondence Committee for all socialists in Europe. Later, this became the Communist League. While in England in December 1847, they attended a meeting of the Communist League Central Committee. It was decided that in order to remove the bourgeoisie from power, the proletariat must control the economy; eliminate the current society, which was established on class antagonisms; and create a new society without classes or private property. Engels and Marx wrote a pamphlet explaining their philosophy; the first draft was called *The Principles of Communism.* Later, Marx finished the pamphlet, calling it *The Communist Manifesto,* which summarized the forthcoming revolution and the nature of the communist society.

Together, these two men claimed that class societies were specific to a restricted historical situation. The history of any class society is one of class struggle. Each class has its own unique interests; this conflicts with the interests of other classes in society. This conflict sooner or later leads to revolution. One of Engels's and Marx's main premises was that the big changes in history were the triumph of one class over another.

Source: Courtesy, Wikipedia.

As Engels and Marx explained it, the *bourgeoisie* (capitalists) were the owners of all the raw materials and means of production. The *proletariat* (workers) owned only their labor power and were required to sell their labor power to the capitalists in order to live. With the vanishing of the bourgeoisie as a class, *class society* would cease to exist. The class-based state is then no longer needed to control the producers, and it withers away."

With the publication of the *Manifesto*, Engels and Marx were forced to flee from Belgium to London. Engels continued to support Marx both financially and philosophically. To do this, Engels returned to work for his father in Germany until 1869, when he was able sell off his share of the family business. The two kept in constant contact over the next 20 years.

Karl Marx died in London in March 1883. Engels devoted the rest of his life to editing and translating Marx's writings. This included the second volume of *Capital* (1885). Engels then used Marx's notes to write the third volume of *Capital* (1894). Friedrich Engels died in London on August 5, 1895.

Engels was a major Marxist theorist in his own right, contributing much to Marxism. Several of his major works are seen as classics in Marxist anthropology, sociology, and economic history. The partial list that follows has made a major contribution to anthropology.

Peasant War in Germany, written in 1850, was inspired by the failure of the revolution of 1848, which strongly resembled the peasant revolutions of 1525. To have a deeper understanding of these histories, the researcher must examine the class grouping in both histories. Both revolutions proved that class alliances are required if there is to be any hope of success in any political revolution.

Engels wrote *Anti-During* in 1878 and *Dialectics of Nature* in 1873 to 1884 to explain materialism and dialectics. Matter in motion is self-creating, with everything in the universe, including life, developing out of already-existing natural forces. Life originates from a complex natural interaction of physical, chemical, and biological materials and evolves from one form into another. Materialism, being dialectical, becomes science without a need for philosophy. Anthropology, being interdisciplinary, can use Engels's work as a bridge between the physical, biological, and social sciences.

Socialism, Utopian and Scientific, 1882 to 1892, was written as a summary of *Anti-During* in pamphlet form. One of Engels's major points was that the three origins of Marxism were French socialism, German philosophy, and English economics. In this pamphlet, Engels clarified that most socialism of the past had been utopian. In the past, in most political history, class analysis was absent. There was a very slow maturity of the dialectical philosophy over thousands of years; this philosophy was what allowed Marx to see and explain the materialist conception of history. This means that the first principle of historical sociology is the mode of producing the necessities of life. This, in turn, is controlled by the distribution of the needed resources and the products created through labor among the members of society. After capitalism took off in Europe in the late 18th century, it rapidly replaced existing class societies around the world. Ranking by birth was replaced by free trade, legal equality, individualism, and competition. Capitalism controlled the economic resources, and the workers had no choice but to sell their labor power to any employer they could find. The state represented the interest of the ruling class. The republic became a dictatorship of the bourgeoisie. With mass production of goods, the means of production became socialized. The working class was then in a position, through revolution, to replace capitalism with socialism.

According to *Origin of the Family, Private Property, and the State*, 1884, state society and class society are two sides of the same category. The first form of exploitation was within the family. The exploitation of women was the first form of inequality. With each further evolution of inequality, class structure is further developed, and the changes in the family reflect these evolving inequalities. With capitalism, the capitalist controls the opportunities for working-class survival. With the family, the husband has authority over the wife in the contemporary capitalist families. To have any real social equality, there must be total equal rights by law. This requires not only legal and political rights, but the woman would have to also be economically independent of her husband. As such, this solution for social equality could lead to the abolition of the monogamous family as the economic unit of society.

Friedrich Engels was known mostly for his close association with Karl Marx. However, Engels made many valuable contributions to Marxist theory in his own right. While Marx had a strong background in philosophy and later political economy, Engels kept Marx abreast of the latest changes in the natural sciences and anthropology.

— *Michael Joseph Francisconi*

See also **Marxism; Political Economy**

Further Readings

Cameron, K. N. (1995). *Dialectical materialism and modern science.* New York: International Publishers.

Engels, F. (1975). *Origin of the family, private property, and the state.* New York: International Publishers.

Engels, F. (1977). *Dialectics of nature.* New York: International Publishers

Engels, F. (1978). *Anti-during.* New York: International Publishers.

Marx, K., & Engels, F. (1970). *The German ideology.* New York: International Publishers.

McLellan, D. (1977). *Friedrich Engels.* New York: Penguin Books.

ENLIGHTENMENT, AGE OF

As a historical epoch, "The Age of Enlightenment" comprises the crucial developments of Western civilization in the 18th century. In France, which is considered the cradle of the Enlightenment, this period included the time from the death of Louis XIV (1715) until the coup d'état of Napoleon Bonaparte (1799). But Enlightenment was spread also over Europe, involving a range of developments in Germany, Britain, Scotland, and Russia, and crossed even further over the Atlantic to influence the substantial events in the history of North America. The founding fathers of the United States were devoted followers of either British or French Enlightenment thought.

The Enlightenment is generally known as a broad social, political, cultural, and intellectual movement, which had been the culmination of a longer period, initiated by the Renaissance and Humanism of the 14th and 15th centuries and followed by Reformation and the natural philosophy and science revolutions of the 16th and 17th centuries. This latter era as a whole, including the Enlightenment as its pinnacle, is described as "The Age of Reason." At the same time, the Enlightenment marked a new beginning. New ideas and approaches to old institutions set the stage for great revolutions to come. Politically, this period included the revolutions both in France (1789–1799) and America (1763–1793). In terms of social development of humanity, the Enlightenment marked the decisive turn to modernity, with its ideals of *liberté, egalité, fraternité,* all destined to have been split up into the opposite ideologies of capitalism and socialism; these too are the emanations of the Enlightenment, with their shared goal to transform the human world, even though pursued by radically different means of liberal democracy versus social revolution. In terms of cultural and intellectual paradigms, the Enlightenment marked the advent of the reign of rationality, science, education, and progress. The movement's intention was to lead humanity out of a long period of irrationality, superstition, and tyranny of the Dark Ages (the Middle Ages). Individualism, freedom, and change replaced community, authority, and tradition as core European values. In fact, the Enlightenment intellectuals themselves were those who coined the name for their era and project. They believed that human reason could be employed in order to build a better world. However, the Enlightenment was the age of reason, which could not eliminate faith as such, despite all its efforts; rather, it replaced the religious faith with the secular faith in reason itself. The essence of the Enlightenment in such a sense was best formulated by Immanuel Kant (1724–1804) in his famous short essay titled "*Was ist Aufklärung?*" (1784), who gave the motto of enlightenment as "*Sapere aude!* Have courage to use your own intelligence!" However, Kant made a distinction between the "Age of Enlightenment" and the "enlightened age," while associating the former with the public and the latter with the private spheres of human life. The full triumph of the Enlightenment principles he could see only in the public.

Intellectually, philosophy can be said to represent the heart of the Enlightenment. The philosophy of the Enlightenment had continued in the belief in a rational, orderly, and comprehensible universe and put forward the claim for a rational and orderly organization of the state and knowledge in a way expressed in the doctrine of Deism. The idea of universal rational order, either found in nature or made in human society, can be seen as the core of this philosophy. Thus, rationalization, standardization, and the search for universal unities are the hallmarks of the Enlightenment. This idea, as applied to social and political order, found its many ways of expression in the "rationalization" of governments in England, Austria, Prussia, and, in particular, in the ideals of the American Declaration of Independence, the Jacobin program of the French Revolution, as well as the American Constitution of 1787. The figure who had become the icon of the age owing to his best representation of such a line of thought was the elitist French philosopher François-Marie Arouet Voltaire (1694–1778). Voltaire had personally served as a counselor to several European rulers in order to achieve the enlightened state of governance. According to him, freedom and tolerance are the companions of human reason. His slogan "*Écrasez l'infâme!*" directed at the traditional Catholic Church and its followers, may serve also as a battle cry against all kinds of human stupidities and for the ideal of a rational society. Voltaire believed in the republic of scholars and in the primacy of ideas in historical evolution. Ideas were for him the motive force. Thus, he became the prophet of progress, which also is the gradual assertion of reason. Voltaire and his rationalistic followers have put much hope in the powers of reason to solve all human problems. One of the most optimistic of them was the Marquis de Condorcet (1743–1794), who in his posthumously published work *Esquisse d'un tableau historique des progrès de l'esprit humain* (1795) provided what can be regarded as the most radical advocacy of human progress based on the power of reason and science in the history of thought. Nonetheless, it was Jean-Jacques Rousseau (1712–1778), the second important Enlightenment philosopher next to Voltaire and his chief adversary, who started to oppose in many respects such overly constructionist prospects, while inclining more to naturalism, which would, eventually, lead to the Romantic movement. Whereas Voltaire insisted on the supremacy of the intellect, Rousseau emphasized the emotions; whereas Voltaire emphasized social, Rousseau emphasized natural forces. The Romantics represented a sort of internal declination within the Age of Enlightenment, which from Rousseau to German thinker J. W. von Goethe (1749–1832) adopted the naturalistic intuition of self-organization and evolutionary forces. The Romantics intuited the unhappy opposition between the naturalness of self-ordering of nature and the artificiality of rational ordering imposed on an organic world. Rousseau even went so far as to advocate a return to primitive simplicity. The modern dualism of culture versus nature has been born with Rousseau, who also applied it to the sphere of education in his famous novel *Émile* (1762).

The idea of universal rational ordering was also implemented in the domain of human knowledge and science. The group of intellectuals calling themselves "*Encyclopédistes*" came up with the idea to bring together all scientific knowledge of all fields in one comprehensive multivolume edition. From this publication, they expected the regeneration of humanity. Denis Diderot (1713–1784) and Jean le Rond d'Alembert (1717–1783) sought the liberation of the mind and education of humanity via the spread of knowledge. Under the editorship of these two, *The Encyclopédie ou Dictionnaire Raisonné des Sciences, des Arts et des Métiers* was published in 17 volumes between 1751 and 1765. The aim of this Enlightenment project was to provide information on every sphere of knowledge and to promote the application of science in industry, trade, and the arts. *Encyclopédie* can be seen as a true manifesto and epitomizing of the spirit of the Enlightenment. In this spirit Baron D'Holbach (1723–1789) wrote his *Systèm de la Nature* (1770), in which he firmly asserted that explanations of nature should not be sought in traditional beliefs or the "revelations" of the Bible, but through the application of scientific method. The Enlightenment thinkers replaced the universalism of theology with the universalism of scientific conceptions.

Such an approach supported the empirical understanding of human nature in the Enlightenment. Etienne Bonnot de Condillac (1715–1780), the most important French Enlightenment empiricist, believed that moral reasoning was susceptible to the same exactitude as geometry and also identified the association of ideas as the key to the study of human nature. Even though Rousseau and the *Encyclopédistes* succumbed to the idea of a "noble savage," according to himself as well as to Voltaire and many others, there is no such thing as godly created nor naturally given unchanging human nature. Rather, it is substantially and almost completely the product of culture and education, as if humans could mold themselves in an arbitrary way. However, there is a problem with human beings here, since the science suggests the doctrine of determinism, effective also in the social realm. Human beings are not exempt from determination even by their biological makeup, and if we accept the naturalist empirical view that human beings are organized systems of matter, as J. O. de La Mettrie (1709–1751) did claim in his work *L'Homme Machine* (1747), and that our minds are formed as a result of experiences, then we may try to explain human behavior in terms of cause and effect. If we knew enough about the biological makeup of an individual, his early childhood experiences, and the social and historical circumstances he was born into, then perhaps we could predict all of his actions. From this point of view, the idea of free will or the ability to choose is simply the result of or ignorance of all of the causal factors. Thus, the idea of determinism, both natural and social, sometimes understood in a very mechanistic way, gave rise to social engineering and started the reign in the realm of anthropology for centuries to come. This has been regarded as the epitome of a scientific approach to human nature, knowledge of which has had to serve as the guidance for rational human action and the building of the rational social order.

The legacy of the Enlightenment can be seen in the set of ideas centralized around rationality and freedom: To be rational is to be free to pursue the scientific truth wherever it may lead us, and to be free is to be rational in the practical pursuing of individual ends and rights. Liberal democracy has been proposed as the best political framework for such a combined application of reason and freedom. However, the history since the 18th century, and in particular the history of the 20th century, has shown that reason is not always the sufficient guarantee of freedom, and vice versa. Without any charge of antihuman intentions placed against the Enlightenment thinkers, it is historical evidence that the atrocities committed in the post-Enlightenment era have also been backed by both the ideologies of rationality and emancipation. It seems as if the Enlightenment has missed some important point in the nature of human nature. The unbound reason can be dangerously intolerant itself, so the problem unresolved has remained, whether reason can be directed from within or not. Furthermore, another problem has remained open, namely how reason can avoid its inclinations to uniformity and preserve diversity. It seems that liberation from tyrannies of blind dogmas and traditions could not save humanity completely from new rationalistic trappings. Thus, there have been many controversies over the interpretations of the "Enlightenment project." Already in the 18th century and later in the 19th century, the movement of counter-Enlightenment had appeared (particularly in Germany), but only more recently, later in the 20th century, did it become evident that the main currents of Western civilization have their roots in the Enlightenment. Undoubtedly, the Enlightenment occupies a central role in the justification of the movement known as "modernism" as well as the era known as "modernity." However, the substantial critique of such trends, based on the failed Enlightenment concept of instrumental rationality, was initiated by philosophers, such as the Germans T. Adorno and M. Horkheimer, in their book *Dialectics of Enlightenment* (1944). Furthermore, at the turn of the 20th century, a cultural and intellectual movement of "postmodernism," drawing on such philosophers as Nietzsche and represented by the radical critic of the Enlightenment Foucault (1926–1984) and many others, started to invoke the terms "postmodernity" and "post-Enlightenment." This has brought up the controversy of whether the legacy of the Enlightenment is to be preserved and continued or rather reassessed and abandoned. It is by no means clear whether humanity is to turn to the search for completely new ideals, or to return to the pre-Enlightenment era, or perhaps attempt a New Enlightenment, in the style of the "New Age" movement. There are some, such as German philosopher J. Habermas (b. 1929), who consider the Enlightenment project unfinished and suggest its completion under some revisions. Thus, judging the Enlightenment shows that it can be both praised and blamed for many things to which it has given an impetus for arising in the modern world.

— *Emil Visnovsky*

See also **Kant, Immanuel; Postmodernism**

Further Readings

Dupre, L. (2004). *The Enlightenment & the intellectual foundations of modern culture.* New Haven, CT: Yale University Press.

Gray, J. (1995). *Enlightenment's wake: Politics and culture as the close of modern age.* London: Routledge.

Himmelfarb, G. (2004). *The roads to modernity: The British, French, and American Enlightenments.* New York: Knopf.

Kramnick, I. (Ed.). (1995). *Enlightenment reader.* Harmondsworth, UK: Penguin Books.

Munck, T. (2000). *Enlightenment: A comparative social history, 1721–1794.* London: Oxford University Press.

Osborne, T. (1998). *Aspects of Enlightenment.* London: UCL Press.

Outram, D. (1995). *The Enlightenment.* Cambridge: Cambridge University Press.

Schmidt, J. (Ed.). (1996). *What is Enlightenment? Eighteenth-century answers and twentieth-century questions.* Berkeley: University of California Press.

ENLIGHTENMENT VERSUS POSTMODERNISM

Among the most dynamic and most alarming developments of postmodern culture has been the growth, especially in the United States and the United Kingdom, of what could be called the "skinhead" culture. Beginning in the early 1980s in both countries, this cultural phenomenon was a direct refutation of the cultural and enlightened norms of the day. Its causes were deeply rooted by fears of unemployment among unskilled, White youths and of large-scale, largely non-White immigration, which White youths feared would submerge them and their way of life. It was caused too by a fear that rising technology would marginalize them, since they did not have the skills needed to compete in an increasingly technological world.

The fact that many immigrants, especially from Pakistan and India, were skilled in modern technology, especially computer science (information technology at its highest level) only served to exacerbate the racism that was a blatant part of the youth ideology). Anti-Semitism was also an important part of their beliefs.

According to the Anti-Defamation League (ADL), the skinhead culture was a British import to the United States. The uniform spread as well: usually T-shirts, very close haircuts (hence the term "skinheads"), jeans or overalls, and heavy workboots, which were used as weapons in fights. Their music, called "oi" music, was loud and reflected their racial prejudices. Once such song "The Voice of Britain," as noted by Bill Buford in *Among the Thugs,* described Jews: "They're the leeches of the nation/but we're going to stand and fight." In America, skinhead music as well was overtly racist and nationalistic. In England, the skinheads adopted the Manchester United Soccer Club as their favorite team (although Manchester played absolutely no role in encouraging this development). On both sides of the Atlantic, the skinheads also brought their hatred to bear on sexual minorities, including lesbians, bisexuals, transgendered, and the intersexed.

The tendency of the skinheads to resort to violence was a fact that was not lost on the organizers of the extreme right wing, such as Tom Metzger of the American White Aryan Resistance (WAR), who attempted to use their free-floating hatred to groom skinheads as the new storm troopers of the White Supremacy movement. Metzger founded WAR in 1983. The ADL noted that, "On November 12, 1988, skinheads from the Portland, Oregon, group East Side White Pride, attacked three Ethiopian immigrants with a baseball bat and steel-toed boots. One of the immigrants—Mulugeta Seraw—was killed. Investigation into the murder resulted in three convictions and revealed close connections between the skinhead gang and White Aryan Resistance. The jury ultimately awarded $12.5 million in damages to the Seraw family ($5 million from WAR; $3 million from Tom Metzger; $4 million from John Metzger; $500,000 from two of the murderers). Upheld on appeal in April 1993, the judgment was one of the largest civil verdicts of its kind in United States history."

Although the lawsuit effectively brought an end to any large-scale organizing that Metzger was able to do, he continued in his role as a leader of the extreme right in the United States. In an update in March 2002, the ADL noted that there were lessons Metzger felt that could be learned from the Palestinian terrorists.

— John F. Murphy Jr.

 ## ENTELECHY

Coined by Aristotle in the 4th century BCE, *entelechy,* or *entelecheia* in classical Greek, originally meant "being complete," or having the end or purpose internally. Two thousand years later, Leibniz found it necessary to reintroduce the term to describe the principle and source of activity, the primitive force, in his "monads," or real, substantial unities. In the beginning of the 20th century, entelechy was again revitalized through the writings of Hans Driesch, who used it to point to an immaterial "thing" that distinguishes the organic from the inorganic. Today, entelechy has come to be associated with the largely discredited or defunct theory of vitalism in the philosophy of biology.

To understand Aristotle's use of this term, it is necessary to see it in relation to two other terms: *dunamis,* often translated as "potentiality," and *energeia,* which is sometimes translated as "activity," sometimes as "actuality." Puzzled by how one can correctly say something like "That is a human," when pointing at an infant or newborn, Aristotle distinguished between a thing's potentiality (dunamis), and a thing's realized potentiality (energeia), that is, what it is or what it is doing relative to a particular potentiality. For example, there is a sense of "human" that is rightly predicated of an infant, since that infant has the potentiality to be a mature human being (i.e., a *rational* animal); likewise, to point to a human adult and

say "That is a human being" is correct, since the thing one is pointing at—a human—has the energeia of being a human (again, it *is* a rational animal). Now, what exactly energeia is, and how it is to be distinguished from entelecheia has puzzled not a few. While Aristotle may have come to use the two terms interchangeably, at times at least, he seems to have used energeia to mean the internal *activity* that a thing has (in its primary sense, the internal activity of a *living* thing) when its potentiality has been realized, and entelecheia to mean the *state* of having that potentiality realized. As the Aristotelian scholar George Blair has put it, in a way they mean the same thing, insofar as the referent (say, a mature human) is the same; but entelecheia points to the fact that the human has "humanity" within it internally (as opposed to having it outside it as it would if it were an infant or a small child), and energeia points to the fact that the human has the internal activity of a mature human. For Aristotle, this means having the soul functions of a mature human (for example, self-nutritive, growth, reproductive activities, sensation and rationality).

In his attempt to understand what must be so, Leibniz postulated his theory of monads. We see around us composite substances. Insofar as these are compound, they are made up of simpler substances. What, then, are the simplest substances? What are the most simple things that exist on their own? They cannot be physical or corporeal things, for all physical things, insofar as they have extension are divisible and so are not, by definition, the most simple. Thus, Leibniz argued, the simplest substances must be incorporeal (without parts or extension), metaphysical points analogous to soul. But while they have no quantity, these most simple substances, or "monads" as he called them, must each have their own inner constitutions. If not, there is no possibility of an explanation for the plurality of perceptible phenomena in the world. Thus, each monad has a principle or source of its own distinctive activities within it, its own primitive force, energy, or activity. This principle or source is what Leibniz called a monad's "entelechy." Monads, then, are the ultimate constituents of compound substances. What we perceive are aggregates of these monads. Each monad has, with its entelechy, a corresponding passivity that limits its activities. Taken together, these active and passive principles result in what Leibniz calls "secondary matter," "mass," or "body" and as such is perceptible and resists penetration. What we call "substances" in the physical world, then, are these aggregates of secondary matter or body, which, in turn, comprise active force (entelechy) and passivity (what Leibniz calls "prime matter"). Each perceptible organic substance is a unity (as opposed to a heap or mere collection of monads), however, insofar as it possesses a dominant monad, the entelechy of which acts as the entelechy of the whole.

Both Aristotle and Leibniz come to speak of entelechy so as to make sense of the world. As such, for both, entelechy is a nonempirical concept. It is not something that can be discovered by experimentation or other scientific means, nor is it meant to explain causal events. For Aristotle, paying careful attention to how we use certain words can show us something about the world we live in and make sense of (i.e., there *are* natures or essences); for Leibniz, in order to make sense of compound substances and the orderliness of the universe, again, something like entelechies must exist. The starting point or question of Hans Driesch, however, was slightly different, as he wondered whether there are events that "cannot be reduced to otherwise known natural phenomena" but are "a law unto themselves and autonomous." His answer, supported by both the results from his experiments on developing organisms as well as by argumentation regarding the compatibility of his ideas with chemistry and physics, was in the affirmative, and this led him to speak (descriptively, he believes) of entelechy as the natural constant and that which differentiates organic phenomena from the inorganic. In essence, his theory of vitalism is based upon two things: first, his observations of certain living creatures able to reproduce their heads and other limbs when cut off and, second, his arguments that the organic being as a whole has certain qualities that are not only not shared by its parts but also are not derivable or reducible to the qualities of any of the parts. What he means by entelechy is just that which the organic whole has that none of its physicochemical constitutents does. Today, Driesch's entelechy and theory of vitalism are held in low repute, but the significance of the differences between the properties of parts and wholes continues to be debated under the title of "emergent properties," "reductionism," and "physicalism."

— *Heidi M. Northwood*

See also **Aristotle; Teleology**

Further Readings

Blair, G. A. (1992). *Energeia and entelecheia: "Act" in Aristotle.* Ottawa, Canada: University of Ottawa Press.

Schröder, J. (1998). Emergence: Non-deductibility or downward causation? *The Philosophical Quarterly, 48,* 433–452.

 # ENVIRONMENTS

The relationship between culture and nature is on assault on many fronts. Researchers argue that environmental degradation is the single most important problem affecting the quality of life across the globe. Author Manjara Mehta quotes from her research on environmental change and gender in the Himalayan Valley: "Our lives are no different from that of our buffaloes." The meaning of this becomes clear when we address the reliance on the physical environment for all of our needs. In a slightly different context, the following passage illustrates this intricate connection and daily struggle for survival. "She walked her daily path to the river. When she arrived, she noticed the water looked different today. A bit cloudier than the day before. The sun was shining and it was incredibly hot. The dry season was approaching and the need to store water was more important than ever. With each day, the presence of clean water became more and more vital to the survival of her family. She took what she needed from the river and headed back to her village. The water would suit her needs for today. She would be able to cook, clean, bathe, and drink from the water she collected every day. However, with the uncertain condition of the water, she had no idea of knowing what effects may result from its consumption. Her family's survival depends on their ability to use and consume clean water. The reliance on this resource directly connects her to the physical environment." This brief vignette only scratches the surface of the human-environment relationship. The mysticism and complexity of the natural environment has often been associated with women. In many cultures, women are responsible for the everyday maintenance of the family and community. Much of this responsibility relies on their daily interaction with the physical environment. The connection between gender and the environment is but one area where culture plays a role in understanding environmental issues.

Assessing the state of the physical environment is an important factor toward a clear understanding of the cultural and social problems of a society. The environment is not simply a space for cultures to grow and emerge but also serves to provide necessities and natural resources vital for a culture to survive. When environments are out of balance with the life they are supporting, problems emerge. Ecologically, habitats achieve and try to maintain equilibrium in order to continue to function. When systems are stressed, levels of natural resources and vital support for animals and humans become impacted. The idea of maintaining equilibrium can be better understood through the concept of carrying capacity and population. Carrying capacity relates the maximum population an environment can support while being able to support that population. When an environment exceeds its carrying capacity, the population can no longer be adequately supported. This results in a decline in available resources and other problems for the population. This ecological description can be translated to human culture as well.

As important as it is to recognize culture as primary in anthropologic studies, it is also important to reference the physical environments that support various cultures. The natural environment shapes and influences global cultural development. Each aspect of culture is impacted by its natural surroundings. From dress to diet, the environment determines what resources will be available for cultural development.

Both environmental anthropology and environmental sociology have emerged as subfields within their respective disciplines to address the role of the environment from both social and cultural aspects. A key point addressed in each field is the relationship that humankind establishes and maintains with the physical environment. Research questions range from discussion of pollution, resource extraction, and desertification, to social concerns of human rights through environmental justice struggles, occupational health and safety, and the environmental movement. The role of the physical environment must be considered in each of these research areas. Problems affect different environments in various ways. Environmental problems span the range of natural environments, including but not limited to tropical rain forest, savanna, desert, temperate, and arctic regions. The following serves as a brief introduction to different ecological areas.

Ecological Types

Ecology is the science that encompasses the study of how organisms interact in and with the natural world. Darwin emphasized the conditions of the struggle for existence and identified the complex relationships through ecology. Throughout his work, the physical environment's influence on the biological condition points to the importance of understanding both dimensions.

Understanding how physical environments are classified helps to make sense of environmental interactions. A biome is a major ecological region within which plant and animal communities are broadly similar in terms of general characteristics and relationship to the physical environment.

Tropical Rain Forest

The biome closest to the equator is distinguished by exuberant plant growth in response to year-round rainfall. The tropical rain forest is marked by little variation in day length or seasonal change. Tropical species may only be found in specific areas of the rain forest; however, it is the greatest space for species diversity. Two of the primary ecological problems facing this region are loss of rain forest due to clear-cutting and loss of species diversity.

The need for open grazing land has led to the disappearance of thousands of acres of rain forest. Worldwide consumption of dairy and meat has led farmers and industry to expand the areas needed for grazing cattle. In addition, demand for resources harvested from the rain forests has also increased. Besides the obvious effects, including loss of habitat for native species, elimination of the rain forest canopy may contribute to global climate change. Researchers note that loss of tree coverage reduces the planet's ability to absorb carbon dioxide burned from fossil fuels. This in turn adds to the increase of greenhouse gases that have been documented to cause an increase in global temperature.

Savanna

The savanna is characterized by extreme rainy and dry seasonal change. This bioregion experiences very heavy summer rain and very dry winters. The terrain shifts from woodland areas with grass to open grassland spaces and deciduous trees.

Some argue that the savanna did not derive from natural processes but from human fire. Following this explanation, the savanna is the oldest human-shaped landscape. The history of environmental problems can begin with this transformation of the natural landscape. Even seemingly natural terrain change can be traced back to human intervention.

Desert

Desert landscapes are found in two primary global locations. Desert landscapes mark both the subtropics, through high-pressure atmospheric conditions, and the mid-latitudes. Found in continental interiors, deserts vary from no recordable rainfall per year to an annual rainfall of 4 to 12 inches. Vegetation in the desert varies from shrublike plant life to cacti and succulents. These plants are able to store moisture for long periods, allowing a high survival rate despite dry conditions. Because of their extreme conditions, desert environments are not able to sustain much in the way of animal or plant life. The desertification of the Earth's other bioregions through erosion, clearcutting, and resources extraction is of global concern. With once fertile regions becoming desertlike, the opportunity for cultures to sustain themselves agriculturally substantially decreases.

Temperate

Temperate zones, once found 30 to 50 degrees North and South latitude, are marked by warm summers and cold winters. Environmental issues that affect this area include but are not limited to deforestation. Deforestation remains the primary issue altering the landscape in this region. Much of the woodland forest cover that once characterized this region has been removed. Our demand for natural resources found in this region continues to grow. Cultural reliance on lumber as a construction material is but one example of resource extraction.

Arctic/Tundra

Known as the tundra biome, this region is characterized by a seasonal temperature that does not exceed 50 degrees Fahrenheit. In addition, most of the area is underlain by permafrost, or permanently frozen ground. Often referred to as the frozen desert, the tundra environment does not offer a variety of animal or plant life. Environmental problems that face this area are similar to those of the desert landscape. The ground is such that it is unavailable for agricultural use. Lack of available water and food create a challenge for any sort of sustainable use of this region.

Because there is not much human activity in this region, resource extraction in vast open spaces is another problem facing this area. For example, the controversial push to explore oil-drilling options in Alaska without a full understanding of the range of use or consequences of drilling characterizes the issues facing the region.

Problems and Solutions

Marked by the first Earth Day, 35 years ago, the environmental movement has developed from a mere acknowledgment of environmental issues in the United States to a global phenomenon. The environmental movement is charged with spreading awareness and working toward solutions for issues facing the environment. Those working within the environmental movement work both sociologically and culturally to promote environmentally friendly policy worldwide. Some key issues facing the global environmental challenge are the development of risk assessment to measure global environmental and societal impact, defining sustainability and developing global environmental policy, and understanding environmental impact in terms of population and technology.

Understanding Risk Assessment

Risk assessment is often used in environmental science to determine risk and calculate possible exposure costs. It is considered somewhat problematic in that many times true risk cannot ever be known. This is the equivalent to trying to calculate the future or probability of certain events happening. For one, individuals have different biological responses to environmental exposure. It would be difficult to say that the same affect would occur each time an exposure response was measured. Political and medical responses to risk will not be the same across populations or cultures. How do we ensure that societies will take measures to ensure the safety of their citizens if risk is left to interpretation? Some may consider a certain event a public health risk, while others may not—leaving populations with different levels of vulnerability.

Uncertainty of the risk outcome is a natural part of this process, and it is something even the most diligent scientific methods can get around. Risk assessment is still our best guess many times. Risk assessment is defined as identifying hazards and calculating adverse consequences, while risk evaluation is the process of determining acceptability of defined risks in order to guide policy decisions. Some questions that must guide our thinking in risk perception include the following: What are some ways of locating risk? How do we identify hazards to humans? How do we calculate acceptable risk in terms of human and nonhuman life? How is scientific knowledge contested? How do members of a community know they are safe or at risk? How do they identify risk and feel safe?

The sociological perspective of risk includes the modernization of a risk society, organizational behavior, and institutional response to risk. The human context in which perceptions are formed involves how constructions are filtered through lenses by social and cultural meanings. For example, research in institutional and technology addresses "normal accidents," or the routine failure of organizations, as well as institutional failures. In essence, this argument claims that accidents are normal and that the relative probability of their occurrence should simply be accepted in society. We should not be surprised at their happening. Other theorists claim that accidents are preventable depending on the quality of leadership and the priority that prevention takes over capital accumulation and profit making.

Sustainability and Global Environmental Policy

In an effort to stall the current rate of environmental degradation, current policy development is guided more and more by the idea of sustainability. In some sense, this is problematic because the definition of sustainability is rarely agreed upon. Generally, sustainable development entails development practices that consider the availability of current resources levels and consider future use of these resources for generations to follow. Resource use and extraction becomes a primary focus in policy design. Many feel that as a society we have exceeded our ability to correct or even attempt to stall the problems that we already face, while others feel that the state of the environment has been overreported as negative and our real conditions are not as bad as once thought. Either way, knowing that much of our resource use is based on the extraction or processing of nonrenewable resources is cause for concern. There have been small strides to address this through the development of alternative fuels, renewable energy, and hybrid vehicles; however, consumption patterns have not changed enough to see that these efforts make an impact yet.

Population, Technology, and Environmental Justice

Issues of population, technology, and environmental justice connect to form an important aspect of the human cultural/environment relationship. Global population is ever increasing, causing more and more strain on the physical environment's ability to sustain human, nonhuman, and plant life. The carrying capacity of the Earth is a formulaic determination that considers population density and available resources for an absolute level of survival. If the population exceeds this level, problems such as disease and starvation, among other things, may occur. One such formula to determine environmental impact is known as IPAT or environmental impact = population $\times$ affluence $\times$ technology. This takes into account the relative level of consumption, population density, and technological promise of a designated area. Determining environmental impact in this way can assist decision makers when they need to consider potential affects of development projects or environmental legislation.

The environmental justice movement emerged in an effort to protect the rights of citizens to live in a healthy, safe setting, free from environmental toxics. Since the 1980s, global strides for environmental justice have focused on the presence of chemical contaminants in communities. Contaminants range from airborne pollution output from nearby factories to the presence of chemical toxins found in soil. Much of the work in the environmental justice movement has been centered on marginalized populations such as minority groups, women and children, and working-class and impoverished members of society.

Work in the environmental justice movement began in the southern region of the United States, where African American communities were carrying the burden of chemical pollution as compared to Caucasian communities. Research in this area has drawn controversial conclusions, but does show a statistically significant correlation between location of chemical waste and race. A similar relationship exists between chemical pollution and class.

Classic works in this area stem from Rachel Carson's alert in the 1962 publication of *Silent Spring*. Following that call to action, environmentalists began to recognize the potential problems of chemical contaminants. Love Canal, in Niagara Falls, New York, served as another wake-up call to communities. Citizens were made aware that chemical contaminants resided in the soil, silently existing among them. Lois Gibbs describes her struggle for recognition of the problem and relocation in her 1982 book *Love Canal, My Story*. Other works in environmental justice include Bullard's account of environmental racism in *Dumping in Dixie*.

Today, environmental justice research spans the globe. Development issues in peripheral nations have emerged as primary in the fight for global environmental equities. As basic as they may be, the fight for the right to clean water, available fertile land, and disease control encompasses much of the global environmental struggle.

The degree to which we concentrate on the preservation of our natural environment will inevitably determine how cultures progress into the future. Culture and environment are inextricably connected. We need to preserve the balance between our human footprint and the natural world. This relationship must be recognized in order to curtail the current path to environmental degradation that is seemingly inevitable.

— *Erin Elizabeth Robinson-Caskie*

Further Readings

Bullard, R. (2000). *Dumping in Dixie: Race, class and environmental quality*. Boulder, CO: Westview Press.

Carson, R. (1962). *Silent Spring*. Boston: Houghton Mifflin.

Cutter, S., Renwick, H. L., & Renwick, W. (1991). *Exploitation, conservation, preservation* (2nd ed.). New York: John Wiley.

Gibbs, L. (1982). *Love Canal: My story*. Albany: State University of New York Press.

Hannigan, J. A. (1995). *Environmental sociology: A social constructionist perspective*. New York: Routledge.

Humphrey, C. R., Lewis, T. L., & Buttel, F. H. (2003). *Environment, energy, and society: Exemplary works*. Belmont, CA: Wadsworth.

Rocheleau, D., Thomas-Slayter, B., & Wangari, E. (Eds.). (1996). *Feminist political ecology*. New York: Routledge.

Townsend, P. (2000). *Environmental anthropology: From pigs to policies*. Long Grove, IL: Waveland Press.

Wilson, E. O. (1988). *On human nature*. Cambridge, MA: Harvard University Press.

GLOBAL WARMING

Global warming is the term used by scientists to describe changes in the climate of the Earth involving increasing temperature. The Earth's climate has become 1 degree Fahrenheit warmer in the past 100 years. The exact reasons are not known by scientists, but their working hypothesis is that it is due to human activity.

Changes in the Earth's climate occur naturally. Not longer than 14,000 years ago, the Earth was experiencing the latest of the planet's Ice Ages. Millions of years before that, it had experienced a much warmer climate. The changes in Earth's climate today are an important research area, as scientists seek to understand whether global warming is mainly a natural or human-caused phenomenon.

Earth's atmosphere is composed of a number of gases: nitrogen, oxygen, carbon dioxide, water vapor, argon (an inert gas), methane, varying amounts of ozone, and other gases such as nitrous oxide. These gases retain energy from the sun and cause the "greenhouse effect," which is a natural phenomenon of the Earth's atmosphere. Without this effect, the biosphere of earth would not exist because the Earth's climate would be too cold.

Global warming is believed to be caused by variations in the quantity of these gases and the amount of energy from the sun that is trapped in Earth's biosphere and atmosphere. For example, the more plants there are, the more carbon dioxide will be locked out of the atmosphere. Potentially, with enough plant growth, the climate could become cooler.

Human energy consumption since the beginning of the Industrial Revolution has caused vast quantities of wood and fossil fuels—coal, oil, and natural gases—to be burned. This activity has increased the amount of carbon dioxide in the atmosphere. As a consequence, the increased carbon dioxide levels are believed to have caused the increase in the temperature of Earth's climate.

An increase in global warming means changes in the climate are occurring that can have significant effects upon both nature and humans. Global warming is melting glaciers. It is raising sea levels in coastal areas and threatening sea life in estuaries and coastal dwellings. It heats the oceans, increases the size of storms such as hurricanes, and shortens winters and prolongs summers.

Global warming threatens humans by increasing drought in some areas, endangering human health with heat stress, and threatening food supplies. The effects upon nature can be catastrophic, even involving the disappearance of whole species.

— Andrew J. Waskey

ENVIRONMENTAL PHILOSOPHY

Environmental philosophy is a branch of systematic philosophy that started addressing the global environmental situation in the second half of the 20th century. Environmental philosophy appears as a philosophical reaction to the worldwide deterioration in the environment and to its partial analysis by biologic and system sciences. This is, for example, a reaction to the general system theory (L. von Bertalanffy); new ethic and axiologic challenges of the so-called Earth ethics (A. Leopold); the first studies of the Roman Club authors (*The Limits to Growth*, 1972); and, indirectly, older concepts of life philosophy (H. Bergson) and process philosophy (A. N. Whitehead). The most influential forms of environmental philosophy comprise ecosophy, that is, the deep ecology (A. Naess); various forms of environmental ethics (J. B. Callicott, J. Passmore, C. E. Haergrove); and social ecology (M. Bookchin). Development of this philosophy is supported by the annually published studies (State of the World) of the WorldWatch Institute in Washington, D.C.

Even though the deep ecology and ecologic ethics achieved decent popularity due to their emphases upon the nonanthropocentric values and upon changes in the orientation of life from nature control and property amassing toward inclusion of man into the biotic community, they are weak in their insufficient ontologic anchoring. The systematic ontical conflict between culture and nature hasn't been clearly philosophically formulated yet, and therefore it hasn't also been accepted as the currently most serious philosophical problem. Except for evolution ontology, the

relationship between culture and nature hasn't become a part of a wider philosophic ontology. The general public still lacks a generally understandable philosophical concept of the global environmental crisis, but there hasn't yet been processed the necessary ontological minimum for its understanding.

Philosophical analysis of the global environmental crisis requires interpreting man, nature, and culture from the viewpoint of the evolution ontology. This viewpoint implies that the current people, who appeared on the Earth at the very end of the Tertiary period, cannot be the climax and meaning of the natural evolution of the biosphere. The unfinished evolution of the life on the Earth still faces a few billion years of future development: It is hardly directed toward any climax, and therefore it cannot culminate in any biologic species. All of the currently living species, including the oldest ones (e.g. bacteria), are mutually interconnected, functionally cooperate, and complement one another, but they also fight each other, because many survive at the expense of the others. Therefore, the currently living individuals, populations, and species, as temporary elements of a higher system of life on Earth, establish the conditions for a slow evolution of the biosphere and, consequently, also for a comparatively stable frame of the human culture's existence and development. Because man, as the first biologic species, has succeeded in starting a cultural revolution, it is apparent that this species' peculiarity isn't based only in speaking ethnic languages, thinking, acting morally, learning, and believing. This peculiarity is best expressed in the thesis that man has established himself on the Earth as the second ontically creative force, *as a small god, as an originator and creator of the nonbiological system of the culture.*

If the natural biotic evolution cannot culminate in man, then even the culture, which is a human product, cannot be a continuation of the natural evolution of life. The system of the culture, which originates within highly organized live nature and draws its nourishment from this nature, must be established in conflict with the natural biotic order. It is an artificial nonbiologic system with dispersed internal information. This internal information cannot really be the biotic genetic information, integrating the biosphere, but the ethnic-language-encoded epigenetic information, the neuronal–spiritual culture. Similarly to the biosphere, the human culture is an open, nonlinear system integrated by internal information. Only when we are able to understand that the spiritual and material cultures belong to each other and that they establish a functional system of the particular culture will we be able to correctly understand not only the role and character of the spiritual culture but also the conflict between the culture and nature. Nevertheless, until the appearance of the global culture of the current technical and consumer type, we couldn't have known anything specific about the character of science, philosophy, and other ideas and values of the spiritual culture. Only now are we starting to realize that our spiritual culture isn't as grand and magnificent as we had believed: It is significantly antinatural and anthropocentric.

Thinking about evolutionary ontology, you can quite easily see that there are just two basic means of origination and maintenance for all current systems and structures: The first means is represented by the natural evolution of nature, and the other is the man-generated evolution of the culture. Disagreement and conflicts between these two creative processes are the roots of the current global environmental crisis. Culture can rearrange and newly shape the highly organized surface of the Earth only by breaking the original natural order, destroying a part of the creative work of the natural evolution, of the capitalized God. Putting it less poetically, the more culture—cities, motorways, fields, cars, and computers—the less nature—rain forests, biological species, and human physical and psychical health.

Only in this context is it possible to understand the impact of the knowledge that man is not just a thinking observer of the surrounding world, but a highly active animal species who is the only one to temporarily manage to deceive the biosphere and, within this biosphere, to start one more still life-dependent but structurally different and ontically constitutive process: the antinatural cultural evolution. We are discovering that this evolution started not only a remarkable human epoch but also a sad period in the Earth's history. Expansion of the systems and structures of the cultural existence results in the suppression and disappearance of the natural existence and causes the sixth stage of the mass extinction of species. Since the cultural evolution rather quickly spoiled the Earth, we are currently facing not only the problem of an adequate theoretical understanding of the substance of this process but also the serious ethical problem of human responsibility and guilt for the lost natural order.

Formally, a simple thesis of the evolutionary ontology, stating that the global environmental crisis is a physical conflict between human culture and the Earth and that culture is the endangered species, shows quite explicitly what is endangered and partially even what should be done about it. For example, there is no point in trying to change human nature. Human nature is as old as man himself, as the culture. It is biologically (genetically) fixed, and we cannot and must not change it in the course of a short time. Also, the Earth's nature (biosphere) as a system that is a part of the universe and that has been established in the course of billions of years cannot be really adapted to human culture, that is, to a comparatively young, dependent and temporary structure (existentially dependent on man). At this civilization crossroads, there is therefore probably only one direction for the future positive development of the culture: an effort to build a biofile culture that would carefully guard the Earth's fitness for habitation.

The secret of the human cultural rise was once connected with the fact that man as a species was able to change the type of his adaptation in a comparatively short time. Possibly under the pressure of extreme external influences, man switched from the prevalence of adjusting his own biological structure, which is slow and genetically limited, to an aggressive adaptive strategy, to an intentional transformation of external environmental conditions. These days, though, this highly efficient strategy, which has included human claim of the whole Earth, has met its own finality.

Yet strategy is just the means, not the ends. Even very different strategies can be equifinal (i.e., they can reach the same goal). Therefore, if we don't want to become prematurely extinct, along with other endangered species, we will have to change the adaptive strategy type, once again. It's an advantage that this time the circumstances make us change something that we can really change: the type of the adaptive strategy of the culture. All of the current culture, as a human-made system that has mostly aggressively adapted nature, pushed her back, reduced, and transformed her so that she would comply with the expansionist claims of his little-adaptable antinatural structure, must turn to an opposite adaptive strategy: to its own adaptation to nature by means of internal organizational transformations without any further growth. This culture can save its indispensable host environment only by making way for nature, only by a biofile transformation of its spiritual and material elements.

Spatial expansion of the material culture elements, which are as objective and spatial as the animate and inanimate nature elements, proceeds only by the culture's limiting or destroying the original natural order. Even though slow-developing culture was advantageous for man (for example, the first cities were rather suitable for easier meeting of cooperating people), the fast-expanding technical civilization is becoming dangerous: It expands too radically the biologically adverse, artificial environment and a differently structured sociocultural space.

The culture-nature conflict doesn't, therefore, culminate either by the "failure" of man or by the "failure" of culture. Quite the contrary, it culminates due to the successful growth of the current antinatural culture, the planetary interconnection of the originally local human cultures. Dispersed, regionally specific cultures, which still prevail in this world, push nature back slowly and invisibly, and therefore the crisis, whose substance we cannot directly see, originates as a result of the decline in naturally organized structures, locations, and regions of the finite surface of the Earth. This crisis originates as a result of a dangerous extinction of the original, man-homogeneous, natural existence. And because the devastation of the Earth's natural order is not just a limited and accidental but a global and dominant result of the cultural spatial expansion, it follows that it is necessary to philosophically consider not only what culture brings to man in the current, narrowly intellectual meaning but also what it brings in a perspective, biological outlook: by radically changing the Earth, natural ecosystems, and the way of humans living within the culture.

The biosphere, as the only earth-based system capable of an independent, long-term existence and evolution, is currently in the state of a critical dynamical imbalance. The biological species extinction rate is about 1,000 times faster than the natural extinction rate. And since an open, nonlinear Earth system is not subject to mechanic causality, even a small impetus could turn it into a new, unbalanced state. We are almost certain that this planetary system, which is capable of self-regulation, will "sacrifice" most of the current higher life forms to maintain its own integrity in new conditions because these life forms will not be currently needed.

Even though this "allergic reaction" of the biotic system of our planet is generally caused only by the human species, we can see a certain, higher, and abstract justice in the fact that even this species is subordinated to the unforgiving logic of maintaining the stability and integrity of life. Man becomes an endangered species. For the first time in history, man and his culture are endangered by their maternal planet environment, which had nourished their rise a long time ago. The central topic of philosophic thinking, which was astonishment in the Antique period, humility in the Middle Ages, and doubt in the Modern Times, is slowly turning toward the feeling of responsibility and guilt.

The conflict between culture and nature has also its gnoseologic roots, connected with human knowledge. All of our conceptual interpretations are influenced by our interests, not only by the individual and group ones, as generally accepted, but also by the generally human ones and species-selfish that aren't usually much talked about. Nature has always been for us just what our conservative biologic equipment has mediated to us in the particular historical era and what part of the external reality we have understood due to our forefathers, training, and education. Not even man as a species learns primarily for the purpose of enjoying the truth, but mostly for the purpose of his own active (aggressive) adaptation to nature by means of culture.

Each particular piece of knowledge about a live or a cultural system (every information revealed within the environment) is not just information about external reality but also an attempt at reconstructing its structure. Learning is possibly ontically creative; it occurs in order that an ontically active system could use it for its own survival, reproduction, and evolution. Therefore, within live or cultural systems, the information acquired from the environment can not only be inscribed and compressed into their internal memories, it can also be retrieved and embodied in ontical structures (in biotic or cultural structures). Considering the similar ontical functions of learning, both the live systems and culture grow in an analogous way: Elements of the external environment are included in their own systems, their learning is materialized, and their own internal information is ontologized. And we could even extend this analogy: The natural biotic knowledge, which is inscribed in the genetic memory, divides the terrestrial nature into animate and inanimate sections; it integrates the biosphere and provides for its evolution. Social-cultural knowledge, which is actually inscribed in the human neuronal memory (in the social-spiritual culture), even without drawing any attention, ontically divides the Earth: into the culture and nature. It integrates the culture, and for the time of the human existence, it participates in its evolution.

Yet despite this similarity, the most important fact still remains hidden. Knowledge of a particular system arises for the purpose of allowing this system's existence, adaptation, and evolution. Contents of the biotic learning is objective to such an extent that it was able to participate in the biosphere creation, the ontical layer of reality interconnected with the abiotic universe by means of substance and energy. By animating some inanimate terrestrial structures, the natural biotic evolution establishes emerging live systems compatible with the evolutionally older processes and structures of the Earth. Even though the social-cultural knowledge whose growing objectivity and exactness were the bases for the Modern Age culture provided for the origination of an emerging ontical layer of the terrestrial reality (culture), the abiotic structures of the culture (for example, the micro-electronic technics) were only pseudoanimated. And worse, so far, they cannot be channeled in the direction of life, but only against it.

Therefore, we have to try to establish the biofile planetary culture that we couldn't have built directly due to our biologic settings, on the basis of our negative experience with the antinatural culture, on the basis of a theoretically sound reconstruction of the current, spontaneously originated culture. The character of this historically unprecedented task implies that its solution can be started only with the help of an adequate ontological increase in wisdom of the philosophy proper, only with the use of a theoretically competent and publicly comprehensible understanding of the crisis. And such a transparent view of the terrestrial existence, an ontological and axiological minimum adjusted to the current world, is needed because the environmental transformation of the culture must proceed both from above and from below, by means of coordinated professional and civil efforts.

— *Josef Šmajs*

See also **Culture Change; Ecology and Anthropology; Gaia Hypothesis; Globalization**

Further Readings

Bookchin, M. (1981). *The ecology of freedom.* Palo Alto, CA: Cheshire Books.

Capra, F. (1982). *The turning point.* New York: Simon & Schuster.

Devall, B., & Sessions, G. (1985). *Deep ecology.* Salt Lake City, Utah. Peregrine Smith.

Gore, A. (1992). *Earth in the balance.* New York: Houghton Mifflin.

Neass, A. (1989). *Ecology, community, and lifestyle. Outline of an ecosophy.* Cambridge: Cambridge University Press.

Skolimowski, H. (1992). *Living philosophy: Eco-philosophy as a tree of life.* London: Arkana.

Smajs, J. (1997). *The threatened culture.* Presov, Slovakia: Dobromysl & Slovacontact.

ENVIRONMENTAL ETHICS

Environmental ethics has been a strong part of the movement to save our environment since its debut in the culture wars of the 1970s. The debate has pitted two equally committed and partisan groups. On one hand are those who view the environment as a field for greater development for the benefit of mankind, as well as a source of increased economic profit. On the other are those groups, like Greenpeace, that feel the environment is a treasure, which must be handed down to later generations pristine and untouched. Most times, such debates have been carried on in reasonably restrained conditions and in acceptance of the other side's point of view. Yet, as the riots in Chile at the meeting of the World Trade Organization (WTO) in 2004 attest, the dispute can become violent. In February 2005 (not for the first time), the debate became deadly.

On February 12, 2005, Sister Dorothy Stang, 73, a nun in the Roman Catholic order of the Sisters of Notre Dame de Namur, was murdered, shot six times at close range as she read from her Bible. She was killed in Anapu, Para State, in Brazil. Serving in Para since 1972, she had carried on a campaign against the logging magnates who had sought to reap a windfall profit from the vast reserves of timber in the Amazon region of Brazil. In doing so, they had intimidated—and even killed—both environmental activists and those who sought to defend them. It was 16 years earlier that the native Brazilian activist Chico Mendez had also been slain by the loggers.

According to Greenpeace, "Para is the Amazon state with the highest murder rate related to land disputes. Some 1,237 rural workers died in Brazil from 1985 to 2001 and 40% of these occurred in Para." Sister Stang's murder had taken place only days after her meeting with Brazil's human rights secretary. While believed to have been on "death lists" for years, Sister Stang had courageously continued her work defending the Amazonian environment and those people who were being terrorized by companies determined to exploit the Amazon at all costs.

As an answer to the outcry following Sister Stang's assassination, the president of Brazil, Luiz Inacio Lula de Silva, sent 2,000 troops of specially trained jungle infantry to restore order in the region. Also, in order to preserve the natural resources for which the nun had been killed, he ordered the creation of two large protected areas, hopefully to be secure from the uncontrolled logging of the past.

— John F. Murphy Jr.

EOLITHS

Eoliths are chipped flint nodules formerly believed to be the earliest stone tools dating back to the Pliocene (in modern terms, a period dating from 2 million to 5 million years ago). These were regarded as crudely made implements that represented the most primitive stage in the development of stone tool technology prior to the appearance of Paleolithic tools, which show definitive evidence of standardized design and manufacture by humans. Given their crudeness, eoliths were considered barely distinguishable from naturally fractured and eroded flints. This led to

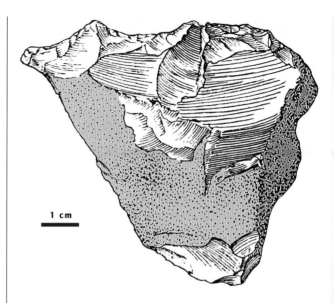

Flint eolith discovered by Benjamin Harrison from the Plateau gravel at Ash in Kent, England

Source: Adapted from K. P. Oakley (1972) *Man the Tool-Maker.* London: Trustees of the British Museum (Natural History).

heated debates between prehistorians and geologists at the end of the 19th and beginning of the 20th centuries about whether or not eoliths did indeed represent human artifacts.

Benjamin Harrison, an amateur archaeologist and naturalist, collected the first eoliths in 1885 while exploring the Chalk Plateau of Kent in southern England (see figure). With the publication in 1891 of Harrison's discoveries by the eminent scientist Sir Joseph Prestwich, eoliths were widely accepted as the earliest known stone tools. A previous report of primitive stone tools from the Miocene of France by Abbé L. Bourgeois in 1867 had already been discounted. The term *eolith* (from the Greek *eos* + *lithos*, "dawn stone") was first coined by J. Allen Brown in 1892. Further discoveries of eoliths were made during the early years of the 20th century by J. Reid Moir below the Red Crag of East Anglia, England, and by A. Rutot and H. Klaatsch in continental Europe. The occurrence of eoliths in Western Europe provided confirmation that humans had occupied the region prior to the oldest known fossil finds. This was important evidence that helped contribute to the acceptance of the fossil remains from Piltdown in southern England as early human ancestors. These latter finds were described in 1912 as a new species of extinct human, *Eoanthropus dawsoni*, but were later found to be a hoax.

In 1905, the French archaeologist M. Boule published one of the earliest critiques of the authenticity of eoliths, claiming that it was impossible to distinguish between intentional chipping of flints by humans and damage caused by natural phenomena. This view was substantiated by S. Hazzledine Warren, based on his experiments and observations, which demonstrated that eoliths can be matched exactly by stones chipped as a result of geological processes, such as glacial movements. The debate continued into the 1930s, but support for the artifactual nature of eoliths in Europe waned with the accumulation of a wealth of evidence from geology and archaeology to show that eoliths are consistent with rocks that are naturally fractured, as well as the discovery of undoubted simple stone tools of late Pliocene age in Africa (i.e., Oldowan tools) associated with the earliest members of the genus *Homo*.

— *Terry Harrison*

Further Readings

Klein, R. G. (1999). *The human career: Human biological and cultural origins* (2nd ed.). Chicago: University of Chicago Press.

Oakley, K. P. (1972). *Man the tool-maker*. London: Trustees of the British Museum (Natural History).

 # ESKIMO ACCULTURATION

The indigenous Arctic peoples are the *Yuit/Yup'ik* of Siberia and Alaska, the Inupiat of Alaska, and Inuit of Canada, Greenland, and Iceland; they have also been generically called *Inuit*. The term *Eskimo* is a name derived from an Algonquin word meaning "to eat it raw" and has been considered by many Arctic people to be an uncomplimentary name, much like the term "Indian" for the indigenous peoples south of the Arctic Circle. From ancient times, these people of the north lived a nomadic to seminomadic lifestyle, which was close to nature, in harmony with their unique environment, and aware of the seasons and the subsistence that was available throughout the year. Survival-appropriate technology was the way of life, and whatever was hunted or gathered was completely utilized, and there was little if anything wasted; for example, walrus intestines were dried and made into waterproof clothing. Their religion was animistic; their belief is that all creation, whether animate or inanimate, has souls, and thus all creation is to be treated with respect and to share a good life.

When the Europeans arrived and exercised their more dominant technology, a disruptive acculturation was attempted to bring about the evisceration and absorption of the Inuit culture. Due to the remoteness and harsh winters, many of the Arctic people did not experience European "conversions" of their homeland until the 20th century. Whether the colonization of the "White men" came in the 1720s, as experienced of the Inuit in Greenland by the Danish, or in 1950s, by the Inuit of Alert Bay, the result has been similar to their culture and environment. The changes that occurred became forms of cultural genocide as the acculturation oppression of the gamut of cultural expression ensued as follows: Drum songs and festivities were outlawed and replaced by Christian music and holidays; the separate accommodations of men's houses and the women and children's houses ceased; the sharing of wives to create a kinship between families stopped; the nomadic lifestyle was replaced by permanent housing; the semi-submerged houses were replaced by drafty houses, requiring oil to heat and money to pay for the oil; "good Christians" didn't have tattoos and labrets, and so they were prohibited; the hierarchies ceased as a result of the declining numbers due to infectious diseases, with which shamans were ill-prepared to deal. The respect of animals' spirits was replaced with Christianity and the medical system, since the missionaries threatened eternal sanctions against all those who professed or practiced a faith in anything outside the religious confines of the church; the ravages of alcohol created ripples of pain and sorrow throughout the indigenous people's lives and communities, as they struggled to adapt to these foreign ways while their world was constantly changing, on multiple levels at an incredible speed. The contacts and settlements of Euro-Americans and the enforcement of "civilization" tactics on the northern aboriginal people have come full circle as these indigenous people have learned to defend their aboriginal homeland and rights in the political arena, bringing about beneficial changes like the Alaska Native Land Claims and the Land Claims Agreement in Canada.

Their traditionally remote homeland has been exposed to the modern luxuries and conveniences of life that is much different than what is within reach in the Arctic regions, training them in the mercantile tradition of commerce, first by trade and trading posts, and then within the newly formed cities; as well as myriad catalogs and magazines, the radio and television brought the world to their living room; and finally the Internet is bringing the Inuit's culture and products to the world. What will be the culmination of cultural ancestry and the impending conglomeration of a working-class identity for the Arctic peoples?

Religion Enforcement and Consequences

The missionaries, shocked by the lifestyle of the "Eskimos," brought the greatest changes to the lives of these Arctic people, which attacked the very core of their lives: their spousal exchange, the practice of polyandry and polygyny, and the practice of families only living together when they were at camp and not at their villages. To remedy these situations, missionaries were known to arrive at a camp or village and quickly marry the couples who were together in bed, whether or not the couples were already traditionally married or intended to marry, and announce that these "Christian" marriages were binding. The next step was to abolish the gender-separate living quarters; their semi-submerged houses were abandoned as planks and shipped in to make houses the missionaries felt the "Eskimos" should live in. These turned out to be little one-room homes, occupied by usually more than one family. This sudden rearrangement brought much confusion and unhappiness to those who felt that their traditional way of life was better.

In the gender-separate living quarters, the young women shouldered many of the daily activities as they were being instructed by their female elders. Like many aboriginal communities, the children were tended to by all of the women, but especially instructed by the elder women. This system gave time for the younger women to learn the responsibilities and knowledge of all the survival skills prerequisite to living in the Arctic environment. The relocation of young Inuit families in Canada to work on the railroads and mines disrupted the traditionally honored training system. This degeneration of the societal fabric was observed and reported by David S. Stevenson in his study of the *Problems of Eskimo Relocation for Industrial Employment*, wherein he found heavy alcoholism occurred, as children were "left to themselves." Compared to the various relocations Stevenson observed, there was one mining area that did experience some success, due to the presence of elder Inuit women who trained the younger women in a trade, which made the relocation bearable.

With the pressing onslaught of modern development, there were also simple pleasures and benefits that came to the Arctic people's lives due to Christianity; for example, a young woman was allowed to marry a young man of her own age and her own choosing, instead of being bound to a prearranged marriage with someone who was usually older than she; also, both twins were now able to live, instead of one being

Campfire on the beach of Nuchek Island of the Chugach People. The Chugach are a mix of Aleuts, Alutiiq, Eyak, and Tlingit. Their language, Alutiiq, is more closely related to the Yup'ik.

Source: Photograph courtesy of John F. C. Johnson, Chugach Alaska Corporation.

A traditional Chugach 3-holed Bidarka kayak

Source: Photograph courtesy of John F. C. Johnson, Chugach Alaska Corporation.

Affiliated Sheldon Jackson; but in the 1970s, a law passed to have high schools in the individual villages, because it was a hardship to have young people return to school during the hunting seasons, when they were most needed at home. Difficulties had also developed with the new environment, for example, coming from the wide-open spaces of the Arctic to the "suffocating" confines of being surrounded by the forests of southeast Alaska. Another contributing factor to some of the students' failure was that the provincial curriculum taught in the village schools failed to adequately prepare them for the broader scope of the larger school's curriculum. There was also a tendency for the students to leave school and return home due to loneliness.

Cognitive studies of Inuit children reported by Judith Kleinfeld found they have innately strong skills in the following: the ability to remember complex images, which facilitates a person's mapmaking and drawing ability, as well as being a natural at mechanical skills. Through the years, as these young people have found their academic strengths and gone on to college, they have seldom returned to the villages, due to a shortage of jobs in their career fields and the modern advantages that they had become adapted to.

chosen to ride in the mother's hood; the infanticide of summer babies also ceased, who before would have slowed down the band during the busiest time. Another valuable contribution has been education, although it came at a heavy price in the beginning stages, empowering the indigenous people in their right to have their own culture and become innovators and leaders in this ever-changing world.

Schooling Among the People

Throughout Alaska and Canada, children were taxied out of their villages and camps by planes, to attend school from fall to spring. During this time, the spread of various diseases, such as measles, whooping cough, and the like, nearly decimated the Arctic people, wiping out nearly half of some villages. This prompted some families to move near the schools to be with their children and medical care; missionary boarding schools also turned into orphanages when the children's families died and there was no one to go home to.

In the villages of Alaska, it had been a practice to send high school children to schools, such as the Presbyterian

The Land and Its Subsistence

Family lifestyles shifted as the fur traders altered the hunters' goals from subsistence to profit motive. Traditional subsistence foods such as seals, whales, and fish were also desired for commercial purposes. At first, these provided the Arctic peoples avenues to acquire the much-needed money that was becoming part of their lives. Transitions were made in the hunting and fishing gear from the poles and boats in fishing, to guns and snowmobiles for hunting. The transition from the dogsleds to snowmobile transportation was a difficult experience for some of the Inuit, when laws were imposed requiring their dogs be tied down and resulted in depriving them of essential exercise they needed to pull the sleds. For a time, there were no hunters in some villages, as the elders lamented over the lack of meat in their diet. When the snowmobiles arrived, they were a mixed blessing, because they were unreliable, broke down, required money for gas to and from the hunting grounds, and, unlike their faithful dogs, could not detect seal breathing holes.

Smoking salmon in a traditional Chugach smokehouse

Source: Photograph courtesy of Darin Yates, Chugach Alaska Corporation.

Although modern food is increasingly consumed, subsistence has been a prevalent mainstay in the Inuit diet. The act of distribution to the families after a catch has seen these people through survival since ancient times. Today, there is a new element to hunting preparation, the pooling of resources acquired through the workforce, to afford the hunting trips. Another important factor negatively affecting their livelihood is the regulation of their fish and game. Prior to the Euro-American government creating these regulations, the Arctic people gathered what they needed, when they needed it, and this system worked, with no overharvesting. Respect was shown for the animals, which meant they only took what was needed. However, in today's regulated society, should a person be apprehended for taking an animal or the herring spawn out of season, for example, there is not only a fine, but the much needed food is confiscated.

From after World War II to the 1960s, the Inuit people began assertively expressing themselves within the political system, due to their appearance in the political spotlight as they defended their aboriginal homeland against the encroachment of the powerful developers and tried to keep their right to subsistence, for example, to preserve their land from the devastation of oil-drilling exploration and exploitation, to control external wild life abuse and taking, to exercise the franchise to vote, and to continue to participate in whale and seal harvests. With the realization that all of the Inuit people were experiencing the same problems, various indigenous organizations began forming, like COPE (Committee for Original People's Entitlement), Inuit Tapirisat (Inuit Brotherhood) in Canada, and the Inuit Circumpolar Conferences, to name a few.

Pollution is a growing concern for the hunters of today, as it falls upon the land and water in which the animals live and are nourished, to be consumed by the Inuit hunter's families. When the Russians did nuclear testing during the cold war, it contaminated the land and reindeer populations from Russia to Scandinavia. There is also an "Arctic haze," a smoke from the industrial plants of the southern regions, that accumulates in the Arctic, as well as the airborne radioactive waste from the 1986 Chernobyl nuclear meltdown. This has resulted in a drastic decline in the birthrate and a rise in cancer-related problems, as well as the increased mortality among the people. The Greenland Inuit breastmilk and muscle tissue, for example, has been analyzed, and the results were determined to be contaminated and equivalent to toxic waste. Considering the plight of our ecosystem and how it is adversely effecting a people who are not contributing to its demise, what would be the next step in healing this world that we all share, for all of the people concerned?

Sunset at Nuchek Island in Prince William Sound, Alaska

Source: Photograph courtesy of Darin Yates, Chugach Alaska Corportation.

European Work Schedule

These traditional Arctic peoples were, and still are, in tune with the rhythm of the seasons and the hunting, fishing, and gathering subsistence lifestyle. Their semi-nomadic lifestyle slowly faded as they made way for whaling ships, fur trapping, and then the workforce. Some found it difficult to adapt and to acclimate to a way of life that required unreasonable rigid work schedules, which appeared to have little relevance to survival in their traditional milieu and were in conflict with the time and availability to prepare for the year-round subsistence that had once been their way of life. Those who have sought a career in carving, for example, have found a way to keep their own lifestyles and schedules and still acquire an inflow of cash funds.

Substance Abuse

An altered state of consciousness was an acceptable practice with many indigenous peoples. Many shamans throughout the world were able to connect with the spirit world via plants, such as peyote for the southern indigenous tribes. Tobacco was used by the Alaskan Inupiats prior to contact with Europeans, through trade with the Siberian Yup'iks. One explorer went into detail describing the various methods of uses for tobacco, for example, holding the smoke in the lungs for long periods of time, which was practiced by the adults and the children. It is surmised that tobacco was the first substance abused by the Inuits. When tobacco was first introduced, was it substance abuse, or was it a means of acquiring an altered state, which facilitated a feeling of connectedness with the spirit world? The tribes in North America cultivated this plant for ceremonies, as far north as the western coast of Canada and southeast Alaska by the Haida and Tlingit.

Alcoholism has been noted since the introduction of liquor among the indigenous people of North America and the Arctic regions. There were records by early sea captains of those who became incapacitated due to their inebriation. This resulted in their failure to make the traditional subsistence gathering, preparation, and preservation of supplies to meet the winter demands. There were disastrous results of starvation in not having enough food to last through the winter. Some villages could become dangerous, as fights, murders, suicide, and domestic violence escalated. Still later, many villages in Alaska became "dry," yet cases of liquor were shipped in; some entrepreneurs would sell bottles at high prices to fund their own uses.

In Joe McGinniss's documentation of his statewide trip to Alaska, he found alcoholism of both "White people" and "Natives," as this land of the "last frontier" was dealing with the new "oil rush" of the 1970s. The various drinking populations who entered the northern regions—sailors, whalers, fur traders, gold prospectors, imported prostitutes, miners, fishermen, construction workers, oil drillers, and the like—have for the most part been models of heavy drinking to the indigenous people. This begs the question of the double standard: "Why was it okay for the 'White man' to drink unto excess, but not for them?" The continued heavy stereotyping of alcoholism among indigenous people fails to recognize the growing numbers of those who are not only abstaining, but are returning to their culture and reidentifying with their ancestral past, on their own power.

The Language

The Inuit language has three main dialects: *Inupiaq* for the western Yup'ik and Inupiat people of Siberia and Alaska, *Inuktitut* for the Canadian Inuits, and *Kalaallisut* for those in Greenland and Iceland. The missionaries tried to prohibit the Inuit language, yet unlike some of the tribes to the south, who had lost their language altogether, the Inuit retained their lan-

A Chugach man carving a kayak paddle

Source: Photograph courtesy of Darin Yates, Chugach Alaska Corporation.

guage. Although in Alaska, the younger generations speak more English than Inupiaq, with their elders, it is the opposite. For the Canadian Inuits, the language is evolving, and for the most part, only the elders speak and understand the old dialect. Books are written in all three dialects, and many are used in the schools for the new generations of Inuit people. In Canada, there are Inuktitut radio and television programs, as well as an Inuktitut production company from which came the movie *Atanarjuat: The Fast Runner* (2003), which became the unprecedented accomplishment as the first Inuit-written, -directed, and -acted movie in the spoken Inuit language of Inuktitut.

The Artists

Ivory carvers were the first to start creating a new trade from their aboriginal lifestyle. During the gold rush in Nome, Angokwaghuk (aka "Happy Jack") studied the sailors' scrimshaw art as a member of a whaling crew and created the first commercial Eskimo art to meet the demands of the changing market. Although he died in the Nome epidemic in 1918, today, his legacy is continuing through the talented Arctic aboriginal carvers, sculptures, print-makers, painters, writers, musicians, and actors who are following in his footsteps and creating art for a new time, a new people, and yet one that still speaks of the northern aboriginal Arctic people.

The Music

Most of the drumming and singing occurred in the winter, during seal-hunting time. After a long day of hunting, the men returned to celebrate their accomplishments with their drumming, dancing, and singing. They sang hunting songs, reverting back to an ancient past and their connection with the spirit world. At times when the festivities were over, the intricately carved masks worn by the dancers were cast into a sacrificial fire. Explorer Roald E. G. Amundsen made reports in his travels of the Arctic (1908) of the "Eskimo" people singing whenever they worked and how their rhythm and tone were "strange" to him.

Not understanding the "savages," the missionaries forbade these Arctic peoples to practice their winter festivals, and their traditional music underwent tremendous upheaval due to the "civilizing" of the

Source: Photograph courtesy of Darin Yates, Chugach Alaska Corporation.

population. The traditional music of drum songs and throat games (singing) within the celebrations that had been practiced since time immemorial were forbidden, and for a time ceased. The Monrovian missionaries had thought they had abolished the "masquerades" in the late 1800s, though they continued until the 1920s incognito in remote areas.

In time, new instruments were introduced, and songs were translated into the various Arctic dialects. Today's drum songs have evolved and reflect the modern Inuit lifestyle: hunting songs have elements of a motor that gave out; a victory song may be about a sport game won; story songs reflect the modern-day parent's pride and patriotism when their child returns safely home from military service. Mainstream music began to appear in the repertoire of the musicians as well, and there is an Inuit record label, Inukshuk Productions, Inc., which features many genres of music by Inuit musicians. Bjork, the internationally celebrated Inuit singer from Iceland, has become one of the most innovative musicians of her time, and her album *Medulla* (2004) features throat singing from Inuit Tanya Tagaq Gillis, of Nunavut.

Future of the Arctic Peoples

The elders have experienced dramatic changes in their lifetime, extending from the traditional survival lifestyle they were born into, mandated by their unique environment, to the culture eradicating actions of Euro-American newcomers into their lands. They have struggled to adapt to changing economic conditions as their subsistence gathering has changed from a full-time occupation to only certain foods and portions, enough to supplement store-bought foods. The hunting-and-gathering areas have diminished, and recently the summers have been longer and the winters shorter, resulting in not only less ice but also thinner ice, which is negatively impacting the wildlife. The elders have also witnessed the tragic breakdown of their family structure, as their children were removed from the camps and villages to attend the government and religiously affiliated schools, only to return and struggle with their identities. They have seen the destruction of their communities from the ravages of drug and alcohol abuse. Recently, they have watched their grandchildren and great-grandchildren; some are discovering the many facets of their culture; some are caught up in the new technology and living far away from home; and others are like a "lost people," not listening to their elders, not knowing how they "fit in."

Through all of the changes that have faced these aboriginal people of the Arctic, they have grown stronger by fighting for their rights as a people. Their cultural identity is growing stronger, and they are bringing their story to the world, in their own words, through the various media. Regardless of the modern homes and conveniences that surround today's Yup'ik, Inupiat, and Inuit, there is a developing bond with the past, as well as a great intent to preserve and perpetuate their culture for posterity. They are courageously meeting the future, not as a people from a faraway place, but as a people known and respected by the world.

— *Pamela Rae Huteson*

See also **Eskimos; Inuit**

Further Readings

Barker, J. H. (1993). *Always getting ready: Upterrrlainarlut: Yup'ik Eskimo subsistence in southwest Alaska.* Seattle: University of Washington Press.

Cavanagh, B. (1982). *Music of the Netsilik Eskimo: A study of stability and change.* Ottawa, Canada: National Museums of Canada.

Cowan, S. (Ed.). (1976). *We don't live in snow houses now: Reflections of Arctic Bay.* Ottawa, Canada: Canadian Arctic Producers.

Hall, E. S. (1975). *The Eskimo storyteller: Folktales from Noatak, Alaska.* Knoxville: University of Tennessee Press.

Hensel, C. (1996). *Telling our selves: Ethnicity and discourse in southwestern Alaska.* New York: Oxford University Press.

Klausner, S. Z., & Foulks, E. F. (1982). *Eskimo capitalist: Oil, politics, and alcohol.* Totowa, NJ: Allanheld, Osmun.

Oswalt, W. H. (1990). *Bashful no longer: An Alaskan Eskimo ethnohistory, 1778–1988.* Norman: University of Oklahoma Press.

Ray, D. J. (1980). *Artists of the tundra and the sea.* Seattle: University of Washington Press.

ESKIMOS

Eskimo, more commonly called *Inuit,* is a term used to describe people who primarily live in the far north, usually the Arctic. The Arctic is located north of the Arctic Circle, and although it has extreme cold temperatures, Eskimos have adapted to the harsh environment both physically and culturally. Most Eskimos are compactly built, having a barrel-shaped torso and short arms and legs, which minimize heat loss. In addition, it is only in the last 50 to 100 years that the Eskimo way of life, which remained virtually unchanged for tens of thousands of years, has become more "modern." Before the 1900s, the Eskimo lifestyle mainly varied depending on the environment and season. The most important aspects of Eskimo life at that time included shelter, food, clothing, and transportation.

In the winter months, some Eskimos built igloos or snowhouses, while others lived in sod houses. The igloos were built for temporary shelter while the Eskimos moved to find food. During the summer, they lived in tents made of seal or caribou skin, depending on which animal was readily available.

Eskimos also hunted seal and caribou and fished for food. Seals were hunted year-round, while caribou were hunted only during the summer and fall. Eskimos hunted seals using different techniques depending on the season. In the fall and winter, seals were taken from the sea ice close to shore. During the spring, hunters killed seals as they slept on the ice, and during the summer, Eskimos hunted seals with harpoons from kayaks. When hunting caribou, women and children helped by chasing the animals toward the waiting men, who then used spears or bows and arrows to make the kills.

Fishing was also common in Eskimo culture. Eskimos fished with forked spears that had hooks made of bone or antler. Salmon, cod, and seal provided the majority of the nutrients from the sea. Many Eskimos preferred to eat meat raw, because otherwise it took a long time to cook over small flames. In addition, raw meat provided Eskimos with essential nutrients that cooking destroyed. This is one of the theories of how Eskimos got their name, which in Abenaki means "eaters of raw meat." Others believe that Eskimo is a Montagnais word that refers to the way Eskimo snowshoes were laced.

Hunting and fishing provided Eskimos not only with food but also clothing. Clothes were made from animal skins, usually caribou because it was lightweight and warm. The style of dress varied between regions, but all Eskimo clothing was similar. The general attire consisted of a hooded jacket, trousers, socks, boots, and mittens. Many women decorated their clothing with beads and furs. Sealskin was used for soles because it allowed moisture to escape, but it kept in heat. During the winter months, it was common for Eskimos to wear two suits of clothing. An inner suit with fur was worn next to the skin, while an outer suit with fur facing outside was worn on top. The air between the suits kept body heat in and allowed perspiration to evaporate. When the weather was warmer, only the inner suit was worn.

To make hunting easier, various types of transportation were used. The Eskimos used dog sleds, which were especially helpful when traveling long distances on snow and ice. Also, boats were used to sail across water, and walking was common during the summer months.

Dog sledding is the method of transportation most commonly attributed to Eskimos. There were two

Source: © Galen Rowell/CORBIS.

charge of making sure that the rules were followed and that people who committed serious crimes were executed.

Religion played an important role in Eskimo culture. Eskimos believed that spirits controlled nature and the forces of life, such as the wind, weather, sun, and moon. Eskimos felt that the souls of the dead lived in another world. After a death, the body was wrapped in animal skins, laid on the tundra, and surrounded by a circle of stones. Tools and other items were placed next to the body for the soul to use in the next world.

For the majority of Eskimos, many of the traditional ways of life ended in the 1900s. Today, most Eskimos live in towns or small settlements and eat food purchased from stores. They live in wooden homes and wear modern clothing. In addition, technological advances allowed Eskimos to replace dog sleds with snowmobiles, and kayaks with motorboats. For many, traditional beliefs have melded with or been substituted by Christianity. Also, most Eskimos now compete with the economy instead of nature. Some work in labor-intensive jobs, while others do not. There is, however, a high unemployment rate among Eskimos, and many use financial assistance from the government.

The majority of Eskimo peoples currently inhabit four countries: the United States, Greenland, Canada, and the Soviet Union. The United States has about 57,000 Eskimos, or Inupiaq and Yupik, who began U.S. citizenship in Alaska in 1924. During World War II, many of them worked at U.S. military bases. Although education is available for all in the United States, most Eskimos do not finish high school.

The total population of Greenland is 56,309, of which 87% (48,989) are Eskimo or Inuit and Kalaadlit. In Greenland, although most Eskimos work in the manufacturing and service industries, unemployment is still high. Greenland has programs to assist Eskimos with education, housing, and health care.

Canada has a population of 33,000 Eskimos or Inuit. The Canadian government offers assistance in

types of wooden sleds: plank sleds and frame sleds. The plank sled was used mainly in Canada and Greenland, and it resembled a long ladder. The Eskimos of Alaska and Siberia used frame sleds that had a basketlike frame built on runners and slanted from the front to the back of the sled. The sleds were propelled using a team of dogs tied to the front. However, the Eskimos were able to keep only as many dogs as food would allow, and in some regions this meant only one or two.

Eskimos also used kayaks and umiaks for transportation across the sea. The kayak was similar to a canoe, with a deck and a wooden frame covered with sealskin, usually made for one person. A long paddle with a blade at both ends was used for propulsion. The umiak was an open boat with a wooden frame, also covered with sealskin, which could hold up to 12 people. These boats were used to hunt large sea animals and for long trips.

Group life was an important aspect of Eskimo culture. Eskimo group size varied and was usually related to type of hunting. Large Eskimo groups usually split into smaller groups when it was time to move in search of food. The subgroups usually consisted of a husband and wife, their children, and the married children's families. In addition, some Eskimos practiced infanticide to keep the population from outgrowing the available resources. Also, Eskimos did not have a formal system of government, but instead followed very strict rules rather than laws. Generally, the elder men were in developing commercial fishing cooperatives and handicrafts to help lower the high Eskimo unemployment rate. Last, the Soviet Union has a population of 1,500 Eskimos on the northeastern tip of Siberia.

No matter where they're found, Eskimos embody a unique coalescence of cultures. Whether they live in igloos or wood houses, hunt or buy commercially manufactured foods, use dog sleds or snowmobiles, Eskimos have remained a people of mystery until recently. Because of their isolation in the far north, Eskimos arrived late in their adoption of modern goods and customs. In the last 50 to 100 years, this modern adoption has demystified Eskimo culture and permitted a better understanding of the Eskimo people, both past and present.

—*Lisa M. Paciulli and Justine B. Movchan*

See also **Eskimo Acculturation; Inuit**

Further Readings

Barker, J. H., & Barker, R. (1993). *Always getting ready, Upterrlainarluta: Yup'Ik Eskimo subsistence in southwest Alaska.* Seattle: University of Washington Press.

Burch, E. S. (1998). *The Inupiaq Eskimo nations of northwest Alaska.* Fairbanks: University of Alaska Press.

Fienup-Riordan, A., Kaplan, L. D., & Silook, S. (2001). *Inupiaq and Yupik people of Alaska.* Anchorage, Alaska Geographic Society.

Molnar, S. (2002). *Human variation.* Upper Saddle River, NJ: Prentice Hall.

Moran, E. (2000). *Human adaptability.* Boulder, CO: Westview Press.

Steltzer, U. (1985). *Inuit: The north in transition.* Chicago: University of Chicago Press.

ESSENTIALISM

Essentialism is a philosophical doctrine that each object has an essence that makes that object what it is. Essence can be seen as a set of properties of a thing, which that thing must possess to be that particular thing.

The word *essence* is the English translation of a Latin term *essentia,* by which Roman translators tried to render the obscure original Aristotelian phrase *ti*

ên einai, which literally means "the what it was to be" for a thing. For Aristotle, the essence of a thing is both the cause of existence of that thing and a set of properties that defines the identity of the thing. A thing cannot change its essential properties as long as it exists or as far as it belongs to a particular *kind,* in contrast to nonessential, accidental properties, the loss of which affects neither existence nor kind-membership of a thing.

For Aristotle, essence is as important for ontology as for epistemology, because true knowledge (*epistémé,* science) of something means to know the essence of a thing by grasping it with words in a specific way called *definition.* A definition is an account ˙(*logos*) that signifies an essence, but we have to keep in mind that for Aristotle, definition is not about the meaning of something, but about what it is to be a something. It is important to point out that according to Aristotle, science is about kinds and the essences that define them, not about individuals, for science cannot be about accidental, random properties. Essence is thought to be common to all members of a kind, and as immutable and everlasting as kinds themselves. That is why true knowledge is possible: There is no reason for later revisions once true essences are discovered. This doctrine of essences and kinds is often called "Aristotelian essentialism."

In many aspects, Aristotelian essences are similar to Platonic forms, with the one important difference, that essences dwell inside the things of this material world, not in a separate immaterial world of forms. This fusion of Platonic forms with Aristotelian essences started with neo-Platonism and was much more elaborated through the Middle Ages period by scholastics in a way to fit within Christian theology. Essences are seen by scholastic philosophy as eternal forms dwelling in God's mind as paradigms according to which things are created (essence precedes existence), and are, of course, immutable and everlasting.

Critics of essentialism have attacked the immutability of essences, refuting the reality of essences as such. Locke rejected Aristotelian essentialism, but at the same time, he suggested two new types of essences: real and nominal. Real essences of material things are, according to Locke, their deep atomic structures, hidden to the naked eye. They are different from Aristotelian essences, for they are not eternal and immutable; they can be changed, as, for example, an internal frame of watch. But there are also nominal essences. Nominal essences are general names that relate to complex ideas, which we develop from experience by sorting things based on various perceivable qualities. Locke holds that there is no single, true sorting of things; there is no single, natural classification that reflects the relationship between natural kinds. In fact, according to Locke, there are many possible ways to classify the world.

The antiessentialist mood of today's social and human scientists is mostly based on empirical studies of race, ethnicity, nationalism, and gender, and it refutes essentialism in general. Support for this general antiessentialism can be found in the philosophy of the 20th century. For example, logical positivists believed that the very idea of essential property is incoherent and that essentialism itself is outmoded intellectual past. Recently, essentialism in philosophy received a new impetus, with interest in modal logic (S. Kripke), but this did not have any impact on antiessentialism of contemporary social and human sciences.

A completely different approach to essentialism came from empirical studies in cognitive and developmental psychology during the last quarter of the 20th century. It was discovered that, from early childhood, the human mind develops essentialist biases. Developmental psychologist Susan Gelman contends that the bias of essentialism influences the way humans categorize things. Based on empirical studies with children, she believes that this "essentializing bias" is not directly taught, but rather occurs early in children as a way of making sense of their natural surroundings. These predispositions are shaped by language and intuitive folk theories about the world. It seems that people unconsciously believe in hidden essences responsible for observable similarities in members within a kind. They also believe in the real existence of natural kinds and a direct correspondence between language and basic categories of natural and social kinds.

Experiments demonstrate that we apply cognitive bias mostly to animal and plant species; to natural substances such as water and gold; and to social kinds such as race and gender. But we do not apply it to artificial kinds, such as tables or socks. These findings are in contrast with the opinion that essentialism itself is culturally constructed by historical coincidence like Western philosophy.

— *Peter Sykora*

See also **Aristotle**

Further Readings

Atran, S. (1998). Folk biology and the anthropology of science: Cognitive universals and cultural particulars. *Behavioral and Brain Sciences, 21,* 547–609.

Gelman, S. A. (2003). *The essential child: Origin of essentialism in everyday thought.* Oxford: Oxford University Press.

Gil-White, F. J. (2001). Are ethnic groups biological "species" to the human brain? *Current Anthropology, 42,* 515–554.

ETHICS AND ANTHROPOLOGY

Concepts

The term *ethics* was first coined by the philosopher and physician Aristotle (384–322 BC), in his book *Ethika Nikomacheia* (ethics for his son Nikomachos). Ethics has its roots in the noun *ethos*, which means "custom." Aristotle understood it as the rational study of custom which, methodically, as a practical science has not the exactness of the theoretical sciences. Today "ethics" is used in a manifold way. The public often uses the term synonymously with moral behavior: Someone is called ethical if they behave morally. In philosophy, ethics is synonymous with "moral philosophy" and deals with questions of how we can justify norms, distinguish "good" and "evil," or develop consistent ethical theories. In Christian theology, ethics is synonymous with "moral theology," reflecting the moral precepts of the Bible and the Church. The term *anthropology* is ambiguous in a similar way. It covers a range from biological anthropology as well as cultural and social anthropology, to philosophical and theological anthropology, each with their different methodologies and scopes.

Let us focus on the fundamental anthropological-ethical question of whether or not there is free will, then turn to the important question of ethical relativism and some topics of professional ethics concerning social and cultural anthropologists.

The Question of Free Will

Neurobiological discoveries in combination with modern genetics have led some to the conviction that human beings are biological machines determined by the biological hardware, especially their brains and genes, combined with influences from outside. So there is no room for free will: The basket of motivations that move us may be fixed. We just do what we are determined to do. If ethics develops moral norms of what we ought to do, this seems to be contradicting the assumption that we are determined. We need the ability to act in accordance or disaccordance with the "ought," not by determination, but by free will. Otherwise, the concept "ought" becomes meaningless.

There are different solutions to this problem. Philosophical anthropology often suggests a version of free will in terms of modular brain functions that is compatible with determinism. We are seen as a complex, determined, neurophysiological system. Data are taken in and alternatives generated and ranked. Eventually, an output initiates an action. This action is considered free, if the following is valid:

> The subject acted freely if she could have done otherwise in the right sense. This means that she would have done otherwise if she had chosen differently *and,* under the impact of other *true and available* thoughts or considerations, she *would* have chosen differently. True and available thoughts and considerations are those that represent her situation accurately, and are ones that she could reasonably be expected to have taken into account. (Blackburn, 1999, p. 102)

Theological anthropology often offers an incompatibilist version; that is, free will is not compatible with determinism. For strict Calvinists, for example, there is no freedom of (the) will. God predetermines what we do. The Roman Catholic Church explains freedom of the will by introducing an inner self, the soul. It is the soul that decides what to do. The question of how different thoughts are evaluated by the soul and why some act in accordance and some in disaccordance with the "ought" is answered by introducing the concepts of grace and sin and the mystery of evil.

Ethical Universalism Versus Cultural Relativism

Social and cultural anthropology has discovered a huge variety of customs among different populations and tribes. The Greek historian Herodotus reports one of the most famous examples. Darius, king of Persia, once asked Greeks who burned the dead bodies of their relatives how much he would have to pay them to eat their fathers' dead bodies. They refused to do it at any price. Then, Darius offered a huge amount of money to some Indians, who by custom ate the bodies of their parents, in order to make them willing to burn their fathers' bodies. The Indians, according to their convictions, refused to accomplish so horrid an act. Herodotus drew the obvious moral conclusion: Each nation considers its own customs as morally right and the opposite customs as morally wrong. Social and cultural anthropology, up to the present day, has discovered huge differences among societies in their moral evaluation of such matters as euthanasia, infanticide, permission of sexual relationship, the question of duties to support children, the poor, the status of women, slave labor, and so on. Philosophical and theological anthropologies differ so much in their theories about men and women that they are one more example of the diversities of different cultures. A very important question arises from these discoveries: Does a cultural relativism entail an ethical relativism? Is morality only a matter of what is customary, relative to a particular society? If this is so, then words such as "good" and "bad" just mean "approved in a certain society" or "disapproved in a certain society." Even if there are common moral convictions across cultures, this does not mean that ethical relativism is proved wrong. There was a time in which slavery was not questioned by any known society. Today, we do not accept slavery as morally right. Although the populations of the great powers were excited about going to war in 1914, we do not claim today that World War I was morally "good."

From a logical point of view, ethical relativism cannot be proved wrong, but the examples of slavery and of World War I show that this ethical position is highly problematic: We do not accept slavery today because *our* society disapproves of slavery. We (do) reject slavery because we are convinced that slavery was wrong and is wrong and will be wrong. And we have good reasons to do so in order to defend human dignity and human rights, which through the experience of the atrocities of the 20th century became the fundament of a common universal ethical bond among human beings. Alan Gewirth developed a rational argument for an ethical universalism concerning human dignity and human rights. This argument rationalizes the experience: I do (or intend to do) "X" voluntarily for a purpose that I have chosen.

There are generic features of agency in a deep sense of the word *agency*. My having the generic features is good for my achieving the purpose I have chosen. I ought to pursue my having the generic features of agency. Other agents categorically ought not to interfere with my having the generic features *against my will* and ought to aid me to secure the generic features when I cannot do so by my own unaided efforts *if I so wish*. I have both negative and positive claim rights to have the generic features. If I have these rights, all agents have these generic rights, and I have to respect their rights. Who does not accept this reasoning contradicts himself or herself, because then it is possible to interfere with his or her generic features against his or her will. But even if this argument gives good reason for an ethical universalism, it does not entail what generic features exactly are. Therefore, on one hand the different results of social, cultural, philosophical, and theological anthropologies do not necessarily lead to an ethical relativism. On the other hand, they help to become careful not to claim a norm as universal too early. For example, the final report of the commission to review the American Association of Anthropologist's statements on ethics states

> Acceptance of "cultural relativism" as a research and/ or teaching stance does not mean that a researcher or a teacher automatically agrees with any or all of the practices of the people being studied or taught about, any more than any person is required to accept each practice of his or her own culture as morally acceptable.

It seems to endorse ethical relativism, but at the same time relativizes the relativism that clearly is the case when the same committee states as a *universal* principle: "Anthropologists must respect, protect, and promote the rights and the welfare of all those affected by their work."

Professional Ethics of the Different Anthropologies

The professional ethics of the different anthropologies have common features with all sciences and humanities. They are bound to good scientific practice. This means that they have to develop an ability to distinguish important from unimportant results. The publications should be scientifically important. This excludes, for example, plagiarism, manipulating research material, and similar kinds of frauds. They have to struggle not to be compromised by research funds they get from "parties with a vested interest," for example, if the ministry of defense of a country pays for anthropological studies in a certain area. Theological anthropologists have to be careful not to present personal opinions as statements of their religious communities. Instead, their research has to be a service to God. Philosophical anthropologists have to reflect the implications of their "image" of human beings for society (cf. the discussion of free will). Theologians and philosophers also have to take into account what the sciences develop. If their results are incompatible with the results of science (to distinguish from transcending the results of science), for example, in stating that the earth is flat or that the species are created distinctly, excluding a creation by means of evolution, they become close to superstition. Biological anthropologists have to be careful not to confuse science with philosophy. If someone speaks of a "selfish gene," he is not speaking as a scientist, but as a philosopher or poet. Social and cultural anthropologists often face ethical dilemmas. If the "universal" principle to promote the welfare of all those affected by their work, mentioned above, is the guideline, there are situations that do not allow a simple solution. This always is the case when the welfare of some is promoted but at the same time the welfare of others is endangered. Therefore, in many cases, ethical codes, for example, for anthropologists in the field, can offer only a framework for decision making. Nevertheless, they are helpful tools in the development of a professional ethics.

— *Nikolaus Knoepffler*

See also **Anthropology, Philosophical**

Further Readings

Blackburn, S. (1999). *Think: A compelling introduction to philosophy.* Oxford: Oxford University Press.

Cantwell, A. E., Friedlander, E., & Tramm, M. L. (Eds.). (2002). *Ethics and anthropology: Facing future issues in human biology, globalism, and cultural property.* New York: New York Academy of Sciences.

Caplan, P., & Caplan, P. (Eds.). (2003). *Ethics of anthropology. Debates and dilemmas.* Oxford: Routledge.

ETHNOCENTRISM

Ethnocentrism is the term used to describe the phenomenon of people from a certain group seeing all other groups in comparison to their own as the ideal. *Ethnos* is the Greek word for "nation," so ethnocentrism literally means nation-centered. *Ethnicity* itself is a word that is broad enough to include any number of features that differentiate a group, such as ancestry, language, religion, culture, or geographic proximity. Ethnocentrism should not be confused with nationalism or patriotism (loyalty and pride in one's nation). Instead, ethnocentrism usually is used negatively in the social sciences.

Because anthropology is the study of human development, those undertaking the study are vulnerable to unfairly comparing other groups to their own. It is impossible, however, to step completely outside of one's own perspective, and the ethnocentric view is not always a distinction of superiority. National holidays in the United States, for example, were based upon Christian ideologies for many years, perhaps not intentionally to neglect other religions such as Judaism, Islam, or Hinduism, but rather based on the assumption that the majority of citizens were Christian. Sometimes certain assumptions are imposed concerning the behavior of other groups. Americans may question the Spanish or Italian siesta when businesses close mid-afternoon for a break after lunch, thinking this a prime time to be working and keeping shops open. Europeans likewise may question the average 2-week American vacation (compared to nearly a month for many European countries), wondering if Americans prefer to be earning money rather than spending quality time at home with their families. Language and concepts that incorporate knowledge are also influenced by culture-specific ideas. What one group identifies as "blue" or "love" might mean different things to members of different groups. Through recognizing that one's observations about the world begin from within a particular cultural position, the anthropologist can gain a better understanding of both one's own and other cultures.

The attitude characterized by ethnocentrism is probably as old as human civilization; traditionally, other cultures were seen as people to be conquered or demonized, often for differences of religion. It was not until the 20th century that anthropology began to integrate the concept into theory and methodological practice, however. In his 1906 book *Folkways,* William Graham Sumner first used the word "ethnocentrism" to explain the way of seeing the world as surrounding one's own group, which is in the center. As humans observe others humans, groups of people are seen as either "us" or "them." Studies of one's own people, also called the "in-group," are informed by the researcher's personal experiences and understanding of cultural values. Studies of other people, or the "out-group," automatically place the observer outside of the culture being observed. Despite intentions to collect fact-based data, the "affectivity in cognition" theory suggests it is difficult, if not impossible, to completely step aside from one's vantage point. When data are analyzed with the assumption that one's home culture is *superior,* the study is tainted with a sort of collective egoism, and that attitude is what we call ethnocentrism.

Ethnocentrism is one of several subclasses of sociocentrism, which, as the name implies, is a central focus around one's own society. Other subclasses include nationalism, class sociocentrism, and specific heritage-focused attitudes like Eurocentrism or Afrocentrism. All of these positions feature two major elements. There is positive valorization, or the presumption of an especially high value on the accomplishments of the in-group. There is also the perspective of evaluating the out-group by comparing those values to one's own. Whatever is praised, or positive, within the in-group is considered to be the normal way of behaving. Whatever is criticized, or negative, is seen as an exception to the norm. An ethnocentric observer will compare the out-group to the norms and exceptions already determined for the in-group. If the observer sees no difference, then the out-group is considered to be identical to the in-group. If differences are noted, they are weighed according to positive and negative assumptions. When the out-group positively values something determined to be negative in the in-group, or the out-group negatively values something determined to be positive in the in-group, the ethnocentric member of the in-group considers the out-group to be developmentally inferior.

Such condemnation can be behind negative cultural attitudes like racism, discrimination, and ethnic cleansing. Ethnocentric behaviors are easily observed in the way the German Nazi regime sought to exterminate the Jewish people, and even through eugenics, the goal of perfecting a breed of human through sterilization and genetic manipulation. In eugenics the intention is less to distinguish people according to ancestry than rather by mental, physical, or health characteristics, such as preventing diseases spread through natural reproduction. Taken to an extreme, however, the ethnocentric group increasingly identifies as "negative" the characteristics that perhaps occur in healthy people. The Western nations of Sweden and the United States forced sterilization on mentally ill citizens well into the 20th century—many of whom were institutionalized for the equivalent of what is called "depression" today. This practice forfeited individual reproductive rights for the betterment of the larger cultural group. When value judgments are placed on what makes someone human or healthy or worthy of propagating the species, those passing judgment are centering their opinions of worth around themselves. By suppressing the outside or inferior group, the status of the in-group is further elevated.

It is natural for people to associate with a group and to find value in the self through pride in one's culture. Furthermore, the awareness of others is fostered by the groups people live within, so an individual's concept of right, wrong, appropriate, and offensive will usually reflect the values of the group as a whole. The anthropologist is interested in recognizing this tendency in the people studied as well as limiting its negative effects within the field. In an effort to overcome ethnocentrism in academic practice, contemporary anthropology has advanced a position of cultural relativism. By recognizing that the individual is influenced by the in-group's cultural values, the anthropologist is able to step back to appreciate the unique characteristics of every culture without judgment. Such a position also encourages the observer to understand behaviors and values for the roles that they serve for that culture. By acknowledging and accounting for ethnocentrism, the study of anthropology allows a deeper understanding of the adaptations made within diverse cultural groups and within one's own.

— *Elisa Ruhl*

Further Readings

LeVine, R. A., & Campbell, D. T. (1972). *Ethnocentrism: Theories of conflict, ethnic attitudes and group behavior.* New York: John Wiley.

McGrane, B. (1989). *Beyond anthropology: Society and the other.* New York: Columbia University Press.
Preiswerk, R., & Perrot, D. (1978). *Ethnocentrism and history: Africa, Asia and Indian America in Western textbooks.* New York: Nok.

 ## ETHNOECOLOGY

Ethnoecology is the study of human knowledge, perception, classification, and management of natural environments. Work in ethnoecology synthesizes the ecologist's understanding of the relationships between biological and physical components in ecosystems with the cognitive anthropologist's focus on the acquisition and expression of cultural information. For ethnoecologists, culture is seen as the knowledge necessary for ecologically adaptive behavior. Accordingly, culture is understood as an evolutionary process transmitted and replicated through language. Ethnoecologists emphasize the symbolic and functional roles of language, the analysis of which allows access to ecological knowledge. Research in ethnoecology integrates the empiricism of ethnoscience with the functionalist perspective of ecological anthropology to understand fully the adaptive significance of cultural knowledge and the ecological relevance of human behaviors.

The term "ethnoecology" was first coined in 1954 by Harold Conklin, who conducted a systematic study of plant-naming strategies among the Hanunóo, a small-scale horticulture society in the Philippines. By examining the content and structure of Hanunóo plant nomenclature, Conklin demonstrated the hierarchical nature of ethnobotanical classification. Conklin's dissertation, though never published, was the first of its kind to adopt an empirical approach to understanding traditional ecological knowledge. While previous ethnobiological studies were concerned primarily with documenting human uses for living things, Conklin's research provided the first real insight into human conceptualization of a natural resource.

Throughout the 1950s and early 1960s, efforts to examine human ecological interactions proceeded within the rubric of ethnobotany, the study of relationships between people and plants, and to a lesser extent, ethnozoology, the study of human-animal relationships. Much of this early work was descriptive in nature and utilitarian in scope, devoted largely to building lists of plant and animal names and their corresponding cultural uses. Although these studies lacked a theoretical framework, they yielded essential discoveries about the common features used in traditional systems of plant and animal nomenclature.

By the mid-1960s and 1970s, ethnoecological research came under the influence of the cognitive theory of culture as a shared system of knowledge. Anthropologists interested in traditional environmental knowledge turned to the ethnoscientific approach, which regards the individual as the culture bearer and language as the medium in which information is encoded. Ecological resources were envisioned as semantic domains, constructed and categorized with reference to the shared similarity between constituent items. This approach, also called the *particle model* of cultural knowledge, focused on the construction of semantic domains according to imagistic associations. This process of "mapping" knowledge and classification of cultural categories ultimately resulted in folk taxonomies of numerous ecological domains, such as firewood in rural Mexico, birds of the Indonesian forests, soils in the Peruvian Andes, and ice in the Canadian Arctic. Subsequent cross-cultural research into folk classification has largely confirmed the existence of a finite set of principles governing human categorization of the living world.

More recently, the analysis of ecological domains has demonstrated how environmental knowledge is distributed among members of a cultural group. Studies of traditional ecological knowledge have found that some individuals know more than others about various plants, animals, and other natural resources, which is the result of *intracultural* factors such as age, gender, occupation, interest, education, and experience. For example, in societies where women control the cultivation and management of food crops, women are more likely to hold more detailed knowledge of cultivars. Conversely, where men participate as hunters in local subsistence, men generally control and communicate information about wild animals. Ethnoecologists have benefited from these discoveries by learning to identify those respondents who are most knowledgeable about specific resources. Variation in ecological knowledge may also stem from *intercultural* differences, such as religion, subsistence, acculturation, and species

diversity in local habitats. Understanding cultural variation is crucial for ethnographers interested in devising strategies for protecting endangered biota from disappearing altogether from local ecosystems and from the cognitive inventory of a society's natural resources.

A complementary approach to ethnoecology is the ethnographic perspective, also referred to as the *wave model* of cultural knowledge. Using participant observation and other qualitative data collection techniques, ethnoecologists have successfully generated behavioral models (also called scripts and schemas) by assessing the perceived consequences of various decisions in the context of relevant ecological variables. This approach has been invaluable for determining and predicting the impact of human behaviors, particularly in unstable ecosystems such as those affected by deforestation. It has been determined, for example, that indigenous communities can and do practice subsistence strategies that maximize the productivity of all available landscapes and resources. Such practices may include the adoption of multiple survival mechanisms, including foraging, fishing, animal husbandry, and the cultivation of home gardens. By defining the parallels between the behavioral and spatial dimensions of the human landscape, ethnoecologists have advanced anthropological understanding of the adaptive significance of cultural knowledge.

Ethnoecology has witnessed significant advancements during the last two decades. Motivated by the urgent need to safeguard biological and cultural diversity in developing regions of the world, ethnoecologists are presently constructing new protocols for protecting indigenous knowledge of agricultural crops. This form of "memory banking" has recently been used in tandem with germplasm conservation to ensure that local crops and heirloom varieties are sustained for posterity, in addition to the cultural knowledge necessary to cultivate and sustain these species. Ethnoecologists have also used their findings to strengthen the productivity of agricultural systems and to engender awareness on a community level of the various medical and economic applications of local species.

Because of its holistic vision of the changing character of indigenous environmental knowledge, ethnoecology is presently informed and guided by a variety of frameworks and methodologies. A number of professional academic organizations, such as the

Society for Ethnobiology and the International Congress for Ethnobiology, have helped to promote the visibility of ethnoecology by providing collaborative venues and publications for anthropologists, ecologists, environmental scientists, and other scholars engaged in ethnoecological research. Multidisciplinary efforts in the field have made considerable progress in documenting and sustaining traditional ecological behaviors and praxis. Presently, the challenges facing ethnoecologists include the development of policies to protect the intellectual property rights of native peoples, the appropriation of funding to support natural resource conservation, and the implementation of local, national, and international strategies to engender cultural support and responsibility for ecological knowledge for the benefit of present generations and those yet to follow.

— *Justin M. Nolan*

See also **Ecology and Anthropology**

Further Readings

Gragson, T. L., & Blount, B. G. (Eds.). (1999). *Ethnoecology: Knowledge, resources, and rights.* Athens: University of Georgia Press.

Nazarea, V. (Ed.). (1999). *Ethnoecology: Situated knowledge/located lives.* Tucson: University of Arizona Press.

Toledo, V. (2002). Ethnoecology: A conceptual framework for the study of indigenous knowledge of nature. In J. R. Stepp, R. S. Wyndham, & R. K. Zarger (Eds.), *Ethnobiology and biocultural diversity* (pp. 511–522). Athens: University of Georgia Press.

 # ETHNOGENESIS

The term *ethnogenesis* is derived from the Greek *ethnos*, signifying a people sharing a same language and culture. The term ethnos is synonymous with the Latin *gens* (*gentes* in the plural) and the less common *natio*. The Greek and the Latin words worked their way into the English language as *nation* in Middle English and *ethnic group* in modern English. Both are used to signify a group of people sharing a common language, common ancestry, common culture, and common territory (though the territory may be an ancestral homeland). The term ethnogenesis is used to describe the process by which an ethnic group or nation (in the older sense of "people" and not "state") is formed. There are many cases of ethnogenesis recorded in history. A case in point is the emergence of the Métis, in the valley of the Red River in what is now Manitoba. The descendants of 18th-century French-speaking fur traders working for the trading companies plying the Canadian and American interior for furs and indigenous wives, the Métis emerged as a distinct cultural entity in the 18th century, with a distinct culture that was a hybrid of French-Canadian and indigenous culture and a distinct language that was a Creole admixture of the French and Cree language. By the mid-18th century, the Métis were referring to themselves as a "new nation," and the ethnogenesis of a new ethnic group or nation was complete.

The Métis are an exceptional group in that their emergence is clearly documented and happened within the last few centuries. In certain cases, the origins of a group are known only in their myths. This is the case with Judaism, and the biblical account of the origin of the Jewish population is traced back to Adam and Eve in the book of Genesis. However, other cultures have accounts of their ethnogeneses. One of the oldest creation accounts is the *Rig Veda*, which was written down 3,500 to 4,000 years ago and recounts the creation of the world. Along with the other Vedas, it recounts the history of the Aryan invaders who came to settle in northern India.

Having a name is often central to determining whether ethnogenesis has occurred. Quite often, a population defines itself as being "human." The term *Inuit* is used by the Inuit (Eskimo) as an ethnonym meaning "people" and is the plural of *Inuk*, or "person," and this term would not have been applied to neighboring indigenous populations. In a similar vein, the original meaning of the word *barbarian* in the Greek language simply signified an individual from another ethnos who did not speak Greek. Likewise, by the 14th century, the inhabitants of the principalities of Eastern Rus (what is now central Russia) were calling their land "the Russian land" and saw themselves as having a distinct language and identity. This was the result of a centuries-long process of ethnogenesis in which they saw their nation or people emerging out of an older Slavic people. In each case, you have the emergence of nations or ethnic groups with their own origin myth.

— *Michel Bouchard*

See also **Ethnohistory**

Further Readings

Hastings, A. (1997). *The construction of nationhood: Ethnicity, religion, and nationalism.* Cambridge: Cambridge University Press.

Smith, A. D. (2004). *The antiquity of nations.* Malden, MA: Polity Press.

 # ETHNOGRAPHER

An ethnographer, most typically a cultural anthropologist, sometimes a sociologist, or another type of social scientist, educator, or humanist, is a person who writes a description of a cultural group or situation using participant observation and informant interviews. The product of the research is the ethnography, or written account of that particular culture. Using all senses, but especially observational skills, the ethnographer spends weeks to months to years in the field collecting data, eventually compiling descriptions of events, people, and activities through what can be a lengthy writing process into publications for student, general, or scholarly audiences. Although they may use laptop computers, tape recorders, and cameras, ethnographers themselves are the primary research instruments in their work.

As part of the fieldwork process, ethnographers establish important relationships with the people they interview. The ethnographer/informant bond is crucial for successful collaborative work. Known as "building rapport," the ethnographer seeks to establish trust and cooperation with individuals from the culture who are interested and knowledgeable about the research topic.

While qualitative and quantitative research methods are taught in many university courses today, ethnographers frequently still develop their own ways of taking and organizing the notes, which contain their field data. There are at least four kinds of notes maintained in the field. Brief or preliminary jottings are quick reminders of what is currently happening, which then can be used as the basis for a fuller account written up later. This full or complete daily account depends on the trained memory of the researcher as well as the preliminary notes. In addition, ethnographers keep a field diary or journal in which they reflect on personal and emotional experiences that may impact their research. Finally, many ethnographers develop interpretive notes, in which they attempt to synthesize and integrate patterns in behavior or ideas that have emerged from their data collection.

As ethnographic fieldwork developed in the first quarter of the 20th century, European ethnographers frequently conducted research in African or Asian colonies of their home countries, while Euro-American researchers visited American Indian reservations. However, social science research including ethnographic fieldwork increasingly attracted native participants in the latter half of the 20th century. Countries such as India have produced many eminent ethnographers. European and American ethnographers also frequently study their own societies today—whether these are unique subcultural studies, such as "tramp" culture or studies of "mainstream" culture, like waitress-customer interaction in bars. The feminist movement of the last quarter of the 20th century not only increased the number of women ethnographers but also produced a variety of ethnographies on women's experiences cross-culturally, ranging from the lives of Bedouin women to Japanese geishas.

Ethnographers influenced by postmodernism and postcolonial criticism often include personal, political, and reflexive writing in their publications. Neutrality and objectivity are no longer the only positions considered legitimate by ethnographers. Balancing the goals of cultural description with political concern and self-awareness is the goal of many. Ethnographers today experiment with many forms of writing and struggle to represent the cultures they study sensitively as well as accurately.

— *Audrey C. Shalinsky*

See also **Ethnographic Writing; Fieldwork, Ethnographic; Participant-Observation**

Further Readings

Golde, P. (1970). *Women in the field.* Chicago: Aldine.

Rose, D. (1990). *Living the ethnographic life* (Qualitative Research Methods Series, 23). Newbury Park, CA: Sage.

Van Maanen, J. (1995). *Representation in ethnography.* Thousand Oaks, CA.: Sage.

OBJECTIVITY IN ETHNOGRAPHY

Objectivity is held as an ideal in ethnography, but most people now agree that complete objectivity is impossible. Ethnography, by its nature, is a subjective study, because it is a study carried out by people who record their observations. Accuracy is a goal of ethnography. It can be furthered by use of photography and tape recordings, as well as personal observations.

Cultural biases, gender biases, and racial biases can influence ethnography. People don't usually realize they have these biases until they are confronted with them. The final product of ethnography is a result of complex interaction between the informants and the field researcher. Methods have been constructed to help the researcher be as objective as possible. That way one who reads the ethnography may better understand the "native" point of view.

There are several reasons why ethnography cannot be wholly objective. The fact that it is an interpretive endeavor attempted by human beings, each bringing his or her own background and experiences to the endeavor, will affect the questions asked and the observations made.

Sometimes, we assume that it is difficult for the ethnographer to be objective because he or she is in a foreign culture. That is not always the case. Ethnographers sometimes work within their own cultures. Also, ethnography is not based on a large number of cases from which generalities may be drawn. It is a descriptive study of one culture in one small area.

It is important for the ethnographer not to assume that his or her culture is the best and the way things are done in it are the way they should be done everywhere. This can lead to a condescending attitude toward the culture being studied. While it is impossible to be completely objective in every way, it is the duty of the ethnographer to try to achieve as impartial a perspective of the culture as possible. This can be aided by using scientific standards and proven procedures.

Ethnography is a qualitative research method, as opposed to quantitative research, which yields statistics based on a large number of cases. Ethnographic research takes place over a long period of time, often months or years.

— Pat McCarthy

VERIFICATION IN ETHNOGRAPHY

Ethnography produces studies of a particular human society. Contemporary ethnographic work is based almost entirely on fieldwork, thus requiring the complete immersion of the anthropologist in the culture and everyday life of the people who are the subject of his or her study. Ethnography is also comparative in nature, because of the cultural and ideological biases that the researcher maintains when doing fieldwork. This central technique in anthropology requires the observer to make a large number of inferences about the meaning of the phenomena under scrutiny. Ethnography is thus a selective process of interpretation that depends on the role and the position that the researcher takes while observing.

The position adopted by observers can result in their becoming more full members than an objective observer of the group under examination. Yet, postpositivist anthropologists have stressed the importance of producing accounts that the observed would recognize as accurate stories of their lives. This has led many ethnographers to check with the group under observation for their interpretations. In his *Social Research Methods* (1992), R. M. Hessler describes this technique as "touching base." This involved going over the more general recordings of his fieldwork on the Mexican American community he was observing with his informant: "I would ask him if I had observed the particular event or confrontation between a neighbourhood resident and the medical director correctly. I even checked my interpretations." In *Interpretation of Cultures,* Clifford Geertz has stressed the importance of describing a given culture in terms we imagine that culture to construct itself. Taking as an example Berber, Jewish, and French cultures, Geertz states that we should cast their descriptions in terms of "the formulae they use to define what happens to them." Yet this is not to say that our accounts are authentically Berber, Jewish, or French, as they are not part of the culture under observation. They are anthropological, "part of developing system of scientific analysis." All anthropological writing is thus fictitious, in the sense that it is constructed, not in the sense that it is based on unreal events.

According to Geertz, the line dividing the mode of representation and substantive content is "as undrawable in cultural analysis as it is in painting," as the source of anthropology can both be in social reality as much as in scholarly artifice. "Although culture exists in the trading post, the hill fort, or the sheep run, anthropology exists in the book, the article, the lecture, the museum display, or sometimes, nowadays, the film." If this seems to threaten the objective status of ethnography, "The threat is hollow." Verification must not be carried out "against a body of uninterpreted data, radically thinned descriptions." The cogency of ethnographic accounts must be measured "against the power of the scientific imagination to bring us into touch with the lives of strangers."

— Luca Prono

ETHNOGRAPHIC WRITING

Ethnography is an in-depth description of a culture or group of people sharing a culture. It is a fairly straightforward idea until one begins to ask troubling questions, such as: What is a culture? What are the boundaries of the group of people we are describing? Who describes them and upon what terms? What is the point of view of the description? The questions can become more difficult and even esoteric: "Who is privileged? Is it the narrator or the people?" "How objective or subjective can the narrator be?" "Should the narrator attempt to be objective?"

The entire issue of reflexivity has come to the fore in ethnographic writing over the past 20 years or so. The need for the ethnographers to put themselves into perspective regarding social position (gender, social class, age, ethnicity, and so on) has became an imperative for ethnographic presentation, as has the need to produce "texts," often verbatim, undigested interviews and descriptions from the field. The influence of literary criticism on this movement is apparent. The philosophical positions and techniques of postmodernism, deconstruction, psychoanalysis, and other relativistic ideas and methods are obvious.

What many people ignore is the fact that many of these questions have troubled ethnographers for many years. Certainly, Franz Boas and his disciples in the United States and Bronislaw Malinowski and his followers in the United Kingdom produced "texts" and described real life people conducting their everyday business. Their papers are filled with such examples, and their letters attest to their interests in producing accurate pictures of societies.

Moreover, major disputes within anthropology between competing pictures of cultures further attracted attention of people to reasons for discrepancies in description. The disputes between Robert Redfield and Oscar Lewis and Ruth Benedict and a young Chinese scholar, Li An-Che, are but two of many disagreements over "ethnographic reality." For example, long before the Margaret Mead-Derek Freeman controversy over Samoa, in which Freeman waited until Mead was dead, there was the dispute between Mead and Jesse Bernard over New Guinean material, a gentler difference of opinion and one of interpretation, not the gathering of information. However, the Lewis-Redfield differences led to a productive exchange of views in which the importance of the position of the observer was taken into account. The consensus was that it would be good to have a team of ethnographers work in an area. This team could compare its divergent views from various perspectives to present a truer picture of the whole.

Certainly, disputes continue to the present day regarding not only sensitivity and "voice" but also accuracy and consequences of description. The most recent of these disputes has been that over the Yanomami as described by Napoleon Chagnon. The ethical implications of the dispute are serious, as are questions regarding the methods and techniques for gathering information. However, many of the questions regard the description of the Yanomami of Venezuela and Brazil as "fierce people," as well as the personality of the ethnographer itself. The issue came to a head with the publication of Patrick Tierney's book *Darkness in El Dorado,* which made serious accusations against Chagnon's field methods and portrayal of the Yanomami.

Recent Developments

Clifford and Marcus (1986) in *Writing Culture: The Poetics and Politics of Ethnography* focused many movements that had been addressing the issues of ethnography over the years. It presented a coherent postmodern, reflexive, politically correct, and literary critical approach to the texts of ethnography wrapped in a neo-Marxist package. It drew careful attention to issues of power in fieldwork and the privileging of Western ideas, tying in carefully not only with French grand theory but also with the works of third-world critics of anthropology, such as Edward Said.

The book also drew needed attention to the obligation for presenting the viewpoint of those who live the culture, what had come by then to be termed the *emic perspective,* and allowing the people to speak for themselves. The Boasian tradition, often without crediting Boas, of collecting texts in the indigenous language regained popularity. The subjective nature of fieldwork, something Joseph Casagrande (1960) in his edited collection *In the Company of Man* had noted, was also given great attention.

In stressing the relativity of fieldwork and the role of the reader in drawing meaning from the "texts," the new relativizing, deconstructionist movement, in the judgment of many, runs the danger of reducing anthropology to a branch of literature in which one opinion is as good as another and in which there are "truths" but no search for "truth." This flirtation with solipsism in which nothing is privileged but only sensitivity matters is also nothing new. It is not the skepticism that demands proof of, say, Raymond Firth or Franz Boas, but rather the reflection of old Greek and Roman strands of philosophy stemming from the Sophists, in which the individual becomes the measure of all things.

The various techniques of ethnography taught in departments of anthropology attempt to incorporate the best of the old and new. For example, here is a sample of guidelines from Michael Stone's course on ethnography at Hartwick College.

In research, you need to identify your personal assumptions, preconceptions, experiences, and feelings that affect your perceptions as a researcher. Hence, you will need to reflect upon them and incorporate them into your thinking and writing throughout the project. You are the essential instrument of the research process. In short, you will learn to be more conscious of your positioning as a researcher. Why have you chosen your site or subject? Which of your fixed positions (personal facts such as your age, gender, race, class and nationality) may affect your continuing perceptions, and how? What subjective positions (life history and personal experiences) may inform your ability to carry out research? What textual positions (the language choices you make in conveying what you perceive) may affect *the way you know* what you know about your research?

In common with other such courses, Stone blends the ethics of the American Anthropological Association with old and new techniques and approaches in a thoroughly professional and useful course. These are highlighted with practical exercises, giving future anthropologists a taste of the field and sharpening their ability to provide what is the building block of anthropological science and humanism: ethnography.

— *Frank A. Salamone*

See also **Boas, Franz; Darkness in El Dorado Controversy; Emics; Ethnographer; Mead, Margaret; Participant-Observation**

Further Readings

Behar, R., & Gordon, M. (Eds.). (1995). *Women writing culture.* Berkeley: University of California Press

Chiseri-Strater, E., & Sunstein, B. S. (1997). *Fieldworking: Reading and writing research.* Upper Saddle River, NJ: Blair Press.

Clifford, J., & Marcus, G. (Eds.). (1986). *Writing culture: The poetics and politics of ethnography.* Berkeley: University of California Press.

Emerson, R. M., Fretz, R. I., & Shaw, L. L. (1995). *Writing ethnographic fieldnotes.* Chicago: University of Chicago Press.

Kirsch, G. (1999). *Ethical dilemmas in feminist research: The politics of location, interpretation, and publication.* Albany: SUNY Press.

Sanjek, R. (Ed.). (1990). *Fieldnotes: The makings of anthropology.* Ithaca, NY: Cornell University Press.

Stoller, P. (1989). *The taste of ethnographic things.* Philadelphia: University of Pennsylvania Press.

van den Hoonaard, W. (Ed.). (2002). *Walking the tightrope: Ethical issues for qualitative researchers.* Toronto, Canada: University of Toronto Press.

 # ETHNOGRAPHY

Ethnography, the study of people in a natural setting, provides an opportunity for researchers to conduct a detailed study of a group of people while being immersed in the culture of that group. Ethnography (*ethno,* "people" or "folk," and *graphy,* "to describe something"), sometimes referred to as participant observation or field research, involves the study of people or an organization though face-to-face interactions in a real-life social setting. There is no deductive hypothesis to follow or any statistical formula. Over time, this interaction yields a rich and detailed account of the culture, history, and characteristics of a social phenomenon.

Ethnography has a rich history. We can see it in the travel logs of early explorers and in the diaries of settlers. In sociology, ethnography is connected to the developments of the early Chicago School, with three primary ideas that emerged from it. First, researchers need to gain access to populations in their natural settings so that they capture the essence of human behavior without it being tainted in a false setting, such as a laboratory experiment. Second, ethnography allows researchers to become intimately familiar with their subjects by talking directly with them. And third, ethnographers gain an understanding of the social world and make theoretical statements about the subjects' perspective, which is the goal of ethnography as a research method.

Ethnography is ideally suited for research topics that are very broad, ambiguous, or have poorly defined boundaries. Topics such as these allow researchers to define the limits of the study, which is sometimes difficult after spending time in the field and continuing to collect data. Topics that are best suited to field research are attitudes and behaviors that we can understood more readily when they unfold over time in their natural settings.

The Practice of Ethnography

We can consider ethnography a collection of techniques rather than a single technique. In-depth interviews, life histories, unobtrusive measures, secondary analysis of text, and historical comparative methods are a few of the techniques enthographers use.

Grounded in an approach called *naturalism,* ethnographies involve observing ordinary events in natural settings rather than in contrived, invented, or researcher-created settings. This approach emphasizes that, to be successful, researchers must consider numerous forms of data collection. Ethnographers try to establish themselves in a community and become a natural part of the setting at the same time they take on the role of researcher. How, then, do ethnographers remain loyal to their research agenda and to living their everyday lives among those they are studying?

Dualistic Nature of Ethnography

The nature of qualitative research is nonlinear and flexible. Rather than focusing on the end results, field researchers may let the situation dictate the direction of their research and thus may follow a loose set of steps.

First, ethnographers select a topic. As with most research, personal interests provide the seed for research topics, as being close to the subject and having a strong interest in the topic are advantages for field researchers.

Second, researchers must distance themselves from the subject of their research, including the results that other researchers have reported in literature on the subject. As researchers defocus, they let go of preconceived stereotypes about their subjects and tell themselves to observe everything, not just what they may consider important at the onset.

Third, successful ethnography involves research strategies. Field researchers must consider how to enter the group, organization, or society they intend to study, including finding gatekeepers and various informants. Ethnographers must decide how much to tell the subjects about their own personal lives, experiences, interests, and belief systems. The very role of researchers might cause the group members to behave differently than if they believed they were simply welcoming a new member. This presents an ethical dilemma. Do researchers disclose nothing at all, deceive the subjects, and get better data? Or do researchers risk affecting the subjects and tell them about the research agenda? As field researchers gain more trust, are exposed to more sensitive information, and become parts of the groups, this issue must be resolved.

Throughout the ethnography, researchers act as both members and scientists. The dualistic nature of this work forces ethnographers to be constantly aware of their roles as participants and as observers. This can affect reliability and validity in terms of overall generalizability. Are the researcher's observations about an event or member consistent and accurate to the meaning put forth by the group's members? Does it make a coherent picture of the situation and setting? Do the data and conclusions fit with the overall context of the study?

Qualitative researchers are more interested in depth of knowledge than breadth of knowledge. Ethnography often involves not simply what is said or done but the underlying context of what is expected or assumed. This highly depends on researchers' insights, awareness, suspicions, and questions.

Classic Ethnographies

A number of ethnographies emerge as classics in the field of anthropology. Among these are the works of Malinowski (*The Trobriand Islands,* 1915; *The Argonauts of the Western Pacific,* 1922), Radcliffe-Brown (*The Andaman Islanders,* 1922), Mead (*The Coming of Age in Samoa,* 1928), Turnbull (*The Forest People,* 1962), and Evans-Pritchard (*The Nuer: A Description of the Modes of Livelihood and Political Institutions of a Nilotic People,* 1968). These researchers develop stories of the cultures and situations in which they studied, and thus have provided insights into specific cultures that may have otherwise gone unnoticed.

Ethnographies expand awareness of global culture, reduce ethnocentric views, and establish significance for ritual, practice, and cultural idiosyncrasies.

— *Erin Elizabeth Robinson-Caskie*

See also **Participant-Observer**

Further Readings

Agar, M. H. (1985). *Speaking of ethnography.* Beverly Hills, CA: Sage.
Clifford, J., & Marcus, G. E. (1986). *Writing culture: The poetics and politics of ethnography.* Berkeley: University of California Press.
Fetterman, D. M. (1989). *Ethnography: Step by step.* Newbury Park, CA: Sage.
Glaser, B. G., & Strauss, A. E. (1967). *The discovery of grounded theory: Strategies for qualitative research.* Chicago: Aldine.
Goodall, H. L. (2000). *Writing the new ethnography.* Walnut Creek, CA: AltaMira.
Goodall, J. (1988). *In the shadow of man.* Boston: Houghton Mifflin.
Kutsche, P. (1997). *Field ethnography: A manual for doing cultural anthropology.* Englewood Cliffs, NJ: Prentice Hall.
Van Maanen, J. (1988). *Tales of the field: On writing ethnography.* Chicago: University of Chicago Press.
Vincent, J. (2002). *The anthropology of politics: A reader in ethnography, theory, and critique.* Malden, MA: Blackwell.

ETHNOHISTORY

Ethnohistory refers in general terms to the study of the history of a social group from an anthropological perspective. Frequently, this involves using a variety of sources, such as oral history, missionary documents, and travel accounts, to reconstruct the social history of the marginalized peoples who tend to form the subject matter of most anthropological accounts. Historians and anthropologists generally undertake ethnohistorical analysis, and the results are published not just in the journal *Ethnohistory* but also in a wide variety of other scholarly publications. Ethnohistorical research is often used in the legal system, particularly in cases regarding Native American property claims.

Ethnohistory's Beginnings

From its origins, ethnohistory has been an interdisciplinary endeavor. Anthropology and history are the primary contributors, both methodologically and theoretically, to the development of the field. From the perspective of history as a discipline, the interest of the Annales School in reconstructing social institutions, broadly speaking, prefigured the interest and development of ethnohistory within history departments. Within anthropology departments, a concern with historical analysis was evident, to a greater or lesser extent, in different kinds of anthropological research from early on (see below, particularly with respect to the Boasians).

Ethnohistory became a clearly demarcated field of inquiry in the 1940s. Initially, ethnohistory was conceived as a way to supplement archaeological research through the use of documentary evidence. As a concern with acculturation processes became more prevalent in the sociocultural anthropology of the 1940s and 1950s, ethnohistory increasingly fell under the rubric of cultural anthropology. Ethnohistory became a truly recognized field of study after it was institutionalized in the form of the 1954 Ohio Valley Historic Indian Conference, which became the American Society for Ethnohistory in 1966, and through publication of the journal *Ethnohistory*.

The Historical Axis in Sociocultural Anthropology

It is, in general, a mistake to argue that "time" or "history" never existed as operational concepts in sociocultural anthropology. The earliest anthropologists in the United States, the Boasians, were quite concerned to trace the diffusion of cultural, linguistic, or other traits over time among native populations. In this respect, they share the legacy of the German diffusionists, who performed the same type of reconstruction in the Pacific, India, and Africa. In general, the Boasians were interested in the study of human pasts to the extent they were interested in the holistic reconstruction of human societies.

However, it is also clear that the Boasians were not engaged in the study of history for its own sake. They never fully reconstructed the past of a culture, and they did not use extensive documentary evidence to aid in their research on the recent past. Indeed, many Boasians, as well as structural functionalists, felt that the documentary evidence would not support research into the cultural phenomena they hoped to study. This thinking ignores the incipient ethnohistorical research present since the "discovery" of the New World, in the work of Landa, Sahagún, and Las Casas. This theoretically subservient use of history characterizes most of the ethnography before the 1950s and not an insignificant amount of it since.

Nor was history of great relevance to the neoevolutionists. Edward Tylor, like the American Lewis Henry Morgan before him, viewed culture in a unilinear evolutionary paradigm. A straightforwardly developmental model that placed Western civilization at the end point of an inexorable cultural movement, Tylor's anthropology and that of contemporary social anthropologists maintained little to no interest in the documentary evidence as a way into understanding the past of cultural groups. In contrast to Émile Durkheim's mechanical/organic typology, which in principle allowed for variation and erratic movement between its end points, the unilinear view held that development proceeded through a series of already well-defined stages.

Those following in the Durkheimian paradigm also generated ahistorical analyses. Interested in the structure of primitive society, they were perhaps not as explicitly evolutionist as Tylor, but neither were they diffusionist Boasians. The *Année Sociologique* tradition referenced the Durkheimian typology of mechanical/organic, which was also a typology of primitive/modern and thus implicitly evolutionist. The French tradition marks the beginning of the study of culture internally—largely free from contextualizing features such as time and place. The social body is understood to structure everything from totemic classifications to religious experience.

With the advent of functionalism and structural functionalism, the general disinterest in time and history continued. For example, Bronislaw Malinowski ignored the study of history in his attempt to elucidate the structure of Trobriand social life. Alfred R. Radcliffe-Brown's biological metaphor of culture as organism naturally developed from Durkheim's interest in social structure. And indeed, Radcliffe-Brown argued explicitly against historical research in anthropology.

Claude Lévi-Strauss's structuralism is the most clearly ahistorical of the models of culture discussed so far. Taking inspiration from de Saussure's structuralist view of language, Lévi-Strauss's binarism effectively ignores the passage of time. Still, this is not to say that history does not play any role whatsoever in his thinking. Indeed, his massive *Mythologiques* series is devoted to tracing out myths of the Americas in a fashion that is not historical, though certainly implies the passage of time in the comparison of versions of myths. That is, Lévi-Strauss is primarily concerned with the binary mental processes revealed by the study of myth and so partially ignores the question of temporality at the same time that it is suggested in his analysis.

Lévi-Strauss's dominance in the discipline of anthropology in the 1950s and 1960s is usefully seen as the general theoretical background to which many of the first ethnohistorians were responding. It should not be surprising that just as a particular conception of anthropology (as the synchronic study of cultural structure) takes hold, there would be some reaction. This is particularly true of anthropology in the Boasian tradition, which was interested in history and the temporal perspective (if only nominally) from its inception. Hence, ethnohistory, if viewed against the intellectual history of anthropology, is a logical development.

The Practice of Ethnohistory

Ethnohistory, as a subfield of sociocultural anthropology, developed out of, and in reaction to, strands of anthropological encounters with historical method. This is why it could be claimed, in the first issue of *Ethnohistory*, that anthropologists needed to incorporate history into their descriptions, whether through the use of archival work or archaeological analysis. Soon, ethnohistorians began to grapple with the use of other types of information as well, such as oral histories. Jan Vansina and others working in Africa had made persuasive arguments that oral history is a genuine type of history and should be accorded a great deal of importance in reconstructing a group's past, although one did need to question the details of the storytelling event—who was telling the story, for what purpose. This example highlights a major difference with the (U.S.-conceived) ethnohistorical approach outlined above, because initially, members of the newly founded subdiscipline were interested more in documentary evidence than in oral history. It is worth noting the similarity between Vansina's and Boas's approach. Ultimately, Vansina's goal was a more complete picture of the past than Boas, the latter using

discrete myths in order to trace diffusion, but both accepted that there is truth in an oral narrative.

In addition to documentary evidence, archaeological reconstruction played an important role in ethnohistorical analysis. Perhaps due to the greater presence of archaeological research efforts in North America (and the Americas generally) than in sub-Saharan Africa, the written and material records were combined to yield rich, diachronic pictures of ethnic groups. Another striking characteristic of ethnohistory is that it was conceived in a consciously political environment: the fight for Native American rights. The drafting of the Indian Claims Commission Act (ICCA) of 1946 allowed groups of Native Americans to sue the U.S. government for compensation for land that was taken illegally (see Indian Claims Commission Act, 25 U.S.C.A. sec. 70 *et seq.*). The journal *Ethnohistory* was a forum in which scholars, who were occasionally called as expert witnesses in these ICCA cases, could present their material, although the practice does not seem to have been frequent (but see *Otoe and Missouria Tribe of Indians v. The United States*, 1955; *Sioux Tribe of Indians v. The United States*, 1985).

The legal background to ethnohistory likely explains the ethnohistorian's initial predilection for documentary evidence, where written evidence is held up to closer scrutiny in a court of law. Even before the ICCA, individuals, often trained by Boas or in the Boasian tradition, completed extensive reports on the Northwest Coast, Siouan and Muskohegean (Southeast), and Cherokee (Southeast) Indians on behalf of the Bureau of American Ethnology. These reports, some of which remain classic statements even today, were used not just to support theoretical arguments but also to demonstrate migration routes and to document Native American ownership of land.

Studies on acculturation have been influenced by the development of ethnohistory. As discussed above, there was always a conscious temporality in anthropological theory, but it was of time as a series of self-contained stages of cultural development. Only in the research on acculturation did diachrony as an active process begin to appear in anthropological analyses. World system theorists and others, such as Immanuel Wallerstein and Eric Wolf, elaborated further methods of acculturation insofar as they analyzed processes by which European politico-economic forces have influenced societies typically seen as isolated—an inherently temporal approach. Still other anthropologists (for example, Marshall Sahlins) have argued for the mutual dependence of (cultural) structure and history by insisting that only through the historical reproduction of cultural structure is structure understood by the observer and altered by those living within it. Put more generally, culture makes sense of history just as history causes the reproduction and reorganization of culture. Thus, ethnohistory has helped to refashion our understanding of the relationship between history and anthropology.

Modern Ethnohistorical Approaches

Ethnohistory demonstrates the fruitful engagement of anthropology and history. Historical scholarship contained a critique of anthropology, at least the kind of anthropological work that theorizes culture as a synchronic whole, such as structural functionalism, structuralism, and even some semiotic approaches. Historically nuanced studies of anthropological topics have shown that things as they are (in the ethnographic present) fit the logic of history just as well as, if not better than, any cultural constraint. At the same time, anthropology has broadened the scope of many historical analyses to include not just descriptions of kings and wars but also investigations of social history and cultural patterning as well. Today, ethnohistorical approaches are used almost instinctively by many historians and anthropologists, as well as scholars in related fields, such as cultural studies.

— *Michael W. Hesson*

See also **Anthropology, Cultural**

Further Readings

Fogelson, R. D. (1989). The ethnohistory of events and nonevents. *Ethnohistory, 36*(2), 133–147.
Shepard, K. III. (1991). The state of ethnohistory. *Annual Review of Anthropology 20*, 345–375.
Trigger, B. (1982). Ethnohistory: Problems and prospects. *Ethnohistory, 29*, 1–19.

 # ETHNOLOGY

The word *ethnology* comes from the Greek words *ethnos,* meaning "people" and *logia,* meaning "study of." Franz Boas said the goal of ethnology was first to describe and explain culture, and then formulate laws about it. While some anthropologists use this term as synonymous with sociocultural anthropology, more often, it means one of the two branches of sociocultural anthropology, the other being ethnography. While ethnography deals with a society in depth, ethnology uses a comparative approach to analyze culture (because of this, in much of the 20th century, social anthropologists concentrated most on ethnography, while cultural anthropologists concentrated most on ethnology). Two current popular ways anthropologists have classified societies is in terms of different modes of production and political organization. In terms of mode of production, one such classification would be in terms of foraging societies, agricultural societies, pastoral societies, traditional states, and industrial societies. In terms of political organization, one such classification would be in terms of band, tribe, chiefdom, and state. Ethnology looks at how people relate to their environment and to other people around them. Ethnologies also do not only describe but also attempt to explain something about culture. While in the past, ethnologists, under the direction of Franz Boas, tried to look at all aspects of culture, many ethnologists today focus on issues of their own specific concern to explain similarities and differences between cultures. Ethnologists often concentrate on specific subfields of anthropology, like psychological anthropology, anthropology of religion, economic anthropology, political anthropology, gender studies, folklore, and the study of kinship.

Three types of ethnology are evolutionary ethnology, comparative ethnology, and historical ethnology. The first anthropologists of the 19th century thought cultures evolved from simpler, more primitive forms to more complex advanced forms. They drew diagrams to show the evolutionary development of societies in terms of things like how people evolved from prerational to scientific, and from magic to religion to science. They also classified societies from least developed to most developed. A chart might then be made of least developed to most developed in this way: Aboriginals, Africans, American Indians, Chinese, Japanese, and English. Two of the most important of the evolutionary ethnologists were Edward Tylor (1832–1917) and Lewis Henry Morgan (1818–1881). Tylor talked about the evolution of religion from animism to polytheism to monotheism, but he said that more advanced civilizations retained primitive features in the form of survivals. He wrote that all societies could evolve in the same way because of a psychic unity of mankind. This meant that all people would find the same answers to problems independently. Morgan talked about the evolution of the family from promiscuity to monogamy. While evolutionary ethnology remains popular in anthropology, particularly archaeology, which looks at typologies of cultural development such as the band, tribe, chiefdom, and state example, most anthropologists reject the idea of progressive evolution where societies evolve from inferior societies to superior ones. They say people who live in bands may have some advantage over people who live in states.

One of the most important early ethnologies was Ruth Benedict's *Patterns of Cultures,* written in 1934. She wrote about cultures as having a particular psychological character in terms of the United States, Zuni, Dobu, and Kwakiutl. Similarly, Margaret Mead looked at Samoa and New Guinea in part to deal with issues in the United States. Malinowski had also done ethnology by showing how Freud's oedipal complex could vary across cultures. In the 1950s, many anthropologists used the Human Relations Area Files to do ethnology, in what is called "holocultural comparison." Other types of ethnology included the structuralism made popular by Claude Lévi-Strauss and regional and local-level comparison among cultural ecologists, ethnoscientists, and some functionalists. In recent years, anthropologists have used ethnology to deal with issues of how to understand "big men" in Melanesia.

Comparative ethnology tends to be more theoretical compared to ethnography, which tends to be more descriptive. Theory influences how anthropologists understand particular cultures. We can see this in terms of two accounts of the village of Tepotzlan in Mexico and two accounts of Samoa. Robert Redfield, who did research in the Mexican village of Tepotzlan in 1926, wrote that folk communities had more harmony than cities. He described Tepotzlan as a harmonious place. Oscar Lewis visited Tepotzlan in 1943 and found discord. Lewis saw the discord in a relatively peaceful village because he was looking for things that Redfield was not. In 1925, Margaret Mead did research in Samoa and said Samoan adolescents had much more sexual freedom than Western ones. Derek Freeman, who had done research in Western Samoa in 1940 and 1943 and did research where Mead had done from 1963 to 1965, said that the Samoans Mead had seen had lied to her. Other anthropologists who have

conducted research in the area, Lowell and Ellen Holmes, say that Mead was basically correct, though she had exaggerated some things. While this matter is not settled, Mead and Freeman both had different theories, and their theories definitely influenced what they said about this part of Samoa. One of the most important theoretical debates today in anthropology is whether anthropology is more a science or a humanity. Various theories, including cultural materialism and hermeneutics, have entirely different answers to these questions. Comparative ethnology is also sometimes used to oppose theory, so that ethnology has been used to show limits of the theories of Wallerstein's world systems theory and Said's concept of orientalism.

Historical ethnology deals with ethnohistories. Ethnohistories look at how a particular culture has changed over time. To do this type of ethnology, an anthropologist has to look at written records and try to reconstruct what a particular culture looked like during different points of time. Generally, anthropologists have to use records not written by anthropologists and deal with the biases of those recording the accounts. Ethnologists act like historians except that they generally deal with the records written about the people rather than records written by the people themselves. Some historical ethnologists looked at transformations of a specific movement, such as the Ghost Dance Movement of Native Americans. Recently, anthropologists like Eric Wolf, Clifford Geertz, and Marshall Sahlins have focused on the changes that take place as cultures have come in contact with Western culture and capitalism.

— *Bruce R. Josephson*

See also **Anthropology, Cultural; Benedict, Ruth; Ethnographer; Ethnohistory; Ghost Dance; Mead, Margaret**

Further Readings

Barnouw, V. (1977). *An introduction to anthropology: Ethnology.* Homewood, IL: Dorsey Press.
Geertz, C. (1973). *The interpretation of cultures.* New York: Basic Books.
Gingrich, A., & Fox, R. (2002). *Anthropology, by comparison.* New York: Routledge.
Holy, L. (Ed.). (1987). *Comparative anthropology.* Oxford: Blackwell.
Vogt, F. (1975). *A history of ethnology.* New York: Holt, Rinehart, & Winston.

ETHOLOGY AND ETHNOLOGY

Among students of early humans in the Americas, the theory that the first hominids had come across a land bridge over the Bering Strait from Siberia was a reliable way of answering the question of how human groups first reached North, Central, and South America. Although the time span varied, this theory had stood the passage of time. However, in July 1996, the discovery of skeletal remains in Washington State posed an interesting—and controversial—challenge to the accepted theory.

As Andrew Slayman wrote in *Archaeology* magazine, "The skeleton came to light in Kennewick, Washington, during a hydroplane race on the Columbia River. Will Thomas and Dave Deacy, residents of nearby West Richland, stumbled across the skull while wading at the edge of the river." While the discovery, in and of itself, seemed not to be the stuff of heated controversy, what followed became just that. As Slayman noted, CT-scans of the skeleton, which was some 8,400 years old, showed that the point of origin had been Europe—not Siberia or Asia. The scientists who came to this conclusion were Catherine J. MacMillan, a professor emeritus at Central Washington University, and the anthropologist James Chatters.

The discovery, and the conclusion of the scientists, raised a telling challenge to the accepted theory. Even more, it offered a challenge of even deeper immediacy to the Native Americans, who, if this discovery were accepted, would suffer severe loss of self-esteem by being displaced as the true, original inhabitants of the Americas. Even more alarming news came when Grover S. Krantz of Washington State University observed that the skeleton, dubbed "Kennewick Man," "cannot be anatomically assigned to any existing tribe in the area, nor even to the Western Native American type in general . . . It shows some traits that are more commonly encountered in material from the eastern United States or even of European origin, while certain other diagnostic traits cannot presently be determined."

The Native American tribes, especially those living in the Pacific Northwest, became outraged at the thought that the central part of their heritage might be denied them. Supporting the tribes, the U.S. secretary of the interior, Bruce Babbitt, offered his opinion. According to Jeff Benedict in *No Bone Unturned,* Babbitt determined that Kennewick Man "was Native American and belonged with the five tribes in the Northwest." The U.S. Army Corps of Engineers, with Babbitt's approval, planned to turn the remains over to the tribes for burial. While this would have satisfied a deep need among Native Americans, it also would have deprived science of a rare opportunity to study the earliest days of human habitation in North America. For 6 years, attorneys Paula Barran and Alan Schneider carried on a legal battle to prevent the federal government from giving Kennewick Man to the tribes. Finally, on August 30, 2002, federal Judge John Jelderks ruled against the government in the case. Although the case ended on a sad note for Native Americans, it did give scientists a chance to perhaps rewrite the early history of mankind in the Americas.

– John F. Murphy Jr.

 ## ETHNOMEDICINE

The nature and experience of affliction and the causes and consequences thereof vary from culture to culture and, over time, within a culture. Cultures have developed more or less organized approaches to understand and treat afflictions, and identify the agents, forces, or conditions believed responsible for them. Ethnomedicine is that branch of medical anthropology concerned with the cross-cultural study of these systems. While medical systems or elements thereof were foci of research early in the 20th century in the work of W. H. Rivers, the study of popular systems of health and illness did not coalesce into a field of study in anthropology until the 1980s. Foundational formulations of the field of medical anthropology appeared in the 1950s and 1960s, in the works of such writers as William Caudill and Steven Polgar.

Indigenous medical beliefs and practices appeared earlier in works focused thereon, as well in ethnographies of religion and culture and personality. Ethnomedicines were conceptualized in terms of an idealized Western medicine, *biomedicine.* Anthropologists considered it to be of an entirely different order than medicines of other cultures, and the term *ethnomedicine* reflected this radical dichotomy.

Ethnomedicine–Old

Ethnomedical beliefs and practices were the products of indigenous cultural developments outside of "modern medicine." Writers unabashedly referred to such systems as "primitive," and "irrational." Because these systems were assumed to be based upon custom, they were, by definition, inefficacious "beliefs" in contrast to the putatively certain "knowledge" of biomedicine. Whether they were the ultimately biological theories of misfortune (witchcraft, as among the Azande) or the diagnosis of skin maladies among the Subanun, any reported ethnomedical efficacy derived "coincidentally" when their beliefs paralleled those of "scientific" medicine.

Early researchers, from Rivers forward, recognized the intimate interconnections of medical with other cultural ideas; no separation existed between medicine and other cultural domains such as religion, gender, or social structure. Researchers assumed this separation held for biomedicine.

Ethnomedical studies' central foci of concern were systems of classification of illness and etiological theories. Researchers developed broad generalizations that often served to bolster the dichotomy between "primitive" or folk medical systems and "scientific medicine." These etiological theories were dichotomized and classified as concepts as "naturalistic" (caused by outside forces and events such as ecological changes) or "personalistic" (caused by specific agents such as witches or sorcerers) or "externalizing and internalizing" medical systems. Such notions dichotomized ethnomedical systems in terms of their logic.

Diagnosis and therapeutic approaches to illness, including rituals, pharmacopoeias, and body manipulation, attracted attention as did the healers themselves. Shamans as well as sorcerers and diviners received considerable interest, including research on recruitment. A research staple was the plethora of folk, or culturebound, disorders (for example, susto, amok, latah, koro). Ethnomedical nosologies are not universal, as biomedicine asserts with respect to its own classifications. Rather, such systems are local, as are many of the illness entities they classify. An example is the well-studied system of humoral pathology in the Americas. As well, what is regarded as a symptom of illness or health varies from culture to culture. Signs of sickness in one culture are signs of health in another. This is the case with depressive ideation, which is seen as troubling in the United States but suggests growing enlightenment in Buddhist cultures.

Ethnomedicines have a wide variety of healing strategies. They include magical/religious means as well as mechanical (body manipulation) and biochemical agents and compounds (for example, purgatives, poultices, drugs). Biomedical compounds also may be employed within a folk medical system, where criteria of usage diverge from that of biomedicine. Therapies may integrate biomedical ideas into traditional practices or reconceptualize such ideas in light of local realities, as with folk systems in the U.S. South. Of concern, too, are indigenous preventive measures. These measures take specific, local forms, depending on indigenous etiological theories. Encounters and transactions in the context of healing were central and have renewed interest due to the increasingly sophisticated semantic, narrative, and linguistic analyses in all medical contexts.

Ethnomedicine–New

The anthropology of biomedicine in the late 1970s and early 1980s permanently altered the perception of biomedicine. The view of it as acultural, rational, and scientific rapidly became unsustainable. The theory and practice of biomedicine is thoroughly cultural and local, with distinct local biologies underlying biomedical research and practice in the West and beyond, as with the notions of "race," that shape scientific/medical research and practice. Biomedical theory and practice is also gendered and generally ignores differential social status and its attendant differences in mortality and morbidity and the geography of affliction.

The term *ethnomedicine* originally included the professional medicines of other cultures, suggesting that these were merely more formalized folk medicines, with rare exception. These professional medicines include Ayurvedic (India), Unani (Middle East), traditional Chinese medicine (TCM), and Kanpo in Japan.

Such medicines evidence all of the features that earlier writers suggested distinguished biomedicine from them: dedicated educational institutions, formal curricula, licensing, pharmacopoeia, divisions of labor and specialization, experimentation, change over time, and written texts.

Biomedicine now is seen as one of a number of professional ethnomedicines. Instead of asserting that "we" have (bio)medicine and "they" have ethnomedicine, we now recognize that all medical systems are medicines. Now, issues of difference and power are foci of research in studies of practice as well as the new biomedical technologies and procedures (for example, definitions of death, organ transplantation).

The new ethnomedicine allows us to examine health and illness experientially, phenomenologically, and in terms of social causes of illness and distress and to dispense with the biased implicit suppositions that framed the early medical anthropological gaze on non-Western medicines.

— *Atwood D. Gaines*

See also **Ethnopharmacology; Ethnopsychiatry; Health Care, Alternative; Medicine Man; Shaman**

Further Readings

Bird, C., Conrad, P., & Fremont, A. (Eds.). (1999). *Handbook of medical sociology* (5th ed.). Englewood Cliffs, NJ: Prentice Hall.

Casey C., & Edgerton, R. (Eds.). (2005). *Companion to psychological anthropology.* Oxford: Blackwell.

Ember, M., & Ember, C. (Eds.). (2004). *Encyclopedia of medical anthropology.* Dordrecht, The Netherlands: Kluwer Academic/Plenum.

Gaines, A. D. (1992). *Ethnopsychiatry: The cultural construction of professional and folk psychiatries.* Albany: State University of New York Press.

Kleinman, A., Das, V., & Lock, M. (Eds.). (1997). *Social suffering.* Berkeley: University of California Press.

Lock, M., Young, A., & Cambrosio, A. (Eds.). (2000). *Living and working with the new medical technologies: Intersections of inquiries.* Cambridge: Cambridge University Press.

Post, S. G. (Ed.). (2004). *Encyclopedia of bioethics* (3rd ed.). New York: Macmillan.

ETHNOPHARMACOLOGY

Ethnopharmacology is the cross-cultural study of how people use plants, animals, fungi, or other naturally occurring resources for medicinal purposes. Such knowledge provides the basis for the herbal remedy industry and has led to the development of at least 121 pharmaceuticals. Often, this involves observation of how a traditional remedy is used; then, the effective chemical compound is isolated in a laboratory for commercial production. In an early example, the French naturalist Jean B. C. T. Leschenault de la Tour brought a plant of the genus *Strychnos* to France in 1805, based on its indigenous use in poison arrows in the South Pacific. French chemists isolated strychnine, an alkaloid still widely used in medicine. Pharmacologists have investigated thousands of different plants to derive drugs used for birth control, surgery, malaria, asthma, heart disease, and many other medical applications.

Ethnopharmacology is used as an argument for conserving cultural and biological diversity. "Bioprospecting" refers to collaboration among drug companies, anthropologists, or biologists searching for new drugs. Some human rights organizations call this "biopiracy," because indigenous knowledge is exploited for profit, and they have succeeded in stopping research projects. The search for new drugs using indigenous knowledge may become obsolete due to new technologies that allow pharmacologists to rapidly isolate chemical compounds from natural sources and screen them for medicinal potential regardless of their use as folk remedies. Also, traditional medicinal knowledge may be disappearing as indigenous populations integrate with the global economy.

Not all anthropologists or pharmacologists believe that indigenous knowledge is useful for finding medical cures. Some argue that there are too many symbolic treatments targeted at satisfying emotional needs that have no biochemical basis—known as the "placebo effect." Alternatively, Makoto Taniguchi and Isao Kubo showed that knowledge of traditional African healers was at least four times more likely to produce useful compounds than a random selection of plants from the same environment. Anthropologist Nina L. Etkin argued that a fundamental cross-cultural problem is that indigenous peoples often have different symbolic interpretations of an illness that may be biologically identical to a medically defined illness. She suggested that ethnopharmacologists analyze the complete cultural process of curing, rather than focusing only on which plants are used.

Ethnopharmacology has important implications for evolutionary theory. Plants evolve toxic chemicals as defenses against herbivores. Kenneth E. Glander,

Barry A. Bogin, and Timothy A. Johns have argued that higher primates evolved in biologically diverse environments and used taste to optimize nutritional intake, while minimizing toxins. Knowledge of beneficial toxins that reduce parasites is transmitted through primate troops. Higher cognitive abilities of humans allow for symbolic interpretation of taste and illness symptoms and more complex cultural transmission. Johns argues that agriculture reduced dietary diversity, increasing the need to culturally identify beneficial toxins. Contrary to the popular notion that rain forests harbor the greatest medicinal potential, John R. Stepp and Daniel E. Moerman have shown that indigenous people rely heavily on weeds growing in agricultural areas or near houses for medicines.

— *David G. Casagrande*

See also **Ethnomedicine; Ethnopsychiatry; Tropical Rain Forests**

Further Readings

Berlin, B., & Berlin, E. A. (2004). Community autonomy and the Maya ICBG project in Chiapas, Mexico: How a bioprospecting project that should have succeeded failed. *Human Organization 63,* 472–486.

Etkin, N. L. (1993). Anthropological methods in ethnopharmacology. *Journal of Ethnopharmacology 38,* 93–104.

Johns, T. A. (1990). *With bitter herbs they shall eat it: Chemical ecology and the origins of human diet and medicine.* Tucson: University of Arizona Press.

 # ETHNOPSYCHIATRY

Ethnopsychiatry is that branch of medical anthropology focally concerned with mental health and illness. Historically, ethnopsychiatry studied the theories and practices of "primitive" or folk psychiatries. Such work generally involved the application of then current western "psychiatric" (unmarked) "knowledge" and practice to the ethnopsychiatries of other cultures. The field of ethnopsychiatry was first delineated by Hungarian-born, French-educated and U.S.-trained psychoanalytic anthropologist and classicist George Devereux (né György Dobó) (1908–1985). His colleague, Dr. Louis Mars, a Haitian psychiatrist, coined the term.

In Devereux's original conception, ethnopsychiatry is double sided. First, it is " the systematic study of the psychiatric theories and practices of a primitive [sic] tribe. Its primary focus is, thus, the exploration of (a) culture that pertains to mental derangements, as (locally) understood" (Devereux, 1961, p. 1). Second, the field is the study of "culture and the abnormal."

The ethnopsychiatric rubric now subsumes a wide variety of studies. They include works from the history and philosophy of medicine and psychiatry as well as from anthropology and allied social sciences. The merging of once distinct disciplines has been occasioned by the interpretive turn in the social sciences. The semantic or hermeneutic and cultural constructivist positions have served to deconstruct dominant discourses of Western medicines and open them to far-ranging analyses that expose the reality of the variety of professional psychiatries and their respective cultural cores. Early on, colonialist psychological projections could be seen as the bases of ethnopsychiatric investigations serving to (re)create notions of otherness of the externally and internally colonized.

Psychiatrists have assumed that Western nosologies and disease entities are universal. Whereas traditionally, ethnopsychiatry focused on folk systems almost exclusively, the "New Ethnopsychiatry" took as its subject all forms of ethnopsychiatric theory and practice, whether folk or professional, in the East or West. It further redefined the clinical encounter as an engagement between healer and sociocultural, historical representative rather than patient-as-biological-unit. This perspective represented an updating and a localizing of Devereux's original conception and sees professional systems of medicine as equally culturally constructed and situated in local cultural historical and moral contexts.

Ethnopsychiatric research now includes the application, as well as study of Western psychological, psychiatric, and psychoanalytic theories themselves in the investigation of psychic lives. Ethnopsychiatry today recognizes that a cultural, rather than a universal, psychology underlies specific folk or professional psychiatries. In anthropology and in professional ethnopsychiatries, the terms *cross-cultural* or *cultural psychiatry* are often used to refer to work at the interface of culture and mental illness and health.

In the New Ethnopsychiatry, the application of German, U.S., or French psychiatric knowledge to another culture provides insight and data both on the psychiatric system from whose perspective the study is conducted as well as that system or systems serving as the object of study. The distinction between folk and professional ethnopsychiatries is now seen as one of degree, not of kind. The former term applies to an informal system that concerns an abnormal ethnopsychology and its treatment, while the latter refers to a formal such system that evidences licensing, educational institutions, written texts, and so on.

The New Ethnopsychiatry, unlike the old, has direct relevance to the theory and practice of professional ethnopsychiatry as well as to anthropology. Increasingly, from within psychiatry, there is recognition of the central role of culture and cultural identity. One here notes the ethno- (or cultural) psychiatry clinics established in Montréal, Paris, Cambridge, Massachusetts, and San Francisco.

In the fourth edition of the *Diagnostic and Statistical Manual of the American Psychiatric Association* (1994) and its text revision (2000), there appears an "Outline for Cultural Formulation and Glossary of Culture-Bound Syndromes." The American Psychiatry Association has published a manual on culture assessment that covers individual cultural identity, etiological theories, culture-specific stressors and supports, cultural features of the patient/physician relationship, and a section on overall cultural assessment for therapy and planning.

However, there is yet the tendency in professional U.S. ethnopsychiatry, in line with its "biological essentialism," one of its two main orientations, among others, to biologize and, therefrom, to create notions of fundamental differences among social categories. With respect to ethnic populations, the biological essentialism reproduces cultural notions of "race" to the detriment of these populations. Gender also plays a role, often negative, in biomedical and psychiatric practice, as does age and social standing. These cultural features demonstrate the validity of the conception of psychiatry as ethnopsychiatry.

A key focus, past and present, has been on local cultural understandings of mental disorder and signs thereof. Such considerations focus on all ethnopsychiatries.

The personal meanings embodied in and the experience of such disorders, illness narratives, more recently have become foci of research. Also of interest are diagnostic and therapeutic practices, including psychopharmacology. Pharmacology studies now include constructions of ethnicities that are allegedly biologically distinct (i.e., like "races"), which "may benefit" from different dosages or different agents.

The study of illness course and outcomes has been important for demonstrating the cultural and social bases of even the major psychiatric illnesses. Work also demonstrates that institutions reflect cultural values and in turn influence the experience and behavior of those living in them, whether hospitals or today's prisons.

The New Ethnopsychiatry incorporates into the clinical setting and psychiatric thinking previously excluded domains of experience. These include the suffering of those subjected to illness and violence and marginal social status (for example, refugees, immigrants).

The New Ethnopsychiatry engages ethnopsychology because of the intimate relationship of the medical/psychiatric with nonmedical notions of self and person, identity, gender, emotion, and cultural history from which notions of affliction derive. Central conceptions of person continue to attract attention in folk psychiatries, as they have in professional psychiatries since its introduction into that literature.

A new area of interest is that of psychiatric bioethics and geropsychiatric bioethics incorporating studies of bioethics.

Chronic ethnopsychiatric conditions, some new to the gaze (and how these are endured and managed by self and others) differ from our usual focus on acute problems. Increasingly, we see interest in geropsychiatry, especially the dementias, such as Alzheimer's disease (AD). This research brings aging into ethnopsychiatry's gaze. The interest in dementia entails the study of the sciences involved in the construction of AD as a disease (and not brain aging).

A stock-in-trade of ethnopsychiatry has been the study of culturebound syndromes. Now, however, researchers often consider Western disorders as culturebound. This perspective actually began in the work of this field's founder, George Devereux, and his analysis of schizophrenia as a culturebound syndrome, in 1963.

— *Atwood D. Gaines*

See also **Dementia; Ethnomedicine**

Further Readings

Desjarlais, R., Eisenberg, L., Good, B., & Kleinman, A. (Eds.). (1995). *World mental health: Problems and priorities in low income countries.* Oxford: Oxford University Press.

Devereux, G. (1961). *Mohave ethnopsychiatry.* Washington, DC: Smithsonian Institution, Government Printing Office.

Fernando, S. (2003). *Cultural diversity, mental health, and psychiatry: The struggle against racism.* London: Brunner/Routledge.

Gaines, A. D. (Ed.). (1992). *Ethnopsychiatry: The cultural construction of professional and folk psychiatries.* Albany: State University of New York Press.

Gaw, A. (2001). *Cross-cultural psychiatry.* Washington, DC: American Psychiatric Association.

Good, M. D., Brodwin, P. E., Good, B. J., & Kleinman, A. (Eds.). (2002). *Cultural assessment in clinical psychiatry.* Washington, DC: American Psychiatry Association.

Jenkins, J. H., & Barrett, R. (Eds.). (2003). *Schizophrenia, culture, and subjectivity: The edge of experience.* Cambridge: Cambridge University Press.

Lebra, W. (Ed.). (2000). *Cultural psychiatry and medical anthropology.* London: Athlone.

Tseng, W.-S., & Streltzer, J. (2004). *Cultural competence in clinical psychiatry.* Washington, DC: American Psychiatric Association.

Whitehouse, P. J., Maurer, K., & Ballenger, J. F. (Eds.). (2000). *Concepts of Alzheimer disease: Biological, clinical, and cultural perspectives.* Baltimore: Johns Hopkins University Press.

 # ETHNOSCIENCE

Ethnoscience is the study of what native people know about the world around them, including biology, zoology, and astronomy. This discipline is concerned with the cultural knowledge and classification systems in a given society. An ethnography, from this methodology, would include all the rules and ideas that a member of a society would need in order to function within its own culture. Ethnoscience began in the mid-1950s as a reaction to traditional ethnographic work, which was thought to be biased toward Western conceptual classifications. The goal of ethnoscientists was to "reproduce a cultural reality as it was perceived and lived by members of a society." In 1956, Floyd Lounsbury and Ward Goodenough published information regarding the semantic analysis of kinship terms. It compared the American Indian Pawnee system with the Truk of the Pacific. These papers presented a method for identifying ideal units and analyzing the organization in structure of classificatory terms. While developed specifically for the purpose of analyzing kinship terms, the general principles can be extended to other domains. During the 1970s, Berlin, Breedlove, and Raven applied this methodology to the way in which people organize knowledge about plants and animals. Their theory emphasized the need to reduce the number of characteristic features used to differentiate species. One technique thought to be used by informants was *attribute reduction,* which simply limits the number of criterial attributes. More simply, "If it quacks, it's a duck." The greater focus for the researchers was *configurational recoding,* where features are chunked together to form a single attribute recognized as a definitive characteristic. In other words, this technique relates "kinds of things"; for example, a husky is a kind of dog because it holds the essence of dogginess. In this system of organization, there are a limited number of levels, and each has a rank determined by what it classifies. The *unique beginner* is a general term encompassing all things included in the taxonomy, for example, the term *plant.* This category can be broken down into life forms, such as "trees," "flower plants," and "vines." Furthermore, there is the level of generic terms, which distinguishes type, such as "palm." The next level determines the specific attributes of the generic term, for instance a "peach palm." The last level is *varietal,* which is rare and used to delineate items of cultural importance. Robert Randall faults this form of analysis by arguing that the anthropologist may be creating the structure by leading the informant's response by the way in which the questions are formed. Despite its criticisms, today, this methodology is used to compare languages through color classifications, as well as influence the development of the discipline of ethnobotany.

One aspect of the emerging field was the adaptation of the methods used in ethnoscience, first employed by Harold Conklin in 1954, with his history work among the Hanunóo. He found that the people had an incredibly rich vocabulary to distinguish their plants containing more than 1,800 specific plant terms. His study involved how the people organized this information.

— *Luci Fernandes*

See also **Ethnosemantics**

Further Readings

Dandridge, R. (1995). *The development of cognitive anthropology.* Cambridge: Cambridge University Press.

McGee, J. R., & Warms, R. L. (2004). *Anthropological theory: An introductory history.* Boston: McGraw-Hill.

Randall, R. (1976). How tall is a taxonomic tree? Some evidence of dwarfism. *American Ethnologist, 3,* 545–546.

 # ETHNOSEMANTICS

Ethnosemantics, sometimes called "ethnoscience," is the scientific study of the ways in which people label and classify the social, cultural, and environmental phenomena of their world. Beginning in the 1960s, ethnosemantics continued the Boasian tradition of focusing on linguistic relativity and the importance of native language terms, with a focus on developing theories of particular cultures, rather than an overarching theory of culture in general. Nevertheless, ethnosemantic studies have contributed to the latter by making it possible to find universal constraints on the ways in which humans deal linguistically with their environments.

One of the best examples of this is the terminology people use for naming colors. Studies have shown that while color-naming systems vary, the different systems can be organized into an implicational scale. All languages appear to have terms for black/dark, white/light, and red. If a language has four terms, it adds either green or yellow; the fifth term added is the missing yellow or green; the sixth is blue; and so on. Because color varies continuously along a spectrum, the boundaries between colors tend to be arbitrary: For example, the boundary between English green and blue is not the same as the boundary between Spanish *verde* and *aula*.

The scope of red, however, is relatively uniform, a result of the biology of color perception that makes the wavelengths in the red area of the spectrum the most neurologically salient part of the spectrum.

Many ethnosemantic studies have focused on folk taxonomies, especially folk biology and botany. In taxonomy, the dominant relationship between categories is hyponymy. For example, *animal* is a hypernym or superordinate category; *mammal, fish,* and *bird* are hyponyms, or *kinds of* animal. One interesting find is that folk biological taxonomies tend to correspond fairly well to the Linnaean system at the level of genus and species. A related problem in ethnosemantics involves the ways in which people classify other people and themselves into putative biologically based "racial" categories; these categories may be relatively crisp (the U.S. hypodescent rule) or fuzzy (as in most of Latin America).

Another important domain of ethnosemantic study is kinship, the way in which people who are considered relations are classified and labeled. At their extremes of complexity, kinship terminologies may be minimally descriptive, as in Hawaiian, in which aunts and uncles are lumped with "mothers" and "fathers," and cousins are "sisters" and "brothers." Or they may be maximally descriptive, as in the Sudanese system, where each position has a unique label.

A technique sometimes used in ethnosemantics is componential analysis, which analyzes the meaning of a term into its components. For example, a componential analysis of the Aymara (Bolivia) pronoun system would take the speaker and the hearer as separate components, with each being either present or absent:

	speaker	*hearer*	
jiwasa	+	+	(you and I)
naya	+	−	(I/we, not you)
juma	−	+	(you, not me)
jupa	−	−	(neither you nor me; they)

Ethnosemantic studies continue to be relevant as anthropologists and linguists investigate the relationships between language, thought, and behavior.

— *Ronald Kephart*

See also **Ethnoscience; Language**

Further Readings

Berlin, B., & Kay, P. (1969). *Basic color terms: Their universality and evolution.* Berkeley: University of California Press.

Lucy, J. A. (1992). *Language diversity and thought: A reformulation of the linguistic relativity hypothesis.* Cambridge: Cambridge University Press.

Medin, D. L., & Atran, S. (Eds.). (1999). *Folkbiology.* Cambridge: MIT Press.

 # ETHOLOGY

Ethology is a subdivision of biology that focuses on animal behavior that is innate—a study of animal behavior that holds the belief that most of what animals know is instinctive, not learned. Instincts are genetically programmed behaviors; they generally serve to galvanize the mechanisms that evoke the animal to act or react. Ethology, as a discipline, developed in Europe and became popular in the early 1900s. As a study of animal behavior, ethology also deals with the question of nurture versus nature, focusing on the natural environment and the physiological aspects in that environment. Unlike animal behaviorists, who are generally interested in learned behaviors, ethologists focus on innate behaviors—that is, the behavior developed during ontogenetic development. According to one theory, for example, ducks learn to "quack" like ducks and don't "honk" like geese because the chicks hear their parents while in the egg; thus, they learn to "quack." Early ethologists noted for their work were Herbert Spencer, Charles Darwin, G. J. Romanes, and William James. Major modern ethologists include Konrad Lorenz, Nikolaas Tinbergen, and Karl von Frisch. These modern ethologists unveiled four basic strategies by which genetic programming directs the lives of animals: sign stimuli, motor programs, drive, and imprinting.

Sign Stimuli: A sign stimulus is an external sensory stimulus that triggers a typical, innate behavior (fixed-action pattern). It allows animals to recognize and react appropriately to important objects or individuals they interact with for the first time. For example, baby herring gulls know from birth to whom they direct their begging calls in order to be fed. They also know how to trigger the regurgitation action in their parents in order to receive the food. However, the chick does not recognize the parent itself. It solely relies on the sign stimulus of the vertical line of the herring gull bill and the red spot on the tip of the bill (pecked at to induce regurgitation). Almost any model presenting this visual image would evoke the same reactions from the chicks. Another example involves the graylag goose and its unaltered egg-retrieval pattern. If it sees an egg outside of the nest, the goose rolls the egg with its beak back to the nest using side-to-side head motions. However, the fixed-action pattern is such that any object resembling an egg is rolled to the nest even though it may not be incubated. Fixed-action patterns are innate behavioral patterns that are triggered by sign stimuli. They are carried out to completion even if other stimuli are present or if the behavior is inappropriate (the graylag goose and nonegg objects).

Sign stimuli aren't solely visual. They may be tactile or olfactory, such as in the case of pheromones. The most customary uses of sign stimuli in wildlife are in communication, food gathering, and in warning signals. The various types of communication include visual, chemical, and mechanical communications. Mechanical communication is primarily performed through vibrations through the ground or air. Chemical communication largely includes pheromones that one animal emits to influence the behavior of another species or that of the other gender. Sign stimuli are also used in courting and mating. They are especially prevalent among animals that are usually solitary except during the sexual part of their lives. Sticklebacks, for example, use a system of interlocking releasers to organize their mating. When the sticklebacks' breeding season arrives, the male's underside turns bright red. While the color attracts females, it also provokes other males to attack. As a female approaches the "red" male, she reveals her belly, which is swollen with eggs. This rouses the male to perform the mating dance and then lead the female to his nest. Through a series of movements, the male induces the female to release her eggs so he can fertilize them. If the female is induced in any other way other than the specific movements of the fertilizing male, the male stickleback will not fertilize the resulting eggs, but will eat them instead.

Motor Programs: Motor programs are chained sequences of specific muscles coordinated to perform a single task. Mating dances, stinging actions, and nest making are all examples of motor programs. There are two classes of motor programs. One is entirely innate (fixed-action patterns), and the other is learned. The first class of motor programs is largely applicable to animals, while the second is largely applicable to humans. The egg-rolling mechanism in geese has been a source of great curiosity to ethologists. The sign stimulus is the egg (or any other round, egglike object); however, the actual act of rolling the egg to the nest is a motor program. It has been recorded that the goose will continue rolling the egg cautiously into the nest even after the egg has been removed. The goose itself does not "think" about performing this act, rather it is inclined to it by the sign stimulus of a round object.

The second class of motor programs includes those that are learned. For example, in humans, bike riding, shoe tying, speaking, swimming, and walking are all learned. However, after a certain amount of time and practice, they become so much part of the norm that they can be performed without full conscious attention. They become so almost innate that they can be performed without normal feedback. An example of this class of motor programs in animals is that of the songbird. Though the songbird needs its audio abilities to sing, once it has learned the "songs," it no longer needs to hear what it is singing. This also applies to humans. Once a person learns to speak, no matter if he goes deaf, he can still speak. These motor programs need to be wired early on in development, so that later in life, they become nearly instinctive.

Drive: The third general strategy of ethology is drive. Drives are generally defined as desires or subconscious instincts that are switched on and off depending on inborn timers and chemical releasers. The stickleback, for example, normally is a solitary creature that neither lives with other individuals of its species, nor wishes to. However, at the stage of sexual reproduction, a sign stimulus is formed (the red belly), a drive to reproduce is created, and a motor program is carried out (the series of movements the male performs to induce the releasing of eggs). Drives are the inborn senses that are awakened when animals need to migrate or hibernate. In some frogs and reptiles, for example, as the weather becomes colder, the blood cells perform reverse osmosis in which the cells become extraconcentrated with salt as the diluted water outside of the cells freezes. In essence, these animals freeze during the winter and thaw out once the weather turns favorable. Other stimuli that trigger drives are lengthening or shortening of days. Spring migration and courtship behavior are triggered by the lengthening of daylight, while the shortening of daylight triggers winter migrations and certain cryogenic methods in animals.

While drives are put to sufficient use in the wild, in domestic animals, they are usually pent-up. The effect of this unused motivation is evident in cats. Even though these animals are well fed, they chase and stalk small animals, insects, or toys. In severe cases, they might even attempt to kill, devour, or disembowel imaginary targets. This behavior can occur without a proper stimulus or, in some cases, without even an apparent stimulus. However, as the desires and motivations of wild animals are exercised, they "learn" to ignore normal, repetitious stimuli if no threat or reward exists. Then, as soon as an abnormal stimulus occurs, normal reactions take place.

Imprinting: Imprinting is an example of programmed learning. It is described as the capacity to learn specific types of information at certain critical periods in development. This method of learning is displayed in the young of certain species. Ducks and other bird chicks must be able to recognize their own parents from other adults of the same species. This is also apparent in humans. Babies seem to know their mothers within a few months of birth. They cry and bring attention to themselves when they know they are being held or coddled by unknown persons. While in humans, this process can actually be described as learning and can afford to take a few months' time, in animals, this process of recognition must occur from birth. This immediate identification is accomplished through evolutionary wiring. Ducklings, for example, are wired to follow the first object they see moving that produces the species-specific call. The call triggers a drive in the duckling to follow the object. As long as the object makes the right calls and moves, the ducklings will follow a varied list of objects, such as rubber balls, cans, and humans.

The parental-imprinting phrase is brief, about 36 hours after birth. Another phase of imprinting occurs when the newborn matures and is about to begin mating. While some of the imprinting is helped along by genetics, most is learned, thus making imprinting the only ethological strategy that relies heavily on learning.

Other Areas of Research in Ethology

There are many strategy specific branches in modern ethology. The new areas of research include comparative ethology, analysis of behavioral patterns, and human ethology.

Comparative ethology is a field that tries to find relations in common behavior between animals with a common ancestor that performed this behavior. The primary mission is to investigate biological and behavioral similarities and differences between two different species and make a connection as to why either occurs.

Analyses of behavioral patterns are prevalent not only among animals, but among humans as well. Analysis has been taking place on the observational, neural, and molecular levels. Sensatory learning abilities have been proposed and tested. Mating behaviors and aggressive behaviors have also been thoroughly researched and explained.

Human ethology is a field that compares our own behavior to that of our closest evolutionary relatives, and through a roundabout way, comes to understand our own behavior. Human ethology is also closely related to comparative psychology, a field that discusses the psychological patterns and relations among our genus. Origins of such phenomenon, including origins of nonverbal communication, social behavior, and grooming are explored by human ethologists. New aspects of human ethology include human behavior, genetic psychology, psychobiology, and behavior evolution. The evolutionary basis of human behavior and methods of how to observe and record human behavior are also addressed by this subject. Thus, human ethology goes hand in hand with psychology but has a biological twist. It focuses on evolutionary and genetic traits that are species specific, and on other behaviors that humans have in common with other animals.

— *Komanduri S. Murty and Ashwin G. Vyas*

See also **Ethology, Cognitive; Lorenz, Konrad**

Further Readings

Eibl-Eibesfeldt, I. (1975). *Ethology: The biology of behavior* (2nd ed.). New York: Holt, Rinehart & Winston.

Hailman, J. P. (1967). *An introduction to animal behavior: Ethology's first century.* Englewood Cliffs, NJ: Prentice Hall.

Lorenz, K. Z. (1981). *The foundations of ethology.* New York: Springer-Verlag.

Lorenz, K. Z. (1996). *The natural science of the human species: An introduction to comparative behavioral research.* Cambridge: MIT Press.

ETHOLOGY, COGNITIVE

Cognitive ethology is the study of higher mental functions in animals. Until about 1980, the possibility of cognitive powers in animals was largely denied. This aversion to thinking about the animal mind was rooted in the deeply embarrassing "Clever Hans" incident.

In the early 1900s, a horse known as "Clever Hans" was apparently taught language, mathematics, and music by a retired German schoolmaster. Hans answered questions by pointing or by tapping his hoof. Thorough tests showed that no trickery was involved. Only after months of experimentation did Oskar Pfungst find the actual source of Hans's cleverness: The horse had discovered that as the tapping or pointing neared the correct answers, members of the audience would tense in anticipation. After the correct number of taps or when the nose had swept to the appropriate object, the observers relaxed.

In an unsurprising wave of overreaction, researchers concluded that animals in general, and horses in particular, had no cognitive powers. Behaviorists, who came to dominate American psychology from 1915 until about 1970, went so far as to deny thinking even in humans; instead, all behavior grew out of conditioning. The other major school studying animal behavior, ethology, accounted for essentially all of behavior on the basis of instinct and innately directed learning; they had little interest in humans. Neither group, then, worried much about thinking.

Telling exceptions to this dominant dismissal of higher mental processes in animals continued to turn up. In 1917, Wolfgang Köhler found evidence of planning in chimpanzees, as did Paul Schiller when he repeated this work 25 years later. In the 1930s and 1940s, Edward Tolman documented several cases of apparent planning in rats, coining the term "cognitive map" to describe the mental manipulations necessary to formulate a novel course of action. Around 1960,

D. S. Olton demonstrated that rats have a maplike maze memory. In the wild, ethologists were finding more and more behavior that seemed to require at least a partial understanding of the problems animals were facing.

Cognitive ethology got its start in 1976, when ethologist Donald Griffin wrote *The Question of Animal Awareness.* His argument was that because evolution predicts continuity between species, and humans have cognitive abilities like planning, thinking, and awareness, then if these mental operations are adaptive, why should we assume that no nonhuman animals can think? The major possible objection to this line of thinking is that some unique human adaptation—most likely language—makes cognition possible. Griffin attempted to show that human mental experience does not inevitably require language and that numerous examples from animals seem to involve analogous—presumably qualitatively similar—cognitive operations. At the same time, work on human language uncovered a widespread set of innate, species-specific circuits that help make it possible.

The ensuing debate sparked research that leaves no doubt that much of the behavior we take as cognitive is routine among animals. Planning novel routes, for instance, is seen in nearly any species with a need, including honeybees and hunting spiders. Mirror-image recognition is evident in chimpanzees, gorillas, and dolphins. Problem solving by thinking rather than trial and error is found in at least chimpanzees and ravens. Honeybees, parrots, and pigeons are among the species that can form concepts. The list goes on and on. Most researchers now agree that the human mind and animal minds have more in common that had been formerly assumed.

— *James L. Gould*

See also **Chimpanzees; Ethology; Instincts; Intelligence**

Further Readings

Gould, J. L., & Gould, C. G. (1999). *The animal mind* (2nd ed.). New York: Freeman.

Griffin, D. R. (1976). *The question of animal awareness.* New York: Rockefeller University Press.

Pfungst, O. (1911). *Clever Hans.* New York: Holt, Rinehart & Winston.

 # ETICS

Etics is a term used by some cultural anthropologists to denote descriptions and explanations of human beliefs and behaviors that are presented in terms relevant to an outside analyst or observer but not necessarily meaningful or relevant to the native practitioners of the culture in question. The linguist Kenneth Pike coined the term etics from the linguistic term *phonetics,* the articulatory, acoustic, or auditory study of the sounds used by speakers of human languages. Pike used etics to represent a level of description of human behavior based on categories meaningfully relevant to scientists but not necessarily to the people performing the behavior.

Marvin Harris and other cultural materialists popularized the term within anthropology by using it to refer to explanations for cultural beliefs and behaviors constructed by objective, scientifically oriented analysts and separate from native explanations. One of Harris's best-known examples is his analysis of the Hindu Indian cattle complex. Hindus revere cattle as sacred and claim that their religion prevents them from killing cattle. However, Harris identified what he saw as objective reasons for not killing cattle, related to their usefulness for pulling plows in the fields and also as producers of dung, which was used as fuel and fertilizer. Furthermore, despite their emic beliefs and behaviors regarding cattle, cattle do in fact end up being killed, particularly male cattle. Thus, the etic level of explanation can be further divided into two categories: *etic-mental* ("Let the male calves starve to death when food is scarce") and *etic-behavioral* ("Male calves are starved to death").

It is important to emphasize that in Pike's original formulation, etics represented a level of description. Pike saw physical behavior, like speech, as composed of waves; humans, however, perceive, categorize, and react to behavior in terms of particles, or contrastive units, which in the case of language correspond to phonemes. Pike's goal of an etic description of any human behavior was to present that behavior in terms of categories relevant to the scientific analysts. Harris and other anthropologists have used the term to represent a level of explanation. Etic explanations correspond very approximately to what some anthropologists refer to as analytic models.

— *Ronald Kephart*

See also **Emics; Models, Anthropological; Phonetics**

Further Readings

Harris, M. (1987). *Cultural materialism: The search for a science of culture.* New York: Random House.

Headland, T. N., Pike K. L., & Harris, M. (Eds.). (1990). *Emics and etics: The insider/outsider debate.* Newbury Park, CA: Sage.

Pike, K. L. (1971). *Language in relation to a unified theory of the structure of human behavior.* The Hague: Mouton.

 # EUDYSPHORIA

Eudysphoria is a neologism coined by A. Gaines to represent and characterize *dysphoric* (the Greek meaning "hard to bear") affect that is ego-syntonic and positively experienced in particular cultural contexts. The term critiques U.S. ethnopsychiatry's uniformly negative conception of dysphoric affect and highlights the existence of distinct, positive cultural evaluations thereof.

Psychiatry interprets dysphoric affect in the form of depression as the most common major mental disorder and asserts it is largely biological in etiology. However, sophisticated psychiatric epidemiological studies regularly yield incomparable incidence, prevalence, and/or lifetime incidence rates for depression and dysthymia. Some of the varying results derive from "the rhetoric of complaint," a Mediterranean self-presentation style stressing misfortune and suffering that enhances self- and social esteem.

Patterned configurations and modes of expression of eudysphoria are found in several culture areas. In the Latin world, they are labeled *peña, dano, tristitia, débilidad, saladera,* and *nervios.* We find *stenohorias* and *nevra* in Greece and *fatigué/triste touts le temps* in France and among immigrant groups from these areas.

The history of Mediterranean religions exhibits an association of dysphoric affect/suffering and religious piety that has led to its positive evaluation and social utility. In this context, those who suffer or who are blessed equally exhibit the grace of divine attention.

As well, the ability to deeply experience suffering and sadness is a mark of a mature personality. Discursive practices and rituals foster this capacity, which can lead to the popular conferral of the title of "saint."

A second cultural system exhibiting eudysphoria is the Buddhist. Here, what Westerners regard as noxious, dispiriting thoughts of worthlessness, meaninglessness, and futility indicate instead deep insight demonstrative of burgeoning enlightenment and transcendence.

While some authors argue for the importance of culture in shaping depression, they yet commonly assume an acultural, biological substrate. Gaines demonstrated the logical problem with this view. Allowing B = biology and C = culture, and D = depression/dysphoria, as "it" is experienced in a specific culture, we find that Western (ethno)psychiatry presumes that universally, $B + C = D$.

However, the equation's factors are not single entities. Rather, they are heterogeneous *categories,* comprising various cultures' notions of biology and of distinct cultures, respectively. Biology is a category constituted by a number of the world's distinct *biologies.* Gaines groups these under the general rubric of *local biology.* The second term of the equation, C, is also problematic because the great heterogeneity of cultures is well established. Thus, the equation cannot hold. For a given culture, $C1$, the formula yields: $B1 + C1 = Dl$, while for a second, the equation is $B2 + C2 = D2$. For n cultures, the formula is: $Bn + Cn = Dn$. However, since $D1\ D2\ Dn$, it is illogical to assert that dysphoria or depression (as emotion, mood, or disorder) has either biological or experiential universality.

— *Atwood D. Gaines*

See also **Buddhism; Ethnopsychiatry**

Further Readings

Casey, C., & Edgerton, R. (Eds.). (2005). *Companion to psychological anthropology.* Oxford: Blackwell.

Gaines, A. D. (Ed.). (1992). *Ethnopsychiatry.* Albany: State University of New York Press.

Horwitz, A. V., & Scheid, T. L. (1999). *A handbook for the study of mental health.* Cambridge: Cambridge University Press.

Kleinman, A., & Good, B. J. (Eds.). (1985). *Culture and depression.* Berkeley: University of California Press.

EUGENICS 871

Leslie C., & Young, A. (Eds.). (1992). In *Paths to Asian medical knowledge.* Berkeley: University of California Press.

Pfleidere, B., & Bibeau, G. (Eds.). (1991). *Anthropologies of medicine.* Wiesbaden, Germany: Vieweg & Sohn Verlag.

 # EUGENICS

Concept

The term *eugenics* was coined by Sir Francis Galton in his book *Inquiries into Human Faculty* (1883). The term is taken from two Greek words: *eu,* which is the Greek word for the adverb "well," and *gen,* which has its roots in the verb *gignesthai,* meaning "to become." Galton described with this word the program of improving the human stock by giving the "more suitable races or strains of blood a better chance of prevailing speedily over the less suitable."

It was the Greek philosopher Plato (427–347 BC) who first developed the idea, which Galton later labeled eugenics. Plato wrote about improving the human stock. He took this idea directly from the successes of animal breeders, especially breeders of hounds and noble poultry. Already in his times, they increased desirable features in livestock by selectively mating only those specimens with the desired trait. In his classical work *Republic* (Book V), Plato proposed measures enforced by the state to foster the procreation of the "best" and to prevent the "worst" becoming parents. Thereby, he did not hesitate to recommend that the philosophical kings, as the leaders of the state, should use lies and deception to convince the people in following their proposals.

Eugenicists at the beginning of the 20th century, following Galton's terminology, used the term "positive eugenics" for the idea of fostering the procreation of the "best" by measures of the state and "negative eugenics" for the idea of preventing the "worst" becoming parents.

Toward Realization and the Discreditation of the Idea

In 1900, three scientists, Correns, Tschermak, and de Vries, independently rediscovered Mendel's "laws of inheritance," written in 1866. They recognized its implications for the study of heredity and the theory of evolution. With this rediscovery, the idea of eugenics became so powerful that a number of leading scientists all over the world started advocating eugenics. New steps were to be taken.

To identify "good" and "bad" genes, research programs were first pursued in both state-supported and private laboratories. Concerning "positive eugenics," the United States enacted the Immigration Act of 1924, reducing the immigration of eastern and southern Europeans to the United States. Britain and Germany changed their family allowance policies in the 1930s. The true topic of the political agenda was "negative eugenics." People with certain forms of diseases, handicaps, or criminal attitudes were sterilized by force. Laws of this kind were declared constitutional in the 1927 U.S. Supreme Court decision of *Buck v. Bell.* By the late 1920s, some two-dozen American states had enacted sterilization laws.

The political agenda of the German National Socialist government included a mixture of racist, ideological, and eugenic ideas. Laws discriminating against handicapped people were introduced as early as 1933. Laws discriminating against Jews were introduced in 1935, and millions of Jews were killed in the gas chambers during World War II. A similar attempt was made against Sinti and Roma. The T4 program (1939–1941 officially, afterwards unofficially) led to the killing of hundreds of thousands of people labeled "unworthy to live," especially those who were mentally handicapped. To foster "positive eugenics" in the Nazi sense, programs like Lebensborn ("spring of life"), in which SS officers mated with selected Aryan women, were undertaken. With the end of the Nazi regime in 1945, eugenics as a term and idea was discredited.

The Reappearance and Reformulation of the Idea of Eugenics

In 1962, with the Ciba-Symposion "Man and His Future," 27 prominent scientists reassessed the original idea of eugenics and spoke openly about improving mankind by genetic diagnosis (negative eugenics) and genetic engineering (positive eugenics). The conference was heavily criticized for its purposes. As a result, instead of fostering the idea of programs to improve mankind, the idea of eugenics was reformulated: The focus is now on the question of whether parents have the right to use genetic diagnosis and genetic engineering to avoid having children with certain genetic traits and to increase the probability of having children with preferred traits. Especially, technologies like preimplantation genetic diagnosis have the potential to fulfill some of these expectations. This is often called the question of whether liberal eugenics is allowed, and if so, to what extent. On the other hand, genetic screening of whole populations (Iceland, Estonia), together with the Human Genome Project led to a new discussion of the idea of eugenics in the classical sense.

Ethical Considerations

Eugenics initiatives can be divided in two categories: *classical eugenics*, as a program of states or supranational institutions to improve the human gene pool, and *liberal eugenics*, as decisions of individuals or couples to control or improve the genetic makeup of their children. Classical and liberal eugenic initiatives can have a twofold aim: "positive eugenics," in which the frequency of genes presumed "good" is increased, and "negative eugenics," in which the frequency of genes presumed "bad" is diminished. Different methods are available or imaginable to reach these aims: On a macroeugenic level, "positive eugenics" could be put into practice through financial incentives for couples with "good genes," whereas "negative eugenics" could include sterilization laws for couples with "bad genes." Programs could also give incentives for preimplantation genetic diagnosis and prenatal diagnosis in order to prevent the presence of certain genes in the next generation. Even the method of germ line treatment is imaginable to introduce "better genes" and extirpate "bad genes." Couples could use the same technologies for their purposes. An ethical evaluation has to take into consideration the difference between decisions of states and decisions of individuals, between different aims and different methods.

Arguments against classical eugenics revolve around the primacy of privacy: Considering the difficulty, if not to say impossibility, of a precise definition of "disease" and "good and bad genes," every couple should have the right to decide on their own over such issues. This affirmation is correct, but at the same time misleading. We may discuss whether a certain genetically altered genotype should be considered a disease, but we have to acknowledge that there are genetic alterations that are life threatening, such

as trisomy 18. However, even if we acknowledge that an alteration of genes causes a life-threatening condition like Chorea Huntington, we have to answer the question of whether a state is allowed to implement a program of "negative eugenics." The question arises because there is an overlapping consensus not to kill a baby with this genetic trait. The reason for this consensus consists in the fact that the newborn can expect about 40 "good" years before the disease will manifest itself. Therefore, we have good reasons to be very careful with political agendas fostering eugenics both negative and positive.

On the other hand, there is a question of how far the freedom to reproduce may go. For example, if human beings who are severely mentally handicapped are not able to take responsibility for their offspring, who are very likely to have a similar mental handicap, then sterilization laws have to be considered. Also for discussion is the question of whether the state is responsible for reducing environmental mutagens to avoid harmful genetic alterations or to give incentives to procreate earlier in life to reduce the risk of children with trisomies. It is a very important point for further ethical discussion whether states have a right to enact laws obliging women to undergo certain forms of prenatal diagnosis or, in the future, preimplantation genetic diagnosis if in vitro fertilization treatment is the case. There will also be forms of gamete selection possible. Some are convinced that these possibilities raise the specter of a political eugenic agenda in which women will be passive recipients of artificially selected embryos. On the other hand, the practically worldwide prohibition of incest shows to a certain extent a common human awareness of genetic risks of relationships between close kin. This prohibition is accepted and rarely questioned.

Concerning liberal eugenics, some forms seem to be accepted in most countries. Abortion after prenatal diagnosis discovering genetic alterations is very common. Even if in some countries, like Germany, these abortions are allowed only because of the risk for the life or health of the mother, in practice, the reason for the abortion is mostly a genetic trait of the child. The huge gap between different aims of liberal eugenics from alterations of chromosomes as trisomy 18 to alterations of genetic traits causing harelip is just as ethically noteworthy as the difference between prenatal and preimplantation genetic diagnosis. This raises the question concerning the moral status of human preembryos, embryos, or fetuses. It is noteworthy: On one hand, prenatal diagnosis concerns a human being with a beating heart. Preimplantation genetic diagnosis concerns a human morula. In addition, the latter is outside the mother. On the other hand, the possibility of choosing between different human morulas (preembryos) presents an option for prospective parents to choose the morula with certain qualities. This opens a wide field for ethical reflections.

Some methods in eugenics result in the destruction of human preembryos, embryos, or fetuses. Whoever considers the moral status of human preembryos, embryos, and fetuses as in principle (right to live) equal to the moral status of born human beings is obliged to reject any destruction of human preembryos after preimplantation genetic diagnosis or any form of abortion undertaken for genetic purposes. The only exception would be made when the preimplantation genetic diagnosis shows that the preembryo has an alteration of chromosomes that would cause its death during pregnancy or immediately after birth (for example, trisomy 15). An obligation would also exist to reject germ line treatment insofar as the establishment of this technology needs experiments, in which preembryos and embryos would be destroyed. Whoever, instead, considers the moral status of human preembryos, embryos, or fetuses as not equal to the moral status of born human beings has a wide range of moral options depending on his or her ethical framework. In this case, the ethical consideration has to take into account that on the one hand, there is a kind of vertical escalation from "negative eugenics" by individual couples—to "positive eugenics" as a political agenda. On the other hand, there is a horizontal escalation from destroying preembryos, embryos, and fetuses for the reasons that they will not survive their first months after birth—to destructions for reasons that these human beings have certain genetic traits that are not accepted by their parents or the society (highest form of escalation). Answers to the different questions arising from these many forms of eugenics possibilities depend on an ethical framework. A utilitarian will answer them differently from someone in the tradition of Immanuel Kant, and even religions answer them differently.

— *Nikolaus Knoepffler*

See also **Euthenics; Galton, Francis; Genetic Engineering**

Further Readings

Buchanan, A., Brock, D. W., Daniels, N., & Wikler, D. (2000). *From chance to choice: Genetics & justice.* Cambridge: Cambridge University Press.

Kevles, D. J., & Lappé, M. (1995). Eugenics. In W. T. Reich (Ed.), *Encyclopedia of bioethics* (Rev. ed., Vol. 2, pp. 765–777). New York: Simon & Schuster Macmillan.

Winnacker E. L., Rendtorff, T., Hepp H., Hofschneider, P. H., & Korff, W. (2002). *Gene technology: Interventions in humans. An escalation model for the ethical evaluation* (English and German 4th ed.). Munich: Utz.

 # EUTHENICS

Euthenics is a branch of art and science that deals with the improvement of human functioning, efficiency, and well-being by modifying controllable environmental factors such as living conditions and education. The word *euthenics* is derived from the Greek word *euthenein,* which means, "to thrive or flourish."

One of the first known authors to make use of the word *euthenics* was Ellen Swallow Richards (1842–1911) in her book *The Cost of Shelter* (1905). She used the word euthenics to mean "the science of better living." In 1926, the *Daily Colonist* summarized euthenics as "efficient living." In 1967, *Technology Week* went on to define euthenics as "man's environmental opportunity," "his education." In all of these nascent definitions, the idea of improving humankind and human functioning by the concept of modifying controllable conditions, such as better shelter, efficient living, and education, is present.

In 1869, an English scientist, Sir Francis Galton (also cousin of Charles Darwin) coined the phrase *eugenics,* which is now defined as the study of human genetics and of particular methods to improve mental and physical characteristics that are inherited. In his book *Hereditary Genius* (1869), he upheld his hypothesis that human mental abilities and personality traits were essentially inherited, in the same manner that hair color, height, and so forth are inherited. This hypothesis was supported by his collection of data and also by analyzing the obituaries in the newspaper, where he traced the lineage of eminent men in Europe and ascribed their success to superior genetics that were inherited. These findings provided the formative years of the eugenics movement.

A modern adaptation of Galton's view of eugenics is directed toward the discouragement (usually forceful) of the propagation among the "unfit," for example, individuals with traits such as dwarfism or Down syndrome. This is defined as "negative eugenics." Conversely, the encouragement of the procreation of those individuals who are healthy and intelligent would be defined as "positive eugenics."

The encouragement of positive eugenics was seen in societies as early as ancient Sparta. In this culture, the strongest and best warriors were arranged to breed with women who were also strong and skillful warriors, or with the daughter of another powerful warrior. In this way, Sparta's people gave birth to some of the toughest and fiercest armies in the ancient world. It was also no coincidence that Sparta was the only city that did not have a wall around it, because they did not need one.

More modern examples of positive eugenics were applications of such principles that included enforced sterilization of the insane in the United States. Even more recently, in 1994, the Republic of China enacted restrictions on marriages involving persons with disabilities and diseases.

Darwin's theory of "natural selection" is also implicitly a form of natural positive eugenics, in that the dominant males will have more opportunity to breed with the females and thus propagate their more favorable genetics. In addition to this, the females of a species are naturally more attracted to the more dominant male or the "alpha male." Both of these natural methods work to ensure the survival and improvement of the species.

The idea of eugenics differs from euthenics in that eugenics makes a direct attempt to ensure a favorable inheritance of good or desirable genetics. This is demonstrated by the act of selective breeding that is seen in dog or horse breeding, and in plant breeding as well. In selective breeding, the breeder will take top-quality stock that contains the favorable genetics desired in that particular species and breed those animals or plants together. This will directly increase the chances of offspring inheriting favorable genetics.

More recently, with the completion of the Human Genome Project and new advances in biogenetic engineering, attempts can be made to manipulate and potentially improve a species' genetics on a molecular level. Technology can be developed to delete or modify (or turn on/off) genes that are associated with undesirable genetic diseases. The major ethical concern is that the technology can be taken too far in an attempt to create a "super human." Additional concerns deal with the uncertainty of the consequences involved in "playing God."

Euthenics differs from eugenics in that euthenics strives to make improvements in human functioning by altering the controllable environment around the individual. There is no attempt to improve or influence the genetic makeup; rather, the improvement is made after birth. However, both euthenics and eugenics share one theme in common: the amelioration of the species by altering controllable factors, whether genetic or environmental.

It is also worth pointing out another difference in approach between euthenics and eugenics. Euthenics uses education to allow an individual to make a choice about whether to reproduce or not. Eugenics on the other hand, makes the decision and eliminates any choice, for example, through legislation or selective breeding.

The attempt to improve humankind, either via euthenics or eugenics, gives rise to serious philosophical questions, such as: "What do societies value in an individual, or what physical inheritable traits are deemed as an advantage or disadvantage in the human species?" In addition, other perplexing questions will need to be evaluated, such as: "What are the moral guidelines (if any) for improving the species, or how much is too much improvement?" and "Who will make these types of decisions, the government, scientific/ medical specialists, ethicists, or religious leaders?" Answers to these questions will only give rise to further questions.

All of these ethical questions will also (and already have) meet with religious conflicts of interest. For example, some people believe that what you are born with is sacred, and therefore alterations of any type are an offense to God. Of course, with the many diverse types of religions worldwide, euthenics and eugenics will be approached differently.

Legal questions will also arise. For example: "What is the legality of inducing sterilization in individuals with undesirable genetics?" and "What are the legal rights of an individual in regard to prenatal and postnatal alterations?" In addition, the cost to society as a whole has to be considered, such as "Who will be able to afford this type of improvement, and who will ultimately benefit from this?"

The future of euthenics will have a direct impact on modern health care. Improvement of human functioning can be attainable by providing education about genetic diseases. Therefore, if the population is made aware of inheritable traits that are undesirable and detrimental to health and quality of life, then perhaps those people may be convinced not to reproduce if they possess those traits, thereby preventing them from being passed on. For example, if two individuals both have a moderate or severe form of epilepsy, those two individuals may decide to not reproduce, to prevent passing on this medical condition to their offspring. This would in effect reduce the prevalence of inherited genetic diseases in the population. In addition, society can be given greater scientific education as to what technologic interventions exist and how they can be beneficial, for example, the existence of reliable prenatal screening and other forms of genetic testing.

Besides improving the environment and increasing education, medical interventions after birth will also play a significant part in euthenics. For example, pharmacological advances in new medications, antibiotic therapy, and nutrition can better improve a person's well-being by directly improving physical health in general and without intentional modification of the genetic makeup.

— *John K. Grandy*

See also **Eugenics; Galton, Francis; Genetic Engineering**

Further Readings

Bennett, J. H. (1983). *Natural selection, heredity, and eugenics.* New York: Clarendon Press.
Carlson, E. (2001). *The unfit: A history of a bad idea.* New York: Cold Spring Harbor Laboratory Press.
Galton, F. (1990). *Hereditary genius: An inquiry into its laws and consequences.* New York: Peter Smith.
Richards, E. (2004). *The cost of shelter.* New York: IndyPublish.com.

EVANS-PRITCHARD, EDWARD (1902–1973)

Edward Evan Evans-Pritchard was a British social anthropologist known for his ethnographic work among the various tribes of Africa. Evans-Pritchard was born in England in 1902. He studied at the Exeter School, Oxford, and the London School of Economics, under Charles Seligman. In 1945, Evans-Pritchard was appointed reader in anthropology at Cambridge University. In 1946, he was appointed professor of anthropology at Oxford, following the departure of A. R. Radcliffe-Brown. He continued as professor and fellow of All Souls College until his retirement in 1970. The following year, he was knighted.

Evans-Pritchard was a significant figure in the development of British social anthropology. First, and foremost, Evans-Pritchard was a brilliant ethnographer, who carried out fieldwork among the Azande and Nuer of the southern Sudan. His field notes contained detailed descriptions of every aspect of life, ranging from religion to political organization to kinship relations. Evans-Pritchard argued that to fully understand another culture, anthropologists must accurately translate and understand the concepts of another unfamiliar culture. This, he argued, was often accomplished by learning another culture's language and using concepts relevant to that group instead of the anthropologist's own culture. Many of his ethnographies, including *The Nuer: A Description of the Modes of Livelihood and Political Institutions of a Nilotic People* (1940), *Kinship and Marriage Among the Nuer* (1951), and *Nuer Religion* (1952), were written with these ideas in mind.

In contrast to other anthropologists, Evans-Pritchard argued that anthropology was not a natural science, but was most closely aligned with humanities. In an article titled "Social Anthropology: Past and Present" (1950), he argued that anthropology is closely related to history due to similarities in theory and method.

During the 1950s and 1960s, much of his research was focused on the study of religion. In *Theories of Primitive Religion* (1965), he argued against prior notions that religion was constructed for sociological and psychological reasons. Instead, he argued that this idea was biased toward the views of the anthropologist, since quite often they were unable to accurately understand the concepts behind another culture's motivations. This was most readily demonstrated by his juxtaposing of the religious views of believers and nonbelievers. For a nonbeliever, the cultural beliefs of others are often explained as a result of sociological, psychological, or existential phenomena. These phenomena are often seen as unreal and have limited behavioral consequences.

Believers view religion in terms of their reality and the ways in which they should relate or organize their daily activities around these ideas. They generally develop concepts and social institutions that help them to relate these phenomena to reality and deal with the consequences that result from undesirable situations.

Evans-Pritchard continued to work on his ethnographic notes until his death on September 11, 1973. Decades later, his ethnographies remain classic texts that inform us about the non-Western populations of the world.

— *Christina B. Rieth*

See also **Anthropology, Cultural; Anthropology, History of**

Further Readings

Bohannan, P., & Glazer, M. (1988). *High points in anthropology.* New York: Knopf.

Evans-Pritchard, E. E. (1937). *Witchcraft, oracles, and magic among the Azande.* Oxford: Oxford University Press.

Evans-Pritchard, E. E. (1940). *The Nuer: A description of the modes of livelihood and political institutions of a Nilotic People.* Oxford: Oxford University Press.

Evans-Pritchard, E. E. (1951). *Kinship and marriage among the Nuer.* Oxford: Oxford University Press.

Evans-Pritchard, E. E. (1956). *Nuer religion.* Oxford: Oxford University Press.

EVE, MITOCHONDRIAL

Mitochondrial Eve is the name given to the idea that the mitochondrial DNA in all modern humans can be traced back to a single genetic lineage, carried by a woman who lived in Africa approximately 250,000 to 150,000 years ago. This idea has been misunderstood by people who incorrectly think that it means that all modern humans can be traced exclusively to one single human ancestor, like the biblical "Eve." This is incorrect because "mitochondrial Eve" is not the ancestral person from whom we can trace our entire nuclear DNA, the DNA that carries the codes to make humans.

Mitochondrial DNA

Mitochondria are small, energy-producing organelles found in eukaryotic cells. They have their own DNA (called *mitochondrial DNA* or *mtDNA*), separate from nuclear DNA, and replicate by themselves. They are thought to have entered into a symbiotic relationship with protoeukaryotic cells earlier than 1.5 billion years ago.

MtDNA is much easier to study than nuclear DNA. There are hundreds of mitochondria in the cytoplasm of each cell, making it easy to extract DNA for study. Human nuclear DNA contains the instructions to make a human being and is 3 billion base pairs long; mtDNA, which primarily contains the information to make the mitochondria, is much shorter, only 16,000 base pairs long (about 0.05% as long). However, there are two major features of mtDNA that make it particularly useful for evolutionary analysis. First, mtDNA accumulates mutations at a faster (but fairly constant) rate than nuclear DNA; these mutations may more often be neutral, instead of advantageous or disadvantageous, so mutations persist instead of being deleted. Second, mtDNA is inherited solely from the mother, so it does not recombine like nuclear DNA.

This latter point requires some explanation. A person inherits nuclear DNA equally through the egg and sperm of the parents. When sperm fertilizes an egg, it contributes almost exclusively nuclear material; any mitochondria-containing cytoplasm from the sperm does not survive entry into the mother's egg. The two nuclei combine to create a person equally related to each parent. However, the parental mitochondria do not combine; the person inherits mtDNA exclusively from the mother.

Matrilines and "Mitochondrial Eve"

So, while males and females inherit nuclear DNA equally from each parent and pass it on equally, both males and females get their mtDNA only from their mother. Going back one generation, a person is equally related to all four grandparents through nuclear DNA, but only one grandparent through mtDNA (the maternal grandmother). This direct inheritance of the mtDNA lineage makes it possible to reconstruct phylogenetic (or evolutionary) trees using these lineages. This means that the mtDNA of all living people are copies (with some mutations) of the mtDNA from one woman who lived thousands of generations ago.

Sometimes, lineages can be lost. In each generation, some women will not leave mtDNA descendants, as they will have either no children or exclusively sons. This lineage loss is analogous to the family name loss experienced in some cultures where women take their husband's family name; if she has no children or exclusively daughters, the name does not continue. As mtDNA lineages slowly die out over time, there are fewer lineages; eventually, there will be only one lineage remaining: the originator of this lineage has been dubbed "mitochondrial Eve." This name is misleading: "Mitochondrial Eve" may be the most recent common ancestor of our mtDNA, but in the grandparents example above, she is only one of our countless other nuclear DNA ancestors who lived alongside her.

Of course, the picture is muddied because new mtDNA lineages can be added over time. When mutations occur in the mtDNA, these mutations are transmitted down the generations as new lineages. Because of these mutations, modern mtDNA has diverged from the original mtDNA from "mitochondrial Eve." Since these mutations occur at a fairly constant rate, the amount of divergence is roughly proportional to the amount of time that has passed. This helps to calibrate the molecular clock used to determine when "mitochondrial Eve," and her population, lived.

The Molecular Clock

The hypothesis behind the molecular clock is that genetic change occurs at a relatively constant rate and therefore can be used to measure the time elapsed since two species (or two populations) diverged from a common ancestor. Because mtDNA accumulates mutations at a higher rate than nuclear DNA, it is used to calibrate a molecular clock to track recent evolutionary changes occurring from several hundred thousand to a few million years ago.

Comparisons of the mtDNA variation in many species indicate that humans are less variable than many other species, most notably chimpanzees. This suggests that humans have undergone a population bottleneck sometime in the past, followed by a rapid population explosion. For mtDNA, this would mean a large number of lineages were lost quickly, followed by a slow buildup of new lineages. Since modern African populations are more variable than other populations, containing more mtDNA lineages, it is thought that the population explosion began in Africa. Using the molecular clock concept, the evidence suggests that "mitochondrial Eve" lived between 250,000 and 150,000 years ago in Africa.

There are several issues involved in assessing the meaning and significance of the genetic data. To explore modern human origins, the mtDNA is used to track past population movements and to determine when and where the earliest modern human ancestor lived. To do this, one must model gene flow between past populations in different geographic regions, which has proven difficult. Another issue is that of stochastic lineage loss; it is possible to remove old mtDNA lineages from a population while retaining the nuclear DNA material. A third problem is that the assumption that the mtDNA mutations are selectively neutral might not be correct. If natural selection favors one or more of the mtDNA lineages, that can create inaccuracies in the molecular clock. Finally, it has been challenged that mitochondria carried by sperm sometimes make it into the fertilized egg, making it possible for some male mtDNA to occasionally be passed on; if this is found to happen more than just rarely, it would throw into question the idea that mtDNA is a pure matrilineal marker and invalidate the concept of a "mitochondrial Eve."

"Mitochondrial Eve" and Modern Human Origins

Was "mitochondrial Eve" a modern human? Some of the oldest fossils that are considered to be anatomically modern humans do date from around this time, in Africa. Most phylogenetic trees constructed using mtDNA show that the earliest branches occur in modern Africans and all other modern human groups branch from them. It is possible, then, that "mitochondrial Eve" lived in the population that later left Africa to colonize the rest of the world. Many researchers cite this evidence as support for a recent African origin model of modern human origins. However, critics of this model cite problems with the calibration of the molecular clock and suggest that "mitochondrial Eve" lived much earlier, during a period that predates anatomically modern humans in Africa. This, they argue, is evidence that modern humans share a common mtDNA ancestor as old as *Homo erectus,* which refutes a recent African origin of our species.

"Mitochondrial Eve" and "Y-Chromosomal Adam"

Recent research has suggested that there is a male analog to "mitochondrial Eve," known as "Y-chromosomal Adam." Humans have 23 pairs of chromosomes; one of these is known as the "sex chromosome," which has two forms, X and Y. Females have two copies of the X chromosome, while males have one X and one Y. So, sons inherit the Y chromosome exclusively from their fathers.

Studies indicate that the common ancestor of Y-chromosome lineages lived in Africa between 90,000 and 60,000 years ago, much later than "mitochondrial Eve." If both sets of dates are correct, this may be evidence that the human species experienced another, more recent bottleneck. It also suggests that the creation and loss of some genetic lineages depends on chance. Alternatively, human behavior may play a role; the practice of polygamy may restrict offspring to a smaller set of all males in the group, which might speed up the loss of some Y-chromosome lineages.

The concept of "mitochondrial Eve," that all modern humans share mtDNA descent with one African woman, is compelling. Rather than imagining our ancestors as fossils, it encourages us to imagine the lives of our great-great-grandmothers, thousands of generations ago.

— *Cathy Willermet*

See also **DNA, Recombinant; Evolution, Molecular; Gene Flow; Genetics, Human**

Further Readings

Dawkins, R., & Ward, L. (1996). *River out of Eden: A Darwinian view of life.* New York: HarperCollins.
Sykes, B. (2001). *The seven daughters of Eve: The science that reveals our genetic ancestry.* New York: Norton.
Wells, S. (2003). *The journey of man: A genetic odyssey.* Princeton, NJ: Princeton University Press.

 # EVIL

The Nature of Evil

The notion of evil is complex but usually involves some combination of or interplay between four basic categories, consisting of two sorts of effect and two sorts of cause or origin. The two sorts of effect are *suffering* and *metaphysical evil,* and the two sorts of cause are *moral* and *natural evil.*

Suffering includes both physical and psychological pain and distress, while *metaphysical evil* involves facts such as the impermanence of the world and the things in it, and especially human death (for simplicity's sake, in what follows, the term *suffering* will generally be used to include *metaphysical evil*). *Moral evil* is roughly what the Christian, for example, would call "sin," the Hindu "p~pa" or "adharma": deliberate actions, typically of human beings, but sometimes of other creatures or of supernatural beings. *Natural evil* is the result of the workings of the natural world as left to itself, without outside or supernatural intervention; it involves natural disasters such as earthquakes, floods, and famines but also individual events such as lightning strikes and sickness. While much if not most discussion in Western traditions of thought has concentrated on the issue of moral evil, other traditions have often been more concerned with the occurrence and degree of suffering and of metaphysical evil. For example, in the Buddhist tradition, Siddhartha was led to give up his life of princely luxury in order to seek enlightenment (the Great Renunciation) when, for the first time in his life, he encountered old age, sickness, and death and realized that suffering (*dukkha*, which is founded in *anicca*, "impermanence") is universal among human beings. In fact, whatever philosophers, theologians, and other thinkers have taken as central, ordinary people in most cultures generally see as problems arising out of the effects rather than out of the causes; in religious terms, especially, it's the occurrence and quantity of pain and suffering, the cutting short of lives, and so on, that causes people to question their faith.

A further important distinction should be drawn between the view that evil is a positive property or entity in itself and the view that evil is a mere privation or absence of goodness. In different cultures this takes very different forms, ranging from a conceptual distinction between kinds of property to a concrete distinction between the presence of a malevolent, evil supernatural being and the absence of a benevolent one. In whatever form, the distinction is especially relevant to the categories of moral evil and suffering, of course, though it can also be applied to the other two categories. The distinction is important, for those who view evil as something positive are usually thought to be under particular pressure to explain its origin.

Different cultures have developed various accounts of the nature and origin of evil, accounts that perform a variety of functions. These include the provision of psychological comfort in the face of suffering or perceived unfairness and the reconciling of evil with other aspects of the culture's belief system, especially with religious beliefs; the latter, of course, will generally also encompass the former.

The Problems

The chief questions asked by cultures throughout the world and over the millennia have centered on two main concerns: first, what are the origin and justification of evil, and second, why is suffering distributed so unfairly? In the Abrahamic religious traditions of Judaism, Christianity, and Islam, the first of these concerns generally takes the form of what is known as the Problem of Evil—the apparent inconsistency between the fact that the world contains (a great deal of) evil and the existence of a god who created the world and who has the attributes of omnipotence, omniscience, and benevolence (in fact, there is a problem concerning the existence and quantity of evil in the world even for those who believe in the existence of benevolent but less than omnipotent, omniscient deities); attempts to resolve this inconsistency are known as "theodicies." In both cases, the concern is sometimes with the mere existence of evil, sometimes with its quantity, and sometimes with the existence of certain kinds of evil (for example, it might be held that moral evil but not natural evil can be accounted for). With specific regard to moral evil, one can also ask why people are sometimes evil, or why normally good people sometimes do evil things; those who believe that people are inherently evil can ask why that should be. Whereas the Problem of Evil and its polytheistic counterparts are bound up with religious beliefs, the question of individual moral evil needn't be; it arises for naturalistic psychology too.

The second general concern is with the fact that suffering is so unfairly distributed. Why, that is, do the good or the innocent so often suffer and the bad or guilty so often prosper? Like the various versions of the Problem of Evil, this sort of question is most natural—perhaps only really makes sense—if asked in the context of a view of the world that involves more than just a naturalistic network of causes and effects. One needs to have some reason to suppose that the world *shouldn't* contain evil or that suffering *should* be distributed according to our deserts. Without such suppositions, there is no ground for surprise when we discover that the world isn't like that.

The Origins of Moral Evil

Here there are two main questions: What is the source of evil in general, and what is the source and nature of evil in the individual person?

With regard to the source of moral evil in general, there are three main views: that human beings are naturally evil, that human beings are naturally good, and that human beings are morally neutral or mixed. The first of these fits naturally with the view that evil is something positive, involving selfish aggression; the second fits with the view that evil is merely negative, an absence of good, so that human evil is the result of our falling away from our original nature; the third is more or less neutral between the two views, though it is most often associated with the former. If the second or third view is accepted, we're faced with questions such as, Why are some people evil? and Why do people sometimes do evil things? Some cultures respond in terms of outside influences, such as demons and witches, or aspects of the natural world; others appeal to the workings of human psychology.

With regard to the three categories of natural evil, suffering, and metaphysical evil, there are three main views: first, the world came about naturally the way it is, so that the occurrence of natural evil is a brute fact, needing no further explanation; second, the world was created by a malevolent being—a god or other powerful supernatural entity (in other words, natural evil is interpreted as a special kind of moral evil, the result of supernatural intentional acts); third, the world was created by a benevolent being, but the occurrence of natural evil can be reconciled with this.

There are two main ways in which people have attempted to reconcile the occurrence of natural evil with a good creator. The first depends upon the notion that a malevolent being or beings, such as fallen angels or demons, interferes in the world; this is of course similar to the notion that the world was created by such a being. The second involves the claim that it's impossible to create a world without the possibility of natural evil (that is, necessarily any set of natural laws will sometimes lead to natural disasters; in our world these include floods, disease, and lightning strikes, but in any possible world without these phenomena, there will always be other evils arising out of the particular structure of that world).

Cultural Relativism

With relevance especially to moral evils, there is a reasonably common view, associated in anthropology especially with the name of Franz Boas, that every culture is structured according to its own logic and so has to be understood in terms of that logic. As a methodological tool, this is unexceptionable; in order to understand any culture in itself rather than as viewed from another culture, one must do one's best to be objective, to get to grips with the culture on its own terms. This approach, central to any scientific endeavor, can, however, slide into the philosophical position that there is no objective truth about cultures and particularly about moral values. In its crudest form, this is of course self-contradictory, for it presents as objectively and universally true the claim that nothing is objectively or universally true. It's not

clear, though, that a consistent form of relativism can be developed, as it can be argued that any relativized notion of truth or morality depends for its meaning on a nonrelativized notion.

The Origins of Natural Evil, Suffering, and Metaphysical Evil

There are three main kinds of explanation of such evils as illness, injury, and natural disasters and for the occurrence of suffering and metaphysical evil such as death. First, one can attribute them to the causal workings of the world; second, one can attribute them to malicious natural beings such as sorcerers, witches (including possessor of the evil eye), or little green men in flying saucers; third, one can attribute them to a supernatural being or beings. All of these approaches divide into many, often very different variations.

Appeals to the causal nature of the world include, aside from scientific accounts, various notions of *karma* (operating within and across a person's lifetime), more or less fatalist systems such as astrology, and metaphysical claims that any physical world with the regular laws needed for life must by its very nature be impermanent and prone to undesirable but inevitable inconveniences. Appeals to the actions of either human or supernatural agents can also vary enormously. For example, misfortune can come from a divinity as a way of reminding the victim of some religious or moral duty or as punishment for some trespass or as a way of building character; on the other hand, the misfortune can be undeserved, caused by a malicious being such as the Tibetan *klu,* the Burmese *nats,* the Scandinavian *black elves,* or (as in the case of HIV–AIDS) government scientists doing secret weapons research.

—*Peter J. King*

See also **Aggression; Boas, Franz; Conflict; Crime; Mores; Taboos; Witchcraft**

Further Readings

Babuta, S., & Bragard, J.-P. (1985). *Evil.* London: Weidenfeld & Nicolson.
Garrard, E. (2002). Evil as an explanatory concept. *The Monist 85,* 320–336.
Herman, A. L. (1976). *The problem of evil and Indian thought.* Delhi, India: Motilal Banarsidass.

King, P. J. (1998). The problem of evil. *Philosophical Writings, 9.*

Midgley, M. (1979). *Beast and man.* Ithaca, NY: Cornell University Press.

Morton, A. (2004). *On evil.* New York: Routledge.

Obeyesekere, G. (1968). Theodicy, sin, and salvation in a sociology of Buddhism. In E. R. Leach (Ed.), *Practical religion.* Cambridge, UK: Cambridge University Press.

Parkin, D. J. (1985). *The anthropology of evil.* Oxford, UK: Blackwell.

Rorty, A. O. (2001). *The many faces of evil.* New York: Routledge.

Sharma, R. P. (1977). The problem of evil in Buddhism. *Journal of Dharma, 2.*

Sharma, U. M. (1973). Theodicy and the doctrine of karma. *Man, 8,* 347–364.

EVOLUTION, ARC OF

One must distinguish between the fact of organic evolution and those different interpretations of this process that are offered in the world literature. The arc of interpretations ranges from materialism, through vitalism and spiritualism, to mysticism. Furthermore, perspectives vary from population dynamics to cosmic history. The interpretation may give preference to science, philosophy, or theology. Emphasis may be placed on facts, concepts, or beliefs, respectively. Essentially, an interpretation of evolution will favor materialism or spiritualism.

Each interpretation of evolution includes a view of humankind within this universe. Our species may be seen as a recent product of primate evolution that is totally within nature and therefore a complex animal that is only distinct from the great apes; that is, our species differs merely in degree (rather than in kind) from the pongids. Or our species may be seen as a special animal that is somehow separated from the natural world in terms of both its rational intellect and immortal soul.

A systematic interpretation of organic evolution is grounded in metaphysical assumptions about ontology and cosmology, whether they are implicit or explicit in the presentation. Likewise, an epistemological stance and an ethical framework are taken (or at least value judgments are made). Obviously, not all evolutionists will take the same perspective, have the same values, or agree on the same interpretation of our species and its place within organic history and this universe.

Charles Darwin (1809–1882) had been greatly influenced by the writings of Lyell and Malthus, and his global voyage as a naturalist aboard HMS *Beagle.* Particularly significant was his 5-week visit to the Galapagos Islands in 1835. Darwin became acutely aware of both the awesome multiplicity of life forms on the earth and the incredible variability existing in individuals both within and among populations. Acknowledging the mutability of species throughout organic history as clearly documented in the fossil record of the geological column, he explained biological evolution in terms of natural selection and sexual selection favoring some individuals over others in the struggle for existence. Over vast periods of time and change, in order to adapt and survive and reproduce under challenging situations or in new environments, most species evolve into new life forms, or they become extinct.

Darwin presented his facts and concepts in two pivotal books, *On the Origin of Species* (1859) and *The Descent of Man* (1871). His scientific interpretation of biological evolution is strictly naturalistic, grounded in mechanism and materialism. Consequently, our human species is seen as an evolved ape with no claim to a special position in dynamic nature that separates it from the rest of the animal world. This scientific interpretation is now defended by Richard Dawkins, whose writings are a rigorous representation of neo-Darwinism.

Henri Bergson (1859–1941) accepted evolution, but he rejected Darwin's materialism, claiming that it does not sufficiently account for the diverging novelty that emerges throughout organic history. Bergson's philosophical orientation gives preference to time, consciousness, and intuition. It maintains that a life force causes biological evolution. Bergson presented his vitalistic interpretation of the living world in his major work, *Creative Evolution* (1907).

Ultimately, Bergson's vitalism supports a dualistic view of dynamic nature that is not in step with the ongoing advances in evolutionary science and rational philosophy. Another vitalistic interpretation of organic evolution had been offered by the philosopher Friedrich Nietzsche, who argued that a will to power pervades the history of life and will eventually bring about the emergence of the future overman (a being that will be as superior to the human animal of today as our species is now superior to the lowly worm).

Pierre Teilhard de Chardin (1881–1955) accepted the fact of evolution while attempting to reconcile science and theology within a process view of this universe. The renowned geopaleontologist and controversial Jesuit priest focused his attention on the earth, maintaining that planetary history represents three major but distinct stages of evolution: geogenesis, biogenesis, and noogenesis. Teilhard believed that evolution is a directional, converging, and spiritual process that will result in the formation of a unified humankind in terms of global thought. Eventually, as he saw it, this developing layer of mind (the noosphere) will detach itself from the earth, transcend space-time, and become united with a personal God at the "omega point"; this future event is the final end goal of human evolution on earth.

Teilhard presented this mystical vision of involuting evolution in his major work, *The Phenomenon of Man* (1938–1940, 1948). Although this fascinating and provocative interpretation of cosmic evolution is essentially both geocentric and anthropocentric, it does deal with those philosophical questions and theological issues surrounding evolution that are usually ignored by traditional thinkers.

Presently, both religious creationism and biblical fundamentalism challenge science and reason. Yet for the arc of evolution, which spans from materialism to mysticism, ongoing discoveries in the special sciences favor an interpretation of evolving life (including our own species) that is grounded in naturalism rather than spiritualism.

— *H. James Birx*

See also **Bergson, Henri; Creationism, Beliefs in; Darwin, Charles; Teilhard de Chardin, Pierre**

Further Readings

Bergson, H. (1998). *Creative evolution.* Mineola, NY: Dover. (Original work published 1907)

Birx, H. J. (1991). *Interpreting evolution: Darwin & Teilhard de Chardin.* Amherst, NY: Prometheus Books.

Darwin, C. (2000). *The voyage of the Beagle.* Amherst, NY: Prometheus Books. (Original work published 1839)

Teilhard de Chardin, P. (1975). *The phenomenon of man* (2nd ed.). New York: Harper & Row/Harper Colophon/Perennial Library. (Original work written 1938–1940, 1948)

INTERPRETING EVIDENCE

Anthropology is a social science that studies the origin and nature of human beings. It gathers data and organizes it into knowledge using the scientific method. Consequently, anthropology's method is naturalistic because it does not use methods taken from sources other than human reason.

As a science, anthropology uses the empirical method to gather evidence. The empirical method may be quantitative or qualitative (objective or subjective). In quantitative studies, the number of behaviors or other features of the object of study are counted. With the advent of computers, quantitative studies of family or group relations, marriage, divorce, and interrelations have been made.

Anthropological data, to be useful, must be converted into scientific knowledge. Interpretation of evidence occurs as field studies are checked for accuracy. For example, did a linguistic study capture the sound or the meaning of a word in the object language?

Interpretation of evidence also requires careful avoidance of prejudice or bias so that unusual human behaviors are not misinterpreted for some reason. The goal is to interpret the evidence so that it explains the seemingly irrational and therefore explains how a people under study developed. As more evidence is gathered, it is placed into increasingly more general categories. Interpretation at this stage allows masses of evidence to be put into a unified model that explains the origin and nature of humans.

Anthropology, until the middle of the 19th century, was a part of natural history, which put an emphasis upon biology. Many aspects of anthropology still use this approach, interpreting data about intelligence, race, and biological features and fossil records of human origins.

After Charles Darwin, cultural anthropology used an evolutionary model. In the 20th century, the focus shifted to studying the function of cultural practices. It also interpreted human nature as infinitely malleable rather than fixed. The functionalist school focused on the function of customs, beliefs, material culture, and other features of a group of people. Structuralists, in contrast, interpreted field studies as part of a hidden-meaning system that could be interpreted by understanding myths and symbols.

An anthropologist, like all scientists, makes a number of decisions before beginning a study. These all require interpretations of evidence. Choosing the object of study, making assumptions about the object of study, choosing the best method for study, and coming to decisions about the meaning of the data all involve interpreting the evidence.

— Andrew J. Waskey

EVOLUTION, DISBELIEF IN

The Abrahamic religions (that is, Christianity, Judaism, and Islam) all have fundamentalist schools and denominations that believe in the inerrancy of the Bible. Because of the belief in the infallibility of the Bible, the fundamentalists reject evolution and believe in the literal truth of the origin accounts as told in Genesis. The fundamentalist Christians, mainly Protestants and some charismatic Catholics, are more numerous and better known, and the consequences of their rejection of evolution are more important for public education in the United States than the fundamentalist schools and denominations of the other Abrahamic religions. Fundamentalist Christians have attempted to pass laws to prohibit the teaching of evolution in the public schools. Having failed to prohibit the teaching of evolution, the fundamentalists have either tried to have the Genesis story told alongside the teaching of the principles of evolution or downplay the centrality of evolutionary theory to the modern life sciences in K–12 textbooks.

There is, however, variation in the explanations of the origin of species offered by the antievolutionists.

The Institute for Creation Research and Answers in Genesis maintain, for example, that the universe, earth, and all species were created less than 10,000 years ago, as described in Genesis. The less literal Christians have proposed the gap theory and the day-age theory. The gap theory sees God as modifying species in the gaps in the fossil record and the day-age theory posits that one day in the Genesis might be longer than a 24-hour day as we know it. More recently, the old idea of the English theologian William Paley (ca. 1802) has been revived in the form of Intelligent Design, or ID. The proponents of ID accept that species undergo small changes and the earth is older than 10,000 years. They argue, however, that living creatures are too complex to have evolved without the planning and intervention of an intelligent designer.

The leaders of antievolutionary organizations are educated. Many have doctorate degrees. While they have thus far presented no research that confirms creationism, many do believe that the widespread acceptance of evolution has led to social ills. In the absence of published research in recognized and accepted scientific and academic journals, it is difficult for creationists to participate in a serious debate on the importance of evolutionary theory to the life sciences.

— Linda D. Wolfe

See also **Creationism, Beliefs in; Darwin, Charles**

Further Readings

Alters, B. J., & Alters S. M. (2001). *Defending evolution: A guide to the creation/evolution controversy.* Boston: Jones & Bartlett.
Number, R. L. (1993). *The creationists: The evolution of scientific creationism.* Berkeley: University of California Press.
Scott, E. C., & Branch, G. (2003). Antievolutionism: Changes and continuities. *BioScience, 53,* 282–285.

EVOLUTION, HUMAN

Inspired by the scientific framework of organic evolution, paleoanthropologists continue to be very successful in discovering the diversified remains of fossil hominids at sites in eastern and southern Africa. This growing evidence represents the very long, branching, and complex process of human emergence from Pliocene apelike forms, through protohominids and then hominids, to the present human species.

The evolution of efficient bipedalism separated humankind's earliest terrestrial ancestors from arboreal quadrupedal pongids; the adaptive and survival advantages of sustained bipedal locomotion for the emerging hominids are still very debatable. Plio-Pleistocene hominids (early australopithecines) were followed by *Homo habilis* with a Paleolithic culture of cores and flakes, then the migrations of *Homo erectus* with bifacial hand axes, and eventually the appearance of *Homo sapiens* with a modern cranial capacity, an advanced material culture, and increasing cognitive abilities in a social group (especially the use of symbolic language as articulate speech).

Darwin's Influence

After waiting 20 years, the great naturalist Charles Darwin finally published *On the Origin of Species* (1859). This book argued for the mutability of species over time by means of variation and selection, that is, organic evolution as a result of the survival of the fittest in the struggle for existence. Knowing how controversial his scientific theory of biological evolution would be for science, philosophy, and theology, Darwin deliberately left out of this pivotal work a discussion on the origin and history of the human species. However, any critical reader could easily see that the Darwinian theory can be extended to also include the evolution of the human animal from an apelike form in the remote past to *Homo sapiens sapiens* of today. In fact, after 1859, both Thomas Huxley in England and Ernst Haeckel in Germany were quick to lecture on and write about human evolution (although early fossil hominid evidence outside of Europe was lacking at that time).

Darwin's writings represent one long argument for organic evolution in terms of both science and reason. Grounded in a mechanistic and materialistic interpretation of nature, his books maintain that natural selection is the basic principle to explain the evolution of all species throughout geological time. The fact that species are mutable challenged traditional science, philosophy and theology; it had been held since antiquity that plant and animal types are eternally fixed within a single hierarchy of static forms from minerals, through plants and animals, to the human being at the apex of this so-called great chain of being or ladder of nature.

The Darwinian conceptual revolution of biological evolution in science gave priority to change over permanence; it also supported mechanism and materialism over Aristotelian teleology and essentialism, while discrediting vitalism and challenging spiritualism.

Twelve years after the appearance of his *Origin* volume, Darwin published *The Descent of Man* (1871). In this work, he focused on human evolution. Darwin claimed that the human species is closest to two African great apes (chimpanzee and gorilla), with which it shares a common fossil ancestor that would be found in Africa; although at that time, it was generally held by naturalists that Asia was the birthplace of humankind. Unfortunately, during Darwin's own life, no fossil hominid specimens older than the Neandertals of Europe had been found, and the bonobo, the third great ape (or pongid) of Africa, was still unknown to science.

As had Huxley and Haeckel, Darwin also maintained that the difference between the human animal and the living pongids is merely one of degree rather than one of kind, there being no structure or function in the human species that does not already exist to some extent in the great apes. Furthermore, Darwin held that the human species is closer to the pongids than they are to the hylobates (gibbon and siamang); evidence from comparative studies in biochemistry, genetics, embryology, immunology, anatomy, physiology, psychology, and behavior now support this scientific generalization.

Today, the discovery and examination of the bonobo, or pygmy chimpanzee, in Central Africa adds a fourth great ape species to the pongids (which include the African gorilla and the common chimpanzee, as well as the Asian orangutan). In fact, in terms of biology and behavior, *Homo sapiens* is very close indeed to both chimpanzees. As a result, it becomes futile to draw a sharp line between the earliest hominid implement-making behavior and the making of tools or weapons by living bonobos and chimpanzees.

The idea that the human species evolved from an apelike ancestor did not settle well with the Victorian worldview. Nevertheless, naturalists could not ignore the growing facts in geology, paleontology, biogeography, botany, and zoology that gave empirical support to the fact of biological evolution. Essentially, the bitter controversy surrounding Darwinism was clearly due to the far-reaching implications and disquieting consequences that scientific evolution held for interpreting the place that the human animal occupies within the primate order and organic history. Evolution claims that the human species is a product

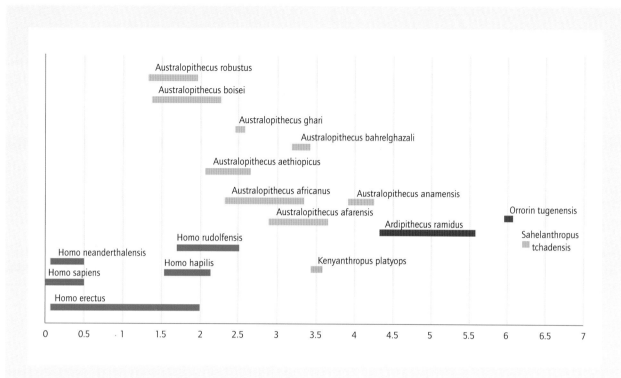

Hominid Evolution: Since the writings of Charles Darwin, Thomas Huxley, and Ernst Haeckel, paleoanthropologists have searched for fossil hominid remains in Africa and Asia to substantiate the scientific theory of human evolution. Although interpretations of particular specimens may vary among physical anthropologists, a century of discoveries now offers an overview of the evidence thus far. The evolution from quasi-bipedal protohominids to our big-brained and culture-bound species with sustained bipedality and articulate speech was a long and complex process. We have uncovered many fossil hominid species that existed during the past four million years, and no doubt many more will be. But all of these species became extinct except our own. Furthermore, the emergence of *Homo sapiens* was not an inevitable outcome of directional evolution, but the result of chance genetic variations and natural/social selection within changing environments over millions of years

Source: Courtesy of Minka Kudrass, Phyletic Museum, Jena.

of, dependent upon, and totally within dynamic nature. The writings of Huxley, Haeckel, and Darwin himself inspired several naturalists to speculate seriously on human evolution and to begin searching for fossil hominids (first in Asia and then in Africa).

Major Discoveries

The framework of evolution provided a new paradigm for understanding and appreciating the human species in terms of science and reason. If primate evolution is true, then fossil hominid specimens should be found to substantiate the emergence of the human animal from a prehistoric apelike form that once existed outside of Europe millions of years ago.

Oddly enough, in his book *Arboreal Man* (1916), the comparative anatomist F. Wood Jones presented a "tarsoid hypothesis" to account for the origin of the human animal. He argued that the human species had descended from an early tarsier-like form independent of the lines leading to the Old World monkeys and six apes. Modern physical anthropology now recognizes that the human animal is closest to the chimpanzees and bonobos. Of course, earlier evolutionists had recognized the glaring similarities between the pongids and the human species in terms of general morphology and social behavior.

Near the end of the 19th century, naturalists began to search for fossil jaws, teeth, crania, and other skeletal bones at hominid sites, first in Asia and then in Africa. Their impressive successes during the past 120 years clearly demonstrate the awesome power of scientific inquiry, particularly when it incorporates a team effort and a multidisciplinary approach in modern paleoanthropology. Furthermore, the shift from merely relative to more exacting (radiometric) dating techniques during this time has resulted in far more accurate models for and better interpretations of hominid evolution.

Inspired by the "missing link" hypothesis of Ernst Haeckel, the naturalist Eugene Dubois left Europe and went to Indonesia in order to search for a fossil apelike form ancestral to the human species and the pongids. Erroneously, Haeckel had maintained that an ape-man without speech (*Pithecanthropus alalus*) had existed between fossil pongids and the present human animal. He further claimed that Asia was the cradle of human evolution, speculating that a landmass he referred to as "Lemuria" (assumed to have once existed) was the geographical location where the human species had its origin from such an ape-man species.

During the early 1890s, at the Trinil site on the island of Java, Dubois was fortunate enough to discover the fossil hominid bones of *Pithecanthropus erectus* ("Java man"). These remains are over 500,000 years old. This evidence suggested that Asia may have been the birthplace of hominids.

During the first two decades of the 20th century, additional Neandertal and Cro-Magnon specimens were being found in Europe. However, none of this hominid evidence dated back earlier than about 200,000 years. Nevertheless, discoveries made of much earlier fossil hominid forms at sites in the Transvaal area of South Africa did substantiate Darwin's claim that this continent (not Asia) was the cradle of humankind.

Of special significance are the fossil hominids found at five sites in the Transvaal area of South Africa. In 1924, anatomist Raymond A. Dart analyzed a fossil juvenile skull from the Taung site; amazingly, it was over 1 million years old. Dart correctly interpreted this specimen as representing a hominid form that was clearly separated from the fossil apes of that time. Subsequently, important discoveries were made of several adult individuals found at other sites in this area (Kromdraai, Swartkrans, Sterkfontein, and Makapansgat). These adult specimens clearly justified giving a hominid status to all this fossil evidence from the Transvaal sites.

Collectively referred to as the "southern apes" or australopithecines of South Africa (although they are hominids, not pongids), these specimens are from 1 to 3 million years old. They represent at least two different species: the large *Australopithecus robustus* and the small *Australopithecus africanus*. There is no conclusive evidence that either form made stone implements. Still, they were the earliest fossil hominids known to paleoanthropology before the middle of the 20th century. However, it is now held that these two species represent side branches in hominid evolution that became extinct about 1 million years ago, long before the most recent Ice Age.

Beginning in 1928, geopaleontological research in the Western Hills near Zhoukoudian, China, was directed first by Davidson Black and then by Franz Weidenreich; both were anatomists from the Cenozoic Laboratory of the Peking Union Medical College. Over several years, scientific excavations unearthed fossil hominid evidence referred to as *Sinanthropus pekinensis* ("Peking man"). These specimens are at least 350,000 years old. The geopaleontologist Pierre Teilhard de Chardin became famous for his research at and popularization of this important site that helped to establish the scientific fact of human evolution. Today, both Java man and Peking man, as well as the hominid skeleton of a boy (specimen KNM-WT 15000) 1.6 million years old from Nariokotome on the western shore of Lake Turkana in central East Africa, are now relegated to the *Homo erectus* phase of human evolution. This stage of hominid development lasted over 1.5 million years, spanning between the earlier *Homo habilis* form and the later *Homo sapiens* species.

Darwin's idea that the earliest humans would be found in Africa greatly inspired the anthropologist Louis S. B. Leakey, who dedicated his entire career to searching for the first fossil hominid specimen to be discovered in central East Africa. Undaunted by his lack of success for three decades, Louis concentrated his research at Olduvai Gorge in the Gregory Rift Valley of Tanzania. Although he found fossil ape specimens, no hominid evidence was discovered during his 30-year search in this part of the world. Even so, Louis continued his quest along with his second wife Mary, an anthropologist specializing in the prehistoric archaeology of central East Africa.

In 1959, ironically, it was Mary Leakey who found the first fossil hominid specimen in central East Africa: the cranium of *Zinjanthropus boisei* (as it was classified at that time), belonging to a 1.75 million-year-old robust hominid form found in the lowest rock strata at Olduvai Gorge. The "Zinj" skull was a major turning point in paleoanthropology because it inspired other physical anthropologists to concentrate their search for other similar hominids (if not even earlier forms) in central East Africa. Today, the famous "Zinj" specimen

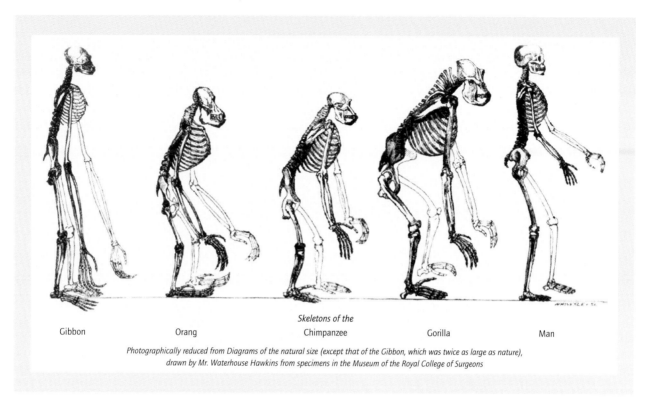

Skeletons of the

Gibbon   Orang   Chimpanzee   Gorilla   Man

Photographically reduced from Diagrams of the natural size (except that of the Gibbon, which was twice as large as nature), drawn by Mr. Waterhouse Hawkins from specimens in the Museum of the Royal College of Surgeons

Source: T. H. Huxley (1863), *Evidence as to Man's Place in Nature.*

is classified as *Australopithecus boisei*, a brutish hominid form, with both large premolars and molars, that became extinct before the most recent Ice Age.

Just 2 years later, Louis himself found the skull of *Homo habilis* in the same rock strata at Olduvai Gorge; it is a far more hominid form than "Zinj" and is directly associated with the pebble culture of the Oldowan tradition, consisting of the earliest human-made stone implements of cores and flakes known at that time (although it is arbitrary when the designation "human" may be first applied to the very long, branching, and complex process of hominid evolution).

In 1972, at Koobi Fora on the eastern shore of Lake Turkana in northwestern Kenya, Richard Leakey discovered the famous *Homo habilis* skull 1470, dating back about 1.9 million years. Therefore, both at the Olduvai Gorge and Koobi Fora sites, the larger-brained *Homo habilis* is associated with the dawn of human-manufactured Paleolithic culture.

In 1974, at the Hadar site in the Afar Triangle of northern Ethiopia, Donald C. Johanson found the fossil hominid "Lucy" skeleton. This specimen was dated at over 3 million years old. Although the skull and teeth of *afarensis* have apelike characteristics, the postcranial skeleton is truly hominid. An analysis of the postcranial

bones revealed that "Lucy" stood erect and walked upright with a bipedal gait. Classified as *Australopithecus afarensis*, this remarkable discovery clearly demonstrated that bipedalism had been established in hominids before the end of the Pliocene epoch.

In 1978, at the Laetoli site, south of Olduvai Gorge, Mary Leakey had the incredible good fortune to find three tracks of hominid footprints about 3.6 million years old. According to Johanson, these Laetoli tracks were made by *Australopithecus afarensis* (for him, the common ancestor of all later hominids). In 1995, these Pliocene footprints were reexcavated and reexamined. Then, the three Laetoli tracks were carefully reburied in order to preserve this unique discovery for centuries to come.

In science, nothing succeeds like success. The more paleoanthropologists search for fossil hominids in central East Africa, the more evidence they find. Recent discoveries by Tim White and Meave Leakey have pushed back the beginning of hominid evolution to over 4.4 million years ago. These earliest bipedal hominid forms are represented by *Ardipithecus ramidus* (a side branch in hominid evolution found in Ethiopia) and the later *Australopithecus anamensis* from Kenya, a species ancestral to *Australopithecus afarensis*.

In 1999, fossil hominid evidence from the Bouri site, south of Aramis, in Ethiopia, was dated to about 2.5 million years old. This latest discovery is designated *Australopithecus garhi* and is another illustration of Plio-Pleistocene hominid species diversity in Africa.

Also, in 1999, at a site in Northern Kenya near the western shore of Lake Turkana, a research team headed by paleontologist Meave Leakey discovered an unusual million-year-old skull. The near-complete cranium shows both hominid-like and pongidlike characteristics: small brain, small teeth, and human-looking but flat face. It is classified *Kenyanthropus platyops*, denoting both a new genus and new species among the early fossil hominids of central East Africa (thereby separating this form from the *Australopithecus afarensis* specimens found at Hadar and Laetoli). If more fossil hominid species from this time period are found, then those complex questions that still concern the direct ancestor to *Homo habilis* may be answered in the future.

One generalization is clear: The very earliest hominid forms emerged in central East Africa long before later hominids, representing *Homo erectus*, migrated north into Europe and east into Asia. Consequently, both Charles Darwin and Louis Leakey are vindicated in light of the growing empirical evidence for the birth of humankind's most remote bipedal ancestors in central East Africa. Of course, models and interpretations of hominid evolution vary among physical anthropologists. And there is no common consensus concerning the classification and interpretation of the growing fossil evidence for hominid evolution. Remaining questions about the origin and emergence of humankind will be answered by the discovery of more fossil hominid specimens and prehistoric stone artifacts in Africa and elsewhere.

Near the famous Hadar site, in Ethiopia, a recent fossil hominid discovery that is 4 million years old could shed more light on the emergence of bipedality (particularly in terms of what the evolving ankle joint contributed to walking upright). Furthermore, at Liang Bua cave, on the Indonesian island of Flores, scientists discovered individual skeletal remains representing a diminutive human species, named *Homo floresiensis*, that lived for thousands of years in isolation from *Homo sapiens;* the age of the bones spans a period from 95,000 to 13,000 years ago. This provocative find illustrates the surprising diversity of early hominids, as well as the enormous influence that geographical isolation has on both the genetic makeup of a remote population and its probable extinction.

The Pongid-Hominid Split

The simplistic three-stage sequence of fossil apes/hominid ancestors/*Homo sapiens,* which was offered at the beginning of the 20th century, has now been necessarily expanded. Present taxonomic schemes account for the ever-growing hominoid and hominid evidence as a result of ongoing research by paleoanthropologists, particularly since the discovery of the "Zinj" skull in 1959. In fact, both the diversity of hominids and the complexity of their evolution is far greater than was imagined in the middle of the 20th century.

The Miocene hominoids represented a large, diversified group of apelike forms that survived and thrived for millions of years throughout the eastern hemisphere. Just several decades ago, fossil hominoid evidence suggested that the split between fossil apes and the earliest hominids had occurred before the end of the Miocene epoch at least 12 million years ago. However, upon careful reexamination of the fossil specimens, all these hominoids were found to be pongidlike rather than hominid-like (suggesting that the pongid-hominid split had occurred much later than was first thought to be the case). A reevaluation of the later Pliocene fossil hominoid evidence places the emergence of protohominids about 5 to 7 million years ago in Africa.

Early hominoid forms ranged from *Proconsul* of Rusinga Island, in Africa, and *Sivapithecus* of the Siwalik Hills, in India and Pakistan (both from the Miocene epoch), to the later *Oreopithecus* of Europe and the huge Pleistocene fossil ape *Gigantopithecus,* of India and China.

About 10 million years ago in central Turkey, the fruit-eating fossil ape *Ankarapithecus meteai* roamed the woodlands long before the pongid-hominid split. Although such forms were once numerous during the Miocene adaptive radiation of hominoid genera and species in Africa and Asia, these fossil apes were becoming extinct during the Plio-Pleistocene time. Insufficient evidence prevents determining which hominoid form is a definite common ancestor of the later African fossil apes and the first protohominids.

The earliest-known hominid, *Ardipithecus ramidus* of Ethiopia, lived about 4.4 million years ago. This form was followed by *Australopithecus anamensis* of Kenya, about 4.2 million years ago, which was later replaced by the emergence of *Australopithecus afarensis* of central East Africa.

The incredible similarities between the human species and the great apes, particularly both the common chimpanzee (*Pan troglodytes*) and the pygmy chimpanzee or bonobo (*Pan paniscus*), argue for a far more recent pongid-hominid split than was once maintained. With the serious consideration of comparative biochemistry and genetics, as well as molecular dating to determine the evolutionary relationships among different primate species, it became clear that protohominid evolution probably diverged from fossil apelike forms only about 5 to 7 million years ago. If this is true, then the common ancestor shared by apes and the human animal should be found somewhere in central East Africa, the fossil remains being only about 6 million years old.

The various fossil hominoid forms during the Plio-Pleistocene age reflect the diversified habitats of the central East African environment during that time. Through the mechanisms of genetic variation and natural selection (including sexual selection), hominoid populations in a variegated environment gave rise to the pongid-hominid split, which resulted in the apes remaining primarily quadrupeds, on one hand, and the emergence of quasi-bipedal protohominids, on the other; with the latter forms leaving quadrupedal locomotion behind as they ventured out of the forests and jungles for a more and more terrestrial social life in the open woodlands and on the grassy savannahs. (A recent theory maintains that bipedality emerged among the protohominids while they evolved in the forests and jungles.)

There were probably numerous attempts at bipedalism. For whatever reason or reasons, there was an adaptive, survival and, therefore, a reproductive advantage to becoming more and more bipedal as the protohominids evolved into terrestrial hominids. Although a long, branching, and complex process, the evolution of protohominids paved the way for the appearance of the earliest true hominid forms as bipeds over 4 million years ago, for example, the species *ramidus* and *anamensis.*

Even though they stood erect and walked upright with a bipedal gait, the early hominid forms of central East Africa (including *afarensis* and *habilis*) probably returned to the security of the trees during the night in order to escape ground predators.

Human Evolution

In modern physical anthropology, the *habilis-erectus-sapiens* sequence is now well documented in the fossil hominid record, although this history is far more complex than was once maintained. Furthermore, there is no common consensus concerning the taxonomy of the early hominids, and no doubt additional species will be found. Nevertheless, for over 2 million years, human evolution shows an increase in the size and complexity of the brain, a reduction in the size of the face and teeth, and an ever-increasing reliance on cultural adaptations (especially symbolic language, manufactured stone technology, and social patterns of cooperative behavior). Although speech, consciousness, and behavior are not preserved in the fossil record, they may be inferred from osteological and archaeological remains.

Like other emerging groups of animals, the early hominids underwent adaptive radiation. To date, over 500 fossil hominid specimens have been found from sites in Africa. This diversity among the early and then later australopithecines resulted in many genera and species. No doubt, many other forms of early and later australopithecines will be found as future paleoanthropologists continue searching for fossil evidence at sites ranging from 1 to 5 million years ago in Africa.

About 2.8 million years ago, a population of *Australopithecus africanus* inhabited subtropical woodlands in South Africa. These bipedal hominid individuals had a small brain, long arms, and short legs; they may have coexisted with *Australopithecus afarensis,* with the probability that both species once shared a common ancestor. This hominid evidence suggests that perhaps the transition from *africanus* to *habilis* may have taken place in South Africa (rather than in central East Africa), followed by the *habilis* species migrating northward.

Within this diversity of australopithecines, it is the bigger-brained, implement-making, and wider-ranging *Homo habilis* that was successful in terms of adapting, surviving, and reproducing over 2 million years ago. Other hominid forms became extinct (for example, *Australopithecus aethiopicus, Australopithecus africanus, Australopithecus boisei,* and *Australopithecus robustus*). Because of its superior brain and Paleolithic culture, *Homo habilis* not only survived, but, more important, it gave rise to the next stage of hominid evolution, *Homo erectus,* about 2 million years ago. This transition was not sudden, for the *habilis* and *erectus* phases overlapped in central East Africa.

The emergence of *Homo erectus* from *Homo habilis* represented a major change both in the biological and sociocultural advances in hominid evolution. Compared to *habilis, erectus* was taller and had a larger brain. It even migrated both north into Europe and east into Asia, although populations of *erectus* remained in Africa. For almost 2 million years, *erectus* survived and thrived throughout the eastern hemisphere. Its culture consisted primarily of stone Acheulean bifacial hand axes, along with cleavers and scrapers in Africa and stone chopper/chopping implements in Asia. From an evolutionary viewpoint, *Homo erectus* represented a long and successful stasis in hominid biocultural evolution. Even so, recent fossil hominid evidence suggests that the *erectus* stage of human evolution may actually represent a diversity of forms (perhaps even different species).

With the extinction of all other hominid genera, *Homo erectus* is directly ancestral to *Homo sapiens.* Before the emergence of the human species, the average hominid brain evolved slowly for about 2 million years, from about 630 cc in *habilis* to about 900 cc in *erectus.* Then, both the size and complexity of the hominid brain evolved faster, reaching an average of 1,400 cc in *sapiens* today. With the appearance of *Homo sapiens,* the human species manifested far greater self-consciousness, along with the emergence of symbolic language as articulate speech (although a crude form of symbolic speech as protolanguage may be over 1 million years old).

About 400,000 years ago, with the extinction of *Homo erectus,* the archaic *Homo sapiens* form first appeared (this stage of hominid evolution probably emerged in Africa before spreading north into Europe and east into Asia). In South Africa, about 120,000 years ago, an early member of the human species left fossil footprints at Langebaan Lagoon and cultural remains (ashes, mussel shells, and animal bones) in caves at Klasies River Mouth. This evidence suggests that South Africa may have been the birthplace of modern *Homo sapiens,* or at least a species anatomically like humans.

The later *Homo sapiens neandertalensis* populations represent a complex and elusive phase of human evolution, showing great regional variation until about 35,000 years ago. They were hunters, gatherers, and scavengers who occupied caves and used fire. More advanced both biologically and culturally, the classic Neandertal people had a modern cranial capacity and the far more sophisticated culture of the Mousterian tradition, including the deliberate burial of their dead with ritual (suggesting the emergence of

magico-religious beliefs and practices). In some areas of the eastern hemisphere, the Neandertals were contemporary with the even more advanced Cro-Magnon people, with the two forms intermittently occupying the same sites. Apparently, the two subspecies seldom, if ever, mixed their gene pools. Any *neandertalensis-sapiens* overlap was relatively brief. For whatever reason or reasons, the Neandertals would eventually disappear, thereby setting the stage for the success of the Cro-Magnon people as *Homo sapiens sapiens* (early phase).

The Cro-Magnons had even greater self-consciousness, and it was expressed in the creative explosion of tools (for example, blades and burins) and works of art (for example, stone sculptures and, in particular, the painted cave murals at Altamira in Spain and Lascaux in France). Surely, the Cro-Magnon people were far more sophisticated than the Neandertals in terms of thought and behavior. The Cro-Magnons built shelters and had articulate speech; perhaps their greater social intelligence and advanced symbolic language (rather than genetic makeup) separated them from the rapidly vanishing Neandertals. Moreover, the Cro-Magnon people are directly related to *Homo sapiens sapiens* (present phase); that is, they were the immediate ancestors to modern humans.

Following the most recent Ice Age, *Homo sapiens sapiens* has been enormously successful in adapting to different environments around the world as a result of the evolution of culture, especially accelerating advances in science and technology. Yet despite sociocultural diversity, the human species has remained a biological unit on this planet. At this present stage of hominid evolution, through genetic engineering, the human animal is becoming more and more capable of directing the further development of itself as well as the ongoing evolution of other plant and animal species. One may argue that the human species, as the bipedal ape or third chimpanzee, is becoming the cosmic primate. In fact, humankind's self-imposed destiny may require adapting to habitats on other worlds.

At present, several different interpretations of human evolution are possible. For example, conflicting phylogenetic models depicting the relationship between humankind's common hominid ancestor and later hominid forms are presented by Donald C. Johanson and Richard Leakey. One may even argue that each of the major phases of hominization first appeared in Africa. Yet the earliest making of fire and the origin of symbolic language as articulate speech may always elude the paleoanthropologists. For the rigorous evolutionist, explaining the long and complex emergence of the human species (strictly in terms of a naturalistic worldview) requires no appeal to a divine plan or predetermined direction or necessary end goal.

The human species is not nailed to this planet, but it is tied to life on earth through genetic evolution. Likewise, the human animal is always subject to the threat of extinction, which remains a possibility in light of the fact that most of the billions of species that have inhabited this planet are now extinct. Ironically, the evolutionary success of the human species in terms of sheer numbers may well be the cause of its future demise (in sharp contrast to humankind's population explosion, the small wandering bands of our earliest bipedal ancestors had been successful for millions of years). Furthermore, there is the ever-increasing possibility that the human species' modern technology (which represents extraordinary progress from the manuports and eoliths of remote hominid ancestors to the stealth jet and space shuttle of today) will in the future either destroy or supersede humankind as now known. Or, in time, the human species may give rise to a new form of life.

In short, hominid evolution has been about a 5-million-year journey from our earliest ancestral form in central East Africa to the self-reflective global species that it represents today. As a result of ongoing research in paleoanthropology, a much clearer and more complete picture of human evolution will emerge in light of the discovery and interpretation of additional fossils and artifacts. With the use of sophisticated computer simulations, future paleoanthropologists will provide science with a better understanding of and deeper appreciation for the emergence of the human species.

Hominid evolution has been a far more complex process than was thought just a few decades ago. The growing fossil evidence clearly documents the past existence of many hominid forms. Yet only one species has been successful, and this form represents the present biological unity of humankind.

About 3.6 million years separate the fossil hominid tracks at Laetoli from Neil Armstrong's footprints on the moon. Overcoming incredible odds and the threats of extinction, hominid evolution has been a remarkable success story. No doubt, in the distant future, humankind's descendants will leave both their bipedal impressions and cultural achievements on the surfaces of remote planets.

— H. James Birx

See also **Hominids; Homo Erectus; Homo Habilis; Human Paleontology; Leakey, Louis S. B.; Leakey, Mary; Leakey, Meave Epps; Leakey, Richard E. F.; Oldowan Culture**

Further Readings

Birx, H. J. (1988). *Human evolution.* Springfield, IL: Charles C Thomas.

Campbell, B. G., & Loy, J. D. (2000). *Humankind emerging* (8th ed.). Boston: Allyn & Bacon.

Darwin, C. (1998). *The descent of man* (2nd ed.). Amherst, NY: Prometheus Books. (Original work published 1871)

Johanson, D. C., Johanson, L., & Edgar, B. (1994). *Ancestors: In search of human origins.* New York: Villard Books.

Leakey, R. E. F. (1994). *The origin of humankind.* New York: BasicBooks/HarperCollins.

Tattersall, I., & Schwartz, J. H. (2000). *Extinct humans.* New York: Westview Press/Nevraumont Books.

de Waal, F. B. M. (2002). *Tree of origin: What primate behavior can tell us about human social evolution.* Cambridge, MA: Harvard University Press.

Walker, A., & Shipman, P. (1996). *The wisdom of the bones: In search of human origins.* New York: Vintage Books/Random House.

Whitehead, P. F., Sacco, W. K., & Hochgraf, S. B. (2005). *A photographic atlas for physical anthropology.* Englewood, CO: Morton.

Wolpoff, M. H. (1999). *Paleoanthropology* (2nd ed.). New York: McGraw-Hill.

EVOLUTION EDUCATION CONTROVERSY

Eighty years after the famous Scopes "Monkey Trial" in 1925, in 2005, American education received a surprise as the controversy over evolution in textbooks was revived. This time it was not in the "Bible Belt" state of Tennessee, but in progressive Pennsylvania. Among religious conservatives, the "theory of intelligent design" has grown up, asserting that the universe was simply too complex to emerge from a single, atypical cosmic big bang. (In fact, intelligent design is itself only a modern fugue on the far older theory of a first cause for the universe, as taught by generations of priests of the Roman Catholic Jesuits, or Society of Jesus.) Intelligent design, while gaining many adherents, has never actually been considered as part of any school biology curriculum.

However, things changed dramatically in November 2004. In that month, the school board in rural Dover, Pennsylvania, voted that biology teachers had to inform their classes that "evolution may not, after all, explain how we all got here," explained ABC News. The decision of the school board made national news, rapidly thrusting the controversy over evolution versus intelligent design into the headlines as it has not been since John Thomas Scopes was brought to trial in Tennessee for teaching evolution.

Immediately, the issue became a cause with both the religious right, whose contribution was important to President George W. Bush's 2004 presidential campaign, and liberal activist groups like the American Civil Liberties Union (ACLU). The ACLU paid prime attention to the developing case in Dover, providing massive legal support to fight the school board's decision. Indeed, into early 2005, the controversy was unresolved; similar scenarios were also being played out in the states of Georgia and Ohio.

— John F. Murphy Jr.

FUTUROLOGY

There have been few "students" of the future with the impact of Alvin and Heidi Toffler, whose previous works *Future Shock, The Third Wave,* and *Powershift* focused the attention of Americans on serious consideration of the future. Their most recent book, *War and Anti-War,* brought attention to a new aspect of the future: the shape and conduct of warfare. In their book, published in 1993, they foresaw the development of electronic warfare, as we see today in the use of Predator drone aircraft.

The Tofflers also wrote of the rise of religious extremism, which in February 1993 saw the first terrorist bombing of New York's World Trade Center. "A minority of Islamic extremists," they warned, "conjure up fantasies of a New Crusade, with the entire Muslim world united in a jihad, or Holy War, against Judeo-Christianity." Even more, they foresaw the dangers of nuclear proliferation. They wrote, "prior to the Gulf War [of 1991], the IAEA (International Atomic Energy Agency) used the equivalent of only 42 full-time inspectors to check on 1,000 declared nuclear energy plants around the world." That figure did not take into account clandestine, or hidden, ones.

Even more, *War and Anti-War* focused on what is known today as electronic warfare or information warfare. Information warfare involves the use of computers to not only plan a country's military campaigns—but also to frustrate an enemy's "cyber-warriors," with such things as "Trojan Horses" and other computer weapons. Indeed, both the United States and the People's Republic of China today emphasize information warfare as a weapon that may indeed one day decide the outcome of a battle. In 1993, the Tofflers wrote how "with only a limited grasp of its implications, nations everywhere are preparing, as best they can, to exploit knowledge-intensivity."

Yet with some of the new technologies have come new risks. The Tofflers wrote of lasers being used to guide bombs and missiles, a significant part of the deadly accuracy of the bombardments that preceded the invasions of Afghanistan in 2001 and Iraq in 2003. However, in the new field of nonlethal weaponry that has developed since the Tofflers' book, lasers are now seen as battlefield weapons that can be used against enemy troops to not only disorient them but blind them as well. As with all else in modern weaponry, including biological weapons, there is a fear that such weapons may reach the hands of terrorists. In the waning months of 2004, there were several reported incidents of laser beams being directed into the eyes of civilian airline pilots. There is evidence that terrorists have explored using lasers as weapons, though there is no specific intelligence indicating al Qaeda or other groups might use lasers in the United States.

— John F. Murphy Jr.

MONOGENESIS VERSUS POLYGENESIS

The theories of monogenesis and polygenesis set forth opposite theories of how the human race evolved. Those who believe in monogenesis say that all humans share the same origin. Polygenesis asserts that at least some of the races had a separate origin. It maintains that different races have different origins, different characteristics, and different histories.

Monogenesis was widely adhered to in Christian Europe through most of its history. This was mainly because the Bible was believed to say that all humans descended from Adam and Eve, giving them all a common origin. Belief in polygenesis became widespread in the United States during the middle of the 19th century. This was in part because it was becoming difficult to reconcile the biblical account with new scientific evidence.

The early polygenists relied mainly on scientific evidence and ignored biblical arguments that the monogenists used. For a while, the pendulum swung toward belief in polygenesis. Some believe that polygenesis was used to further racism in the United States. Charles Darwin was a believer in monogenesis and believed that polygenesis was just an excuse for racism. When interest in polygenesis was at its height in the United States, some of the leading American polygenists shifted the focus of their beliefs. Rather than concentrating on proving that different races had different origins, they began to focus their efforts on proving that the then current differences in the races would continue unchanged.

The theories of monogenesis and polygenesis are also debated by linguists trying to determine the origin of languages. Approximately 5,000 languages are spoken in the world today. Did all of those languages spring from one original language? Or did many languages develop in many different locations? Linguists analyze languages to find systematic differences and similarities. They believe that those with similar structures may have evolved from a common ancestor. There is even debate among linguists about whether or not certain languages should be grouped together in families. Linguists divide into the lumpers and the splitters. Lumpers believe that there are only approximately two dozen languages. Splitters believe that there are many times that number of basic groupings.

Joseph Greenberg of Stanford University is convinced that the original language developed in Africa among early *Homo sapiens.* He believes that the original language, which he calls the Mother Tongue, diverged eventually over time into the several thousand languages spoken today.

So the debate goes on. No one has proven conclusively that either monogenesis or polygenesis is correct.

— Pat McCarthy

IAN TATTERSALL

Paleontologist, evolutionary biologist, and primate behaviorist Ian Tattersall is curator of anthropology at the American Museum of Natural History in New York and adjunct professor of anthropology at the City University of New York. Tattersall's biography is as diverse and varied as his academic interests. He was born in England but grew up in East Africa and received his professional training at Cambridge (archaeology and anthropology) and at Yale (geology and vertebrate paleontology). His fieldwork has taken him to countries such as Madagascar, Vietnam, Surinam, Yemen, and Mauritius.

Tattersall has focused on two main areas of research, in which he has achieved international fame: the analysis of the human fossil record, and the study of the ecology and systematics of the lemurs of Madagascar. His many books, including *Becoming Human: Evolution and Human Uniqueness* (1999) and *Extinct Humans* (2001), have popularized scientific findings on evolution and primates for a general readership. His studies have proved extremely readable, yet other scholars in the field have criticized them for their lack of academic references and sustained evidence.

Source: Denis Finnin/AMNH.

Tattersall argues that in the evolutionary process, there is "continual evolutionary experimentation, with constant origins of new species, triage among those species by competition, and the extinction of the unfortunate." He also asserts that humans owe much to chance and opposes the theory of modern evolutionary synthesis, which brings together Darwinian evolution and the laws of Gregor Mendel. Tattersall has revised the straight-line progression of the human "family tree," which would take the human race from the apelike *australopithecines* to the mysterious *Homo habilis* to the legendary Neandertals and culminate in the superior *Homo sapiens.* According to his theory, many different types of extinct species have coexisted during the evolutionary process.

Tattersall has identified the Cro-Magnons as the ancestors of humans, claiming that the Neandertals were replaced by them. The defining feature, which differentiates the two hominids and which makes humans unique, was the development of symbolic thought that is clearly shown in the elegant artworks found in the Cro-Magnon caves. "Art, symbols, music, notation, language, feelings of mystery, mastery of diverse materials and sheer

cleverness: all these attributes, and more, were foreign to the Neandertals and are native to us," Tattersall concluded in *Becoming Human.* Yet, in spite of his celebration of human abilities, Tattersall seems to have doubts about the potential of contemporary humankind for further evolution: "Everything we know about evolution suggests that to get true innovation, you need small, isolated populations, which is now unthinkable."

— Luca Prono

 ## EVOLUTION, MODELS OF

Several major models have been used to represent organic evolution on earth. These models include the arc, line, spiral, circle, pyramid, and tree or bush or coral of life forms throughout biological history.

Aristotle (384–322 BCE), the father of biology, including morphology and taxonomy, taught that plants and animals represent a hierarchical line of eternally fixed forms. These kinds of life range from the simplest plant to the most complex animal, with our own species, as the only rational being, at the apex of this planetary ladder of the living world. Aristotle's great chain of being, from global minerals to celestial stars, was not an evolutionary interpretation of this universe.

Aristotle's worldview is grounded in the assumption that each type of life has a fixed essence. Consequently, this natural philosophy contributed to an antievolutionary view of organic history for nearly 2,000 years.

Carolus Linnaeus (1707–1778), the father of modern taxonomy, classified the living world into groups of similar life forms (for example, the primate order includes our species, apes, monkeys, and prosimians). Linnaeus was not an evolutionist, although he did admit that a species may produce varieties of itself.

As the first serious evolutionist, Lamarck (1744–1829) interpreted organic history as an escalator of evolving species. He wrote that the human being has evolved from the chimpanzee in Africa and the orangutan in Asia. With little empirical evidence and no explanatory mechanism that could be tested, Lamarck was unable to convince other naturalists that species are mutable and evolve throughout vast periods of time.

Charles Darwin (1809–1882) wrote about the evolving tree of life in order to represent the branching out of successive species over eons of organic time. To also include the fact that plant and animal forms have become extinct throughout biological history, he preferred to interpret organic evolution as the coral of life. Darwin's empirical evidence, from paleontology to morphology, and explanatory mechanism of natural selection convinced several important naturalists that species either evolve or become extinct over time. His own sketch of evolving species illustrates the principle of divergence, thereby challenging all straight-line interpretations of organic history.

Ernst Haeckel (1834–1919) was the first evolutionist to draw a detailed picture of the tree of life. In fact, he drew several illustrations to demonstrate the historical relationships among groups of species as a branching tree of organic evolution. These illustrations may be seen in his home Villa Medusa, now a museum in Jena, Germany.

Several thinkers have interpreted evolving nature as a circle. Herbert Spencer (1820–1903) saw the universe in general and earth history in particular as a returning circle, each cycle representing the three basic stages of evolution, equilibrium, and devolution; yet each cycle would be different in its content.

However, Friedrich Nietzsche (1844–1900) held that given enough time, the identical cosmic cycle would return. In fact, for him, this same cycle would repeat itself forever. Nietzsche's awesome idea of the eternal recurrence of this same universe is the quintessential assumption of his metaphysical position.

Critical of Darwinian mechanistic materialism, Henri Bergson (1859–1941) argued that a vital force is necessary to account for the pervasive creativity throughout organic evolution. For him, this vital force has caused the creative divergence of plants, insects, and animals within biological history. In his interpretation of reality, our species now represents the apex of organic evolution in terms of consciousness. Yet, in the final analysis, Bergsonian philosophy gives preference to metaphysics and intuition rather than science and reason.

Although influenced by Henri Bergson, the geopaleontologist and Jesuit priest Pierre Teilhard de Chardin (1881–1955) emphasized global convergence rather than planetary divergence. Teilhard saw earth history in terms of three successive circles: the inorganic geosphere, the organic biosphere, and the human noosphere. Seeing things within the framework of a spiraling and involuting pyramid, he believed that the further evolution of our species on planet earth will result in a mystical unity of humankind with God. Teilhard referred to this final end goal for our species as the "omega point."

Today, most neo-Darwinians reject both teleology and essentialism. They interpret organic evolution and our species within a strictly naturalistic framework. Earlier models of evolution have been modified in light of the growing fossil and genetic evidence, as well as the use of computers to understand and appreciate the patterns in biological history. Ongoing inquiry will generate new models of organic evolution.

One may speak of emerging teleology as scientists genetically engineer new life forms and, through human intervention, more and more direct the continuous evolution of our own species and others. Furthermore, empirical evidence documenting exobiology and exoevolution would result in a conceptual revolution concerning interpreting the place of life and humankind within this dynamic universe.

— *H. James Birx*

See also **Evolution, Human; Evolution, Organic; Evolutionary Epistemology**

Further Readings

Bergson, H. (1998). *Creative evolution.* Mineola, NY: Dover. (Original work published 1907)

Birx, H. J. (1991). *Interpreting evolution: Darwin & Teilhard de Chardin.* Amherst, NY: Prometheus Books.

Darwin, C. (2000). *The autobiography* (F. Darwin, Ed.). Amherst, NY: Prometheus Books. (Written in 1876, first published in 1887)

Teilhard de Chardin, P. (1975). *The phenomenon of man* (2nd ed.). New York: Harper & Row/Harper Colophon/Perennial Library.

EVOLUTION, MOLECULAR

Theories of molecular evolution try to explain the natural history of deoxyribonucleic acid (DNA), which is the material carrier of genetic information.

Evolutionarily relevant variations between organisms must be implemented in the biochemical structure of DNA sequences. Otherwise, those variations

Source: © iStockphoto/Andrei Tchernov.

would not be genetically transmitted from an organism to its offspring, so they would disappear from nature after one generation. Molecular evolution is thus the foundation of evolution on all higher levels of biological organization, like the organism, the population, or the species.

After the famous discovery of the double-helical structure of DNA by James D. Watson and Francis H. Crick in 1953, it was known that genetic information is stored in sequences of four DNA building blocks, the nucleotides. That parts of the linear structure of DNA store genetic information means that those parts can instruct the biosynthesis of proteins, which are the most important macromolecules for cellular metabolism. More concretely, the specific succession of nucleotides can encode the primary structure of a protein, that is, the linear sequence of amino acids linked by peptide bonds. In the information bearing parts of DNA, three nucleotides (a codon) encode one amino acid. A gene is the informational unity the function of which is to encode the complete primary structure of a protein. The set of rules that relate each of the 64 possible codons (one has to take the number of nucleotides, which is four, to the power of the number of nucleotides in a codon, which is three) to an amino acid residue constitutes the genetic code. Those rules cannot be deduced from the laws of biochemistry alone. The molecular evolutionist must also reconstruct the historical and contingent physico-chemical context in which the genetic code originated.

The biological disciplines that are involved in discovering the laws of molecular evolution and in reconstructing its course are, above all, biochemistry, molecular and population genetics, systematics, and general evolutionary theory.

Biochemistry and molecular genetics analyze the material structures and the physico-chemical mechanisms that realize the storage, replication, variation, transmission, and reading of genetic information. The success of this project is evident from the enormous technical progress that was made during the last 30 years in the development of genetic engineering.

Population genetics studies the evolutionary dynamics by which the relative frequency of genes changes with time in populations of organisms. Mathematical models were developed that describe different types of evolutionary dynamics in a more and more realistic way. These models can be tested against empirical data gathered by systematic analyses of wild-living populations.

Systematics classifies the rich variety of species, which lived and live on Earth, in order to reconstruct their evolutionary relationships in so-called "phylogenetic trees." Such a tree shows graphically how some species, with which we are concerned, are related to each other by placing their common ancestor at its root and by illustrating the separation of a new species with a branching point. Finally, the species in question are to be found at the top of the resulting branches. Before the advent of automated DNA-sequencing techniques, morphological descriptions were the most important data on which phylogenetic trees were based. Nowadays, molecular data of DNA sequences are of equal importance for the reconstruction of natural history.

General evolutionary theory tries to synthesize the insights of the before-mentioned biological disciplines in an all-embracing picture of molecular evolution. This integration is to be accomplished by discovering the causal mechanisms that can explain the facts of natural history.

What mechanisms are responsible for molecular evolution? Of course, the answer that first comes to mind is natural selection, the evolutionary mechanism that stands in the center of Charles Darwin's research on the origin of species. His theory can be applied to the molecular level, if we remember that the differences between individual organisms and therefore also between species are caused by differences in their genetic material, which are, in turn, caused by mutations in the nucleotide sequences of their DNA.

Since those mutations are inherited by offspring, fitness as the measure for the evolutionary success of an organism can be redefined on the molecular level as the replication rate of its genes in the gene pool of its population. The struggle for life described by Darwin is thus the struggle of genes to raise the number of their copies in the next generation. The more copies of a DNA sequence that are successfully transmitted to offspring, the fitter it is.

But there is another theory that claims also to contribute important insights to the explanation of the course of molecular evolution. This claim is laid by the neutral theory of molecular evolution, which the Japanese population geneticist Motoo Kimura has developed since the 1960s. He postulates that most genetically transmitted mutations are selectively neutral; they do not have any positive or negative consequence on the fitness of the organism in which they occur. The spread of neutral mutations in the gene pool of a population, called "genetic drift," has then nothing to do with natural selection. It is a process that follows, from the perspective of natural selection, a completely random course.

Today, even staunch Darwinians accept that genetic drift constitutes an important mechanism that is effective in natural history. On the other hand, it seems to be also clear that randomness cannot explain everything in evolution. Kimura's neutral theory does not completely replace Darwin's selection theory, but it describes an explanatory scheme that supplements traditional Darwinian reasoning. In concrete cases of explaining a molecular evolutionary process that happened between kindred species, it is often very difficult—and perhaps impossible—to decide which of the two theories proves to be right.

How difficult it is to develop a general evolutionary theory on the molecular level will be clear after one has realized that it has to address not only the evolution of DNA. Molecular evolution also encompasses the evolution of precursors of DNA and, last but not least, the origin of the first material carrier of genetic information. Since the existence of genetic information presupposes the existence of a genetic code, the origin of the latter belongs to the main problems of research into molecular evolution, too.

— *Stefan Artmann*

See also **DNA Testing; Gene Flow; Genetic Drift; Genetic Engineering**

Further Readings

Graur, D., & Wen-hsiung, L. (2000). *Fundamentals of molecular evolution* (2nd ed.). Sunderland, MA: Sinauer.

Kimura, M. (1983). *The neutral theory of molecular evolution.* Cambridge: Cambridge University Press.

Küppers, B.-O. (1985). *Molecular theory of evolution: Outline of a physico-chemical theory of the origin of life* (2nd ed.). Berlin: Springer.

EVOLUTION, ORGANIC

Evolution, in the modern sense, refers to changes in the genetic composition of populations over time and is the result of natural selection and/or genetic drift acting on population variation. In this Darwinian paradigm, species may change or split into more than one species (speciation). All extant species are descendants of a common ancestor (descent with modification). Definition of the term in this framework encompasses the gene-frequency changes of population microevolution, anagenetic changes within a lineage, cladogenesis, and the appearance of evolutionary novelties. The present diversity of organisms was produced by change within species (anagenesis) and splitting of species (cladogenesis) through geological time, in contrast to the explanations offered by separate creation and Lamarckian transformism. The former denies both the mutability and common ancestry of species, and the latter invokes change within species but denies the splitting and common ancestry of species. Historically, the term *evolution* was also used to describe development of the embryo and in the theory of embryonic recapitulation.

Evolution is a process that occurs in populations rather than in individuals: The genetic composition of a population changes, but that of the individual does not. Evolution occurs in populations by changes in the frequencies of alleles and genotypes. The changes at the genetic level are observed in the phenotypes of individuals (e.g., protein structure, individual morphology, behavior).

Ernst Mayr identifies five major postulates that form the foundation of the Darwinian paradigm: (1) organisms change through time, (2) all organisms have a common ancestor, (3) species multiply by

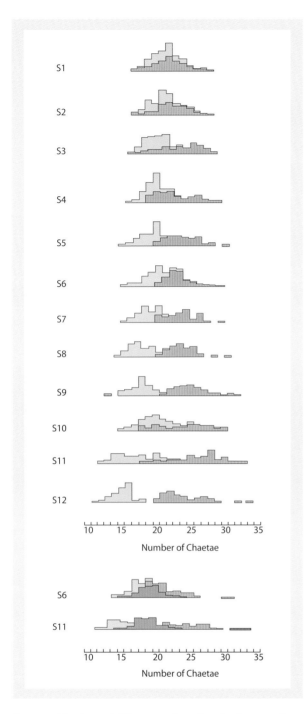

Figure 1 Thoday and Gibson conducted a selection experiment on a number of sternopleural chaetae (stout hairs, bristles) in *D. melanogaster*. The histograms depict distribution curves for each generation S1-S12. Green is progeny of low number females and orange is progeny of high number females. Disruptive selection caused the high chaetae group to diverge from the low chaetae group.

Source: From *Nature, 193*, pp. 1164–1166, "Isolation by Disruptive Selection" by Thoday, J. M., & Gibson, J. B., et al. Copyright © 1962, reprinted by permission of *Nature*.

splitting or budding, (4) gradualism, and (5) natural selection. It should be pointed out that the Darwinian concept of gradualism is not that evolutionary change is necessarily slow and steady. Rather, it is that evolution does not occur by saltations, the results of macromutations that render offspring reproductively isolated from the parental generation, *sensu* the writings of Richard Goldschmidt.

Evidence for Evolution

Matt Ridley points out that two fundamental questions need to be answered to demonstrate evolution. Do populations and species change through time? And do living organisms share a common ancestor? The evidence used to answer these questions in the affirmative comes from a number of sources, including observation of evolution on a small scale, the presence of extensive variation among populations and subspecies, homology, adaptive radiation, and the fossil record.

Evolution "on a small scale," over a number of generations rather than over millions of years, has been achieved under domestic and experimental conditions and observed in the wild. The origin and development of domestic breeds of animals and plants has been a topic of interest to anthropologists and clearly demonstrates that species change. In *On the Origin of Species* (1859), Charles Darwin discusses the production of domestic breeds as the result of "accumulative selection" by humans and points out that breeders and horticulturalists intentionally modify breeds within a human lifetime. He particularly concentrates on the origin of pigeon breeds. Darwin also addresses "unconscious selection," in which a breed is altered simply by breeding the "best" individuals (for example, the English pointer dog). In both techniques, the breeder is allowing only those individuals with extreme values of a particular character to produce offspring during each consecutive generation (the "traditional breeder's approach"). This shifts the mean value for the selected characteristic during successive generations in the descendants: The breeder is applying directional selection to the particular trait of interest (the somewhat unfortunate term "artificial selection" is often applied to this methodology, which could be misconstrued). Darwin expands upon this discussion in *The Variation of Animals and Plants Under Domestication* (1883) and states that domestication is a gigantic experiment in selection. Modern discussions of the principles and results of plant and animal breeding are couched in terms of genetics.

In an experimental context, both the traditional breeders' approach and natural selection in a controlled environment have been employed to demonstrate change in populations. Well-known examples of the former have focused on disruptive selection on the number of sternopleural chaetae (stout hairs) in the fly, *Drosophila melanogaster.* These experiments not only sought to demonstrate that change in mean population chaetal number would result from differential reproduction but also tested whether disruptive selection could overwhelm the results of gene flow—a central issue in sympatric and parapatric speciation models. The general approach was to allow flies with low chaetal number and flies with high chaetal number to breed, but not allow breeding by those with intermediate numbers. The results consistently showed shifts in mean population numbers over time. The same approach was employed in a behavioral context by J. C. Tryon, a pioneer of behavioral genetics, in his famous experiment on maze-running ability in rats. Later applications include the work of Rodriquez-Ramilo and associates on the effects of inbreeding and selection on *D. melanogaster.*

In experiments that employ natural selection in a controlled environment, subjects are exposed to a predetermined environmental regimen for one or more generations, but the experimenter does not directly determine which individuals breed. D. N. Reznick and associates used this approach in field experiments in which guppies were moved from areas where they were subject to predation by cichlid fishes to sites where they were not; the descendants of guppies from sites with less predation matured later and at a larger size than descendants of those from high predation sites. The approach is particularly valuable for the study of niche dimensions, range limits, and character displacement.

Demonstration of the occurrence of evolution in the wild often falls within the discipline termed *ecological genetics,* a combination of naturalistic observation, experimentation in the field, and the use of laboratory genetics. Ecological genetics seeks to establish that change occurs within populations and species, to demonstrate that there is a hereditary basis to phenotypic variation, and to identify the agent of change. The work of J. H. Gerould on color polymorphism in caterpillars is cited as an early example.

Figure 2 Industrial melanics from a variety of moth genera. The *typica* variety of the peppered moth is in the upper left (1) and the *carbonaria* form (2) is below it.

Source: Plate 5.6 (p. 62) from *The Evolution of Melanism* by Kettlewell, B. (1973). By permission of Oxford University Press.

A common methodology employs the following components: (1) observations and collections made to establish that distinct phenotypes (generally of a trait that manifests clear polymorphism) are found in the wild, (2) establishing that there is a change in the proportions of the phenotypes over time or geographic distance, (3) determination that there is a genetic basis to the various phenotypes, and (4) identification of the agent that is responsible for altering the frequencies of phenotypes and genotypes. The latter step is often the most difficult, because the occurrence of a feature may be influenced by more than one process. In *Ecological Genetics,* Edmund B.

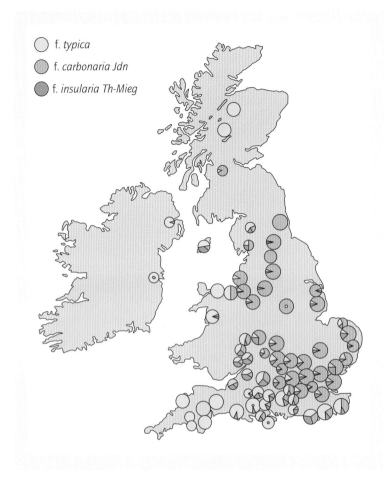

f. *typica*

f. *carbonaria* Jdn

f. *insularia* Th-Mieg

Figure 3 The frequencies of *carbonaria* (blue areas) and *typica* (green areas) in Britain. Shaded segments represent the *insularia* variety, which is not discussed in this entry. There is a strong correlation between pollution levels and frequency of *carbonaria*: High frequencies were close to, or east of, polluted industrial districts; in contrast, Scotland and southwest England show virtually no *carbonaria*.

Source: Plate 5.4 (p. 113) from *Melanism: Evolution in Action* by Majerus, M. E. N. (1998). By permission of Oxford University Press.

Ford synthesizes the extensive literature on shell polymorphism in *Cepaea nemoralis*, chromosome polymorphisms in *Drosophila*, mimetic polymorphism in butterflies such as *Papilio dardanus*, and industrial melanism.

Industrial melanism is generally cited in discussions of evolution demonstrated on a small scale. A classic example has been that of wing and body color polymorphism in the English peppered moth, *Biston betularia*. Michael Majerus states that melanism occurs whenever there is a pervasive darkening of the ground color or patterning of an organism. The term *industrial melanism* applies to darkening as a result of industrial pollution of the environment. The

first-known melanic specimen of the peppered moth was captured in 1848, in Manchester, and melanics rapidly increased to 98% to 99% of the population by 1895 to 1898. The books of Ford, Bernard Kettlewell, and Majerus summarize literature on the phenomenon dating back to 1864. It is often held that the origin of the melanic *carbonaria* was a single point mutation in the region around Manchester, with subsequent migration to other areas, but Majerus indicates that there may have been more than one mutational event. Early explanation of the occurrence of melanism invoked Lamarckian transformism. A mutation pressure explanation was advanced by J. W. H. Harrison in 1928. He argued that melanism was induced in adults as a consequence of larvae feeding on leaves contaminated with mutagens that increased the mutation rate of genes associated with melanin production. However, it has never been confirmed that the influence of environmental stimuli during development can induce melanism in adult Lepidoptera.

The Darwinian natural selection explanation replaced those of the inheritance of acquired characteristics and mutation pressure. The primary explanation of the geographic spread, and numerical increase of *carbonaria* became that of selective advantage of the melanic form over that of the lighter *typica* in areas of industrial air pollution, because of camouflage from insectivorous birds. The occurrence of industrial melanism in Lepidoptera gave rise to a series of elegant studies of *Biston betularia*, summarized by Ford, Kettlewell, and Majerus, and Kettlewell's work had a significant impact on the acceptance of natural selection as an agent responsible for evolution. His investigations included a controlled experiment on bird predation on moths in an aviary to construct quantitative degrees of camouflage effectiveness, field experiments in polluted (Christopher Cadbury Bird Reserve, Birmingham) and unpolluted (Deanend Wood, Dorset) localities, and surveys of peppered-moth frequencies throughout Britain. The fieldwork included mark-recapture, studies to determine whether moths released in early morning were still at the release point later in the day, and (with Niko Tinbergen) filming of actual bird predation on moths. Kettlewell concluded that differential selective predation by birds was responsible for differences in the relative frequencies of *typica* and *carbonaria* in areas that had become polluted.

It has been realized that the classic exposition of natural selection on *Biston betularia* is too simple, in part because camouflage and predation do not seem to be important in maintaining melanism in some other taxa. A variety of workers have studied industrial melanism in the ensuing decades since Kettlewell's landmark work. The term industrial melanism is now applied to taxa such as the two-spot ladybird and the pale brindled beauty moth, without the implication that predation is responsible for maintaining the polymorphism. Kettlewell himself pointed out that melanism affects many aspects of an organism's life, including behavior, sexual selection, temperature tolerance, and physiology of pigment production; natural selection could potentially affect the moth population through any of these features, among others. Publications by Bruce R. Grant and Majerus review many of the major criticisms, including that large numbers of released moths produced artificially high prey densities and may have attracted birds; moths settled on tree trunks, but it is unclear whether this is a natural hiding place for *B. betularia;* moths released during daylight hours do not behave normally; a combination of lab-raised and wild-caught moths were used; there are differences between human and bird vision; and there was no evidence that typicals and melanics prefer to rest on different backgrounds—contra Kettlewell's barrel experiments. However, these authors conclude that such shortcomings do not jeopardize the principal conclusions that the intensity of bird predation varies according to habitat and that industrial melanism in the peppered moth is a valid example of natural selection and evolution in the wild. There was a solid correlation between pollution levels and the frequency of the melanic form. Kettlewell compared the relative success of the morphs on the same parts of trees in different areas (not different parts of trees in the same area), and he showed that moths that were most conspicuous to humans were also eaten first by birds. Kettlewell's conclusions are bolstered by recent studies of predation on male mosquitofish by Lisa Horth.

Geographic variation in intraspecific phenotypes and proportions of genotypes provides evidence for evolution. If a species is studied in the wild, it will generally be found that there are phenotypic variants in different geographic areas. Often, these variants are designated as subspecies of the species; variation is often so extensive that small differences in samples of populations have been used to assign subspecific rank, and some have argued that the subspecies category has been overutilized. Examples of variation within the primates include the geographic variants found within sub-Saharan vervet monkeys (*Cercopithecus aethiops*), South American white-fronted capuchins (*Cebus albifrons*), tufted capuchins (*Cebus apella*) and common squirrel monkeys (*Saimiri sciureus*), and the northern greater galago (*Otolemur garnetti*). Interpopulation variability is often readily interpreted in terms of environmental factors to which each population has adapted, as in the cases of *Peromyscus* mouse populations to substrate color and cyanogenic clover (*Trifolium repens*) to probability of frost. The latter also illustrates that interpopulation variation can be distributed in the form of a cline, a gradual change in a phenotypic character or genotypic along a geographic transect. In humans, there is a cline in the frequency of B type blood across Eurasia. A cline may be formed by interbreeding between formerly isolated populations or by geographic variation in selection pressures on a character. Descent from a common ancestor and subsequent local evolution are the most logical and parsimonious explanations for geographical variants. Special creation and transformism would have to explain each local variant as having a separate origin. Explanation by Lamarckian transformism would be particularly hard to envision, as it would necessitate separate origin by spontaneous generation for each population, followed by the inheritance of acquired characteristics that would make populations separated by hundreds of miles sufficiently different to be distinguished only at the subspecies level.

Powerful evidence from geographic variation comes from ring species, in which there is an almost continuous set of intermediates (cline) between two sympatric species, and the intermediates are arranged in a ring. The set of intermediates between the lesser black-backed gull (*Larus fuscus*) and herring gull (*L. argentatus*) is distributed around the North Pole. As one moves along the ring, there is only one species present in any local area. However, there are

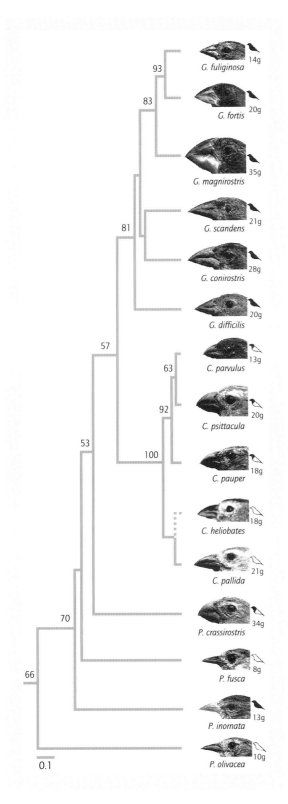

Figure 4a Phylogeny of Darwin's finches based on microsatellite length variation

Source: Adapted from Grant, Peter R., *Ecology and Evolution of Darwin's Finches.* © 1986 Princeton University Press. Reprinted by permission of Princeton University Press.

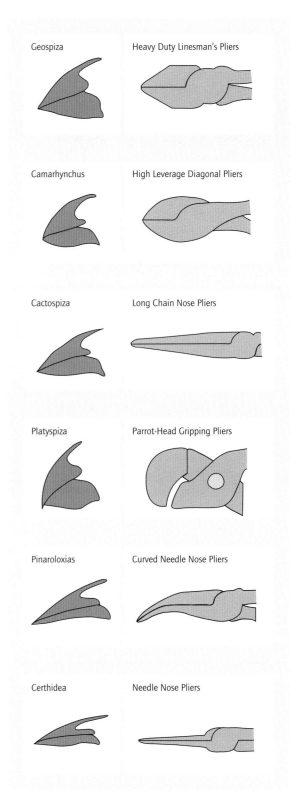

Figure 4b Analogy between beak shapes and pliers

Source: Adapted from Grant, Peter R., *Ecology and Evolution of Darwin's Finches.* © 1986 Princeton University Press. Reprinted by permission of Princeton University Press.

reproductively and ecologically separate species where the two end points of the ring meet in Europe. Mayr terms this "speciation by distance." Ring species demonstrate that intraspecific variation can be great enough to make two species and that there is a continuum from interindividual to interspecific variation. Recent research on greenish warblers (*Phylloscopus trochiloides*) by Darren E. Irwin and colleagues, using amplified fragment length polymorphism markers, provides evidence that speciation by distance can produce distinct species despite gene flow along the ring.

Homology is the possession by two or more species of a trait derived, with or without modification, from a common ancestor. Gunter P. Wagner terms it the central concept of comparative morphology. It is also robust evidence for evolution, for structures are homologous because of common descent, not because of close similarity in function. Wagner explains that homologous structures (homologs) are those that have been acquired only once in the history of a group of organisms possessing the character; those features of a development system that cause restriction in phenotypic consequences of genetic variation are important in determining that features are homologs. Well-known examples are the pentadactyl hand of a primate and the pentadactyl wing of a bat: They both possess five digits because of descent from a common ancestor, not because of close similarity in function.

Wagner also points out that the study of homologs is the basis for the reconstruction of phylogenetic history by morphological methods. This has historically been true in the study of adaptive radiations before the advent of molecular phylogenetic approaches. An adaptive radiation occurs when a single ancestral species diversifies into a large number of descendant species that occupy a variety of ecological niches and differ in traits used to exploit those differing niches. Articles in *Molecular Evolution and Adaptive Radiation* (1997), edited by Thomas J. Givinish and Kenneth J. Sytsma, give alternate definitions. Well-known examples include the radiations of placental and marsupial mammals, Hawaiian silversword plants, African cichlid fishes, and Caribbean *Anolis* lizards. All 14 species of Galapagos finches share finch homologies and are members of the single subfamily Emberizinae of the finch family Fringillidae. In the even more diverse radiation of Hawaiian honeycreepers, all species share finch homologies. Although beak size is a continuously varying character governed by both genetic and environmental factors, Galapagos finch and Hawaiian honeycreeper species manifest beaks adapted to particular foraging strategies and diverse niches.

The evidence for evolution that is most often cited is from the fossil record. Four aspects of the fossil record are particularly important: Many species are extinct; fossil and extant forms in the same geographic region are related to each other (law of succession); the history of the Earth has been one of environmental change; and species have changed through time and there are transitional forms in the fossil record. The latter aspect of the fossil record is one that receives particular attention, in terms of both describing forms that are transitional between major taxa and in documenting evolution within lineages and clades.

One of the presumed problems with using the fossil record as evidence for evolution is that there are gaps between fossil forms and a smooth transition is not always documented. Darwin listed this as the first difficulty of the theory of descent with modification in *On the Origin of Species* (1859) and sought to answer the objection by pointing out the imperfect and intermittent nature of preservation of "parent-forms" and intermediate links. This explanation has been used subsequently on many occasions, and workers have sought to chronicle the resolution of the fossil and archeological records.

A particularly well-known fossil history is that of horses. Since the early work of Kovalevsky, many eminent paleontologists (including the rivals O. C. Marsh and Edward Drinker Cope) have studied horse evolution. The writings of George Gaylord Simpson have made the evolution of the horses one of the best-known, and debated, examples of long-term evolution. Simpson's work has sometimes been characterized as advocating that the morphological trends in dental morphology, crown size, body size, skull size, preoptic dominance, brain size, and limb ratios were the result of phyletic evolution within a direct phylogenetic lineage, that is, a single line of gradual transformation from Eocene *Hyracotherium* to modern *Equus*. However, in *The Major Features of Evolution* (1953), Simpson points out that horse evolution is characterized by repeated and complex splitting (he specifically states that it is "bush-like"). He notes that there were no trends that continued throughout the history of the family in any line.

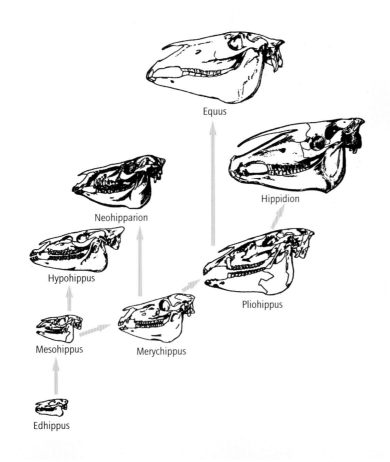

Figure 5a   Trends in the evolution of horses. Simpson termed the early Miocene "the great transformation" of horse anatomy correlated with the spread of grassland. 5A presents the evolution of the skull, showing the increase in size and changes in cranial proportions including lengthening of the preorbital region; 5B depicts the trend toward increased brain size and complexity; 5C shows the trend toward increased crown height in upper molar teeth; 5D illustrates the molarization of premolars in the Eocene; 5E further depicts evolution of horse cheekteeth from brachydont, browsing teeth to hypsodont, grazing teeth for transverse shearing of abrasive grasses; 5F provides selected stages in the evolution of the forefoot, with a reduction of metapodials from 4 in *Hyracotherium* (eohippus) to 3 in *Mesohippus* and eventually to 1 in "Pliohippus" and *Equus*. Simpson viewed each column as a distinct mechanical type.

Contrary to creationist views, horse fossils chronicle large-scale evolutionary change even if the various genera were separated from one another by tens of millions of years. This is true regardless of whether horse evolution is interpreted in the context of anagenesis or as an example of "bushy," cladogenetic evolution. Controversies regarding whether evolution has occurred within a lineage or clade by phyletic evolution or punctuated equilibrium are debates regarding the tempo and pattern of morphological change, not whether change has occurred—both patterns document evolution. The same is true of contrasting interpretations of hominin evolution. However, creationist tracts sometimes cite sources emphasizing rectangular patterns of evolution to argue that evolution does not occur because of a purported lack of transitional forms; they demand evidence of phyletic evolution to support evolution as a fact.

Robert L. Carroll summarizes several well-documented cases of phyletic, directional evolution in late Cenozoic mammals in *Patterns and Processes of Vertebrate Evolution* (1997), including increase in length of limb bones and in the number of osteoderms in the giant armadillo (*Homesina*) lineage from Florida, morphology of the upper and lower molars in the sagebrush vole (*Laqurus curtatus*) over 287,000 years, and change in size and thickness of enamel in the molars of the water vole (*Arvicola cantiana*) over 300,000 years.

Examples of phyletic evolution have been chronicled for the primate fossil record, including within the Eocene *Cantius* lineage by W. C. Clyde and P. D. Gingerich and the Eocene *Tetonius-Pseudotetonius* lineage by Kenneth Rose and Thomas Bown. Meave Leakey discusses phyletic evolution in the *Theropithecus oswaldi* baboon lineage, from the upper Burgi Member Koobi Fora Formation to upper Bed II of Olduvai Gorge, in characters such as increase in complexity of molars and their size compared with those of anterior teeth, decrease in size of canines and in the sectorial cusp of P_3, development of a "reversed cusp of Spee" on cheekteeth, increase in size of the glenoid process, and increase in estimated body weight. She interprets the evidence as representing an unbranched, evolving lineage that can be divided into the three subspecies: *T. oswaldi darti* (earliest in time and

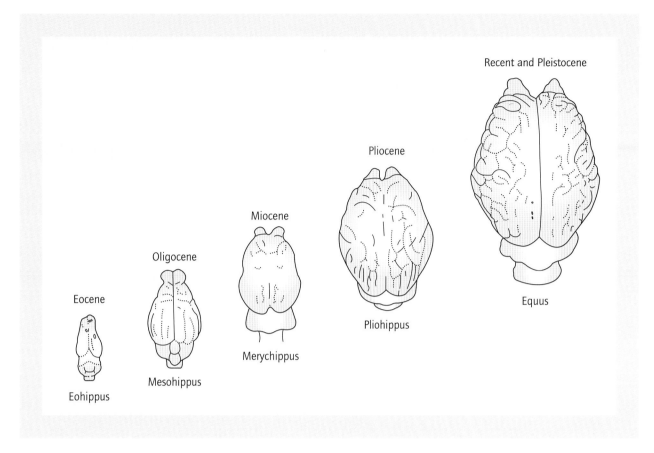

Figure 5b

smallest in size), *T. o. oswaldi* (intermediate) and *T. o. leakeyi* (latest and largest). Gerald G. Eck also interprets it as a phyletically evolving lineage but prefers to assign the earliest material, from Hadar and Makapansgat, to the species *T. darti* rather than using subspecific designation.

The recording of the tempo and pattern of change in individual characters is the methodology used in the studies cited above. It is preferable to plotting the range of species to document the pattern of evolution. The results produced by the latter often depend on the degree of variability in morphological parameters of each named species or genus, as well as on whether species are recognized on the basis of meristic characters or on those that vary continuously. Carroll states that the character-based approach often shows that evolution occurs in a mosaic manner: that different characters, or the same character at different stratigraphic levels, will show different tempos and patterns of evolution—an observation also discussed by Simpson in reference to horse evolution.

Variation and the Processes That Affect It

Genetic variation in characters is the raw material for evolution. As pointed out by Ronald Fisher in the fundamental theorem of natural selection and supported by subsequent experimentation by Francisco Ayala, evolution can occur only in populations that manifest genetic variation. Population geneticists have therefore spent considerable amounts of effort to measure variation. Since the pioneering work of Richard Lewontin and J. L. Hubby, gel electrophoresis has often been the technique employed, and estimates of genetic variation have been made by electrophoresis of proteins and both mitochondrial and nuclear DNA. Mean heterozygosity and the percentage of polymorphic loci are then calculated. Although John H. Gillespie argues that electrophoretic studies of enzymes may overestimate the amount of protein variation (because these proteins may be more polymorphic than are "typical" protein loci), the basic conclusion has been that natural populations are very

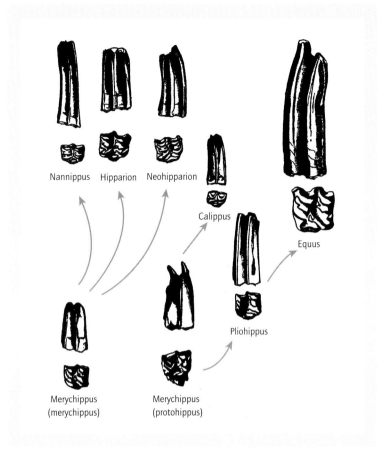

Nannippus   Hipparion   Neohipparion

Calippus

Equus

Pliohippus

Merychippus
(merychippus)

Merychippus
(protohippus)

Figure 5c

Source: From *Horses* by George Gaylord Simpson, copyright © 1951 by Oxford University Press, Inc. Used by permission of Oxford University Press, Inc.

new mutation arises, it eventually becomes the new wild type. A population would evolve, but there would not be much genetic variation at any one time in the population. Mutations would be deleterious or have adaptive value, but would not be neutral in their effects.

With the discovery of large amounts of genetic variation in populations, two major competing models (balance and neutral mutation) sought to explain the maintenance of variation. The balance model, associated with Theodosius Dobzhansky, observes that many individuals are heterozygous at many loci: No single allele is best, and balancing selection would prevent a single allele from reaching very high frequency. Evolution would occur by gradual shifts in the frequency of alleles. Examples of heterozygote advantage, in which the heterozygote is fitter than is either homozygote (as in sickle-cell trait), bolster this argument. The neutral-mutation hypothesis (termed by Mark Ridley, the "purely neutral" theory) states that much, if not most, variation is selectively neutral because different genotypes are physiologically equivalent. Evolution is not driven so much by natural selection acting on alternate phenotypes/genotypes, but by genetic drift. The purely neutral hypothesis predicts that larger populations will contain more genetic diversity than smaller ones, a prediction that appears to be contradicted by evidence.

Five processes influence the amount of variation in a population: mutation, recombination, gene flow, genetic drift, and natural selection. Mutation is any heritable change in the DNA, including both point mutations (for example, alleles that produce the varieties of hemoglobin) and chromosomal mutations (for example, polyploidy, polysomy). Recombination (crossing over), a process by which segments of homologous chromosomes are exchanged during Prophase I of meiosis, produces new combinations of alleles on chromosomes. Gene flow is the incorporation of alleles into the gene pool of a population from one or more other populations. The archetypal view is that it homogenizes genetic composition if it is the only operating factor; that is, the amount of gene flow between local populations influences the

variable. Jeffrey B. Mitton, in *Selection in Natural Populations* (1997), states that 33% to 50% of enzyme loci are polymorphic and the average individual is polymorphic for 4% to 15% of its genes, but there is considerable variety in the percentage of genes that are polymorphic, from 0% in the modern cheetah and northern elephant seal to 100% in the mussel *Modiolus auriculatus*. Studies of plants and of *Peromyscus* mice suggest that the amount of genetic variation increases with the size of the geographic range.

High levels of variation counter the "classical model," associated with Herman J. Muller, which held that populations in the wild would manifest little genetic variation: The model postulated that one allele of each gene would function best in each deme and would therefore be favored by natural selection. Almost all members of the population would be homozygous for this "wild-type" allele. If a superior degree to which each deme is an independent evolutionary unit, for if there is little gene flow, then each deme evolves independently from others. Gene flow would not only deter genetic drift but also potentially constrain the adaptive divergence of populations living in different environments. This issue is important because models of sympatric and parapatric speciation assume that if selection is strong enough, it can overwhelm the effects of gene flow and adaptive divergence and speciation can occur. Recent work by Andrew P. Hendry and Eric B. Taylor on lake and stream populations of the threespine stickleback fishes (*Gasterosteus aculeatus*) suggests that gene flow may constrain adaptive divergence, but to varying degrees, and that different traits do not respond in the same way to the same amount of gene flow.

Genetic drift (the "Sewall Wright effect") is the random fluctuation of allele frequencies in effectively small populations: populations in which the number of individuals that actually breed is small. The basic premise is that small samples are often not representative of the range of genetic variation within a population and that the frequency of an allele in a small sample is unlikely to be equal to its frequency in the entire gene pool of a large population. Genetic drift is sometimes subdivided into continuous drift, intermittent drift, and the founder principle. The founder principle refers to situations in which populations are begun by a small number of colonists, which carry a fraction of the variability of the parental population, and allele frequencies differ from those of the parental population. When a population is subject to drift, the frequency of an allele will randomly change from one generation to the next until the allele is either fixed or lost (see Figure 7). It, therefore, reduces the amount of genetic variation within a population. Genetic drift has been produced in experimental populations of *Drosophila*, extensively treated mathematically, and modeled by computer simulation. It has been discussed in the microevolution of aboriginal Australians, the high incidence of hereditary eye disease and clinodactyly in the human island population of Tristan da Cunha, Ellis-van Creveld dwarfism in eastern Pennsylvanian Amish, and oculocutaneous albinism Type 2 in the Navajo.

Natural selection was defined by Darwin as the preservation of favorable individual differences and variations and the destruction of those that are disadvantageous. Selection acts directly on the phenotypes

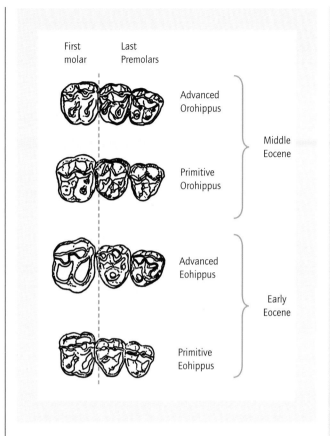

Figure 5d

Source: From *Horses* by George Gaylord Simpson, copyright © 1951 by Oxford University Press, Inc. Used by permission of Oxford University Press, Inc.

of organisms and indirectly on their genotypes. In a genetic sense, alleles that promote greater ability to survive and reproduce in a particular environment (higher fitness) will leave more offspring than do less fit genotypes. The difference in frequency between various genotypes and phenotypes is a result of differences in ecology and not because of chance. Selection can occur at any stage of the life span, but it has maximal evolutionary impact when it acts on those age classes with the highest reproductive values. There are several basic premises: Phenotypic variation exists between individuals in a species; species have more offspring than can survive and reproduce; individuals with different phenotypes vary in their ability to survive and reproduce in a particular environment; and a portion of the ability to survive and reproduce is hereditary. While selection can cause evolution to occur in a population, a population may be at equilibrium as a result of natural selection and other processes.

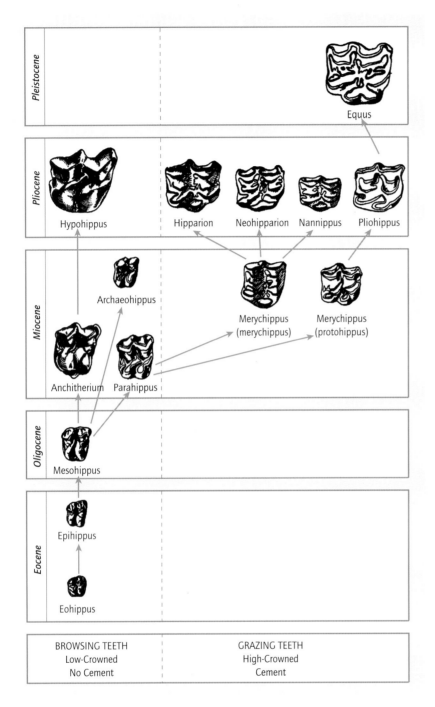

Figure 5e

Source: From *Horses* by George Gaylord Simpson, copyright © 1951 by Oxford University Press, Inc. Used by permission of Oxford University Press, Inc.

generally focused on kin selection), and entire species (species selection, a tenant of punctuated equilibrium and a proposed mechanism to explain evolutionary trends without invoking phyletic evolution). Most of the naturalistic, experimental, and theoretical work centers on selection at the level of the individual. A number of well-known naturalistic cases are cited: melanism in peppered moths, survival of English sparrows during the winter of 1898, shell color polymorphism in British populations of European landsnails, water snakes on islands in western Lake Erie, heavy metal tolerance in the grass *Agrostis tenuis* on mine tailings, stolon length in populations of *Agrostis stolonifera* that grow in different environments, Batesian mimicry in Lepidoptera, and immunity to malaria in human populations with sickle-cell trait.

Neutral Theory and the Molecular Clock

While it is clear that the above five processes affect the amount of variation in populations, there is considerable debate over which mechanisms are most important in maintaining and changing the amount of genetic diversity. Natural selection and adaptation have received considerable attention, as has the purely neutral theory of molecular evolution (termed the "neoclassical theory" by Lewontin). In this hypothesis, most evolutionary changes in the DNA do not result from the action of natural selection on variation. Rather, the mechanism of change is the random fixation of neutral or almost neutral mutants by the action of genetic drift. The probability of fixation of a neutral allele in a finite population is equal to the initial gene frequency (p); the rate of gene substitution is equal to the mutation

It has been posited that selection can occur at any level of organization that fulfills the above premises: individual genes or larger parts of the genome (for example, meiotic drive in *Drosophila* and other taxa), individual organisms that have different genotypes and phenotypes, groups of organisms (discussion rate per locus. Most intraspecific protein and DNA polymorphisms are selectively neutral, and polymorphic alleles are maintained by a balance between origination by mutation or introduction into a population by gene flow and elimination by random extinction. Therefore, most molecular polymorphisms are not maintained by selection. It is predicted that genes that evolve rapidly will manifest high degrees of intraspecific variability.

Masatoshi Nei, in *Molecular Evolutionary Genetics* (1987), summarizes major points in the neutralist theory: many mutations at the nucleotide level are apparently neutral or nearly neutral; only a small proportion of mutations are advantageous; natural selection is a process that preserves advantageous mutations and eliminates disadvantageous ones; new mutations spread by genetic drift or by natural selection, but a large proportion of new mutations are eliminated by chance; and populations do not always have the genetic variation for new adaptation. In the neutralist paradigm, natural selection is invoked to explain the *loss* of disadvantageous mutations, but genetic drift to account for *fixation* of mutations. This differs from the selectionist approach, which invokes the effects of natural selection to explain both fixation and loss.

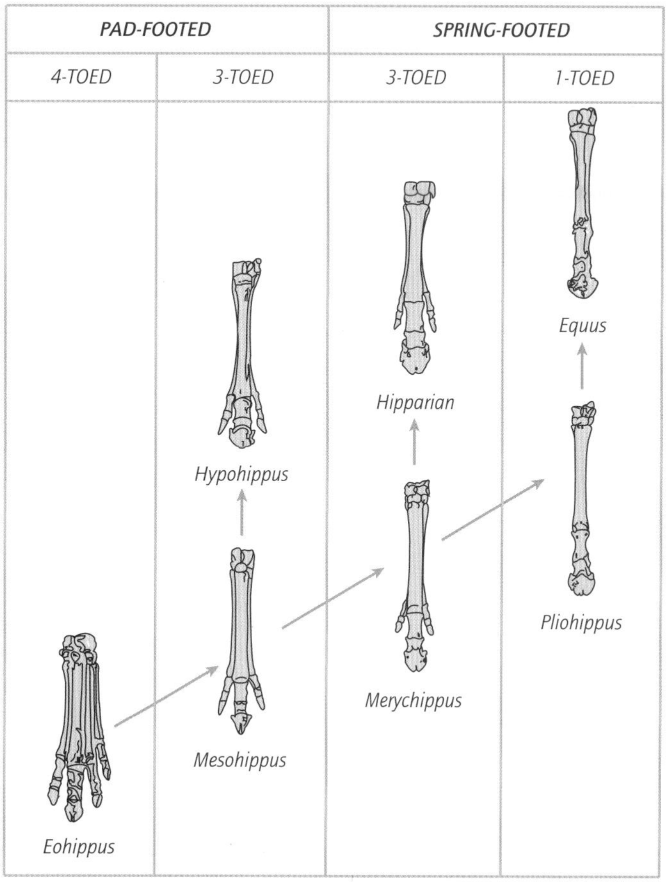

Related to the idea of selective neutrality is the molecular clock hypothesis, in which the rate of nucleotide or amino acid substitution is constant per site per year. The clock predicts a stochastically, not absolutely, constant rate of change. In his writings, Moto Kimura assumes that the rate of neutral mutation per year is almost constant among different organisms with very different generation spans, a conjecture that appears to depend on whether mutations are synonymous (silent) or nonsynonymous (replacement). The application of the molecular clock achieved notoriety by the work of Vincent Sarich, in which he concluded that the earliest possible date of divergence of the African apes and hominins was slightly more than 4 million years ago. This suggestion strongly contradicted the dominant paradigm of the period, which placed the divergence in the Miocene with the identification of *Ramapithecus* as a hominin, and Sarich made the extreme statement that morphology was an unreliable indicator upon which to base estimates of dates of divergence. "Universal" rate calibrations have been suggested for mitochondrial DNA, albumin immunological distances, codon substitutions for cytochrome, myoglobin, alpha and beta hemoglobin, fibrinopeptides A and B and insulin, and the 16S rRNA gene.

The purely neutral and molecular clock hypotheses have received both support and criticism. In *The Genetic Basis of Evolutionary Change* (1974), Richard Lewontin extensively reviews the evidence for the maintenance of genetic variation available

PAD-FOOTED		SPRING-FOOTED	
4-TOED	*3-TOED*	*3-TOED*	*1-TOED*

Figure 5f

Source: From *Horses* by George Gaylord Simpson, copyright © 1951 by Oxford University Press, Inc. Used by permission of Oxford University Press, Inc.

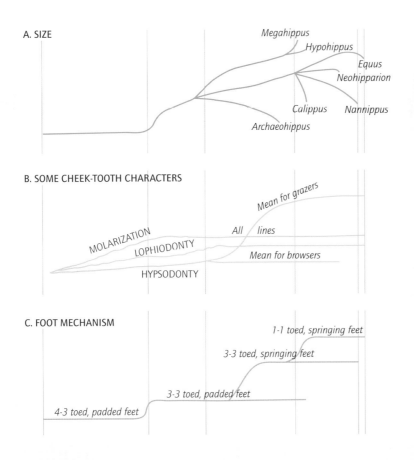

A. SIZE

Megahippus
Hypohippus
Equus
Neohipparion
Calippus   Nannippus
Archaeohippus

B. SOME CHEEK-TOOTH CHARACTERS

Mean for grazers
MOLARIZATION   All   lines
LOPHIODONTY
Mean for browsers
HYPSODONTY

C. FOOT MECHANISM

1-1 toed, springing feet
3-3 toed, springing feet
3-3 toed, padded feet
4-3 toed, padded feet

Figure 6 Diagram of the evolution of characters in horses. Vertical lines are not proportional to the size of the changes, and the curves show rates, times, and directions of change in a relative way. Simpson's commentary states that trends were often different in rate and direction in different lines and in the same lines at different times, different trends occurred at different times and rates within a single functional system, a character may not show any trend for a long period even though it may have manifested a trend earlier or later in the fossil record, and a character may change from one "stable adaptive level" to another by a unique sequence of step-like shifts.

Source: Adapted from *The Major Features of Evolution* by George Gaylord Simpson. Copyright © 1953.

to that date, including the neutralist explanation and the suggestion that variation is maintained by frequency-dependent selection. More recent reviews include those by John C. Avise (*Molecular Markers, Natural History, and Evolution,* 1994), Gillespie (*The Causes of Molecular Evolution,* 1991), Roger Lewin (*Patterns in Evolution: The New Molecular View,* 1997), Nei (*Molecular Evolutionary Genetics,* 1987), and Ridley (*Evolution,* 2004), as well as many professional papers. Discussion can be divided into that which deals with the relative importance of selective neutrality in evolution and that which is aimed at

the assumptions and application of the molecular clock.

Because of the large amount of electrophoretic work that has been done on allozymes, examples of protein variation that can be shown to have important physiological effects and impact on fitness are used to counter the neutralist hypothesis. Different allozymes should work better in different environments: It should be possible to discover the kinetic and thermostability properties that make one variant work better than others in a particular environment and to find higher percentages in areas where it works better than other variants. There should also be increases and decreases in the relative percentages of allozymes as environments change. Studies that have sought to understand enzyme variation in an adaptive context include those of J. E. Graves and G. N. Somero on lactate dehydrogenase in four barracuda species, Ward Watt and colleagues on phosphoglucose isomerase in *Colias* butterflies, and D. A. Powers and P. M. Schulte on lactate dehydrogenase-B in the fish *Fundulus heteroclitus*.

Of particular interest are studies that have examined species on either side of the Isthmus of Panama, as the date of the origin of the isthmus is considered to be well established at about 3 to 3.1 million years ago. Results have been used to counter both the interpretation of allozyme variants as selectively neutral and the application of the molecular clock. Gillespie, citing the work of Graves and colleagues on pairs of fish species that are separated by the isthmus, argues that adaptive changes in the enzyme lactate dehydrogenase occur with only a 2-to-3-degree difference in average environmental temperature between the Atlantic and Pacific. Application of

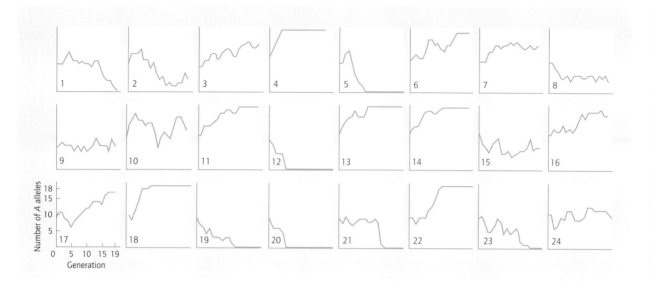

Figure 7   Computer simulation of genetic drift over 19 generations in 24 hypothetical populations, each of 9 individuals. Note that the allele frequency changes at random from one generation to the next. If the simulation was continued, allele frequency would change erratically until the allele was either fixed ($p = 1$) or lost ($p = 0$) in each population.

Source: Adapted from D. L Hartl, *A Primer of Population Genetics, 2/e* (1988, Fig. 1, p. 72). Reprinted by permission from Sinauer Associates.

Atlantic and Pacific comparisons to the molecular clock has yielded contradictory results, at least in the study of mtDNA. Avise and associates find that there is a definite separation in the mtDNA phylogeny of the Atlantic and Pacific populations of the green turtle (*Chelonia mydas*) but that the extent of the sequence divergence is 10 times lower than expected if the mammal-derived evolutionary rate of 2% divergence per million years is applied (Allan Wilson argues that this rate should be applicable to all animals). Avise concludes that mtDNA evolution is slower in turtles than in mammals. In contrast, a study by E. Bermingham and H. A. Lessios finds that the rate of divergence per million years for sea urchins is close to that calculated for mammals. Further complicating the molecular clock debate, Nancy Knowlton examined mtDNA and allozymes for snapping shrimp and concluded that the age of the biogeographic vicariance event probably does not accurately document the point at which gene flow stopped between the Atlantic and Pacific sides of the isthmus.

A revision of the original selective neutrality hypothesis is the "nearly neutral theory," associated with T. Ohta, in which there are small positive or negative selection coefficients associated with mutations. In this paradigm, nearly neutral mutations are affected more by drift when populations are small, but more by natural selection when populations are large. It may be argued that these effects of population size are true regardless of whether the mutation is nearly neutral or has a substantial positive or negative selection coefficient. Ridley extensively discusses this paradigm and perceives several advantages in comparison with the "purely neutral" hypothesis, including the prediction of a more erratic, less constant rate of evolution based on the influence of population size on whether slightly disadvantageous mutations will be affected by drift or selection.

Recent attention has also focused on microsatellite analysis rather than on the more traditional allozymes, mtDNA and RFLPs. Microsatellites are short, repeated sequences that are usually found in noncoding regions of nuclear DNA. They manifest a Mendelian pattern of inheritance, unlike mtDNA. Because of the large amount of variability in microsatellite arrays, researchers have used them in identification of parents/offspring and in forensic applications. It has also been suggested that they may show selective neutrality because their function is currently unknown. John Hawks and colleagues incorporate microsatellites in their discussion of population bottlenecks and Pleistocene hominin evolution: Variation in microsatellite base pairs should reflect population size expansions if the loci are selectively neutral. However, as the authors point out, if it can be demonstrated that selection affects microsatellites, then variability in these regions need not indicate population expansions.

Evolution and Physical Anthropology

The Darwinian paradigm of evolution provides a conceptual framework in which the fossil record, primate behavior/ecology, and human and nonhuman primate population biology can be interpreted. While it was possible for Linnaeus to assign formal taxonomic names to primates (for example, *Cercopithecus aethiops*) and Baron Cuvier to describe *Adapis parisiensis* from the Montmartre gypsum quarries prior to Darwinism, the evolutionary paradigm provides a unifying, explanatory framework for physical anthropology. In their recent edition of *Principles of Human Evolution* (2004), Roger Lewin and Robert A. Foley discuss the four types of biological explanation; two varieties that are relevant to our discussion are explanations about adaptive value and evolutionary history. The former inquiries about the function of a trait or behavior and the latter about evolutionary history; both are central to the investigations conducted by physical anthropologists. It is not adequate to simply describe a morphological feature or behavior. Rather, it is crucial to (1) understand how that feature or behavior allows the individual to successfully interact with its environment and (2) to understand the diversity of extinct and extant primates in the context of common descent.

Physical anthropology has borrowed from other disciplines of evolutionary biology and ecology in these endeavors and, increasingly, contributed to the formulation of evolutionary concepts with application beyond the primates. Examples of concepts and techniques adapted from other areas of evolutionary biology and ecology are too numerous to completely enumerate here. The study of variation was a major contribution of the New Synthesis of evolutionary biology and was emphasized by papers in the seminal *Classification and Human Evolution* (1963), edited by Sherwood L. Washburn; it has formed a major aspect of primate taxonomy in both neontological and paleontological settings. Paradigms of phyletic evolution and punctuated equilibrium have been used in the interpretation of the primate fossil record. Various species concepts, such as the biological species concept, the phylogenetic species concept, and the recognition species concept, have been applied to primates. Cladistic taxonomic philosophy and methodology, initially invented by the entomologist Willi Hennig, has been widely adopted and applied by physical anthropologists. The idea of the ring species (speciation by distance) was discussed by Yoel Rak to analyze hominin evolution in the Levant. It has been suggested that the phenomenon of nanism (dwarf forms), observed in island forms of ducks, hippopotami, elephants, and deer, may have occurred in hominin evolution, as documented by the recent discovery of *Homo floresiensis*. The ideas of sociobiology, employed outside of physical anthropology to explain social systems as diverse as eusocial insects and naked mole rats, are widely employed in modern primatology. And formulations associated with population genetics (such as the Hardy-Weinberg equilibrium and effective population size) are routinely used in the study of human and nonhuman primate population biology.

Physical anthropologists have been somewhat slower to apply their findings to larger evolutionary issues and concepts. This is unfortunate, because primate morphology, ecology, population biology, and behavior have been studied with an intensity that is unequalled in mammalogy. Long-term field studies, such as those of the Awash and Amboseli baboons, provide a wealth of detailed data that are of great benefit to the specialties of speciation research and behavioral ecology.

— *Paul F. Whitehead*

See also **DNA, Recombinant; Evolution, Molecular; Gene Flow; Genetic Drift; Mutations; Selection, Natural**

Further Readings

Avise, J. C. (1994). *Molecular markers, natural history, and evolution.* New York: Chapman & Hall.

Carroll, R. L. (1997). *Patterns and processes of vertebrate evolution.* Cambridge: Cambridge University Press.

Conner, J. K. (2003). Artificial selection: A powerful tool for ecologists. *Ecology, 84,* 1650–1660.

Freeman, S., & Herron, J. C. (2001). *Evolutionary analysis.* (2nd ed.). Upper Saddle River, NJ: Prentice Hall.

Gillespie, J. H. (1991). *The causes of molecular evolution.* New York: Oxford University Press.

Givnish, T. J., & Sytsma K. J. (1997). *Molecular evolution and adaptive radiation.* Cambridge: Cambridge University Press.

Kimura, M. (1983). *The neutral theory of molecular evolution.* Cambridge: Cambridge University Press.

Majerus, M. E. N. (1998). *Melanism: Evolution in action.* Oxford: Oxford University Press.

Mayr, E. (1991). *One long argument: Charles Darwin and the genesis of modern evolutionary thought.* Cambridge, MA: Harvard University Press.

Ridley, M. (2004). *Evolution* (3rd ed.). Malden, MA: Blackwell.

EVOLUTIONARY ANTHROPOLOGY

In a famous manifesto, the geneticist Theodosius Dobzhansky (1900–1975) claimed in 1973 that "nothing in biology makes sense except in the light of evolution." One could also wonder if anything in anthropology makes sense except in the light of evolution. Indeed, there is a part of anthropology that does not deal with evolutionary issues. This is true for most of cultural anthropology, especially on the fringe of the sociology domain. It is even true for some aspects of physical anthropology. Medical anthropology deals with the health status of different populations in relation to different geographical and sociocultural environments. Forensic anthropology focuses mostly on identification of body remains, as well as of living subjects. It should be also underlined that anthropology was born and developed as a science in a preevolutionist period. Although the word *anthropologos* was used in antiquity, it is not before the Renaissance that it was used in a context involving goals of knowledge. Until the Classical Age, it was mostly centered on the "knowledge of one's self." However, dissertations on the moral nature of humans developed in parallel to studies of character and anatomical descriptions. From the middle of the 16th century, surgeons such as André Vesale (1514–1564) put emphasis on the anatomical determination of the human body. The word *anthropologia* appears for the first time in its anatomical meaning in a German book by Magnus Hundt (1449–1519),

published in 1501, *Anthropologium, de hominis dignitate, natura et proporietatibus.* In the 17th century, anthropology, the science of the study of humans, was divided between anatomy, addressing the body structure, and psychology, which speaks about the soul. In the 18th century, the first anthropological syntheses were developed, including the *Treaty of Man* by Georges-Louis de Buffon (1707–1788) and *The Anthropology or General Science of Man* published in 1788 by Alexandre Cesar Chavannes (1731–1800). Under the influence of the 18th-century naturalists such as Carl Linnaeus (1707–1778) and Buffon, anthropology became the natural history of humans. It was defined as such in 1795 by Johann Friedrich Blumenbach (1752–1840). The middle of the 19th century is marked by the creation of anthropological institutions, faculty chairs, and scientific societies in France, England. Germany, and the United States.

Revolutionary Perspectives on Anthropology

Anthropology was already established as an official science when three major events revolutionized perspectives on the place of humans in nature. In 1856, fossil remains of an extinct form of humans were discovered in the site of Feldhofer (Neandertal, Germany). Discoveries of fossil humans had already occurred in 1830 in Belgium (Engis) and in 1848 in Gibraltar (Forbe's Quarry). However, although these specimens were later identified as genuine fossil hominids, the finding of Neandertal was the first recognized as such. It is not before the latter part of the 19th century that the concept of Neandertals as a distinct and extinct form of humans was universally accepted. Second, in 1859, Charles Darwin (1809–1882) published his master work, *On the Origin of Species by Means of Natural Selection.* The notion of evolutionary change in living species predated Darwin, and the French scientist Jean-Baptiste Lamarck (1744–1829) can be considered the father of the evolution concept in its biological meaning. However, Lamarck failed to propose a valid mechanism to explain the mechanism of evolutionary processes. The primary contribution of Darwin was the identification of natural selection as a major force driving evolutionary changes. The third event of major importance also occurred in 1859. English archaeologists and geologists including Hugh Falconer (1808–1865), Joseph Prestwich (1812–1896), and Sir John Evans (1823–1908) accepted the association of human-made Paleolithic flint implements with extinct fauna in geological ancient deposits that had been described by Jacques Boucher de Perthes (1788–1868) in northern France. Although a large portion of anthropological studies still remained out of the evolutionary perspective, beginning with this period, prehistoric archaeology and human paleontology became important topics of research for cultural and physical anthropologists. Because of the complexity of the roots of anthropology, this science is the crossing point of several distinct fields of knowledge and is multidisciplinary in nature. Evolutionary anthropology can be defined more as a perspective than as a science. It is the synthesis of the various fields of anthropological studies addressing the behavioral and biological nature of humans and their mechanisms of emergence through time.

Human Evolutionary Processes

Looking at the anatomical changes of humans in a remote past, and at the changes in technical skills, is the most obvious way to approach human evolutionary processes. Indeed, paleoanthropology represents the core of evolutionary anthropology and is essentially the field that unites all the others. The term *paleoanthropology* is sometimes understood as a synonym of *human paleontology*; however, more often it encompasses paleontological and archaeological studies. In the course of their evolution, humans have combined biological and cultural adaptations while they geographically expanded. Even if technical responses to the challenges offered by the conquest of new geographic and ecological niches became preponderant, it is most important to consider the two aspects of human adaptation and their complex interactions. One defining aspect of human paleontology lies in the fact that the study of rare and precious specimens remains the core of the discipline. The fossil hominids give a very fragmentary and discontinuous picture of the past evolution of humans. Traditionally, they have been described and compared in order to provide a picture of the phylogenetic tree of our ancestors and direct relatives. One major problem in this process is related to the difficulty in accessing specimens. After discovery, they can remain unpublished for long periods, and later, they can be possibly under the care of curators more preoccupied by conservation than by scientific studies. Since the

1990s, new techniques, primarily from medical imaging (for example, CT scanning) have allowed development of new approaches for the study of these fossils. "Virtual paleoanthropology" is based on the utilization of 3-D images that allow virtual extraction and reconstruction, precise quantitative analyses of internal structures, and also mathematical analyses of the shape through 3-D morphometrics and the modelling of ontogenetic processes, biomechanical properties, and evolutionary changes themselves. Although the resolution of these 3-D images is still far from perfect, one can expect that in the future their use will reduce the need to access the specimens. Work on the original specimens will be restricted to specific issues such as the analysis of fine anatomical details, cut marks, microstructure, and chemical composition.

A new series of approaches have developed, inherited primarily from histology, geochemistry, and biochemistry. With the rise of non- (or less) destructive methods, this field is rapidly expanding. In parallel, it should be noted, there have been growing interests in biological issues, for example, diet or growth processes, that are not directly related to phylogentic issues. Microstructural studies have developed mostly in the field of dental anthropology. Several types of incremental mineralized structures, to date, represent the primary way to assess life history in extinct species. This emergence of microstructural analyses has been made possible by large technological advances in microscopy.

Chemical analyses of fossil specimens aimed to reconstruct paleobiological features are mostly concerned with extraction of organic molecules. The sequencing of small fragments of mitochondrial DNA extracted from fossil remains of humans and animals has opened a new area of paleobiological study. The analysis of stable isotopes, mostly carbon, oxygen, and nitrogen, represents another major field of research in paleoanthropology. Stable isotope rate is an essential source of information about the environment and the diet of individuals during their lifetimes. In the future, issues such as migration and seasonality will become accessible through these kinds of studies. These methods may also provide a better knowledge of the environmental conditions of humans in the continental environment.

Paleoanthropologists place a great deal of emphasis on the understanding of evolutionary processes. Important methodological progress was made in the 1970s with the rise of cladistic methods. However, specialists still investigate the significance of the features used in phylogenetic analysis. To what extent are they genetically determined, or depend on environmental conditions and behaviors? Are they homologous from one species to another? These are the questions that need resolution in order to gain better insight into phylogenetic relationships. Among the paleobiological issues, changes in growth and development processes along life history are increasingly seen as a powerful mechanism to explain evolutionary changes. A consistent effort is applied to the

Photo by H. Moll, Max-Planck-Institute, Leipzig, Germany

establishment of developmental trajectories in extant hominoids and extinct hominins. Other aspects of the biology of extinct species are also accessible through the progress of archaeological sciences. Proteins and lipids are extracted with increasing frequency from fossil bones and may give us access to physiological features that have been inaccessible to date. Paleodemographic questions related not only to life history and longevity but also to population size and their fluctuations through environmental changes are also of high interest.

Importance of Fieldwork

A very important aspect of paleoanthropological studies is related to fieldwork. The spectacular increase of fossil material in the last two or three decades, resulting in a much better understanding of human evolutionary history, is mainly the consequence of the development of field surveys and excavations. This is also where, often, human paleontologists and prehistoric archaeologists meet. Contrasting with the rarity of ancient human remains, artifacts are found in large numbers in areas where humans have lived in the past. The occurrence of stone artifacts is the most reliable parameter to assess the occupation of given geographical areas through geological time. However, the abundance of stone artifacts provides a biased picture of ancient behaviors and technologies.

The evidence for the "Stone Age" comes mostly from the fact that tools manufactured by flaking of hard stones are virtually indestructible and can accumulate in very large numbers over long periods of time. Most of the Pleistocene was actually, rather, a "Wood Age," at least in some parts of the world. The study of archaeological sites with mixed artifacts, faunal remains, and sometimes structures such as fireplaces left by humans aim to separate human activities from natural processes. Most of the time, it is a somewhat naïve view to assume that these accumulations represent "habitats." In many cases, human occupation was discontinuous and other mammals such as carnivores may have played a major role in the accumulation and alteration of the faunal remains. The artifacts themselves could be displaced in a secondary accumulation. Finally, the whole site may have undergone significant geological modifications. Site formation and taphonomical studies are important issues in the interpretation of archaeological sites. The density and distribution of the human occupations in the landscape are related to environmental factors that one tries to discriminate. These data help us to understand the history of the peopling, past demographic fluctuations and the way ancient humans could exploit the environment. Zooarchaeology research aims to analyze the faunal remains in order to reconstruct hunting (or scavenging) strategies, carcass processing, and transportation and, in a broader context,

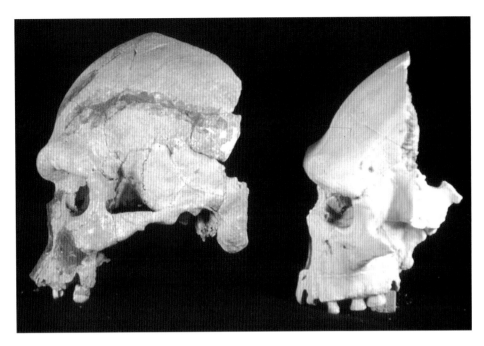

Photo courtesy of Max-Planck-Institute, Leipzig, Germany

physiology. Attention has also been paid to differences in the process of growth and development among different species of monkeys and apes. Primate paleontology is an important field of research, as it brings light on the phylogenetic relationships of living and extinct species and also on the adaptive strategies of the different groups. However, with respect to phylogeny, molecular studies and genetics have as well made a very significant contribution in the last decade. Finally, social organization and behavior of living apes and monkeys is also an important field of research that aids in understanding the emergence of hominin societies.

how ancient hunter-gatherers interacted with the animal world. The stone and bone artifacts themselves are the objects of many studies. They were, in the past, considered as chronological markers, but today the technology leading to their production has become of greater interest and gives us some clues about the skills and cognitive abilities of ancient humans. The raw materials that have been used by ancient humans also inform us about the patterns of land occupation and possible long-distance exchanges between human groups. For the most recent periods of prehistory, the occurrence of symbolic manifestations such as body ornaments, geometric signs, paintings, engravings, and sculptures reveals the development of modern thinking. It can give some clues on the major changes in the social organization in humans and, likely also, in the development of modern language. For these late periods, it is possible to use the archaeological evidence to identify ancient ethnocultural entities.

Study of Nonhuman Primates

Because evolutionary anthropology is mainly concerned with the question, "What makes humans different?," the study of nonhuman primates represents an important part of its scope. In this perspective, primate studies focus on biological and behavioral aspects. A large proportion of evolutionary studies have been dedicated to comparative anatomy and

Among the primates, the species that are the closest to our own are classified together with humans and their ancestors into the superfamily of hominoids. This is the reason that many studies put emphasis on the gibbons, the orangutans, and our even closer relatives, the African apes: gorillas, common chimpanzees, and bonobos. One major problem faced by evolutionary anthropology lies in the fact that, in the wild, these species are greatly endangered. Although they may survive only in zoos in the near future, there is still a lot to learn from them. This is especially true in the areas of development, genetics, and ethology (the science of animal behavior). Unfortunately, life in captivity will make many questions regarding these issues inaccessible. In the past, hominoids have been a much more successful group than they are today. The human species, which covers an entire planet, represents an exception. In fact, the number of species of hominoids has been reduced since the Miocene period. Other groups of primates (cercopithecoids), on the contrary, have undergone an expansion during the same period. Hominoids represent a group of middle- to large-bodied primates, primarily adapted to forested or semiforested environments. Analyzing the anatomy of the living and fossil species is of crucial interest to understand human origins. Indeed, hominins achieved a very unique adaptive model. They adapted to a new evological niche for hominoids, in particular the open environments of the middle and high latitudes. They adapted to an entirely new locomotor repertoire with the development of bipedalism. They accessed new diets with the developments of carnivory and hunting. Finally, they developed cultural and technical adaptations to a level unequalled in the primate world. In an evolutionary perspective, primatology is interested in analyzing these differences between humans and apes but also in the separate emergence of some features once considered unique to humans in the other hominoids. In terms of behavior, it is important to understand how the variety of social systems developed by apes responds to different adaptative strategies. This includes social organization and reproductive patterns that can be quite different from one species to another. The types of cognitive abilities that have been developed by these different species are under the scrutiny of primatologists. Sociocognitive processes, including communication, cooperation, social interactions, and learning, are also very important to analyze.

It is fascinating to consider the behavioral diversity that can exist between different populations of the same species of apes. One of the most important discoveries of the last decades has been the revelation of "ape cultures." Different groups within the same species can develop "traditions." This issue has been studied especially in common chimpanzees in which technical skills involving the use of tools such as hammers and anvils, but also "fishing sticks" to acquire insects, have been described. These technologies, as well as specific behaviors such as hunting strategies for a spectrum of prey, are transmitted between generations and vary from one group to another. Wherever possible, wild apes are studied by direct observation in the field, which implies long-term projects dedicated to the follow groups and individuals over long periods of time. In the course of these field projects, some biological aspects are also analyzed, and molecular geneticists analyze samples of feces and hair collected noninvasively to address questions concerning paternity, reproductive strategies, relatedness between and within social units and phylogeny.

Evolutionary anthropological genetics investigates the genetic history of primates in general and humans in particular. This field of evolutionary anthropology focuses on the processes directly affecting the evolution of the genome, such as mutation, recombination, natural selection, and genetic drift. Rebuilding the detailed history of different lineages in terms of demographic evolution and phylogenetic relationships is also of great interest in this discipline. With increasing frequency, studies are dedicated to living great apes, which provide a very important comparative model for the evolution of early hominids even if, in general, their demographic and genetic evolution differed in important ways from our own over the course of the last 2 million years. Molecular phylogeny has provided invaluable information on the origin, relationships, and times of divergence for the different species of hominoids, including humans. Another important aspect of genetic studies is dedicated to examining the ways in which the genome determines development and function of organisms. The comparison of the gene expression patterns in various tissues in primates has given us a greater understanding of many biological aspects of the human nature. The history of ancient populations, or even extinct species, can be approached by using genetic analyses. It is possible to extract, amplify, and sequence mitochondrial DNA fragments from fossils, such as Neandertals 40,000 years old. This genetic information helps us to establish the phylogenetic status and times of divergence of such an extinct species. It provides insights into the variation of the size of these ancient populations throughout their evolution. Fossil DNA is as well extracted from nonhuman mammals, which were the hunted game or the competitors of our ancestors and relatives. Such genetic material is extracted from bone remains but also from coprolites (fossil feces). It provides data for interesting comparisons, as animal material is much more abundant that are human fossils. A major challenge faced by paleogenetics results from the problem of contamination of ancient samples by modern human DNA, which is abundant in our present environment. Paradoxically, it is easier to identify genuine fossil DNA in extinct humans such as Neandertals than in more recent modern populations.

Population Genetics

Since the 1980s, population genetics has emerged as a major methodological framework in which to understand the origin, migration, and evolutionary history of the modern humans and their direct ancestors.

The analysis of genetic variation in living populations has been intensively explored in evolutionary anthropological research. This is particularly true for research examining variation in the mitochondrial DNA, transmitted from mother to offspring, and in the Y chromosome, exclusively transmitted from fathers to sons. Most of these studies establish a recent origin of modern humans (between 200,000 and 100,000 BP), most likely in Africa. They suggest past bottlenecking of ancient populations and indicate a late dispersal of modern populations throughout Eurasia and Australia, and even more recently, throughout the Americas and the Pacific Islands. Genetic analysis provides not only a general tree for human populations but also some indications of the timing of colonization by modern humans. In the details, it can bring some light on interactions between groups, mating strategies, differences in mobility between genders, or the geographical origin of pioneer groups like those that colonized the Pacific. Population genetics often interacts with linguistics in order to elucidate the detailed history of human groups. Like genes, languages are transmitted from parents to their children. Words and grammatical structures also undergo "mutations," which result in a diversification and divergence of numerous linguistic groups.

Language is indeed a unique feature of humans, and a great deal of effort is dedicated to the study of its structure and evolution. Although "communication" is common among other animal species, human language distinguishes itself by the complexity of sounds that the human vocal tract is capable of producing, as well as the control of sound production at a rapid time scale. It is also characterized by the complexity of its syntax, which facilitates the organization of concepts in a way that goes much further than the simple combination of vocal signals. The question of the origin of language is difficult and much debated. Anatomical features allowing the physical production of human languages, as well as the cerebral abilities necessary for its manifestation, may well have been selected independently and for other needs in the course of hominin evolution. Linguists are very much interested in establishing the common features of all human languages ("language universals"). Some have even tried to delineate some traits of an original language ancestral to all the others. Language universals may result primarily from the way the human mind is able to conceptualize ideas and articulate them into speech. Other aspects of linguistic studies are dedicated to the way languages can differ from each other and how they vary over the course of time. Understanding these processes allows the construction of language trees at different scales. Families of languages descending from a single ancestor have been established. Sometimes they present distribution that can be related to the spread, development, or movement of large human groups. Establishing the relationships between these families into larger units has proven to be a more difficult task. The fact that linguistic traits can be imposed or adopted from one group to another through complex historical processes greatly complicates comparisons of archaeological, genetic, and linguistic features in order to rebuild the history of different populations.

Developmental and Comparative Psychology

Developmental and comparative psychology is also crucial to the understanding of what makes humans different. This field of research investigates cognitive and social features of humans and compares them to those of other primates. These studies aim to establish the abilities that have been uniquely developed by humans. Studies on large apes are generally conducted through experiments exploring the abilities of the different species. The field also explores individual variation within groups. Several types of cognition are explored and are generally grouped into two areas referred to as social cognition and physical cognition. The first is relevant to how individuals are able to understand the actions and intentions of other individuals. Analyzing the learning and imitation processes is a main issue in the analysis of social cognition. Physical cognition is implemented by individuals in their interactions with their environment. Experimental psychology is also much interested in the development of human children. Humans contrast with other primates with an extended period of brain maturation occurring after birth while the individual is already interacting with his or her physical and social environment. The learning period is longer in humans than in any other species of primates. The acquisition of language is one of the most spectacular changes during this period. Psychologists are interested in how humans read and understand the minds of other people and develop social skills during the first year of life. Techniques of medical imaging have opened the possibility to connect the brain development with the acquisition of specific abilities. In older children, the development of social and physical cognition is also explored. The acquisition of language is, of course, a main focus of interest. Its learning processes are investigated in a clinical way, as well as cross-culturally.

Evolutionary psychology also analyzes human behavior in adults. The reproductive strategies, mating patterns, and parental investment in children have played a particularly important role in the past and present evolution of human groups. However, the field extends to many other behaviors, such as reciprocity and cooperation between individuals, or even violence and homicide. The determinism of these behaviors and/or of their transmission is often difficult to clarify, as they are also depending on cultural and economical conditions. Ultimately, cultural features in past and present societies can also be assessed in an evolutionary perspective.

The animal nature of humans has always been a matter of fascination, if not of anxiety, for us. For centuries, philosophers, writers, and scientists have tried to define the unique nature of humans and to separate them from the animal world. Evolutionary anthropology deals with the oldest origins of humans, among the primates, and utilizes our closest relatives as comparative models. It interprets the complex features of human behavior in the light of adaptation and faces the challenge of unweaving the complex interactions between biology and culture at work in the course of human evolution.

— *Jean-Jacques Hublin*

Further Readings

Barrett, L., Dunbar, R., & Lycett, J. (2002). *Human evolutionary psychology.* New York: Palgrave.

Boesch, C. (2000). *Behavioral diversity in chimpanzees and bonobos.* Cambridge, UK: Cambridge University Press.

Cavalli-Sforza, L. L. (2000). *Genes, peoples and languages.* Berkeley: University of California Press.

Delson, E., Tattersall, I., van Couvering, J. A., & Brooks, A. S. (Eds.). (2000). *Encyclopedia of human evolution and prehistory.* New York: Garland.

Klein, R. (1999). *The human career: Human biological and cultural origins* (2nd ed.). Chicago: University of Chicago Press.

Photo courtesy of Max-Planck-Institute, Leipzig, Germany

Spencer, F. (Ed.). (1997). *History of physical anthropology* (Vols. 1–2). New York: Garland.

Tomasello, M. (2003). *Constructing a language: A usage-based theory of language acquisition.* Cambridge, MA: Harvard University Press.

 ## EVOLUTIONARY EPISTEMOLOGY

Evolutionary epistemology considers the scientific processes and bounds of *knowledge,* with an emphasis on natural selection as the crucial source of sensate cognition by which organisms adapt to their environments. This mode of naturalistic epistemology contrasts significantly with the traditional *transcendant*

formulation, which presupposes no particular format of knowledge. The traditional approach traces to Plato, who sought to differentiate knowledge from true belief insofar as the true belief does not require *justification.* Later rational empiricists, notably Descartes, sought to identify and further systematize the bounds and processes of human knowledge, particularly as it is organized in neuromental assemblages. Ultimately, the two approaches converge in the aim of traditional epistemology to reconstruct human knowledge via justification that separates knowledge from merely true beliefs.

However, Darwinian insights of the 19th century cast humans as natural beings arising in the course of evolution. As means of human knowledge and belief are likewise expressions of natural selection, they are perhaps best analyzed and systematized by the scientific method in general and the principles of evolution more specifically. Hence, there is a pragmatic, not transcendant, basis for epistemics rooted in a priori facts of evolutionary biology and psychology.

Evolutionary epistemology has two main component interests: adaptation as it occurs both through phylogeny or within individual development and understanding the legacy of ideas, concepts, and cultural tropes in which knowledge exists. With respect to adaptation, the phylogenetic analysis of evolutionary epistemology takes up how the mechanisms of sentience *fit* the world. This is a direct extension of Darwinian concepts to philosophy insofar as the heuristic function of knowledge is to enhance reproductive fitness. Thus, evolutionary epistemology of adaptation posits, in the first instance, that the processes and bounds of knowledge accumulate and evolve as the result of variation and selection. Otherwise, the ontogenic aspect of adaptation takes up how individual ontogeny of knowledge is also an expression of processes in which variation and selection play a central role. Trial-and-error learning or the development of scientific theories are obvious examples of this second element in the evolutionary epistemology of adaptation.

These direct correspondences between mechanisms of evolution with those of ideation were noted by Darwin, Spencer, Romanes, Poincaré, Dewey, William James, and others. However, it was only more recently that evolutionary epistemology was systematized as a cogent philosophical approach to knowledge, first by Karl Popper and then by Donald T. Campbell and others.

Popper emphasized *conjecture* and *refutation* as key elements of valid science and also noted that every scientific theory must be *falsifiable;* that is, it must be subject to deselection. Such an iterative trial-and-error process accumulates knowledge about the world. In his later work, Popper emphasized analogies between this iterative conjecture/refutation process and the very similar operations of natural selection, in what he deemed evolutionary epistemology.

Campbell greatly elaborates this approach to take in the whole of evolutionary neuromental processes subserving knowledge in sentient beings. Campbell's project directly applies Darwinian principles to educe three main provisos:

1. *Blind variation and selective retention:* Primitive processes for new knowledge are *blind.* However, even without foresight as to what may be learned, ineffective elements are deselected whereas adaptive elements are retained.

2. *Vicarious selector:* Trial-and-error processes recede as "fit" knowledge accumulates and functions as a selector predictive of environmental selective pressures.

3. *Nested hierarchy:* Retained selectors may also be subject to variation and selection at a higher level. This fosters cognitive-emotive-rational assemblages at higher levels of ever-more-intelligent adaptive systems.

But there is another strand of evolutionary epistemology beyond this cognitive neurobiological perspective, as there is a need to explain the evolution of epistemic norms of ideation itself. To this end, models of scientific theory and human culture are constructed in a manner compatible with evolutionary neurobiology. Ultimately, this other main component relates to semiotics and meaning making as it analyzes the scientific method itself in evolutionary terms as varying hypotheses are selected on the accumulation of useful information.

These two interrelated but quite different aspects of the field have become known, respectively, as the *evolution of epistemological mechanisms* (EEM) and *evolutionary epistemology of theories* (EET). Valid EEM selectionist explanations (for example, how the brain works) do not in themselves explicate how systems of human knowledge are assembled.

Conversely, valid EET explanations of how human knowledge systems are selected do not in themselves explicate the neurobiological mechanisms of perception or cognition.

Indeed, one major criticism of evolutionary epistemology is that it traverses and perhaps conflates several levels and domains of evolution—biological, sensory, perceptual, cognitive, emotional, social, and linguistic—even as it also addresses the rather different realm of the evolution of scientific concepts. A more complete epistemology of human knowledge must explain how these processes interact within both phylogeny and individual development as well as with respect to the evolution of scientific culture. Thus, some argue that neither EEM nor EET analyses are proper works of epistemology, at least as epistemology is traditionally a normative discipline. However, the rigorous consideration of evolutionary possibilities and constraints with respect to processes and bounds of knowledge has greatly enriched traditional epistemology. It has also brought attention to important issues of practical importance in an era marked by major progress in neuromental sciences.

Evolutionary epistemology may best offer descriptive accounts of knowledge mechanisms, whereas traditional epistemology attends to the resolution of prescriptive issues of continuing philosophical interest. At the very least, evolutionary epistemology enhances traditional methods as it helps identify implausible normative prescriptive notions that are inconsistent with evolutionary perspectives concerning human understanding.

— *Daniel R. Wilson*

See also **Popper, Karl**

Further Readings

Bradie, M. (1986). Assessing evolutionary epistemology. *Biology & Philosophy, 1,* 401–459.

Campbell, D. (1960). Blind variation and selective retention. Creative thought as in other knowledge processes. *Psychological Review, 67,* 380–400.

MacLean, P. (1990). *The triune brain in evolution.* New York: Plenum.

Popper, K. (1972). *Objective knowledge: An evolutionary approach.* Oxford: Clarendon Press.

EVOLUTIONARY ETHICS

The obvious as well as the ideal place from which to begin a consideration both of social Darwinism and of evolutionary ethics is the work of Charles Darwin and the ideas he developed and presented in *On the Origin of Species* (1859), which advocates both of social Darwinism and of evolutionary ethics have tried to apply more widely. This is not, of course, to say that Darwin had no intellectual ancestors, any more than it is to say that biological theory has stood still since his death. To say or to suggest either of these things would be wrong.

It would not even be true to say that nothing was published with any claim to the label "evolutionary ethics" until after the first appearance of *On the Origin of Species.* Herbert Spencer was strictly correct when, in the general preface to *The Principles of Ethics,* he claimed that the "doctrine of organic evolution" as it applied to humans had come earlier than that. Spencer was on this occasion referring to his *Social Statics,* first issued at the end of 1850 and containing an outline of the ethical ideas he was about to develop. He could also have claimed, and elsewhere did claim, to have been the first to use the notion of the "survival of the fittest" in an evolutionary context, in an article in the *Westminster Review* for 1852.

The very phrase a "struggle for existence," which epitomizes the gladiatorial view of human life so often taken to be the true moral to be drawn from *On the Origin of Species,* is to be found already, in a similar context, in 1798, in what should be called "the first essay of Malthus on *The Principle of Population,*" in order to distinguish it from the substantially different work Malthus issued in 1803 as if it were merely a second edition. Darwin himself acknowledges his debt to this first essay of Malthus in *On the Origin of Species.* Nevertheless, after all due cautions have been given, it is *On the Origin of Species* that is, and must be, the reference point here. It was the ideas of that work which the forerunners foreran. It was the triumph in biology of the theory that it presented which lends vicarious prestige to whatever can be put forward as Darwinism.

Since many sharp things need to be said about some particular sorts of attempts to develop an evolutionary ethic, it becomes important to emphasize from the beginning that the desires to connect, to see microcosms in relation to the macrocosm, are in

themselves excellent; and certainly, they should be shared and not despised by anyone who aspires to the title of "philosopher." It is therefore neither surprising nor discreditable that in every generation since Darwin, some of the liveliest and least blinkered of students of biology have wanted to explore the possibility of connections between Darwinian evolution and ethics.

The main reason why professional philosophers are apt very brusquely to dismiss all such efforts is that we mistake it that they must involve the committing of what philosophers call the "naturalistic fallacy." The nerve of this fallacy is the attempt to deduce a conclusion about what either *ought* to be or *ought to have been* the case from premises stating only, in morally neutral terms, what either *actually is* or *actually was* the case. Once this fallacy has been recognized for what it is, it may seem that with evolutionary ethics, this is both the heart of the matter and the end of the affair.

This is not good enough. Certainly, the first necessity when a logical fallacy has been committed is to show what was going wrong in that particular case and then perhaps to reinforce the lesson by citing a few further cases of committing the same fallacy in various other areas of discourse. But to stop there would be to fail to appreciate that the source of the very idea of an evolutionary ethic, which Darwin himself did not accept, lies in *On the Origin of Species.* The danger of Darwin's pointedly paradoxical expression "natural selection," and this danger has often been realized, is that it can mislead people to overlook that this sort of selection is blind and nonrational, which is precisely the point. Once this point is missed, it is easy, especially if you are already apt to see nature as a mentor, to go on to take natural selection as a sort of supreme court of normative appeal—and this despite, or in many cases doubtless because of, the time-serving character of the criterion of fitness by which this sort of selection operates. Such ideas may then be, and often have been, regarded as the biological application of the Hegelian slogan, "World history is the world's court of judgment."

These apotheoses of natural selection take many forms. Perhaps the most interesting and important of such misconceptions, and one from which Darwin himself was not altogether free, is that the deductive argument that was the core of his theory proves some sort of law of progressive development. Thus, Darwin concludes his chapter on instincts with the sentence:

"Finally, it may not be a logical deduction, but to my imagination it is far more satisfactory to look at such instincts as the young cuckoo ejecting its foster brothers, ants making slaves . . . not as specially endowed or created instincts, but as small consequences of one general law leading to the advancement of all organic beings—namely multiply, vary, let the strongest live and the weakest die."

Again in the penultimate paragraph of the whole book, Darwin writes: "As all the living forms of life are the lineal descendents of those which lived long before the Cambrian epoch we may feel certain that . . . no cataclysm has desolated the whole world. Hence we may look with some confidence to a secure future of great length. And as natural selection works solely by and for the good of each being, all corporeal and mental endowments will tend to progress towards perfection."

The first of these two passages is not, perhaps, as clear and explicit as one could wish. But in the light of the unhesitating concluding sentence of the second, we may perhaps take it that "what may not be a logical deduction" is not the "one general law leading to the advancement of all organic beings," but rather its implications as regards the more unattractive instincts. Certainly Darwin here was offering natural selection as a guarantee of progress and as both a descriptive and a prescriptive law. Equally certain is that this guarantee was not in fact warranted by his theory. Indeed, neither of the conclusions of this second passage can be justified as deductions from the theory alone.

The first was, on the evidence available to Darwin, an entirely reasonable inductive extrapolation. It is only since the beginning of the atomic era that we humans have acquired any grounds for anxiety about the survival prospects of our own species. The second conclusion never was justified. To choose is necessarily to exclude, and there would seem to be no reason at all, and certainly none within the theory, for saying of every individual who loses out in the struggle for existence that that must be for its own good. Applied not to individuals but to species, the statement might seem to find some justification in the now notorious fact that most actual variations are unfavorable. But because survival is, in theory, the criterion of fitness, and hence of what counts as favorable, the only good that is guaranteed is the survival of whatever makes for survival; and this good is not necessarily good by any independent standard.

Although we would be mistaken if we believed that Darwin's theory implies a general law of progressive development, the idea that it does has been perennially tempting. Since it surely is the case that in every epoch of the fossil record, fresh possibilities of life have been realized, and since it also seems that the most complex of these in each epoch have been more elaborate than the most sophisticated achievements of the previous period, and since we ourselves are among the latest products of such development, it is easy to pick out a trend that we can scarcely regard as anything but progressive.

To pick out a progressive trend is, of course, made still easier if we allow ourselves to misconstrue in a normative sense the paleontologists' purely spatio-temporal use of the terms "higher" and "lower" to characterize first the strata and then the creatures that first appear in those strata. It was not for nothing that Darwin pinned into his copy of *Vestiges of the Natural History of Creation* the memorandum slip, "Never use the words *higher* and *lower*."

Once a trend has been thus identified it may seem a short step from a trend to *the* trend, another equally short step from *the* trend to a *law of tendency,* and so again finally, from a law of tendency to a universal overriding *law of development*. This slippery slope is greased by the fact, first, that the crucial mechanism is called natural selection or the survival of the fittest and, second, that the core of Darwin's theory is a deductive argument that certainly does prove that natural selection is operating and is therefore ensuring the survival of the fittest.

But a trend is a very different thing from a law of tendency. There is a trend if there has been a direction in the development so far, whether or not there is any reason to think that things will continue to develop along this line. But to assert a law of tendency is to say that something always has occurred and always will occur, except in so far as this tendency was or will be inhibited by some overriding force. Furthermore, a law of tendency is a very different thing from an absolute law of development. The former may obtain even though the tendency in question is never in fact fully realized; the first law of motion and Malthus's principle of population are not disproved by the observations that in fact there always are impressed forces and countervailing checks. But an absolute law of development would state that some particular line of evolution is absolutely inevitable, that it neither will or would be prevented by any counteracting causes.

Darwin himself seems never to have gone further than to suggest (as in the two passages already quoted) that his theory might warrant a conclusion of the first and weaker kind: that there is in the evolution of all living things an inherent tendency to progress. It was left to others reviewing evolutionary biology in the light of their own various preconceptions about the (supposedly) predestined lines of nonhuman development to discern in Darwinism the deeper foundation for, or the wider background of, their own supposedly discovering absolute laws of human progress.

By far the most interesting and most important case is that of the two most famous young Hegelians, Karl Marx and Friedrich Engels. In his preface to the first German edition of *Das Kapital*, Marx wrote, "When a society has got upon the right track for the discovery of the natural laws of its movement—and it is the ultimate aim of this work to lay bare the economic law of motion of modern society—it can neither clear by bold leaps, nor remove by legal enactments, the obstacles offered by the successive phases of its normal development. But it can shorten and lessen the birth pangs." And in his speech at Marx's graveside, Engels claimed, "Just as Darwin discovered the law of development of organic nature, so Marx discovered the law of development of human history."

The crucial distinctions between actual trends, laws of tendency, and absolute laws of development can be instructively applied to the writings of two 20th-century British social Darwinists: Julian Huxley, who, after first acquiring his Fellowship of the Royal Society as a result of his biological research, eventually went on to become the first director of UNESCO (United Nations Educational, Scientific, and Cultural Organization), and Joseph Needham, who, after first acquiring his Fellowship of the Royal Society in the same way, went on, with considerable assistance from Chinese colleagues, to produce his massive study, *Science and Civilization in Ancient China.*

Huxley in a famous essay on "Progress, Biological and Other" quoted one of the sentences from Darwin we have just quoted: "As natural selection works solely by and for the good of each being, all corporeal and mental endowments will tend to progress towards perfection." It is, I think, clear that Huxley, if pressed, would never claim to be revealing more than a law of tendency, and usually only an actual trend.

Huxley starts by urging that the most fundamental need of man as man is "to discover something, some being or power, some force or tendency . . . moulding the destinies of the world—something not himself, greater than himself, with which [he can] harmonize his nature . . . repose his doubts . . . achieve confidence and hope." He then offers "to show how the facts of evolutionary biology provide us, in the shape of a verifiable doctrine of progress, with one of the elements most essential to any such externally-grounded conception of God." He later concludes that "the fact of progress emerging from pain and imperfection . . . is an intellectual prop which can support the distressed and questioning mind, and be incorporated into the common theology of the future."

Although Julian Huxley is certainly not adequately insistent upon the first crucial distinction between an actual trend and a force, he does in the following essay on "Biology and Sociology" fairly clearly repudiate the suggestion that the actual progressive direction of development to be discerned in evolutionary biology and elsewhere necessarily reveals an absolute law of progressive development: "When we look into the trend of biological evolution, we find as a matter of fact that it has operated to produce on the whole what we find good . . . This is not to say that progress is an inevitable "law of nature," but that it has actually occurred. . . ." This strongest idea of a law of inevitable development, rejected by Huxley, is in fact urged, eloquently and unequivocally, by Joseph Needham in two books of essays, *Time: The Refreshing River* and *History Is on Our Side*. Much of their interest for us lies in the attempted synthesis of biological science, Marxist historical pseudoscience, and ritualistic Christian religion. For the author was at the time of writing a leading biochemist, an active member of the Communist Party, and a practicing Christian.

Thus, Needham was able to write that the historical process was the organizer of the City of God. "The new world-order of social justice and comradeship, the rational and classless world state, is not a wild idealistic dream, but a logical extrapolation from the whole course of evolution, having no less authority than that behind it, and therefore of all faiths the most rational."

— *Antony Flew*

See also **Darwin, Charles; Malthus, Thomas; Spencer, Herbert**

Further Readings

Farber, P. L. (1998). *The temptations of evolutionary ethics.* Berkeley: University of California Press.
Katz, L. D. (Ed.). (2000). *Evolutionary origin of morality: Cross-disciplinary perspectives.* Exeter, UK: Imprint Academic.
Nitecki, M. H., & Nitecki, D. V. (1993). *Evolutionary ethics.* Albany: State University of New York Press.
Thompson, P. (Ed.). (1995). *Issues in evolutionary ethics.* Albany: State University of New York Press.

EVOLUTIONARY ETHICS

An *Encyclopedia of Philosophy* writes of evolutionary ethics: "Morality is universal, whereas biologically useful altruism is particular favoring the family or the group over others. Evolutionary ethics is, on a philosopher's time-scale, a very new approach to ethics. Though interdisciplinary approaches between scientists and philosophers have the potential to generate important new ideas, evolutionary ethics still has a long way to go."

One area in which evolutionary ethics has been set on its head is in Africa, where AIDs has devastated the population of the continent. In South Africa, for example, which has tended to be reticent about divulging its losses due to AIDs, the loss of life has been staggering. The *Washington Post* noted, "South Africa reported a 57 percent jump in deaths between 1997 and 2002, providing a startling—if indirect—picture of the rocketing toll of the country's AIDS epidemic. Releasing figures from a widely awaited national mortality study, Statistics South Africa reported deaths had leapt to 499,268 in 2002 from 318,287 in 1997. Among those older than 15, deaths increased by 62 percent."

The disease, which has completely changed the face of health in Africa, spread largely in the 1980s over the Trans-Africa highway, which had opened up vast areas of the continent to commerce. AIDs was carried over wide distances by truck drivers who passed it to roadside prostitutes, who were driven by rural poverty to the African cities that served the trucking trade, like Kinshasa in the Congo. Ironically, in a situation where the ravages of AIDs are aggravated by the spread of modern commerce, the disease's toll is only made higher by traditional African tribal practices. In much of West Africa, tribal custom has held that abstinence from sexual intercourse marked the period after a wife gave birth to a child, a custom rooted in helping the new mother recover her health from the ordeal of child bearing. Of course, implicit too was that if she recovered in a healthy state, she would be able to bear more children to ensure the survival of the tribe. However, recent studies have shown that while husbands abstain from sex with their wives, they have sexual relations with other women, among whom there could be carriers of HIV, the virus which causes AIDs. In various studies, this situation was essentially unchanged after controlling for marriage type, age, education, urban-rural residence, income, and household wealth.

The report concluded with the observation that the potentially protective effect of prolonged abstinence after childbirth in Benin (and probably in much of West Africa) is offset by an increased probability that husbands will seek extramarital partners without using condoms. The implication is clear that to curtail new cases of AIDs, the old tribal customs will have to change and the population educated: What once helped the evolution of the species now hurts it. But such customs rooted in the past are difficult to alter. Thus, an ancient taboo, designed to promote the health of the mother and the ultimate survival of the tribe, has come to threaten tribal extinction from a modern nemesis: AIDs.

— John F. Murphy Jr.

EVOLUTIONARY PSYCHOLOGY

In *Evolutionary Psychology: A Primer,* Leda Cosmides and John Tooby write that "The brain is a physical system. It functions as a computer. Its circuits are designed to generate behavior that is appropriate to your environmental circumstances." During

recent years, this theory has led to a new trend in psychology and psychiatry: the use of new psychiatric medications. Increasingly during the 1990s and the early 2000s, Ritalin, or its generic form, methylphenedate, has been prescribed for the conditions known as attention deficit disorder (ADD) and attention deficit hyperactivity disorder (ADHD) among children, including elementary school age children. It was hoped that such medication would help to control or modify students whose behavior was considered disruptive to their teachers and classmates.

However, concern over the use, and possible misuse, of such a drug among young patients caused almost immediate concern from parents and medical personnel. The concern was underscored by the U.S. Congress Subcommittee on Early Childhood, Youth, and Families holding hearings on the subject in May 2000. Congressman Michael Castle, who chaired the hearings, noted in his opening remarks that "A news report on the increasing use of Ritalin caught my attention. I was particularly alarmed by the finding that for the years 1991 to 1995, the number of children ages two to four, who were prescribed psychotropic drugs, including Ritalin, increased by 50 percent. The researchers commented that these findings were 'remarkable' given the lack of research on the drug's effect on children." Such prescription of psychotropic medication also opened up another serious problem—those for whom the drug was prescribed were also selling it or giving it to their peers, either to increase performance in school or for recreational abuse.

The mounting concern over Ritalin and its possible abuses spurred further legislative attention, as legislators on all levels of government responded to the rising level of concern. The *State Health Lawmaker's Digest* for March 10, 2005, noted, "The results show that psychotropic medication prevalence varied across the three sites. Stimulant treatment in preschoolers increased approximately threefold during the early 1990s. During the late 1980s and 1990s, there was a dramatic increase in the use of psychotropic medications by children in the United States. This increase cuts across age, racial/ethnic, geographic, gender and insurance groups. Stimulants are often used as part of treatment for attention deficit-hyperactivity disorder (ADHD). Example: Ritalin."

One of the conclusions of the report was alarming: "Thus, there are still many unresolved questions involving the long-term safety of psychotropic medications in young children and the possible effects on a developing brain." While the debate over the use of stimulant drugs for the young continues, as does that for the prescribing of antidepressants, ongoing public interest ensures that the most important part of the dialogue will remain at center stage: the psychological health of young people.

— John F. Murphy Jr.

 # EVOLUTIONARY ONTOLOGY

Ontology is that branch of philosophy that asks what exists. Traditionally, this has been understood to mean what kinds of things exist in general, but in recent times, it has also been applied to mean what objects a scientific theory requires to actually exist if it is to explain the phenomena. We must therefore ask what things evolutionary theory requires to exist. This is, of course, distinct from the question of what things we can *observe* or *measure,* which is a matter of epistemology, not ontology.

In metaphysics, a distinction is sometimes made between *types* of things, and *tokens* of the types. A similar and related issue is whether things are *classes* that can be defined or *individuals* that can only be described or ostensively defined (i.e., pointed at). Most evolutionary objects have been interpreted to be either types and classes or tokens and individuals. Part of the problem is that since evolution by definition involves a lack of stability in the objects it explains and covers, it is hard to clearly define the types of objects.

Universal Darwinism

Evolution is usually understood as a biological process, but following Richard Dawkins, and with antecedents well before him, attempts have been made to formulate what is called by Dawkins "universal Darwinism." This is a generalized model of evolution that is independent of the physical substrate—a kind of general theory of any possible evolutionary process that might be called "Darwinian." Philosopher David Hull has applied it most extensively to the evolution of science, for example. We will consider biological evolution, but with an eye to the generalized ontological implications.

When we ask what "evolutionary theory" requires, of course we must take some representation of it, as that theory is itself evolving over time. The most widely discussed form is, of course, the conception of Richard Dawkins, sometimes called the "selfish-gene perspective," after his seminal book, or the "received view." Out of this and later works, a distinction was refined by David Hull, which has become known as the "Hull-Dawkins distinction," between *replicators* (genes and anything that is copied accurately like genes, including cultural items, called *memes*) and the economic systems they are part of and are reproduced when they are copied, which Hull calls *interactors* (organisms and anything like them that are differentially successful at getting the resources needed to replicate), although Dawkins prefers a less voluntaristic term, *vehicles.* Replicators are defined in Dawkins's *The Selfish Gene* as being those entities that are *fecund* (make more of themselves), *faithful* (have a high fidelity of replication), and are *long-lived* (persist over evolutionary time frames). Organisms do not persist over intergenerational time frames and so are not significant in evolutionary terms. Replicators are divided into "dead-end" replicators (for example, somatic genes), and germ line replicators (gamete genes).

The received view has been opposed or modified by critics, particularly Ernst Mayr (1988), who asserts that the objects subject to selection are organisms, not genes, which are "hidden" from evolution. Another critical stream is called "developmental systems theory," and its adherents hold that the evolutionary objects subjected to selection are *developmental systems* and life cycles. It is worth noting that Dawkins's view is a reworking and development of George C. Williams's notion of an *evolutionary gene,* which is, as he called it, a "cybernetic abstraction," defined as "any inherited information for which there is a favorable or unfavorable selection bias equal to several or many times its rate of endogenous change." A primary feature of evolutionary theory is that what is hereditable, whether they are replicators or not, must have variant forms (in genetics, *alleles*) that can be in competition for resources in order for selection to occur.

Sewall Wright suggested a metaphor of an *adaptive landscape,* which is the fitness value of each possible allele of each locus in the genome. This is sometimes taken literally, as a description of the values of genes in an environment. The adaptive landscape is itself constituted by the states of other organisms and their genes, as well as by the physical environment in which all these organisms exist. The sum total of these features is called the *ecosystem,* which is arranged into classes called *ecotypes.* A particular role in an ecotype is referred to as a *niche.* These properties of evolving things are primarily economic; they refer to the physical resources required by interactors to persist until reproduction. William Wimsatt has influentially defined *reproducers* as the key object in evolution viewed from an economic aspect, instead of replicators. This has given rise to the distinction made by Stanley Salthe and Niles Eldredge between the *genealogical hierarchy* and the *economic hierarchy.* Genes apply only to the genealogical hierarchy.

Phylogenetic Objects

A major set of disputes has arisen over the *phyletic* (that is, the evolutionary-tree level) entities in evolution. These include questions about the ontological standing of *species* and other *taxa,* whether lower than species or higher. Mayr asserts the ontological primacy in evolution of the *population,* which is a group of interbreeding organisms, or a Mendelian gene pool. Populations are understood to be primarily statistical in nature, with properties distributed over modal curves. It is expected that most populations will be polymodal (in biology, *polytypic*). On this view, a species is the set of all populations (the *metapopulation*) that exchange genes. Asexual (nonreplicator exchanging) species have to be defined in another way, usually based on their genome clustering about a "wild-type" mode that is at an adaptive peak.

A somewhat different approach derives from the taxonomic discipline of *cladistics.* This approach of classification is by genealogy (*clades,* meaning branches) rather than by grades or overall similarities. The fundamental object of cladistics is the *lineage,* which is variously understood as a sequence of populations or as the parent-child relationship of any organic entity. Lineages that split (*cladogenesis*) form clades, which are the ancestor and all descendent lineages of a particular branch. Such groups of taxa are called *monophyletic* and are the only natural group

allowed in cladistic methodology. However, while clades are taxonomic groups based around species, cladistic methods also apply to genetic lineages, and the resulting trees of genes are considered to support phylogenetic trees if they agree. If they do not, a consensus of gene trees is held to give the taxonomic, or phylogenetic, tree.

Part of the problem with an evolutionary perspective for taxonomy is that the entities are not stable, and they are not all commensurate. While in the older Linnaean system, there were absolute ranks such as genus, family, order, class, kingdom, and so on, in the cladistic view, these are arbitrary and relative, and the only "natural rank" is the species, in part because the assignment of groups of species to these ranks is a subjective one. Cladistics is therefore a rankless system.

Beneath the level of species, there are smaller entities. In biology, there are subspecific groups known as geographical races, although the term *race* is now often avoided in favor of some other term, such as *variety.* Geographical groups are specified by a correlation of traits with distinct ranges. However, varieties can also be found across ranges, and in this case these are referred to as *subtypes, varieties,* or *trait* groups.

Group Selection

While the level of the individual organism (the interactor) is considered to be the primary focus of selection, another level is the *kin group,* in which the genetic fitness of a gene is the average fitness of all copies of the gene in all interactors (*inclusive fitness*). This allows selection to make individuals altruistic toward their kin, without making their genes less fit. However, it does not allow for altruism (in which a replicator makes its vehicle behave in ways that benefit other vehicles and not itself) to evolve toward nonkin, that is, those who do not share that gene.

Some have proposed *group selection,* in which the larger scale groups behave as the "fitness bearers." Many think this is inconsistent with the replicator-interactor distinction or its precursors, while others seek to find analogues at higher levels to the canonical replicators and interactors. Group selection has been proposed for trait groups, temporary populations competing against each other, for species, and even for larger-scale clades. Even the classical argument of Williams against group selection allowed it could occur.

Some have also argued for the reality of *body plans*, or generalized structural arrangements of organisms, in evolution acting as constraints on the possible evolutionary trajectories in a "space" of morphologies (*morphospace*), although others consider this to be an artifact of the modeling methodology.

Ontologies and the Metaphysics of Evolution

Overall, evolutionary ontologies have been divided into those that are historical (process based) and those that are ahistorical (pattern based). Things that are defined ahistorically, such as some definitions of species, tend to rely on the characters or propositions used to define them. These things form *classes*, and they do not change, although a lineage might change into a class from another class or grade. A more recent approach is to see evolutionary objects as *individuals*, meaning not individual organisms or cohesive systems, but historical objects with a boundary in space and time. Michael Ghiselin and David Hull defined species as individuals in this way (although they have also defined species as cohesive individuals as well). Similar considerations apply to other evolutionary objects, such as genes; they can be classes on one account or individuals on another, but not both in the same account.

— *John S. Wilkins*

See also **Cladistics; Dawkins, Richard; Evolutionary Epistemology; Memes**

Further Readings

Dawkins, R. (1989). *The selfish gene.* Oxford and New York: Oxford University Press.

Gee, H. (2001). *Deep time: The revolution in evolution.* London: Fourth Estate.

Gould, S. J. (2002). *The structure of evolutionary theory.* Cambridge, MA: Belknap/Harvard University Press.

Hull, D. L. (1988). *Science as a process: An evolutionary account of the social and conceptual development of science.* Chicago: University of Chicago Press.

Oyama, S. (2000). *The ontogeny of information: Developmental systems and evolution.* Durham, NC: Duke University Press.

Sober, E., & Wilson, D. S. (1998). *Unto others: The evolution and psychology of unselfish behavior.* Cambridge, MA: Harvard University Press.

Sterelny, K., & Griffiths, P. E. (1999). *Sex and death: An introduction to philosophy of biology.* Chicago: University of Chicago Press.

Williams, G. C. (1966). *Adaptation and natural selection: A critique of some current evolutionary thought.* Princeton, NJ: Princeton University Press.

Wilson, R. A. (Ed.). (1999). *Species: New interdisciplinary essays.* Cambridge: Bradford/MIT Press.

 # EXCAVATION

Excavation is one of the most commonly known and used techniques of archaeological investigation. It involves the systematic removal of data from the ground. Excavation provides the most complete evidence for human activity during a particular period and how these activities changed over time. There are many approaches to excavation, but at its most basic, the method involves looking at activities horizontally in space and vertically through time.

By its very nature, excavation is a destructive and costly process. It is an unrepeatable experiment that requires precise methods of data extraction and recording. Before excavating a site, it is essential to understand how sites are formed. Sites are what remains from settlements and other structures. The residues of a past social system will change over time due to decay, erosion, robbing, and the effects of plant and animal action. It is thus important to recognize these processes and distinguish them from the past actions that led to the creation of the site.

To understand this, it is essential to understand the principle of stratigraphy. This is a geological principle that states that layers of strata are laid down according to processes: The layer at the bottom is the oldest layer, while the topmost layer is the most recent. This is called the *law of superposition.* Understanding this process is crucial for interpretation and dating purposes.

The archaeologist, then, must carefully remove and record each layer and understand the stratigraphic sequence. He or she must be able to recognize how the process works. For example, a pit dug from a higher into a lower layer may lead to later materials being found in lower levels. Strata can also become inverted; for example, a series of strata can be eroded to the bottom of a valley. To this, one must add what Michael Schiffer calls "N-transforms," natural processes which affect the archaeological record, for example, burrowing by animals and seismic activity. Changes brought about by humans are called "C-transforms" (cultural transforms).

Source: © iStockphoto/Tina Rencelj.

Sampling Strategies

The first requirement, however, is identifying the survey area in which to operate. Once that is accomplished, the archaeologist must then break down the region into smaller units in order to test the viability of any sampling strategy, particularly in little-explored areas. The major problem with this is in extrapolating whether the validity of results are representative of the survey region as a whole.

Such sampling techniques include systematic, random, and stratified random sampling. Systematic sampling can be thought of like alternating black-and-white pieces on a chessboard, which assumes that the sites themselves were laid out in a gridlike format approaching a modern city square layout. The pitfall is that the excavators may hit or miss everything if the layout of the site in question does not correspond to the idealized, superimposed excavation grid.

An alternative, random sampling uses a method whereby the sample squares in the survey region are fixed by randomly chosen coordinates. This method ignores known material culture distributions and environmental boundaries. While it might appear that such randomly chosen squares will be distributed widely, in practice, it is more common for tight clusters of squares to appear, leaving large sections of the surveyed region unsampled. Thus, this method does not take into account any knowledge of the landscape and the impact this may have had on the distribution of settlement and material culture remains.

As a result, the most commonly used sampling method is *stratified random sampling*. The survey area is first divided up according to its environmental or topographic layout, and sampling is then undertaken within each of the zones as deemed appropriate. This method has the advantage of combining ecological knowledge with the power of random test excavations.

However, even stratified random sampling has its problems. Although it attempts to balance statistical variability with representativeness, the region chosen for sampling is determined both by financial considerations and a degree of expectation on the part of the archaeologist about the nature and size of the site or sites expected. Therefore, the interplay between practical and theoretical considerations is a reflection of the research designs undertaken.

An example of good surveys is to be found in rock art studies. Many rock paintings are present in rocky terrain, which makes targeted surveying a necessity. Not all geological formations are suitable either for painting or for long-term survival of art, and field teams will normally focus on those geological zones that maximize the potential for mapping new occurrences of rock art sites.

Excavation Techniques

The focus on the methodology of excavations is far later in the history of archaeology. Early approaches simply involved the extraction of material deemed interesting by the excavator. While many such endeavors are accompanied by accounts, these are very different from the site reports familiar to students and archaeologists. The birth of modern techniques dates to the 19th century. The British Lieutenant-General Pitt Rivers developed a precise methodology during excavations on his estate, Cranborne Chase. His meticulous attention to detail was simply groundbreaking.

Archaeological excavation methodology and its procedures are typical of sampling. Factors of preservation, together with the economics involved in setting up the research project, result in excavators adopting sampling procedures that are best targeted toward achieving the objectives of the mission.

Attention also is paid to other pragmatic considerations, like natural formation processes, as archaeological sites can have complex physical and organic environments. These include water and wind actions, animal depositions and interference, as well as plant growth. The impact of these actions could disturb the site in such a way that detailed reconstruction is required in order to interpret the original material traces in a meaningful fashion.

The reasons behind why a particular site was chosen to be excavated, and the manner in which it was, must be recorded. A test of good record keeping is replicability, which permits another archaeological mission to accurately track the steps taken by its predecessor and enables participants to access the excavation strategies employed and to reconstruct the contexts of the material culture unearthed. Although this attention to detail is important, as with all archaeological work, there is a continual interplay occurring between research aims, technical developments, and theoretical perspectives.

Vertical Dimensions

The interplay between cultural and natural formation processes, operating between when the site was first used and the time of excavation, potentially renders the stratigraphy of sites complicated. Repeated uses of a site by hunter-gatherers, for example, are difficult to separate out into their discrete visits. However, archaeological traces of fireplaces and food refuse are manifested through localized, subtle alterations in soil color. These are called *lenses,* which are present within the stratigraphic layer.

At sites that have been visited repeatedly for a lengthy period of time, it is often difficult to distinguish between the complex series of lenses and layers that develop. The archaeologist records such stratigraphies through the use of sections: the stratigraphy of a straight side in a designated trench.

In situations where there are no discernable differences in soil color or texture, the archaeologist still needs to maintain vertical control and therefore may elect not to try and excavate according to faint stratigraphic layers, but instead in arbitrary vertical units called "spits."

Underwater Excavation

Horizontal and vertical control of deposits becomes even more paramount when dealing with sites under bodies of water; indeed, this is what distinguishes archaeological research from treasure scavenging.

Excavation underwater is rendered problematic by the presence of multiple hazards not encountered on the surface: seabeds of various textures exposed to currents, depth of sediments accumulated on top of the archaeological deposit, and the quality of visibility. Grid squares, made of rope, need to be placed over the designated area of the site and secured in place by concrete sinkers. Additional sinker markers are required for assisting in laying out the quadrants, which are buoyed and mapped using theodolites from the surface.

Thus, excavation techniques vary widely and are adapted according to the research requirements and the physical nature of the site in question. Despite the differing views held by archaeologists on the nature of the interaction between theory and data, the central tenet is to accurately establish the context in which the assemblages excavated occurred.

Stratigraphy as Dating

When deciding on what form of stratigraphic units to follow in an excavation, the archaeologist is also effectively deciding on the type of chronology to employ. Different, and sometimes discrete, human actions get compacted together by soil color and texture into layers. At Stone Age sites, many hundreds of individual actions and occupations may be compacted into a layer. Thus, archaeologists are confronted with the tangle of dealing with compacted human actions through artificially dividing the actions into discrete slices.

In this way, stratigraphy is at the heart of the archaeological concept of time, enabling reconstructions of chronologies to be undertaken through relative and absolute dating techniques. Examples of relative dating include analyzing and comparing the faunal compositions of neighboring or faraway sites, constructing pottery seriation sequences, and more specialized techniques, such as contrasting the chemical composition of fossil bone material. Absolute dating techniques, providing age estimates that refer to a calendrical time scale, are based either upon radioactive decay or other natural processes.

Beyond Excavation

Excavation is the most visible part of archaeology. In the public mind, it is what archaeologists do. However, as any dig participant can attest, postexcavation is a far more time-consuming and equally important activity. Excavation is not meant to stand alone; the processing and publication of material is equally important.

Moreover, it is not always possible to fund excavation projects and/or obtain legal permits. For this reason, surveys have become increasingly important, for example, in the Mediterranean. While surveys potentially offer a broad range of information in a relatively shorter space of time, excavation remains the best way to uncover and document the past.

On another level, excavation provides an excellent opportunity to create dialogue with the nonarchaeological community. Ian Hodder's excavations at Catal Hoyuk are an example of reflexive archaeology and dialogue with various communities. Finally, the material culture recovered must be handled and conserved appropriately. Excavation also raises many contentious issues, including repatriation and claims to land rights.

— *Isabelle Vella Gregory*

See also **Archaeology; Stratigraphy**

Further Readings

Barker, P. (1993). *Techniques of archaeological excavation* (3rd ed.). London and New York: Routledge.
Hall, M. (1996). *Archaeology Africa.* Cape Town, South Africa: David Philip.
Renrew, C., & Bahn, P. (2004). *Archaeology: Theory, methods, and practice.* London: Thames & Hudson.
Roskams, S. (2001). *Excavation* (Cambridge Manuals in Archaeology). Cambridge: Cambridge University Press.
Schiffer, M. B. (1996). *Formation processes of the archaeological record.* Salt Lake City: University of Utah Press.

EXOBIOLOGY AND EXOEVOLUTION

Exobiology is the scientific search for life-forms existing elsewhere in this universe, whereas exoevolution involves speculating on the adaptive histories of organisms on other worlds.

It is not generally known that, at least once in his life, Charles Darwin envisioned the existence of plants and animals on another world. In 1836, having returned to a Brazilian rain forest and being impressed with its luxurious life-forms, he thought how great it would be if it were possible to admire the scenery of another planet. Darwin recorded this speculation in Chapter 21 of his first book, *The Voyage of the Beagle* (1839).

Do life-forms exist on other worlds? Are there intelligent beings living among the galaxies? Have advanced civilizations emerged elsewhere in this universe? These questions were asked by a few major thinkers in antiquity, but now these same questions are being taken seriously by many distinguished scientists and philosophers. The answers will have a direct bearing on the place life itself and the human species occupy within dynamic nature.

In particular, is the human animal unique and alone in this material cosmos? Or is the human species just one of many similar sentient beings inhabiting unknown worlds throughout sidereal reality? The science of exobiology intensifies human curiosity and challenges the imagination, while the quest to find forms of life and intelligence beyond the Earth requires a multidisciplinary approach that involves scientific specialists in various fields, from astronomy and biochemistry to biology and engineering, as well as the latest advances in space technology.

Exobiology

If life emerged from matter on the Earth, then is it not possible that organisms have appeared elsewhere in this universe? From ancient speculations to modern hypotheses, some of the greatest minds in the history of philosophy and science have grappled with the idea of exobiology (the existence of life-forms beyond this planet), for example, Cusa, Leibniz, and Kant.

In antiquity, Anaxagoras and Lucretius maintained that life does exist beyond the Earth. During the Italian Renaissance, the daring philosopher Giordano Bruno (1548–1600) argued for an eternal, infinite, endlessly changing, and inhabited universe. He even held that intelligent beings, superior to the human species, exist on planets elsewhere in dynamic reality. Of course, his iconoclastic framework challenged the earthbound and human-centered worldview entrenched in Western philosophy and theology. In fact, Bruno was burned alive at the stake in Rome (near the Vatican) because of his unorthodox worldview.

In the 20th century, although a silenced evolutionist, the geopaleontologist and Jesuit priest Pierre Teilhard de Chardin (1881–1955) failed to take seriously the probability of life-forms and intelligent beings existing on planets elsewhere. Instead, he focused on this Earth and the human species. Actually, his cosmology is merely a planetology. In his major work, *The Phenomenon of Man* (1955), Teilhard believed that the final goal of human evolution is a spiritual Omega Point at which time the united human species will merge with a personal God at the end of Earth history in terms of a converging and involuting collective consciousness. It is not surprising that his mystical vision satisfied neither religious creationists nor scientific evolutionists, although the courageous Teilhard is to be greatly admired for his serious introduction of the fact of evolution into modern theology

Going beyond the ideas of Galileo and Darwin, one may anticipate an exobiology revolution in scientific cosmology. The impact would be awesome for the human species. No longer would the Earth or the organisms on this planet, including humankind, be unique in this universe.

In the United States, astronomers Frank Drake and Carl Sagan took the emerging science of exobiology seriously. In 1961, Drake proposed a mathematical equation to determine the number of detectable civilizations in this universe. His calculations suggest that there may be thousands of civilizations similar to those of humankind in the Milky Way galaxy. And in his popular writings and television series, Sagan brought the exciting probabilities of exobiology to the general public. Modern technology now makes the search for life and intelligence elsewhere possible, particularly in terms of space probes and radio telescopes, for example, the Arecibo Observatory in Puerto Rico.

Concerning civilizations with advanced technologies, physicist Freeman Dyson speculates that superior beings could use planetary matter to build an energy-capturing sphere ("Dyson Sphere") around their star.

In Russia, the scientists Nikolai S. Kardashev and Iosif Shklovskii have proposed the construction of several huge radio telescopes in the Earth's solar system, in order to detect extrasolar planets. Actually, modern astronomers have already discovered over 60 planets existing in other solar systems. Kardashev has classified civilizations into three energy output types: Type 1 is planetary, Type 2 is solar, and Type 3 is galactic. Going beyond this scheme, one could even imagine a supercivilization utilizing the power output of a cluster of galaxies.

Considering the age and size of this expanding universe, with its billions of years and billions of nebulas, there has probably been all the time and space necessary for life (as now known) to have emerged more than once in nature. The general uniformity of both physical laws and chemical elements throughout reality increases the probability that life, that is, the RNA or DNA molecule, has appeared on other worlds. In fact, carbon and water are plentiful in this universe. Furthermore, organic molecules (amino acids) exist in comets, meteors, cosmic gas/dust clouds, and planetary atmospheres. Therefore, the conditions for the origin of life do exist elsewhere in reality. Surely, the discovery of the RNA or DNA molecule in the sidereal depths of outer space would give exobiology an empirical foundation it now lacks, and it would intensify further scientific investigation for conscious observers and intelligent machines elsewhere in this cosmos.

All living forms need not be restricted to only this planet. Because there are billions of galaxies, each with billions of stars, it seems reasonable to assume that there are millions of solar systems with planets similar to the Earth. No doubt, at least some of these planets would resemble the Earth in size, chemistry, temperature, and atmosphere. Thus, it is highly probable that zones with the necessary conditions for the origin of life exist elsewhere. Of course, extraterrestrial organisms need not be similar to those plants and animals that have inhabited and now exist on the Earth. As a result, alien forms of galactic life could be so different from known organisms that they may not be recognized by the human species or detected by its technology.

Is life a unique miracle or random accident or statistically inevitable, given enough time and the right situation? Actually, the origin of life on this planet was remarkably swift from the geological perspective. It appeared about 4 billion years ago, only 600 million years after the formation of the Earth. Surely, if the origin of life happened once, then it can happen again elsewhere under similar conditions; recall that the prebiotic chemistry for life pervades this universe.

Logic does not dictate that this planet or life on Earth or the human species must be unique in all reality (although religionists and theologians may still believe each of these claims to be true).

At this time, there is no direct empirical evidence to support exobiology. Because of the awesome cosmic distances among the stars and nebulas, one may never discover the existence of life on other worlds in this universe (even if it does exist). Life-forms may have emerged and vanished before the existence of this solar system, or organisms will appear on other planets in the remote future. Another possibility is that superior beings elsewhere may not be interested in the human species; if they are intelligent enough to discover humankind, then they are wise enough to stay away. The human animal has nothing to offer such superior visitors from deep space.

Furthermore, it is possible that other universes with life-forms have existed before this one, are coexisting with this world, or will exist after this particular cosmic epoch has ended. Consequently, the questions raised by exobiologists may never be answered in the affirmative, even if life does exist elsewhere. The same is true for questions concerning exoevolution.

Perhaps numerous inhabited planets do orbit stars in this galaxy and in others. Concerning the organic evolution of life-forms on other worlds, what is possible? If planetary systems are common, then do Earthlike worlds elsewhere harbor biological activity needing carbon and liquid water (or is life elsewhere based on another element, for example, silicon or boron)? The human quest for cosmic life and intelligence may even find fossils and artifacts on other worlds.

Exoevolution

Four billion years of biological evolution on this planet have produced a staggering spectra of organisms, ranging from bacteria and plants to invertebrates and vertebrates. This creative unity of global life includes such diverse life forms as worms, sponges, sharks, turtles, snakes, and elephants. Among the very social creatures are species of insects, birds, and primates (especially the pongids and hominids). Yet, most of the species that have inhabited this world are now extinct, for example, all the trilobites, ammonites, and dinosaurs have vanished from the biosphere.

As if organic evolution on Earth is not difficult enough for many to accept, especially biblical fundamentalists, then the discovery of exoevolution will challenge all thinkers to seriously reassess the place that humankind occupies in dynamic reality.

The only process of organic evolution that is now known to science is the one taking place on Earth. However, exobiology infers exoevolution. Environments are never fixed anywhere in nature. No doubt, the struggle for existence pervades this universe. As on this planet, life-forms elsewhere would have evolved to meet the challenges of their changing habitats. One can only speculate on what directions organic evolution and adaptive radiation have taken on other worlds. Perhaps human explorers will find species similar to ants, whales, and the apes; and maybe even the technological remains of past civilizations, or the existence of cognitive biorobots of superior intelligence, will be discovered in this cosmos.

If life-forms are found elsewhere, then future scientists and philosophers would participate in the critical study of comparative exoevolution. Or if human beings send themselves and other life-forms into outer space, then these plants and animals will evolve in strange new habitats (thereby making the study of exoevolution a certainty). In fact, the human species itself may evolve into a new form of life as it adapts to living among the distant stars.

Are we completely alone in this material universe? If not, then contact with extraterrestrials will be the most momentous event in human history. In fact, the Nietzschean Overman may have already emerged somewhere in this universe. Cosmic aliens with superior intelligence could be wise, benign, creative, and compassionate, or they could be indifferent and evil. Certainly, their achievements in science and technology will be far beyond our comprehension.

Moreover, cosmic microbes may cause diseases that could bring the human species (if not all terrestrial life-forms) to extinction. The cosmic quest for life elsewhere is not to be taken lightly.

Exobiology and exoevolution directly challenge geocentrism, zoocentrism, and anthropocentrism. The discovery of organic evolution beyond the Earth will make this planet and the human species even less significant than they now are. If intelligent beings are discovered elsewhere, then the human animal will no longer be something special in this universe. Such an incredible event would have an awesome and lasting impact on humankind's science, philosophy, and theology (not to mention the inevitable psychological and sociocultural changes to the self-centered human species). Giving priority to science and reason, and with courage and humility, future naturalists will need to accept the true place of our human species in material reality from a cosmic perspective and within the evolutionary framework.

For most scientists, the origin of life on Earth was a strictly materialistic event. The subsequent history of living forms on this planet has been a long, complex, contingent, unpredictable, opportunistic, and inefficient process of biological evolution. Organic evolution is also nonrepeatable, irreversible, and subject to material constraints.

Homo sapiens sapiens is a product of, dependent upon, and totally within evolving nature. Because of the staggering necessary sequence of improbable events that had to occur in order to bring human beings into existence, it is unlikely that the human species will meet its exact duplicate on a remote world. Nevertheless, at least once, with the recent emergence of the human being, this dynamic universe became aware of itself.

Rational speculations are very important, but there is no substitute for evidence, observation, and communication. It is conceivable that processes of evolution elsewhere in this universe have produced forms of life similar to, or remarkably different from, those species that have emerged on the Earth over billions of years. In fact, the possibilities for life-forms inherent in exoevolutions on other planets seem endless.

Of course, extinction and evolution are two sides of the coin of life. A comet strike or global plague or nuclear war could wipe out the human animal and most, if not all, of the other species on Earth. In fact, this vulnerable planet has already experienced at least five mass extinctions. Similar horrific events may have already eliminated all life-forms on some other worlds.

There is no evidence of a preestablished direction or preconceived purpose or preordained goal for this cosmos that gives the human species a central position in material nature. This universe is clearly independent of and utterly indifferent to humankind; until now, the human species has played no special role in the existence of reality. There was cosmic time before the appearance of the human animal, and material nature will endure after the extinction of life and consciousness on this planet.

At some time in this millennium, reminiscent of the young Charles Darwin in a Brazilian rain forest, a naturalist may stand on another world and marvel at forms of life beyond humankind's present imagination. Another intriguing possibility remains: the survival and fulfillment of the human species may depend on its working in consort with sentient life-forms still to be encountered elsewhere in this universe.

— *H. James Birx*

Further Readings

Davies, P. (1995). *Are we alone? Philosophical implications of the discovery of extraterrestrial life.* New York: HarperCollins.

Dick, S. J. (1996). *The biological universe: The Twentieth-century extraterrestrial life debate and the limits of science.* Cambridge, UK: Cambridge University Press.

Drake, F., & Sobel, D. (1992). *Is anyone out there: The scientific search for extraterrestrial intelligence.* New York: Delacorte.

Ferris, T. (2000). *Life beyond earth.* New York: Simon & Schuster.

Koerner, D., & LeVay, S. (2000). *Here be dragons: The scientific quest for extraterrestrial life.* Oxford, UK: Oxford University Press.

Lamb, D. (2001). *The search for extraterrestrial intelligence: A philosophical inquiry.* New York: Routledge.

Lemonick, M. D. (1998). *Other worlds: The search for life in the universe.* New York: Simon & Schuster.

Sagan, C., & Shklovskii, I. S. (1966). *Intelligent life in the universe.* San Francisco: Holden-Day.

Webb, S. (2002). *Where is everybody? Fifty solutions to the Fermi Paradox and the problem of extraterrestrial life.* New York: Copernicus/Springer-Verlag.

Zubbay, G. (2000). *Origins of life on earth and in the cosmos.* San Diego, CA: Academic Press.

 # EXOGAMY

From the Greek εντὸζ + γαμώ ("out" + "to marry"), exogamy is the marital rule according to which the spouse must be sought outside the social group (e.g. kindred, totem, royal) one belongs to. It is the opposite of endogamy.

The explanation of exogamy has been a major concern for anthropologists. In addition, as it has been mainly linked to the interdiction of incest, which constitutes the most important form of exogamy, exogamy as a social phenomenon was considered to be of natural origin. However, Lévi-Strauss theorized that the interdiction of incest, and therefore exogamy, is not of natural but of cultural origin. Based on a quote from Tylor, he proceeded to give the succinct interpretation that man very soon realized that he needed to choose "between marrying-out and being killed-out." Under these conditions, no society can exist without exogamy.

Just as social groups aim to preserve and transmit their constitutive elements (for example, power, wealth, religion, language) to the following generations through endogamy in order to perpetuate their existence, exogamy aims at forming alliances between the groups connected through marriage for the same purpose. This perpetuation is achieved as well through biological replenishment as well as any sort of strengthening (financial, military, etc.) and the resolution of enmities, and so on, as has been and is the case with royal families, for which exogamy is the norm. An example of this is the marriage of Eric Tudor, heir of the house of Lancaster from his mother's side, with Elisabeth from the house of York. Eric was crowned king by setting an end to the War of the Two Roses (1455–1458), fought between the houses of Lancaster and York over the throne of England. The war took its name from the crests of the houses, Lancaster's being a red rose and York's a white one. With his marriage, Eric united the two roses on his crest and became the head of a new dynasty.

Consanguinity Kindred Exogamy

The most common form of exogamy occurs with the selection of the spouse outside the kindred group within which marriage would constitute incest. The stringency of the universal rule forbidding incest (and thereby enforcing exogamy) varies for different societies, ranging from the interdiction of marriage between parents and children as well as between brothers and sisters to the interdiction of marriage if even a single common ancestor is discovered.

For instance, the Greek Orthodox Church allows marriage between relatives beyond the fourth degree (i.e., the first cousins) for consanguinity kindred. However, custom appears to be stricter than religion, as it only allows marriage between relatives past the second cousins most of the time, or even past the third cousins on more rare occasions. Elsewhere, as in for example, the Aborigines in Australia, marriage is forbidden between parallel cousins, that is, children

of two siblings of same sex, which are considered to be siblings (a case of exogamy). Conversely, it is allowed and even largely enforced between cross cousins, that is, children of two siblings of different sex (brother and sister), this being a case of endogamy.

Lineage and Clan Exogamy

Exogamy is also a very frequent phenomenon on a *clan* (a social group the members of which acknowledge a common ancestry and whose relationships are ruled by solidarity) or *lineage* (the group of individuals who are interconnected through consanguineal kinship either patrilineally or matrilineally and who acknowledge a common ancestor) level. In northern Albania and parts of southern Albania, the fis, a large group of men of patrilineal descent with a common ancestor (lineage), follows a strict exogamy. The obstacles to marriage derive from the state of consanguinity the members of the same fis share because of their "blood link," originating from their patrilineal affiliation. If a marriage within the fis was discovered, the "culprits" were subjected to persecution and could even be assassinated. The *clans* in southern Mani (Greece) were also exogamic for the same reason.

A strict exogamy is obeyed by most totem *clans*, that is, clans bearing the names of plants, animals, or natural processes that they usually treat as their ancestors and protectors (totems). The members of the clan with this common ancestry consider each other relatives. This results in exogamy, as in the Ojibwa Native North Americans, where the term *totem* originates (*ototeman* means "is my friend or relative" in their language).

Fictitious (or Ritual) Kindred Exogamy

Apart from consanguineal (or by affinity) relatives, individuals related by *fictitious* (or *ritual*) *kinship* are also usually subject to exogamy. This term covers social bonds equivalent to consanguineal or affinity kinship, often using the terminology of kinship (or cognate terms, for example, father-godfather) and usually necessitating a ritual for their creation (such as godparenthood, adoption, or fraternization).

The rule of exogamy is thus particularly stringent for godparenthood in the Greek Orthodox Church, where marriage is forbidden between the godparent and the godchild as well as the godparent and the godchild's parent. This is because the godparents are considered to be spiritual parents and the godchild their spiritual child. In order to remove the risk of such a marriage, custom dictates that men only baptize boys and women only baptize girls. This practice has yet another purpose: it eliminates the possibility of a marriage between godchildren baptized by the same godparent. The godchildren are considered siblings by custom and for whom marriage is forbidden. The danger of a marriage of this kind is particularly evident in endogamic societies. Still according to custom, marriage is also forbidden between the natural children of the godparent and their godchildren, who are considered siblings as well.

Exogamy usually applies between an adopting parent and an adopted child in most societies, as the adopted child takes the place of a natural child. In some cases, for example, in Albania, a powerful *lineage* could adopt a weaker one by adopting one of its children. The members of both lineages would then be subject to exogamy.

Interdiction of marriage also stands between individuals who have become siblings following a ritual (fraternization), although these individuals are most often of the same gender (usually men). Fraternization is encountered in many African and Balkan societies, where exogamy can apply to the families of the individuals linked by fraternization and often to the members of both their lineages.

— *Maria Velioti-Georgopoulos*

See also Endogamy

Further Readings

Goody J. (1983). The spiritual and the natural. In *The development of family and marriage in Europe* (pp. 194–221). Cambridge, UK: Cambridge University Press.
Lévi-Strauss, C. (1949). Endogamy et xogamy. In *Les structures élémentaires de la parenté* (pp. 49–60). Paris: PUF.
Lévi-Strauss, C. (1962). *Le totémisme aujourd'hui*, Paris: PUF.

 # EXTINCTION

Extinction is a word commonly associated with undesirable, catastrophic loss of entire populations or species. However, extinction is as much a part of the cycle of life on Earth as is evolution. Indeed, extinction and evolution together form the cycle responsible for the ever-increasing complexity of life on Earth. From the earliest evidence in the fossil record, we see populations and species disappear, to be replaced by other populations and species. In most cases, this occurs as the more complex organism replaces the simpler one. However, there have been several times in the Earth's history when mass extinctions occurred that wiped out the complex forms but allowed simpler forms to survive.

It is human nature to seek ways to forestall or avoid the inevitable concerning human extinction, and thus the study of extinction has earned high priority in scientific circles. This heightened interest has led to significant research on the topic. A true understanding of the processes of extinction requires a detailed understanding of most facets of the Earth's history, including climate shifts, tectonic movements, atmospheric conditions and content, sea level changes, and the flora and fauna itself. The geologic and fossil records are notoriously incomplete, making this research difficult. Even the tidbits that have been discovered, however, provide tantalizing glimpses into the intricate and complex patterns and processes of extinction.

Extinction can best be defined as the condition that exists when the last remaining individual of a population or species dies. Since this death can be caused by any number of factors and since extinction is inevitable for every species on Earth, understanding the causes, patterns, and processes involved can be daunting.

Types of Extinction

Extinction events can generally be divided into two types: background extinction and catastrophic, or mass, extinction. Background extinction follows the concept of Darwin's "survival of the fittest," perhaps better expressed as "survival of the luckiest." For one reason or another, groups of living organisms regularly pass into oblivion. These reasons include lack of nutrients, disease, genetic anomalies, unusual weather conditions, and being out-competed for existing resources. Changes in climate seem to play the largest role in this type of extinction. Very minor changes, as small as having a drought in a region for a few years, can cause an extinction event.

Background extinction seems to be part of a cycle most species of organisms follow. Initially, a species comes into existence from organisms occupying a new environment or following a new life style compared with their ancestors'. These organisms typically exhibit few specializations, and they are generally not very well suited to the new environment or lifestyle. Through successive generations, the organisms become more specialized and better able to exist in the new environment, but this comes at the cost of being less able to cope with changes to the new environment. Finally, the organism faces the problem of a change in its new environment, and because it no longer has the ability to adapt and change rapidly, it dies out. If the species is not an evolutionary dead end, somewhere in this process, some of the offspring were either born defective, forcing them to move into a different environment to survive, or perhaps a small group was merely trapped in an area where the environment was somewhat different. In any case, the demise of the parent species leaves behind one or more daughter species, and the cycle continues. Throughout the history of the Earth, this pattern has produced a gradual increase in both the number of different species and the complexity of organisms on Earth.

Catastrophic extinction often has the opposite effect on the number and complexity of Earth's species. Catastrophic extinctions, as far as is currently known, are always related to a massive, rapid change in the Earth's global environment. Such extinctions tend to affect the most complex and specialized organisms more rapidly and seriously. Simpler, generalized forms are usually better able to survive catastrophic events. There have been numerous catastrophic extinction events throughout Earth's history. Although there are many references to the "Big 5" and the current extinction as the sixth, there have actually been more than 20 times when mass extinction has occurred. Catastrophic extinction is defined as the extinction of a large number of species in a short time interval. It is easy to see that extinction events may be included or excluded from this category based simply on what one decides is a "large number of species" and a "short time interval."

There have been at least 5 major catastrophic extinction events and at least 14 more events that saw losses of more than 20% of species of organisms on the Earth. In addition, there may be as many as a dozen more extinction periods in the fossil record that are potentially this severe. However, due to the incomplete nature of the rock and fossil records, these events may or may not have occurred, and the actual number of Earth's catastrophic extinction events may never be known. Also, the classification of extinction events is arbitrary; there are no sharp separations in severity of extinction events. Extinctions of virtually every resolvable magnitude have occurred, from one species to virtually all species wiped out in a single event or time period.

Benefits of Extinction

Most of the research concerning extinction is concerned with the harmful effects to living species and the best means of preventing their extinction. A major force in human politics today is maintaining the current "status quo." Humans do not like to see change, especially when it concerns the loss of species that humans value. However, the history of hominids would be quite different were it not for the driving forces of extinction and adaptation. The last few million years of Earth's climate history have been unusually variable. The Earth has gone from very warm to very cool several times during this period. We are currently experiencing a moderate global temperature that is unusual from a geologic perspective. In fact, scientists are divided over whether we are on the brink of another ice age or a severe greenhouse event.

Such fluctuations of global climate have undoubtedly been responsible for the "weeding out" of hominid species such as *Australopithecus* in favor of the more intelligent *Homo habilis*. Had the climate not changed and the forests of the Pliocene given way to savannah grasslands, the australopithecines would likely still abound. The global cooling of the climate during the early Pleistocene caused the loss of the forest habitat of *Australopithecus*, and the species most likely died out as a result of this loss of habitat. However, the ability to use tools and the addition of meat to the diet allowed at least some members of *Homo* to survive and thrive long after the extinction of *Australopithecus*.

Similar climatic variation throughout Earth's history is likely the single most important mechanism behind the evolution of increasingly more complex species. An event that spells disaster for one population or species is likely to provide an opportunity for another group to change, adapt, and grow. From the current data, it seems that only the most cataclysmic events in Earth's history reverse this trend and cause the loss of the more complex species.

Major Extinction Events

The earliest-known, well-documented catastrophic extinction occurred near the end of the Precambrian, approximately 670 million years ago. This event wiped out approximately 70% of Earth's species; stromatolites and acritarchs were especially hard-hit. This extinction likely produced the conditions needed for the Vendian fauna, a series of soft-bodied animals, to appear and evolve. In turn, the Vendian fauna were largely wiped out approximately 520 million years ago, and the Cambrian hard-shelled fauna appeared. Other events documented by major faunal turnovers include the end-Cambrian (488 mya), end-Ordovician (438 mya), late Devonian (360 mya), end-Permian (251 mya), end-Triassic (200 mya), end-Cretaceous (65 mya), and end-Pleistocene (the last 10,000 years).

Five of these extinction events have been recognized as the "Big 5": the late Ordovician event, when 84% of animal species went extinct; the late Devonian extinction, when 79% of existing species were lost; the end Permian extinction, when over 95% of all species died out; the late Triassic extinction, when 79% of species vanished (this actually turned out to be two closely timed but separate events; however, it is still considered one of the "Big 5"); and the Cretaceous Tertiary (K/T) extinction, which ended the reign of the dinosaurs and over 70% of animal species disappeared. It is likely that more taxa were lost from the Vendian and Cambrian extinctions than from some of the "Big 5" events, but the paucity of the fossil record prevents truly accurate determinations. Also, please note that the numbers of missing species supplied here are calculations and estimates from studies mostly concerned with hard-shelled invertebrates. Other organisms either preserve poorly (small vertebrates, soft-bodied invertebrates, unicellular and colonial organisms) or are primarily nonmarine (plants, higher vertebrates) and thus are preserved only under fortuitous circumstances. These factors severely limit the accuracy of the numbers listed above but should not significantly affect the relative severity comparisons.

The most severe extinction event was the Permo/Triassic (P/T) extinction. It is estimated that the Earth was virtually sterilized at that time, with over 99% of all life being wiped out. Because it takes only a small surviving population of any taxon to preserve that taxon, the extinction percentages are largest at the lowest taxonomic levels. For instance, over 99% of individuals were lost during the Permo/Triassic event, but only 95% of species, 70% of genera, and 50% of family-level taxa were lost. It should also be noted that such a massive disruption to global ecology is also seen in the rocks themselves. The Paleozoic rocks of the world are noted for their abundance of marine, coral reef structures, and even amateur geologists easily recognize the red sandstones of the early Triassic in outcrops around the world. Only one family of coral survived. There has not been one fossil reef structure found in rocks dating to the first 10 million years after the Permo/ Triassic extinction event, and it took 100 million years for corals to again create significant reefs worldwide.

Causes of Extinction

Causes of catastrophic extinction, except in the current instance, are speculative at best. One observation that has troubled researchers for a long while now is the periodicity of extinctions and how this periodicity may correlate with astronomical events. There seems to be statistically significant regularity in the timing of extinctions, and this observation has spawned several hypotheses concerning causes for increased large meteor, asteroid, or comet impacts during those periods. As of this time, there is no conclusive evidence of this being the case, but the hypothesis does coincide with the K/T extinction being caused by asteroid impact. Unfortunately, the cycle is 26 or 27 million years in duration, and most evidence of impacts vanishes in only a few thousand years due to erosion and redeposition. Most recently, this line of investigation has led to the suggestion of a hypothetical binary sun (Shiva or Nemesis) or 10th planet (Planet X) that has an orbit that passes through the Oort Cloud, disturbing orbits and sending an increased amount of comets and other objects hurtling toward the Earth. It is well documented that a magnetic anomaly affects Uranus, Neptune, and Pluto, and this is the primary evidence that some large celestial body exists in the distant reaches of our solar system. Without precise measurements of this object and its orbit (its very existence is conjectural at this point), its effect on other objects in our solar system is impossible to accurately predict.

There are, however, several well-documented causes of worldwide catastrophe that don't involve a hypothetical planetary body. Every major extinction event and most of the minor ones have been associated with one or more known climate-altering events. In fact, of the "Big 5," all but the late Ordovician extinction are time equivalent, with massive extrusive volcanics and large meteor craters. Also, all of the "Big 5" are associated with large-scale glaciation except the K/T event. Trying to sort out the relative importance of these factors contributing to Earth's extinctions has been the focus of much research, speculation, argument, and frustration. It is likely that every major extinction event involved a variety of factors that combined to create inhospitable, often uninhabitable, environments over large portions of the Earth's surface.

It is now known that many of the recorded extinction events are correlated with changes in sea level. When glaciers cover significant portions of the Earth, virtually all continental shelf environments are brought to the surface, severely reducing the amount of available primary marine habitat. Likewise, when sea levels rise, major portions of the most habitable continental lowlands are inundated. This rise and fall of sea level is largely responsible for most documented extinctions, because the preserved sediments are primarily marine and show the loss of these types of life. Sessile organisms abound in continental shelf environments, but they are very susceptible to extinction through loss of habitat. It is possible that current research is skewed in overreporting (or underreporting) the seriousness of an event because most of the data gathered to date are from these marine environments.

The Current and Future Extinction

Compared with past extinction events, the current rate of species loss is very high. Should this rate continue for more than a few thousand years, the current event will easily rival the "Big 5" when it comes to number of species lost. However, it is beyond human experience to be able to recognize if this loss is comparable to other minor events or if it is truly a major catastrophe for life on Earth. The fossil and geologic records provide us with glimpses in time, but the records are of instants that are usually hundreds or thousands of years apart. If we were looking at the fossil record of this time from the vantage point of several million years in the future, we would not be able to separate those species lost during the last ice age from those lost last year.

The one comparison that can be made is how, in general terms, the current conditions on Earth match up with conditions during, or just prior to, any other extinction event. The Earth is recovering from an ice age, which matches the conditions found at the onset of at least four major extinctions. This is significant in that every documented ice age event is observed to coincide with an extinction event, and ours is no exception. When combined with a dramatic rise in temperature, as in a virtually instantaneous global-warming event, the matching situations found in the geologic record indicate a severe extinction. This, in fact, was the situation that was thought to have existed at the time of the P/T extinction event.

Unlike the P/T event, however, the Earth is not currently experiencing massive volcanic eruptions, nor is the Earth experiencing sizable asteroid impacts. Should both of these events happen, the Earth would undoubtedly see a repeat of the P/T extinction and most life would cease to exist. On the other hand, the P/T event was mitigated somewhat by the amount of carbon removed from the system through the reef-building processes of the Paleozoic. The Earth is currently experiencing a reintroduction of massive amounts of carbon previously removed from the system, and this is creating a carbon overload and atmospheric carbon dioxide spike.

On the whole, many scientists see many similarities between the Earth's final minutes before the P/T extinction and the present. The two questions, "Do we need to stop this pattern?" and "Can we stop this pattern?" are likely to plague scientists for the foreseeable future. Unfortunately, the answers to these questions may determine the cause and severity of the next extinction event on Earth.

— *David Trexler*

See also **Fossil Record**

Further Readings

Benton, M. J. (2003). *When life nearly died: The greatest mass extinction of all time.* New York: Thames & Hudson.

Cockell, C. (2003). *Impossible extinction: Natural catastrophes and the supremacy of the microbial world.* Cambridge: Cambridge University Press.

Hallam, T. (2004). *Catastrophes and lesser calamities: The causes of mass extinctions.* Oxford: Oxford University Press.

Leakey, R., & Lewin, R. (1995). *The sixth extinction: Patterns of life and the future of humankind.* New York: Anchor Books.

Macdougall, D. (2004). *Frozen earth: The once and future story of ice ages.* Berkeley: University of California Press.

McGhee, G. R. Jr. (1996). *The Late Devonian mass extinction: The Frasnian/Famennian crisis.* New York: Columbia University Press.

MASS EXTINCTIONS

The earth has an enormous biodiversity. However, many scientists, biologists, oceanographers, zoologists, and numerous others who work in scientific disciplines are very concerned that the earth may soon experience a catastrophic loss of a great number of species.

There are an estimated 2 million plants and animals known today. Some scientists estimate that as many as 50 times that number may exist. However, the danger is that a great number of species may disappear before they are even discovered.

There is geological evidence from fossils that during previous geological eras many species vanished within a short period of time. There may have been as many as five major extinctions that occurred during the earth's history. Fossil evidence strongly suggests that massive dying of species occurred during the Ordovician, Devonian, and Permian geological eras. The most obvious example is the disappearance of the dinosaurs. However, the concern today is that another "great dying" of species is being caused not by nature but rather by humans.

Polls taken of biologists, environmentalists, naturalists, and other scientists report concern not only that numerous species are now threatened with extinction but also that a massive extinction is under way. Some have estimated that 20% of all species could disappear by 2040. The estimate of extinction by some scientists is as high as 50,000 species each year.

The single major cause of massive species extinction is widely believed to be human activities. These activities include the thinning of the ozone layer, global warming, hunting, farming, mining, pollution from industry, deforestation and logging, the introduction of invasive species, habitat loss, and degradation. Evidence for species extinction that scientists offer includes the great declines in populations of plants, fish, and frogs as well as the decline in living corals in coral reefs.

The International Union for Conservation of Nature and Natural Resources is a global organization networking thousands of scientists. It has issued a "Red List" of species that are extinct, threatened, or endangered as well as those that are in satisfactory condition.

Critics charge that the claims of massive extinction are exaggerated and alarmist and that these overestimations are falsely derived from extrapolations based on the destruction of rain forests or other rich habitats. When asked in opinion polls, many laypeople do not believe that mass extinctions are likely to occur.

— Andrew J. Waskey

◇ ◇ ◇ ◇ ◇
INDEX

Atheistic naturalism, 1697

Athena Nike, 7

Athletic competition, 1218–1219

Atlatls, 523

Atomistic philosophy, 422

Attention-deficit hyperactivity disorder (ADHD), 407, 925

Attractors, 480

Auel, Jean Marie, 299–300

Augustine, 1307–1308, 1830

Aum Shin Rikyo, 624

Aunjetity culture, 1341

Aurignacian culture, 300–301, 525, 1208, 1723

Aurobindo, Sri, 1284

Austin, John, 1440

Australia, 301–305, 307

    creationism debate, 587

    women and anthropology, 305–306

Australian Aborigines, 1–3, 304–305, **306–311**

    body painting, 1791

    collector culture, 530

    domestic violence, 306

    ecology, 307

    economy, 308

    face painting, 1548

    identities, 308–309

    kinship, 309

    language, 1

    marriage and exchange of women, 309–310

    Mungo Lady/Man, 1645–1646

    plant use, 622

    polygyny, 1883–1884

    population, 307

    putative hominid ancestors, 1740

    racist evolutionary interpretations, 2092

    religion and cosmology, 309

    rock art at Ubirr, 2237–2238

    sacred landscapes, 574

    study of, 2–3

    technologies, 307–308

    white Australian society and, 310–311

    women's ethnography, 136

Australian women anthropologists, 305–306

Australoid, 569

Australopithecines, 271, **311–317**, 675–676, 886, 886, 887–889

bipedalism, 373–377

brain structure, 564, 1307

climate change and extinction, 938

fossil footprints, 996

group behavior, 2303

Homo habilis distinctions, 1189

Johanson's work, 1347–1349

Kenyanthropus and, 1363–1364

orangutan similarities, 205–206, 1780–1782

tool use, 1190, 2311–2312

    See also Ardipithecus; Orrorin; Sahelanthropus; specific species

Australopithecus aethiopicus, 315, 889

Australopithecus afarensis, 315, 401, 886, 887, 1456–1457

    bipedalism, 373–377

    footprint impressions, 1808

    Johanson's work, 1347–1349

    "Lucy," 887, 1348, 1349

    Lucy reconstruction models, 1500–1503, 1781–1782

    proposed evolutionary lineage, 1457

    tree-climbing ability, 1210

Australopithecus africanus, 271, 315–316, 354, 401, 675, 886, 887, 889

    proposed evolutionary lineage, 1457

    speech organs, 1423

Australopithecus anamensis, 219, 315, 317, 886, 1180

Australopithecus boisei, 315, 885, 889, 1450, 1451, 1453, 2329, 2364

    proposed evolutionary lineage, 1457

Australopithecus garhi, 316, 317, 885, 2311–2312

Australopithecus "*habilis*," 316. *See also Homo habilis*

Australopithecus robustus, 316, 884, 889

    proposed evolutionary lineage, 1457

Autism, 407

Automation, 2167

Avarna, 2248–2251

Avery, Oswald, 1036

Avunculocal families, 945, 947, 1538

Axelrod, Robert, 483

Axes, hand, 317–318. *See also* Hand axes

Aye-aye, 1959

Ayers Rock, 302

Aymara, 319–320

Ayoreo, 1113

Azande. *See* **Zande**
Aztecs, 1552, 1589, 1591
   Aztec agriculture, 320–322
   cannibalism, 1144
   temples, 2175
   Tenochtitlan, 2175–2178
Azusa Street Revival, 1836

Baba, Marietta, 100, 101
Babbage, Charles, 552
Baboons, 323–326, 466–468, 1617,
   1930, 1932, 2138, 2329
   aggressive behavior, 33, 325
   bipedalism, 375
   cladistics, 515
   communication, 325
   diseases, 326
   locomotion study, 1949–1954
   social system, 323–324
   types, 323
   vocalization and communication, 1420
Baby talk, 1405
Babylon, 326–328, 1583, 1584–1585
   temples, 2174
Bachofen, Adolphe, 1439–1440
Bachofen, Johann Jakob, 535, 1553
Bacon, Francis, 1268
Baer, Karl E., 659
Bakhtin, Mikhail, 328–329
Balinese culture, 2199
Balkanization, 330
Balkans, 329–331
Baluchi language, 331
Baluchistan, 331
Bambuti, 1558–1562
Bands, 1871
Bankes, William, 804–805
Bantu-speaking people, 2230–2232
Banyang medicine man, 332–336
Baoulé, 292
Barbados, 103
Barham, Lawrence, 2211
Barnett, Steve, 111–112
Barnouw, Victor, 1604
Barnum, P. T., 1655
Bärsch, Claus-Ekkehard, 1272

Basic personality structure, 613–614, 1358–1359,
   1603–1605
Basket Maker culture, 69–70
Basque language, 1489
Bass, William, 365–366
Bastian, Adolf, 1252, 1255
Bastide, Roger, 2151
Batchelor, John, 265
Bates, Daniel G., 332
Bateson, Gregory, 181, 188, 643–645, 657, 1569
Bateson, William, 1058
Battered child syndrome, 489
Baudrillard, J., 2088
Bauer, Bruno, 1860
Baugh, Carl, **1818**
Beadle, George, 1045
Beads, 292, 297, 524, 2182
Bear Feast, 297
Beauty, 609, 648, 2335
Beauvoir, Simone de, 2330
Becker, Gary S., 336–337
Becker, Howard, 740
Behar, Ruth, 137
Behavior, collective, 337–339
Behavior norms. *See* **Norms**
Behavioral ecology, 770, 771–773, 2303. *See also*
   Human behavioral ecology; Primate behavioral
   ecology
Behavioral genetics, 811, 899, 1964–1970
   evolutionary behavioral sciences, 1967–1969
   molecular genetics, 1967
   quantitative behavioral genetics, 1966–1967
   See also **Psychology and genetics**
Behavioral observation, 964–965
Behavioralism, 1879
Behaviorism, 731, 1299
Being and non-being, 663–664
Bell, Diane, 136
Bell, Gertrude Margaret Lowthian, 2329
Bella Coola, 954
The Bell Curve (Murray & Herrnstein),
   1052–1053
Beltran, Gonzalo Aguirre, 1589
Benedict, Ruth, 169, **339–342**, 555, 632,
   1470, 1493, 1568, 1569, 2328
   cultural relativity of deviance, 1962

Cicero, 1074, 1307

Cimmerians, 457, 458

Circumcision, 1562, 2023–2024

Cities. *See* **City, history of**

Cities of ancient Egypt, 2258–2259

Citizenship and migrations, 1599

City, history of, 509–511
 early Mediterranean, 510
 early New World, 509–510
 early Old World, 509
 global city, 511
 industrial, 510
 urban planning, 510
 See also Urbanism

Civil disobedience, 513–514

Civil rights movement, 28, 338, 1368–1369

Cladistics, 229, 515–516, 914, 927, 1226, 1631.
  See also specific applications

Clans, 73, **516–518**, 1370
 Aborigines, 1
 exogamy, 934–936, 1441, 1765
 Haida, 1126
 Hopi, 1202
 Iroquois, 1330
 Ojibwa, 1765
 Omaha Indians, 1772
 Tlingit, 2202

Clans, totems and. *See* **Totem poles; Totemism**

Clark, Grahame, 250

Clark, Wilford, 232

Class, 2115
 consciousness, 1108, 1541, 2101
 multiculturalism and, 1640–1641
 rank societies, 2104–2105
 state power and, 1870
 voluptuousness and, 648

Class conflict, 556, 557, 815–816, 2099, 2113

Class societies, 2099–2101

Classical Period Near Eastern culture, 248

Cleavers, 317

Clements, Tad, 1696–1697

Clever Hans, 868

Clifford, J., 852

Climate change, 826–827, 938
 geomythology, 1066–1071

Clines, 518–519, 901

Clinical genetics, 519–520, 1223–1226. *See also* Gene therapy

Clinically applied anthropology, 144–149
 biomedical culture, 145–146
 education, 146–147
 See also Medical anthropology

Clocks, 2197

Cloning, 759–761, 1053, 2015

Closed society, 1075, 2285

Clothing. *See* **Textiles and clothing**

"Cloud People" (Chachapoya), 469–477

Clovis culture, 520–527, 977, 1494–1495, 1680, 1684
 Beringia and origins, 525–527, 1684
 environmental context, 527
 lifeways, 522–525
 origins, 525–527

Cocaine, 1984

Cocco, Louis, 2350

Coevolution, 484, 603, 1211

Cognates, 1351, 1486

Cognatic descent, 1370

Cognition
 bilingualism and, 1311
 definition, 207
 Haeckel's panpsychism, 1121–1122
 primitive mentality, 1467
 symbolism and, 2150
 Yerkes' intelligence studies, 2352
 See also **Intelligence**

Cognition, ape. *See* **Ape cognition**

Cognitive criteria, 2066

Cognitive ethology, 868–869

Cognitive map, 868, 2296

Cognitive-behavioral theories, 577

Cohn, Norman, 1270

Coliseum, 527–529

Collective bargaining, 91

Collective behavior, 337–339, 2116

Collective consciousness, 174, 1442

Collective unconscious, 1255

Collectors, 529–530. *See also* Hunter-gatherers

Colobines, 530–533

Colobus monkeys, 530, 1617, 1933, 1937–1938, 1948–1949
 Himalayan fossil sites, 2090

Iroquois, 1325–1326
primate adaptive strategies, 713–714
role, 2028
xenophobia and, 2342
See also **Aggression**; Warfare
Conflict resolution. *See* **Dispute resolution**
Conflict theory of justice, 1352, 2113
Conflictual modernization theory, 781
Confucianism, 558–562, 1843
challenges to, 561–562
doctrine of the mean, 559–560
humanism, 1249
naturalism, 1695
neo-Confucianism, 560
philosophical tradition, 558
rectification of names, 559
self-cultivation, 558–559
spiritual tradition, 560–561
Congoid, 569
Conjugal family form, 946
Conklin, Harold, 846, 864
Consanguine family form, 946, 1625
Conscience, 1006
Consciousness, 563–566, 711
altered states, 565, 2318
anthropistic theory, 563
biological factors, 564–565
Cartesian dualism, 563–564
class, 1108, 1541, 2101
definition, 563
Dennett's evolutionary framework, 730–733
evolution of, 564
Freud and, 1006
internal conversation, 607
stream of, 2198
Consciousness, collective, 174, 1442
Consciousness, social, 630, 647–648
Conservation, cultural, 625–626
Conservative Judaism, 1344
Consortium of Practicing and Applied
Anthropology
Programs (COPAA), 178
Consumer behavior, 111–116
Consumption, 777
Continental drift, 566–568, 2305–2306.
See also Plate tectonics

Contraceptive technology, 2016
Contraselection, 677, 678
Convergent evolution, 224, 481, 895
Cook Islands, 1887, 1990–1993
Cook, James, 304, 1798, 1986, 1992, 2154, 2207
Coon, Carlton S., 568–569
Cooperative learning, 784–785
Copan, 236
Copernicus, Nicholas, 345–346
Copi, M., 2066
Copper Age, 570–571
Copper-Bronze Age Celtic Europe, 456–457
Coprolites, 1808, 2161
Coptic language, 572, 793
Coptic monasticism, 571–573
Coptic Orthodox Church, 479, 571–573
Corporate culture, 99–102, 1408
Corporate descent groups, 1370
Corrective rituals, 2013
Cortés, Hernán, 2362
Cortisol levels, 1217, 1218
Cosmic evolution, 881, 949–951, 1120–1125
Cosmological anthropocentrism, 82
Cosmological naturalism, 1696
Cosmology, 573
ancient Greek, 810
anthropic principle, 352
Australian Aborigines, 309
biblical creationism versus geology, 585–587
Big Bang theory, 345, 347–354
Bruno and, 420–423
Copernicus, Galileo, and Newton, 345–346
Da Vinci's studies, 1464
Einstein, 346–347
Gaia hypothesis, 1015–1016
Haeckel's evolutionary monism, 1120–1125
Hinduism, 1279
Kwakiutl, 1392
legends, 1457–1459
life on other worlds, 422
Mayan, 1556
origins of life, 352–353
sacred landscapes and, 573–574
Teilhard de Chardin and, 2170
Cosmology, biblical creationism. *See* Creationism
Cotton, 321–322

forensic applications, 1970–1971
Gestalt, 1378
human factors, 108
Psychology, evolutionary, 609–610, 811, 919,
925–926, 1867, 1965, 2315
Psychology, Soviet, 2291. *See also* **Vygotsky,
Lev Semenovich**
Psychology and genetics, 1964–1970
eugenics and, 1969
evolutionary behavioral sciences, 867, 1964,
1967–1969
personality research, 1968
quantitative behavioral genetics, 1966–1967
See also Eugenics; Molecular genetics; Social
Darwinism
Psychology of culture, 641–642
Pterosaurs, 584
Puberty, 2073
Puberty rites, 289, 2013
Puebloan cultures (Anasazi), 69–72
Pueblo I, 70–71
Pueblo II, 71
Pueblo III, 71
Pueblo IV, 71
Puerto Rico, 1601
Punctated equilibrium theory,
695–696, 904, 2061
Punishment, 998
Purification and pollution
death, 75
Gypsy culture and, 1116
rituals, 2011
Purushardha, 1275
Putnam, Frederick Ward, 238
Puuc-Chenes style, 2260
Pu'uhonua o Honaunau, 1971
Pygmies, 1558–1562, 2232
Pygmy chimpanzees. *See* Bonobos
Pyramid texts, 2258
Pyramids, 798, 802, 803, **1972–1975**
archaeologists of, 1972
construction methods, 1975
Egyptian religion and, 1974
history of, 1973–1974
origin and development of, 1972–1973
Pytheas of Marseille, 457, 458

Qafzeh, 1109, 1110, 1191
Qi, 560, 663, 665, 1525
Qijia culture, 570
Qin state, 1849
Qing Dynasty, 1977–1979
Quadrupedalism. *See* **Primate quadrupedalism**
Qualitative research methods, 2019–2020
Quantitative research methods, 2018
Quantitative trait loci (QTLs), 1967
Quantum mechanics, 1702–1710
Quechua, 62, 319, 474, **1979–1980**
Queer Nation, 2335
Quine, William Van Ormand, 117, 2064
Quintessential feeling of freedom, 2000
Qur'an (Koran), 1237–1242, 1334.
See also **Islam**

Ra expeditions, 1157
Race, 519, 568–569, 928, 2115, 2302
academic achievement and, 1757
amity-enmity principle, 1360–1361
Blumenbach's varieties of humankind, 385
caste, 1276
categories in Brazil, 1143–1144
intelligence and, 1966
involuntary and voluntary minorities, 1757
Jews and, 1346–1347
Montagu's criticism, 1620–1621
multiculturalism and, 1640–1641
polygenesis and monogenesis, 893
social construct, 398, 1669, 2308, 2342
xenophobia and, 2342
Race memory, 226
Race relations, Brazilian studies, 1143–1144
Racial/ethnic differences in intelligence, 1050,
1052–1053
Racial hygiene. *See* Eugenics
Racism, 699
Australian Aborigines and, 2–3
Boas and, 387, 388
early evolutionists and, 2092
Jews and pseudo-anthropology, 1346–1347
Muller and Aryan culture, 1635–1636
skinhead culture, 820–821
Social Darwinism and eugenics,
698–699, 701